The 24th Annual International Symposium on

COMPUTER ARCHITECTURE

June 2-4, 1997
Denver, Colorado

Sponsored by

ACM—The First Society in Computing, SIGARCH

IEEE Computer Society TCCA

CONFERENCE PROCEEDINGS

ACM PRESS
ACM—The First Society in Computing

The Association for Computing Machinery
1515 Broadway
New York, N.Y. 10036

ACM ISBN: 0-89791-901-7

Additional copies may be ordered prepaid from:

ACM Order Department
P.O. Box 12114
Church Street Station
New York, N.Y. 10257

Phone 1-800-342-6626
(U.S.A. and Canada)
+1-212-626-0500
(All other countries)
Fax: +1-212-944-1318
E-mail: acmpubs@acm.org

ACM European Service Center
108 Cowley Road
Oxford OX 4 1 JF UK

Phone: +44-1-865-382338
Fax: +44-1-865-381338
E-mail: acm_europe@acm.org
URL: http://www.acm.org

ACM Order Number: 415974

Printed in the U.S.A.

Message from the General Chair and the Program Chair

It is a great pleasure to welcome you to Denver, Colorado, the "Mile-High City," for the 24th Annual International Symposium on Computer Architecture. We hope that your stay in Denver will be a most enjoyable and productive one.

The area around the conference hotel is known locally as Lower Downtown or LoDo. This area has changed significantly in recent years, experiencing a dramatic rebirth and making it a vibrant part of the city. In part this renewed vigor is due to the construction of the new baseball field, Coors Field, home the Colorado Rockies. But is it also due to a very healthy business climate in which Denver, due to its geographically central location, is becoming increasingly important to many international businesses. This increased international exposure is evidenced by the G7 meeting which will be held in Denver just prior to the symposium.

We believe this high-energy locale is an appropriate setting to highlight the continuing dynamic and vibrant quality of computer architecture research evident in the quality and variety of the papers in this year's symposium proceedings. For close to 25 years, our computer architecture community has been the source of many of ideas and concepts that have contributed to the incredible performance improvements in computing technology. We believe this trend continues with the papers found in this set of proceedings.

A critical component to maintaining this excellence is the care and effort that so many from the computer architecture research community are prepared to spend on the reviewing process. This year's call for papers resulted in 147 submissions. Over 600 written reviews were obtained by the program committee for these papers—about 4 reviews per paper. On January 17th the program committee met in Ann Arbor, Michigan to select a program based on these reviews. The high quality of the papers made this a difficult task, nevertheless, the meeting ran smoothly and 30 papers were selected for the final program.

We would like to thank the members of the Program Committee and the reviewers for their unselfish efforts, and to Denise DuPrie and Laura Falk who handled the electronic submission process, web page creation, and the production of the proceedings. We would also like to thank several people who helped with the conference organization. First, Guri Sohi who, more than two years ago, offered the initial encouragement to proceed with having this conference in Denver; Mike Smith for organizing the tutorials and workshops; Dirk Grunwald for his incredible help with local arrangements and many day to day details; and finally, Matt Farrens, who provided a great deal of moral support and valuable ideas.

We hope you will find Denver an interesting and exciting place to visit, whether you only visit Denver or if you stay on to explore the many camping, hiking and recreational opportunities in the Rockies.

Andrew Pleszkun
Trevor Mudge

Organizing Committee

for

The 24th Annual International Symposium on Computer Architecture

General Chair: Andrew R. Pleszkun, Department of ECE University of Colorado-Boulder
Program Chair: Trevor Mudge, Department of EECS, The University of Michigan
Local Arrangements Chair: Dirk Grunwald, University of Colorado-Boulder
Publicity Chair: Matthew Farrens, University of California-Davis,
Tutorials Chair: Mike Smith, Harvard University

Steering Committee

Joel Emer, Digital Equipment Corporation
Mike Flynn, Stanford University
Allan Gottlieb, New York University
Yale Patt, The University of Michigan
Guri Sohi, University of Wisconsin-Madison

Program Committee

Gul Agha, Illinois

Anant Agarwal, MIT

Forrest Baskett, SGI

Brian Bershad, Washington

Laxmi Bhuyan, Texas A&M

Peter Chen, Michigan

Tom Conte, North Carolina State

Joel Emer, DEC

Joel Emer, DEC

Matt Farrens, UC Davis

Dirk Grunwald, Colorado

John Gurd, Manchester

Mark Hill, Wisconsin

Wen-mei Hwu, Illinois

Monica Lam, Stanford

Steve Melvin, Zytek

David Nagle, CMU

Lionel Ni, Michigan State

Kunle Olukotun, Stanford

David Patterson, UC Berkeley

Stuart Sechrest, Michigan

Mike Smith, Harvard

Per Stenstrom, Chalmers

Nigel Topham, Edinburgh

Mateo Valero, Politecnica de Catalunya

David Wood, Wisconsin

Robert Yung, Sun Microsystems

Willy Zwaenepoel, Rice

List of Reviewers

Abdel-Shafi, Hazim
Adiletta, Matthew
Adve, Sarita
Agarwal, Anant
Akella, Venkatesh
Anderson, Eric
Andersson, Per
Arpaci-Dusseau, Remzi
Arvind, D. K.
Asami, Satoshi
August, David I.
Austin, Todd M.
Ayguade, Eduard
Baer, Jean-Loup
Banerjia, Sanjeev
Baskett, Forest
Basu, Sujoy
Becker, David
Bershad, Brian
Betz, Vaughn
Black, Bryan
Braun, Jaymie
Calder, Brad
Callahan, Timothy J.
Cardwell, Neal
Chamdani, Joseph
Chang, Fay
Cheatham, Thomas
Chen, Brad
Chen, I-Cheng Kevin
Chen, Peter M.
Cheng, Ben-Chung
Chong, Fred
Chou, Yuan
Chow, Paul
Chun, Brent N.
Connors, Daniel A.
Conte, Marie
Conte, Tom
Cormen, Tom
Davis, Mark
DeHon, Andre
Deitrich, Brian
Ding, Jason
Dundas, Jim
Dusseau, Andrea C.
Edmondson, John H.
Edwards, Bruce
Eichenberger, Alexandre
Emer, Joel
Espasa, Roger
Evers, Marius
Falsafi, Babak
Farkas, Keith I.
Farrens, Matthew
Fernandes, Marcio
Flautner, Krisztian
Fossum, Tryggve
Frank, Matthew
Franklin, Manoj
Friendly, Dan
Fromm, Richard
Gammack, Richard
Garrett, Charlie
Giacalone, Glenn
Gloy, Nikolas
Gonzalez, Antonio
Gonzalez, Jose
Goodman, James
Gross, Thomas
Grunwald, Dirk
Gurd, John
Gyllenhaal, John C.
Hamacher, Carl
Havanki, Bill
Hicks, Jamey
Hill, Mark D.
Hirsch, Mary Ann
Ho, Sam
Horowitz, Mark
Hsieh, Cheng-Hsueh
Hsieh, Wilson
Hsu, Liang-Chuan
Huang, Andrew
Ibbett, Roland
Indiresan, Atri
Iyer, Ravishankar
Jacob, Bruce
Jacobson, Quinn
Jennings, Matt
Joerg, Chris
Joersz, Rob
John, Lizy
Johnson, Teresa L.
Jones, Graham
Juan, Toni
Keckler, Stephen W.
Keeton, Kimberly
Kessler, Richard E.
Kim, Sang wook (Peter)
Kim, WooYoung
Koopman, Philip
Koufaty, David
Kozyrakis, Christoforos E.
Kubiatowicz, John
Kumar, Akhilesh
Lam, Monica
Lang, Tomas
Larin, Sergei
Larus, James
Lauterbach, Gary
Lavery, Daniel M.
Lee, Corinna G.
Lee, Dennis
Lefurgy, Charles
Lewis, Brian
Li, Kai
Lick, Kelsey
Lipasti, Mikko
Llosa, Josep
Lowney, Geoff
Lynch, William
Mackenzie, Kenneth
Mangione-Smith, Bill
Manjikian, Naraig
Manoharan., S
Martorell, Xavier
Mattews, John
McLellan, Ed
Menezes, Kishore
Mishra, Amitabh
Mitrevski, Jovan
Mowry, Todd C.
Mukherjee, Shubu
Nagle, David
Navarro, Juan J.
Newburn, Chris
Nguyen, Anthony-Trung
Nguyen, Thu
Ni, Lionel
Nikhil, Rishiyur S.
Nisbet, Andy
Nishtala, Satya
Noonburg, Derek B.
Olukotun, Kunle
Other, A. N.
Pai, Vijay S.
Patterson, David
Pirvu, Marius
Pleszkun, Andrew R.
Postiff, Matt
Quong, Russell
Racunas, Paul
Rajamony, Ram
Ramanathan, Parmesh
Ranganthan, Parthasarathy
Rauchwerger, Lawrence
Reilly, Matthew
Reinhardt, Steven K.
Rich, Kevin
Rogers, Anne
Romer, Theodore
Root, Stephen C.
Rosenblum, Mendel
Rudolph, Larry
Sargeant, John
Sarrazin, David
Sathaye, Sumedh
Sathaye, Sumedh
Sawdon, Wayne A.
Schechter, Stuart
Schoinas, Ioannis
Seltzer, Margo
Shen, John
Sirer, Emin Gun
Sivasubramaniam, Anand
Slob, A.
Smith, J. E.
Smith, Michael D.
Snelling, Dave
Sohi, Guri
Soundararajan, V.
Stamm, Rebecca
Stark, Jared
Steely, Simon
Stenstrom, Per
Stricker, Thomas M.
Stumm, Michael
Talagala, Nisha
Talluri, Madhu
Thomas, Randi
Topham, Nigel
Torrellas, Josep
Tyson, Gary
Uhlig, Richard
Vahid, Frank
Vaidya, Nitin H.
Valero, Mateo
Valero, Mateo
Valero-Garcia, Miguel
Vijaykumar, T.N.
Voelker, Geoff
Walton, Robert
Watson, Ian
Welch, Brent
Wilkes, John
Wolman, Alec
Wong, Wayne
Wood, David
Woods, Viv
Wu, Le-Chun
Wu, Michael
Yang, Qing
Yang, Woodward
Yeung, Donald
Young, Cliff
Yung, Robert
Zaky, S. G.
Zekauskas, Matthew J.
Zwaenepoel, Willy

Table of Contents

Improving Instruction Level Parallelism

NUMA and COMA Architectures

Prefetching and Prediction

Branch Prediction

Managing the Memory Hierarchy and Memory-Centric Architectures

Improving Superscalar Instruction Dispatch and Issue by Exploiting Dynamic Code Sequences

Sriram Vajapeyam
Supercomputer Education and Research Centre
and
Dept. of Computer Science & Automation
Indian Institute of Science
Bangalore, INDIA 560012
sriram@csa.iisc.ernet.in

Tulika Mitra[1]
Dept. of Computer Science & Automation
Indian Institute of Science
Bangalore, INDIA 560012
tul@csa.iisc.ernet.in

Abstract

Superscalar processors currently have the potential to fetch multiple basic blocks per cycle by employing one of several recently proposed instruction fetch mechanisms. However, this increased fetch bandwidth cannot be exploited unless pipeline stages further downstream correspondingly improve. In particular, register renaming a large number of instructions per cycle is difficult. A large instruction window, needed to receive multiple basic blocks per cycle, will slow down dependence resolution and instruction issue. This paper addresses these and related issues by proposing (i) partitioning of the instruction window into multiple blocks, each holding a dynamic code sequence; (ii) logical partitioning of the register file into a global file and several local files, the latter holding registers local to a dynamic code sequence; (iii) the dynamic recording and reuse of register renaming information for registers local to a dynamic code sequence. Performance studies show these mechanisms improve performance over traditional superscalar processors by factors ranging from 1.5 to a little over 3 for the SPEC Integer programs. Next, it is observed that several of the loops in the benchmarks display vector-like behavior during execution, even if the static loop bodies are likely complex for compile-time vectorization. A dynamic loop vectorization mechanism that builds on top of the above mechanisms is briefly outlined. The mechanism vectorizes up to 60% of the dynamic instructions for some programs, albeit the average number of iterations per loop is quite small.

1. INTRODUCTION

A significant amount of recent research in superscalar processors has been directed at increasing the effective instruction fetch bandwidth[Rot96a, Con95a, Yeh93a, Hao96a]. Fetching a larger number of instructions per clock enables the processor to step through the program quicker and thus find more independent instructions for issue. However, increased fetch bandwidth can lead to the later pipeline stages of the processor becoming bottlenecks. Typical pipeline stages in an aggressive superscalar processor capable of out-of-order instruction issue are depicted in Figure 1. After instructions are fetched and decoded, source and destination registers are renamed before instructions are dispatched to the instruction window, where they wait until their source operands are ready. Increasing the fetch bandwidth could result in the following bottlenecks in the subsequent pipeline stages:

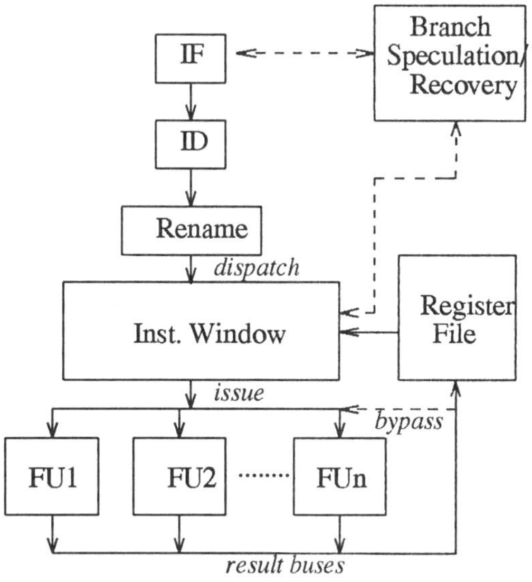

Figure 1. A Typical Superscalar Processor Pipeline

(1) The register renaming bandwidth has to grow proportionally with the fetch bandwidth. The register renaming process has a sequential component[Wei95a] involving determining data dependencies amongst the instructions that are simultaneously being renamed. Even when partially parallel methods are used for dependence checking [Pal96a], the rename stage latency is limited by the number of read ports needed for the register map table,

[1] Tulika Mitra's current address: Graduate Student, Dept. of Computer Science, SUNY at Stony Brook, NY 11794-4400. email : mitra@cs.sunysb.edu.

Benchmark	Fetch Bandwidth (Instructions/Cycle)							
	8		16		32		64	
	Win.Size (Avg.)	ILP	Win.Size (Avg.)	ILP	Win.Size (Avg.)	ILP	Win.Size (Avg.)	ILP
Bubsort	18	8.0	149	16.0	424	31.8	989	63.2
Eqntott (short input)	28	8.0	1095	15.6	5714	27.8	6496	51.2

Table 1. Impact of Fetch Bandwidth on Instruction Window Size and Performance. The study assumes 100% branch prediction accuracy, unlimited number of functional units, and unlimited maximum window size. The results are for short inputs, and indicate that large windows are needed even with relatively limited fetch bandwidths.

which is proportional to the number of operands being simultaneously renamed. These issues make renaming more than a few instructions per clock difficult.

(2) The instruction window could grow very large if the sustained instruction issue rate does not keep up with the instruction fetch/dispatch rate. Preliminary studies show (Table 1) that the window size grows large with fetch bandwidth even as performance increases, despite assumptions of unlimited functional units and unlimited instruction issue bandwidth. (Several previous studies[Aus92a, Lam92a, Wal91a] have directly or indirectly reported the performance improvements shown by large window sizes when *unlimited* fetch bandwidth is assumed.) This scenario is possible when sequential and highly parallel code segments are interspersed in the program trace. A larger window can increase the time needed to (i) feed a result/result tag to all waiting instructions in the window, and (ii) select and issue *n* instructions in a cycle from amongst all the ready instructions in the window.

(3) The physical register space needed to support a large instruction window could slow down register access time to more than one clock cycle. Each instruction in the instruction window needs a unique destination physical register, as physical registers are single-assignment registers. Thus a 256-entry instruction window is likely to use a 256-entry register file.

(4) A large instruction window needs a large number of functional units to exploit the exposed parallelism. The complexity of full bypassing of results grows quadratically with functional units since each functional unit output has to be provided data paths to the inputs of all other functional units.

A recent study [Pal96a] of the logic complexity of various superscalar pipeline stages identifies the instruction window logic for large windows as potentially the key limiting factor for processor clock speed. The next slowest stage is the register renaming stage when renaming multiple instructions per cycle. The register file access time for large files is also shown to be a problem. Full bypassing within a clock cycle is shown to be impossible for large windows.

We propose a set of mechanisms to address the above problems in superscalar processors. First, we partition the instruction window into blocks on instruction-fetch boundaries, allowing instruction selection logic and result bypassing to be simplified. Next, the register file is partitioned into a global register file and local register files, one per block, that hold registers that are strictly local to the instructions in the block. Third, we propose the recording of register renaming information in the trace cache[Rot96a], allowing rename requirements to be considerably reduced on a trace cache hit and thus increasing the effective rename bandwidth.

We next observe that several loops in ordinary programs exhibit vector-like behavior at runtime despite possibly having complex control paths in the static loop body. Complex static loop characteristics will preclude compile-time vectorization. We describe a *dynamic vectorization* mechanism that detects vectorizable behavior and alleviates the problems of large instruction windows by executing such loops in vector mode.

Performance studies show that the increased effective dispatch bandwidth and improved issue, bypass, and register access operations of the first set of proposed mechanisms provide significant performance improvements (ranging from 1.5 to 3 times) over a traditional superscalar processor model. Further, the proposed dynamic vectorization mechanism can capture as much as 60% of the dynamic instructions for some of the programs.

We describe the instruction window organization and related mechanisms in section 2. A performance study of the proposed mechanisms is presented in section 3. The dynamic vectorization scheme is described in section 4. We summarize and draw conclusions in section 5.

2. TRACE WINDOW

A large traditional instruction window can slow down the processor clock cycle, as discussed in the introduction. We propose the organization of the instruction window into *trace lines*, where each trace line is the logical equivalent of a line in the recently proposed trace cache [Rot96a]. Figure 2 depicts such an instruction window. A trace line consists of a small number of dynamically successive basic blocks in the program's execution, and is uniquely defined [Rot96a] by the address of the first instruction and outcomes for each of the branches in the dynamic sequence. Trace lookup in the trace cache consists of obtaining a match on both the address and the prediction bits. Multiple trace lines can originate at the same instruction address and can be present simultaneously in the trace cache. The trace window essentially partitions a traditional instruction window into blocks that can hold trace lines. A block is filled when a

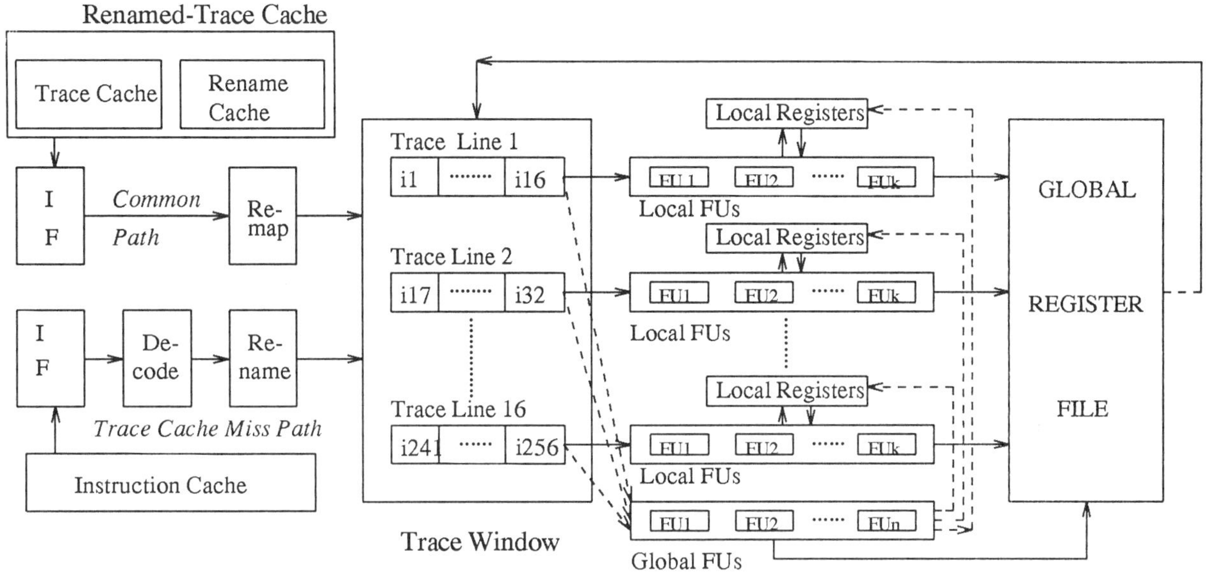

Figure 2. Instruction Window Organized into Trace Lines

trace line is dispatched to it, and freed when all instructions in the trace line have issued.

We describe further the organization of the trace window into trace lines in subsection 2.1. A mechanism for partitioning the large physical register file into a global file and several local files is described in subsection 2.2. Recording and reuse of register renaming is described in subsection 2.3. Subsection 2.4 describes a simple adaptation of the 2-level adaptive block-predictor[Fra95a] (proposed for use with restricted static program subgraphs having multiple targets) for use in conjunction with dynamic traces. We describe related work on instruction window organizations in subsection 2.5.

2.1. TRACE LINES

Each trace line fetched from the trace cache is decoded, renamed, and dispatched to a single trace line in the instruction window (termed trace window, Figure 2). Traditional window operations such as result forwarding and instruction selection are speeded up by this organization. The example configuration in Figure 2 shows each trace line with its own copy of each integer functional unit type, and costlier floating-point units shared across trace lines. Result bypassing is restricted to within the functional unit group associated with the instruction's trace line, and thus to dependent instructions from the same trace line. Previous work [Fra92a] shows that most instruction destinations are consumed within the next 32 dynamic instructions after being produced. This indicates that a trace line size of 32 instructions with restricted bypassing can capture a large fraction of the benefits of full bypassing without incurring the clock cycle penalty[Pal96a] of the latter.

Instructions that depend only on other instructions within the same trace line can have their dependencies quickly resolved due to the presence of local bypassing. Such intra-trace line dependence resolution can proceed in parallel and independently across the trace lines; it is also fast due to the small size of each trace line (i.e. a small subwindow). Dependencies across trace lines will be resolved relatively slowly, and will likely involve centralized logic.

Instruction issue bandwidth is restricted to a small number of instructions per cycle per trace line (e.g. 2 instructions/cycle per trace). This reduces the number of datapaths needed for simultaneously transmitting multiple instructions (i.e., opcodes and operands) to the functional units. Large peak issue rates can slow down window operations indirectly by increasing the window silicon area. The average ILP within a basic block is known to be around 2, and the ILP is not much higher across a few dynamically successive basic blocks. A trace line size of 16 instructions will typically hold about 3 dynamically successive basic blocks.

Further, it might be sufficient to issue instructions in-order from a trace line, assuming good compile-time instruction scheduling within basic blocks. This simplifies instruction selection logic by reducing the number of instructions that need to be examined each cycle to just the two at the head of the trace line. (The trace line then has to be treated as queue, with instructions at the head departing after issue and further instructions moving to the head.)

The trace window thus enables decentralisation of instruction issue operations (identifying ready instructions and arbitrating among them for issue). This avoids the bottleneck centralized issue logic would become [Pal96a] for large windows.

2.2. REGISTER FILE DECOMPOSITION

Each instruction in the instruction window, excepting branch and store instructions, needs a destination register, thus increasing the physical register size for large windows. In conjunction with the likelihood that bypassing has to be limited, register file access time can become a bottleneck. A solution to this problem lies in exploiting the fact that not all physical registers are live beyond the trace line that produce them. Table 2 shows the average number of live-on-exit registers and locally

Benchmark	Trace-Line Size (Instructions)									
	8		16		24		32		64	
	LoEx	Local	LoEx	Local	LoEx	Local	LoEx	Local	LoEx	Local
cc1	3.52	1.09	5.56	3.66	6.95	6.87	8.08	10.35	11.07	25.80
comp	3.55	1.06	5.66	3.56	7.05	6.79	7.97	10.47	10.09	26.79
eqntott	3.87	1.26	4.73	5.52	5.03	10.34	5.28	15.22	6.15	34.86
esp	4.22	1.79	5.77	6.24	6.64	11.37	7.24	16.78	8.01	40.04
xlisp	3.46	0.87	5.38	3.29	6.66	6.34	7.60	9.74	9.59	25.08

Table 2. The average number of Live-On-Exit and Local Destination Registers per trace line, for different trace line sizes. About half the registers are strictly local for the smaller trace lines (16 and 24 insts). The proportion of local registers increases for larger trace lines. The IBM RS6000's 1-bit condition-code registers are excluded in the above measurements; they have negligible impact[Mit97a]. Floating-point registers are rarely used by the benchmarks.

```
i1: R1 <- R2 + R3
i2: R4 <- R4 * R1
i3: R1 <- R1 + R5
i4: Branch TARGET
```

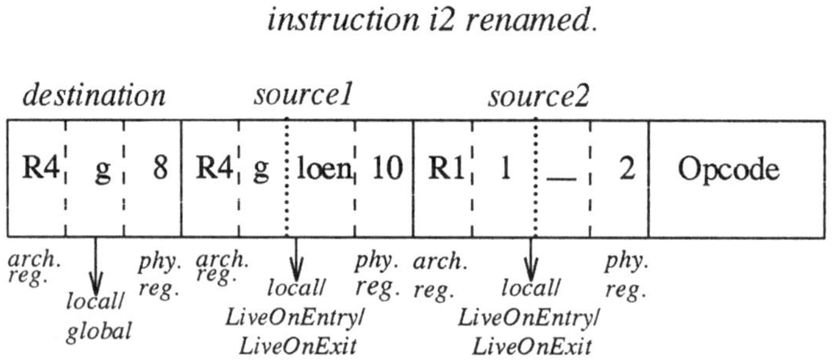

Figure 3. Renaming of Registers into Local and Global Physical Register Files. Register R4 is both live-on-entry to and live-on-exit from this block, and instruction i2 is appropriately renamed. Instruction i1's destination is strictly local to this code block.

consumed registers for the SpecInt92 benchmarks for different choices of trace line size. Typically, around half the registers written by a small trace line (say of size 16 or 24 instructions) are not live beyond the trace line. The proportion of such local registers increases for larger trace lines.

Locally live destination registers can be renamed to a physical register file local to the trace line; live-on-exit destination registers are renamed to a global register file. A single bit tagged to each destination operand identifier in the renamed trace line indicates whether the specified physical register is from the local or the global register file. Source operands can be classified as live-on-entry (produced by another trace line), local (produced by the local trace line and available in the local register file), or live-on-exit (produced locally, but live-on-exit and hence available in the global register file). Live-on-entry source registers have to use old mappings of the global register file; live-on-exit source registers use new global register file mappings produced after renaming the destinations of their trace line. Two bits are tagged to each source operand to allow this classification. Figure 3 illustrates such renaming using a 4-instruction trace line. The local register file size needed is typically[2] no more than the number of instructions in the trace line. The local file is flushed when the corresponding trace line is removed from the window. The global register file size needed is proportional to the total number of live-on-exit registers in the entire window.

[2] Some instructions have multiple destinations — for example, the LoadUpdate instruction in the IBM RS6000.

Traditional register renaming involves looking up a map table to pick up current mappings for architectural registers and, in parallel, true-dependence checking, followed by a modification of the mappings for source registers that were produced by earlier instructions in the current rename group (Figure 4a). To identify live-on-exit registers, output-dependence checking is done in parallel with the true-dependence checking (Figure 4b). In parallel, a unique local physical register is also tentatively picked up for each destination. (A simple scheme uses the instruction position in the trace as the destination register identifier for the instruction.) If the check logic indicates that an instruction's output is overwritten by a later instruction in the current rename group, the destination's local mapping is forwarded to the subsequent map modification stage instead of the mapping picked up from the global free list (the latter is then returned to the free list). This involves just an additional 2-to-1 mulitplexor latency per destination register, and is unlikely to affect the rename stage latency since the dependence check logic is faster than the map table lookup[Pal96a]. The tagging of register identifiers with the local/global bit and the live-on-entry/live-on-exit bit is achieved trivially by appropriately tagging the inputs to the 2-to-1 multiplexors.

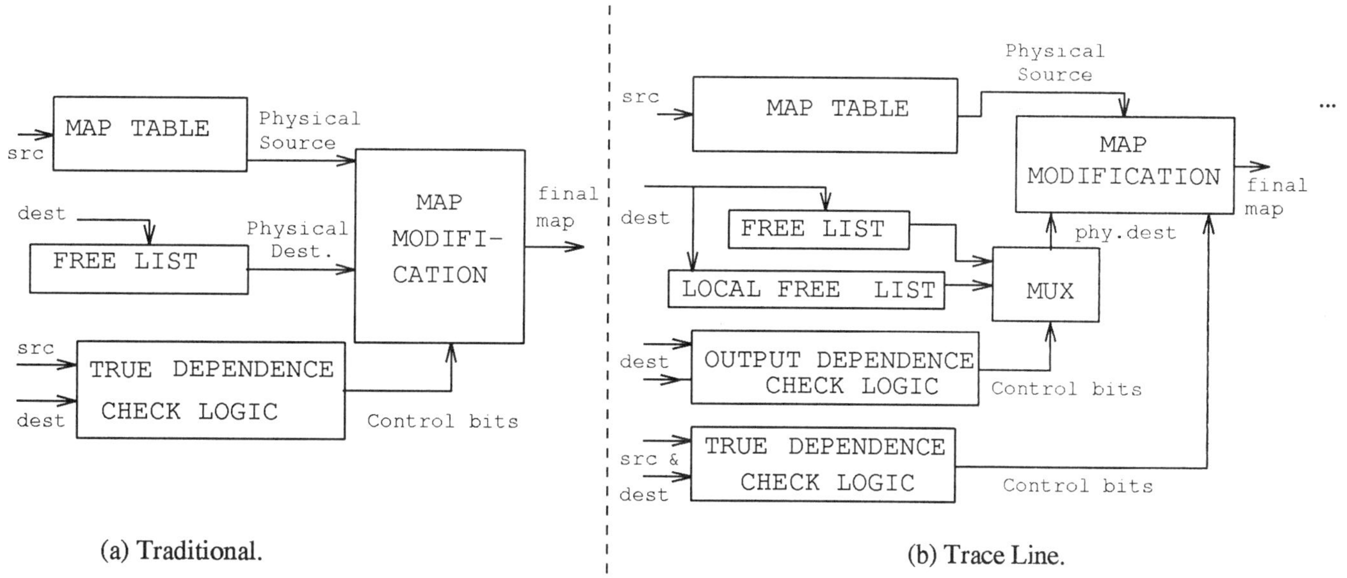

(a) Traditional. (b) Trace Line.

Figure 4. Register Renaming.

Assuming register rename bandwidth is 4 instructions per cycle, a 16-instruction trace line would ordinarily be renamed and dispatched as four 4-instruction chunks, one chunk per cycle. However, in order to rename registers into local and global physical files, all the chunks are buffered at the rename stage's output until the last chunk is renamed, and the entire trace line is dispatched at the end of 4 clocks. This is necessary because a register that is live on exit from an earlier chunk of the trace line might be overwritten by a later chunk and thus not be live on exit from the trace line. Identification of the trace line's live-on-exit registers is pipelined, just as the renaming. All previously renamed chunks are output-dependence checked against the chunk currently being renamed, in parallel with intra-chunk dependence checking. A match results in the mapping for the previous chunk being changed in the map modification stage. Checking for inter-chunk dependences thus increases the dependence checking hardware in the rename stage but not the latency. When all four chunks are renamed, the buffer holding the trace line is flushed to the instruction window.

Register renaming of a trace line restricts dispatch bandwidth, and identification of live-on-exit registers makes instruction dispatch bursty. The next section proposes a mechanism for alleviating these problems considerably when trace lines are reused (i.e., when a control path is revisited).

2.3. RENAMED-TRACE CACHE

Register renaming bandwidth is unlikely to keep up with fetch bandwidth for superscalar processors dispatching more than a few instructions per cycle. We avoid full renaming on trace reuse by capturing in the trace cache renamed trace lines, obtained from the output of the register rename stage, rather than raw instructions. Figure 5 shows a typical entry in the trace cache. Additional bits are used with each trace line to record the live-on-entry and live-on-exit registers for the line. Each line also holds the instructions in decoded form, thus allowing the instruction decode stage to be skipped on a renamed-trace cache hit. Only the live-on-entry and live-on-exit registers for a reused line need to be remapped, allowing the line to go through a lower-bandwidth renaming stage in a single cycle. Each identifier in the "live-on-entry" tag of the trace line looks up the map table to pick up the current mapping. Each identifier in the "live-on-exit" tag of the trace line picks up a new physical register from the free list. Subsequently, operand specifiers that have the global bit set copy the new mappings in parallel (Figure 6), except for live-on-entry source operands which use old mappings. Operands marked as "local" use the previously recorded mappings. We observe that dependence checking logic is eliminated. A trace line appears to the rename stage as a single CISC instruction with multiple sources and multiple destinations, and only a mapping from architectural to physical registers is required.

The rename stage latency is determined by the number of operands looking up the map table and possibly by the number of operands querying the free list. The copying of the mappings into the instructions is similar to the map modification stage (Figure 4) of traditional renaming. Table 3 indicates that typically less than 6 map table lookups are involved per trace line of 16 instructions; table 2 indicates about 6 free list queries correspondingly. This demand is less than that for renaming 4

Benchmark	Trace-Line Size (Instructions)				
	8	16	24	32	64
cc1	3.79	5.19	5.99	6.55	7.83
comp	4.95	6.80	7.90	8.62	10.21
eqntott	3.43	4.10	4.38	4.65	5.54
esp	4.14	5.68	6.90	7.72	8.39
xlisp	3.65	4.81	5.47	5.89	6.86

Table 3. The average number of unique Live-On-Entry source registers for different trace line sizes.

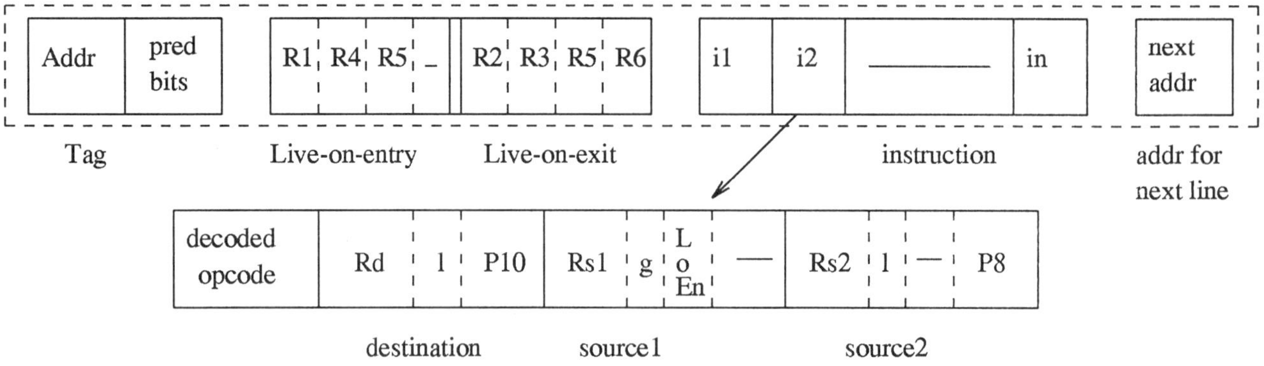

Figure 5. A block in the Renamed-Trace Cache. Live-on-entry and live-on-exit registers have to be renamed before use.

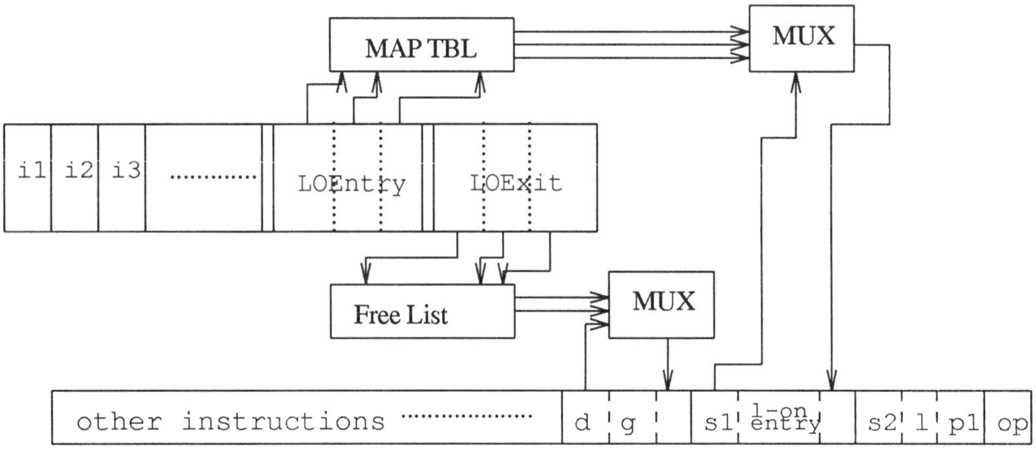

Figure 6. Single-Cycle Renaming of a Trace Line from the Renamed-Trace Cache. Source S1 and the destination for the depicted instruction pick up new mappings, but source S2 is local and uses the recorded mapping P1.

instructions simultaneously and thus can be accomplished in one cycle.

2.4. BRANCH PREDICTION BANDWIDTH

Several extensions to two-level adaptive branch predictors have been proposed to allow the prediction of more than one branch per cycle, an essential requisite for high instruction-fetch bandwidth. We adapt the 2-level adaptive block predictor [Fra95a] for the proposed architecture to obtain multiple predictions quickly. A trace line fetched from the trace cache provides the address of the next trace line in dynamic program order. The global history table corresponding to the next address indexes into a pattern history table, which provides the prediction bits to be tagged on to the next address prior to looking up the trace cache in the next cycle. Each entry in the pattern history table is a simple fixed-size bit pattern holding prediction bits, plus a mask indicating the number of valid prediction bits. The trace cache is indexed using the trace line address tagged with the prediction bits (masked to the correct size). Since the trace cache provides the next address for each trace line, the pattern history table can be enhanced to provide an alternate address usable when a prediction bit returned by the table resolves as incorrect. This can help speedup recovery from mispredictions.

2.5. PREVIOUS WORK

Decoupled access-execute architectures and their variants (for example, [Smi84a, IBM90a]) partition the instruction window into an integer queue, a floating-point queue, and in some cases a branch queue. This reduces result forwarding across the three queues as well as speeds up instruction selection since each queue has an independent set of functional units. However, some data forwarding and dependence checking is often still needed between the queues, complicating and slowing down the issue logic[Wei95a]. The register file is naturally partitioned into an integer file and a floating-point file, thus speeding up register access potentially by a factor of two. Tomasulo's algorithm [Tom67a] physically partitions the instruction window, by associating reservation stations with functional units. This speeds up instruction selection since only the reservation stations associated with a functional unit have to be checked for ready instructions. However, results still have to be forwarded to the entire instruction window.

Dependence-based architectures[Pal96a], being proposed simultaneously and independently, come closest to the trace window approach. Here the large instruction window is partitioned into multiple queues, each queue holding a chain of dependent instructions rather than a trace line. Instruction dispatch logic steers each instruction to the window partition holding its dependence-ancestors. The key differences of the dependence-based architecture are (i) the register file is not separated into local and global files, and (ii) register renaming information is not reused, thus having the same instruction dispatch rate as traditional superscalar processors. The Multiscalar architecture[Fra92b, Fra93a] takes a different approach to window partitioning and achieving large windows. Here code segments identified at compile-time are executed in parallel on multiple PEs organized as a circular chain. The program's instruction window consists of the combined instruction windows of all the PEs. Finding appropriate static program chunks, and load balancing across the PEs are some of the issues that arise in this approach.

Instruction caches that hold decoded instructions have been proposed in a variety of contexts (for example, [Dit82a, Hwu87a, Mel88a, Pat85a, Pat85b]). Static, compile-time partial renaming of individual basic blocks has been proposed in [Spr94a]. The scheme proposed in this paper records and reuses dynamic renaming done across a set of basic blocks. Recording and reuse of dynamic renaming has been proposed in the context of renaming the micro-operations of a CISC instruction[Smo95a]. The register file is partitioned into one for use across the CISC instructions and one for use by micro-operations (from multiple CISC instructions), in the context of speeding up CISC instruction decoding. The renaming mechanism requires a fairly large (for example, 512 registers) micro-operations register file. Recording of dynamic instruction issue order to achieve VLIW-like issue has been proposed in [Fra94a].

3. PERFORMANCE OF TRACE WINDOW

We evaluate the performance of the proposed trace window via trace-driven simulations with appropriate timing assumptions for the various instruction window operations. We first describe the experimental setup and then present results.

3.1. EXPERIMENTAL SETUP

Benchmarks

We use the Spec92 Integer benchmarks to capture the behavior of programs with relatively unpredictable control flow. We simulate the first 100 million instructions from each trace, except for compress which executed only 73 million instructions. (The benchmark sc is not simulated due to a problem with generating traces on our platform). The benchmarks were compiled for an IBM RS/6000 using the IBM XLC compiler, version 3.1, running under the AIX operating system version 4.1. The standard optimization flags distributed in the SPEC suite makefiles (-O2) were used. We note that not using any optimization flags would have biased the study in favor of the trace window. Lack of appropriate optimization settings considerably restricts register allocation, producing code that frequently stores and reloads variables that could have continued to reside in registers. This would have resulted in a spuriously higher proportion of local registers.

Machine Models

We simulate the performance of a representative Trace Window model (TW) and compare it primarily with that of (i) a superscalar model (SUPER) and (ii) a trace window model with ideal instruction fetch (IF). We further study the effect of the renamed-trace cache by simulating a trace window model without the renamed-trace cache (TW-NoRTC). We also consider an impossibly good superscalar model, 8SUPER. To better understand the potential for performance benefits, we consider a TW model with oracle branch prediction (TW-Oracle) and a TW model with a more restrictive trace cache (TW-LockupCache). We first mention the common machine parameters used across the models, and then describe the individual models.

All models use a trace cache of 256 lines and a perfect instruction cache. To remove the effects of limited resources on instruction window size and thus highlight the impact of pipeline latencies, we assume an unlimited number of functional units and memory ports. A 64KB 4-way set associative data cache is simulated (by interfacing Dinero [Hil84a] to our simulator) for all benchmarks except Espresso which used a 16KB cache. (The working set size of Espresso is known [Bur96a] to be significantly smaller). The functional unit and cache latencies assumed are shown in Table 4. A 2-level adaptive GAg(18)[Yeh93b] branch predictor with adequate prediction bandwidth is simulated rather than the block-level predictor based scheme described in section 2.4. The block-level predictor is known to be as accurate[Fra95a] as the GAg predictor. We assume perfect memory disambiguation in all models.

The TW model assumes 16 trace lines of length 16 instructions each, resulting in an instruction window of 256 instructions. No limit is imposed on the number of branches in a trace line. A renamed-trace cache is assumed; no limit is imposed on the number of live-on-entry/live-on-exit registers that can be remembered in a renamed trace line[3] (Figure 5). For renamed-trace cache misses, instructions are fetched from the instruction cache, renamed, and dispatched at the rate of 4 per

Function Unit	Latency (cycles)	Function Unit	Latency (cycles)
Load (Cache hit)	2	Load (Cache miss)	12
Conditional Branch	1	Uncnd. Branch.	1
Logic	1	FP Add	3
Integer Add	1	FP Mult	4
Integer Mult	4	FP Div	8
Integer Div	8		

Table 4. Functional Unit and Data Cache Latencies. The floating point functional units are rarely exercised by the benchmarks.

[3] This can be implemented by using a 1-bit mask per architectural register in the trace cache for live-on-entry information and another 1-bit mask for live-on-exit information. If the alternate implementation of explicitly storing a limited number of register identifiers is used, trace line building can be terminated when a trace line's live-on-entry/live-on-exit registers exceed the limit. The former implementation is preferable.

cycle into the corresponding trace line in the window. For renamed-trace cache hits trace lines can be dispatched to the window at the rate of one per cycle. The renamed-trace cache is implemented as an unlimited lockup-free cache, as described shortly. An instruction can start execution no earlier than the clock cycle subsequent to its entry into the window. A maximum of 2 instructions can be issued per cycle (out of order) from each trace line, resulting in a total peak issue bandwidth of 32 instructions. (The issue bandwidth is kept higher than the fetch bandwidth to allow for bursty parallelism.) Results can be bypassed between instructions from the same trace line. Instructions that write global registers spend an additional clock in the Write Back (WB) stage before dependent instructions from a different trace line can be issued. This implies bypassing from the write ports to the read ports of the global register file. We assume sufficient result buses and write ports. Upon resolution of a mispredicted branch, instruction fetch from the correct path can be initiated in the subsequent cycle.

Unlimited lockup-free operation during trace misses is supported by separating the renamed-trace cache into a trace cache storing raw trace lines (plus rename information associated with individual instructions) and a smaller, higher-associativity rename cache holding critical rename information, specifically the identities of the live-on-entry and live-on-exit registers of the trace line as well as the next address field (Figure 2). The lines in the rename cache have to always be a superset of the raw trace cache. A trace line miss in the raw trace cache miss could still be a hit in the rename cache, allowing register renaming for the missing trace line to be done even before it is fetched from the instruction cache. This allows subsequent renamed-trace cache lookups while the previous miss is being satisfied over 4 clock cycles (i.e. lockup-free operation). Assuming each renamed-trace line holds 5-bit identities of 6 live-on-entry and 6 live-on-exit registers (Tables 2 and 3) and a 12-bit next-address offset, each rename cache line is 9 bytes long compared to the corresponding trace cache line size of at least 112 bytes (4 bytes of raw instruction plus 3 bytes of local rename information associated with the instruction, for 16 instructions in the trace line). Thus the rename cache can be much smaller and of much higher associativity to provide better hit rates. We model a sufficiently large fully-associative rename cache that has only compulsory misses. The fraction of unique trace lines referenced by a program is usually less than 0.1%[Mit97a], thus keeping the required rename cache size small.

The IF model assumes 100% hit rate in the trace cache and 100% branch prediction accuracy to study the performance of the TW model under ideal instruction fetch conditions. This represents an upper bound on the performance of TW.

The TW-NoRTC model assumes that the trace cache does not record renaming and decoding information. Thus all instructions have to be renamed before dispatch, reducing the effective dispatch bandwidth to 4 instructions per cycle (the rename bandwidth). This also increases the branch misprediction penalty since in the TW model the correct path might be present in the renamed-trace cache and thus dispatched at the rate of 16 instructions per cycle. TW-NoRTC uses the same assumptions as the TW model otherwise, thus serving to isolate the benefits of the renamed-trace cache.

The SUPER model simulates a traditional superscalar processor. The improvement shown by the TW model over SUPER represents the performance benefits of the proposed architecture over traditional approaches. The cost of traditionally organizing a large window is captured by assuming that no bypassing is possible, thus incurring a 1-clock penalty of the write-back stage for dependencies. An instruction dependent on a single-cycle operation can thus start execution only 1 clock after the latter starts execution and not on the immediately subsequent cycle. We note that this assumption is optimistic, as result forwarding to a large instruction window is unlikely to be possible in a single-cycle write-back stage. We assume that any 32 instructions can be issued from the window each cycle, as opposed to the restrictions in the trace window models. In addition, we simulate an impossibly good superscalar model, 8SUPER, that has twice the register renaming bandwidth of SUPER and TW-NoRTC but is similar to SUPER otherwise.

We consider two additional machine models to better understand the performance of TW. The TW-Oracle model assumes perfect branch prediction. This model represents the improvements possible to TW by better branch handling; the difference between IF and TW-Oracle lies in the trace cache. The TW-LockupCache model differs from the TW model in that the renamed-trace cache does not support lockup-free operations. A trace-cache miss in the TW-LockupCache model results in a 5-cycle dispatch penalty (refer Figure 2).

3.2. RESULTS

Table 5 shows the instruction level parallelism sustained in the different primary machine models. The first observation is that significant speedups are provided by the TW model over the TW_NoRTC model and the SUPER superscalar model. (All speedups are with respect to the TW-NoRTC model rather than the SUPER model since the former is a more realistic machine model.) This indicates that the additional dispatch bandwidth made possible by the renamed-trace cache increases the effective instruction window available for finding independent instructions. While the speedup is significant for all benchmarks, speedups for eqntott and compress are relatively limited due to the dominating effects of branch mispredictions and cache misses. Mispredictions reduce the dispatch bandwidth by wasting cycles on the wrong control path. Data cache misses increase the lifetime of dependent instructions in the instruction window, thus reducing the effective window size. Table 6 shows that compress has the worst prediction accuracy, trace cache miss rate, and data cache miss rate of the five benchmarks, while eqntott has a significantly poorer data cache miss rate than the other three benchmarks. Further, the average lifetime of a mispredicted branch is the highest for these two benchmarks.

The significant gap between the IF model and the TW model shows the scope for improving performance through a better trace cache and through reducing the branch misprediction penalty (given the fairly high prediction accuracies). Several possible avenues for increasing the trace cache hit rate have been outlined by the trace cache proposers[Rot96a]. Compress accesses relatively few unique dynamic trace lines. We suspect pathological conflicts in the trace cache for those trace lines; this might be alleviated for example by using some of the prediction bits of the address to index the trace cache.

The branch misprediction penalty includes the delay in branch scheduling after dispatch, and the refill time from the correct path after branch resolution. The former is dependent on early scheduling of instructions that compute the condition register tested by the branch. Table 6 shows that the average lifetime (after dispatch) of a mispredicted branch is quite high for many of the bennchmarks. The hardware scheduling

Machine	IF (Peak ILP 16)		TW (Peak ILP 16)		TW-NoRTC (Peak ILP 4)		SUPER (Peak ILP 4)		8SUPER (Peak ILP 8)	
	ILP	Speedup	ILP	Speedup	ILP	Speedup	ILP	Speedup	ILP	
cc1	10.80	(5.40)	4.40	(2.20)	2.00	(1.0)	2.20	(1.10)	3.01	(1.51)
compress	7.93	(4.99)	2.25	(1.42)	1.59	(1.0)	1.78	(1.12)	2.17	(1.37)
eqntott	11.31	(5.36)	3.65	(1.73)	2.11	(1.0)	2.39	(1.13)	3.35	(1.59)
espresso	14.96	(6.31)	7.42	(3.13)	2.37	(1.0)	2.53	(1.07)	3.66	(1.54)
xlisp	11.91	(5.13)	6.17	(2.66)	2.32	(1.0)	2.44	(1.05)	3.54	(1.53)

Table 5. Performance of the various Machine Models. The sustained instructions/cycle and the speedup over a Trace Window model with no Renamed-Trace Cache and limited result bypassing (TW-NoRTC) are shown. The SUPER model has less restricted instruction issue than the TW-NORTC model, and the 8SUPER model has twice the rename bandwidth of SUPER and TW-NORTC. IF models perfect instruction fetch. The significant performance benefits of the TW model over TW-NoRTC and SUPER show the effectiveness of the proposed mechanisms.

Bench-mark	Branch Mispred. Rate (%)	Trace-Cache Miss Rate (%)	Data-Cache Miss Rate (%)	Avg. Mispred. Lifetime (Cycles)
cc1	6.00	55.06	0.51	7.9
compress	9.39	56.0	12.00	19.6
eqntott	3.53	21.87	4.24	14.2
espresso	2.43	46.87	0.51	6.8
xlisp	3.18	32.31	0.01	12.1

Table 6. Factors contributing to the lowering of effective instruction fetch bandwidth. Trace-cache miss rates model interference from fetching the wrong control path (all branches along the wrong path are modeled as predicted not taken). The average lifetime of a mispredicted branch indicates the large cost (in fetch/dispatch cycles) of the relatively few mispredictions.

considered in this paper does not give higher scheduling priority to branch deciding instructions.

The SUPER model performs 7% to 13% better than the TW-NoRTC model despite lack of bypassing. This can be attributed to the ability of SUPER to select any 32 instructions from the window for issue in a clock cycle. Experiments show that the additional penalty incurred due to lack of bypassing does not significantly affect SUPER's performance[Mit97a]. The impossibly good superscalar model 8SUPER performs almost as well as the TW model for compress and eqntott (which have orthogonal factors limiting performance), but performs well below TW for the other three programs.

Table 7 further investigates the performance of the TW model. The TW-Oracle model performs considerably better than the TW model due to perfect branch prediction; in fact it attains a very large fraction of the benefits of perfect instruction fetch (the IF model). This suggests that the relatively poor miss rates of the trace cache are overshadowed by the much longer branch misprediction lifetimes of the benchmarks. This is particularly so since the TW model assumes a perfect lockup-free trace cache and thus reduces the penalty on a trace cache miss. The results for the TW-LockupCache bear this out; the penalty for a trace cache miss is 5 clock cycles in this model. The performance drop due to the lack of the lockup-free feature supported by a lockup-free cache is as dramatic as the performance improvement of TW-Oracle due to removal of long-lifetime branch mispredictions. In fact, we had incorporated the lockup-free cache in our first simulations of the TW model, prior to simulating the TW-LockupCache model, and were surprised to discover its beneficial role. Experiments show that the lockup-free feature provides most of the benefits of a perfect (100% hitrate) trace cache for a machine with realistic branch prediction (i.e. for the TW model)[Mit97a]. Both these results point to the enormous cost of each stall cycle in a highly parallel processor organization.

Overall, the results demonstrate the benefits of the improved dispatch bandwidth provided by the proposed trace window schemes. This increase in dispatch bandwidth increases the costs associated with other sources of pipeline bubbles, such as branch mispredictions and cache misses, pointing to the importance of reducing those costs.

4. DYNAMIC VECTORIZATION

Vector instructions [Rus78a] save instruction fetch bandwidth and reduce demands on instruction window size by fetching a loop body just once and issuing multiple iterations using fairly simple issue logic. Vectorization also allows subsequent sequential code to be fetched and executed in parallel with the loop's execution. Vector instructions provide several other performance improvements which we do not elaborate. In this section, we briefly outline a hardware mechanism for vectorizing dynamic loops that fit into a single trace line of the trace window. A detailed description is not presented in this paper due to space constraints. The fraction of dynamic instructions vectorized by the mechanism is subsequently presented. A more detailed performance evaluation of dynamic vectorization is in progress.

The vectorization mechanism relies on status bits and tags associated with each trace line in the trace window. The default settings of the status bits and tags correspond to normal operation of the trace window, without the vectorization capability.

Machine	TW-Oracle (Peak ILP 16)		TW (Peak ILP 16)		TW-LockupCache (Peak ILP 16)	
	ILP	Speedup	ILP	Speedup	ILP	Speedup
cc1	9.74	(2.21)	4.40	(1.00)	2.58	(0.59)
compress	7.52	(3.34)	2.25	(1.00)	1.98	(0.88)
eqntott	10.44	(2.86)	3.65	(1.00)	2.88	(0.79)
espresso	13.97	(1.88)	7.42	(1.00)	3.72	(0.50)
xlisp	11.12	(1.80)	6.17	(1.00)	3.50	(0.57)

Table 7. Performance of the two variants of the TW machine model. The TW-Oracle model assumes perfect branch prediction. The TW-LockupCache model assumes that the renamed-trace cache does not support lockup-free operation, thus increasing the effective penalty of trace misses.

Benchmark	Fraction of Insts. Vectorized	Avg. Loop Size (Dyn. Insts.)	Loop Limit		
			(Avg.)	(Median)	(Max)
cc1	18.15%	15.12	9.75	4	1031
compress	33.38%	32.95	4.46	3	4311
eqntott	61.73%	7.11	12.38	10	2131
espresso	61.30%	14.29	6.69	3	1075
xlisp	6.20%	8.32	2.81	2	999

Table 8. Dynamic Vectorization. The fraction of dynamic instructions vectorized by the proposed hardware mechanism.

4.1. TRACE LINE VECTORIZATION

Vectorization depends on the detection of a trace line that ends in a (predicted) taken backward branch to (the beginning of) itself. To facilitate this, the occurrence of a (predicted) taken backward branch terminates the current trace line, the target of the backward branch thus starting a new trace line. Each trace line in the trace window is tagged with its address and the address of its immediate predecessor in the trace dispatch order. During trace fetch, the trace window is looked up in parallel with the trace cache to determine whether the current fetch address corresponds to the start of a dynamic loop. A hit occurs if a trace line's address *and* its predecessor tag match the current fetch address. The match of the predecessor tag is necessary to ensure correct renamed-register semantics, not discussed here due to space constraints. On a hit, a copy of the corresponding trace line is sent to the register rename stage, instead of the copy from the trace cache.

A trace line received from the trace window is renamed and dispatched to the trace window with its VECTOR status bit set, indicating to the issue logic that multiple iterations of each instruction in the trace line have to be issued. Thus the entire loop has now been dispatched in a single cycle after loop detection. On subsequent clocks, instruction fetch proceeds down the fall-through path[4] of the loop-terminating backward branch. A DISPATCH COUNTER, initialized to a maximum value, is associated with a vectorized trace line to indicate the number of loop iterations. An ISSUE COUNTER associated with each instruction indicates the number of iterations issued for that instruction. A branch instance that is resolved as mispredicted determines loop termination for the trace line. The DISPATCH COUNTER for the trace is then set to the ISSUE COUNTER of the mispredicted branch. Already issued instances beyond the loop limit are squashed; instructions and results are tagged with their ISSUE COUNTER until committed to machine state to facilitate such squashing.

We observe that different instances of a vectorized instruction refer to the same physical register identifiers. Correctness is maintained by dynamically associating queues with each operand. A queue map table, queried for each instance of a vectorized instruction, maps operands to a hardware pool of queues. When a vectorized instruction finishes execution, the corresponding queue is freed, and its tail entry is copied to the global register file.

Architectural registers that are live-on-entry and those that are modified by the vectorized trace are handled specially to insure correctness. The live-on-exit physical registers are marked busy on vector trace dispatch, and are freed only when the corresponding vector instruction's last iteration completes. Registers that are both live-on-entry and live-on-exit from a vectorized trace indicate recurrences and are appropriately handled.

Once a trace line is vectorized, most of the associated instruction issue and queue operations involved are similar to those in vector machines[Rus78a]. In this subsection we have

[4] The fall-through address for the trace-line terminating branch can be stored with the trace line in the trace cache, or in the branch predictor as the predicted fall-through address.

restricted ourselves to outlining the detection of a vectorizable trace line due to space limitations.

4.2. FRACTION OF INSTRUCTIONS VECTORIZED

We have enhanced the TW machine model to simulate the dynamic vectorization scheme. In this paper, we limit performance studies to determining the fraction of program instructions vectorized by the mechanism. The results reported in Table 8 are collected assuming unlimited size trace lines. The first observation is that a significant fraction of the dynamic instructions are captured in vector mode for all benchmarks except xlisp. For eqntott and espresso, the fraction is more than 60%. Next, the average loop limit (vector length) is fairly short, and about half the loop visits (the median loop limit) have vector lengths of 4 or less, except for eqntott with a median of 10 iterations. The maximum loop limit encountered is much larger. We draw the following conclusions. Phases of the programs around the loops with maximum loop limit will benefit from the vectorization scheme. Second, the trace cache can record the vectorized version of each trace line just as it records renaming information, and thus can reduce any vector detection overheads for repeated visits to short loops. Third, some loops (for example, the main loop in compress) repeatedly execute just two control paths within a loop a large number of times. This encourages the exploration of simple enhancements to the vectorization mechanism for capturing such loops.

4.3. PREVIOUS WORK

The CONDEL architecture[Uht92a] proposed by Uht captures a single copy of complex loops in a static instruction window. It uses state bits per iteration to determine the control paths taken by the loop and to correctly enforce dependencies. Two key differences exist between the CONDEL approach and dynamic vectorization. CONDEL captures the entire static loop body, which may not be possible if the loop body exceeds the implemented window size. We find several loops have large static body but much smaller dynamic size. Second, the CONDEL architecture does not fetch instructions from beyond the loop during loop execution. The dynamic vectorization scheme overlaps post-loop code's execution with the loop.

5. CONCLUSIONS

We have proposed a set of mechanisms to alleviate the problems caused by large instruction windows and limited register rename bandwidth in superscalar processors with large instruction fetch bandwidths. The mechanisms include partitioning of the instruction window, corresponding partitioning of the register file, and reuse of rename information to improve effective dispatch bandwidth. We find a resulting performance improvement between 1.5 to 3 times over a traditional superscalar processor for the SpecInt92 benchmarks.

Second, we observe that several loops in ordinary programs exhibit vector- like behavior at runtime. We outlined a hardware mechanism for detecting vector behavior and executing loops in vector mode. A significant fraction of the dynamic instructions are vectorized by the mechanism, up to 60% for two benchmarks. This encourages further investigation of dynamic vectorization even though the average and median loop limits (vector length) are small.

Overall our results show that capturing and exploiting dynamic behavior can considerably improve the performance of ordinary programs on superscalar processors. Further, our results also indicate that improved instruction dispatch mechanisms increase the penalties associated with disruptions to pipeline flow such as branch mispredictions, data cache misses, and instruction/trace cache misses. With improved instruction fetch and dispatch bandwidth and increasing speculation levels, we expect attention to shift from reducing the frequency of these disruptions to techniques for reducing the cost of disruptions. Previously considered techniques include prefetching for caches and fetching along multiple paths for control predictions. Squashing only control-dependent and (indirectly) data-dependent instructions on a misprediction is another previously identified direction for reducing misprediction penalty.

Acknowledgements

We thank Ravi Nair for the IBM RS6000 tracing tool. The first author would like to thank Jim Smith for his feedback on early versions of the dynamic vectorization idea.

REFERENCES

[Aus92a]
T. M. Austin and G. S. Sohi, "Dynamic Dependency Analysis of Ordinary Programs," in *The 19th Annual International Symposium on Computer Architecture*, Gold Coast, Australia, May 1992.

[Bur96a]
D. Burger, J. R. Goodman, and A. Kagi, "Quantifying Memory Bandwidth Limitations of Current and Future Microprocessors," *23rd Int'l Symposium on Computer Architecture*, 1996.

[Con95a]
T. Conte, K. N. Menezes, P. M. Mills, and B. Patel, "Optimization of Instruction Fetch Mechanisms for High Issue Rates," *22nd Annual Int'l Symposium on Computer Architecture*, June 1995.

[Dit82a]
D. R. Ditzel and H. R. McLellan, "Register Allocation for Free: the C Machine Stack Cache," *Proc. Int. Symp. on Arch. Support for Prog. Lang. and Operating Sys.*, March 1982.

[Fra92a]
M. Franklin and G. S. Sohi, "Register Traffic Analysis for Streamlining Inter-Operation Communication in Fine-Grain Parallel Processors," *25th Annual Symposium on Microarchitecture*, Dec. 1992.

[Fra92b]
M. Franklin and G. S. Sohi, "The Expandable Split Window Architecture for Exploiting Fine-Grain Parallelism," in *The 19th Annual International Symposium on Computer Architecture*, Gold Coast, Australia, May 1992.

[Fra93a]
M. Franklin, "The Multiscalar Architecture," *Ph.D. Thesis, University of Wisconsin-Madison*, 1993.

[Fra94a]
M. Franklin and M. Smotherman, ''A Fill-Unit Approach to Multiple Instruction Issue,'' *27th Int'l Symposium on Microarchitecture*, Dec. 1994.

[Fra95a]
M. Franklin and S. Dutta, ''Control Flow Prediction with Tree-Like Subgraphs for Superscalar Processors,'' *28th Annual Symposium on Microarchitecture*, Nov. 1995.

[Hao96a]
E. Hao, P-Y. Chang, M. Evers, and Y. Patt, ''Increasing the Instruction Fetch Rate via Block-Structured Instruction Set Architectures,'' *29th Annual Int'l Symposium on Microarchitecture (to appear)*, Dec. 1996.

[Hil84a]
M. D. Hill and A. J. Smith, ''Experimental Evaluation of On-Chip Microprocessor Cache Memories,'' *Proc. 11th Annual Symposium on Computer Architecture*, June 1984.

[Hwu87a]
W. W. Hwu and Y. N. Patt, ''Design Choices for the HPSm Microprocessor Chip,'' in *Proc. 20th Annual Hawaii International Conference on System Sciences*, Kona, HI, January 1987.

[IBM90a]
IBM, ''Special Issue on the IBM RISC System/6000 Processor,'' *IBM Journal of Research and Development*, January 1990.

[Lam92a]
M. S. Lam and R. P. Wilson, ''Limits of Control Flow on Parallelism,'' *Proc. International Symposium on Computer Architecture*, May 1992.

[Mel88a]
S. W. Melvin, M. C. Shebanow, and Y. N. Patt, ''Hardware Support for Large Atomic Units in Dynamically Scheduled Machines,'' in *Proc. 21st Annual Workshop on Microprogramming and Microarchitecture*, San Diego, CA, November 1988.

[Mit97a]
Tulika Mitra, ''Performance Evaluation of Improved Superscalar Issue Mechanisms,'' in *M.E. Project Report*, Dept. of Computer Science, Indian Institute of Science, January 1997.

[Pal96a]
S. Palacharla, N. Jouppi, and J. E. Smith, ''Quantifying the Complexity of Superscalar Processors,'' *Univ. of Wisconsin-Madison Technical Report*, vol. CS-TR-96-1328, November 1996, (Available at http://www.cs.wisc.edu/trs.html; a version to appear in ISCA'97).

[Pat85a]
Y. N. Patt, W. W. Hwu, and M. Shebanow, ''HPS, A New Microarchitecture: Rationale and Introduction,'' in *Proc. 18th Annual Workshop on Microprogramming*, Pacific Grove, CA, December 1985.

[Pat85b]
Y. N. Patt, S. W. Melvin, W. W. Hwu, and M. Shebanow, ''Critical Issues Regarding HPS, A High Performance Microarchitecture,'' in *Proc. 18th Annual Workshop on Microprogramming*, Pacific Grove, CA, December 1985.

[Rot96a]
E. Rotenberg, S. Bennett, and J. E. Smith, ''Trace Cache: A Low Latency Approach to High Bandwidth Instruction Fetching,'' in *29th Annual Int'l Symposium on Microarchitecture*, Paris, Dec. 1996.

[Rus78a]
R. M. Russel, ''The Cray-1 Computer System,'' *Communications of the ACM*, vol. 21, pp. 63-72, Jan. 1978.

[Smi84a]
J. E. Smith, ''Decoupled Access/Execute Architectures,'' *ACM Transactions on Computer Systems*, Nov. 1984.

[Smo95a]
M. Smotherman and M. Franklin, ''Improving CISC Instruction Decoding Performance Using a Fill Unit,'' *28th Annual Symposium on Microarchtecture*, Dec. 1995.

[Spr94a]
E. Sprangler and Y. N. Patt, ''Facilitating Superscalar Processing via a Combined Static/Dynamic Register Renaming Scheme,'' *27th Annual Int'l Symposium on Microarchitecture*, Dec.1994.

[Tom67a]
R. M. Tomasulo, ''An Efficient Algorithm for Exploiting Multiple Arithmetic Units,'' *IBM Journal of Research and Development*, January 1967.

[Uht92a]
A. K. Uht, ''Concurrency Extraction via Hardware Methods Executing the Static Instruction Stream,'' *IEEE Transactions on Computers*, vol. 41, July 1992.

[Wal91a]
D. Wall, ''Limits of Instruction Level Parallelism,'' *4th International Conf. on Arch.Support for Prog.Langs. and Op.Sys.*, April 1991.

[Wei95a]
Shlomo Weiss, ''Implementing Register Interlocks in Parallel-Pipeline, Multiple Instruction Queue, Superscalalr Processoors,'' *Proc. First Int'l Symposium on High Performance Computer Architecture*, 1995.

[Yeh93b]
T-Y. Yeh and Y. N. Patt, ''A Comparison of Dynamic Branch Predictors that use Two Levels of Branch History,'' *20th Int'l Symposium on Computer Architecture*, 1993.

[Yeh93a]
T-Y. Yeh, D. MArr, and Y. Patt, ''Increasing the Instruction Fetch Rate via Multiple Branch Prediction and a Branch Address Cache,'' *Proc. 7th ACM Int'l Conference on Supercomputing*, July 1993.

Exploiting Instruction Level Parallelism in Processors by Caching Scheduled Groups

Ravi Nair and Martin E. Hopkins
IBM Thomas J. Watson Research Center
P. O. Box 218, Yorktown Heights, NY 10598.

Abstract

Modern processors employ a large amount of hardware to dynamically detect parallelism in single-threaded programs and maintain the sequential semantics implied by these programs. The complexity of some of this hardware diminishes the gains due to parallelism because of longer clock period or increased pipeline latency of the machine.

In this paper we propose a processor implementation which dynamically schedules groups of instructions while executing them on a fast simple engine and caches them for repeated execution on a fast VLIW-type engine. Our experiments show that scheduling groups spanning several basic blocks and caching these scheduled groups results in significant performance gain over fill buffer approaches for a standard VLIW cache.

This concept, which we call DIF (Dynamic Instruction Formatting), unifies and extends principles underlying several schemes being proposed today to reduce superscalar processor complexity. This paper examines various issues in designing such a processor and presents results of experiments using trace-driven simulation of SPECint95 benchmark programs.

1: Introduction

The tremendous advance in the performance of microprocessors in recent years is due largely to improved lithography and circuit techniques. However, a significant role is also being played by the organization and exploitation of functional units in modern processors. Compared to the early microprocessors, modern superscalar processors [1] attempt to dispatch and retire multiple instructions every cycle in a sustained manner. In order to do this they provide multiple functional units along with hardware to keep these units busy. They provide larger sets of registers than that required by the instruction set architecture and use dynamic renaming to exploit these larger register files. They allow instructions to execute out-of-order, but provide mechanism to give the appearance of in-order completion to the program. Additionally, modern superscalar processors speculate on the path taken by the program, for example by predicting the targets of conditional branches.

Most of the code executed by modern superscalar processors is non-vector code, sometimes referred to as unstructured code. There is parallelism to be exploited from such code as studies [2] have shown. However, a large moving window of instructions is needed to extract this parallelism; resource limitations and the inability to predict the path with full accuracy result in the machine achieving only a fraction of the available parallelism.

It is becoming evident that the complexity of superscalar processors is increasing disproportionately with the scale of techniques mentioned in the opening paragraph. Tremendous strain is placed on the design, verification, and manufacture of these processors. This complexity also invariably causes the clock frequency of these processors to be lower than that of processors which use such techniques sparingly. This reduction in clock frequency diminishes some of the performance gained through parallelism.

Very Long Instruction Word (VLIW) architectures [3] have been proposed as a potential way to attack these problems. These architectures lay the responsibility of detecting instruction-level parallelism on the compiler, thereby virtually eliminating the complex hardware needed in superscalar machines to detect parallelism. The detection and exploitation of this parallelism is aided by new compiler techniques, although at some cost in compilation time and compiled code size. The clock frequency of a VLIW machine is not limited by the complexity of instruction dispatch, register renaming, or out-of-order execution. Thus the proponents of VLIW architectures argue that it should be possible to build processors which not only are far less complex than superscalar processors, but also ones which have a higher clock frequency.

1.1: Dynamic Scheduling -- The DIF concept

The main disadvantage of the pure VLIW concept is that it is not capable of either adjusting to the dynamic variations in program behavior, or of exploiting parallelism across code partitions unavailable at compile time. For example, dynamic shared libraries which form the framework of most commercial programs today, consist of many separately compiled modules. The amount of parallelism that exists in each compiled routine may be only a fraction of the amount of parallelism that can be exploited if the run-time context of the routine were also available. This limitation of the VLIW concept is a principal focus of the microarchi-

ISCA '97 Denver, CO, USA
© 1997 ACM 0-89791-901-7/97/0006...$3.50

tecture proposed in this paper, which we call *Dynamic Instruction Formatting*, or *DIF*.

The DIF machine incorporates a parallel engine, similar to the VLIW, but operating as an additional execution engine or accelerator. The primary engine in a DIF machine is a processor which is simple and less aggressive in exploiting parallelism. Instructions, when first encountered, are executed in this primary engine. Simultaneous with the execution of a code sequence, this engine determines dependences between instructions, and reformats them in a form convenient for direct execution by the parallel engine. The reformatted sequence is placed in a separate cache, the DIF cache, from where the instructions are fetched for parallel execution if they are encountered again. Figure 1 shows a schematic for a machine employing the DIF architecture.

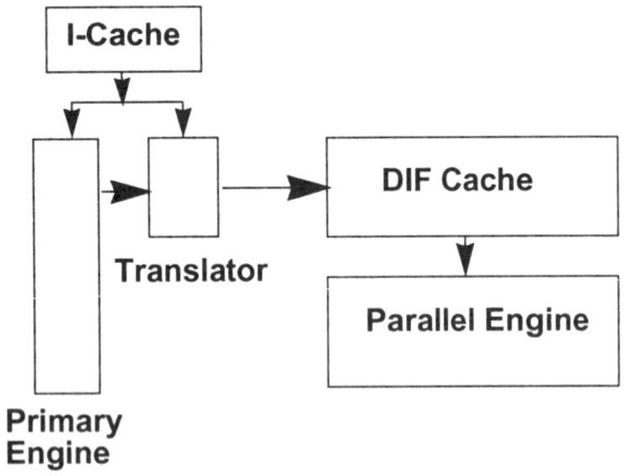

Figure 1: The DIF microarchitecture

The DIF concept, like the concept of a traditional cache, relies on dynamic reuse of code sequences. Such reuse is, in some sense, fundamental to the performance of all modern processors. Branch prediction, which basically attempts to predict the path through a program, relies for its accuracy on such code sequence reuse. Similarly, the performance of VLIW processors is largely dependent on the ability of the compiler to construct a large enough window to reschedule for parallelism. To limit the complexity of compilation and the size of the compiled code, the compiler restricts this scheduling to commonly executed paths determined either through program analysis or through execution profiles. Thus the reliance on code reuse is evident even in this case.

Superscalar processors work hard to determine the dependence between instructions and to dispatch instructions to functional units for each encounter of a sequence of instructions. In this respect, they do not take advantage of code sequence reuse manifest in most application programs. They compensate for this by making the hardware for scheduling sophisticated and fast. The DIF machine, on the other hand, sacrifices the exploitation of parallelism on first invocation of a sequence, expecting to make up the loss by faster execution during repeated invocations. The primary engine is kept simple, for example by superpipelining, while the parallel engine is kept simple by implementing the simple pipeline of a classic VLIW machine.

Compared to the VLIW machine the DIF has two main advantages. First, it separates implementation of the parallel engine from the instruction set architecture. This allows the same binary executable to work on multiple implementations of the parallel engine, each having a different mix of parallel functional units. In fact, it allows existing binaries to work without modification on new DIF implementations. Second, the DIF machine is better able to both exploit dynamic variations in code behavior, and schedule across dynamic subroutine and library boundaries.

1.2: Related studies

The idea of reformatting instructions in hardware and caching them has been proposed by other researchers. Melvin, Shebanow and Patt [4] proposed the concept of a *fill unit* which basically accepts microinstructions generated from instructions in memory and saves them for reuse. They argued that more parallelism can be extracted by making the cached set larger. Execution was always directly from the fill unit. In the DIF machine, formatting occurs only at one unit, but in contrast to the fill unit approach, execution of an instruction may occur either in the primary engine or in the parallel engine (In Section 2.2 we will detail several benefits to be gained from having a separate processor that can execute instructions in order). Further, unlike the fill unit approach, the DIF machine also schedules the code before caching. The pipeline organization of the DIF parallel engine is greatly simplified by eliminating the need to schedule operations after fetching them from the DIF cache.

Rechtschaffen and Ekanadham [5] propose a *self-parallelizing computer system,* which "learns" how to execute an instruction sequence in parallel while executing it the first time. This is cached for possible re-execution in a parallel mode. The target organization for parallel execution in their proposal is a multithreaded processor with threads operating independently in several full-function processors, and with communication between threads occurring through send and receive messages between registers. Unlike this approach, the target for translation in the DIF machine is akin to a VLIW engine. We feel that, for a uniprocessor a single program counter implementation with shared register files greatly simplifies the problem of communication and synchronization between units.

Franklin and Smotherman [6] suggest an implementation of the fill-unit concept for a VLIW target. As in [4], even in the learning mode, they execute instructions only after translating them into VLIW form. An important difference in their approach compared to the DIF approach is that their unit of caching is a single VLIW instruction. Hence they are unable to extract the additional parallelism that could be extracted by having a larger unit for a cache entry as in the DIF machine.

Several other studies, including Yeh, Marr and Patt [7], Johnson [8], Dutta and Franklin [9], and Rotenberg, Bennett and Smith [10] address the problem of caching path information for simplified instruction fetching when code is reused. The DIF machine goes beyond these proposals and actually caches instruction schedules for more efficient parallel execution.

1.3: Organization of this Paper

This paper is organized as follows. In Section 2 we discuss various issues arising in the design of a DIF machine and suggest hardware structures. In Section 3 we describe tools and benchmarks that were used in simulating and evaluating the performance of the DIF concept. The results of our simulation study are presented in Section 4. Finally, in Section 5 we present our conclusions.

2: Hardware Organization of a DIF Machine

There are several issues which need to be examined in designing a DIF machine. In this section we describe the hardware organization of a machine employing such a microarchitecture and explain the design tradeoffs.

2.1: Concept of a Group

In [4], Melvin, Shebanow and Patt suggest that for high performance it is necessary for execution atomic units to be large, because more concurrency can be exploited by issuing a larger amount of work as a single unit. Shown in Figure 2 is a sequence

#	Address	Instruction	
0	117fe8	cmpi	CR0 <- R15,0
1	117fec	stw	R17 -> 120(R31)
2	117ff0	addi	R25 <- R17,0
3	117ff4	ble	CR0,*+508
4	117ff8	lwz	R6 <- 856(R3)
5	117ffc	lwz	R25 <- 1472(R2)
6	118000	addic	R26 <- R6,-48
7	118004	lwzu	R6,R26 <- 48(R26)
8	118008	addi	R4 <- R18,0
9	11800c	lwz	R28 <- 8(R6)
10	118010	lwz	R27 <- 4(R6)
11	11801c	addi	R3 <- R28,0
12	118020	stw	R27 -> 172(R31)
13	118024	bl	*+39008

Figure 2: Section of trace from *gcc*

of PowerPC instructions from a frequently executed piece of code in *gcc*, one of the programs in the SPECint95 benchmark suite. Figure 3 shows a graphical representation of the dependence between instructions in this sequence. Each level in the figure represents instructions which are independent of each other and which could be represented as a single VLIW instruction.

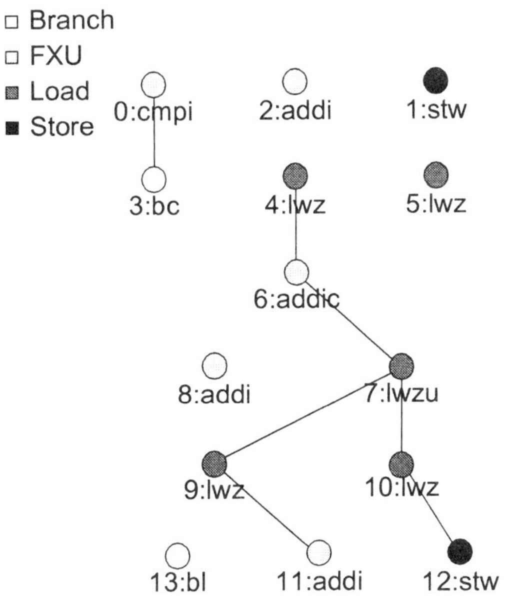

Figure 3: Inorder scheduling of instruction sequence of Figure 2

Figure 4 shows another scheduling for the same sequence

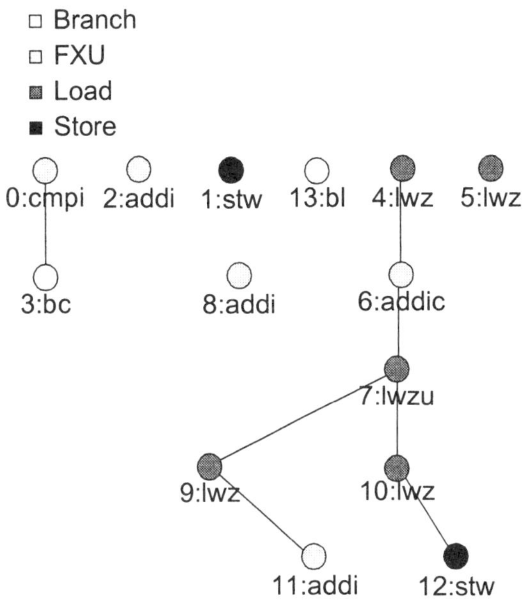

Figure 4: Out-of-order scheduling of instruction sequence of Figure 2

requiring fewer VLIW instructions. The key to achieving this improved performance is the freedom given to instructions to move past each other, commonly referred to as executing *out-of-order*. The principal effect of executing out-of-order is that a functional unit that is not busy could be used to execute an instruction whose inputs are ready, even though there may be intervening instructions ahead of it waiting for their inputs to become available. Care must be taken that the result of the instruction moved up in this manner is not used by the intervening instructions. Register renaming [11] is an effective way of taking care of such write-after-read and write-after-write hazards that accompany out-of-order execution.

Executing instructions out-of-order introduces three additional difficulties. Most instruction set architectures require that when an interrupt occurs, the state of the machine must be restored to what it would have been, were all instructions in the program executed in order. This essentially requires that an out-of-order machine be able to compute the state at every possible interruptible instruction and save it in a way that it can use on interrupts.

We define the notion of a DIF group to simplify this problem of precise interrupts. A *group* is simply the unit formed by the translator and stored in a DIF cache entry. It is organized as a sequence of long words with a single unique entry address. Each long word comprises a set of parallel operations that can be performed simultaneously as in a VLIW instruction. (We will refer to each long word in a group as a LIW, and reserve the use of the term VLIW specifically to the instruction unit in a VLIW machine.) Execution proceeds from one LIW in the group to the next sequential LIW. The last LIW in the group specifies a group exit address, which could be the entry address of either an existing group in the DIF cache or the address of an instruction which needs to be executed in the primary engine. Groups may span several basic blocks. Hence additional exits will be associated with conditional branches encountered in a group. Only the state of the machine at the entry to the group will be checkpointed. No attempt is made to save the state at interruptible instructions in a group. When an interrupt occurs, the state will be restored to that at the beginning of the group and execution control will be transferred to the primary engine. The primary engine re-executes the instructions in a precise interrupt mode, perhaps by executing them in order.

The second difficulty with executing out-of-order is the possibility that a load from a memory location may move ahead of a store to the same location, resulting in a wrong value being loaded. By saving additional information in each group as described in Section 2.8 it is possible to detect and correct such rare occurrences while allowing the maximum parallelism to be exploited in common cases.

The third difficulty occurs when instructions are moved across branches. If the branch is a conditional branch, a superscalar out-of-order machine typically chooses one path and allows instructions from that path to be reordered. If this is not the path actually taken, the machine must execute compensating code to undo the actions of the moved instructions. More typically, the superscalar machine saves information during execution which allows it to reset the state back to the point of the branch. A DIF group therefore contains information associated with each conditional branch that allows control flow to resume at the branch when the learnt direction differs from the actual. This information is computed at learning time and saved with the group in the DIF cache, in contrast to the superscalar machine where it is recomputed dynamically for every speculated branch.

Thus a DIF group, in addition to being a scheduled sequence of instructions, contains additional information (a) to assist in the detection of possible aliasing during loads and stores, and (b) to recover from mispredicted branches.

Since the DIF group is not used outside the processor chip, the encoding of the LIW may be designed to maximize the efficiency of operation of the parallel engine. Different implementations may have different organizations of the LIW. In fact, it is not necessary for all operations and all auxiliary fields in a LIW to be physically adjacent as long as the relationship between the operations and fields can be deciphered.

Similar to an entry in the trace cache described in [10] and in the expansion cache of [8], the group has the property of alignment not found in a traditional I-cache entry. Execution always begins at the beginning of an entry. This simplifies the operation of fetching a group from the DIF cache. Because groups are designed to execute over multiple cycles, the alignment also permits overlap of the fetch of a group with its execution.

2.2: Role of the Primary Engine

We have noted two roles that the primary engine plays in the DIF microarchitecture, that of determining cacheable sequences of operations to be scheduled by the translator, and that of re-executing instructions in a group during recovery from generally unexpected conditions. We envision a third role for the primary engine: that of executing certain complex and infrequently occurring instructions which would be inconvenient to execute on the parallel engine.

The DIF organization allows the parallel engine to implement just a subset of the instruction set, leaving the remaining instructions to be executed in the primary engine. However, in order to keep the two engines decoupled, a group is terminated when such a complex instruction is encountered. Whenever possible, the translator should convert such complex instructions to simpler primitives which are scheduled along with other instructions in a group. If the group were terminated early because of a complex instruction, not only is there a possibility of reduced parallelism due to smaller group size, there is also the possibility of increased misses in the DIF cache because of underutilized groups. The IBM PowerPC architecture, for example, has a *load-update* instruction which updates one of the registers used in address computation as a side-effect of performing of the load. This instruction, while complex by some standards, occurs commonly enough in code compiled for existing machines that breaking it up into two operations prior to scheduling is more reasonable than terminating the group when it is encountered.

On the other hand, there are several instructions in any instruction set architecture that are rarely executed, and which are good candidates for execution exclusively in the primary engine. Examples of these in the PowerPC domain include instructions involving special system registers, trap instructions, instructions which assist in storage control, and instructions which support cache coherence and multiprocessing.

Load-multiple and *load-string* instructions in the PowerPC present an interesting case. These instructions allow multiple registers to be loaded by a single instruction, requiring renaming of potentially large numbers of registers at the same time. As shown in Figure 5 below, the load-string instructions are rare and the average number of registers loaded by these instructions is typically small. However, the load multiple instructions, typically used to restore registers before returns from subroutines, could potentially pose problems. It may be worthwhile therefore to treat each occurrence of such an instruction according to the number of registers loaded. When the number is small it may be reasonable to break up such an instruction into multiple operations and schedule them into a group. When the number is large they should be executed exclusively in the primary engine. In *vortex*, for example, a load multiple is encountered every 80 instructions, though 69% of these load-multiple instructions load 4 or fewer registers. By incorporating these into the group, we reduce the frequency of group closing load-multiple instructions to about 1 in 300.

	% load-complex instructions		Average number of regs. loaded	
Benchmark	**multiple**	**string**	**multiple**	**string**
compress	0.36	0.00	3.0	2.3
gcc	0.73	0.02	10.5	2.9
go	0.35	0.00	11.2	2.3
ijpeg	0.13	0.04	8.7	3.8
m88ksim	0.63	0.02	4.5	4.0
perl	0.99	0.94	7.1	2.5
vortex	1.24	0.12	4.5	3.0
xlisp	1.13	0.00	6.4	3.4

Figure 5: Statistics for complex load operations in PowerPC applications

Perhaps the best way to view the primary engine is that it serves as a safety net. It should be used sparingly, but its existence allows the resources in the DIF cache and the parallel engine to be utilized more effectively.

2.3: Register Renaming

As mentioned in Section 2.1, the ability to rename registers is key to executing instructions out-of-order. Typically, register renaming involves mapping an architected register to a new physical register whenever it is the target of some instruction. This physical register becomes the source for all uses of the architected register until it is written again, at which point it is returned to a free pool of registers. The bookkeeping associated with such renaming involves looking up a table to determine the current mapping of a register whenever the contents of the register are used, and updating the table whenever the register is written. When several instructions are executed simultaneously, a large number of ports is needed to satisfy the lookup and update requirements for this table.

One way of circumventing this problem in DIF is to use a two-level renaming scheme.[1] The first renaming is done during translation. Each register field in the translated format has two components, the architected register name and a suffix denoting the number of times that register has been written in the current group. Each time a register is written, the suffix for the register is incremented. The translator keeps track of the suffix and uses it to modify those instruction fields where the register appears as a source. Let us illustrate this with an example.

Figure 6 shows the result of the first level of renaming on the

#	Address	Instruction	
0	117fe8	cmpi	CR0.1 <- R15.0,0
1	117fec	stw	R17.0 -> 120(R31.0)
2	117ff0	addi	R25.1 <- R17.0,0
3	117ff4	ble	CR0.1,*+508
4	117ff8	lwz	R6.1 <- 856(R3.0)
5	117ffc	lwz	R25.2 <- 1472(R2.0)
6	118000	addic	R26.1 <- R6.1,-48
7	118004	lwzu	R6.2,R26.2 <- 48(R26.1)
8	118008	addi	R4.1 <- R18.0,0
9	11800c	lwz	R28.1 <- 8(R6.2)
10	118010	lwz	R27.1 <- 4(R6.2)
11	11801c	addi	R3.1 <- R28.1,0
12	118020	stw	R27.1 -> 172(R31.0)
13	118024	bl	*+39008

Figure 6: Sequence of Figure 2 with resources renamed

sequence of instructions in Figure 2. Two sets of resources are renamed in this figure, the condition registers, CR0 through CR7, and the general purpose registers, R0 through R31. All registers have a suffix of 0 entering the group. In instruction 0, the condition register CR0 is renamed to CR0.1, which is used in instruction 3 for the conditional branch. Registers 6, 25 and 26 are renamed twice in the group. Two renames are needed for the load-update instruction 7: the address for the load is computed by adding 48 to the contents of register R26.1, the resulting value being stored in renamed register R26.2, while the loaded value is written into renamed register R6.2.

The group scheduled according to the graph in Figure 4 along with the annotated register fields is shown in Figure 7. The first long instruction word (LIW) consists of 5 instructions. Two simultaneous write operations are performed on register 25 in slot 0. This became possible only because instructions were allowed to move across the conditional branch. One of these values will be discarded depending on the outcome of the conditional branch.

This static renaming scheme is sufficient if it can be guaranteed that at the entry to each group, the correct values for the registers

Slot	#	Instruction	
0	0	cmpi	CR0.1 <- R15.0,0
	1	stw	R17.0 -> 120(R31.0)
	2	addi	R25.1 <- R17.0,0
	4	lwz	R6.1 <- 856(R3.0)
	5	lwz	R25.2 <- 1472(R2.0)
	13	bl	*+39008
1	3	ble	CR0.1,*+508
	6	addic	R26.1 <- R6.1,-48
	8	addi	R4.1 <- R18.0,0
2	7	lwz	R6.2 <- 48(R26.1)
	7#	addi	R26.2 <- R26.1,48
3	9	lwz	R28.1 <- 8(R6.2)
	10	lwz	R27.1 <- 4(R6.2)
4	11	addi	R3.1 <- R28.1,0
	12	stw	R27.1 -> 172(R31.0)

Figure 7: Group of Figure 2 with 5 LIWs after translation

are available in the physical registers associated with a suffix of 0. In other words, copy 0 of each register should contain the architected state of that register at the beginning of execution of a group. This however could involve expensive register copy instructions at the exit of each group. For example, if the conditional branch in instruction 3 were taken, only CR0 and R25 would have to be copied from their values in CR0.1 and R25.1. A much larger set of registers as shown in Figure 8 would have to be copied if the branch were not taken and execution proceeded to the end of the group. Such a map, which we call the *exit map*, completely defines which physical registers contain the current architected value at each exit.

ble taken	CR0.1, R25.1
end of group	CR0.1, R3.1, R4.1, R6.2, R25.2, R26.2, R27.1, R28.1

Figure 8: Map representing architected state at end of group

(All other registers have their architected state unchanged from that at beginning of execution of the group.)

Rather than take extra cycles on completion of a group to perform this copy operation, we propose a second level of renaming. Instead of moving values among registers we provide a hardware *group map* which points to the actual physical registers containing the current architected state, i.e. the state at the beginning of execution of a group. At the end of execution of a group, the information in the exit map is used to update the group map before starting execution of the next group. This can be accomplished by allocating a fixed number of physical registers for each architected register and cycling through these in a fixed order. For a given register then, the group map points to a set of physical registers, and each renaming thereafter refers to the next physical register in the set in order.

Figure 9 shows the hardware needed to accomplish the renaming as just described. The suffix associated with a register in the LIW is added to the number pointing to the current architected value in the group map. This addition is performed modulo the

1. This "rotational remap" renaming scheme was proposed by Greg Grohoski.

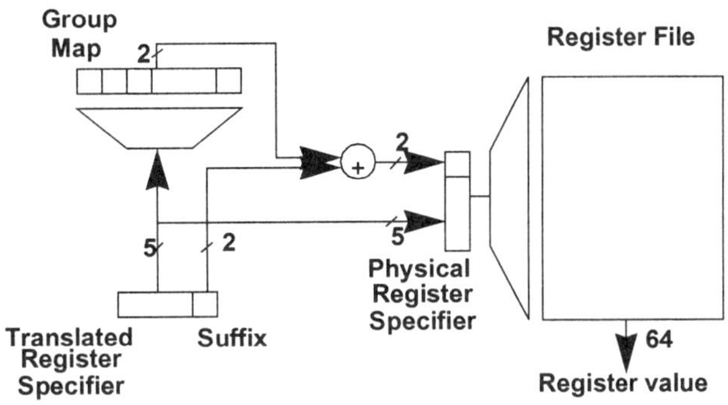

Figure 9: Schematic for GPR renaming, assuming 32 registers and 4 renames per register

number of physical registers available for that register. When the number available is a power of 2, an exclusive-OR could be used instead of a full adder.

The two-level renaming scheme just described is considerably simpler than renaming in a superscalar machine. A superscalar machine typically keeps a list of free physical registers. In each cycle, for all registers renamed in that cycle, the machine has to determine availability of free registers, allocate an appropriate one, and update the rename map. In contrast, most of this work is performed at translation time in the DIF and can be done at the rate of approximately one rename per cycle. Updating the group map itself occurs only once per group.

When instructions are executed in the primary engine, the register fields are assumed to have a suffix of 0. The physical registers used both for reading and writing in the primary engine are directly those specified by the group map. The group map therefore is unchanged during execution in this mode.

The DIF renaming scheme incurs an overhead in the space occupied by a group. Besides the space occupied due to longer register fields, additional space is taken up in each group for the exit map. Updating is facilitated if the exit map were available in the same format as a group map, so that all entries in the group map can be updated in parallel. The PowerPC architecture defines 76 registers, including the general purpose, floating-point, condition, link, count, and exception registers. Therefore, assuming 4 renames per register, each exit contributes 19 bytes to the exit map. We could eliminate a large fraction of this overhead by allowing the exit map information to be reconstructed at run time; this becomes possible if each instruction in the group is tagged simply with the serial number of the next exit.

By taking advantage of the additional time available during translation in the DIF engine, therefore, we rename in the DIF engine with hardware of considerably less complexity compared to that required by highly superscalar machines.

2.4: Organization of the Parallel Engine

There are two fundamentally different organizations possible for the DIF parallel engine. In the first, the functional units of the parallel engine are homogeneous, each one capable of executing all types of operations. Such an engine presents an easy target for scheduling of the original instruction. The space occupied by each unit on the chip is identical. All registers are shared by all units and bypasses are implemented between units to ensure timely availability of results.

In the other organization, the functional units are typed, so that each functional unit or set of functional units performs some subset of all operations expected of the parallel engine. Each functional unit takes up a fraction of the space needed by a full functional unit. This allows more units to be accomodated on a chip; more effective utilization of these units could be made by matching the distribution of unit types with the characteristics of the target workload of the machine. Moreover, register files can be placed close to those functional units that use them more: the general purpose registers can be placed close to the fixed point units, the floating point registers close to the floating point units, and the condition registers close to the branch unit. The port requirements for each type of register file and the bypass requirements between units are less stringent in such an organization compared to one with homogeneous units. In general, the typed design should lead to a smaller and faster implementation of the parallel engine.

Another advantage of a typed design is the possibility of separating the DIF cache into several smaller caches, each one serving a group of functional units as shown in Figure 10. Such an organi-

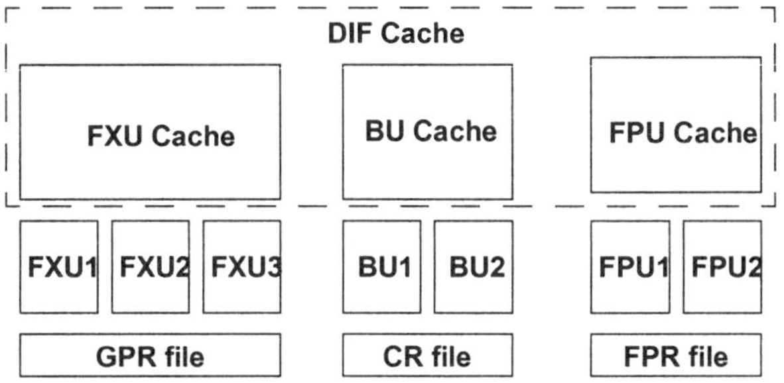

Figure 10: Schematic for a DIF parallel engine with typed functional units

zation allows shorter communication paths between the cache, the functional units and the register file. Among other advantages, this layout reduces the complexity of clock distribution which is increasingly becoming problematic at smaller lithographies.

2.5: Scheduling Hardware

We have described how the parallel engine operates and what information it expects for its operation. This information is constructed in parallel with the first execution of the sequence. In this section we will describe the operations involved in scheduling a group.

Scheduling instructions basically involves examination of resources needed by each instruction and determining an ordering for the instructions. This is similar to the task performed in software by a compiler. The space available on a chip and the time available in a cycle however constrain the sophistication of hardware scheduling. The most straightforward scheduling in terms of ease of implementation is *greedy* scheduling. In greedy scheduling, an instruction is placed in a slot corresponding to the earliest time that it can be executed.

The computation of this earliest time is facilitated by a hardware table with as many entries as resources that are kept track of. In the case of architected registers, each entry consists of a *rename* field and a *ready slot* field. The rename field for a register keeps track of the number of times that register has been written in the current sequence. The ready slot field specifies the earliest time that the current value of the register is available for use by a subsequent instruction. If unit clock latency is assumed for all operations, this field specifies the earliest LIW slot in the group that can be used for an instruction dependent on this result.

Let us examine the actions to be taken by the translator when it encounters an instruction. At the beginning of group formation, all entries in the table are set to 0. If the instruction is a primary-only instruction, e.g., a complex load operation, the group is closed. (Closing a group involves saving the group in the DIF cache and resetting it for use in constructing the next group.) An instruction to be scheduled may need to be broken up into simpler operations, each having no more than one register that is written. By examining the ready slot for each resource used in an operation, the earliest slot at which the operation could be placed is determined. If the slot is not available, consecutive slots are examined until an available slot is found. If unit latency is assumed, the result of the operation is available for use in the next slot. Hence the ready slot field in the entry corresponding to the result register is set to the new value and its rename field is incremented. If no slot is available for an instruction, the group is closed.

For illustration, the state of the table at the end of instruction 7 in the sequence of Figure 2 is shown in Figure 11 assuming unit latency for all operations. Instruction 8 depends on R18, which has

	CR			GPR							
	0		7	0		6		25	26		31
Rename	1					2		2	2		
Ready Slot	1					3		1	3		

Figure 11: Status at end of instruction 7 while forming group of Figure 6

All other fields remain 0

a value 0 in the ready slot. Since the parallel unit in the example can accomodate only 5 fixed point instructions, this instruction will have to go into slot 1. The ready slot for R4 is set to 2, and the rename value for R4 is set to 1.

During execution of a group the program counter remains pointing to the first instruction in the sequence comprising the group. Hence, along with each group it is necessary to append the address of the next group. This is done by inserting in the last slot of the group an unconditional branch to the next address to be executed. Further, the exit map set for the group as shown in Figure 8 must also be saved. The information for each of the exit maps is readily available from the rename fields in the table used during translation; for each conditional branch, its exit map is constructed when the branch is encountered during execution.

The operations mentioned in this section are fairly simple to implement in hardware. Considering the amount of work done in a cycle at dispatch time in modern superscalar processors, it should be easy to translate instructions in this manner at the rate of one per cycle. Since the primary engine is likely to be pipelined, the translator itself could be pipelined to further reduce the work done in each cycle stage.

2.5.1: Scheduling for non-unit latencies

We now examine the case when the latency of an operation is more than one cycle. Two options are available. We could schedule operations in those slots determined by taking this latency into account, or we could schedule for unit latency and stall operations in a LIW when needed. The two cases are illustrated through the example of Figure 12. In the example, the multiply operation is

0	0: xori R11.1 <- R10.0,1	
1	1: slwi R12.1 <- R11.1,4	2: mulli R15.1 <- R11.1,7
2		4: ori R12.2 <- R12.1,3
3	3: stw R15.1 -> 16(R5.0)	5: stw R12.2 -> 12(R5.0)

Figure 12: Scheduling for multi-cycle latency

Operation 3 depends on the 2-cycle operation 2

assumed to take 2 cycles to complete. Since instruction 3 depends on the result of the multiply operation, it is placed in slot 3 in Figure 12 leaving slot 2 unused. A subsequent instruction which does not depend on the result of the multiply instruction is later placed in slot 2. When executed, each slot in the group will complete in a single cycle.

In contrast, the scheduling obtained assuming unit latencies, shown in Figure 13, will cause a stall of a cycle in slot 2, resulting

0	0: xori R11.1 <- R10.0,1	
1	1: slwi R12.1 <- R11.1,4	2: mulli R15.1 <- R11.1,7
2	3: stw R15.1 -> 16(R5.0)	4: ori R12.2 <- R12.1,3
3		5: stw R12.2 -> 12(R5.0)

Figure 13: Scheduling for unit latency

Operations 3 and 4 in slot 2 both stall because of the dependence of operation 3 on the 2-cycle operation 2

in the group taking an additional cycle overall.

Skipping slots for multi-cycle latency operations may not always be the right strategy. As the latency of an operation becomes larger, the likelihood increases that intervening slots are more sparsely utilized, or not utilized at all. When an intervening slot is completely empty at the end of group formation, it may be eliminated and the group collapsed. Collapsing groups increases utilization of a group, but it requires a group to provide during translation more slots than the maximum permissible.

Sparsely utilized slots pose a more difficult problem because the maximum slot limit for a group may be reached well before a sizable number of instructions is accomodated. Thus, there appears to be a tradeoff between the execution time of a group and the utilization of the group. A compromise solution is to treat all non-unit latencies as having a latency of 2, and take the occasional stall for the entire LIW when the latency of an operation is greater than 2.

2.6: Closing Conditions for a Group

In the previous section we described how the translator works to form a group. An important task of the translator is that of deciding when a group should be closed. While the decision is easy in most cases, there are situations where this decision is not as obvious.

The obvious situations when the translator decides on closing a group are those which are forced by resource limitations. Two cases were mentioned in the previous section. When a complex instruction is encountered, the group must be closed because execution of the instruction must take place on the primary engine.

The second case occurs when no slots are available to place the next instruction in the sequence. This may be due to several reasons, for example,

- when dependences force the next instruction to a slot beyond the maximum allowed in a group,
- when the appropriate functional unit type for an instruction is not available,
- when rename registers are not available for the next instruction, and
- when the number of conditional branches encountered is equal to the maximum number of exits allowed in a group.

Besides unconditional and conditional branches, most instruction sets also include an *indirect* branch, whose target is determined at run time from the contents of some register. In the PowerPC, this register is one of two special registers, the link register or the count register. When a code sequence is speculated past such a branch, it is necessary at run time to confirm that the target address is indeed identical to the one that was encountered during translation. In many types of code the frequency of such indirect branches is low. So it may be appropriate to close the group at such instructions. However, in some types of code, especially object-oriented code, it may be more appropriate to schedule these instructions with the rest of the group and provide additional information in the group to verify the speculated path.

In the absence of any additional hardware, a group will continue to grow until one of the above conditions is encountered. Thus a group may include instructions which are already at the head of some previously formed group. This duplication could be avoided if a group is closed when an instruction is encountered during translation that is the starting instruction of an already formed group in the DIF cache. However, this has the effect of reducing the extent of parallelism exploited, as demonstrated below in a loop that moves a series of words from one location in memory to another.

```
loop:  bdz    out
       lwzu   R0 <- 4(R10)
       stwu   R0 -> 4(R11)
       b      loop
out:
```

The *bdz* instruction in the loop decrements a special register called the count register and branches when the value in this register reaches 0. Figure 14 below shows that if the group is closed

Slot 1	bdz	lwzu		
Slot 2	stwu	b		
Slot 3				
Slot 4				

Figure 14: Group formed when translation is stopped at end of iteration

when the first statement of an existing group is encountered, only one iteration of the loop is contained in the group. Ignoring memory effects, two operations are completed every cycle in the steady state. In contrast, 12 instructions can be completed every 4 cycles if group formation is continued as shown in Figure 15. Thus, while the group of Figure 14 prevents duplication of code and allows group sizes to be kept small, better parallelism can be exploited by learning longer paths as in Figure 15. This phenomenon is analogous to the improved scheduling possible in compilers through software pipelining [12].

	Group at loop			
Slot 1	bdz	lwzu		
Slot 2	stwu	bdz(2)	lwzu(2)	
Slot 3	stwu(2)	bdz(3)	lwzu(3)	
Slot 4	stwu(3)	bdz(4)	lwzu(4)	b loop+8

Figure 15: Group formed when translation is continued to fill the available slots

Besides the space taken up by the larger group, there appears to be another potential problem with this approach. As shown in Figure 16, a new group would be created starting at the address corresponding to the *stwu* instruction at the address **loop+8.** Again, our experiments appear to indicate that this is not usually a problem, and that the gain due to increased parallelism outweighs the loss due to capacity misses in the DIF cache. In fact, in the example above, a least-recently-used replacement scheme for the DIF cache would eliminate the first group from the cache because it is not used after first formation. We intend in the future to study the role that a compiler could play in the determination of appropriate group starting and stopping points with a view to reducing cache pollution, especially in applications where the working set is large.

	Group at loop+8			
Slot 1	stwu	bdz(2)	lwzu(2)	
Slot 2	stwu(2)	bdz(3)	lwzu(3)	
Slot 3	stwu(3)	bdz(4)	lwzu(4)	
Slot 4	stwu(4)	bdz(5)	lwzu(5)	b loop+8

Figure 16: Second group formed when translation is continued to fill the available slots

2.7: Behavior of Branches

Since the program counter in a DIF machine points to the entry address of a group during parallel execution, unconditional branches encountered during translation may be omitted from the group. Similarly, in the case of unconditional *branch-and-link* instructions on the PowerPC, it is sufficient to have just one operation in the LIW corresponding to the save of the return address in the link register. For conditional branches, the displacement field could be encoded for efficient address computation.

Mispredictions of conditional branches within a group could have been treated the same way as interrupts, i.e., the group could have been re-executed on the primary engine till the point of misprediction. It is important though to limit the penalty due to mispredicted branches because there are several situations where large misprediction penalties could degrade performance severely. The saving of exit maps for each conditional branch in the group is motivated precisely by this need to make recovery from mispredictions fast. It is also important in the DIF machine for prediction to be reasonably accurate because an incompletely executed group is likely to exhibit less parallelism compared to a completely executed group.

The default path taken after a conditional branch is the one that was learnt at translation time, not the fall-through path in the executable. Thus, as long as the learnt path continues to be executed, no additional fetches are needed. This is in contrast to a traditional I-cache, where even a correctly predicted taken branch always implies a cache fetch. The DIF machine dynamically achieves the effect of profile-based code reorganization which has been explored, for example, by Krall [13]. In fact, an advantage that DIF has over such software schemes is that it can react to changing dynamic behavior, rather than depend on summary behavior across the entire program.

The prediction implicit in the DIF group is a *path prediction*, rather than a branch prediction. Previous studies have pointed to the fact that path-based prediction is really more effective than traditional branch direction prediction. There is a difference between hardware path correlation as described in [14] and path prediction as done by the DIF machine. The former predicts the direction of the next branch based on the path through which it arrived, while DIF predicts the direction of a series of branches once it gets to a certain point. With additional hardware the two approaches may be combined; multiple groups could be associated with the same entry point, each representing a different arrival path.

It may still be necessary to "unlearn" a group, especially when it is observed that some group exits prematurely and seldom proceeds to completion. By introducing counters with each conditional branch in a group, it becomes possible to decide whether a group should be discarded from the cache. The act of discarding forces a retranslation at the entry address of the group when it is reencountered, thereby forcing the scheduling of a sequence hopefully leading to fewer mispredicted branches.

2.8: Out-of-Order Memory Accesses

Load and store instructions are associated with memory addresses which are computed using register values known only at run time. The phenomenon of two load or store instructions referring to the same location is termed *memory aliasing*. Except for trivial cases, it is not possible to determine during translation whether two such instructions could be referring to the same location. The fact that they refer to different locations during translation does not guarantee that these instructions will not be aliased during subsequent group executions.

Alias detection is important because it limits the reordering of loads and stores. If a store is moved ahead of another store, the value written to memory will be wrong if the two stores write to the same location. Similarly, if a load is moved ahead of a store, a problem arises if the store writes to the same location as the load. If the value written by the store is not the same as the existing value in that location, the load would have placed the incorrect value in a register.

Store buffers help in reducing the aliasing problem. In modern processors the number of cycles needed to put a set of results into memory often exceeds the number of cycles needed to produce these results. The store buffer is essentially a buffer to interface between the processor and the cache or memory bus. When stores are speculative the results in the store buffer are not committed to memory until it can be determined that the speculated path is valid. In a DIF machine, the store buffer can be used to detect aliasing by tagging the order in which the values should be updated to memory. The sequence number of the original instruction is used for tagging. Correct operation of a program is ensured by writing values from the store buffer to memory in the order indicated by the tags. Speculative stores can be accomodated by including the exit number of the instruction in the tag. When an exit occurs in a group at a conditional branch, only those stores occurring before the exit are committed to memory from the store buffer.

Load aliasing, i.e. the problem associated with moving loads ahead of stores, can be handled by implementing an associative memory containing the address and sequence numbers of each load encountered in a group. When a store occurs, the address of the store is used as an index into this memory. If there is a match, the sequence numbers of the load and store are compared. A conflict is confirmed if the sequence number of the load is higher than the sequence number of the store. Variations of this scheme have been described by Franklin and Sohi [15]. The hardware needed could be simplified if additional information is provided in the group indicating which load or store instructions have been moved ahead of a given store.

While no guarantee can be made about the aliasing property of any given pair of load or store instructions, it is usually the case that if a pair in a sequence is aliased, it will continue to be aliased in subsequent invocations of the sequence, whereas if it were not aliased at first occurrence, it is unlikely to be aliased at subsequent invocations. Thus information gathered during the learning phase could be used to decide whether or not loads/stores should be allowed to move ahead of stores. In the event that an aliasing does occur during later execution of a group, the entire group is re-executed in the primary engine as in the case of interrupting instructions. The previously learnt group is replaced from the DIF cache by a new one which does not allow the offending move for future invocations.

We note that a lot of the techniques mentioned in this section will be needed by any future processor that attempts to exploit instruction-level parallelism. The DIF group provides a framework to simplify the hardware needed for alias detection.

3: Performance Analysis

The principal tool used to evaluate the DIF concept was a timing simulator. The simulator, while not a faithful reproduction of the hardware, models the behavior of the main hardware components of a DIF machine, including the I-cache, the DIF cache, the D-cache, an inorder primary engine, a translator and a parallel engine. The simulator permits extensive exploration of the design space by parametrizing the number and type of functional units available in the parallel engine, the number of LIW slots in a group and the number of renames allowed per register. While it does not model the pipelines in the machine in great detail, it allows specification of penalties for various events, e.g., conditional branch mispredictions and transitions between the primary and the parallel engines.

The input to the simulator was a set of instruction and memory reference traces obtained by executing application programs from the SPECint95 suite. Each of the benchmarks was run to completion on a data set chosen in such a way as to ensure that a reasonable sized trace was obtained. A very large trace limits our ability to explore the design space because of computing requirements, whereas a very small trace may not amortize the warm-up phase of the caches in the machine. After some experimentation we arrived at a set of inputs which yielded traces containing between 30 and 120 million instructions for each benchmark.

In presenting our results we will refrain from averaging the behavior on the benchmarks. The SPECint95 benchmarks, as a whole, may not be representative of the characteristics presented in real user situations. However, the results of individual programs in the SPEC suite allow a better evaluation of the strengths and weaknesses of a design point. For example, the behavior in commercial and object oriented environments is fairly well captured by the *gcc* benchmark which with its large footprint stresses the instruction cache and branch prediction mechanisms of modern processors.

The simulator presents a graphic interface to the user allowing the user to select a hardware configuration and an application. The program searches the database of previously executed simulations to determine whether the results of this design point are already available. This avoids expensive duplication of runs of the same configuration. If the result does not exist, the tool provides the user with the option of either browsing through results for design points which are close to the one desired, or of actually performing the simulation for the new design point. As the database grows, the user is able to extrapolate the results from what is already available in the database without actually performing the simulation.

4: Results

This section presents results obtained from simulating the benchmarks as described in Section 3.

4.1: Effect of out-of-order execution

The discussion in Section 2.1 hinted at the potential performance gain from scheduling instructions out-of-order. Figure 17 confirms that this is indeed the case, and that the advantage due to out-of-order scheduling is greater when more instructions can be placed in a group. To ensure the absence of extraneous effects, the experiments leading to the results in this figure were performed with infinite I- and D-caches and a very large (2048 x 4) DIF cache. The parallel engine was assumed capable of handling 2 branch operations and 4 operations of any other type in one cycle.

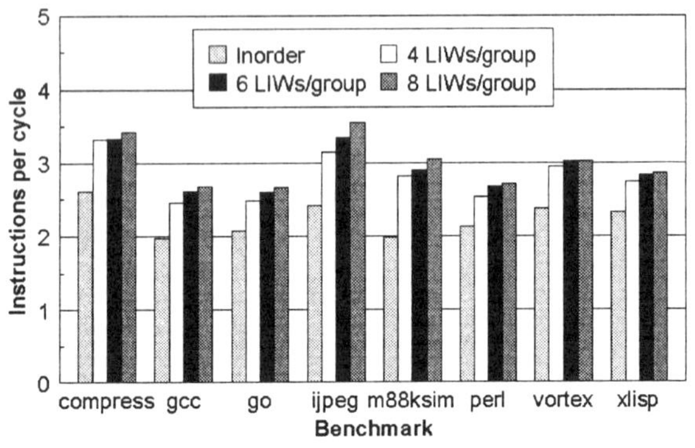

Figure 17: Parallelism through out-of-order execution

Homogeneous parallel unit with 2 branch units and 4 general functional units per LIW

In the inorder case, ignoring cache effects, there is no advantage in forming groups with more than one LIW in a group. On the other hand, Figure 17 shows that the out-of-order performance increases considerably as the group size is increased. In one case, *m88ksim*, the out-of-order performance with 8 LIWs per group is as much as 50% better than the inorder performance.

Figure 18 shows that there is additional parallelism to be gained by increasing the width of the parallel engine. However, the gain due to the larger number of units diminishes as the width gets large. In particular, there does not appear much to be gained in *gcc* and *go* by increasing the number of functional units beyond 4.

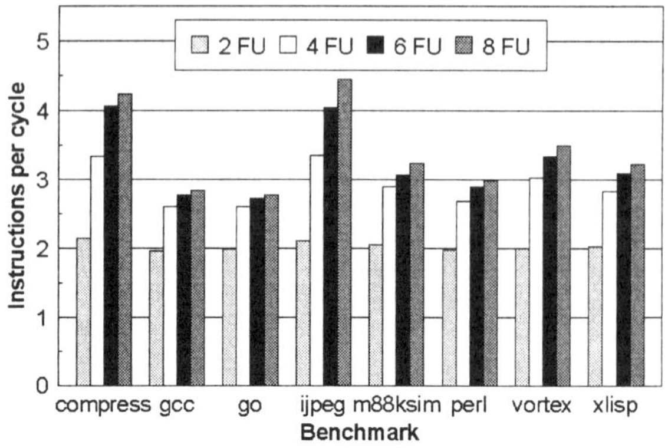

Figure 18: Increased parallelism through larger number of functional units

6 LIWs per group, 2 branch units in each LIW in addition to functional units

Increasing the number of functional units is more expensive than increasing the number of LIWs in a group, because entire functional units have to be replicated, additional ports need to be provided to register files, and additional bypass paths have to be routed.

As the size of a group is increased, the actual window over which the translator performs scheduling increases. Figure 19 shows a distribution of the useful instructions executed in a group for *gcc*. The percentage of instructions which are executed in groups having at least 20 instructions grows considerably as the number of LIWs available in the group increases. This implies that even in *gcc* which has a large percentage of subroutine calls and a large percentage of complex instructions, there is potential for scheduling over large windows of instructions.

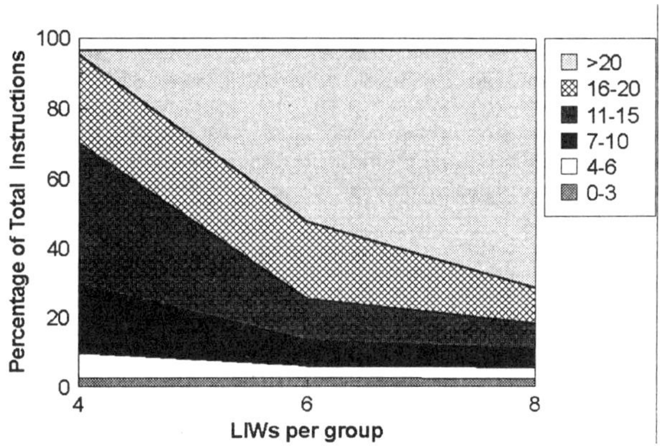

Figure 19: Distribution of useful instructions in groups for various group sizes

2 branch units and 4 general functional units per LIW. The remaining instructions were executed in the primary engine.

Figure 20 plots the actual parallelism achieved for *gcc* for each range of dynamic group size. The combination of higher parallelism in larger groups with the larger percentage of instructions executed in the larger groups results in a higher overall performance

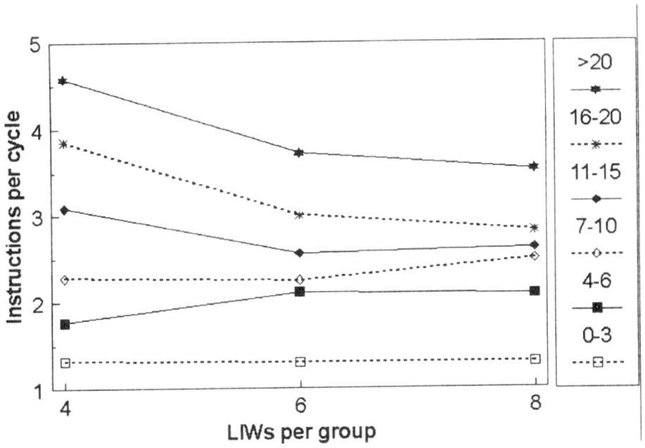

Figure 20: Variation of parallelism with number of useful instructions in a group

2 branch units and 4 general functional units per LIW

for larger groups. What was unexpected was the tendency for the average parallelism in larger groups to decrease as their number increases. The reason for this is interesting. When any group is executed to completion, all the work done in a group is useful work. Hence the total parallelism (for all the work done in a group) is the same as the useful parallelism. On the other hand, when there is misprediction in a group, some work associated with the wrongly speculated path may be thrown away. The result is that the useful parallelism is lower than the parallelism as seen by the engine. When more LIWs are available in a group as in the right side of the graph, a larger fraction of the executed groups of size 20 or more instructions constitute groups with mispredictions, exhibiting lower useful parallelism. On the other hand, on the left side of the graph, there is a higher likelihood that a group with 20 instructions is executed to completion.

4.2: Effect of DIF cache size

The results of the previous section, in some sense, represent the highest achievable parallelism on existing code. When the DIF cache is smaller the parallelism is expected to be lower because collision and capacity misses in the cache result in premature flushing of useful translations. The parallelism achieved by the parallel engine itself may remain constant; however, the repeated translations of the same sequences cause the overall parallelism in the workload to be lower. Figure 21 shows the results of simulating various sizes of the DIF cache with each entry being a group of instructions. It is interesting that except for *gcc* and *go*, the benchmarks do not show tremendous sensitivity to the size of the DIF cache. This is attributable to the generally small instruction working set of benchmarks in the SPEC95 suite. Thus even with a 2-way set associative DIF cache having only 256 entries, the premature replacement of useful paths does not occur often.

The shaded region behind each set indicates the parallelism achieved by the parallel engine alone. This is the parallelism that would have been seen if the time for translation and the time spent in complex instructions dropped to 0. The parallel mode performance is somewhat higher than the overall performance in *gcc*, *perl*, *vortex* and *xlisp*. Looking back at the table of Figure 5 we see that these benchmarks spend a significant amount of time executing complex instructions. Better performance may be possible by breaking up some of the load-complex instructions into individual loads as described in Section 2.2.

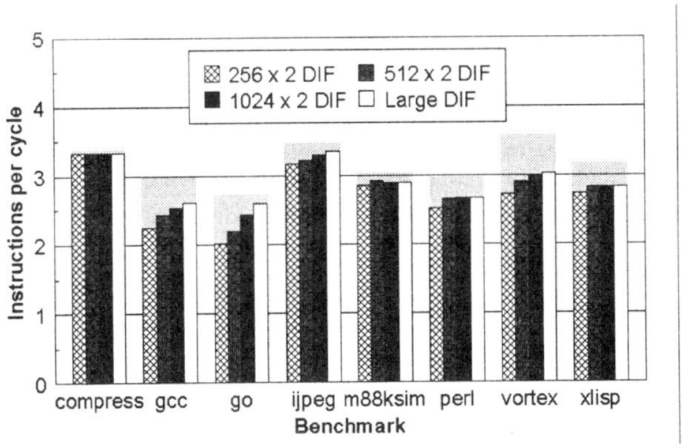

Figure 21: Variation of parallelism with size of DIF cache

Homogeneous parallel unit with 2 branch units and 4 general functional units per LIW, 6 LIWs/group

4.3: Effect of stopping at cache hits

The loop example of Section 2.6 suggests that better parallelism is possible if translation is continued beyond an instruction that is already the start of a sequence in the DIF cache. Figure 22 confirms that there is no advantage in any of the benchmarks by restricting duplication of basic blocks in a DIF group. Moreover, the hardware required to restrict this duplication is greater because the DIF cache directory would need to be accessed every cycle. In loop-intensive scientific applications the unrolling effect due to duplication could be even more beneficial.

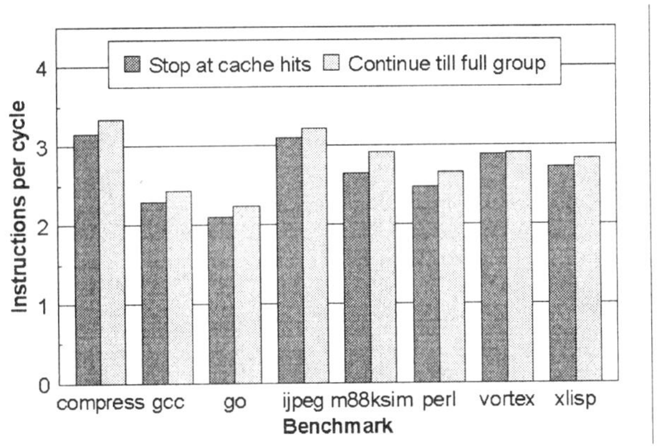

Figure 22: Effect of continuing group formation past existing DIF entry point

Homogeneous parallel unit with 2 branch units and 4 general functional units per LIW, 6 LIWs/group, 512 x 2 DIF cache

4.4: Effect of typed functional units

In Section 2.4 we indicated that a better organization from the hardware point of view would be one which types the functional units, rather than one which has homogeneous functional units as assumed so far. We performed a set of experiments constraining the units to 2 branch units plus *n* units of each of the following types: fixed point, load, store, floating-point, where *n* was varied from 1 to 4. Figure 23 shows that the performance of the typed case, for example when $n = 2$, is considerably better than the performance of the homogeneous case with 2 full functional units, and almost the same as the performance with 4 full functional units. The $n = 2$ typed case occupies more DIF cache space, but is less complex in register port requirements and in the space occupied by the units compared to the 4 full functional unit design.

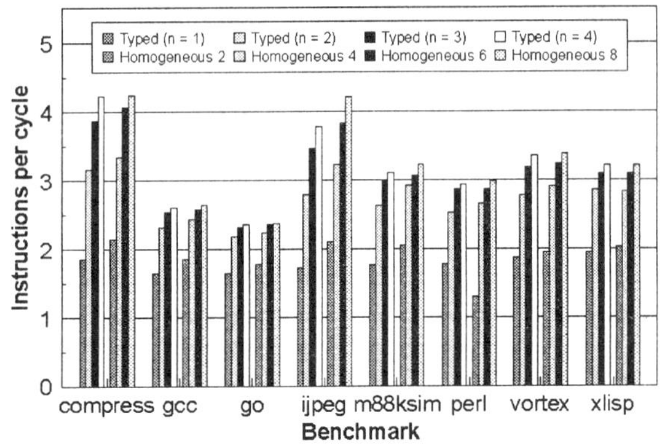

Figure 23: Variation of parallelism with number of functional units

2 branch units per LIW, 6 LIWs/group, 512 x 2 DIF cache

4.5: Effect of I-cache size

In the ideal steady state, the DIF cache should contain the instruction working set of a program. The I-cache therefore serves only to satisfy the compulsory misses occurring during translation. We can therefore expect I-cache requirements in a DIF machine to be fairly minimal. Figure 24 plots the I-cache miss rates for two

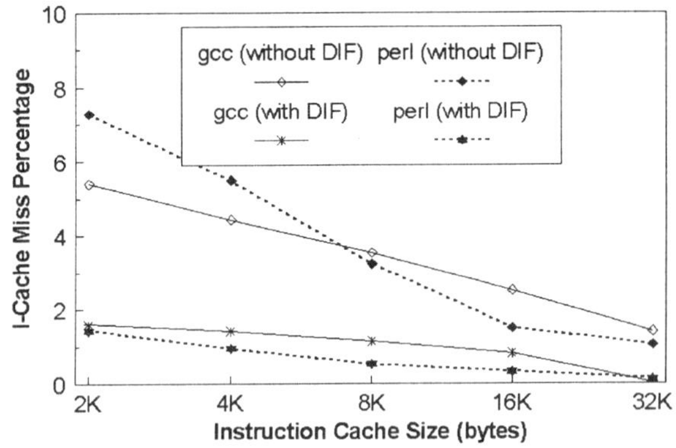

Figure 24: Comparison of I-cache performance with and without DIF

Homogeneous: 2 branch units and 4 general functional units per LIW, 6 LIWs/group, 512 x 2 DIF cache

cache-intensive programs in the SPECint 95 suite, *gcc* and *perl*. The miss percentage with a very small 2K I-cache is practically the same as what would have been observed with a very large 32K cache in a standard superscalar processor. With the potential for including large level 2 caches on chip using modern process technology, the first level I-cache in a DIF machine could probably be dispensed with altogether.

4.6: Performance of a simple DIF machine

We now present the results from simulating a simple first generation DIF machine. The machine is assumed to have a typed parallel engine with 2 functional units of each type, a 512 x 2 DIF cache, a 2-way set-associative I-cache with 128-byte lines and 16 lines per set, 2 cycle miss penalty, and a direct-mapped D-cache with 128 lines each of length 32 bytes, and a 2-cycle miss penalty. Since the D-cache is small and direct-mapped, we assume that results of load instructions can be used in the immediately following cycle.

In Figure 25 we show the performance of the simple machine

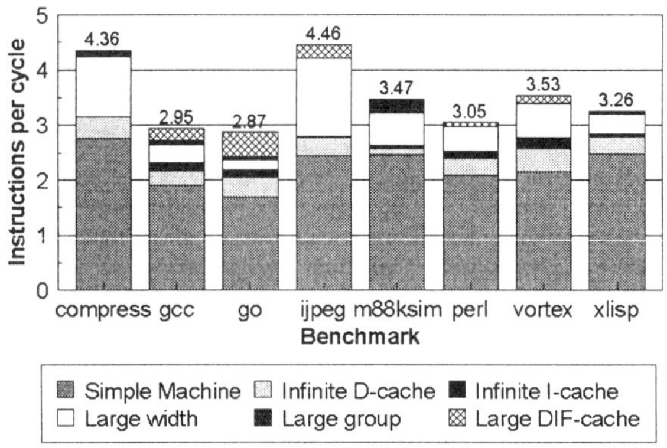

Figure 25: Breakup of effect of resource limitations on parallelism in simple DIF machine

Homogeneous parallel unit with 2 branch units and 4 general functional units per LIW, 6 LIWs/group

and also give an idea of what causes the difference between the performance it achieves and the theoretically achievable parallelism. We observe that two of the principal contributors to the reduction in parallelism are the small D-cache and the small width of the parallel engine.

One way to improve the D-cache performance is to incorporate a larger D-cache with a 2-cycle access latency. This would require uses of loads to be scheduled with a delay slot as described in Section 2.5.1. We expect all future machines exploiting instruction-level parallelism to pay considerable attention to the data access problem. Most solutions to this problem in other types of high-performance machines would also be useful for the DIF machine. Examples include data reorganization through the compiler, and data prefetching techniques, both in hardware and in software.

The reduction in parallelism due to the limited number of functional units is actually a pleasant surprise. It confirms the observation made by other researchers [2] that there is parallelism to be exploited even in unstructured integer programs.

5: Concluding Remarks

In this paper we introduced a new approach to exploiting instruction-level parallelism in programs. The approach, called Dynamic Instruction Formatting (DIF), involves discovering sequences of instructions spanning multiple basic blocks while executing them on a primary engine and caching a scheduled version of the sequence for execution on a parallel engine. The experiments in the paper used instruction streams compiled to the PowerPC instruction set, although the fundamental approach could be used for other source architectures. The target architecture was VLIW-like. It differed from a pure VLIW architecture in that each unit of execution was essentially a sequence of VLIWs, rather than a single VLIW.

A unique feature of the DIF approach is the availability of a primary engine which can execute the complete source architecture, although at a lower rate than that achievable in the parallel engine. By actually executing code on the primary engine, the translator is able to capture a window containing several basic blocks for scheduling. The availability of the primary engine also simplifies the parallel engine which delegates to the primary engine hard but infrequent tasks like recovery from exceptions and the execution of complex instructions.

We also introduced the concept of a group. Because of its larger granularity, the DIF group allows code to be ordered better to exploit parallelism. This paper discussed groups with a single sequence of instructions; however the notion may be extended to a VLIW execution tree incorporating both taken and fall-through paths as described in [16].

A typical DIF implementation has a clean partitioning of function that lends itself well to VLSI chip layout. Moreover, the control logic to execute in the parallel mode is considerably simpler compared to a superscalar implementation with a similar number of functional units. Both these factors suggest that it would be easier to implement a high clock frequency DIF compared to a superscalar processor with similar clock frequency.

The paper described results of simulating the DIF architecture on the SPECint95 suite of benchmarks. The results indicate that even for existing code, compiled without instruction-level parallelism considerations, there is a fair amount of parallelism that can be exploited by simple DIF implementations. The experiments also showed that with advances in technology and looser resource constraints, there is a good amount of parallelism that can be exploited from these programs. These results are encouraging considering the commercial importance of being able to execute existing code on new implementations.

There appears to be even greater potential in the DIF machine to exploit parallelism from recompiled programs. There are several compiler optimizations that could yield more parallelism from ordinary programs. For example, our results showed that when the percentage of useful instructions performed in large groups increases, more parallelism can be exploited. One way to achieve this is through the use of techniques like static correlated branch prediction [17] which determine frequently executed paths through programs and treat them as schedulable units. By providing this information to the translator, it should be possible to reduce not only mispredictions in groups, but also retranslations due to cache pollution. We hope to study compiler techniques for DIF to a greater extent in the future.

The DIF concept brings together several ideas that are being proposed today to bridge the mismatch between instruction set architectures and the exploitation of instruction level parallelism. It builds on thc concept that execution atomicity of an implementation may be larger than the architectural atomicity. It embodies the concept of path correlated branch prediction in the way groups are formed. It emulates the alignment properties of the trace cache. Finally, it provides structure to ideas like register renaming and memory alias resolution that will be commonplace in future machines exploiting instruction-level parallelism.

6: Acknowledgments

The authors wish to express their appreciation for the work done by Erdem Hokenek, Bob Meade, Greg Grohoski, Abe Mammen, Al Chang, Craig Chase and Cliff Young, and for valuable discussions with Marc Auslander, Kemal Ebcioglu, Eric Kronstadt, Jaime Moreno, Mayan Moudgill and Dan Prener. Thanks are due also to Mark Charney for the SPECint95 binary executables, and for the *xsample* tool used in the I-cache simulations of Figure 24.

7: References

[1] M. Johnson, *Superscalar Microprocessor Design*, Prentice-Hall, Englewood Cliffs, NJ, 1991.

[2] E.M. Riseman and C.C. Foster, "The Inhibition of Potential Parallelism by Conditional Jumps," *IEEE Transactions on Computers*, vol. C-21, pp. 1405-1411, Dec. 1972.

[3] J.A. Fisher, "Very Long Instruction Word Architectures and the ELI-512," *Proc. 10th Annual Intl. Symp. on Computer Architecture*, pp. 140-150, June. 1983.

[4] S. Melvin, M. Shebanow and Y. Patt, "Hardware Support for Large Atomic Units in Dynamically Scheduled Machines," *Proc. 21st Intl. Symp. on Microarchitecture*, Dec. 1988.

[5] R.N. Rechtschaffen and K.Ekanadham, "Self-parallelization of Sequential Object Codes," *Proc. PACT95, Intl. Conf. on Parallel Architectures and Compilation Techniques*, 1995.

[6] M. Franklin and M. Smotherman, "A Fill Unit Approach to Multiple Instruction Issue," *Proc. 27th Intl. Symp. on Microarchitecture*, Nov. 1994.

[7] T.-Y. Yeh, D.T. Marr and Y. Patt, "Increasing the Instruction Fetch Rate via Multiple Branch Prediction and a Branch Address Cache," *Proc. 7th Intl. Conf. on Supercomputing*, July 1993.

[8] J.D. Johnson, *Expansion Caches for Superscalar Processors*, Tech. Report CSL-TR-94-630, Computer Science Laboratory, Stanford, CA, June 1994.

[9] S. Dutta and M. Franklin, "Control Flow Prediction with Tree-Like Subgraphs for Superscalar Processors," *Proc. 28th Intl. Symp. on Microarchitecture*, Nov. 1995.

[10] E. Rotenberg, S. Bennett and J.E. Smith, "Trace Cache: a Low Latency Approach to High Bandwidth Instruction Fetching," *Proc. 29th Intl. Symp. on Microarchitecture*, Nov. 1996.

[11] R.M. Keller, "Look-Ahead Processors," *Computing Surveys*, vol. 7, no. 4, pp. 177-195, December 1975.

[12] M. Lam, "Software Pipelining: An Effective Scheduling Technique for VLIW Machines," *Proceedings of the SIGPLAN '88 Conference on Programming Language Design and Implementation*, June 1988.

[13] A. Krall, "Improving Semi-static Branch Prediction by Code Replication," *Proc. ACM SIGPLAN '94 Conf. on Programming Language Design and Implementation*, June 1994.

[14] R. Nair, "Dynamic Path-Based Branch Correlation," *Proc. 28th Intl. Symp. on Microarchitecture*, Nov. 1995.

[15] M. Franklin and G. Sohi, "The expandable split-window paradigm for exploiting fine-grain parallelism," *Proc. 19th Annual Intl. Symp. on Computer Architecture*, June 1992.

[16] K. Ebcioglu, "Some Design Ideas for a VLIW Architecture for Sequential Natured Software," in M. Cosnard et al, *Proc. IFIP WG 10.3 Working Conference on Parallel Processing*, Pisa, Italy, 1988.

[17] C. Young and M.D. Smith, "Improving the Accuracy of Static Branch Prediction Using Branch Correlation," *Proc. , Sixth Intl. Conf. on Architectural Support for Programming Languages and Operating Systems*, Oct. 1994.

DAISY: Dynamic Compilation for 100% Architectural Compatibility

Kemal Ebcioğlu and Erik R. Altman
IBM Thomas J. Watson Research Center
Yorktown Heights, NY 10598
{kemal,erik}@watson.ibm.com

Abstract

Although VLIW architectures offer the advantages of simplicity of design and high issue rates, a major impediment to their use is that they are not compatible with the existing software base. We describe new simple hardware features for a VLIW machine we call **DAISY** (**D**ynamically **A**rchitected **I**nstruction **S**et from **Y**orktown). **DAISY** is specifically intended to emulate existing architectures, so that all existing software for an old architecture (including operating system kernel code) runs without changes on the VLIW. Each time a new fragment of code is executed for the first time, the code is translated to VLIW primitives, parallelized and saved in a portion of main memory not visible to the old architecture, by a *Virtual Machine Monitor* (software) residing in read only memory. Subsequent executions of the same fragment do not require a translation (unless cast out). We discuss the architectural requirements for such a VLIW, to deal with issues including self-modifying code, precise exceptions, and aggressive reordering of memory references in the presence of strong MP consistency and memory mapped I/O. We have implemented the dynamic parallelization algorithms for the *PowerPC* architecture. The initial results show high degrees of instruction level parallelism with reasonable translation overhead and memory usage.
Keywords: INSTRUCTION-LEVEL PARALLELISM, OBJECT CODE COMPATIBLE VLIW, DYNAMIC COMPILATION, BINARY TRANSLATION, SUPERSCALAR

1 Background and Motivation

Very Long Instruction Word (VLIW) architectures offer the advantages of design simplicity, a potentially short clock period, and high issue rates. Unfortunately, high performance is not sufficient for success. One of the major impediments to using a VLIW (or *any* new ILP machine architecture) has been its inability to run existing binaries of established architectures. It was argued (and not facetiously) in a recent keynote speech [11], that architectures which do not run *Intel x86* code may well be doomed for failure, regardless of their speed!

To solve the compatibility problem efficiently, there have been several proposals beyond plain or caching interpreters [10]. One has been the object code translation approach (e.g. [20, 21, 22, 23]), where a software program takes as input an executable module generated for the old machine, and profile directed feedback information from past emulations, if available. It then generates a new executable module that can run on the new architecture (resorting to interpretation in some difficult cases), and that gives the same results that plain interpretation would. Although many of the nasty challenges to static object code translation (programs printing their own checksum, shared variables, self modifying code, generating a random number and using it as a branch target address, and so on) have been addressed, the static object code translation solution still has some problems.

If object code translation is used to emulate applications written for one existing machine on another ([22, 23]), then many primitives may need to be generated to emulate one old architecture instruction, or unsafe simplifying assumptions may need to be made (e.g. about ordering of shared variable accesses, or the number of bits in the floating point representation) to get more performance, in which case full compatibility is sacrificed. This is typically because hardware features to help compatibility with an "important" old architecture were not designed into the new fast machine; compatibility was just not emphasized, or came as an afterthought. For example, the set of condition codes maintained is often quite different in different architectures. This object code translation approach does allow the convenience of running many important applications of the old architecture on the new machine, but does not provide a replacement for the old machine in terms of speed and range of applications.

If the new architecture is fully binary compatible with the old one by hardware design, but does not run with the best performance on old binaries, ([20, 21]), and the new features of the new architecture that improve performance can be utilized only by object code translation, or recompilation, the solution is still not perfect. Rapid adoption of new architectural features for higher performance may be possible under certain circumstances; scientific and technical computing is an example. But computer designers often underestimate the strong inertia of the user community and software vendors at large, and their resistance to change.

Another approach is to translate the old architecture instructions to a new internal representation (e.g. VLIW) at Icache miss time, by hardware [9, 14, 19]. This approach is robust in the sense that it implements the old architecture completely. But the optimizations that can be performed by the hardware are limited, compared to software opportunities. Also the conversion from the old architecture representation in memory to the internal Icache representation is complex (especially if one attempts to do re-ordering) and can require substantial hardware design investment, and VLSI real estate.

As an alternative we present **DAISY** (**D***ynamically* **A***rchitected* **I***nstruction* **S***et from* **Y***orktown*). **DAISY** employs software translation, which is attractive because it dispenses with the need for complex hardware whose sole purpose is to achieve compatibility with (possibly ugly) old architecture(s). Given the appropriate superset of features in the new architecture (e.g. condition codes in *x86*, *PowerPC*, and *S/390* format), **DAISY** can be dynamically architected by software to efficiently emulate any of the old architectures. Assuming that we can begin with a clean slate for both hardware and emulation software, and adopt a simple design philosophy, what architectural features and compilation techniques are required to make software translation efficient and 100% compatible with existing software? We attack this problem in the current paper.

While **DAISY** and this paper focus mainly on a VLIW as the new architecture, the same ideas can be applied any new superscalar design, and potentially to other new ILP architectures that break binary compatibility as well. Current compiler techniques for attaining high ILP are unacceptably slow for dynamic parallelization, which requires real-time performance from a compiler, in order to make the overhead imperceptible to the user. To this end, we describe a new, significantly faster parallelization technique. We have implemented this technique for the *PowerPC* and we report the initial encouraging ILP results. Another feature of the new compilation technique is the ability to maintain precise exceptions, so the original instruction responsible for an exception can be identified, whenever an exception occurs. While out-of-order superscalars use elaborate hardware mechanisms to maintain precise exceptions, in our case this is done by software alone.

The paper is organized as follows: We first give an example illustrating the new fast dynamic compilation algorithm used by **DAISY**. Next, various architectural features to support high performance translation are described. We then describe the dynamic translation mechanism whereby **DAISY** runs the old software with minimal hardware support. Next we discuss the mapping mechanisms from the old code to VLIW code and back. We then provide some experimental results and conclude.

2 The Compilation Algorithm

In this paper, we call the original, old architecture that we are trying to emulate, the *base architecture*. The VLIW which emulates the old architecture we called the *migrant architecture*, following the terminology of [20]. The base architecture could be any architecture, but we will be giving examples mostly from the *IBM PowerPC*.

Traditional caching emulators may spend under 100 instructions to translate a typical base architecture instruction (depending on the architectural mismatch and complexity of the emulated machine). So caching emulators are very fast, but do not do much optimization nor ILP extraction. Traditional VLIW compiler techniques, on the other hand, extract considerable ILP at the cost of much more overhead.

The goal in **DAISY** is to obtain significant levels of ILP while keeping compilation overhead to a minimum, to meet the severe time constraints of a virtual machine implementation. Unlike traditional VLIW scheduling, **DAISY** examines each operation in the order it occurs in the original binary code, converting each into RISC primitives (if a CISCy operation). As each RISC primitive is generated, **DAISY** immediately finds a VLIW instruction in which it can be placed, while still doing VLIW global scheduling on multiple paths and across loop iterations and while maintaining precise exceptions.

Figure 1 shows an example of *PowerPC* code and its conversion to VLIW code [1]. This conversion uses the algorithm described in [6]. However, the discussion below should make the main points clear. We begin with four major points:

- Operations 1–11 of the original *PowerPC* code are scheduled in sequence into VLIW's. It turns out that two VLIW's suffice for these 11 instructions, yielding an ILP of 4, 4, and 3.5 on the three possible paths through the code.
- Operations are always added to the end of the last VLIW on the current path. If input data for an operation are available prior to the end of the last VLIW, then the operation is performed as early as possible with the result placed in a renamed register (that is not architected in the original architecture). The renamed register is then copied to the original (architected) register at the end of the last VLIW. This is illustrated by the `xor` instruction in step 4, whose result is renamed to `r63` in VLIW1, then copied to the original destination `r4` in VLIW2. By having the result available early in `r63`, later instructions can be moved up. For example, the `cntlz` in step 11 can use the result in `r63` before it has been copied to `r4`. (Note that we use parallel semantics here in which all operations in a VLIW read their inputs before any outputs from the current VLIW are written.)
- The renaming scheme just described places results in the architected registers of the *base architecture* in original program order. Stores and other operations with

[1] For an animated version of this example, please visit `http://www.research.ibm.com/vliw`.

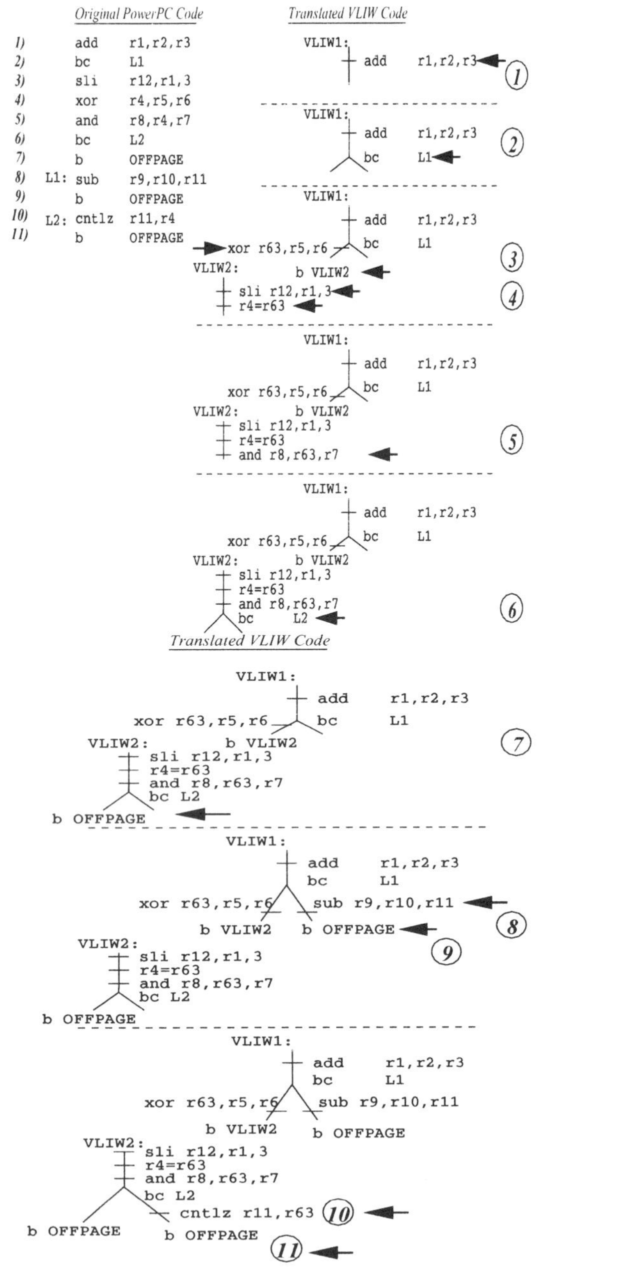

Figure 1: Example of conversion from *PowerPC* code to VLIW tree instructions.

non-renameable destinations are placed at the end of the last VLIW on the current path. In this way, precise exceptions can be maintained.

For example, assume an external interrupt occurs immediately after VLIW1 finishes executing, and prior to the start of VLIW2. The interrupt handler is just an incrementally compiled version of the standard *PowerPC* interrupt handler. Hence it looks only at *PowerPC* architected registers. These registers appear as if instruction 2, bc has just completed execution and control is about to pass to instruction 3, sli. (The instruction address register is even set to the proper *PowerPC* address of the sli, as will be described in Section 3.3.) Since VLIW2 expects the value of the speculatively executed xor to be in non-architected register r63, it is not a valid entry point for the interrupt handler to return to: the value of r63 is not saved by the *PowerPC* interrupt handler, and hence its value may be corrupted upon return from the interrupt. Thus the **VMM** must either (1) interpret *PowerPC* instructions starting from instruction 3, sli, until reaching a valid entry into VLIW code (which depends only on values in *PowerPC* architected registers), or (2) it must compile a new group of VLIW's starting from instruction 3, so as to create a valid entry point.

- VLIW instructions are trees of operations with multiple conditional branches allowed in each VLIW [5]. All the branch conditions are evaluated prior to execution of the VLIW, and ALU/Memory operations from the resulting path in the VLIW are executed in parallel.

Note that this approach works even if data is misinterpreted as code and aggressively scheduled. As we discuss more in Section 2.1, no side effects to architected resources occur until the point in the original program at which they would occur. However, we can and do limit scheduling of data by halting translation at unconditional branches. If the address following such a branch is indeed code, it must be reachable in one or more of the following ways: (1) by some other path on the page, (2) some branch from another page, or (3) by an indirect jump. In case (1), the address will be properly translated when encountered on the other path. For cases (2) and (3), the address will be translated when the executing program actually attempts to branch to that address. In Section 3.2, we discuss VLIW branch instructions which facilitate cases (2) and (3).

As this example suggests, the instruction set of the *migrant VLIW architecture* should be a superset of the *base architecture* for efficient execution. [2] This example also raises several questions. How is an OFFPAGE branch handled? How and why is it different than an ONPAGE branch? How are indirect branches handled? These questions are addressed in Section 3.

2.1 Essential Architectural Features for Aggressive Reordering

The VLIW must have the usual support for speculative execution and for moving loads above stores optimistically, even when there is a chance of overlap, as discussed in (e.g. [13, 12, 20, 5, 8]). Furthermore, data intermingled with code, and (unknowingly) scheduled as code must not cause errant execution. In order to keep the paper self contained, we briefly mention here how we address these problems.

Each register of the VLIW has an additional exception tag bit, indicating that the register contains the result of an operation that caused an error. Each opcode has a speculative version (in the present implementation, operations that set a

[2] Complex and/or infrequent instructions such as Load Multiple Registers or Decimal Divide can be decomposed into simpler primitives.

non-architected register such as `r63` will be speculative). A speculative operation that causes an error does not cause an exception, it just sets the exception tag bit of its result register. The exception tag may propagate through other speculative operations. When a register with the exception tag is used by a non-speculative commit operation, or any non-speculative operation, an exception occurs. This is illustrated below:

```
        ORIGINAL CODE              VLIW CODE
                                load  r63<-[Addr]
     bc    L1                   bc    L1
     load  r3<-[Addr]           copy  r3<-r63
```

Register `r63` is not architected in the *base architecture*. Hence when it is `load`ed, no exception occurs, even if this `load` would normally cause a page fault or segmentation violation. Instead the exception tag bit of `r63` is set. If the `bc` falls through, the attempt to `copy r63` to `r3` will result in an exception since `r3` is architected in the *base architecture*. However, if `bc` is taken, then execution continues apace and no exception is ever taken. This mechanism allows the **VMM** to move loads aggressively above conditional branches without changing the exception behavior of the original program.

As discussed above, loads may be moved above stores that cannot be proven not to store into the same location. If there does turn out to be aliasing between a speculative load and a store it passed, or some other processor changed the memory location, the code must be retranslated starting at the load. This allows both the optimistic execution of loads on a single program, and also strong multiprocessor consistency (assuming the memory interface supports strongly consistent shared memory).

It is not always possible to distinguish at dynamic compile time which loads refer to I/O space (I/O references should not be executed out of order). A speculative memory mapped I/O space load, will be treated as a no-op, but the exception tag of the result register of the load operation will be set. When the load is committed, an exception will occur and the load will be re-executed — non-speculatively this time.

Note that neither exception tags nor the nonarchitected registers are part of the *base architecture* state; they are invisible to the *base architecture* operating system, which does not need to be modified in any way. With the precise exception mechanism, there is no need to save or restore non-architected registers at context switch time.

Finally, for this paper, we assume that the *base architecture* machine is a "standard" register oriented machine with sequential semantics. This need not be the case. For example, [7] outlines how the **DAISY** approach could be implemented for a *Java* stack machine. If the *base architecture* is a VLIW with parallel semantics, where `x = y; y = x;` means exchange `x` and `y`, the code must first be converted to sequential code by introducing temporaries. The exchange then becomes the sequential code,
`t = x;    x = y;    y = t;`.

3 Page and Address Mapping Mechanisms

In this section, we describe the address space layout of the VLIW or *migrant architecture* and how it compares to that of the *base architecture*. We then describe why this layout allows a translation mechanism whereby the *migrant architecture* runs the old *base architecture* software with minimal hardware support. We also discuss why with this layout, a page is a useful unit of translation for dynamic translation. Finally we describe why **DAISY** is robust in the presence of self-modifying or self-referential code and why all possible entry points to a page need not be known when translating from a particular entry point to that page.

The VLIW (*migrant architecture*) has a virtual memory that is divided into 3 sections, as illustrated in Figure 2. The low portion, starting from address 0, is mapped with the identity mapping, where *VLIW virtual address = VLIW real address*, and is identical to the *base architecture's* physical address space. (i.e., "real memory" for *PowerPC*, "absolute memory" for *S/390*, "physical memory" for *x86*). In Figure 2, for example the *base architecture* virtual page at virtual address `0x30000` is mapped to the *base architecture* physical page at physical address `0x2000` (which is the same as VLIW virtual address `0x2000` in the low portion of the VLIW virtual memory), through the normal virtual memory mechanism of the *base architecture*.

The next, middle portion of the VLIW virtual memory address space, comprises of (1) a read only store (ROM), which contains the Virtual Machine Monitor (**VMM**) software (that accomplishes the dynamic translation between *base architecture* code and VLIW code), (2) a read/write area to store various data structures needed by the **VMM**, and (3) a nonexistent memory area (a hole in VLIW virtual address space). The middle section (where present) is also mapped with the identity mapping, *VLIW virtual = VLIW real*.

The third and top section is the translated code area, and starts at a large power of 2 address called VLIW_BASE (e.g.`0x80000000`). There are at least two ways in which this section can be mapped:

- For each page in the physical memory of the *base machine*, (= the low portion of VLIW virtual memory) there is an N times larger page in the translated code area of the VLIW virtual address space. To achieve an efficient mapping between the *base architecture* code and VLIW code, N should be a power of 2, so $N = 4$ seems a reasonable value for *PowerPC*, *S/390* or *x86*. (The actual code expansion can be larger or smaller, as described in later sections.) The translation of a page at physical address n in the base architecture physical memory, is at VLIW virtual address $n \times N +$ VLIW_BASE. The translated code area is not mapped *VLIW virtual = VLIW real* (since that would require a VLIW real memory area N times larger than the *base architecture* memory). Instead, the **VMM** translates pages when the first execution attempt occurs, and maps it to a real VLIW page frame from a pool of page frames in the upper part of VLIW real storage (discarding the least recently used ones in the pool if no more page frames are available).

- An alternative is to maintain the top section of memory as a hash table of translated entries. The hash table is indexed by the *base architecture* physical address and contains the real address of translated VLIW code. This hash table is maintained by the **VMM**, which adds entries to the hash table as page entry points are translated, and removes them as translations of new pages need the space. This approach has the advantages (1) that code for a translated page can be contiguous, (2) that code need never be moved when a new entry point is discovered, and (3) that there is less wastage — no portion of a VLIW real memory page need be wasted if the actual translation requires less than an $N\times$ expansion. However, this second mapping is more complicated than the first approach, and hence slower.

For simplicity, we shall discuss only the mechanisms first mapping in the Sections below. However, the second approach can be extended in a straightforward manner to accomplish the actions described.

3.1 Creation of a Page Translation

Suppose a program running on the base architecture branches offpage to a *base architecture* instruction, whose physical address is n. In the translated version of the same program running on the VLIW, this branch will be executed by branching into VLIW virtual address $n \times N+$VLIW_BASE in upper area of the VLIW virtual address space. Assume the beginning physical address of this 4K byte *base architecture* physical page was $n_0 = (n\&$`0xfffff000`$)$ (in C notation). If this *base architecture* page has never been executed before, then the corresponding $N\times$ 4K byte page at VLIW virtual address ($n_0 \times N +$ VLIW_BASE) is not mapped, and therefore a "VLIW translation missing" exception occurs, which is handled by the **VMM**. The **VMM** creates a translation for the *base architecture* physical page at physical address n_0, and makes the corresponding translated code area page map to some $N\times$ 4K byte page frame in the upper area of VLIW real memory. Then the interrupted translated program will be resumed to redo the branch to address ($n \times N+$VLIW_BASE), which will now succeed. When that first page of the *base architecture* program branches to a physical address n' in a second, different *base architecture* physical page that has not yet been executed, that page will in turn be translated and mapped in the same manner.

As a concrete example, as shown in Figure 2, suppose the *base architecture* program begins when the operating system branches to *base architecture* virtual address `0x30100` (part of the 4K page at `0x30000 - 0x30fff`).

- The *base architecture* virtual address `0x30100` has been mapped (via *base architecture* page tables) to *base architecture* physical address `0x2100` (part of the 4K page frame `0x2000 - 0x2fff`).
- The VLIW translation of `0x2100` is at VLIW virtual address `4 x 0x2100` + VLIW_BASE = `0x80008400` (part of the 16K page `0x80008000 - 0x8000bfff`).
- In the translated code, the branch to *base architecture* virtual address `0x30100` is really executed as a branch to VLIW virtual address `0x80008400`, which belongs to a 16K VLIW virtual page that is not yet mapped. So this branch initially causes a *translation missing* interrupt to the **VMM**. The **VMM** creates the translation of the *base architecture* 4K physical page frame `0x2000 - 0x2fff` and writes it into the VLIW 16K page frame at (say) VLIW real address `0x02000000 - 0x02003fff`,
- Finally the **VMM** maps the VLIW 16K virtual page `0x80008000 - 0x8000bfff` to this page frame at `0x02000000 - 0x02003fff`.

The interrupted translated program is then restarted, and now the branch to VLIW virtual address `0x80008400` succeeds without an interrupt, and starts executing the translated VLIW code for the first page.

We emphasize that the contents of the upper portion of the VLIW Real Memory are managed by the **VMM** and are not paged. When room is needed for newly translated code, the **VMM** discards the least recently used translation to make space. At some point it may be desirable to page translations to disk so as to save them for later use, but initially we wish to develop an architecture that requires no base software or system changes.

All exceptions are fielded by the **VMM**. When an exception occurs, the VLIW branches to a fixed offset (based on the type of exception) in the **VMM** area. So far we have described the *VLIW translation not present* and *code modification* interrupts, that are handled directly by the **VMM**. Another type of exception occurs when the translated code is executing, such as a page fault or external interrupt. In such cases, the **VMM** first determines the *base architecture* instruction that was executing when the exception occurred. (The translation is done maintaining precise interrupts as was described in Section 2, so this is possible.) The **VMM** then performs interrupt actions required by the *base architecture*, such as putting the address of the interrupted `base architecture` instruction in a specific register. Finally the **VMM** branches to the translation of the base operating system code that would handle the exception. When the base operating system is done processing the interrupt, it executes a `return-from-interrupt` instruction which resumes execution of the interrupted code at the translation of the interrupted instruction.

We still need to address the problem of how to handle an offpage branch in the *base architecture* to an address q on the same 4K page as n, but where q was not identified as a possible entry point during the translation starting from n. This problem is addressed in Section 3.2. Another concern is self-referential code such as code that takes the checksum of itself or code with floating point constants intermixed with real code or even pc-relative branches. These are all transparently handled by the fact that all registers architected in the *base architecture* — including the *program counter* or *instruction address register* — contain the values they would

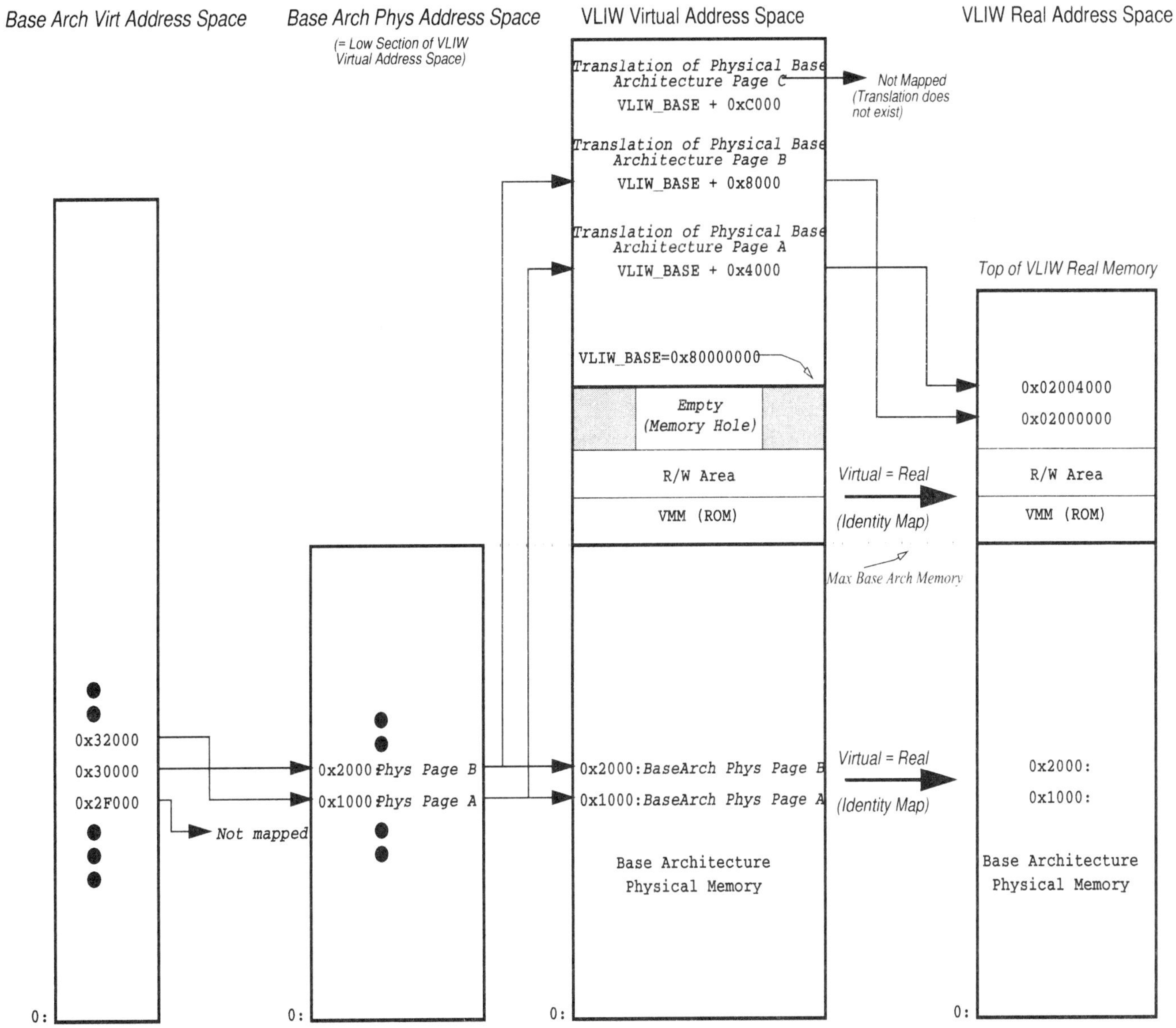

Figure 2: VLIW Address Space Layout

contain were the program running on the *base architecture*. The only means for code to refer to itself is through these registers, hence self-referential code is trivially handled.

A final major concern is self modifying code. Each "unit" of *base architecture* physical memory (low section of VLIW virtual memory) has a new read-only bit, not known to the *base architecture*. (The unit size is 4K for *PowerPC*, ≥ 2 bytes for *S/390*, ≥ 1 byte for *x86* — perhaps 8 for both.) Whenever the **VMM** translates any code in a memory unit, it sets its read only bit to a 1. Whenever a store occurs to a memory unit that is marked as read-only (by this or another processor, or I/O) an interrupt occurs to the **VMM**, which invalidates the translation of the page containing the unit. The exception is precise, so the *base architecture* machine state at the time of the interrupt corresponds to the point just after completing the *base architecture* instruction that modified the code (in case the code modification was done by the program). After invalidating the appropriate translation, the program is restarted by branching to the translation of the *base architecture* instruction following the one that modified the code. If the page currently executing was modified, then retranslation of the page will occur before the program can be restarted.

The above paragraphs describe the logical behavior of the address mappings. In the actual implementation, these multiple levels of address mapping are collapsed to one level, so cross-page branches can execute very efficiently, as will be seen in section 3.2.

3.2 VLIW Branch Instructions

We described in Section 3.1 how one could find the translation of a *base architecture* instruction at physical address n, by branching to VLIW virtual address $n \times N +$ VLIW_BASE. So, if an instruction is at offset n in the *base architecture* page, its translation is at offset $n \times N$ in the VLIW translated code page. In reality, not all entry points are valid all the time in the VLIW page, a fact with which cross-page branches must deal. There are multiple ways of implementing cross-page branches, and we first describe a high-performance alternative. We then describe two lower performance and cheaper alternatives.

High Performance Branches

The VLIW primitive to perform a cross-page branch is:

`(GO_ACROSS_PAGE reg offset)`

The `offset` is added to the register `reg` to obtain an effective address of the *base architecture*. That effective address is first translated to a physical address of the *base architecture*; then it is multiplied by N and VLIW_BASE is added to it; then it is translated to a VLIW real address, which is finally the address of the branch target VLIW. If the *base architecture* physical address is not available, a *base architecture instruction page fault* exception occurs (to a handler in the **VMM** — all exceptions are fielded by the **VMM**). If the translated VLIW code for this page is not available, a *translation missing* exception occurs. If the target VLIW is not marked as a valid entry, an *invalid entry* exception occurs. Otherwise execution proceeds with the target VLIW instruction.

The above description may give the impression of a daunting CISC instruction, but here is how it can be implemented: Assume the VLIW Instruction Translation Lookaside Buffer (ITLB) maps the *base architecture* 4K virtual page numbers directly into VLIW $N\times$ 4K real page frame numbers that contain the translated code. The software could guarantee that the low order 12 bits of `reg` is 0, or the `offset` is 0, so the low order 12 bits of the effective address `reg+offset` is immediately available. The low order 12 bits of the effective address are shifted left by $log2(N)$ bits, and applied to the Icache (14 bits allows a 64K cache, if 4 way associative). At the same time the upper bits of the effective address are sent to the ITLB. If a VLIW real address that comes out of the Icache directory matches the VLIW real address that comes out of the ITLB, no miss occurs. The target VLIW is then checked for an valid entry marker on the next cycle, while optimistically executing the target VLIW as if it were a valid entry (and recovering before any side effects occur, and causing an exception, in case the target VLIW is an invalid entry).

If only an Icache miss occurs, hardware handles it. One could handle an ITLB miss by hardware sequencers, but using a yet lower level of software to implement a "micro-interrupt" ITLB miss handler is simpler, and more in line with the philosophy of the present design. (Note that all software in a VLIW is like horizontal microcode, so no part of the VLIW software is necessarily slower than horizontal microcode.)

Other types of branches are:

- `(GOTO offset)` just branches to the VLIW at `offset` in the current page (no check for a valid entry). Ordinary intra-page branches between VLIW's use this branch.
- `(GOTO lr)`, `(GOTO long_offset)` branch to the VLIW at the real address given by a link register, `lr` or the `long_offset`. There is no check for a valid entry, and the ITLB is bypassed. Branches to an overflow area may use these primitives.

The cross-page branch, ITLB, and valid entries mechanism described above are intended for reducing the latency of a cross-page branch. If we give up the simultaneous ITLB lookup, we could first do the address translation in a prior VLIW, and then send a VLIW real address to the Icache, which has some advantages in Icache design.

```
  ; reg + offset is translated to physical address n.
  ; The VLIW real address for VLIW virtual address
  ; n*N + VLIW_BASE is then placed in lr1.
(LRA reg offset (lr1))

  ; Goto VLIW real addr in lr1. Check if valid entry
(GO_ACROSS_PAGE lr1)
```

Simpler Cross Page Branches

As noted earlier, we can also give up the valid entry

point approach. Let the translated code page for a *base architecture* page consist of a vector of pointers. For a base instruction at offset n in the *base architecture* page, vector element n will contain the real address of the VLIW code, or in case the entry at offset n has not yet been created for this page, the real address of a translator routine, that will create the corresponding VLIW code. This costs another level of indirection, but is simpler to manage.

```
  ; Put translated reg + offset in t1 ==> t1 contains
  ; real address of ptr to VLIW code for this entry.
(LRA reg offset (t1))

  ; Load ptr to real addr of VLIW code into lr1.
(LOAD_REAL t1 0 (lr1))

  ; Goto VLIW code. Make no valid entry chk
(GOTO lr1)
```

For additional simplicity, we could even give up the ITLB and simulate a big direct mapped ITLB in VLIW real memory by software. In many cases the operations for doing the cross-page branch may be moved up into previous VLIW's, and their latencies hidden.

3.3 Finding Exception-Causing Instruction in Base Architecture

As we mentioned in Section 3.1, when an exception occurs in VLIW code, the **VMM** should be able to find the *base architecture* instruction responsible for the interrupt, and the register and memory state just before executing that instruction.

A **Virtual Page Address (VPA)** register is maintained. The **VPA** contains the address of the current page in the original code, and is updated in the translated code whenever a cross-page branch is executed. The simplest way to identify the original instruction that caused an exception is to place the offset of the base instruction corresponding to the beginning of a VLIW as a `no-op` inside that VLIW, or as part of a table that relates VLIW instructions and base instructions, associated with the translation of a page. For example, the offset within a page could be kept in a 10-bit field in each VLIW instruction. (10 bits assumes a 4096 byte page aligned on a 4-byte boundary.)

If the VLIW has an exception semantics where the entire VLIW appears not to have executed, whenever an error condition is detected in any of its parcels, then the offset identifies where to continue from in the base code. Interpreting a few base instructions may be needed before identifying the interrupting base instruction and the register and memory state just before it.

If the VLIW has a sequential semantics (like an in-order superscalar, where independently executable operations have been grouped together in "VLIW's") so that all parcels that logically preceded the exception causing one have executed when an exception is detected, the identification of the original base instruction does not require interpretation. Assuming the *base architecture* code page offset corresponding to the beginning of the VLIW is available, the original base instruction responsible for the exception can be found by matching the assignments to architected resources from the beginning of the VLIW instruction, to those assignments in the base code, starting at the given base code offset.

One way to avoid extra fields, tables, and pointers to the original *base architecture* instructions altogether is as follows: Let us assume the VLIW has sequential semantics, and exceptions occur at a parcel of VLIW, (as opposed to a VLIW boundary). In this scheme there are no offsets in the VLIW code that relate it to the *base architecture*, nor any tables. This scheme relies on the fact that the entry point of the group of VLIW's, is known to have an exact correspondence with a *base architecture* instruction. (If the beginning of the group is at offset $N \times n$ in the translation page, the original base instruction must be at offset n in the *base architecture* page).

We describe the scheme with the help of the example in Figure 3. Assume that the `load` at address 0x8 causes a page fault. To determine the *base architecture* address of the exception-causing instruction, the **VMM** finds the backward path from the exception causing parcel to the entry point of the group of VLIW's. The exception is registered in `VLIW2` in the `copy r5=r5'` instruction, when the exception bits associated with `r5'` are acted upon. Thus the **VMM** traces from this parcel to the start of `VLIW1`, the entry point of this group of VLIW's. If VLIW's are laid out in a topological order from the entry point, a backward scan in the binary code from the interrupting parcel to the nearest entry point should be able to rapidly identify the path from the entry point to the interrupting parcel.

As the backward path is scanned, {`copy, bc, VLIW2, b VLIW2, load, cmpi, VLIW1`}, the **VMM** remembers the branch directions taken by conditional branches, in this case the fact that `bc cr0.eq` is not taken. Upon reaching the top of the backwards path, the *base architecture* address corresponding to `VLIW1` is calculated: **VPA** + $\texttt{VLIW1}_{\text{offset}}/4$, if the code has $4\times$ expansion. In this case the calculation yields address 0 in the *base architecture*. Now the same path is followed in forward order, {`VLIW1, cmpi, load, b VLIW2, VLIW2, bc, copy`}. There has to be a one to one correspondence between assignments to architected registers, conditional branches and stores in the VLIW code path, and assignments to architected registers, conditional branches and stores in the *base* code path. Thus the `cmpi` assignment to `cr0` is matched first. The `load` to `r5'` is passed over since `r5'` is not architected in the `base architecture`. The next correspondence is the `bc` at address 0x4 in the *base architecture*. The **VMM** recorded that this branch was not taken, so the **VMM** moves to instruction at 0x8 in the *base architecture*. The `load` to `r5` in the *base architecture* is matched to the `copy` to `r5` in the VLIW. Since the **VMM** recorded that this `copy` caused the exception, it determines that the `load` at 0x8 is the offending instruction. The **VMM** then puts 0x8 in the register used by the *base architecture* to identify the exception, and branches to the VLIW translation of the exception handler.

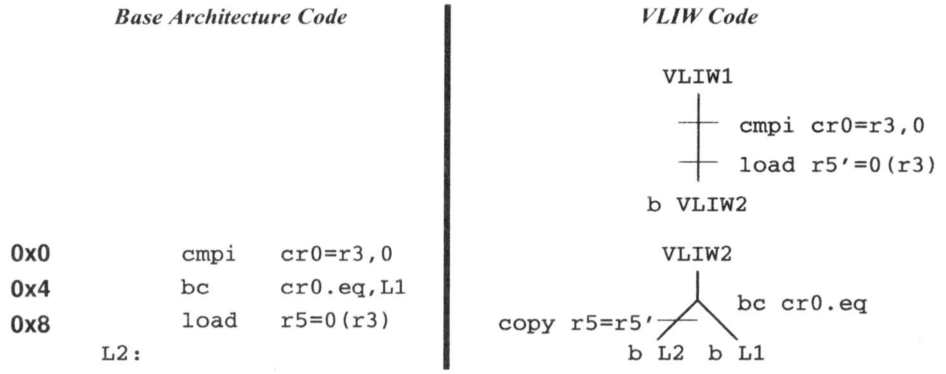

Figure 3: Finding the *base architecture* instruction responsible for an exception

4 Experimental Results

We have implemented the incremental compilation technique for the *RS/6000*, which is essentially the same as *PowerPC* for our purposes. The present version of the incremental compiler is incomplete in a number of ways. For example, the "combining" optimization includes only a small subset of all combining possibilities, and software pipelining is not implemented. Nevertheless, we provide here some preliminary results on the **SPECint95** benchmarks, as well as a few AIX utilities, and an Erastothenes' Sieve program for finding prime numbers (a Stanford integer benchmark).

Since our implementation of **DAISY** runs on RS/6000 machines, a set of RS/6000 simulation instructions (in direct binary form) is also generated for each VLIW. These RS/6000 instructions emulate the actions of each VLIW. In effect we use a *compiled simulation* method similar to *Shade* [3] for simulating our VLIW machine on the RS/6000. During transitions between VLIW's, a counter is incremented for each VLIW flowgraph edge. From the edge counts and from information about the static properties of each edge, ALU usage histograms and other statistical data can be obtained at the end of the run. A call to a kernel routine is translated to a real call, so kernel routines are not simulated in the current implementation. But since many applications that spend most of their time in user and library code, we can learn significantly about available ILP, and tradeoffs in compiler techniques, from the current implementation.

Table 1 contains the pathlength reductions achieved on the **SPECint95** benchmarks for an 8-issue machine. These numbers were obtained by executing the benchmarks with the full **SPECint95** reference inputs, with a resulting execution of more than 500 billion *PowerPC* operations, or about 200 billion VLIW instructions, as can be discerned from the mean infinite cache pathlength reduction of 2.5. (The pathlength reduction is equal to the number of operations in the RS/6000 execution trace divided by the number of VLIW instructions in the VLIW execution trace.) The pathlength reduction can be viewed as an abstract measure of the infinite cache instruction level parallelism for the program.

The VLIW machine has primitives similar to the *PowerPC*, but with 64 integer and floating point registers, rather than 32 in *PowerPC*. Operation latencies are the same as in the *PowerPC-604*. A total of 8 operations (out of which 4 can be memory accesses), and a total of 3 conditional branches (4-way branching) can be executed in each VLIW, which follows the tree instruction model. Efficient hardware implementations of the tree VLIW have been described elsewhere (e.g. [5]). The implemented incremental compilation algorithm is similar to the one discussed in this paper, although instead of generating binary VLIW code, an assembly level listing is produced.

Program	*PowerPC* Ins *per VLIW*	Average Size of Translated Page
compress	2.6	9K
gcc	2.3	24K
go	2.4	36K
ijpeg	2.7	14K
li	2.5	10K
m88ksim	2.1	14K
perl	2.4	11K
vortex	2.9	12K
MEAN	**2.5**	**16K**

Table 1: Pathlength reductions and code explosion moving from *PowerPC* to VLIW.

DAISY's performance was achieved at quite low cost. In the current experiments, **DAISY** required an average of 4315 *RS/6000* instructions to compile each *PowerPC* instruction. Furthermore, we found that **DAISY** comes within 20% of a more traditional static VLIW compiler [16] which implements a large number of sophisticated optimizations and takes approximately 100,000 instructions to compile each instruction. By way of comparison, the *gcc* compiler executes an average of 65,000 RS/6000 instructions to generate each machine instruction in its output. Finally, our implementation is a research prototype intended for flexible experimentation. We expect to reduce our translation overhead significantly with straightforward tuning, and further with an eventual rewrite of the incremental compiler, when the de-

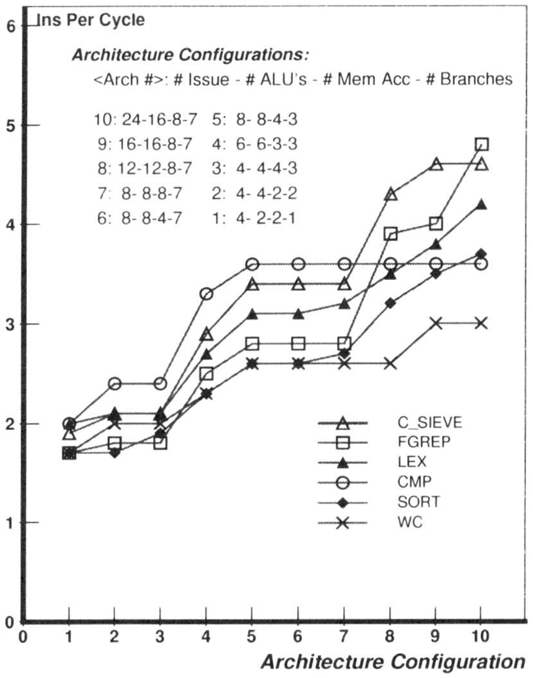

Figure 4: Pathlength reductions for Different Machine Configurations

sign matures. As a rough guess, under 1000 base instructions per base instruction seems achievable for implementing our aggressive compiler techniques.

Code explosion statistics for the benchmarks are also in Table 1. The average code expansion per actually translated page is 16K/4K = 4× (this is just the VLIW code size; empty wasted space on pages due to the 4× fixed expansion may lead to additional overhead, unless used for something else). We have placed little emphasis in our implementation on controlling code explosion and expect to reduce the explosion in future implementations. Notice that only the actually executed pages get translated, so code explosion may be less than that of a static VLIW compiler that translates all pages of the executable.

Figure 4 indicates, for several small utilities [3], how the pathlength reduction changes with the number of resources available in the *migrant* VLIW machine. These benchmarks all achieved ILP around 2 for the most primitive machine, with 4-wide VLIW instructions, 2 of whose ops may be ALU operations, and 2 of which may be memory ops, with only 1 branch allowed per cycle. Performance diverges for a 24-wide high end machine, with ILP of close to 5 achieved for `fgrep`.

Another measure of interest is the number of crosspage branches executed. As discussed in Section 3.2 crosspage branches can be expensive, particularly in low-end imple-

[3] Time constraints did not permit us to obtain the corresponding numbers for **SPECint95**.

# Ins to Compile an Instruction	*Unique Code pages*	*Reuse Factor*	Time Change
4000	200	39000	***-47%***
4000	1000	7800	***14%***
4000	10000	780	***707%***
1000	200	39000	***-59%***
1000	1000	7800	***-43%***
1000	10000	780	***130%***

Table 3: Overhead of Dynamic Compilation

mentations of the VLIW. Table 2 breaks down the number of crosspage branches in the seven benchmarks. *PowerPC* has 3 distinct types of crosspage branches: (1) direct branches, (2) branches via the `Link Register`, and (3) branches via the `Counter Register.` Notice that there is wide variety among the different benchmarks as to the fraction of instructions which are crosspage branches.

Analysis of Compiler Overhead

Table 3 indicates the extra runtime of a two second program, due to dynamic compilation, assuming a VLIW machine running at 1 GHz and assuming that both the incremental compiler and the program have an average ILP of 4 instructions per cycle. Table 3 was devised using a rough formula for relating the amount of reuse needed of each page (or instruction) in order to make a VLIW with an incremental compiler faster than the *base architecture* in executing a particular program. [6]. By *reuse*, we mean the number of times each translated instruction executes.

Table 4 gives an idea of the reuse factor for large programs such as those in the **SPEC95** benchmark suite. Table 4 indicates that they have very high reuse factors with a mean of over 500,000. The static code sizes were obtained on an *RS/6000* using the installed C compiler. [4].

A final example further supports the fact that dynamic compilation can be practical. Consider a worst case program that jumps from page to page, never repeating code. If the number of unique code pages executed is reasonable (say 200), the large percentage increase in time is probably imperceptible, as we expect only a millisecond will be required to translate each page. If the number of unique code pages is large, the overhead is likely to be dominated by the *base architecture* OS paging activity. Of course, thrashing due to a translated code area that is not large enough, will lead to extreme slowdown, and must be prevented.

5 Previous Work

Virtual machine concepts have been used for many years, for example in IBM's VM operating systems [2], but virtual machines have so far implemented a virtual architecture on almost the same architecture (e.g. *S/360* on *S/370*, *8086* on *486*, whereas in **DAISY** we support a very different virtual

[4] We thank Mark Charney, Tom Puzak, and Ravi Nair for these numbers and constructing the tools with which to obtain them.

Program	Branch Type: Direct	via `Linkreg`	via `Counter`	**Total**	Total VLIW's Exec / Total Crosspage Branches
compress	456M	1149M	96	**1605M**	*11*
gcc	771M	620M	69M	**1461M**	*10*
go	1325M	949M	39K	**2273M**	*15*
ijpeg	218M	179M	20M	**416M**	*60*
li	25M	31M	1M	**57M**	*468*
m88ksim	1326M	1072M	667M	**3065M**	*12*
perl	434M	376M	30M	**840M**	*25*
vortex	2076M	1515M	12M	**3603M**	*8*

Table 2: Number of crosspage branches in different benchmarks.

	Dynamic Ins Executed	Static Size *Ins Words*	Ins Reuse Factor
INTEGER			
go	80.8 billion	135,852	*594,764*
m88ksim	74.3 billion	84,520	*879,081*
cc1	34.1 billion	357,166	*95,474*
compress	46.4 billion	52,172	*889,366*
li	66.7 billion	67,084	*994,276*
ijpeg	68.5 billion	88,834	*771,101*
perl	48.7 billion	138,603	*351,363*
vortex	81.8 billion	212,052	*385,754*
FLOATING POINT			
tomcatv	19.8 billion	81,488	*243,003*
swim	23.2 billion	81,041	*287,324*
su2cor	24.9 billion	94,390	*263,911*
hydro2d	35.1 billion	95,668	*367,106*
mgrid	52.1 billion	83,119	*626,519*
applu	36.2 billion	99,526	*363,890*
turb3d	61.1 billion	90,411	*675,320*
apsi	21.2 billion	119,956	*176,690*
fpppp	98.0 billion	91,000	*1,076,624*
wave5	25.3 billion	120,091	*210,390*
MEAN	**49.9 billion**	**116,276**	***513,998***

Table 4: Reuse factors for **SPEC95** benchmarks

architecture on a VLIW. Caching emulators are commonly used for speeding up emulation. For example, each instruction is individually translated and the translation is cached for re-use when the instruction is emulated again [10]. However, in this approach, there is no sophisticated reordering, and thus no consequent difficult issues to deal with, for maintaining precise exceptions. We are also inspired by VLIW compiler research (e.g. the Moon-Ebcioglu compiler techniques [15] and Rau's work [18]), but in this paper we have proposed a new dynamic compilation algorithm that is much faster than existing VLIW compilation techniques, and which achieves good run-time performance.

Our initial page-based translation ideas were inspired by the work of Conte and Sathaye [4] who proposed a translation at page fault time. However, their approach is intended for achieving object code compatibility between different generations of the same family of VLIW machines, and is not intended for emulating an existing architecture. Conte and Sathaye's approach has a clever encoding which guarantees that the size of the code does not change during translation. However this guarantee does not hold for general virtual machine implementations. Dynamic translation by hardware to an internal VLIW-like representation at Icache miss time [9, 14, 19, 17] achieves a similar purpose, but requires complex Icache miss processing hardware and more hardware design investment, and does not allow sophisticated compiler techniques that can be implemented in software. Static translation of executable modules such as *FX!32*, was done in [20, 22, 23]. However, static translation does not address the problem of achieving 100% compatibility with the old architecture, including operating system code, debuggers, device drivers, etc.. So, although there are many influences to our line of thought, we believe that the combination of the ideas presented here constitute a new solution for an important compatibility problem.

6 Conclusion

We have described **DAISY**, an approach for making VLIW's and other novel architectures fully compatible with existing software for *base architecture(s)*. **DAISY** achieves this without any special hardware for emulation. Our approach could be important in the future for making an ultimate open system, where a single hardware chip can run multiple operating systems and *base architectures*. It is only necessary that the chip be constructed with an appropriate superset of the primitive operations of the multiple *base architectures*, e.g. *x86*, *PowerPC*, and *S/390*. A similar technique can be applied to aid migration to other new ILP architectures, that would otherwise break binary compatibility.

Although space constraints do not permit us to elaborate here, a novelty of **DAISY** is that it affords a practical means to achieve oracle parallelism (at high compilation cost): the first time an entry point to a page is encountered, the instructions in the page starting at the entry point are interpreted and the execution path revealed by the interpretation (say path A) is compiled into VLIW's, until a stopping point is encountered on path A. If the group is entered again, and it takes the same path A, performance will be high since it executes VLIW code solely. Further details may be found in [6]

Acknowledgements

We wish to thank the anonymous referees for their many useful suggestions. We also wish to thank Jaime Moreno, Mayan Moudgill, Arkady Polyak, and many of our other colleagues at IBM for their observations and discussion about this work.

References

[1] J. Auslander, M. Philipose, C. Chambers, S.J. Eggers and B.N. Bershad, *Fast, Effective Dynamic Compilation*, PLDI '96.

[2] J.P. Buzen and U.O. Gagliardi. *The Evolution of Virtual Machine Architecture* National Computer Conference, pp.291-299, 1973.

[3] R.F. Cmelik and D. Keppel, *Shade: A Fast Instruction-Set Simulator for Execution Profiling*, Technical Report UWCSE 93-06-06, University of Washington Computer Science and Engineering Department, 1993, `http://www.cs.washington.edu/research/compiler/papers.d/shade.html`

[4] T.M. Conte and S.W. Sathaye *Dynamic Rescheduling: A Technique for Object Code Compatibility in VLIW Architectures* Proc. MICRO-28, pp. 208-217, 1995.

[5] K. Ebcioğlu, *Some Design Ideas for a VLIW Architecture for Sequential-Natured Software*, In Parallel Processing (Proceedings of IFIP WG 10.3 Working Conference on Parallel Processing), edited by M. Cosnard et al., pp. 3-21, North Holland. Available at `http://www.research.ibm.com/vliw`

[6] K. Ebcioğlu and E.R. Altman, **DAISY:** *Compilation for 100% Architectural Compatibility*, Report No. RC 20538, IBM T.J. Watson Research Center. Available at `http://www.watson.ibm.com:8080`

[7] K. Ebcioğlu, E.R. Altman, and E. Hokenek, *A JAVA ILP Machine Based on Fast Dynamic Compilation*, Proceedings of (IEEE MASCOTS) International Workshop on Security and Efficiency Aspects of Java, Eilat, Israel, January 9-10, 1997, Available at `http://www.watson.ibm.com:8080`

[8] K. Ebcioğlu and R. Groves, *Some Global Compiler Optimizations and Architectural Features for Improving the Performance of Superscalars*, Report No. RC 16145, IBM T.J. Watson Research Center. Available at `http://www.research.ibm.com/vliw`

[9] M. Franklin and M. Smotherman. *A Fill-unit Approach to Multiple Instruction Issue* Proc. MICRO-27, 1994.

[10] T.R. Halfhill, *Emulation: RISC's Secret Weapon* BYTE, April 1994.

[11] W.M. Hwu *VLIW: Is It For Real This Time?* Keynote Speech in MICRO-27, November 1994. The foils are currently in: `http://american.cs.ucdavis.edu/Micro27`

[12] V. Kathail, M. Schlansker, and B.R. Rau, *HPL PlayDoh Architecture Specification Version 1.0*, Technical report HPL-93-80, Hewlett-Packard Laboratories, Technical Publications Department, 1501 Page Mill Road, Palo Alto, CA 94304, Feb. 1994.

[13] Scott A. Mahlke, William Y. Chen, Wen-mei W. Hwu, B. Ramakrishna Rau, and Micheal S. Schlansker, *Sentinel Scheduling for VLIW and Superscalar Processors*, Proceedings of the Fifth Int'l Conference on Architecture Support for Programming Languages and Operating Systems (ASPLOS-V), Boston, MA, Oct. 12-15, 1992, pp.238-247

[14] S. Melvin, M. Shebanow, and Y. Patt, *Hardware Support for Large Atomic Units in Dynamically Scheduled Machines*, In Proceedings of the 21st Annual International Symposium on Microarchitecture, December 1988.

[15] S.M. Moon and K. Ebcioğlu, *An Efficient Resource-Constrained Global Scheduling Technique for Superscalar and VLIW Processors*, Proc. MICRO-25, pp. 55-71, IEEE Press, December 1992.

[16] M. Moudgill, J.H. Moreno, K. Ebcioğlu, E.R. Altman, S.K. Chen, and A. Polyak, *Compiler/Architecture Interaction in a Tree-Based VLIW Processor*, Report No. RC 20694, IBM T.J. Watson Research Center. Available at `http://www.watson.ibm.com:8080`.

[17] R. Nair and M. Hopkins, *Exploiting Instruction Level Parallelism in Processors by Caching Scheduled Groups*, In Proceedings of the 24th Annual ACM/IEEE International Symposium on Computer Architecture, Denver, Colorado, June 2-4, 1997.

[18] B.R. Rau, *Dynamically Scheduled VLIW Processors*, Proc. MICRO-26, IEEE Press, December 1993.

[19] E. Rotenberg, S. Bennett, and J.E. Smith, *Trace Cache: A Low Latency Approach to High Bandwidth Instruction Fetching*, In Proceedings of the 29th Annual International Symposium on Microarchitecture, November 1996.

[20] G.M. Silberman and K. Ebcioğlu, *An Architectural Framework for Supporting Heterogeneous Instruction-Set Architectures*, IEEE Computer, Vol. 26, No. 6, June 1993, pp. 39-56.

[21] G.M. Silberman and K. Ebcioğlu, *An Architectural Framework for Migration from CISC to Higher Performance Platforms*, Proc. 1992 International Conference on Supercomputing, pp. 198-215, ACM Press, 1992.

[22] R. Sites et al. *Binary Translation*, CACM, Vol. 36, no.2, pp. 69-81, Feb. 1993.

[23] T. Thompson *An Alpha in PC Clothing* BYTE, February 1996.

On Deadlocks in Interconnection Networks*

Timothy Mark Pinkston   Sugath Warnakulasuriya
SMART Interconnects Group
EE-System Dept., University of Southern California, Los Angeles, CA 90089-2562
{*sugath@scf, tpink@charity*}*.usc.edu; http://www.usc.edu/dept/ceng/pinkston/SMART.html*

Abstract

Deadlock avoidance-based and deadlock recovery-based routing algorithms have been proposed in recent years without full understanding of the likelihood and characteristics of actual deadlocks in interconnection networks. This work models the interrelationships between routing freedom, message blocking, correlated resource dependencies and deadlock formation. We empirically show that increasing routing freedom, as achieved by allowing unrestricted routing over multiple virtual channels, makes deadlocks highly improbable and reduces the likelihood of other types of correlated message blocking behavior that can degrade performance. Our results further substantiate that recovery-based routing algorithms have a higher potential performance advantage over deadlock avoidance-based routing algorithms which, inherently, allow less routing freedom.

1 Introduction

Interconnection network routing algorithms aim to minimize message blocking by efficiently utilizing network virtual channel and physical channel resources while en uring deadlock freedom. Routing approaches to accomplish this can be based on avoiding deadlock or on recovering from deadlock. Avoidance-based routing algorithms enforce certain routing restrictions in order to altogether avoid deadlocks [1, 2, 3]. Recovery-based routing algorithms relax routing restrictions but must provide a means for recovering from potential deadlocks that may form [4, 5, 6]. Thus, the main distinction between these two approaches is the decision made in trading off routing freedom and deadlock formation.

Recent work on characterizing deadlocks in k-ary n-cube networks ($n > 1$) with unrestricted use of two or more virtual channels per physical channel concludes that deadlocks are highly improbable, indicating that deadlock recovery-based routing is *viable* [7]. However, the circumstances under which either routing approach is *preferable* depend both on the frequency with which deadlocks occur and on the degradative effects of correlated message blocking behavior which can precipitate deadlock formation. Correlated message blocking and deadlock may be so infrequent for some network configurations that avoidance-based routing could use network resources inefficiently, resulting in poorer performance. On the other hand, precipitous message blocking leading to deadlock may be so frequent and costly in other network configurations that avoidance-based routing might outperform recovery-based routing.

In this paper, we identify network design parameters which significantly influence deadlock formation, and we model the frequency and characteristics of deadlock forming phenomena in wormhole and cut-through k-ary n-cube networks. We empirically quantify the model using an interconnection network simulator that implements accurate deadlock detection capabilities. From this, we gather useful information that allows us to determine under what circumstances recovery-based routing algorithms are preferred over avoidance-based algorithms and to understand how networks should be designed to optimize the performance of recovery-based routing algorithms. We investigate the effect that routing freedom has on deadlock formation by varying routing adaptivity and the number of virtual channels supported by the network. We investigate the effect that different channel buffer configurations with fixed aggregate capacity have on deadlock formation by varying buffer width and depth. Finally, we investigate the effect that routing freedom has on the formation of non-deadlocked correlated resource dependencies by comparing message blocking behavior of well-known avoidance-based and recovery-based routing algorithms.

This work can be used to better understand the nature and likelihood of deadlock forming phenomena in interconnec-

*This research was supported in part by an NSF Research Initiation Award, grant ECS-9411587, and an NSF Career Award, grant ECS-9624251.

tion networks and their implications on network and routing algorithm design. These results provide valuable insight into the design of more efficient interconnection networks and routing algorithms, whether they be based on deadlock avoidance or deadlock recovery. Our objective is not to directly compare the performance (i.e., latency and throughput) of the two routing approaches but, rather, to compare the causal effects of various network parameters and routing approaches on message blocking behavior. To our knowledge, this study is the first of its kind to provide such insight into network and router design from the perspective of factors influencing message blocking and deadlock.

The next section provides background on deadlocks in interconnection networks and classifies deadlocks based on channel wait-for graph dependencies. Section 3 identifies key factors which influence deadlock and provides an intuitive model relating these factors to the formation of deadlocks. Section 4 presents our evaluation approach and gives empirical simulation results. Section 5 discusses related work. Finally, conclusions and future directions are presented in Section 6.

2 Deadlock Formation in Interconnection Networks

Deadlocks occur when cyclic resource dependencies are formed by consumers holding onto some resources while waiting to acquire others. In wormhole-switched interconnection networks, messages are the consumers and virtual channels are the resources. As a message travels through the network, it acquires exclusive use (ownership) of a virtual channel prior to each hop. If the first flit (header) of a message blocks, it can be thought of as requesting the exclusive use of one of possibly many alternative virtual channels in order to progress to the next hop. A blocked message can resume once a new virtual channel is acquired. As the last flit (tail) of a message moves through the network, it releases the previously acquired virtual channels which then become available for other messages to acquire. The "exclusive ownership" and "resource wait-for" conditions along with the condition that messages are not preempted makes cyclic dependencies, and therefore deadlock formation, possible.

2.1 Depicting Deadlocks

In order to depict deadlock formation, a representation which captures resource dependencies within an interconnection network is needed. We use *channel wait-for graphs* (CWGs) for this purpose [8]. Channel wait-for graphs are used to depict network state reflecting resource allocations and requests existing at a particular point in time as opposed to resource allocations allowed by the routing algorithm as in [3, 9, 10]. In this context, channel wait-for graphs are not necessarily connected.

Figures 1 through 3 show examples of messages being routed in *k*-ary n-cube wormhole networks, along with the corresponding CWGs. In the network illustrations (Figures 1a, 2a, and 3a), the source and destination nodes of message m_i are labelled s_i and d_i, respectively. In the CWGs (Figures 1b, 2b, and 3b), vertices represent virtual channels. Outgoing arc(s) at each vertex are labelled with the message which currently owns that virtual channel. A path formed by a series of solid arcs with the same label implies the temporal order in which virtual channels were acquired and continue to be owned by a particular message. Blocked messages are represented by connecting the ends of such paths to one or more desired virtual channels using dashed arcs. At any vertex, the labels of incoming dashed arcs represent the group of messages that desire to use that virtual channel at this instant in time.

Consider the scenario in Figure 1a which shows five messages (m_1, m_2, m_3, m_4, and m_5) being routed minimal adaptively in a network with a single virtual channel per physical channel. Message m_1 has acquired channels vc_0 and vc_1, and requires vc_3 to continue. Similarly, message m_2 has acquired channels vc_2 and vc_3, and requires vc_5 to continue; message m_3 has acquired channels vc_4 and vc_5, and requires vc_7 to continue; message m_4 has acquired channels vc_6 and vc_7, and requires vc_1 to continue. All four of these messages are blocked and will wait indefinitely for one of the other messages in the group to release an owned virtual channel. Message m_5 has acquired channels vc_8 and vc_9, and requires vc_4 to continue, so it is also forced to wait indefinitely.

Figure 1b shows the CWG for the scenario in Figure 1a. There is a single cycle in this graph consisting of vertices vc_1, vc_3, vc_5, and vc_7. Given the set of all vertices involved in this cycle, $R = \{vc_1, vc_3, vc_5, vc_7\}$, observe that the set of vertices that can be reached by each and every member of R is R itself. This type of relationship formed by vertices in one or more cycles is referred to as a *knot* [11]. A knot is a necessary and sufficient condition for deadlock [8]. Hence, we depict deadlocks as knots in CWGs.

2.2 Classifying Deadlocks

A deadlock can be characterized by three attributes: *deadlock set*, *resource set*, and *knot cycle density* [7, 8]. The deadlock set is the set of messages which own the virtual channels involved in the knot. The resource set is the set of all virtual channels owned by members of the deadlock set. The knot cycle density represents the number of unique cycles within the knot. For example, the deadlock in Figure 1 involves four messages in its deadlock set $\{m_1, m_2, m_3, m_4\}$, occupies eight channels in its resource set $\{vc_0, vc_1, vc_2, vc_3, vc_4, vc_5, vc_6, vc_7\}$, and has a knot cycle density of one cycle.

Message m_5, although waiting for a virtual channel owned by message m_3 and not able to proceed until the deadlock

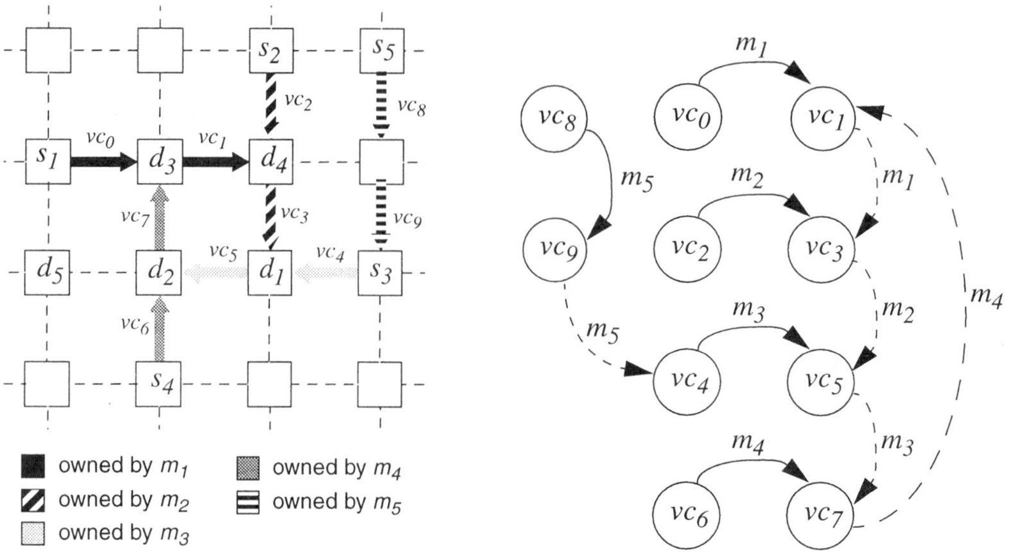

Figure 1. (a) A "single-cycle deadlock" (consisting of messages $\{m_1, m_2, m_3, m_4\}$) formed under minimal adaptive routing in a network with 1 virtual channel per physical channel in each direction. (b) The set of vertices $\{vc_1, vc_3, vc_5, vc_7\}$ forms a knot in the channel wait-for graph.

is resolved, is not considered to be in the deadlock set as its resources (vc_8 and vc_9) do not meet the condition for participation in the knot. We refer to this type of message as a *deadlock dependent message* [8] and distinguish it from those messages actually in the deadlock set. The usefulness of this distinction is evident when developing deadlock detection mechanisms for deadlock recovery-based routers. The detection mechanism must be careful not to incorrectly identify deadlock dependent messages as being among those properly in the deadlock set as removing them from the network will not resolve the deadlock. Moreover, deadlock dependent messages may be transient in that they may be able to proceed using an alternate resource not owned by one of the messages in the deadlock set.

Below, we classify deadlocks based on knot cycle density– one of the deadlock attributes which indicates complexity in correlated resource dependency required for deadlock. Classification is important because various types of deadlock (and precipitation leading to deadlock) may have different degrading effects on overall network performance. For instance, deadlocks with smaller knot densities are likely to effect local regions of the network only whereas those having larger knot densities are likely to effect more global regions of the network and, therefore, be more harmful.

2.2.1 Single-Cycle Deadlocks

Deadlocks having a knot cycle density of one cycle are what we refer to as *single-cycle deadlocks*. Single-cycle deadlocks can only occur in networks having minimal resources and/or highly restrictive routing options on available resources. For example, single cycle deadlocks can form under minimal adaptive routing only when all but one routing option is available to *all* messages comprising the deadlock set, as illustrated in Figure 1 (e.g., all messages have exhausted their adaptivity, only one virtual channel per physical channel is implemented, etc.). Single-cycle deadlocks can also form under static routing for similar reasons. In both cases, the routing function returns at most a single channel option which is reflected in the CWG by a single dashed outgoing arc at any vertex, as shown in Figure 1b (maximum "fan-out" of one). A single cycle is sufficient to form a knot. Nonetheless, in order for a knot comprised of a single cycle to form, a highly correlated pattern involving multiple messages must exist. With adaptive routing, messages must completely exhaust their adaptivity in order to form such a single-cycle deadlock. Hence, the degree of correlation required for single-cycle deadlock to form under adaptive routing is much greater than that under static routing.

2.2.2 Multi-Cycle Deadlocks

Deadlocks having a knot cycle density greater than one cycle are what we refer to as *multi-cycle deadlocks*. Figure 2 depicts a network and CWG for this more complex type of deadlock—one comprised of multiple resource dependency cycles. The network uses minimal adaptive routing and two virtual channels per physical channel per direction (bidirectional). Once again for deadlock to occur, all messages in the deadlock set must be blocked waiting to acquire any virtual channel needed to continue routing, all of which are owned by other members of the deadlock set. There are multiple unique cycles in the CWG depicting this situation. In Figure 2b, the set of all vertices involved in this group of cycles,

$R = \{vc_1, vc_3, vc_5, vc_7, vc_9, vc_{11}, vc_{13}, vc_{15}\}$, meets the requirement for a knot. The deadlock set contains eight messages $\{m_1 \ldots m_8\}$, the resource set contains 16 virtual channels $\{vc_0 \ldots vc_{15}\}$, and the knot cycle density is 24 cycles.

Channel wait-for graphs which have multiple outgoing dashed arcs per blocked message (i.e., vertex fan-out > 1) are indicative of networks which allow a greater degree of routing freedom. The fan-out reflects routing freedom which is determined, among other things, by routing adaptivity across dimensions and virtual channel selectivity within dimensions. This greatly influences the number of unique cycles that can form. More importantly, increasing the routing freedom exponentially increases the degree of correlation of resource dependency required for multiple cycles to form knots, as discussed in later sections.

2.2.3 Cyclic Non-Deadlocks

A scenario in which multiple cycles exists but which does not result in deadlock is referred to as a *cyclic non-deadlock*. Such a situation is depicted in Figure 3. This is similar to the previous example except that message m_4's destination is changed so that it can now wait for two additional channels (vc_{16} and vc_{17}) which are owned by two non-blocked messages (m_9 and m_{10}). There are still 24 unique cycles in the CWG (same as in Figure 2b), and the set of all vertices in this group of cycles is $\{vc_1, vc_3, vc_5, vc_9, vc_{11}, vc_{13}, vc_{15}\}$. However, although the vertices vc_{16}, vc_{17}, vc_{18}, and vc_{19} are reachable from members of this set, the opposite does not hold. This set (or any subset thereof) does not meet the conditions for a knot; therefore, there is no deadlock in this network. This is because message m_4 will eventually acquire vc_{16} or vc_{17} to reach its destination and subsequently release vc_7, which will allow one of the two messages waiting for this channel (m_3 or m_7) to continue (see Figure 3b). Other messages will then be able to follow in a similar fashion.

Cyclic non-deadlocks are instantiations of those cyclic dependency situations described by Duato which are allowed by his theory for deadlock-free adaptive routing [3]. Duato formally proves that cycles are necessary but not sufficient for deadlock to occur. Deadlock avoidance routing algorithms based on Duato's theorem may have resource dependency graphs with multiple cycles but always have an escape resource available to packets to avoid deadlock (such as vc_{16} or vc_{17} in Figure 3b). The elimination of cycles to avoid deadlock (as required by some avoidance-based routing schemes [1, 2, 12]) is overly restrictive. Similarly, eliminating cycles in a packet wait-for graph to avoid deadlock as in [13] is also overly restrictive—the packet wait-for graph for this example clearly contains multiple cycles, yet no deadlocks exist.

Cyclic non-deadlocks involving many correlated cycles can precipitate the formation of multi-cycle deadlocks and, as such, can degrade performance. Even if they do not lead to deadlock formation, cyclic non-deadlocks can lead to situations where messages block cyclically faster than they can be drained and, therefore, remain blocked for extended periods of time causing increased latency and reduced throughput [3] (note the drainage dependency depicted in Figure 3b). Hence, this is an important class of deadlock-forming phenomenon that must be examined to fully understand its impact on routing approaches (see Section 4.4).

3 Factors Influencing Deadlock

An intuitive model which identifies and describes the interrelationships of key factors which influence deadlock is presented. While closed-form expressions that estimate the probability of deadlock as a function of various network design parameters may provide added rigor, deriving such expressions is very complex and beyond the scope of this work. It is sufficient to simply understand the relationship between these factors qualitatively to gain insight as to how to design more optimal networks and routing algorithms.

The following interrelated factors influence the probability of deadlock formation: *routing freedom*, the number of *blocked messages* within the network, and the number of *resource dependency cycles* (as depicted in a CWG). Table 1 summarizes the interrelationships. Table 1a relates those network factors affecting routing freedom and the *capacity* for blocked messages in a network. Table 1b describes how the collective effects of the key network factors given in Table 1a influence key deadlock forming phenomena such as the *number* of blocked messages in the network, the *potential* for resource dependency cycles to form, and the *probability* of deadlock formation.

Routing freedom corresponds to the number of routing options available to a message being routed at a given node within the network. As shown in Table 1a, it can be increased by adding physical channels (i.e., increase alternative paths *available* across directions and dimensions of the network with bidirectional, higher node-degree networks), adding more virtual channels per physical channel (i.e., increase routing options *available* within each dimension), and/or increasing the adaptivity of the routing algorithm (i.e., increase routing options *allowed* within and across each dimension). Routing freedom is reflected in CWGs by the fan-out of vertices, which can be location dependent for packets enroute in the network—smaller fan-out than that maximally allowed by the routing algorithm can result if adaptivity is exhausted, as shown in Sections 2.2.1 - 2.2.3.

Blocked messages are those messages in the network which cannot acquire any of the alternative channels required to make progress at a given point in time. The capacity for blocked messages increases as the network's capacity to hold messages increases. Hence, as shown in Table 1a, it can be increased by adding physical channels, adding virtual channels, increasing virtual channel buffer depth, and/or decreasing message (packet) length. Affecting these network param-

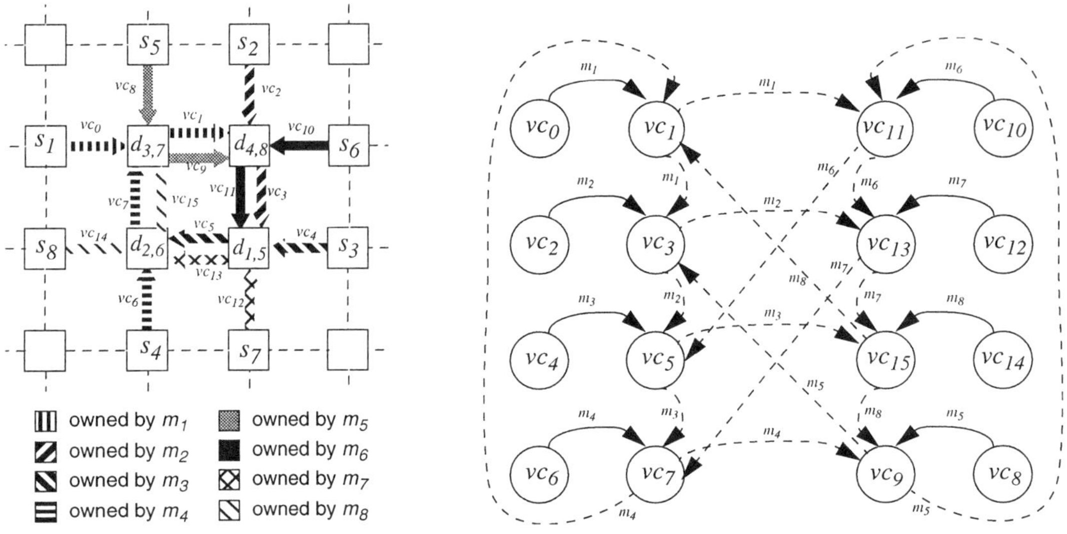

Figure 2. (a) A "multi-cycle deadlock" (consisting of messages $\{m_1, m_2, m_3, m_4, m_5, m_6, m_7, m_8\}$) formed under minimal adaptive routing with 2 virtual channels per physical channel in each direction. (b) The set of vertices $\{vc_1, vc_3, vc_5, vc_7, vc_9, vc_{11}, vc_{13}, vc_{15}\}$ forms a knot in the channel wait-for graph.

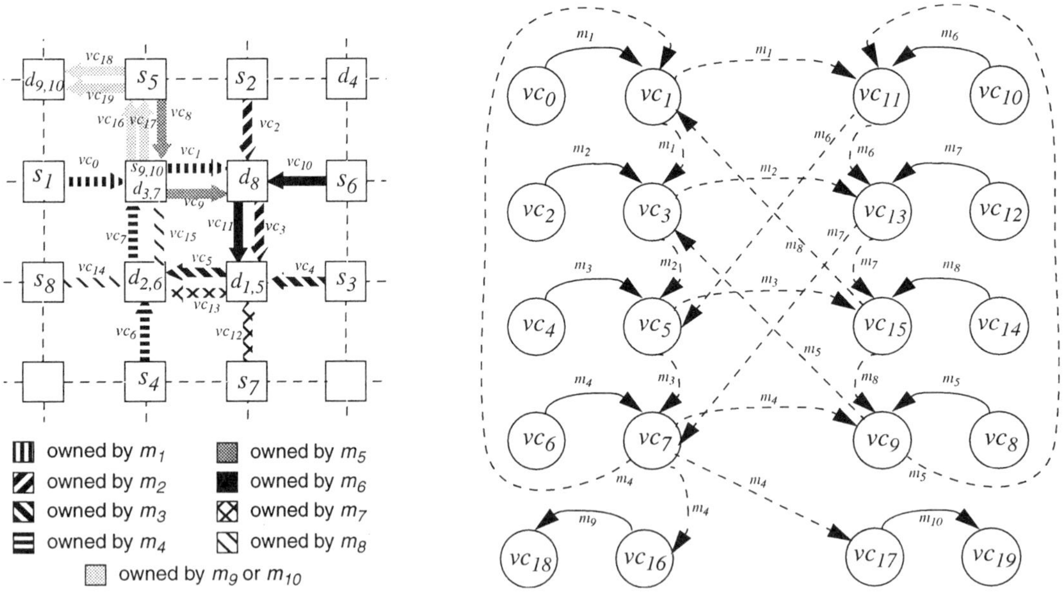

Figure 3. (a) A "cyclic non-deadlock" network state under minimal adaptive routing with 2 virtual channels per physical channel in each direction. (b) There are multiple cycles but no knots in the channel wait-for graph.

eters as such increases the number of messages which can enter the network and, subsequently, the number of messages that can potentially block at saturation. Correlated message blocking can result in resource dependency cycles described in the previous section.

As shown in Table 1b, increasing routing freedom exponentially decreases the likelihood of messages blocking in the network but exponentially increases the potential number of cycles that can form when messages block (first row of the table). The exponential relationships are due to the involutional effects of routing freedom with the number of network hops experienced by messages (for the former) and with the number of blocked messages in the network (for the latter). For instance, given an average distance of n hops each allowing a routing freedom of F, the theoretical upper bound on routing freedom of a message from source to destination is F^n, whereas blocking opportunity is only n. The upper bound can be further limited by the fact that F can decrease as hops are taken. Likewise, given B blocked messages each with a routing freedom of F, the theoretical upper bound on the number of unique cycles which can form is F^B. This can be further limited by the topological connections possible. Hence, as the number of blocked messages increase (i.e., due to lack of sufficient routing freedom), the potential for cycle formation increases exponentially, which can increase the probability of deadlock (second row of the table). The third row of the table indicates that an increase in the number of cycles actually formed increases the number of blocked messages in the network and the probability of deadlock. As described previously in the context of cyclic non-deadlocks, blocked messages involved in cycles persist in the network due to slow drainage from dependent resources, causing other messages to block.

Routing freedom has an opposite and more influential effect on deadlock probability than the number of blocked messages and cycles. As routing freedom is increased, the number of blocked messages decreases exponentially and, more importantly, the degree of correlation required among blocked messages to form a knot increases exponentially. This decreases the likelihood of deadlock exponentially as shown in the first row of Table 1b. Given enough routing freedom, this correlation factor offsets the opposing effect on deadlock probability caused by the potential exponential increase in the number of cycles. For instance, networks with minimal routing freedom may not offset the opposing effects as there may exist a one-to-one correspondence between cycles and deadlocks (e.g., single-cycle deadlocks). However, networks with greater routing freedom can offset the opposing effects as a large number of cycles can exist without deadlock formation (e.g., cyclic non-deadlocks). Confirmation of some of the interrelationships given by our model is provided in previous work [7]. Below, we further substantiate our intuitive model by empirically quantifying the influence of routing freedom and other network design parameters on deadlock forming phenomena through simulation.

4 Empirical Results of Network Factor Influences on Deadlocks

The previous section presents an intuitive model relating key influential factors of deadlock forming phenomena. Using simulation, we quantify these effects for torus connected k-ary n-cube networks by first examining the effect that routing freedom has on deadlock formation. We then examine the effect that different channel buffer configurations with fixed channel capacity have on deadlock formation. Finally, we examine the effect that routing freedom has on cyclic non-deadlock phenomena by comparing correlated message blocking behavior caused by recently proposed deadlock avoidance-based and deadlock recovery-based adaptive routing schemes.

4.1 Simulation Methodology

Our approach for precisely detecting deadlocks is based on a theoretical framework which defines a deadlock as a knot within a CWG [8]. We implement a deadlock detection algorithm that is able to identify knots within the CWG of an ongoing network simulation. The deadlock detection algorithm involves maintaining a CWG, detecting cycles within this graph, and identifying a group of cycles which form a knot. It is implemented in a flit-level simulator called *FlexSim* (an extension of *FlitSim 2.0*).

All simulations are run for normalized loads up to full network capacity or until the network saturates with respect to the number of resource dependency cycles (shown in the figures by a vertical line). In most cases, this saturation load exceeds the loads at which network performance (latency and throughput) saturates. Observing simulation results beyond performance saturation loads is necessary since, in many cases, deadlocks may not begin to form until the network is deeply saturated. Initially, each simulation was run for a duration of 20,000 simulation cycles beyond steady state. For those experiments which resulted in no deadlock, simulation was extended for a duration of 200,000 cycles in order to provide greater opportunity for deadlock to occur.

Unless otherwise stated, all simulations are performed using a torus-connected 16-ary 2-cube with bidirectional channels, a fixed message size of 32 flits, a virtual channel buffer depth of two flits, and a channel selection policy which favors continuing routing in the current dimension over turning. Random traffic patterns are simulated. A minimal *true fully adaptive routing* (TFAR) algorithm is used unless otherwise specified. This algorithm allows unrestricted routing in any profitable dimension using any available virtual channel. Deadlocks are possible since no other restrictions are enforced. Dimension-ordered routing (DOR) is used for

Network Factors	Routing Freedom	Capacity for Blocked Messages
Increased Routing Adaptivity	↑	
Increased Physical Channels	↑	↑
Increased Virtual Channels	↑	↑
Increased Buffer Depth		↑
Increased Message Length		↓

Effects of Network Factors	Number of Blocked Messages	Potential for Cycles	Probability of Deadlock
Increased Routing Freedom	▼	▲	▼
Increased Num. of Blocked Msgs.		▲	↑
Increased Number of Cycles	↑		↑

↑ Increases ▲ Exponentially Increases
↓ Decreases ▼ Exponentially Decreases

Table 1. (a) How key network factors directly affect routing freedom and the capacity for blocked messages, and (b) how they indirectly influence the probability of deadlock.

deadlock-susceptible static routing (i.e., no virtual channel class ordering is enforced). The deadlock detection algorithm is invoked every 50 simulation cycles. When a deadlock is detected, it is immediately "broken" by removing a message in the deadlock set flit-by-flit from the network so as to synthesize a recovery procedure. Deadlock set, resource set, and knot cycle density measures are used to describe the size and complexity of deadlocks. If no deadlocks are detected for a given simulation run, we use the total number of resource dependency cycles formed and the number and percentage of blocked messages to represent the conditions that could lead to deadlock formation.

4.2 Effect of Routing Freedom on Deadlock Formation

We investigate the effects of increasing routing freedom on deadlock by varying routing adaptivity and the number of virtual channels. To examine the effects of routing adaptivity, we compare DOR with TFAR. To examine the effects of increasing the number of virtual channels, we allow the *unrestricted use* of 1, 2, 3, and 4 virtual channels within each network dimension.

Figure 4a plots deadlocks versus load rate for DOR with 1 and 2 virtual channels. *No deadlocks occurred for DOR with 3 or 4 virtual channels* (so they do not show up in the figure). Deadlocks in DOR1 begin to appear at much lower load rates than for DOR2 (50% of its saturation load versus 87% of the saturation load for DOR2), and for any given load rate, DOR2 results in fewer deadlocks than DOR1. This suggests that the greater routing freedom provided by the second virtual channel, even though its use is inherently restricted to only within the current dimension by DOR, exponentially increases the degree of correlation required by messages to form deadlock, thereby reducing the likelihood of deadlock exponentially.

Figure 4b plots deadlock set size, resource set size, and knot cycle density for the deadlocks. The average deadlock set size for DOR2 is roughly two to three times larger than for DOR1. DOR1 has a maximum routing freedom of one, which leads to single-cycle deadlocks (knot cycle density of one is not plotted). In contrast, DOR2 leads to multi-cycle deadlocks with knot densities ranging from 20 to 400 cycles. The small increase in deadlock set size (at saturation load) causes this exponential increase in knot cycle density, which corresponds to the relationship between blocked messages and cycles described by our model in Section 3. Deadlocks in DOR are generally isolated to within a row or column in our two dimensional torus network, and, therefore, the factor of two difference in the resource set size of DOR1 and DOR2 simply corresponds to the number of virtual channels in a particular direction within a row or column of the network. These characteristics further suggest that in networks with greater routing freedom, deadlocks, when formed, tend to be large and complex due to the requisite higher degree of correlation among messages comprising them.

TFAR leads to a few single-cycle deadlocks and a large number of multi-cycle deadlocks when only a single virtual channel is used (about 1 deadlock for every 100 messages delivered at saturation and 1 for every message delivered in deep saturation). These deadlocks involve (on the average) deadlock sets of 20-30 messages, resource sets of 150-250 virtual channels, and densities ranging from 1 to 247 cycles (with an average density of about 20 cycles). While one virtual channel does not provide enough routing freedom to offset opposing effects, *2 virtual channels with TFAR provide enough routing freedom to virtually eliminate all deadlock.* Because deadlocks did not form in our TFAR2, TFAR3, and TFAR4 simulations, we examine message blocking and cycle

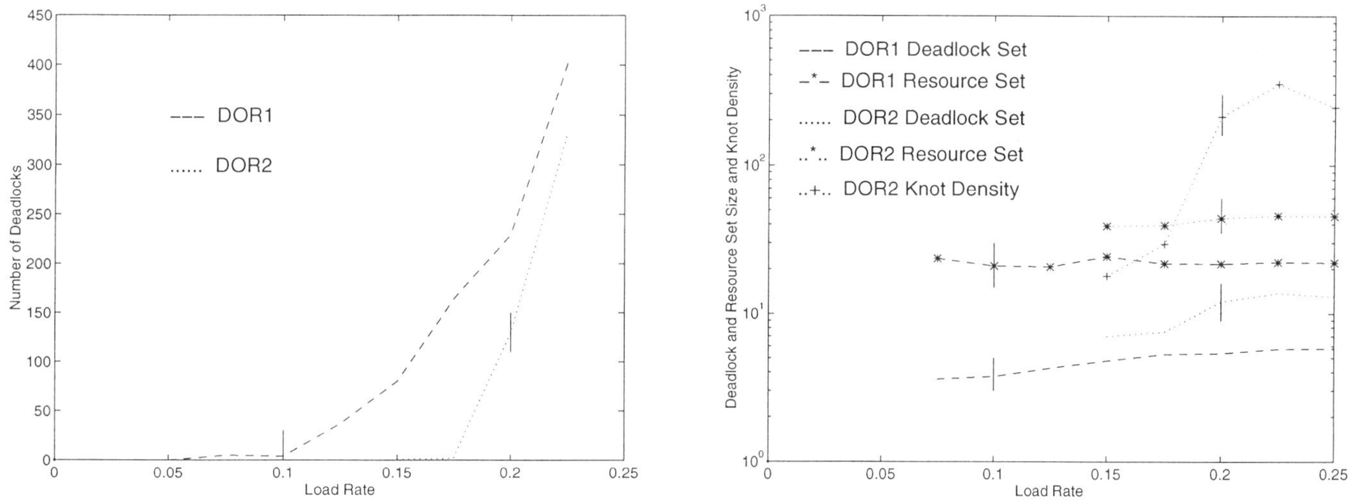

Figure 4. (a) Number of deadlocks versus load rate and (b) deadlock and resource set size and knot cycle density versus load rate for DOR with 1 and 2 virtual channels per physical channel in a 16x16 bidirectional torus under uniform traffic. A message length of 32 flits and a buffer depth of 2 flits is assumed. Vertical lines indicate performance saturation.

formation instead, both of which directly influence the precipitation of deadlock.

Figure 5a plots the number of messages in the network (upper curve) and the number of messages blocked within the network (lower curve) versus load rate. As shown, the second virtual channel increases the load at which TFAR saturates by more than a factor of two. The third and fourth virtual channel improves the saturation load by 22% and 18%, respectively. Before saturation, the number of blocked messages decreases as the number of virtual channels is increased. As described in Section 3, increasing the number of virtual channels helps to reduce the number of messages that block, causing fewer cycles to form thereby reducing the likelihood of deadlock. However, the primary deadlock reducing benefit of increasing the number of virtual channels is the increased routing freedom, which decreases the likelihood of deadlock exponentially due to the correlation in resource dependency required.

Figure 5b plots the number of cycles formed versus load rate for TFAR with 1, 2, 3, and 4 virtual channels. The number of cycles begin to grow rapidly at the point where the number of blocked messages increase, which agrees with our intuitive model. This rapid growth is caused by both the sharp increase in the number of messages which block at saturation as well as the greater routing freedom achieved through the addition of virtual channels. The absence of deadlock notwithstanding, the large number of cycles suggests the formation of large cyclic non-deadlocks at saturation, which can be potentially harmful. We examine this further in Section 4.4.

In summary, these results indicate that increasing routing adaptivity and the number of virtual channels reduce the number of blocked messages in the network, as predicted by our intuitive model. This effect, along with the higher degree of correlation of message dependencies required for deadlock due to the greater routing freedom, *greatly* diminishes the likelihood of deadlock. We find that with unrestricted routing, deadlocks tend to be eliminated with only a few virtual channels (2 virtual channels in our simulations), which confirms previous results [7]. We also find that cyclic non-deadlocks begin to grow rapidly at network saturation. This can lead to persistent blocking. Therefore, to improve performance, operating the network below saturation can make cyclic non-deadlocks less likely. These interesting results provide valuable insight as to how recovery-based routing networks should be designed to optimize performance.

4.3 Effect of Wider versus Deeper Channel Buffers on Deadlock Formation

The intuitive model presented previously indicates that increasing channel buffers either in terms of the number of virtual channel buffers (width) or the capacity of virtual channel buffers (depth) has an influential effect on the number of messages which can potentially block and cause deadlock. We now investigate the effects of wider versus deeper channel buffers on deadlock *for a fixed network capacity* by configuring channel buffers as *many but shallower virtual channels* such as in wormhole networks [12] or as *fewer but deeper virtual channels* such as in virtual cut-through networks [14]. It has been shown previously that wormhole networks are more susceptible to deadlock than cut-through networks when a fixed number of virtual channels are used [7]. However, from an implementation standpoint, this is an unfair comparison as aggregate channel capacity is higher for cut-through net-

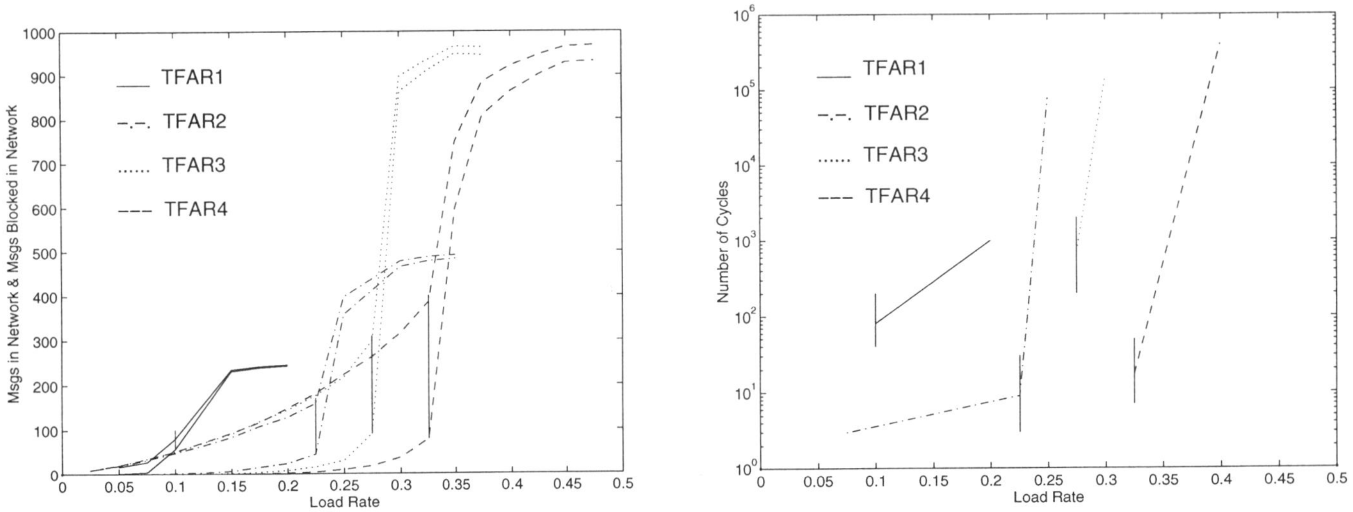

Figure 5. (a) Average number of messages (in network and blocked) versus load rate and (b) number of cycles versus load rate for TFAR with 1, 2, 3 and 4 virtual channels per physical channel in a 16x16 bidirectional torus under uniform traffic. A message length of 32 flits and a buffer depth of 2 flits is assumed. Vertical lines indicate performance saturation. The curves for the number of cycles begin with the first non-zero data point.

works under the assumption of constant aggregate number of virtual channels. Here, we wish to identify which channel buffer configuration is preferred under the fairer assumption of constant aggregate channel capacity by examining which configuration has a more beneficial effect on reducing the likelihood of deadlock and correlated message blocking when buffer costs remain fixed.

As shown in Table 1 of Section 3, configuring flit buffers as many but shallower virtual channels increases routing freedom as messages have a larger pool of resources from which to choose during routing. In contrast, fewer but deeper virtual channel buffers provide less routing freedom but allow for "message compaction" resulting in each message spanning fewer nodes on blockage. This relationship between channel buffer configuration, routing freedom, and resource coupling is illustrated in Figure 6 using CWGs. In our simulations, we assume 32 flit buffers per channel and compare the effectiveness of the following four channel buffer configurations in reducing deadlock: 1 virtual channel 32 flits deep (i.e., supports cut-through switching), 2 virtual channels each 16 flits deep, 3 virtual channels each 11 flits deep, and 4 virtual channels each 8 flits deep (i.e., supports wormhole switching and buffered wormhole switching [15]).

Our simulations show that some deadlocks occurred for the 1 virtual channel (32 flit) configuration (approximately one deadlock for every two messages delivered at deep saturation), but *no deadlocks formed for the configurations with 2 or more virtual channels for up to and beyond saturation.* Both single-cycle and multi-cycle deadlocks were found for the 1 virtual channel (32 flit) configuration. Their deadlock set sizes ranged from 4 to 200 messages, resource set sizes

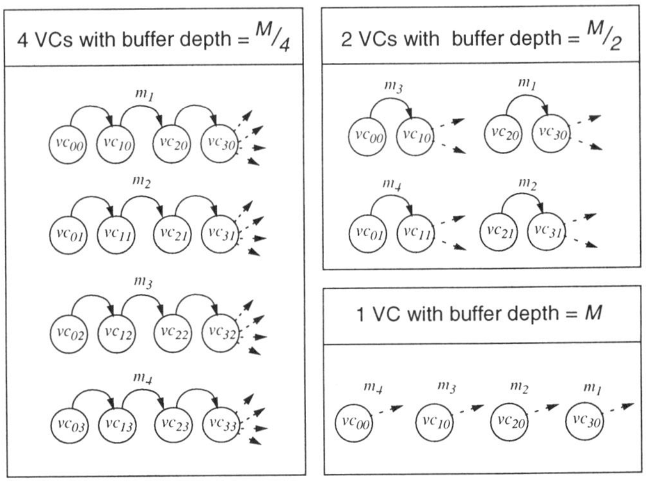

Figure 6. The effect of varying the number of virtual channels and virtual channel buffer depth for a fixed channel buffer capacity as depicted in a CWG. In this example, M = message length, m_n represents message number, and vc_{ij} are virtual channels, where i represents node number and j represents virtual channel number. Under the constant channel capacity assumption, shallower buffers allow more routing freedom but deeper buffers allow less resource coupling.

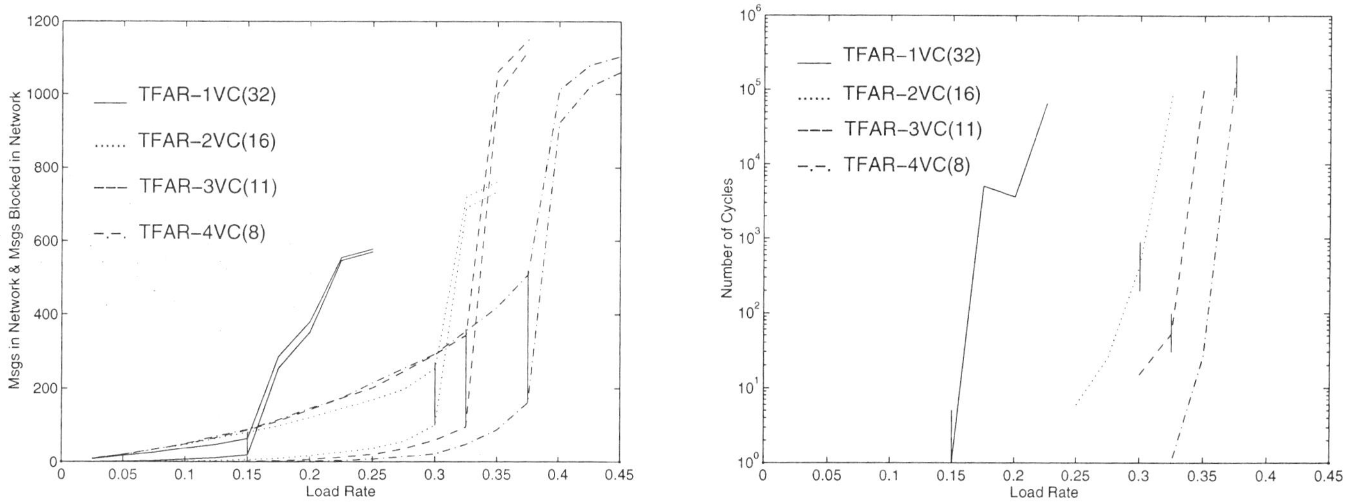

Figure 7. (a) Messages in the network and messages blocked in the network versus load rate and (b) number of cycles versus load rate for channel buffer configurations with 32 flit total capacity: 1 virtual channel (32 flits deep), 2 virtual channels (16 flits deep), 3 virtual channels (11 flits deep), and 4 virtual channels (8 flits deep). A 16x16 bidirectional torus with uniform traffic and a message length of 32 flits is assumed. Vertical lines indicate performance saturation. The curves for the number of cycles begin with the first non-zero data point.

from 18 to 250 channels, and knot densities from 1 to 105,000 cycles.

Because no deadlock formed for configurations with two or more virtual channels, we examine message blocking and cycle formation. Figure 7a shows the number of messages which enter the network and the number of messages which block versus load rate for the four router configurations. The second virtual channel increases the load supported before saturation by 83%, and the third and fourth virtual channel increase this further by 18% and 31%, respectively. When considering their respective saturation points, the TFAR-2VC(16) is able to support 210% more messages than TFAR-1VC(32), TFAR-3VC(11) is able to support 50% more messages than TFAR-2VC(16), and TFAR-4VC(8) is able to support 75% more messages than TFAR-3VC(11). In terms of the percentage of messages blocked at saturation, TFAR-1VC(32) results in 30% of messages being blocked, TFAR-2VC(16) in 30%, TFAR-3VC(11) in 21%, and TFAR-4VC(8) in 32%.

Figure 7b shows the formation of cycles for the four configurations. The number of cycles begins to grow rapidly at or near saturation, suggesting the formation of large cyclic non-deadlocks. As shown in our model, both wider and deeper buffers lead to an increased capacity for blocked messages (third and fourth rows of Table 1a). Wider buffers, however, allow the fixed capacity network to support a larger number of messages before cyclic non-deadlocks form, thereby suggesting that increased routing freedom provided by the wider buffers has a more significant effect on reducing message blocking than does the compaction resulting from deeper buffers. However, when a large number of messages block at saturation, the increased routing alternatives provided by the wider buffers contributes significantly to the rapid growth in the number of cycles as shown in our model.

In summary, results indicate that even though the capacities of the four channel buffer configurations are roughly equal, each additional virtual channel allows substantially more messages to be serviced by the network prior to saturation and fewer of them to block, making deadlocks less likely. This suggests that scarce channel buffer capacity is more effectively used as multiple shallow virtual channels than as a singular deep virtual channel. This reduces the likelihood of deadlock and cyclic non-deadlock blocking behavior considerably.

4.4 Effect of Routing Freedom on Cyclic Non-Deadlocks

Previous sections indicate that increasing routing freedom makes deadlock highly improbable even beyond network saturation, but this does not completely eliminate the formation of resource dependency cycles which cause correlated message blocking behavior. We investigate the effects of increasing routing freedom on cyclic non-deadlock phenomena by comparing deadlock avoidance-based routing—which, to some degree, limits routing freedom in order to always avoid deadlock—with deadlock recovery-based routing which allows complete routing freedom with the caveat that deadlocks are possible. We wish to identify which approach is more effective at reducing cyclic non-deadlocks and concomitant correlated message blocking assuming sufficient routing freedom is provided to make deadlock highly improbable (as assumed by deadlock recovery-based routing schemes [4, 5, 6]).

We compare *Duato*'s avoidance-based adaptive routing algorithm [3] with *Disha* [5], a recently proposed recovery-based adaptive routing algorithm. Three and four virtual channels are assumed for both, along with the other default network parameters. *Duato*'s algorithm restricts routing on two of the virtual channels in order to avoid deadlock but allows unrestricted routing on the third and fourth virtual channels. *Disha* allows unrestricted routing (minimal as well as non-minimal) on all four virtual channels, but we simulate *Disha* assuming minimal TFAR.

Figure 8a plots the percentage of messages blocked in the network for the two algorithms with 3 and 4 virtual channels. Both *Duato4* and *Disha3* improve the saturation load of *Duato3* by 50%. This is further improved upon by *Disha4* by 20%. At their respective saturation points, *Disha3* results in 50% less congestion than does *Duato3* assuming the same number of virtual channels. Similarly, *Disha4* results in 30% less congestion than does *Duato4*. The greater routing freedom allowed by *Disha* on all virtual channels can be used by messages to circumvent blockage exponentially, as represented in our model (first row of Table 1b). *Disha*'s advantage over *Duato*, however, decreases incrementally with each additional virtual channel because both algorithms allow TFAR on each new virtual channel.

Figure 8b plots the number of cycles formed versus load rate for *Duato* and *Disha* with 3 and 4 virtual channels. Cycles begin to appear and grow rapidly at saturation. This point occurs sooner for *Duato*, resulting in the formation of cyclic non-deadlocks in *Duato3* and *Duato4* prior to that for either *Disha3* or *Disha4*. As represented by our model, the increased number of blocked messages in *Duato* contributes to an exponential increase in the potential for cycles to form (second row of Table 1b). The greater routing freedom provided by *Disha* has a more significant effect on reducing message blocking than it does in contributing to highly correlated resource dependencies that lead to cyclic non-deadlocks. However, once cycles do begin to form in *Disha*, the combined effects of increased routing alternatives and message blocking on many of the alternatives tend to make the number of cycles that eventually form greater than that which can occur in *Duato*.

In summary, these results suggest that routing algorithms designed primarily to maximize routing freedom tend to cause less cyclic non-deadlock dependencies and concomitant correlated message blocking than algorithms designed primarily to avoid deadlock (and secondarily to maximize routing freedom). Hence, if the network supports sufficient routing freedom to make deadlock highly improbable, deadlock recovery-based routing algorithms should outperform deadlock avoidance-based routing algorithms as resources are used more efficiently.

5 Related Work

Previous studies have measured deadlock frequency in interconnection networks using crude approximations based on network congestion and message blocking via time-outs as the primary means for detecting deadlocks [4, 5, 16]. In contrast, our work provides insight into not only the frequency of true routing deadlocks detected accurately but also the characteristics of deadlocks and phenomena precipitating deadlock. Channel wait-for graphs have previously been used to represent connections allowed by deadlock-free routing algorithms as opposed to being used to depict and detect deadlocks as is done here. A summary of work characterizing deadlocks as knots in generalized resource graphs intended to describe deadlocks in operating systems is presented in [11]. The work presented here uses similar resource models proposed in [8] to characterize interconnection network deadlocks. Our previous work [7] precisely quantifies the frequency and characteristics of deadlocks and concludes that recovery-based routing is viable. The work presented here, however, expands upon this by relating key network parameters to possible deadlock forming phenomena as well as identifying the circumstances under which recovery-based routing is preferred over avoidance-based routing.

6 Conclusions and Future Work

This work describes the interrelationships between routing freedom, blocked messages, correlated resource dependencies, and deadlock formation. An intuitive model is developed and quantified through simulation that characterizes how key network design parameters affect routing freedom which, in turn, affects message blocking and cyclic resource dependencies which, in turn, affects routing deadlock probability. As the number of network resources (physical and virtual channels) and the routing options allowed on them by the routing algorithm increase, routing freedom increases; as routing freedom increases, the number of messages which tend to block decreases; as the number of blocked messages decrease, the number of resource dependency cycles decrease; as the number of cycles decrease, the probability of deadlock decreases exponentially owing to the fact that multi-cycle deadlocks require highly correlated patterns of cycles—the complexity of which increases with routing freedom. This leads us to conclude that *deadlocks in interconnection networks can be highly improbable when sufficient routing freedom is provided by the network and fully exploited by the routing algorithm.*

Networks which maximize routing freedom have the additional benefit of reducing the probability of cyclic non-deadlock resource dependencies which cause correlated message blocking that severely degrades network performance.

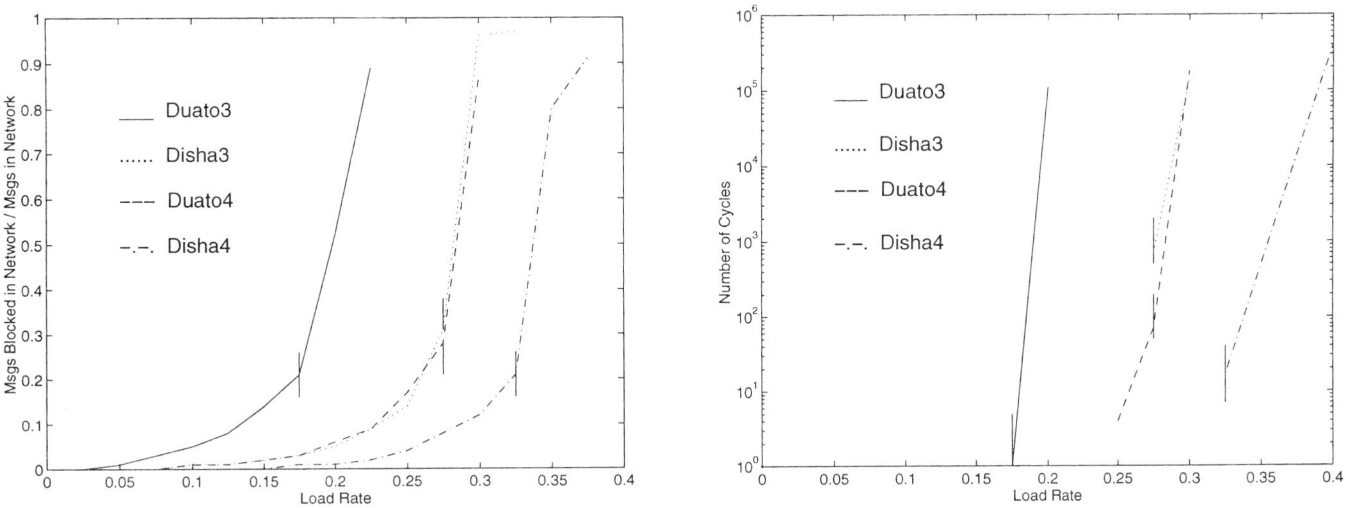

Figure 8. (a) Percentage of messages blocked in the network versus load rate and (b) number of cycles versus load rate for Duato with 3 and 4 virtual channels and Disha with 3 and 4 virtual channels in a 16x16 bidirectional torus under uniform traffic. A message length of 32 flits and buffer depth of 2 flits is assumed. Vertical lines indicate performance saturation. The curves for the number of cycles begin with the first non-zero data point.

This leads us to conclude that, given sufficient routing freedom provided by the network, *deadlock recovery-based routing algorithms have a higher potential performance advantage than deadlock avoidance-based routing algorithms.*

Further implications of our results on network and routing algorithm design will be explored in future work. We will investigate the effectiveness of throttling mechanisms [17] that limit the injection of messages into the network as a means of limiting the exponential growth rate in cyclic non-deadlock formation beyond network saturation. We will continue to characterize the interrelationship of other network factors which may affect message blocking and deadlock formation. We also plan to extend our deadlock characterization work to irregular network topologies and to hybrid, non-uniform traffic loads generated by real parallel processor applications.

References

[1] Andrew A. Chien and J. H. Kim. "Planar-Adaptive Routing: Low-Cost Adaptive Networks for Multiprocessors". In *Proc. of the 19th Symposium on Computer Architecture*, pp 268-277, May 1992.

[2] L. Ni and C. Glass, "The Turn Model for Adaptive Routing", In *Proc. of the 19th International Symposium on Computer Architecture*, IEEE Computer Society, pages 278-287, May 1992.

[3] J. Duato. "A New Theory of Deadlock-free Adaptive Routing in Wormhole Networks". *IEEE Transactions on Parallel and Distributed Systems*, 4(12):1320-1331, December 1993.

[4] J. Kim, Z. Liu, and A. Chien. "Compressionless Routing: A Framework for Adaptive and Fault-tolerant Routing". In *Proc. of the 21st International Symposium on Computer Architecture*, pp 289-300, April 1994.

[5] Anjan K.V. and Timothy M. Pinkston, "An Efficient, Fully Adaptive Deadlock Recovery Scheme: Disha", In *Proc. of the 22nd International Symposium on Computer Architecture*, pp 201-210, June 1995.

[6] Anjan K.V., Timothy M. Pinkston, and Jose Duato, "Generalized Theory for Deadlock-Free Adaptive Wormhole Routing and its Application to Disha Concurrent", In *Proc. of the 10th International Parallel Processing Symposium*, pp 815-821, April 1996.

[7] Sugath Warnakulasuriya and Timothy Mark Pinkston. "Characterization of Deadlocks in Interconnection Networks", To appear in *Proc. of the 11th International Parallel Processing Symposium*, April 1997.

[8] Sugath Warnakulasuriya and Timothy Mark Pinkston. "Implementation of Deadlock Detection in a Simulated Interconnection Network Environment", Technical Report CENG 97-01, University of Southern California, January 1997.

[9] J. Duato. "A Necessary and Sufficient Condition for Dead lock-free Adaptive Routing in Wormhole Networks". *IEEE Transactions on Parallel and Distributed Systems*, 6(10):1055- 1067, October 1995.

[10] Loren Schwiebert, D.N. Jayasimha, "A Necessary and Sufficient Condition for Deadlock-Free Wormhole Routing", *Journal of Parallel and Distributed Computing*, 32, 103-117 (1996).

[11] Mamoru Maekawa, Arthur E. Oldehoft, and Rodney R. Oldehoft, *Operating Systems: Advanced Concepts*, Benjamin Cummings, 1987.

[12] William J. Dally and Charles L. Seitz, "Deadlock-Free Message Routing in Multiprocessor Interconnection Networks", *IEEE Transactions on Computers*, Vol. C-36, No. 5, pp 547-553, May, 1987.

[13] William J. Dally and Hiromichi Aoki, "Deadlock- Free Adaptive Routing in Multicomputer Networks Using Virtual Channels", *IEEE Transactions on Parallel Distributed Systems*, Vol. 4, No. 4, April, 1993.

[14] Parviz Kermani and Leonard Kleinrock. "Virtual cut- through: A new computer communication switching technique", *Computer Networks*, pages 267-286, 1979.

[15] C.B. Stunkle et al. "The SP2 high-performance switch", *IBM Systems Journal*, vol. 34, no. 2, pp. 185-204, 1995.

[16] D. Reeves, E.Gehringer, and A. Chandiramani. "Adaptive Routing and Deadlock Recovery: A Simulation Study", In *Proceedings of the 4th Conference on Hypercube Concurrent Computers and Applications*, 1989.

[17] J. Duato. "Deadlock-Free Adaptive Routing Algorithms for the 3D-Torus: Limitations and Solutions". In *Proceedings of Parallel Architectures and Languages Europe 93*, June 1993.

Implementing Multidestination Worms in Switch-Based Parallel Systems: Architectural Alternatives and their Impact *

Craig B. Stunkel† Rajeev Sivaram‡ Dhabaleswar K. Panda‡

†IBM T. J. Watson Research Center
P. O. Box 218
Yorktown Heights, NY 10598
stunkel@watson.ibm.com

‡Dept. of Computer and Information Science
The Ohio State University
Columbus, OH 43210
{sivaram,panda}@cis.ohio-state.edu

Abstract

Multidestination message passing has been proposed as an attractive mechanism for efficiently implementing multicast and other collective operations on direct networks. However, applying this mechanism to switch-based parallel systems is non-trivial. In this paper we propose alternative switch architectures with differing buffer organizations to implement multidestination worms on switch-based parallel systems. First, we discuss issues related to such implementation (deadlock-freedom, replication mechanisms, header encoding, and routing). Next, we demonstrate how an existing central-buffer-based switch architecture supporting unicast message passing can be enhanced to accommodate multidestination message passing. Similarly, implementing multidestination worms on an input-buffer-based switch architecture is discussed. Both of these implementations are evaluated against each other as well as against a software-based scheme using the central buffer organization. Simulation experiments under a range of traffic (multiple multicast, bimodal, varying degree of multicast, and message length) and system size are used for evaluation. The study demonstrates the superiority of the central-buffer-based switch architecture. It also indicates that under bimodal traffic the central-buffer-based hardware multicast implementation affects background unicast traffic less adversely compared to a software-based multicast implementation. Thus, multidestination message passing can easily be applied to switch-based parallel systems to deliver good collective communication performance.

1 Introduction

The wormhole-routing switching technique is the current trend in building parallel systems due to inherent advantages such as low-latency communication and reduced communication hardware overhead [9, 23]. This switching technique is being used with a wide variety of topologies. Examples include k-ary n-cube networks (Cray T3D [7], Intel Paragon [11], Ncube [10]), fat-tree networks (CM-5 [16], Meiko CS2 [4]), and multistage interconnection networks (IBM SP1/SP2 [35, 36]). All of these systems are being used to support either the distributed-memory or distributed-shared memory programming paradigms. For efficient support of either paradigm, these systems require fast collective communication [2, 20] support, as defined by the Message Passing Interface (MPI) Standard, from the underlying communication subsystem. Among the set of collective communication operations, *broadcast* and *multicast* are fundamental and they are used in several other operations like barrier synchronization and reduction [25]. Thus, it is essential to reduce latency of broadcast and multicast operations on these systems to achieve high performance parallel computation.

Many software schemes have been recently proposed in the literature to efficiently implement broadcast and multicast in wormhole-routed k-ary n-cube networks [3, 21], multistage interconnection networks [38], and irregular networks[14]. All of these schemes use point-to-point (*unicast*) message passing and require multiple *contention-free* phases to achieve fast broadcast and multicast. For multicasting to d destinations, these schemes typically require $\lceil \log_2(d+1) \rceil$ communication phases. Since the ratio of communication start-up time to propagation time is quite high on current parallel systems [7, 11, 35], such a software-based unicast message-passing approach leads to very high latency for broadcast and multicast operations. In addition, under hybrid unicast and multicast traffic, the software-based approach leads to low throughput from the network. This is due to increased network contention because of multi-phase implementation of a multicast. Such performance degradation has forced researchers and designers of parallel systems to investigate hardware support for multicast [22].

A new concept, *multidestination* wormhole message passing, has been introduced recently [18, 26] for efficient implementation of collective communication operations using a fewer number of communication phases. Unlike a unicast message which has a single destination, such a mechanism allows a message to have multiple destinations. A multidestination worm provides the flexibility to distribute data to multiple nodes or to gather data from multiple nodes using a single message and a single communication start-up. These worms get routed on the data network together with the unicast messages. Using such worms it has been shown that broadcast and multicast operations on k-ary n-cube networks with different routing schemes (e-cube, adaptive, Hamiltonian, etc.) can be implemented with significantly reduced latency [18, 26] compared to unicast-based schemes. This mechanism and the associated schemes were specifically developed for direct networks with k-ary n-cube topologies in mind and thus cannot be easily extended to switch-based systems.

In our recent work [32, 33], we have extended the multidestination message passing concept to multistage interconnection networks. This extension involves a new concept called *multiport en-*

*This research is supported in part by NSF Grant MIP-9309627, NSF Career Award MIP-9502294 and an IBM Cooperative Fellowship.

coding and an asynchronous replication mechanism at the input buffers of a switch to implement deadlock-free multicast. Using this new encoding, a set of algorithms for multicast/broadcast have been developed and evaluated. In this work, it has been shown that the latency of a single multicast/broadcast operation can be reduced up to a factor of 4 compared to the software-based scheme using unicast messages.

The results in [32] show the proof-of-concept of multidestination message passing in MINs. However, the paper does not explore other architectural alternatives and their impact. For example, the IBM SP2 [36] uses a central-buffer-based buffer organization in a switch for unicast message passing, and this potentially provides a powerful basis for worm replication. Similarly, the multiport-based encoding in [32] allows a multicast to be implemented in multiple phases. Even though this approach requires fewer phases than the unicast-based software scheme, a challenging problem is to implement multicast in even fewer phases using better encoding schemes.

In this paper, we address these challenges and consider architectural alternatives and their impact on the implementation of multidestination worms for multicast/broadcast on switch-based parallel systems. We consider a *bit-string encoding* scheme to implement multidestination worms. This encoding allows a multicast/broadcast to be implemented using a single communication phase. Two alternative switch architectures, central-buffer and input-buffer, are considered. Detailed designs for implementing multidestination worms on these two switch architectures are derived. It is shown that multidestination worms can be implemented on both switch architectures with very little additional hardware. These designs also provide realistic timing parameters for routing and propagation of multidestination worms.

Next, the implementations on both switch architectures are evaluated under different traffic scenarios. Two performance measures (latency vs. throughput and received vs. applied load) are studied for multiple multicast traffic as well as hybrid traffic consisting of both multicasts and unicasts. The hardware-based implementations are also compared with the software-based multicast scheme using unicast messages. The results demonstrate the benefits of the hardware-based multicast schemes compared to the software-based scheme. Furthermore, with equal amount of buffer space in a switch, the central-buffer-based implementation shows an improvement up to a factor of 1.3–2 compared to the input-buffer-based implementation. These results clearly demonstrate the superiority of the central-buffer-based scheme to support multidestination worms for fast multicast/broadcast on switch-based parallel systems.

The paper is organized as follows. Section 2 provides an overview of switch-based parallel systems. Issues related to implementing multidestination worms are presented in Section 3. Detailed designs to implement multidestination worms on central-buffer-based and input-buffer-based switch architectures are presented in Sections 4 and 5, respectively. A comparison of these two implementations is carried out in Section 6. Section 7 shows performance evaluation results. Related work is reviewed in Section 8.

2 Switch-Based Parallel Systems

In this section we briefly describe the various categories of switch-based parallel systems and define the scope of this work. Switch-based parallel systems fall into two broad classes: (i) systems based on regular interconnects and (ii) systems based on irregular interconnects.

Communication and synchronization issues on parallel systems based on regular interconnects have been studied quite extensively. Architectures using unidirectional multistage interconnection networks (MINs) and bidirectional MINs (bidi-MINs) or fat-tree networks [16, 29] fall into this category. In such networks, the regular pattern of interconnection between switches allows for simple routing functions to be defined for routing messages between nodes. In unidirectional MINs, messages must traverse all switch stages to reach the destination processors. In bidirectional MINs on the other hand, *turnaround* routing can be used, which rewards local communication. Figures 1(a) and (b) show examples of unidirectional and bidirectional MIN networks respectively.

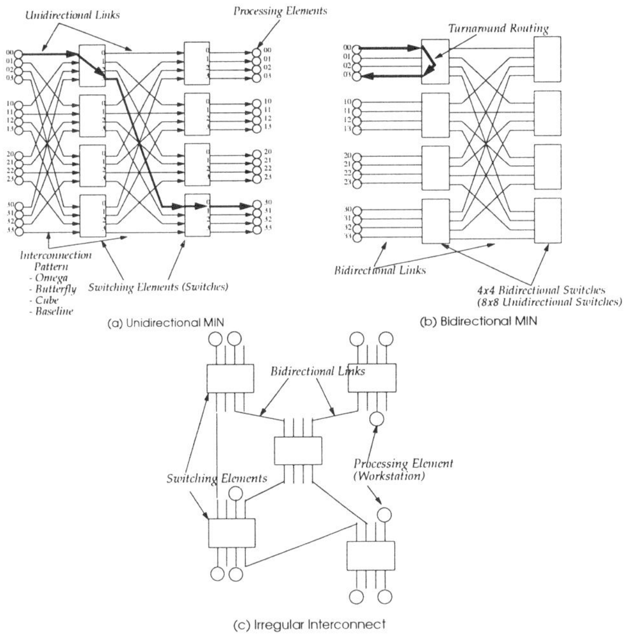

Figure 1: Examples of switch-based parallel systems.

Another class of switch-based parallel system that is becoming popular is networks of workstations (NOWs/COWs). These systems typically consist of workstations interconnected with switches in irregular topologies. Deadlock free routing of messages in such networks is a challenging problem [28, 30]. Figure 1 (c) shows an example of an irregular network of workstations.

The schemes and designs proposed in this paper are applicable to all categories of switch-based parallel systems. However, for performance comparisons we restrict ourselves to bidirectional MIN topologies. In the next section, we introduce the concept of multidestination worms in the context of switch-based parallel systems and discuss some of the issues to be considered in implementing them.

3 Issues in Implementing Multidestination Worms

The path-based multicast proposed for direct networks [18, 26] has been shown to lead to deadlock in unidirectional MINs [6]. Even without this constraint, path-based multicast is highly inefficient because the network has to be traversed multiple times, and flits of the message have to be copied and forwarded by the network interface associated with the nodes.

An alternative method for implementing multidestination worms is to augment switches with replication capability. A switch replicates flits of an arriving multidestination worm to one or more of its output ports. In strict or pure wormhole routing, switches buffer only a single flit of an arriving worm and cannot accept the next flit until this buffer is freed. For a multidestination worm that has to be forwarded to multiple output ports, this buffer cannot be freed until the switch can forward the flit to all (required) output ports. Thus deadlock can easily occur if two multidestination packets that must be forwarded to the same set of output ports arrive at a switch with one of the worms reserving a subset of the output ports and the other worm reserving the rest. This deadlock problem exists even if the switch can buffer more than one flit. Figure 2 presents an example of such a deadlock scenario. In the next section we describe two replication mechanisms that have been proposed in the literature and the methods that they adopt to overcome this deadlock problem.

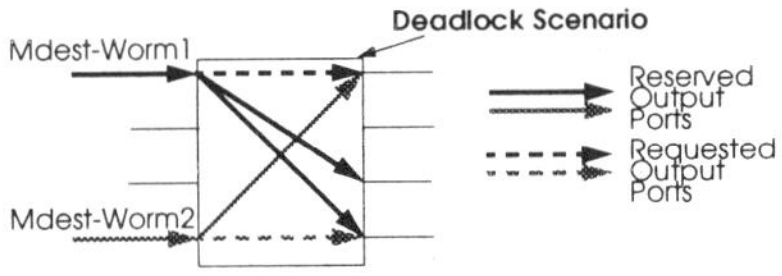

Figure 2: Typical case of deadlock for multidestination worms that use replication at the switches.

3.1 Deadlock-free Replication

Two replication methods have been proposed in the literature. *Synchronous* replication requires that flits of a multidestination worm proceed in lock-step. Thus any *branch* of the multidestination worm that is blocked can block all other branches. This replication mechanism was originally proposed in the context of pure wormhole routing and is susceptible to deadlock. Furthermore it requires some kind of feedback architecture to ensure that the flits proceed in lock-step [6].

Asynchronous replication [6, 27] is an alternative mechanism that allows flits of a multidestination worm to be forwarded to the subset of requested output ports that the worm successfully reserves. If a switch is equipped with a buffer of size f flits, under asynchronous replication at most f flits can be forwarded to the output ports that have been reserved by the multidestination worm before the worm is blocked because of the required output ports which it could not reserve. This is because none of the f flits in the buffer can be freed as they haven't been forwarded to all of the required output ports, and more flits cannot enter the full buffer. *Bubbles* are therefore introduced if the remaining requested output ports cannot be obtained before the input buffer fills up. Even this method of replication is susceptible to deadlock.

To prevent deadlock under synchronous replication, deadlock avoidance schemes have been proposed that arbitrate between multidestination packets at a switch to prevent cyclic wait [6]. To prevent deadlock under asynchronous replication, switches must be equipped with buffers large enough to store the largest packet in the system. Deadlock is prevented if the switches can guarantee that a packet accepted for transmission can be *eventually* completely buffered at the switch [32], a requirement that is weaker than virtual cut-through [13].

Asynchronous replication may be preferred for a practical implementation due to the following reasons. Firstly, it does not require the costly feedback architecture required under synchronous replication. Secondly, it is more efficient because blocked branches don't block other branches (in fact, there is no dependence across branches). Finally, many current day switches already provide for relatively large buffers at the switches [4, 36] making the satisfaction of the deadlock-freedom requirement under asynchronous replication easier.

In this paper we present two alternative implementations of multidestination worms with asynchronous replication. The two implementations differ primarily in the way they guarantee that an arriving multidestination worm can eventually be completely buffered. One of the implementations uses a central-buffer-based switch architecture. This architecture uses an output queuing technique similar to the ones used in switches of the IBM SP2 [36] for unicast message passing. The other implementation uses an input-buffer-based switch architecture. Detailed designs to implement multidestination worms on these two switch architectures are discussed in Section 4 and 5 respectively. In the remaining part of this section we discuss two additional issues related to implementing multidestination worms: header encoding and routing.

3.2 Header Encoding

A variety of header encoding mechanisms for routing multidestination headers have been proposed in the literature. These schemes differ in the following characteristics: size of the header required for encoding, knowledge required at the switches about the system topology, complexity and speed of the decoding logic required at the switches, and the multicast sets that can be covered using these schemes [5, 32]. It must be emphasized that the encoding and decoding mechanism used for routing a multidestination worm is independent of the scheme adopted for replicating a multidestination worm at a switch.

In [32] we have proposed a multiport encoding scheme for multidestination worms. This encoding mechanism allows extremely simple decoding logic at the switches. In addition, switches are not required to know the topology of the MIN network. Depending on the network topology, the source node encodes the header of a multidestination worm based on the path that needs to be followed to reach a set of destinations. However, all arbitrary multicast destination sets cannot be encoded in a single worm using multiport encoding. Instead, given an arbitrary multicast destination set, a set of multiport encoded worms are required to cover the destinations. A multi-phase multinomial tree based approach is adopted to perform multicast using this set of multiport encoded worms. Even though this scheme performs better than software-based multicast using unicast message passing, a multi-phase implementation may not be desirable for system level multicasts such as cache invalidation traffic in distributed shared memory systems. This is because with cache invalidation only the source node has information about the destination set [8]. Thus, a single phase implementation may be preferable in such systems, perhaps at a slight additional decoding logic cost.

One form of header encoding that accomplishes multicast to arbitrary multicast destination sets in a single communication phase is *bit-string encoding* [5, 27]. The encoding consists of N bits where N is the system size, with a '1' bit in the ith bit position indicating that processor i is a multicast destination.

To decode a bit-string encoded header a switch must possess knowledge about the processors that can be reached through each of its output ports. This *reachability information* [27] can be encoded using a similar N bit string for each output port with '1' bits denoting processors that are reachable via the output port. Such an N-bit string is associated with each output port. For some unidirectional MINs, the space required to store this information can be reduced by taking into account the fact that a processor may be reached from only one of the switch's output ports because of the unique path property possessed by some of these networks. The reachability information can be set up at the switches at the time of system startup or reconfiguration. Figure 3 shows a bidirectional

MIN network along with the reachability information associated with some of the output ports. The figure also shows a bit string encoded header and the path followed by the corresponding multidestination worms.

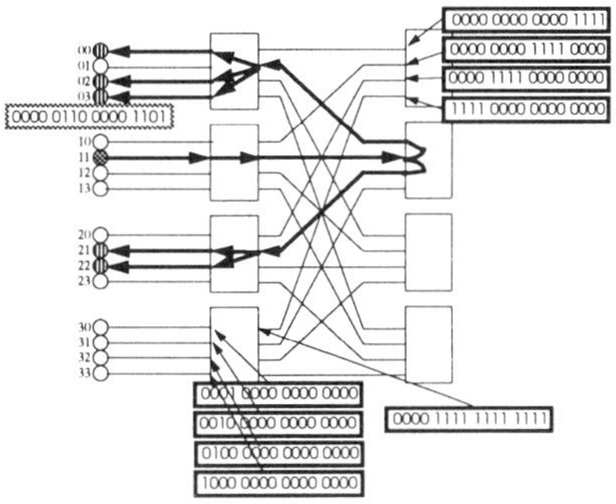

Figure 3: An example of a bidirectional MIN network with 16 processors, bit-string encoded header with the path of the corresponding multidestination worm, and the reachability strings associated with some of the output ports.

When a multidestination worm with a bit-string encoded header arrives at a switch, the switch compares the bit-string in the header with the reachability information associated with every one of its output ports. The output ports required by the worm can thus be determined. The logic required to compare these bit-strings is quite simple and thus, we do not present it in detail.

3.3 Routing

Although the bit-string encoding presented in the previous section allows a multidestination worm to be replicated along a fixed path from a source to its destinations, the presence of alternative paths between nodes in some switch-based networks may not be adequately exploited using the bit-string encoding alone. In networks like the bidi-MINs, there exists considerable choice in the way a multidestination message can get routed. A multidestination message could replicate downwards on its forward path while going to the *least common ancestor* (LCA) [29] stage of the source and destinations and then cover the remaining destinations by replicating on the way back from the LCA stage[1].

Alternatively a multidestination worm could just travel to the LCA stage and then cover all the destinations by replicating on the way back [27]. Since the same set of destinations can be reached from any switch in the LCA stage, choice exists in both methods for determining the path taken upto the LCA stage—one can decide to deterministically route messages to the LCA stage or to make the choice adaptively.

In this paper, we assume that multidestination worms travel adaptively up to the LCA stage and that the destinations are covered by replicating on the downward path from the LCA stage. In addition to the bit-string encoded header, the worm may carry a count field which is initialized to the LCA stage. The count is decremented at each switch on the worm's forward path and the worm begins its backward journey when the count value becomes zero. It is to be noted that such choices of path do not exist for unidirectional MINs with the unique path property.

[1]Such a method allows replication to proceed in both directions within a switch. This introduces deadlock problems because of multidestination packets traveling in one direction using up the entire buffer space at a switch that uses a shared central buffer for replication. Such deadlock can be avoided by ensuring that at all times there exists at least one packet's space in the buffer for multidestination packets traveling in either direction.

For irregular topologies, routing can be performed much like the routing described for bidi-MINs by assuming a tree structure superimposed on the irregular network. Such tree structures are typically used in irregular networks to provide deadlock-free routing of unicast messages. For example, in the up*/down* [30] routing algorithm, a tree structure is imposed on the networks and links are uniquely identified as 'up' links or 'down' links depending on whether they take you closer or farther away from the root. Such a tree can be used to determine reachability information for the 'down' links of the switches. Multidestination routing can then be performed by adaptively routing a message to a LCA switch by following 'up' links and then replicating the message on the 'down' path at the intermediate switches using the reachability information associated with each of the switches' 'down' links.

In this section, we have described some of the issues with respect to implementing multidestination worms in switch-based architectures. In the next two sections we discuss how asynchronous replication of multidestination worms can be implemented on two alternative switch architectures: central-buffer-based (output-queue-based) and input-buffer-based.

4 Central Buffer (Output Queue) based Switch Architecture

We now describe a switch architecture with output buffering modified for implementing multidestination worms. We first describe an output buffer based switch architecture very similar to the high performance switch in the IBM SP2 [36]. We then present modifications that could be made to this architecture to implement multidestination worms.

4.1 Buffered Wormhole Routing

The *buffered wormhole routing* used in the IBM SP2 is a variation of wormhole routing wherein every switch in the network is equipped with a central buffer and a crossbar, as illustrated in Figure 4. When a packet arrives at an input port and encounters no

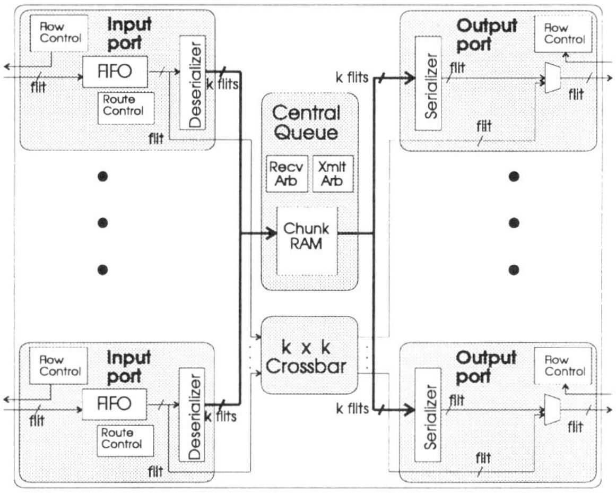

Figure 4: A switch equipped with a central buffer

contention for the chosen output port, the packet uses the crossbar path for minimal delay. However, when packets are blocked at an input port due to a busy output port, the switch attempts to store the packet in this central buffer, thus freeing the links held by the trailing packet flits. There may be enough space in the central buffer to store the entire packet. However, there is *no guarantee* that a packet arriving at a switch will find enough space in the central buffer to be completely stored. If the central buffer does not have adequate space to store the entire blocked packet, as many as possible of the packet flits are stored in the central buffer and the remainder of the packet is blocked in place. Note that in the absence of contention, packets may propagate through the network just as in a purely wormhole routed network, and the central buffers will remain empty.

An SP2-like central buffer is an extremely attractive resource for packet replication because multiple output ports can retrieve the identical packet flits from the same shared buffer. However, because there is no assurance that this central buffer can store an entire multidestination packet, the central buffer as described cannot guarantee to prevent multicast deadlock. To address this problem, we will describe minor modifications to the basic central buffer free-space logic that are similar to virtual cut-through operation. Specifically, these changes guarantee that any packet admitted to the central buffer can (eventually) be entirely stored. This guarantee effectively decouples the interdependence of the replicated output packets at a switch, eliminating the cause of multicast wormhole routing deadlock.

In the SP2 buffered wormhole implementation, the central buffer effectively forms a separate FIFO queue of packets for each output port. Each input port can write flits into the buffer, and each output port can read flits. Central buffer space is dynamically allocated to requesting input ports on a least-recently-served basis.

For a k-port switch, k flits are buffered (deserialized) by an input port into a k-flit *chunk* before being written into the central buffer. These k-flit chunks are read from the central buffer and are disassembled (serialized) into k flits again by the intended output port. This reduces the number of central buffer RAM read and write ports required. As an example, in the 8-port SP2 switches, up to 1 flit is received (transmitted) at each input (output) port every cycle. An SP2 chunk is therefore 8 flits, and the central buffer only requires 1 RAM write port and 1 RAM read port to match the input and output bandwidth of the switch. In general, for a switch with k input and k output ports, a chunk size of k flits is required for a 2-port RAM to match the input and output bandwidth of the switch. The central buffer logic maintains a list of free chunk locations. A central buffer write allocates a free chunk, and a read returns a free chunk.

There must be a mechanism—the next-packet list—to order the packets within each packet queue. Each packet is divided into chunks, and thus there is also a mechanism—the next-chunk list—to order the chunks within a packet.

To record these two types of linking information, two pointer fields are associated with each chunk of data: the next-packet (NP) field and the next-chunk (NC) field (see Figure 5). In addi-

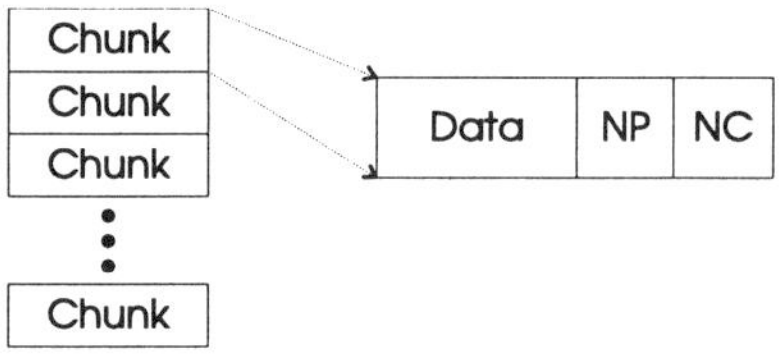

Figure 5: Organization of a central buffer

tion, each output port o maintains first-packet ($firstP[o]$) and last-packet ($lastP[o]$) pointers into its packet queue, and a first-chunk ($firstC[o]$) field that points to the next chunk to be read if output port o has not read the last chunk of the current packet. Each input port i maintains a last-chunk ($lastC[i]$) field that points to the last chunk written by input port i. All pointers are assumed to be nil when invalid. In the following discussion, we shall assume input port i is writing chunks to output port o.

The next-packet list is updated each time the first chunk (the *header chunk*) of a packet is written. If no packets are currently on the destination output port's packet queue ($firstP[o] \equiv nil$), then $firstP[o] \leftarrow writeloc$, where $writeloc$ is the address where the header is written. Otherwise, $NP[lastP[o]] \leftarrow writeloc$. The last-packet pointer is updated ($lastP[o] \leftarrow writeloc$), and the packet-list is terminated ($NP[writeloc] \leftarrow nil$).

The logical structure of a typical output port queue within the central buffer is shown in Figure 6. There are two packets shown,

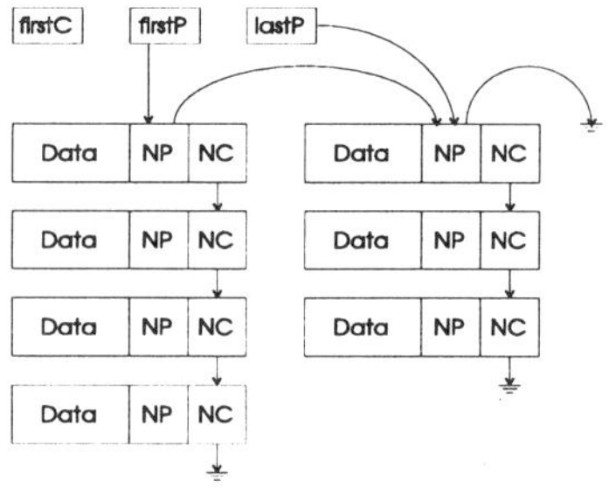

Figure 6: Structure of an output port queue within the central buffer

each with its associated chunks displayed in a column. Pointer fields with no arrows emanating from them are currently invalid (e.g., next-packet fields are not used except for header chunks).

When a header chunk is read from the central buffer, the next-packet list must also be updated ($firstP[o] \leftarrow NP[readloc]$). It should be evident that the order of packets on a queue is entirely determined by the order of header chunk writes.

The next-chunk fields provide a similar linking function between packet chunks. On a write, when a valid last-chunk pointer exists, the central buffer next-chunk location pointed to by last-chunk is updated with the location of the currently written chunk (if $lastC[i] \neq nil$, then $NC[lastC[i]] \leftarrow writeloc$). When an input port writes a chunk, it also updates its last-chunk pointer with the write location ($lastC[i] \leftarrow writeloc$).

On the output port side, except for when a header chunk is being read, the output port first-chunk field is used to determine the location of the next central buffer chunk read ($readloc \leftarrow firstC[o]$). For header chunk reads, the first-packet pointer is used ($readloc \leftarrow firstP[o]$). On every chunk read, the output port's first-chunk pointer is updated with the associated central buffer next-chunk pointer ($firstC[o] \leftarrow NC[readloc]$).

Figure 7 shows the structure of the queue from Figure 6 after the first two chunks of the first packet in the queue have been read by the output port. Note that $firstP$ and $firstC$ have been updated, and $firstC$ is now a valid pointer field required for retrieving the next chunk from the queue.

4.2 The Shared Central Buffer Replication Method

We desire a replication method that requires only one copy of the packet to be transmitted from the input port, and a method which acquires the deadlock-avoidance advantages of virtual cut-through operation. This goal can be achieved via the central buffer, with replication occurring during the *read* of the chunk out of the central buffer by the output port.

In this single-copy replication method, the input port writes each chunk into the central buffer once, but also initializes an associated counter c to k_s, where k_s is the degree of replication required

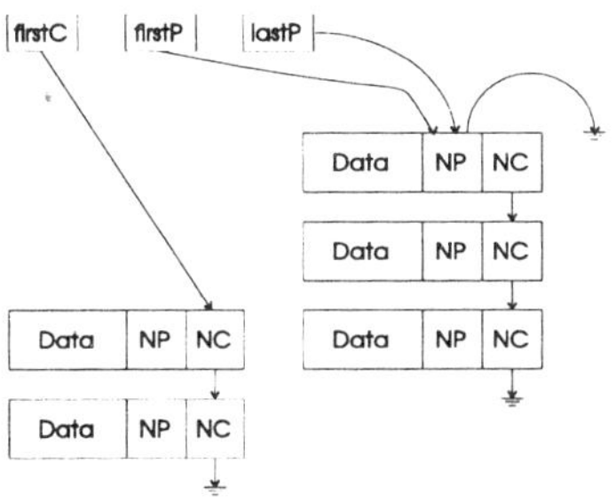

Figure 7: Structure of the same output port queue after two chunk reads

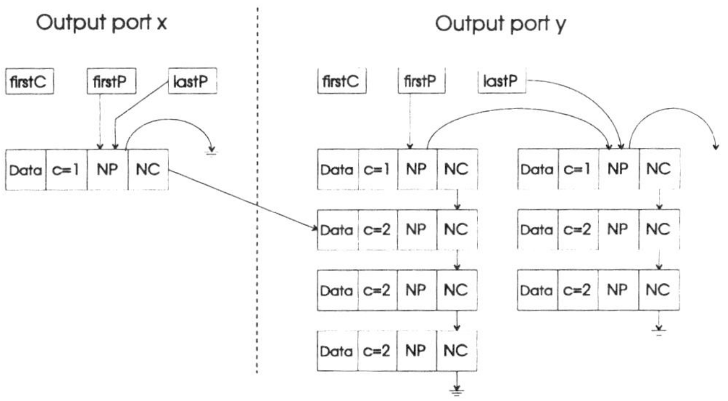

Figure 8: Replicated header chunks pointing to the same second chunk

at that switch. When an output port reads the chunk from the central buffer, it checks c. If $c \equiv 1$, then the chunk is thrown away. Otherwise, c is decremented.[2] The relatively large size of a chunk minimizes the impact of adding a counter c to the storage space for each central buffer chunk.

The multiple-flit size of a chunk provides another striking advantage for this method: an input port can write a multidestination packet into the central buffer at full bandwidth, while simultaneously all k_s output ports are reading the packet at full bandwidth. Thus latency *and* required buffer space are minimized. We have established the motivation for the single-copy replication method; in the next section we examine the implementation issues.

4.2.1 Replication Implementation

In this section we describe modifications to the basic buffered wormhole strategy that provide efficient single-copy replication. The basic change is to provide a counter, c, with each chunk that indicates the number of output ports that have not yet read the chunk from the central buffer, as introduced in the preceding section.However, there remains a problem with the next-packet lists.

If a single header chunk is written to the central buffer, then there exists only a single next-packet pointer associated with this header chunk. Therefore, even if the last-packet and appropriate next-packet pointers are updated for every destination output port, the next-packet lists will be converged, an unacceptable situation.

One solution is to write k_s copies of the header chunks, one for each destination output port. This immediately provides a distinct next-packet pointer for each queue, maintaining their disjoint nature. All other chunks of the multidestination packet are written once. This method requires $k_s - 1$ more chunks of central buffer space. Because it requires several cycles for the header write, this temporarily reduces the achievable total bandwidth into (but not of) the central buffer. Figure 8 illustrates this solution. Output ports x and y share the same packet at the start of their queues, yet their next-packet lists remain separate.

4.2.2 Emulating Virtual Cut-Through

As explained before, the equivalent of virtual cut-through (VCT) operation is required to avoid the dependence between output ports which can lead to multicast deadlock. VCT designs perform flow-control on a packet basis, allowing transmission of a packet from a switch only when the entire packet can be buffered at the downstream switch or node. Wormhole flow-control designs can be augmented to provide the aspects of VCT that are essential for multicasting, given sufficient buffering capability within each switch. To use a central buffer for emulating VCT, the total central buffer size must be as large or larger than the largest packet to be buffered.

When a multicast packet is replicated at a switch, each chunk of this packet must be stored in the central buffer before being read by all destination output ports. The packet header chunk is not allowed to enter the central buffer until there is a *guarantee* that the entire packet will *eventually* obtain space within the central buffer. This does not necessarily require that space for the entire packet exists *prior* to writing the header chunk.[3] When the header chunk is written (at least before any other chunk from any input port is subsequently written) the required number of chunks are reserved for use by that multicast packet only. In designs that maintain a "free chunk counter," this is most easily accomplished by decrementing the free space count by the total number of multicast packet chunks to be written.

To summarize, although the normal wormhole switch-to-switch flow-control is used between switches, the multicast packet header chunk is prevented from entering the central buffer until the entire multicast is guaranteed to fit within this buffer. This is a weaker requirement than VCT, and is only applied to multicast packets which are to be replicated within that switch. Thus, multidestination worms can be implemented in central buffer-based switch architectures with very little additional hardware support.

If some or all of the destination output ports are idle, it is possible to forward flits directly to these idle ports via the crossbar to minimize latency. However, because the idle ports could soon block from downstream traffic congestion, these ports might eventually require use of the central buffer as well. Conversely, a full central buffer could prevent the multicast packet from being written into the buffer (for the "busy" output ports) at full bandwidth, and this would slow the progress of succeeding flits destined for the idle ports. To simplify the accompanying design issues, we did not consider forwarding multicasts through the crossbar.

5 Input Buffer based Switch Architecture

In this section we describe an input-buffer-based switch architecture for implementing multidestination worms. The crucial step is to increase the size of the input buffers in the switch so that they are larger than the largest multicast packet allowed in the system. Any multicast packet that arrives at an input port is thus guaranteed to be

[2] An implementation need not strictly follow this convention. For instance, c could initially be set to $k_s - 1$, in which case if $c \equiv 0$ then the last output port is reading the chunk. This choice might allow c to be implemented with 1 less bit.

[3] If the designer can identify cases in which chunks currently within the central buffer are guaranteed to be read and freed, then these chunks may be able to be counted toward the available buffer space. These cases will vary from design to design and may also be topology-dependent.

completely buffered eventually (the packet at the head of the buffer will definitely be eventually freed implying that packets behind it will definitely progress one by one to the head of the buffer).

Just as with the previous architecture, flits of an arriving multidestination worm are assembled into chunks and stored in a chunk-wide RAM that constitutes the input buffer. When a multidestination worm arrives at the switch, a count value is associated with every one of its chunks. The switch decodes the multidestination worm header to determine the output ports to which the worm should be forwarded. A request is then enqueued for each of these output ports and the idle output ports begin reading chunks of the message from the appropriate input ports. As a chunk is read, the count value associated with it is decremented and the chunk is discarded once all output ports have read it. The chunk that is read is stored in an output buffer from where it is transmitted onto the next link on a flit by flit basis. Note that the header chunk is also read by each of the output ports as part of the message—every branch of the multidestination worm carries the same bit string header implying that no header manipulation needs to be done at the intermediate switches. As discussed in the previous section, chunking allows output ports to maintain a flit per cycle rate while requiring only a 2 port (1 read, 1 write) RAM. Figure 9 shows a snapshot of a multidestination worm with asynchronous replication making progress in an input-buffer-based switch architecture. In the figure, the multidestination worm enqueues a request for a busy port, while the ports that are available read chunks of the worm from the input buffer, simultaneously decreasing the associated count value. The ports take turns reading from the input buffer.

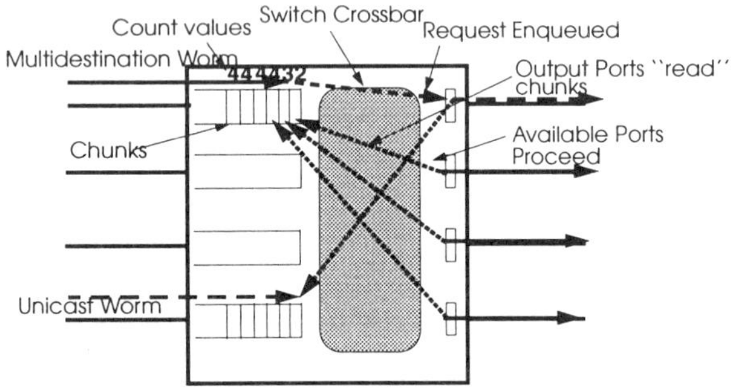

Figure 9: Snapshot of a multidestination worm making progress through a switch with an input buffer based architecture.

An implication from the above description is that a chunk is transmitted in a single cycle across the switch crossbar. This would require a chunk-wide crossbar in a naive implementation, which would increase the wiring complexity within the switch chip. To alleviate this problem we have proposed alternative implementations which perform as well as an implementation with a chunk-wide crossbar [33]. These implementations pipeline the transfer of flits in a chunk from the input to output by either (i) using k separate flit-wide RAMs instead of a single chunk-wide RAM (where k is the number of input and output ports in the switch, which defines the chunk size as described before) or (ii) using a series of registers to pipeline the transfer of the flits from the chunk-wide RAM. Alternatively the pipelined memory outlined in [12] may also serve the same purpose. Interested readers are requested to refer to [33] for further details on the approaches using the flit-wide RAMs and the register pipeline.

Another important design decision in this architecture is whether packets at different points in the input buffer should be allowed to make progress or whether progress should be restricted to the packet at the 'head' of the input buffer. The former option implies that a fairly complex next packet list must be associated with every output port, much like the next packet list described in the context of the central buffer in the previous section. While this list is associated with the single central buffer in the previous section, the presence of multiple input buffers complicates the structure of this list. This complexity is eliminated if only packets at the head of the input buffer are allowed to make progress—an output port need only know which input port it must serve next, the location to read from to begin transfer is implicit. We therefore decided to adopt the approach with packets being processed in FIFO order for our study.

6 Comparing the two architectures

In this section we qualitatively examine the two proposed architectures before comparing them to software multicasting in the next section. Both schemes will benefit from using fewer links overall for a multicast, compared to the links used by the $\lceil \log_2(m+1) \rceil$ messages required for the software multicast. The central buffer approach is significantly more complex, thus it is not worth considering unless it is expected to provide better performance. It is well-known that shared central buffers provide superior performance for most unicast traffic [37, 36].

The central buffer based architecture provides a dynamically-shared resource for input and output ports. In contrast, the input buffer implementation statically and evenly divides the available storage among the input ports. If the load among the input ports is unbalanced, the central-buffer-based scheme is likely to benefit because the ports have shared access to a larger buffer and can potentially use nearly the entire space available even when some or all of the intended output ports are busy with other traffic. In a bidi-MIN network, multidestination worms adaptively travel from the source to the least common ancestor and then turn back. They then replicate on their downward path, tending to cause more blocking on the "right" input ports than on the "left" input ports, and a centrally-buffered scheme can adjust to this imbalance.

Another expected drawback of the input buffer based implementation is head-of-the-line blocking: a blocked packet at the head of the FIFO blocks all packets behind it. Multicast is likely to exacerbate this problem, as the packet at the head of the input FIFO will not be dislodged until all destination output ports have read the entire packet. In the next section, our simulation experiments attempt to quantify these comparisons.

7 Performance Evaluation

To assess the performance impact of input FIFO replication and central buffer replication schemes, we conducted simulations on a C++/CSIM-based model incorporating these options. To judge hardware multicasting versus software multicasting methods, we also implemented the binomial tree-based U-Min algorithm [38] that eliminates link contention among the unicast messages of a software multicast.

7.1 Simulation parameters and methodology

The default performance parameters and the central buffer model were based roughly on a contemporary switch: the SP Switch of the IBM RS/6000 SP systems which is a successor to the SP2 High Performance Switch [36]. Each switch in these systems has 8 input ports and 8 output ports, where input and output ports are typically paired and connected to another switch's input/output port pair over a bidirectional link. Each output (input) port can send (receive) a 2-byte flit every 13.33 nsec cycle, for a maximum of 300

MB/s of bidirectional traffic over the link. For our simulations, we count latency in cycles and we assume 2-byte flits. Minimum latency through each switch is assumed to be 6 cycles, with 4 cycles required for reading data out of the input FIFO, determining the route, requesting output port(s), and granting the request. For input port FIFO replication or for traversing the switch via the central buffer, flits are deserialized into a chunk, requiring 7 extra cycles for the 8-flit chunks.

As in the SP Switch, we assume the central buffer accommodates 256 chunks, each of which contains eight 2-byte flits, for a total of 4 Kbytes of storage. In the central buffer model, each of the 8 input FIFOs contains 64 flits, for a total on-chip packet buffer space of 5 Kbytes. To equalize storage between the central buffer and input buffering models, we assume 640 bytes (320 flits) of storage for each input FIFO in the input buffering model.

We assume that packet flits are immediately pulled from the network upon arrival at a node. As with most network simulations, in our experiments we measure latency vs. applied load and received vs. applied load (under both switch architectures). We simulated random traffic for 128-byte and 512-byte messages, and we assumed that both of these message sizes fit within a single packet. For an m-way multicast simulation on an n-node system, for each message we randomly chose m uniformly distributed destinations among the $n-1$ non-source nodes. Message transmission times for each node were exponentially distributed. Latency results include queuing time at the source node, and latency curves are not plotted above the saturation bandwidth (latency is infinite in a stable but saturated system). To create a stable environment for statistics collection, we typically ran the simulations with 100,000–150,000 cycles (or more) of cold start time before commencing data collection.

7.2 Multicast simulation issues

Multicast traffic evaluation raises new issues beyond unicast traffic. The definition of multicast latency is problematic: latency can be defined as (a) the latency of the last received message of the multicast, or (b) as average of the latencies of each received message of the multicast. Nupairoj and Ni [24] argue that (a) is the more important term in assessing message-passing collective communication performance. In another example, shared-memory systems multicasts might be used for cache line invalidations to multiple destinations, and the source must wait for the last received (and acknowledged) invalidation before modifying the cache line. Except for graphs in which we directly compare definition (a) with (b), we choose definition (a) for recording latency.

A second issue: when the network is operating below the saturation bandwidth for m-way hardware multicasts, the packet injection bandwidth B_i does not equal the packet receive bandwidth B_o. Instead, $B_o = mB_i$. Thus mB_i is effectively the load being injected into the network. One is tempted to simply plot latency versus B_o, but we prefer to plot performance measures against a stimulus, not a response. Most of our graphs display "effective input load" (mB_i) on the x-axis. Let a load of 1 for B_o represent full bandwidth received at each node. Although it is possible that $mB_i > 1$, a stable system will already be in saturation for $mB_i = 1$ anyway. Thus we do not show results for $mB_i > 1$.

A final issue is message startup overhead. In network simulations, unicast messages are typically assumed to have negligible startup overhead. With this assumption the network can easily be stressed beyond saturation during simulation, yielding more insights into its behavior. In implementing software multicast, most real systems have a non-negligible overhead between receiving a multicast packet and forwarding the packet along the next stage of the binomial tree. In our simulations we "zero" this overhead—minimizing the latency of software multicasting—to give it the best chance of competing against hardware multicasting.

We conducted simulations for both 16-node and 64-node fat-trees constructed from switching elements with 4 parents and 4 children (8 ports). Our default message size is 128 bytes (64 flits), which could correspond roughly to message sizes of request and reply packets for shared-memory systems. To further stress the network, we also plot performance for 512-byte messages. In the rest of this section we discuss the effects of varying a number of input loading and network characteristics.

7.3 Impact of multicast degree

To understand the effect multicast on network performance, we begin by varying the degree of the multicast m for a 16-node system, for switches with and without central buffers.

The top graph in Figure 10 compares software versus hardware multicasting latency using centrally-buffered switches in both cases. As m increases, the software multicast latency increases and

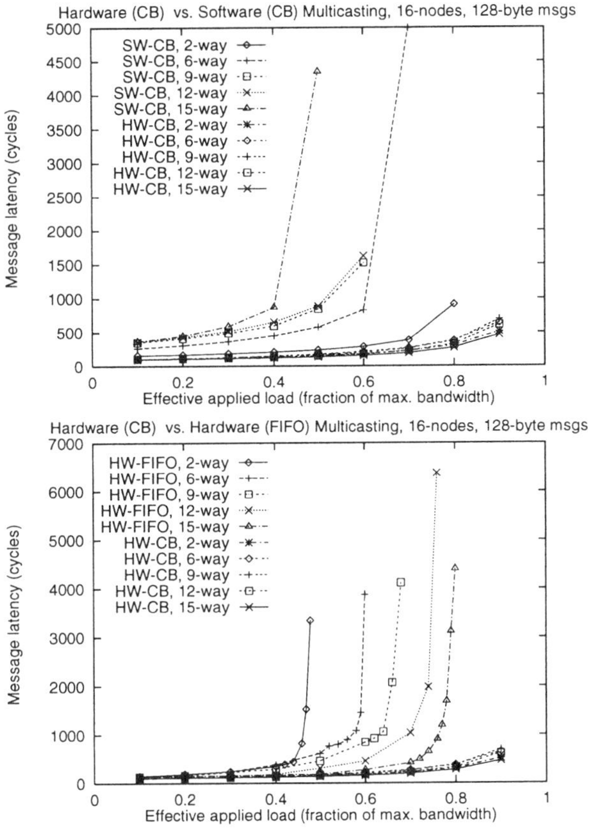

Figure 10: Latency vs. Effective applied load for software multicast, hardware multicast with central buffering, and hardware multicast with input buffering.

saturates more quickly. The hardware multicast latency is much lower and increases much less dramatically.

The bottom plot of Figure 10 compare our two proposed hardware replication methods. Comparing the top and bottom graphs, we can observe that for small m, input FIFO replication actually performs worse than software multicasting with a central buffer. This follows from the superiority of central buffer queuing over input queuing for unicast packets. However, in contrast to software multicasting, input FIFO replication latencies *decrease* with increasing m, and saturation bandwidth increases. As m increases, a larger percentage of the replication occurs late on the paths to the destination nodes. For example, for $m = 2$ in a 16-node system, most replication occurs at the 2nd-level switches, whereas for $m = 15$ most replication occurs at the 1st-level switches just before reaching the nodes. And as noted before, for $B_o = mB_i$, increasing m decreases B_i.

Figure 11 allows a better inspection of saturation bandwidth by plotting output bandwidth B_o versus effective input bandwidth mB_i. The bottom graph confirms that for input FIFO replication,

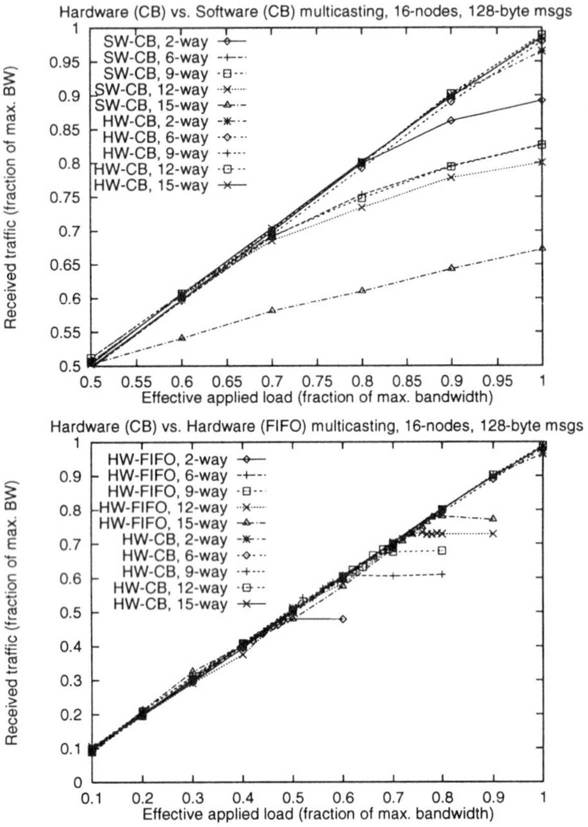

Figure 11: Received vs. Effective applied load for software multicast, hardware multicast with central buffering, and hardware multicast with input buffering.

saturation bandwidth increases with m. For the software multicasts shown in the top graph, the opposite is true. Unlike the characteristic flattened B_o lines for the bottom graph, the software multicast B_o does not flatten out after B_o becomes less than mB_i. This is because the software forwarding of messages is happening less frequently as latency increases, and this acts as a drag on the input bandwidth. Thus it may not be appropriate to characterize the software multicast as in saturation; the centrally-buffered switches continue to increase delivered bandwidth for this message size. In fact, for the central buffer replication scheme, saturation bandwidth is near enough to 100% that it is hard to distinguish the curves, although the highest bandwidth is achieved for large m. To better see the impact of m on saturation for central buffer replication, we increase the message size in the next section.

7.4 Impact of message size

The graphs we have shown thus far use 128-byte messages, which the large central buffers typically handle quite easily to over 90% of the maximum load. In this section, to stress the network further we examine the impact of a larger message size: 512 bytes.

Figure 12 is a latency graph for a 16-node system for small hardware and software multicasts. The 2-way and 4-way hardware

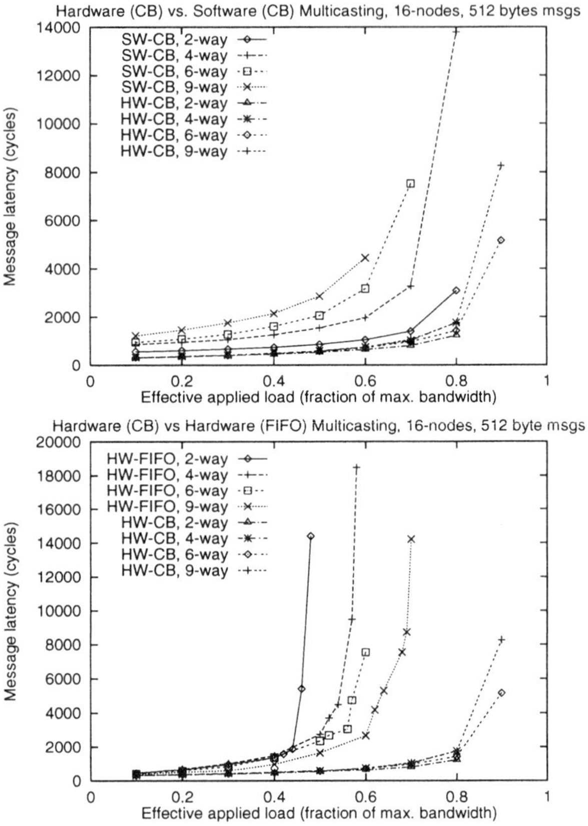

Figure 12: Latency vs. Effective applied load for a 16-node system, 512-byte messages

central buffer based multicasts now saturate before 0.9 effective load, although the 6-way and 9-way multicasts do not. Again this is because, for equivalent $B_o = mB_i$, larger m implies smaller B_i, resulting in less packets traversing the first stages of the network, although in the last stage of the network bandwidth is equivalent.

The software multicasts also saturate more quickly than for the 128-byte case. Just as for the 128-byte messages, saturation bandwidth decreases as m increases, because for software multicasts, $B_o = B_i$.

The results for 128-byte and 512-byte simulations are qualitatively similar, and throughout the rest of the paper we shall choose message size arbitrarily.

7.5 Impact of system size

To this point we have relied on 16-node simulations to test various parameters. To assess whether lessons learned from 16-node simulations are applicable to larger systems, we now compare 16-node and 64-node hardware multicasting experiments for the central buffer model. We do not show software multicast results for 64-node systems, because they grow even worse as m increases.

Figure 13 shows latency and bandwidth for low, medium, and high values of m for each system size. The 64-node system exhibits

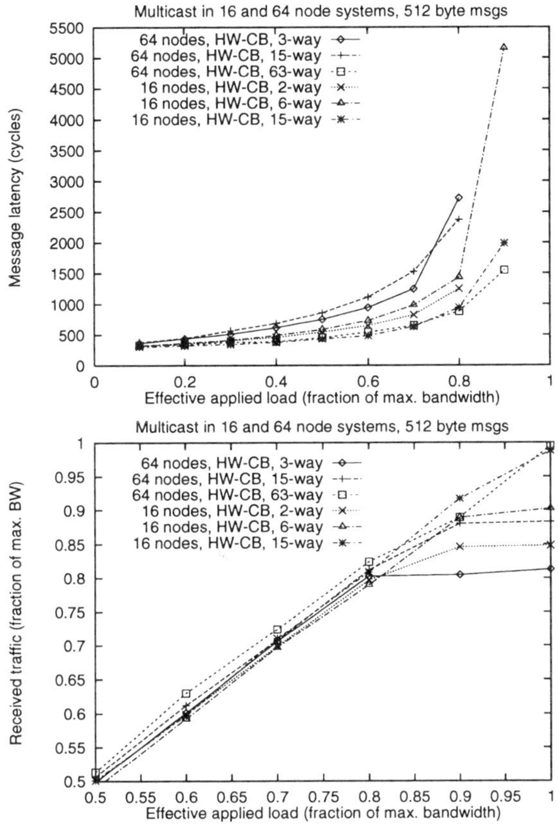

Figure 13: Performance of 16-node and 64-node systems with central buffers, 512-byte messages

higher latency and slightly lower saturation bandwidth than the 16-node system for comparable multicasts. This fits well with experience from unicast simulations on fat-trees: although fat-trees theoretically scale bandwidth linearly, in a larger network random traffic requires more hops on average and therefore encounters more contention, lowering achievable bandwidth. Just as for the 16-node system, the low m multicast has low latency but saturates earliest.

7.6 Interaction between multicast and unicast traffic

The experiments so far have stressed the network applying a single mode in traffic input: random m-way multicast traffic. In a typical parallel application, however, message traffic will not be entirely multicast or entirely unicast at any moment.

To better understand the interaction of multicast and unicast traffic, we simulate random *bimodal* traffic in which 20% of the received load is due to multicasts. Thus B_o consists of two components B_{ou} and B_{om} (where B_{ou} and B_{om} are the packet receive bandwidths of the unicast and multicast messages respectively), and $B_{om} = 0.2B_o$. For example, if $B_o = 0.7$, then $B_{om} = 0.14$ and $B_{ou} = 0.56$. Figure 14 shows the result of combining unicasts with 4-way multicasts.

For 80% unicast traffic, it is natural that the average latency should closely follow the unicast message latency unless multicast latency grows disproportionately large. Hardware multicasts perturb unicast traffic much less than do software multicasts, resulting in a lower combined latency. This is because hardware multicasts occupy network links for less time than software multicasts, due to both lower latency and a lower number of links traversed during the multicast.

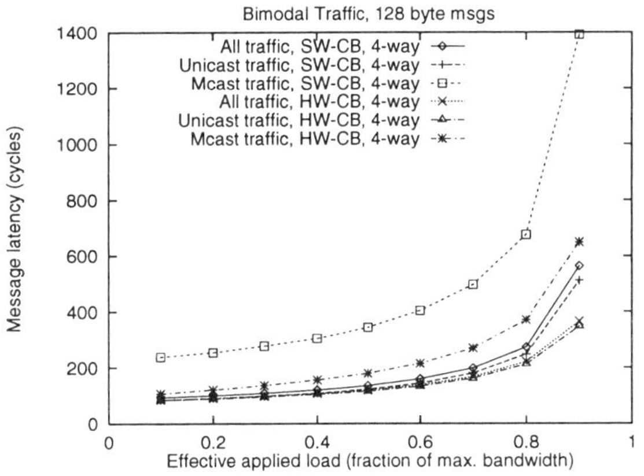

Figure 14: Bimodal latency for a 16-node system with central buffers, 128-byte messages

7.7 Measuring latency in an alternate way

We mentioned in Section 7.2 that there are two alternatives for calculating the average latency of multicasts. To this point, we have chosen definition (a): the latency of the last received message of the multicast. In this section we compare (a) to (b): the average of the latencies of each received message of the multicast.

Figure 15 displays this comparison for $m = 6$ on the top, and $m = 15$ on the bottom. For the $m = 6$ case, (a) and (b) are nearly equal for the hardware central buffer multicast at low loads, but for higher loads (a) exceeds (b) by almost 60%. For hardware input FIFO replication, the difference between (a) and (b) grows more rapidly, as does the magnitude of the latencies. For the software multicast, there is always a significant difference. As noted in Section 7.3, for small m software multicasting with central buffers actually saturates later than hardware multicasting with input FIFO replication, hence the crossovers in the graph.

For the $m = 15$ hardware multicast cases, the (a) and (b) definitions match closely throughout a large load range. Software multicast has no such property due to the $\lceil \log_2(m+1) \rceil$ steps required to complete it.

To summarize, when (a) and (b) definitions are nearly equal, it indicates that different branches of the multicast messages are arriving nearly synchronously. This is an attractive property for loosely synchronous algorithms and collective operations such as barrier synchronization that can be aided by multicasting. Hardware multicasting displays this nearly synchronous behavior for low loads or high degree of multicast (when all other traffic is multicast traffic of similar degree, and the network is not saturated).

7.8 Summary

Here we summarize our simulated performance results. The central-buffer-based hardware replication scheme exhibited a number of desirable characteristics in comparison to software multicasting. Latency was much lower and saturation bandwidth was higher for the entire range of multicast degree m, system size n, and message size. When random multicasts are part of bimodal traffic along with random unicast messages, the hardware multicasts perturb the unicasts less than do the software multicasts. Hardware multicast

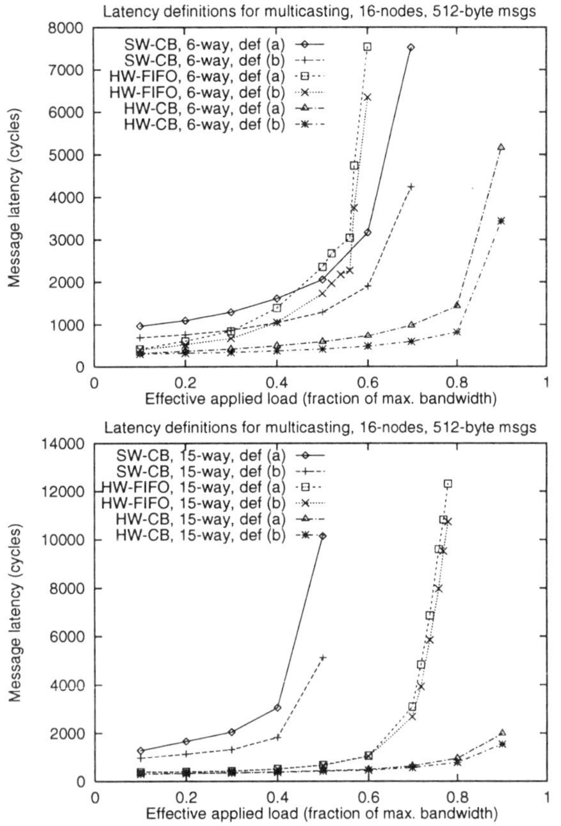

Figure 15: Comparing latency definitions for a 16-node system, 512-byte messages

latency varies less over the range of destinations of a particular multicast, especially for light loads or large m.

The input-FIFO-based hardware replication scheme did not fare as well, especially at high loads, but for large m this scheme outperformed the software multicasting with a central buffer. This is significant considering that central buffers perform much better than input FIFOs for unicast traffic. Obviously a software multicast scheme using switches with no central buffers would perform worse than any option simulated.

8 Related Work

Other recent research has focussed on hardware multicasting schemes. As mentioned before, a path based model was proposed for multicasting on two dimensional mesh networks by Lin and Ni [18, 17]. This work was extended to a Base Routing Conformed Path (BRCP) model by Panda et al. [26] applicable to any k-ary n-cube network. Kesavan and Panda [15] have studied the problem of multiple multicast for meshes using both software based and hardware path based multicasts.

In the context of switch based parallel systems, Chiang and Ni have proposed a method for synchronous replication of multidestination worms [6] adopting a deadlock avoidance scheme at the switches. A somewhat related multicasting technique proposed in the context of DSM systems based on direct networks is the tree based multicasting scheme proposed in [19]. Instead of guaranteeing freedom from deadlock, a deadlock recovery scheme is proposed that "prunes" blocked branches. This method is effective only for short messages as prevalent in a distributed shared memory system. The architectures proposed in the current paper allow multicast for packets as large as the buffer size at the switches and the technique works well for both long and short messages. Andrews et al. [1] have proposed a method for tree based multicast using bit-string encoding in the context of dance-hall architectures. However this work only focuses on store and forward networks and short message lengths.

Some parallel systems like the CM-5 [16], Meiko CS2 [4] etc. provide facilities for multicasting. However, the CM-5 uses a separate network for multicast operations and only one multicast is allowed in this network at any given time. Data-less multicasts or eurekas are supported in the Cray T3E [31] in the same network used for normal data communication. Using data-less multicast packets avoids the deadlock scenarios outlined in this paper and the solution does not extend to multicast of data packets. The approach presented in this paper allows arbitrary numbers of multicasts, each of size upto the maximum packet size allowed in the system, to proceed concurrently while using the same network as all other data to achieve multicast communication. Furthermore, unlike the approach proposed for the Meiko CS2, multicast to arbitrary destination sets is allowed.

9 Conclusion

In this paper we have presented two switch architectures with differing buffer organizations for implementing multidestination worms in switch-based parallel systems. We have described in detail how a central-buffer-based switch architecture that supports only unicast message passing can be modified to support multidestination message passing at very little additional cost. We then performed extensive simulations to evaluate the relative performance of our proposed switch architectures and to compare the achieved hardware multicast performance with the best software multicast algorithm. To make the comparisons more interesting, we factored out the high start-up overhead associated with the software schemes in our performance comparisons. The performance achieved by such a software multicast algorithm is the best that can be achieved using point to point communication primitives alone.

Our performance studies have shown that central-buffer-based switch architectures prove extremely beneficial in improving hardware multicast performance. Such architectures can deliver good performance across an entire range of applied loads, message lengths, multicast degrees and system sizes. Although the alternative implementation using an input FIFO delivers multicast performance similar to the central-buffer-based implementation for single multicasts and multiple multicasts at low loads, the degradation in performance is rapid and occurs at relatively light loads. *If the associated start-up overhead is neglected*, the central-buffer-based software multicast outperforms hardware multicast using the input-FIFO-based implementation for low multicast degrees on a 16 node system. This implies that software multicast, using efficient messaging layers and support at the network interfaces to reduce start-up overhead, has the potential to offer good performance when used in conjunction with central-buffer-based switches.

We are currently studying the impact of enhancements to the switch architecture to support reliable barrier synchronization [34]. The relative performance of such a scheme compared to an efficient software-based scheme in terms of absolute barrier latency and in terms of their impact on other network traffic is being evaluated. We are also studying the the impact of hot spot traffic and other traffic patterns. Finally, we will also be working on measuring the impact of these enhancements to the communication subsystem on benchmark application performance in the DM and DSM domains.

References

[1] ANDREWS, J. B., BECKMANN, C. J., AND POULSEN, D. K. Notification and multicast networks for synchronization and coherence. *Journal of Parallel and Distributed Computing 15* (Aug. 1992), 332–350.

[2] BALA, V., BRUCK, J., CYPHER, R., ELUSTONDO, P., HO, A., HO, C.-T., KIPNIS, S., AND SNIR, M. CCL: A Portable and Tunable Collective Communication Library for Scalable Parallel Computers. In *Proceedings of the International Parallel Processing Symposium* (1994).

[3] BARNETT, M., PAYNE, D. G., AND DE GEIJN, R. V. Optimal Broadcasting in Mesh-Connected Architectures. Tech. Rep. TR91-38, Dept. of Computer Science, Universityof Texas at Austin, Dec 1991.

[4] BEECROFT, J., HOMEWOOD, M., AND MCLAREN, M. Meiko CS-2 Interconnect Elan-Elite Design. *Parallel Computing 20* (Nov 1994), 1627–1638.

[5] CHIANG, C. M., AND NI, L. M. Multi-Address Encoding for Multicast. In *Proceedings of the Parallel Computer Routing and Communication Workshop* (May 1994), pp. 146–160.

[6] CHIANG, C. M., AND NI, L. M. Deadlock-Free Multi-Head Wormhole Routing. In *Proceedings of the First High Performance Computing-Asia* (1995).

[7] CRAY RESEARCH, INC. *Cray T3D System Architecture Overview*, 1993.

[8] DAI, D., AND PANDA, D. K. Reducing Cache Invalidation Overheads in Wormhole DSMs Using Multidestination Message Passing. In *International Conference on Parallel Processing* (Chicago, IL, Aug 1996), pp. I:138–145.

[9] DALLY, W. J., AND SEITZ, C. L. Deadlock-Free Message Routing in Multiprocessor Interconnection Networks. *IEEE Transactions on Computers* (May 1987), 547–553.

[10] DUZETT, B., AND BUCK, R. An Overview of the Ncube-3 Supercomputer. In *Proceedings of the Frontiers of Massively Parallel Computation* (1992), pp. 458–464.

[11] INTEL CORPORATION. *Paragon XP/S Product Overview*, 1991.

[12] KATEVENIS, M., VATSOLAKI, P., AND EFTHYMIOU, A. Pipelined Memory Shared Buffer for VLSI Switches. In *Proceedings of ACM SIGCOMM* (August 1995), pp. 39–48.

[13] KERMANI, P., AND KLEINROCK, L. Virtual Cut-Through: A New Computer Communications Switching Technique. *Computer Networks 3*, 4 (Sept. 1979), 267–286.

[14] KESAVAN, R., BONDALAPATI, K., AND PANDA, D. K. Multicast on Irregular Switch-based Networks with Wormhole Routing. In *Proceedings of the International Symposium on High Performance Computer Architecture (HPCA-3)* (1997), pp. 48–57.

[15] KESAVAN, R., AND PANDA, D. K. Minimizing Node Contention in Multiple Multicast on Wormhole k-ary n-cube Networks. In *Proceedings of the International Conference on Parallel Processing* (Chicago, IL, Aug 1996), pp. I:188–195.

[16] LEISERSON, C. E., ET AL. The Network Architecture of the Connection Machine CM-5. In *Proceedings of the ACM Symposium on Parallel Algorithms and Architectures* (1992), pp. 272–285.

[17] LIN, X., K.MCKINLEY, P., AND NI, L. M. Deadlock free multicast wormhole routing in 2-D mesh multicomputers. *IEEE Trans. on Parallel and Distributed Systems 5*, 8 (Aug. 1994), 793–804.

[18] LIN, X., AND NI, L. M. Deadlock-free Multicast Wormhole Routing in Multicomputer Networks. In *Proceedings of the International Symposium on Computer Architecture* (1991), pp. 116–124.

[19] MALUMBRES, M. P., DUATO, J., AND TORELLAS, J. An Efficient Implementation of Tree-Based Multicast Routing for Distributed Shared-Memory Multiprocessors. In *Proceedings of the Eighth IEEE Symposium on Parallel and Distributed Processing* (New Orleans, LA, October 1996), pp. 186–189.

[20] MCKINLEY, P. K., AND ROBINSON, D. F. Collective Communication in Wormhole-Routed Massively Parallel Computers. *IEEE Computer* (Dec 1995), 39–50.

[21] MCKINLEY, P. K., XU, H., ESFAHANIAN, A.-H., AND NI, L. M. Unicast-based Multicast Communication in Wormhole-routed Networks. *IEEE Transactions on Parallel and Distributed Systems 5*, 12 (Dec 1994), 1252–1265.

[22] NI, L. Should Scalable Parallel Computers Support Efficient Hardware Multicasting? In *ICPP Workshop on Challenges for Parallel Processing* (1995), pp. 2–7.

[23] NI, L., AND MCKINLEY, P. K. A Survey of Wormhole Routing Techniques in Direct Networks. *IEEE Computer* (Feb. 1993), 62–76.

[24] NUPAIROJ, N., AND NI, L. M. Performance Metrics and Measurement Techniques of Collective Communication Services. In *First International Workshop on Communication and Architectural Support for Network-Based Parallel Computing (CANPC '97), Lecture Notes in Computer Science 1199* (February 1997), pp. 212–226.

[25] PANDA, D. K. Issues in Designing Efficient and Practical Algorithms for Collective Communication in Wormhole-Routed Systems. In *ICPP Workshop on Challenges for Parallel Processing* (1995), pp. 8–15.

[26] PANDA, D. K., SINGAL, S., AND PRABHAKARAN, P. Multidestination Message Passing Mechanism Conforming to Base Wormhole Routing Scheme. In *Proceedings of the Parallel Computer Routing and Communication Workshop* (1994), pp. 131–145.

[27] PANDA, D. K., AND SIVARAM, R. Fast Broadcast and Multicast in Wormhole Multistage Networks with Multidestination Worms. Tech. Rep. OSU-CISRC-4/95-TR21, Dept. of Computer and Information Science, The Ohio State University, April 1995.

[28] QIAO, W., AND NI, L. M. Adaptive Routing in Irregular Networks Using Cut-Through Switches. In *Proceedings of the International Conference on Parallel Processing* (Chicago, IL, Aug 1996), pp. I:52–60.

[29] SCHERSON, I. D., AND CHIEN, C.-H. Least common ancestor networks. In *Proc. 7th Int. Parallel Processing Symp.* (1993), pp. 507–513.

[30] SCHROEDER, M. D., ET AL. Autonet: A High-speed, Self-configuring Local Area Network Using Point-to-point Links. Tech. Rep. SRC research report 59, DEC, Apr 1990.

[31] SCOTT, S. L. Synchronization and communication in the T3E multiprocessor. In *ASPLOS-VII* (Sept. 1996).

[32] SIVARAM, R., PANDA, D. K., AND STUNKEL, C. B. Efficient Broadcast and Multicast on Multistage Interconnection Networks using Multiport Encoding. In *Proceedings of the 8th IEEE Symposium on Parallel and Distributed Processing* (Oct 1996), pp. 36–45.

[33] SIVARAM, R., PANDA, D. K., AND STUNKEL, C. B. Efficient Broadcast and Multicast on Multistage Interconnection Networks using Multiport Encoding. Tech. Rep. OSU-CISRC-3/96-TR15, The Ohio State University, March 1996.

[34] SIVARAM, R., STUNKEL, C. B., AND PANDA, D. K. A Reliable Hardware Barrier Synchronization Scheme. In *Proceedings of the 11th IEEE International Parallel Processing Symposium* (April 1997).

[35] STUNKEL, C. B., SHEA, D., GRICE, D. G., HOCHSCHILD, P. H., AND TSAO, M. The SP1 High Performance Switch. In *Scalable High Performance Computing Conference* (1994), pp. 150–157.

[36] STUNKEL, C. B., SHEA, D. G., ABALI, B., ET AL. The SP2 High-Performance Switch. *IBM System Journal 34*, 2 (1995), 185–204.

[37] TAMIR, Y., AND FRAZIER, G. L. High-performance multi-queue buffers for VLSI communication switches. In *Proc. 15st Ann. Int. Symp. on Computer Architecture* (May 1988), pp. 343–354.

[38] XU, H., GUI, Y.-D., AND NI, L. M. Optimal Software Multicast in Wormhole-Routed Multistage Networks. In *Proceedings of the Supercomputing Conference* (1994), pp. 703–712.

Tolerating Multiple Failures in RAID Architectures with Optimal Storage and Uniform Declustering

Guillermo A. Alvarez Walter A. Burkhard Flaviu Cristian

Department of Computer Science and Engineering
University of California, San Diego
La Jolla, CA 92093–0114, USA
{galvarez, burkhard, flaviu}@cs.ucsd.edu

Abstract

We present DATUM, a novel method for tolerating multiple disk failures in disk arrays. DATUM is the first known method that can mask any given number of failures, requires an optimal amount of redundant storage space, and spreads reconstruction accesses uniformly over disks in the presence of failures without needing large layout tables in controller memory. Our approach is based on information dispersal, a coding technique that admits an efficient hardware implementation. As the method does not restrict the configuration parameters of the disk array, many existing RAID organizations are particular cases of DATUM. A detailed performance comparison with two other approaches shows that DATUM's response times are similar to those of the best competitor when two or less disks fail, and that the performance degrades gracefully when more than two disks fail.

1 Introduction

Disk arrays [15] offer significant advantages over conventional disks. Fragmentation of the total storage space into multiple inexpensive disks allows cost-effective solutions that benefit from the aggregate bandwidth of the component disks, and from the smaller seek latencies associated with shorter arms. The mean time between failures (*MTBF*) for the array as a whole decreases linearly with the number of independent component disks, possibly resulting in mere days before catastrophic failure and loss of data.

It is therefore necessary to store, along with the data, redundant information in order to recover from disk failures. Most existing approaches like RAID-5 [15] and parity declustering [10] rely on parity calculations to provide tolerance against a single disk failure. However, there are several reasons for considering architectures capable of masking multiple simultaneous disks failures [3, 4, 7, 9]:

- Applications are placing stronger demands on storage subsystems as a result of manipulating large audio and video objects in real-time. Existing analyses [4] show that increasing the number of check sectors per stripe is a better (i.e. more cost-effective) approach to improving reliability than increasing the number of reliability groups or relying on the likely improvements of each disk's MTBF.
- Disks can exhibit latent sector failures, in which an unavailable group of sectors is detected only when trying to access these sectors. Data are irretrievably lost if the array tolerates a single failure and a latent sector failure is detected when trying to reconstruct a crashed disk.
- Safety-critical applications can require large MTTDLs that can not be achieved by tolerating single failures.
- Some approaches [5, 6] distribute the controller's functionality among loosely coupled nodes (to avoid the centralized controller as a single point of failure). In such scenarios, the contents of one or more correct disks may become inaccessible because some other component has failed, e.g. the communication network. Communication failures often are much more likely to happen than several actual disk crashes. Storage systems must continue to provide correct service in these situations.

This work was partially supported by grants from the Air Force Office of Scientific Research, California MICRO, Oakland, and Symbios Logic, Wichita.

In this paper we present DATUM (Disk Arrays with opTimal storage, Uniform declustering and Multiple-failure tolerance), a novel declustering method that tolerates multiple disk failures in a disk array. DATUM allows the user ample freedom in configuring the disk array, without constraining the values of array parameters; up to $n-1$ failures can be tolerated in an array of n disks. DATUM uses the theoretical minimum amount of storage space for storing redundant data in the array. Sectors containing redundancy are uniformly distributed over all disks, thereby eliminating bottlenecks when failures occur and easing the burden on surviving disks during on-line reconstruction [10]. Our approach can accommodate distributed sparing as well, with similar benefits. Datum also performs the minimal number of disk accesses to implement small writes. Thus, DATUM is the first known method for tolerating an arbitrary number of failures that is optimal with respect to both storage space and write overhead, and that distributes redundant data uniformly by using a set of layout functions that can be evaluated efficiently with very low memory requirements.

Our approach is based on the information dispersal algorithm (*IDA*) [17], a coding technique for which a fast VLSI implementation exists [2]. We tested an implementation of DATUM against implementations of parity declustering [10] and EVENODD [3], by utilizing a very accurate disk array simulator [8]. Our results show that despite its generality, DATUM has the same performance as its best competitor method for the failure scenarios they have in common, and that response times continue to degrade gracefully beyond that point: the scenarios tolerated only by DATUM having more than two failures.

Section 2 describes the system model, terminology, and failure assumptions for the rest of the paper. In Section 3, we describe the basics of the IDA and its application to DATUM. The location functions that result in the uniform, declustered layout of data and redundancy are presented in Section 4. Section 5 evaluates DATUM's performance for diverse workloads and failure scenarios. Related studies are described in Section 6, and a conclusion is offered in Section 7.

2 System Model

A disk array has a total of n identical disks. Each disk has an independent controller. Different disks can service independent requests in parallel. Each controller provides the abstraction of a linear address space of sector numbers within the disk it controls, thus hiding bad media portions and the position of each sector in terms of surface, track and sector within track. For simplicity, we assume that each disk has the same number of usable sectors.

There is also an *array controller*, that translates user requests into individual operations on the disks of the array, supervises their completion, and reconfigures the array in the presence of failures. It can be implemented in software, in hardware, or as a hybrid. It also provides a linear address space to the disk array *clients*. Disks can fail during their operation; the failure of a disk is detected when a read or write operation on it fails. We assume the array controller can identify a failed disk. We do not discuss how to tolerate failures in other components of the system, such as interconnection buses or array controllers [6, 12].

Disk space is logically structured into *stripe units*; each stripe unit has a fixed number of sectors, and contains either user data or redundant data. DATUM services accesses involving an integral number of stripe units at the client level. A *stripe* consists of a fixed number of user data stripe units, plus a number of redundant stripe units computed from the user data units. The existence of redundant units is transparent to the clients, that have access to a linear address space containing only user data.

3 Information Dispersal

The information dispersal algorithm (*IDA*) [17] encodes a sequence $F = (d_1, d_2, \ldots, d_m)$ of m integers into a sequence of $m+f$ integers in such a way that any m of the $m+f$ integers suffice to recover F. The IDA transformation is linear and of the form

$$(d_1, d_2, \ldots, d_m) \cdot T = (e_1, e_2, \ldots, e_m, e_{m+1}, \ldots, e_{m+f}) \quad (1)$$

where T is an $m \times (m+f)$ matrix having the property that any m columns are linearly independent. IDA can recover the user data F from any m of the $m+f$ values as follows: Suppose we have access to the sequence $(e_{i_1}, e_{i_2}, \ldots, e_{i_m})$. We know that

$$(d_1, d_2, \ldots, d_m) \cdot (t_{i_1}\, t_{i_2}\, t_{i_3} \cdots t_{i_m}) = (e_{i_1}, e_{i_2}, \ldots, e_{i_m})$$

where t_i denotes the ith column of transformation T and the appropriate columns of T are shown. Since these m columns are linearly independent, we can invert this matrix and obtain F from the m integers.

In our application of IDA, the sequence F represents m equal-sized portions of user data (disk array stripe units) and the $m+f$ values represent encoded

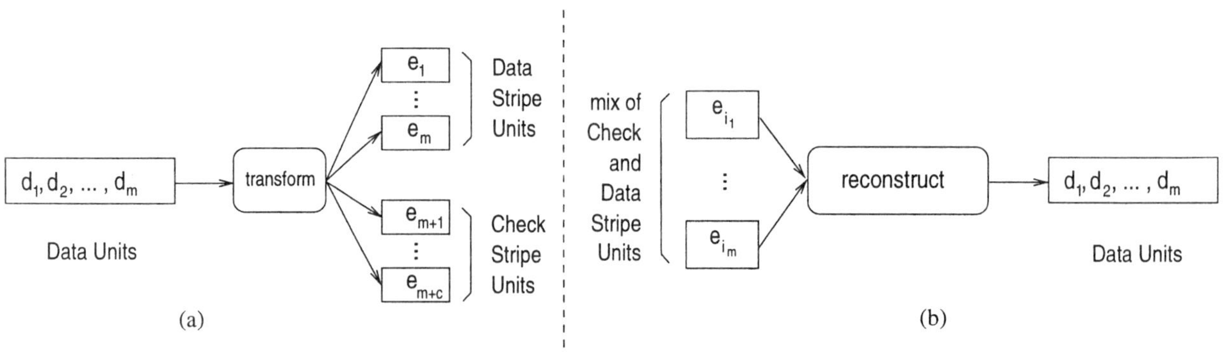

Figure 1: Information Dispersal Algorithm: (a) Encoding; (b) Decoding

data including the redundant data (again stripe units.) Each stripe unit is stored on a different disk in the array. Any data stripe can be reconstructed if m or more disks are correct; that is, if f or fewer disks have failed. Figure 1(a) illustrates how redundancy is calculated when writing a whole stripe of client data to the array; part (b) shows how the whole stripe is reconstructed from any m encoded stripe units. We require an additional property for DATUM to obtain RAID Level 5-like behavior: m of the encoded stripe units must be identical to the m client data stripe units. This can be done only if the whole user data portion of the stripe is also recorded in the array in the clear; that is, the encoding must be *systematic* [11]. The matrix T, shown in Equation (2), consists of the identity matrix and f more columns so that the set of $m+f$ columns satisfies the linear independence condition.

$$T = \begin{pmatrix} 1 & 0 & \dots & 0 & t_{1,m+1} & t_{1,m+2} & \dots & t_{1,m+f} \\ 0 & 1 & \dots & 0 & t_{2,m+1} & t_{2,m+2} & \dots & t_{2,m+f} \\ \vdots & \vdots & \ddots & \vdots & \vdots & \vdots & \ddots & \vdots \\ 0 & 0 & \dots & 1 & t_{m,m+1} & t_{m+2} & \dots & t_{m,m+f} \end{pmatrix} \quad (2)$$

Rabin [17] and Preparata [16] describe ways of constructing T that result in low computational costs; however, none achieves the systematic property yielding m clear stripe units. We can always obtain a matrix T with the desired structure using elementary row operations on a candidate matrix obtained by any method.

IDA makes no assumption regarding the amount of space required to represent the encoded values. Maximum distance separable (*MDS*) error-correcting encoding [11], which is similar to IDA, ensures that the representation of m stripe units, each of size s bytes, as $m+f$ stripe units will require exactly $(m+f) \times s$ bytes. This is accomplished by using finite fields to represent the values. In fact, with this additional requirement, the IDA transformation matrix becomes the codeword generator matrix for an MDS code; thus IDA generalizes MDS encoding. DATUM uses only the theoretical minimum amount of disk space to store each stripe in such a way that its contents are recoverable even if f stripe units are missing.

DATUM's application of IDA is based on the $GF(256)$ finite field. Elements of our transformation matrices range over $GF(256)$, so we can represent any element in a single byte without wasting space. The encoding and decoding operations are done one byte at a time in each stripe unit. When we denote client data stripe unit i in terms of byte values as follows $(d_{1,i}, d_{2,i}, \dots, d_{s,i})$, Equation (1) yields the jth byte for each of the encoded stripe units.

$$(d_{j,1}, d_{j,2}, \dots, d_{j,m}) \cdot T = (e_{j,1}, e_{j,2}, \dots, e_{j,m}, e_{j,m+1}, \dots, e_{j,m+f}) \quad (3)$$

The two field operations can be implemented very efficiently: addition is the bitwise exclusive-or operation, and multiplication can be implemented using fast table lookups using a discrete logarithm [11] table of size 256 bytes. In general, for a finite field of η elements we can store the logarithm table with η elements rather than the structure with $\Theta(\eta^2)$ elements that the full multiplication table requires.

A *small write* occurs when a single stripe unit is written by a client application. Small writes are typically expensive in RAIDs as the redundant data must be updated as well; our byte-wise interleaving scheme of Equation (3) allows us to process them in the following manner. We denote components of redundant stripe unit j as $(e_{1,m+j}, \dots, e_{s,m+j})$ (where s is the size of the stripe unit, and $1 \leq j \leq f$) and the elements of T by $t_{i,j}$. Assume, without loss of generality, that data stripe 1 has been updated yielding $(d'_{1,1}, \dots, d'_{s,1})$ as the result of a small write. Each of the f check stripe units must be updated as well: for $i = 1, \dots, s$ and $j = 1, \dots, f$ we have

$e_{i,m+j} = d_{i,1}t_{1,m+j} \oplus d_{i,2}t_{2,m+j} \oplus \cdots \oplus d_{i,m}t_{m,m+j}$ (previous values), and
$e'_{i,m+j} = d'_{i,1}t_{1,m+j} \oplus d_{i,2}t_{2,m+j} \oplus \cdots \oplus d_{i,m}t_{m,m+j}$ (only data stripe 1 changed),

thus we obtain the update expression:

$$e'_{i,m+j} = d'_{i,1}t_{1,m+j} \oplus d_{i,1}t_{1,m+j} \oplus e_{i,m+j}. \tag{4}$$

Therefore, to implement a small write, it is necessary to: *i)* read the old values of the data unit being written and the f redundant units, *ii)* recompute the check stripe unit values as in Equation (4), and finally *iii)* write the new data stripe value as well as the f check stripe units. As a consequence of the Singleton bound [11], it is not possible to write less than $f+1$ stripe units if the array is to tolerate up to f failures. Accordingly, DATUM performs the optimal number $f+1$ disk writes per small write operation. The literature discusses system-level optimizations that do not require the user to wait until the $f+1$ writes complete successfully. For instance, updates to redundant stripes can be deferred while logging them to disk [22], while writing them to non-volatile cache [12], or by doing nothing at all [18]. These optimizations are in principle applicable to any disk array architecture, including DATUM, and we do not consider them here.

4 Layout Functions

One of the contributions of this work is a suite of functions that map each client address to the set of disks and sectors (i.e. offsets within each participating disk) where the corresponding user data and redundant data are stored in the array. In general, performance under failure is better when the units of each stripe are written in a subset of the n disks of the array. Our layout functions meet the first five layout goals set forth by Holland and Gibson [10]. When a disk fails and each stripe is distributed over all the disks of the array (like in RAID-5 [15]), an access to a random stripe unit has probability $1/n$ of hitting the failed disk, thus resulting in $n-1$ accesses to all the other stripe units. On the other hand, when each stripe is laid out over $k \leq n$ disks, the probability of hitting the failed disk remains the same, but the overhead is only $k-1$ accesses when a request to the failed disk is served. Similar arguments show that client applications also experience a much less substantial performance degradation during on-line reconstruction of a failed disk, as only some of the stripes being reconstructed will have units in each of the surviving disks.

In the remaining part of this section we present the functions that convert between client-level addresses and disks and sectors in DATUM. After that, we discuss some of the properties of our functions.

4.1 Set of Disks for a Stripe

Given an address for a stripe unit, it is necessary to compute the set of disks that have fragments of the corresponding stripe (in case the access being serviced involves on-the-fly reconstruction). Space has to be allocated uniformly over all disks to avoid bottlenecks. We represent the disks that store units for a given stripe with a *k-combination*: a tuple $< X_1, \ldots, X_k >$ where each $X_i \in [0, n-1]$ (a disk identifier). Furthermore we require that in each k-combination: $X_i < X_{i+1}, i = 1, \ldots, k$. This is to avoid ambiguity as we intend to use k-combinations as sets. There are $num\_combs = \binom{n}{k}$ possible k-combinations.

We define the total order $\succ$ over the set of combinations as: $< X_1, \ldots, X_k > \succ < Y_1, \ldots, Y_k >$ if and only if either $X_k > Y_k$, or there exists a $j < k$ such that $X_i = Y_i$ for $k \geq i > j$ and $X_j > Y_j$. Given a k-combination $c =< X_1, \ldots, X_k >$, its position in the total order is given by (the reader interested in the proofs of the results mentioned in this paper is directed to [1]):

$$loc(< X_1, \ldots, X_k >) = \binom{X_k}{k} + \binom{X_{k-1}}{k-1} + \cdots + \binom{X_1}{1}$$

Since the *loc* mapping is a bijection, we can compute its inverse *invloc*. The following algorithm computes the k-combination given its position in the order $\succ$; the answer resides in integer array c.

```
invloc(position)
   for (int i=k; i≥1; i--)
      l = i;
      while (choose(l,i) ≤ j)
         l = l+1;
      c[i] = l-1;
      position = position - choose(l-1,i);

   return(c)
```

Stripe unit *addr* as seen by the user is contained in stripe number $str = \lfloor addr/m \rfloor$ of the DATUM array, since each stripe has m data units—the existence of redundant units is transparent to users. Given that in general there will be more stripes than k-combinations, we map *str* into the disks of the k-combination $invloc(str \bmod num\_combs)$. That is, the mapping from stripes into disks repeats cyclically every *num_combs* stripes.

4.2 Allocation of Redundant and Data Stripe Units

Given the disks $c =< X_1, \ldots, X_k >$ corresponding to a stripe *str*, we must choose m of these disks to hold the data units, and the remaining $k - m$ will hold the redundant units. This choice must be made in such a way that the redundant units are evenly distributed among disks to maximize available disk bandwidth in the failure-free case (when redundant units are never accessed for reconstruction, so a disk containing more redundant data than data units would be underutilized).

We take disks in positions

$\lfloor str/num\_combs \rfloor f, (\lfloor str/num\_combs \rfloor f{+}1) \bmod k, \ldots,$
$(\lfloor str/num\_combs \rfloor f + f - 1) \bmod k$

for the redundant units, and the remaining disks for data units. That is, we take the first f disks of each tuple for the first *num_combs* stripes, then move on to the next f positions of c, and so on. It is easy to see that the same positions will be used for redundant units after $lcm(k, f)/f$ iterations of this procedure, where $lcm(k, f)$ denotes the least common multiple of k and f. k/f iterations are enough in the best case, and at most k in the worst case. This generalizes the function of [10] for $f = 1$, that takes in turn each of the disks of the tuple to hold the parity redundant unit.

4.3 Offset of Stripe Units within Disks

Once we have found the set of disks $c =< X_1, \ldots, X_k >$ corresponding to a stripe *str*, we have to determine the offsets at which each stripe unit of *str* is stored in each X_i. We start using each disk at offset 0 in its address space, and from then on we allocate each unit to the lowest free offset in the disk where it must be stored. Therefore, the sector offset in disk X_i where *str*'s unit is allocated equals the number of times X_i appeared in k-combinations smaller than $< X_1, \ldots, X_k >$, times the number of sectors per stripe unit (that is a constant of the array).

We need to determine the number of times $\#X_i$ that the value X_i has appeared in k-combinations c' such that $c \succ c'$. It turns out that $\#X_i$ can be computed in the following way:

$$\#X_k = loc(c) - \binom{X_k}{k},$$

$$\#X_j = \sum_{i=1}^{j-1} \binom{X_i}{i} + \sum_{i=j+1}^{k} \binom{X_i - 1}{i - 1},$$

$$\text{for } j = 1, \ldots, k-1.$$

Figure 2 shows the first iteration of our layout functions for $n = 4, k = 3, m = 2$ (i.e. $f = 1$, a single failure is tolerated). The figure displays the assignment of stripe units to disks. For this example, there are four 3-combinations, so each of the three cycles in Figure 2 contains four stripes. In the first cycle we map each stripe's redundant unit to the first element of each 3-combination, in the second cycle we take the second, and in the third cycle we take the last. The figure shows that each disk contains the same number of redundancy units in each iteration.

To illustrate the application of our layout functions, consider how the stripe unit with $addr = 9$ in the user's address space is located in the array. This unit forms part of stripe $\lfloor addr/m \rfloor = 4$ in the array's address space. Stripe 4 is mapped according to the 3-combination $invloc(4 \bmod \binom{n}{k}) = invloc(0) =< 0, 1, 2 >$. Of the three disks of the 3-combination, redundant information will be in the position $\lfloor 4/\binom{n}{k} \rfloor f = 1$, that corresponds to disk number 1 in the 3-combination. Since each stripe contains 2 data units and $9 \bmod 2 = 1$, the desired unit is the second data unit of the stripe—therefore, it is mapped to disk 2 (the last component of the 3-combination). It remains to determine the offset of disk 2 that must be accessed: this equals $\#(2, < 0, 1, 2 >) + \binom{n}{k} \lfloor stripe\_num/\binom{n}{k} \rfloor$. The first term equals 0, the second term equals 3; thus the stripe unit is located at disk 2, offset 3 as shown in the figure.

4.4 Properties of the Layout Functions

The set of layout functions used in DATUM can tolerate multiple failures: each stripe is split into k stripe units, and units of the same stripe are never stored in the same disk. The data in every stripe is recoverable even if up to f disks of the array become unavailable.

In order to reconstruct the L bytes of a stripe, DATUM reads L/m bytes from each of any m surviving disks. The bytes needed from any disk are contiguous (because sectors of the same stripe unit are contiguous on disks), so the seek delays are minimal. Therefore, reconstruction accesses (either to service a client request or to reconstruct a failed disk) in DATUM are minimal and contiguous.

Redundant units are uniformly distributed on all the disks. Since these must be updated during every user write, the aggregate load is shared equally among all disks. During degraded-mode operation, the additional load of reconstructing stripe units on failed disks is evenly distributed among the surviving disks. Similarly when a failed disk is replaced by a spare, it must be

Offset	Disk 0	Disk 1	Disk 2	Disk 3
0	S0,R	S0,U0	S0,U1	S1,U3
1	S1,R	S1,U2	S2,U4	S2,U5
2	S2,R	S3,R	S3,U6	S3,U7
3	S4,U8	S4,R	S4,U9	S5,U11
4	S5,U10	S5,R	S6,R	S6,U13
5	S6,U12	S7,U14	S7,R	S7,U15
6	S8,U16	S8,U17	S8,R	S9,R
7	S9,U18	S9,U19	S10,U21	S10,R
8	S10,U20	S11,U22	S11,U23	S11,R
	...	...	...	...

Sn,Um: Data unit with address m, contained in stripe n
Sn,R: Redundant unit of stripe n

Figure 2: Sample Layout for $f = 1$

reconstructed to leave the array in a failure-free state. Reconstruction is often performed on-line, i.e. while the array is servicing user requests. In order to avoid the presence of bottlenecks and to minimize the degradation of the service, reconstruction accesses are also evenly spread—because every pair of disks appears together in the same number of k-combinations. Also, *large writes* (when the access updates all the data portion of a stripe) are serviced without reading the previous contents of any disk sector.

The layout functions have low computational and memory requirements. It is convenient to store a few binomial coefficient values in memory for improving efficiency, as one or more of these functions are in the critical path of every request sent to the array.

5 Performance

We report the results of a performance comparison made by running DATUM, EVENODD [3], and parity declustering [10] under a highly-concurrent workload of small reads and writes. Our goal is to compare how these different methods perform under a spectrum of failure scenarios, from failure-free operation to three unavailable disks. We chose parity declustering as a basis for comparison because it distributes data onto disks using balanced block designs, and it uses the same encoding (parity) as the RAID family [15]. EVENODD was considered because it is the only existing scheme that can tolerate two failures while using the same minimal amount of redundant storage, regardless of array size. The redundant units are rotated cyclically over the different disks of the array in our implementation of EVENODD, as suggested in [3].

The experiments were run on RaidFrame [8], a tool where implementations of RAID architectures can be tested and evaluated. RaidFrame's synthetic workload generator generates concurrent sequences of requests for disk accesses, from multiple client threads. Each RAID architecture converts each individual user requests into sets of read and write accesses on specific disks of the array; our implementations of DATUM, parity declustering, and EVENODD are at this level in the hierarchy. Individual disk accesses are serviced by an event-driven disk simulator, calibrated to several choices of real disks. The current release of RaidFrame consists of approximately 50,000 lines of C code.

In our case, array parameters were configured as follows. The array had a total of $n = 15$ disks in every case, so all measurements are normalized to cost. Each stripe unit consisted of eight 512-byte sectors, for a total of 4Kbytes. The individual disks of the array were HP2247s, with a total storage of approximately 900 Mbytes, average seek time 10 milliseconds, and revolution time 11 milliseconds. Each disk's controller used the shortest-seek-time-first queueing policy in a queue that can hold 10 outstanding requests. Regarding the synthetic workload, it consisted of random, independent 4-Kbyte accesses (the size of one stripe unit) uniformly distributed over the user's address space. There was no caching or read-ahead used in our simulations; these optimizations are up to the client applications (e.g. a file system manager). Accesses were aligned to a stripe unit

	DATUM	EVENODD	Parity decl.
Failure-free	$m = 9$ $k = 10$	$m = 13$ $k = 15$	$m = 9$ $k = 10$
$f = 1$	$m = 9$ $k = 10$	$m = 13$ $k = 15$	$m = 9$ $k = 10$
$f = 2$	$m = 9$ $k = 11$	$m = 13$ $k = 15$	N/A
$f = 3$	$m = 9$ $k = 12$	N/A	N/A

Table 1: Experiment Configurations

boundary. We chose these workloads because small accesses (particularly writes) are typically most demanding for RAID architectures. The same disk array simulator and similar synthetic workloads have been used a number of times in the literature [8, 10, 22]. For larger accesses, there are a number of possible optimizations that can be implemented for any of the three schemes discussed in this section. Our implementation of the DATUM array architecture took about 2,400 lines of code.

For each failure scenario, we report the average response times for each request under workloads of pure reads and pure writes, as a function of the number of array access requests per second. Table 1 shows the configurations used for each method under each failure scenario. Each simulation ran until the size of the 95% confidence interval was within a 2% of the reported values; therefore, 95% confidence intervals are fairly small and we do not include them in the graphs. DATUM's configuration depends on the number of failures we want to tolerate.

Bestavros reports in [2] times of approximately 100 nanoseconds/byte for the VLSI implementation of IDA. Since his design does not allow pipelining, this amounts to less than 0.5 milliseconds for a 4096-byte stripe. This has been added wherever necessary to the times spent by DATUM in disk accesses. According to [2], it is possible to design a more sophisticated chip that can support pipelining and be driven by a clock ten times faster.

5.1 Failure-free Operation

For these experiments, the DATUM array was configured with $k = 10$ and $m = 9$, i.e. a single redundant unit per stripe. Figure 3 shows the performance of read and write operations for the three RAID architectures under consideration. The read operations have roughly the same performance, as each of them implements small reads in the failure-free case by simply reading the stripe unit requested by the user. The cost of writes is similar for DATUM and parity declustering; in both cases the array reads the old value of the data unit being written and the redundant unit of its stripe, recalculates the redundant unit, and writes both units back to the disks. The cost of small writes in EVENODD is substantially larger since the array needs to read, recompute and write *two* redundant units for each small write; this makes the array reach its point of saturation at about 180 reqs/sec, compared to 280 reqs/sec for the other two architectures.

5.2 Single Disk Failure

The DATUM array has the same configuration as in the previous section, as it must tolerate a single failure. Figure 4 shows the performance of read and write operations for the three RAID architectures.

The execution times for read operations are larger than in the failure-free. When a disk is unavailable, the reads directed to it must be implemented by reading all the remaining units of the stripe and reconstructing the missing data. EVENODD would have a better response time if stripe units were three or four times larger in this same configuration because each stripe spans the 15 disks of the array (as opposed to a subset of 10 disks for DATUM and parity declustering), so reads in parallel from different disks would make a difference. As in the failure-free case, EVENODD writes are slower because two redundant units must be updated. The performance difference is due to the fact that EVENODD can always tolerate two failures, while DATUM can be configured to the reliability requirements of each installation For every architecture, the writes are slower than in the failure-free case because a reconstruction must be made when writing an unavailable data unit.

5.3 Double Disk Failure

We compare DATUM with EVENODD only, as parity declustering does not tolerate more than one failure. The DATUM array is configured as $m = 9, k = 11$—with two redundant units per stripe. Figure 5 depicts the response times for DATUM and EVENODD.

A larger fraction of the small reads require a reconstruction here, increasing the average response time. The read performance of the two schemes is quite similar, even though EVENODD seems to be able to sustain a slightly larger arrival rate before saturation. We attribute this fact to the larger stripe size that places less load on each individual disk. Regarding writes, the performance of the two schemes is also very similar. EVENODD's performance is almost the same in the single- and double-failure scenarios; we attribute this to the fact

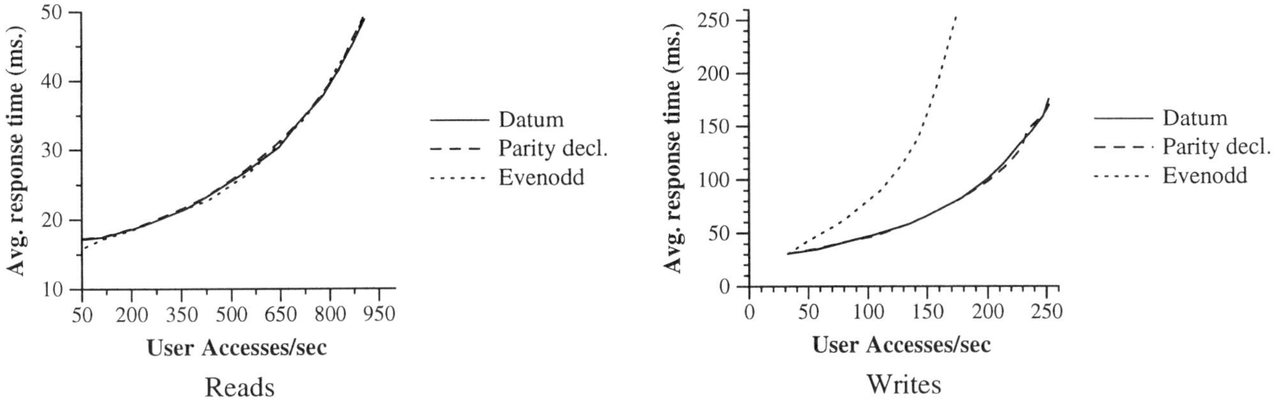

Figure 3: Response times, failure-free case

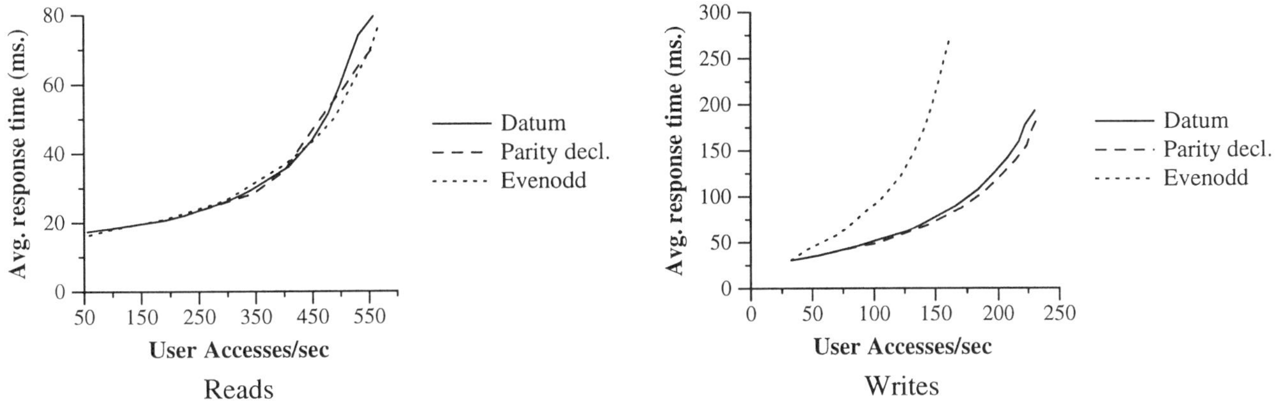

Figure 4: Response times, one failure

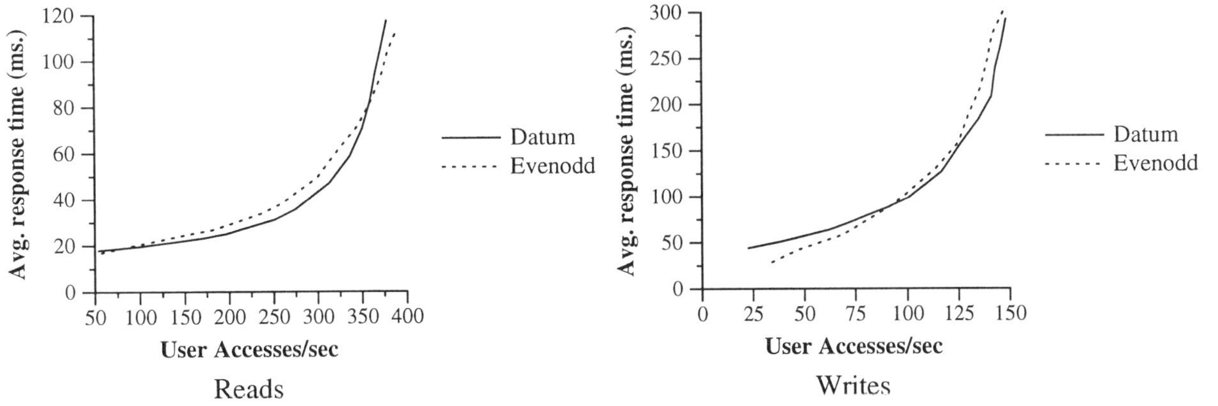

Figure 5: Response times, two failures

that each stripe spans all the disks, so the reconstructions that must be performed when an unavailable data unit is written place additional demands on every surviving disk.

5.4 Triple Disk Failure

DATUM is the only method among the three considered that can tolerate three or more failures. The DATUM array is configured as $m = 9, k = 12$—with three redundant units per stripe.

The response times are shown in Figure 6. They are naturally larger than in the previous failure scenarios; but the response curves have similar characteristics. Moreover, for each failure scenario, the DATUM curves have a first derivative that is roughly within a constant factor of the first derivative of the previous scenario. This constant rate of degradation suggests that DATUM degrades gracefully as more failures occur; we plan to make additional measurements to test the accuracy of this conjecture.

6 Related Work

We discuss three main groups of relevant studies, although some of them belong to more than one category: coding methods, parity declustering, and RAID architectures. Coding methods for tolerating multiple failures have been proposed by Gibson *et al* [9]; their f-dimensional parity method can tolerate multiple failures, but it achieves the optimal redundancy only when $k = i^f$ for some integer i, and in that case it needs fi^{f-1} separate disks for storing redundant information. The other codes also require an increasing number of redundant disks as a function of the reliability group size, unlike DATUM where the size of a redundant unit is independent of the number of units per stripe. EVENODD [3] tolerates two disk failures, and can be efficiently implemented on existing controller hardware. Even though EVENODD does not inherently prevent declustering, the layout proposed in [3] makes every disk a member of every stripe; this limits the array to a maximum of 259 disks, and is likely to result in performance degradation during on-line reconstruction [10]. Burkhard and Menon [4] analyze the additional dependability gained by using MDS codes to tolerate multiple failures; that paper concentrates on reliability calculations, and does not address the issues of run-time performance or array layout. They conclude that increasing the fault-tolerance within each reliability group is more cost effective than partitioning the array into more groups, or relying on improvements to the reliability of each disk. Their conclusions are applicable to DATUM, as our IDA is an MDS code as well.

Several existing studies investigate parity declustering, i.e. the uniform distribution of data and parity redundancy over the array when each stripe uses a subset of the disks. Muntz and Lui [14] suggest balanced incomplete block designs (BIBDs) to achieve uniform distribution; Holland and Gibson [10] implemented the scheme and evaluated its performance. BIBDs have two main drawbacks: they do not exist for every array configuration (thus only certain values of the array parameters can be implemented), and they can require substantial amounts of controller memory for table storage, of the order of several Mbytes. To address the first problem, Schwabe and Sutherland [19] have extended the BIBD generation techniques, and bounded the degradation in uniformity incurred when using approximate block designs. Unlike these approaches, DATUM does not place restrictions on the configuration parameters of the array, and does not need to store a block design in memory as the location functions implement the mappings (our mappings are equivalent to a complete block design that is not stored in memory). Pseudo-random permutation declustering has been proposed by Schwarz and Burkhard [21] as well as Merchant and Yu [13]. ACATS declustering, proposed by Schwarz and Burkhard [20], works deterministically for any array configuration thus avoiding the need for a pseudo-random generator and explicit BIBD configuration storage.

RAID architectures were originally proposed by Patterson *et al* in [15]. From the solutions presented there, RAID-5 provides tolerance against a single failure and does not decluster the parity information. Multiple-erasure SID [7] is a RAID scheme for multimedia workloads that can tolerate an arbitrary number of failures while performing contiguous accesses to the disks. Solutions for the layout constraints exist only for some array configurations, and the fraction of the storage devoted to redundant information is at least $f/(\sqrt{m}+f)$, compared to the optimal $f/(m+f)$.

7 Conclusions

We presented DATUM, an architecture for redundant declustered disk arrays that can tolerate an arbitrary number of simultaneous disk failures. Since the trend for the coming years dictates larger number of smaller disks at each installation and/or distributed striping approaches, there is a pervasive need for going beyond the reliability provided by schemes that can tolerate single

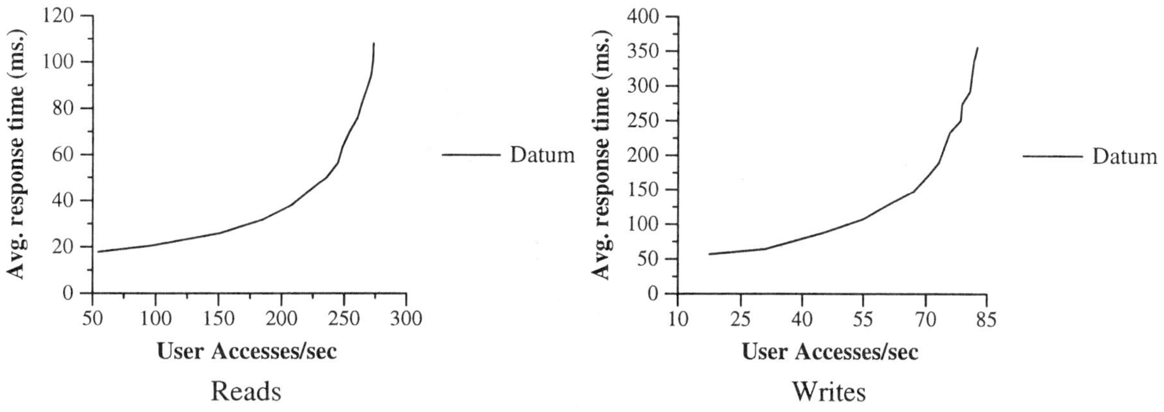

Figure 6: Response times, three failures

or even double failures. DATUM relies on information dispersal as a coding method. The layout functions presented achieve uniform declustering of the user data and redundant data over the disks, and they place no restrictions on the configuration parameters of the array. The functions can be evaluated efficiently, and have very low memory requirements. Several existing layout policies are special cases of DATUM.

DATUM is the only existing method that requires the optimal amount of redundant storage, generalizes to any number of failures and any array configuration, and declusters uniformly user data and redundant data over the disk array. It also accommodates distributed sparing. The number of disk accesses performed on writes are also minimal. A VLSI implementation of the coder and decoder already exist, and its speed is adequate for this purpose. We compared the performance of DATUM with two other RAID architectures, and found that it performs as well as the best of its competitors for the common failure scenarios they can tolerate. Moreover, DATUM degrades gracefully as the number of failures increases beyond the number of failures tolerated by the other two architectures.

Acknowledgements

We want to thank Jim Zelenka and William Courtright for supporting RaidFrame, and the anonymous reviewers for contributing to improve the presentation.

References

[1] G. Alvarez, W. Burkhard, and F. Cristian. Tolerating multiple failures in raid architectures with optimal storage and uniform declustering. Technical report CS96-500, UCSD–CSE, November 1996. Also available by anonymous `ftp` from `elm.ucsd.edu/pub/galvarez/datum.ps.Z`.

[2] A. Bestavros. SETH: A VLSI chip for the real-time information dispersal and retrieval for security and fault-tolerance. In *Proc. Intl. Conf. on Parallel Processing*, 1990.

[3] M. Blaum, J. Brady, J. Bruck, and J. Menon. Even-odd: An efficient scheme for tolerating double disk failures in RAID architectures. In *Proc. of the Annual International Symposium on Computer Architecture*, pages 245–54, 1994.

[4] W. Burkhard and J. Menon. Disk array storage system reliability. In *Proc. of the International Symposium on Fault-tolerant Computing*, pages 432–41, 1993.

[5] L. Cabrera and D. Long. Swift: Using distributed disk striping to provide high I/O data rates. *Computing Systems*, 4(4):405–39, 1991.

[6] P. Cao, S. Lim, S. Venkataraman, and J. Wilkes. The TickerTAIP parallel RAID architecture. In *Proc. of the Annual International Symposium on Computer Architecture*, pages 52–63, 1993.

[7] A. Cohen and W. Burkhard. SID for efficient reconstruction in fault-tolerant video servers. In *Proc. of ACM Multimedia*, pages 277–86, November 1996.

[8] W. Courtright, G. Gibson, M. Holland, and J. Zelenka. A structured approach to redundant disk array implementation. In *Proc. of the International Symposium on Performance and Dependability*, 1996.

[9] G. Gibson, L. Hellerstein, R. Karp, R. Katz, and D. Patterson. Coding techniques for handling failures in large disk arrays. In *Proc. of the International Conference on Architectural Support for Programming Languages and Operating Systems*, pages 123–32, 1989.

[10] M. Holland and G. Gibson. Parity declustering for continuous operation on redundant disk arrays. In *Proc. of the International Conference on Architectural Support for Programming Languages and Operating Systems*, pages 23–35, 1992.

[11] F. MacWilliams and N. Sloane. *The Theory of Error-Correcting Codes*. North-Holland, The Netherlands, 1977.

[12] J. Menon and J. Cortney. The architecture of a fault-tolerant cached RAID controller. In *Proc. of the Annual International Symposium on Computer Architecture*, pages 76–86, 1993.

[13] A. Merchant and P. Yu. Performance analysis of a dual striping strategy for replicated disk arrays. In *Proc. of the Second International Conference on Parallel and Distributed Information Systems*, pages 148–157, San Diego, January 1993.

[14] R. Muntz and J. Lui. Performance analysis of disk arrays under failure. In *Proceedings of the 16th VLDB Conference*, pages 162–173, Brisbane, June 1990.

[15] D. Patterson, G. Gibson, and R. Katz. A case for redundant arrays of inexpensive disks (RAID). In *Proc. of the ACM SIGMOD International Conference on Management of Data*, pages 109–116, 1988.

[16] F. Preparata. Holographic dispersal and recovery of information. *IEEE Transactions on Information Theory*, 35(5):1123–4, September 1989.

[17] M. Rabin. Efficient dispersal of information for security, load balancing, and fault tolerance. *Journal of the ACM*, 36(2):335–48, April 1989.

[18] S. Savage and J. Wilkes. AFRAID— a frequently redundant array of independent disks. In *Proc. of the USENIX 1996 Annual Technical Conference*, January 1996.

[19] E. Schwabe and I. Sutherland. Improved parity-declustered layouts for disk arrays. In *Proc. of the Symposium on Parallel Algorithms and Architectures*, pages 76–84, Cape May, N.J., June 1994.

[20] T. Schwarz and W. Burkhard. Almost complete address translation (ACATS) disk array declustering. In *Proceedings of the Eighth IEEE Symposium on Parallel and Distributed Processing*, pages 324–331, New Orleans, June 1996.

[21] T. Schwarz and W. Burkhard. Reliability and performance of RAIDs. *IEEE Transactions on Magnetics*, 31:1161–1166, March 1995.

[22] D. Stodolsky, G. Gibson, W. Courtright, and M. Holland. A redundant disk array architecture for efficient small writes. Technical report CMU-CS94-170, Carnegie Mellon Univ., July 1994.

Hardware Fault Containment in Scalable Shared-Memory Multiprocessors

Dan Teodosiu, Joel Baxter, Kinshuk Govil, John Chapin*, Mendel Rosenblum, and Mark Horowitz

Computer Systems Laboratory
Stanford University, Stanford, CA 94305
http://www-flash.stanford.edu

Abstract

Current shared-memory multiprocessors are inherently vulnerable to faults: any significant hardware or system software fault causes the entire system to fail. Unless provisions are made to limit the impact of faults, users will perceive a decrease in reliability when they entrust their applications to larger machines. This paper shows that fault containment techniques can be effectively applied to scalable shared-memory multiprocessors to reduce the reliability problems created by increased machine size.

The primary goal of our approach is to leave normal-mode performance unaffected. Rather than using expensive fault-tolerance techniques to mask the effects of data and resource loss, our strategy is based on limiting the damage caused by faults to only a portion of the machine. After a hardware fault, we run a distributed recovery algorithm that allows normal operation to be resumed in the functioning parts of the machine.

Our approach is implemented in the Stanford FLASH multiprocessor. Using a detailed hardware simulator, we have performed a number of fault injection experiments on a FLASH system running Hive, an operating system designed to support fault containment. The results we report validate our approach and show that in conjunction with an operating system like Hive, we can improve the reliability seen by unmodified applications without substantial performance cost. Simulation results suggest that our algorithms scale well for systems up to 128 processors.

1 Introduction

Scalable shared-memory multiprocessors are becoming an increasingly common computing platform. Several companies, including HP-Convex [20], Sequent [11], and Silicon Graphics [10], are shipping multiprocessor systems with configurations of up to a few hundred processing nodes.

However, current shared-memory multiprocessors are inherently vulnerable to faults: any significant hardware or system software fault will cause the entire system to fail. Unless provisions are made to limit the impact of faults, users will perceive a decrease in reliability when they entrust their applications to larger machines. This is an important problem for the viability of large-scale shared-memory multiprocessors as general-purpose compute servers.

Fault containment is a reliability technique widely used in distributed systems, in which the effects of a fault are limited to a small portion of a system [15]. In a computing system that provides fault containment, the chance of failure for a task depends only on the amount of resources that the task uses, not on the size of the entire system.

When running on a large-scale shared-memory multiprocessor, applications of small to moderate size will benefit from the increased reliability offered by fault containment. Since these applications only require a limited amount of resources, they will be protected from failures that occur in the parts of the machine they do not use. Fault containment can also provide benefits to large parallel applications that use a substantial fraction of the machine, if these applications are structured to cope with the loss of some of their resources.

Several challenging issues arise when one tries to implement fault containment on a shared-memory machine. The tight coupling provided by shared memory allows the effects of hardware faults to spread much faster and to more nodes than in a traditional distributed system. In addition, many of the fault containment techniques used in distributed systems (such as performing consistency checks on all incoming messages) appear to be prohibitively expensive given the low latency requirements of a high-performance memory system.

This paper describes one method for implementing fault containment in a scalable shared-memory multiprocessor without substantially reducing its performance or increasing its cost. Rather than relying on expensive techniques that mask the effects of data loss, our approach is based on limiting the impact of faults and running a distributed algorithm to bring the machine back to an operational state after a failure. We have added support to the FLASH multiprocessor [7][9] to confine the effects of most hardware and system software faults. Using the SimOS simulation environment [19], we have validated our approach by performing a number of fault injection experiments on a detailed simulation of the machine.

Achieving fault containment in a shared-memory multiprocessor requires careful design of both its hardware and its operating system. Current multiprocessor operating systems are unable to cope with the loss of any essential hardware resource, such as the failure of a processor or a memory board. This issue has been addressed in our previous work on the Hive operating system [3][18] that was developed in conjunction with the FLASH multiprocessor. This paper focuses on the hardware and firmware support required for an operating system such as Hive that provides fault containment. The experimental results reported in the paper show that, in conjunction with Hive, our implementation offers fault containment benefits to unmodified applications running on FLASH.

*Author's present address: Laboratory for Computer Science, Massachusetts Institute of Technology, Cambridge, MA 02139.

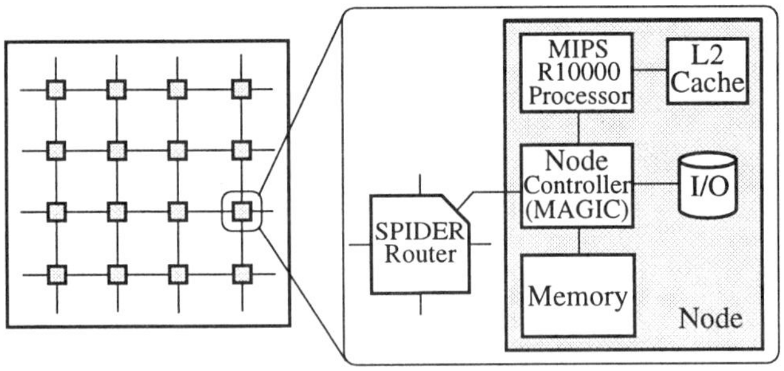

FIGURE 2.1. Overview of the FLASH multiprocessor. FLASH consists of a set of nodes connected through a point-to-point interconnect. Each node contains a portion of the distributed main memory and a node controller that handles cache coherence and other communication within the node and with other nodes.

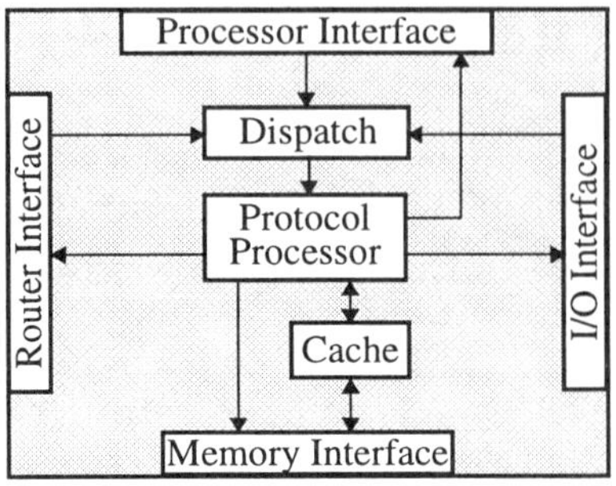

FIGURE 2.2. The MAGIC programmable node controller. The programmable node controller in FLASH contains a RISC processor core that executes handlers to process incoming messages. Handlers are efficiently dispatched by a configurable dispatch mechanism.

The remainder of the paper is organized as follows. In Section 2 we summarize the relevant architectural features of FLASH. Section 3 describes the impact of hardware and firmware faults on the machine, and the features we have added to FLASH to limit this impact. Section 4 presents the distributed recovery algorithm that is run after a failure to restore normal operation on the functioning parts of the machine. We conclude with an experimental evaluation of the effectiveness and scalability of our approach.

2 FLASH Architecture Overview

The FLASH multiprocessor currently being built at Stanford is a CC-NUMA (Cache-Coherent with Non-Uniform Memory Access time) machine that can accommodate up to 512 processors in its largest configuration (Figure 2.1). Each node in the machine contains a MIPS R10000 processor [25] and its second-level cache, a portion of the machine's distributed main memory, a programmable node controller, and attached I/O devices such as disks or network adapters.

The programmable node controller, called MAGIC, manages cache coherence between nodes, as well as all other communication within the node and with other nodes [9]. MAGIC (Figure 2.2) contains a statically scheduled, dual-issue RISC processor core that executes code sequences called *handlers*. The handlers update protocol state, control communication, and manage MAGIC's resources. On receiving a request from the processor, the interconnect, or the node's I/O devices, MAGIC uses a configurable hardware dispatch mechanism to efficiently select the proper handler to respond to that request. The code and data for the protocol processor are stored in a reserved portion of the node's main memory, and may be cached on MAGIC.

By changing the MAGIC handlers it is possible to use a variety of different cache coherence protocols in FLASH. In this paper we assume the use of a directory-based protocol [9] which assigns each 128-byte memory line to a fixed *home node*, where the protocol state for that line is stored. Memory data from one node may be cached by the processor of any other node. Handlers running at the home node for a cache line manage the cache coherence protocol state of that line.

Nodes in FLASH communicate through a high-speed, reliable, flow-controlled interconnect that is based on Silicon Graphics's CrayLink technology and SPIDER router chip [4]. For simplicity, in this paper we shall assume that the nodes are arranged in a two-dimensional mesh. Although such a topology could be realized with the SPIDER routers, FLASH actually uses a hierarchical fat hypercube topology that has a smaller diameter than a mesh with the same number of nodes. The algorithms described in the paper are independent of the actual topology of the machine.

3 Fault Containment in FLASH

Our strategy for coping with hardware failures in FLASH is based on limiting the amount of state lost after a failure and ensuring that the functioning parts of the system are brought back to an operational state. When a fault occurs, the operation of the system is disrupted for a brief period of time to perform the required clean-up and recovery actions. This approach makes it possible to provide undiminished performance during normal operation.

Our fault containment design can thus be broken down into a *set of features* that limit the impact of faults and allow the system to operate despite missing hardware resources, and a *recovery algorithm* that is executed to restore the system to normal operation after a hardware failure. The set of features is introduced in this section, while Section 4 discusses the recovery algorithm.

Figure 3.1 is a roadmap of our presentation of the impact of faults on the system and of the features needed to limit this impact. We start with an overview of the effect of node and interconnect faults on the operation of the machine (a discussion of low-level hardware issues has been relegated to Section 6). We then show how disruptions in the operation of the hardware or firmware can affect the shared memory system, and point out what corrective actions have to be taken. Finally, we discuss how these failures can affect the operating system. The impact of operating system software errors lies beyond the scope of this paper; see [3] and [18] for a detailed treatment of this topic.

3.1 Direct Impact of Faults

As shared-memory multiprocessor systems scale to larger numbers of processors, the probability of a hardware fault increases. The problems we expect to see in practice include partial power supply or cooling system losses, disconnected inter-cabinet cables, node controller firmware errors, and memory failures. For the purpose of this discussion, the direct impact of faults on the machine can be divided into node failures and interconnect failures. Although we discuss the two types of failures separately, a combination of these effects may occur after any given hardware fault.

Node failures: When a node fails, the node's MAGIC controller, processor, portion of main memory, and attached I/O devices all become unavailable. Any information stored in the failed node's processor and MAGIC caches is lost. A node failure may affect the rest of the system by causing other processors to stall and the interconnect to become congested:

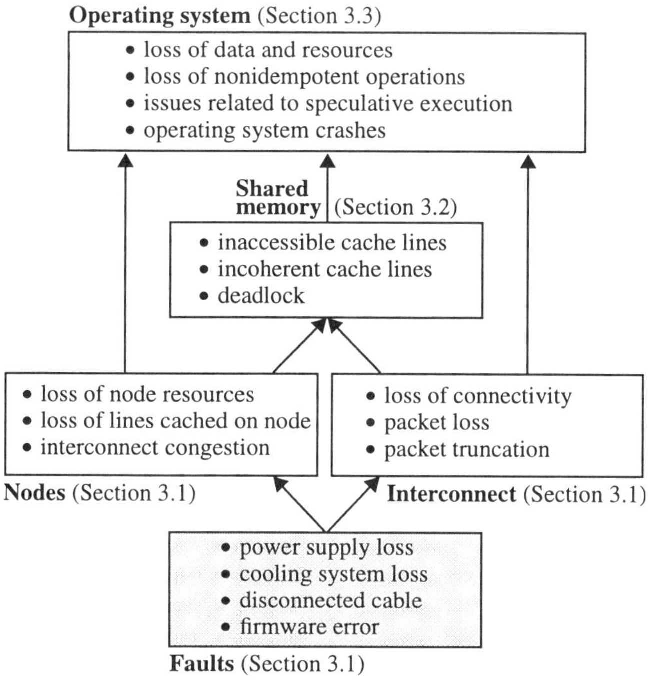

FIGURE 3.1. Impact of hardware and firmware faults. In a scalable shared-memory multiprocessor, hardware and firmware faults may disrupt the functioning of the machine's interconnect, nodes, shared memory, and operating system.

- If a processor sends a coherence request to a failed node, the processor may stall waiting for the request to complete. Note that even if the system software carefully avoids sending any requests to failed nodes, it cannot fully control what references the processors issue. Dynamically scheduled out-of-order execution processors, such as the MIPS R10000 used in FLASH, may speculatively execute code at the predicted target of a branch before it is known whether or not that branch will be taken (the R10000 can speculate through up to four branches). If a branch prediction turns out to be incorrect, the processor discards the results of the speculation, but has already issued any speculatively executed memory references. This means that during incorrect speculation, the processor can issue a memory request for an address that the code does not actually intend to access.
- A node failure has the potential to disrupt the functioning of the whole interconnect. Consider the case in which due to a firmware bug one of the MAGIC handlers enters an infinite loop. After its buffers fill up, the node controller stops accepting packets from the interconnect. If requests continue to be sent to the failed node, traffic will start backing up into the interconnect. As router buffers fill up, the congestion may eventually prevent other interconnect traffic from being delivered. Within a brief time after the failure, coherence traffic throughout the system may come to a standstill.

Limiting the impact of node failures: To avoid sending messages to failed nodes during normal operation, MAGIC uses a configurable hardware table, called the *node map,* that records the availability of all nodes in the system. Each node checks its local node map before sending a request out over the interconnect. The information in the node map is kept up-to-date by the recovery algorithm. The node map checks are implemented entirely in MAGIC hardware and do not add any latency to MAGIC handlers.

Node failures caused by MAGIC firmware faults can cause congestion of the interconnect. If this occurs, it is the responsibility of the recovery algorithm to restore normal network operation by reprogramming the routers bordering the failed area to discard packets routed into it.

Interconnect failures: Having a reliable, flow-controlled interconnect is critical for good performance during normal operation of the multiprocessor. Unfortunately, designing the rest of the system to take advantage of these interconnect features implies that an interconnect failure can disrupt the functioning of the system, by causing loss of connectivity and packet loss or truncation:

- In the interconnect used in FLASH, packets sent between two given nodes travel along a static route that is defined by routing tables programmed into the individual SPIDER routers. Therefore, loss of links and routers (for example after a cabinet power failure) can reduce the connectivity of the interconnect. After a failure, any messages routed through the failed portion of the system will not reach their destinations, even if alternate paths around the faulty area exist.
- During normal operation, the CrayLink interconnect guarantees that no messages are lost or corrupted. However, packets may be dropped or truncated as a result of a failure. For instance, if the power supply to a part of the interconnect goes down, any messages that were in transit through that part of the interconnect will be lost. If the link a message is currently traversing fails, the message will be truncated and a truncated packet will be delivered to the destination.

Limiting the impact of interconnect failures: Connectivity between the functioning nodes can be restored by reprogramming the routing tables so that packets are routed around the failed areas. Loss of connectivity is thus a temporary condition that can be corrected by the recovery algorithm.

For efficiency reasons, we have chosen to let the cache coherence protocol and the operating system deal with packet loss and truncation rather than hiding those effects through the use of a reliable end-to-end transmission protocol. An end-to-end protocol that would buffer messages and perform all necessary retransmissions for coherence traffic would be prohibitively expensive to implement in MAGIC firmware. It takes MAGIC less than 120 nanoseconds, or 24 protocol processor instructions, to execute the handler for processing a read request from a remote node. Any instructions added to this handler for end-to-end checks would slow it down considerably and degrade the performance of the machine. On the other hand, a hardware implementation of end-to-end reliability can be quite effective, as shown in [23].

If a truncated message is received by a node controller, it is not generally possible to discard the message. To reduce the latency of memory operations in FLASH, data is pipelined as it passes through the memory, the interconnect, and MAGIC. When a node controller detects a truncated message, it may have already fed part of that message to the processor. In those cases, MAGIC completes the message, setting the parity error bits on all data words that were lost, and initiates the recovery algorithm.

3.2 Impact of Faults on Shared Memory Operation

Node failures and packet loss or truncation can damage the correctness of the cache coherence protocol. These effects depend on the type of coherence protocol used. In the case of the directory-based protocol currently used in FLASH, a failure can have the following impacts:

- Any cache line whose home is on a failed node becomes *inaccessible.* Even if this line happened to be cached elsewhere in the system at the time its home node failed, it can no longer be used because all cache misses to it are directed to and must be serviced by its home node.

- A cache line can become *incoherent* in two cases: if the line was cached exclusive by a failed node, or if a message containing the only valid copy of the line is dropped or truncated. Although the home node (as well as the coherence protocol state) of an incoherent line remains accessible after a failure, the only valid copy of that line has been lost. For example, a cache line can become incoherent if a cache writeback message is lost, since the cache coherence protocol used in FLASH entrusts the only valid copy of that line to the writeback message for efficiency reasons.
- Memory operations may *deadlock* after a failure. The cache coherence protocol used in FLASH sometimes locks a memory line to prevent access when the line is in a transient state. (This can occur, for instance, when the home node is waiting for invalidate acknowledgments from the nodes sharing a line.) An access to a locked line fails and is retried until it succeeds. If the unlocking message is lost or if the sender of this message fails, a node trying to access the locked line will spin indefinitely waiting for the lock to be released.

Limiting the impact of faults: In order to allow normal shared memory operation to resume after a failure, the recovery algorithm must determine exactly what data has been lost and reset the state of the cache coherence protocol to break any deadlock that may have occurred. After resumption of normal operation, the processors must be prevented from using lost or incoherent data. The following support is needed:

- Any memory references to inaccessible cache lines must be caught and terminated immediately. This is done by having the node map mechanism described previously act as one of the inputs to the MAGIC dispatch table. If a node tries to reference an inaccessible line, an error handler is dispatched on that node's MAGIC. Rather than relaying the memory request to the failed home node, the error handler terminates the reference by raising a bus error.

  Special treatment is required for the set of cache lines corresponding to low physical addresses in FLASH. This is due to the fact that for most processors, including the R10000, exception vectors are located at a fixed range of physical addresses. Requiring all processors in the machine to fetch their vectors from the same memory range would introduce a single point of failure into the system. We have avoided this problem in FLASH by replicating the address range containing the exception vectors. The node controllers contain a hardware *remap* mechanism that converts all references to the vector address range into node-local references.
- Processors must be prevented from using incoherent lines. These lines are identified by the recovery algorithm and marked as incoherent in the cache coherence protocol state. When a processor sends a request to the home node of a line, the handler servicing the request checks the protocol state of that line. If the line is marked incoherent, the handler sends back a special reply that terminates the access by raising a bus error. The additional checks for incoherent lines do not add any latency to common handlers since we were able to insert these checks in unused MAGIC instruction slots.

3.3 Impact of Faults on the Operating System

Traditional multiprocessor operating systems cannot fully benefit from the hardware fault containment support available in FLASH, since in most cases they are unable to recover from the loss of any of their resources. To provide fault containment benefits to applications running on FLASH, we have developed the Hive

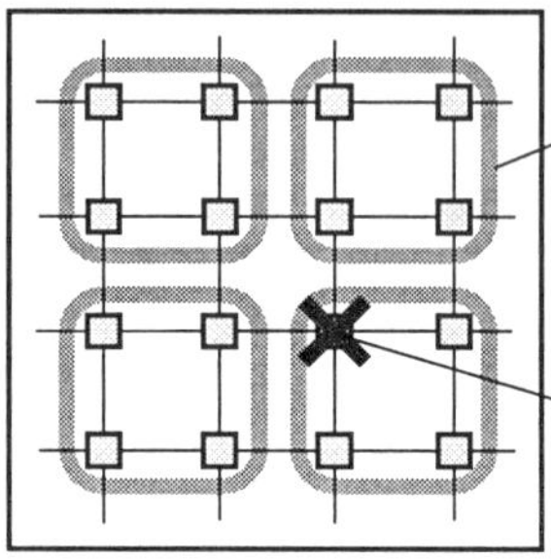

FIGURE 3.2. Partitioning the multiprocessor into Hive cells. The Hive operating system provides fault containment by partitioning the machine into failure units and running a separate kernel (a *cell*) in each unit. Cells are able to survive most hardware or system software faults occurring outside of their failure units.

operating system [3][18], a binary-compatible extension of Silicon Graphics's IRIX 5.2.

Hive is structured as an internal distributed system of *cells*, as shown in Figure 3.2. Each cell is a multiprocessor operating system kernel that manages a separate partition of the machine. The cells communicate to provide the user with the usual single system image expected from a shared-memory multiprocessor operating system. Hive provides fault containment by limiting the effects of most faults to one or a few cells.

Hardware faults have several types of impacts on Hive:

- A failure that causes cache lines to become inaccessible or incoherent can cause a cell to crash if the lost data included kernel text or data structures of that cell. Similarly, the failure of a node may cause a cell to deadlock if the failed node was holding one of the cell's system locks (such as the run queue lock) at the time of the failure.
- Traffic loss as the result of a failure can damage I/O operations. If an operation such as an uncached read or write to an I/O device register is lost, it is difficult to determine whether the request has actually been serviced or not. Since those requests are in general nonidempotent, retrying them is not appropriate.
- An incorrectly speculated write may cause a processor to fetch some arbitrary line into its cache in exclusive mode. If that processor fails, the data is lost. Therefore, a node failure could destroy arbitrary data that happened to be cached exclusive on that node as a result of incorrect speculation. This effect can cause multiple cells to crash after a single hardware fault.

Limiting the impact of faults: To limit vulnerability to failures occurring in other parts of the system, each Hive cell must carefully control which resources it uses for its kernel text and data structures, and must defend those resources from outside corruption. FLASH provides the following support:

- The recovery algorithm enforces the abstraction that each partition of the machine behaves as a hardware *failure unit*. The shape of failure units is carefully chosen so that all coherence traffic inside a unit stays within the portion of the interconnect allocated to that unit. This allows the recovery algorithm to guarantee that no intra-cell memory traffic is lost as long as there are no faults in the hardware of the corresponding failure unit. If any component in a failure unit fails, the recovery algorithm stops all the nodes in that failure unit, thereby ensuring a clean shutdown of the affected cell.

  To prevent its critical data from becoming inaccessible or incoherent, a cell only stores this data in memory belonging to its own failure unit. Cells are allowed to read the kernel data structures of other cells, but not to modify them directly. If a cell needs to change the state of some other cell (for instance, when forking a process to the other cell), it makes a remote procedure call (RPC) to ask the other cell to perform the operation.

- Hive cells prevent damage caused by the loss of nonidempotent operations by avoiding uncached accesses to I/O devices across cell boundaries. If a cell needs to access an I/O device belonging to a different cell, it sends an RPC to the other cell and asks it to perform the operation. This inter-cell RPC mechanism is itself vulnerable to packet loss, but the Hive RPC subsystem uses an end-to-end protocol to guarantee exactly-once semantics.

  MAGIC supports this design by terminating with a bus error any uncached accesses to I/O devices that come from outside the local failure unit. This has the additional benefit of defending against software errors in other cells.

- MAGIC provides a hardware access control mechanism called the *firewall* that enables each cell to control precisely which of its data structures can be fetched exclusive by nodes outside the cell. The firewall associates an access control list with every 4KB memory page that specifies which nodes in the machine have write access to that page. If a node tries to fetch a line exclusive from a page to which it does not have write permission, MAGIC will issue a bus error.

  The firewall allows cells to protect their data against speculative writes, and helps defend against wild writes resulting from system software crashes in other cells [3].

- A wild write issued by the processor has the potential to disrupt the operation of that node's MAGIC, as the node controller's code, internal data structures, and cache coherence protocol state are all stored in a region of the node's memory. To defend against operating system software errors, this region is only writable by the protocol processor of the local MAGIC. The node controller prevents accidental modification using a configurable *range limit* implemented for efficiency in dedicated logic and set at protocol firmware boot time. Accesses from any R10000 processor, including the local one, that violate the range limit are terminated with a bus error by MAGIC.

4 Fault Recovery in FLASH

Many of the features described in Section 3 rely on the existence of a recovery algorithm that is executed after a fault has occurred. The purpose of this algorithm is to determine which parts of the machine have remained operational after a fault, and to reconfigure the multiprocessor so that normal operation can be resumed on the functioning parts. Table 4.1 summarizes the conditions that trigger the recovery algorithm and the tasks that it performs.

We start by giving an overview of the recovery algorithm, after which the presentation follows the phases of the algorithm shown in Figure 4.2. For completeness, at the end of the section we have included a brief discussion of operating system recovery.

4.1 Overview of the Recovery Algorithm

The recovery algorithm is divided into the four phases shown in Figure 4.2: recovery initiation, information dissemination, interconnect recovery, and recovery of the cache coherence protocol state. After the recovery algorithm completes it is possible to resume normal operation in the functioning parts of the machine; the operating system is informed that the recovery algorithm has run and performs its own recovery actions [3] before allowing user-level processes to continue execution.

TABLE 4.1. Recovery algorithm triggers and tasks.

Events that trigger hardware recovery	
memory operation timeout	Section 4.2
NAK counter overflow	Section 4.2
MAGIC firmware assertion failure	Section 4.2
reception of truncated interconnect packet	Section 4.2
Tasks performed by the recovery algorithm	
update node map	Section 4.3
implement hardware failure units	Section 4.3
recover interconnect	Section 4.4
mark incoherent cache lines	Section 4.5
resolve coherence protocol deadlock	Section 4.5

To avoid single points of failure, the recovery algorithm runs as a distributed algorithm over all the functioning nodes in the machine. The algorithm is able to cope with additional hardware failures that occur during its execution by restarting whenever a new fault is detected.

Under some pathological overload conditions, recovery might be triggered even in the absence of a hardware fault. The algorithm has been carefully designed so that normal execution can be resumed after a false alarm without any data loss. The sole effect of a false alarm is a brief interruption in the operation of the machine.

The remainder of this subsection provides some background for the presentation of the recovery phases by discussing the types of failures recognized by the recovery algorithm, the way nodes communicate during recovery, and the implementation of the algorithm.

Failure types: We simplify the design of the recovery algorithm by considering only two abstract classes of failures, and by mapping all actual faults that can occur in the real system onto a combination of those two abstractions. A comprehensive diagnosis of the cause of the failure need not be done by the recovery algorithm, but can instead be performed off-line. The two abstract failure classes are node failures and link failures:

- A *node failure* affects the node's controller, processor, and memory, but not the router to which the failed node is connected. For most node failures, any packets that are sent to the failed node are discarded. The only exception is the case of a MAGIC firmware error in which a handler enters an infinite loop and causes the node controller to stop accepting packets.
- A *link failure* prevents transmission of interconnect traffic. In the CrayLink interconnect, failed links act as "black holes" by sinking any traffic that is directed through them. The recovery algorithm does not distinguish between the failure of a router and the failure of all the links connected to that router.

A hardware failure in the real machine will usually result in several link or node failures that occur almost simultaneously. For instance, a power supply loss may manifest itself as the failure of a set of routers and all of their connecting links; a disconnected cable between two cabinets appears as multiple link failures.

Inter-node communication during recovery: For the reasons discussed in Section 3.1, the recovery algorithm cannot use the normal CrayLink communication mechanisms when sending information between nodes. To avoid these problems, FLASH dedicates two virtual lanes of the interconnect for recovery traffic. When it starts, the recovery algorithm can assume that the dedicated lanes are not clogged with backed-up traffic.

Recovery packets use a source-routing mechanism provided by the CrayLink interconnect that allows the sender of a message to

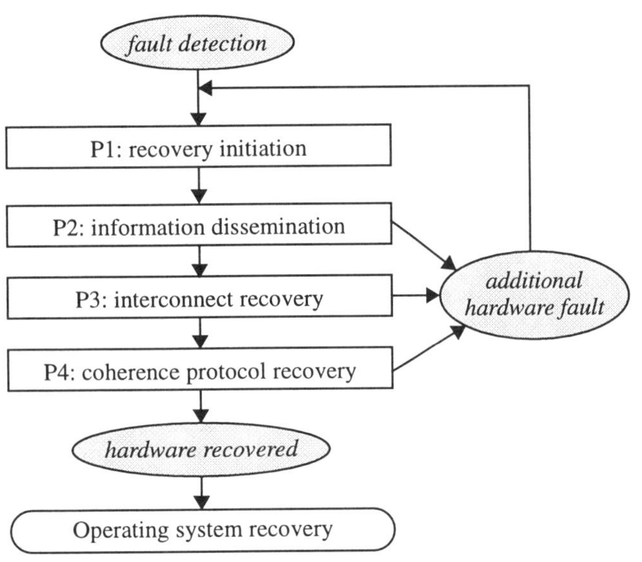

FIGURE 4.2. Hardware fault recovery algorithm in FLASH. After a hardware fault is detected, a distributed algorithm is executed on all the functioning nodes in the machine. The algorithm diagnoses the system, reconfigures the interconnect and resets the state of the cache coherence protocol.

specify on a link-by-link basis the exact route the message will take to its destination. This allows nodes to route messages around the failed areas. The number of hops that a source-routed packet can traverse is limited, so the initial phases of recovery use only local communication (exchange of messages between neighboring functioning nodes).

An important characteristic of the source-routing delivery mechanism is that packets do not back up indefinitely. If a source-routed packet has been stalled in a router for more than a specified time, subsequent source-routed packets sent to that router are automatically discarded. This prevents the virtual lanes used for recovery from becoming congested.

Recovery algorithm implementation: Given that the node controllers in FLASH are programmable, one could imagine implementing most of the recovery algorithm in node controller firmware. However, this would be a poor system design decision, since keeping the node controller as simple as possible helps increase the level of confidence in its correctness. Instead, most of the recovery algorithm, about 6,000 lines of C code, executes on the R10000 processors. Only the strictly necessary support was added to MAGIC firmware, contributing about 2,000 new lines to the existing 12,000 lines of node controller code.

Since the recovery algorithm temporarily suspends all normal memory system operations, it is essential that the code executed on the R10000 does not cause any coherence traffic. Therefore, for the duration of hardware recovery the processors fetch their code and data from uncached space only. In this mode, the overhead of performing a bus transaction and running a MAGIC handler for every instruction fetch slows the R10000 processor down to under 2.5 MIPS.

4.2 Recovery Initiation Phase

The first phase of the recovery algorithm is initiated when a failure is detected in the system. After starting the recovery code on the R10000, a node diagnoses the resources in its immediate vicinity and triggers recovery on the surrounding nodes.

Failure detection: As shown in Table 4.1, there are four mechanisms in FLASH that can trigger the recovery algorithm:

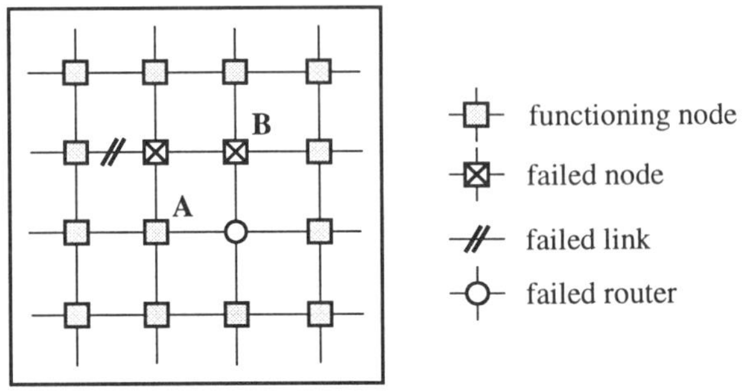

FIGURE 4.3. Failure detection in FLASH.
In this example, *A* receives no reply to a memory request it has sent to *B*, since *B* has failed. Eventually, *A* times out and triggers the recovery algorithm.

memory operation timeouts, NAK counter overflows, firmware assertion failures, and reception of truncated packets.

Memory operation timeouts signal that the home node to which a memory request has been sent has failed, or that one of the request or reply messages has been delayed or lost. Consider the example shown in Figure 4.3. Node *A* has sent a cache coherence request to node *B*, but node *B* has failed and hence cannot satisfy the request and send back a reply. Eventually, node *A*'s controller notices that the request has timed out and triggers recovery.

The second failure detection mechanism is implemented with NAK counters. Requests to a memory line are answered with a NAK reply whenever that line is locked by some other memory operation. Each node controller maintains a hardware NAK counter that keeps track of the number of times a given memory request has been unsuccessfully retried. A *NAK counter overflow* is an indication that deadlock may have occurred as the result of a failure. The node controller implements NAK counters as dedicated logic in its processor interface. Updating the counters does not add any latency to MAGIC operation.

The third mechanism is implemented with *assertions* in the MAGIC firmware that check for firmware errors. Assertions can only be used sparingly, since it is important to avoid slowing down the normal operation of the machine. The primary use of assertions is during the debugging of the cache coherence protocol implementation.

Since the CrayLink interconnect guarantees the integrity of packets during normal operation, the *reception of a truncated packet* by a node controller indicates that a failure has occurred. The next handler that is dispatched on that MAGIC is a special error handler that triggers recovery.

Initiating recovery code on the R10000: After a failure is detected, the node controller causes the node's R10000 processor to start executing the recovery code. The initiation of the recovery code must not depend on the correctness of the system software running on that processor, given that the operating system is far too complex to be trusted to react promptly and reliably. This creates two problems. First, initiation must use a non-maskable interrupt (NMI). Not all processors provide a restartable NMI[1] (in particular, the R10000 NMI is not always restartable). Second, posting the non-maskable interrupt is not by itself sufficient for dropping the processor into recovery, as the processor may be waiting for some memory requests to complete.

Rather than using an NMI on the R10000, MAGIC forces a processor interface bus parity error which raises a Cache Error that has most of the necessary properties. This solution is not optimal,

1. An example of appropriate support is the RED_state found in the UltraSPARC architecture [22].

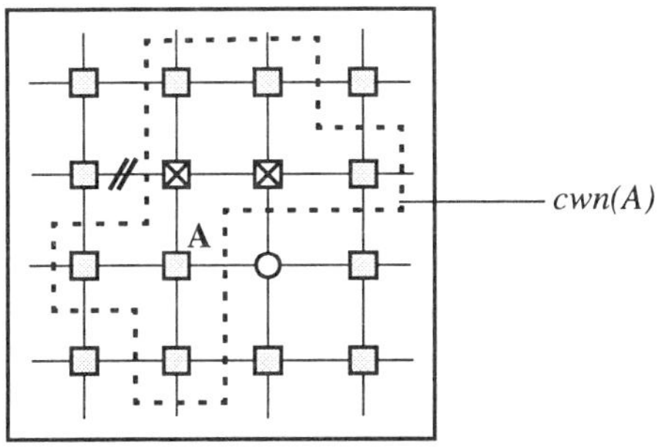

FIGURE 4.4. The set of closest working neighbors.
Every node exchanges information on the state of the system with all other functioning nodes that are closest to it. The set of closest working neighbors (*cwn*) is determined during recovery initiation.

since fielding of the exception may be delayed if another (genuine) Cache Error is being handled; we rely on the fact that the latter is a low-probability event. To make sure that the processor starts executing the recovery code immediately, any pending requests to cacheable addresses are NAK'ed by MAGIC. These requests will be reissued by the processor after recovery completes.

Outstanding uncached operations require a different treatment as they have exactly-once semantics and must not be retried. If an uncached read operation is pending at the time of recovery initiation, the recovery code running on MAGIC terminates the read by returning a NAK, but also allocates an internal buffer in MAGIC memory to save the result of the read when it arrives from the network. (As discussed in Section 3.3, a remote uncached read can only be an intra-cell one. Thus, either the read succeeds, or the failure unit corresponding to the cell goes down entirely.) Prior to resuming normal operation, the recovery code emulates the read instruction and advances the saved program counter past it.

Determining the set of closest working neighbors: After the processor has started executing the recovery code, it probes its neighboring routers and node controllers to determine which resources in its vicinity are reachable and functioning. Each node *A* determines its set of *closest working neighbors, cwn(A)*, which includes all the functioning nodes that can be reached from *A* through a path that does not contain other nodes in *cwn(A)*. An example *cwn* set is shown in Figure 4.4.

The determination of *cwn(A)* is an iterative process that probes nodes located further and further away from *A* until every path starting at *A* either ends in a failed link or contains a functioning node. At each step, *A* first probes the unexplored links by interrogating the routers at the end of those links. *A* then sends ping packets to the node controllers at the end of the unexplored links. A ping reply will only be received if the pinged node has successfully started executing the recovery code on the R10000 processor. While arbitrarily complex self-diagnostics could be run on a node before responding to a ping reply, successfully dropping the node's processor into recovery is complicated enough to provide evidence that the node is functioning correctly.

Triggering recovery on all good nodes: Typically, an anomalous condition in the operation of the machine is brought to the attention of a node by one of the mechanisms shown in Table 4.1. After a node has detected a hardware problem and started executing the recovery algorithm, it will send ping packets to all the nodes in its *cwn* set, dropping those nodes into recovery, too. A wave of ping packets spreading from each node to its immediate functioning neighbors will eventually cause all the good nodes in the system to enter recovery.

As an optimization to speed up recovery triggering, nodes speculatively send ping packets to their immediate neighbors before performing the *cwn* exploration. We have found that in FLASH this heuristic can lead to a fivefold increase in the speed at which recovery is triggered.

We assume the redundancy in the machine's interconnect is high enough that a partitioning of the system ("split-brain syndrome") is unlikely to occur. A heuristic such as shutting down the whole machine if more than a given fraction of its nodes have failed may help avoid split-brain behavior. The subsequent phases of the recovery algorithm assume that the interconnect remains connected.

4.3 Information Dissemination Phase

At the end of the initiation phase, each node *A* knows only the state of the links and nodes in its immediate vicinity, namely *cwn(A)*. The purpose of the dissemination phase is to ensure that every functioning node in the machine learns the global system state.

The dissemination phase proceeds in a number of rounds. During each round, each node *A* exchanges its current knowledge about the state of the machine with all the nodes in *cwn(A)*. As information propagates between neighboring nodes, each node gains a more complete picture of the state of the system.

```
LState = {info about links in cwn(A)}
NState = {info about nodes in cwn(A)}
round = 1
repeat
    for all n in cwn(A) do
        send (LState, NState) to n
        get (LS, NS) from n
        LState = merge(LState, LS)
        NState = merge(NState, NS)
    done
    round = round+1
until COND
```

A node gains full knowledge about the system after a number of rounds equal to the height of the BFT (breadth-first tree) rooted at that node. From this point on, `LState` and `NState` remain unchanged even if additional rounds are executed. However, the BFT height is not the same for all nodes, meaning that for different nodes, `LState` and `NState` may stabilize after a different number of rounds. To keep the nodes synchronized, we need a condition *COND* that terminates the above loop after the same number of rounds on all nodes, while guaranteeing that their information has stabilized.

One such loop termination condition could check that the number of rounds executed equals the maximum height of a BFT rooted at any node in the graph. This maximum height corresponds to the diameter of the interconnection graph. Note that the diameter depends on what parts of the system are working, and may change as the result of a failure. Unfortunately, the diameter is expensive to compute precisely since the best known algorithm is quadratic in the number of nodes.

As a simple approximation to the diameter, all nodes use the same algorithm to choose one of the functioning nodes, compute the height *h* of the BFT rooted at that node (in linear time), and terminate the dissemination algorithm after *2h* rounds (*2h* is an upper bound to the diameter). Still better approximations to the diameter can be computed in linear time, as shown in [1].

The BFT computations have to be carefully scheduled in order to avoid slowing down the dissemination phase. If every node computes the BFT as soon as its knowledge about the state of the system has stabilized, BFT computations on neighboring nodes will be chained during consecutive rounds instead of proceeding in parallel. To avoid the serialization of those computations, during the dissemination phase we only compute the BFT on a few nodes

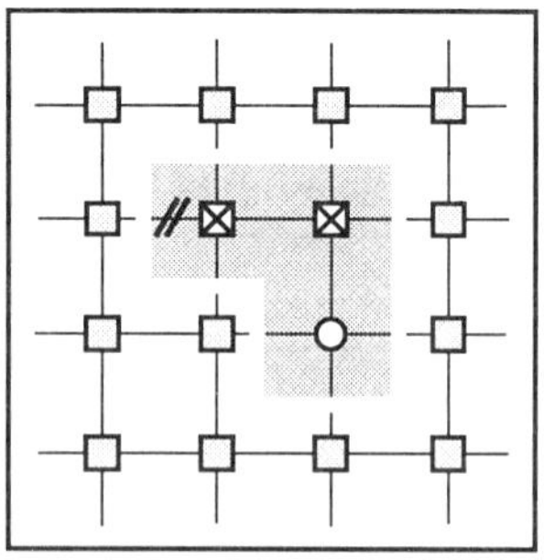

FIGURE 4.5. Interconnect recovery.
Each faulty region is isolated by discarding any traffic that tries to enter the region. After the interconnect has drained, the routing tables are reprogrammed such that normal coherence traffic will be routed around the failed regions.

for which `LState` and `NState` stabilize first. Those nodes send the resulting diameter estimation as a hint to their neighbors during subsequent rounds. Nodes that receive a hint defer their BFT computation until the end of the dissemination phase, when all the deferred computations occur in parallel.

Nodes use the knowledge gained during the information dissemination phase to update the node maps of their individual node controllers. If a node finds out that it is part of a failure unit in which some other resources have failed, the node shuts itself down after the cache coherence protocol recovery phase completes.

4.4 Interconnect Recovery Phase

The common knowledge about the state of the system gained during the dissemination phase allows the nodes to recover the interconnect with only minimal communication between them. Recovering the interconnect (Figure 4.5) involves three steps: isolating the failed regions, draining any stalled interconnect traffic, and reprogramming the routing tables.

In the first step all the routers bordering the failed parts of the system are reprogrammed to discard coherence traffic that is stalled trying to enter the failed region. As a side effect of discarding these packets, other stalled traffic makes forward progress and eventually reaches its destination. During this step the node controllers keep fielding coherence messages until the interconnect has drained. To avoid generating new traffic, the node controllers switch to a mode where incoming requests do not generate the replies or invalidates that would normally be sent.

To determine when the interconnect has drained, we rely on the existence of a small upper bound τ for the delay between two consecutive deliveries of stalled packets (the packets do not have to be delivered to the same node). The nodes go through a two-phase agreement protocol. During the first phase, all the notes vote to proceed after they have not seen any delivery of stalled traffic to their node controllers for at least τ time units. In the second phase, nodes can either vote to proceed, if they still haven't seen any delivery of stalled traffic, or they can request that the agreement protocol be restarted, if any delivery of stalled traffic took place since their first vote. The two phases are implemented as (fault-tolerant) barriers using the BFT computed during dissemination [6]. In practice, we have not observed any case in which the agreement protocol did not commit in the first round.

After all the traffic has drained out of the interconnect, it is safe to reprogram the routing tables so that new traffic will be routed around the failed regions. Stalled traffic must be drained first since otherwise we may introduce loops and cause traffic deadlock while reprogramming the routers. When computing the new routing tables, the key problem is to avoid introducing potential loops that could lead to deadlock. We use the turn method and an approach similar to the one described in [5] and [21] to guarantee that the routing is deadlock free. Although this approach is able to produce a deadlock-free rerouting for many of the common failure cases, a general solution is still an open research issue; the details are outside the scope of this paper.

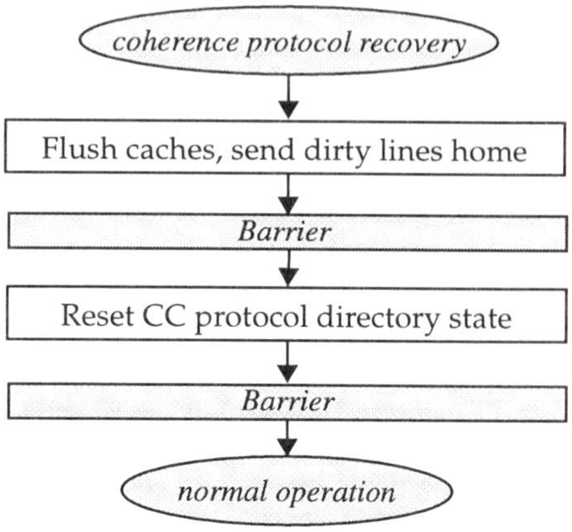

FIGURE 4.6. Cache coherence protocol recovery.
To determine what cache lines have become incoherent, all the functioning nodes flush their processor caches and send dirty lines back home. After the flush completes, each node examines the state of the cache lines it owns. Any line that hasn't made it home is marked as incoherent.

The reconfiguration phase ends with a global barrier that guarantees that all routers have been reprogrammed before any new coherence traffic is injected into the interconnect. After the barrier, the interconnect is again ready to carry normal coherence traffic; this is essential for the last phase of the recovery algorithm, during which communication between nodes is not local.

4.5 Cache Coherence Protocol Recovery Phase

The purpose of the final recovery step (Figure 4.6) is to reset the state of the cache coherence protocol and to determine which cache lines have become incoherent. Since there is no *a priori* way to know which coherence messages have been lost, the system first returns all dirty remote data to its home node. This is implemented by having all nodes flush their processor caches and send all dirty cache lines back to their homes. (It is not necessary to send any coherence message to the home for lines that are not dirty, since for those lines the copy at the home is valid.) After flushing their caches, the nodes join a global barrier. This barrier is implemented as an all-to-all send and relies on the in-order delivery of packets provided by the interconnect to guarantee that all writebacks have made it to their destinations.

Following the barrier, each node resets the state of its cache coherence protocol data structures. To determine which cache lines have been lost, each node scans its protocol directory state. Any line that still appears to be cached exclusive must have been lost. Incoherent lines are marked so that future accesses to those lines will be bus-errored by MAGIC. For all other lines, the protocol state is reset to "clean and not cached" since after the cache flush step all processor caches in the system are empty.

After the reset of the directory state, the nodes join another global barrier. At this point, the machine's interconnect and shared memory system are ready to resume normal operation, and the node controllers will again dispatch the normal handlers to service coherence requests.

4.6 Operating System Recovery

Prior to resuming normal operation, each node controller raises an interrupt to inform the operating system that hardware recovery has taken place in the machine. This interrupt causes Hive to activate its own recovery mechanisms before allowing user-level processes to continue execution.

The functioning cells adjust their internal kernel data structures to reflect the new machine configuration and to preserve the single system image semantics. User applications that had any essential dependencies on the failed cells are terminated, while other applications are allowed to continue unaffected. Normal system operation resumes after operating system recovery has completed.

The operating system must be able to cope with incoherent lines, since any access to those lines will give rise to a bus error. After Hive removes all the mappings to a page, it uses a special MAGIC service to check whether the page contains any incoherent lines and to reset the state of the cache coherence protocol for those lines before reusing the page.

5 Experimental Results

In this section we report experimental results for our hardware fault containment implementation in FLASH. We start by describing the simulation environment used for our experiments. Next we present the results of 1000 validation runs that we performed in order to verify the correctness of our implementation. To demonstrate that our solution provides end-to-end fault containment, we ran an additional batch of experiments in which we injected a fault during the execution of a workload running on top of the Hive operating system. We conclude this section with scalability results.

5.1 Simulation Environment

We debugged and tested our implementation of fault recovery using the SimOS [19] and FlashLite [7] simulators, since the FLASH hardware is not available at the time of writing. FlashLite is an accurate model of the FLASH memory system that models in detail both the node controllers and the CrayLink interconnect.

In the experiments reported below, we used an R4000 processor model, rather than the R10000 simulator which is significantly slower. The simpler model does not expose any of the effects related to incorrect speculation, but should otherwise demonstrate all the effects seen on the real machine.

The machine configurations used in our experiments are shown in Table 5.1. For the end-to-end recovery experiments we booted the Hive operating system [3] in an 8-cell configuration with one processor and 16 MB of main memory per cell. We ran a parallel make benchmark that compiles eight of the GnuChess 4.0 files, with each compile executing on a different cell. The benchmark generates a large amount of coherence traffic, since one of the cells acts as a file server for the other cells and the Hive file system uses shared memory for all file data transfers across cell boundaries.

Table 5.2 shows the types of faults we have simulated in our experiments. All the faults shown in this table correspond to possible occurrences on a real system.

5.2 Experimental Validation

In the first batch of validation experiments we did not boot an operating system, but used a stand-alone test program to create a controlled sharing pattern before injecting a fault. In each run, all the processors start by filling up their caches with lines chosen at random from the range of valid system addresses. For each line, we randomly decide whether it will be fetched in shared or exclusive mode. After all the processors have filled up at least half of their caches, we inject a fault. Upon completion of the hardware recovery algorithm, the processors read all of the system's memory and check, for each cache line, whether it contains the correct data or has become incoherent. We keep track in the simulator of the lines that may have become incoherent, either because they were cached on a failed node or because they were in a transitional state when we injected the fault. This allows us to verify that our recovery algorithm does not mark more lines as incoherent than necessary. The results of the validation experiments are shown in Table 5.3. We did not observe anomalies in any experiment.

End-to-end recovery experiments: For the end-to-end recovery experiments we injected the types of faults shown in Table 5.2 into an 8-processor system running a parallel make workload on top of the Hive operating system. We performed the experiments listed in Table 5.4, injecting the faults while all of the eight compiles were running, and checked the results of the completed compiles. In all experiments, the system correctly ran the hardware recovery algorithm and underwent operating system recovery. 91.6% of the

TABLE 5.1. Simulated hardware configurations for the fault injection experiments.

Component	Characteristics
Processors	8 × MIPS R4000 @ 200 MHz
Node controllers	8 × MAGIC @ 100 MHz
Memory / node	1-16 MB
L2 cache size	1 MB

TABLE 5.2. Fault injection experiment types.

Fault type	Description
Node failure	MAGIC fails, but the router stays up. Any packets sent to the node controller are discarded.
Router failure	Any packets sent to the router are discarded.
Link failure	Packets that try to traverse the link are dropped.
Infinite loop	MAGIC stops accepting packets. Traffic directed to this node backs up into the interconnect.
False alarm	Recovery triggered by an exceptional overload condition in the absence of a fault.

TABLE 5.3. Validation experiments.

Injected fault type	# of experiments	# of failed experiments
Node failure	200	0
Router failure	200	0
Link failure	200	0
Infinite loop in MAGIC handler	200	0
Recovery triggered by false alarm	200	0

TABLE 5.4. End-to-end recovery experiments.

Injected fault type	# of experiments	# of failed experiments
Node failure	310	29
Router failure	215	20
Link failure	268	22
Infinite loop in MAGIC handler	394	28
Total	1187	99

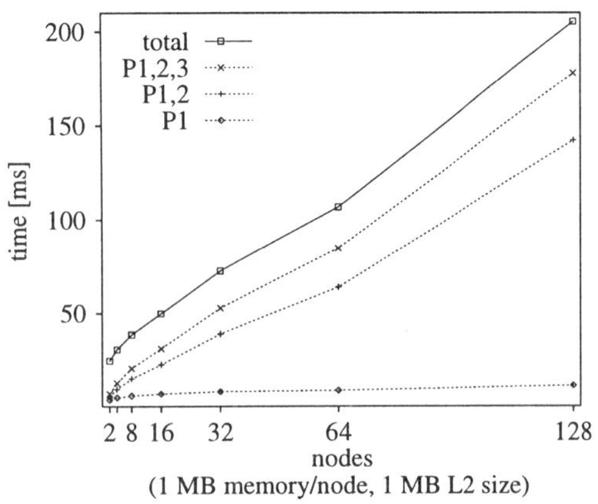

FIGURE 5.5. Total hardware recovery times.
The times shown for the four phases of the recovery algorithm are for a mesh configuration. The time required for the information dissemination phase (*P2*) grows slower for a hypercube topology.

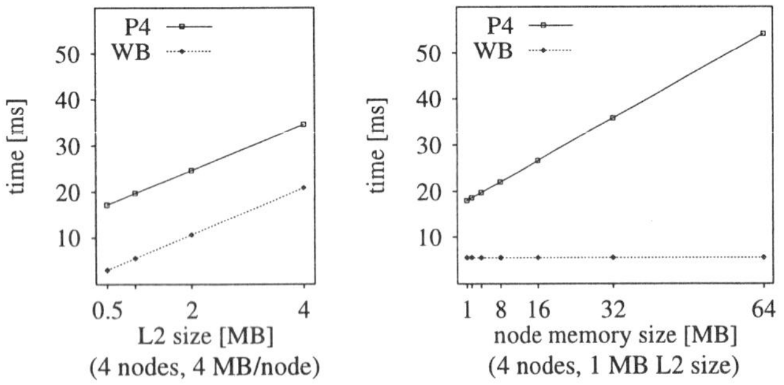

FIGURE 5.6. Cache coherence protocol recovery times.
In the last phase (*P4*) of the hardware recovery algorithm, the processors flush their caches (*WB*) and then reset the state of the cache coherence protocol. Assuming no interconnect contention during the flush, these steps scale linearly with the second level cache size and the amount of memory per node, respectively.

runs correctly finished executing the compiles that were not affected by the fault. Investigation of the failed runs shows that the problems are caused by a few operating system bugs rather than incorrect hardware recovery. All the OS bugs are related to the presence of incoherent lines after a fault; these cases were not exercised in our previous experiments [3][18], which were performed using a less detailed simulator.

5.3 Scalability Results

The time required for the hardware recovery algorithm to complete depends on the number of processors in the system, the second level cache size, and the amount of memory per node.

Figure 5.5 shows how the hardware recovery time scales with the number of processors. For large systems, hardware recovery is dominated by the time required for the dissemination phase. This phase scales better (both asymptotically and for a moderate number of nodes) on the fat hypercube topology used in FLASH than on the mesh interconnect we have simulated in these experiments, since its running time is proportional to the diameter of the interconnect.

Both components of the last recovery phase (flushing the caches and recovering the state of the cache coherence protocol) scale linearly with the size of the second level cache and the amount of memory per node, respectively (see Figure 5.6). On large

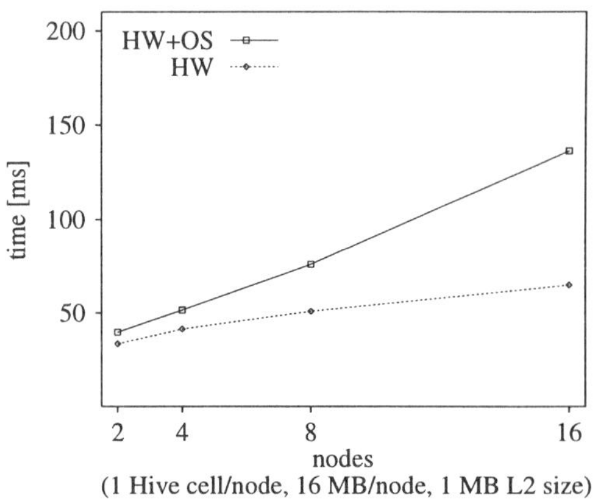

FIGURE 5.7. End-to-end recovery times.
Applications that continue running after a fault will be suspended for the duration of the hardware recovery algorithm (*HW*) and of the Hive operating system recovery phase (*OS*).

machines, the cache flush time may be higher if the flood of writebacks leads to interconnect contention or memory hot spots.

The duration for which user processes are suspended after a hardware fault is shown in Figure 5.7. These times include both hardware and operating system recovery, and should be acceptably fast for most applications. Operating system recovery time should be significantly faster on large machines than this graph suggests, since it scales with the number of cells rather than the number of nodes and large systems are likely to run with multiple nodes per cell. Furthermore, we have identified several ways to reduce Hive recovery time.

To gauge the precision of the above scalability figures, we simulated a few dozen R10000 instruction fetches from uncached space using a cycle-accurate RTL model of the R10000 processor and a Verilog model of the MAGIC chip. The only significant deviation we observed was in the time required for fetching and executing an uncached instruction on the R10000. In the precise simulation this time is 390 ns, while SimOS/FlashLite report only 320 ns. The discrepancy is primarily due to the fact that the R4000 simulator used in our experiments does not accurately simulate the execution pipeline and the bus interface of the R10000. The overall impact of this imprecision on our scalability results is small, since a significant fraction of the recovery algorithm is spent executing protocol processor code for which the time required is accurately simulated by FlashLite.

6 Discussion

We begin this section by discussing some low-level hardware design considerations for providing fault containment. Next we evaluate the performance impact of fault containment on normal operation, and address the issues related to implementing fault containment on a machine with hardwired node controllers. We conclude with an overview of related work.

6.1 Low-Level Support for Fault Containment

To make effective fault containment possible, the hardware of the machine must be designed to provide the following three properties: no single point of failure, *fail-fast* failure behavior, and *monotonic* failures. Components are fail-fast if after a fault they stop working without generating erroneous outputs. Components fail monotonically if they remain halted until repaired or reset.

The requirement concerning the absence of a single point of failure is obvious, and is the main reason that fault containment cannot be easily provided in bus-based shared-memory multiprocessors. Fortunately, scalable shared-memory systems have a structure that lends itself naturally to this design goal.

The fail-fast and monotonic failure properties are important since it is in general impossible to design a recovery algorithm that can cope with arbitrary Byzantine failures. In practice, however, neither the fail-fast nor the monotonic failure property can be guaranteed in all cases. Occasionally, components can be expected to generate bad outputs (due to a firmware error, for instance) or to suffer from intermittent faults (such as a wiring problem). In these cases our fault-containment approach may break down and the whole machine may fail. This is acceptable as long as the probability of a such a fault is small enough to have no significant impact on the overall reliability of the machine. Careful design of the hardware and of the node controller firmware can minimize this probability.

6.2 Costs and Benefits of Flexibility

Table 6.1 summarizes the hardware features that support fault containment in FLASH. We believe that similar mechanisms will be required to provide fault containment in other scalable multiprocessor architectures. This is an area for future research, as only an explicit design of a fault containment solution for an architecture will bring out all the significant details.

It is simple to evaluate the performance cost of most node controller features that were added to FLASH. The node map, truncated message dispatch, remap, range check, memory operation timeout, and NAK counter mechanisms are implemented in dedicated logic in the MAGIC interfaces or dispatch mechanism. Careful design ensures that these features do not increase the number of MAGIC clock cycles required to dispatch and execute handlers during normal operation.

The firewall mechanism is more intrusive, since our implementation requires adding access permission checks to the handlers that service intercell writes. Detailed system simulations show that the average increase in intercell write cache miss latency due to the firewall is less than 7% of the fastest internode write cache miss [3]. Since intercell write cache misses make up a small fraction of the cache coherence operations and since the R10000 processors provide latency-hiding mechanisms, the degradation in application performance lies in the noise for most workloads.

An important issue for fault containment solutions on other scalable multiprocessor architectures is the flexibility of the node controller. Unlike MAGIC, node controllers in most current commercial scalable multiprocessors are hardwired, not programmable. Whether or not it is possible to implement fault containment in a machine with hardwired node controllers without impacting performance is a topic for future research. However, our experience with FLASH provides insights for such a development.

The main difference between hardwired and programmable controllers, as far as fault containment is concerned, lies in the support they can offer for the recovery algorithm. Design complexity limits a hardwired controller to a significantly lower level of support than is implemented in MAGIC. The minimum support required is: (1) mechanisms for detecting hardware failures, (2) mechanisms for unstalling the processor and initiating recovery, and (3) a mode in which the processor performs all node controller functions except for processing the uncached reads and writes needed to access the recovery code and data. This solution requires exposing most of the state of the node controller to allow the processor to take control of its operation during recovery.

6.3 Related Work

An early effort at recovering from failures in the C.mmp multiprocessor is described in [24]. C.mmp attempted to diagnose the system after a fault and excluded any failed resources before resuming the unaffected processes. However, C.mmp did not have to deal with most of the issues described in this paper, since it did not use caches and since it had a crossbar interconnect. Furthermore, due to an *ad-hoc* design of the error recovery component, C.mmp was not able to handle many errors.

TABLE 6.1. Summary of features used for hardware fault containment in FLASH.

Node controller	
node map	Section 3.1
handling truncated messages	Section 3.1
remap exception vectors	Section 3.2
firewall	Section 3.3
range check	Section 3.3
memory operation timeouts	Section 4.2
NAK counter overflow	Section 4.2
assertions on protocol state	Section 4.2
Routers and interconnect	
reprogrammable routing tables	Section 3.1
detection of truncated messages	Section 3.1
dedicated virtual lanes for recovery	Section 4.1
source-routed message option	Section 4.1
Processor	
non-maskable restartable interrupt	Section 4.2

The Sequoia shared-memory multiprocessor [2] provided fault tolerance by using a checkpointing scheme. In this scheme, main memory stores two copies of all application data. Any writeback requires the entire cache to be flushed twice (under OS control), once to each memory copy. For a high-performance system like FLASH, such an approach would come at a very high cost, and would run contrary to our driving goal of leaving the normal mode performance of the system intact.

An approach for fault tolerance in COMA (Cache Only Memory Architecture) systems has been proposed in [13], but has not been implemented. The foremost drawback of this scheme is the high overhead for maintaining copies of memory lines. A further difficulty consists in determining whether non-idempotent operations (such as uncached I/O operations) have completed before a fault since rolling back to a previously saved state and reissuing those operations may violate their exactly-once semantics. The approach described in [13] can only cope with the failure of one processor, requires a spare processor to resume operation, and cannot handle interconnect failures.

A general survey of checkpointing techniques for distributed shared memory can be found in [14].

Fault containment has been implemented in several network operating systems such as Locus [16], Sprite [17], and Solaris MC [8]. Due to a much weaker coupling between nodes and to the absence of shared memory, these systems do not have to cope with the problems described in Section 3.1 and Section 3.2. Node failures are detected in a lazy fashion, while transient network problems are handled by an end-to-end transmission protocol.

The HAL multiprocessor provides an efficient hardware implementation of an end-to-end reliable protocol for coherence traffic [23]. The advantage of end-to-end reliability for fault containment consists in eliminating the loss of coherence packets that try to traverse a failed area, since these packets are resent by the hardware after the connectivity of the interconnect is restored. A recovery algorithm similar to the one described in this paper could be used for the HAL system. With a reliable interconnect, the cache flush step could be eliminated, but the directories would still have to be scanned and their state updated to reflect the loss of memory lines cached either shared or exclusive in the failed portion of the machine.

7 Conclusions

Fault containment has been used in many distributed systems, but to our knowledge has not been previously implemented in a high-performance shared-memory multiprocessor. While providing weaker guarantees than fault tolerance, fault containment avoids the expensive duplication of resources required by fault tolerance.

In this paper we have shown that fault containment techniques can be successfully applied to scalable shared-memory multiprocessors. We have added fault containment support to the FLASH multiprocessor without significantly affecting its performance, at least as measured through detailed simulation.

Our approach to providing fault containment in FLASH includes implementing a set of features that limit the impact of faults and a distributed recovery algorithm that is executed after a fault to restore the normal operation of the system. The experimental results reported in the paper indicate that this approach is effective and leads to acceptably short failure recovery times for systems up to 128 nodes.

Adding support for fault containment in FLASH was made easier by the existence of a programmable node controller whose behavior can be easily extended without hardware modifications. Much of the necessary support was added in the form of node controller software extensions. This approach was essential to our design process, since it allowed us to incrementally add functionality to the recovery algorithm without having to change the design of the MAGIC hardware.

The implementation of fault containment in FLASH should offer valuable information to those considering adding similar support to other scalable multiprocessors. Hardware fault containment provides an attractive way to increase the reliability and usability of these machines.

Acknowledgments

Rajeev Motwani contributed to the design of the second phase of the recovery algorithm. Mark Heinrich implemented the simulator for the CrayLink interconnect used in FlashLite. We are grateful to John Heinlein for running the detailed R10000 RTL model and MAGIC Verilog simulation. John Keen kindly provided feedback on an earlier draft of this paper. We thank Silicon Graphics for giving us access to the IRIX 5.2 source code.

This work was supported in part by ARPA contract DABT63-94-C-0054. Mendel Rosenblum is partially supported by a National Science Foundation Young Investigator award.

References

[1] D. Aingworth, C. Chekuri, and R. Motwani. "Fast Estimation of Diameter and Shortest Paths (without Matrix Multiplication)." In *Proceedings of the Seventh Annual ACM-SIAM Symposium on Discrete Algorithms*, pp. 547-553, 1996.

[2] P. Bernstein. "Sequoia: A Fault-Tolerant Tightly Coupled Multiprocessor for Transaction Processing." *IEEE Computer* 21(2), February 1988.

[3] J. Chapin, M. Rosenblum, S. Devine, T. Lahiri, D. Teodosiu, and A. Gupta. "Hive: Fault Containment for Shared-Memory Multiprocessors." In *Proceedings of the 15th ACM Symposium on Operating Systems Principles*, pp. 12-25, December 1995.

[4] M. Galles. "Scalable Pipelined Interconnect for Distributed Endpoint Routing: The SGI SPIDER Chip." Presented at *Hot Interconnects Symposium IV*, August 1996.

[5] C. Glass and L. Ni. "Fault-Tolerant Wormhole Routing in Meshes without Virtual Channels." *IEEE Transactions on Parallel and Distributed Systems* 7(6), pp. 620-636, June 1996.

[6] J. R. Goodman, M. K. Vernon, and P. J. Woest. "Efficient Synchronization Primitives for Large-Scale Cache-Coherent Multiprocessors." In *Proceedings of the 3rd International Conference on Architectural Support for Programming Languages and Operating Systems*, pp. 64-73, April 1989.

[7] M. Heinrich, J. Kuskin, D. Ofelt, J. Heinlein, J. Baxter, J.P. Singh, R. Simoni, K. Gharachorloo, D. Nakahira, M. Horowitz, A. Gupta, M. Rosenblum, and J. Hennessy. "The Performance Impact of Flexibility in the Stanford FLASH Multiprocessor." In *Proceedings of the 6th International Conference on Architectural Support for Programming Languages and Operating Systems*, pp. 274-285, October 1994.

[8] Y. A. Khalidi, J. M. Bernabeu, V. Matena, K. Shirriff, and M. Thadani. "Solaris MC: A Multi Computer OS." In *Proceedings of the USENIX 1996 Annual Technical Conference*, pp. 191-204, January 1996.

[9] J. Kuskin, D. Ofelt, M. Heinrich, J. Heinlein, R. Simoni, K. Gharachorloo, J. Chapin, D. Nakahira, J. Baxter, M. Horowitz, A. Gupta, M. Rosenblum, and J. Hennessy. "The Stanford FLASH Multiprocessor." In *Proceedings of the 21st International Symposium on Computer Architecture*, pp. 302-313, April 1994.

[10] J. Laudon, and D. Lenoski. "The SGI Origin 2000: A ccNUMA Highly Scalable Server." In *Proceedings of the 24th Annual International Symposium on Computer Architecture*, June 1997.

[11] T. Lovett and R. Clapp. "STiNG: A CC-NUMA Computer System for the Commercial Marketplace." In *Proceedings of the 23rd Annual International Symposium on Computer Architecture*, pp. 308-317, May 1996.

[12] N. Lynch. *Distributed Algorithms*. Morgan Kaufmann Publishers, 1995.

[13] C. Morin, A. Gefflaut, M. Banatre, and A. Kernarrec. "COMA: an Opportunity for Building Fault-tolerant Scalable Shared Memory Multiprocessors." In *Proceedings of the 23rd Annual International Symposium on Computer Architecture*, pp. 56-65, May 1996.

[14] C. Morin, and I. Puaut. "A Survey of Recoverable Distributed Shared Memory Systems." IRISA Technical Report 975, December 1995.

[15] V. P. Nelson. "Fault-tolerant computing: fundamental concepts." *IEEE Computer* 23(7), pp. 19-25, July 1990.

[16] G. Popek and B. Walker. *The LOCUS Distributed System Architecture*. MIT Press, 1985.

[17] J. K. Ousterhout, A. R. Cherenson, F. Douglis, M. N. Nelson, and B. B. Welch. "The Sprite network operating system." *IEEE Computer* 21(2), pp. 23-36, February 1988.

[18] M. Rosenblum, J. Chapin, D. Teodosiu, S. Devine, T. Lahiri, and A. Gupta. "Implementing Efficient Fault Containment for Multiprocessors." *Communications of the ACM* 39(9), September 1996, pp. 52-61.

[19] M. Rosenblum, S. Herrod, E. Witchel, and A. Gupta. "Complete Computer Simulation: The SimOS Approach." *IEEE Parallel and Distributed Technology* 3(4), pp. 34-43, Winter 1995.

[20] T. Sterling, P. Merkey, and D. Savarese. "Improving Application Performance on the HP/Convex Exemplar." *IEEE Computer* 29(12), pp. 50-55, December 1996.

[21] J. Vounckx et al. "Fault-Tolerant Compact Routing based on Reduced Structural Information in Wormhole-Switching based Networks." In *Proceedings of the Colloquium on Structural Information and Communication Complexity*, May 1994.

[22] D. Weaver and T. Germond, eds. *The SPARC Architecture Manual, Version 9*. Prentice-Hall, Inc., 1994.

[23] W. Weber et al. "The Mercury Interconnect Architecture: A Cost-effective Infrastructure for High-performance Servers." In *Proceedings of the 24th Annual International Symposium on Computer Architecture*, June 1997.

[24] W. Wulf, R. Levin, and S. P. Harbison. *HYDRA/C.mmp: An Experimental Computer System*. McGraw-Hill, 1981.

[25] K. Yeager. "The MIPS R10000 Superscalar Microprocessor." *IEEE Micro* 16(2), pp. 28-41, April 1996.

Effects of Communication Latency, Overhead, and Bandwidth in a Cluster Architecture

Richard P. Martin, Amin M. Vahdat, David E. Culler and Thomas E. Anderson
Computer Science Division
University of California
Berkeley, CA 94720

Abstract

This work provides a systematic study of the impact of communication performance on parallel applications in a high performance network of workstations. We develop an experimental system in which the communication latency, overhead, and bandwidth can be independently varied to observe the effects on a wide range of applications. Our results indicate that current efforts to improve cluster communication performance to that of tightly integrated parallel machines results in significantly improved application performance. We show that applications demonstrate strong sensitivity to overhead, slowing down by a factor of 60 on 32 processors when overhead is increased from 3 to 103 μs. Applications in this study are also sensitive to per-message bandwidth, but are surprisingly tolerant of increased latency and lower per-byte bandwidth. Finally, most applications demonstrate a highly linear dependence to both overhead and per-message bandwidth, indicating that further improvements in communication performance will continue to improve application performance.

1 Introduction

Many research efforts in parallel computer architecture have focused on improving various aspects of communication performance. These investigations cover a vast spectrum of alternatives, ranging from integrating message transactions into the memory controller [5, 10, 29, 41] or the cache controller [1, 20, 32], to incorporating messaging deep into the processor [9, 11, 12, 17, 22, 23, 36, 40], integrating the network interface on the memory bus [7, 31], providing dedicated message processors [6, 8, 37], providing various kinds of bulk transfer support [5, 26, 29, 37], supporting reflective memory operations [7, 21], and providing lean communication software layers [35, 43, 44]. Recently, we have seen a shift to designs that accept a reduction in communication performance to obtain greater generality (e.g., Flash vs. Dash), greater opportunity for specialization (e.g. Tempest [38]), or a cleaner communication interface (e.g., T3E vs. T3D). At the same time, a number of investigations are focusing on bringing the communication performance of clusters closer to that of the more tightly integrated parallel machines [3, 12, 21, 35, 43]. Moving forward from these research alternatives, a crucial question to answer is how much do the improvements in communication performance actually improve application performance.

The goal of this work is to provide a systematic study of the impact of communication performance on parallel applications. It focuses on a high performance cluster architecture, for which a fast Active Message layer has been developed to a low latency, high bandwidth network. We want to quantify the performance impact of our communication enhancements on applications and to understand if they have gone far enough. Furthermore, we want to understand which aspects of communication performance are most important. The main contributions of this work are (i) a reproducible empirical apparatus for measuring the effects of variations in communication performance for clusters, (ii) a methodology for a systematic investigation of these effects and (iii) an in-depth study of application sensitivity to latency, overhead, and bandwidth, quantifying application performance in response to changes in communication performance.

Our approach is to determine application sensitivity to machine communication characteristics by running a benchmark suite on a large cluster in which the communication layer has been modified to allow the latency, overhead, per-message bandwidth and per-byte bandwidth to be adjusted independently. This four-parameter characterization of communication performance is based on the LogP model [2, 14], the framework for our systematic investigation of the communication design space. By adjusting these parameters, we can observe changes in the execution time of applications on a spectrum of systems ranging from the current high-performance cluster to conventional LAN based clusters. We measure a suite of applications with a wide range of program characteristics, e.g., coarse-grained vs. fine-grained and read vs. write based, to enable us to draw conclusions about the effect of communication characteristics on classes of applications.

Our results show that, in general, applications are most sensitive to communication overhead. This effect can easily be predicted from communication frequency. The sensitivity to message rate and data transfer bandwidth is less pronounced and more complex. Ap-

This work was supported in part by the Defense Advanced Research Projects Agency (N00600-93-C-2481, F30602-95-C-0014), the National Science Foundation (CDA 9401156), Sun Microsystems, California MICRO, Hewlett Packard, Intel, Microsoft, and Mitsubishi. Anderson was also supported by a National Science Foundation Presidential Faculty Fellowship. The authors can be contacted at {rmartin, vahdat, culler, tea}@cs.berkeley.edu.

plications are least sensitive to the actual network transit latency and the effects are qualitatively different than what is exhibited for the other parameters. Overall, the trends indicate that the efforts to improve communication performance pay off. Further improvements will continue to improve application performance. However, these efforts should focus on reducing overhead.

We believe that there are several advantages to our approach of running real programs with realistic inputs on a flexible hardware prototype that can vary its performance characteristics. The interactions influencing a parallel program's overall performance can be very complex, so changing the performance of one aspect of the system may cause subtle changes to the program's behavior. For example, changing the communication overhead may change the load balance, the synchronization behavior, the contention, or other aspects of a parallel program. By measuring the full program on a modified machine, we observe the summary effect of the complex underlying interactions. Also, we are able to run applications on realistic input sizes, so we escape the difficulties of attempting to size the machine parameters down to levels appropriate for the small problems feasible on a simulator and then extrapolating to the real case [45]. These issues have driven a number of efforts to develop powerful simulators [38, 39], as well as to develop flexible hardware prototypes [24].

The drawback of a real system is that it is most suited to investigate design points that are "slower" than the base hardware. Thus, to perform the study we must use a prototype communication layer and network hardware with better performance than what is generally available. We are then able to scale back the performance to observe the "slowdown" relative to the initial, aggressive design point. By observing the slowdown as a function of network performance, we can extrapolate back from the initial design point to more aggressive hypothetical designs. We have constructed such an apparatus for clusters using commercially available hardware and publicly available research software.

The remainder of the paper is organized as follows. After providing the necessary background in Section 2, Section 3 describes the experimental setup and our methodology for emulating designs with a range of communication performance. In addition, we outline a microbenchmarking technique to calibrate the effective communication characteristics of our experimental apparatus. Section 4 describes the characteristics of the applications in our benchmark suite and reports their overall communication requirements, such as message frequency, and baseline performance on sample input sets. Section 5 shows the effects of varying each of the four LogP communication parameters for our applications and, where possible, builds simple models to explain the results. Section 6 summarizes some of the related work and Section 7 presents our conclusions.

2 Background

When investigating trade-offs in communication architectures, it is important to recognize that the time per communication operation breaks down into portions that involve different machine resources: the processor, the network interface, and the actual network. However, it is also important that the communication cost model not be too deeply wedded to a specific machine implementation. The LogP model [14] provides such a middle ground by characterizing the performance of the key resources, but not their structure. A distributed-memory multiprocessor in which processors physically communicate by point-to-point messages is characterized by four parameters (illustrated in Figure 1).

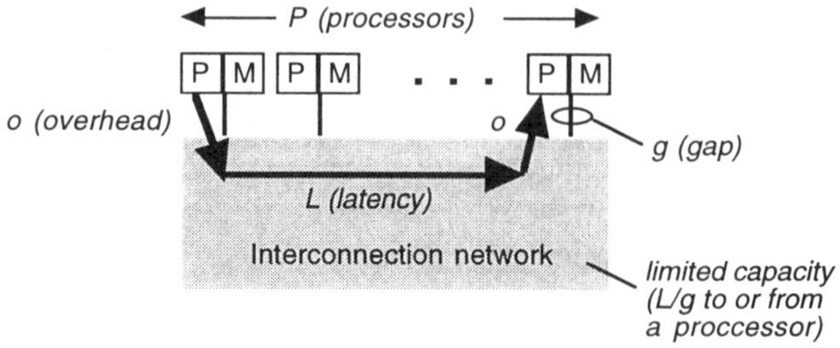

Figure 1: **LogP Abstract Machine.** *The LogP model describes an abstract machine configuration in terms of four performance parameters: L, the latency experienced in each communication event, o, the overhead experienced by the sending and receiving processors, g, the gap between successive sends or successive receives by a processor, and P, the number of processors/memory modules.*

L: the *latency*, or delay, incurred in communicating a message containing a small number of words from its source processor/memory module to its target.

o: the *overhead*, defined as the length of time that a processor is engaged in the transmission or reception of each message; during this time, the processor cannot perform other operations.

g: the *gap*, defined as the minimum time interval between consecutive message transmissions or consecutive message receptions at a module; this is the time it takes for a message to cross through the bandwidth bottleneck in the system.

P: the number of processor/memory modules.

L, o, and g are specified in units of time. It is assumed that the network has a finite capacity, such that at most $\lceil L/g \rceil$ messages can be in transit from any processor or to any processor at any time. If a processor attempts to transmit a message that would exceed this limit, it stalls until the message can be sent without exceeding the capacity limit.

The simplest communication operation, sending a single packet from one machine to another, requires a time of $L + 2o$. Thus, the latency includes the time spent in the network interfaces and the actual transit time through the network, which are indistinguishable to the processor. A request-response operation, such as a read or blocking write, takes time $2L + 4o$. The processor issuing the request and the one serving the response both are involved for time $2o$. The remainder of the time can be overlapped with computation or sending additional messages.

The available per-processor message bandwidth, or communication rate (messages per unit time) is $1/g$. Depending on the machine, this limit might be imposed by the available network bandwidth or by other facets of the design. In many machines, the limit is imposed by the message processing rate of the network interface, rather than the network itself. Because many machines have separate mechanisms for long messages(e.g. DMA), it is useful to extend the model with an additional gap parameter, G, which specifies the time-per-byte, or the reciprocal of the bulk transfer bandwidth [2]. In our machine, G is determined by the DMA rate to or from the network interface, rather than the network link bandwidth.

Platform	o (μs)	g (μs)	L (μs)	MB/s(1/G)
Berkeley NOW	2.9	5.8	5.0	38
Intel Paragon	1.8	7.6	6.5	141
Meiko CS-2	1.7	13.6	7.5	47

Table 1: **Baseline LogGP Parameters.** *This figure shows the performance of the hardware platform used, the Berkeley NOW. Two popular parallel computers, the Intel Paragon and the Meiko CS-2 are included for comparison.*

The LogGP characteristics for our cluster, the Berkeley NOW, are summarized in Table 1. For reference, we also provide measured LogGP characteristics for two tightly integrated parallel processors, the Intel Paragon and Meiko CS-2 [15].

3 Methodology

In this section we describe the empirical methodology of our study. The experimental apparatus consists of commercially available hardware and system software, augmented with publicly available research software that has been modified to conduct the experiment. The experimental apparatus is calibrated using a simple microbenchmarking technique.

3.1 Experimental setup

The apparatus for all our experiments is a cluster of 32 UltraSPARC Model 170 workstations (167 MHz, 64 MB memory, 512 KB L2 cache) running Solaris 2.5. Each has a single Myricom M2F network interface card on the SBUS, containing 128 KB SRAM card memory and a 37.5 MHz "LANai" processor [8]. This processor plays a key role in allowing us to independently vary LogGP parameters. The machines are interconnected with ten 8-port Myrinet switches (model M2F, 160 MB/s per port).

All but two of the applications are written in an SPMD model using Split-C [13], a parallel extension of the C programming language that provides a global address space on distributed memory machines. Split-C (version 961015) is based on GCC (version 2.6.3) and Generic Active Messages (version 961015), which is the base communication layer throughout the study. While the programming model does not provide automatic replication with cache coherence, a number of the applications perform application-specific software caching. The language has been ported to many platforms [2, 34, 43, 44]. The sources for the applications, compiler, and communication layer can be obtained from a publically available site [1].

3.2 Technique

The key experimental innovation is to modify the communication layer so that it can emulate a system with arbitrary overhead, gap, or latency. We then vary these parameters independently and observe the effect on application performance. Our technique is depicted in Figure 2 which illustrates the interaction of the host processor, the LANai (network interface processor) and the network for communication between two nodes.

[1] `ftp.cs.berkeley.edu/pub/CASTLE/Split-C/-release/sc961015`

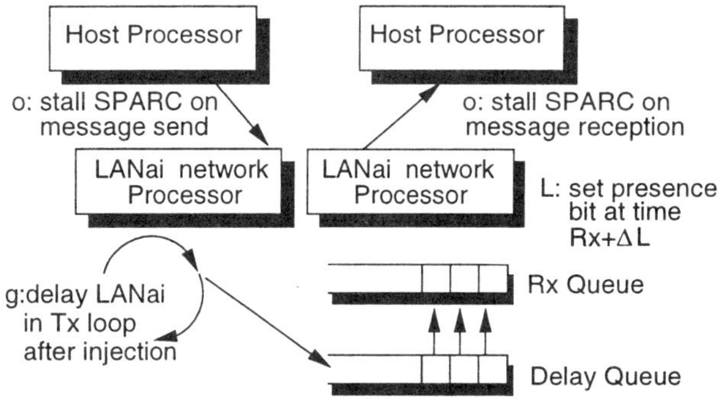

Figure 2: **Varying LogGP Parameters.** *This figure describes our methodology for individually varying each of the logP parameters. The interaction between the host processor, the network processor (LANai) and the network is shown for communication between two nodes.*

The majority of the overhead is the time spent writing the message into the network interface or reading it from the interface. Thus, varying the overhead, o, is straightforward. For each message send and before each message reception, the operation is modified to loop for a specific period of time before actually writing or reading the message.

The gap is dominated by the message handling loop within the network processor. Thus, to vary the gap, g, we insert a delay loop into the message injection path after the message is transferred onto the wire and before it attempts to inject the next message. Since the stall is done after the message is actually sent the network latency is unaffected. Also, since the host processor can write and read messages to or from the network interface at its normal speed, overhead should not be affected. We use two methods to prevent excessive network blocking from artificially affecting our results. First, the LANai is stalled at the source rather than the destination. Second, the firmware takes advantage of the LANai's dual hardware contexts; the receive context can continue even if the transmit context is stalled. To adjust G, the transmit context stalls after injecting a fragment (up to 4KB) for a period of time proportional to the fragment size.

The latency, L, requires care to vary without affecting the other LogGP characteristics. It includes time spent in the network interface's injection path, the transfer time, and the receive path, so slowing either the send or receive path would increase L. However, modifying the send or receive path would have the side effect of increasing g. Our approach involves adding a delay queue inside the LANai. When a message is received, the LANai deposits the message into the normal receive queue, but defers setting the flag that would indicate the presence of the message to the application. The time that the message "would have" arrived in the face of increased latency is entered into a delay queue. The receive loop inside the LANai checks the delay queue for messages ready to be marked as valid in the standard receive queue. Modifying the effective arrival time in this fashion ensures that network latency can be increased without modifying o or g.

3.3 Calibration

With any empirical apparatus, as opposed to a discrete simulator, it is important to calibrate the actual effect of the settings of the in-

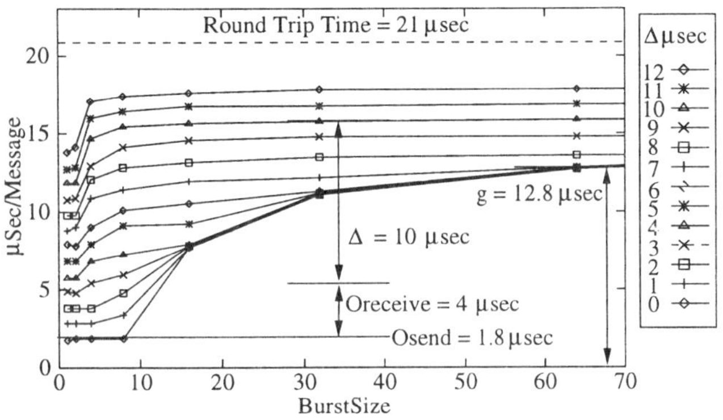

Figure 3: **Calibration of LogP Parameters.** *The LogP signature is visible as the isobaric plot of burst size vs. fixed computational delay, Δ. This signature was a calibration made when the desired g was 14 µsec. The send overhead, receive overhead and gap can be read from the signature. Overhead is modeled as the average of the send and receive overhead. Latency is computed as $\frac{1}{2}$(round trip time)-2o.*

put parameters. In this study, it is essential to verify that our technique for varying LogGP network characteristics satisfies two criteria: first, that the communication characteristics are varied by the intended amount and second that they can be varied independently. Such a calibration can be obtained by running a set of Active Message micro-benchmarks, described in [15]. The basic technique is to measure the time to issue a sequence of m messages with a fixed computational delay, Δ between messages. (The clock stops when the last message is issued by the processor, regardless of how many requests or responses are in flight.) Plotting the average message cost as a function of the sequence size and delay generates a LogP *signature*, such as that shown in Figure 3. Each curve in the figure shows the average initiation interval seen by the processor as a function of the number of messages issued, m, for a fixed Δ. For a short sequence, this shows the send overhead. Long sequences approach the steady-state initiation interval, g. For sufficiently large Δ the bottleneck is the processor, so the steady state interval is the send overhead plus the receive overhead plus Δ. Finally, subtracting the two overheads from half the round-trip time gives L.

Table 2 describes the result of this calibration process for three of the four communication characteristics. For each parameter, the table shows the desired and calibrated setting for that parameter. For overhead, the calibrated value is within 1% of the desired value. Observe that as o is increased, the effective gap increases because the processor is the bottleneck, consistent with the LogP model. As desired, the value of L is independent of o. The calibrated g is somewhat lower than intended and varying g has little effect on L and no effect on o. Increasing L has little effect on o. A notable effect of our implementation is that for large values of L, the effective g rises. Because the implementation has a fixed number of outstanding messages independent of L, when L becomes very large the implementation is unable to form an efficient network pipeline. In effect, the capacity constraint of our system is constant, instead of varying with L and g as the LogGP model would predict.

To calibrate G, we use a similar methodology, but instead send a burst of bulk messages, each with a fixed size. From the steady-state initiation interval and message size we derive the calibrated bandwidth (not shown). We increase the bulk message size until we no longer observe an increase in bandwidth (which happens at a 2K byte message size). The calibrated values are used in the analysis done below.

4 Applications and Baseline Characteristics

With a methodology in place for varying communication characteristics, we now characterize the architectural requirements of the applications in our study. To ensure that the data is not overly influenced by startup characteristics, the applications must use reasonably large data sets. Given the experimental space we wish to explore, it is not practical to choose data sets taking hours to complete; however, an effort was made to choose realistic data sets for each of the applications. We used the following criteria to characterize applications in our benchmark suite and to ensure that the applications demonstrate a wide range of architectural requirements:

- **Message Frequency:** The more communication intensive the application, the more we would expect its performance to be affected by the machine's communication performance. For applications that use short messages, the most important factor is the message frequency, or equivalently the average interval between messages. However, the behavior may be influenced by the burstiness of communication and the balance in traffic between processors.
- **Write or Read Based:** Applications that read remote data and wait for the result are more likely to be sensitive to latency than applications that mostly write remote data. The latter are likely to be more sensitive to bandwidth. However, dependences that cause waiting can appear in applications in many forms.
- **Short or Long Messages:** The Active Message layer used for this study provides two types of messages, short packets and bulk transfers. Applications that use bulk messages may have high data bandwidth requirements, even though message initiations are infrequent.
- **Synchronization**: Applications can be bulk synchronous or task queue based. Tightly synchronized applications are likely to be dependent on network round trip times, and so may be very sensitive to latency. Task queue applications may tolerate latency, but may be sensitive to overhead. A task queue based application attempts to overlap message operations with local computation from a task queue. An increase in overhead decreases the available overlap between the communication and local computation.
- **Communication Balance**: Balance is simply the ratio of the maximum number of messages sent per processor to the average number of messages sent per processor. It is difficult to predict the influence of network performance on applications with a relatively large communication imbalance since varying LogP parameters may exacerbate or may actually alleviate the imbalance.

4.1 Benchmark Suite

Table 3 summarizes the programs we chose for our benchmark suite as run on both a 16 and a 32 node cluster. Most applications are well

Desired	Observed			Desired	Observed			Desired	Observed		
o	o	g	L	g	g	o	L	L	L	o	g
2.9	2.9	5.8	5.0	5.8	5.8	2.9	5.0	5.0	5.0	2.9	5.8
4.9	5.1	10.1	5.0	8.0	7.5	2.9	5.1	7.5	8.1	2.9	6.3
7.9	8.1	16.0	4.7	10	9.6	2.9	5.5	10	10.3	2.9	6.4
12.9	13.0	26.0	5.0	15	14	3.0	5.5	15	15.5	2.9	7.0
22.9	23.1	46.0	4.9	30	29	3.0	5.5	30	30.4	2.9	9.6
52.9	52.9	106.0	5.4	55	52	2.9	5.5	55	55.9	3.0	15.5
77.9	76.5	151.0	5.3	80	76	2.9	5.5	80	80.4	2.9	21.6
102.9	103.0	205.9	6.0	105	99	3.0	5.5	105	105.5	3.0	27.7

Table 2: **Calibration Summary.** *This table demonstrates the calibration of desired LogP parameter values versus measured values. The table also shows that the LogP parameters can be varied independent of one another.*

Program	Description	Input Set	16 node Time (sec)	32 node Time (sec)
Radix	Integer radix sort	16 Million 32-bit keys	13.66	7.76
EM3D(write)	Electro-magnetic wave propagation	80000 Nodes, 40% remote, degree 20, 100 steps	88.59	37.98
EM3D(read)	Electro-magnetic wave propagation	80000 Nodes, 40% remote, degree 20, 100 steps	230.0	114.0
Sample	Integer sample sort	32 Million 32-bit keys	24.65	13.23
Barnes	Hierarchical N-Body simulation	1 Million Bodies	77.89	43.24
P-Ray	Ray Tracer	1 Million pixel image 16390 objects	23.47	17.91
Murφ	Protocol Verification	SCI protocol, 2 procs, 1 line, 1 memory each	67.68	35.33
Connect	Connected Components	4 Million nodes 2-D mesh, 30% connected	2.29	1.17
NOW-sort	Disk-to-Disk Sort	32 Million 100-byte records	127.2	56.87
Radb	Bulk version of Radix sort	16 Million 32-bit keys	6.96	3.73

Table 3: **Applications and Data Sets.** *This table describes our applications, the input set, the application's communication pattern, and the base run time.*

parallelized when scaled from 16 to 32 processors. Each application is discussed briefly below.

- **Radix Sort:** sorts a large collection of 32-bit keys spread over the processors, and is thoroughly analyzed in [19]. It progresses as two iterations of three phases. First, each processor determines the local rank for one digit of its keys. Second, the global rank of each key is calculated from local histograms. Finally, each processor uses the global histogram to distribute the keys to the proper location. For our input set of one million keys per processor on 32 processors the application spends 98% of its time in the communication phases.

  The communication density plot of Figure 4a is useful in understanding the communication behavior of this application. The darkness of cell i, j indicates the fraction of messages sent from processor i to processor j. The dark line off the diagonal reflects the global histogram phase, where the ranks are accumulated across processors in a kind of pipelined cyclic shift. The grey background is the global distribution phase. Overall, the communication is frequent, write-based and balanced.

- **EM3D:** EM3D [13] is the kernel of an application that models propagation of electromagnetic waves through objects in three dimensions. It first spreads an irregular bipartite graph over all processors. During each time-step, changes in the electric field are calculated as a linear function of the neighboring magnetic field values and vice versa. We use two complementary versions of EM3D, one write-based and the other read-based. Both versions contain relatively short computation steps. The write-based EM3D uses pipelined writes to propagate updates by augmenting the graph with special boundary nodes. EM3D(write) represents a large class of bulk synchronous applications, alternating between local computation and global communication phases. The read version uses simple blocking reads to pull update information locally and

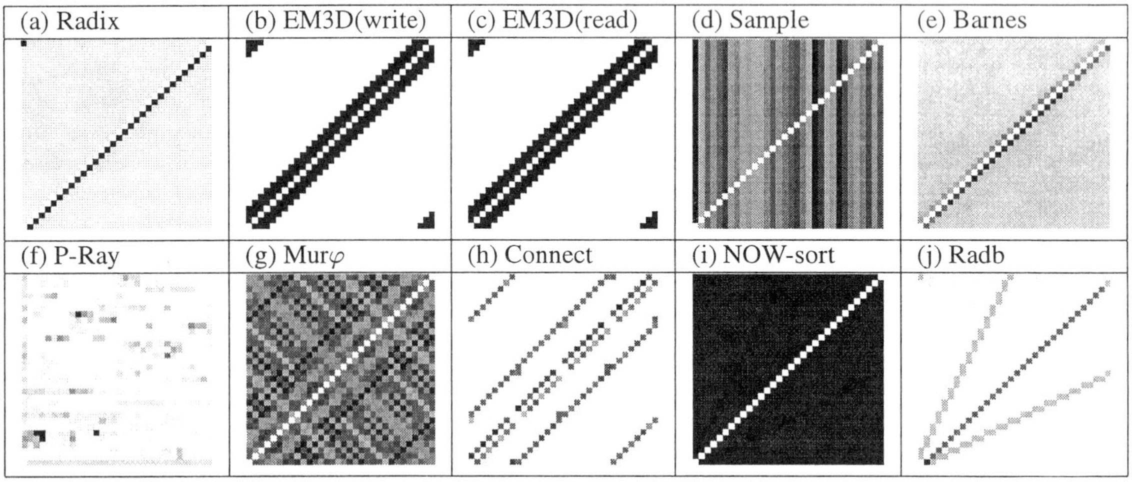

Figure 4: **Communication Balance.** *This figure demonstrates the communication balance between each of the 32 processors for our 10 applications. The greyscale for each pixel represents a message count. Each application is individually scaled from white, representing zero messages, to black, representing the maximum message count per processor as shown in Table 4. The y-coordinate tracks the message sender and the x-coordinate tracks the receiver.*

does not need to create special boundary nodes. The locality of connectivity in the graph for both versions is indicated by the dark swath in Figures 4b and 4c.

- **Sample Sort:** is a probabilistic algorithm which sorts a large collection of 32-bit keys by first choosing $p - 1$ "good" splitter values and broadcasting them to all processors. Every processor distributes its keys to the proper destination processor, based on the splitter values, and finally, a local radix sort is performed on the received keys. An interesting aspect of this application is the potential for unbalanced all-to-all communication as each processor potentially receives a different number of keys. This is reflected in the vertical bars in Figure 4d. For our input size, the local sort time is dominated by the distribution of keys to their proper destinations. For our input of 16 million keys Sample sort spends 85% of the time in the two communication phases.
- **Barnes:** Our implementation of this hierarchical N-Body force calculation is similar to the version in the SPLASH benchmark suite [45]. However, the main data structure, a spatial oct-tree, is replicated in software rather than hardware. Each timestep consists of two phases, a tree construction phase and an interaction phase among the simulated bodies. Updates of the oct-tree are synchronized through blocking locks. During the interaction phase, the processors cache oct-tree nodes owned by remote processors in a software managed cache. Communication is generally balanced, as the solid grey square shows in Figure 4e.
- **P-Ray:** This scene passing ray tracing program distributes a read-only spatial oct-tree over all processors. The processors evenly divide ownership of objects in the scene. When a processor needs access to an object stored on a remote processor, the object is cached locally in a fixed sized software-managed cache. Communication thus consists entirely of blocking read operations; the frequency of such operations is a function on the scene complexity and the software caching algorithm. The dark spots in Figure 4f indicate the presence of "hot" objects which are visible from multiple points in the scene.
- **Parallel Murφ:** In this parallel version of a popular protocol verification tool [18, 42], the exponential space of all reachable protocol states are explored to catch protocol bugs. Each processor maintains a work queue of unexplored states. A hash function maps states to "owning" processors. When a new state is discovered, it is sent to the proper processor. On reception of a state description, a processor first checks if the state has been reached before. If the state is new, the processor adds it to the work queue to be validated against an assertion list.
- **Connected Components:** First, a graph is spread across all processors [33]. Each processor then performs a connected components on its local subgraph to collapse portions of its components into representative nodes. Next, the graph is globally adjusted to point remote edges (crossing processor boundaries) at the respective representative nodes. Finally, a global phase successively merges components between neighboring processors. The communication to computation ratio is determined by the size of the graph.
- **NOW-sort:** The version of NOW-sort used in this study sorts records from disk-to-disk in two passes [4]. The sort is highly tuned, setting a the MinuteSort world record in 1997. The sorting algorithm contains two phases. In the first phase, each processor reads the records from disk and sends them to the final destination processor. The perfectly balanced nature of the communication of phase 1 is shown by the solid black square in Figure 4i. The sort uses one-way Active Messages directly, sending bulk messages at the rate the records can be read from disk. Phase 2 of the algorithm consists of entirely local disk operations. Unlike the other applications, NOW-sort performs a large amount of I/O, so can overlap communication overhead with disk accesses.
- **Radb:** This version of the radix sort [2] was restructured to use bulk messages. After the the global histogram phase, all keys are sent to their destination processor in one bulk mes-

Program	Avg. Msg./ Proc	Max Msg./ Proc	Msg./ Proc/ms	Msg. Interval (μs)	Barrier Interval (ms)	Percent Bulk Msg.	Percent Reads	Bulk Msg. KB/s	Small Msg. KB/s
Radix	1,278,399	1,279,018	164.76	6.1	408	0.01%	0.00%	26.7	4,612.9
EM3D(write)	4,737,955	4,765,319	124.76	8.0	122	0.00%	0.00%	0.6	3,493.2
EM3D(read)	8,253,885	8,316,063	72.39	13.8	369	0.00%	97.07%	0.0	2,026.9
Sample	1,015,894	1,294,967	76.76	13.0	1,203	0.00%	0.00%	0.0	2,149.2
Barnes	819,067	852,564	18.94	52.8	279	23.25%	20.57%	110.4	407.1
P-Ray	114,682	278,556	6.40	156.2	1,120	47.85%	96.49%	358.5	93.5
Connect	6,399	6,724	5.45	183.5	47	0.06%	67.42%	0.0	152.5
Murφ	166,161	168,657	4.70	212.6	11,778	49.99%	0.00%	3,876.6	65.8
NOW-sort	69,574	69,813	1.22	817.4	1,834	49.82%	0.00%	3,125.1	17.2
Radb	4,372	5,010	1.17	852.7	25	34.73%	0.04%	33.6	21.4

Table 4: **Communication Summary**. *For a 32 processor configuration, the table shows run times, average number of messages sent per processor, and the maximum number of messages sent by any processor. Also shown is the message frequency expressed in the average number of messages per processor per millisecond, the average message interval in microseconds,the average barrier interval, the percentage of the messages using the Active Message bulk transfer mechanism, the percentage of total messages which are read requests or replies, the average bandwidth per processor for bulk messages, and the average bandwidth per processor for small messages.*

sage. Depending on network characteristics, use of these bulk messages can speed up the performance of the sort relative to the standard radix sort.

4.2 Characteristics

As summarized in Table 3, the applications represent a broad spectrum of problem domains and communication/computation characteristics. To quantify the differences among our target applications, we instrumented our communication layer to record baseline characteristics for each program (with unmodified LogGP parameters) on 32 nodes. Table 4 shows the average number of messages, maximum number of messages per node (as an indication of communication imbalance), the message frequency expressed in the average number of messages per processor per millisecond, the average message interval in microseconds, and the average interval between barriers as a measure of how often processors synchronize. Table 4 also shows the percentage of the messages using the Active Message bulk transfer mechanism, the percentage of the total messages which are a read request or reply, the average bandwidth per processor for bulk messages, and the average bandwidth per processor for small messages. Note that the reported bandwidth is for bytes transmitted through the communication layer as opposed to bandwidth delivered to the application.

Table 4 shows that the communication frequency of our applications varies by more than two orders of magnitude, and yet none of them are "embarrassingly parallel." This disparity suggests that it is quite difficult to talk about typical communication behavior or sensitivity. Most of the applications have balanced communication overall, whereas others (Sample, P-Ray) have significant imbalances. Barnes and EM3D(write) are bulk synchronous applications employing barriers relatively frequently. Barnes, Murφ, P-Ray, Radb and NOW-sort utilize bulk messages while the other applications send only short messages. Finally, EM3D(read), Barnes, P-Ray, and Connect do mostly reads, while the other applications are entirely write based. Applications doing reads are likely to be dependent on network round trip times, and thus sensitive to latency, while write based applications are more likely to be tolerant of network latency. Most of the applications demonstrate regular communication patterns. However, Connect and P-Ray are more irregular and contain a number of hot spots. While these applications do not constitute a workload, their architectural requirements vary across large classes of parallel applications.

5 Sensitivity to Network Performance

Given our methodology and application characterization, we now quantify the effect of varying LogGP parameters on our application suite. To this end, we independently vary each of the parameters in turn to observe application slowdown. For each parameter, we attempt to explain any observed slowdowns based on application characteristics described in the last section. Using this intuition, we develop models to predict application slowdown.

5.1 Overhead

Figure 5(b) plots application slowdown as a function of added overhead measured in microseconds for our applications run on 32 nodes. The extreme left portion of the x-axis represents runs on our cluster. As overhead is increased, the system becomes similar to a switched LAN implementation. Currently, 100 μs of overhead with latency and gap values similar to our network is approximately characteristic of TCP/IP protocol stacks [27, 28, 43]. At this extreme, applications slow down from 2x to over 50x. Clearly, efforts to reduce cluster communication overhead have been successful. Further, all but one of our applications demonstrate a linear dependence to overhead, suggesting that further reduction in overhead will continue to yield improved performance. Qualitatively, the four applications with the highest communication frequency, Radix, Sample, and both EM3D read and write, display the highest sensitivity to overhead. Barnes is the only application which demonstrates a non-linear dependence to overhead. Instrumentation of Barnes on 16 nodes revealed that as overhead is increased, lock contention causes the program to go into livelock. With zero added overhead, the average number of failed lock attempts per processor is 2000 per timestep. At 13 μs of overhead, the number of failed lock attempts per processor per timestep skyrockets to over 1 million. This implementation of Barnes does not complete for overhead values greater than 13 μs on 16 nodes and 7 μs on 32 nodes.

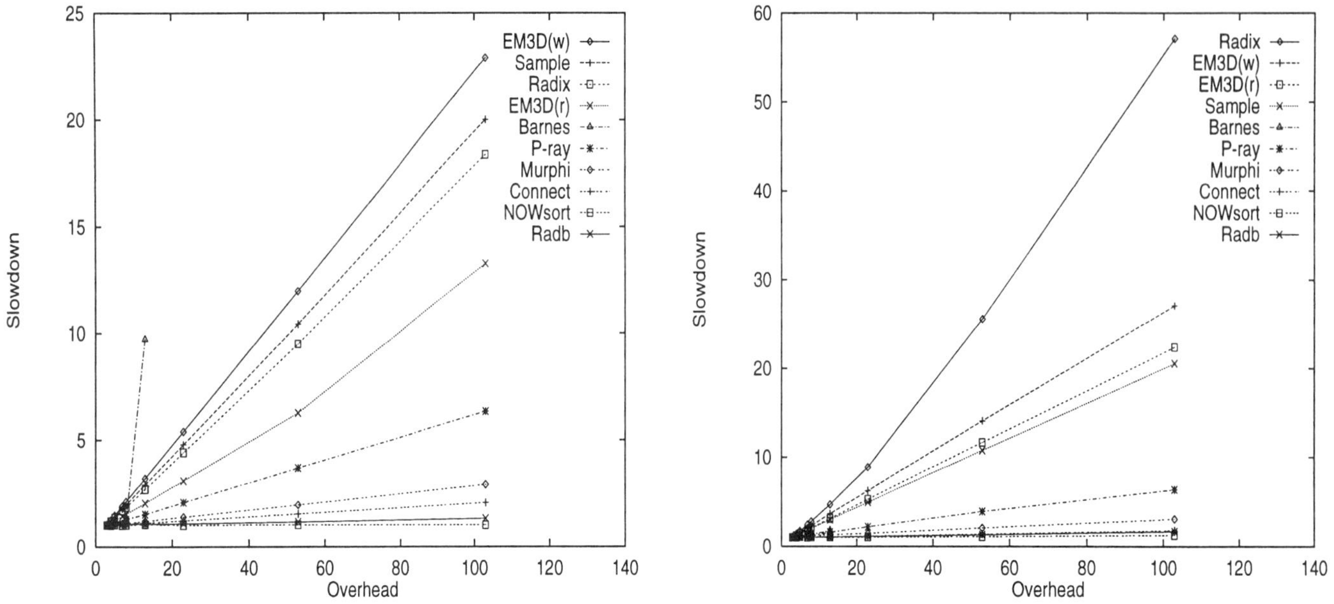

(a) (b)

Figure 5: **Sensitivity to Overhead for 16 and 32 Nodes.** *This figure plots application slowdown as a function of overhead in microseconds. Slowdown is relative to application performance with our system's baseline LogGP parameters. Measurements for the graph on the left were taken on 16 nodes, while measurements for the graph on the right were taken on 32 nodes with a fixed input size.*

To determine the effect of scaling the number of processors on sensitivity to overhead, we executed our applications on 16 nodes with fixed inputs. Figure 5(a) plots the resulting slowdown as a function of overhead for runs on 16 nodes. With the exception of Radix, the applications demonstrate almost identical sensitivity to overhead on 16 processors as they did on 32 processors, slowing down by between a factor of between 2 and 25. Recall that Radix contains a phase to construct a global histogram. The number of messages used to construct the histogram is a function of the radix and the number of processors, not the number of keys. For a constant number of keys, the relative number of messages per processor increases as processors are added. Radix thus becomes more sensitive to overhead as the number of processors is increased for a fixed input size. In addition, the difference in sensitivities between 16 and 32 nodes is exacerbated by a serial phase in program, which is described below.

To develop insight into our experimental results, we develop a simple analytical model of application sensitivity to added overhead. The model is based on the fact that added overhead is incurred each time a processor sends or receive a message. Thus, given an processor's base runtime, r_{orig}, the added overhead, Δo, and m, the number of communication events for each processor, we expect runtime, r_{pred}, to be:

$$r_{pred} = r_{orig} + 2m\Delta o$$

The factor of two arises because, for Split-C programs, all communication events are one of a request/response pair. For each request sent, the processor will incur an overhead penalty receiving the corresponding response in addition to the overhead for the sent request. If the processor is sending a response, it must have incurred an overhead penalty when it received the request message.

Given this model for the overhead sensitivity of individual processors, we extrapolate to predicting overall application runtime by making the following simplifying assumptions. First, applications run at the speed of the slowest processor, and second, the slowest processor is the processor that sends the most messages. Thus, by replacing m in the equation with the maximum number of messages sent by a processor from Table 4, we derive a simple model for predicting application sensitivity to added overhead as a function of the maximum number of messages sent by any processor during execution.

Table 5 describes how well this model predicts application performance when compared to measured runtimes. For two applications which communicate frequently, Sample, and EM3D(write), our model accurately predicts actual application slowdown . For a number of other applications, most notably Radix, P-Ray and Murφ, the sensitivity to overhead was actually stronger than our model's prediction; the model consistently under-predicts the run time. To explain this phenomenon, we turn back to the assumptions in our model.

Recall in the simple overhead model, we assume that P_m, the processor which sent the most messages, m, is the slowest processor. In addition, we implicitly assume all work in the program is perfectly parallelizable. It is this second assumption which leads to under-predicted run times. If a processor, P_n, serializes the program in a phase n messages long, when we increase o by Δo, then the serial phase will add to the overall run time by $n\Delta o$. However, the simple model does not capture this "serialization effect" when $P_m \neq P_n$.

A more important result of the of the serialization effect is that it reduces speedup as a function of overhead, i.e. speedup gets worse the greater the overhead. Thus, parallel efficiency will decrease as overhead increases for any applications which have a serial portion.

o μs	Radix		EM3D(write)		EM3D(read)		Sample		Barnes	
	measure	*predict*	*measure*	*predict*	*measure*	*predict*	*measure*	*predict*	*measure*	*predict*
2.9	7.8	7.8	38	38	114	114	13.2	13.2	43.2	43.2
3.9	10.5	10.3	48.1	47.5	138.7	130.7	16.1	15.8	50.1	44.9
4.9	13.2	12.9	58.1	57.0	161.6	147.3	18.7	18.4	56.3	51.8
6.9	18.7	18.0	77.4	76.1	208.8	180.5	23.8	23.6	76.1	60.3
7.9	21.5	20.5	87.4	85.6	232.9	197.2	26.5	26.2	N/A	N/A
13	36.3	33.3	138.5	133.3	354.4	280.3	39.3	39.1	N/A	N/A
23	68.9	58.9	236.2	228.6	600.1	446.7	65.2	65.0	N/A	N/A
53	198.2	135.7	535.9	514.5	1332.5	945.6	142.7	142.7	N/A	N/A
103	443.2	263.6	1027.8	991.0	2551.7	1777.2	272.1	272.2	N/A	N/A

o μs	P-Ray		Murφ		Connect		NOW-sort		Radb	
	measure	*predict*	*measure*	*predict*	*measure*	*predict*	*measure*	*predict*	*measure*	*predict*
2.9	17.9	17.9	35.3	35.3	1.17	1.17	56.9	56.9	3.73	3.73
3.9	19.0	18.5	37.1	35.7	1.19	1.18	56.7	57.0	3.77	3.74
4.9	19.6	19.0	37.7	36.0	1.20	1.19	61.2	57.1	3.77	3.75
6.9	22.0	20.1	41.8	36.7	1.23	1.20	57.9	57.4	3.82	3.77
7.9	20.8	20.7	41.9	37.0	1.24	1.21	58.3	57.6	3.83	3.78
13	28.2	23.5	46.2	38.7	1.31	1.25	58.1	58.3	3.93	3.83
23	39.0	29.1	51.2	42.1	1.44	1.34	58.3	59.7	4.10	3.93
53	69.7	45.8	72.6	52.2	1.85	1.61	61.7	63.9	4.81	4.23
103	114.0	73.6	107.8	69.1	2.52	2.08	71.1	70.8	6.19	4.73

Table 5: **Predicted vs. Measured Run Times Varying Overhead.** *This table demonstrates how well our model for sensitivity to overhead predicts observed slowdown for the 32 node runs. For each application, the column labeled* `measure` *is the measured runtime, while the column labeled* `predict` *is the runtime predicted by our model. For frequently communicating applications such as Radix, EM3D(write), and Sample, the model accurately predicts measured runtimes.*

Notice how for Radix, parallel decreases as a function of overhead when scaled from 16 to 32 nodes.

Radix sort demonstrates a dramatic example of the serialization effect. The sensitivity to overhead for Radix on 32 processors is over double that of 16 processors. When overhead rises to 100μs, the slowdown differential between 16 and 32 processors is a factor of three. The global histogram phase contains a serialization proportional to the radix and number of processors [19]. In the unmodified case, the phase accounts for 20% of the overall execution time on 32 processors. When the overhead is set to 100μs, this phase accounts for 60% of the overall execution time. However, on 16 processors with 100μs of overhead, the histogram phase takes only 16% of the total time.

5.2 Gap

We next measure application sensitivity to gap. Figure 6 plots application slowdown as a function of added gap in microseconds. The programs demonstrate widely varying reactions to gap, ranging from being unaffected by 100 μs of gap to slowing down by a factor of 16. The qualitative difference between application sensitivity to gap and sensitivity to overhead can be explained by the fact that sensitivity to gap is incurred by the program only on the portion of the messages where the application attempts to send at a rate greater than the gap. The rest of the messages are not sent quickly enough to be affected by the gap. Thus, infrequently communicating applications can potentially ignore gap entirely, while overhead is incurred independent of message frequency. The four applications with the highest communication frequency, Radix, EM3D(write) and read, and Sample, suffer the largest slowdowns from added gap. The other applications are much more tolerant to gap, slowing down by no more than a factor of 4 even in the presence of 100 μs of added gap.

Developing a model for application sensitivity to gap presents more difficulties than developing the model for sensitivity to overhead. A processor is not affected unless it attempts to send messages more frequently than the gap. At this point, the processor must stall for a period waiting for the network interface to become available. Without more precise knowledge of inter-message intervals, the model for gap sensitivity depends on assumptions made about these intervals. At one extreme, the uniform model assumes that all messages are sent at the application's average message interval, I, from Table 4. In this case, the predicted runtime, $r^{(u)}_{pred}$, can be predicted as a function of total gap, g, the average message interval, I, the base runtime, r_{base}, and the maximum number of messages sent by any node, m:

$$r^{(u)}_{pred} = \begin{cases} r_{base} + m(g - I) & \text{if } g > I \\ r_{base} & \text{otherwise} \end{cases}$$

At the other extreme, the burst model assumes that all messages are sent in discreet communication phases where the application attempts to send as fast as the communication layer will allow. Under this model, the added gap, Δg, is incurred for each communication event. This second model again assumes that the applications runs at the speed of the processor sending m messages, the maximum number of messages per processor from Figure 4, and would predict runtime, $r^{(b)}_{pred}$, as:

g μs	Radix		EM3D(write)		EM3D(read)		Sample		Barnes	
	measure	*predict*	*measure*	*predict*	*measure*	*predict*	*measure*	*predict*	*measure*	*predict*
5.8	7.8	7.8	38	38	114	114	13.2	13.2	43.2	43.2
8	10.2	11	46.1	49.9	119	134.8	14.8	16.5	44.1	45.4
10	13	14.2	56.5	61.8	129.7	155.6	17.5	19.7	50.2	47.5
15	19.2	20.5	78.5	85.6	164.7	197.2	24.2	26.2	55.3	51.8
30	38.1	39.7	150.3	157.1	289.3	321.9	42.9	45.6	61.6	64.6
55	69.9	71.7	273.1	276.2	523	529.8	75.1	78	99.1	85.9
80	101.9	103.7	394	395.4	756.9	737.7	107.5	110.4	157.3	107.2
105	133.8	135.7	515.6	514.5	993.1	945.6	139.7	142.7	207.9	128.5

g μs	P-Ray		Murφ		Connect		NOW-sort		Radb	
	measure	*predict*	*measure*	*predict*	*measure*	*predict*	*measure*	*predict*	*measure*	*predict*
5.8	17.9	17.9	35.3	35.3	1.17	1.17	56.9	56.9	3.73	3.73
8	18.1	18.6	37.4	35.8	1.19	1.18	57.9	57.0	3.77	3.74
10	17.8	19.3	36.1	36.2	1.21	1.19	57.6	57.2	3.78	3.75
15	17.9	20.7	36.2	37.0	1.24	1.23	60.9	57.6	3.80	3.78
30	19.1	24.9	38.4	39.5	1.34	1.32	57.3	58.6	3.86	3.85
55	23.2	31.8	37.5	43.8	1.51	1.50	57.2	60.4	3.96	3.98
80	29.0	38.8	39.3	48.0	1.68	1.69	56.9	62.1	4.08	4.10
105	35.5	45.8	39.9	52.2	1.85	1.88	57.4	63.9	4.25	4.23

Table 6: **Predicted vs. Measured Run Times Varying gap.** *This table demonstrates how well the burst model for sensitivity to gap predicts observed slowdown. For each application, the column labeled* measure *is the measured runtime, while the column labeled* predict *is the runtime predicted by our model.*

$$r_{pred}^{(b)} = r_{base} + m\Delta g$$

Application communication patterns determine which of the two models more closely predicts actual application runtime. The uniform model predicts that applications ignore increased gap until reaching a threshold equaling the application's average message interval. At this threshold, the applications should slowdown linearly with increasing gap. The burst model predicts a linear slowdown independent of average message interval. Given the linear dependence to gap demonstrated by the applications in Figure 6, we believe that for our applications, the burst model more accurately predicts application behavior. Table 6 depicts how well the burst model predicts actual program slowdown. As anticipated, the model over predicts sensitivity to gap since not all messages are sent in bursts. The model works best for heavily communicating applications, as a larger percentage of their messages are slowed by gap.

The two models considered demonstrate a range of possible application behavior. Applications communicating at very regular intervals would follow the uniform model, while applications communicating in discreet phases would track the burst model.

5.3 Latency

Traditionally, most attempts at improving network performance have focused on improving the network latency. Further, perceived dependencies on network latencies have led programmers to design their applications to hide network latency. Figure 7 plots application slowdown as a function of latency added to each message. Perhaps surprisingly, most of applications are fairly insensitive to added latency. The applications demonstrate a qualitatively different ordering of sensitivity to latency than to overhead and gap. Further, for all but one of the applications the sensitivity does not appear to be strongly correlated with the read frequency or barrier interval, the operations most likely to demonstrate the strongest sensitivity to latency.

The sensitivity of EM3D(read), Barnes, P-Ray, and Connect to latency results from these applications' high frequency of read operations (see Figure 4). Read operations require network round-trips, making them the most sensitive to added latency. However, for all but one of these applications, the observed slowdowns are modest (at most a factor of four in the worst-case) even at the latencies of store-and-forward networks (100 μs).

EM3D(read) performs a large number of blocking reads; it represents a "worst-case" application from a latency perspective because it does nothing to tolerate latency. It is also the only application for which a simple model of latency is accurate. Interestingly, for equal amounts of added "work" per message (100 μs of latency and 50 μs of overhead), the simple latency model for EM3D(read) is quite accurate yet the simple overhead model under predicts the run time.

The applications which do not employ read operations largely ignore added latency. The small decrease in performance at the tail of the slowdown curves is caused by the increase in gap associated with large latencies as the Active Message flow control mechanism limits the network capacity (see Table 2).

5.4 Bulk Gap

Only applications attempting to send large amounts of data in bursts should be affected by reductions in bulk transfer bandwidth. Note that we do not slow down transmission of small messages, but rather add a delay corresponding to the size of the message for each bulk message. Further, applications should tolerate decreases in available bulk bandwidth until the bandwidth dips below the application's requirements at any point during its execution.

Figure 8 plots application slowdown as a function of the maxi-

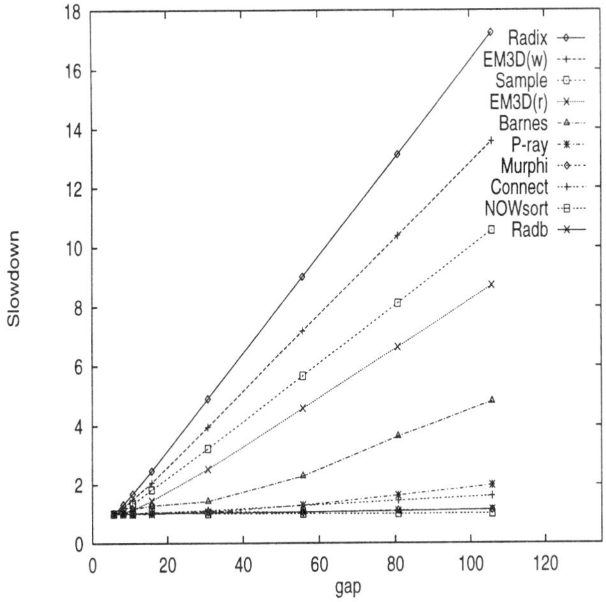

Figure 6: **Sensitivity to gap.** *This figure plots slowdown as a function of gap in microseconds.*

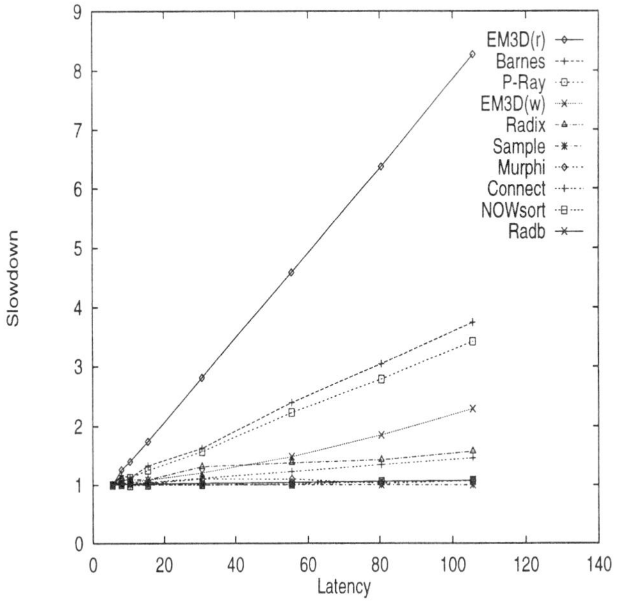

Figure 7: **Sensitivity to Latency.** *This figure plots slowdown as a function of latency in microseconds.*

mum available bulk transfer bandwidth. Overall, the applications in our suite do not display strong sensitivity to bandwidth. No application slows by more than a factor of three even when bulk bandwidth is reduced to 1 MB/s. Further, all of the applications, including Radb, which moves all of its data in a single burst using bulk messages, do not display sensitivity until bulk bandwidth is reduced to 15 MB/s. Surprisingly, the NOW-sort is also insensitive to reduced bandwidth. This version of the NOW-sort uses two disks per node. Each disk can deliver 5.5 MB/s of bandwidth [4], and during the communication phase a single disk is used for reading and the other for writing. As Figure 8 shows, NOW-sort is disk limited. Until the network bandwidth drops below that of a single disk, NOW-sort is unaffected by decreased bandwidth.

5.5 Summary

Varying the LogGP parameters for our cluster of workstations and benchmark suite lead to a number of interesting results. Applications displayed the strongest sensitivity to network overhead, slowing down by as much as a factor of 50 when overhead is increased to roughly 100 μs. Even lightly communicating processes suffer a factor of 3-5 slowdown when the overhead is increased to values comparable to many existing LAN communication stacks. Frequently communicating applications also display strong sensitivity to gap suggesting that the communication phases are bursty and limited by the rate at which messages can be injected into the network. For both overhead and gap, a simple model is able to predict sensitivity to the parameters for most of our applications. Perhaps most interesting is the fact that all the applications display a linear dependence to both overhead and gap. This relationship suggest that continued improvement in these areas should result in a corresponding improvement in application performance (limited by Amdahl's Law). In contrast, if the network performance were "good enough" for the applications, (i.e. some other part of the system was the bottleneck), then we should observe a region were the application did not slow down as network performance decreased.

The effect of added latency and bulk gap is qualitatively different from the effect of added overhead and gap. Further, the effects are harder to predict because they are more dependent on application structure. For example, applications which do not perform synchronization or read operations (both of which require round trip network messages) can largely ignore added latency. For our measured applications, the sensitivity to overhead and gap is much stronger than sensitivity to latency and available bandwidth. Thus, efforts in improving overhead and gap will result in the largest performance improvements across a wide class of applications demonstrating diverse architectural requirements.

Finally, this study demonstrates an interesting tradeoff between processor performance and communication performance. For many parallel applications, relatively small improvements in network overhead and gap can result in a factor of two performance improvement. This result suggests that in some cases, rather than making a significant investment to double a machine's processing capacity, the investment may be better directed toward improving the performance of the communication system.

6 Related Work

The Flash team recently conducted a study with very similar goals under simulation [25]. This study focuses on understanding the performance requirements for a communication controller for a cache-coherent distributed memory machine. It is difficult to make a direct quantitative comparison with their results because of differences in the simulated machine, the application sets, the small problem sizes used for simulation, and the metrics used. Still, a qualitative comparison is useful. The Flash study introduces a concept of occu-

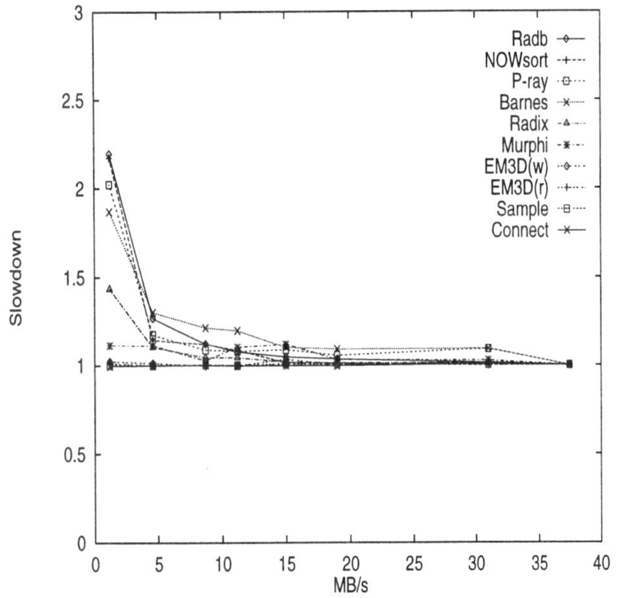

Figure 8: **Sensitivity to Bulk Gap.** *This figure plots slowdown as a function of maximum available network bandwidth.*

pancy, the cycles spent in the communication controller on each end of a message event. In their study, the message request and response is free from the processor's viewpoint. From the processor's viewpoint, occupancy adds to both the round-trip time and also slows the rate at which requests can be serviced, i.e., occupancy is part of our latency as well as gap. Their study also shows that many applications are surprisingly sensitive to occupancy. The Flash hardware prototype should provide an ideal testbed to perform a systematic *in situ* study like the one reported here in the DSM context.

The Wind Tunnel team has explored a number of cooperative shared memory design points relative to the Tempest interface through simulation and prototyping [30, 38], focused primarily on protocols. In principle, the wind tunnel provides enough power to systematically determine application sensitivity to the LogGP parameters within a given protocol, although the small local memory of the underlying CM5 may limit the study to small data sets.

Cypher [16] described the characteristics of a set of substantial message passing applications also showing that application behavior varies widely. The applications were developed in the context of fairly heavy weight message passing libraries and are more heavily biased to bulk transfers. The average message intervals are much larger than what our applications exhibit. Calculations on the data shows that actual data transfer rate is quite low. However, it is difficult to predict from the reported data how the performance would be affected with changes in the underlying message layer.

7 Conclusions

We have developed a simple empirical method for exploring the sensitivity of parallel applications to various aspects of communication performance. Using a high performance cluster as a baseline, we are able to increase each of the four communication parameters of the LogGP model — latency, overhead, message bandwidth and byte bandwidth — independently, and we have observed the effects on a broad range of applications. In general, we see that efforts to improve communication performance in a cluster architecture beyond what would be expected of a well-designed LAN are well rewarded. Applications are most sensitive to overhead, and some are hyper-sensitive to overhead in that the execution time increases with overhead at a faster rate than the message frequency would predict. Many applications are also sensitive to message rate or to message transfer bandwidth, but the effect is less pronounced than with overhead. The linear response to increased gap suggests that communication tends to be very bursty, rather than spaced at even intervals. Applications are least sensitive to network latency, the effects are uncorrelated with message frequency, and they appear complex to predict. Overall, the considered applications are surprisingly tolerant to latency.

The results suggest that there is considerable additional gain to be obtained by further reducing the communication overheads in clusters. Ongoing architectural efforts which integrate the network interface closer to the processor, either by placing the network interface onto the memory bus [11, 12, 38], into the memory controller [29], or by minimizing the number of stores and loads required to launch a communication event will continue to improve application performance.

Acknowledgments

We would like to thank Bob Horst for motivating this study. We would also like to thanks those people who provided us valuable assistance understanding the applications: Steve von Worley for P-Ray, Remzi Arpaci-Dusseau and Andrea Arpaci-Dusseau for Now-sort, Eric Anderson for Barnes, Ulrich Stern for Murφ, Chris Scheiman for Bulk Radix and Steve Lumetta for Connect and EM3D.

References

[1] A. Agarwal, R. Binchini, D. Chaiken, K. Johnson, D. Kranz, J. Kubiatowicz, B. Lim, K. Mackenzie, and D. Yeung. The MIT Alewife Machine: Architecture and Performance. In *Proceedings of the 22nd International Symposium on Computer Architecture*, pp. 2–13, May 1995.

[2] A. Alexandrov, M. Ionescu, K. Schauser, and C. Scheiman. LogGP: Incorporating Long Messages into the LogP model - One step closer towards a realistic model for parallel computation. In *7th Annual Symposium on Parallel Algorithms and Architectures*, May 1995.

[3] T.E. Anderson, D.E. Culler, D.A. Patterson, and the NOW Team. A Case for NOW (Networks of Workstations). *IEEE Micro*, vol. 15, pp. 54–64, Feb. 1995.

[4] A. C. Arpaci-Dusseau, R. H. Arpaci-Dusseau, D. E. Culler, J M. Hellerstein, and D. A. Patterson. High-Performance Sorting on Networks of Workstations. In *Proceedings of 1997 ACM SIGMOD International Conference on Management of Data*, May 1997.

[5] R. Arpaci, D.E. Culler, A. Krishnamurthy, S. Steinberg, and K. Yelick. Empirical Evaluation of the CRAY-T3D: A Compiler Perspective. In *Proceedings of the 22nd International Symposium on Computer Architecture*, 1995.

[6] E. Barton, J. Crownie, and M. McLaren. Message Passing on the Meiko CS-2. In *Parallel Computing*, vol. 20, pp. 497–507, Apr. 1994.

[7] M.A. Blumrich, K. Li, R. Alpert, C. Dubnicki, E.W. Felten, and J. Sandberg. Virtual Memory Mapped Network Interface for the

SHRIMP Multicomputer. In *Proceedings of the 21st International Symposium on Computer Architecture*, Apr. 1994.

[8] N.J. Boden, D. Cohen, R.E. Felderman, A.E. Kulawik, C.L. Seitz, J.N. Seizovic, and W. Su. Myrinet—A Gigabet-per-Second Local-Area Network. *IEEE Micro*, vol. 15, pp. 29–38, Feb. 1995.

[9] S. Borkar. Supporting Systolic and Memory Communication in iWarp. In *The 17th Annual International Symposium on Computer Architecture*, pp. 70–81, Seattle, WA, USA, May 1990.

[10] E. D. Brooks III, B. C. Gorda, K. H. Warren, and T.S. Welcome. *BBN TC2000 Architecture and Programming Models*.

[11] J.B. Carter, A. Davis, R. Kuramkote, C. Kuo, L.B. Stoller, and M. Swanson. Avalanche: A Communication and Memory Architecture for Scalable Parallel Computing. Technical Report UUCS-95-022, University of Utah, 1995.

[12] D. Chiou, B.S. Ang, Arvind, M.J. Beckerle, G.A. Boughton, R. Greiner, J.E. Hicks, and J.C. Hoe. StarT-NG: Delivering Seamless Parallel Computing. In *EURO-PAR'95 Conference*, Aug. 1995.

[13] D.E. Culler, A.C. Dusseau, S.C. Goldstein, A. Krishnamurthy, S. Lumetta, T. von Eicken, and K. Yelick. Parallel Programming in Split-C. In *Proceedings of Supercomputing '93*, pp. 262–273, 1993.

[14] D.E. Culler, R.M. Karp, D.A. Patterson, A. Sahay, K. E. Schauser, E. Santos, R. Subramonian, and T. von Eicken. LogP: Towards a Realistic Model of Parallel Computation. In *Fourth ACM SIGPLAN Symposium on Principles and Practice of Parallel Programming*, pp. 262–273, 1993.

[15] D.E. Culler, L.T. Liu, R.P. Martin, and C.O. Yoshikawa. Assessing Fast Network Interfaces. In *IEEE Micro*, vol. 16, pp. 35–43, Feb. 1996.

[16] R. Cypher, A. Ho, S. Konstantinidou, and P. Messina. Architectural Requirements of Parallel Scientific Applications with Explicit Communication. In *Proceedings of the 20th International Symposium on Computer Architecture*, pp. 2–13, May 1993.

[17] W. J. Dally, J. S. Keen, and M. D. Noakes. The J-Machine Architecture and Evaluation. In *COMPCON*, pp. 183–188, Feb. 1993.

[18] D.L. Dill, A. Drexler, A.J. Hu, and C.H Yang. Protocol Verification as a Hardware Design Aid. In *International Conference on Computer Design: VLSI in Computers and Processors*, 1992.

[19] A.C. Dusseau, D.E. Culler, K.E. Schauser, and R.P. Martin. Fast Parallel Sorting Under LogP: Experience with the CM-5. In *IEEE Transactions on Parallel and Distributed Systems*, vol. 7, pp. 791–805, Aug. 1996.

[20] S. Frank, H. Burkhard II, and J. Rthnie. The KSR 1: Bridging the Gap Between Shared Memory and MPPs. In *COMPCON*, pp. 285–294, Feb. 1993.

[21] R. B. Gillett. Memory Channel Network for PCI. In *IEEE Micro*, vol. 16, pp. 12–18, Feb. 1996.

[22] V. G. Grafe and J. E. Hoch. The Epsilon-2 Hybrid Dataflow Architecture. In *COMPCON*, pp. 88–93, Mar. 1990.

[23] J. R. Gurd, C. C. Kerkham, and I. Watson. The Manchester Prototype Dataflow Computer. In *Communications of the ACM*, vol. 28, pp. 34–52, Jan. 1985.

[24] M. Heinrich, J. Kuskin, D. Ofelt, J. Heinlein, J. Baxter, J. P. Singh, R. Simoni, K. Gharachorloo, D .Nakahira, M. Horowitz, A. Gupta, M. Rosenblum, and J. Hennessy. The Performance Impact of Flexibility in the Stanford FLASH Multiprocessor. In *Proceedings of the 6th International Conference on Architectural Support for Programming Languages and Operating Systems*, pp. 274–285, Oct. 1994.

[25] C. Holt, M. Heinrich, J. P. Singh, E. Rothberg, and J. Hennessy. The Effects of Latency, Occupancy, and Bandwidth in Distributed Shared Memory Multiprocessors. Technical Report CSL-TR-95-660, Stanford University, Jan. 1995.

[26] R. W. Horst. TNet: A Reliable System Area Network. *IEEE Micro*, vol. 15, pp. 37–45, Feb. 1994.

[27] J. Kay and J. Pasquale. The Importance of Non-Data-Touching Overheads in TCP/IP. In *Proceedings of the 1993 SIGCOMM*, pp. 259–268, San Francisco, CA, Sept. 1993.

[28] K. Keeton, D. A. Patterson, and T. E. Anderson. LogP Quantified: The Case for Low-Overhead Local Area Networks. In *Hot Interconnects III*, Aug. 1995.

[29] J. Kuskin, D. Ofelt, M. Heinrich, J. Heinlein, R. Simoni, K. Gharachorloo, J. Chapin, D. Nakahira, J. Baxter, M. Horowitz, A. Gupta, M. Rosenblum, and J. Hennessy. The Stanford FLASH Multiprocessor. In *Proceedings of the 21st International Symposium on Computer Architecture*, pp. 302–313, Apr. 1994.

[30] A. R. Lebeck and D. A. Wood. Dynamic Self-Invalidation: Reducing Coherence Overhead in Shared-Memory Multiprocessors. In *Proceedings of the 22nd International Symposium on Computer Architecture*, June 1995.

[31] C. E. Leiserson, Z. S. Abuhamdeh, D. C. Douglas, C. R. Feynman, M. N. Ganmukhi, J. V. Hill, W. D. Hillis, B. C. Kuszmaul, M. A. St. Pierre, D.S. Wells, M. C. Wond, S. Yang, and R. Zak. The Network Architecture of the CM-5. In *Symposium on Parallel and Distributed Algorithms*, pp. 272–285, June 1992.

[32] D. Lenoski, J. Laudon, T. Joe, D. Nakahira, L. Stevens, A. Gupta, and J. Hennessy. The DASH Prototype: Implementation and Performance. In *Proceedings of the 19th Annual International Symposium on Computer Architecture*, pp. 92–103, May 1992.

[33] S. Lumetta, A. Krishnamurthy, and D. E. Culler. Towards Modeling the Performance of a Fast Connected Components Algorithm on Parallel Machines. In *Proceedings of Supercomputing '95*, 1995.

[34] R. P. Martin. HPAM: An Active Message Layer for a Network of Workstations. In *Proceedings of the 2nd Hot Interconnects Conference*, Aug. 1994.

[35] S. Pakin, M. Lauria, and A. Chien. High Performance Messaging on Workstations: Illinois Fast Messages (FM) for Myrinet. In *Supercomputing '95*, 1995.

[36] G. M. Papadopoulos and D. E. Culler. Monsoon: An Explicit Token-Store Architecture. In *Proceedings of the 17th Annual International Symposium on Computer Architecture*, pp. 82–91, May 1990.

[37] P. Pierce and G. Regnier. The Paragon Implementation of the NX Message Passing Interface. In *Proceedings of the Scalable High-Performance Computing Conference*, pp. 184–190, May 1994.

[38] S. K. Reinhardt, J. R. Larus, and D. A. Wood. Tempest and Typhoon: User-Level Shared Memory. In *Proceedings of the 21st International Symposium on Computer Architecture*, pp. 325–336, Apr. 1994.

[39] M. Rosenblum, S. A. Herrod, E. Witchel, and A .Gupta. Complete Computer Simulation: The SimOS Approach. In *IEEE Parallel and Distributed Technology*, Fall 1995.

[40] S. Sakai, Y. Yamaguchi, K. Hiraki, Y. Kodama, and T. Yuba. An Architecture of a Dataflow Single Chip Processor. In *Proc. of the 16th Annual Int. Symp. on Comp. Arch.*, pp. 46–53, June 1989.

[41] S. L. Scott. Synchronization and Communication in the T3E Multiprocessor. In *Proceedings of the 7th International Conference on Architectural Support for Programming Languages and Operating Systems*, Oct. 1996.

[42] U. Stern and D. L. Dill. Parallelizing the Murphi Verifier. Submitted for publication.

[43] T. von Eicken, A. Basu, V. Buch, and W. Vogels. U-Net: A User-Level Network Interface for Parallel and Distributed Computing. In *Proceedings of the Fifteenth SOSP*, pp. 40–53, Copper Mountain, CO, Dec. 1995.

[44] T. von Eicken, D. E. Culler, S. C. Goldstein, and K. E. Schauser. Active Messages: a Mechanism for Integrated Communication and Computation. In *Proc. of the 19th Int'l Symposium on Computer Architecture*, May 1992.

[45] S. C. Woo, M. Ohara, E. Torrie, J. P. Singh, and A. Gupta. The SPLASH-2 Programs: Characterization and Methodological Considerations. In *Proceedings of the 22nd International Symposium on Computer Architecture*, pp. 24–36, June 1995.

The Mercury Interconnect Architecture: A Cost-effective Infrastructure for High-performance Servers

Wolf-Dietrich Weber, Stephen Gold, Pat Helland†, Takeshi Shimizu, Thomas Wicki, and Winfried Wilcke

HAL Computer Systems
1315 Dell Ave, Campbell, CA 95008

† Microsoft Corporation
One Microsoft Way, Redmond, WA 98052

Abstract

This paper presents HAL's Mercury Interconnect Architecture, an interconnect infrastructure designed to link commodity microprocessors, memory, and I/O components into high-performance multiprocessing servers. Both shared-memory and message-passing systems, as well as hybrid systems are supported by the interconnect. The key attributes of the Mercury Interconnect Architecture are: low latency, high bandwidth, a modular and flexible design, reliability/availability/serviceability (RAS) features, and a simplicity that enables very cost-effective implementations. The first implementation of the architecture links multiple 4-processor Pentium® Pro based nodes. In a 4-node (16-processor) shared-memory configuration, this system achieves a remote read latency of just over 1 µs, and a maximum interconnect bandwidth of 6.4 GByte/s. Both of these parameters far outpace comparable SCI-based solutions, while utilizing much fewer hardware components.

1 Motivation

The Mercury Interconnect Architecture was developed in response to the need for a flexible, high-performance interconnect for large-scale multiprocessor systems. The advent of cheap and powerful microprocessors promises the delivery of the compute power of mainframe- and supercomputer-class machines at the cost structure of workstations. The missing piece to turn this potential into reality is an interconnect capable of harnessing the collective power of the individual processors and integrating them with memory and I/O components into a high-performance system. That is the motivation for the Mercury Interconnect.

The remainder of this paper is split into two major areas: a description of the Mercury Interconnect Architecture (sections 2 through 5), and the details of the first implementation (sections 6 and 7). Section 8 discuss the scalability of the architecture and implementation. The final section summarizes the paper and analyzes how well the first implementation met the goals of the architecture.

2 Mercury Architecture

Figure 1 shows the picture of a general interconnect, which is also the highest-level view of the Mercury Interconnect. A collection of processor/memory and I/O nodes are plugged into the interconnect and communicate with one another using the network services. The depiction of the interconnect as a cloud symbolizes the fact that the attached nodes do not need to know about the internal features of the interconnect to make use of its services.

ISCA '97 Denver, CO, USA
© 1997 ACM 0-89791-901-7/97/0006...$3.50

Figure 1: A general interconnect.

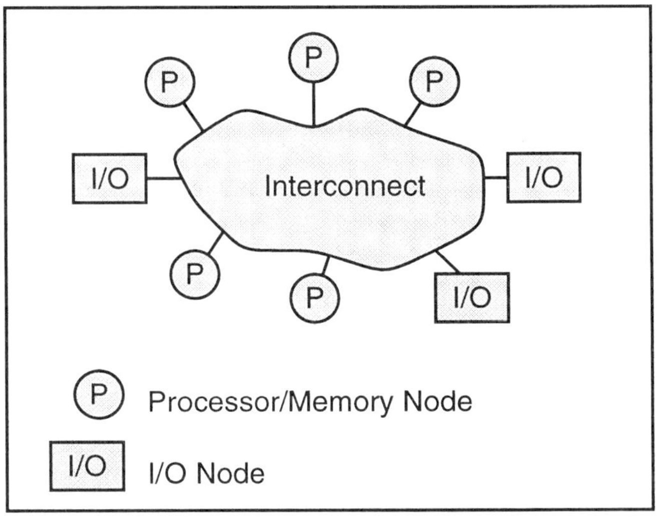

2.1 Goals

When setting out to define an architecture, a set of goals is required to allow the architects to make a consistent set of trade-offs which in turn leads to a balanced design. The key goals of the Mercury Interconnect Architecture are as follows:

- lowest possible communication latency between nodes
- communication bandwidth between nodes comparable to local memory bandwidth of state-of-the-art systems
- flexible and scalable interconnect topology
- enough reliability, availability, and serviceability features to build commercial servers
- cost effectiveness

Each of these goals is discussed in further detail below.

Achieving a low inter-node communication latency is absolutely vital for any multiprocessor interconnection network. Given that the Mercury Interconnect might be used to link processors to memory, the required node-to-node latencies have to be in the range of a few multiples of normal memory system access times.

Equally important to low inter-node communication latency is high inter-node communication bandwidth. If the interconnect is used to link a processor to memory, the interconnect should not represent a bandwidth bottleneck in that path.

In terms of topology, the goal is for the interconnect to have a flexible topology and to be readily scaled from a size that interconnects just a handful of nodes to the huge size required to link many hundreds of nodes. The interconnect should be modular to ensure that small systems can be built at a low cost, with the construction of large systems also possible. As the network grows, the bisection bandwidth should grow as well, in order to prevent bandwidth bottlenecks in the interconnect.

Since the Mercury Interconnect might be used as the basis for a large commercial server system, it must support the reliability, availability, and serviceability features that such a server demands. Data must be reliably transmitted. The topology must allow for redundancy. The network must support runtime re-configuration in order to route around failures and to allow for the addition or removal of nodes.

The goal of cost-effectiveness needs almost no explanation. For the interconnect it means that components should stay away from exotic (i.e. expensive) technologies. For example, this means that custom chips must use standard CMOS processes.

2.2 Achieving the goals

The following sections discuss the approaches used for achieving the goals set out at the start.

2.2.1 Packet switching

The nature of processor-to-memory communication leads to the exchange of short (cache-line sized) data blocks with rapidly changing communication patterns. This property alone immediately forces a packet-switched rather than a circuit-switched network transport mechanism.

2.2.2 Cascadable routers

The goal of a flexible and scalable interconnect topology leads to an interconnect architecture that is made up of a number of independent switching units (called *routers*). As shown in Figure 2, each node incorporates a network interface that connects the node to a router in the interconnect switch fabric. Two nodes can be connected back-to-back without a router, a small network can consist of a single router, and multiple routers can be cascaded to form very large networks.

Figure 2: Network Interfaces and Routers.

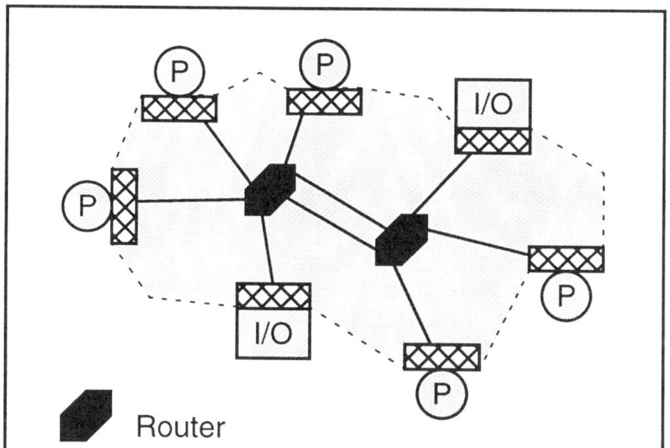

2.2.3 Plesiochronous clocking

Having a potentially large collection of communicating routers and nodes leads to the problem of clock distribution for such a physically large collection of hardware. For the Mercury Interconnect, a plesiochronous clocking strategy was adopted to avoid all clock synchronization issues. Each node and each router can have its own clock source. The clocks are all nominally running at the same frequency, but since they are derived from different oscillators they are expected to drift in phase over time. The interconnect is designed to easily tolerate the small inaccuracies in the clock frequency of off-the-shelf crystal oscillators.

2.2.4 Source routing

In order to keep the network latency low, routing decisions at each hop in the interconnect have to be made very quickly. In the Mercury Architecture, this is achieved by pre-determining the route from a given node to any other node on the network and storing those routes at the source node. Network routing then simply consists of picking up the route at the source and following that route through the network to the destination. At each routing step, a router determines the next link to traverse and then discards that step from the route (prefix routing), making the routing task itself extremely fast.

2.2.5 Layering of functionality

The functionality of the Mercury Interconnect Architecture is distributed over three layers. Layering allows a clean division of functions which in turn makes the design and verification easier. Each layer provides a well-specified set of services to the layer above it, making use of the services of the layer below it. As shown in Figure 3 the layers from bottom to top are: the fast frame mover (FFM), the reliable packet mover (RPM) and the interconnect services manager (ISM). The FFM layer is present in both the network interface of the nodes and in the router. The RPM and ISM layers are present only in the nodes.

The FFM layer is responsible for managing the data transport between different nodes and routers. It accomplishes link-level buffer management and flow control between the two ends of the link, as well as the routing through the network from source node to destination node. In the framework of the OSI reference model, this corresponds roughly to the physical, data link, and networking layers. The key concept behind the FFM is speed. This demands high clock rates and reduced logic functionality.

Figure 3: Interconnect layers.

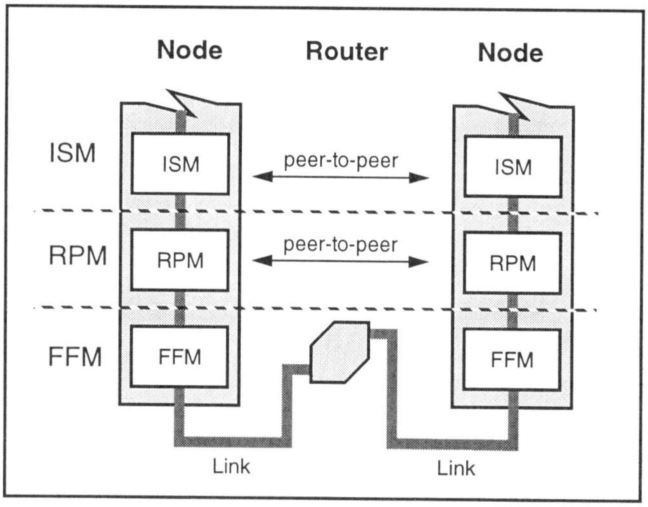

The RPM layer is responsible for providing end-to-end reliability for transfers between node pairs. The FFM may occasionally corrupt data, misroute transfers, or drop them altogether. The RPM layer recovers failures and provides an ordered stream of transfers between any pair of communicating nodes. The RPM corresponds to the transport layer of the OSI reference model.

Finally, the ISM layer interfaces to the rest of the node and maps the node's communication requirements into the services provided by the RPM. There can be different ISM layers for different purposes. Examples are a cache-coherence ISM for a shared-memory machine, or a messaging ISM for a distributed memory message-passing machine.

The following sections discuss each of the three layers in greater detail.

3 Fast Frame Mover (FFM) layer

A Mercury network link consists of two unidirectional connections. Each connection is made up of 34 data bits, a set of voltage reference signals, a differential clock, and two control signals (see Figure 4). A link thus consists of about 90 conductors.

Signalling over the Mercury link is accomplished using low swing signals. Clocks are transmitted along with the data in order to eliminate any dependence on cable length. While the clock lines are fully-differential, the data and control lines are pseudo-differential: they have one reference signal per 7 or 8 data/control signals. Data is transferred on both edges of the clock, i.e. two bits of information are transferred per wire per clock period.

Figure 4: Mercury network link.

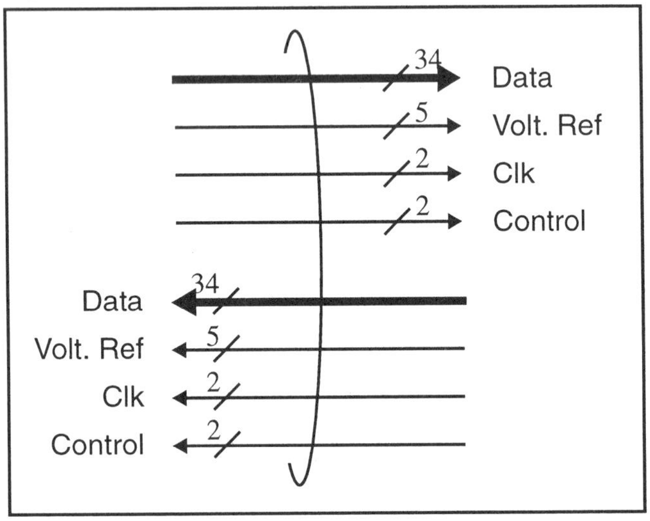

The FFM layer is responsible for moving a frame (Figure 5) of information between two nodes that are connected to the interconnect. A frame consists of a 68-bit frame header and a frame body that has between 1 and 18 68-bit words. The frame header mainly contains the frame route which controls the path that a frame will take through the network. The contents of the frame body are ignored by the FFM layer. The frame is not protected by any error code.

A route consists of an ordered list of routing steps. When a frame enters a router, the routing step at the head of the list tells the router which port to exit through. This routing step is then removed from the frame header, all remaining routing steps are shifted over by one, and a null routing step is concatenated to the end of the route list. In this manner, a frame makes its way through the network, until it reaches its final node destination.

The FFM implements three distinct channels through the interconnect. There is a high-, a medium-, and a low-priority channel. The higher priority channels have reserved buffer capacity, which allows them to make progress even if the lower priority channels are completely blocked. The FFM provides these channels as a service to the RPM and has no control over how they are used.

Figure 5: A Frame.

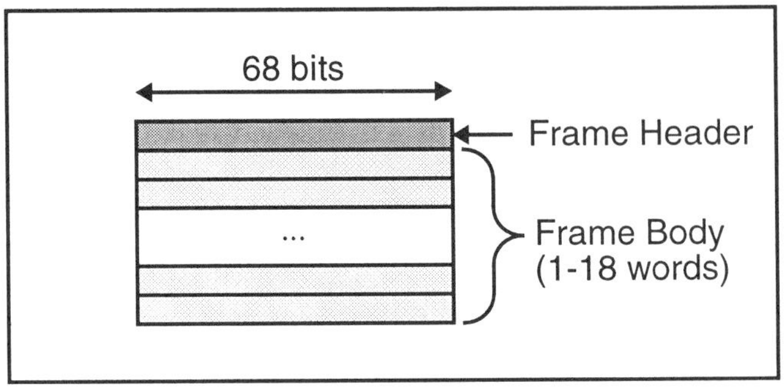

The FFM layer is also responsible for buffering and flow control on a per-link basis, i.e. between the two routers/nodes connected at the opposite ends of a single link. The routers employ virtual cut-through routing, which allows them to process and transmit the head of a frame while the body is still arriving, thus reducing fall-through latency. However, if a frame is blocked and cannot make progress through the router, there is enough input buffering to allow all of the frame to be "sucked" into the router rather than congesting the inbound link. The buffers at the receiving end of a link are allocated at the sending end of the link. Enough buffering is provided to completely hide the round-trip latency of the link, thus allowing a link to achieve 100% of its maximum transmission capacity.

Since network errors can corrupt frames and hence routes, it is possible for deadlock cycles to be set up by corrupted frames. The FFM incorporates a buffer lifetime time-out mechanism which allows a frame to live in a given buffer for only so long. When a buffer lifetime time-out occurs, the frame is simply discarded, thus freeing the FFM buffer.

A final function that resides in the FFM domain is the synchronization between different clock domains. As mentioned before, each router and node can have its own local clock. On each incoming link, the arriving data is clocked in with the link clock and is then synchronized into the local clock domain. The flow control mechanism between each end of the link prevents overrun conditions due to a sender's clock being slightly higher in frequency than the corresponding receiver's clock.

The key concept behind the FFM is speed. It is imperative to keep the latency through each router as small as possible and to attain the highest possible link bandwidth. To this end, FFM functionality is reduced to a bare minimum, and the FFM is allowed to occasionally corrupt a frame leading to a misroute or the transfer of corrupted data. These failures are recovered in the RPM layer above. Not having to guarantee error-free transmission within a wide margin of process technology and environmental conditions allows the FFM to be run at a more aggressive clock frequency than would otherwise be possible, and hides any meta-stability problems.

4 Reliable Packet Mover (RPM) layer

The RPM layer is responsible for reliable end-to-end communication between node pairs. The unit of transfer for the RPM is a packet (Figure 6), which fits into the frame body at the FFM layer.

A packet consists of a 128-bit RPM header and an RPM body that is made up of between 0 and 8 128-bit words. The packet header contains source, destination, sequence number, and packet type information. It also has enough room for the ISM layer to transport a 64-bit address and 18-bit command.

Figure 6: A packet (transported as a frame body).

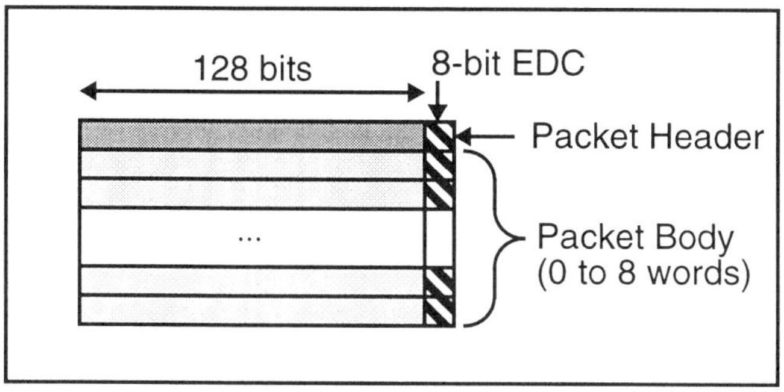

Each 128-bit word of the packet is annotated with an 8-bit error detection code (EDC). Another coding mechanism provides block protection in addition to the line protection provided by the EDC. This division allows for the use of a packet's data before the entire packet has been received.

The RPM uses the FFM to rapidly move packets from the source node to the destination node, but it must cover for the occasional transmission errors in the FFM layer. Errors are not expected to be frequent, so the RPM is optimized for the common non-error case.

In order to turn an unreliable stream of unordered frames into a reliable stream of ordered packets the RPM uses the following techniques:

- source node buffering with time-out and retransmission
- acknowledgments
- reordering and duplicate suppression

The basic feature that these techniques build upon is the use of sequence numbers. Each packet that is sent between a pair of nodes receives a unique sequence number. Sequence numbers are used end-to-end between RPM peers, rather than at intermediate points in the interconnect, making the FFM simpler and faster. Sequence numbers allow the receiver to deliver packets in the order they were sent, even in the face of occasional reordering by the FFM layer. Since the FFM guarantees a maximum frame lifetime in each router, there is a system-wide maximum frame lifetime. The sequence numbers are large enough to assure that they cannot wrap around during a frame lifetime, thus eliminating the possibility of sequence number aliasing.

A copy of each packet is kept at the sending node at the time that the packet is sent into the network. The copy is kept in a "transmission buffer" at the sender until it is guaranteed that the destination node has received an error-free copy of the packet.

Acknowledgments are used by the receiver to indicate to the sender that a packet has been received successfully. Acknowledgments always use the high-priority FFM channel, allowing them to make progress through the network even if the entire network is clogged. When an acknowledgment is received by the sender, it can discard its copy of the packet and reuse the transmission buffer for another packet that needs to be sent. Transmission buffers are not dedicated to a particular destination. Only a small number of transmission buffers are required, because the round-trip network latency for a packet to be sent and an acknowledgment to be returned is very small.

When a frame arrives at a node it may be corrupted in some way. Corrupted frames are simply discarded by the receiver. Negative acknowledgments are not used because they cannot be reliably generated, and also because frame corruption is expected to be so rare that the time-out and retransmission mechanism is sufficient.

In the case that a packet or acknowledgment is lost in the network, the sender never receives an acknowledgment for a packet that it sent. In this case, the sender eventually times out. Since it has retained a copy of the packet in a transmission buffer, it can simply retransmit the packet.

Time-out and retransmission can lead to the problem of duplicate packets. For example, even though a packet may have been received properly, the acknowledgment could be lost. Eventually the sender times out and sends another copy of the packet. The receiver thus sees two copies of the same packet. Such duplicates are suppressed with the help of the sequence number. The receiver can tell that the packet is a duplicate and simply discards the second copy. However, it does acknowledge it, so as to allow the sender to advance to the next packet and free up its transmission buffer.

The use of sequence numbers and enough transmission buffers to cover the round-trip latency of the network allows the RPM to fully utilize the capacity of the underlying FFM layer. This is similar to a traditional sliding window flow control protocol, but differs in the important way of buffer allocation. In the sliding window protocol, enough buffering for the entire window is provided for each reliable connection, i.e. for each node-pair at both the sender and the receiver. This means that the number of buffers per node grows with the square of the total number of nodes in the system. In contrast, the shared transmission buffer scheme requires buffers only at the sending side, and needs only enough buffers to cover the round-trip latency of the network, regardless of the total number of nodes connected.

The RPM provides an error-free FIFO channel from each node to every other node on the network. This property is very powerful and makes protocol design in the higher ISM layer significantly easier.

5 Interconnect Services Manager (ISM) layer

The ISM layer is the highest protocol layer in the Mercury Interconnect Architecture. It maps the node's communication requirements into the services provided by the RPM. While the FFM and RPM layers are largely independent of the node's implementation details, the ISM layer naturally depends heavily on these details because it is the ISM layer that interacts closely with the remainder of the node's hardware. As of this writing, a cache-coherent ISM has been defined that allows multiple nodes containing processors, memory, and I/O to be connected into a globally cache coherent non-uniform memory access (CC-NUMA) machine [7], or a shared-nothing message-passing machine.

The cache coherence protocol chosen for the cache-coherent ISM is a directory-based protocol [1]. A directory-based protocol is a good match for an interconnect-based CC-NUMA machine, because the directory information is distributed in a manner similar to the distribution of main memory. Each node contains a portion of the globally accessible main memory space and the associated directory.

The coherence directory is a sparse directory [11, 7], i.e. there is not a one-to-one relationship between cache lines held in main memory and directory entries. Instead, the directory is sized as a function of the remote processor caches, since only remotely cached memory lines require a directory entry. This directory organization reduces the required directory size dramatically over more conventional directory structures.

The coherence protocol itself consists of a set of messages that is exchanged between nodes to keep the caches globally coherent. The protocol is loosely based on that of the Stanford DASH multiprocessor [5, 6]. Features that are common are the three major states (invalid, shared, dirty) and optimizations for low-latency replies to read and write misses when the cache line is dirty in another node (3-way transfers). Modifications were made mostly to take advantage of the underlying features of the RPM, and to make transient states explicit.

Making all transient states explicit makes the protocol more tractable and easier to verify. Instead of having states overloaded with different meanings depending on what messages are in flight, each state that has a different behavior gets a different name. In addition, a given protocol state transition has to be finished completely, before another transition on the same cache line can start. While this may impact performance slightly, it makes the protocol much more robust because the protocol does not have to deal with late arrival of stale messages from earlier protocol transactions.

The coherence protocol uses a single channel between nodes. Deadlock avoidance is achieved by providing enough buffering at each node to make deadlock cycles impossible.

6 Implementation

Although the original implementation of the Mercury Interconnect Architecture was targeted at a high-performance server using SPARC architecture processors, it was readily re-targeted to interconnect standard high-volume SMP servers employing Intel's Pentium® Pro processors. The first implementation of the Mercury Interconnect Architecture is known as the S1 System.

6.1 The HAL S1 System

The HAL S1 System is a shared-memory or message-passing machine consisting of standard high volume Intel processor-based SMP nodes linked together with the Mercury Interconnect. Figure 7 shows one node, and a portion of the interconnect. Each node contains four Pentium® Pro processors, up to 1 GByte of DRAM, and two PCI buses for attaching I/O. The interconnect implementation supports up to 32 nodes (128 processors), of which any 4-node subsets can make up 16-processor cache-coherent systems.

Figure 7: Architecture of the HAL S1 System.

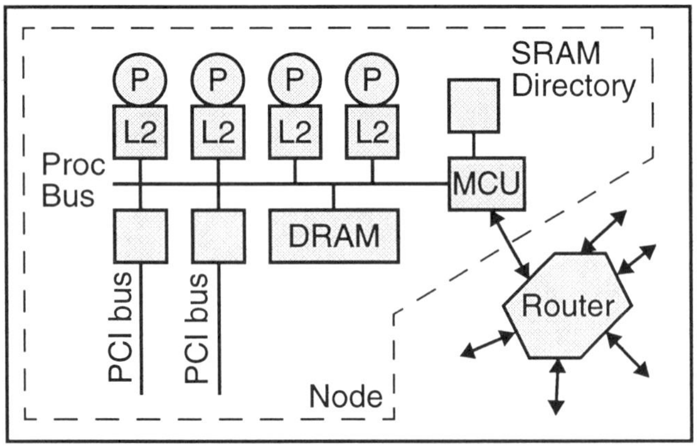

Cache-coherent systems run the SCO UnixWare™ operating system. This OS is NUMA-aware and contains features that localize memory references, thus allowing standard shared-memory applications to capitalize on the higher bandwidths and lower latencies to local memory in NUMA architectures.

Non-coherent systems can run any operating system that runs on the standard 4-way node, thus allowing many different forms of message-passing (clustered) machines to be built. Clustering works well for exploiting coarse-grain parallelism and is also a good way to achieve system fault-tolerance without having to build very expensive fault-tolerant hardware. To this end, the hardware allows hot plugging of the interconnect links.

The hardware implementation supports hybrid coherent/message-passing machines as well as pure coherent and pure message-passing systems.

The S1 System uses two custom chips: the Router [9, 10] and the Mesh Coherence Unit (MCU). The Router is a six-ported full crossbar implementing the FFM layer. The MCU acts as the bridge between the coherent processor bus and the interconnect. It implements a cache-coherent and message-passing ISM layer, as well as the RPM and FFM layers of the interconnect. The two custom chips are discussed in detail below.

6.2 Router

The Router for the S1 System is a symmetrical 6-ported crossbar. It is built out of standard 0.35 μm, 5-layer metal CMOS technology, has a die size of 14 mm by 13 mm and 1.9 million transistors. It implements the routing functions with three different priority channels, link-level flow control, and synchronization between different clock domains.

The Router includes six buffers per input port to allow full-bandwidth transfer and flow control on each link. Coupled with a dedicated input line into the crossbar per buffer element, the only arbitration that has to take place is for the output lines of the crossbar. This arbitration is very fast.

The simplicity of the FFM layer of the architecture coupled with an aggressive Router microarchitecture and smart circuit techniques allow the Router to achieve a clock frequency of 285 MHz. The Router uses 300 mV low-swing signals, with data being transferred on both edges of the clock. In the S1 System, the network is clocked at 200 MHz, leading to a usable link bandwidth of 1.6 GByte/s per link per direction. The maximum bandwidth through the Router is thus 9.6 GByte/s. The fall-through latency (without contention) from any port to any other port is 42 ns.

The Mercury links can be built out of a variety of technologies. Multiple Routers could be placed on a single circuit board, and interconnected via PCB traces. The Router also supports cables of up to 2 m in length, allowing interconnection of larger systems. Mercury links can be hot-plugged, enabling reconfiguration of a running system.

The Router also includes numerous performance monitoring and error recording features to aid in interconnect monitoring and failure analysis.

6.3 Mesh Coherence Unit

The Mesh Coherence Unit (MCU) for the S1 System acts as the network interface for the nodes. It is also built out of 0.35 μm, 5-layer metal CMOS, has a die size of 14 mm by 10 mm, and 1.6 million transistors. The MCU provides the following functions to the processors: a global cache-coherent address space, global inter-processor interrupts and bus error mechanisms, efficient memory copy (DMA) between nodes, message-passing support for nodes that do not share memory, and extensive performance monitoring. Each of these functions is explained in further detail below.

The MCU's primary function is to provide a global cache-coherent address space. It achieves this by extending the bus-based snoopy coherence protocol used on each node with a directory-based point-to-point coherence protocol between nodes. The sparse coherence directory is stored in standard off-the-shelf SRAM chips. Only three 1 Mbit chips are required, for a total directory size of less than 0.5 MByte. A comparable full-directory design with 6 bits of state for every cache line would require 24 MByte of storage per GByte of main memory.

Global interrupts are achieved via interconnect messages. Interrupts are launched from one node via a write to a special MCU register. They are delivered at the destination node via the APIC bus [4], which is the standard interrupt delivery vehicle for Intel Pentium® Pro processors.

Bus error mechanisms are also extended via the interconnect and echoed on all nodes participating in a coherent address space. In this manner all processors running a single copy of the operating system are notified of error conditions.

To aid the OS in its task migration and load balancing functions that are important for NUMA localization, the MCU includes a memory copy (DMA) engine. It can be used to copy chunks of main memory from one node to another at the granularity of a cache line. The most likely use of this memory copy engine is to achieve high-performance page copy between clusters without involving the processors themselves or destroying the processors' cache state. Memory copy is a simple extension of the coherence protocol, which already provides for the efficient movement of cache-lines around the machine.

The Mercury Interconnect can be used for message-passing (clustered) architectures as well as shared-memory architectures. The support required for message-passing falls out once the coherence mechanisms have been implemented. The MCU supports both small messages (up to 24 bytes) that have been optimized for low-latency, and high-bandwidth bulk transfer via the memory copy engine. The MCU includes a protection mechanism that eliminates the chance of accidental reading/writing of the wrong memory section in a message-passing system.

Finally, extensive performance monitoring features have been included in the MCU. Events can be counted on the bus and in the interconnect. In addition, remote latencies and buffer utilizations can be measured. The performance monitoring hardware permits the measurement of the characteristics of real applications. The measured data is used to tune the operating system and applications, as well as to help guide future architectural trade-offs.

6.4 Performance

The performance data presented in this section was gathered using a simulation model of a 4-node (16-processor) system using a single Router. The processors are running at 200 MHz, the processor bus at 66 MHz, and the interconnect at 200 MHz. The simulation model includes hardware models of existing chips (Pentium® Pro and memory controller) and RTL software models of our own chips (Router and MCU). Hardware models consist of a real chip encapsulated in a layer of software that allows it to be linked with other software simulation models.

Given that entire applications cannot be run on this simulation environment due to time constraints, we focus on some vital performance characteristics: latency, bandwidth, and synchronization overhead. Small programs (micro-benchmarks) were run on the system to measure these characteristics. We now look at each of them in turn.

6.4.1 Latency

In order to measure latencies from the processor all the way through the memory system and back to the processor, we use a string of dependent loads to a large stride vector and measure the repetition rate in the absence of other activity (unloaded). Table 1 shows the results.

Table 1: Unloaded 4-node latencies.

Type of access (after L2 cache miss)	Latency [ns]
local memory read (base SMP)	240
remote memory read, clean	1065
remote memory read, dirty at third node	1365

The latency of a load that misses all caches in the base node is 240 ns. When remote memory is accessed, this latency is just over 1 µs, i.e. about 4 times as large as the local latency. If the data happens to be dirty in a third node, a 3-way transfer takes place and the latency becomes 1365 ns.

6.4.2 Bandwidth

Bandwidth is measured by copying a region of memory (4 KByte) from one place in memory to another. Regions are arranged so as to maximize the chance of a DRAM page hit. We look at processor-initiated transfers (using the *movsl* opcode with the target region mapped as *write combining*), and transfers that use the memory copy engine in the MCU. The results are presented in Table 2. Note that the bandwidth number listed is the actual copy bandwidth achieved, not the sum of the read and write bandwidths. "Local copy" is a transfer from local to local memory. "Remote copy pull" involves reading in a remote node and writing in the local node. "Remote copy push" reads in the local node and writes in the remote node.

Table 2: 4-node transfer bandwidths (single agent).

Type of transfer	Agent	Bandwidth [MByte/s]
local copy	processor	105
remote copy pull	processor	67
remote copy push	processor	73
remote copy pull	mem copy	270
remote copy push	mem copy	275

For the local copy case, the achieved bandwidth of 105 MByte/s is limited by the memory controller. Both reads and writes are in the same controller and switching between them lowers the efficiency of the DRAM access. For remote copy (both push and pull) the reads and writes are now on two different nodes and hence in different memory controllers. At this point, the bandwidth achieved is limited by the processor architecture (each processor can only have a small number of operations outstanding) and the fact that half the operations are seeing the remote memory latency. Nonetheless, both processor-initiated push and pull still achieve around 70 MByte/s transfer bandwidth, which is about 2/3 of the local copy bandwidth. When we use the memory copy engine incorporated in the MCU, the transfer bandwidth increases to about 270 MByte/s. This is about 4 times the bandwidth that can be achieved with a processor alone and has the additional benefit of not polluting the processor's cache. There are three reasons why the memory copy engine can achieve a much higher transfer bandwidth than a single processor. First, it can have more operations outstanding than the processor. Secondly, data occupies the bus on the initiating node only once, whereas it has to go on the bus twice when using the processor. Finally, additional bus bandwidth is consumed for split transactions on the initiating node when the processor is used.

The second set of bandwidth experiments involve multiple agents reading from a single region (for pull) or writing to a single region (for push). The purpose of these runs is to place a lot of stress on a single node's bus and memory controller. Table 3 shows the results. For these runs the amount of memory that each agent copies has been reduced to 1 or 2 KByte to allow multiple agents to access the same DRAM page.

Table 3: 4-node transfer bandwidths (multiple agents).

Type of transfer	Agents	Bandwidth [MByte/s]
local copy	4 processors	121
remote copy pull	4 processors	173
remote copy push	4 processors	141
remote copy pull	12 processors	359
remote copy push	12 processors	405
remote copy pull	3 mem copy	356
remote copy push	3 mem copy	428

For 4 processors copying from/to local memory, we are still limited by the read/write switching of the single memory controller. The resulting bandwidth is 121 MByte/s, hardly larger than the copy bandwidth achieved by a single processor. For the 4-processor remote cases, this restriction is lifted and we see a corresponding increase in copy bandwidth. However, the bandwidth is still considerable lower than what can be achieved with a single memory copy engine, because of the inefficiencies of using the processor for copying (described above). For the 12-processor remote cases, all processors in three nodes are copying to/from memory in the fourth node. With this arrangement, close to the 530 MByte/s full capacity of the processor bus can be attained (359 MByte/s for pull and 405 MByte/s for push). If the memory copy engines in the three nodes are used, the achieved bandwidth is very similar. In either case we are limited by the memory controller and processor bus in the target node.

In summary, the bandwidth experiments show that remote access does not present a bandwidth bottleneck, other than that induced by the combination of a larger remote latency and a limited number of operations outstanding in the processor. The memory copy engine does not have this problem and achieves about 4 to 6 times the transfer bandwidth of a processor.

6.4.3 Synchronization overhead

Synchronization overhead determines the grain size of parallelism that can be efficiently exploited in an application running on that machine. If synchronization overhead is very large (such as in typical message-passing architectures) good parallel speedup can be obtained only on applications that have very large independent grains of computation. Conversely, a low synchronization overhead allows parallelism to be exploited both for coarse- and fine-grain computations.

In order to assess what the synchronization overhead is, we run a simple program that simulates a central task queue. Processors obtain a task from the queue by doing an atomic fetch&increment on the task queue index. Each task is a spin loop of fixed size. The grain size of the tasks is adjusted by changing the length of the spin loop.

Let us first look at the synchronization overhead obtained when the task size is minimized (Figure 8). In this experiment, we are thus measuring the time it takes to pass the synchronization variable between processors. In the standard node with 4 processors on a snoopy bus, it takes on average 227 ns to synchronize and execute a null task. When we go to 8 processors connected via the Mercury interconnect, this number increases to 411 ns. Finally, with 16 processors, the synchronization overhead is 490 ns. The increase in synchronization overhead over the base node is only 81% for a 2-node system and slightly over a factor of 2 for a 4-node system.

Figure 8: Synchronization overhead.

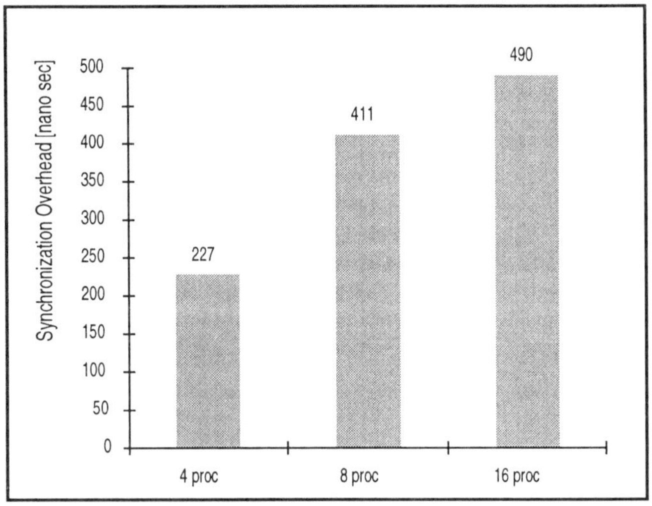

To find out what grain size is needed to obtain good speedup we now look at parallel efficiency as the grain size of the tasks is varied. For each run with a certain number of processors, only the task size is adjusted, while the number of tasks per processor remain constant. Parallel efficiency is calculated as:

$$\text{Efficiency (n procs)} = \frac{t_{\text{single proc}}}{t_{n \text{ procs}} \cdot n}$$

Where $t_{\text{single proc}}$ is the time needed to execute a task on a single processor, and $t_{n \text{ procs}}$ is the time needed to execute that task on n processors. The resulting efficiencies are shown in Figure 9.

The 4-processor runs show the synchronization overhead for a single node, i.e. the synchronization overhead of the snoopy coherence protocol on the processor bus. Above a grain size of about 0.8 µs, efficiency in excess of 80% is obtained. Smaller grain sizes lead to a rapid decrease in parallel efficiency. As we go to 8 processors, two effects reduce the parallel efficiency. The first is that the interconnect introduces extra synchronization latency (as shown above). However, there is an additional effect that reduces efficiency when increasing the number of processors, even if the synchronization overhead were to stay unchanged. This is due to the fact that the task throughput keeps increasing as the work is divided between more processors, while the synchronization overhead does not decrease. The net result of the two effects is that a task size of about 4 µs is needed to get to the 80% efficiency mark with 8 processors. For 16 processors, 80% efficiency is reached with 6 µs tasks. Overall, we see that while the larger systems require somewhat larger grain sizes to achieve good parallel efficiency, the growth in grain size is gradual. Even on the larger systems, good efficiency can be obtained on parallel codes that have a very small grain.

Figure 9: Parallel efficiency as a function of grain size.

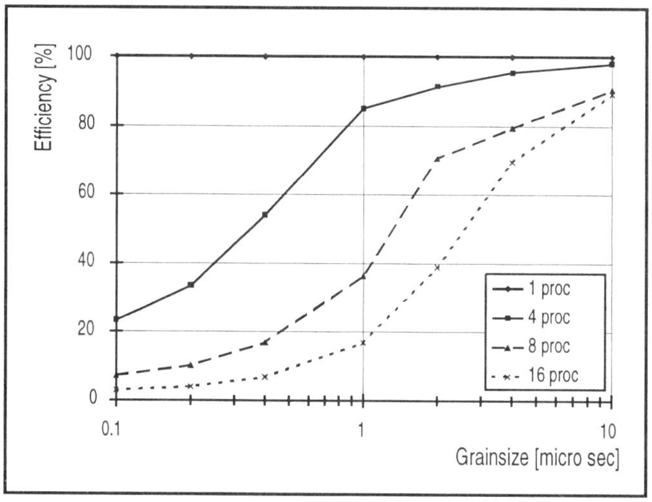

7 Comparison with related systems

Two other companies have recently presented machines that interconnect multiple quad Pentium® Pro nodes into a single shared-memory system: Sequent [8] and Data General [2]. These two systems are very similar to each other. They both use an SCI-based interconnect [3], a microcoded controller, and a large per-node cache. They differ primarily in the fact that Sequent uses a higher-performance SCI link implementation.

Comparing the amount of hardware used to connect the nodes together, we find that the SCI-based systems both use a large DRAM-based L3 (node-level) cache, several custom control and data path chips, and a large amount of SRAM and DRAM to hold coherence state/tag information. In contrast, the HAL S1 System uses a single custom chip and three standard 1 Mbit SRAMs.

The difference in the hardware required to link the nodes together is attributed primarily to the requirements of SCI. The coherence structures and protocol used by SCI are not a very good match to the snoopy coherence protocol of the Pentium® Pro bus. The cache line size is different (64 bytes instead of 32 bytes), and the processor caches do not implement the tags and links that SCI requires. The matching between the two protocols is done via a large L3 cache. This cache maintains inclusion of remote data with the processor caches on one side, and implements the SCI coherence structures on the other. The L3 cache is large (16 MByte or more) in order not to cause too many evictions from the L2 caches and to reduce the number of inter-node operations.

Figure 10 compares the remote latencies achieved by the different systems, and also includes the single-node local latencies for reference. The loaded latencies for the S1 System were obtained with a detailed analytical queueing model of the hardware, driven by a set of workload parameters that are representative of a transaction processing application. Both the Data General [2] and Sequent [9] loaded latencies are also for a transaction processing workload.

Figure 10: Remote latencies of different systems.

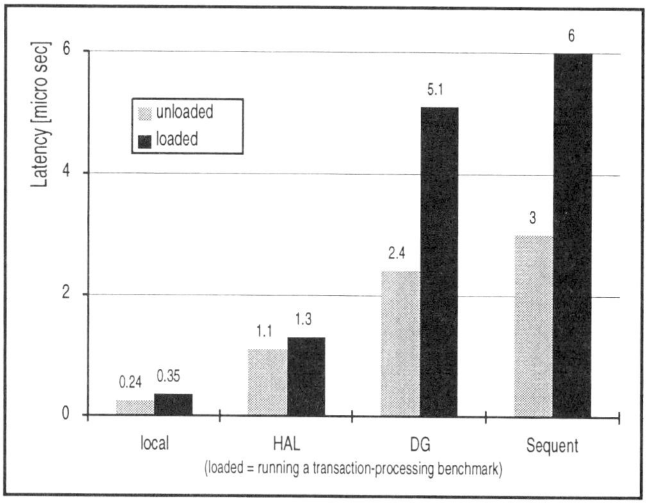

As seen in Figure 10, the unloaded remote latency of the S1 System is less than half of that of the Data General machine, and just over a third of that of the Sequent machine. When running a transaction processing benchmark the remote latency of the Data General machine degrades from the 2.4 µs unloaded number to 5.1 µs, while the Sequent machine degrades from 3 µs to 6 µs. In contrast, the S1 System remote latency increases only slightly from 1.1 µs to 1.3 µs. The link level is unlikely to be the culprit for the large latency in the SCI-based systems. In both of these machines the link transfer latency is only a small fraction of the overall remote latency [2, 8]. The majority of time is spent on protocol processing. Both Sequent and Data General decided to use a micro-coded processor to run the SCI coherence protocol. Not only does this coherence controller add significantly to the unloaded remote latency, but it can also become a major bottleneck in the system when the load increases. It likely accounts for the large difference between unloaded and loaded latency in the SCI-based systems. The S1 System, on the other hand, incorporates a hard-wired and pipelined protocol engine that is very tightly coupled to the snoopy bus of the node. The results are a low unloaded remote latency and very little latency degradation under loading.

For simplicity reasons, the S1 System does not include a per-node L3 cache. It is interesting to look at the average L2 miss latency to study the trade-off between the SCI-based systems that incorporate an L3 cache but have much longer remote latencies, versus the S1 System with shorter latencies but no L3 cache. The key parameter that determines this trade-off is the fraction of L2 misses that are satisfied locally (i.e. by local memory or the L3 cache) called the *locality fraction.* Figure 11 plots equivalent average L2 latency (i.e. equivalent performance) for different locality fractions in the S1 System and the Data General system. For this graph, the following L2 miss penalties are used: 350 ns (local), 1.3 µs (remote S1), 5.1 µs (remote DG).

We see that for a locality fraction of 80% in the Data General system, a locality fraction of 0% (i.e. all remote) achieves the same performance in the S1 System. For points below a locality fraction of 80%, the Data General system cannot match S1 System performance. For a transaction processing workload, Data General expects the locality fraction with L3 cache to be about 90% [2], yielding an average L2 miss latency of 825 ns. The estimate for a similar workload on the S1 System is a 60% locality fraction[1], leading to an average L2 miss latency of 730 ns. Even though the S1 System has no L3 cache, it achieves about 12% better memory system performance. It is unlikely that the SCI-based systems can improve their performance by increasing the L3 cache size, because these caches are already very large and most misses are likely to be coherence misses.

Figure 11: Locality fractions for equal performance.

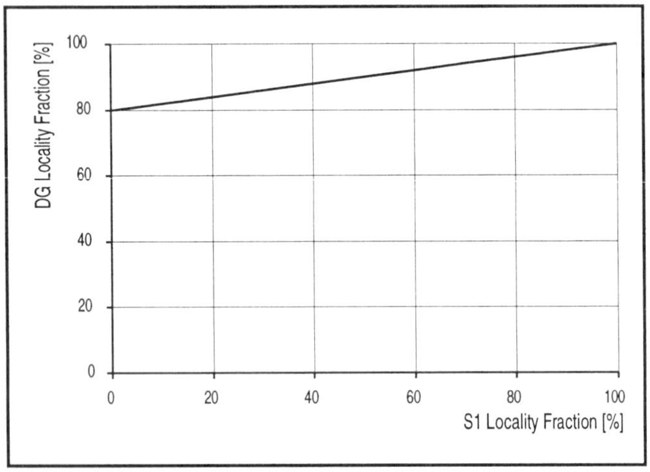

Looking at raw interconnect bandwidth, Data General uses dual SCI rings for a total bandwidth of 1 GByte/s. Sequent uses a single, higher performance ring which also achieves 1 GByte/s. By comparison, a 4-node S1 System built with a single Router has an interconnect bandwidth of 6.4 GBytes/s. The interconnect fabric itself is unlikely to become a bottleneck in either system: in the SCI-based systems the coherence controller is likely to throttle traffic, and in the S1 System the processor buses remain the bottleneck.

8 Scalability of the Mercury Architecture

The original goal of the Mercury Interconnect Architecture was to allow the construction of systems with several hundreds of nodes. Different layers of the interconnect architecture impose different limits to the building of large-scale systems. This section discusses these scaling limits from the lowest to the highest interconnect layer.

At the lowest level, one of the most important parameters is the physical length of a link. The length of a link is limited by two factors: the electrical properties of the chosen implementation technology, and the buffering/flow-control strategies required to support the round-trip latency resulting from the physical link length. The S1 link implementation allows for 2 m links at a bandwidth of 1.6 GByte/s per direction. The primary limits to increasing this length are inter-bit skew margins and signal attenuation over the cable. The flow control scheme of the Mercury Architecture guarantees that the full link bandwidth can be attained, as long as enough receiver-side input buffers are provided. If either the link length or bandwidth are increased, the number of buffers has to be increased to keep up. The current implementation uses 6 input buffers, and the architecture supports up to 32.

Routing also presents a scaling limit. The FFM frame header that holds the route contains up to 60 bits of routing information. The implementation has some flexibility on the use of these routing bits. In the S1 System, routing steps are 3 bits each (6-ported router) and there is a limit of at most 10 steps per route. This places an upper limit of several thousand nodes for a star-like topology. Topologies with high bisection bandwidths, such as meshes and hypercubes, can support several hundred nodes.

Source routing requires each node to store a route to all of the other nodes in the system. The size of each node's routing table thus grows linearly with the total nodes in the system. At first glance this may appear to be a severe scalability limit. However, the amount of storage required per node is very small. In the S1 System, the routing table entries are 30 bits wide. By limiting the system to a maximum of 32 nodes, the amount of storage required per node is only 120 bytes.

The table holding per node-pair sequence numbers scales in the same manner as the routing table. In the S1 System, 128 bytes of storage is required for this table.

Reliable node-to-node communication requires each node to keep a copy of all packets sent until an acknowledgment arrives from the receiver. The number of transmission buffers required for full-bandwidth transmission grows linearly with the link bandwidth and the acknowledgment latency of the network. In the S1 System, 10 transmission buffers are required. Since each packet can be at most 48 bytes in size, the transmission buffers take up 480 bytes of storage.

At the ISM layer, the cache coherence directory limits the number of nodes in a cache-coherent group. The processors used in the S1 System have a 32-bit virtual address space. We thus decided to limit the number of nodes sharing memory to 4 (16 processors), believing that there is not much of a market for larger shared-memory systems using this processor. By limiting a cache-coherent group to 4 nodes, we were able to use a very simple bit-vector scheme for the coherence directory. More complicated, scalable directory organizations exist [7], so Mercury Architecture shared-memory systems with several hundreds of processors are feasible.

In this section we have discussed the scaling limits of the Mercury Architecture and its first implementation. While the S1 System is limited to 32 nodes total, and up to 4 nodes per cache-coherent group, these limits are features of the implementation. The fundamental limits of the architecture allow for much larger systems.

9 Summary

The Mercury Interconnect Architecture was developed as an infrastructure for high-performance multiprocessor systems constructed out of commodity microprocessors, memory and I/O components. The first implementation uses two custom VLSI components to connect multiple standard 4-processor Pentium® Pro SMPs into large shared-memory and/or message-passing multiprocessors.

1. This number was derived by taking a cache miss trace of a transaction processing workload and dividing the misses into the following categories: code, private data, and shared data. Code and private data are assumed to be always local while shared data is distributed randomly.

The interconnect achieves very low latencies and high communication bandwidths. For a 4-node (16-processor) shared-memory system, the remote memory access latency is just over 1 µs which is about 4 times as long as the local access latency. The use of a hard-wired and pipelined protocol engine ensures that there is very little latency increase when a load is applied. The maximum interconnect bandwidth is 1.6 GByte/s per link per direction and 9.6 GByte/s through a single Router. In the S1 System the interconnect utilization is thus expected to be very low, yielding good predictable performance.

Our goal of flexibility and scalability in the interconnect is achieved by the modular nature of the interconnect, using the cascadable 6-port Router, and allowing free topologies. A small and cheap interconnect can be made up of a single Router, while large systems can grow to accommodate up to 32 nodes. If a suitable topology (such as a hypercube or mesh) is used, bandwidth increases as the size of the interconnect is scaled up. At the same time, latency through the interconnect increases very slowly, because the Router fall-through latency is only 42 ns.

The Mercury Interconnect features reliable transport of data between nodes, allows multiple redundant paths between nodes, and supports hot-plug capability of interconnect links. These features make it a good infrastructure for commercial multi-processing servers.

We believe cost-effectiveness has been achieved in the implementation of the interconnect. The Router is a single-chip solution built out of standard CMOS. Similarly, the MCU is a complete single-chip bridge between the Pentium® Pro bus and the Mercury Interconnect. For coherent operation the only additional hardware required are three off-the-shelf 1 Mbit SRAM chips.

Comparison with Pentium® Pro based systems using an SCI interconnect shows that the S1 System achieves a higher performance while utilizing a fraction of the hardware required by these other systems.

Acknowledgments

The work presented here was the result of the co-operation of many individuals at HAL, too numerous to mention here. The authors would like to acknowledge the hard work of the Router and MCU teams that have turned this architecture into reality, and the integration team for all those hours spent in the lab. Special thanks goes to Frank Chen whose unwavering commitment and effort enabled real hardware to see the light of day.

References

[1] L. Censier and P. Feautrier. A New Solution to Coherence Problems in Multicache Systems. *IEEE Transactions on Computers* C-27, 12 (December 1978), pages 1112-1118.

[2] R. Clark and K. Alnes. An SCI Interconnect Chipset and Adapter. In *Symposium Record, Hot Interconnects IV*, pages 221-235, August 1996.

[3] IEEE Computer Society. *IEEE Standard for Scalable Coherent Interface (SCI)*, IEEE Standard 1596-1992, New York, August 1993.

[4] Intel. *Pentium® Pro Family Developer's Manual Volume 3: Operating System Writer's Guide*. Intel Corporation, 1996.

[5] D. Lenoski, J. Laudon, K. Gharachorloo, A. Gupta, and J. Hennessy. The Directory-Based Cache Coherence Protocol for the DASH Multiprocessor. In *Proceedings of the 17th International Symposium on Computer Architecture*, pages 148-159, May 1990.

[6] D. Lenoski, J. Laudon, K. Gharachorloo, W.-D. Weber, A. Gupta, J. Hennessy, M. Horowitz, and M. Lam. The Stanford DASH Multiprocessor. In *IEEE Computer* 25, 3 (March 1992), pages 63-79.

[7] D. Lenoski and W.-D. Weber. *Scalable Shared-Memory Multiprocessing*. Morgan Kaufmann Publishers, San Francisco, CA, 1995.

[8] T. Lovett and R. Clapp. STiNG: A CC-NUMA Computer System for the Commercial Marketplace. In *Proceedings of the 23rd International Symposium on Computer Architecture*, pages 308-317, May 1996.

[9] T. Lovett and R. Clapp. Private correspondence, February 1997.

[10] A. Mu, B. Chia, S. Kondapalli, C. Koo, J. Larson, L. Nguyen, R. Sastry, Y. Satsukawa, H.-C. Shih, T. Wicki, C. Wu, K. Yu, and X. Zhang. A 285 MHz 6-port Plesiochronous Router Chip with Non-Blocking Cross-Bar Switch. In *1996 Symposium on VLSI Circuits: Digest of Technical Papers*, pages 136-137, 1996.

[11] A. Mu, J. Larson, R. Sastry, T. Wicki, and W. Wilcke. A 9.6 GigaByte/s Throughput Plesiochronous Routing Chip. In *Digest of Papers of the 41st IEEE Computer Society International Conference (Compcon)*, pages 261-266, February 1996.

[12] W.-D. Weber. *Scalable Directories for Cache-Coherent Shared-Memory Multiprocessors*. Ph.D. Thesis, Stanford University, January 1993. Also available as Stanford University Technical Report CSL-TR-93-557.

The Design and Analysis of a Cache Architecture for Texture Mapping

Ziyad S. Hakura and Anoop Gupta

Computer Systems Laboratory
Stanford University
Stanford, CA 94305

Abstract

The effectiveness of texture mapping in enhancing the realism of computer generated imagery has made support for real-time texture mapping a critical part of graphics pipelines. Despite a recent surge in interest in three-dimensional graphics from computer architects, high-quality high-speed texture mapping has so far been confined to costly hardware systems that use brute-force techniques to achieve high performance. One obstacle faced by designers of texture mapping systems is the requirement of extremely high bandwidth to texture memory. High bandwidth is necessary since there are typically tens to hundreds of millions of accesses to texture memory per second. In addition, to achieve the high clock rates required in graphics pipelines, low-latency access to texture memory is needed. In this paper, we propose the use of texture image caches to alleviate the above bottlenecks, and evaluate various tradeoffs that arise in such designs.

We find that the factors important to cache behavior are (i) the representation of texture images in memory, (ii) the rasterization order on screen and (iii) the cache organization. Through a detailed investigation of these issues, we explore the best way to exploit locality of reference and determine whether this technique is robust with respect to different scenes and different amounts of texture. Overall, we observe that there is a significant amount of temporal and spatial locality and that the working set sizes are relatively small (at most 16KB) across all cases that we studied. Consequently, the memory bandwidth requirements of a texture cache system are substantially lower (at least three times and as much as fifteen times) than the memory bandwidth requirements of a system which achieves equivalent performance but does not utilize a cache. These results are very encouraging and indicate that caching is a promising approach to designing memory systems for texture mapping.

1 Introduction

Computer graphics is becoming an increasingly important application. Consequently, there has been much interest from designers of general-purpose microprocessors, media processors, and specialized hardware to provide cost-effective real-time computer graphics capabilities. Examples of recent developments in this area are the Visual Instruction Set (VIS) in UltraSPARC™ [16] and FBRAM [18] from Sun Microsystems, MMX™ Technology [19] and Accelerated Graphics Port (AGP) [1] from Intel Corporation, Magic Carpet [12] from MIPS Technologies, and Talisman [13] from Microsoft Corporation. In this paper, we focus on one challenging aspect of graphics architecture, the design of a memory system for texture mapping.

The mapping of images onto the surfaces of three-dimensional objects is known as texture mapping. Texture mapping has earned the role of a fundamental drawing primitive for its ability to substantially enhance the realism and visual complexity of computer-generated imagery [23, 22]. Examples of this technique include the mapping of a 2D color image of a wooden texture to the surface of a guitar, a road image to a highway, or a grassy plot image to a mountain. In addition to the mapping of surface color [5], texture mapping has been used for mapping a myriad of other surface parameters including reflection of the environment [21], bumps [9], transparency [7], and shadows [20, 25].

One characteristic of texture mapping is that texture images often require large amounts of memory (typically in the range of a few megabytes to tens of megabytes). The amount of memory is dependent upon the number of textures in a scene and the size of each texture. It is generally accepted that the usefulness of texture mapping hardware increases with the amount of memory dedicated for textures. Another characteristic of texture mapping is that it requires many calculations and texture lookups. This characteristic causes it to be the main performance bottleneck in graphics pipelines. For each screen pixel (fragment) that is textured, the calculations consist of generating texture addresses, filtering multiple texture samples to avoid aliasing artifacts, and modulating the texture color with the pixel color. (Throughout this paper we will use the terms *fragment* and *screen pixel* interchangeably.) Since the number of fragments that are textured can be quite large (typically tens to hundreds of millions per second), and each textured fragment requires multiple texture lookups (usually 8), the memory bandwidth requirements to texture memory can be very large (typically several gigabytes per second). In addition, to achieve the high clock rates required in graphics pipelines, low-latency access to texture memory is needed.

The Silicon Graphics' RealityEngine [14] is an example of a high-end parallel graphics architecture that can support real-time texture mapping. This system uses multiple engines (also called fragment generators) for texture mapping fragments. Each engine has an 8-way banked DRAM memory system that is dedicated for textures (total 16 MB), and can perform eight independent texture lookups in parallel. Since there are multiple fragment generators (between 5 and 20) and each one has its own dedicated memory, the texture images must be replicated in each memory. One problem with this architecture is that an application running on a 20 fragment generator system is limited to 16 MB of unique memory for textures even though there is a total of 320 MB of texture memory in the system. Therefore, the domain of applications that can utilize the texture mapping hardware is constrained by the limited amount of unique memory.

An alternative approach for providing fast texture accesses and high bandwidths is to use an SRAM cache with each fragment generator instead of a dedicated DRAM memory. The premise of this idea is that there is a substantial amount of locality of refer-

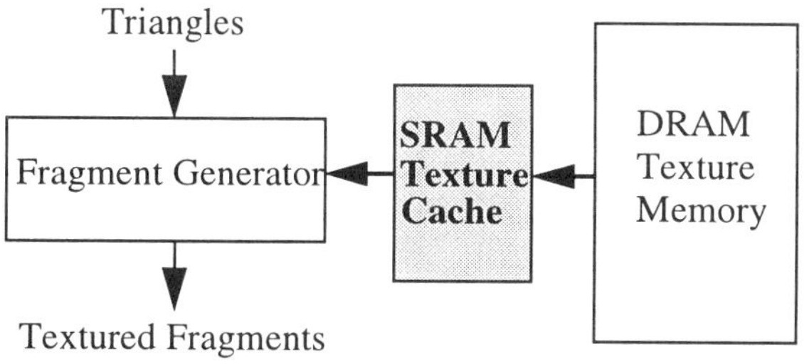

FIGURE 2.1. Block diagram of texture mapping hardware.

ence in texture mapped scenes. Thus, the cache size can be relatively small compared to a dedicated memory. The cache would be backed by a shared pool of DRAM. One advantage of this solution is that there is no need for texture replication for each fragment generator and the amount of unique memory for textures can be much larger. Another advantage is that the lower cost of a small cache compared to a much larger dedicated memory makes this architecture more scalable. A final advantage is that the latency of access to texture memory can be much lower and the access bandwidth can be substantially higher due to the use of SRAM.

In this paper, we focus on a system that uses a single fragment generator and study the implications of a texture cache on memory bandwidth and rendering performance. Particularly important to the cache behavior are the representation of textures in memory, the rasterization order on screen and the cache organization. Through a detailed investigation of these three issues, we explore the best way to exploit temporal and spatial locality and determine whether this technique is robust with respect to different scenes and different amounts of texture. It is interesting to note that current graphics pipelines do not use caches for texture mapping and no serious evaluations have been published. Our simulation indicates that there is a significant amount of temporal and spatial locality and that the working set sizes are relatively small (at most 16KB) across all cases that we studied. As a result, we find that even small caches of 32KB can offer substantial cost/performance benefits. With respect to the representation of textures in memory, we find that a blocked representation is required to fully exploit spatial locality and to avoid any dependency on the orientation of textures as they appear on the screen. When the texture images are large, the image arrays must be either padded or blocked at a coarser level to avoid conflicts between texture blocks. Finally, we find that a tiled rasterization order is useful for reducing the working set size and for avoiding conflicts between texture blocks.

The remainder of the paper is structured as follows. The next section provides background information on texture mapping. The motivation for a texture cache and its potential benefits are described in Section 3. Section 4 explains our experimental methodology and describes the benchmarks used in the study. Section 5 introduces two representations of textures in memory and evaluates their miss rate characteristics and interactions with the cache organization. Section 6 introduces tiled rasterization and evaluates its effect on working set size and conflict misses. Section 7 relates the miss rate results from Section 5 and Section 6 to memory bandwidth and rendering performance. Finally, Section 8 summarizes the results and presents conclusions.

2 Background

To understand where texture mapping fits in a real-time rendering system, we briefly describe the four major functions of a traditional graphics pipeline [11]: geometry processing, fragment generation, hidden surface removal, and framebuffer display. The 3D geometries of scenes are commonly defined in terms of triangles. In the first stage, matrix transformations are applied to the triangle vertices, resulting in a perspective mapping of the triangles to the 2D display. The second stage is fragment generation consisting of rasterization, shading, and texture mapping of fragments. The third stage is hidden surface removal, accomplished using a z-buffer algorithm and the final stage is the display of the rendered image stored in the framebuffer.

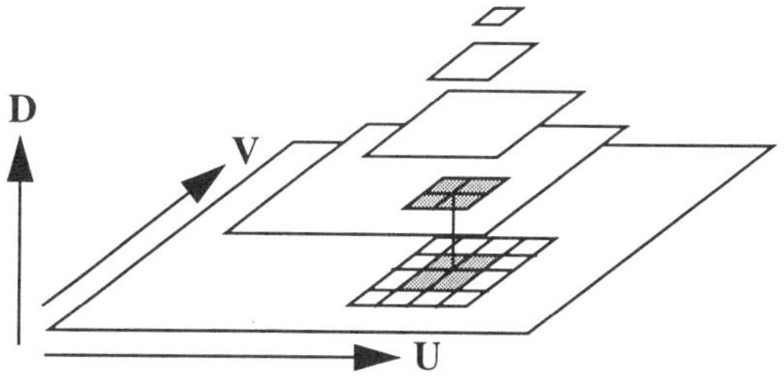

FIGURE 2.2. Illustration of a Mip Map. Eight texels (shaded) from two adjacent levels of the pyramid are used in a Trilinear Interpolation.

Of the four stages in a graphics pipeline, we are primarily interested in the second stage. A block diagram of the second stage is shown in Figure 2.1. The fragment generator is responsible for rasterizing the input triangles into fragments and performing the shading and texture mapping calculations. Rasterization involves interpolating screen coordinates, depth, texture coordinates and shading color across the surface of each triangle, and identifying the screen pixels (also called fragments) that lie inside the triangles. The color applied to the fragments is usually a function of both the shading and texture mapping calculations. Before we can describe how the fragments are texture mapped, we must first discuss the concept of Mip Mapping.

The goal of Mip Mapping, introduced by Williams [15], is to efficiently avoid aliasing artifacts by quickly filtering the texture image. It involves representing a texture as an image pyramid as illustrated in Figure 2.2. The bottommost level of the pyramid is the original texture image and each subsequent level is a filtered and down-sampled version of the previous level. Consider an example in which a texture mapped triangle is being viewed from far away, so that there is low resolution of image details. In this case, an area of texture can be represented by one screen pixel. Instead of re-filtering the image based on the level-of-detail required, we can use the pre-computed image from the appropriate level of the Mip Map. Each level of the Mip Map corresponds to a particular screen pixel to texture pixel ratio, where a screen pixel refers to the pixel on the screen itself and texture pixel, or *texel*, refers to the pixel in the texture image being depicted on the screen.

When applying texture, we compute the texture coordinates (u,v) and the screen pixel to texel ratio d. In practice, the u,v, and d coordinates do not exactly map to a single texel. Consequently, we must take the weighted average of the eight texels closest to the (u,v,d) coordinates, four texels each from the two levels whose d values most closely approximate the desired d value. This is known as trilinear interpolation. A special case arises if the screen pixel to texel ratio is less than one. This occurs when a texture mapped triangle is being viewed from very close and causes the original texture image to be magnified. In this case, we take the weighted average of the four texels closest to the (u,v) coordinates in the bottommost level of the image pyramid. This is known as bilinear interpolation. The result of the trilinear or bilinear interpolation is usually modulated with the color computed from the shading calculations to obtain the final color for the textured fragment.

In summary, the fragment generator is responsible for rasteriz-

Phase of Fragment Generator Computation	Precision	Add/Subtract/ Shift	Multiply	Divide	Number of Texture Memory Accesses
Per Triangle Setup	Fixed/Floating	89	64	1	-
Per Fragment Rasterization and Shading	Fixed/Floating	11		1	-
Level-of-detail, d	Fixed/Floating	9	9		-
Texel coordinates nearest (u,v,d)	Fixed Integer	5 14	5		-
Texel address calculation	Integer	Dependent upon Memory Representation. See Section 5.			-
Trilinear Interpolation/ Bilinear Interpolation	Fixed	56 24	28 12		8 4
Modulation with fragment color	Fixed	8	4		-

TABLE 2.1. Computational costs of the operations of a fragment generator. Apart from triangle setup, all the costs are on a per fragment basis.

ing triangles into fragments, computing level-of-detail and Mip Map texture addresses for each fragment, filtering the texels that are accessed using either trilinear or bilinear interpolation, and finally applying the texture color to the fragments. Typical unoptimized computational costs for each of the operations of a fragment generator are shown in Table 2.1. Since these costs are quite high, fragment generators often exploit deep pipelining and parallelism. In fact, most of the costs are incurred by texture mapping.

3 Texture Cache: Motivation and Benefits

In this section, we identify the types of locality of reference that are present in texture accesses and discuss the benefits of adding an SRAM texture cache between the fragment generator and DRAM texture memory.

3.1 Locality of Reference in Texture Mapping

The effectiveness of a memory hierarchy depends on locality of reference in data accesses. Both spatial and temporal locality are present in texture mapping.

3.1.1 Spatial Locality

The representation of textures as Mip Maps contributes to spatial locality in texture accesses. The Mip Map accesses have a high degree of spatial locality since the level of the map is selected to closely match the level-of-detail that is being drawn on the screen. In essence, this means that movements of one pixel in screen space roughly correspond to movements of one texel in texture space, hence the spatial locality in texture space. The spatial locality in Mip Map accesses is thus present irrespective of the scene.

3.1.2 Temporal Locality

Temporal locality in accesses to texture data is present when rendering a single frame and between consecutive frames. We generally do not expect our caches to exploit temporal locality between consecutive frames because the cache sizes that we consider are much smaller than the amount of texture data that is typically used by a single frame. Between memory and disk, however, this kind of temporal locality is of interest. Within a single frame, two types of temporal locality are present: locality arising from overlap of accesses needed for filtering between neighboring fragments and locality arising from repeated texture. Below, we discuss each of these two types of temporal locality in more detail.

Overlap of Accesses between Neighboring Fragments

Temporal locality is present between the texel accesses of neighboring fragments. Since each textured fragment must access multiple texels for trilinear or bilinear interpolation, it is expected that some of these accesses will overlap with the texel accesses of neighboring fragments. We measured the average number of accesses per texel made by a spatially contiguous group of fragments across all four benchmark scenes, which are described in Section 4. The results for trilinear interpolation (lower level), trilinear interpolation (upper level) and bilinear interpolation are 4, 14 and 18, respectively. For trilinear interpolation, we distinguish between texel accesses that are to the more detailed level, lower level, and the less detailed level, upper level, of the two adjacent levels of the Mip Map that are used in the interpolation. These results clearly show that the texels in the upper level of a trilinear interpolation are accessed a larger number of times than the texels in the lower level. Since the lower level is more detailed than the upper level, it is traversed more rapidly and this leads to fewer accesses per texel. In general, we expect texels in the lower level of a trilinear interpolation to be accessed an average of four times and the texels in the upper level to be accessed an average of sixteen times. For bilinear interpolation, the number of accesses per texel is directly related to the amount of texture magnification and this can vary widely depending on the scene.

Repeated Texture

Temporal locality is also present when a texture is repeated across the surface of an object. An example application is a wall that is textured by repeating a 2D texture image of an individual brick. Since the amount of repetition is a function of the texture coordinates defined in the high-level geometric description of the scene, this type of temporal locality is very scene dependent. We measured the average number of times a texel is repeated in the benchmark scenes. The results for the Town, Guitar, Goblet and Flight scenes are 2.9, 1.7, 1.1 and 1.0 times, respectively.

3.2 Texture Cache Benefits

The evolution of DRAM technology motivates the use of an SRAM texture cache. The rapid growth in DRAM density has meant that fewer DRAM chips are needed to construct a memory of a fixed size. The use of higher density memory chips has led to a decline in bandwidth per Megabyte of memory [24]. An SRAM texture cache can exploit locality of reference to hide most of the texture accesses from reaching memory, thus lowering the bandwidth requirements.

Another reason for adding an SRAM cache is that block transfers of cache lines between the cache and memory make it possible to get the most bandwidth out of the memory. Present-day DRAM architectures are optimized for long burst transfers to microprocessor caches since this amortizes the setup costs of the transfer over many bytes and leads to the most efficient memory bus utilization.

A third reason for having an SRAM texture cache is that static memories typically have shorter access latencies than dynamic memories. The SRAM cache can be tightly coupled with the fragment generator which makes it possible to run the fragment generator at higher clock rates. This is an incentive for integrating the SRAM cache onto the same chip as the fragment generator.

Finally, a recent trend in computer graphics has been the use of rendered images as textures [3]. As a result, it has become desirable to unify the framebuffer and texture memories to avoid copy-

Scene	Image Resolution (Pixels)	Number of Triangles	Average Triangle Area (Pixels)	Average Triangle Width (Pixels)	Average Triangle Height (Pixels)	Number of Textures	Texture Storage (MB)	Texture Used (MB)	Texture Used (%)	Pixels Textured (millions)
Flight	1280x1024	9152	294	38	20	15	56	6.3	11%	1.4
Town	1280x1024	5317	1149	67	23	51	4.7	1.8	38%	2.1
Guitar	800x800	719	1867	72	94	8	4.9	1.1	23%	0.7
Goblet	800x800	7200	41	25	14	1	1.4	0.78	56%	0.3

TABLE 4.1. Texture Mapping Benchmarks.

ing data between the two. A fragment generator connected to an SRAM texture cache does not necessarily require a dedicated texture memory. This makes it possible to fetch the texture data as it is needed from whichever DRAM buffer it is stored in. In fact, multiple fragment generators can share the same DRAM memory system and no cache coherence is needed since the texture data is mostly read-only. The caches can be flushed if necessary when the textures change.

The organization of the texture cache is characterized by three parameters: cache size, line size and associativity. The choice of cache size is related to the working set sizes of texture mapped scenes. The line size depends on the amount of spatial locality that can be exploited. As noted earlier, larger line sizes can elicit a larger fraction of the peak memory bandwidth. Finally, the cache associativity is related to the kinds of conflicts that can occur.

4 Methodology

Doing performance studies for graphics architectures is a difficult endeavour. The primary reasons are the lack of well-established benchmark programs and the lack of tools for obtaining traces of graphics commands. In this section, we discuss how we address these and additional issues.

4.1 Simulation Environment

The simulation environment consists of three components. The first component is a software implementation of a three-dimensional polygonal graphics pipeline. This is responsible for geometry, clipping, lighting of vertices, rasterization, shading, texture mapping and finally Z-buffering. The pipeline is similar to the one described in [14]. Specifically, the texture mapping implementation is based on the OpenGL specification document [17]. Since the pipeline is implemented in software, we can easily experiment with different representations of texture in memory and can rasterize the triangles in either the horizontal or vertical direction. The textures are assigned memory using the malloc() system call and we allocate 32 bits per texel. The triangles are rasterized in the same order that they are specified in the input.

The second component is a capability to trace the GL calls that are made by a graphics application while it is running in real-time on a hardware-based renderer. This was done using a standard utility program called gldebug, intended for debugging GL programs, and a parser that parses the GL calls while the application is running. This technique can be applied to any binary executable that makes GL calls. The trace is then fed to our software implementation of the graphics pipeline which executes equivalent procedures and generates images as output. The images allow us to verify that the interpretation of the trace is accurate.

The third component is a trace-driven cache simulator that can model different cache sizes, line sizes and associativities. Whenever the software-based fragment generator accesses a texel from memory, it also makes a call to the cache simulator passing the address of the texel as a parameter. The cache simulator runs concurrently with the graphics pipeline.

4.2 Benchmarks

We study four benchmarks that are applications of color texture mapping. The characteristics of these benchmarks are summarized in Table 4.1. Because the cache sizes that we consider are much smaller than the amount of texture used in each benchmark, we do not expect to exploit temporal locality between consecutive frames. For this reason, we have selected a single frame per benchmark.

The first two benchmarks, shown in Figure 4.1 and Figure 4.2, are taken from the Silicon Graphics Reality Engine Demo Suite and are representative of present-day applications of texture mapping. The Flight scene, shown in Figure 4.1, uses several 1024x1024 pixel satellite images as textures and maps these textures onto a geometric model of the terrain. An important characteristic of the Flight scene is that it has large variations in level-of-detail as a result of the mountainous terrain. In comparison, the Town scene, shown in Figure 4.2, maps many smaller textures onto flat surfaces and these textures appear upright in the image of the scene. The Guitar scene, shown in Figure 4.3, is another application where textures are mapped onto flat surfaces. It differs from the Town scene in that the textures are larger and they do not appear uniformly oriented in the image of the scene. Finally, the fourth benchmark, shown in Figure 4.4, consists of a single texture wrapped around a goblet. The Goblet benchmark is characterized by its use of small triangles to make up the curved surface and by the variations in level-of-detail that occur when the surface becomes 90 degrees to the viewing angle. In all four benchmarks, the textures are stored as Mip Maps and trilinear interpolation is used for filtering the images.

5 Representation of Texture Maps in Memory

The representation of texture maps in memory is important to the cache behavior because it effects where texture data is placed in the cache. In this section, we study the interaction between the texture representation and the parameters of the cache organization. We examine two representations: a Nonblocked representation and a Blocked representation.

5.1 Previous Work

In [15], Williams also described a clever memory organization and addressing scheme for two-dimensional textures which is illustrated in Figure 5.1(a). At each level of the pyramid, the image is separated into its red, green, and blue color components. The filtered and down-sampled levels of the pyramid are stored above and to the left of their predecessor levels. Once the u, v, and d coordinates are calculated, indexing the Mip Map is a simple matter that involves binary operations since the individual images are sampled at powers of two.

Although this representation makes addressing very inexpensive, it is prone to several problems from a caching perspective. The most serious problem is that the individual color components

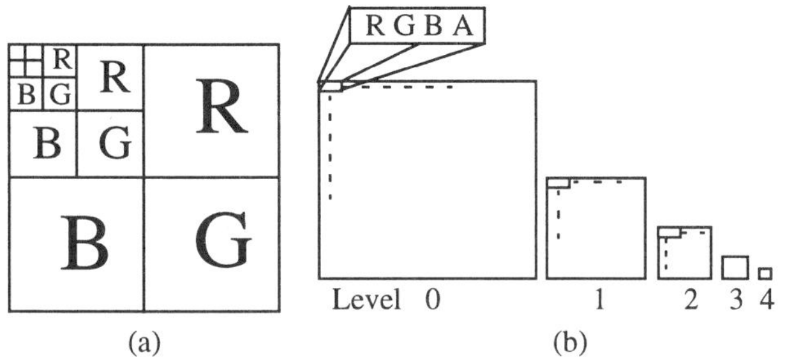

FIGURE 5.1. (a) Mip Map representation proposed by Williams. (b) Base nonblocked representation.

of a texel are always separated by powers of two bytes in memory since the texture image dimensions are powers of two. (Note that in most graphics libraries including OpenGL, the texture image dimensions are either restricted to be powers of two or the images are padded so that the dimensions are powers of two.) Thus, it is very likely that the individual color components will map to the same line in the cache resulting in conflicts. Another problem is that the representation does not exploit spatial locality that would be present if the color components were stored contiguously in the same cache line. Finally, since the image is separated by component, reading a texel from the cache requires three separate accesses with tag comparisons for each access.

5.2 Base Nonblocked Representation

An alternative representation is illustrated in Figure 5.1(b). In this representation, the red, green, blue and alpha components are stored contiguously. Each level of the pyramid is represented by its own two-dimensional array and each array is stored in row-major order. We will consider this representation as the base representation for the remainder of this paper since it is not prone to the problems mentioned previously.

5.2.1 Texel Addressing

The main advantage of the base representation is that it requires the fewest number of addressing calculations. The addressing calculations, shown below, assume that the dimensions of the texture arrays are powers of two. The texel addressing calculations must be performed eight times per fragment since a trilinear interpolation requires eight texture samples.

All variables are a function of the Mip Map level.
tu, **tv**: texel u- and v-coordinates
base: starting address of 2D texture array
lw: $\log_2$(width of 2D texture array in pixels)

Texel address = base + (tv << lw) + tu

5.2.2 Cold Misses

Cold misses cannot be avoided and so they represent the lower bound for miss rates in the cache. Figure 5.2 shows graphs of miss rate versus cache size measured for fully associative caches with an LRU replacement policy. These graphs assume a line size of 32 bytes and fully associative caches so that we can ignore conflict misses. We study the effect of line size on cold misses and defer the discussion of conflict misses to Section 5.3.3.

Cold misses typically occur in two places: along triangle edges where the textures are first accessed, and in the interior of large triangles when the texture accesses cross cache line boundaries. The cold miss rates can be deduced from the miss rates for the large caches since they do not include capacity misses. (Note that the cold miss rates are the same regardless of whether rasterization is horizontal or vertical; we discuss the effect of rasterization direction on working set size in Section 5.2.3). The cold miss rates for the Town, Guitar, Goblet and Flight scenes are 0.55%, 0.87%, 1.5%, and 2.8% respectively. These miss rates are quite low considering that the line size of 32 bytes holds just eight texels.

One factor that contributes to differences in cold miss rate is the amount of temporal locality in the form of repeated texture. As previously noted in Section 3.1.2, the amount of repetition of textures is very scene dependent. Another factor is the frequency of changes in level-of-detail across the surfaces that are textured. In the Town and Guitar scenes, the surfaces are predominantly flat causing the variations in level-of-detail to be gradual. As a result, we find that a large fraction of each line of texture data that is fetched into the cache is used. In comparison, the mountainous terrain in the Flight scene causes frequent changes in level-of-detail. Consequently, the accesses are fragmented across different levels of the Mip Map and a smaller fraction of each line of texture data that is fetched into the cache is used. Since more lines are needed for texturing, the cold miss rates are higher.

We also measured the cold miss rates for caches with a larger 128 byte line size. The results for the Town, Guitar, Goblet and Flight scenes are 0.15%, 0.25%, 0.42%, and 1.1% respectively. We see that the cold miss rates are much reduced with increasing line size, indicating the presence of substantial spatial locality.

5.2.3 Working Set Size

The working set size is a measure of the amount of data that is actively in use at a particular time. Most applications have a hierarchy of working sets [6]. In a graph of miss rate versus cache size, the different levels of the working set hierarchy can be seen as plateaus followed by sharp reductions in miss rate at particular cache sizes.

One can consider the coarsest level of the working set hierarchy in texture mapping to consist of all the texture data required to render an image. The *Principle of Texture Thrift* [4] defines the minimum amount of data required to render an image:

Given a scene consisting of textured 3D surfaces, the amount of texture information minimally required to render an image of the scene is proportional to the resolution of the image and is independent of the number of surfaces and the size of the textures.

This principle is a consequence of the fact that each pixel of the image can represent at most one filtered sample of texture. The advantage of representing textures in the form of Mip Maps is that the amount of data used in filtering for each pixel is fixed regardless of the level-of-detail.

We are interested in understanding the makeup of the first significant working set because it corresponds to the smallest cache size that one would consider using for caching texture images. We are also interested in making a worst-case estimate of the size of the first significant working set to generalize our analysis beyond the benchmarks that we study. We define the first significant working set as the first level of the working set hierarchy and begin by noting that a triangle is rasterized one scan line at a time, where a scan line consists of either a horizontal or vertical span of pixels in screen space. We assume for our worst-case analysis that the triangle being rasterized is large and spans the entire area of the screen. We have shown that there is spatial and temporal locality in the accesses to texture data, especially by accesses from adjacent scan lines. A cache that is large enough to hold the texture data needed for an entire scan line can exploit such localities of reference to significantly reduce miss rates. Thus, we see that the first level working set consists of the texture data needed for an entire scan line, and a significant reduction in miss rate occurs when the cache is large enough to hold this working set. Two parameters that can place a bound on the worst-case working set size are the texture image size and the screen size. If the texture image size is less than

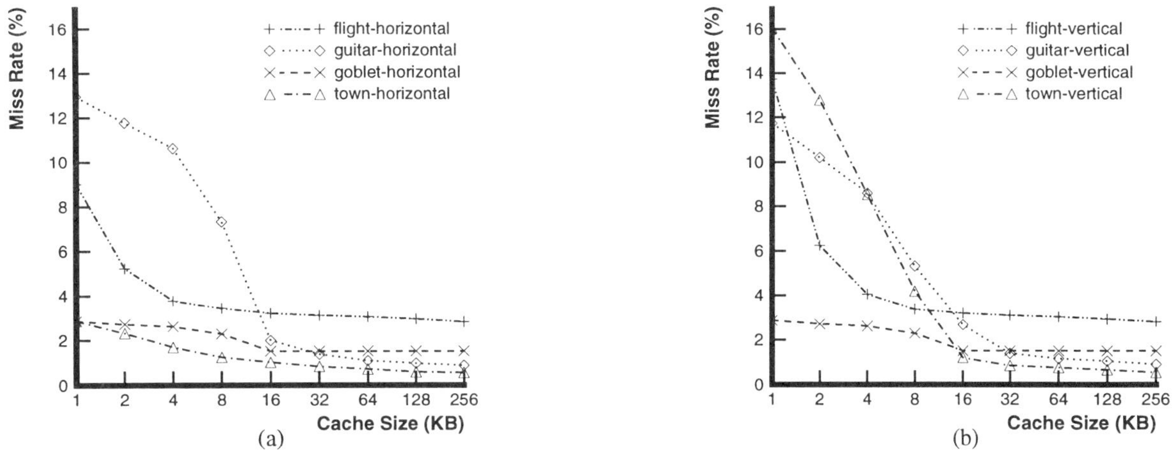

FIGURE 5.2. Results for the base representation using fully associative caches. The line size is 32 bytes (8 texels). (a) Horizontal rasterization (row major order). (b) Vertical rasterization (column major order).

the screen size, the texture is wrapped around and repeated. In this case, the worst case working set size is bounded by the cache line size multiplied by the length of the diagonal of the texture image, since this is the maximum length through the texture and the texture can appear in an arbitrary orientation on the screen. On the other hand, if the texture image size is greater than the screen size, the worst case working set size is bounded by the cache line size multiplied by the maximum width or height of the screen, depending upon whether we rasterize horizontally or vertically[1].

We have measured the average runlength of texel accesses from the same texture. The results for the Town, Guitar and Flight scenes, which are applications of more than one texture, are 223,629, 553,745 and 562,154, respectively. An underlying assumption is that the triangles are processed in the same order that they are specified in the high-level geometric description of the scene. These long runlengths demonstrate that the working set is limited to one texture at any point in time.

When rendering a span of pixels in screen space, texels (texture pixels) may be traversed in arbitrary orientations on the screen. In the worst case, the texture accesses can be streaming vertically through the texture causing only a fraction of each cache line that is brought into the cache to be actively used. The net effect is that the working set size is larger than it needs to be. This is a shortcoming of the base representation that we have chosen.

Figure 5.2(a) shows the miss rate results versus cache size when the scenes are rasterized horizontally. The first level working set sizes for the Flight, Town, Guitar and Goblet scenes are 4KB, 8KB, 16KB, and 16KB respectively. These working set sizes are a very small fraction of the total amount of texture that is used to render each scene (please see Table 4.1 for the full texture content used) and indicate that texture caching can be effective with relatively small cache sizes.

Figure 5.2(b) shows the miss rates versus cache size when the scenes are rasterized vertically. Compared to Figure 5.2(a), the miss rates for the Town scene have substantially increased for small cache sizes, whereas the miss rates for the other scenes have not changed quite as much. The first level working set size for the Town scene has grown from 8KB to 16KB because of a mismatch between the base representation and the rasterization direction. In fact, since most of the textures appear upright in the image of the Town scene, vertical rasterization causes the direction in which the texels are accessed to be perpendicular to the direction in which the texels are stored leading to worst-case behavior. In the Flight scene, the effect is less pronounced because the triangles are moderately sized. The Goblet scene results do not change because the triangles are relatively small. The results for the Guitar scene do not change very much because the textures in this scene are not uniformly oriented in any particular direction. From an architectural perspective, the important point is that the base representation is sensitive to the direction of texture accesses. For the remainder of this paper, we report results using vertical rasterization for the Town scene since this leads to worst-case behavior, and report results using horizontal rasterization for the Flight, Guitar and Goblet scenes.

In summary, we have shown that the cold miss rates are very low and can be further reduced with larger line sizes. The long texture runlengths, measured with the same rendering sequence as that taken by actual hardware engines that do texture mapping, indicate that the working set is limited to one texture. In addition, the working set sizes are very small compared with the amount of texture that is used to render each scene, justifying the use of relatively small texture caches. Finally, we found that the base representation is sensitive to the orientation of textures on the screen.

5.3 Blocked Representation

A blocked representation can be used to reduce the dependency on the orientation of textures, as seen by the viewer, and to exploit more spatial locality. A blocked representation of a 5-level Mip Map is illustrated in Figure 5.3. In this representation, also commonly known as Tiled, texels that are within a square region (block) of a two-dimensional image are ordered consecutively in memory. The idea of texture blocking is previously discussed in [4] and [10]. There are several issues that are raised by this representation. First, what is the addressing overhead associated with blocking? Second, how do we select the block size and is it related to the cache line size? Third, what are the improvements in miss rate as we increase the cache line size? Finally, what is the effect of blocking on conflict misses? In the following subsections, we discuss each of these issues in turn.

5.3.1 Texel Addressing Overhead

The blocked representation converts two-dimensional texture arrays into four-dimensional arrays. Therefore, the texel addressing calculations must be done in a two-step process which is illustrated below. We assume that the blocks are square and have dimensions that are powers of two. Furthermore, we assume that the blocks have the same dimensions across all Mip Map levels.

1. The screen rasterization path that would lead to the smallest working set would follow a Peano-Hilbert order since this would traverse a region of the texture in a spatially contiguous manner.

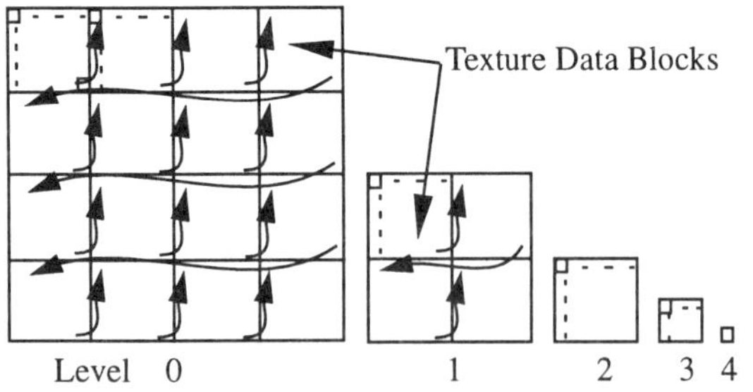

FIGURE 5.3. An illustration of the blocked representation for a texture Mip Map.

bw, **bh**: block width and height in texels. These are equal and are powers of two.
lbw, **lbh**: $\log_2$(bw or bh)
bs: $\log_2$(bw * bh)

The following variables are a function of the Mip Map level.
rs: $\log_2$(width of texture array in texels * bh)
tu, **tv**: texel u- and v-coordinates
bx, **by**: block coordinates
sx, **sy**: sub-block coordinates in texels
base: starting address of 4D texture array

bx = tu >> lbw
by = tv >> lbh
Block address = base + (by << rs) + (bx << bs)

sx = tu & (bw - 1)
sy = tv & (bh - 1)
Texel address = Block address + (sy << lbw) + sx

The variables bx, by, sx, and sy are simply bit-fields of the u- and v- texel coordinates, tu and tv. Furthermore, two of the shift operations shown above, involving the variables bs and lbw, have constant shift amounts assuming that the block dimensions remain fixed. Hence, the aggregate hardware overhead of the blocked representation compared to the base representation simply consists of two additions. These operations are incurred in the calculation of the block address.

5.3.2 Selecting a Block Size and Cache Line Size

The next question we would like to answer is whether there is any interaction between the block size used in the representation and cache line size. Figure 5.4 shows miss rate versus cache line size for a variety of block sizes. We chose a 32KB cache for our measurements because this cache size is larger than the working set sizes which we noted earlier. The graph in Figure 5.4(a) is for the Town scene. It shows that the lowest miss rates occur when the block size most closely matches the cache line size. For example, the lowest miss rate for a 64 byte cache line is for a 4x4 block which has a block size of 64 bytes. This effect can be explained by observing that individual cache lines that hold square regions of texture are most effective at exploiting spatial locality. When the block sizes greatly differ from the cache line sizes, we find that the working set sizes can become unnecessarily large leading to many capacity misses. The results for the Guitar scene, shown in Figure 5.4(b), are very similar.

We would like to quantify the extent of reduction in miss rate as the line size is increased. Figure 5.5 shows the effects of line and block size on miss rate for a fully associative 32KB cache. At 32KB, the primary misses that remain are cold misses and these misses are independent of the orientation of textures as viewed on the screen. The miss rates for the Flight, Goblet, Guitar and Town scenes at a line size of 32 bytes are 2.8%, 1.5%, 1.2% and 0.8% respectively. The miss rates at a line size of 128 bytes are 0.87%,

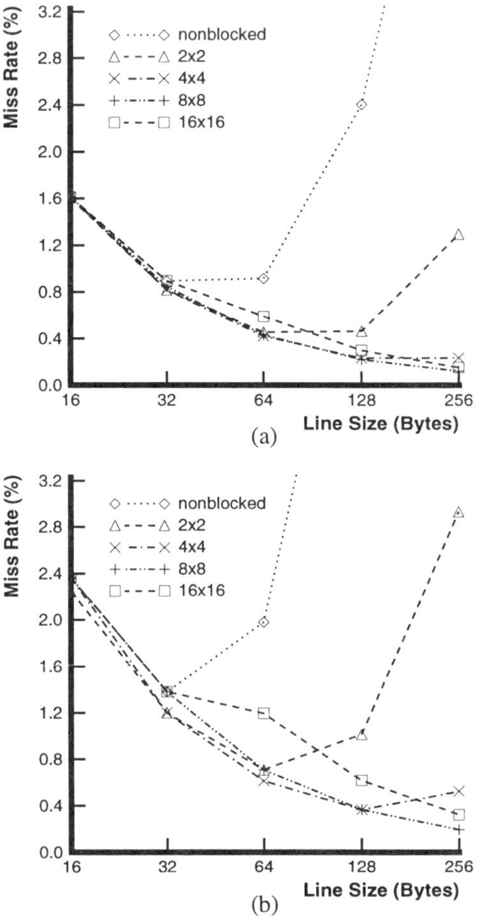

FIGURE 5.4. The interaction between block size and cache line size. These results were measured using fully associative 32KB caches. The block dimensions are given in texels.
(a) Town-vertical. (b) Guitar-horizontal.

0.41%, 0.36% and 0.21%. There appears to be a significant reduction in miss rate as the line and block sizes are increased.

Thus far, we have presented results for a 32KB cache and we have found that this cache size is adequate for holding the working sets of all four scenes. In Figure 5.6, we show results specific to the Guitar scene for different cache sizes. These graphs demonstrate that the blocked representation when coupled with larger line and block sizes, leads to a reduction in the number of capacity misses for cache sizes that are smaller than the working set size. In Figure 5.4 we saw that increasing the line size alone, without blocking, leads to worse miss rates. We can conclude that the blocked representation is an essential component for reducing the frequency of capacity misses. We have found that the other benchmark scenes experience similar reductions in capacity misses (although not shown here due to space reasons) when the cache sizes are smaller than the working set sizes.

In summary, we can conclude that the best block size to use for texturing corresponds to when the memory required to store one block of texture is the same as the cache line size. Furthermore, for scenes that we evaluate, there is enough spatial locality that larger line sizes can be used.

5.3.3 Conflict Misses

Thus far, we have ignored conflict misses and have only shown results for fully associative caches. In this section, we identify the

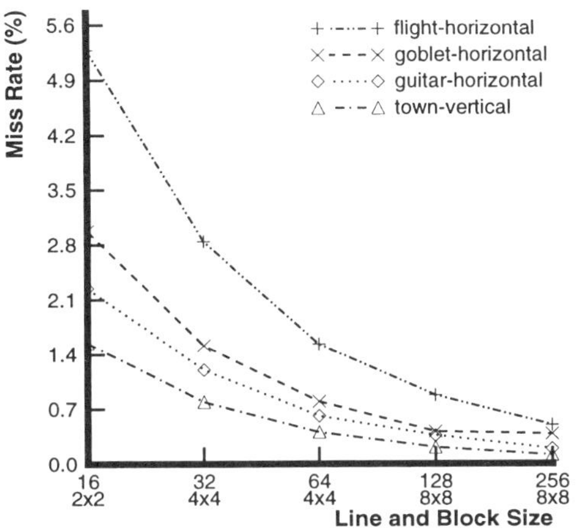

FIGURE 5.5. Effect of changes in line and block size on miss rates for all four scenes. These results were measured using fully associative 32KB caches. The block dimensions are given in texels.

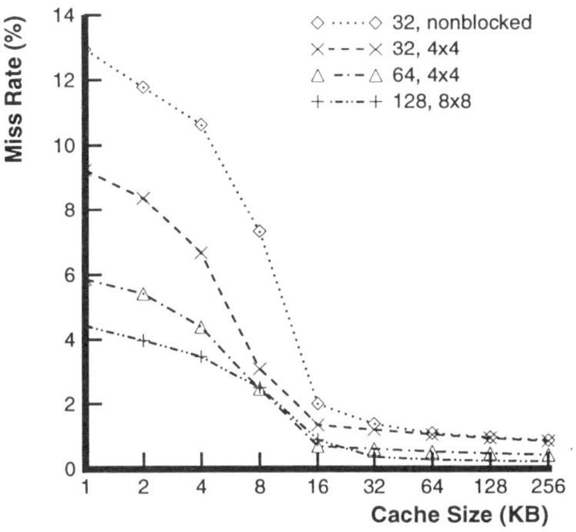

FIGURE 5.6. Effect of blocked representation on miss rates for different cache sizes. These results were measured for the Guitar scene using fully associative caches. The lines are labeled with the line size and block dimensions given in texels.

kinds of conflict misses that can occur and discuss how they can be avoided.

In Figure 5.1(b), we showed that in the base nonblocked representation, the levels of a Mip Map are stored separately in memory as two-dimensional arrays. Since these arrays are usually restricted to have dimensions that are powers of two, conflicts are prone to occur between neighboring texels that are in the same column. This kind of conflict miss can be avoided with the use of a blocked representation. The texels that lie within a block are guaranteed not to conflict in the cache since they are stored consecutively in memory. Moreover, since the block size is selected to be the same as the cache line size, the group of texels that lie within a block would be held by the same cache line.

Conflicts can also occur between blocks which are in different levels of a Mip Map. These conflicts are likely to be avoided with a two-way set-associative cache since trilinear interpolations simultaneously access at most two levels of a Mip Map.

Figure 5.7 shows graphs of miss rate versus cache size for different cache associativities. A relatively large line size of 128 bytes was selected for these experiments because conflict misses are more likely to occur when there are fewer lines in the cache. Thus, these results are indicative of the worst-case effect of conflicts on miss rate. The results in Figure 5.7(a) are for the Goblet scene and show that there is a significant difference in miss rates between the direct-mapped caches and the two-way set-associative caches. Since the triangles in the Goblet scene have fairly small areas, it is unlikely that conflicts will occur between blocks that are in the same level of a Mip Map. Hence, we attribute this difference in miss rates to conflicts between blocks that are in different levels of a Mip Map. The graph also shows that the two-way set-associative caches have the same miss rates as the fully associative caches indicating that increasing the associativity beyond two-way does not lead to any further improvement in miss rates.

The results in Figure 5.7(a) for the Goblet scene assumed a blocked representation. Had the representation been nonblocked, an eight-way associative cache would have been required to achieve the same miss rates as a fully associative cache among the small cache sizes. This result demonstrates that the blocked representation is useful for avoiding conflicts between neighboring texels in different rows of a 2D array.

The results in Figure 5.7(b) are for the Town scene. In this graph, we also find that two-way set-associativity is useful for eliminating conflicts between adjacent levels of a Mip Map. However, unlike Figure 5.7(a), there is a notable difference between the miss rates for the two-way set-associative caches and the fully associative caches. Vertical rasterization through the upright textures in the Town scene leads to conflicts between multiple blocks which lie within the same 2D array. The graph for the Town scene also shows that limited cache associativities beyond two-way are beneficial for small cache sizes, but are ineffective at avoiding this kind of block conflict miss among large caches. The results for the Guitar scene are similar since the textures are accessed along a variety of paths and the triangles are large. The results for the Flight scene are also similar except that most of the conflicts are avoided when the caches are eight-way set-associative and this is attributed to the fact that the triangles are moderately sized.

In summary, the blocked representation prevents conflicts from occurring between neighboring texels. Conflicts are also prone to occur between blocks. Conflicts between blocks at adjacent levels of the Mip Map can be successfully eliminated with two-way set-associative caches. Conflict misses that occur within the same 2D array are harder to prevent because the textures can be accessed along any path. In the next section, we discuss a tiled rasterization order that has the effect of reducing the number of blocks in the working set that can conflict with each other.

6 Rasterization Order and Tiling in Screen Space

The order in which screen pixels are traversed to determine whether they lie within the boundary of a triangle is the rasterization order. The rasterization order effects the texture access pattern and consequently, it can influence the cache behavior. As can be seen in Figure 6.1(a), the rasterization path of row major order spans the entire width of the triangle. As a result, the working set size for row major order is proportional to the amount of texture needed for an entire row of fragments; thus the working set size is related to the dimensions of the triangles that are mapped onto the screen. We propose reducing this variance, and thus the cache size needed for textures, by the use of a tiled rasterization order.

In a tiled order, a spatially contiguous block of screen pixels is traversed consecutively. Figure 6.1(b) illustrates a tiled rasterization path where the screen is statically decomposed into tiles. The cost associated with tiling depends on the rasterization algorithm. Additional setup computations for each tile may be required if the rasterization, shading and texture parameters are computed incre-

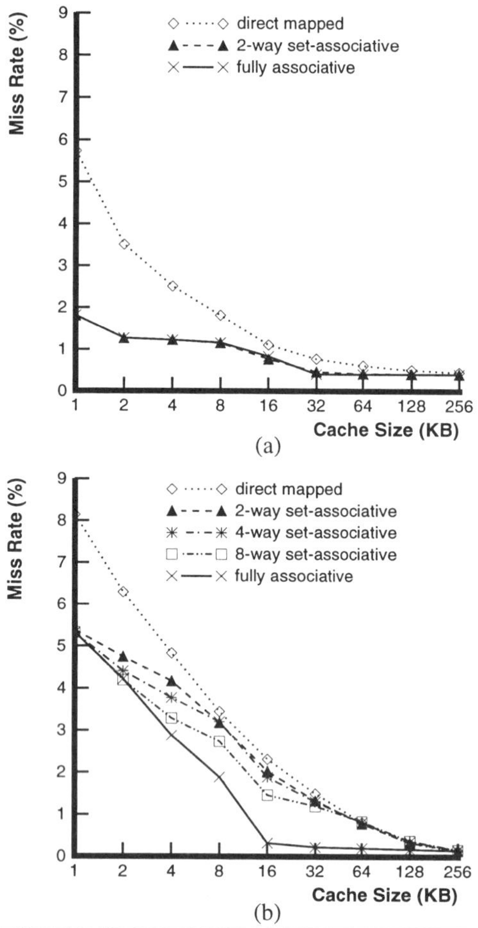

FIGURE 5.7. Effect of cache associativity on conflict misses. The textures are stored in blocks of 8x8 texels and the cache line size is 128 bytes. (a) Goblet-horizontal. (b) Town-vertical.

mentally across the surface of a triangle. One factor that has considerable influence on the texture access pattern is the tile size. In the following two sections, we address the issues of selecting a tile size and study the implications of tiled rasterization with respect to texture representation and cache organization.

6.1 Selecting a Tile Size

To understand the interaction between the tile dimensions and the working set size, we show miss rate results versus cache size in Figure 6.2 for the Guitar scene. The measurements were taken with a blocked texture representation and a relatively large line size of 128 bytes to take advantage of spatial locality. In Figure 6.2(a), we find that as we progress from very small tiles to medium tiles, there are significant reductions in miss rate amongst cache sizes that previously did not fit the working set. It is evident that tiling causes the working set size to be reduced and this shows up as fewer capacity misses. Figure 6.2(b) shows that the opposite effect occurs as we progress from medium tiles to very large tiles for the same scene. When the tiles are very small, the texture access patterns converge towards the access pattern of a nontiled rasterization order. On the other hand, when the tiles are very large, the working sets are larger than the cache size and capacity misses dominate the cache behavior.

We have found that tiled rasterization has a similar effect on the results of the Town scene. One characteristic that is common to both the Guitar and Town scenes is that they include large triangles that span significant areas of the screen. When the triangles are moderately sized, as in the Flight scene, the effect of tiled rasterization on the working set size is less pronounced, and when the triangles are small, as in the Goblet scene, the working set size becomes completely unaffected by the tile dimensions. For scenes with small triangles, it is advantageous to render neighboring triangles that lie in the same tile consecutively to exploit spatial locality and thus ensure that the working set size is minimized. We can conclude that tiled rasterization does not hurt when the triangles are small (and is thus robust), while in frequently occurring situations where the triangles are large it helps substantially in reducing working set size.

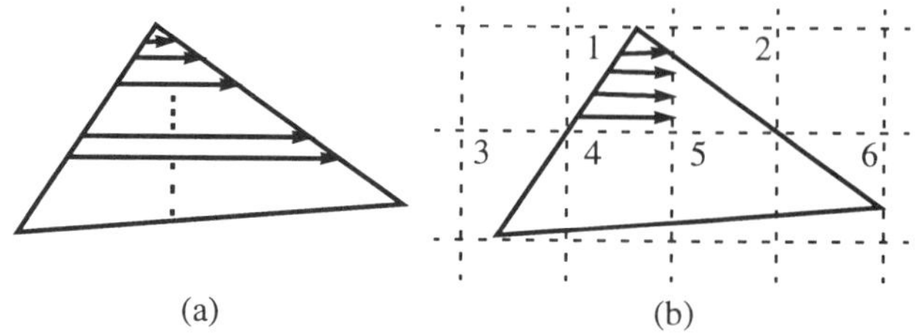

FIGURE 6.1. (a) Illustration of nontiled horizontal rasterization, (b) Illustration of tiled rasterization. The arrows indicate the rasterization path within a tile and the numbers indicate the order in which the tiles are rasterized.

6.2 Effect of Tiling on Conflict Misses

In Section 5.3.3, we found that conflicts between blocks that are in the same level of a Mip Map are difficult to avoid because the direction of texture accesses can be arbitrary. Assuming that neighboring blocks do not map to the same line in the cache, tiled rasterization can reduce the occurrence of this kind of block conflict since it confines the working set to a spatially contiguous region of texture. Unfortunately, because the texture image dimensions are powers of two and the memory required for a single row of texture blocks can be a multiple of the cache size, it is likely that conflicts will arise between neighboring blocks in the same column. One way to ensure that neighboring blocks do not conflict is to place a number of unused pad blocks at the end of each row of blocks as illustrated in Figure 6.3(a). This scheme requires additional texel addressing calculations which are shown below.

bw, bh: block width and height in texels. These are equal and are powers of two.

ps: $\log_2$(bw * bh * number of pad blocks). Number of pad blocks is a power of two.

by: block row coordinate

Texel address = Texel address computed for blocked representation + (by << ps)

The shift operation shown above has a constant shift amount assuming that the block dimensions and the number of pad blocks remain fixed. Hence, the additional hardware overhead of padding is just one addition per texel addressing calculation. Padding also incurs a memory overhead, though this overhead tends to be negligible for large textures where padding is most needed.

Another way to ensure that neighboring blocks do not conflict is to use another level of blocking in the representation of the texture images as illustrated in Figure 6.3(b). In this scheme, the two-dimensional texture arrays would effectively be stored as six-dimensional arrays. The size of the coarser blocks should be equal to the cache size since this ensures that a square region of blocks can be mapped into the cache without any conflicts. The additional hardware overhead of another level of blocking is two additions per texel addressing calculation.

Figure 6.4 shows the effect of tiled rasterization on conflict

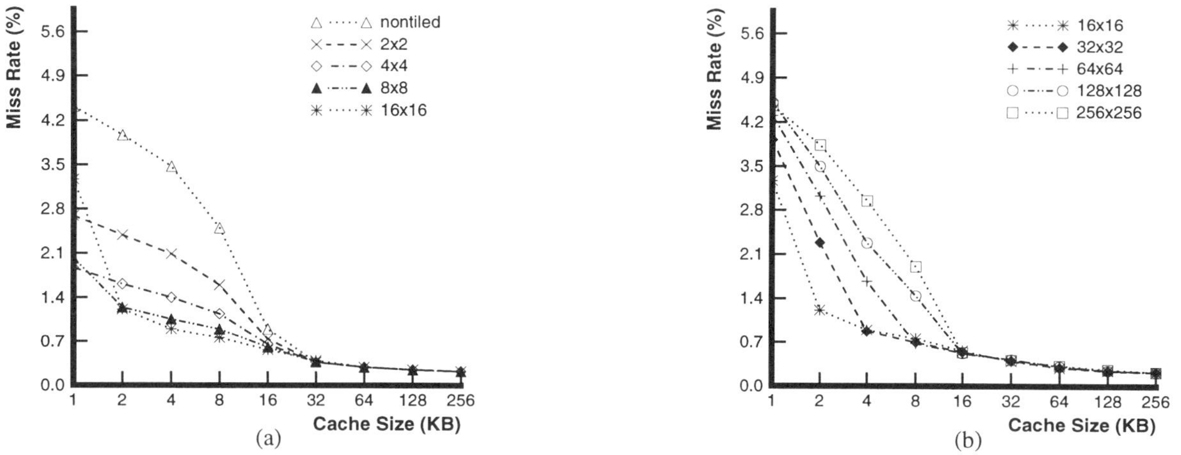

FIGURE 6.2. Effect of tiled rasterization on the working set size. These results were measured for the Guitar scene using fully associative caches. The textures are stored in blocks of 8x8 texels and the cache line size is 128 bytes. The tile dimensions are given in pixels. (a) Small to medium tile sizes. (b) Medium to large tile sizes.

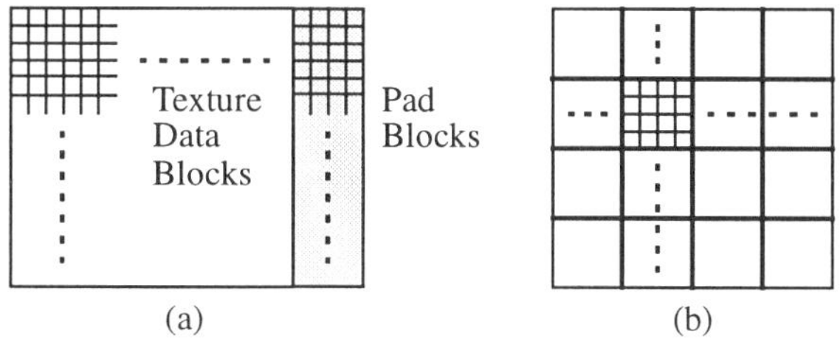

FIGURE 6.3. (a) Illustration of a 4D blocked and padded representation for one level of a Mip Map. We use the same number of pad blocks at the end of each row of blocks for all levels of a Mip Map. (b) Illustration of a 6D blocked representation for one level of a Mip Map. The size of the finer 2D blocks is selected to be equal to the cache line size and the size of the coarser 4D blocks is selected to be equal to the cache size.

misses for the Town and Flight scenes. Comparing the tiled rasterization results for the Town scene in Figure 6.4(a) with the non-tiled rasterization results previously shown in Figure 5.7(b), we find that the rate of conflicts is quite diminished with tiled rasterization. As expected, the effect of tiled rasterization on block conflict misses in the Guitar scene is very similar. Even though the Flight scene uses moderately sized triangles, it is highly prone to conflicts between neighboring blocks that lie in the same column because of the relatively large textures used for the terrain images. Indeed, Figure 6.4(b) for the Flight scene shows that tiled rasterization by itself is not sufficient for avoiding block conflict misses. However, when tiled rasterization is combined with either padding or 6D blocking, the rate of block conflict misses is significantly reduced. We can conclude that tiled rasterization effectively limits the number of blocks in the working set that can conflict with each other and that either padding or 6D blocking is needed to ensure that conflicts do not occur between neighboring blocks.

7 Memory Bandwidth and Rendering Performance

Perhaps the two most important metrics that characterize a texture mapping system are rendering performance and memory bandwidth. In this section, we discuss the issues in texture caching that effect rendering performance and after making some assumptions about the machine model, we relate the miss rates to memory bandwidth.

7.1 Machine Model

As previously shown in Figure 2.1, the texture mapping hardware consists of two components: a fragment generator and an SRAM texture cache. We discuss the details of each of these components separately.

7.1.1 Fragment Generator

The fragment generator is responsible for performing a fairly large number of calculations. As mentioned earlier, these include rasterizing triangles into fragments, computing level-of-detail and texture addresses for each fragment, trilinear interpolation of texels accessed from a Mip Map, and finally, applying the filtered texture to the fragments. To accomplish all of these tasks, we assume that the fragment generator exploits parallelism and pipelining to a great extent. We also assume that the clock frequency is 100 MHz since this is representative of present-day ASIC technology.

An appropriate measure of rendering performance is the number of textured fragments per second. One factor that can limit the maximum bandwidth achieved is the number of texels that can be accessed from the cache per cycle. Considering that a trilinear interpolation requires eight distinct texels to be accessed from the cache, a system that accessed just one texel per cycle would be limited to 12.5 million textured fragments per second. It is apparent that to achieve higher performance, more than one texel must be accessed per cycle. This issue is discussed further in Section 7.1.2. For now, we assume that the machine can read four texels per cycle, leading to a maximum bandwidth of 50 million textured fragments per second. The computation time is factored out by the pipelined nature of the system.

Another factor that can effect the performance of the system is the latency associated with filling a cache line from memory when a cache miss occurs. Even though the memory latency tends to be very long (roughly fifty 10ns cycles for a 128 byte cache line), it still must be completely hidden to achieve the maximum rate of fragments textured per second. Note that the memory latency would constrain the performance of the system if it were not hidden and that this reduction of fragment bandwidth becomes more pronounced as we increase the clock rate or the number of texel accesses per cycle. Another incentive for hiding the memory latency is the notion of robustness of performance with respect to different scenes. Some applications of real-time graphics require a high level of performance even under the worst-case conditions. A texturing system can sustain the maximum rate if the memory

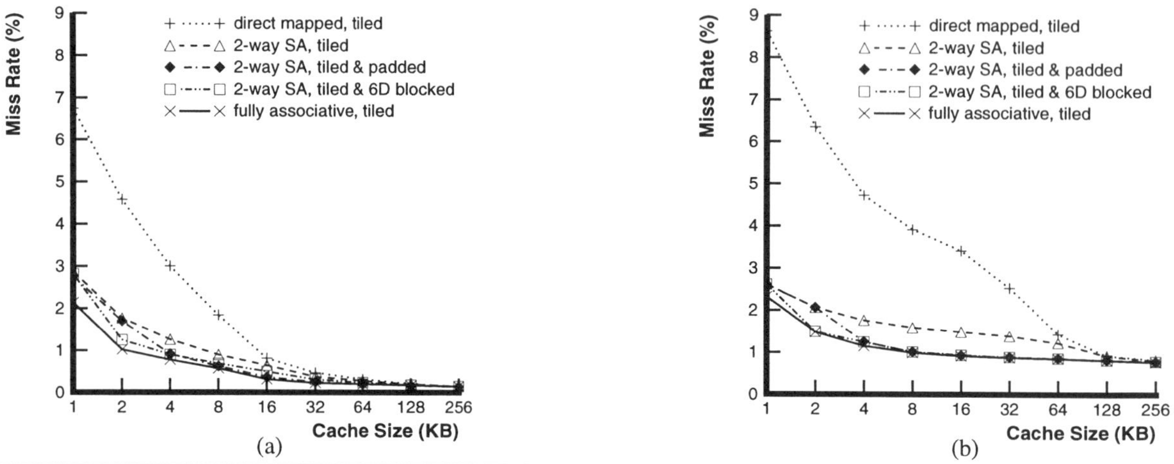

FIGURE 6.4. Effect of tiled rasterization on conflict misses. The textures are stored in blocks of 8x8 texels and the cache line size is 128 bytes. The tiles are 8x8 pixels. The padded results use a pad of four blocks at the end of each row of texture blocks. For the 6D blocked results, we use the largest block size for the coarser blocks that is less than or equal to the cache size.
(a) Town scene (rasterization is in column major order within and between tiles). (b) Flight scene.

latency is completely hidden and the memory bandwidth is met.

One solution for hiding the memory latency is proposed in [13]. The basic idea is to compute the texel addresses far in advance of the cache accesses by rasterizing the triangles twice: the first time to compute the texel addresses and to prefetch the lines that are missing in the cache and the second time to perform fragment texturing and shading. Since the texel addresses are needed by both rasterizers, they can either be computed independently by each rasterizer or they can be passed from the first rasterizer to the second by means of a FIFO buffer. The former approach is likely to be more costly because of the large number of calculations needed to compute the texel addresses (please refer to Table 2.1).

7.1.2 SRAM Texture Cache

As mentioned in the previous section, it is important to be able to access more than one texel from the cache in the same cycle. A common way of designing a multi-ported cache is to interleave the cache lines across multiple independently addressed banks [8]. Since a trilinear interpolation involves accessing neighboring texels, the interleaving across banks in a texture cache must be at the granularity of a texel rather than a cache line. A conflict-free address distribution which allows up to four texels to be accessed in parallel is possible if the texels are stored in a morton order within the cache lines [3]. Morton order implies that the texels are stored in 2x2 blocks. The texels within each 2x2 block are interleaved across the four banks and the same interleaving pattern is used for all 2x2 blocks that lie within a cache line to ensure that adjacent texels in abutting blocks are assigned to different banks.

While it may seem from Table 2.1 that the number of calculations for texture mapping is sufficiently high that the computation rather than cache bandwidth is the bottleneck, in practice this is not the case. Comparing the number of calculations required in each phase of texture mapping, we note that the trilinear interpolation portion is the most computationally-intensive. The nature of this computation is such that cache bandwidth is critical to performance. Consider the core of a trilinear interpolation, which must be performed separately for each R,G,B,A color component:

Interpolated value = Texel(n) + Weight * (Texel(n+1) - Texel(n))

We observe that this calculation requires pairs of texel values before it can proceed. Limiting the number of texel accesses to one per cycle constrains the rate of subtractions to one every other cycle. In contrast, a two-ported cache would allow subtractions every cycle. One might also consider adding more than two cache ports so that this calculation can be performed in parallel on different pairs of texels. Since the trilinear interpolation phase is the bottleneck in the fragment generator pipeline, improving its performance would directly impact the overall performance of a fragment generator. While we have been mostly focussing on special-purpose hardware, recent additions of visualization instructions such as MMX [19] and VIS [16] and deep pipelines have shifted the bottleneck away from computation in microprocessors.

7.2 Memory Bandwidth

The memory bandwidth results assuming that the system operates at peak bandwidth of 50 million textured fragments per second are shown in Table 7.1. We report results for three different cache sizes: 4KB, 32KB, and 128KB. The 4KB cache is representative of a very small on-chip cache. The 32KB cache is large enough to hold the working sets, yet it can also be placed on-chip. Both the 4KB and 32KB caches are two-way set-associative. The 128KB cache size provides a measure of how low the miss rates and memory bandwidths can become if a very large cache is used. This cache is direct mapped since associativity makes little difference in miss rates at this size. The results were measured for the blocked representation since we previously found this texture representation to be most suitable. In addition, the texture arrays are padded and the rasterization in screen space is tiled to reduce conflict misses and working set size.

One trend that can be seen in these results is that the memory bandwidth requirements are much reduced in the transition from the 4KB cache to the 32KB cache for all scenes except the Flight scene where the reductions are more modest. The transition to the 128KB cache leads to less drastic reductions in memory bandwidths demonstrating that fairly small cache sizes are adequate for texture mapping. Another trend is that the memory bandwidth requirements increase very slightly with increasing line size for the 32KB and 128KB caches. This result is encouraging because larger line sizes can elicit a larger fraction of the peak memory bandwidth.

We would like to compare the memory bandwidth requirements discussed above for a fragment generator that uses an SRAM texture cache with the memory bandwidth requirement of a fragment generator of equivalent performance that directly accesses a dedicated DRAM memory system for all texel lookups. For the latter system, which does not use a cache, the memory bandwidth

Cache Size Associativity		4KB 2-way Set-Associative			32KB 2-way Set-Associative			128KB Direct Mapped		
Line Size Block Size		32 4x4	64 4x4	128 8x8	32 4x4	64 4x4	128 8x8	32 4x4	64 4x4	128 8x8
Scene	Flight	**396** (3.24)	**447** (1.83)	**610** (1.25)	**355** (2.91)	**386** (1.58)	**435** (0.89)	**339** (2.78)	**366** (1.50)	**425** (0.87)
	Town	**233** (1.91)	**271** (1.11)	**444** (0.91)	**99** (0.81)	**103** (0.42)	**122** (0.25)	**77** (0.63)	**78** (0.32)	**88** (0.18)
	Guitar	**319** (2.61)	**371** (1.52)	**552** (1.13)	**154** (1.26)	**161** (0.66)	**215** (0.44)	**120** (0.98)	**125** (0.51)	**137** (0.28)
	Goblet	**385** (3.15)	**566** (2.32)	**596** (1.22)	**189** (1.55)	**212** (0.87)	**225** (0.46)	**194** (1.59)	**215** (0.88)	**229** (0.47)

TABLE 7.1. Memory bandwidth requirements in MBytes/second for different cache and line sizes. The performance of the system is 50 million textured fragments/second. The miss rates are also shown in parentheses. The texture maps are stored in a blocked and padded representation in memory. The block dimensions are given in texels and the pad is four blocks at the end of each row of texture blocks. The rasterization is tiled in screen space using 8x8 pixel tiles. Texels are 32-bits.

requirement is 1.5 GBytes/second (4 bytes/texel * 8 texels/fragment * 50M fragments/second). On the other hand, the memory bandwidth requirement for a system that uses a 32KB cache is between 100 and 450 MBytes/second. We see that there is a three to fifteen times reduction in memory bandwidth requirements due to caching.

Although the main focus of this paper has been on a graphics rendering system with a single fragment generator, it is interesting to note that the memory bandwidths are low enough that a parallel system could be built with multiple fragment generators sharing a single texture memory, each with their own cache. As mentioned earlier, this makes it possible to avoid replicating the textures in each fragment generator memory as is done in the RealityEngine.

8 Conclusions and Future Work

As we move into the era of the Internet with 3-D virtual chat groups, realistic visualization of scientific phenomenon, photorealistic computer games, the need to provide high performance yet cheap computer graphics is becoming critical. While much attention has been given in the past to design of memory hierarchies for general-purpose computers using the SPEC benchmarks and transaction processing benchmarks, so far there is little published data available on core graphics algorithms like texture mapping. This paper attempts to fill that gap.

We have built a sophisticated environment in which computer graphics workloads can be rendered, and our simulation results show that caches can be highly effective for texture-mapped graphics. Traditionally, caches have not been used in computer graphics systems where the philosophy has been to provide guaranteed performance under worst-case conditions, although this philosophy is beginning to change [13]. By using techniques such as (i) block-based representation of Mip-Mapped textures, (ii) tiled rendering in the screen space itself, and (iii) padded or six-dimensionally blocked texture arrays, we can robustly reduce the miss rates. We study the relationship between block size in texture representations and cache line size, and also discuss which tile sizes are appropriate. We observe that caches as small as 16 KBytes with 2-way associativity (to reduce conflict miss rates for Mip Map levels) can reduce the effective bandwidth needed from the memory system by a factor of three to fifteen, while also reducing the latency of access. Because of the above tiling techniques, the performance can be made robust regardless of the scenes that are being texture mapped.

A promising approach for rendering directly from compressed textures has been proposed in the literature [2]. In future work, it would be interesting to study the interaction between compressed representations of textures and cache architectures. Another area which we have not studied in detail is the use of texture caching in parallel architectures. One of the interesting questions that must be addressed in this area is how to balance the work among multiple fragment generators without reducing the spatial locality in each reference stream.

Acknowledgments

We would like to thank Vijayaraghavan Soundararajan, Gordon Stoll, and especially Pat Hanrahan for helpful discussions and valuable comments on earlier drafts of this paper. We are also grateful to John Gerth for his help and to Homan Igehy for contributing the Guitar scene. The Flight and Town scenes appear courtesy of Silicon Graphics and Paradigm Simulation. This work was partly supported by DARPA under grant No. DABT63-95-C-0085-P00000.

References

[1] Accelerated Graphics Port (AGP). *Accelerated Graphics Port Interface Specification*, Revision 1.0. Intel Corporation, 1996.

[2] A. C. Beers, M. Agrawala, and N. Chaddha. Rendering from Compressed Textures. In *Proceedings of SIGGRAPH'96*, pages 373-378, August 1996.

[3] A. Schilling, G. Knittel, and W. Strasser. Texram: A Smart Memory for Texturing. In *Computer Graphics and Applications*, pages 32-41, May 1996.

[4] Darwyn Peachey. Texture on Demand. Technical Report, Pixar, 1990.

[5] Ed Catmull. *A Subdivision Algorithm for Computer Display of Curved Surfaces*. PhD thesis, University of Utah, Dec. 1974.

[6] E. Rothberg, J. P. Singh, and A. Gupta. Working Sets, Cache Sizes, and Node Granularity Issues for Large-Scale Multiprocessors. In *Proceedings of the 20th Annual International Symposium on Computer Architecture*, pages 14-25, May 1993.

[7] Geoffrey Y. Gardner. Visual Simulation of Clouds. In *Proceedings of SIGGRAPH'85*, pages 297-303, July 1985.

[8] Gurindar S. Sohi and Manoj Franklin. High-Bandwidth Data Memory Systems for Superscalar Processors, In *Fourth Int'l. Conference on Architectural Support for Programming Languages and Operating Systems*, pages 53-62, April 1991.

[9] James F. Blinn. Simulation of Wrinkled Surfaces. In *Proceedings of SIGGRAPH'78*, pages 286-292, August 1978.

[10] James F. Blinn. The Truth About Texture Mapping. In *Computer Graphics and Applications*, pages 78-83, March, 1990.

[11] J. Foley, A. van Dam, S. Feiner, J. Hughes. *Computer Graphics Principles and Practice*, Second Edition. Addison-Wesley Publishing Company, Inc., 1990.

[12] James L. Turley. Action-Packed Fray for Newest Video Games. *Microprocessor Report*, pages 15-20, May 30, 1995.

[13] Jay Torborg, and James T. Kajiya. Talisman: Commodity Realtime 3D Graphics for the PC. In *Proceedings of SIGGRAPH'96*, pages 353-363, August 1996.

[14] Kurt Akeley. RealityEngine Graphics. In *Proceedings of SIGGRAPH'93*, pages 109-116, August 1993.

[15] Lance Williams. Pyramidal Parametrics. In *Proceedings of SIGGRAPH'83*, pages 1-11, July 1983.

[16] L. Kohn, G. Maturana, M. Tremblay, A. Prabhu, and G. Zyner. Visual Instruction Set (VIS) in UltraSPARC™. In *Proceedings of COMPCON'95*, pages 462-469, March 1995.

[17] Mark Segal, and Kurt Akeley. *The OpenGL Graphics System: A Specification*, Version 1.0. Silicon Graphics, Inc., 1992.

[18] M. F. Deering, S. A. Schlapp, and M. G. Lavelle. FBRAM: A new Form of Memory Optimized for 3D Graphics. In *Proceedings of SIGGRAPH'94*, pages 167-174, July 1994.

[19] MMX™ Technology. *Intel Architecture MMX Technology Programmer's Reference Manual*. Intel Corporation, March 1996.

[20] M. Segal, C. Korobkin, R. van Widenfelt, J. Foran, and P. Haeberli. Fast Shadows and Lighting Effects Using Texture Mapping. In *Proceedings of SIGGRAPH'92*, pages 249-252, July 1992.

[21] Ned Greene. Applications of World Projections. In *Proceedings of Graphics Interface '86*, pages 108-114, May 1986.

[22] Paul Haeberli and Mark Segal. Texture Mapping as a Fundamental Drawing Primitive. In *Proceedings Fourth Eurographics Workshop on Rendering*, pages 259-266, June 1993.

[23] Paul S. Heckbert. Survey of Texture Mapping. In *Proceedings of Graphics Interface '86*, pages 207-212, May 1986.

[24] Steven A. Przybylski. *New DRAM Technologies: A Comprehensive Analysis of the New Architectures*, Second Edition. MicroDesign Resources, 1996.

[25] W. T. Reeves, D. H. Salesin, and R. L. Cook. Rendering Antialiased Shadows with Depth Maps. In *Proceedings of SIGGRAPH'87*, pages 283-291, July 1987.

Designing High Bandwidth On-Chip Caches

Kenneth M. Wilson and Kunle Olukotun

Computer Systems Laboratory
Stanford University
Stanford, CA 94305
{kwilson, kunle}@ogun.stanford.edu

Abstract

In this paper we evaluate the performance of high bandwidth caches that employ multiple ports, multiple cycle hit times, on-chip DRAM, and a line buffer to find the organization that provides the best processor performance. Processor performance is measured in execution time using a dynamic superscalar processor running realistic benchmarks that include operating system references. The results show that a large dual-ported multi-cycle pipelined SRAM cache with a line buffer maximizes processor performance. A large pipelined cache provides both a low miss rate and a high CPU clock frequency. Dual-porting the cache and the use of a line buffer provide the bandwidth needed by a dynamic superscalar processor. In addition, the line buffer makes the pipelined dual-ported cache the best option by increasing cache port bandwidth and hiding cache latency.

1. Introduction

It is well known that the on-chip memory system of a microprocessor is a key determinant of microprocessor performance. Previously, the main concerns of memory designers were cache size, associativity, and line size. As the performance of microprocessors increases, instruction and data bandwidth demands lead chip designers to create more complicated on-chip memory systems. Currently, designers are considering multi-ported caches, multi-cycle caches, multi-level caches, and even caches made with on-chip DRAM. Though each of these has been covered individually in previous work [Joup94, MIPS94, Oluk92, Saul96, Shim96, Sohi91, Wils96], there are no papers that investigate the interaction of these different methods to find the organizations that work well together.

There are many options available for increasing cache bandwidth. One straightforward way of increasing cache bandwidth is to provide multiple cache ports that can be independently addressed by the processor's load/store unit in the same cycle. Ideally, each cache port operates independently, with no increase in hit time and only a small increase in chip area. Another way to increase memory bandwidth is to enlarge the primary data cache. Enlarging the primary data cache decreases the cache's miss rate, thereby decreasing the average response time of the processor's memory system. Increasing the size of the primary data cache causes the hit time of the cache to increase. Since accessing the data cache is usually on the processor's critical timing path, the hit time of larger caches may be pipelined to avoid increasing the processor's cycle time. The extra processor cycles can be partially hidden by the use of a dynamic superscalar processor. If a very large on-chip cache is desired, the designer may choose to use DRAM in place of SRAM. With improvements in DRAM technology it is now possible to include DRAM memory on-chip [Saul96][Shim96]. Caches containing DRAM can have much larger capacities than standard SRAM cache designs for equal processor die area.

One way to increase memory bandwidth and at the same time hide the increase in hit time needed by a larger cache is to add a small buffer with a one cycle access time to the processor's load/store execution unit. This level zero cache can be implemented as a small line buffer [Wils96]. A line buffer holds cache data inside the processor's load/store unit to allow a load to recently accessed data to be satisfied from the line buffer instead of from the cache. This prevents the load from occupying the primary data cache ports, allowing other loads to access the cache earlier. When a line buffer is added to a processor with a multi-cycle cache, not only does the line buffer reduce the utilization of the cache ports, but the line buffer also reduces the average latency of load instructions by returning data in a single cycle.

To understand the interaction between different high bandwidth cache organizations, we evaluate the performance of caches that employ combinations of multi-port, multi-cycle access, on-chip DRAM, and a line buffer. In the course of this evaluation we find the combination of features and cache parameters that provides the best processor performance. To determine processor performance we use an accurate model of a four issue dynamic superscalar processor with non-blocking caches. The rest of this paper is organized as follows: The high bandwidth on-chip cache designs for this investigation are described in section 2. The experimental methodology for simulating the architectures is discussed in section 3. The results that characterize the design space by looking at the interactions between different on-chip cache configurations are presented in section 4. First, the processor instructions per cycle (IPC) results show the effect of the different cache configurations on processor performance when changes in cycle time are not taken into account. Second, we combine the IPC results with the processor cycle times determined in section 2 to find the application execution times of our benchmarks for various cache size and structure. Section 5 gives our conclusions.

2. High Bandwidth Cache Design

In this section we describe alternative high bandwidth cache designs and look at their impact on cache access time. The impact on cache access time is important because we are interested in the largest cache which has an access time within the processor's cycle time. We assume that the hit time of the cache is on the critical timing path of the processor and therefore directly impacts the processor's cycle time. If this is not the case, a larger slower cache should be built to improve the processor's performance.

To measure cache access time we use the technology independent delay measurement technique called *fan-out of four* (FO4) [Horo92]. One FO4 is the delay of a signal passing through an inverter driving a load capacitance that is four times larger than its input (e.g. driving four equivalently sized gates). Circuits can then be judged by comparing their delay to the delay of the inverter with a fan-out of four. Once FO4 is used to calculate the change in delay for a new cache structure, we find the resulting cache access time by using the fact that a processor with a single-ported single-cycle 8 Kbyte primary data cache on the processor's critical timing path has a cycle time of 25 FO4 [Horo96].

A modified version of *cacti* [Wilt96] is used to quantify the relationship between cache size and cache hit time. Cacti models a 0.5um CMOS process to find the cache access time for SRAM cache sizes varying from 4 Kbytes to 256 Kbytes. Even though cacti produces cache access times for larger caches, cacti does not produce the best cache design due to restrictions on cacti's design space. Since we are interested in SRAM cache sizes of up to 1 Mbyte, we modified cacti to support larger caches by changing cacti's parameters to increase the size of its design space. For instance, we increased the possible number of cache sub-arrays from eight to thirty-two. The resulting cache access times are converted to FO4 and graphed under the label "Single-Ported Cache" in Figure 1. Note that the shape of the curve for the cache access times is as expected and is just an extension to the cache access curve found in [Wilt94]. The cacti results for eight-way banked caches are also shown in Figure 1 and will be explained in the next section.

2.1 Multi-Ported Caches

Multiple cache ports are required to satisfy the bandwidth demands of modern superscalar processors. In a four issue dynamic superscalar processor with a 32 Kbyte primary data cache, adding a second cache port increases processor performance by an average of 25% [Wils96]. As expected, there are diminishing returns in performance from increasing the number of cache ports beyond two. Increasing the number of cache ports to three and four increased processor performance by only four and one percent respectively. For this reason we concentrate on caches with two ideal ports. An ideal cache port operates independently of any other cache port, is accessible every cycle, and has a cache hit time of one cycle. In reality multiple cache ports are usually implemented by banking or duplicating the primary data cache.

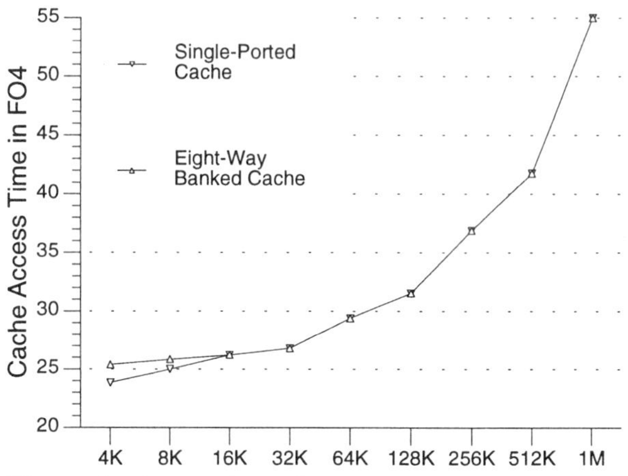

Figure 1: Access times for single-ported and eight-way banked caches.

Banked caches consist of multiple independently addressed banks [Sohi91]. Recent microprocessors have used this technique to improve memory bandwidth. The MIPS R10000 [MIPS94][Yeag96] implements a two-way banked cachc. Splitting cache accesses into two banks allows two cache accesses to be overlapped if the two cache accesses are to different banks. Given an ideal cache access stream, this technique can double the bandwidth of the primary data cache. However, in practice this technique suffers from bank conflicts and may not increase performance if enough references address the same bank.

One drawback of implementing a banked cache is an increase in the number of wires required to interconnect the banks. This increases both the area consumed by the cache and the wire delay. The delay due to the increased wire lengths is offset by the decrease in delay required to address the smaller cache array. In the case of small caches, banking results in an increase in both cache access time and cache area. For larger caches banking becomes a trade-off between processor die area and cache access time. In fact the cache designs produced by cacti are already eight-way banked internally for cache sizes of 16 Kbytes and greater.

We use cacti to find the cache access times of eight-way banked caches that vary in capacity from 4 Kbytes to 1 M byte. Cacti considers cache organizations within a design space and picks the best organization. We force cacti to consider only caches that contain eight or more banks. This produces the access times for eight-way or greater internally banked SRAM caches graphed in Figure 1. As expected, the access times presented in Figure 1 for eight-way banked caches are greater than the access times for single-ported cache sizes of less than 16 Kbytes. The eight-way banked and single-ported caches have the same access times for cache sizes of 16 Kbytes and greater because single-ported caches of 16 Kbytes and greater are already at least eight-way internally banked. Assuming there is no timing penalty for changing an internally banked cache to an externally banked cache, the eight-way banked curve of Figure 1 can be used to represent the cache access times for externally eight-way banked caches.

Another way to build a multi-ported cache is to duplicate the primary data cache such as in the DEC Alpha 21164 [Edmo95]. The Alpha contains two copies of the primary data cache. The dual-ported cache of the DEC Alpha has the performance drawback that all stores must be sent to both cache ports simultaneously so that both copies of the data cache are consistent. Using both cache ports for each store should not significantly degrade performance because stores can be buffered and bypassed to allow loads to access the cache first. We make the assumption that stores can be buffered until both cache ports are not servicing load instructions. This means that stores do not degrade machine performance; therefore ideal multiple cache ports are used to model duplicate caches.

Even though duplicating the data cache causes a doubling of the die area needed for the primary data cache, the only timing cost is the added delay due to adding one more write port to the load/store buffer. Since adding an additional write port causes only a small increase in delay, we assume that the added delay can be eliminated with increased effort spent on the circuit design. This means that the access times for single-ported caches shown in Figure 1 can also be used for duplicate caches.

2.2 Pipelined Caches

With application working sets increasing and the gap between memory access time and processor cycle time expanding, some chip designers will decide to implement larger caches that require multi-cycle hit times. Using multi-cycle hit times allows the use of larger and more complicated primary caches without impacting processor cycle time. This is especially important for primary data caches. The extra hit time of a multi-cycle cache can be partially hidden by pipelining the cache [Oluk92], and using a dynamic superscalar processor [Wils95].

The size of a cache that can be accessed in two or three processor cycles can be determined from the cycle times shown in Figure 1. If a processor has a cycle time of 25 FO4, an 8 Kbyte cache can be accessed in one processor cycle, a 512 Kbyte cache can be accessed in 1.67 cycles, and a 1 Mbyte cache can be accessed in 2.20 cycles. Pipelining requires the addition of a latch with a delay of 1.5 FO4, to create a 512 Kbyte cache that can be implemented on-chip and be accessed in two processor cycles. Further, Figure 1 shows that if a 1 Mbyte cache is desired, either the processor cycle time has to be increased to make this cache fit into a two cycle hit time, or the hit time of the 1 Mbyte cache must be increased to three processor cycles. In this study we do not consider on-chip SRAM caches larger than 1 Mbyte.

2.3. Increasing Cache Port Efficiency

A line buffer is a small fully-set-associative multi-ported level-zero cache located within the processor's load/store execution unit [Wils96]. When a line buffer is added to a processor's load/store execution unit, it reduces the number of accesses to the cache ports by satisfying a large percentage of the load instructions before they access a cache port. By decreasing the number of accesses to the cache ports, the line buffer reduces the need for multiple cache ports. Another advantage of a line buffer is that it returns recently accessed cache data in a single cycle, which helps hide the additional latency of pipelined caches.

2.4. DRAM Caches

A fairly recent proposal for building an on-chip cache is to use DRAM on the processor die [Saul96][Shim96]. The main advantage of DRAM is that it allows much larger caches to be constructed on-chip. The chief disadvantage is longer cache hit times. Much of the performance effect of the longer hit times can be hidden through the addition of a small first level cache and the latency hiding abilities of a dynamic superscalar processor. The extra latency can be further reduced by using a line buffer to return data with high spatial and temporal locality in a single processor cycle.

The biggest hurdle to placing DRAM caches on the processor die is that the technologies to create DRAMs and processors are completely different. With today's technologies, it is only possible to build a low performance processor on a DRAM die; this might be useful for microcontrollers and low-end CPUs. High-end CPUs are more likely to use the option of building DRAM on the processor die. Due to the differing technologies this will make the DRAM consume about twice the die area and decrease the DRAM performance.

One advantage of using DRAM for on-chip caches is that the row buffers of the DRAM can be combined to make a first level data cache. In [Saul96], two row buffers for every DRAM bank were used to make a 16 Kbyte primary data cache with two-way-set-associativity. The disadvantage to using the row buffers as a primary data cache is that each row buffer contains 512 bytes. This means that the line size of the 16 Kbyte data cache is 512 bytes. The longer line size reduces the hit rate of the row buffer data cache, but should not have too great an impact since the miss time of the row buffers is the time to access the DRAM cache. For this study, we use a DRAM cache size of 4 Mbytes and do not use a secondary off-chip cache due to the large size of the DRAM cache.

The on-chip DRAM hit time is not completely understood at this time, but [Saul96] predicts a six cycle hit time is possible for a 200MHz processor. They also predict that using the DRAM's row buffers as a first level cache allows a cache hit time of one processor cycle if the data is in the row buffer. These hit times are very aggressive. An actual implementation of a processor in a DRAM technology [Shim96] used a separate 2 Kbyte SRAM data cache with a one cycle hit time and a miss time to DRAM of five cycles, but with a processor frequency of only 66 Mhz. It takes a DRAM cache design similar to [Saul96] to provide enough bandwidth to compete with standard on-chip SRAM caches. Due to our concern for adequate bandwidth we use a one cycle hit time 16 Kbyte two-way-set-associative row buffer cache, but vary the hit time of the DRAM cache from six to eight cycles to get an idea of how processor performance decreases as the hit time of the DRAM increases.

3. Simulation Methodology

This section describes the dynamic superscalar processor used to evaluate the different on-chip memory structures, and the SimOS [Rose95b] environment under which the processor is simulated. We also discuss the simulation methods and benchmarks used to produce the results presented in this study.

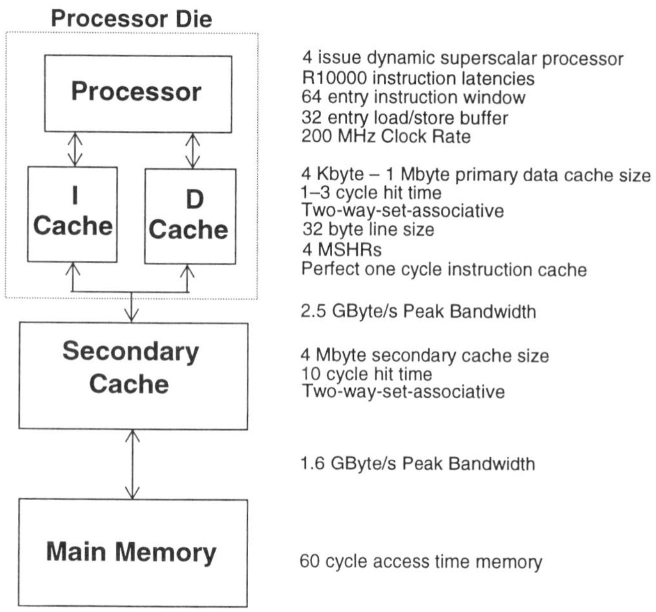

Figure 2: Processor and memory subsystem.

3.1. Processor and Memory Subsystem

The processor used for this study is a four issue dynamic superscalar processor with R10000 instruction latencies and a 200 Mhz clock rate [Yeag96, Gwen94, MIPS94]. The processor and memory subsystem are summarized in Figure 2. Unlike the R10000, our processor model has a 64 entry reorder buffer and a 32 entry load/store buffer. To focus the study on the performance of the memory subsystem, there are no restrictions on the type of instructions that can be issued each cycle.

The memory subsystem consists of separate primary instruction and data caches, a unified secondary cache, and main memory. The primary instruction cache is a perfect cache that always hits and responds in a single cycle. The primary data cache is a two-way-set-associative cache with 32 byte lines and a single cycle access time, or a fully pipelined multi-cycle access time. Note that the load latency is actually one cycle greater than the cache access time due to the load's address calculation. The data cache is lock-up-free, but the cache size is not fixed, allowing us to investigate the performance effects of various cache sizes. The second level cache is a 4 Mbyte two-way-set-associative cache with 64 byte lines and a ten cycle (50ns) access time. Four miss status handling registers (MSHR) [Fark94] implement the lock-up-free cache and are located in the primary data cache to support misses for up to four data cache lines. Main memory has a sixty cycle (300ns) access time.

For some applications high performance off-chip memory bandwidth is critical for good performance. Our memory organization supports a bandwidth of 1.6 GBytes/second peak between the second level cache and main memory, and 2.5 GBytes/second peak between the processor chip and the second level cache. Though these memory bandwidths may seem very impressive, the DEC Alpha 21264 [Kell96] supports even greater bandwidths of 2 GBytes/second from the second level cache to memory and 4 GBytes/second from the processor die to the second level cache.

3.2. SimOS Environment

SimOS [Rose95b] is a complete machine simulation environment containing models of all the hardware present on modern computer systems including the CPU, memory subsystems, and I/O devices. It can simulate the hardware with enough speed and detail to boot and run a commercial Unix-based operating system, Silicon Graphics IRIX version 5.3, and arbitrary application programs that run on IRIX.

This study uses the MXS [Benn95] CPU simulator running under SimOS. MXS is a detailed CPU simulator that simulates the machine model described earlier in this section. This CPU simulator models a dynamic superscalar processor that supports multiple instruction issue, out-of-order execution, hardware branch prediction, and lock-up-free caches. The simulator's operation is parameterized and can be configured to accurately model a variety of machines.

SPEC95 integer benchmarks

gcc	Builds SPARC code
li	LISP interpreter
compress	Compresses and decompresses file in memory

SPEC95 floating point benchmarks

tomcatv	Mesh-generation program
su2cor	Quantum physics; Monte Carlo simulation
apsi	Solves problems regarding temperature, wind, velocity, and distribution of pollutants

SimOS multiprogramming benchmarks

pmake	Two compilation processes for 17 files
database	Sybase SQL server using bank/customer transaction processing modeled after the TPC-B transaction processing benchmark [Gray93]
VCS	Simulates the FLASH MAGIC chip [Kusk94] using the Chronologics VCS simulator

Table 1: The nine benchmarks.

3.3. Benchmarks

The performance of nine realistic benchmarks is used to evaluate the high bandwidth cache designs that are proposed in section two. Table 1 shows that the nine benchmarks are made up of three integer SPEC95 benchmarks, three floating point SPEC95 benchmarks, and three multiprogramming applications. The newer SPEC95 benchmarks were chosen over SPEC92 because their larger working set sizes stress the memory system much more than the SPEC92 benchmarks. The three SimOS benchmarks were chosen because they represent realistic multiprogramming workloads from the areas of programming, database transaction processing, and engineering simulation.

Each benchmark is simulated for over 100 million instructions within an interesting portion of its execution. The breakdown of execution time spent in kernel, user, and idle for each benchmark is shown in Table 2. Idle is a result of waiting for I/O, and applications such as database spend a large portion of their execution in this mode. Since the processor is spinning in a tight loop in idle mode, the instructions per cycle (IPC) for this mode could skew the results for benchmarks with significant idle time. For this reason, the IPC of the benchmarks during idle time is not factored into our performance measurements.

	Kernel	User	Idle	Load	Store
gcc	10.0	90.0	0.0	28.1	12.2
li	0.2	99.8	0.0	33.2	13.0
compress	8.4	91.6	0.0	34.5	8.0
tomcatv	0.4	99.6	0.0	26.9	8.5
su2cor	0.5	99.5	0.0	28.0	6.3
apsi	2.2	97.8	0.0	40.0	11.7
pmake	8.9	86.0	5.1	25.8	11.9
database	18.4	17.0	64.6	24.8	13.6
VCS	9.9	90.1	0.0	25.7	15.1

Table 2: Execution time percentages plus percentages of loads and stores in the instruction stream.

It is interesting to note that the floating point benchmarks almost never execute in kernel mode, while the integer benchmarks spend up to ten percent of their execution time in kernel mode. In addition to improving the accuracy of simulation results for integer benchmarks, the simulation of kernel mode, as well as user mode, allows the simulation of multiprogramming benchmarks such as pmake and kernel intensive benchmarks like database which spend 9% and 52% of their non-idle time in kernel mode respectively.

4. Results

To characterize the performance of the different on-chip cache designs we simulate them with cache sizes varying from 4 Kbytes to 1 Mbyte. The simulation results are shown for one representative benchmark from each of the three groups. Gcc represents the integer SPEC95 benchmarks, tomcatv the floating point SPEC95 benchmarks, and database the multiprogramming benchmarks. The results are presented in two stages. First, to understand how IPC changes with cache structure, we present results for a processor with a fixed processor cycle time. We consider the effect that pipelining has on IPC for an ideal 32 Kbyte multi-ported cache as the pipeline depth of the cache is increased from one to three cycles. We also perform the same study with banked caches and compare the results to ideal multi-ported caches. Then we show how the addition of a line buffer increases IPC by hiding memory latency. To conclude our study of IPC we look at DRAM caches. Second, using our knowledge of IPC we investigate which memory organization provides the smallest application execution time for different processor cycle times.

Before we begin looking at the high bandwidth memory organizations, we look at the miss rates per instruction of our nine benchmarks. The miss rates give an idea of the application working set size and the changes in benchmark performance with cache size. Figure 3 shows the effect on the cache misses per instruction of increasing the primary data cache size for each of the nine benchmarks used in this study. Note that the miss rates for each of our representative benchmarks are consistent with those of the other two benchmarks within their grouping.

From Figure 3 we see that the integer SPEC95 benchmarks have the lowest miss rates, the multiprogramming benchmarks have much larger miss rates, and the floating point SPEC95 benchmarks have slightly lower miss rates on average than the multiprogramming benchmarks. The integer benchmarks have the smallest miss rates because they have working sets that fit into smaller caches. We also see that for integer benchmarks changes in miss rate due to increases in cache size tend to be incremental. The multiprogramming benchmarks are integer applications with larger working sets than the integer SPEC95 benchmarks, so the change in miss rate with increasing cache size responds similarly for both; however the multiprogramming application's miss rates are greater. The floating point applications have large working sets and radical drops in miss rates at specific cache sizes. Their response to increasing cache size is different from the integer applications because floating point applications tend to access their data in more regular patterns than integer applications.

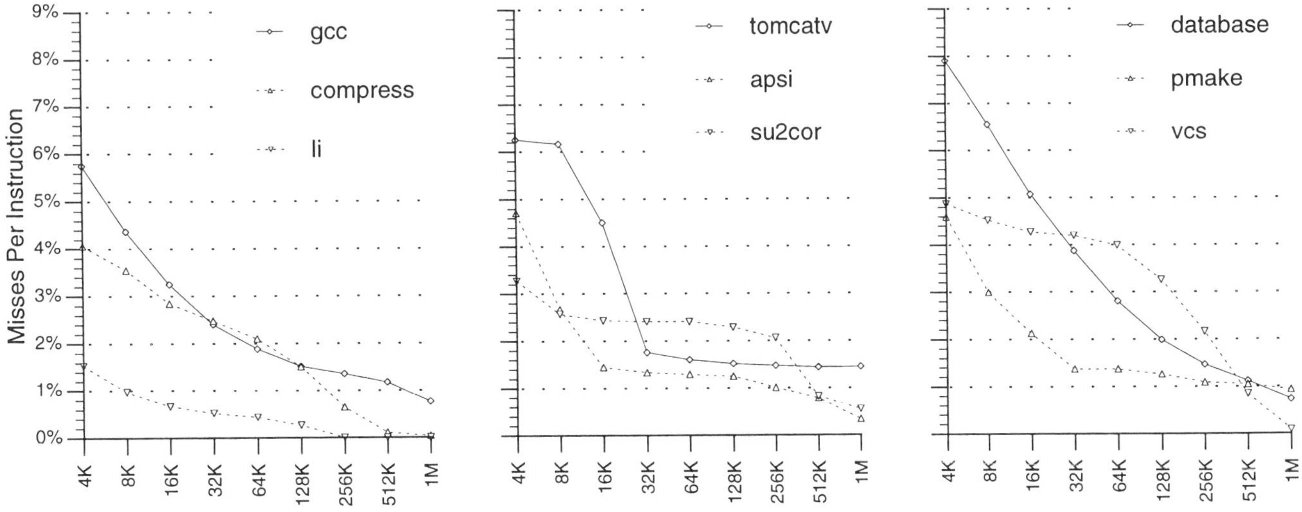

Figure 3: Benchmark miss rates in misses/instruction for single-ported caches.

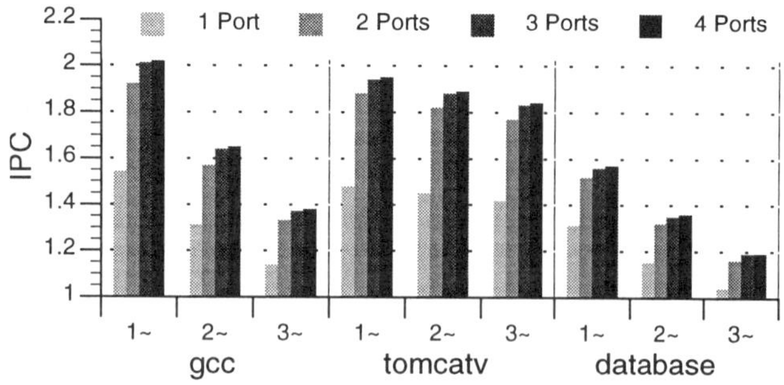

Figure 4: The performance of ideal multi-cycle multi-ported 32 Kbyte caches with a fixed processor cycle time. A "~" is used to denote cycle

4.1. Multi-Cycle, Multi-Ported Caches

We begin by presenting the IPC results of ideal multi-cycle caches with a fixed processor cycle time. For caches with multi-cycle hit times, a key question is: How much performance is lost as the hit time, measured in processor cycles, increases? Figure 4 shows how machine performance decreases with increasing hit time for one to four ideal cache ports with a 32 Kbyte primary data cache for gcc, tomcatv, and database. We see from Figure 4 that the decrease in performance for the benchmarks with multi-cycle hit times is almost independent of the number of ideal cache ports. In the case of integer applications, multi-cycle hit times degrade machine performance considerably. For the integer application gcc with two ideal cache ports, performance declines by 18% when the cache hit time is increased to two cycles, and performance declines another 15% when the cache hit time is increased to three cycles. Without the use of a dynamic superscalar processor there would be a larger performance decrease given the frequency of loads. The dynamic superscalar processor is able to hide a portion of the additional latency of the pipelined cache by reordering instruction execution to start the cache accesses as early as possible and rescheduling the load uses when necessary. For floating point applications, machine performance does not decrease nearly as much due to the large amount of instruction level parallelism (ILP) available. The dynamic superscalar processor uses the ILP available in tomcatv to hide a greater portion of the multi-cycle hit time than is possible for integer applications. Tomcatv shows only a 3% drop in performance for a two cycle hit time cache and another 3% drop in performance for a three cycle hit time. For database, a larger integer application, the performance decrease is 13% and 12% for two and three cycle hit times respectively. The smaller decline compared to gcc is due to database's larger working set which causes a higher miss rate and therefore reduces the performance impact due to increases in cache hit time.

Figure 5 shows the performance that results with banked caches of 1 to 128 banked ports and one to three cycle hit times for a 32 Kbyte primary data cache and fixed processor cycle time. By comparing Figure 5 with Figure 4, we see that a four-way banked cache provides lower performance than a cache with two ideal cache ports, while an eight-way banked cache provides higher performance than a cache with two ideal cache ports. The 128-way banked cache results show that the performance difference between an eight-way banked cache and a cache with a large number of banks is small.

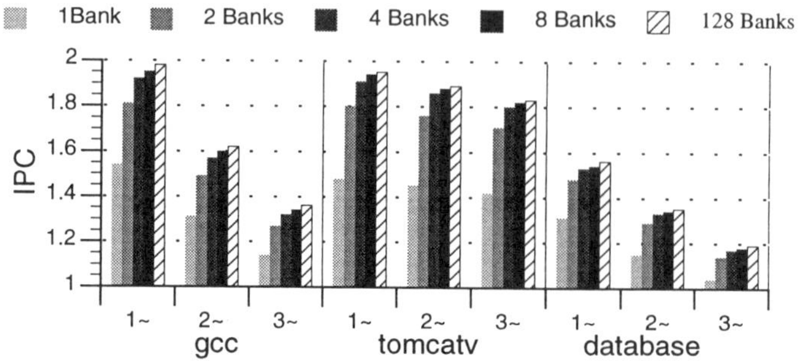

Figure 5: The performance of 32 Kbyte multi-cycle banked caches with a fixed processor cycle time.

Note that where banked caches are discussed we are interested in the number of external banks where each external bank has its own cache port. These results hold for all nine benchmarks and validate our focus on eight-way banked caches in this study.

By comparing Figure 5 to Figure 4, we see that the decrease in performance for multi-cycle hit times is about the same for an eight-way banked cache as it is for caches with two ideal cache ports. In addition, the slope of the performance decrease shown in Figures 4 and 5 is fairly constant for each benchmark as the hit time is increased from one to three cycles. The results in Figures 4 and 5 are for a fixed cache size of 32 Kbytes. In section 4.4 we investigate the performance effect of changes in cache size, processor cycle time, and cache hit time.

4.2. Line Buffer with Multi-Ported Multi-Cycle Caches

The use of a 32 64-bit entry fully-set-associative multi-ported line buffer allows a large percentage of load instructions to be satisfied from the buffer in a single cycle instead of from the data cache. Figure 6 shows the IPC of the three representative benchmarks for 32 Kbyte eight-way banked and duplicate caches of one, two, and three cycle hit times with and without a line buffer. In the legend of Figure 6, the label "LB" is added to show when a line buffer is included in the processor's load/store execution unit. In all cases the addition of a line buffer increases machine performance, but for the eight-way banked cache with a single cycle hit time the increase in machine performance is only about one-half of a percent. The reason for this small increase is that the line buffer was originally proposed to decrease the cache port access pressure when there is only one cache port. In a four issue processor with more than two cache ports, the load/store unit does not tend to get backed up with loads waiting to access the cache port; therefore, there is little performance gain due to the addition of a line buffer. The only exception is for very small caches, where the extra associativity provided by the line buffer increases processor performance.

On the other hand, a single cycle duplicate cache only contains two cache ports; therefore decreasing the cache port access pressure with a line buffer provides a greater processor performance increase of three percent. A previous study [Wils96] showed that using four ideal cache ports instead of two ideal cache ports increased performance by less than five percent for a one cycle 32 Kbyte cache. A line buffer achieves over 60% of that performance improvement without increasing the number of cache ports from two to four.

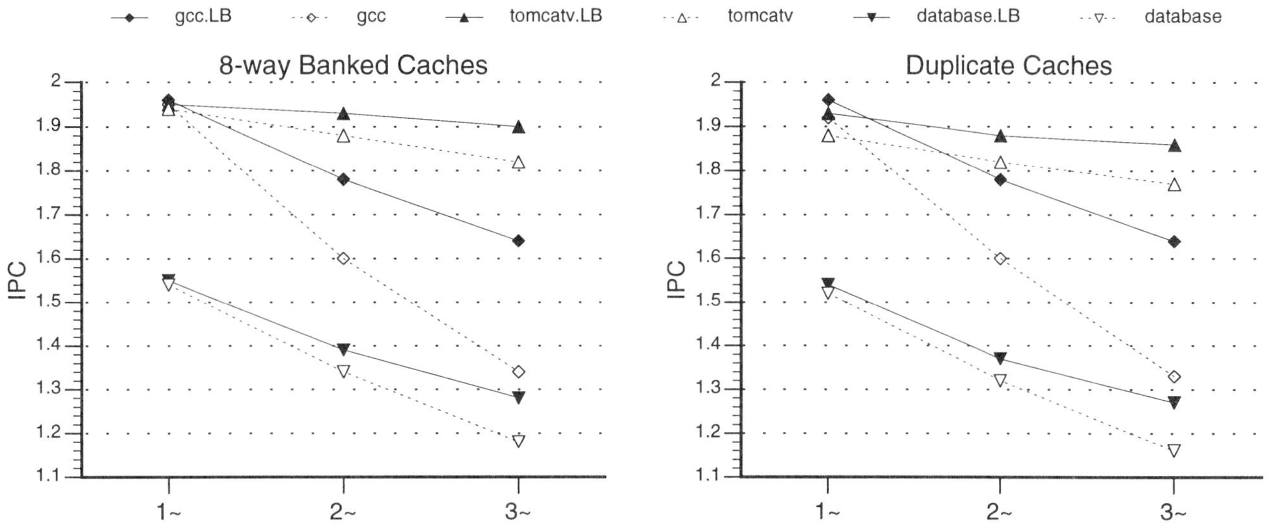

Figure 6: 32 Kbyte multi-cycle eight-way banked and duplicate caches with a line buffer and fixed processor cycle time.

Even though a line buffer is useful for multiple cache ports, it shows even more promise for pipelined caches. The line buffer hides a portion of the latency of a pipelined cache by returning data in a single cycle, thereby reducing the number of loads that need to wait for the multi-cycle hit time of the pipelined cache. As the degree of pipelining increases, the line buffer offers greater performance advantage. The use of a line buffer with an eight-way banked (duplicate) cache improves gcc's processor performance by 11% (11%) for a two cycle pipelined cache, and 22% (23%) for a three cycle pipelined cache. The database application sees a significant though smaller performance gain of 4% (4%) and 8% (9%) for two and three cycles of pipelining. Even though database is an integer application like gcc, it has a much larger working set than gcc and therefore a higher miss rate. Since the line buffer improves the performance of cache hits and not misses, we anticipate a smaller performance gain from database. Tomcatv has the smallest performance gain of only 3% (3%) and 4% (5%) for two and three cycles of pipelining. Figures 4 and 5 show that tomcatv has only a small drop in performance when a pipelined cache is used with a dynamic superscalar processor. Therefore the extra cache latency is already being hidden, providing less opportunity for the line buffer to improve processor performance. The line buffer causes a 50% reduction in the performance drop due to pipelining the cache for gcc, 50% for tomcatv, and 28% for database. Considering that the addition of a line buffer does not impact the processor's cycle time [Wils96] and machine performance is always increased, the rest of the results presented in this paper are for memory subsystems that include a line buffer.

4.3. Performance of DRAM Caches

Figure 7 presents the performance results for our dynamic superscalar processor with a 4 Mbyte DRAM on-chip data cache, a 16 Kbyte two-way-set-associative single-cycle cache created from the DRAM row buffers, and no 4 Mbyte SRAM off-chip cache. The hit time of the DRAM is varied from six to eight cycles to show how longer DRAM latencies will affect machine performance. Only the results for eight-way banked DRAM caches are presented because a 4 Mbyte cache is large and the DRAM's row buffers act as banks.

The performance results for the banked DRAM cache without a line buffer are added to show how much difference a line buffer makes as the hit time of the DRAM is increased from six to eight cycles. With the database application, the performance of the banked DRAM cache with and without a line buffer is identical.

Compared to [Shim96] the hit time of the row buffers and DRAM are very optimistic. This is necessary to make a DRAM cache that could compare to on-chip SRAM caches. We find that if the row buffers have a two cycle hit time (not shown on graph), the performance of the DRAM cache does not perform well enough to merit implementation on the processor die.

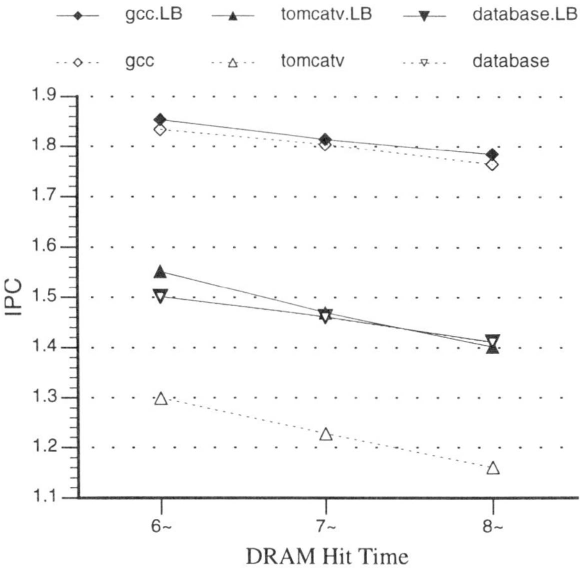

Figure 7: Multi-cycle 4 Mbyte DRAM cache with an eight-way banked 16 Kbyte row buffer cache and fixed processor cycle time.

Figure 7 shows that a line buffer provides a negligible improvement in the performance of gcc and database but drastically increases the performance of tomcatv. For an eight-way banked one cycle hit time cache, a line buffer is not really needed to reduce the access pressure on the cache ports. Therefore, we do not expect an improvement from the line buffer unless very small caches are used or there are a great number of conflict misses that can take advantage of the extra associativity provided by the line buffer. Database shows no performance increase due to the line buffer, but gcc gains more incremental performance from adding a line buffer to DRAM caches than to SRAM caches. This occurs because the use of 512 byte cache lines reduces processor performance by increasing the number of conflict misses and therefore increasing the importance of the extra associativity added by the line buffer. The line buffer increases the performance of tomcatv 18% by reducing the conflict misses that are caused both by the increase in line size, and the small size of the 16 Kbyte cache. With a line buffer, the performance cost of using the 16 Kbyte two-way-set-associative 512 byte line row buffer cache instead of an equivalent SRAM cache with 32 byte lines is 17%, 6%, and 6% for tomcatv, gcc, and database respectively.

Note that the decrease in processor performance due to increasing the hit time of the DRAM cache is not that significant because of the single-cycle hit time row buffer cache. The same amount of performance is lost with an increase in DRAM hit time of six to seven cycles as is lost for an increase in hit time from seven to eight cycles. On average for all nine benchmarks, the processor performance drops by 3% for each one cycle increase in the DRAM hit time.

4.4. Comparing Design Alternatives

To determine which on-chip memory organization provides the best IPC, we simulate the nine benchmarks with cache sizes ranging from 4 Kbytes to 1 Mbyte, and cache hit times of one to three processor cycles. As expected, the best performing organizations are single cycle access duplicate caches and eight-way banked caches with a line buffer inside the processor's load/store execution unit.

Figure 8 shows how the IPC of the processor increases with increasing cache size for gcc, tomcatv, database, and the average of the nine benchmarks. This is done for duplicate and eight-way banked pipelined caches of one to three cycles with a line buffer. The datapoint for the 4 Mbyte DRAM cache with a one cycle 16 Kbyte row buffer cache and a six cycle DRAM hit time is also shown. The curves for both gcc and database have the same characteristics as the curves for the average of the nine benchmarks. Tomcatv behaves slightly differently. For larger cache sizes, the eight-way banked cache just barely outperforms the duplicate cache. Large eight-way banked caches perform better because floating point applications, like tomcatv, are more likely than integer applications to take advantage of the extra cache ports by having more than two non-conflicting load instructions ready to access the cache in a single cycle. On the other hand, for a small cache tomcatv performs significantly better with a duplicate cache than an eight-way banked cache. The higher miss rate of the small cache causes cache lines to be replaced more frequently. For tomcatv, the banked cache tends to group cache accesses to different cache lines within a single cycle. This increases the rate of cache line replacement, lowering the cache's ability to take advantage of spatial locality and therefore increasing the miss rate. As the miss rate decreases with larger caches, the chance of replacing a cache line decreases, and the performance advantage of more cache ports allows the eight-way banked cache to outperform the duplicate cache.

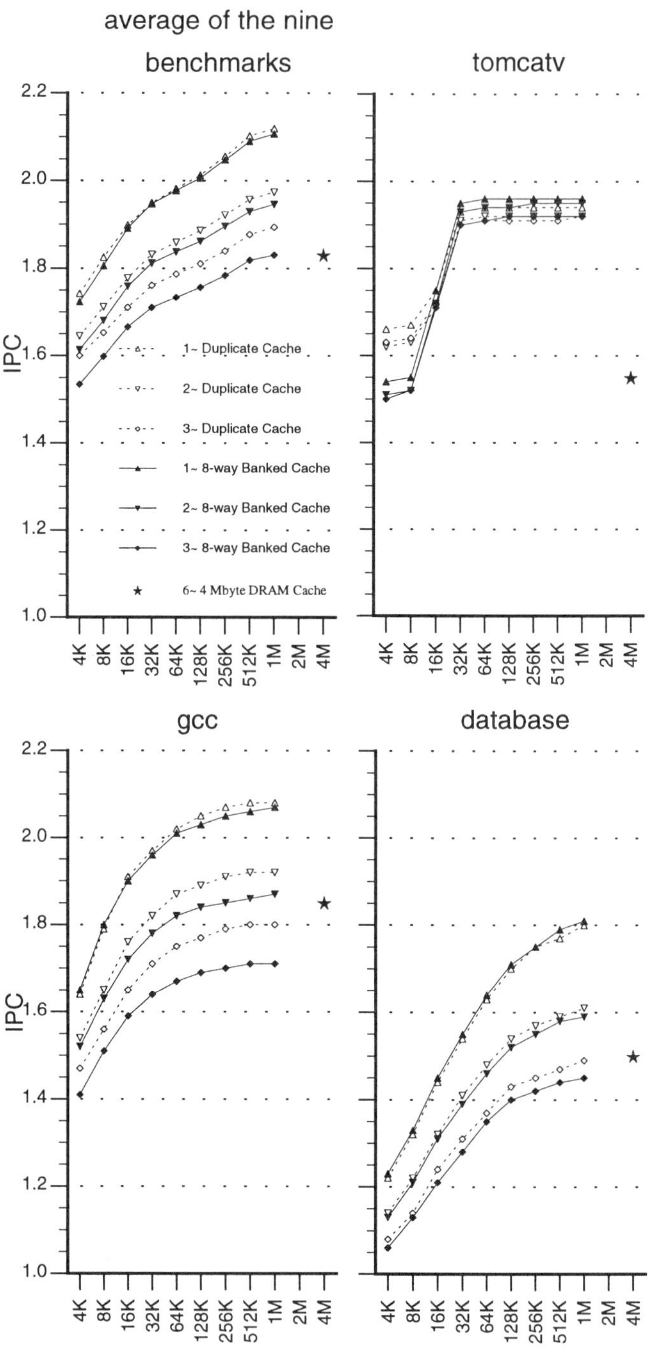

Figure 8: IPC of multi-cycle banked and duplicate caches with a line buffer and fixed processor cycle time.

In Figure 8 we see that on average the performance of a duplicate cache is greater than that of the equivalent eight-way banked cache even though Figures 4 and 5 show us the opposite result. The change is due to the inclusion of a line buffer within the load/store execution unit of the processor. Earlier in this study we showed that without the line buffer, eight-way banked caches always outperform duplicate caches. Although an eight-way banked cache has the drawback of bank conflicts, the performance penalty is not as severe as being restricted to two cache ports. Adding a line buffer does not significantly reduce bank conflicts, but does reduce port contention; therefore, a duplicate cache with a line buffer can outperform an eight-way banked cache with a line buffer. Furthermore, the cache access time of an eight-way banked cache is always greater or equal to the cache access time of a duplicate cache of the same size. Consequently, on average a duplicate cache with a line buffer will outperform an eight-way banked cache with a line buffer. For this reason we only examine duplicate caches to find the best cache organization for a given processor cycle time.

The IPC of a six cycle hit time DRAM cache with a one cycle row buffer cache and a line buffer is also included in Figure 8. Even with the optimistic hit time simulated for the DRAM cache, on average the DRAM cache does not perform as well as a 16 Kbyte SRAM cache. The reasons for this are first, the 512 byte lines of the row buffer cache cause a significant degradation in processor performance due to conflict misses that is only partially alleviated by the use of a line buffer, and second, the 16 Kbyte row buffer cache is not large enough to make up for the six cycle latency of the DRAM. A DRAM cache can only compete with a SRAM cache if the row buffer cache is increased to 32 Kbytes and the performance degradation due to the use of 512 byte lines can be hidden.

Up to this point we have considered the processor's cycle time fixed and presented performance in terms of IPC results, whereas the real measure of performance is application execution time. To determine execution time, we use the cache access times shown in Figure 1 to find the maximum size duplicate SRAM cache that can be built with hit times of one, two, and three processor cycles for a given processor cycle time. We then use these cache sizes and cycle times to find the execution time of applications running on a processor with the corresponding dual-ported cache. However, we cannot use the IPC results shown in Figure 8 because they are from simulations of the different cache structures with a fixed level two cache hit time of ten cycles and a memory access time of sixty cycles. Different simulations using the correctly scaled level two cache hit time and memory access time are used in Figure 9 to present the execution time of our applications. Figure 9 shows how the execution times for gcc, tomcatv, database, and the average of all nine benchmarks vary with cache size and hit time for different processor cycle times. The curves for each benchmark are normalized to the execution time of the processor with a cycle time of 10 FO4 and a 32 KByte three-cycle pipelined cache.

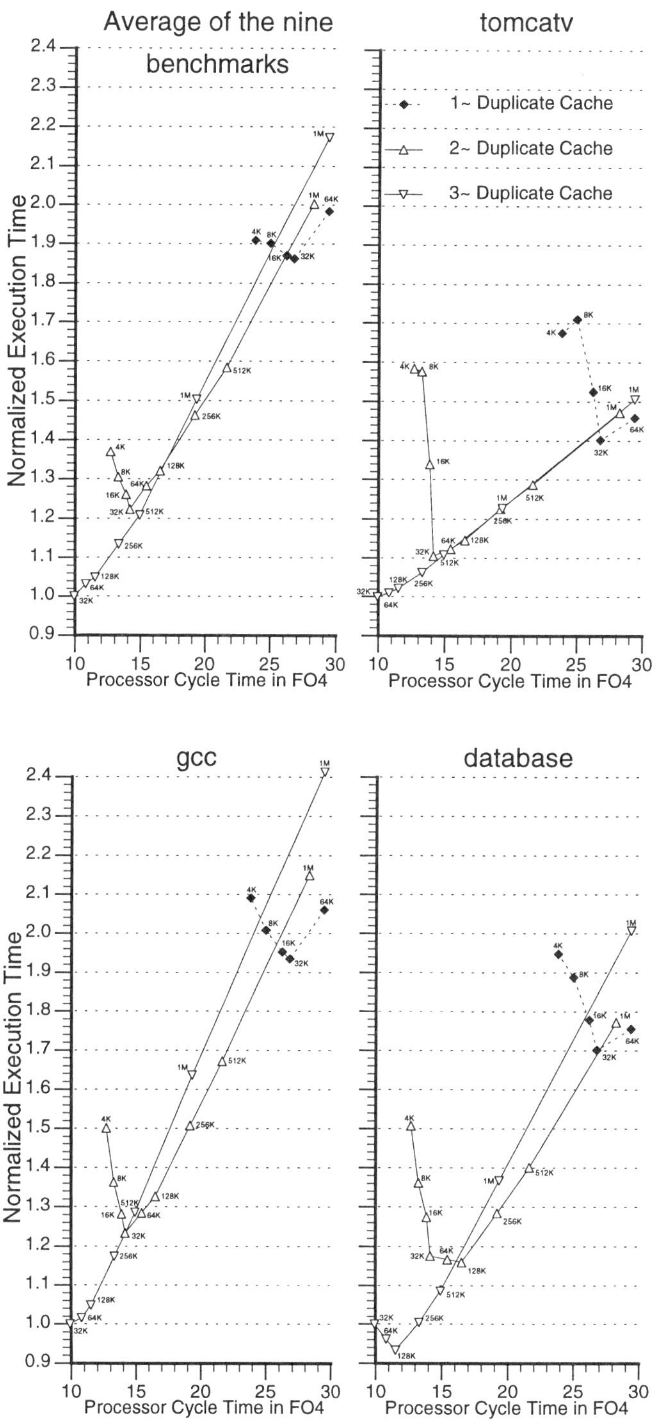

Figure 9: Normalized execution time for multi-cycle duplicate caches with a line buffer.

Notice that the execution time curves for the duplicate caches have similar shapes for one and two cycle hit time caches. The curve for the three cycle cache is also comparable, but only the region from a 32 Kbyte cache to a 1 Mbyte cache is shown. The shape of the curves for gcc and database is the same as for the average of the nine benchmarks, but the slope of the curve for database is flatter than the curve for gcc. The slope of the database curve is flatter since the miss rates are greater; therefore the effect of increasing the frequency of the processor is less. In the case of tomcatv, we see very little difference between the performance of one to three cycle pipelined caches in the range of 32 Kbytes to 1 Mbyte because the IPC of tomcatv does not vary in this range of cache sizes, and tomcatv loses very little performance with increasing cache pipeline depth.

One thing to note from Figure 9 is that even with a fixed cache size, a given percentage reduction in processor cycle time results in a smaller percentage reduction in execution time. This is due to the fact that a significant portion of an application's execution time is spent in the memory system. For example, the performance of tomcatv only increases by a factor of 1.5, even though the processor cycle time is reduced by a factor of three. We find that tomcatv spends roughly half of its execution time in the memory system. Using a speedup of three in processor cycle time and fifty percent of the execution time spent in the processor, Amdahl's Law [Henn96] predicts an overall performance increase of 1.5 times.

The non-pipelined cache results of Figure 9 can be compared to the results of Jouppi and Wilton [Joup94] for single-level on-chip caches. They used cacti for the access times of their caches and a trace driven memory simulator to simulate the performance of 1 Kbyte to 256 Kbyte direct mapped blocking caches. We also use cacti for our cache access times, but we simulate a dynamic superscalar processor with two-way-set-associative non-blocking caches. The dynamic superscalar processor and the non-blocking caches hide part of the performance lost due to small cache sizes, and a two-way-set-associative cache will perform about as well as a direct-mapped cache of twice its size [Henn96]. These differences tend to increase the processor's performance for smaller size caches and decrease the incremental performance gained from doubling the cache size.

Our two studies overlap for gcc and tomcatv executed with single-cycle single-level caches varying in size from 4 Kbytes to 256 Kbytes. Jouppi and Wilton show that the best performance with a single level of cache is achieved for SPEC92 gcc with a 32 Kbyte direct mapped primary data cache. For SPEC95 gcc, we find that for an aggressive dynamic superscalar processor, the best performance for gcc is obtained with a two-way set-associative 32 Kbyte duplicate cache. In the case of SPEC92 tomcatv, Jouppi and Wilton found that only a 16 Kbyte data cache was required, but we find that a 32 Kbyte duplicate cache is needed to provide the best execution times. Larger set-associative caches are required due to the larger working set sizes of the SPEC95 benchmarks. Our caches are also multi-ported to support the additional cache bandwidth required by a dynamic superscalar processor.

The amount of cache pipelining that optimizes performance depends on both the working set size of the applications that are executed on the dynamic superscalar processor and the processor's cycle time. Executing with larger application working sets increases the cache miss rate, requiring a larger cache to minimize execution time. Refer to Figure 3 to see how the larger cache sizes available due to pipelining reduce miss rate. Decreasing the processor's cycle time makes it harder to build a cache large enough to minimize execution time without pipelining the cache. Therefore, the combination of a large working set size and a small processor cycle time require large pipelined caches to produce the best processor performance.

In Figure 9 we see that the best performing cache organization is indeed based upon both processor cycle time and working set size. If the processor's cycle time is large enough, a single-cycle 64 Kbyte duplicate cache will provide the best performance, but if the processor's cycle time is less than 25 FO4, a pipelined cache is always the best performer. In between these two extremes the best organization is dependent upon both cycle time and working set size. For gcc we see that if the processor can accommodate a single-cycle 16 Kbyte cache then the cache should not be pipelined; however database has a larger working set than gcc, so its results lead to a different conclusion. In fact, if we simulate only small applications with working sets that can fit in a 4 Kbyte cache, there is be no point in using pipelined caches unless the processor's frequency is so fast that a one cycle 4 Kbyte cache cannot be built. Only applications with large realistic working sets need the larger caches that are possible with pipelining.

From Figure 9 we see that a processor cycle time of 29 FO4 can accommodate a one cycle 64 Kbyte duplicate cache. Even with database's working set size, a 64 Kbyte single cycle cache outperforms any pipelined cache that can be built. For processor cycle times of less than 29 FO4, the larger pipelined cache maximizes processor performance. In the unlikely event that a dynamic superscalar processor can be built in 15 FO4, a 1 Mbyte three cycle cache provides the best performance, but a two cycle 32 Kbyte cache should be considered for its smaller die area at the cost of a small drop in performance. If a processor can be built with a cycle time of 10 FO4, then at least three cycles of pipelining are required.

Figure 9 shows the best cache size and pipelining necessary to minimize application execution time for a given processor cycle time. When the processor cycle time is not fixed, we find that on average a 32 Kbyte cache minimizes execution time for each cache pipeline depth. This shows that on average our application working sets fit well enough within a 32 Kbyte cache that increasing the cache size does not sufficiently decrease the cache miss rate to compensate for the resulting increase in cycle time.

5. Conclusion

In this study we have investigated a number of on-chip data cache organizations that include multi-ported caches, multi-cycle caches, line buffers, and DRAM caches. We have evaluated these cache organizations with simulations that include operating system references for nine realistic benchmarks with primary data cache sizes ranging from 4 Kbytes to 4 Mbytes. A dynamic superscalar processor with a lockup-free fully-pipelined cache was used to maximize the bandwidth demands on the cache. The processor cycle times were varied from a cycle time of 29 FO4, that can accommodate a 64 Kbyte one cycle single-ported primary data cache, to extremely fast processors that have a processor cycle time of only 10 FO4.

For a fixed cache size and processor cycle time, increasing the number of cache ports through cache banking and cache duplication increases processor performance, while increasing the amount of pipelining in the cache decreases processor performance. In the case of ideal cache ports, increasing the number of ports from one to two results in a 25% increase in processor performance. An increase in the number of cache ports from two to three achieves a 4% increase in performance and an increase from three to four ports increases performance by less than 1%. Duplicating the cache results in processor performance comparable to a cache with two ideal cache ports. Adding extra cache ports by banking the cache also increases processor performance, but much more slowly than adding ideal cache ports. We used cacti to analyze an eight-way banked cache and demonstrated that banking the cache increases the hit time for small cache sizes. Larger caches, however, already use an internal banking structure. Looking at IPC and ignoring changes in cycle time, we found that a processor with a duplicate cache will always outperform a four-way banked cache but that an eight-way banked cache will always outperform a duplicate cache. For this reason we concentrate on eight-way banked caches and duplicate caches in this study. When pipelining is added to the cache with cache size and cycle time held constant, we see a 12-23% decrease in IPC per pipeline stage for integer applications but only a 3-9% decrease for floating point applications.

Since adding additional cache ports can be expensive both in die area and cache cycle time, a line buffer can be used to reduce the performance loss due to building fewer cache ports. The use of a line buffer with a duplicate cache improves processor performance by 3%, while a line buffer with an eight-way banked cache improves performance by only 0.5%. In fact, the performance improvement due to a line buffer used with a duplicate cache changed the results so that the IPC of a duplicate cache with a line buffer is on average always greater or equal to the IPC of an eight-way banked cache with a line buffer. In addition, the use of a line buffer with pipelined multi-ported caches decreases the performance drop due to pipelining by 28%-61% for integer applications and 50%-74% for floating point applications.

Combining cycle time, cache size, and cache structure to find the cache organization with the best performance on our nine benchmarks, we found that the use of a large pipelined duplicate cache with a line buffer almost always results in the best processor performance. Since the use of a line buffer always increases processor IPC without a corresponding increase in processor cycle time and the cycle time of a duplicate cache is always less than or equal to the cycle time of an eight-way banked cache, a processor performs better with a duplicate cache instead of an eight-way banked cache as long as a line buffer is included within the load/store execution unit of the processor. We also found that the use of an aggressive six cycle hit time 4 Mbyte DRAM cache with a one cycle eight-way banked 16 Kbyte two-way-set-associative primary row buffer cache and a line buffer, on average, provides less processor performance than an equivalent 16 Kbyte SRAM cache with a ten cycle hit time 4 Mbyte secondary cache.

To minimize application execution time, the pipeline depth of the cache must be determined by the processor's cycle time. For a processor with a slow cycle time of 29 FO4, a 64 Kbyte dual-ported single-cycle cache provides the best processor performance. On the other hand, for processor cycle times between 29 FO4 and 24 FO4, a two cycle cache delivers the best performance if there is enough room on the processor die for the larger two cycle cache. For processor cycle times of less than 24 FO4, the cache must be pipelined since the processor cannot support a single-cycle non-pipelined cache of even 4 KBytes.

Acknowledgments

We would like to thank Mendel Rosenblum, Steve Herrod, Edouard Bugnion, and Robert Bosch for their help with SimOS, Mark Horowitz for his help with cache design, and the reviewers for their insightful comments. This work was supported by ARPA contract DABT63-94-C-0054.

References

[Aspr93] Tom Asprey, Gregory S. Averill, Eric DeLano, Russ Mason, Bill Weiner, and Jeff Yetter, "Performance Features of the PA7100 Microprocessor", *IEEE Micro*, June 1993, pp. 22-35.

[Benn95] James Bennett and Mike Flynn, "Performance Factors for Superscalar Processors", Technical Report CSL-TR-95-661, Computer Systems Laboratory, Stanford University, Feb. 1995.

[Bowh95] William J. Bowhill, et al, "Circuit Implementation of a 300-MHz 64-bit Second-generation CMOS Alpha CPU", *Digital Technical Journal*, Special 10th Anniversary Issue, Vol. 7, No. 1, 1995, pp. 100-118.

[Chap91] Terry I. Chappell, Barbara A. Chappell, Stanley E. Schuster, James W. Allen, Stephen P. Klepner, Rajiv V. Joshi, and Robert L. Franch, "A 2-ns Cycle, 3.8-ns Access 512-kb CMOS ECL SRAM with a Fully Pipelined Architecture", *IEEE Journal of Solid-State Circuits*, Vol. 26, No. 11, November 1991, pp. 1577-1585.

[Chen92] Tien-Fu Chen and Jean-Loup Baer, "Reducing Memory Latency via Non-blocking and Prefetching Caches", *ASPLOS-V*, Boston, Massachusetts, October 12-15, 1992.

[Chen94] Chung-Ho Chen and Arun K. Somani, "A Unified Architectural Tradeoff Methodology", *Proceedings of the 21st Annual International Symposium on Computer Architecture*, Chicago, Illinois, April 18-21, 1994, pp. 348-357.

[Conte92] Thomas A. Conte, "Tradeoffs in Processor/Memory Interfaces for Superscalar Processors", *Proceedings of the 25th Annual International Symposium on Microarchitecture*, Portland, Or 1992.

[Cvet94] Zarka Cvetanovic and Dileep Bhandarkar, "Characterization of Alpha AXP Performance Using TP and SPEC Workloads", *Proceedings of the 21st Annual International Symposium on Computer Architecture*, Chicago, Illinois, April 18-21, 1994, pp. 60-70.

[Edmo95] John H. Edmondson, et al, "Internal Organization of the Alpha 21164 a 300-MHz 64-bit Quad-issue CMOS RISC Microprocessor", *Digital Technical Journal*, Special 10th Anniversary Issue, Vol. 7, No. 1, 1995, pp. 119-135.

[Fark94] Keith I. Farkas and Norman P. Jouppi, "Complexity/Performance Tradeoffs with Non-Blocking Loads", *Proceedings of the 21st Annual International Symposium on Computer Architecture*, Chicago, Illinois, April 18-21, 1994, pp. 211-222.

[Farr94] Mathew Farrens, Gary Tyson, and Andrew R. Pleszkun, "A Study of Single-Chip Processor/Cache Organizations for Large Numbers of Transistors", *Proceedings of the 21st Annual International Symposium on Computer Architecture*, Chicago, Illinois, April 18-21, 1994, pp. 338-347.

[Gee93] Jeffrey D. Gee, Mark D. Hill, Dionisios N. Pnevmatikatos, and Alan Jay Smith, "Cache Performance of the SPEC92 Benchmark Suite", *IEEE Micro*, August 1993, pp. 17-27.

[Gray93] Jim Gray, Ed., "The Benchmark Handbook for Database and Transaction Processing Systems", Morgan Kaufmann Publishers, 1993.

[Gwen94] Linley Gwennap, "MIPS R10000 Uses Decoupled Architecture", *Microprocessor Report*, Volume 8, Number 14, October 24, 1994, pp. 18-22.

[Henn96] John L. Hennessy and David A. Patterson, "Computer Architecture a Quantitative Approach", Morgan Kaufmann Publishers, Inc, Second Edition, 1996.

[Horo92] M. Horowitz, S. Przybylski, and M. D. Smith, "Tutorial on Recent Trends in Processor Design: Reclimbing the Complexity Curve", *Western Institute of Computer Science*, Stanford University, 1992.

[Horo96] M. Horowitz, "High Frequency Clock Distribution", High Frequency Digital Logic Design and Clocking Strategies, *1996 Symposium on VLSI Circuits*, June 13-15, 1996.

[Hunt95] Doug Hunt, "Advanced Performance Features of the 64-bit PA-8000", *Digest of papers COMPCON '95*, IEEE Computer Society Press, San Francisco, CA, March 5-9, 1995, pp. 123-132.

[John91] Mike Johnson, "Superscalar Microprocessor Design", Prentice-Hall Inc, 1991.

[Joup90] Norman P. Jouppi, "Improving direct-mapped cache performance by the addition of a small fully-associative cache and prfetch buffers", *Proceedings of the 17th Annual Int'l Symposium on Computer Architecture*, IEEE Computer Society Press, Seattle, May 28-31, 1990, pp. 364-373.

[Joup93] Norman P. Jouppi, "Cache Write Policies and Performance", *Proceedings of the 20th Annual International Symposium on Computer Architecture*, San Diego, California, May 16-19, 1993.

[Joup94] Norman P. Jouppi and Steven J. E. Wilton, "Tradeoffs in Two-Level On-Chip Caching", *Proceedings of the 21st Annual International Symposium on Computer Architecture*, Chicago, Illinois, April 18-21, 1994, pp. 34-45.

[Krof81] David Kroft, "Lockup-Free Instruction Fetch/Prefetch Cache Organization", *Proceedings of the 8th Annual International Symposium on Computer Architecture*, 1993 pp. 81-87.

[Kell96] Jim Keller, "The 21264: A Superscalar Alpha Processor with Out-of-Order Execution", *Microprocessor Forum*, October 22-23, 1996.

[Kusk94] Jeff Kuskin, et al, "The Stanford FLASH multiprocessor", *Proceedings of the 21st International Symposium on Computer Architecture*, pp. 302-313, April 1994.

[Mayn94] Ann Marie Grizzaffi Maynard, Colette M. Donnelly, and Bret R. Olszewski, "Contrasting Characteristics and Cache Performance of Technical and Multi-User Commercial Workloads", *ASPLOS-VI*, San Jose, CA, October 4-7, 1994.

[McLe93] Edward McLellan, "The Alpha AXP Architecture and 21064 Processor", *IEEE Micro*, June 1993, pp. 36-47.

[MIPS94] MIPS Technologies, Incorporated, "R10000 Microprocessor Product Overview", MIPS Open RISC Technology, MIPS Technologies, Incorporated, October 1994.

[Naff96] Samuel Naffziger, "SP 22.5: A Sub-Nanosecond 0.5 um 64b Adder Design", *1996 IEEE International Solid-State Circuits Conference Digest of Technical Papers*, Volume 39, February 1996, pp. 362, 363.

[NEC94] NEC Corporation, "16M bit Synchronous DRAM, preliminary data sheet", NEC Corporation, March 1994.

[Oluk92] Kunle Olukotun, Trevor Mudge, and Richard Brown, "Performance Optimization of Pipelined Primary Caches", *Proceedings of the 19th Annual International Symposium on Computer Architecture*, Gold Coast, Australia, May 19-21, 1992, pp. 181-190.

[Przy88] Przybylski, S., M. Horowitz, and J. Hennessy, "Performance Tradeoffs in Cache Design", *Proceedings of the 15th Annual International Symposium on Computer Architecture*, June 1988, pp.290-298.

[Rau93] B. Ramakrishna Rau and Joseph A. Fisher, "Instruction-Level Parallel Processing: History, Overview, and Perspective", *Journal of Supercomputing*, 7, 1993, pp. 9-50.

[Rose95] Mendel Rosenblum, Edouard Bugnion, Stephen Alan Herrod, Emmett Witchel, and Anoop Gupta, "The Impact of Architectural Trends on Operating System Performance", *Proceedings of the 15th ACM Symposium on Operating Systems Principles*, Copper Mountain Resort, Colorado, Dec. 3-6, 1995.

[Rose95b] Mendel Rosenblum, Stephen A. Herrod, Emmett Witchel, and Anoop Gupta, "Complete Computer System Simulation: The SimOS Approach", *IEEE Parallel and Distrubuted Technology*, Volume 3, Number 4, Fall 1995.

[Saul96] Ashley Saulsbury, Fong Pong, Andreas Nowatzyk, "Missing the Memory Wall: The Case for Processor/Memory Integration", *Proceedings of the 23rd Annual International Symposium on Computer Architecture*, May 22-24, 1996, pp. 90-101.

[Shim96] Toru Shimizu, et al, "A Multimedia 32b RISC Microprocessor with 16Mb DRAM", *1996 IEEE International Solid-State Circuits Conference Digest of Technical Papers*, Volume 39, IEEE Catalog Number 96CH35889, February 1996, pp. 216, 217.

[Sohi91] Gurindar S. Sohi and Manoj Franklin, "High-Bandwidth Data Memory Systems for Superscalar Processors", *ASPLOS-IV*, Santa Clara, CA, April 8-11, 1991.

[SPEC95] SPEC, "SPEC Benchmark Specifications - 101.tomcatv", SPEC95 benchmarks release, 1995.

[Toma67] Tomasulo, R. M., "An Efficient Algorithm for Exploiting Multiple Arithmetic Units.", *IBM Journal of Research and Development*, Vol. 11 (January 1967), pp. 25-33.

[Uht86] Uht, A. K., "An Efficient Hardware Algorithm to Extract Concurrency from General Purpose Code", *Proceedings of the Nineteenth Annual Hawaii International Conference on System Sciences*, 1986, pp. 41-50.

[Upto94] Michael Upton, Thomas Huff, Trevor Mudge, and Richard Brown, "Resource Allocation in a High Clock Rate Microprocessor", *ASPLOS-VI*, San Jose, CA, October 4-7, 1994, pp. 98-109.

[Wall93] David W. Wall, "Limits of Instruction-Level Parallelism", *WRL Research Report 93/6*, Western Research Laboratory, November 1993.

[Wilk95] Maurice V. Wilkes, "The Memory Wall and the CMOS End-Point", *ACM Computer Architecture News*, Vol. 23, No. 4, September 1995, pp. 4-6

[Wils95] Kenneth M. Wilson and Kunle Olukotun, "High Performance Cache Architectures to Support Dynamic Superscalar Microprocessors", Technical Report CSL-TR-95-682, Computer Systems Laboratory, Stanford University, June 1995.

[Wils96] Kenneth M. Wilson, Kunle Olukotun, and Mendel Rosenblum, "Increasing Cache Port Efficiency for Dynamic Superscalar Microprocessors", *Proceedings of the 23rd Annual International Symposium on Computer Architecture*, May 22-24, 1996, pp. 147-157.

[Wilt94] Steven J. E. Wilton and Norman P. Jouppi, "An Enhanced Access and Cycle Time Model for On-Chip Caches", *WRL Research Report 93/5*, Western Research Laboratory, 1994.

[Wilt96] Steven J. E. Wilton and Norman P. Jouppi, "CACTI: An Enhanced Access and Cycle Time Model", *IEEE Journal of Solid-State Circuits*, Volume 31, Number 5, May 1996, pp. 677-688.

[Witc96] Emmett Witchel and Mendel Rosenblum, "Embra: Fast and Flexible Machine Simulation", *Proceedings of the ACM SIGMETRICS '96: Conference on Measurement and Modeling of Computer Systems*, Philadelphia, PA, 1996.

[Wulf95] Wm. A. Wulf, Sally A. McKee, "Hitting the Memory Wall: Implications of the Obvious", *ACM Computer Architecture News*, Vol. 23, No. 1, March 1995, pp. 20-24.

[Yeag96] Kenneth C. Yeager, "MIPS R10000", *IEEE Micro*, Vol. 16, No 2, April 1996, pp. 28-40.

Memory-System Design Considerations for Dynamically-Scheduled Processors

Keith I. Farkas[†] farkas@eecg.toronto.edu

Paul Chow[†] pc@eecg.toronto.edu

Norman P. Jouppi[‡] jouppi@pa.dec.com

Zvonko Vranesic[†] zvonko@eecg.toronto.edu

[†]Electrical and Computer Engineering
University of Toronto
10 Kings College Road
Toronto, Ontario M5S 3G4 Canada

[‡]Digital Equipment Corporation
Western Research Lab
250 University Avenue
Palo Alto, California 94301 USA

Abstract

In this paper, we identify performance trends and design relationships between the following components of the data memory hierarchy in a dynamically-scheduled processor: the register file, the lockup-free data cache, the stream buffers, and the interface between these components and the lower levels of the memory hierarchy. Similar performance was obtained from all systems having support for fewer than four in-flight misses, irrespective of the register-file size, the issue width of the processor, and the memory bandwidth. While providing support for more than four in-flight misses did increase system performance, the improvement was less than that obtained by increasing the number of registers. The addition of stream buffers to the investigated systems led to a significant performance increase, with the larger increases for systems having less in-flight-miss support, greater memory bandwidth, or more instruction issue capability. The performance of these systems was not significantly affected by the inclusion of traffic filters, dynamic-stride calculators, or the inclusion of the per-load non-unity stride-predictor *and the* incremental-prefetching *techniques, which we introduce. However, the incremental prefetching technique reduces the bandwidth consumed by stream buffers by 50% without a significant impact on performance.*

1 Introduction

Dynamically-scheduled processors offer much greater tolerance for data-cache misses than do statically-scheduled processors. This increased tolerance is provided by the ability to issue instructions in an order different from that in which they were fetched whenever a hazard prohibits in-order issue. Cache misses may induce data and structural hazards that involve the instructions that are waiting to be issued. The degree of tolerance represents a balance between the number instructions that are not affected by such hazards, and the time required to resolve the miss. This balance exists because the longer a cache miss takes to be resolved, the greater the number of instructions that are required to hide it.

The time required to resolve a miss is determined by the bandwidth of the memory interface that is situated between the data cache and the lower levels of the memory hierarchy, and by the time required to fetch a data item once a request for it has been issued. The ability to hide a cache miss is determined by the ability of the dynamic scheduler to issue unaffected instructions. The likelihood that such instructions are available to the scheduler is determined by a number of factors. Branch prediction is an important factor because its use allows the hardware to continue fetching instructions from beyond a branch for which the direction or destination (address) is not statically known. Speculative fetching of instructions provides the supply of (possibly) unaffected, new instructions. These instructions can be made available to the dynamic scheduler if the required hardware resources for processing the instructions are available.

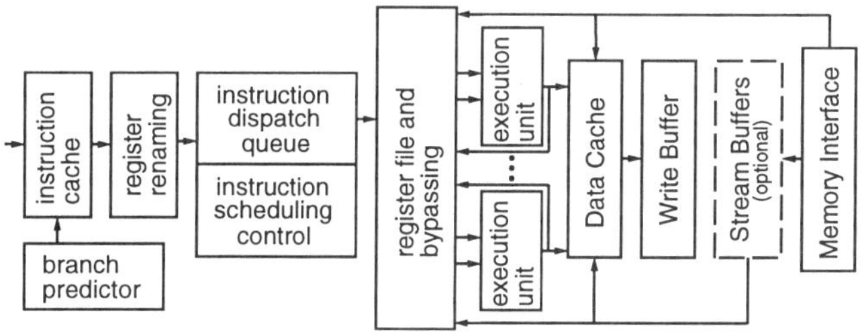

Figure 1: Overview of our dynamic scheduling implementation; only the data path is shown.

In our system model (Figure 1), the *dispatch queue* stores the instructions from which the dynamic scheduler chooses the instructions to issue next. To insert an instruction into the dispatch queue, there must be an available entry, and, if the instruction names an *architectural register* as a destination, there must be a *physical register* available to rename the named architectural register. If one of the required resources is not available, the process of inserting instructions must be stalled until a resource is available.

The availability of dispatch-queue entries and physical registers is affected by the number of miss-processing resources that are provided by the lockup-free data cache. The number of such resources places a limit on the number of cache misses that can be serviced concurrently. If a resource is required and none is available, the dynamic scheduler must stop issuing memory instructions until the required resource is available. Such stalls in the issuing of memory instructions can quickly lead to a full dispatch queue and a decrease in the rate of forward progress.

In this paper, our goal is to provide insight into the effectiveness of hardware-based techniques for reducing the apparent time cost of

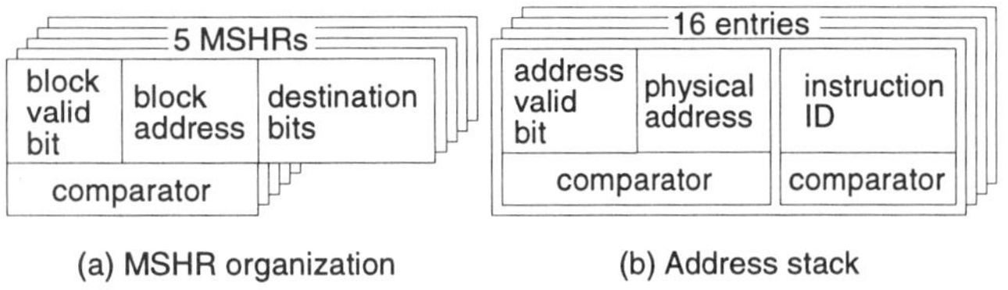

Figure 2: Functional block diagram of the proposed lockup-free cache implementation that supports 16 in-flight memory accesses and five in-flight cache-block fetches.

cache misses or increasing the tolerance for data-cache misses. The memory-system components that we consider are the register file, the lockup-free data cache, and the *stream buffers* [1], a technique for implementing hardware-based prefetching. We also examine the interface between these components and the lower levels of the memory hierarchy.

The presentation begins with a description of the lockup-free cache and stream buffer implementations we consider, followed by an overview in Section 3 of our system model and simulation methodology. Then, we examine the performance of various lockup-free data cache organizations in Section 4, and of various stream-buffer implementations in Section 5.

2 Hardware

This section describes, in the context of a dynamically-scheduled processor, the hardware that is required to implement a lockup-free data cache and the stream buffer implementations that we consider. A more complete discussion of these components is given in [2].

2.1 Lockup-free Cache

When the processor detects a data-cache miss, it must determine whether the cache-block containing the missing data is already being fetched, and it must resolve all pending cache misses when this cache-block is returned from the lower levels of the memory hierarchy. This functionality is provided by *miss status holding registers* (MSHRs) [3], but for dynamically-scheduled processors, additional functionality is required that is not present in statically-scheduled processors. This functionality allows selective cache misses to be suppressed while allowing others to be completed, thereby permitting the cancellation of speculatively executed memory instructions.

To provide the required functionality, we use a set of MSHRs and an *address stack*. The MSHRs are used to determine whether a cache block is already being fetched, whereas the address stack is used to resolve pending cache misses. As shown in Figure 2a, each MSHR has three fields. The "block valid bit" indicates whether the cache block with the address stored in the "block address" field is in the process of being fetched. When a data-cache miss is detected, the MSHRs are associatively searched to determine whether the cache block is already being fetched. If a match is detected, the cache miss is referred to as a *secondary miss*, whereas if no match is detected, the miss is referred to as a *primary miss* [3]. For a primary miss, a free MSHR is allocated, the block address is written, the "block valid bit" set, and a fetch request for the cache block is issued to the next level in the memory system. If there are no free MSHRs, no further memory requests can be issued until an MSHR is released by the return of previously-requested data; the load or store that caused this *structural-hazard-induced stall* will be replayed subsequent to the freeing of an MSHR.

When a cache-block is returned, an associative lookup of the MSHR structure is done to extract the "destination bits" (Figure 2a). This information indicates whether the cache block is to be returned to the data cache, the instruction cache, or perhaps neither because it is to be used to resolve an access to an uncached memory location. Some information must be returned with the data to facilitate this lookup. Since dynamically-scheduled processors often support cache consistency and thus have a mechanism for sending addresses to the processor from the memory system, a reasonable choice is to have the memory return the fetch-request address along with the data. After the destination bits are extracted, the cache-block is sent to the component that requested a copy.

To resolve data-cache misses once a block is returned, the address stack is used. The address stack (Figure 2b) is implemented as a fully associative buffer. After the hardware issues a load or a store and calculates the physical address for the memory access, it writes this address into a free address-stack entry, if there is one available. If there is no free entry, then a structural-hazard-induced stall is mandated, and the instruction will be replayed subsequent to the freeing of an entry. Once an address-stack entry is allocated, should the required data not be found in the cache, the valid bit in the address stack for the instruction is set, and if necessary, a cache-block fetch is initiated. When this block is returned from the lower levels of the memory system, at same time as the hardware writes it into the cache, it does an associative lookup of all the entries in the address stack. For each match, the control logic notes that the corresponding memory instruction can now be replayed. In a complex and more costly design, the address-stack entry allocated to a memory instruction M is freed once M is completed. In a simpler and less costly design, the address-stack entry is freed when M is retired.

In the event that a mispredicted branch or an exception mandates the flushing of M from the processor as part of the flushing process, the address-stack entry held by M is invalidated. Thus, if the instruction was waiting for a cache block to be fetched, when the block is returned, it is guaranteed that the action indicated by M will not be performed, because there is no matching entry in the address stack. If M is a load, the named physical register will not be written, whereas if M is a store, the data will not be written. In this way, the instructions affected by the branch misprediction or exception are suppressed while those preceding the faulting instruction can be completed normally. This ability to easily suppress selective cache misses makes an address stack more attractive for dynamically-scheduled processors than the more conventional methods for recording information about primary and secondary misses [4].

Although not described in the literature, it is likely that lockup-free caches are implemented in this way by the MIPS R10000 [5] using the address queue and address stack, the PA-8000 [6] using the memory buffer and the address-reorder buffer, and in the PowerPC 604 [7] and 620 [8] using the load queue.

2.2 Stream Buffers

A stream buffer is a hardware-based prefetching technique that can be used to prefetch and store data that might be required to resolve future data cache misses. In this paper, we extend the model described in [9] by including the provision for: (1) a new prefetch strategy, called *incremental prefetching*, which reduces the memory traffic generated by stream buffers, and (2) a new method for dynamic calculation of strides, called the *per-load stride predictor*.

Memory-traffic filtering has been implemented using the *allocation filter* technique proposed by Palacharla and Kessler [10]. This filter prevented a stream buffer from being allocated until the second miss to a stream is detected. On the second miss, a stream buffer was allocated and it began prefetching the block subsequent to the one corresponding to the second miss. Our proposed *incremental prefetching* technique differs from the allocation-filter technique in that it limits the number of blocks fetched after a stream buffer has

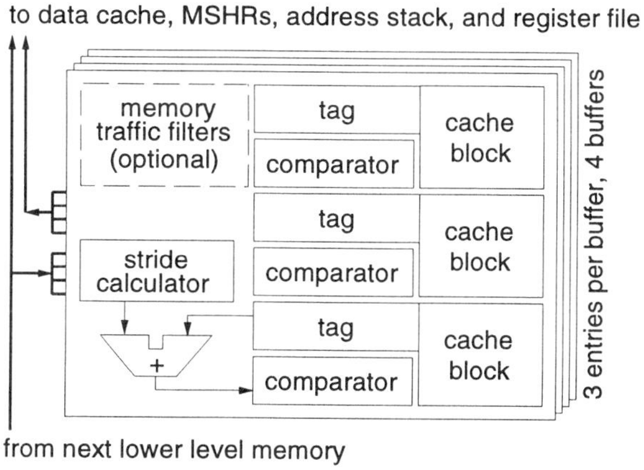

Figure 3: The enhanced stream-buffer model. In this example, there are four stream buffers with three entries each, and any one of the 12 entries can be used to supply the missing data for a cache miss.

been allocated until the stream is found to be useful. With incremental prefetching, when a stream buffer is first allocated, only one block is fetched. If the block is then used to service a cache miss, the next two blocks are fetched. This process of fetching the next $2 \times N$ blocks if one of the last N was used to resolve a cache miss continues until the stream buffer is reallocated.

Dynamic-stride prediction has been implemented using a scheme based on the *minimum delta* scheme proposed by Palacharla and Kessler [10]. With this scheme, on a stream-buffer miss, the allocation filter was applied to determine whether a unit-stride should be used. If there was a filter miss, then the minimum signed difference between the miss address and the last N miss addresses was determined. This minimum delta, which may be positive or negative, was the stride. However, if the stride S was smaller than the size of a cache block, then a unit stride was used with the same sign as S. This strategy guards against the prefetch stream of a stream buffer overlapping with itself. A stream buffer was allocated if the miss was the third miss in a series to blocks that were separated by this stride. The stride predictor is shown in Figure 3, which depicts the enhanced stream-buffer model.

We introduce the *per-load stride predictor*. It differs from the minimum-delta scheme in that a stride is determined for a load instruction L by considering only the previous miss addresses generated by L. This predictor is based on the scheme proposed by Fu et al. [11] for preloading the data cache and is similar to the data prefetching scheme of Chen and Baer [12]. Our predictor uses a fully associative buffer to record the last miss address for N static loads, along with the program-counter address of each load. Thus, a stride prediction is based only on the past memory behavior of the static load for which the prediction is being made. We also implement an enhancement to provide the functionality of an allocation filter. With this enhancement, a stream buffer is allocated with a unit stride the first time a memory instruction M is executed for which there is no entry in the miss-address table and the required data (with address A) is not in the data cache or a stream buffer. Subsequently, a stream buffer is allocated only if $S = A_{n-1} - A_{n-2} = A_n - A_{n-1}$, where A_x is the address of the data for the xth stream-buffer miss generated by M. By default, a stream buffer is not allocated on the second miss. As before, if the stride S is smaller than the size of a cache block, then a unit stride is used with the same sign as S.

3 Simulation Methodology

This section describes our investigation methodology, the system model we assume, and our simulation framework. The methodology was selected to allow us to identify performance trends and design relationships, rather than to estimate the performance of specific system designs.

3.1 System Model

Our system model implements a RISC superscalar processor whose instruction set is based on the DEC Alpha instruction set. We assume that all instructions can be be speculatively executed, and that the processor can issue 4 or 8 instructions per cycle. These issue widths are representative of the current state-of-the art and future processors. The issue rules for the 4-way and 8-way issue processors are given in rows 1 and 2 of Table 1. The processor has a standard four-stage execution pipeline, and, with the exception of the execution stage (stage 3), all stages have a single-cycle latency. The functional unit latencies are given in row 3 of Table 1.

In a clock cycle, the number of instructions that can be inserted into the dispatch queue is equal to 1.5 times the maximum issue width of the processor, while the maximum number of instructions that can be retired is exactly twice the issue width of the processor. These values were chosen to reduce the possibility of either instruction insertion or instruction commitment being a significant bottleneck. Instructions are selected for issuing using a greedy algorithm that issues the earliest instructions in fetch order first. Hardware is included to dynamically disambiguate memory addresses so as to allow memory instructions to issue before those occurring earlier in the program order. The register file includes a configurable and equal number of integer and floating-point registers. The number of registers considered for each issue width are given in Table 2a; this table also specifies the number of dispatch-queue entries. The register file for the four-way issue processor has eight read ports and sufficient write ports to prevent any write-port conflicts arising when registers are filled on the resolution of a cache miss. For the eight-way issue processor, there is twice the number of ports.

The model implements precise exceptions, and uses a branch prediction scheme proposed by McFarling [13] that comprises a bimodal predictor, a global history predictor, and a mechanism to select between them. The prediction scheme is used to predict the direction of conditional branches; all other control flow instructions are assumed to be 100% predictable.

The model includes separate instruction and data caches, and supports non-blocking loads and non-blocking stores. Stores are assumed to be implemented using write-around (i.e., no-write-allocate) and write-through policies with a write buffer situated between the data cache and lower levels in the data memory hierarchy. Since our goal was to include only the important features of a processor that affect the design of the register file and memory system, we assume that the servicing of instruction cache misses does not delay the servicing of data cache misses. Hence, the instruction cache has a fixed miss penalty. Furthermore, we assume that no memory bandwidth is required to retire stores in the write buffer. This assumption prevents any stalls due to a full write buffer and prevents stores from delaying the servicing of cache fetches.

The data cache is assumed to be a 64-KByte, two-way set associative cache that can be configured to be lockup, lockup-free, or perfect; the perfect organization assumes a 100% hit rate. These three organizations are listed in Table 2b. For the lockup-free cache, three types of in-flight miss restrictions are considered. The most restrictive type, designated m_x, limits the number of outstanding cache misses to be at most x, where x is an integer greater than zero. The second type, designated f_x is less restrictive because it imposes no limit on the number of secondary misses. Rather,

#		total	integer total	integer multiply	integer other	floating point total	floating point divide	floating point other	loads & stores	control flow
1	number issued	4	4	4	4	2	1	2	2	1
2	per cycle	8	8	8	8	4	2	4	4	2
3	latency in cycles			6	1		8/16	3	1†	1

Table 1: Instruction-issue rules and functional-unit latencies for the 4-way and 8-way issue processors. All functional units are fully pipelined with the exception of the floating-point divider. The divider is not pipelined and has an eight-cycle latency for 32-bit divides, and a 16-cycle latency for 64-bit divides. †There is a single load-delay slot.

(a) processor details	
issue width	**# registers**
4-way issue with 32-entry dispatch queue	48, 64, 96, or 128
8-way issue with 64-entry dispatch queue	64, 96, 128, or 256

(b) memory details		
cache type	**abbrev.**	**fetch spacing**
lockup	lk	
lockup-free	m_x	0
	f_x	8
	i	
perfect	p	

(c) stream buffer details				
#	**stride predictor type**	**N_s**	**traffic filters**	**abbrev.**
1	no stream buffers			N
2	unit		none (baseline)	S_b
3			incremental fetching	S_i
4			P&K allocation filters	S_f
5			P&K filters & incremental	S_{f+i}
6	min-delta	32	P&K allocation filters	A_d
7			P&K filters & incremental	A_{d+i}
8	per-load	10 or 32	none	P
9			stride filters	P_f
10			incremental fetching	P_i
11			incremental & stride filters	P_{f+i}

Table 2: System designs. A system is defined by selecting specific parameters from the processor, memory, and stream-buffer details tables. N_s in table (c) specifies the number of entries in the table of miss addresses.

it limits only the number of primary misses to be at most x. A cache with this functionality offers greater flexibility than one with the functionality offered by m_x, and therefore has a more aggressive implementation. Because a fetch request is required for each primary miss, the value of x for the f_x restriction also indicates the maximum number of outstanding cache-initiated fetch requests. The third type, designated i, is even less restrictive because it does not impose a limit on the number of primary or secondary misses. In real processors, the value of x for m_x might correspond to the number of address-stack entries, while the value of x for f_x might correspond to the number of MSHRs.

Requests for blocks of data are sent via the memory interface to the next level in the memory hierarchy. The memory interface returns the requested block in a constant number of cycles, called the *fetch latency*; we assume a 32-cycle fetch latency. The bandwidth of the interface is constrained by controlling the number of cycles between the launching of fetch requests. A *fetch spacing* of zero allows requests to be launched as soon as they are submitted, and thus, corresponds to an interface with a very large bandwidth. A *fetch spacing* of one allows the memory interface pipeline to be full whereas a spacing equal to the fetch latency allows at most one in-flight fetch. Thus, the time required to resolve a cache miss is not deterministic for non-zero fetch spacings but has a lower bound equal to the fetch latency; Table 2b specifies the two fetch spacings that we consider.

The 10 stream-buffer implementations (rows 2-11 in Table 2c) each comprise eight, four-entry stream buffers, and optional support for either memory-traffic filters, dynamic-stride prediction, or both. The implementation with none of this optional hardware is referred to as the *baseline* implementation, and for notational convenience it is designated as S_b. The abbreviations used for the other implementations are given in the table. We assume that one cycle is required to extract a block of data from a stream buffer.

When a block is returned to the cache, the cache line is written simultaneously with the writing of the appropriate words into all registers with loads outstanding to this block (updating all pending registers requires the multiple write ports mentioned above). Writing a register or a cache line is assumed to take one cycle.

Figure 4 presents an overview of the just-described system model.

3.2 Simulation Framework

This study is based on execution-driven simulations using an object code instrumentation system called ATOM [14], which is available for Alpha AXP workstations. The results presented correspond to simulations of seven benchmarks, six from the SPEC92 suite and the *appsp* benchmark from the NAS suite. The benchmarks are listed in Table 3 along with some run-time characteristics for the four-way and eight-way issue processors. For each of the six SPEC92 benchmarks, one of the official data sets was used (ref or small), and these are shown in Table 3 in column 2; for *appsp*, the data set that was used is described in the table caption. In all cases, the benchmarks were compiled using the Alpha native C compiler with the global ucode optimizer enabled, and the linker was directed to perform link-time optimizations.

The results in Table 3 are for a four-way issue processor and an eight-way issue processor. Both systems had a lockup-free data cache with no in-flight-miss restrictions, and an eight-cycle fetch spacing. The four-way issue processor had 64 registers (i.e., 64 integer and 64 floating point), while the eight-way issue processor had 96 registers.

Column 3 gives the number of instructions in the trace for each benchmark, which is equivalent to the number that commit. (An instruction is said to *commit* when it has completed *and* all the instructions preceding it in program order have completed.) The number of committed instructions does not necessarily equal the number of instructions that are executed due to mispredicted

bench- mark	data set	com- mit instr.	4-way issue						8-way issue					
			issue instr.		IPC		% load miss		issue instr.		IPC		% load miss	
			total	load	issue	commit	pri.	sec.	total	load	issue	commit	pri.	sec.
(1)	(2)	(3)	(4)	(5)	(6)	(7)	(8)	(9)	(10)	(11)	(12)	(13)	(14)	(15)
appsp	note[a]	319	320	68	1.58	1.57	6.0	6.8	322	68	2.44	2.42	6.0	7.6
compress	ref	86	111	25	1.63	1.27	11.9	3.5	139	31	2.34	1.45	10.7	3.1
hydro2d	note[b]	237	238	54	1.45	1.44	12.6	21.1	240	55	2.52	2.49	12.5	36.4
mdljdp2	small	291	317	47	1.74	1.60	2.3	0.4	352	53	2.84	2.34	2.1	1.9
su2cor	small	417	432	106	1.88	1.81	8.4	8.1	445	109	2.63	2.46	8.2	14.3
swm256	ref	377	378	97	1.77	1.76	6.6	2.6	379	97	2.92	2.92	6.6	10.3
tomcatv	ref	910	911	247	1.63	1.63	11.2	21.1	911	248	2.40	2.40	11.2	28.4

Table 3: Dynamic statistics for each benchmark for both issue widths. Columns 3, 4, 5, 10, and 11 give instruction counts in millions; columns 8, 9, 14, and 15 give the primary and secondary data-cache miss rates for load instructions. Notes: (a) *appsp* was run for 50 iterations with a 12x12x12 grid; (b) *hydro2d* was run for 15 iterations rather than the 400 specified in the official "ref" data set.

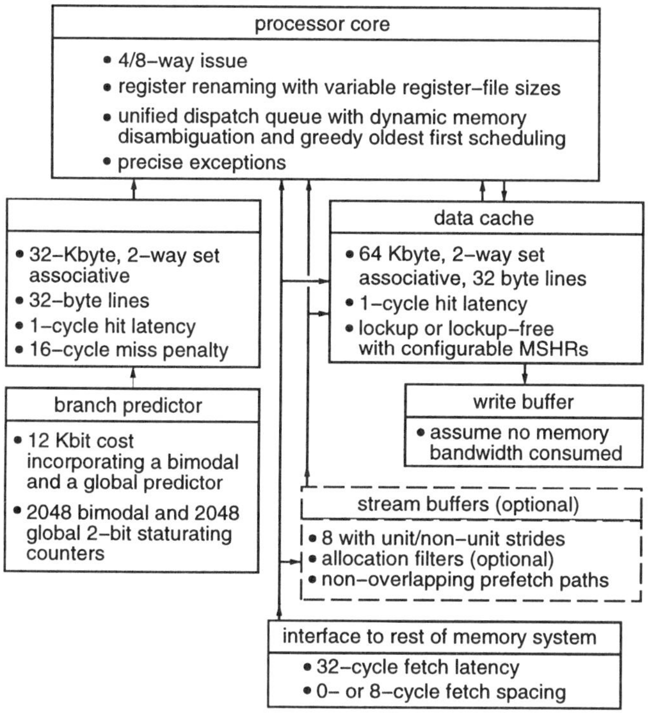

Figure 4: Overview of machine model.

branches (exceptions are not modeled). The number of executed instructions is given under columns 4 and 10 with columns 5 and 11 giving the number of loads. Both the number of committed instructions and the number of executed instructions are dynamic instruction counts.

The average number of instructions per cycle (IPC) for each benchmark and each issue width are given in columns 6, 7, 12, and 13. The *issue IPC*, given in columns 6 and 12, is the ratio of the number of instructions that are *issued* to the total (simulated) run time; the issue IPC measures the rate at which instructions are dispatched to the functional units. In our system model, the difference between the issue IPC and the maximum issue width is due to the dependences in the code and the number and type of functional units. The *commit IPC*, given in columns 7 and 13, is the ratio of the number of instructions that *commit* to the total run time. The difference between the issue IPC and the commit IPC is due to instructions that are incorrectly speculatively executed when following mispredicted branches.

The statistics presented in the table show that the benchmarks generate enough data-cache behavior to affect the performance of the memory-system implementations that we consider. First, the data presented in column 3 suggests that each trace contains a significant number of instructions, and second, the data presented in columns 4 to 5, 8 to 11, and 14 to 15 suggest that the benchmarks have significant data-cache behavior.

4 In-flight Cache Misses

To evaluate the design and performance implications of data-cache misses with different numbers of in-flight-miss resources, we evaluated performance for the system-design space listed in Tables 2a and 2b. Figures 5a and 5b respectively present the (overall) average commit IPC[1] obtained by the benchmarks on the systems with the four-way and eight-way issue processors. In both of these figures, coordinate $(c, r : s)$ gives the average commit IPC for a processor having a cache design c, a register-file size r and a fetch spacing s. The cache designs are mapped on the left-to-right axis with the less restrictive designs located to the left. The register-file sizes and fetch spacings are mapped on the front-to-back axis, with the larger register files located towards the back. For each register-file size, the IPC values for a zero cycle fetch spacing are behind those for an eight-cycle fetch spacing. Thus, the coordinates to the left and towards the back represent more aggressive system implementations.

Examination of the data presented in Figure 5 suggests a number of important relationships. These relationships are discussed below beginning with the relationship between performance, number of registers, and support for in-flight misses.

Consider the commit IPC values given in Figure 5a corresponding to the use of a lockup-free cache with no restrictions on in-flight misses, that is, coordinates $(c = \mathrm{i}, r : s)$. Observe that the average commit IPC increases with the size of the register file. Furthermore, the rate of increase decreases at larger sizes. For instance, for a fetch spacing of eight cycles, doubling the size from 48 to 96 yields an improvement of 70%, while doubling the size from 64 to 128 yields an improvement of only 36%. In general, an increase in the number of registers permits more instructions to be in some stage of execution, thereby better utilizing the available hardware, and thus improving performance. However, this correlation between more registers and better performance is less pronounced for the systems with less support for in-flight misses. For example, if four in-flight fetches are permitted, $(c = f_4, r : s)$, doubling the size from 48 to 96 yields an improvement of 68% while doubling the size from 64 to 128 yields an improvement of 35%. If the support for misses is further reduced by allowing only four in-flight misses,

[1] The (overall) average commit IPC is calculated for each system configuration by first computing the average commit IPC for each benchmark for that system. The per-benchmark average commit IPC is equal to the total number of instructions that are committed when the benchmark is run divided by the total number of (simulated) clock cycles required to run it. Then, these per-benchmark averages are combined using an arithmetic average to obtain the reported (overall) average commit IPC. The commit IPC values for each benchmark are given in [15].

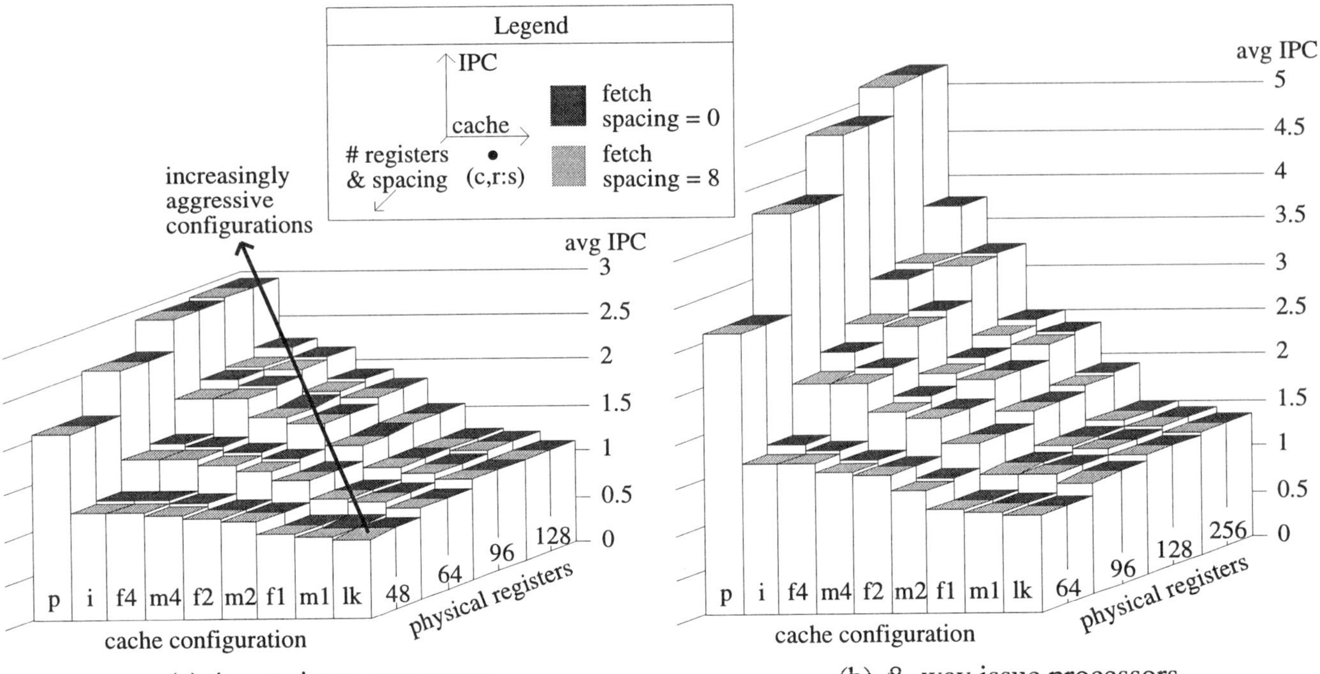

(a) 4–way issue processors (b) 8–way issue processors

Figure 5: Average commit IPC of all benchmarks for their (simulated) execution on the investigated systems.

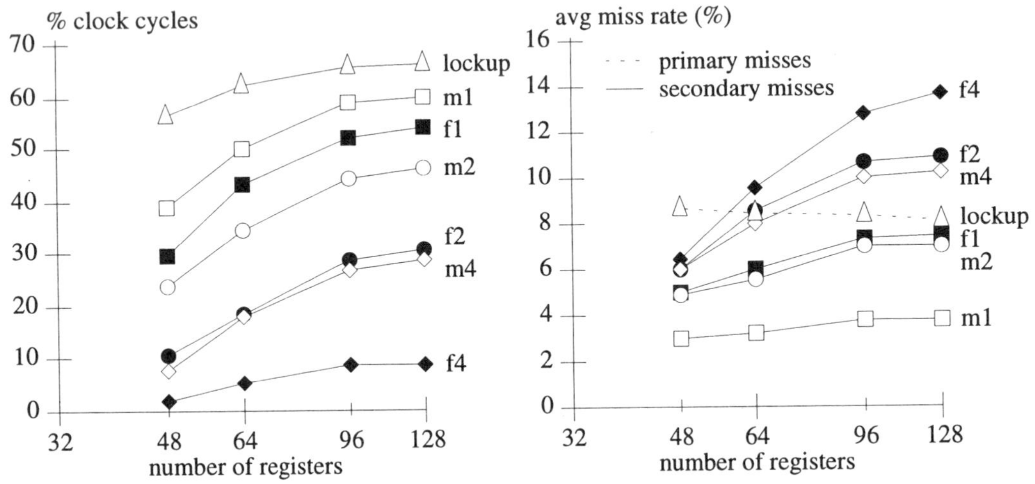

(a) Percentage of (simulated) clock cycles in which a load-miss induced stall was in effect

(b) Primary and secondary load-miss rates. The primary miss rates for all lockup-free cache organizations are coincident with the curve for the lockup cache.

Figure 6: Statistics for load-induced cache misses for the four-way issue processors using an eight-cycle fetch spacing. Each figure contains a curve for each of the seven in-flight miss restrictions that were investigated.

$(c = m_4, r : s)$, the improvement percentages are 53% and 25%, respectively.

The data presented in Figure 5a also suggests that system performance is more heavily affected by increasing the number of registers than providing support beyond four in-flight misses. For example, consider the system $(c = m_4, r = 64 : s = 8)$, that is, one with support for four in-flight misses, 64 registers, and an eight-cycle fetch spacing. Compared to this baseline system, one having twice the number of registers $(c = m_4, r = 128 : s = 8)$ will perform 25% better, while one with no restrictions on in-flight misses $(c = i, r = 64 : s = 8)$ will perform only 5% better.

The above noted relationships between performance, number of registers, and support for in-flight misses are in part due to the increase in the number of structural-hazard-induced stalls that occur when the amount of in-flight miss support is reduced. To illustrate this increase in stalls, Figure 6a presents the percentage of (simulated) clock cycles in which such stalls occur in the systems using the four-way issue processors with an eight-cycle fetch spacing. In the figure, the percentages for each in-flight miss restriction are given by the seven curves as a function of the number of registers[2]. For instance, with 64 registers, the percentage for each in-flight miss restriction is: 5% for f_4, 18% for m_4, 19% for f_2, 34% for m_2, 43% for f_1, 49% for m_1, and 62% for a lockup cache.

The significant difference in the above percentages between f_x and m_x restrictions for the same value of x is due to the benchmarks requiring significant amounts of secondary-miss support. This requirement is suggested by the miss rates presented in Figure 6b. As can be observed, while the primary miss rates for all systems having a given number of registers are sufficiently similar that the data points are coincident, there are significant differences in the secondary-miss rates. With less support for in-flight misses, the load instructions that correspond to these secondary misses must instead be held in the dispatch queue. Moreover, because memory instructions cannot be issued during a structural-hazard-induced stall, the dispatch queue will tend to fill up with memory instructions for which the data is already in the data cache. Thus, the rate at which entries are freed and new instructions are inserted will decrease as the stall progresses. Together, these two effects reduce the demand for registers and the performance gains that accompany increasing the number of registers. As the data in Figure 6 suggests, this reduction is more significant with larger numbers of registers because the secondary miss rates are larger, and because structural-hazard-induced stalls occur for a greater percentage of the (simulated) run-time.

The trend of decreasing performance with less lockup-free support is more pronounced with the systems having eight-way issue processors. Data supporting this trend is presented in Figure 5. Observe that there is less variance in the commit IPC values when more restrictions are imposed on in-flight misses in the systems with four-way issue processors (Figure 5a) than in the systems with eight-way issue processors (Figure 5b). This trend occurs because the performance of systems with wider-issue processors is more sensitive to the design of the memory system. The cause of this increased sensitivity is the ability to issue more instructions per cycle, which tends to reduce the number of clock cycles between the issuing of load instructions. As a result, at any point in the execution of an application, there tends to be a greater number of in-flight fetches and secondary misses.

Additional insight into this difference between the two issue widths is suggested by the differential in the commit IPC values when the fetch spacing is reduced from 8 cycles to 0 cycles. As shown by the data in Figure 5, when the fetch spacing is reduced, there is greater variance in the commit IPC values for the eight-way issue processors, and in particular, for systems with greater support for in-flight misses and a larger number of physical registers.

In summary, a number of observations can be drawn from the above discussion, and these are presented in Section 6.

5 Stream Buffer Implications

To investigate the design and performance implications of stream buffers, the system model was augmented to include the stream-buffer models described in Section 2.2. The system model was then used to evaluate the behavior of the benchmarks on a number of systems that were chosen to capture the behavior at several representative points in the large design space.

5.1 Baseline Stream Buffers

For clarity in presenting key observations, consider first the performance implications of including the baseline stream-buffer implementation in 16 of the systems listed in Table 2. The performance of the benchmarks on the resulting 32 systems (16 without stream buffers and 16 with stream buffers) is presented in Figure 7. This figure gives the average commit IPC for each benchmark as a function of the issue width of the processor, the size of the register files, the type of data cache, the fetch spacing, and the optional use of stream buffers. The lockup-free cache had no restrictions on the number of in-flight misses (type i). The columns with N at their base (e.g., the column marked by [1]) give the commit IPC values for systems without stream buffers, while those with S_b at the base (e.g., the column marked with [2]) give the commit IPC for systems with stream buffers.

One important observation is that if stream buffers are included in a system, there is an overall performance gain, with this gain being bigger for systems having lockup caches and a larger number of registers. To illustrate this relationship, consider the columns marked with [1] and [2] in Figure 7 that correspond to the performance obtained on systems with 48 registers, a fetch spacing of eight cycles, and a four-way issue processor. Comparison of the relative position of the data points in these two columns shows that the data points are generally higher in the second column. The average increase in IPC for systems with the lockup-free cache (the filled circles) is 0.35, while for systems with the lockup cache (the filled squares), the average increase is 0.46. Expressed as speedup ratios, these increases correspond to a speedup of 1.29 for the systems with a lockup-free cache and a speedup of 1.51 for systems with a lockup cache.

The more significant speedup for systems with a lockup cache is a consequence of the hardware being blocked from issuing memory instructions during stalls induced by structural hazards. For systems with this type of cache, stream buffers enhance the performance because they significantly reduce the effective cache-miss penalty. Systems with lockup-free caches, however, can issue unrelated memory instructions during such stalls, and, thus, are both less sensitive to the effective cache-miss penalty, and more tolerant of cache misses. The amount of tolerance such systems have is a function of the number of physical registers, because the number of registers determines how many instructions can be simultaneously in execution. Thus, with more registers, the speedup obtained with stream buffers will decrease. As illustrated in Figure 7, when the number of physical registers is increased from 48 to 64 (columns [3] and [4]), the speedup for systems with lockup-free caches drops to 1.25, while the speedup for systems with lockup caches rises to 1.58.

The above observations suggest that if a system can support a large number of in-flight misses, it is more beneficial to increase the number of registers than it is to include stream buffers. To illustrate this phenomenon, consider again the same four system configurations. When a lockup-free cache is used, a 32% performance improvement is obtained by increasing the number of registers from 48 to 64, but an improvement of only 29% is obtained by using stream buffers. On the other hand, when a lockup cache is used, a 14% performance improvement is obtained by increasing the number of registers from 48 to 64, but an improvement of 51% is obtained by using stream buffers.

The performance gains achieved with stream buffers are a result of the buffers prefetching a significant number of cache blocks that are used to resolve cache misses. Table 4 presents data to quantify the frequency at which cache misses were anticipated. This table provides: in column 2, the run-time speedup due to the use of the stream buffers; in column 3, the primary data-cache miss rate; in column 4, the percentage of primary misses resolved using data either present in a stream buffer, or for which a fetch request had already been launched; and in column 5, the number of cache blocks used to resolve one of these misses as a percentage of the total number of cache blocks returned by the memory system in response to a fetch request from a stream buffer. Ignoring *compress*

[2] These percentages represent the average of the percentages for each benchmark.

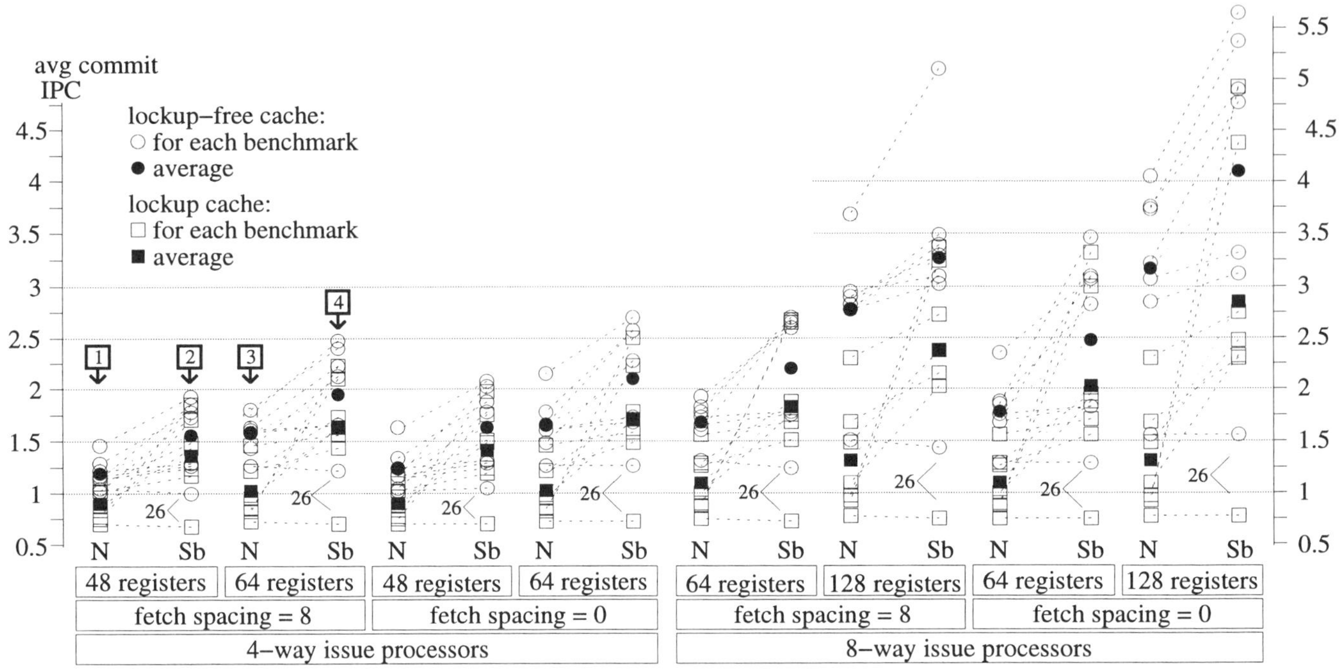

Figure 7: Average commit IPC for systems using either a four-way or an eight-way issue processor and either no stream buffers (N) or the baseline stream-buffer implementation (S_b). The dotted lines connect the data points of each benchmark for each cache implementation. The unfilled circles indicate the IPC for each benchmark obtained with the use of a lockup-free cache having no in-flight miss restrictions, while the filled circles indicate the overall average IPC for all benchmarks. The squares indicate similar information but with the use of the lockup cache.

for the moment, observe that 18% to 98% of the blocks prefetched by the stream buffers (column 5) are used to resolve 29% to 77% of primary misses (column 4).

The statistics presented in the table are sensitive to the number of physical registers. If the number is increased, there is little change in both the number of primary misses, and the number of times data is fetched in response to a stream buffer request. But, there is a significant drop in the number of misses for which the missing data is actually present in a stream buffer. This drop is largely due to the increase in the issue IPC that accompanies the increase in the number of registers. This increase in the issue IPC reduces the time between successive cache misses, and thus reduces the time available for prefetching. *Compress*, however, as already noted, does not benefit from stream buffers. Rather, as shown in Figure 7 by the curves labeled "26", for a fetch spacing of 8 cycles and a four-way issue processor with 48 registers, its performance decreases by

bench-mark	speed-up	primary misses		SB
		%	% resolved by SB	% blocks used
(1)	(2)	(3)	(4)	(5)
appsp	1.09	6.0	28.9	18.1
compress	0.95	12.9	0.2	0.1
hydro2d	1.70	12.6	77.3	97.7
mdljdp2	1.06	2.4	60.6	48.5
su2cor	1.32	8.7	53.1	63.8
swm256	1.36	6.7	44.7	29.3
tomcatv	1.64	11.2	71.6	98.4

Table 4: Effectiveness of the baseline stream-buffer implementation when used in a 4-way issue processor with 48 registers and an 8-cycle fetch spacing.

4% when run on the systems having the lockup cache, and by 5% when run on the systems having the lockup-free cache. This performance decrease is a result of the stream buffers prefetching mostly un-needed cache blocks, thereby delaying the launching of fetch requests that are needed to service cache misses. On these systems, less than 0.2% of primary cache misses are resolved using prefetched cache blocks. The percentages are much higher for the other benchmarks, as shown in Table 4 by the data given in column 4.

A second important relationship that is suggested by the data of Figure 7 is the performance insensitivity of the systems to the bandwidth of the interface. When the fetch spacing is reduced from 8 cycles to 0 cycles, with the exception of *compress*, the commit IPC values change relatively little. This observation suggests that even with a fetch spacing of 8 cycles, contention for the memory interface is not significant. One result of this lack of contention is that with an 8-cycle fetch spacing, when a stream buffer is reallocated, 95 times out of 100, all of its entries contain valid data. Consequently, when the fetch spacing is reduced to 0 cycles, there will not be a large increase in the amount of prefetched data, and hence, only small performance gains are likely. When the fetch spacing is changed to 0 cycles, the least significant change in the speedup ratios is an increase from 1.29 to 1.33 with 48 registers and a lockup-free cache, and the most significant change is an increase from 1.58 to 1.67 with 64 registers and a lockup cache. These speedup ratios are given in Table 5 under the column heading "4-way". Like the other benchmarks, *compress* performs better with a fetch spacing of 0 cycles, but unlike the other benchmarks, it does not achieve a speedup greater than one. This phenomenon is shown in Figure 7 by the curves near the bottom whose right-most data points are labeled with "26". Observe that when a fetch spacing of 0 cycles is used, the curves are nearly horizontal.

When the baseline stream buffers are used in systems with an

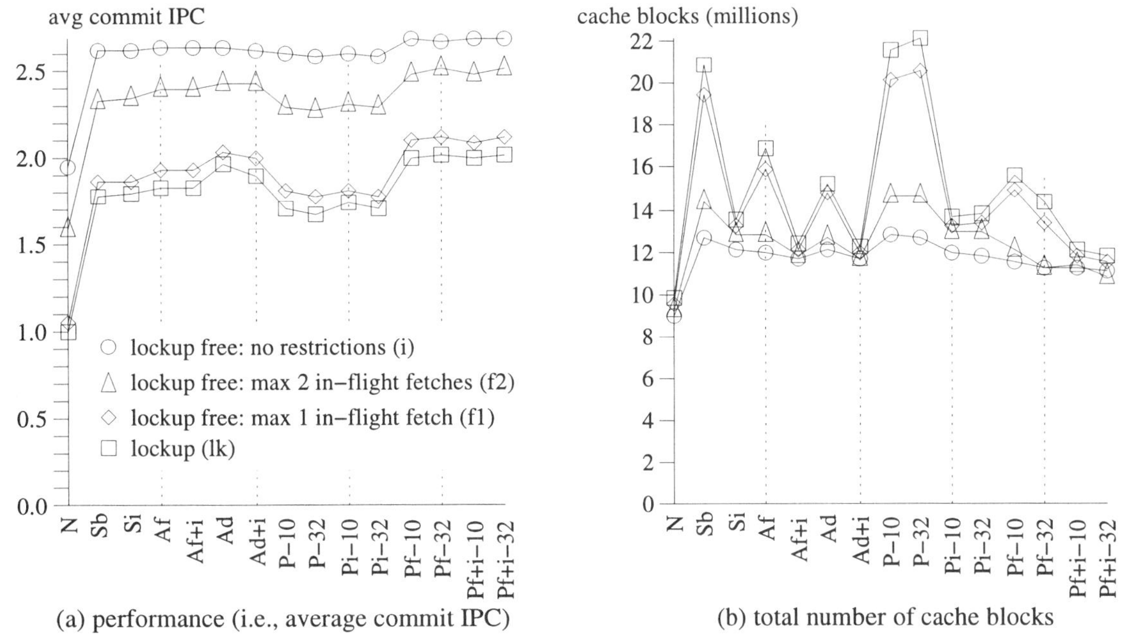

Figure 8: Performance of *su2cor* and the total number of cache blocks supplied by the memory interface when it was run on systems using one of the 15 stream-buffer implementations.

cache type	fetch spacing	4-way # registers 48	4-way # registers 64	8-way # registers 64	8-way # registers 128
lockup	8	1.51	1.58	1.70	1.87
	0	1.57	1.67	1.80	2.15
lockup-free	8	1.29	1.24	1.30	1.18
	0	1.33	1.28	1.38	1.29

Table 5: Average speedup in (simulated) run-time for all benchmarks due to the use of the baseline stream-buffer configurations.

eight-way issue processor and 64 dispatch queue entries, the same trends as those noted for the four-way issue processors occur, but the differences tend to be greater. The increased significance is a consequence of the eight-way issue processor issuing and committing more instructions per cycle thereby resulting in a compression of time. This temporal compression not only reduces the time between the occurrence of cache misses, but also increases the number of secondary cache misses and the instruction cost of servicing all cache misses.

5.2 Memory Traffic and Dynamic Strides

Although the baseline stream-buffer implementation improves the performance of six of the benchmarks, the basic design can be augmented to reduce the possible negative impact of excess memory traffic, unit strides, and the possibility of flushing useful data from a stream buffer when it is reallocated. To counter the negative impact of stream buffers, the enhancements listed in Table 2c can be employed.

The results obtained from the simulated execution of the benchmarks on these systems show a number of common relationships, and these will be illustrated using the *su2cor* benchmark and its execution on 60 systems. These 60 systems had an eight-way issue processor, 64 physical registers and a fetch spacing of 8 cycles. Figure 8a presents the average commit IPC values for these executions, while Figure 8b presents the total number of cache blocks that were supplied by the memory interface. In both figures, each of the curves for the four data-cache configurations (i, f_2, f_1, and k) includes a data point for the 15 stream-buffer implementations. The stream-buffer implementations are listed along the horizontal axes using the abbreviations given in Table 2c. However, the abbreviations used for the designs based on the per-load scheme (e.g., P_f) also include a suffix (e.g., 10) to indicate the number of entries in the missed-load buffer.

An important relationship suggested by the data presented in Figure 8a is that the enhancements to the baseline stream-buffer implementation have at best a small effect on performance, with this effect being more significant for the systems with less aggressive cache configurations. For example, when the implementations are used with the lockup cache (type lk), there are pronounced variations in commit IPC values, but when the implementations are used with the lockup-free cache having no in-flight miss restrictions (type i), the commit IPC values vary very little. The increased performance sensitivity of the more restrictive cache configurations to the stream-buffer implementation is due to two factors. First, systems with more support for in-flight misses have greater tolerance for cache misses. Thus, whether a stream-buffer implementation improves performance by correctly prefetching data that is missing from the cache, or degrades performance by tying up the memory interface with misfetched data, the overall performance impact, be it positive or negative, will be smaller.

Second, systems with more support for in-flight misses tend to require fewer clock cycles to execute an application. Hence, there are fewer clock cycles available for prefetching data, and there is a reduction in the number of clock cycles between the detection of cache misses for which the missing data has not been prefetched. As a result of these two effects, systems with less restrictive cache configurations tend to fetch fewer cache blocks from the memory interface. This trend is suggested by the relative positions of the curves in Figure 8b. The performance differential between the stream-buffer implementations is a reflection of the ability of an implementation to correctly prefetch data and to hold on to the data until it is required. Thus, the implementations with some form of filtering give better performance (Figure 8a) and generate less memory traffic (Figure 8b).

When the number of physical registers is increased and/or the bandwidth-limit on the memory interface is removed, data similar to that presented in Figure 8 is obtained. Due to space constraints, this data is not presented, but the following two relationships are nonetheless noted; the corresponding data is presented in [15].

First, concerning the number of physical registers and the amount of support for in-flight misses, for systems using the type i lockup-free cache, the performance impact of the stream-buffer implementation is even smaller if the number of physical registers is increased. Increasing the number of registers allows more instructions to be simultaneously in some stage of execution, which increases the tolerance for cache misses, and decreases the number of clock cycles required to run the application. Thus, when the number of registers is increased, the commit IPC varies less for the various stream buffer implementations, and the number of blocks fetched from the memory system decreases. However, for the systems with restrictive cache configurations, increasing the number of registers increases the performance sensitivity to the stream buffer implementations. A larger number of registers increases the percentage of clock cycles in which memory instructions cannot be issued (Figure 6a), thus increasing the performance sensitivity to the effective cache-miss latency. Because the performance impact of such stalls is a function of their duration, stream-buffer implementations that are better at lowering the effective cache-miss latency give better performance. Furthermore, the implementations that perform better generate less memory traffic because there is less time to prefetch the data.

Second, concerning the bandwidth of the memory interface, removal of the bandwidth limit leads to a more pronounced difference in the relative performance obtained with the stream-buffer implementations. When memory bandwidth is not limited, the stream-buffer implementations that are more beneficial are those that are better at prefetching and holding onto data that is subsequently required to resolve a cache miss. Thus, while the techniques for filtering stream-buffer allocations have a positive performance impact, the incremental prefetching technique, which serves only to reduce memory bandwidth requirements, has no significant performance impact. However, incremental prefetching reduces the bandwidth consumed by stream buffers by 50%.

Finally, concerning all the benchmarks[3], several comments should be made. On systems with a type i lockup-free cache, the stream-buffer enhancements had less than a 5% impact on performance with the exception of *swm256*. Furthermore, these enhancements had little impact on the performance of *mdljdp2* and *hydro2d* irrespective of the cache organization, while they significantly degraded the performance of *tomcatv* if in-flight miss restrictions existed. *Appsp*, *su2cor*, and *swm256* performed best if the system included one of the following two sets of mutually exclusive enhancements: (1) the PK-allocation filters, and optionally, the min-delta stride predictor; or (2) the per-load stride predictor with filtering, and optionally, incremental prefetching. Finally, for all the systems considered and all benchmarks, the stream-buffer implementations with PK-allocation filters or stride filters generated between 1.5 and 4.2 times less memory traffic. In most cases, the per-load stride predictor with stride filtering generated the least amount of memory traffic.

6 Conclusions

In this paper, we have presented an investigation and analysis of the design of the register file and the other levels of the data memory hierarchy. This analysis has focused on identifying performance trends and design relationships. The components we considered affect the apparent time-cost of servicing cache misses and the tolerance for data-cache misses. The following conclusions can be drawn from the analysis.

First, similar performance was obtained from all systems having support for fewer than four in-flight misses, irrespective of the register-file size, the issue width, and the memory bandwidth. While increasing the hardware support for in-flight misses beyond this point did increase system performance, for the configurations considered, the improvement was less than that obtained by increasing the number of registers.

Second, systems with a greater amount of support for in-flight misses require a greater proportion of the support to be for secondary misses, since the secondary miss rate tends to increase as the amount of in-flight-miss support is increased. Additional registers should also be provided to offset the increase in the average register lifetime that is a result of the ability to support a larger number of in-flight misses.

Third, system performance is relatively unaffected by the bandwidth of the memory interface if the processor can issue a maximum of only four instructions per cycle. But, when the issue width is increased to eight, the bandwidth of the memory interface has a more significant impact on performance, especially in systems with support for at least four in-flight fetches. While the performance sensitivity to the bandwidth is small for all but the most aggressive systems, the reported percentages represent a lower bound due to the assumption that neither the instruction cache nor the write buffer use the memory interface. If these two components were to compete for the bandwidth of the interface, contention would increase, which would increase the performance sensitivity to the bandwidth. The rate of this increase would be greater for systems with the eight-way issue processor since wider issue processors generate more traffic in a given time period than narrower issue processors. Nonetheless, if stream buffers are not included in the system, the bandwidth is unlikely to be a significant factor for the less aggressive systems and the benchmarks discussed in this paper.

Fourth, the addition of stream buffers to a system leads to a more significant performance increase for systems having either more restrictive lockup-free caches, more memory bandwidth, or more instruction issue capability. For the systems investigated, the design of the lockup-free cache had the greatest impact on performance, and the bandwidth of the memory interface had the least impact. Increasing the number of registers results in a more significant performance increase with systems having a lockup cache but a less significant increase with systems having a lockup-free cache. The increase is larger for the systems with the eight-way issue processors.

Fifth, system performance is not significantly affected when stream buffers are used that have traffic filters and dynamic-stride calculators. This observation is not surprising since the performance of the benchmarks is at best 16% better when the memory interface has an infinite bandwidth. In other words, contention for the interface is not a significant problem. This observation also suggests that the address stream generated by cache misses when each benchmark is run is dominated by interleaved unit-stride streams. Thus, the cost of supporting dynamic-stride calculation is not warranted for these seven benchmarks. However, in spite of the similar performance of many of the enhanced stream-buffer implementations, the cost of those that have traffic filters is probably warranted since the system model does not take into account all possible sources of memory traffic. The exact type of filter would have to be determined when a specific system is being considered. A larger set of benchmarks would also be required, as well as including all of the traffic effects into the model.

Finally, the incremental-prefetching technique we introduce reduces the bandwidth consumed by stream buffers by half with little

[3]The data for these benchmarks is given in [15].

performance loss.

Acknowledgments

The research described in this paper has been partially funded by the Natural Sciences and Engineering Research Council of Canada and by Digital Equipment Corporation. We thank Brad Calder and Alan Eustace for helping us with the ATOM simulation infrastructure, Annie Warren and Jason Wold for logistical support while our simulations ran, and the other WRL-ites for putting up with these simulations. Finally, we thank Digital Equipment Corporation for providing us with the Alpha AXP workstations.

References

[1] Norm Jouppi. Improving Direct Mapped Cache Performance by the Addition of a Small Fully Associative Cache and Prefetch Buffers. Technical Report TN-15, Digital Equipment Corporation Western Research Lab, March 1990.

[2] Keith I. Farkas. *Memory-system Design Considerations for Dynamically-scheduled Microprocessors*. PhD thesis, Department of Electrical and Computer Engineering, University of Toronto, Ontario, Canada, January 1997. (URL: http://www.eecg.toronto.edu/~farkas/thesis_phd.html).

[3] David Kroft. Lockup-Free Instruction Fetch/Prefetch Cache Organization. *In the Proceedings of the Eighth International Symposium on Computer Architecture*, pages 81–87, May 1981.

[4] Keith I. Farkas and Norman P. Jouppi. Complexity/Performance Tradeoffs with Non-Blocking Loads. *In the Proceedings of the 21st International Symposium on Computer Architecture*, pages 211–222, 1994.

[5] Kenneth C. Yeager. The MIPS R10000 Superscalar Microprocessor. *IEEE Micro*, 16(2):28–40, 1996.

[6] Linley Gwennap. PA-8000 Combines Complexity and Speed. *Microprocessor Reports*, 8(15):1,6–11, 1994.

[7] S. Peter Song, Marvin Denman, and Joe Chang. The PowerPC 604 RISC Microprocessor. *IEEE Micro*, 14(5):8–17, 1994.

[8] IBM Microelectronics. *PowerPC 620 RISC Microprocessor Technical Summary*, 10 1994. document number: MPR620TSU-01.

[9] Keith I. Farkas, Norman P. Jouppi, and Paul Chow. How Useful Are Non-blocking Loads, Stream Buffers and Speculative Execution in Multiple Issue Processors? *In the Proceedings of the First International Symposium on High Performance Computer Architecture*, pages 78–89, 1995.

[10] Subbarao Palacharla and R. E. Kessler. Evaluating Stream Buffers as a Secondary Cache Replacement. *In the Proceedings of the 21st International Symposium on Computer Architecture*, pages 24–33, 1994.

[11] John W. Fu, Janak H. Patel, and Bob L. Janssens. Stride Directed Prefetching in Scalar Processors. *In the Proceedings of the 25th Annual International Symposium on Microarchitecture*, pages 102–110, 1992.

[12] Tien-Fu Chen and Jean-Loup Baer. Reducing Memory Latency via Non-blocking and Prefetching Caches. *In the Proceedings of the Fifth International Conference on Architectural Support for Programming Languages and Operating Systems*, pages 51–61, October 1992.

[13] Scott McFarling. Combining Branch Predictors. *Digital Equipment Corporation Western Research Lab Technical Note TN-36*, 1993.

[14] Amitabh Srivastava and Alan Eustace. Atom: A system for building customized program analysis tools. *In the Proceedings of the ACM SIGPLAN '94 Conference on Programming Languages*, March 1994.

[15] Keith I. Farkas, Paul Chow, Norman P. Jouppi, and Zvonko Vranesic. Memory-system Design Considerations for Dynamically-scheduled Processors. Technical Report 1, Digital Equipment Corporation Western Research Lab, 1997. (URL: http://www.research.digital.com/wrl/techreports).

The Interaction of Software Prefetching with ILP Processors in Shared-Memory Systems *

Parthasarathy Ranganathan, Vijay S. Pai, Hazim Abdel-Shafi, Sarita V. Adve

Department of Electrical and Computer Engineering
Rice University
Houston, Texas 77005
{parthas|vijaypai|shafi|sarita}@rice.edu

Abstract

Current microprocessors aggressively exploit instruction-level parallelism (ILP) through techniques such as multiple issue, dynamic scheduling, and non-blocking reads. Recent work has shown that memory latency remains a significant performance bottleneck for shared-memory multiprocessor systems built of such processors.

This paper provides the first study of the effectiveness of software-controlled non-binding prefetching in shared-memory multiprocessors built of state-of-the-art ILP-based processors. We find that software prefetching results in significant reductions in execution time (12% to 31%) for three out of five applications on an ILP system. However, compared to previous-generation systems, software prefetching is significantly less effective in reducing the memory stall component of execution time on an ILP system. Consequently, even after adding software prefetching, memory stall time accounts for over 30% of the total execution time in four out of five applications on our ILP system.

This paper also investigates the interaction of software prefetching with memory consistency models on ILP-based multiprocessors. In particular, we seek to determine whether software prefetching can equalize the performance of sequential consistency (SC) and release consistency (RC). We find that even with software prefetching, for three out of five applications, RC provides a significant reduction in execution time (15% to 40%) compared to SC.

1 Introduction

Shared-memory multiprocessors are increasingly built of commodity microprocessors that exploit high levels of instruction-level parallelism (ILP) with techniques such as multiple issue, dynamic scheduling, and non-blocking reads. Such ILP features have the potential for greatly improving system performance. However, recent work has shown that while these features significantly improve the performance of computation, memory system performance remains a key bottleneck in multiprocessors [27].

To reduce memory stall time, many current processors support software-controlled non-binding prefetching. With this technique, the compiler or programmer schedules an explicit prefetch instruction for a location that will be accessed by the processor at a later time, with the goal of bringing the location into the processor's cache before it issues a demand memory access [4]. Previous studies have shown that software-controlled non-binding prefetching can eliminate a large fraction of memory stall time in shared-memory multiprocessors [24, 33]. However, all such studies used previous-generation processors with single-issue, static scheduling, and blocking reads. Consequently, such studies do not account for the interactions between software prefetching and the other latency-tolerating techniques already incorporated in ILP-based multiprocessors. An analysis of these interactions is required to assess the effectiveness of current software prefetching strategies for state-of-the-art shared-memory multiprocessors.

Memory system performance also depends on the consistency model of the system. Relaxed memory consistency models such as release consistency (RC) can potentially tolerate more memory latency than the simple model of sequential consistency (SC), but mandate a more complex programming model. Studies on previous-generation multiprocessors have shown that software prefetching can improve the performance of both SC and RC [14]. Systems with ILP processors, however, can incorporate hardware optimizations such as speculative reads and hardware prefetching from the instruction window to improve the performance of SC [10]. A recent study has shown that such techniques substantially narrow the performance gap between SC and RC, but a significant gap remains for some applications [28]. Since software prefetching targets the same latencies as RC, it is important to determine if software prefetching can eliminate the remaining gap between SC and RC on current multiprocessors, allowing the high performance of RC with the simple programming model of SC.

This paper is the first study of software-controlled non-binding prefetching in shared-memory multiprocessor systems using state-of-the-art ILP processors, and has two goals:

(1) To understand how software prefetching interacts with ILP in multiprocessors, and to identify its limitations.

(2) To understand if software prefetching can equalize the performance of SC and RC.

*This work is supported in part by the National Science Foundation under Grant No. CCR-9410457, CCR-9502500, and CDA-9502791, and the Texas Advanced Technology Program under Grant No. 003604016. Vijay S. Pai is also supported by a Fannie and John Hertz Foundation Fellowship.

ISCA '97 Denver, CO, USA

To achieve these goals, we study the impact of software prefetching on five applications from the SPLASH and SPLASH-2 suites. We insert prefetches in the applications by hand, following the currently best known compiler prefetching algorithm [23]. We run the applications on a detailed execution-driven simulator modeling shared-memory multiprocessors with state-of-the-art ILP processors.

For our first goal, we compare the performance benefits of software prefetching on two multiprocessor systems referred to as `Simple` and `ILP`. These systems are identical in every respect except that `Simple` uses previous-generation processors while `ILP` uses state-of-the-art ILP processors. For this part, we assume RC for both systems since RC has been shown to have the best performance (compared to SC or processor consistency) for these systems [9, 11, 28].

We find that for three out of our five applications, current software prefetching methods achieve a significant reduction in total execution time (12% to 31%) on `ILP`. However, even after applying software prefetching, data memory stall time constitutes a large fraction of the total execution time on `ILP`. Specifically, four out of five applications spend more than 30% of their time in data memory stalls. In contrast, on `Simple`, four out of five applications see less than 17% data memory stall time after applying software prefetching. Overall, we find current software prefetching methods to be significantly less effective in addressing memory stall time in `ILP` than in `Simple`, leaving most of our applications largely memory bound on `ILP`.

Compared to `Simple`, the two primary factors that contribute to the reduced effectiveness of prefetching on `ILP` are an increase in the number of late prefetches and an increase in contention for various resources. These factors occur because `ILP` speeds up computation and thus provides less work with which to overlap prefetch latency. Further, the increased frequency of misses in `ILP` also leads to increased resource contention. This in turn increases the latency of individual misses and further increases the number of late prefetches. Several straightforward modifications to the prefetching scheme to reduce late prefetches and resource contention did not show any appreciable benefits.

For our second goal, we compare the performance benefits of prefetching on ILP multiprocessors that implement SC and RC. For SC, we consider a straightforward implementation as well as an optimized implementation incorporating write buffering, speculative reads, and hardware prefetching from the instruction window [9, 10, 28]. We find that even with software prefetching, for three applications, RC provides significant reductions in execution time (15% to 40%) compared to the most optimized version of SC. The effectiveness of software prefetching in SC implementations is limited for reasons similar to the RC system. These limitations, however, have a larger impact on SC since SC exposes write latencies, which are hidden by RC. Thus, we find that software prefetching is unable to close the performance gap between SC and RC for our applications.

The rest of the paper is organized as follows. Section 2 gives background information on the software prefetching algorithm and the memory consistency implementations evaluated in this study. Section 3 presents our simulated architectures, performance metrics, simulation environment, and applications. Section 4 discusses our results on the interaction of software prefetching with ILP on RC. Section 5 re-examines various assumptions of our prefetching scheme and explores several modifications. Section 6 describes our results on the interaction of software prefetching with consistency models. Section 7 discusses related work. Section 8 concludes the paper.

2 Background

Sections 2.1 and 2.2 respectively describe the base software prefetching algorithm and memory consistency implementations we use in this study.

2.1 Software Prefetching Algorithm

The best known software prefetch insertion algorithm implemented in a compiler is by Mowry et al. [23, 24]. We describe this algorithm below. Section 3.4 describes how we use it to insert prefetches in our applications.

The algorithm is loop-based, and consists of an analysis phase and a scheduling phase. The *analysis phase* identifies the accesses that do not exhibit cache locality, and for which prefetches need to be inserted. When determining locality, this phase assumes a cache size reduced by an appropriate fraction to account for conflict misses. The analysis conservatively assumes that no locality is maintained across synchronization.

The *scheduling phase* follows the analysis phase and uses loop peeling, unrolling, and strip-mining to insert prefetches only for the accesses that are expected to cause cache misses. Accesses to the same cache line are grouped into equivalence classes, and an exclusive prefetch is used to obtain ownership along with the data for the line if at least one member of the equivalence class is a write. The inner-most loop corresponding to an access is software pipelined to schedule a prefetch a certain number of iterations ahead of the demand access. The number of iterations is computed by the formula $\lceil \frac{L}{W} \rceil$, where L is the expected miss latency in cycles and W is an estimate of the shortest possible path through an iteration in cycles. This number is referred to as the *prefetch distance*, and is expected to represent the number of iterations needed to completely overlap the latency of a prefetch. In this paper, we also use the term prefetch distance to refer to the number of instructions needed to overlap the prefetch latency.

The above core algorithm only handles affine accesses. It is further extended to handle indirect accesses when the indirection is through an affine reference. Two prefetches are inserted for each indirect access. The first prefetch is used to fetch the address of the indirect access, and the second uses the address to prefetch the indirect access. Since the second prefetch uses the value of the first, the first prefetch must be scheduled before the second according to the prefetch distance.

2.2 Memory Consistency Models

The memory consistency model of a system determines the extent to which the system can appear to overlap or reorder memory operations to hide memory latency.

Sequential consistency (SC) [18] guarantees that all memory operations appear to execute in program order and hence offers a simple and intuitive programming model. We examine two implementations of sequential consistency – SCplain and SCopt. SCplain is a naive implementation that enforces memory ordering by stalling the issue of a memory operation until the previous memory operation of that processor has completed.

SCopt is a more aggressive implementation that improves performance through three hardware techniques, hardware prefetching of writes from the instruction window [10, 28],

ILP Processor	
Processor speed	300MHz
Maximum fetch/decode/retire rate (instructions per cycle)	4
Instruction window	64 entries
Functional units	2 integer arithmetic 2 floating point 2 address generation
Simultaneous speculated branches	8
Maximum instructions in memory queue	32
Network parameters	
Network speed	150MHz
Network width	64 bits
Flit delay (per hop)	2 network cycles
Bus type	Split transaction
Bus width and speed	128 bits at 100 MHz
Cache parameters	
Cache line size	64 bytes
L1 cache (on-chip)	Direct mapped, 16 KB
L1 request ports	2
L1 hit time	1 cycle
Number of L1 MSHRs	8
L2 cache (off-chip)	4-way associative, 64 KB
L2 request ports	1
L2 hit time	8 cycles, pipelined
Number of L2 MSHRs	8
Memory parameters	
Memory access time	18 cycles (60 ns)
Memory transfer bandwidth	16 bytes/cycle
Memory interleaving	4-way

Figure 1: Default system parameters

speculative reads [10, 28], and write buffering [9]. The first two techniques, hardware prefetching and speculative reads, exploit the instruction-lookahead window and speculation support available in ILP processors. The hardware prefetching technique issues a non-binding prefetch for a decoded memory instruction in the instruction issue window once the address of the instruction is computed. The effectiveness of this technique is primarily constrained by the size of the instruction window and the time for the address to be computed. Speculative reads extend the benefits of hardware prefetching by speculatively using the values of reads brought into the cache, even while previous demand accesses are incomplete. If a possible violation of memory ordering is detected due to early use of such data, the system rolls back the speculative load and all subsequent instructions. The third optimization in SCopt, write buffering, allows writes to retire from the instruction window as soon as they reach the head of the window. Each write is buffered in the processor's memory queue, and is issued to the cache only after the previous write (by program order) has completed. Write buffering allows multiple writes to be retired before issue. A read following such writes, however, must wait for these writes to complete before the read can retire from the instruction window.

The release consistency model (RC) [12] allows more overlap and reordering of memory operations than SC, albeit at the cost of greater programming complexity. RC distinguishes between data and synchronization operations, allowing data operations to be reordered with respect to one another. We only study a straightforward implementation of RC. We do not consider a corresponding RCopt implementation, as previous work has shown that hardware prefetching and speculative reads do not significantly affect the performance of RC for our applications [28], and RC already implements a superset of the write buffering optimization. Writes in RC retire from the instruction window as soon as they reach the head, maintaining a memory queue entry until issue to the cache; unlike SCplain and SCopt, RC allows multiple writes to issue in parallel.

3 Methodology

This section describes the experimental methodology used in this paper. Sections 3.1, 3.2, and 3.3 respectively describe the architectures modeled, our performance metrics, and our simulation environment. Section 3.4 describes the applications used in this study and the prefetches inserted in these applications.

3.1 Simulated Architectures

The first part of this study compares two multiprocessor systems – `ILP` and `Simple`. These systems are equivalent in all respects except for the processor modeled. `ILP` uses state-of-the-art high-performance processors while `Simple` uses previous generation processors. We compare the `ILP` and `Simple` systems not to propose any architectural tradeoff, but rather, to understand how software prefetching interacts with ILP techniques. Therefore, the two systems have identical clock rates, and include identical aggressive memory and network systems suitable for `ILP`.

3.1.1 Processor Models

The `ILP` system uses state-of-the-art processors employing ILP features such as multiple-issue, out-of-order execution, speculative execution, non-blocking reads, and register renaming. Our implementation of the processor core resembles the MIPS R10000 microarchitecture [22], but also includes aggressive features from other architectures. Default parameters for the processor are listed in Figure 1. The `Simple` system uses previous-generation statically-scheduled, single-issue processors with blocking reads.

`Simple` processors rely on compilers to schedule instructions to hide functional unit latencies. In `ILP` processors, the hardware instruction window can serve the same purpose. Since we do not have access to a compiler that schedules instructions according to our `Simple` architecture, we use single-cycle functional unit latencies in both models for a fair comparison of the two systems. To study the impact of this assumption on `ILP` performance, we ran our simulations with realistic functional unit latencies. We found that, except on one application (Water), there was little impact on `ILP` execution time because `ILP` processors successfully overlapped functional unit latencies. Our key findings continue to hold even in Water.

Both processor models include support for software-controlled non-binding prefetching, with both exclusive-mode and shared-mode prefetches. Prefetch instructions retire as soon as they reach the top of the instruction window, but occupy a slot in the processor's memory queue until they are issued. Prefetches are not dropped even if resource constraints block their issue, and prefetched lines are brought into the highest level of the memory hierarchy. These two assumptions follow previous work [23], and are re-evaluated in Section 5.

Both processor models support RC, using the SPARC V9 `MEMBAR` fence instructions to impose ordering at synchronization points [32]. The `ILP` processor additionally supports the two implementations of sequential consistency described in Section 2.2 – SCplain and SCopt. As with software prefetching, we do not drop hardware prefetches in SCopt even if their issue is blocked due to resource constraints. The SCopt processor includes a speculative load buffer to monitor outstanding speculative reads [10] and employs a mechanism similar to that used in the MIPS R10000 [22] to recover when possible consistency violations are detected.

3.1.2 Memory Hierarchy and Multiprocessor Configuration

We simulate a hardware cache-coherent, non-uniform memory access (CC-NUMA) shared-memory multiprocessor using an invalidation-based, three-state directory coherence protocol. Each node in our simulated system includes a processor, two levels of caches, and a portion of the global shared-memory and directory. A split-transaction bus connects the network interface, directory controller, and the rest of the system node. The nodes are connected using a two-dimensional mesh network. Figure 1 summarizes the memory system parameters.

Both caches are non-blocking with 8 miss status holding registers (MSHRs) [17] each. The MSHRs store information about the misses and coalesce multiple requests to the same cache line. In the event of a write request being received for the same line as a pending read, the MSHR blocks the write request and issues an ownership request only after the read returns (we refer to such stalls as write-after-read stalls). This implementation avoids complex races at the MSHRs and directory that can arise from reordering in the network, and resembles several current systems.

The L1 cache is dual-ported, allowing two accesses to be handled simultaneously, and uses a write-allocate write-back policy. We assume a write-back policy for the L1 cache since previous work has shown that SC systems perform best with write-back caches and because several recent systems support write-back L1 caches. The L2 cache is a fully pipelined, write-allocate write-back cache. The L1 cache size is 16 KB and the L2 cache size is 64 KB. These sizes are chosen based on the input sizes of our applications (described in Section 3.4), following the methodology described by Woo et al. [34]. The primary working sets for our applications fit in the L1 cache, while the secondary working sets do not fit in the L2 cache.

The number of processors in our system varies by application and is either 8 or 16 depending on the scalability of the application, as summarized in Figure 3.

3.2 Performance Metrics

In addition to reporting execution times, we consider various components of execution time to enable identification of the performance bottlenecks in our systems. We divide the execution time into three components – CPU, data memory, and synchronization. We use the following convention to account for stall cycles [27, 28, 30]. All cycles where the processor retires the maximum number of instructions allowed by the architecture are considered busy time. Otherwise, we charge the cycle to the stall time component of the first instruction that could not be retired that cycle. We group together the busy time and functional unit stall time as CPU time. We subdivide the data memory stall time into the time spent on L1 hits, L2 hits, local memory accesses, and remote memory accesses, for both reads and writes. Henceforth, we use the term *memory stall time* to denote the data memory stall component of execution time.

We divide prefetches into various categories, as summarized in Figure 2. These categories are *useful*, in which a prefetched line arrives on time and is used by a demand access; *late*, in which a prefetched line arrives after the demand access; *early*, in which the prefetched line is replaced or invalidated before use, or is never used; and *unnecessary*, in which the line being prefetched is already present in either the cache or the MSHRs. We describe prefetches that

Category	Description
Useful	Arrives on time; used by demand access
Late	Arrives after demand access (i.e. latency only partially hidden)
Early	Replaced or invalidated before use (or unused)
Unnecessary	Hits in cache or MSHR

Figure 2: Classification of prefetches

Application	Input Size	Processors
LU	256 by 256 matrix, block 8	8
FFT	65536 points	16
MP3D	50000 particles	8
Water	512 molecules	16
Radix	1024 radix, 512K keys, max 512K	8

Figure 3: Applications, input sizes, and system sizes

result in the replacement of a line needed by a demand access as *damaging*; all prefetch types other than unnecessary prefetches can also be damaging.

3.3 Simulation Environment

We use the Rice Simulator for ILP Multiprocessors (RSIM) [26] to model the `Simple` and `ILP` systems described in the previous sections. RSIM models the processors, memory system, and interconnection network in detail, including contention at all resources. Specifically, unlike current direct-execution simulators, we accurately model the details of the processor pipelines. Our simulator is execution-driven (as opposed to trace-driven) and hence allows the interactions between processors during the simulation to affect the course of the simulation. To speed up our simulations, we assume that all instructions hit in the instruction cache and that all private variables hit in the data cache. However, we do model contention due to private data accesses at various processor and cache resources.

3.4 Applications and Prefetching Methodology

We use five applications in this study – Radix, LU, and FFT from the SPLASH-2 suite [34], and Water and Mp3d from the SPLASH suite [31]. Since we do not have a compiler that implements software-prefetching for C programs, we insert prefetches by hand, following the algorithm by Mowry et al. (Section 2.1) for all applications except Water. Prefetching for Water is described further below.

We assume a default prefetch distance of 200 instructions to model the representative latency seen in the system. In Section 5, we vary the prefetch distance to study the impact of this assumption. To account for conflict misses, our locality analysis assumes a cache size equivalent to a fraction of the L1 cache. We choose a fraction that minimizes the number of unnecessary prefetches for all our applications. We perform loop transformations as required by the prefetching algorithm. Whenever loop-unrolling was used in the prefetch version of an application, we also used it for the base application, as loop-unrolling improves the performance of `ILP`. In addition, since our focus is on the prefetch algorithm and not on a particular compiler implementation, we assume aggressive compiler techniques (e.g., procedure inlining, symbolic loop-bound analysis) to perform locality analysis. For RC, since write latency is already hidden, we do not issue exclusive prefetches for cache lines that are only written; however, we use exclusive prefetches for reads of lines that will also be written. For SC, we additionally issue exclusive prefetches for cache lines that are only written, since SC can expose write latency. We next describe each application and the prefetches inserted.

We study two versions of **LU**. The first, **LUorig**, is the original SPLASH-2 application enhanced by using flags instead of barriers for better load balance. The second version, **LUopt**, additionally uses loop-interchange transformations to move read misses closer to each other. This increases the number of read misses that overlap with each other, better exploiting the support for non-blocking reads in `ILP` [27]. LUopt achieves higher performance than LUorig on `ILP` without prefetching, but is outperformed by LUorig with the addition of prefetching. We therefore report the results of both versions in Section 4; subsequent sections use only LUorig. Prefetching in LU covers all loop nests in the application. The writes in these loop nests follow reads to the same locations, so we insert exclusive prefetches for such read accesses.

We consider two versions of **FFT**, **FFTorig** and **FFTopt**. Analogous to LUopt, FFTopt clusters read misses (in the transpose phase) to increase overlap. We only report results for FFTopt because it outperforms FFTorig on the `ILP` system, both with and without prefetching. Prefetching is used for all read accesses expected to miss; some of these are exclusive prefetches. In the transpose phase, there are write misses for which there are no previous reads in the same phase; these writes are prefetched in the SC version.

In **Mp3d**, all reads to particles are prefetched. These particles are used to generate addresses for cells, which are prefetched using the method for indirect accesses described in Section 2.1. All prefetches are exclusive. Some cell accesses cannot be prefetched because their addresses are known only immediately before their demand accesses.

In **Radix**, prefetches are inserted for all reads that are expected to miss and whose addresses are known sufficiently before the demand access. Exclusive prefetches are used in the prefix-sum phase of this application. The key sort or "permutation" phase consists of writes to lines that are not previously read in the same phase. These writes cannot be prefetched for SC because their addresses are not known early enough before the demand access.

Water is the only application for which we do not strictly follow the algorithm in Section 2.1. The algorithm assumes no locality across synchronization, and thus does not schedule prefetches across synchronization accesses. However, since locks in Water do not have much contention and the critical sections are too small to schedule prefetches, we move prefetches corresponding to accesses within a critical section to before the critical section. This allows these prefetches to overlap with the lock acquire of the critical section, improving the benefits of prefetching. We issue exclusive prefetches in the `UPDATE_FORCES` procedure to prefetch the force data structures before entering the associated critical sections. We also prefetch molecule displacements. These prefetches occur within loops with large bodies, and consequently see prefetch distances much larger than the default 200 instructions in the other applications.

The input sizes for our applications are summarized in Figure 3. These are greater than or equal to the sizes used in the SPLASH and SPLASH-2 distributions for all applications except LU. In the case of LU, owing to higher simulation times with our detailed simulator, we use a problem size one step smaller than recommended, but also scale down the number of processors appropriately. We use 16 processors for applications that scaled well (FFT and Water) and 8 processors otherwise (LU, Mp3d, and Radix). Data layouts for these applications for LU, FFT, and Radix follow the recommendations of the SPLASH-2 distribution; data layouts for Mp3d and Water aim to maximize locality.

4 Interaction of Software Prefetching with ILP

This section evaluates how software prefetching interacts with ILP techniques in shared-memory multiprocessors by comparing its impact on the `ILP` system with that on the `Simple` system. This section uses RC for both `ILP` and `Simple`, since RC has been shown to provide better performance than SC for both types of systems [9, 11, 28].

Figures 4 and 5 present the key results from our experiments. Throughout Figure 4, `+PF` indicates the addition of software prefetching. Figure 4(a) shows the execution times for each application on `Simple` and `ILP`, both with and without software prefetching. The execution times are normalized to the time for the application on `Simple` without prefetching, and are divided into three components – CPU, memory stall, and synchronization stall time. Figure 4(b) magnifies the memory region of Figure 4(a), providing a more detailed characterization of memory latency. Each bar showing memory stall time is separated into read and write components by a horizontal dividing line. With RC, no significant write component time is seen in any application (however, contention caused by writes can impact read time). Read and write stall times are further divided into time spent stalled on L1 cache hits, L2 cache hits, misses to local memory, and misses to remote memory. Figure 4(c) shows the prefetches issued to the L1 cache, and divides them into the categories ***useful***, ***late***, ***early***, and ***unnecessary*** according to the definitions in Section 3.2. The total number of prefetches are normalized to the number in `Simple`.

Figure 5 summarizes the key statistics from Figure 4. The first two rows show the reductions in overall execution time and memory stall time due to software prefetching in both `ILP` and `Simple`. The third row shows the percentage of time an `ILP` or `Simple` execution is stalled for memory with software prefetching. The last row shows the percentage of prefetches that are late in `ILP` and `Simple`. For LU, Figure 5 reports only LUorig since LUorig with software prefetching performs better than LUopt with software prefetching for both `Simple` and `ILP`.

4.1 Overall Results

As shown in the first row of Figure 5, software prefetching achieves an overall reduction in execution time in `ILP` similar to or greater than that in `Simple` for three out of five applications (LU, Water, and Radix). The reductions for `ILP` are significant (12% to 31%) for three applications (LU, Mp3d, and Water). However, focusing on the memory stall time (the execution time component specifically targeted by prefetching), we find that software prefetching is less effective in reducing memory stalls on `ILP` than on `Simple`. Specifically, for our applications, prefetching reduces the absolute memory stall time by an average of 34% in `ILP` compared to 56% in `Simple`. The net effect is that even after prefetching is applied to `ILP`, memory stall time constitutes more than 30% of the total execution time for all applications except Water, and more than 40% of the time for three applications. In contrast, in `Simple`, all applications except Mp3d see less than 17% memory stall time. Thus, for our applications, the `ILP` system remains memory-bound even with software prefetching.

The reasons for the reduced effectiveness of software prefetching on memory stall time in `ILP` and its resulting impact on total execution time are identified in the following subsections.

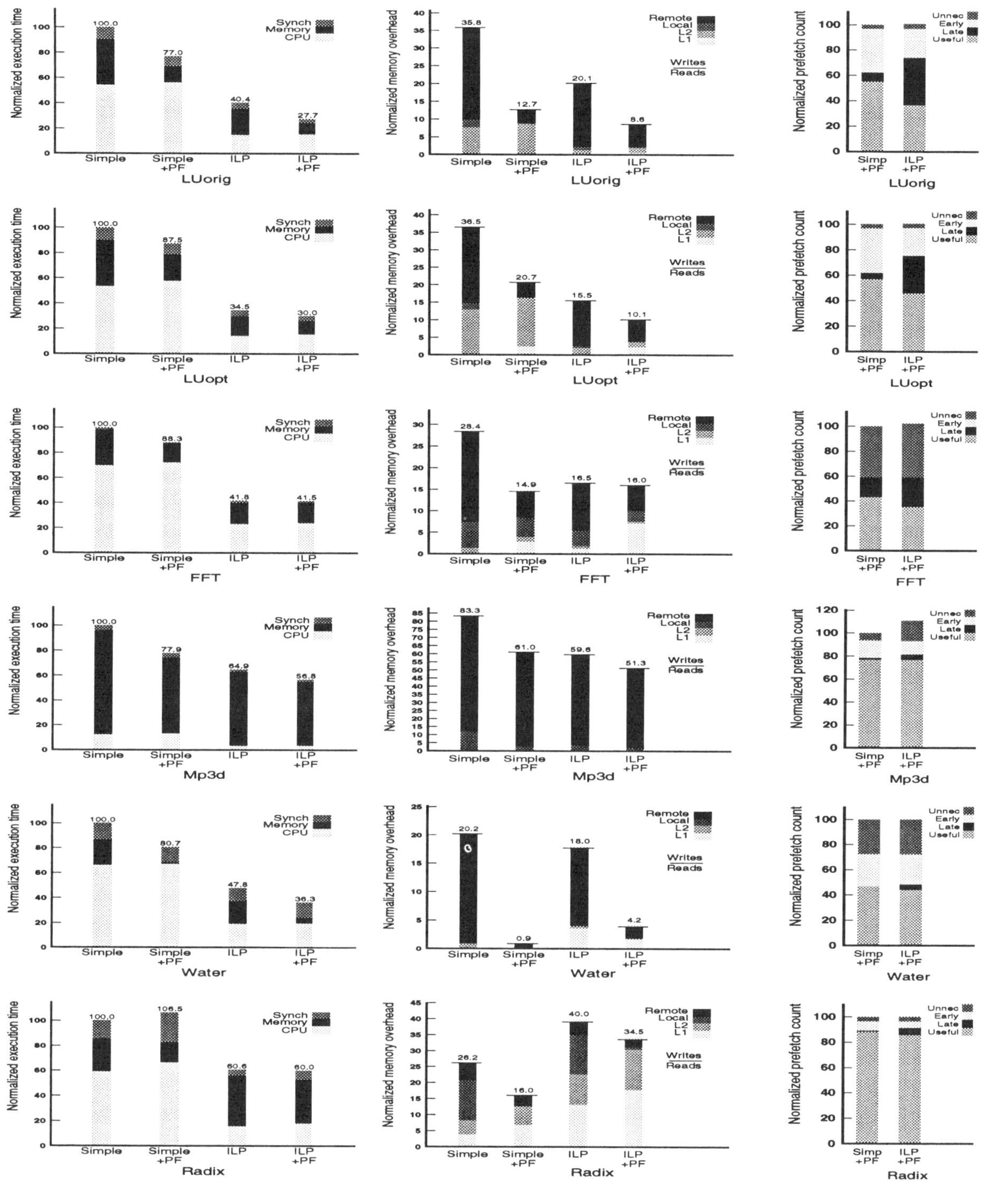

(a) Execution time components (b) Memory stall time (c) Prefetch characterization

Figure 4: Impact of software prefetching on `Simple` and `ILP` performance

Performance Metric	LU		FFT		Mp3d		Water		Radix	
	ILP	Simple	ILP	Simple	ILP	Simple	ILP	Simple	ILP	Simple
% execution time reduced	31	23	2	13	12	22	24	19	1	-7
% memory stall time reduced	57	65	9	53	14	27	77	96	14	39
% memory stall time remaining	31	17	41	15	91	78	12	1	58	15
% prefetches that are late	37	7	23	16	4	1	4	0	5	0

Figure 5: Effectiveness of software prefetching

Factor	LUorig	LUopt	FFT	Mp3d	Water	Radix
Late prefetches	√	√	√	√	√	√
Resource contention		√	√		√	√
Speculative prefetches			√	√		
Overlapped accesses	√	√				
Early prefetches	√	√		√	√	√

Figure 6: Factors shaping the effectiveness of software prefetching for ILP

4.2 Memory Stall Time Reduction

We first identify three factors that make software prefetching less successful in reducing memory stall time in `ILP` than in `Simple`. We then identify two factors that enable `ILP` to achieve benefits in memory stall time reduction not available in `Simple`. Figure 6 summarizes these factors and the applications affected by each factor. Our focus here is on the difference between `Simple` and `ILP`, so we do not discuss issues that are common to both systems.

Increased late prefetches. Figures 4(c) and 5 show that the number of prefetches that are too late to completely hide the miss latency increases in all our applications when moving from `Simple` to `ILP`. One reason for this increase is that multiple-issue and dynamic scheduling speed up computation in `ILP`, decreasing the computation time with which each prefetch is overlapped. In addition, `Simple` stalls on any read misses that are not prefetched or that incur a late prefetch, thereby allowing other outstanding prefetches to complete. `ILP` does not provide similar leeway, as it does not immediately stall the processor on misses. The above reasons also lead to an increased frequency of memory accesses in the `ILP` case, which in turn increases contention for system resources. As a result, misses have longer latency in `ILP`, further increasing the number of late prefetches.

Our results also show that optimizations to cluster read misses for the `ILP` system (described in Section 3.4) can reduce the effectiveness of software prefetching. In the absence of prefetching, LUopt provides a 13% reduction in execution time compared to LUorig for `ILP`. With prefetching, however, LUopt sees 10% *more* execution time than LUorig. The clustering optimization used in LUopt decreases the amount of computation between successive misses. As a result, prefetches require a greater number of iterations in order to completely overlap the expected miss latency. However, the loops in LUopt do not have enough iterations to accommodate the needed prefetch distance, so the prefetches in LUopt are unable to successfully hide their targeted latencies.

Increased resource contention. Even without prefetching, `ILP` processors stress system resources more than `Simple`. These resources include processor functional units, cache ports, cache MSHRs, the memory bus, the memory and directory banks, and the network. Resource contention is less in `Simple` because `Simple` processors stall on read misses, allowing resources used by previous writes and prefetches to free up during these stalls.

Resource contention can result in an increase in each of the components of memory latency, and can be further exacerbated by prefetching. For prefetched accesses, an increase in latency after the L1 cache access can either be successfully overlapped by prefetching or appear as late prefetches, described above. However, prefetching cannot target increased latencies incurred at or before the L1 cache access. We focus on this type of resource contention next.

We recognize contention for resources at or before the L1 cache access in our applications by observing the presence of exposed L1 read hit time, as this time is otherwise hidden in both `Simple` and `ILP`. Additionally, the presence of an exposed L2 read hit component in `ILP` also generally indicates resource contention, since ILP techniques usually hide L2 read hit latencies otherwise. We identify the sources of these types of resource contention by examining MSHR occupancy at the caches and functional unit utilization (not shown here for lack of space).

In our applications, resource contention before the L1 cache particularly limits the `ILP` performance of LUopt, FFT, and Radix. These applications see significant MSHR saturation, caused by overlapped reads in LUopt and FFT and by writes in Radix. When the MSHRs of a cache saturate, subsequent misses stall at the cache ports, eventually blocking even cache hits. This effect is particularly large in FFT and Radix, as evidenced by a significant L1 read hit component. As discussed above, such a component cannot be targeted by software prefetching, and is actually exacerbated by the greater frequency of requests with prefetching. Additionally, for FFT, software prefetching with `ILP` also sees a shortage of ALUs and address generation units needed to calculate addresses for both prefetch and demand accesses.

Water stands as an exception to the above trends, as software prefetching actually relieves some resource contention in this application. Water sees resource contention for the processor's memory queue due to lock releases. Each release is marked with a release memory fence, using a SPARC V9 memory barrier. This fence prevents the issue of all subsequent writes until all previous reads and writes complete. As a result, later writes can fill up the memory queue if earlier accesses do not complete quickly enough. If the memory queue fills up, subsequent accesses (including cache hits and private accesses) are prevented from entering the memory queue or being processed in any fashion. Since prefetching can cause accesses before the release memory fence to complete more quickly, this source of resource contention is actually reduced by software prefetching.

Speculative prefetches. In `ILP`, prefetch instructions can be speculatively issued past a mispredicted branch. Speculative prefetches can potentially hurt performance by bringing unnecessary lines into the cache. Among our applications, only Mp3d experiences a significant number of speculative prefetches, with 11% more total prefetches in `ILP` than in `Simple`. However, most of the speculated prefetches are to lines also prefetched on the correct path, and the correct prefetches either coalesce with the speculative prefetches or hit because of them. Thus, speculative prefetches do not impact performance in our applications.

Overlapped accesses. In `ILP`, accesses that are difficult to prefetch may be overlapped because of non-blocking reads and dynamic scheduling. Thus, overall, prefetching may appear more effective in `ILP` than in `Simple`, as prefetching in `ILP` only needs to target those accesses that are not already overlapped by `ILP`. We see the benefit of overlapped accesses in LUorig and LUopt. In particular, the fraction of remote latency overlapped in these applications is much smaller in ILP than in Simple for the reasons discussed above. Nevertheless, the fraction of overall memory stall time reduced in these applications is similar in both systems. In these applications, the lines to be prefetched suffer from repeated L1 cache conflicts; thus, prefetches can be replaced from the L1 cache before their corresponding demand accesses. In Simple, each of these conflicting accesses must incur at least an L2 access time penalty. In contrast, non-blocking reads and dynamic scheduling allow the ILP system to effectively overlap the latencies of these conflicting accesses, thereby removing a limitation to prefetching experienced by Simple.

Fewer early prefetches. In most of our applications, the number of early prefetches drops in ILP. This reduction occurs because the ILP system allows less time between a prefetch and its subsequent demand access, decreasing the likelihood of an intervening replacement or invalidation. Early prefetches can hinder demand accesses by replacing or invalidating needed data from the same or other caches without providing any benefits in latency reduction. Thus, the reductions in early prefetches seen in ILP can potentially help improve prefetching effectiveness for these applications. However, in our applications, such benefits are offset by an increase in late prefetches with ILP.

4.3 Impact on Total Execution Time

Despite its reduced effectiveness in addressing memory stall time, software prefetching achieves significant execution time reductions with ILP for three of our applications (see Figure 5) for several reasons.

Increased weight of memory stall time. ILP features like multiple issue and dynamic scheduling provide greater improvements for computation time than for the memory stall time on all our applications [27]. As a result, memory stall time contributes far more to execution time in ILP than in Simple. Thus, even a smaller fraction of memory stall time reduced in ILP can lead to a reduction in overall execution time similar to or greater than that seen in Simple.

Reduced prefetch overhead. For all of our applications, the ILP system sees less instruction overhead from prefetching (as a percentage of total execution time) than the Simple system. This is because dynamic scheduling and multiple issue allow many of the additional instructions associated with software prefetching to overlap with other computation or memory accesses.

Effect on synchronization stall time. Prefetching can also impact the synchronization component of execution time. The impact of prefetching with ILP on synchronization time varies among our applications, with both positive and negative interactions. However, the synchronization component contributes little to ILP execution time in all of our applications except Water. In Water, there is a negative interaction because prefetching increases synchronization acquire latency in ILP due to increased contention in the memory system. Thus, synchronization time expands to fill a large part of the reduction in memory stall time with prefetching in the ILP system.

5 Re-examining Assumptions of the Prefetching Scheme

The previous section shows that late prefetching and resource contention are the two key limitations to the effectiveness of prefetching on ILP. This section re-examines several assumptions in our prefetching scheme, with the goal of reducing late prefetches and resource contention in ILP.

5.1 Reducing Late Prefetches

Increasing the prefetch distance. A straightforward way to reduce the number of late prefetches is to increase the prefetch distance. We varied the prefetch distance from our default of 200 instructions to 400 and 800 instructions. Figure 7 shows the results for LU, FFT, Mp3d, and Radix (we henceforth only focus on LUorig since it gives better performance with prefetching). We do not apply this technique to Water because, in this application, prefetches either occur within loops where one iteration already has more than 800 instructions, or occur within control statements where prefetching before the branch can lead to an excessive number of prefetches of lines that are not used by the procesor. In Figure 7, PF, PF2, and PF4 refer to prefetching distances of 200, 400, and 800 instructions respectively. Figure 7(a) shows the execution times for each version normalized to ILP without prefetching, and Figure 7(b) characterizes the types of prefetches seen in each version. The variation in the total number of prefetches in the three versions is due to speculative prefetching (Section 4.2).

As Figure 7 shows, the PF2 and PF4 versions reduce the number of late prefetches in all applications. However, there is no significant improvement in execution time in any of the applications. On the contrary, increased prefetch distances have a negative impact on some applications.

There are three reasons why increased prefetch distances do not improve performance for our applications. First, in Mp3d and Radix, the decrease in late prefetches occurs at the expense of an increase in early prefetches. Many prefetches arrive at the cache much before the demand access. These are vulnerable to cache replacements or invalidations for a longer time, as also observed in studies of previous-generation multiprocessors [33]. In Mp3d, these early prefetches hurt performance because they prematurely invalidate other processors' cache lines (due to false and true sharing). In Radix, most early prefetches are replaced prefetches that do not adversely affect other processors.

Second, on applications that are resource-bound, larger prefetch distances further stress system resources by keeping more prefetches outstanding at a time. Our detailed statistics show that the resultant MSHR saturation exposes additional L1 hit latencies (LU, FFT, and Radix) and L2 hit latencies (LU and Radix), which offset the performance benefits due to reducing late prefetches.

Third, in FFT, some loops containing late prefetches do not have an adequate amount of computation to increase the prefetch distance sufficiently in order to reduce late prefetches.

Latency-sensitive prefetching. When the prefetch distance is increased in LU, Mp3d, and Radix, early prefetches increase primarily because the algorithm makes the approximation that all misses incur a common latency. In NUMA multiprocessors, however, remote memory latencies are significantly larger than local memory latencies. Consequently, it may be beneficial to perform a form of *latency-sensitive* prefetching for such systems. The prefetching algorithm can be modified to determine the prefetch distance for each access based on the predicted latency of the access (e.g., by using information about the data layout). Such an approach has been discussed in other studies for software and hardware prefetching [8, 13, 21]. Our applications, however, did not show much benefit with this modification.

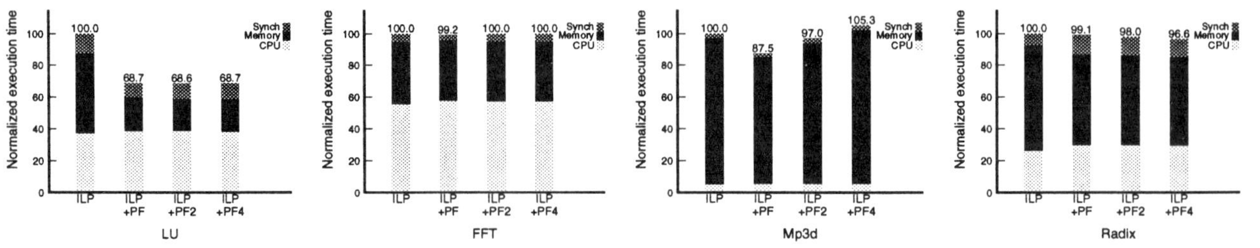

(a) Execution time components

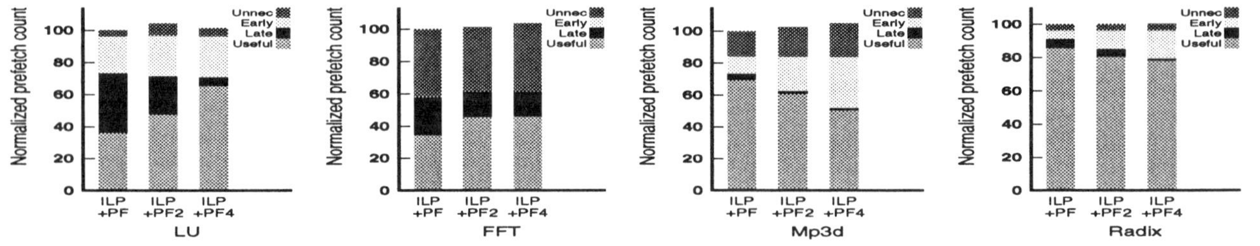

(b) Prefetch characterization

Figure 7: Effect of increasing the prefetch distance

It was difficult to apply latency-sensitive prefetching to LU since different dynamic instances of the same memory instruction in LU can reference both local and remote memory. For Mp3d and Radix, we assumed a prefetch distance of 100 instructions for loops with only local prefetches and the best observed distance (from PF, PF2, and PF4) for loops with remote prefetches. Both Mp3d and Radix achieve negligible improvements (less than 1%). In Radix, there is a significant reduction in the number of early prefetches; however, the demand latencies overlapped by these prefetches contribute only a small part of the total execution time. In Mp3d, the high false and true sharing makes late prefetches preferable to early prefetches.

Outer-loop prefetching. Figure 7(b) shows that FFT continues to see a significant number of late prefetches even in the PF4 version (20% of the total number of prefetches). The prefetching algorithm described in Section 2.1 adds prefetching at the innermost level of the loop nest that causes cache misses. However, the transpose phase of FFT uses a blocked algorithm, and the inner loop of the transpose does not have enough computation or iterations to accommodate a larger prefetching distance. In this case, the outer loop could potentially be software pipelined to prefetch further in advance. Thus, we insert prefetches for a block that will be accessed in a later iteration, rather than for later lines of the same block in the current iteration[1]. We implemented this form of outer-loop prefetching in FFT. However, we observed a 16% slowdown for two reasons. First, the addition of outer-loop prefetching increases the number of prefetches outstanding at a time, further increasing the resource contention in the system (evidenced by a 13% increase in MSHR saturation). Second, adding outer-loop prefetching introduces inter-block cache conflicts.

5.2 Reducing Resource Contention

Although the base architecture used in Section 4 is aggressive in processor, network, and memory system resources, some applications still observe reduced benefits from prefetching on ILP due to increased resource contention. We next re-examine two assumptions in our prefetch strategy that can affect resource contention with ILP.

L2 prefetching. The prefetch strategy used in Section 4 prefetched data into the L1 cache. Prefetching only to the L2 cache can potentially reduce contention in two ways. First, L2 prefetching allows the prefetching algorithm to use the larger L2 cache size in its locality analysis, possibly resulting in fewer prefetches and consequently less contention for address generation units and cache ports. Second, bypassing the L1 cache can potentially reduce resource contention at the L1 cache. However, subsequent demand accesses now see the L2 cache latency, instead of the L1 cache latency. With ILP processors, such L2 cache latencies can be overlapped by non-blocking reads and dynamic scheduling, and thus may not hinder performance.

We find that, for all our applications, the execution time with L2 prefetching is within 1% of the execution time with L1 prefetching. L2 prefetching does not see any performance degradation because ILP techniques are successful in overlapping most of the L2 cache latencies. However, L2 prefetching provides no significant benefits, as the use of the L2 cache size in locality analysis does not reduce the number of prefetches for our applications and input sizes.

Prefetch drop strategy. Following previous work, our base prefetch strategy does not drop prefetches even when resource constraints block their issue [23]. We examined an alternate strategy that drops prefetches when the L1 cache MSHRs are saturated. Our results show less than 2% difference in execution time on all our applications. Dropping prefetches does not give greater performance improvements because any advantages in reducing resource contention are offset by greater latencies seen by subsequent demand misses, as in studies with previous-generation processors [23].

5.3 Summary and Implications

The results of this section show that straightforward modifications to the prefetching algorithm to reduce late prefetches do not necessarily translate to more effective prefetching in

[1]McIntosh has simultaneously developed a similar algorithm for a High Performance Fortran compiler [20].

our applications because of increased early prefetches, inadequate computation, and/or increased stress on system resources. Additionally, alternate prefetch strategies that target L1 resource contention, like L2 prefetching and a simple prefetch drop strategy, do not significantly impact the performance of prefetching for our applications.

These results show that further techniques are needed to alleviate the effects of late prefetches and resource contention. Latency-reducing techniques such as *producer-initiated* communication primitives [1, 15, 29] appear promising. A recent study with simple processors has shown that such primitives can interact positively with software prefetching to reduce the effects of both late prefetches and resource contention [1].

6 Interaction of Prefetching with Consistency Models on ILP Systems

This section evaluates the performance benefits of software prefetching with sequential consistency on ILP multiprocessors and also determines if software prefetching can equalize the performance of sequential consistency (SC) and release consistency (RC). We examine two implementations of sequential consistency – SCplain and SCopt – representing the straightforward and aggressive implementations of SC respectively, and the straightforward implementation of RC, as described in Section 2.2. Figure 8 summarizes the results for this section and is analogous to Figures 4(a) and 4(b).

6.1 Overall Results

We find that the performance benefits of software prefetching vary widely across the consistency implementations. The benefits seen on SCplain are consistently higher than those seen on RC. Consequently, software prefetching reduces the gap between SCplain and RC for all our applications. Nevertheless, RC with software prefetching still shows a substantial reduction in execution time relative to SCplain with software prefetching, ranging from 24% to 65% for our applications.

On SCopt, the addition of software prefetching leads to significant improvements for LU and Water, and small or no improvements for the other three applications; these are comparable to the improvements due to prefetching on RC. Software prefetching significantly decreases the performance gap between SCopt and RC only in LU. RC with software prefetching continues to give significant reductions in execution time compared to SCopt with software prefetching on FFT, Mp3d, and Radix (15%, 35% and 40% respectively).

The addition of software prefetching thus does not entirely eliminate the performance advantages of RC. The following sections respectively analyze the reasons for the remaining memory stall time in SC systems after adding software prefetching and the reasons for the remaining performance difference between SC and RC.

6.2 Memory Stall Time Reduction in SC Systems

Without software prefetching, the SC implementations see larger memory stall time than RC due to consistency constraints [28]. Software prefetching can address much of this additional time and thus can lead to larger reductions in memory stall time than in RC. However, even after adding software prefetching, a significant amount of memory stall time still remains with SC in all our applications except Water (an average of over 58% of total execution time for SCplain and over 43% for SCopt). We next discuss three reasons for the remaining memory stall time in SC systems, focusing on the differences between SC and RC with software prefetching.

Limitations of software prefetching. As in RC, much of the remaining memory stall time in SC is due to the limitations of prefetching stemming from late and early prefetches or resource contention. However, the impact of these limitations is higher on SCplain and SCopt, since they see these effects on writes as well as reads (RC hides the latency of writes). SCplain sees an even higher impact of these limitations since it does not overlap any part of the read latency (unlike SCopt and RC). Additionally, in SC, downgraded prefetches (exclusive prefetches transitioned to shared-state by an external coherence action before the demand access) can further reduce the benefits of prefetching for write accesses.

One or more of the above effects is seen with all our applications in the SC systems. The effect of late prefetches is seen in all applications. The effect of early prefetches is seen in Mp3d (caused by true and false sharing) and LU (caused by conflicts at the L1 and L2 caches). Only FFT sees significant resource contention, evidenced through MSHR saturation. In contrast to RC, Radix does not see resource contention in SC since the writes in the key permutation phase are no longer overlapped, and so do not saturate the MSHRs.

Consistency-related delays. SC with software prefetching also experiences memory stall time owing to the constraints of the consistency implementation.

In SCplain, demand accesses cannot be issued before reaching the head of the memory queue. Consequently, SCplain without software prefetching sees a significant amount of consistency-related read and write hit latency (2% to 17% of execution time). These latencies are not targeted by software prefetching.

In SCopt, write buffering prevents write stall times from being directly exposed to the processor. However, read operations in SCopt cannot retire from the instruction window until all previous writes have completed. Thus, unlike RC, reads can result in stall time if previous writes were not successfully prefetched.

Unamenable accesses. Finally, a significant portion of the memory stall time can still remain because of memory accesses that are not amenable to prefetching. In Mp3d and Radix, addresses of some high-latency memory accesses are determined very close to their use, preventing the prefetching algorithm from issuing prefetches for these accesses. The SC systems expose the latency of both read and write operations that are unamenable to prefetching; RC, on the other hand, generally sees only read latencies.

6.3 Comparison of RC and SC

Comparing RC and SCplain, RC with software prefetching achieves lower execution time than SCplain with software prefetching by hiding the latency of write misses (whether late, early, or unprefetched), and by avoiding consistency-related delays. One or more of these components is substantial in the SCplain executions of all our applications. As a result, the gap in execution time between RC and SCplain RC remains significant, ranging from 24% to 65% for our applications.

Comparing RC and SCopt, RC with software prefetching achieves lower execution time than SCopt with software prefetching if reads in SCopt experience stall time waiting

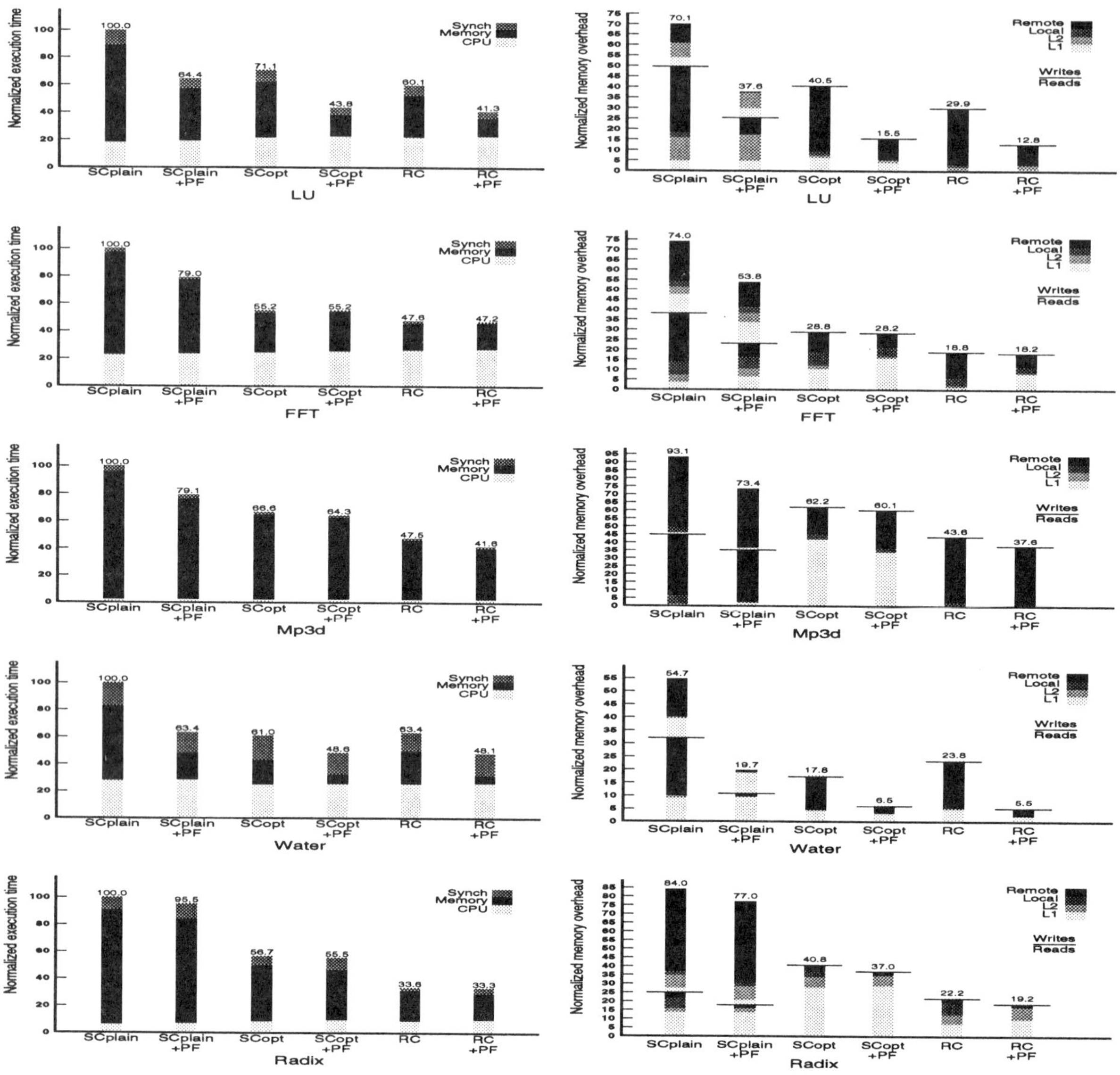

(a) Execution time components

(b) Memory stall time components

Figure 8: Effect of software prefetching on consistency models

for previous write latencies (due to ineffective prefetching or unprefetched accesses). FFT, Mp3d, and Radix see this effect. Consequently, RC with software prefetching shows significantly lower execution times than SCopt with software prefetching for these applications (15%, 35% and 40% respectively). LU and Water have comparable performance with RC with software prefetching and SCopt with software prefetching.

Additionally, as mentioned in Section 4.3, software prefetching can contribute either positively or negatively to the synchronization component of execution time. However, memory stall time dominates the execution times of most of our applications, and subsequently determines the performance difference between SC and RC.

Thus, our results indicate that software prefetching is unable to close the gap between SC and RC. Write latencies that prefetching is unable to hide remain the most important reason for this performance gap. Our results also show that software prefetching alone does not obviate the need for hardware optimizations to SC, since SCopt continues to significantly outperform SCplain for all applications, even with the addition of software prefetching.

7 Related Work

To the best of our knowledge, there have not been any previous evaluations of either hardware or software controlled non-binding prefetching for state-of-the-art ILP multiprocessors.

Gornish evaluated binding prefetching for both single-issue and multiple-issue statically-scheduled multiprocessors with non-blocking reads [13]. The binding prefetches rely on software cache-coherence and require complete cache flushes before and after each parallel loop. Processor pipelines and functional-unit contention are not modeled. This work integrates hardware and software prefetching support, dynamically adapting hardware prefetching distance according to the latency of each reference. The study finds that software prefetching provides execution time improvements on their multiple-issue system similar to or greater than those seen with their single-issue system, but does not analyze the interaction of ILP features with prefetching.

Three recent studies on prefetching in uniprocessors examine state-of-the-art uniprocessors with multiple issue, dynamic scheduling, and non-blocking reads. Luk and Mowry proposed software prefetching algorithms for pointer-based data structures and evaluated their algorithms for an ILP processor similar to the MIPS R10000 [19]. Bennett and Flynn compared stream buffers (a form of hardware-controlled prefetching), hardware stride-based prefetching, and victim caches for state-of-the-art ILP processors [2]. They found that stream buffers and stride-based prefetching do not have much impact on most SPEC92 programs, as these techniques stress bus bandwidth. In another study, Bennett and Flynn proposed a *prediction cache* that dynamically adapts between stream buffer and victim cache functionality based on program miss patterns [3]. The prediction cache dynamically adjusts the stream buffer prefetching distance based on the late prefetch pattern of the program. Although all of the above studies use aggressive ILP uniprocessors, they do not focus on the impact of ILP on prefetching, and so do not relate the results of their studies to the ILP features of the processor.

Other previous studies on prefetching with ILP uniprocessors examine statically-scheduled processors. Chen et al. investigated the use of software-controlled prefetching on statically-scheduled multiple-issue uniprocessors for non-numeric applications [6]. This work seems to allow only one outstanding read (but several outstanding prefetches). Further, they assume a small read latency of 10 cycles. Their results show prefetching to be effective with multiple issue uniprocessors. Chen and Baer compared the performance of non-blocking reads and hardware prefetching on a statically-scheduled single-issue uniprocessor [5]. They found that their hardware prefetching scheme generally performed better than non-blocking reads and is less sensitive to memory latency. They also studied the combination of non-blocking reads and hardware prefetching for two applications and found it to perform better than either technique alone. Farkas et al. studied the impact of non-blocking reads and stream buffers with statically-scheduled multiple-issue uniprocessors [7]. They assumed a small miss latency of 16 cycles. They found that both non-blocking reads and stream buffers improve performance; the best performance is achieved when both are combined.

In the context of previous-generation systems, several studies have proposed algorithms for software-controlled non-binding prefetching [4, 16, 23, 24, 25]. Of these, Mowry et al. developed the most sophisticated algorithm and compiler implementation, with a comprehensive evaluation for both uniprocessors and shared-memory multiprocessors [23, 24, 25]. This algorithm is described in Section 2.1. Tullsen and Eggers evaluated software-controlled non-binding prefetching on a bus-based system [33]. They characterized bandwidth needs of their applications, and found that the benefits of prefetching degrade as bandwidth needs increase. They also found that increasing the prefetch distance can reduce late prefetches but can also increase early prefetches, and thus does not significantly improve performance. We found this to be true for our ILP-based system as well (Section 5.1).

Gupta et al. evaluated the interaction between software-controlled prefetching and straightforward implementations of consistency models for systems with simple processors [14]. They found that prefetching significantly improved the performance of both SC and RC. However, for two out of their three applications, a significant performance gap remained between SC and RC even after adding prefetching.

8 Conclusions

Shared-memory multiprocessors are being increasingly built from commodity microprocessors that aggressively exploit instruction-level parallelism. This paper provides the first study of the effectiveness of software-controlled non-binding prefetching in multiprocessor systems built of state-of-the-art ILP processors. We compared two multiprocessors systems – `ILP` and `Simple` – that are equivalent in every respect except that the former uses state-of-the-art ILP processors while the latter uses previous-generation processors (with single issue, static scheduling, and blocking reads). We found that while software prefetching resulted in substantial reductions in execution time (12% to 31%) for three out of five applications on the `ILP` system, it is significantly less effective in reducing the data memory stall time on the `ILP` system than on the `Simple` system. Even after the addition of software prefetching, memory stall time constituted more than 30% of the execution time for four out of five applications on the `ILP` system. In contrast, on the `Simple` system, memory stall time constituted less than 17% of the execution time for four out of five applications. Thus, software prefetching does not significantly change the memory-bound nature of most of our applications on the `ILP` system.

The key factors that limit the effectiveness of software prefetching on the `ILP` system are an increase in late prefetches and an increase in contention at various resources. Our results thus motivate modifications to prefetching algorithms so that they are more sensitive to resource use and to variations in expected latency for different accesses. Several straightforward enhancements to the prefetching scheme, however, did not show any improvements. An alternative technique to improve memory system performance is the use of latency-reducing (rather than tolerating) techniques. For example, producer-initiated communication primitives may be able to reduce latency and resource contention, while interacting positively with prefetching.

This paper also examines whether software prefetching can equalize the performance of sequential consistency (SC) and release consistency (RC) on ILP multiprocessors. We found that although software prefetching reduces the gap between the straightforward implementations of SC and RC, a significant gap remained between these implementations (ranging from 24% to 65% for our applications). Comparing an optimized hardware implementation of SC to a straightforward implementation of RC, we found that a significant gap remains for three out of five applications (15% to 40%). Write latencies that prefetching does not effectively hide remain the most important reason for the performance gap between SC and RC. Thus, future efforts to provide SC programmability with RC performance need to more effectively address the limitations that write latencies impose on SC.

9 Acknowledgments

We would like to thank Kathi Fletcher, Nat McIntosh, Shubu Mukherjee, Ram Rajamony, and Willy Zwaenepoel for valuable feedback on earlier drafts of this paper.

References

[1] H. Abdel-Shafi, J. Hall, S. V. Adve, and V. S. Adve. An Evaluation of Fine-Grain Producer-Initiated Communication in Cache-Coherent Multiprocessors. In *Proceedings of the 3rd International Symposium on High-Performance Computer Architecture*, 1997.

[2] J. E. Bennett and M. J. Flynn. Latency Tolerance for Dynamic Processors. Stanford University, CSL-TR-96-687, 1996.

[3] J. E. Bennett and M. J. Flynn. Reducing Cache Miss Rates Using Prediction Caches. Stanford University, CSL-TR-96-707, 1996.

[4] D. Callahan, K. Kennedy, and A. Porterfield. Software Prefetching. In *Proceedings of the 4th International Conference on Architectural Support for Programming Languages and Operating Systems*, 1991.

[5] T.-F. Chen and J.-L. Baer. Reducing Memory Latency via Non-Blocking and Prefetching Caches. In *Proceedings of the 5th International Conference on Architectural Support for Programming Languages and Operating Systems*, 1992.

[6] W. Y. Chen et al. Data Access Microarchitectures for Superscalar Processors with Compiler-Assisted Data Prefetching. In *Proceedings of the 24th Annual International Symposisum on Microarchitecture*, 1991.

[7] K. Farkas, N. Jouppi, and P. Chow. How Useful are Non-Blocking Loads, Stream Buffers and Speculative Execution in Multiple Issue Processors? In *Proceedings of the 1st International Conference on High-Performance Computer Architecture*, 1995.

[8] K. Fletcher. Compiler-hardware cooperation in prefetching for shared-memory multiprocessors. Ph.D. Thesis Proposal, Rice University, September 1995.

[9] K. Gharachorloo, A. Gupta, and J. Hennessy. Performance Evaluation of Memory Consistency Models for Shared-Memory Multiprocessors. In *Proceedings of the 4th Inernational Conference on Architectural Support for Programming Languages and Operating Systems*, 1991.

[10] K. Gharachorloo, A. Gupta, and J. Hennessy. Two Techniques to Enhance the Performance of Memory Consistency Models. In *Proceedings of the International Conference on Parallel Processing*, 1991.

[11] K. Gharachorloo, A. Gupta, and J. Hennessy. Hiding Memory Latency Using Dynamic Scheduling in Shared-Memory Multiprocessors. In *Proceedings of the 19th Annual International Symposium on Computer Architecture*, 1992.

[12] K. Gharachorloo, D. Lenoski, J. Laudon, P. Gibbons, A. Gupta, and J. Hennessy. Memory Consistency and Event Ordering in Scalable Shared-Memory Multiprocessors. In *Proceedings of the 17th Annual International Symposium on Computer Architecture*, 1990.

[13] E. H. Gornish. *Adaptive and Integrated Data Cache Prefetching for Shared-Memory Multiprocessors.* PhD thesis, University of Illinois at Urbana-Champaign, 1995.

[14] A. Gupta, J. Hennessy, K. Gharachorloo, T. Mowry, and W.-D. Weber. Comparative Evaluation of Latency Reducing and Tolerating Techniques. In *Proceedings of the 18th Annual International Symposium on Computer Architecture*, 1991.

[15] M. D. Hill, J. R. Larus, S. K. Reinhardt, and D. A. Wood. Cooperative Shared Memory: Software and Hardware Support for Scalable Multiprocessors. In *Proceedings of the 5th International Conference on Architectural Support for Programming Languages and Operating Systems*, 1992.

[16] A. C. Klaiber and H. M. Levy. An Architecture for Software-Controlled Data Prefetching. In *Proceedings of the 18th Annual International Symposium on Computer Architecture*, 1991.

[17] D. Kroft. Lockup-Free Instruction Fetch/Prefetch Cache Organization. In *Proceedings of the 8th International Symposium on Computer Architecture*, 1981.

[18] L. Lamport. How to Make a Multiprocessor Computer that Correctly Executes Multiprocess Programs. *IEEE Trans. on Computers*, C-28(9):690–691, 1979.

[19] C.-K. Luk and T. C. Mowry. Compiler-Based Prefetching for Recursive Data Structures. In *Proceedings of the 7th International Conference on Architectural Support for Programming Languages and Operating Systems*, 1996.

[20] N. McIntosh. Private communication. *Rice University*, February 1997.

[21] N. McIntosh, K. Fletcher, K. Cooper, and K. Kennedy. Compiler Techniques for Software Prefetching on Cache-Coherent Shared-Memory Multiprocessors. Center for Research on Parallel Computation, Rice University, CRPC-TR96675-S, 1997.

[22] MIPS Technologies, Inc. *R10000 Microprocessor User's Manual, Version 1.1*, 1996.

[23] T. Mowry. *Tolerating Latency through Software-Controlled Data Prefetching.* PhD thesis, Stanford University, 1994.

[24] T. Mowry and A. Gupta. Tolerating Latency Through Software-Controlled Prefetching in Shared-Memory Multiprocessors. *Journal of Parallel and Distributed Computing*, 12(2):87–106, 1991.

[25] T. C. Mowry, M. S. Lam, and A. Gupta. Design and Evaluation of a Compiler Algorithm for Prefetching. In *Proceedings of the 5th International Conference on Architectural Support for Programming Languages and Operating Systems*, 1992.

[26] V. S. Pai, P. Ranganathan, and S. V. Adve. RSIM: An Execution-Driven Simulator for ILP-Based Shared-Memory Multiprocessors and Uniprocessors. In *Proceedings of the 3rd Workshop on Computer Architecture Education*, 1997.

[27] V. S. Pai, P. Ranganathan, and S. V. Adve. The Impact of Instruction Level Parallelism on Multiprocessor Performance and Simulation Methodology. In *Proceedings of the 3rd International Symposium on High Performance Computer Architecture*, 1997.

[28] V. S. Pai, P. Ranganathan, S. V. Adve, and T. Harton. An Evaluation of Memory Consistency Models for Shared-Memory Systems with ILP Processors. In *Proceedings of the 7th International Conference on Architectural Support for Programming Languages and Operating Systems*, 1996.

[29] D. Poulsen. *Memory Latency Reduction via Data Prefetching and Data Forwarding in Shared-Memory Multiprocessors.* PhD thesis, University of Illinois at Urbana-Champaign, 1994.

[30] M. Rosenblum, E. Bugnion, S. A. Herrod, E. Witchel, and A. Gupta. The Impact of Architectural Trends on Operating System Performance. In *Proceedings of the 15th ACM Symposium on Operating Systems Principles*, 1995.

[31] J. P. Singh, W.-D. Weber, and A. Gupta. SPLASH: Stanford Parallel Applications for Shared-Memory. *Computer Architecture News*, 20(1):5–44, 1992.

[32] Sparc International. *The SPARC Architecture Manual, Version 9*, 1993.

[33] D. Tullsen and S. Eggers. Effective Cache Prefetching on Bus-Based Multiprocessors. *ACM Transactions on Computer Systems*, 13(1):57–88, 1995.

[34] S. C. Woo, M. Ohara, E. Torrie, J. P. Singh, and A. Gupta. The SPLASH-2 Programs: Characterization and Methodological Considerations. In *Proceedings of the 22nd Annual International Symposium on Computer Architecture*, 1995.

VM-Based Shared Memory on Low-Latency, Remote-Memory-Access Networks*

Leonidas Kontothanassis[†] Galen Hunt, Robert Stets, Nikolaos Hardavellas, Michał Cierniak, Srinivasan Parthasarathy, Wagner Meira, Jr., Sandhya Dwarkadas, and Michael Scott

Department of Computer Science
University of Rochester
Rochester, NY 14627–0226

[†] DEC Cambridge Research Lab
One Kendall Sq., Bldg. 700
Cambridge, MA 02139

Abstract

Recent technological advances have produced network interfaces that provide users with very low-latency access to the memory of remote machines. We examine the impact of such networks on the implementation and performance of software DSM. Specifically, we compare two DSM systems—Cashmere and TreadMarks—on a 32-processor DEC Alpha cluster connected by a Memory Channel network.

Both Cashmere and TreadMarks use virtual memory to maintain coherence on pages, and both use lazy, multi-writer release consistency. The systems differ dramatically, however, in the mechanisms used to track sharing information and to collect and merge concurrent updates to a page, with the result that Cashmere communicates much more frequently, and at a much finer grain.

Our principal conclusion is that low-latency networks make DSM based on fine-grain communication competitive with more coarse-grain approaches, but that further hardware improvements will be needed before such systems can provide consistently superior performance. In our experiments, Cashmere scales slightly better than TreadMarks for applications with false sharing. At the same time, it is severely constrained by limitations of the current Memory Channel hardware. In general, performance is better for TreadMarks.

*This work was supported in part by NSF grants CDA–9401142, CCR–9319445, CCR–9409120, and CCR–9510173; ARPA contract F19628–94–C–0057; an external research grant from Digital Equipment Corporation; and graduate fellowships from Microsoft Research (Galen Hunt) and CNPq–Brazil (Wagner Meira, Jr., Grant 200.862/93-6).

1 Introduction

Distributed shared memory (DSM) is an attractive design alternative for large-scale shared memory multiprocessing. Traditional DSM systems rely on virtual memory hardware and simple message passing to implement shared memory. State-of-the-art DSM systems (e.g. TreadMarks [1, 16]) employ sophisticated protocol optimizations, such as relaxed consistency models, multiple writable copies of a page, and lazy processing of all coherence-related events. These optimizations recognize the very high (millisecond) latency of communication on workstation networks; their aim is to minimize the frequency of communication, even at the expense of additional computation.

Recent technological advances, however, have led to the commercial availability of inexpensive workstation networks on which a processor can access the memory of a remote node safely from user space, at a latency two to three orders of magnitude lower than that of traditional message passing. These networks suggest the need to re-evaluate the assumptions underlying the design of DSM protocols, and specifically to consider protocols that communicate at a much finer grain. The Cashmere system employs this sort of protocol [17, 18]. It uses directories to keep track of sharing information, and merges concurrent writes to the same coherence block via write-through to a unique (and possibly remote) main-memory copy of each page.

In this paper we compare implementations of TreadMarks and a modified version of Cashmere on a 32-processor cluster (8 nodes, 4 processors each) of DEC AlphaServers, connected by DEC's Memory Channel [12] network. Memory Channel allows a user-level application to write to the memory of remote nodes. The remote-write capability can be used for (non-coherent) shared memory, for broadcast/multicast, and for very fast user-level messages. Remote reads are not directly supported. Where the original Cashmere protocol used remote reads to access directory information, we broadcast directory updates on the Memory Channel. Where the original Cashmere protocol would read the contents of a page from the home node, we ask a processor at the home node to write the data to us. In Trcad-Marks, we use the Memory Channel simply to provide a very fast messaging system. Our aim is to compare a more fine-grain approach to shared memory to a state-of-the-art DSM that does not rely on remote memory access. In future work we intend to study alternative fine-grain protocols in more detail; we believe the current version of Cashmere to be a good first cut.

Our performance results compare six specific protocol implementations: three each for TreadMarks and Cashmere. For both systems, one implementation uses interrupts to request information from remote processors, while another requires processors to poll for remote requests at the top of every loop. The third TreadMarks implementation uses DEC's standard, kernel-level implementation of UDP for the Memory Channel. The third Cashmere implementation dedicates one processor per node to handling remote requests. This approach is similar to polling, but without the additional overhead and the unpredictability in response time: it is meant to emulate a hypothetical Memory Channel in which remote reads are supported in hardware. The emulation is conservative in the sense that it moves data across the local bus twice (through the processor registers), while true remote reads would cross the bus only once.

In general, both Cashmere and TreadMarks provide good performance for many of the applications in our test suite. The high remote memory channel interrupt overheads of Digital Unix significantly reduce performance for both TreadMarks and Cashmere. In general, TreadMarks is more sensitive to interrupt latencies since it uses request-response communication for both synchronization and data transfer. The Memory Channel implementation of Cashmere uses interrupts only for page (data) transfers. Cashmere takes advantage of remote memory access for program and meta-data resulting in fewer messages requiring a reply. In our experiments, Cashmere scales slightly better than TreadMarks for applications with false sharing since the use of home nodes reduces the number of request-response messages required to update the local copy of a page. In general, however, performance is better for TreadMarks due to reduced communication requirements. Overall, Cashmere spends less time in protocol code at the expense of extra communication, but is severely constrained by limitations of the current Memory Channel hardware.

Three principal factors appear to contribute to making the differences between TreadMarks and Cashmere on the Memory Channel smaller than one would expect on an "ideal" remote-memory-access network. First, the current Memory Channel has relatively modest cross-sectional bandwidth, which limits the performance of write-through. Second, it lacks remote reads, forcing Cashmere to copy pages to local memory (rather than fetching them incrementally in response to cache misses), and to engage the active assistance of a remote processor in order to make the copy. With equal numbers of compute processors, Cashmere usually performs best when an additional processor per node is dedicated to servicing remote requests, implying that remote-read hardware would improve performance further. Third, our processors (the 21064A) have very small first-level caches. Our write-doubling mechanism increases the first-level working set for certain applications beyond the 16K available, dramatically reducing performance. The larger caches of the 21264 should largely eliminate this problem.

We are optimistic about the future of Cashmere-like systems as network interfaces continue to evolve. Based on previous simulations [18], it is in fact somewhat surprising that Cashmere performs as well as it does on the current generation of hardware. The second-generation Memory Channel, due on the market very soon, will have something like half the latency, and an order of magnitude more bandwidth. Finer-grain DSM systems are in a position to make excellent use of this sort of hardware as it becomes available.

The remainder of this paper is organized as follows. We present the coherence protocols we are evaluating in Section 2. In Section 3, we discuss our implementations of the protocols, together with the mechanisms we employed (write doubling, page copying, directory broadcast, and remote read emulation) to overcome limitations of the hardware. Section 4 presents experimental results. The final two sections discuss related work and summarize our conclusions.

2 Protocols

Both TreadMarks and Cashmere maintain coherence at page granularity, employ a relaxed consistency model, and allow multiple concurrent writers to the same coherence block. There are significant differences, however, in the way sharing information for coherence blocks is maintained, and in the way writes to the same coherence block by multiple processors are merged. Mainly, TreadMarks does not take advantage of remote memory access for anything other than fast messaging, while Cashmere uses remote memory access for fine-grain communication of coherence information and shared data.

2.1 Cashmere

Cashmere maintains coherence information using a distributed directory data structure. Currently, directory entries are organized as a set of eight 4-byte words, one for each SMP node in the system. Each word contains presence bits for each of the four processors within the SMP (4 bits), the id of the *home node* for the page (5 bits), whether the home node is still the original default or has been set as the result of a "first touch" heuristic (1 bit), and an indication of whether a particular CPU within a node has exclusive read/write permission for the page (4 bits). The home node indications in separate words are redundant. Directory space overhead for the 8K pages supported by Digital Unix is about 3% and would be smaller if we did not have to replicate the directory on each of our eight nodes. Directory overhead could be reduced by packing the directory information into a single long word (64 bits). However, this would require locking of the directory entry. The current directory structure does not require the use of locks except to set the home node of a page.

The choice of home node can have a significant impact on performance. The home node itself can access the page directly, while the remaining processors have to use the slower Memory Channel interface. We assign home nodes at run time, based on which processor first touches a page after the program has completed any initialization phase [23]. The home node is set only once during the lifetime of a program, and thus the use of locks does not impact performance.

In addition to the directory data structure, each processor also holds two globally accessible lists, the *write notice list* and the *no longer exclusive (NLE) list*. These globally accessible lists are protected by cluster-wide locks. The *write notice list* contains descriptors (write notices) for pages that are valid on the processor and have been written by remote processors. A bit map is also associated with the *write notice list* in order to avoid duplicate write notices for the same page. The *NLE list* contains descriptors for pages to which the processor once held exclusive access, but which are now shared by multiple processors. A processor can avoid certain overhead for a page so long as it retains exclusive access (see below).

Protocol operations happen in response to four types of events: **read** page faults, **write** page faults, **acquire** synchronization operations, and **release** synchronization operations.

When a processor takes a read page fault, it acquires exclusive access to the directory word representing its SMP node (using *load-linked/store-conditional (ll/sc)* within the node), and adds itself to the sharing set. It then checks to see if the home node has been assigned (valid home node bits). If the home node bits are not valid and home node ownership has already been asserted by another node, the faulting processor sets the home node bits in its node's directory entry. If home node ownership has not been asserted by any other node (checked by examining all other directory words), the faulting processor acquires the directory entry lock to assert home node ownership. It also scans all words in the directory entry to determine if another processor has previously acquired exclusive read/write permission on the page. If so, it appends a descriptor for the page to the *NLE list* of the former exclusive-sharer processor.

Locally, the faulting processor creates a mapping for the page. Ideally, the mapping would allow the processor to load cache lines from the home node on demand. On the Memory Channel, which does not support remote reads, a copy of the page is requested from the home node, and then written into the local copy (see below). A write page fault on an invalid page is treated the same as a read page fault. In addition, on each write page fault, the processor inserts the page number in a local list called the *dirty list*. The faulting operation is then restarted after providing the appropriate (read and write) permissions to the page.

At an acquire synchronization operation, the processor traverses its *write notice list* and removes itself from the sharing set of each page found therein. The removal operation requires that the processor obtain exclusive access (within the SMP node) for the corresponding word in the directory entry, and modify the bitmask of sharing processors.

At a release synchronization operation, the processor traverses its *dirty list* and informs other processors of the writes it has performed since the previous release operation. For each entry in the *dirty list* the processor scans the directory entry for that page. If other processors are found to be sharing the page, the releaser appends a notice to the *write notice list* of every sharing processor, if a write notice does not already exist for the page (checked by examining the bit mask). If no other processor is found sharing the page, the processor indicates that the page is in exclusive mode by appropriately modifying its directory word. If the page does not move to exclusive mode, the processor downgrades its permission to read-only so as to catch subsequent writes. After processing its *dirty list* the processor also traverse its *NLE* list. For each entry listed in the list it takes the same set of actions it took for entries in the *dirty list* with two differences. It sets a flag indicating that this page should never move to exclusive mode again and also avoids moving it to exclusive mode now, even if no other processors are found to be sharing the page.

The final issue to be addressed is the mechanism that allows a processor to obtain the data written by other processors. For each page there is a unique home node to which processors send changes on the fly. Our protocol guarantees that a release operation cannot complete before all its writes have been applied at the unique home node. Future acquires are guaranteed to find data that is in their logical past at the home node. On a network with remote reads there would be only one copy of each page in main memory—namely the copy at the home node. Every page mapping would refer to this page; cache fills would be satisfied from this page; and the collection of changes would happen via the standard cache write-through or write-back. On the Memory Channel, we must create a local copy of a page in response to a page fault. Normal write-back then updates this local copy. To update the copy at the home node, we insert additional code into the program executable at every shared memory write (write doubling).

This protocol differs in a number of ways from the Cashmere protocol employed in simulation-based studies [18]. The most important differences stem from differences in hardware platforms. The ideal simulated hardware (i.e. the one that yields the best performance for Cashmere-like protocols) assumes the ability to map remote pages and service cache misses to them in hardware as well as the ability to forward writes to home nodes using write-through. In the current implementation we were forced to use page copying and doubling of writes in software (see section 3).

We have also made modifications to the protocol itself. In particular we have removed the "weak" state from the implemented protocol. In simulation, any page with at least one writer resided in the weak state. Weak pages were optimistically assumed to be modified during every synchronization interval: all sharers would automatically invalidate the pages during acquire operations. The current protocol opts instead for the exclusive mode and for explicit write notices. Pages in exclusive mode experience only the initial write fault, the minimum of possible protocol overhead. At release operations, processors send write notices for all modified non-exclusive pages that do not already have such a notice pending. These two enhancements improve Cashmere's ability to efficiently handle private pages and producer-consumer sharing patterns.

2.2 TreadMarks

TreadMarks is a distributed shared memory system based on lazy release consistency (LRC) [16]. Lazy release consistency is a variant of release consistency [20]. It guarantees memory consistency only at synchronization points and permits multiple writers per coherence block. Lazy release consistency divides time on each node into intervals delineated by remote synchronization operations. Each interval is represented by a vector of timestamps, with entry i on processor j representing the most recent interval on processor i that logically precedes the current interval on processor j. When a processor takes a write page fault, it creates a write notice for the faulting page and appends the notice to a list of notices associated with its current interval.

When a processor acquires a lock, it sends a copy of its current vector timestamp to the previous lock owner. The previous lock owner compares the received timestamp with its own, and responds with a list of all intervals (and the write notices associated with them) that are in the new owner's past, but that the new owner has not seen. The acquiring processor sets its vector timestamp to be the pairwise maximum of its old vector and the vector of the previous lock owner. It also incorporates in its local data structures all intervals (and the associated write notices) sent by the previous owner. Finally, it invalidates (unmaps) all pages for which it received a write notice. The write notice signifies that there is a write to the page in the processor's logical past and that the processor needs to bring its copy of the page up to date.

To support multiple writers to a page, each processor saves a pristine copy of a page called a *twin* before it writes the page. When asked for changes, the processor compares its current copy of the page to the page's twin. The result of the comparison is a run-length encoding of the changes, called a *diff*. There is one diff for every write notice in the system. When a processor takes a read page fault (or a write page fault on a completely unmapped page), it peruses its list of write notices and makes requests for all unseen modifications. It then merges the changes into its local copy in software, in the causal order defined by the timestamps of the write notices.

Barrier synchronization is dealt with somewhat differently. Upon arrival at a barrier, all processors send their vector timestamps (and intervals and write notices), to a barrier manager, using a conservative guess as to the contents of the manager's vector timestamp. The manager merges all timestamps, intervals, and write notices into its local data structures, and then sends to each processor its new updated timestamp along with the intervals and write notices that the processor has not seen.

The TreadMarks protocol avoids communication at the time of a release, and limits communication to the processes participating in a synchronization operation. However, because it must guarantee the correctness of arbitrary future references, and because all information is local and communication occurs only via messaging, the TreadMarks protocol must send notices of all logically previous writes to synchronizing processors even if the processors have no copy of the page to which the write notice refers. If a processor is not going to acquire a copy of the page in the future (something the protocol cannot of course predict), then sending and processing these notices may constitute a significant amount of unnecessary work, especially during barrier synchronization, when all processors need to be made aware of all other processors' writes. Further information on TreadMarks can be found in other papers [1].

3 Implementation Issues

3.1 Memory Channel

Digital Equipment's Memory Channel (MC) network provides applications with a global address space using memory mapped regions. A region can be mapped into a process's address space for transmit, receive, or both (a single virtual address mapping can only be either for transmit or for receive). Virtual addresses for transmit regions map into physical addresses located in I/O space, and, in particular, on the MC's PCI adapter. Virtual addresses for receive regions map into physical RAM. Writes into transmit regions are collected by the source MC adapter, forwarded to destination MC adapters through a hub, and transferred via DMA to receive regions with the same global identifier (see Figure 1). Regions within a node can be shared across processors and processes. Writes to transmit regions originating on a given node will be sent to receive regions on that same node only if *loop-back* has been enabled for the region. In our implementation of Cashmere, we use loop-back only for synchronization primitives. TreadMarks does not use it at all.

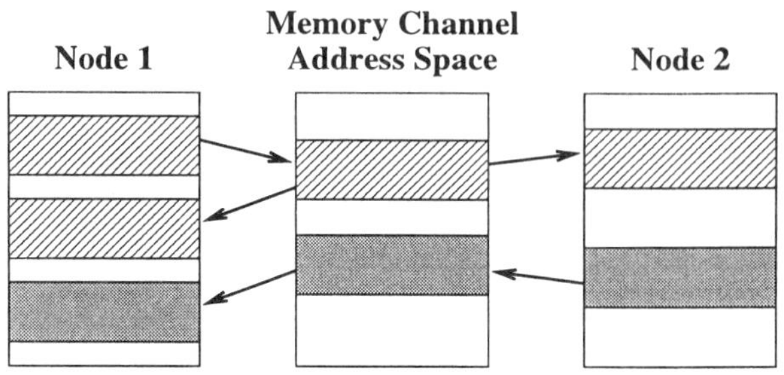

Figure 1: Memory Channel space. The lined region is mapped for both transmit and receive on node 1 and for receive on node 2. The gray region is mapped for receive on node 1 and for transmit on node 2.

```
label:
    ldq   $7, 0($13)        ; Check poll flag.
    beq   $7, nomsg         ; If message,
    jsr   $26, handler      ;   call handler.
    ldgp  $29, 0($26)
nomsg:
```

Figure 2: Polling. Polling code is inserted at all interior, backward-referenced labels. The address of the polling flag is preserved in register \$13 throughout execution.

Unicast and multicast process-to-process writes have a latency of 5.2 μs on our system (latency drops below 5μs for other AlphaServer models). Our MC configuration can sustain per-link transfer bandwidths of 30 MB/s with the limiting factor being the 32-bit AlphaServer 2100 PCI bus. MC peak aggregate bandwidth is also about 32 MB/s due to a limitation on the early implementation of the Memory Channel device driver. We expect that number to get closer to the 100MB/s supported by the hardware with the new driver release.

Memory Channel guarantees write ordering and local cache coherence. Two writes issued to the same transmit region (even on different nodes) will appear in the same order in every receive region. When a write appears in a receive region it invalidates any locally cached copies of its line.

3.2 Remote-Read Mechanisms

Although the first-generation Memory Channel supports remote writes, it does not support remote reads. To read remote data, a message passing protocol must be used to send a request to a remote node. The remote node responds by writing the requested data into a region that is mapped for receive on the originating node.

Three different mechanisms can be used to process transfer requests. The most obvious alternative uses a MC provided inter-node interrupt to force a processor on the remote node into a handler. The second alternative is for processes to poll for messages on a periodic basis (e.g. at the tops of loops). The third alternative is to dedicate one processor on every node to servicing remote requests, and have that processor poll on a continual basis.

Memory Channel allows a processor to trigger an inter-node interrupt by means of a remote write for which the recipient has created a special receive region mapping. This capability is exported to applications as an `imc_kill` function which is called with a remote host name, process identifier and UNIX signal number. The interrupt is filtered up through the kernel to the receiving process only when the receiving process subsequently enters the kernel, resulting in an average inter-node signal cost of almost 1 millisecond.

Polling requires instrumentation that checks the message receive region frequently, and branches to a handler if a message has arrived. Applications can be instrumented either by hand or automatically. We instrument the protocol libraries by hand and use an extra compilation pass between the compiler and assembler to instrument applications[1]. The instrumentation pass parses the compiler-generated assembly file and inserts polling instrumentation at the start of all labeled basic blocks that are internal to a function and are backward referenced—i.e. at tops of all loops. The polling instruction sequence appears in Figure 2.

Dedicating a processor to polling on each node is the least intrusive mechanism: it requires neither application changes nor expensive interrupt handlers. Of course, a dedicated processor is unavailable for regular computation. In general, we would not expect this to be a productive way to use an Alpha processor (though in programs that don't scale well it can actually be better than further parallelism). Our intent is rather to simulate the behavior of a hypothetical (and somewhat smaller) Memory Channel system that supports remote reads in hardware.

3.3 Cashmere

Cashmere takes advantage of MC remote writes to collect shared memory writes, to update the page directory, and to implement synchronization. The Cashmere virtual address space consists of four areas (see Figure 3). The first area consists of process private memory. The second contains Cashmere meta-data, including the page directory, synchronization memory, write notice and NLE lists, and protocol message-passing regions (for page fetch requests). The other two areas contain Cashmere shared memory. The higher of these two contains the processor's local copies of shared pages and the lower contains MC regions used to maintain memory consistency between nodes.

The page directory and synchronization regions are mapped twice on each node: once for receive and once for transmit. Remote meta-data updates are implemented by writing once to the receive region in local memory and again to the write region

[1]We did not use ATOM since the current version can only insert instrumentation in the form of procedure calls incurring singificantly higher overhead

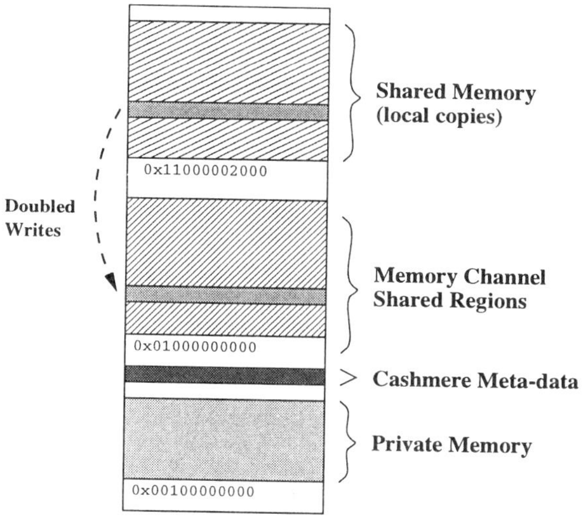

Figure 3: Cashmere process address space. Writes are duplicated from the private copy of a shared memory page to the corresponding page in the MC regions. MC regions are mapped for receive on home nodes and for transmit on all other nodes.

```
srl   $3, 40, $7     ; Create page offset
sll   $7, 13, $7     ;   if shared write.
subq  $3, $7, $7
zap   $7, 0x20, $7   ; Subtract MC offset.
stq   $1, 0($3)      ; Original write.
stq   $1, 0($7)      ; Doubled write.
```

Figure 4: Write Doubling, in this case for an address in register 3 with 0 displacement.

for transmit. MC loop-back is not used because it requires twice the PCI bandwidth: once for transmit and once for receive, and because it does not guarantee processor consistency.

For every actively-shared page of memory, one page is allocated in the process's local copy area and another in the MC area. If a process is located on the home node for a shared page, the MC page is mapped for receive. If a process is not located on the home node, then the MC page is mapped for transmit. In the current version of Digital Unix, the number of separate Memory Channel regions is limited by fixed-size kernel tables. Each MC region in our Cashmere implementation contains a *superpage*, the size of which is obtained by dividing the maximum shared memory size required by the application by the number of table entries. Superpages have no effect on coherence granularity: we still map and unmap individual pages. They do, however, constrain our "first touch" page placement policy: all pages of a given superpage must share the same home node.

3.3.1 Write Doubling

All writes to shared memory consist of an original write to the private copy and a duplicate write to the MC area. The duplicate write and associated address arithmetic are inserted into applications by parsing and updating assembly code, in a manner analagous to that used to insert polling. As in polling, we rely on the GNU C compiler's ability to reserve a register for use in the instrumented code. Single-processor tests confirm that the additional register pressure caused by the reservation has a minimal impact on the performance of our applications. A compiler-supported Cashmere implementation would be able to use one of the registers ($7) for other purposes as well.

Figure 4 contains the assembly sequence for a doubled write. The sequence relies on careful alignment of the Cashmere shared-memory regions. The local copy of a shared page and its corresponding Memory Channel region differ in address by 0x0100 0000 2000. The high bit in the offset places the addresses far enough apart that all of shared memory can be contiguous. The low bit in the offset ensures that the two addresses will map to different locations in the first-level cache on the home node. To obtain the address to which to double a write, we use the value of the 40th bit to mask out the 13th bit. We also clear the 40th bit. For a truly private reference, which should not be doubled, these operations have no effect, because the 40th bit is already 0. In this case, the private address is written twice. By placing the address arithmetic before the original write, so that the writes are consecutive instructions, we make it likely that spurious doubles of private writes will combine in the processor's write buffer. As an obvious optimization, we refrain from doubling writes that use the stack pointer or global pointer as a base.

3.3.2 Page Directory and Locks

Page directory access time is crucial to the overall performance of Cashmere. Directory entries must be globally consistent and inexpensive to access. As mentioned previously, the page directory is mapped into both receive and transmit regions on each node. Each entry consists of eight 4-byte words.

Both application and protocol locks are represented by an 8-entry array in Memory Channel space, and by a test-and-set flag on each node. To acquire a lock, a process first acquires the per-node flag using *ll/sc*. It then sets the array entry for its node, waits for the write to appear via loop-back, and reads the whole array. If its entry is the only one set, then the process has acquired the lock. Otherwise it clears its entry, backs off, and tries again. In the absence of contention, acquiring and releasing a lock takes about 11 μs. Digital Unix provides a system-call interface for Memory Channel locks, but while its internal implementation is essentially the same as ours, its latency is more than 280 μs. Most of that overhead is due to the crossing of thr kernel-user boundary. Application and protocol locks use the same implementation. Application barriers are tree-based. Upon arrival, each processor first waits for all of its children to arrive, then notifies its parent of the sub-tree's arrival, and finally waits for notification from the root of the barrier tree before continuing. All notifications are posted through explicit words in Memory Channel space.

3.4 TreadMarks

We have modified TreadMarks version 0.10.2 to use the MC architecture for fast user-level messages. Only the messaging layer was changed: all other aspects of the implementation are standard. In particular, we do not use broadcast or remote memory access for either synchronization or protocol data structures, nor do we place shared memory in Memory Channel space.

We present results for three versions of TreadMarks. The first uses DEC's kernel-level implementation of UDP for the Memory Channel, with regular `sig_io` interrupts. The second uses user-level message buffers, and sends `imc_kill` interrupts (see Section 3.2) to signal message arrival. The third is built entirely in user space, with polling (see Section 3.2—the polling instrumentation used for TreadMarks and Cashmere is identical) to determine message arrival. Interrupts (and in particular signals) for the first two implementations are expensive in Digital Unix, and are a principal factor limiting scalability. While polling in our implementation makes use of the Memory Channel hardware, it could also be implemented (at somewhat higher cost) on a more conventional network. In our experiments it allows us to separate the intrinsic behavior of the TreadMarks protocol from the very high cost of signals on this particular system.

The UDP version of TreadMarks creates a pair of UDP sockets between each pair of participating processors: a request socket on which processor A sends requests to processor B and receives replies, and a reply socket on which processor A receives requests from processor B and sends replies. The MC version replaces the sockets with a pair of message buffers. Two sense-reversing flags (variables allocated in Memory Channel space) provide flow control between the sender and the receiver: the sender uses one flag to indicate when data is ready to be consumed; the receiver uses the other to indicate when data has been consumed. Reply messages do not require interrupts or polling: the requesting processor always spins while waiting for a reply. Because both DEC's MC UDP and our user-level buffers provide reliable delivery, we have disabled the usual timeout mechanism used to detect lost messages in TreadMarks. To avoid deadlock due to buffer flow-control, we have made the request handler re-entrant: whenever it spins while waiting for a free buffer or for an expected reply it also polls for, and queues, additional incoming requests.

In both TreadMarks and Cashmere each application-level process is bound to a separate processor of the AlphaServer. The binding improves performance by taking advantage of memory locality, and reduces the time to deliver a page fault. To minimize latency and demand for Memory Channel bandwidth, we allocate message buffers in ordinary shared memory, rather than Memory Channel space, whenever the communicating processes are on the same AlphaServer. This is the only place in either TreadMarks or Cashmere that our current implementations take advantage of the hardware coherence available within each node.

4 Performance Evaluation

Our experimental environment consists of eight DEC AlphaServer 2100 4/233 computers. Each AlphaServer is equipped with four 21064A processors operating at 233 MHz and with 256MB of shared memory, as well as a Memory Channel network interface. No other processors are connected to the Memory Channel. Each AlphaServer runs in multi-user mode, but with the exception of normal Unix daemons no other processes were active during the tests. The underlying virtual memory page size is 8 Kbytes. A cache line is 64 bytes.

For Cashmere, we present results for three different mechanisms to handle remote requests—a dedicated "protocol processor" (`csm_pp`), `imc_kill` interrupts (`csm_int`), and polling (csm_poll). The protocol processor option approximates the ability to read remote memory in hardware. For TreadMarks, we present results for three different versions—one that uses DEC's kernel-level MC UDP protocol stack with sigio interrupts (tmk_udp_int), one that uses user-level messaging on MC with imc_kill interrupts (tmk_mc_int), and one that uses user-level messaging on MC with polling (tmk_mc_poll).

4.1 Basic Operation Costs

Memory protection operations on the AlphaServers cost about 62 μs. Page faults cost 89 μs. It takes 69 μs to deliver a signal locally, while remote delivery costs the sender 584 μs and incurs an end-to-end latency of about 1 ms. The overhead for polling ranges between 0% and 36% compared to a single processor execution, depending on the application.

The overhead for write doubling ranges between 0% and 39% compared to a single processor execution for Cashmere, depending on the application. Directory entry modification takes 16 μs for Cashmere, if locking is required, and 5 μs otherwise. In other words, 11 μs is spent acquiring and releasing the directory entry lock, but only when relocating the home node. The cost of a twinning operation on an 8K page in TreadMarks is 362 μs. The cost of diff creation ranges from 289 to 534 μs per page, depending on the size of the diff.

Table 1 provides a summary of the minimum cost of page transfers and of user-level synchronization operations for the different implementations of Cashmere and TreadMarks. All times are for interactions between two processors. The barrier times in parentheses are for a 16 processor barrier.

4.2 Application Characteristics

We present results for 8 applications:

SOR: a Red-Black Successive Over-Relaxation program for solving partial differential equations. The red and black arrays are divided into roughly equal size bands of rows, with each band assigned to a different processor. Communication occurs across the boundaries between bands. Processors synchronize with barriers.

LU: a kernel from the SPLASH-2 [32] benchmark, which for a given matrix A finds its factorization $A = LU$, where L is a lower-triangular matrix and U is upper triangular. The matrix A is divided into square blocks for temporal and spatial locality. Each block is "owned" by a particular processor, which performs all computation on it.

Water: a molecular dynamics simulation from the SPLASH-1 [30] benchmark suite. The shared array of molecule structures is divided into equal contiguous chunks, with each chunk assigned to a different processor. The bulk of the interprocessor communication happens during a computation phase that computes intermolecular forces. Each processor accumulates its forces locally and then acquires per-processor locks to update the globally shared force vectors, resulting in a migratory sharing pattern.

TSP: a branch-and-bound solution to the traveling salesman problem. Locks are used to insert and delete unsolved tours in a priority queue. Updates to the shortest path are protected by a separate lock. The algorithm is non-deterministic in the sense that the earlier some processor stumbles upon the shortest path, the more quickly other parts of the search space can be pruned.

Gauss: a solver for a system of linear equations $AX = B$ using Gaussian Elimination and back-substitution. The Gaussian elimination phase makes A upper triangular. Each row of the matrix is the responsibility of a single processor. For load balance, the rows are distributed among processors cyclically. A synchronization flag for each row indicates when it is available to other rows for use as a pivot.

Ilink: a widely used genetic linkage analysis program from the FASTLINK 2.3P package that locates disease genes on chromosomes. We use the parallel algorithm described by Dwarkadas et al. [8]. The main shared data is a pool of sparse arrays of genotype probabilities. Updates to each array are parallelized. A master processor assigns individual array elements to processors in a round robin fashion in order to improve load balance. After each processor has updated its elements, the master processor sums the contributions. Barriers are used for synchronization. Scalability is limited by an inherent serial component and inherent load imbalance.

Barnes: an N-body simulation from the SPLASH-1 [30] suite, using the hierarchical Barnes-Hut Method. Each leaf of the program's tree represents a body, and each internal node a "cell": a collection of bodies in close physical proximity. The major shared data structures are two arrays, one representing the bodies and the other representing the cells. The Barnes-Hut tree construction is performed sequentially, while all other phases are parallelized and dynamically load balanced. Synchronization consists of barriers between phases.

Em3d: a program to simulate electromagnetic wave propagation through 3D objects [7]. The major data structure is an array that contains the set of magnetic and electric nodes. These are equally distributed among the processors in the system. For each phase in the computation, each processor updates the electromagnetic potential of its nodes based on the potential of neighboring nodes. While arbitrary graphs of dependencies between nodes can be constructed, the standard input assumes that nodes that belong to a processor have dependencies only on nodes that belong to that processor or neighboring processors. Processors use barriers to synchronize between computational phases.

Table 2 presents the data set sizes and uniprocessor execution times for each of the eight applications, with the size of shared memory space used in parentheses. The execution times were measured by running each application sequentially without linking it to either TreadMarks or Cashmere.

4.3 Comparative Speedups

Figure 5 presents speedups for our applications on up to 32 processors. All calculations are with respect to the sequential

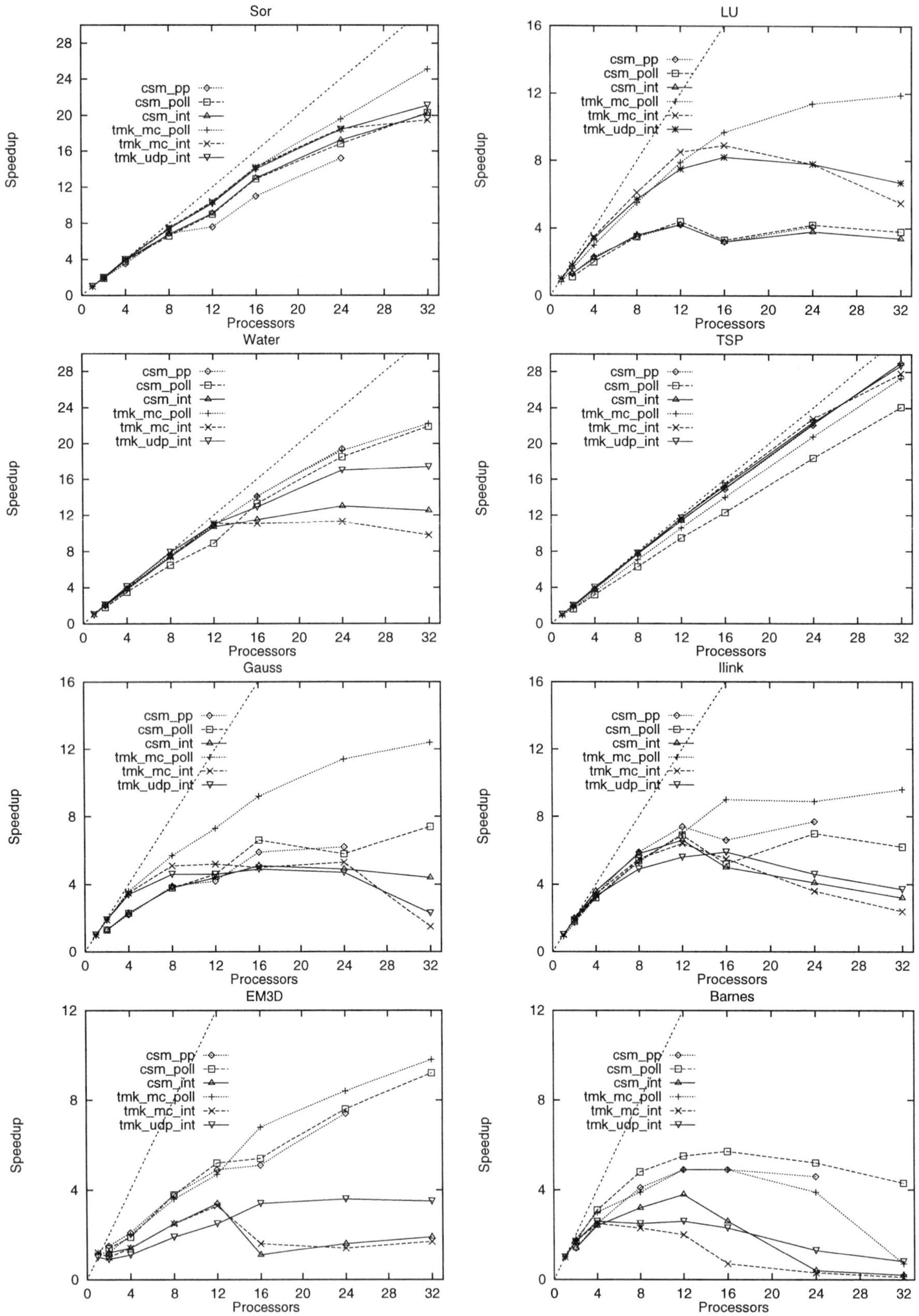

Figure 5: Speedups.

Operation	Time (μs)					
	csm_pp	csm_int	csm_poll	tmk_udp_int	tmk_mc_int	tmk_mc_poll
Lock Acquire	11	11	11	1362	976	79
Barrier	90 (173)	88 (208)	86 (205)	987 (8006)	568 (5432)	75 (1213)
Page Transfer	736	1960	742	2932	1962	784

Table 1: Cost of basic operations.

Program	Problem Size	Time (sec.)
SOR	3072x4096 (50Mbytes)	194.96
LU	2046x2046 (33Mbytes)	254.77
Water	4096 mols. (4Mbytes)	1847.56
TSP	17 cities (1Mbyte)	4028.95
Gauss	2046x2046 (33Mbytes)	953.71
Ilink	CLP (15Mbytes)	898.97
Em3d	60106 nodes (49Mbytes)	161.43
Barnes	128K bodies (26Mbytes)	469.43

Table 2: Data set sizes and sequential execution time of applications.

times in Table 2. The configurations we use are as follows: 1 processor: trivial; 2: separate nodes; 4: one processor in each of 4 nodes; 8: two processors in each of 4 nodes; 12: three processors in each of 4 nodes; 16: two processors in each of 8 nodes; 24: three processors in each of 8 nodes; and 32: trivial, but not applicable to csm_pp.

Table 3 presents detailed statistics on the communication incurred by each of the applications on the polling implementations of Cashmere and TreadMarks at 32 processors, except for Barnes, where the statistics presented are for 16 processors. Since the performance for Barnes drops significantly with more than 16 processors, we present the statistics at 16 processors in order to make a reasonable comparison. The statistics presented are the execution time, the number of lock and barrier synchronization operations, number of read and write faults, the number of page transfers for Cashmere, and the number of messages and data transferred for TreadMarks. Other than execution time, the statistics are aggregated over all 32 (16 in the case of Barnes) processors.

Figure 6 presents a break-down of the execution time processors for each application. The breakdown is normalized with respect to total execution time for Cashmere on 32 processors (16 for Barnes). The components shown represent time spent executing user code (`User`), the overhead of profiling for polling (`Polling`—Cashmere and TreadMarks) and write doubling (`Write doubling`—Cashmere only), time spent in protocol code (`Protocol`), and communication and wait time (`Comm & Wait`). Two of the components—`Comm & Wait` and `Protocol`—were measured directly on the maximum number of processors. The remaining three components—`User`, `Polling`, and `Write Doubling`—could not be measured directly and thus reflect extrapolation from the one-processor case. (On one processor we could turn polling and write doubling on and off and measure the change in execution time. On 32 [or 16] processors we assume that the ratios of user and

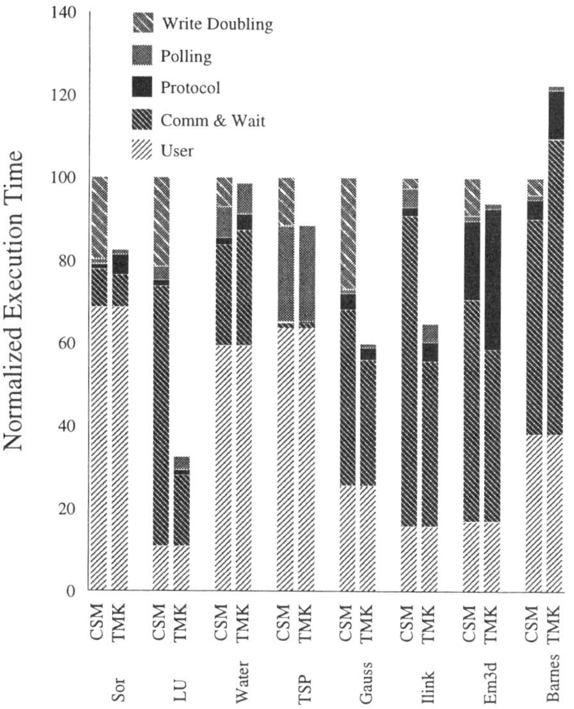

Figure 6: Breakdown of normalized execution time for the polling versions of Cashmere and TreadMarks (Barnes at 16 processors, the others at 32).

polling time remain the same as on a single processor, and use these times (calculated from TreadMarks) to determine the write doubling time for Cashmere).

TSP displays nearly linear speedup for all our protocols. Speedups are also reasonable in SOR and Water. Em3d, LU, Ilink, Barnes, and Gauss have lower overall speedup. Generalizing over varying numbers of processors (see figure 5), performance of Cashmere and TreadMarks is similar for TSP and Water. Cashmere outperforms TreadMarks on Barnes. TreadMarks outperforms Cashmere by significant amounts on LU and Gauss, and by smaller amounts on SOR, Em3d, and Ilink.

For Barnes, where Cashmere performs better than TreadMarks, the differences in performance stem primarily from Cashmere's ability to merge updates from multiple writers into a single home node, as well as to eliminate duplicate write notices for the same page: TreadMarks must generally merge diffs from multiple sources to update a page in Barnes (note the high message count in Table 3, and the larger fraction of communication

	Application	SOR	LU	Water	TSP	Gauss	Ilink	Em3d	Barnes
CSM	Exec. time (secs)	9.6	66.9	84.3	166.8	128.5	145.2	21.9	78.5
	Barriers	48	129	36	2	8	521	250	10
	Locks	0	0	3680	2638	133914	0	0	0
	Read faults	6242	27041	84271	20442	207035	228605	195268	127029
	Write faults	9116	7470	35573	9057	8181	45485	95875	98273
	Page transfers	9312	27046	84272	23805	207037	230010	195268	127032
TMK	Exec. time (secs)	7.8	21.7	83.1	147.8	77.0	94.2	20.6	96.3
	Barriers	48	129	36	2	8	521	250	10
	Locks	0	0	3680	2664	133914	0	0	0
	Read faults	2976	22828	84300	20479	220748	194462	194349	49577
	Write faults	2976	4302	33001	9133	8052	42562	95175	98279
	Messages	8990	83896	217590	57841	1008056	653402	406320	1451167
	Data (Kbytes)	27296	300400	816601	36021	1008820	511804	460774	592509

Table 3: Detailed statistics for the polling versions of Cashmere and TreadMarks (Barnes at 16 processors, the others at 32).

and wait time in Figure 6), and communicate a write notice for each process that writes a page. In addition, Figure 6 shows that TreadMarks spends a larger fraction of time executing protocol code (diffing and twinning). This overhead is avoided in Cashmere through the use of write-through to merge the changes by multiple writers.

For Ilink, where TreadMarks performs better than Cashmere, the differences in performance stem from the sparsity of Ilink's data structures. Only a small portion of each page is modified between synchronization operations. Hence, the diffs of TreadMarks result in less data communication than the page reads of Memory-Channel Cashmere, resulting in a much larger amount of time spent in communication for Cashmere (see Figure 6).

In Water the various competing effects more or less cancel out. TreadMarks spends more time in protocol code in diffing and twinning, while Cashmere spends more time communicating whole pages (the entire molecule data structure is not modified between any two synchronization points). It is difficult to draw conclusions from TSP, because of its non-determinism.

Write doubling to internal rows of an SOR or Em3d band is wasted in Cashmere, since no other processor ever inspects those elements. The impact is reduced to some extent by the "first write" placement policy, which ensures that the doubled writes are local, but the doubled writes affect performance none-the-less. This effect can be seen in Figure 6, where write doubling comprises 19% of the total time in SOR and 8% of Em3d's execution time. Em3d spends significantly more time in protocol code for TreadMarks, performing diffing and twinning, while Cashmere spends more time in communication, once again because entire pages are transferred on a miss even though only part of the page was modified.

The most dramatic differences between Cashmere and TreadMarks occur in LU and Gauss, and can be traced to cache effects. Specifically, the increase in cache pressure caused by write doubling forces the working set of these applications out of the first-level cache of the 21064A. In LU, with a 32X32 block, the primary working set is 16 Kbytes, which fits entirely in the first level cache of the 21064A. Write doubling increases the working set to 24K for Cashmere, forcing the application to work out of the second level cache and thus significantly hurting performance. Gauss exhibits similar behavior. In Gauss the primary working set decreases over time as fewer rows remain to be eliminated. For our problem size the working set starts by not fitting in the first level cache for Cashmere and TreadMarks. As it reduces in size it starts fitting in the cache first for TreadMarks and at a later point for Cashmere. The importance of the effect can be seen in the single-processor numbers. When compiled for Cashmere (with write doubling and protocol operations), Gauss takes about 1750 seconds on one processor. When compiled for TreadMarks, it takes 954. Similarly, LU for Cashmere on one processor takes 380 seconds; for TreadMarks it takes 255. In both cases, modifying the write-doubling code in the Cashmere version so that it "doubles" all writes to a single dummy address reduces the run time to only slightly more than TreadMarks. These effects show up in the write doubling sub-bars of Figure 6. Note that these sub-bars account for 21% of total execution time in LU, and 27% in Gauss. On a machine with a larger first-level cache (e.g. the 21264), we would not expect to see the same magnitude of effect on performance.

In addition to the primary working set (data accessed in the inner loop) Gauss has a secondary working set which affects performance. The secondary working set for our input size is 32Mbytes/P where P is the number of processors. At 32 processors the data fits in the processor's second level cache resulting in a jump in performance for the Cashmere protocols. TreadMarks does not experience the same performance jump due to the memory pressure effects of requiring space in the cache for diffs and twins.

With the possible exception of TSP, whose results are non-deterministic, polling for messages is uniformly better than fielding signals in both TreadMarks and Cashmere for larger numbers of processors (the effect is a function of the number of remote operations). High interrupt latencies also result in a sudden reduction in performance for Em3d and Barnes (the two applications with the most active sharing) for both protocols when we move from 12 processors spread across 4 nodes to 16 processors spread across 8 nodes. At 16 processors in Barnes, the high cost of the *imc_kill* signal results in an 86% drop in performance for `tmk_mc_int` relative to `tmk_mc_poll`, with performance actually being worse than that for `tmk_udp_int`. At small numbers of processors, `tmk_udp_int` does perform worse than `tmk_mc_int` as expected, because of the overhead of executing the `udp` protocol stack. In general, TreadMarks is more sensitive to interrupt latency than is Cashmere, due to the higher number of request-response communications (synchronization and data transfers). Cashmere requires request-response communication only for data transfer. For example, in Gauss at 32 processors, TreadMarks fields 231760 interrupts, while Cashmere fields only 186001 interrupts.

The tradeoff between polling and the use of a "protocol processor" in Cashmere is less clear from our results, and there seems to be no clear incentive for a protocol processor, if the sole use of the protocol processor is to service page requests. Polling imposes overhead in every loop, but often results in page requests being serviced by a processor that has the desired data in its cache. The protocol processor must generally pull the requested data across the local bus before pushing it into the Memory Channel. Hardware support for reads could be expected to outperform either emulation: it would not impose loop overhead, and would use DMA to ensure a single bus traversal.

Additional bandwidth should also help Cashmere since it has higher bandwidth requirements than TreadMarks. While bandwidth effects are hard to quantify, we have observed that applications perform significantly better when bandwidth pressure is reduced. An 8-processor run of Gauss, for example, is 40% faster with 2 processors on each of 4 nodes than it is with 4 processors on each of 2 nodes. This result is consistent with the findings of Erlichson et al. [10]; it indicates that there is insufficient bandwidth on the link between each SMP and the hub, something that should be remedied in the next generation of the network.

5 Related Work

Distributed shared memory for workstation clusters is an active area of research: many systems have been built, and more have been designed. For purposes of discussion we group them into systems that support more-or-less "generic" shared-memory programs, such as might run on a machine with hardware coherence, and those that require a special programming notation or style.

5.1 "Generic" DSM

The original idea of using virtual memory to implement coherence on networks dates from Kai Li's thesis work [21]. Nitzberg and Lo [25] provide a survey of early VM-based systems. Several groups employed similar techniques to migrate and replicate pages in early, cache-less shared-memory multiprocessors [4, 19]. Lazy, multi-writer protocols were pioneered by Keleher et al. [16], and later adopted by several other groups. Several of the ideas in Cashmere were based on Petersen's coherence algorithms for small-scale, non-hardware-coherent multiprocessors [26]. Recent work by the Alewife group at MIT [33] and the FLASH group at Stanford [10] has addressed the implementation of software coherence on a collection of hardware-coherent nodes.

Wisconsin's Blizzard system [29] maintains coherence for cache-line-size blocks, either in software or by using ECC. It runs on the Thinking Machines CM-5 and provides a sequentially-consistent programming model. The more recent Shasta system [28], developed at DEC WRL, extends the software-based Blizzard approach with a relaxed consistency model and variable-size coherence blocks. Like Cashmere, Shasta runs on the Memory Channel, with polling for remote requests. Rather than rely on VM, however, it inserts consistency checks in-line when accessing shared memory. Aggressive compiler optimizations attempt to keep the cost of checks as low as possible.

AURC [14] is a multi-writer protocol designed for the Shrimp network interface [2]. Like Cashmere, AURC relies on remote memory access to write shared data updates to home nodes. Like TreadMarks, however, AURC uses distributed information in the form of timestamps and write notices to maintain sharing information. As a result, AURC has no need for directory, lock, or write notice/NLE list metadata: remote-mapped memory is used only for fast messages and doubled writes. The Shrimp network interface, like that of the Memory Channel, does not support remote reads, presumably because they are significantly more difficult than writes to implement, and less crucial for good performance. Where the Cashmere protocol was originally designed to read lines from remote memory on a cache miss, the AURC protocol was designed from the outset with the assumption that whole pages would be copied to local memory. Because the Shrimp interface connects to the memory bus of its 486-based nodes, AURC is able to double writes in hardware, avoiding a major source of overhead in Cashmere. Experimental results for AURC are currently based on simulation; implementation results await the completion of a large-scale Shrimp testbed.

5.2 Special Programming Models

A variety of systems implement coherence entirely in software, without VM support, but require programmers to adopt a special programming model. In some systems, such as Split-C [7] and Shrimp's Deliberate Update [2], the programmer must use special primitives to read and write remote data. In others, including Shared Regions [27], Cid [24], and CRL [15], remote data is accessed with the same notation used for local data, but only in regions of code that have been bracketed by special operations. The Midway system [34] requires the programmer to associate shared data with synchronization objects, allowing ordinary synchronization acquires and releases to play the role of the bracketing operations. Several other systems use the member functions of an object-oriented programming model to trigger coherence operations [6, 11, 31].

Because they provide the coherence system with information not available in more general-purpose systems, special programming models have the potential to provide superior performance. It is not yet clear to what extent the extra effort required of programmers will be considered an acceptable burden. In some cases, it may be possible for an optimizing compiler to obtain the performance of the special programming model without the special syntax [9].

5.3 Fast User-Level Messages

The Memory Channel is not unique in its support for user-level messages, though it is the first commercially-available workstation network with such an interface. Large shared memory multiprocessors have provided low-latency interprocessor communication for many years, originally on cache-less machines and more recently with cache coherence. We believe that a system such as Cashmere would work well on a non-cache-coherent machine like the Cray T3E. Fast user-level messages were supported without shared memory on the CM-5, though the protection mechanism was relatively static.

Among workstation networks, user-level IPC can also be found in the Princeton Shrimp [2], the HP Hamlyn interface [5] to Myrinet [3], and Dolphin's snooping interface [22] for the SCI cache coherence protocol [13].

6 Conclusion and Future Work

We have presented results for two different DSM protocols—Cashmere and TreadMarks—on a remote-memory-access network, namely DEC's Memory Channel. TreadMarks uses the Memory Channel only for fast messaging, while Cashmere uses it for directory maintenance and for fine-grained updates to shared data. Our work is among the first comparative studies of fine and coarse-grained DSM to be based on working implementations of "aggressively lazy" protocols.

Our principal conclusion is that low-latency networks make fine-grain DSM competitive with more coarse-grain approaches, but that further hardware improvements will be needed before such systems can provide consistently superior performance. TreadMarks requires less frequent communication and lower total communication bandwidth, but suffers from the computational overhead of twinning and diffing, which occur on the program's critical path, and from the propagation of unnecessary write notices, especially on larger configurations. Cashmere moves much of the overhead of write collection off the critical path via write-through, but at the expense of much more frequent communication, higher communication bandwidth, and (in the absence of snooping hardware) significant time and cache-footprint penalties for software write doubling. Unlike TreadMarks, Cashmere sends write notices only to processors that are actually using the modified data, thereby improving scalability (though the use of global time can sometimes lead to invalidations not required by the happens-before relationship).

The fact that Cashmere is able to approach (and sometimes exceed) the performance of TreadMarks on the current Memory Channel suggests that DSM systems based on fine-grain communication are likely to out-perform more coarse-grain alternatives on future remote-memory-access networks. Many of the most severe constraints on our current Cashmere implementation result from hardware limitations that are likely to disappear in future systems. Specifically, we expect the next generation of the Memory Channel to cut latency by more than half, to increase aggregate bandwidth by more than an order of magnitude, and to significantly reduce the cost of synchronization. These changes will improve the performance of TreadMarks, but should help Cashmere more. Eventually, we also expect some sort of remote read mechanism, though probably not remote cache fills. It seems unlikely that inexpensive networks will provide write doubling in hardware, since this requires snooping on the memory bus. The impact of software write doubling on cache footprint, however, should be greatly reduced on newer Alpha processors with larger first and second level caches.

Cashmere and TreadMarks differ in two fundamental dimensions: the mechanism used to manage coherence information (directories v. distributed intervals and timestamps) and the mechanism used to collect data updates (write-through v. twins and diffs). We are currently developing multi-level protocols that take advantage of hardware coherence within each AlphaServer node, and that combine the benefits of the TreadMarks and Cashmere protocols. These protocols will reduce the bandwidth requirements of write-through and eliminate write doubling overhead through the use of diffs and twins, while retaining the ability to merge modifications at a single node and to reduce coherence information by distributing it at a fine grain. Finally, we are continuing our research into the relationship between run-time coherence management and static compiler analysis [9].

References

[1] C. Amza, A. L. Cox, S. Dwarkadas, P. Keleher, H. Lu, R. Rajamony, W. Yu, and W. Zwaenepoel. TreadMarks: Shared Memory Computing on Networks of Workstations. *Computer*, 29(2):18–28, Feb. 1996.

[2] M. Blumrich, K. Li, R. Alpert, C. Dubnicki, E. Felten, and J. Sandberg. Virtual Memory Mapped Network Interface for the SHRIMP Multicomputer. In *Proc. of the 21st Intl. Symp. on Computer Architecture*, pp. 142–153, Apr. 1994.

[3] N. J. Boden, D. Cohen, R. E. Felderman, A. E. Kulawik, C. E. Seitz, J. N. Seizovic, and W.-K. Su. Myrinet: A Gigabit-per-Second Local Area Network. In *IEEE Micro*, pp. 29–36, Feb. 1995.

[4] W. J. Bolosky, M. L. Scott, R. P. Fitzgerald, R. J. Fowler, and A. L. Cox. NUMA Policies and Their Relation to Memory Architecture. In *Proc. of the 4th Intl. Conf. on Architectural Support for Programming Languages and Operating Systems*, pp. 212–221, Apr. 1991.

[5] G. Buzzard, D. Jacobson, M. Mackey, S. Marovich, and J. Wilkes. An Implementation of the Hamlyn Sender-Managed Interface Architecture. In *Proc. of the 2nd Symp. on Operating Systems Design and Implementation*, Oct. 1996.

[6] J. S. Chase, F. G. Amador, E. D. Lazowska, H. M. Levy, and R. J. Littlefield. The Amber System: Parallel Programming on a Network of Multiprocessors. In *Proc. of the Twelfth ACM Symp. on Operating Systems Principles*, pp. 147–158, Dec. 1989.

[7] D. Culler, A. Dusseau, S. Goldstein, A. Krishnamurthy, S. Lumetta, T. von Eicken, and K. Yelick. Parallel Programming in Split-C. In *Proc. Supercomputing '93*, pp. 262–273, Nov. 1993.

[8] S. Dwarkadas, A. A. Schaffer, R. W. Cottingham Jr., A. L. Cox, P. Keleher, and W. Zwaenepoel. Parallelization of General Linkage Analysis Problems. *Human Heredity*, 44:127–141, 1994.

[9] S. Dwarkadas, A. L. Cox, and W. Zwaenepoel. An Integrated Compile-Time/Run-Time Software Distributed Shared Memory System. In *Proc. of the 7th Intl. Conf. on Architectural Support for Programming Languages and Operating Systems*, Oct. 1996.

[10] A. Erlichson, N. Nuckolls, G. Chesson, and J. Hennessy. SoftFLASH: Analyzing the Performance of Clustered Distributed Virtual Shared Memory. In *Proc. of the 7th Intl. Conf. on Architectural Support for Programming Languages and Operating Systems*, Oct. 1996.

[11] M. J. Feeley, J. S. Chase, V. R. Narasayya, and H. M. Levy. Integrating Coherency and Recovery in Distributed Systems. In *Proc. of the 1st Symp. on Operating Systems Design and Implementation*, Nov. 1994.

[12] R. Gillett. Memory Channel: An Optimized Cluster Interconnect. *IEEE Micro*, 16(2), Feb. 1996.

[13] D. B. Gustavson. The Scalable Coherent Interface and Related Standards Projects. *IEEE Micro*, 12(2):10–22, Feb. 1992.

[14] L. Iftode, C. Dubnicki, E. W. Felten, and K. Li. Improving Release-Consistent Shared Virtual Memory Using Automatic Update. In *Proc. of the 2nd Intl. Symp. on High Performance Computer Architecture*, Feb. 1996.

[15] K. L. Johnson, M. F. Kaashoek, and D. A. Wallach. CRL: High-Performance All-Software Distributed Shared Memory. In *Proc. of the Fifteenth ACM Symp. on Operating Systems Principles*, Dec. 1995.

[16] P. Keleher, A. L. Cox, and W. Zwaenepoel. Lazy Release Consistency for Software Distributed Shared Memory. In *Proc. of the 19th Intl. Symp. on Computer Architecture*, pp. 13–21, May 1992.

[17] L. I. Kontothanassis and M. L. Scott. High Performance Software Coherence for Current and Future Architectures. *Journal of Parallel and Distributed Computing*, 29(2):179–195, Nov. 1995.

[18] L. I. Kontothanassis and M. L. Scott. Using Memory-Mapped Network Interfaces to Improve the Performance of Distributed Shared Memory. In *Proc. of the 2nd Intl. Symp. on High Performance Computer Architecture*, Feb. 1996.

[19] R. P. LaRowe Jr. and C. S. Ellis. Experimental Comparison of Memory Management Policies for NUMA Multiprocessors. *ACM Transactions on Computer Systems*, 9(4):319–363, Nov. 1991.

[20] D. Lenoski, J. Laudon, K. Gharachorloo, A. Gupta, and J. Hennessy. The Directory-Based Cache Coherence Protocol for the DASH Multiprocessor. In *Proc. of the 17th Intl. Symp. on Computer Architecture*, pp. 148–159, May 1990.

[21] K. Li and P. Hudak. Memory Coherence in Shared Virtual Memory Systems. *ACM Transactions on Computer Systems*, 7(4):321–359, Nov. 1989.

[22] O. Lysne, S. Gjessing, and K. Lochsen. Running the SCI Protocol over HIC Networks. In *2nd Intl. Workshop on SCI-based Low-cost/High-performance Computing (SCIzzL-2)*, Mar. 1995.

[23] M. Marchetti, L. Kontothanassis, R. Bianchini, and M. L. Scott. Using Simple Page Placement Policies to Reduce the Cost of Cache Fills in Coherent Shared-Memory Systems. In *Proc. of the Ninth Intl. Parallel Processing Symp.*, Apr. 1995.

[24] R. S. Nikhil. Cid: A Parallel, "Shared-memory" C for Distributed-Memory Machines. In *Proc. of the 7th Annual Workshop on Languages and Compilers for Parallel Computing*, Aug. 1994.

[25] B. Nitzberg and V. Lo. Distributed Shared Memory: A Survey of Issues and Algorithms. *Computer*, 24(8):52–60, Aug. 1991.

[26] K. Petersen and K. Li. Cache Coherence for Shared Memory Multiprocessors Based on Virtual Memory Support. In *Proc. of the 7th Intl. Parallel Processing Symp.*, Apr. 1993.

[27] H. S. Sandhu, B. Gamsa, and S. Zhou. The Shared Regions Approach to Software Cache Coherence on Multiprocessors. In *Proc. of the 4th ACM Symp. on Principles and Practice of Parallel Programming*, May 1993.

[28] D. J. Scales, K. Gharachorloo, and C. A. Thekkath. Shasta: A Low Overhead, Software-Only Approach for Supporting Fine-Grain Shared Memory. In *Proc. of the 7th Intl. Conf. on Architectural Support for Programming Languages and Operating Systems*, Oct. 1996.

[29] I. Schoinas, B. Falsafi, A. R. Lebeck, S. K. Reinhardt, J. R. Larus, and D. A. Wood. Fine-grain Access Control for Distributed Shared Memory. In *Proc. of the 6th Intl. Conf. on Architectural Support for Programming Languages and Operating Systems*, pp. 297–306, Oct. 1994.

[30] J. P. Singh, W.-D. Weber, and A. Gupta. SPLASH: Stanford Parallel Applications for Shared-Memory. *ACM SIGARCH Computer Architecture News*, 20(1):5–44, Mar. 1992.

[31] A. S. Tanenbaum, M. F. Kaashoek, and H. E. Bal. Parallel Programming Using Shared Objects and Broadcasting. *Computer*, 25(8):10–19, Aug. 1992.

[32] S. C. Woo, M. Ohara, E. Torrie, J. P. Singh, and A. Gupta. Methodological Considerations and Characterization of the SPLASH-2 Parallel Application Suite. In *Proc. of the 22nd Intl. Symp. on Computer Architecture*, June 1995.

[33] D. Yeung, J. Kubiatowitcz, and A. Agarwal. MGS: A Multigrain Shared Memory System. In *Proc. of the 23rd Intl. Symp. on Computer Architecture*, May, 1996.

[34] M. J. Zekauskas, W. A. Sawdon, and B. N. Bershad. Software Write Detection for Distributed Shared Memory. In *Proc. of the 1st Symp. on Operating Systems Design and Implementation*, Nov. 1994.

Efficient Synchronization: Let Them Eat QOLB[1]

Alain Kägi, Doug Burger, and James R. Goodman

Computer Sciences Department
University of Wisconsin-Madison
1210 West Dayton Street
Madison, Wisconsin 53706 USA
galileo@cs.wisc.edu - http://www.cs.wisc.edu/~galileo

Abstract

Efficient synchronization primitives are essential for achieving high performance in fine-grain, shared-memory parallel programs. One function of synchronization primitives is to enable exclusive access to shared data and critical sections of code. This paper makes three contributions. (1) We enumerate the five sources of overhead that locking synchronization primitives can incur. (2) We describe four mechanisms (local spinning, queue-based locking, collocation, and synchronized prefetch) that reduce these synchronization overheads. (3) With detailed simulations, we show the extent to which these four mechanisms can improve the performance of shared-memory programs. We evaluate the space of these mechanisms using seventeen synchronization constructs, which are formed from six base types of locks (TEST&SET, TEST&TEST&SET, MCS, LH, M, and QOLB). We show that large performance gains (speedups of more than 1.5 for three of five benchmarks) can be achieved if at least three optimizing mechanisms are used simultaneously. We find that QOLB, which incorporates all four mechanisms, outperforms all other primitives (including reactive synchronization) in all cases. Finally, we demonstrate the superior performance of a low-cost implementation of QOLB, which runs on an unmodified cluster of commodity workstations.

1 Introduction

Shared-memory multiprocessors are rapidly becoming the machines of choice for solving large, fine-grained scientific programs. Multiple factors support this trend. The advent of affordable desktop symmetric multiprocessors (SMPs) will increase the application base. The successful development of shared-memory multiprocessing standards [43] reduce the time to market by decreasing design time and by letting manufacturers use commodity parts. Both the Convex Exemplar [7] and the Sequent STiNG [27] relied on these standards. The emergence of low-cost, fine-grain software implementations of shared-memory, such as SHASTA [38] or TO [35] further reduce the cost of supporting the shared-memory model. Finally, successful research prototypes such as the Stanford DASH [25] have shown that this class of machines can obtain excellent speedups for a wide range of programs that use fine-grained communication.

Traditional message-passing programming models force the programmer to embed implicit synchronization with each communication of data. Such a requirement restricts the parallelization strategy—dynamic task distribution becomes extremely difficult, for example. The shared-memory programming model, conversely, uses cache coherence protocols to keep shared data consistent. The programmer judiciously employs explicit synchronization to provide mutual exclusion for data and code, as well as synchronizing processors between phases of computation.

The two major classes of explicit synchronization operations in shared-memory multiprocessors are barriers and locks. Although barriers are important to efficient shared-memory programs, they are well-understood, and many efficient implementations have been proposed and/or built [15, 20, 23, 32, 44]. In this study, we focus on providing more efficient mutual exclusion through better locks.

Locks provide individual processors with exclusive access to shared data and a critical section of code. This exclusive access is particularly well-suited to the fine-grained nature of many shared-memory parallel programs. Fine-grained programs ideally associate as little data or code as possible with a critical section, minimizing serialized processing, thus maximizing available parallelism. Since access to critical sections is by definition serialized among processors, large overheads when accessing a contested critical section degrade both parallel performance and potential scalability. To maximize both the performance of fine-grain parallel applications that use locking, and the potential to scale to larger numbers of processors, we must minimize the delays associated with the transfer of exclusively accessed resources.

The act of transferring control of a critical section is a complex one, that may involve multiple remote transactions. Complex protocols have been proposed that perform this transfer efficiently, allowing reasonable performance when there is high contention for a lock. The complexity of these protocols causes unnecessary delays when accessing a lock that is not held. Conversely, simple locking schemes that can access a free lock quickly may perform poorly in the presence of contention. This fundamental trade-off has resulted in proposals of numerous primitives in the literature [3, 13, 16, 26, 28, 30, 37].

This paper contains a detailed and thorough evaluation of a range of locking primitives. To understand where the opportunities for optimization lie, we first decompose the time associated with a

1. Pronounced "Colby."

This work is supported in part by NSF Grant CCR-9509589 and by the Intel Research Council.

ISCA '97 Denver, CO, USA
© 1997 ACM 0-89791-901-7/97/0006...$3.50

complete locking period into three phases: *Transfer*, *Load/Compute*, and *Release*. Together, these phases form a *synchronization period*, which determines the global throughput of synchronization operations and thus determines scalability for codes that rely heavily on locks. We then describe four mechanisms that locks may incorporate to reduce the time spent in the three phases: *local spinning*, *queue-based locking*, *collocation* (of a lock and data within the same cache line), and *synchronous prefetch.*

Using detailed simulation with both microbenchmarks and real applications (drawn from the SPLASH and SPLASH-2 suites), we measure the performance of six base primitives: TEST&SET, TEST&TEST&SET [37], LH locks [28], M locks [28], MCS locks [30], and QOLB [13]. We extend these primitives with the mechanisms listed above, plus exponential backoff and prefetches inserted automatically by a compiler. We also measure the performance of reactive synchronization schemes. In all, we study a total of seventeen primitive/mechanism combinations. We find that QOLB, which can incorporate all of the mechanisms listed above, outperforms all other locks in all cases (including reactive synchronization). We also see that very efficient locking can *double* the speedup of real applications (for one of the five benchmarks that we measured). Although QOLB outperforms the other primitives, it requires mechanisms that the others do not (which usually implies hardware support). We discuss exactly what support QOLB requires, and show that much of the necessary support already exists in current systems. Finally, we present performance results of an all-software implementation of QOLB running on an unmodified cluster of commodity workstations, and we show that this low-cost implementation still outperforms the alternatives.

In Section 2, we explain our decomposition of a synchronization period in greater detail. In Section 3, we show how the four optimizing mechanisms that we identified can reduce different parts of the synchronization period. In Section 4, we explain the primitives that we study in detail, and discuss how each of them uses a different set of the four mechanisms. In Section 5, we describe our experimental methodology. In Section 6, we present and discuss our performance results from this experimental space. In Section 7, we discuss the cost of hardware-supported synchronization. Finally, in Section 8 we provide a summary of our main results and conclude.

2 Overhead of mutual exclusion

From the perspective of an individual processor, the time associated with an access to a critical section consists of the time from which the processor first requests access to the corresponding lock, to the time at which the processor completes the release on that lock. This time period does not directly correlate with global performance, however. Multiple processors contending for entry to the same critical section may overlap the time from the issue of their requests to the first release of the lock. A good analogy to this distinction is the difference between the latency of an individual request to a memory system, and the throughput achievable by pipelined accesses to that same memory system.

To determine how these critical section accesses limit global performance and ultimately scalability, we define the notion of a *synchronization period.* The synchronization period is the length of time between completion of two successive synchronization operations (e.g., two successive releases) on the same variable. The successive synchronization operations may occur on different processors. This synchronization period is the service time that the processor incurs once the previous processor releases the lock. Since access to this critical section is by definition serialized, the synchronization period will place an upper bound on possible performance (codes that do not access critical sections heavily will see upper bounds on performance from other sources, of course).

We depict our breakdown of a synchronization period in Figure 1. The figure shows events to synchronization variable **X**. The first event depicted is the completion of the release of lock **X** by processor A. Several processors are contending to gain access to **X**. We assume that processor B wins the ensuing arbitration. When the lock acquire completes, processor B enters the critical section. Upon finishing the work in the critical section processor B prepares to release **X**, and eventually completes this operation. Our breakdown of a synchronization period consists of three phases:

- *Transfer*: the time at which processor A completes its release of the lock to the time processor B completes its acquire. At the point that the release completes; the releasing processor has atomically written the "unlocked" value to the lock. The contending nodes may then issue or re-issue requests (depending on the locking primitive) to obtain the lock. A period of arbitration may ensue. Once the next recipient of the lock is determined, the lock must be sent to that node.

- *Load/compute*: the time at which processor B completes its lock acquire to the time processor B issues its lock release. Once a processor obtains the lock, it enters the critical section. The processor will most likely have to read some locked data, perform some computation, and write some locked data. Accessing the data to read and write will likely incur some remote accesses.

- *Release*: which is the time from processor B issuing the lock release to the completion of the lock release. When the processor issues a release operation for the lock, remote accesses may be necessary before that operation may complete. Other processors may have removed the lock from the releasing processor's cache, for example, or the releasing processor may have to re-obtain write permission for the lock's cache line. Some aggressive memory models [1, 12] may allow some overlap between the *Load/compute* and *Release* phases.

In addition to illustrating this decomposition in Figure 1, we also list the components of each phase. The components marked with an asterisk are the only ones that are fundamental, which would be part of a truly minimal synchronization period. The components marked with a "+" are overheads that cannot be eliminated, but whose latencies may be partially or entirely hidden. Unmarked components are ripe for elimination through optimization.

3 Synchronization mechanisms

We have isolated what we believe to be a fundamental set of four mechanisms that synchronization primitives may incorporate. In Table 1 we show the overheads (from Figure 1) reduced by each

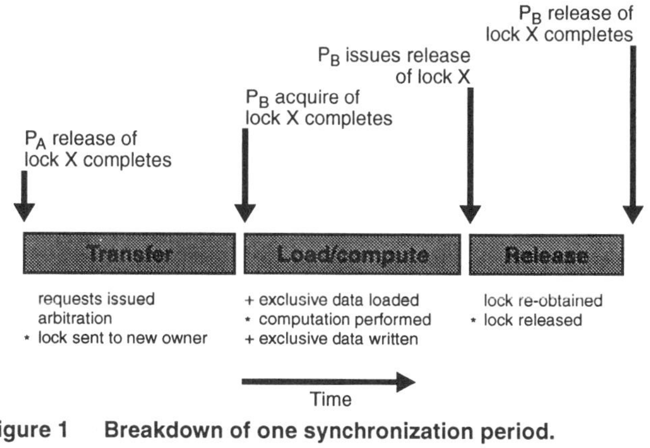

Figure 1 Breakdown of one synchronization period.

SYNCHRONIZATION MECHANISMS	PHASE OF THE SYNCHRONIZATION PERIOD: TRANSFER: Arbitration	TRANSFER: Lock transfer	LOAD/COMPUTE: Data read	LOAD/COMPUTE: Data write	RELEASE: Re-obtain lock
Local spinning					
Queue-based locking	✓	✓			✓
Collocation			✓	✓	
Synchronous prefetch		✓	maybe		

Table 1 How synchronization mechanisms reduce overhead.

of these mechanisms. The definitions and explanations of each mechanism are as follows:

- *Local spinning*: allows a requesting node to spin on a local copy of the lock. Although local spinning does not directly reduce overheads on the critical path of the synchronization period, it does greatly reduce the load on the network, particularly for longer critical sections. When the lock is released, the coherence mechanism will invalidate all local copies (since the releasing node needed an exclusive copy to modify that line), and when they next access the line, one requester will see that the lock has been freed and will acquire the lock.
- *Queue-based locking*: eliminates arbitration overhead and reduces lock transfer time, both in the *Transfer* phase. This mechanism reduces synchronization overhead in the following ways: (i) creates a queue of waiting requesters, thus performing arbitration when the requests are received and not when the current holder releases the lock; (ii) reduces lock transfer time by restricting communication to be between the releasing node and the acquiring node only (although the number of remote accesses required to perform this transfer will vary among different primitives); (iii) eliminates the overhead of re-obtaining the lock in the *Release* phase, since no other nodes access the lock directly until the holder releases the lock.
- *Collocation*:[1] lets protected data be transferred with the transfer of the lock itself. Since the data arrive with the lock, collocation eliminates read and write overheads in the *Load/Store* phase. The implementations we study in this paper achieve collocation by coupling a lock and critical data together in the same transfer block (a cache line). If the critical data are larger than one cache line, collocation will only partly reduce the read and write access overheads. If the critical data are determined dynamically, effective collocation is difficult.
- *Synchronous prefetch*: allows a processor to issue a request for a particular lock in advance of its critical section. The memory system will effect the transfer of the lock from the holder to the prefetching requester only when the holder releases the lock. Thus this mechanism will not impede the current holder's progress in the critical section. If a node prefetches the lock and the holder releases it before the requester reaches its critical section, the requester may be able to hide the lock transfer latency completely.

1. col.lo.ca.tion (n) \.kal-*-'ka-sh*n\: the act or result of placing or arranging together; specif: a noticeable arrangement or conjoining of linguistic elements (as words) [45] (*words* in this context are 4-byte quantities of data).

4 Synchronization primitives

The six base primitives we discuss in this paper are TEST&SET (abbreviated TS), TEST&TEST&SET (abbreviated TTS), MCS locks, LH locks, M locks, and QOLB. Table 2 shows which primitives incorporate which of the mechanisms described in Section 3. In Table 3, we show the minimum number of remote messages required for acquiring a lock. The counts correspond to messages on the critical path only. Each pair of numbers shown represents the number of messages required for a DASH-like [25] and an SCI-like [43] protocol, respectively. In cases where the lock is not held (columns one and two), the number of transactions is from issue to completion of the lock acquire. If another node holds the lock, the number of remote transactions shown is the number from issue of the release by the lock holder to the completion of the acquire by the requester. In the rest of this section, we define each base primitive and describe each in terms of the mechanisms that it incorporates, as shown in Table 2.

4.1 TEST&SET

TEST&SET (TS) was the sole synchronization primitive available on numerous early systems (such as the IBM 360 series [17]). TS performs an atomic read-modify-write on a memory location. It reads the value contained therein, and unconditionally sets the value to be non-zero. TS returns the value that was obtained from the read. It may be implemented with an atomic swap of as little as one bit.

We see in Table 3 that the TS primitive is efficient when a lock is not held; the primitive can immediately load the lock into the processor's cache and lock it. TS is less efficient when there is contention for a lock, since the lock's line is shifted from requester to requester in "exclusive" state. When the holder wishes to release the lock, it must re-obtain the lock from the requester that has moved the line into its cache. Concurrently, all requesters continue to send requests for writable copies of the lock. Although this scheme technically guarantees that some processor makes forward progress, it does not guarantee fairness, nor does it prevent starvation. Worse, it generates continuous remote transactions from the requesters (if there are more than one), even while the lock is being held. We see from Table 2 that the only optimization (of those in

SYNCHRONIZATION PRIMITIVE	SYNCHRONIZATION MECHANISM: Local spinning	Queue-based locking	Collocation	Synchronous prefetch
TS	no	no	optional	no
TTS	yes	no	optional	no
MCS, LH, M	yes	yes	partial	no
QOLB	yes	yes	optional	yes

Table 2 Synchronization primitives. For each synchronization primitive, this table shows which synchronization mechanisms it incorporates. We deemed collocation to be optional, since the programmer may choose not to exercise it.

Synchronization primitive	Minimal number of remote messages			
	Lock idle in memory	Unlocked, cached elsewhere	Locked, single contestant	Locked, N contestants
TS	2, 2	3, 6	5, 11	5, 11
TTS	4, 2	6, 6	8, 11	8, 9+2×N
MCS	2, 2	3, 6	7, 15	5, 9
LH	2, 2	9, 10	5, 11	5, 11
M	2, 2	3, 6	5, 11	5, 11
QOLB	2, 2	3, 4	1, 1	1, 1

Table 3 Number of remote transfers for acquire. The numbers in the table represent the minimal number of messages needed to acquire a lock. The counts correspond to messages on the critical path only. We show numbers for several initial lock states and two cache-coherence protocols. Each number on the left assumes a DASH-like protocol [25], and each number on the right assumes an SCI-like protocol [43]. We assume that the acquiring node, the releasing node (if applicable), and the directory node are all different nodes. In cases where the lock is not held (columns one and two), the number of transactions is from issue to completion of the lock acquire. If another node holds the lock, the number of remote transactions is from issue of the release by the lock holder to the completion of the acquire by the requester.

the table) that TS may implement is collocation. Collocation may be effective if requesters rarely attempt to obtain the lock while held. When a request for a held lock occurs, however, the requester and holder will ping-pong the lock (and collocated data) between their caches, as the holder accesses the data and the requester spins on the lock. The ping-ponging of the block will stall the holder, increasing the length of its critical section and thus increasing the global synchronization period.

A policy often applied to TS is exponential backoff, in which after a failure to obtain the lock a requester waits for successively longer periods of time before issuing another request for a lock [3]. We implemented a backoff scheme closely following the guidelines that appear in the original article: when an attempt to obtain a lock is unsuccessful, the requestor waits for an amount of time randomly selected from a uniform distribution; the algorithm doubles the mean of the distribution after each failed attempt up to a maximum. At the start of a fresh synchronization period the initial mean corresponds to half of the mean used in the previous period. The maximum mean is set to 16K cycles, which is roughly the time required to service a simple write miss (i.e., three network round trips or approximately 600 cycles) times the number of nodes in the system. We initialize the mean to one cycle, which corresponds also to the minimum mean.

4.2 TEST&TEST&SET

Rudolph and Segall first proposed an extension to TS that performs a read of the lock before attempting the actual TS operation [37]. They called this primitive TEST&TEST&SET (TTS). This primitive enables waiting requesters to spin on shared, read-only copies of the lock (local spinning*)*, waiting for the holder to release the lock. When the holder issues the release, the read-only copies are invalidated, the holder obtains a writable copy of the lock, and then releases it. The requesters load readable copies into their caches, and finding the lock released, attempt the TS. One of the requesters will succeed in obtaining a writable copy of the lock and locking it.

Although TTS employs local spinning to reduce interconnect traffic while the lock is held, the time needed to acquire the lock is longer than TS (see Table 3), due to the requesters' initial requests for read-only copies (instead of an exclusive copy, as with TS). The contention when the lock is freed can be substantial, as all requesters attempt to acquire the lock at that point, and then all attempt to upgrade the lock to a writable state. Exponential backoff may therefore improve TTS as well as TS. Collocation with TTS may work better than with TS, since the lock holder can still read data allocated in the lock's cache line, as it is shared with the requesters. TTS collocation is not ideal, however, since the holder will ping-pong the cache line with requesters whenever it writes to the collocated data.

4.3 MCS locks

Several researchers have independently proposed locking primitives that incorporate both local spinning and queue-based locking in software [2, 29, 16]. One of them is the locking primitive called MCS, developed by Mellor-Crummey and Scott [29]. The MCS scheme inserts requesters for a held lock into a software queue at the time of the request, using atomic operations such as SWAP and COMPARE&SWAP to update the list correctly. With queue-based locking, arbitration for the eventual recipient of the lock is therefore performed in advance, first-come, first-serve. Arbitration for TS and TTS, conversely, occurs at the time of lock release, increasing the synchronization period.

The price of maintaining the requester queue in software is larger overhead, especially under contentionless conditions. When a lock is released, however, communication occurs only between the releaser and the requester at the head of the queue. Network traffic is thus reduced to a constant number of network traversals per synchronization access, while the other requesters in the queue continue to spin locally.

Since each requester is spinning on a different address, these software queue-based algorithms cannot easily benefit from collocation. Partial collocation can be achieved by placing protected data along with the data structure that tracks the queue insertion point. If there is little contention, partial collocation may be effective. A more sophisticated approach could better exploit collocation by placing data either with the insertion pointer when there is no contention, or with the appropriate queue element when contention exists. However, this approach requires copying of data which, done carelessly, may sacrifice their integrity (e.g., in the context of recursive data structures). We did not investigate this approach. These algorithms are also unable to prefetch data without significant changes that greatly add to their complexity.

4.4 LH and M locks

Magnusson, Landin, and Hagersten proposed two software queue-based locking primitives, LH and M [28] (Craig independently developed a lock identical to LH [8]). They claimed that their primitives would require one fewer remote access to transfer a lock than does MCS, enabling their schemes to outperform MCS when lock contention exists. The LH lock achieves this behavior at the expense of increased latency to acquire an uncontested lock. The M lock achieves the more efficient lock transfer without increased uncontested lock access latency, at the expense of significant additional complexity in the lock algorithm. We implemented both locks according to the description in their paper, which presents the actual algorithms in detail [28].

4.5 Reactive synchronization

In 1994, Lim and Agarwal proposed "reactive synchronization" schemes [26], which dynamically switch among software locks that perform well under various levels of contention. For instance, it may combine TS for low-contention phases of execution with MCS for periods of high-contention. Reactive synchronization attempts to achieve both low latency lock access and efficient transfer at low cost (e.g., using only all-software primitives).

We implemented reactive synchronization, closely following the guidelines in the paper [26]. For low-contention phases, we used TS with exponential backoff. For high-contention phases, we used MCS (our results show that MCS is the best-performing software lock under high contention, of the locks that we measured). Our implementation switched to MCS after five consecutive lock acquisitions experienced higher levels of contention than a fixed threshold (a mean delay of 32 clock cycles). We switched from MCS to the low-contention lock when the queue was empty upon lock release five consecutive times.

4.6 QOLB

Goodman, Vernon, and Woest proposed the Queue-On-Lock-Bit primitive (QOLB—originally called QOSB) [13], which was the first proposal for a distributed, queue-based locking scheme. QOLB maintains a hardware queue of waiting processors, in which pointers to adjacent queue entries are held in the cache line. Waiting processors spin locally on a "shadow" copy of the lock address, preventing unnecessary network traffic or interference with the lock holder. Because lock requesters spin on the same address as that of the lock, without evicting or downgrading the lock holder's copy, effective collocation is possible (unlike the other primitives that we have discussed). When the holder releases its lock, the lock is sent directly to the requester at the head of the queue, incurring a total of one network crossing to transfer the lock (see Table 3).

In addition to enabling local spinning, collocation, and efficient handoffs through queueing, QOLB is a non-blocking primitive. This characteristic permits a processor to use QOLB for performing synchronous prefetching, allowing the processor to overlap data and lock access times with other useful work. If the prefetch is issued sufficiently far in advance, it is possible for the requester to see *no overhead* associated with the critical section entry, either for accessing the lock or the data. Figure 2 shows an example of how QOLB is used to access data in a critical section. The first call to ENQOLB (a non-blocking operation) allocates a shadow copy of the cache line and sends a message that inserts the requester into the hardware requester queue. This early request allows the processor to overlap the fetch time with useful computation. The subsequent calls to ENQOLB in the loop spin locally until the owner releases the lock and sends it directly to the waiting node. When ENQOLB returns "true," the processor enters the critical section. The processor relinquishes the lock with the call to DEQOLB, at which point both the lock and any data in the lock's cache line are sent directly to the next waiting processor. In this example, we assume that the critical section data can fit in 63 bytes. This will not always be the case, of course. Also, QOLB is fair in general, except in the unusual cases when a processor's shadow copy of the lock is replaced from its cache, forcing the processor to rejoin the queue at its end.

```
struct _locked data {
  char lock;
  char data[63];              /* 64-byte cache line */
};

void
critical_section(struct _locked data *ptr) {
  /* Prefetch lock & data (assumes proper alignment) */
  EnQOLB(&ptr->lock);
  /* Various computation here */
  ...
  while (!EnQOLB(&ptr->lock)) ;              /* Spin */
  /* Critical section here */
  ...
  DeQOLB(&ptr->lock);              /* Release lock */
}
```

Figure 2 QOLB code example.

5 Experimental methodology

We measured the performance of the six synchronization primitives discussed in Section 4, varying mechanisms from Table 2 when possible, except that we did not simulate collocation in conjunction with the LH and M locks (we will show later that MCS generally performs better than LH and M, which are not inherently more amenable to collocation than MCS). We also measured the performance of reactive synchronization (also without collocation since reactive synchronization is not inherently amenable to collocation). Our seven main locking schemes (and their corresponding abbreviations) are thus as follows: TEST&SET (TS), TEST&SET&SET (TTS), MCS locks, LH locks, M locks, reactive synchronization (R), and QOLB. We used the following abbreviations for optional mechanisms or policies: collocation (+C), hand-inserted synchronous prefetch (+P), compiler-generated synchronous prefetch (+CP), and exponential backoff (+E).

5.1 Simulation environment

Our simulation platform was the Wisconsin Wind Tunnel (WWT) [33], which uses a 32-processor Thinking Machines CM-5 [23] as its host machine. WWT executes SPARC binaries in native mode on the CM-5, only trapping into the simulator upon a cache miss. WWT assumes fixed execution time for the instructions (the actual values correspond to the instruction delays listed in the CY701 SPARC user's guide [9]). WWT makes some assumptions about the target system to simplify simulation—it assumes both a perfect instruction cache, and that stack accesses always hit in the data cache.

The default WWT network model assumes a fully connected point-to-point target network, in which messages take a constant number of cycles for a one-way network traversal. A large enough constant latency provides sufficient lookahead for efficient parallel simulation, as nodes stop and synchronize only once every C cycles, where C is the constant network latency. Using a small C (or variable-length messages) reduces the node lookahead, which causes severe increases in simulation time [6].

Although we model contention at the node interfaces, memory, and memory directories, using a constant network latency ignores contention in the network itself. To account for network contention, we used an analytical model [41] (which takes the network load as a parameter) to derive a different constant network latency for each benchmark. We estimated this aggregate network load from the traffic statistics of previous simulations and their total execution times. Since the network latency affects execution time and therefore aggregate load, we iterated this estimation until the difference between the network latency constant and the value produced by the model converged to within one cycle (the final latencies for the benchmarks ranged from 85 to 91 cycles). To validate this methodology, we simulated several points for each benchmark using the WWT extended with a detailed, event-driven SCI network simulator. Our network simulator accurately simulates message buffering, message retransmission, and flow control [5]. The target network that we used to derive the validation is an 8×4 mesh of rings that routes requests in increasing dimension order (x, y) and responses in decreasing order (y, x). The internal details of the simulated network correspond closely to those of the SCI transport layer standard [43]. The mean difference between the execution time of simulations using the constant network model and simulations using the detailed network simulator was 2%. The difference was always under 5% [18].

Using a global mean to model contention tends to underestimate execution time, since traffic often occurs in bursts that add more queueing delay than if the same traffic was evenly distributed over time. With our validation, we have bounded this discrepancy. Even so, since our more aggressive synchronization primitives (MCS, QOLB) generate less traffic than do the alternatives, accurately modeling contention in the network would only serve to increase the reported performance gap between the lower- and higher-performing primitives. Our results are therefore conservative.

5.2 Target systems

The target systems that we simulate are all 32-processor, cache-coherent shared-memory systems that use the Scalable Coherent Interface (SCI) [43] as their base cache-coherence protocol. SCI is a particularly appropriate choice for our base platform, since two of the newest shared-memory multiprocessors on the market implement cache-coherent SCI (the Convex EXEMPLAR [7] and the Sequent STING [27]), and numerous other vendors are exploring SCI as an option. Each node in our CC-NUMA target system is workstation-like, containing a processor, a 1-Mbyte four-way set-associative cache memory with 64-byte lines, a 64-entry transaction queue, a network interface, and some fraction of the distributed, globally-shared memory with the associated directory entries. The transaction queue is similar to a functionally extended write buffer. It supports the following asynchronous operations: writes, prefetches, coherence operations, and cache line flushes caused by replacement (rollouts). A complete description of the system parameters and their associated timings appears elsewhere [18]. WWT allocates private target pages locally, and distributes shared target pages to the target nodes round-robin. Our simulated memory system supports release consistency [12].

5.3 Microbenchmark experiment description

We repeat the method used by both Anderson [3] and Lim and Agarwal [26] to measure raw critical section throughput. We constructed a microbenchmark that accesses a critical section in a loop repeatedly (the benchmark accesses the critical section a total of 3,200 times; these accesses are distributed evenly among the processors). Once in the critical section, a processor waits 800 cycles before releasing the lock (this stall simulates access to, and computation of, protected data). After release, the releasing processor waits for a random amount of time selected from a uniform distribution. The mean of the distribution is five times the critical section delay (4,000 cycles). As the number of nodes is increased, the contention for the lock increases, and eventually the reduction in execution time is stopped (and in some cases reversed) by the increasing lock contention.

For this experiment we assumed a fixed network latency between any two nodes of 100 cycles.

5.4 Macrobenchmark experiment descriptions

The benchmark applications that we used for our experiments are Barnes, Mp3d, Ocean, Pthor, and Raytrace, drawn from the SPLASH and SPLASH-2 suites [42, 46]. Descriptions of these benchmarks appear in the original articles. We compiled all benchmarks using GCC version 2.7.2 with the option -O3. We padded data in each benchmark, where necessary, to eliminate false sharing [14]. We modified Ocean both by translating it to C and by skewing its array storage (slightly increasing the size of the working arrays into arrays of prime size, from 128 to 131 elements in each dimension). We used the locking version of Mp3d for all experiments. Pthor assigns a descriptor to each element of the digital circuit being simulated. Only a few fields of this descriptor are frequently modified in the course of the simulation. To take advantage of automatic replication of read-only data and reduce cache misses, we collocated the frequently modified Pthor fields in a single cache line.

BENCHMARK	TYPE OF SIMULATION	INPUT	SYNCH. PERIOD
Barnes	Barnes-Hut N-body	2,048 bodies, 11 iter.	1,840
Mp3d	Hypersonic flow	24,000 mols, 25 iter.	44
Ocean	Hydrodynamic	98×98, 2 days	17,469
Pthor	Digital circuit	RISC, 1,000 timesteps	7,633
Raytrace	3-D rendering	TEAPOT	490

Table 4 Macrobenchmarks.

We list the problems that the benchmarks solve and the inputs that we used in Table 4. The fourth column of Table 4 lists the period of critical section entry for each benchmark, computed by dividing the benchmark execution time (discounting initialization) by the total number of critical section entries (across all 32 processors). We computed this statistic from the sequentially consistent run of QOLB with all mechanisms enabled. The frequency at which locks are obtained is an important metric, since improving the synchronization primitive will have little benefit for an application that uses locks infrequently.

For these macrobenchmarks, we varied the memory model as well as the synchronization primitive. By using two memory models (sequential consistency and aggressive release consistency), we show that the performance gained by improving the synchronization primitive cannot also be gained solely by making the memory model more aggressive. The memory models that we simulated are two different implementations of release consistency: sequential consistency (denoted SEQ), and an aggressive implementation that attempts to minimize the number of times that the processor is stalled by memory operations (denoted REL). For the latter memory model, we labeled all memory accesses as aggressively as possible according to the structure proposed by Gharachorloo and others [11, 12], and inserted the appropriate memory fences to achieve release consistency on our simulated hardware platform. Although our system assumes blocking loads, we implement a merging write buffer of up to 64 non-blocking stores, which allows multiple stores to be combined and loads to be serviced by stores. This large buffer permits very aggressive relaxation of the consistency model for stores.

5.5 Prefetching compiler algorithm

We used an enhanced version of GCC that automatically inserts prefetch operations, developed locally by Aboulenein. This compiler takes a critical section and the address of the associated lock variable, and automatically inserts the ENQOLB and DEQOLB instructions for the lock. More importantly, the compiler attempts to move an ENQOLB instruction to a prespecified distance above the entry point to the critical section, thus performing a synchronous prefetch.

The compiler uses two methods for trying to insert the prefetching ENQOLB instructions. It first attempts to move the prefetch operation into a basic block that *dominates* [24] the basic block containing the entry point of the critical section. If the compiler is unable to locate a basic block that dominates the critical section entry point, the compiler resorts to a technique similar to trace scheduling [10], which inserts ENQOLB operations in non-dominating basic blocks. To ensure correctness, the compiler must also insert DEQOLB operations along all possible paths that do not include the critical section.

6 Results

In this section we present our microbenchmark and macrobenchmark results. We then compare pairs of macrobenchmark runs in an attempt to identify the effect that the individual synchronization mechanisms have on performance.

6.1 Microbenchmark results

We plot completion time of the microbenchmark loop in Figure 3. Since there is no shared data used in the critical section, we do not explore collocation. We measure the throughput of TS and TTS both with and without exponential backoff, MCS, LH and M locks, QOLB, and reactive synchronization (using TS+E for the low-contention case and MCS for the high-contention case). We see that QOLB performs best in all cases, under both low and high contention. TS and TTS perform second- and third-best under low contention (one or two processors), but their performance quickly degenerates for more than four. Adding exponential backoff makes TS and TTS perform worse under low contention, but prevents a severe performance degradation in the presence of numerous requestors. The LH and M locks outperform all primitives other than QOLB under medium contention (four processors).

Under high contention MCS outperforms both LH and M. The difference in performance is attributable to the cache behavior of these primitives and the cache coherence protocol we simulated. Under MCS, a processor always reuses the same queue element (or memory address) to insert itself in the queue. Under both LH and M, queue elements tend to migrate from releasing to acquiring nodes [28]. In SCI, a write to a migrating cache block requires more network transactions than does a write to a block accessed mostly by one processor. Other cache-coherence protocols may not display this behavior.

Magnusson, Landin, and Hagersten [28] state that under high contention, MCS generates one extra cache miss than do LH or M. Careful collocation of the MCS "next" pointer and the lock bit (as implied in the original article [29]) prevents this extra cache miss. Under high contention, this collocation permits two read accesses to be satisfied by a single miss instead of two. For all our experiments we assumed that the MCS tail pointer is indeed collocated with the lock bit, which improves its performance under high contention but hinders performance slightly under medium contention. In MCS, placing the lock bit and tail pointer together can result in extra remote accesses when a node is adding itself to a two-element queue at the same time the head of the queue is freeing the lock. Finally, we see that our reactive synchronization scheme is successful in that it closely tracks the performance of the best software alternative under both low- and high-contention conditions.

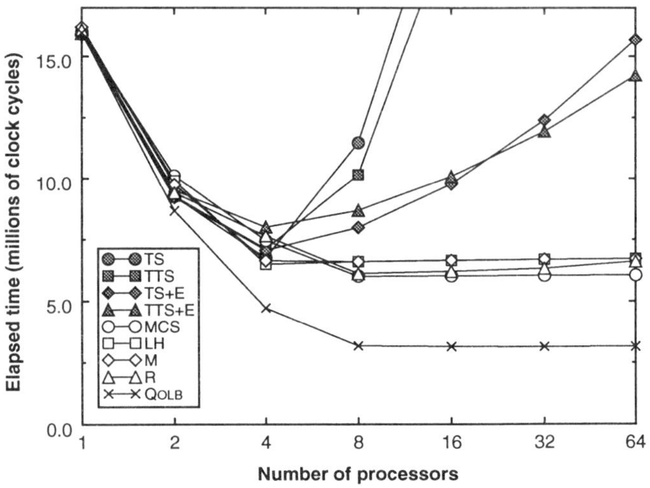

Figure 3 Microbenchmark performance.

6.2 Macrobenchmark results

We present the results of the macrobenchmark experiments in Table 5. TS is the base case for each benchmark and memory model. We list the simulated execution time of each base experiment (in millions of cycles) in parentheses in the TS row and SEQ column of Table 5. The other numbers in Table 5 are all speedups relative to their particular base case. The running times that we present correspond to the entire execution of the benchmarks.

What is most striking about these results is the magnitude of the speedups, considering that the only parameter being varied is the synchronization primitives. Raytrace executes twice as fast in

	Benchmark									
	Barnes		Mp3d		Ocean		Pthor		Raytrace	
Experiment	SEQ	REL	SEQ	REL	SEQ	REL	SEQ	REL	SEQ	REL
TS	(190)	0.94	(231)	1.02	(16.5)	1.19	(221)	1.16	(826)	1.22
TS+C	1.67	1.85	1.03	1.12	1.31	1.69	0.86	1.13	2.47	2.56
TS+E	1.17	1.40	0.86	1.21	1.12	1.37	0.88	1.22	2.06	2.15
TS+E+C	1.31	1.67	0.90	1.29	1.31	1.68	0.93	1.34	2.56	2.65
TTS	1.02	1.11	1.05	1.11	1.02	1.22	1.04	1.23	1.03	1.12
TTS+C	1.72	1.87	1.09	1.18	1.32	1.70	0.95	1.36	2.54	2.61
TTS+E	1.17	1.40	0.83	1.18	1.11	1.40	0.87	1.21	2.03	2.15
TTS+E+C	1.32	1.66	0.87	1.25	1.26	1.70	0.94	1.35	2.56	2.65
MCS	1.57	1.61	1.18	1.30	1.24	1.55	1.06	1.25	2.31	2.26
MCS+C	1.58	1.63	1.25	1.36	1.25	1.65	1.17	1.37	2.29	2.33
LH	1.21	1.48	0.81	1.12	1.24	1.55	0.87	1.22	2.26	2.31
M	1.21	1.47	0.75	1.06	1.24	1.55	0.87	1.18	2.25	2.29
R	1.19	1.47	0.76	1.08	1.19	1.49	0.87	1.20	2.28	2.35
QOLB	1.79	1.83	1.46	1.60	1.31	1.65	1.11	1.34	2.58	2.64
QOLB+C	1.89	1.92	1.65	1.75	1.34	1.70	1.25	1.51	2.62	2.69
QOLB+C+P	1.89	1.92	1.65	1.75	1.31	1.68	1.26	1.54	2.63	2.70
QOLB+C+CP	1.89	1.93	1.64	1.74	1.35	1.70	1.25	1.53	2.63	2.70

Table 5 Speedups of different synchronization primitives. The numbers in parentheses represent the execution time (in millions of clock cycles) for the particular benchmark running on sequentially consistent hardware. The other numbers represent speedups, calculated as the ratio of the execution time of the base run to that of the optimized synchronization primitive.

30 cases. The smallest speedup, with all four mechanisms employed, is sequentially consistent Pthor with 25%. Although Pthor uses locks more than does Barnes or Ocean, Barnes has bursty streaks of accesses to locks. Lock accesses in Pthor are more evenly distributed, so they do not degrade performance nearly so much as in Barnes (thus leaving less opportunity for improvement). The speedups for Ocean are small not because the mechanisms are ineffective, but because Ocean uses locks less frequently than do the other benchmarks (see Table 4). For all benchmarks, however, QOLB with collocation consistently captures the bulk of the performance improvement to be gained. Our implementation of synchronous prefetching is generally ineffective, speeding up or slowing down the execution by at most 2%.

Three of the benchmarks (Barnes, Ocean, and Raytrace) exhibit similar performance for QOLB and TS (or TTS) with collocation. This is untrue for Mp3d and Pthor, however. Using collocation with TTS improves the performance of Mp3d little, and makes the performance of Pthor deteriorate. The lower performance of Pthor with collocation results from the relatively long length of Pthor's critical sections. These long critical sections give requesters the opportunity to attempt to obtain the lock, pulling both the lock and critical section data out of the holder's cache. This behavior does not occur with QOLB because waiting nodes in a QOLB queue spin on shadow lines, not the actual addresses.

Partial collocation with MCS improves the performance of all benchmarks, except for Barnes and the sequentially consistent runs of Ocean and Raytrace. In these cases collocation either has little impact (Ocean and Barnes) or degrades performance slightly (Raytrace). Unlike TS, MCS causes only a fixed number of memory operations to be issued per synchronization access, thus limiting the disturbance caused by collocation.

Raytrace exhibits much larger speedups than does any other benchmark. The Raytrace base case (TS) is extremely slow (as is TTS). Adding any other mechanism besides local spinning improves the performance of Raytrace substantially. These two primitives perform so poorly because much of the locking is for very small critical sections, for which there is heavy contention. Collocation makes the small critical sections extremely fast. Queue-based locking eliminates the large relative overhead that occurs due to contention when the lock is released.

Adding exponential backoff improves performance moderately for all benchmarks but Mp3d and Pthor in the sequentially consistent runs, in which we observed slowdowns of up to 20%.

Reactive synchronization is generally within 25% of the best performing synchronization primitives (disregarding the collocation mechanism and the QOLB runs). The exceptions are the sequentially consistent run of Barnes and Mp3d, where reactive synchronization is 32% and 53% slower than MCS, respectively.

6.3 Individual mechanisms

This section isolates the performance contributions of the individual mechanisms in Section 3. Figure 4 shows performance differences between eight pairs of experiments (for each benchmark). Each pair of experiments isolates one particular mechanism. There is doubtless interaction between an "isolated" mechanism and the other components of the synchronization primitive. This decomposition is not intended to quantify the performance contribution of individual mechanisms definitively, but to aid in understanding of how their combinations affect performance. We also isolate the exponential backoff policy. We list the isolated mechanisms or policies below, along with their corresponding experiment pairs:

	Experiment pair	
Isolated mechanism or policy	With	Without
Local spinning	TTS	TS
Exponential backoff	TTS+E	TTS
Queue-based locking	MCS	TTS
	QOLB	TTS
Collocation	TS+C	TS
	TTS+C	TTS
	QOLB+C	QOLB
Synchronous prefetch	QOLB+C+CP	QOLB+C

All runs in Figure 4 assume a sequentially consistent memory model. The y-axis plots speedup. Figure 4 shows that local spin-

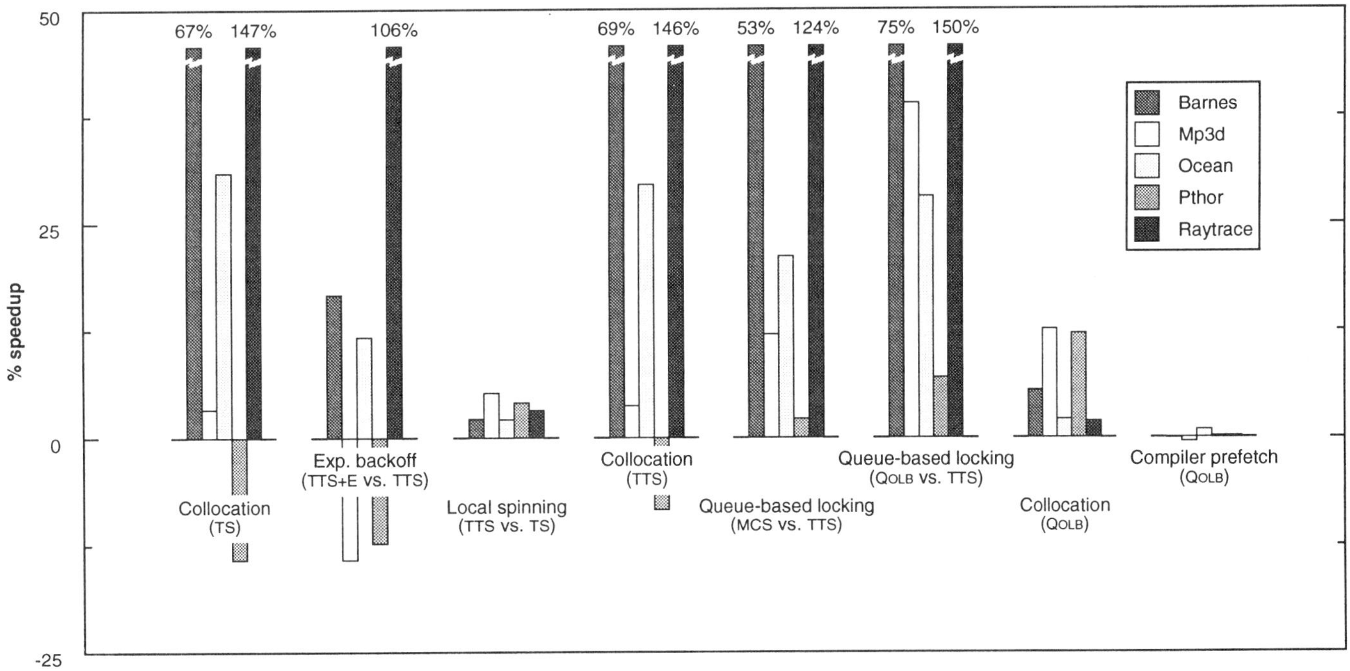

Figure 4 Effects of individual mechanisms.

ning is generally ineffective. Queue-based locking (using MCS) increases speedup for all benchmarks. Using collocation with TS and TTS causes very different behavior across the benchmarks: reducing speedup (Pthor), having a negligible effect (Mp3d), causing a moderate increase (Ocean), and causing a large increase (Barnes and Raytrace). This high variance with collocation exists because requesters may either steal the data from the lock holder, hurting performance, or prevent extra remote transfers into a network filled with arbitration traffic, thus mitigating exceptionally poor performance.

Synchronization prefetching is ineffective, never affecting the running time by more than 2%. We suspect that there is much more opportunity for improvement with synchronous prefetch, as the compiler algorithm was not as aggressive as possible, and we did not restructure the codes or algorithms to exploit the power of the QOLB prefetch operator.

7 Cost of QOLB

In Section 6, we showed that QOLB outperforms all other synchronization primitives in all cases. This performance comes with an associated cost. Most of the other primitives that we discuss can be implemented almost entirely in software, requiring only an atomic memory operation, such as SWAP, in hardware. QOLB, conversely, requires additional hardware support. In this section, we enumerate the additional mechanisms that QOLB requires, discuss the cost spectrum of possible implementations of these mechanisms, and present performance results of a low-cost implementation of QOLB that runs on a cluster of commodity workstations.

QOLB requires four mechanisms for a fully functional implementation: non-blocking synchronizing instructions, direct node-to-node transfer of the lock (from lock releaser to acquirer), storage of the queue state information (such as the next node in the queue), and the capability for multiple nodes to perform operations on the same address without invoking the coherence protocol (the "shadow line" described in Section 4.6). The highest-performance implementation of QOLB requires hardware support in both the processor and the memory system: specialized non-blocking QOLB instructions in the processor, plus extra state, direct cache-to-cache transfer of the lock, and "shadow copy" support in the cache. The SCI standard's implementation of QOLB incorporates the latter three mechanisms,[1] for example, and leaves the processor implementation undefined.

Much lower-cost implementations, which achieve much of the potential performance of QOLB, are possible. QOLB instructions in the processor may be replaced with generic non-blocking loads or stores, eliminating the need to modify a commodity processor. To use generic memory operations, the memory controller must be able to recognize the issued instructions as synchronization operations. These operations may be "flavored," if the processor supports such loads and stores, or they may be memory-mapped into a special "synchronization space." These operations must also be marked uncachable, lest they hit in on-chip caches and never reach the memory controller.

In addition to the processor support, low-cost memory system alternatives for QOLB exist. Recent multiprocessor implementations have begun to use protocol processors at individual nodes to handle inter-node communication. These implementations may use a custom protocol engine, such as Wisconsin Typhoon [34], Stanford FLASH [21], or Sequent STiNG [27], or a commodity protocol processor with some additional off-chip hardware support [35]. These protocol engines can store the QOLB state in either specialized storage or main memory, send direct messages to ship the lock bit to the next waiting processor in a queue, and bypass (or supplement) the global coherence protocol to permit shadow spinning.

To determine if low-cost implementations of QOLB will still outperform other primitives, we compared the performance of QOLB, MCS, and a message-based centralized queue lock (CQL) [39] implemented on an unmodified cluster of commodity workstations. The workstations used the Blizzard run-time system [40] to provide the illusion of shared memory. Blizzard is an implementation of the Tempest interface [34] which, through user-level software, lets users customize the behavior of shared memory to suit the needs of their parallel applications. MCS and CQL are part of the locally available Blizzard distribution and are implemented directly on top of the Tempest interface. We implemented QOLB using the Tempest interface. Our implementation follows closely the QOLB specification in the SCI standard [43]. Specific details on the lock implementations are described elsewhere [19]. Our cluster of workstations consist of 40 unmodified dual processor Sun SPARCStation 20s, each with two 66-MHz HyperSPARC processors [36] and a Myricon Myrinet interface [4]. For our measurements, we used only a single processor per node; that processor is responsible for executing both the program and the Tempest handlers. The detection of message arrival is achieved through polling. A binary rewriting tool [22] automatically inserts polling instructions in the parallel program.[2] The time spent polling is minimized by exploiting the coherence protocol in the memory bus. The polling code checks the status of the network interface through an access to a cachable location, thus limiting the number of these accesses that require the bus to complete. The network interface uses its DMA interface to update the polled location [31]. We set the cache block size to 128 bytes.

To evaluate these implementations, we used a microbenchmark similar to that described in Section 5.3. To explore the impact of collocation, this microbenchmark does not wait a fixed amount of time in the critical section; instead, it writes a value into a shared-memory location. If the synchronization primitive permits collocation, this location may be collocated with the lock. As before, once a processor exits the critical section, it waits for a randomly generated amount of time (selected from a uniform distribution with a mean of approximately 1350μs). The benchmark executes the loop body 100,000 times, divided evenly among the contending nodes.

In Figure 5, we show the elapsed time (in seconds) of the microbenchmark loop under contention levels ranging from one to 16.[3] The figure depicts the elapsed time for four synchronization configurations: MCS, CQL, QOLB, and QOLB with the lock and the variable collocated (QOLB+C). When there is no contention, MCS performs better than either CQL or QOLB. The difference is due to the fact that the latter two implementations require invocation of protocol handlers to acquire or release a lock, while MCS can perform the same operations using simple loads and stores that hit in the cache. Under high contention, QOLB+C outperforms the other primitives. In the 16-node configuration, QOLB+C completes the loop 5.6 as fast as MCS and 2.6 times as fast as CQL. CQL and QOLB perform similarly, with CQL being about 10% faster than QOLB (without collocation) under high contention.

Considering message counts only we could conclude that QOLB should clearly outperform CQL. Indeed, under high contention, QOLB has a single message on the critical path (see Table 3), while CQL has two (one message from the releaser to the lock manager and another one from the manager to the acquirer). The observed behavior is due to the transmission times of the messages used by these implementations; CQL uses short messages to communicate

1. To our knowledge the SCI standard is the only design that includes QOLB.

2. That tool is also responsible for inserting checks before each shared-memory access [39].

3. Due to a shortcoming in the Myrinet interface we could not collect numbers with more than 16 nodes.

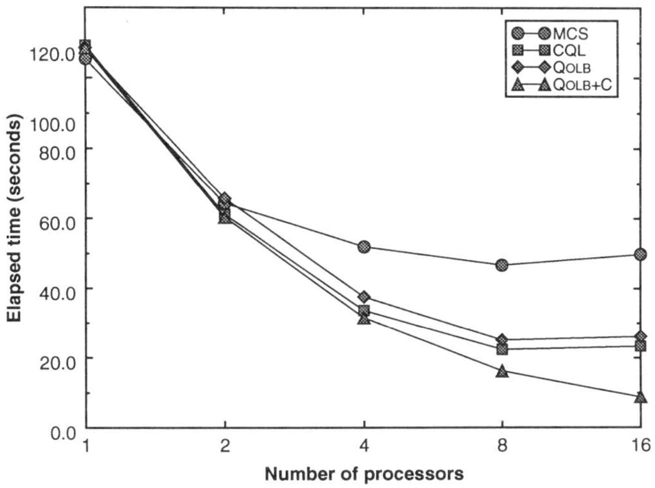

Figure 5 Performance of software QOLB.

with the node managing the centralized queue, while QOLB transfers entire cache lines of 128 bytes. On our system, the round trip time of a message carrying a cache line is roughly twice the round trip of a short message.

8 Summary and conclusion

This paper focused on providing efficient locking primitives to improve the performance and scalability of fine-grain shared-memory parallel programs. Instead of focusing on the individual latencies associated with mutually exclusive accesses to critical sections, we focused on the global throughput of critical section accesses. We defined the notion of a *synchronization period*: one "cycle" of multiple serialized accesses to a critical section. We broke this time into three phases (*Transfer*, *Load/compute*, and *Release*), and classified the components of each of these phases as either unavoidable latencies or removable overheads. We identified four optimizing mechanisms (*local spinning*, *queue-based locking*, *collocation*, and *synchronous prefetch*) that can assist in eliminating the removable overheads of critical section accesses.

We performed a thorough evaluation of this space, simulating the performance of seventeen locking constructs (formed from six base primitives: TEST&SET, TEST&TEST&SET, MCS, LH, M, and QOLB) in detail with both real parallel applications and the more traditional microbenchmarks. We also demonstrated the performance of our synchronous prefetching compiler. Finally, we compared the performance of three queue-based locking schemes running on an unmodified cluster of workstations, the results of which support our simulation results.

Our results showed that local spinning consistently aids performance but not very much. Queue-based locking was very effective, except in the cases where the overhead of MCS, LH, and M locks hurt low-contention critical section access latencies. Collocation of the lock and locked data in the same cache line showed wildly different effects with TEST&SET and TEST&TEST&SET; collocation may greatly increase or decrease performance, depending on the benchmark. Collocation consistently improved the performance of QOLB. Synchronous prefetching was the least effective of any of the mechanisms.

The most important result of our experiments is the consistent and large performance gain that QOLB achieves, which is further increased by collocation. Graunke and Thakkar [16] concluded that "... elaborate hardware [synchronization] schemes are unnecessary even when considering larger non-bus-based [systems]." Mellor-Crummey and Scott stated [30] that "special purpose synchronization mechanisms, such as QOLB, are unlikely to outperform our MCS lock by more than 30%." Our results refute these assertions; QOLB outperforms MCS by 40% for Mp3d.

Lim and Agarwal claimed [26] that reactive synchronization "reduces the motivation for providing hardware support for queue locks." Since QOLB outperforms the best software locks under either low- or high-contention conditions, it should also outperform reactive synchronization schemes. Our results confirm this hypothesis—QOLB speedups were from 10% to 92% higher than reactive synchronization, and this disparity only increased by adding collocation and synchronous prefetch to QOLB.

Finally, we claim that the inherent cost requirements of QOLB are not prohibitive. Hardware queue-based locking is not prohibitively expensive, as DASH implemented one such synchronization scheme [25] (it differs from QOLB in that the centralized memory directory kept track of queued requesters). QOLB is an integral part of the SCI standard [43], and uses many of the same mechanisms needed to implement the coherence protocol. As we showed in Section 7, many current- and next-generation multiprocessors already contain most of the hardware support needed to implement hardware-supported QOLB. We also showed that a low-cost, lower performance version of QOLB can be implemented on current systems with no additional hardware support and still outperform the alternatives.

Acknowledgments

We are also thankful to the following people: David Wood first proposed to decompose synchronization primitives into mechanisms. Mary Vernon commented on drafts of this paper. Satish Chandra, Babak Falsafi, Steve Reinhardt, Ioannis Schoinas, Brian Toonen helped clarify some fine points of Tempest and Blizzard. We benefited from discussions with T. N. Vijaykumar.

References

[1] Sarita V. Adve and Mark D. Hill. Weak Ordering — A New Definition. In *Proceedings of the 17th Annual International Symposium on Computer Architecture*, pages 2–14, May 1990.

[2] Thomas E. Anderson. The Performance Implications of Spin-Waiting Alternatives for Shared-Memory Multiprocessors. In *Proceedings of the 1989 International Conference on Parallel Processing*, volume II Software, pages 170–174, August 1989.

[3] Thomas E. Anderson. The Performance of Spin Lock Alternatives for Shared-Memory Multiprocessors. *IEEE Transactions on Parallel and Distributed Systems*, 1(1):6–16, January 1990.

[4] Nanette J. Boden, Danny Cohen, Robert E. Feldermann, Alan E. Kulawik, Charles L. Seitz, Jakov N. Seizovic, and Wen-King Su. Myrinet: A Gigabit-per-Second Local Area Network. *IEEE Micro*, 15(1):29–36, February 1995.

[5] Douglas C. Burger and James R. Goodman. Simulation of the SCI Transport Layer on the Wisconsin Wind Tunnel. In *Proceedings of the Second International Workshop on SCI-Based High-Performance Low-Cost Computing*, March 1995.

[6] Douglas C. Burger and David A. Wood. Accuracy vs. Performance in Parallel Simulation of Interconnection Networks. In *Proceedings of the Ninth International Parallel Processing Symposium*, pages 22–31, April 1995.

[7] Convex Computer Corporation, Richardson, TX. *SPP1000 Systems Overview*, 1994.

[8] Travis S. Craig. Building FIFO and Priority-Queueing Spin Locks from Atomic Swap. Technical Report 93-02-02, Department of Computer Science and Engineering, University of Washington, Seattle, WA, February 1993.

[9] Cypress Semiconductor, San Jose, CA. *CY7C601 SPARC RISC User's Guide*, second edition, 1990.

[10] Joseph A. Fisher. Trace Scheduling: A Technique for Global Microcode Compaction. *IEEE Transactions on Computers*, C-30(7):478–490, July 1981.

[11] Kourosh Gharachorloo, Sarita V. Adve, Anoop Gupta, John L. Hennessy, and Mark D. Hill. Programming for Different Memory Con-

sistency Models. *Journal of Parallel and Distributed Computing*, 15(4):399–407, 1992.

[12] Kourosh Gharachorloo, Daniel Lenoski, James Laudon, Philip Gibbons, Anoop Gupta, and John Hennessy. Memory Consistency and Event Ordering in Scalable Shared-Memory. In *Proceedings of the 17th Annual International Symposium on Computer Architecture*, pages 15–26, May 1990.

[13] James R. Goodman, Mary K. Vernon, and Philip J. Woest. Efficient Synchronization Primitives for Large-Scale Cache-Coherent Shared-Memory Multiprocessors. In *Proceedings of the Third Symposium on Architectural Support for Programming Languages and Operating Systems*, pages 64–75, April 1989.

[14] James R. Goodman and Philip J. Woest. The Wisconsin Multicube: A New Large-Scale Cache-Coherent Multiprocessor. In *Proceedings of the 15th Annual International Symposium on Computer Architecture*, pages 422–431, May 1988.

[15] Allan Gottlieb, Ralph Grishman, Clyde P. Kruskal, Kevin P. McAuliffe, Larry Rudolph, and Marc Snir. The NYU Ultracomputer–Designing an MIMD Shared Memory Parallel Computer. *IEEE Transactions on Computers*, C-32(2):175–189, February 1983.

[16] Gary Graunke and Shreekant Thakkar. Synchronization Algorithms for Shared-Memory Multiprocessors. *IEEE Computer*, 23(6):60–70, June 1990.

[17] International Business Machines, Inc., Poughkeepsie, NY. *IBM System/360 Principles of Operation*, ninth edition, May 1970.

[18] Alain Kägi, Nagi Aboulenein, Douglas C. Burger, and James R. Goodman. Techniques for Reducing the Overheads of Shared-Memory Multiprocessing. In *Proceedings of the 1995 International Conference on Supercomputing*, pages 11–20, July 1995.

[19] Alain Kägi and James R. Goodman. SoftQOLB: An Ultra-Efficient Synchronization Primitive for Clusters of Commodity Workstations. Technical Report 1327, Computer Sciences Department, University of Wisconsin, Madison, WI, November 1996.

[20] R. E. Kessler and J. L. Schwartzmeier. CRAY T3D: A New Dimension for Cray Research. In *Proceedings of the 38thIEEE Computer Society International Conference (COMPCON)*, pages 176–182, February 1993.

[21] Jeffrey Kuskin, David Ofelt, Mark Heinrich, John Heinlein, Richard Simoni, Kourosh Gharachorloo, John Chapin, David Nakahira, Joel Baxter, Mark Horowitz, Anoop Gupta, Mendel Rosenblum, and John Hennessy. The Stanford FLASH Multiprocessor. In *Proceedings of the 21st Annual International Symposium on Computer Architecture*, pages 302–313, April 1994.

[22] James R. Larus and Eric Schnarr. EEL: Machine Independent Executable Editing. In *Proceedings of the 1995Conference on Programming Language Design and Implementation*, pages 291–300, June 1995.

[23] Charles E. Leiserson, Zahi S. Abuhamdeh, David C. Douglas, Carl R. Feynman, Mahesh N. Ganmukhi, Jeffrey V. Hill, W. Daniel Hillis, Bradley C. Kuszmaul, Margaret A. St. Pierre, David S. Wells, Monica C. Wong, Shaw-Wen Yang, and Robert Zak. The Network Architecture of the Connection Machine CM-5. In *Proceedings of the Fourth Annual ACM Symposium on Parallel Algorithms and Architectures*, pages 272–285, June 1992.

[24] Thomas Lengauer and Robert E. Tarjan. A Fast Algorithm for Finding Dominators in a Flowgraph. *Transactions on Programming Languages and Systems*, 1(1):121–141, July 1979.

[25] Daniel Lenoski, James Laudon, Kourosh Gharachorloo, Wolf-Dietrich Weber, Anoop Gupta, John Hennessy, Mark Horowitz, and Monica Lam. The Stanford DASH Multiprocessor. *IEEE Computer*, 25(3):63–79, March 1992.

[26] Beng-Hong Lim and Anant Agarwal. Reactive Synchronization Algorithms for Multiprocessors. In *Proceedings of the Sixth Symposium on Architectural Support for Programming Languages and Operating Systems*, pages 25–35, October 1994.

[27] Tom Lovett and Russell Clapp. STiNG: A CC-NUMA Computer System for the Commercial Marketplace. In *Proceedings of the 23rd Annual International Symposium on Computer Architecture*, pages 304–315, May 1996.

[28] Peter Magnusson, Anders Landin, and Erik Hagersten. Efficient Software Synchronization on Large Cache Coherent Multiprocessors. Technical Report T94:07, Swedish Institute of Computer Science, Kista, Sweden, February 1994.

[29] John M. Mellor-Crummey and Michael L. Scott. Algorithms for Scalable Synchronization on Shared-Memory Multiprocessors. *ACM Transactions on Computer Systems*, 9(1):21–65, February 1991.

[30] John M. Mellor-Crummey and Michael L. Scott. Synchronization Without Contention. In *Proceedings of the Fourth Symposium on Architectural Support for Programming Languages and Operating Systems*, pages 269–278, April 1991.

[31] Shubhendu S. Mukherjee, Babak Falsafi, Mark D. Hill, and David A. Wood. Coherent Network Interface for Fine-Grain Communication. In *Proceedings of the 23rd Annual International Symposium on Computer Architecture*, pages 247–258, May 1996.

[32] G. F. Pfister, W. C. Brantley, D. A. George, S. L. Harvey, W. J. Kleinfelder, K. P. McAuliffe, E. A. Melton, V. A. Norton, and J. Weiss. The IBM Research Parallel Processor Prototype (RP3): Introduction and Architecture. In *Proceedings of the 1985 International Conference on Parallel Processing*, pages 764–771, August 1985.

[33] Steven K. Reinhardt, Mark D. Hill, James R. Larus, Alvin R. Lebeck, James C. Lewis, and David A. Wood. The Wisconsin Wind Tunnel: Virtual Prototyping of Parallel Computers. In *Proceedings of the 1993 ACM Sigmetrics Conference on Measurements and Modeling of Computer Systems*, pages 48–60, May 1993.

[34] Steven K. Reinhardt, James L. Larus, and David A. Wood. Tempest and Typhoon: User-Level Shared Memory. In *Proceedings of the 21st Annual International Symposium on Computer Architecture*, pages 24–33, April 1994.

[35] Steven K. Reinhardt, Robert W. Pfile, and David A. Wood. Decoupled Hardware Support for Distributed Shared Memory. In *Proceedings of the 23rd Annual International Symposium on Computer Architecture*, pages 35–44, May 1996.

[36] ROSS Technology, Inc., Austin, TX. *SPARC RISC User's Guide: hyperSPARC Edition*, third edition, September 1993.

[37] Larry Rudolph and Zary Segall. Dynamic Decentralized Cache Schemes for MIMD Parallel Processors. In *Proceedings of the 11th Annual International Symposium on Computer Architecture*, pages 340–347, June 1984.

[38] Daniel J. Scales, Kourosh Gharachorloo, and Chandramohan A. Thekkath. Shasta: A Low Overhead, Software-Only Approach for Supporting Fine-Grain Shared Memory. In *Proceedings of the Seventh Symposium on Architectural Support for Programming Languages and Operating Systems*, pages 174–185, October 1996.

[39] Ioannis Schoinas, Babak Falsafi, Mark D. Hill, James R. Larus, Christopher E. Lukas, Shubhendu S. Mukherjee, Steven K. Reinhardt, Eric Schnarr, and David A. Wood. Implementing Fine-Grain Distributed Shared Memory on Commodity SMP Workstations. Technical Report 1307, UWCS, March 1996.

[40] Ioannis Schoinas, Babak Falsafi, Alvin R. Lebeck, Steven K. Reinhardt, James R. Larus, and David A. Wood. Fine-Grain Access Control for Distributed Shared Memory. In *Proceedings of the Sixth Symposium on Architectural Support for Programming Languages and Operating Systems*, pages 297–306, October 1994.

[41] Steven L. Scott, James R. Goodman, and Mary K. Vernon. Performance of the SCI Ring. In *Proceedings of the 19th Annual International Symposium on Computer Architecture*, pages 403–414, May 1992.

[42] Jaswinder Pal Singh, Wolf-Dietrich Weber, and Anoop Gupta. SPLASH: Stanford Parallel Applications for Shared Memory. *Computer Architecture News*, 20(1):5–44, March 1992.

[43] IEEE Computer Society. Scalable Coherent Interface (SCI). ANSI/IEEE Std 1596-1992, August 1993.

[44] Teruo Utsumi, Masayuki Ikeda, and Moriyuki Takamura. Architecture of the VPP500 Parallel Supercomputer. In *Proceedings of Supercomputing '94*, Washington, D.C., November 1994.

[45] Webster. *Webster's Seventh Dictionary*. 1965.

[46] Steven Cameron Woo, Moriyoshi Ohara, Evan Torrie, Jaswinder Pal Singh, and Anoop Gupta. The SPLASH-2 Programs: Characterization and Methodological Considerations. In *Proceedings of the 22nd Annual International Symposium on Computer Architecture*, pages 24–36, June 1995.

Dynamic Speculation and Synchronization of Data Dependences

Andreas Moshovos, Scott E. Breach, T. N. Vijaykumar, Gurindar S. Sohi
Computer Sciences Department
University of Wisconsin-Madison
1210 West Dayton St.
Madison, WI 53706
{moshovos, breach, vijay, sohi}@cs.wisc.edu

Abstract

Data dependence speculation is used in instruction-level parallel (ILP) processors to allow early execution of an instruction before a logically preceding instruction on which it may be data dependent. If the instruction is independent, data dependence speculation succeeds; if not, it fails, and the two instructions must be synchronized. The modern dynamically scheduled processors that use data dependence speculation do so blindly (i.e., every load instruction with unresolved dependences is speculated). In this paper, we demonstrate that as dynamic instruction windows get larger, significant performance benefits can result when intelligent decisions about data dependence speculation are made. We propose dynamic data dependence speculation techniques: (i) to predict if the execution of an instruction is likely to result in a data dependence mis-speculation, and (ii) to provide the synchronization needed to avoid a mis-speculation. Experimental results evaluating the effectiveness of the proposed techniques are presented within the context of a Multiscalar processor.

1 Introduction

Speculative execution is an integral part of modern ILP processors, be they statically- or dynamically-scheduled designs. Speculation may take two forms: control speculation and data speculation. Control speculation implies the execution of an instruction before the execution of a preceding instruction on which it is control dependent. Data speculation implies the execution of an instruction before the execution of a preceding instruction on which it *may be* or *is* data dependent.

To date, much attention has been focused on control speculation. This outlook is natural because control speculation is the first step. Control speculation (or some equivalent basic block enlargement technique such as if-conversion with predicated execution) is required if we want to consider instructions from more than one basic block for possible issue. Given the sizes of basic blocks, the need to go beyond a basic block became apparent some time ago, and several techniques to permit control speculation were developed, both in the context of statically- and dynamically-scheduled machine models. Improving the accuracy of control speculation (especially dynamic techniques) via the use of better branch prediction has been the subject of intensive research recently; a plethora of papers on dynamic and static branch prediction techniques have been published.

Data speculation has not received as much attention as control speculation. The two forms of data speculation that have received some attention are data value speculation and data dependence speculation. In data value speculation an attempt is made to predict the data value that an instruction is going to produce [15,19]. In data dependence speculation, no explicit attempt is made to predict data values. Instead, a prediction is made on whether the input data value of an instruction has been generated and stored in the corresponding named location (memory or register).

Most of the research on data dependence speculation has focused on ensuring correct execution while carrying out this form of speculation [8,9,10,18] and on static dependence analysis techniques [1,2,5,6,21]. So far, no attention has been given to dynamic techniques to improve the accuracy of data dependence speculation. This is because in the small instruction window sizes of modern dynamically scheduled processors [12,11,14], the probability of a mis-speculation is small, and furthermore, the net performance loss that is due to erroneous data dependence speculation is small.

In this paper, we argue that as dynamically-scheduled ILP processors are able to establish wider instruction windows, the net performance loss due to erroneous speculation can become significant. Accordingly, we are concerned with dynamic techniques for improving the accuracy of data dependence speculation while maintaining the performance benefits of aggressive speculation. We propose techniques that attempt: (i) to predict those instructions whose immediate execution is going to violate a true data dependence, and (ii) to delay the execution of those instructions only as long as is necessary to avoid the mis-speculation. A preliminary evaluation of the ideas presented in this paper was first reported in [17].

The rest of this paper is organized as follows: First, in section 2 we review data dependence speculation and discuss how it affects ILP execution. Then in section 3, we discuss the components of a method for accurate and aggressive memory data dependence speculation, while in section 4, we present an implementation framework for this method. In section 5, we provide experimental data on the dynamic behavior of memory dependences and present an evaluation of an implementation of the method we propose within the context of a Multiscalar processor [3,4,7,20]. Finally, in section 6 we list what, in our opinion, are the contributions of this work and offer concluding remarks. In the discussion that follows we are concerned with data dependence speculation; accordingly, we use the terms data dependence speculation, data speculation, and speculation interchangeably.

2 Data Dependence Speculation

Programs are written with an implied, total order. As a program executes, data values are produced and consumed by its instructions. These values are conveyed from the producer to the consumer by binding the value to a named storage location, namely registers and memory.

An ILP or other parallel machine, takes a suitable subset of the instructions (an instruction window) of a program and converts the total order within this subset into a partial order. This is done so that instructions may execute in parallel and/or in an execution order that might be different from the total order. The shape of the

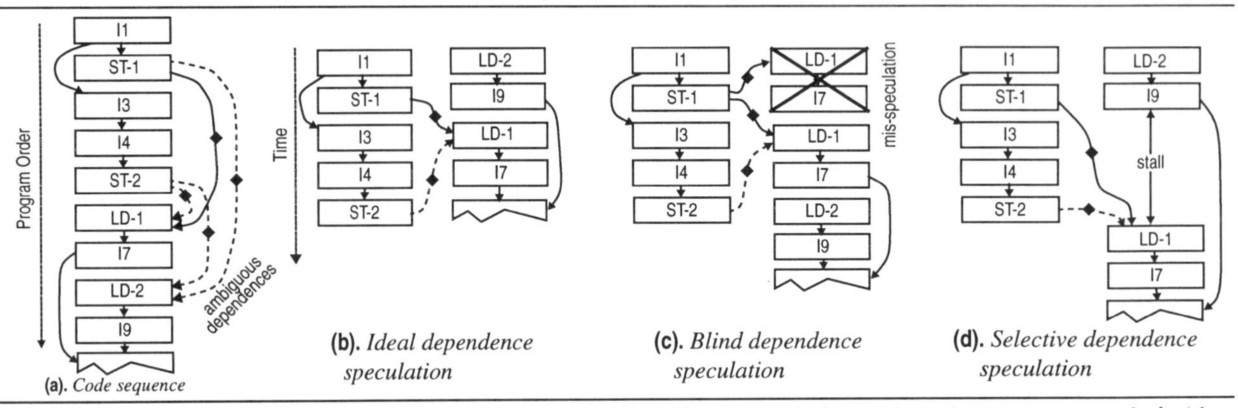

Figure 1. *Data dependence speculation examples. Arrows indicate dependences. Dependences through memory are marked with diamonds. Dotted arrows indicate ambiguous dependences that are resolved to no dependence during execution.*

partial order and the parallelism so obtained are heavily influenced by the dependences that exist between the instructions in the total order. Dependences may be unambiguous (i.e., an instruction consumes a value that is known to be created by an instruction preceding it in the total order) or ambiguous (i.e., an instruction consumes a value that may be produced by an instruction preceding it in the total order). During execution, an ambiguous dependence gets resolved to either a true dependence, or to no dependence.

To maintain program semantics, a producer/consumer instruction pair that is linked via a true dependence has to be executed in the order implied by the program. However, any execution order is permissible if the two instructions are linked via an ambiguous dependence that gets resolved to no dependence. This latter case represents an opportunity for parallelism and hence for higher performance. Unfortunately, the mere classification of a dependence as ambiguous implies the inability to determine whether a true dependence exists without actually executing the program. It is for this reason that ambiguous dependences may obscure some of the parallelism that is available. This problem is most acute in the case where the production and consumption of data is through memory. Thus, in this paper, we restrict our discussion to memory dependences even though all the concepts we present could easily be applied to the speculation of register dependences.

To expose the parallelism that is hindered by ambiguous dependences, data dependence speculation may be used. In data dependence speculation, a load is allowed to execute before a store on which it is ambiguously dependent. If no true dependence is violated in the resulting execution, the speculation is successful. If, however, a true dependence is violated, the speculation is erroneous (i.e., a mis-speculation). In the latter case, the effects of the speculation must be undone. Consequently, some means are required for detecting erroneous speculation and for ensuring correct behavior. Several mechanisms that provide this functionality, in either software and/or hardware, have been proposed [7,8,9,10,16,18].

Though data dependence speculation may improve performance when it is successful, it may as well lead to performance degradation because a penalty is typically incurred on mis-speculation. Consequently, to gain the most out of data dependence speculation we would like to use it as aggressively as possible while keeping the net cost of mis-speculation as low as possible.

The modern dynamically-scheduled processors that use data dependence speculation [11,12,14] do so blindly (i.e., a load is speculated whenever possible). No explicit attempt is made to reduce the net cost of mis-speculation. The reasons are simply that, in this environment, mis-speculations are extremely infrequent, and the cost incurred on mis-speculation is low. Both phenomena are directly attributable to the window sizes that these processors can establish (these are limited to a few tens of instructions in the best case). As window sizes grow larger, however, we argue that minimizing the net cost of mis-speculation becomes important. Under these new conditions, the mis-speculations become more frequent, and the cost of mis-speculations becomes relatively high.

To minimize the net cost of mis-speculation, while maintaining the performance benefits of speculation, we may attempt: (i) to minimize the amount of work that is lost on mis-speculation, (ii) to reduce the time required to redo the work that is lost on mis-speculation[1], or (iii) to reduce the probability of mis-speculation (or, in other words, to reduce the absolute number of mis-speculations). In this work we pursue the third alternative. We elaborate on this in the next section.

3 Components of a Solution

The ideal data dependence speculation mechanism not only avoids mis-speculations completely, but also allows loads to execute as early as possible. That is, loads with no true dependences (within the instruction window) execute without delay, whereas loads that have true dependences are allowed to execute only after the store (or the stores) that produces the necessary data has executed. Equivalently, loads with true dependences are synchronized with the store (or the stores) they depend upon. It is implied that the ideal data dependence speculation mechanism has perfect knowledge of all the relevant data dependences.

An example of how the ideal dependence speculation mechanism affects execution is shown in figure 1. In part (b), we show how the code sequence of part (a) may execute under ideal data dependence speculation as compared to when speculation is used blindly, part (c). The example code sequence includes two store instructions, *ST-1* and *ST-2*, that are followed by two load instructions, *LD-1* and *LD-2*. Ambiguous dependences exist among these four instructions as indicated by the diamond marked arrows. During execution, however, only the dependence between *ST-1* and *LD-1* is resolved to a true dependence (as indicated by the continuous arrow). Under ideal dependence speculation, *LD-2* is executed without delay, whereas *LD-1* is forced to synchronize with *ST-1*.

In contrast to what is ideally possible, in a real implementation, the relevant data dependences are often unknown. Therefore, if we are to mimic the ideal data dependence speculation mechanism, we have to attempt: (i) to predict whether the immediate execution

1. One such technique is Dynamic Instruction Reuse [19].

of a load is likely to violate a true data dependence, and if so, (ii) to predict the store (or stores) the load depends upon, and, (iii) to enforce synchronization between the dependent instructions. However, since this scheme seems elaborate, it is only natural to attempt to simplify it. One possible simplification is to use *selective* data dependence speculation, i.e., carry out only the first part of the (ideal) 3-part operation. In this scheme the loads that are likely to cause mis-speculation are not speculated. Instead, they wait until the data addresses of all preceding stores, that have not yet executed, are known to be different; explicit synchronization is not performed. (We use the term *selective data dependence speculation* to signify that we make a decision on whether a load should be speculated or not. Loads with dependences are not speculated at all, whereas loads with no dependences can execute freely. In contrast, in ideal dependence speculation, we make a decision on when is the right time to speculate a load.) An example of how selective speculation may affect execution is shown in part (d) of figure 1. In this example, *LD-2* is speculated, whereas *LD-1* is not, since the prediction correctly indicates that *LD-2* has no true dependences while *LD-1* does. However, with this scheme, and due to the lack of explicit synchronization, a load may be delayed more than necessary (*LD-1* waits for *ST-2* also). In practice, and as we demonstrate in the evaluation section, selective data dependence speculation can lead to inferior performance when compared to blind speculation (part (c) of figure 1) even when perfect prediction of dependences is assumed. Even though other simplifications to the 3-part ideal operation may be possible, in this paper we restrict our attention to dependence speculation schemes that attempt to mimic the ideal data dependence speculation system. We do so because our primary goal is to demonstrate the potential of dynamic dependence speculation and synchronization mechanisms, rather than to perform a thorough evaluation of a variety of mechanisms.

To mimic the ideal data dependence speculation system, we need to implement all the 3 components of the ideal system as described before. That is, we must: (i) dynamically identify the store-load pairs that are likely to be data dependent (i.e., the dependences that are likely to cause mis-speculation), (ii) assign a synchronization mechanism to dynamic instances of these dependences, and (iii) use this mechanism to synchronize the store and the load instructions.

Dynamically tracking all possible ambiguous store-load pairs is not an option that we consider desirable, or even practical. Fortunately, our empirical observations suggest that the following phenomena exists: *the static store-load instruction pairs that cause most of the dynamic data mis-speculations are relatively few and exhibit temporal locality* (we present empirical evidence in section 5). That is, at any given time, different dynamic instances of a few static store-load pairs, either operating repeatedly on the same memory location (scalar variable) or operating on different memory locations, account for the majority of the mis-speculations. This observation suggests that we may use past history to dynamically identify and track such store-load pairs, and cache this information in a storage structure of reasonable size. The remaining issue is by what means to synchronize the store-load pair.

An apt method of providing the required synchronization dynamically is to build an association between the store-load instruction pair. Suppose this (dynamic) association is a condition variable on which only two operations are defined: *wait* and *signal*, which test and set the condition variable respectively. These operations may be logically incorporated into the dynamic actions of the (dependent) load and store instructions to achieve the necessary synchronization.

The above concept is illustrated in the example of figure 2

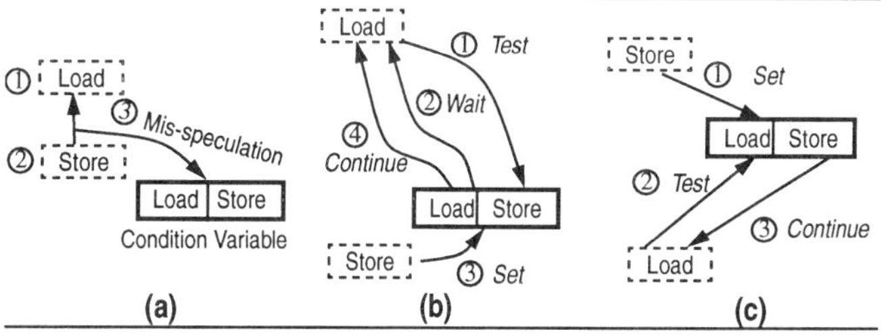

Figure 2. *Synchronization example*

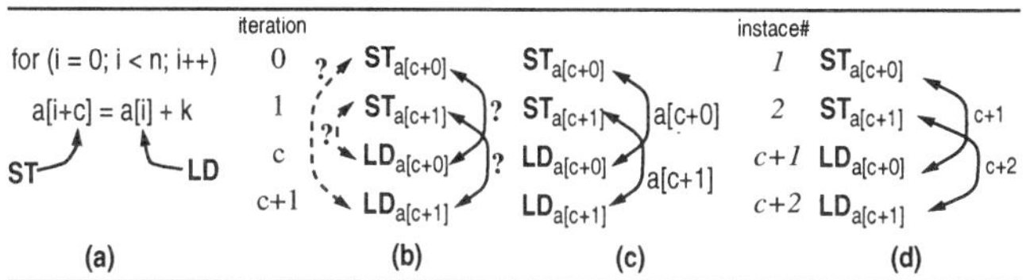

Figure 3. *Example code sequence that illustrates that multiple instances of the same static dependence can be active in the current instruction window. In parts (b), (c), and (d), the relevant store and load instructions from four iterations of the loop of part (a) are shown.*

where we assume that some means exist to dynamically associate store-load instruction pairs with condition variables (we discuss these means later in this section). As shown in part (a), an earlier mis-speculation results in the association of a condition variable with a subsequent dynamic instance of the offending store-load instruction pair. With the condition variable in place, consider the sequence of events in the two possible execution sequences of the load and store instructions. In part (b), the load is ready to execute before the store. However, before the load executes, it tests the condition variable; since the test of the condition variable fails, the load waits. After the store executes, it sets the condition variable and signals the waiting load, which subsequently continues its execution as shown. No mis-speculation is observed, and the sequential order is preserved. In part (c), the order of execution is a store followed by a load. After the stores executes, it sets the condition variable and records a signal for the load. Before the load executes, it tests the condition variable; since the test of the condition variable succeeds, the load continues its execution as shown (the condition variable is reset at this point). One may wonder why synchronization is provided even when the execution order follows the program order (i.e., store followed by load). This scenario represents the case where the dependence prediction correctly indicates that a dependence exists but fails to detect that the order of execution has changed (most likely in response to external events whose behavior is not easy or desirable to track and predict, such as cache misses or resource conflicts). Synchronization is desirable even in this case since, otherwise, the load will be delayed unnecessarily.

Once condition variables are provided, some means are required to assign a condition variable to a dynamic instance of a store-load instruction pair that has to be synchronized. If synchronization is to occur as planned, the mapping of condition variables to dynamic dependences has to be unique at any given point of time. One approach is to use just the address of the memory location accessed by the store-load pair as a handle. This method provides an indirect means of identifying the store and load instructions that are to be synchronized. Unless the store location is accessed only by the corresponding store-load pair, the assignment will not be unique.

Alternatively, we can use the dependence edge as a handle. The dependence edge may be specified using the (full or part of) instruction addresses (PCs) of the store-load pair in question. Unfortunately, as exemplified by the code sequence of figure 3 part (b), using this information may not be sufficient to capture the actual behavior of the dependence during execution; the pair (PC_{ST}, PC_{LD}) matches against all four edges shown even though the dotted ones should not be synchronized. A static dependence between a given store-load pair may correspond to multiple dynamic dependences, which need to be tracked simultaneously.

To distinguish between the different dynamic instances of the same static dependence edge, a tag (preferably unique) could be assigned to each instance. This tag, in addition to the instruction addresses of the store-load pair, can be used to specify the dynamic dependence edge. In order to be of practical use, the tag must be derived from information available during execution of the corresponding instructions. A possible source of the tag for the dependent store and load instructions is the data address of the memory location to be accessed, as shown in figure 3 part (c). An alternate way of generating instance tags is shown in figure 3 part (d), where dynamic store and load instruction instances are numbered based on their PCs[2]. The difference in the instance numbers of the instructions which are dependent, referred to as the *dependence distance*, may be used to tag dynamic instances of the static dependence edge[3] (as may be seen for the example code, a dependence edge between ST_i and $LD_{i+distance}$ is tagged - in addition to the instruction PCs - with the value i+distance). Though both tagging schemes strive to provide unique tags, each may fall short of this goal under some circumstances (for example, the dependence distance may change in a way that we fail to predict, or the address accessed may remain constant across all instances of the same dependence).

Since, our primary goal in this paper, is to introduce and evaluate novel mechanisms (and not to carry out a thorough analysis of a variety of options), we restrict our attention to the second scheme where the dependence distance is used to tag dependences.

4 Implementation Aspects

As we discussed in the previous section, in order to improve the accuracy of data dependence speculation, we attempt: (i) to predict dynamically, based on the history of mis-speculations, whether a store-load pair is likely to be mis-speculated and if so, (ii) to synchronize the two instructions. In this section, we describe an implementation framework for this technique. We partition the support structures into two interdependent tables: a *memory dependence prediction table* (MDPT) and a *memory dependence synchronization table* (MDST). The MDPT is used to identify, through prediction, those instruction pairs that ought to be synchronized. The MDST provides a dynamic pool of condition variables and the mechanisms necessary to associate them with dynamic store-load instruction pairs to be synchronized. In the discussion that follows, we first describe the support structures and then proceed to explain their operation by means of an example.

We present the support structures as separate, distinct components of the processor. We do so, since we believe that the crux of the proposed technique is better described when the support structures are considered in this fashion. However, it is possible and probably desirable in an actual implementation, to combine the prediction and the synchronization structures and/or to integrate them with other components of the processor. For example, a simple extension is to provide the synchronization functionality in the data cache or some other similar storage structure, so that both the data and the necessary synchronization are provided at the same point. Later in this paper, we describe the implementation of a single structure that provides both dependence prediction and synchronization and discuss its advantages and its limitations. However, since our goal is to demonstrate the utility of the proposed technique, we do not consider further integration or any other implementations.

4.1 MDPT

An entry of the MDPT identifies a static dependence and provides a prediction as to whether or not subsequent dynamic instances of the corresponding static store-load pair will result in a mis-speculation (i.e., should the store and load instructions be synchronized). In particular, each entry of the MDPT consists of the following fields: (1) valid flag (V), (2) load instruction address (LDPC), (3) store instruction address (STPC), (4) dependence distance (DIST), and (5) optional prediction (not shown in any of the working examples). The valid flag indicates if the entry is currently in use. The load and store instruction address fields hold the program counter values of a pair of load and store instructions. This combination of fields uniquely identifies the static instruction pair for which it has been allocated. The dependence distance records the difference of the instance numbers of the store and load instructions whose mis-speculation caused the allocation of the entry (if we were to use the data address to tag dependence instances this field would not have been necessary). The purpose of the prediction field is to capture, in a reasonable way, the past behavior of mis-speculations for the instruction pair in order to aid in avoiding future mis-speculations or unnecessary delays. Many options are possible for the prediction field (for example an up-down counter or dependence history based schemes); a discussion is postponed until later in this section. The prediction field is optional since, if omitted, we can always predict that synchronization should take place.

4.2 MDST

An entry of the MDST supplies a condition variable and the mechanism necessary to synchronize a dynamic instance of a static instruction pair (as predicted by the MDPT). In particular, each entry of the MDST consists of the following fields: (1) valid flag (V), (2) load instruction address (LDPC), (3) store instruction address (STPC), (4) load identifier (LDID), (5) store identifier (STID), (6) instance tag (INSTANCE), and (7) full/empty flag (F/E). The valid flag indicates whether the entry is, or is not, in use. The load and store instruction address fields serve the same purpose as in the MDPT. The load and store identifiers have to uniquely identify, within the current instruction window, a dynamic instance of a load or a store instruction respectively. The exact encoding of this field depends on the implementation of the OoO (out-of-order) execution engine (for example, in a superscalar machine that uses reservation stations we can use the index of the reservation station that holds the instruction as its LDID or STID). The instance tag field is used to distinguish between different dynamic instances of the same static dependence edge (in the working example that follows we show how to derive the value for this field). The full/empty flag provides the function of a condition variable.

2. At this point we are not concerned with mechanisms that implement this functionality. However, note that only the difference between the instance numbers is relevant and not the absolute values. As we explain in the evaluation section, in Multiscalar we can approximate the instance numbers by using statically assigned stage identifiers. In a superscalar environment we may use a small associative pool of counters. Load and store instructions can then be numbered based on their PC as they are issued. To support invalidations due to mis-speculation, these counters will have to be treated as registers. Alternatively, a load (store) that has to synchronize, may perform a backward (forward) scan through the instruction window attempting to locate the appropriate store (load) instruction.

3. To aid understanding, this scheme can be viewed as a dynamic, run-time implementation of the linear recurrence dependence analysis done by compilers.

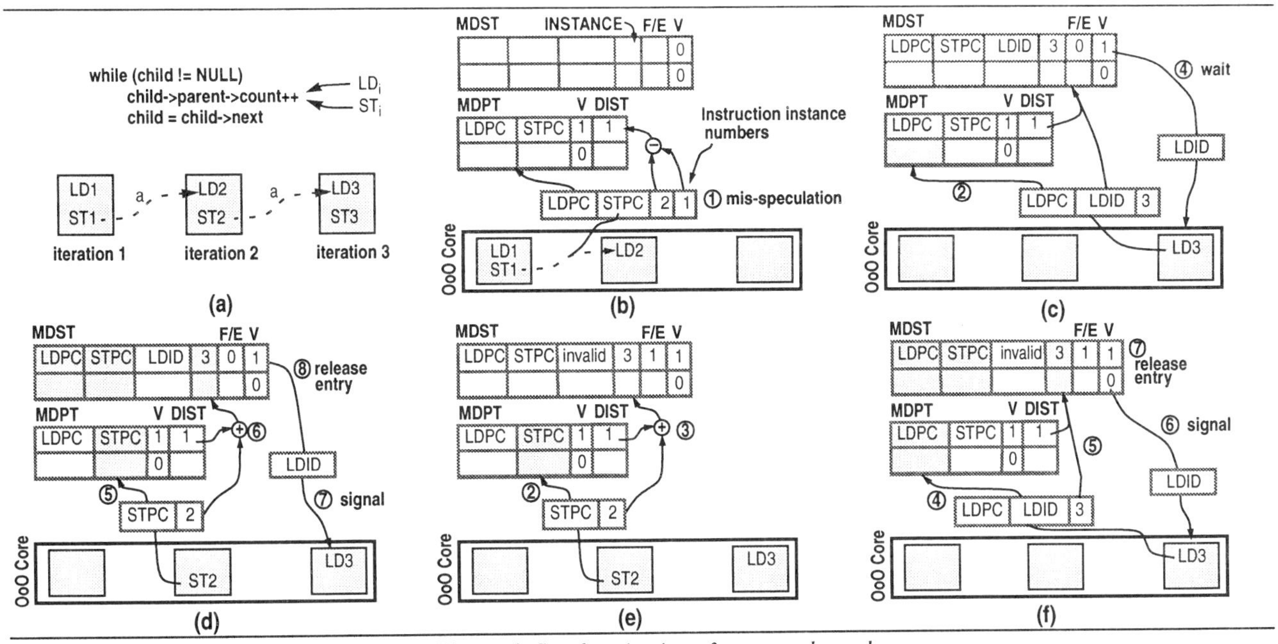

Figure 4. *Synchronization of memory dependences.*

4.3 Working Example

The exact function and use of the fields in the MDPT and the MDST are best understood by means of an example. In the discussion that follows we are using the working example of figure 4. For the working example, assume that execution takes place on a processor which: (i) issues multiple memory accesses per cycle from a pool of load and store instructions and (ii) provides a mechanism to detect and correct mis-speculations due to memory dependence speculation. For the sake of clarity, we assume that once an entry is allocated in the MDPT it will always cause a synchronization to be predicted.

Consider the memory operations for three iterations of the loop, which constitute the active pool of load and store instructions as shown in part (a) of the figure. Further, assume that *child->parent* points to the same memory location for all values *child* takes. The dynamic instances of the load and store instructions are shown numbered, and the true dependences are indicated as dashed arrows connecting the corresponding instructions in part (a). The sequence of events that leads to the synchronization of the ST2-LD3 dependence is shown in parts (b) through (d) of the figure. Initially, both tables are empty. As soon as a mis-speculation (ST1-LD2 dependence) is detected, a MDPT entry is allocated, and the addresses of the load and the store instructions are recorded (action 1, part (b)). The DIST field of the newly allocated entry is set to 1, which is the difference of the instance numbers of ST1 and LD2 (1 and 2 respectively). As a result of the mis-speculation, instructions following the load are squashed and must be re-issued. We do not show the re-execution of LD2.

As execution continues, assume that the address of LD3 is calculated before the address of ST2. At this point, LD3 may speculatively access the memory hierarchy. Before LD3 is allowed to do so, its instruction address, its instance number (which is 3), and its assigned load identifier (the exact value of LDID is immaterial) are sent to the MDPT (action 2, part (c)). The instruction address of LD3 is matched against the contents of all load instruction address fields of the MDPT (shown in grey). Since a match is found, the MDPT inspects the entry predictor to determine if a synchronization is warranted. Assuming the predictor indicates a synchronization, the MDPT allocates an entry in the MDST using the load instruction address, the store instruction address, the instance number of LD3, and the LDID assigned to LD3 by the OoO core (action 3, part (c)). At the same time, the full/empty flag of the newly allocated entry is set to empty. Finally, the MDST returns the load identifier to the load/store pool indicating that the load must wait (action 4, part (c)).

When ST2 is ready to access the memory hierarchy, its instruction address and its instance number (which is 2) are sent to the MDPT (action 5, part (d)). (We do not show the STID since, as we later explain, it is only needed to support control speculation.) The instruction address of ST2 is matched against the contents of all store instruction address fields of the MDPT (shown in grey). Since a match is found, the MDPT inspects the contents of the entry and initiates a synchronization in the MDST. As a result, the MDPT adds the contents of the DIST field to the instance number of the store (that is, 2 + 1) to determine the instance number of the load that should be synchronized. It then uses this result, in combination with the load instruction address and the store instruction address, to search through the MDST (action 6, part (d)), where it finds the allocated synchronization entry. Consequently, the full/empty field is set to full, and the MDST returns the load identifier to the load/store pool to signal the waiting load (action 7, part (d)). At this point, LD3 is free to continue execution. Furthermore, since the synchronization is complete, the entry in the MDST is not needed and may be freed (action 8, part (d)).

If ST2 accesses the memory hierarchy before LD3, it is unnecessary for LD3 to be delayed. Accordingly, the synchronization scheme allows LD3 to issue and execute without any delays. Consider the sequence of relevant events shown in parts (e) and (f) of figure 4. When ST2 is ready to access the memory hierarchy, it passes through the MDPT as before with a match found (action 2, part (e)). Since a match is found, the MDPT inspects the contents of the entry and initiates a synchronization in the MDST. However, no matching entry is found there since LD3 has yet to be seen. Consequently, a new entry is allocated, and its full/empty flag is set to full (action 3, part (e)). Later, when LD3 is ready to access the memory hierarchy, it passes through the MDPT and determines that a synchronization is warranted as before (action 4, part (f)). The MDPT searches the MDST, where it now finds an allocated entry with the full/empty flag set to full (action 5, part (f)). At this point, the MDST returns the load identifier to the load/store pool so the load may continue execution immediately (action 6, part (f)). It also frees the MDST entry (action 7, part (f)).

4.4 Issues

We now discuss a few issues which relate to the implementation we have described.

4.4.1 Intelligent Prediction

Upon matching a MDPT entry, a determination must be made as to whether the instruction pair in question warrants synchronization. The simplest approach is to assume that any matching entry ought to be synchronized (i.e., the predictor field is optional). However, this approach may lead to unnecessary delays in cases where the store-load instruction pairs are mis-speculated only some of the time. Instead, a more intelligent approach may be effective. Any of the plethora of known methods (counters, voting schemes, adaptive predictors, etc.) used to provide the intelligent prediction of control dependences may be applied, with appropriate modifications, to the prediction of data dependences. Regardless of the actual choice of mechanism, the prediction method ought to exhibit the quality that it strengthens the prediction when speculation succeeds and weakens the prediction when speculation fails.

4.4.2 Incomplete Synchronization

So far, it has been assumed that any load, that waits on the full/empty flag of an entry in the MDST, eventually sees a matching store that signals to complete the synchronization. Since an MDPT entry only provides a prediction, this expectation may not always be fulfilled. If this situation arises, the two main considerations are: (i) to avoid deadlock and (ii) to free the MDST entry allocated for a synchronization that will never occur. The deadlock problem is easily solved, as it is reasonable to assume that a load is always free to execute once all prior stores are known to have executed. At that point, the load identifier has to be send to the MDST where it is used to free the entry that was allocated for the particular load.The information recorded in the MDST entry can then be used to locate update the corresponding prediction entry in the MDPT

Under similar circumstances to those described above, a store may allocate an MDST entry for which no matching load is ever seen. Since stores never delay their execution, there is no deadlock problem in this case. However, it is still necessary to eventually free the MDST entry. Unfortunately, we cannot de-allocate this entry when the store retires (recall that in section 3 we explained that we would like to synchronize a store-load pair when the prediction indicates that we should, even if the execution order does not violate the dependence). A possible solution is to free entries whose full/empty flag is set to full whenever an entry is needed and no table entries are not in use. Another possible solution is to allocate entries using random or LRU replacement, in which case entries are freed as needed.

4.4.3 Mis-speculations

In the event of control or data mis-speculation, it is desirable, although not necessary, to invalidate any MDST entries that were allocated to the instructions that are squashed. The LDID and the STID fields can be used to identify the entries that have to be invalidated.

Typically, many instructions continuous in the program order, are invalidated when a mis-speculation occurs. Thus, we may have to invalidate multiple MDST entries on mis-speculation. Fortunately, the MDST has to be notified only of those instructions that have entries allocated to them, which are typically going to be few. To support multiple invalidations per cycle, several options exist such as (i) providing multiple ports to the STID and LDID tags, or (ii) using a suitable encoding of the STID and LDID tags that would allow for the invalidation of a range of instructions. For example, we can use as many bits as the maximum number of simultaneously, unresolved control transfer instructions allowed. This encoding allows us to invalidate at a basic block granularity with an associative lookup.

4.4.4 Multiple Table Entry Matches

Although not illustrated in the examples, it is possible for a load or a store to match multiple entries of the MDPT and/or of the MDST. This case represents multiple memory dependences involving the same static load and/or store instructions (for example in the code *if (cond)* $store_1$ *M else* $store_2$ *M; load M*, there are two dependences *(*$store_1$*, load)* and *(*$store_2$*, load)*). There are several ways of addressing this issue.

A straightforward approach is to ensure, by means of the replacement and allocation policies, that a unique mapping with respect to both loads and stores is maintained in the tables. For example, in the MDPT we may allow a new entry to be created only after any pre-existing entries for the same static load or store are de-allocated. To maintain a unique mapping in the MDST, we may force a load or a store to stall and retry if there is another entry for either of the instructions that have to synchronize (alternatively we may de-allocate the pre-existing entry). This approach is acceptable when: (i) multiple dependences per static load and store are relatively uncommon or (ii) when the dynamic dependence pattern consists of long series during which only one of the many dependences is active for the most part. In both cases, the adaptive nature of the prediction mechanism is likely to discard all but the most frequent mis-speculations. If multiple dependences are relatively common, a more aggressive approach that evaluates multiple entries simultaneously is expedient. One approach is to support multiple stores per load or vice versa. This can be achieved by modifying the entries MDPT and MDST to include multiple fields for store PCs per load (or the other way around).

If multiple dependences are to be fully supported within the implementation framework we presented in this section, the following considerations must be addressed: (i) when multiple dependences are predicted from the MDPT, how to allocate multiple entries, one per predicted dependence, in the MDST, (ii) when synchronization happens on an MDST entry, how to determine whether the particular load has other entries it has to wait for, and (iii) when a store synchronizes simultaneously with many loads in the MDST, how to go about sending all the LDIDs. Again several options exist. For the purposes of this paper, we address all three considerations by combining the two tables into a single structure where each prediction entry carries with it a predefined number of synchronization entries (note that in this organization, the PCs of the instructions need not be recorded in each synchronization entry). We next explain how this organization addresses the aforementioned issues. Allocating multiple synchronization entries, each for a different prediction entry, is straightforward since the prediction and synchronization entries are now physically adjacent. To determine whether a load has other synchronization entries when a synchronization occurs, we do a second associative lookup using the load's LDID. If no other entries are found the load is allowed to continue execution. Finally, when multiple loads are simultaneously synchronized, we allow only up to a predefined number of them to do so at any given cycle (selecting the loads to wake up among those that have been signalled is no different than selecting the instructions to execute from those that are ready in an OoO processor).

4.4.5 Centralized Versus Distributed Structures

So far it has been assumed that the MDPT and the MDST are

centralized structures. However, as greater levels of instruction-level parallelism are exploited, greater numbers of concurrent memory accesses must be sustained. Under such conditions, the support structures are likely to play a key role in execution. As a consequence, it is important to assure that neither structure becomes a bottleneck. The most straightforward way to meet this demand is to multi-port the tables. While such an approach provides the needed bandwidth, its access latency and area grow quickly as the number of ports is increased. It is also possible to divide the table entries into banks indexed by the load and store instruction addresses. This solution is likely to be inadequate since temporal and spatial locality in instruction reference patterns may cause many conflicting bank accesses.

An alternative approach is to actually distribute the structures, with identical copies of the MDPT and the MDST provided at each source of memory accesses (assuming multiple load/store queues, multiple load/store reservation stations, etc.). Each source of memory accesses need only use its local copy of the two tables most of the time. As soon as a mis-speculation is detected, this fact is broadcast to all copies of the MDPT, causing an entry to be allocated in each copy as needed. A load instruction uses both tables in the same manner as described earlier. A store instruction, on the other hand, behaves somewhat differently. In the event a match for a store is found in a local MDPT, all identifying information for the entry is broadcast to all copies of the MDST. Each copy of the MDST searches its entries to find any allocated synchronization entry. The outcomes with respect to whether a match is or is not found are similar to those described earlier. In addition, any prediction update to an entry of a local MDPT must be broadcast in order to maintain a similar view among all of the copies of this table.

5 Experimental Evaluation

In this section we present experimental evidence in support of our observations on the dynamic behavior of memory dependences, and we evaluate the utility of the mechanism we proposed in the previous section. To do so, we require a processing model where dynamic data dependence speculation is heavily used and where the dynamic window size is relatively large. One processing model that satisfies both requirements is the Multiscalar processing model [7, 20]. Accordingly, we use various configurations of Multiscalar processors for most of the experiments we perform. However, for some of our experiments we use an unrealistic OoO execution model. We do so in order to demonstrate that our observations on the dynamic behavior of memory dependences are not specific to the Multiscalar processing model.

The unrealistic OoO execution model we use corresponds to a processor that is capable of establishing a perfect, continuous window of a given size. Under this model and for a window size of n, a load is always mis-speculated if a preceding store, on which it is data dependent, appears within less than n instructions apart in the sequential execution order. This model represents the worst case scenario with respect to the number of mis-speculations that can be observed at run-time since it assumes that every dependence that is visible from within the given instruction window is mis-speculated. We use this model not only to show that our observations about the dynamic behavior of memory dependences hold even under these extreme conditions, but also, to provide some insight on how the number of possible mis-speculations and dependences varies as a function of the dynamic window size.

To demonstrate the utility of the proposed mechanisms, we simulate various configurations of a Multiscalar processors. A Multiscalar processor relies on a combination of hardware and software to extract parallelism from ordinary (sequential) programs. In this model of execution, the control flow graph (CFG) of a sequential program is partitioned into portions called tasks. These tasks may be control and data dependent. A Multiscalar processor sequences through the CFG speculatively, a task at a time, without pausing to inspect any of the instructions within a task. A task is assigned to one of a collection of processing units for execution by passing the initial program counter of the task. Multiple tasks execute in parallel on the processing units, resulting in an aggregate execution rate of multiple instructions per cycle. In this organization, the instruction window is bounded by the first instruction in the earliest executing task and the last instruction in the latest executing task. More details of the Multiscalar model can be found in [3,4,7,8,20].

In a Multiscalar processor, dependences may be characterized as *intra-task* (within a task) or *inter-task* (between individual tasks). The results herein are all simulated executions in which intra-task memory data dependences are not speculated, but inter-task memory data dependences are freely speculated. That is, mis-speculations may only occur for store-load instruction pairs whose dependence edge crosses dynamic task boundaries. Furthermore, the results reflect execution with no compiler supported disambiguation of these memory dependences. This detail implies that even in cases where an unambiguous memory dependence exists, it is treated no differently than an ambiguous memory dependence during execution. At first glance, the reader may be tempted to conclude that the results of this section are not very useful since many dependences could be classified as unambiguous, even with a rudimentary compiler. However, this conclusion is not necessarily correct, and we elaborate on this next.

The goal of any OoO execution processor, be it superscalar or Multiscalar, is to execute a sequential program in parallel. In doing so, any processor of this kind, dynamically converts the sequential program order into a parallel execution order. In this environment, the only condition that prevents the OoO execution of two instructions is the existence of a dependence that the OoO execution engine can detect without executing the instructions. This implies that even if the compiler knows that a particular memory dependence exists, nothing prevents the dynamic speculation of the corresponding load instruction. Consequently, to prevent the speculation of a dependence, the compiler has to identify by some means (for example through ISA extensions) that a load should not be speculated immediately and to enforce synchronization between unambiguously-dependent instructions (perhaps by using signal and wait operations on compiler generated synchronization variables or via full/empty bits). This is not a trivial task and futhermore, a program in which synchronization has been inserted is not a sequential program any more.

5.1 Methodology

The results we present have been collected on a simulator that faithfully represents a Multiscalar processor. The simulator accepts annotated big endian MIPS instruction set binaries (without architected delay slots of any kind) produced by the Multiscalar compiler, a modified version of GNU GCC 2.5.8 compiler (the SPECint95 benchmarks were compiled with the newest Multiscalar compiler which was built on top of GCC 2.7.2). In order to provide results which reflect reality with as much accuracy as possible, the simulator performs all of the operations of a Multiscalar processor and executes all of the program code, except system calls, on a cycle-by-cycle basis. (System calls are handled by trapping to the OS of the simulation host.)

We performed the bulk of our experimentation with programs taken from the SPECint92 benchmark suite (with inputs indicated in parentheses): *compress* (in), *espresso* (ti.in), *gcc* (integrate.i), *sc* (loada1), and *xlisp* (7 queens). However, to demonstrate the utility of the proposed data dependence speculation mechanism, we also report performance results (for one Multiscalar configuration) for the SPECint95 and SPECfp95 suite. However, in order to keep the simulation time of the SPEC95 programs reasonable, we used either the train or the test input data sets (which sometimes are in the order of a few billion instructions). We used the train data set for the following programs: *099.go*, *129.compress*, *132.ijpeg*, *134.perl* (jumble), *147.vortex*, *101.tomcatv*, *110.applu*, *141.apsi*, *145.fpppp*, and *146.wave5*. For *124.m88ksim*, *126.gcc*, *130.li*, *102.swim*, *103.su2cor*, *104.hydro2d*, *107.mgrid*, and *125.turb3d*, we used the test data set. All programs, except 101.tomcatv, 125.turb3d, and 146.wave5, were ran to completion for the input used. Table 1 reports the dynamic, useful (i.e., committed), instruction counts for the corresponding Multiscalar execution. Only one version of a Multiscalar binary is created per benchmark; the same Multiscalar binary is used for all the Multiscalar configurations in these experiments. The Multiscalar binaries are also used by the unrealistic OoO execution model, however in this case, the Multiscalar specific annotations are ignored.

SPECint92		*SPECint95*		*SPECfp95*	
compress	73 M	*099.go*	595 M	*101.tomcatv*	2.8 G
espresso	596 M	*124.m88ksim*	496 M	*102.swim*	776 M
gcc	73 M	*126.gcc*	1.6 G	*103.su2cor*	1.4 G
sc	440 M	*129.compress*	39 M	*104.hydro2d*	1.2 G
xlisp	247. M	*130.li*	1.08 G	*107.mgrid*	5.9 G
		132.ijpeg	1.58 G	*110.applu*	675 M
		134.perl	2.37 G	*125.turb3d*	2.8 G
		147.vortex	3.04 G	*141.apsi*	2.9 G
				145.fpppp	511 M
				146.wave5	2.7 G

Table 1. *Dynamic instruction count per benchmark (committed instructions).*

5.2 Configuration

In this section we give the details of the Multiscalar processor configurations we used in our experimentation. We simulate Multiscalar processor configurations of 4 and 8 processing units (or stages) with a global sequencer to orchestrate task assignment. The sequencer maintains a 1024 entry 2-way set associative cache of task descriptors. The control flow predictor of the sequencer uses the path based scheme described in [13]. The control flow predictor also includes a 64 entry return address stack.

The pipeline structure of a processing unit is a traditional 5 stage pipeline (IF/ID/EX/MEM/WB) which is configured with 2-way, out-of-order issue characteristics. (Thus the peak execution rate of a 4-unit configuration is 8 instructions per cycle). The instructions are executed by a collection of pipelined functional units (2 simple integer FU, 1 complex integer FU, 1 floating point FU, 1 branch FU, and 1 memory FU) according to the class of the particular instruction and with the latencies indicated in table 2. A unidirectional, point-to-point ring connects the processing units to provide a communication path, with a 2 word width and 1 cycle latency between adjacent processing units. All memory requests are handled by a single 4-word, split transaction memory bus. Each memory access requires a 10 cycle access latency for the first 4 words and 1 cycle for each additional 4 words, plus any bus contention.

Each processing unit is configured with 32 kilobytes of 2-way set associative instruction cache in 64 byte blocks. (An instruction cache access returns 4 words in a hit time of 1 cycle, with an additional penalty of 10+3 cycles, plus any bus contention, on a miss.) A crossbar interconnects the processing units to twice as many interleaved data banks. Each data bank is configured as 8 kilobytes

Scalar	*Cycles*	*Scalar*	*Cycles*	*Floating-Point*	*Cycles*
Add/Sub	1	*Store*	1	*Add/Sub SP/DP*	2/2
Shift/Logic	1	*Load*	1	*Multiply SP/DP*	4/5
Multiply	4	*Branch*	1	*Divide SP/DP*	12/18
Divide	12				

Table 2. *Functional Unit Latencies ("SP/DP" stands for "Single/Double precision").*

of direct mapped data cache in 64 byte blocks with a 32 entry address resolution buffer, for a total of 64 kilobytes and 128 kilobytes of banked data storage as well as 256 and 512 address resolution entries for 4-stage and 8-stage Multiscalar processors respectively. (A data bank access returns 1 word in a hit time of 2 cycles, with an additional penalty of 10+3 cycles, plus any bus contention, on a miss.) Both loads and stores are non-blocking.

5.3 Dynamic behavior of memory dependences

As we noted in section 3, the number of mis-speculations increases with the window size. Furthermore, the vast majority of the mis-speculations observed dynamically can be attributed to relatively few static dependences (store-load pairs) that exhibit temporal locality. In this section, we present experimental evidence in support of these observations. To do so, we simulate *data dependence caches*, or *DDCs*, of various sizes. A DDC of size *n*, records the data dependences that caused the *n* most recent mis-speculations. We count two events, hits and misses. These we define as follows: whenever a mis-speculation occurs we search through the DDC using the instruction PCs of the offending store and load instructions. If a matching entry is found, we count a hit, otherwise, we count a miss. A low data dependence cache miss rate implies that the relevant data dependences exhibit temporal locality.

In table 3, we report the number of mis-speculations observed under the unrealistic OoO model for various window sizes (WS column). As it can be seen, moving from a window of 8 instructions to a window of 32 instructions results in a dramatic increase in the number of mis-speculations. It is implied that most of the dynamic dependences are spread across several instructions (which may include many unrelated stores). This observation provides a hint to why selective data dependence speculation (i.e., not speculating the loads with dependences within the current window) may cause performance degradation when compared to blind speculation; when a dependence is spread across several, unrelated stores, it is often the case that it takes more time to wait until all the unrelated stores are resolved than to incur a mis-speculation and re-execute the load and the instructions that follow it.

In table 4, we show the number of static dependences that are responsible for 99.9% of all dynamic mis-speculations. Note that as the window size increases more static dependences are exposed. These newly exposed dependences may be far more frequent than the dependences observed when the window is smaller. This explains, for example, why in *compress* fewer dependences are responsible for the vast majority of mis-speculations when the window increases from 8 to 16 or 8 to 32. Finally, in table 5 we show the miss-rate of DDCs of 32, 128, and 512 entries. As it can be seen, even when all the dynamic dependences (that are visible from within the given instruction window) are mis-speculated, only a few static dependences cause most of the mis-speculations. Furthermore, DDCs of moderate size capture most of these dependences.

For the Multiscalar model we use two configurations, one with four stages and one with eight stages. The number of mis-speculations observed for these configurations are shown in table 6. As it

WS	compress	espresso	gcc	sc	xlisp
8	33	47.45 K	276.08 K	2.99 M	2.03 M
16	857.05 K	1.01 M	602.73 K	6.09 M	5.35 M
32	2.46 M	1.41 M	1.57 M	11.38 M	8.67 M
64	3.74 M	7.25 M	2.51 M	13.73 M	13.85 M
128	4.31 M	10.87 M	3.33 M	26.91 M	19.79 M
256	5.42 M	14.15 M	4.26 M	32.18 M	23.93 M
512	6.05 M	17.19 M	5.02 M	35.59 M	26.66 M

Table 3. *Unrealistic OoO model: Number of dynamic memory dependences observed as a function of window size (WS).*

WS	compress	espresso	gcc	sc	xlisp
8	6	33	255	46	31
16	2	104	704	127	73
32	5	291	1753	250	105
64	9	429	2967	380	167
128	18	848	4446	589	266
256	25	1500	6083	722	333
512	26	2021	8001	851	367

Table 4. *Unrealistic OoO model: number of static dependences responsible for 99.9% of all mis-speculations observed ("WS" stands for "window size").*

WS	CS	compress	espresso	gcc	sc	xlisp
8	32	18.1818	0.1317	2.2430	0.8489	0.0275
8	128	18.1818	0.1194	0.8645	0.0034	0.0027
8	512	18.1818	0.1194	0.1252	0.0034	0.0027
16	32	0.0028	0.3331	18.3372	5.5203	1.5507
16	128	0.0028	0.0190	1.5781	0.0445	0.0026
16	512	0.0028	0.0178	0.7249	0.0043	0.0026
32	32	0.0020	1.9247	33.0022	6.6796	4.8927
32	128	0.0020	0.1128	4.3829	1.7359	0.0033
32	512	0.0020	0.0343	1.0176	0.0045	0.0028
64	32	0.0034	2.3540	44.4893	11.1012	19.7762
64	128	0.0023	0.2453	10.5860	3.3251	0.1762
64	512	0.0023	0.0142	1.2652	0.0062	0.0028
128	32	0.0269	17.3775	52.1914	21.5784	37.8038
128	128	0.0027	0.6911	20.5244	3.7346	2.6479
128	512	0.0027	0.0389	2.2264	0.1043	0.0029
256	32	0.0274	20.8417	56.0067	29.7778	55.9566
256	128	0.0026	3.5985	27.4677	4.4675	5.2390
256	512	0.0026	0.1261	3.6096	0.3614	0.0034

Table 5. *Unrealistic OoO model: Miss-Rate (percentage) of DDC as a function of window size and DDC size. WS stands for "window size", and CS stands for "DDC size".*

Stages	compress	espresso	gcc	sc	xlisp
4	1.04 M	2.38 M	285 K	2.57 M	2.18 M
8	1.99 M	2.86 M	464 K	4.81 M	2.76 M

Table 6. *Multiscalar model: number of mis-speculations observed.*

can be observed, mis-speculations are more frequent when the window size is larger (8 stages as opposed to 4 stages). In table 7, we report the miss-rates of DDCs of various sizes for the 8-stage configuration only (i.e., for this experiment we use the configuration with the higher number of mis-speculations). As it can be seen, even a DDC of 64 entries exhibits a miss rate of less than 10% for all benchmarks. Furthermore, a DDC with 1024 entries captures virtually all static dependences for all benchmarks except gcc. For the Multiscalar model, we do not show measurements on the number of static dependences that cause most of the mis-speculations. That these dependences are few is implied by the results of the next section.

CS	compress	espresso	gcc	sc	xlisp
1	50.970	16.68	85.20	73.74	68.29
2	31.470	11.18	75.59	28.16	39.82
4	11.240	9.74	62.96	16.22	18.77
8	0.660	4.28	45.84	14.45	4.40
16	0.020	1.10	31.93	6.46	1.59
32	0.002	0.36	18.05	2.96	0.31
64	0.002	0.10	8.92	0.88	0.01
128	0.002	0.05	4.55	0.17	.0004
256	0.002	0.03	3.16	0.02	.0004
512	0.002	0.02	2.93	0.01	.0004
1024	0.002	0.02	2.40	0.01	.0004

Table 7. *8-stage Multiscalar: DDC miss-rates (percentage) as a function of the DDC size ("CS" stands for DDC size).*

5.4 Comparison of dependence speculation policies

In this section we: (i) demonstrate that selective speculation may lead to inferior performance when compared to blind speculation and (ii) obtain an upper bound on the performance improvement that is possible through the use of the data dependence prediction and synchronization approach we described in section 3.

To do so, we compare the following four data dependence speculation policies: (i) NEVER, (ii) ALWAYS, (ii) WAIT, and (vi) PSYNC (for perfect synchronization). Under NEVER, no data dependence speculation is performed. Under ALWAYS, dependence speculation is used blindly (this is the policy used in the modern ILP processors that implement dependence speculation). Under policy WAIT, data dependence speculation is used selectively, that is loads with true dependences are *not* synchronized; instead they are forced to wait until the addresses of all previous stores are known to be different. Finally, under PSYNC, loads with no dependences execute as early as possible, whereas loads with true dependences synchronize with the corresponding stores. Policy PSYNC provides an upper limit on the performance improvement that is possible through the use of the mechanisms we presented in section 3. For PSYNC and WAIT we make use of perfect dependence prediction.

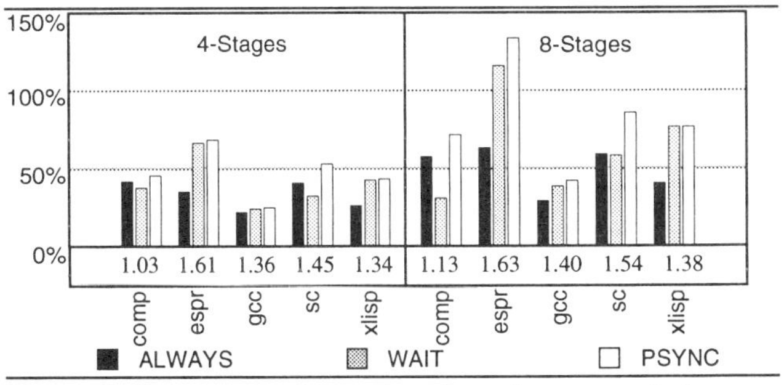

Figure 5. *Comparison of three data dependence speculation policies. Speedups (%) are relative to policy NEVER.*

In figure 5, we report (along the X-axis) the IPC of Multiscalar processor configurations that do not use data dependence speculation (policy NEVER) and the speedups obtained when policies ALWAYS, WAIT, or PSYNC are used instead. Since the dynamic window size is an important consideration we simulate Multiscalar configurations of four and eight stages. It can be observed that even blind data dependence speculation (policy ALWAYS) significantly improves performance in all cases. Furthermore, in contrast to when dependence speculation is not used, increasing the window size results in sizeable performance benefits.

Focusing on policy PSYNC, we can observe that it constantly improves performance over policy ALWAYS, sometimes significantly and furthermore, that the difference between PSYNC and ALWAYS becomes greater as the window size increases (8 stages compared to 4 stages). In addition, under policy PSYNC, increasing the window size typically results in higher performance. The results about policy PSYNC demonstrate that the technique we described in section 3 has the potential for performance improvements that are often significant (even when compared to blind speculation). Finally, selective data dependence speculation (policy WAIT) generally outperforms blind speculation (policy ALWAYS) and performs comparably to policy PSYNC in the 4-stage configuration for three of the benchmarks (espresso, gcc, and xlisp). However, for compress and sc, it performs worse than both PSYNC and ALWAYS (the cause of this phenomenon we explained in section 3, figure 1). As we move to larger windows (8 stages) the difference between PSYNC and WAIT becomes more significant for all benchmarks except xlisp.

5.5 Evaluation of the proposed mechanism

In the previous section we demonstrated the performance potential of our data dependence speculation technique. In this section we evaluate an implementation of this technique. The implementation we simulate is based on the mechanism we detailed in section 4. In this implementation, the MDPT and MDST are combined into a single structure where each MDPT entry carries as many MDST entries as there are stages. This implementation allows us to support multiple dependences per static store or static load as we explained in section 4. However, with this organization, only a single synchronization entry is allowed per static dependence and per stage. The simulated structure is a centralized, fully associative resource that provides as many ports as need for a particular Multiscalar processor configuration. For prediction purposes, each entry contains a 3-bit up-down saturating counter which takes on values 0 through 7. The predictor uses a threshold value of 3 for prediction; values less than the threshold predict no dependence, and values greater than or equal predict dependence and consequent synchronization. We also maintain LRU information for purposes of replacement. An entry within the table may be allocated speculatively without cleanup if bogus, but updates to the prediction mechanism within an entry only occur non-speculatively when a stage commits. To distinguish between instances of the same static dependence we use a variation of the instance distance scheme which we discussed in section 3. In this scheme we approximate the instance numbers via the use of stage identifiers which are statically assigned to each stage. A load that is forced to synchronize on multiple dependences is allowed to execute only after all of them are satisfied. All simulation runs are performed for the Multiscalar processor configurations described earlier, and unless otherwise noted, the MDPT/MDST structure we simulate has 64 entries.

The results presented in this section are in support of a new concept. Consequently, our primary goal is to demonstrate the utility of the proposed mechanism. Though a thorough evaluation of the design space is highly desirable, it is not possible to include in this paper since the design space is vast, and the simulation method that is necessary (instruction driven, timing simulation) is extremely time consuming.

Even though we do not attempt an exhaustive evaluation of the design space, we do simulate two different dependence predictors which we refer to as (i) SYNC and (ii) ESYNC (the "E" is for enhanced). SYNC is our baseline predictor that uses an up/down saturating counter (as described in the beginning of this section). ESYNC, in addition to the up/down counter, also records for each dependence the PC of the task that issued the corresponding store instruction. Synchronization is enforced on a load that matches a MDPT entry only if the task PC of the stage at distance DIST (as recorded in the MDST entry) matches the task PC recorded in the predictor. This enhancement targets loads that have multiple static dependences which occur via different execution paths. In this case, the load does not have to wait for all the dependences, only for the dependence that lies on the proper execution path. However, since the task PC represents only minimal control path information, this predictor may fall short of its goal under some circumstances.

In the rest of this section, we first present and discuss results on the SPECint92 programs. We report the accuracy of the dependence prediction mechanism, the mis-speculation rate, and the performance improvement obtained. The speedups reported are relative to blind speculation (policy ALWAYS of section 5.4), which is the policy currently implemented in several modern processors. We later present and discuss results on the SPEC95 programs. For the latter programs, we report only performance numbers (due to space limitations).

In table 8, we report the breakdown of the dynamic dependence predictions for the SPECint92 programs. Since a load on which a dependence prediction is made may not necessarily have a dependence, a single number cannot be used to describe the accuracy of dependence prediction (in contrast to what is possible in control prediction). Instead, a dependence prediction has to be classified into one of four possible categories depending on whether a dependence is predicted and on whether a dependence actually exists. In the results shown, we count the dependence predictions done on loads that were either committed or have been issued from tasks that were squashed as a result of a dependence mis-speculation (we do not count predictions on loads that were squashed for other reasons). Predictions are recorded only once per dynamic load and at the time the load is ready to access the memory hierarchy. Furthermore, for those loads on which a dependence is predicted, the prediction is recorded after we have checked the synchronization entries for the first time. That is, in the case when a dependence is predicted, we count a "no dependence" outcome if a pre-existing, matching, synchronization entry allows the load to continue execution without delay, otherwise we count a "dependence" outcome. A dependence prediction is correct when the predicted and the actual outcomes are the same (rows *"N/N"* and *"Y/Y"*), otherwise the prediction is incorrect (rows *"N/Y"* and *"Y/N"*). An incorrect dependence prediction may result in mis-speculation (*"N/Y"*), or it may unnecessary delay the load (*"Y/N"*). We will refer to the latter predictions as *false dependence predictions*.

In table 9, we report how the mis-speculation frequency (defined as the number of mis-speculations over committed loads) improves when the proposed mechanism is in place for 4 and 8 stage configurations. In nearly all cases, the proposed prediction/synchronization mechanism reduces the number of mis-speculations by an order of magnitude. Furthermore, mis-speculations are typically reduced to less than 1% of useful loads. However, note that a decrease in the number of mis-speculations does not necessarily translate directly into a proportionate increase in performance (after all, if we did not use speculation, the mis-specula-

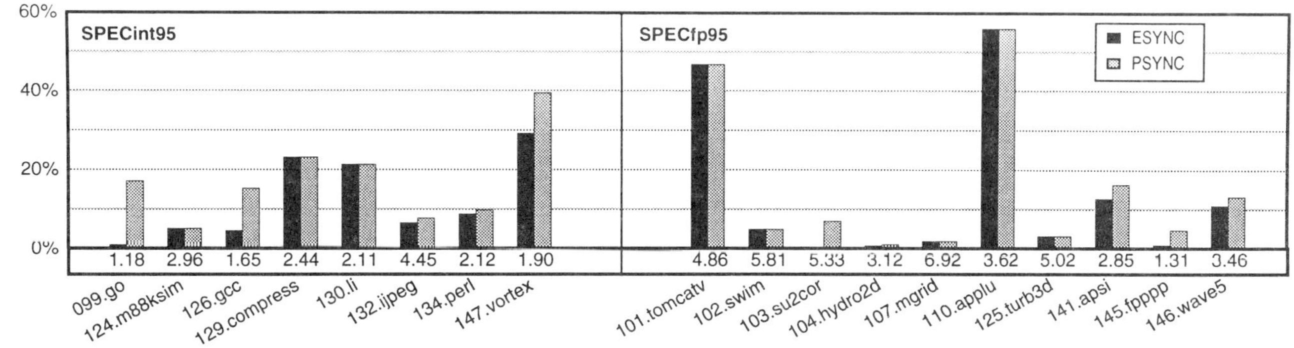

Figure 7. *Performance of our data dependence speculation mechanism for the SPEC95 programs. We simulate an 8-stage Multiscalar processor and we report speedups relative to blind speculation (policy ALWAYS) for the ESYNC predictor and for perfect dependence speculation (policy PSYNC). Along the X-axis we report the IPC obtained when the ESYNC predictor is in use.*

		P/A	*compress*	*espresso*	*gcc*	*sc*	*xlisp*
4-Stages	SYNC	N/N	81.62	98.62	95.56	97.19	95.99
		N/Y	0.18	0.02	1.38	0.26	0.08
		Y/N	4.17	0.03	0.80	0.14	0.06
		Y/Y	14.03	1.33	2.27	2.41	3.86
	ESYNC	N/N	85.79	98.63	96.06	97.40	96.07
		N/Y	0.09	0.01	1.20	0.24	0.00
		Y/N	0.30	0.03	0.07	0.08	0.00
		Y/Y	13.81	1.33	2.67	2.28	3.92
8-Stages	SYN	N/N	73.60	95.52	93.60	95.00	94.99
		N/Y	0.15	0.20	1.65	0.62	0.08
		Y/N	4.95	0.18	1.61	0.26	0.14
		Y/Y	21.31	4.09	3.15	4.11	4.79
	ESYNC	N/N	79.57	95.54	94.85	95.35	95.12
		N/Y	0.07	0.05	1.48	0.66	0.00
		Y/N	0.00	0.07	0.09	0.04	0.01
		Y/Y	20.37	4.34	3.58	3.95	4.87

Table 8. *Dependence prediction breakdown (%). "N" and "Y" stand for "No dependence" and "Dependence" respectively, whereas "P/A" stands for "Predicted/Actual".*

	Policy	*compress*	*espresso*	*gcc*	*sc*	*xlisp*
4-Stages	*ALWAYS*	0.07312	0.02178	0.02007	0.02089	0.03556
	SYNC	0.00083	0.00016	0.00650	0.00271	0.00055
	ESYNC	0.00001	0.00013	0.00434	0.00250	0.00001
8-Stages	*ALWAYS*	0.13567	0.02613	0.03162	0.03891	0.04436
	SYNC	0.00205	0.00137	0.01428	0.00747	0.00069
	ESYNC	0.00004	0.00046	0.01159	0.00698	0.00002

Table 9. *Mis-speculations per committed load.*

tion rate would be zero). The main cause is twofold. First, the synchronized instructions may only represent a shift of cycles from time lost due to mis-speculations, to stall time in the overall picture of execution. That is, even though a load is not mis-speculated, there may be little other work to do while the load is waiting to synchronize. Second, false dependence predictions may impose unnecessary delays.

In figure 6, we show how the performance varies when our mechanism is in place, as compared to the base case Multiscalar processor that speculates all loads as early as possible (policy ALWAYS of figure 5). For almost all cases, the proposed mecha-

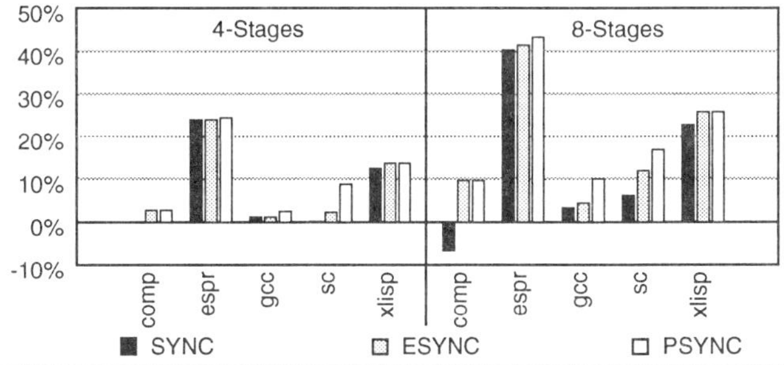

Figure 6. *Performance of our data dependence speculation mechanism on the SPECint92 programs. Speedups (%) are relative to policy ALWAYS.*

nism with the ESYNC predictor, not only improves performance, but also performs close to what is ideally possible (PSYNC columns). The SYNC predictor also improves performance for most of the programs. However the SYNC predictor never outperforms the ESYNC predictor. The SYNC predictor also offers virtually no performance improvement (over blind speculation) for compress and sc in the 4-stage configuration. Furthermore, performance degradation is observed for compress on the 8-stage configuration. False dependence predictions ("YN" marked rows in table 8) are responsible for this poor behavior. The counter based SYNC predictor fails to capture the data dependence patterns exhibited by this program. The ESYNC predictor, however, is able to successfully capture these patterns, since the dependences occur only via specific execution paths. There are two causes for the marked improvement demonstrated for espresso: (i) the average, dynamic task size is about 100 instructions, and (ii) most of the mis-speculations are the result of simple recurrences that occur most of the time (note however that the memory locations involved are often accessed via pointers). Consequently, for this program, the cost of mis-speculations is relatively high, whereas, even a simple up/down counter based predictor can capture the dynamic behavior of the most important dependences.

In figure 7, we report the performance results for the SPEC95 programs on an 8-stage Multiscalar processor. Along the X-axis we report the IPC obtained when our data dependence speculation/synchronization is used. The ESYNC bars represent the speedup obtained relatively to blind speculation (policy ALWAYS of section 5.4), whereas the PSYNC marked bars represent the speedup possible when ideal speculation and synchronization is used (policy PSYNC of section 5.4). Overall, our dependence speculation/synchronization mechanism improves performance, often significantly, for almost all the programs studied. Furthermore, our mechanism quite often performs close to what is ideally possible for the given configuration.

For the SPECint95 programs, the potential performance improvement is appreciable, ranging from 5% to almost 40%. For 124.m88ksim, 129.compress, and 130.li, our mechanism performs comparably to the ideal mechanism. Though the mechanism does not perform as well for 132.ijpeg, 134.perl, and 147.vortex, it does capture a significant amount of the gain that is possible. Nevertheless, both 099.go and 126.gcc fall short of this potential as compared to the ideal dependence speculation. The dependence patterns of these programs are quite irregular and exhibit relatively poor temporal locality as compared to the other programs. In particular, the performance of 099.go is limited by poor control prediction (even with the fairly sophisticated control prediction scheme used) and instruction supply.

For the SPECfp95 programs, most of the dependences we capture are loop recurrences. However, for 145.fpppp and 103.su2cor our mechanism is unable to synchronize some of the dependences. For these two programs, the size of the working set of dynamic dependences exceeds the capacity of our dependence prediction structures. Closer examination reveals that the instruction window established by 145.fpppp can grow to be as large as a few thousand instructions. (Most of the time is spent in a loop whose iterations execute each around 1000 instructions. With the greedy task partitioning policy currently used by the Multiscalar compiler, each iteration executes as a single task.) Tasks of similar size are also experienced in part of 103.su2cor. With the given instruction window size, it is no surprise that the working set of dependences is quite large. Increasing the size of the dependence prediction structures or breaking up each iteration to several tasks are two possible solutions. For 101.tomcatv and 110.applu, our mechanism performs very close to what is ideally possible. Our mechanism is also able to synchronize dependences that would otherwise cause performance degradation for 141.apsi and 146.wave5, but to a lesser extent. It should be noted that we simulated the first 2.8 billion instructions for 101.tomcatv and 146.wave5. Performance improves when these programs are simulated to completion. For example, at 10 billion instructions, the IPC for 101.tomcatv with the ESYNC mechanism is 5.68, whereas the IPC for 146.wave5 at completion (6.4 billion instructions) is 3.79. For 102.swim, 104.hydro2d, 107.mgrid, and 125.turb3d, there is little to be gained from dependence speculation and synchronization for the given configuration. For those programs, some other part of the processor (for example the functional units or the memory system) is saturated.

6 Implications and Conclusions

We make the following contributions in this paper:

- We demonstrate that, as the dynamic window sizes get larger, the net performance loss due to data dependence mis-speculations becomes significant.
- We identify three possible directions that can be followed to minimize this performance loss: (1) minimizing the work lost on mis-speculation, (2) minimizing the time required to redo this work, and (3) improving the accuracy of speculation.
- We observe that the static data dependences that are responsible for the majority of mis-speculations are few and dynamically exhibit temporal locality. The latter observation applies even when all dependences visible from within the dynamic instruction window are considered.
- We propose the concept of dynamic dependence prediction and synchronization and use it to reduce the net performance loss due to data dependence mis-speculation. We also identify the key issues involved in designing such data dependence speculation structures.
- We describe a microarchitectural technique that can be used to implement dynamic data dependence prediction and synchronization. Further, we demonstrate that for a specific OoO processor this technique can provide significant performance improvements. We finally identify most of and address some of the key design issues.

Our experimental results confirm the efficacy of the technique we propose. However, since this work introduces a new concept, we were not able to do a thorough evaluation of the design space and to explore many alternatives and other possible applications of the proposed technique. We believe that this fact does not diminish the importance of our results and observations. In our opinion, this work represents only a first step towards improving the accuracy of data dependence speculation and towards using dynamic dependence speculation and synchronization. Several directions for future research exist in improving the mechanisms we presented, in using the proposed technique in other processing models, and in using data dependence speculation in ways different than those we have discussed.

Though we have worked with memory dependences, the proposed techniques are general and applicable to a range of other uses of data speculation. Such uses include register dependences (this is mostly relevant to multiple program counter execution models such as Multiscalar) and value prediction (for example in a data speculation approach that uses value prediction only when dependences are likely to exist). We also believe that exposing the dependence prediction (MDPT) and/or the synchronization (MDST) structures to the compiler (perhaps via ISA extensions) opens new possibilities for statically orchestrated dependence speculation. (For example the synchronization variables can be allocated by the compiler to enforce synchronization of unambiguous dependences, whereas the prediction can be probed by the program during run-time to make on-the-fly decisions on when and which dependences to speculate.)

Even though in this work we considered fairly simple dependence predictors, any of the plethora of predictors used for branch prediction may be used, with appropriate modifications, to improve the accuracy of dependence prediction. Further improvement of our mechanisms may be possible by considering alternative dependence tagging schemes and synchronization primitives. Furthermore, it would be interesting to consider integrating the dependence prediction and synchronization structures with other components of the processor (for example, we may implement the synchronization functionality in the data cache or in a similar structure so that both the data and the necessary synchronization are provided from the same structure).

The techniques we proposed are applicable to processing models other than Multiscalar. However, further study is necessary, since differences in the instruction window size and in the granularity of checkpointing may influence the relative performance of various dependence speculation and synchronization schemes. We maintain that as ILP processors continue to become more aggressive, the use of data speculation will become even more widespread, and techniques (especially dynamic ones) to improve the accuracy of data dependence speculation, such as those proposed in this paper, will become important.

Acknowledgments

This work was supported in part by NSF Grants CCR-9303030 and MIP-9505853, ONR Grant N00014-93-1-0465, and by U.S. Army Intelligence Center and Fort Huachuca under Contract

DABT63-95-C-0127 and ARPA order no. D346. The views and conclusions contained herein are those of the authors and should not be interpreted as necessarily representing the official policies or endorsements, either expressed or implied, of the U. S. Army Intelligence Center and Fort Huachuca, or the U.S. Government.

We thank Jim Smith, Todd Austin, Andy Glew, Sridhar Gopal, Stefanos Kaxiras, and Dionisios Pnevmatikatos for their valuable comments and suggestions on this work.

References

[1] R. Allen and K. Kennedy. Automatic Translation of FORTRAN Programs to Vector Form. *ACM Transactions on Programming Languages and Systems*, 9(4):491–452, Oct. 1987.

[2] U. Banerjee. *Dependence Analysis for Supercomputing*. Boston, MA: Kluwer Academic Publishers, 1988.

[3] S. E. Breach, T. N. Vijaykumar, and G. S. Sohi. The anatomy of the register file in a multiscalar processor. In *Proc. of the 27th Annual International Symposium on Microarchitecture*, pages 181–190, Dec. 1994.

[4] B. Case. *What's next for Microprocessor Design*. Microprocessor Report, Oct. 1995.

[5] J. R. Ellis. *Bulldog: A Compiler for VLIW Architectures*. Ph.D. thesis, Yale University, Feb. 1985.

[6] M. Emami, R. Ghiya, and L. J. Hendren. Context-sensitive interprocedural points-to analysis in the presence of function pointers. In *Proc. SIGPLAN Conf. on Programming Language Design and Implementation*, pages 242–256, June 1994.

[7] M. Franklin. *The Multiscalar Architecture*. Ph.D. thesis, University of Wisconsin-Madison, Madison, WI 53706, Nov. 1993.

[8] M. Franklin and G. S. Sohi. ARB: A Hardware Mechanism for Dynamic Memory Disambiguation. *IEEE Transactions on Computers*, 45(5):552–571, May 1996.

[9] D. M. Gallagher, W. Y. Chen, S. A. Mahlke, J. C. Gyllenhaal, and W. W. Hwu. Dynamic Memory Disambiguation Using the Memory Conflict Buffer. In *Proc. ASPLOS VI*, pages 183–193, Oct. 1994.

[10] A. S. Huang, G. Slavenburg, and J. P. Shen. Speculative disambiguation: A compilation technique for dynamic memory disambiguation. In *Proc. 21st Annual Symposium on Computer Architecture*, pages 200–210, May 1994.

[11] D. Hunt. Advanced performance features of the 64-bit PA-8000. In *IEEE CompCon*, pages 123–128, 1995.

[12] *PowerPC 620 RISC Microprocessor Technical Summary*, IBM Order number MPR620TSU-01, Motorola Order Number MPC620/D, Oct. 1994.

[13] Q. Jacobson, S. Bennett, N. Sharma, and J. Smith. Control Flow Speculation in Multiscalar Processors. In *Proc. 3rd Annual International Symposium on High-Performance Computer Architecture*, Feb. 1997.

[14] J. Keller. The 21264: A Superscalar Alpha Processor with Out-of-Order Execution. *Digital Equipment Corp., Hudson, MA*, Oct. 1996.

[15] M. H. Lipasti and J. P. Shen. Exceeding the dataflow limit via value prediction. In *Proc. of the 29th Annual International Symposium on Microarchitecture*, Dec. 1996.

[16] S. A. Mahlke, W. Y. Chen, W. W. Hwu, B. R. Rau, and M. S. Schlansker. Sentinel scheduling for VLIW and superscalar processors. In *Proc. ASPLOS V*, 1992.

[17] A. I. Moshovos, S. E. Breach, T. N. Vijaykumar, and G. S. Sohi. A dynamic approach to improve the accuracy of data speculation. Technical Report 1316, Computer Sciences Dept., University of Wisconsin-Madison, March 1996.

[18] A. Nicolau. Run-time disambiguation: Coping with statically unpredictable dependencies. *IEEE Transactions on Computers*, 38(5):663–678, May 1989.

[19] A. Sodani and G. S. Sohi. Dynamic Instruction Reuse. In *Proc. 24th Int. Symposium on Computer Architecture*, June 1997.

[20] G. S. Sohi, S. E. Breach, and T. N. Vijaykumar. Multiscalar processors. In *Proc. 22nd Int. Symposium on Computer Architecture*, pages 414–425, June 1995.

[21] R. P. Wilson and M. S. Lam. Efficient Context-Sensitive Pointer Analysis for C Programs. In *Proc. SIGPLAN Conf. on Programming Language Design and Implementation*, pages 1–12, June 1995.

Dynamic Instruction Reuse

Avinash Sodani and Gurindar S. Sohi

Computer Sciences Department
University of Wisconsin-Madison
1210 West Dayton Street
Madison, WI 53706 USA
{sodani,sohi}@cs.wisc.edu

Abstract

This paper introduces the concept of dynamic instruction reuse. Empirical observations suggest that many instructions, and groups of instructions, having the same inputs, are executed dynamically. Such instructions do not have to be executed repeatedly — their results can be obtained from a buffer where they were saved previously. This paper presents three hardware schemes for exploiting the phenomenon of dynamic instruction reuse, and evaluates their effectiveness using execution-driven simulation. We find that in some cases over 50% of the instructions can be reused. The speedups so obtained, though less striking than the percentage of instructions reused, are still quite significant.

1 Introduction

There are three parameters that influence the execution time of a program. Microarchitecture has concentrated on two of them: (i) the number of instructions executed per clock cycle, i.e., the IPC, and (ii) the clock cycle time. The third parameter: (iii) the total number of instructions, has been considered the domain of software. In this paper we address the following question: "Can we develop microarchitectural techniques to reduce the number of instructions that have to be executed dynamically, and what are the potential benefits of such techniques?''

Just as caches reduce the number of memory accesses made dynamically if a memory location is going to be accessed repeatedly, the number of instructions executed dynamically can be reduced if an instruction is going to produce the same value repeatedly. We have observed many instructions, and groups of instructions, having the same inputs (consequently producing the same output) when executed dynamically. This observation can be exploited to reduce the number of instructions executed dynamically as follows: by buffering the previous result of the instruction, future dynamic instances of the same static instruction can use the result by establishing that the input operands in both cases are the same. We call this *dynamic instruction reuse*.

Dynamic instruction reuse can benefit performance in two main ways. First, by not having to pass through all the phases of execution (e.g., issue, execute, result bypass) dynamically, utilization of machine resources could be reduced, alleviating resource conflicts. Second, and more important, the outcome of an instruction can be known much earlier, allowing instructions

ISCA '97 Denver, CO, USA

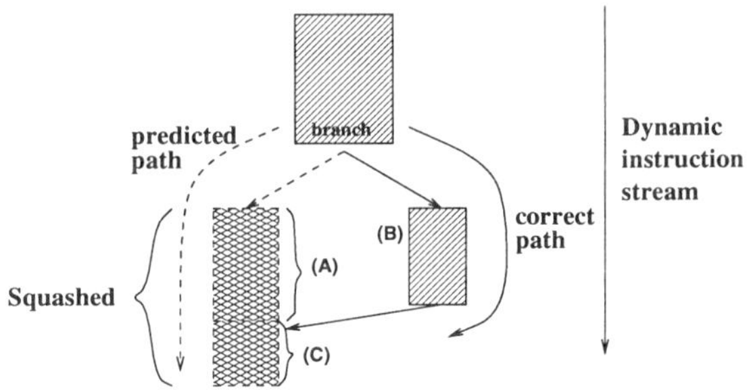

Figure 1. *Scenario where execution on the (mis)predicted path converges with the execution on the correct path. In such cases certain instructions from part (C) need not be re-executed when encountered on the correct path.*

that are dependent upon the outcome to proceed sooner. As we shall see, the results of chains of dependent instructions could all be generated in a single cycle, short-circuiting dependence chains, and reducing the lengths of critical paths of execution.

This paper is concerned with exploiting the phenomenon of dynamic instruction reuse. Towards this end, we develop microarchitectural mechanisms that allow the outcome of an instruction to be known earlier than it would had the instruction have to pass through all the phases of its execution. We describe the concept of dynamic instruction reuse in section 2, and present scenarios to illustrate why it occurs and why might it be a useful phenomenon to exploit. In section 3, we present three different schemes for instruction reuse. Each scheme employs a *reuse buffer*, a buffer of previous outcomes of instruction execution. In section 4 we show how a reuse buffer can be incorporated into a generic superscalar processor. In section 5 we provide a quantitative evaluation, and in section 6 we discuss related work. Finally section 7 presents some concluding remarks.

2 Scenarios for Dynamic Instruction Reuse

Before developing mechanisms to allow dynamic instruction reuse, we need to understand why this phenomenon occurs. What causes instructions to be executed with the same input operands? Why are such instructions in the program in the first place? Are such instructions needed? Why might it be better to obtain the outcome of an instruction from a buffer rather than recompute it? In order to answer these questions, we look at a couple of scenarios

The first scenario involves speculative execution in a dynamically scheduled processor. As illustrated in Figure 1, when a branch instruction is encountered, its outcome is predicted, and instructions from the predicted basic block (block A) are executed speculatively. In addition to executing instructions from

```
main_func(a, b, c) {
    ...
    func(a, list, size);
    ...
    func(b, list, size);
}
```
(a)

```
int func(x, list, size) {
    int i;
    for(i=0; i<size; i++) {
     if(x==list[i]) return i;
    }
    return -1;
}
```
(b)

```
1    i = 0
2    if(i >= size) jump out
3    p = list + i
4    val = Memory[p]
5    if(x == val) jump found
6    i++
7    jump 2
```
(c)

```
*1   i = 0
*2   if(i >= size) jump out
*3   p = list + i
*4   val = Memory[p]
 5   if(a == val) jump found
*6   i++
*7   jump 2
*2   if(i >= size) jump out
*3   p = list + i
*4   val = Memory[p]
 5   if(a == val) jump found
*6   i++
     ...
```
(d)

```
*1   i = 0
*2   if(i >= size) jump out
*3   p = list + i
*4   val = Memory[p]
 5   if(b == val) jump found
*6   i++
*7   jump 2
*2   if(i >= size) jump out
*3   p = list + i
*4   val = Memory[p]
 5   if(b == val) jump found
*6   i++
     ...
```
(e)

Figure 2. *Scenario illustrating that instructions often perform the same computation repeatedly. The dynamic instructions marked "*" would perform the same computation for both the calls to function* `func` *shown in the figure.*

block A, the processor may execute instructions from another block (C), which is control independent of the branch. If the branch was mispredicted, instructions executed from both blocks A and C are discarded, execution resumes at block B, from where it proceeds to block C. Instructions in block C that were discarded, but whose operands are not affected by instructions in either blocks A or B, would end up being re-executed. If the results of such instructions were buffered, and we could detect that their operands values are the same, their results could be reused, thereby reducing the squash penalty. We term this scenario as *squash reuse*.

Our initial goal for developing an instruction reuse mechanism was to reduce the branch mis-prediction penalty, especially for short forward branches, as described above. However, when we were studying the effectiveness of the mechanisms that we developed for the above case, we discovered that the concept was much more powerful. Other scenarios where instructions can be reused dynamically also arise frequently. These scenarios are a result of two important artifacts of how the dynamic computation is expressed statically. First, programs are written to be generic, i.e., operate upon a variety of input data sets — we don't write programs that operate on only a single input data set. Starting out with a single static program, different inputs will cause different instructions to be executed dynamically, resulting in a different dynamic operation stream for each input data set. For a particular input set, operands for some of the instructions may not change dynamically (they would in another execution with a different input data set). Second, programs are written to express a desired computation in a concise manner. For example, the computation to carry out operations on each element of a 1000-element data structure is expressed using a loop structure; we don't write separate instructions for each element of the data structure. In the process of recreating the dynamic sequence of operations from the static representation, many operations may be repeated, as we shall see shortly.

The above situations are best illustrated by an example. Consider the example of Figure 2. The function `func` searches for a value in a `list` of a particular `size`. The function `main_func` calls `func` several times, searching for a different element in the same list with each call. When `func` is called, it iterates through the `list`, element by element, searching for the value until the end of the `list`, exiting when the value is found. Instructions corresponding to the loop in `func` are shown in Figure 2(b). Figure 2(d) shows the dynamic instances of these instructions which are generated by the first call to `func`. In each iteration of the loop, the instruction 2 is dependent upon the `size` parameter, the instructions 3 and 4 are dependent upon the `list` parameter, instruction 5 is dependent upon both the `list` as well as the value being searched for, and instruction 6 is dependent on the induction variable. If `func` is called again (Figure 2(e)) on the same `list` (and same `size`), but with a different search key, then all the different dynamic instances of instructions 1-4 and 6 produce the same outcomes as they did the last time the function was called (a total of `size` dynamic instances of instructions 2-4 and 6). Only the dynamic instances of instruction 5 produce results that might be different from what they were in the previous call to `func`. This "reuse'' of the results of the dynamic instances of instructions 1-4 and 6 is directly attributable to the fact that `func` was written to be a generic list search function, but in this particular case, only one of its parameters changed between different calls to it. Even if `func` was called with all its parameters being different for each call, the different dynamic instances of the instruction 6 (i=0, i=1, i=2, ..) in the second call to `func` would end up producing the same values as they did in the first call to `func`, a consequence of using loops to express the desired computation in a concise manner. (Actually, if the `size` parameter was also different, then only *min*(`size1,size2`) dynamic instances of instruction 6 would produce the same values.)

How might performance benefit if we buffered the (`size`)

dynamic instances of instructions 1-4 and 6 in the above example, and reused them? First, the dynamic instances of instructions 1-4 and 6 do not have to pass through all the different phases of execution (ALU, issue, result bus, etc.), thereby reducing the demand for processor resources. (In the above case, accesses to the data cache are also eliminated — these end up becoming accesses to the buffer which holds previous instruction results.) Second, the critical path to carry out the total computation involved in `func` can be reduced considerably. Without dynamic instruction reuse, the critical path through the computation, as expressed above, would be `size+3` steps (assuming that the loop executes all `size` iterations), `size` steps to generate all the dynamic instances for the induction variable `i`, plus 3 steps to execute instructions 3, 4, and 5 of each iteration (which form a dependence chain). In other words, the height of the dataflow graph for the above computation is `size+3` steps. With instruction reuse, in the best case, the critical path, i.e., the height of the dataflow graph through the computation, is reduced to only 1 step. This is because the outcomes of all the dynamic instances of instructions 1-4 are already known, and all the dynamic instances, being independent of one another, could all execute at the same time. In other words, dynamic instruction reuse allows us to *exceed the dataflow limit* that is "inherent'' in the program. Of course, in an actual execution other constraints will prevent us from achieving the dataflow limit in either case, but concentrating on the dataflow limit illustrates the potential power of the concept. We call this second scenario *general reuse.*

The above example shows that the potential for instructions to be reused dynamically exists. As we shall see in section 5, in some cases over 50% of all executed instructions produce results that they produced earlier, suggesting a need to exploit the phenomenon. Our objective is to develop dynamic techniques to exploit repetitive behavior of the above type. While not impossible, doing the same statically in the compiler would require a tremendous (and very likely impractical) effort in the above case: constant propagation, function in-lining, loop unrolling `size` times, common sub-expression elimination, all carried out globally (and possibly inter-procedurally), sufficient registers to store `size` elements, as well as alias analysis to allow register allocation of the list elements. In the above example, to achieve the same effect as dynamic instruction reuse, the compiler would essentially have to end up putting the `size` elements of list in registers, and in-lining `func` as a sequence of `size` static instructions, each of which compares value with a register. This is a tall order, given the current state of the art. Accordingly we concentrate on developing dynamic schemes for instruction reuse.

3 Schemes for Instruction Reuse

In this section, we describe three hardware schemes to implement dynamic instruction reuse. To reuse an instruction we need to determine that its outcome is going to be the same as a previous outcome, and reuse the previous outcome. The reuse schemes described in this section implement this determination in different ways. In each scheme we store the result(s) of a previously-executed instruction in a hardware structure called *Reuse Buffer (RB)* (Figure 3).[1] When an instruction is encountered, the RB is queried to see if it contains a reusable result for the instruction. Three issues need to be dealt with: (i) how the information in the RB is accessed, (ii) how we know that the accessed RB entry (or entries) has reusable information, and (iii) how the buffer is managed.

The first issue is easily dealt with: the program counter (PC) of the instruction provides a convenient index for searching the RB. The RB could be organized with any degree of associativity, the larger the associativity, the larger the number of dynamic instances of an instruction that can be held in the RB at a given time.

To deal with the second issue, we need to develop a *reuse test* which checks information accessed from the RB to see if there is a reusable result. Details of the test depend upon the reuse scheme, as we describe shortly.

There are two aspects to RB management: (i) deciding which instructions get placed in the buffer, and (ii) maintaining the consistency of the buffer. The decision as to what to place in the buffer can range from no policy, i.e., place all recently executed instructions in this buffer (if they aren't already present), to a more judicious policy that filters out instructions that aren't likely to be reused.[2] Maintaining the consistency of information in the RB depends upon the reuse scheme, as we see shortly.

Next, we present details of three schemes for reusing instructions. These schemes mainly differ in the way in which reusable results are identified. The first scheme (S_v) tracks operand values for each instruction, the second scheme (S_n) tracks only operand names (register identifiers), and the third scheme (S_{n+d}) tracks dependence relationships among the instructions. For each scheme, we discuss the following issues:

- What information is stored in the RB?
- How is the reuse test performed?
- How is the information in the RB updated/invalidated?

In practice, the reuse schemes would be implemented in a variety of different ways. In this paper we concentrate on the functionalities required by each reuse scheme instead of their implementations.

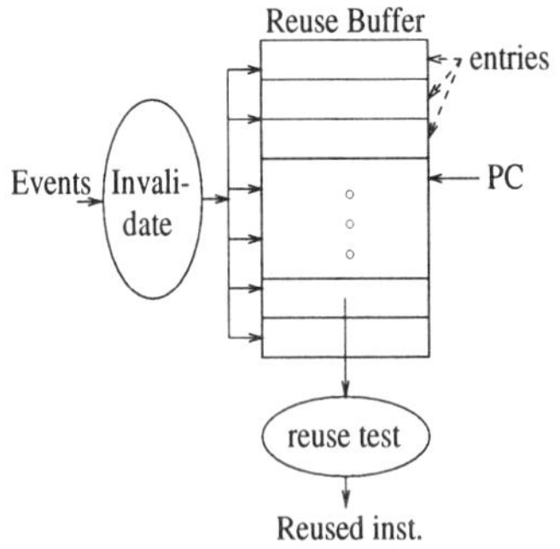

Figure 3. *Generic Reuse Buffer. It is indexed by the PC and it has mechanism for selectively invalidating entries based on some event.*

1. Depending upon the buffer mapping and management policy, the RB could contain the outcomes of many previous dynamic instances of the same instruction. For example, in Figure 2, the buffer could contain all the `size` dynamic instances of the instruction updating the induction variable, with each dynamic instance producing a different value.

2. In this paper, we do not explore this aspect of the problem — in our discussions and experiments we assume that all recently executed instructions are placed in the RB.

tag	operand1 value	operand2 value	address	result	mem valid

(a)

tag	operand1 reg name	operand2 reg name	address	result	result valid	mem valid

(b)

tag	operand1		operand2		address	result	result vaild	mem vaild
	src-index	reg name	src-index	reg name				

(c)

Figure 4. *RB entry (a) Scheme S_v (b) Scheme S_n (c) Scheme S_{n+d}*

3.1 Scheme S_v: Reuse based upon operand values

Scheme S_v is a straightforward implementation of the reuse concept. The operand values of an instruction are stored along with its result. Since the reuse test is based on operand values, as we will see shortly, we call this scheme S_v, where 'v' stands for *value*.

When an instruction is decoded, its current operand values are compared with those stored in the RB. If they are the same, then the result stored in the RB is reused. Loads, being a two-operation instruction, need special handling. Address-calculation can be reused if the operands for the address calculation did not change. However, the actual outcome of the load can only be reused if the addressed memory location was not written into by a store instruction. Information in the RB has to distinguish between the two. Likewise, stores are also special. While reusing the address calculation part of a store presents no problems (we treat it no differently from the address calculation for a load) we make no attempt to reuse the actual memory write — the memory write could have side effects outside the domain of the processing node (similar restrictions would apply to other instructions with side effects, e.g. loads in the I/O space).

- **RB entry:** An entry in RB for this scheme is shown in Figure 4(a). The *tag* field stores part of the PC. The *result, operand value1,* and *operand value2* store the result and the operand values of the instruction. These fields are used to identify the instruction (or address calculation in case of a load/store) that can be reused. The *memvalid* bit and the *address* field are used to determine if the actual memory access for a load instruction can be reused; the *memvalid* bit indicates whether the value loaded from memory (present in the *result* field) is valid, and the *address* field stores the memory address (i.e., the outcome of the address calculation).

- **Reuse test:** For testing reuse, the operands of an instruction are compared with the values in the *operand value* fields of the RB entry. A match indicates that *result* is valid (for non-load/store instructions) or *address* is valid (for loads and stores). For loads, in addition to testing the validity of the *address* bits, we also need to test the *memvalid* bit to see if the outcome of the load (in the *result* field) can be reused. If the operand values are not known at the time of the reuse test then the instruction is not reused.

- **Invalidation:** For non-load operations, the reuse test works because the operands uniquely determine the result and therefore invalidations are not needed to maintain the integrity of the test. For loads, a store to the same address invalidates the value in the *result* field. Accordingly, on a store the *address* field of each RB entry is searched for a matching address, and the *memvalid* bit reset for matching entries.

Note that the *address* field, *memvalid* field, and the associative search for invalidations are required only to maintain the integrity of load values. The RB can be split into two buffers: one for storing load values and another, the main RB, for storing everything except the load values (including entries for load addresses). This RB organization has two advantages: first, *address* and *memvalid* fields need not be maintained for entries storing non-load instructions, reducing the overall storage required for the reuse scheme; second, the main RB need not have invalidation logic, this logic would only be present in the buffer for load values, which probably would be much smaller compared to the main RB. Nevertheless, since our goal is to demonstrate the potential of instruction reuse, and not to compare the merits of different implementations, we assume a unified RB for our experiments presented in this paper.

3.2 Scheme S_n: Reuse based upon register names

In scheme S_n, we attempt to trivialize the reuse test (and also to reduce the size of each RB entry). Rather than store operand values, we store operand (architectural) register identifiers in the RB. When an instruction writes into a register, all instructions with a matching (source) register identifier in the RB are invalidated. Since the reuse test is based on operand names (and not value), we call this scheme S_n, where 'n' stands for *name*. The remaining details are:

- **RB entry :** An RB entry for this scheme is shown in Figure 4(b). Differences from scheme S_v are: (i) the *operand1* and *operand2* fields contain register names of the operands instead of actual operand values, (ii) there is a *resultvalid* bit, which indicates whether the result is valid. (This bit was not required in scheme S_v because the reuse test detected the stale results). This bit is set when an entry is first inserted into the RB.

- **Reuse test:** The reuse test is as simple as testing the state of *resultvalid* and *memvalid* bits. Address calculation for load/store instructions and results for all other instructions can be reused if the *resultvalid* bit is set; the result of a load instruction can be reused if both *resultvalid* and *memvalid* are set.

- **Invalidations :** As before, stores invalidate the loads from the same address (*memvalid* bit is reset). Moreover, when a register is written, the RB is searched for entries whose operand field matches the name of the register. The entries which match are marked invalid (*resultvalid* bit is reset).

Note that the effect of invalidations (which is to purge stale results) can be obtained in other ways too, e.g., using *timestamps* for the operands. As mentioned earlier, in this paper we focus on the required functionality and leave the task of exploring different implementations as a future work.

3.3 Scheme S_{n+d}: Reuse using register names and dependence chains

Scheme S_{n+d} extends scheme S_n by attempting to establish chains of dependent instructions, and to track the reuse status of such instruction chains. Since in this scheme the reuse status of an instruction in the RB is established based on its operand names and/or its dependence information, we call this scheme S_{n+d} (the letters ‘n’ and ‘d’ stand for *name* and *dependence* respectively).

Figure 5(a) motivates scheme S_{n+d}. The figure shows a dynamic stream of instructions on the left and the contents of the RB at different point in time on the right. I, J, K is a chain of dependent instructions; I_1, J_1, K_1 and I_2, J_2, K_2 are the dynamic instances of this instruction chain. With scheme S_n, only instruction I_2 could reuse the result of I_1, because results of J_1 and K_1 are invalidated by instruction R. Scheme S_{n+d} instead tries to establish the fact that instruction J_2 (J_1) depends solely upon instruction I_2 (I_1), and instruction K_2 (K_1) depends solely upon instructions I_2 and J_2 (I_1 and J_1) (Figure 5(b)). If instruction I_2 can be reused, so can instructions J_2 and K_2. Furthermore, if I_2, J_2, and K_2 are all fetched simultaneously from the RB, the reuse status of all three could be established simply by establishing the reuse status of I_2, and verifying the dependence relationship (as we elaborate below). This is tantamount to obtaining the result(s) of chains of dependent operations in a single cycle. Scheme S_v, which does not maintain instruction dependence relationships, can't establish the reuse status of a dependence chain as easily. In our example, the reuse status of I_2 would have to be established; the result of I_2 would be needed to establish the reuse status of J_2; and J_2's result would be needed to establish the reuse status of K_2.

For the ensuing discussions we define the following terms

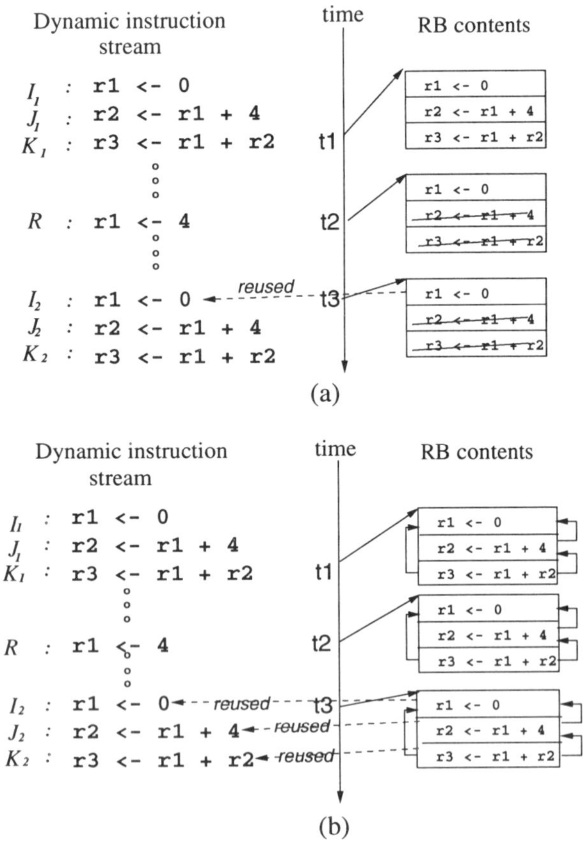

Figure 5. *Dependent sequence of instructions (a) not handled in Scheme S_n, but (b) handled in Scheme S_{n+d}.*

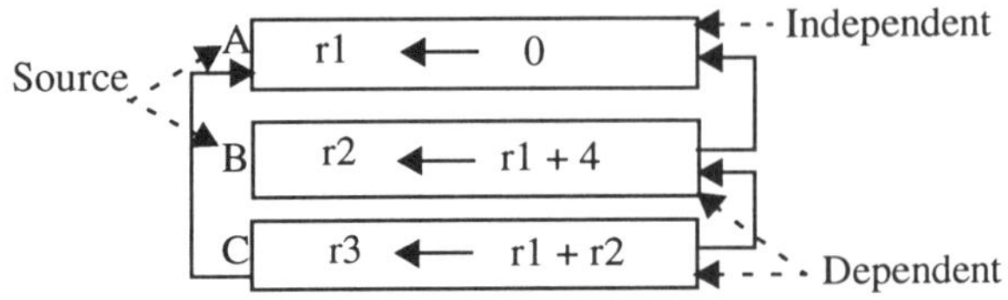

Figure 6. *Instructions with data dependence links. The arrows point from the instruction using the value to the instruction producing the value.*

(illustrated in Figure 6). Instructions that produce values used by other instructions in the chain are called *source* instructions (e.g. A and B in the figure). Instructions whose source instructions are not in the chain, which implies that their data dependence information is not available, are called *independent* instructions (e.g. A). Finally, instructions whose source instructions are in the chain are called the *dependent* instructions (e.g. B and C).

Dependence chains are created as entries are inserted into the RB. To facilitate this process, we use a mapping table called a *Register Source Table (RST)*. The RST has an entry for each architectural register; it tracks the RB entry which has (or will have) the latest result for that register. When an entry is reserved in the RB for an instruction, the RST entry for its destination register is updated to point to the reserved entry. If the instruction which is the latest producer of a register is not in the RB, then the RST entry for that register is set to invalid. The RST is similar in spirit to the rename map used in register renaming. In essence, the RST is used to link a consumer instruction to the latest producer instruction by pointing to the "physical register" (RB entry) of the producer. Accordingly, another way of looking at scheme S_{n+d} is to consider it as a "physical register" version of scheme S_n, which tracks dependences using architectural registers. We now present details of this scheme's operation.

- **RB entry:** An RB entry (shown in Figure 4(c)) is similar to that of scheme S_n, except for the addition of a *src-index* field. The dependence links are created by storing the RB index of the source instructions in this field. An invalid value is inserted in this field if the source doesn't exist in the RB.

- **Reuse test:** The reuse status of independent instructions is established as it was in scheme S_n (*resultvalid* bit is set; *memvalid* is set in the case of load instructions). A dependent instruction is reused if its source instructions (in the RB), as indicated by the *src-index* field of its operands, are indeed the latest producers for its operands. This fact is established with the help of the RST, as we shall illustrate below with the help of an example (Figure 7).

- **State updates:** As in schemes S_v and S_n, stores invalidate the loads to the same address (*memvalid* is reset). As in scheme S_n, independent instructions are invalidated when their operands registers are overwritten (*resultvalid* is reset). Dependent instructions need not be invalidated on operand overwrites because their reuse status can be established using their dependence information. Instead, they are invalidated when their source instructions are evicted from RB, i.e., when the dependence information is lost.[3] To perform this operation the RB needs to be searched for entries whose *src-index* field matches the index (in RB) of the source instruction being evicted. The entries which result in a match are invalidated (*resultvalid* bit is

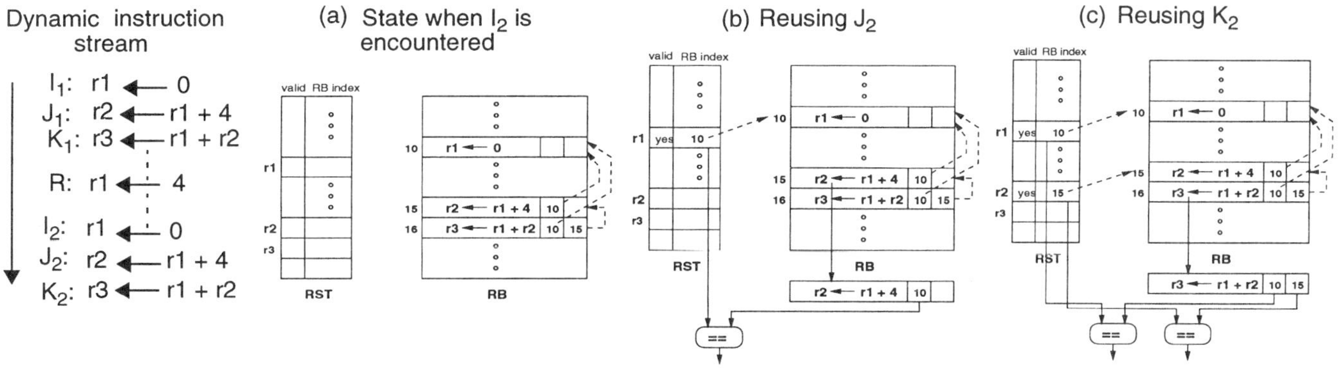

Figure 7. *Illustrating the reuse test for dependent instructions. (a) State when I_2 is encountered. (b) Testing r2 <- r1 +4 for reusability. (c) Testing r3 <- r1 + r2 for reusability. (Instruction R is not shown in RB for clarity).*

reset).

We illustrate the working of this scheme using the example shown in Figure 7 with the same dynamic stream of instructions as in Figure 5. Figure 7(a) shows the state of the RB and RST at the time when I_2 is encountered in the dynamic instruction stream. At this time, the results of instructions I_1, J_1 and K_1 are present in the RB with appropriate data dependence information (indicated by the links in RB and the index values in the *src-index* field). Since instructions J_1 and K_1 are stored in the RB as dependent instructions, their results are not invalidated by instruction R (unlike scheme S_n). Instruction I_2 reuses the result of I_1 (since it is independent and valid) and the RST entry for *r1* is updated to point to RB entry 10 (the latest producer for *r1*)(Figure 7(b)). To establish the reusability of J_2, the *src-index* field for *r1* is compared with the RST entry for *r1* (Figure 7(b)). The match indicates that the source for *r1* in the dependence chain (which is I_1) is also the current producer for *r1*; hence the result is reusable. Instruction K_2 gets reused in a similar fashion (Figure 7 (c)). The instructions I_2, J_2, K_2 can be reused simultaneously if encountered in the same cycle. While performing the reuse test on each one, interdependence among them needs to be considered. The interdependence check is similar to what is done while renaming registers for multiple dependent instructions in the same cycle.

4 Microarchitecture with a Reuse Buffer

Figure 8 shows a generic microarchitecture with an RB. Except for the RB (and the datapaths associated with it), the rest of the microarchitecure is similar to what is found in a generic dynamically-scheduled superscalar processor.

The *Instruction Fetch Unit* fetches and places the instructions in the *Instruction Queue*. Instruction decode and register renaming is done in the *Decode and Rename Unit*. At this point, the RB is accessed to see if a reusable result for the instruction can be found. If a reusable result is found, the instruction does not need to be operated upon any further; it bypasses the *Instruction Window* (IW), and proceeds directly to the *Reorder Buffer* (ROB) [8]. Loads bypass the IW only if both micro-operations, address calculation and the actual memory operation, can be reused. If a reusable result is not found in the RB, an entry is reserved in the RB where the result of the instruction will be placed after it is executed, setting it up for future reuse (in scheme S_{n+d}, the RST has to be updated accordingly). Once in the IW, instructions proceed as they would in any generic superscalar processor. After an instruction has executed, its results are stored in the reserved RB entry. In scheme S_v, the operand values are also stored in the entry at this time. When an instruction commits, depending on the reuse scheme, it invalidates appropriate results in the RB.

Since the RB contains state that will determine the outcome of future instructions, it needs to be maintained precisely (just like a register file). The straightforward way to do this is to update the RB only when an instruction is committed. However, this approach prevents speculatively-executed instructions from being entered into the RB, making it ineffective for one of our purposes, that of recovering squashed work. Accordingly, we must allow the RB to be updated speculatively, and take necessary actions (depending upon the reuse scheme) to ensure correct behavior. For scheme S_v, inserting instructions into the RB speculatively requires no special actions — the reuse test ensures that the correct result is obtained. For scheme S_{n+d}, the RST controls the reusability of instructions. Just like the rename map in a superscalar processor, checkpoints of the RST have to be taken when a speculation decision is made, and it has to be repaired in the case of an incorrect speculation.

Other issues, such as interlocks to ensure correct operations, flushing on context switches, etc., are fairly routine, and we don't discuss them further.

Though in all previous discussions we assumed that an RB

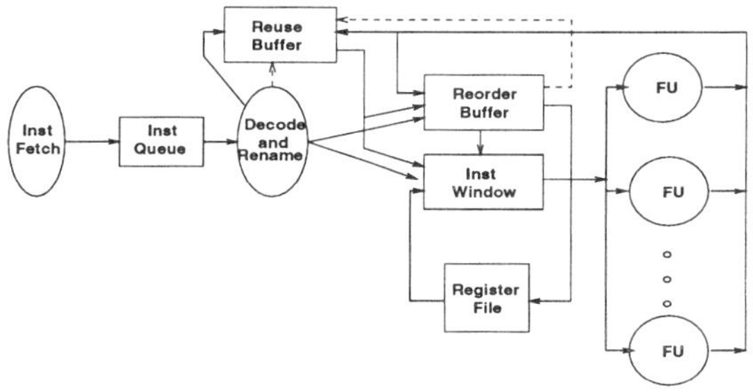

Figure 8. *Generic microarchitecture with a reuse buffer.*

3. An optimization to this approach is to check whether the source instruction is the current producer for its destination register (this can be done using the RST); if so, then the dependent instructions are not invalidated, instead they are treated as independent instruction thereafter. In our simulations we implemented this optimization.

access takes a single cycle, there is no need for this timing constraint since accesses may be pipelined. For example, the access can begin in the fetch stage of the pipeline after the PC of the instruction is available (since only the PC is required for indexing the RB, the RB access can begin as early as in fetch stage); then only the reuse test needs to be performed in the decode stage. Other operations, like invalidations, evicting entries to make way for new instructions etc., can be pipelined as well. For example, when the RB gets full, entries can be freed for future inserts. This will ensure that free RB entries are always available, eliminating the search for a victim entry from the critical path. Thus, despite its size, the RB seems unlikely to be the structure that determines the cycle time.

5 Experimental Evaluation

Our simulator is built on top of the *SimpleScalar toolset* [1], an execution-driven simulator based upon the MIPS-I ISA. The base simulator models in detail a 4-way dynamically-scheduled processor with its first level of instruction and data cache memory. The parameters for the base out-of-order simulator are listed in Table 1. We extended this base simulator to incorporate the RB and the three instruction reuse schemes described earlier. The RB is integrated with the processor pipeline as described in section 4. In our simulations, the RB is capable of supporting 4 reads, 4 writes, and 4 independent invalidations simultaneously. We also assume that all RB accesses — read, write or invalidate — complete in one cycle, and that, like scheme S_{n+d}, scheme S_v can reuse multiple dependent results in a single cycle (the maximum length of a dependence chain reused in a cycle is equal to the read bandwidth of RB, which is 4 in the simulated configuration). This configuration of the RB, though aggressive, allows us to study the concept of instruction reuse without been limited by any particular implementation.

5.1 Benchmarks

The benchmark programs analyzed are listed in Table 2 along with their inputs and number of dynamic instructions executed on the timing simulator. There are five integer programs from SPEC '92 benchmark suite (*gcc, compress eqntott, espresso, xlisp*) and five integer programs from the SPEC '95 benchmark suite (*go, m88ksim, vortex, ijpeg* and *perl*). Other integer programs analyzed are: *Yacr2*, a VLSI channel router routing a channel with 230 terminals, and *Mpeg*, a mpeg decoder which decodes a mpeg file with 71 frames. Except for *go, m88ksim, vortex* and *ijpeg*, all programs were run to completion. These four programs were run for first 1 billion instructions on a functional simulator (so that we do not do all our measurement in the initialization phases) and for the next 500 million cycles (or completion) on the timing simulator. The exact number of instructions simulated in a fixed number of cycles is dependent on the microarchitectural enhancements applied. Thus, for these programs (except *ijpeg* which ran to completion) in Table 2 we show the approximate number of instructions executed on the timing simulator. All the benchmark programs were compiled using GNU *gcc* (version 2.6.3), *gas* (version 2.5.2) and *gld* (version 2.5) with maximum optimizations (-O3).

Benchmarks	**Input**	**Inst. count (Mil.)**
Gcc	1stmt.i	116.2
Compress	in	66.4
Eqntott	int_pri_3.eqn	1117.3
Espresso	bca.in	458.4
Xlisp	li-input.lsp	967.8
Go	null.in (reference)	~750.0
M88ksim	ctl.in (reference)	~1050.0
Vortex	vortex.in (training)	~900.0
Ijpeg	vigo.ppm(training)	442.2
Perl	scrabbl.in(training)	555.6
Yacr2	input2	397.5
Mpeg	foot.mpeg	385.9

Table 2: *Benchmark programs, inputs and instruction count.*

5.2 Experiments and Results

We performed several experiments to evaluate the concept of dynamic instruction reuse. Being the first paper on the concept (and mechanisms to exploit it), an exhaustive evaluation of all interesting cases is not possible. Furthermore, we also don't evaluate the concept in the abstract. Rather, we concentrate on

Instruction fetch	4 instructions per cycle. Aggressive: can fetch beyond multiple branches and across cache line boundaries. Fetch stops only on I-cache misses.
Instruction cache	16K bytes, direct mapped, 32 byte cache line, 6 cycles miss latency
Branch predictor	2048 BTB entries with 2-bit saturating counters.
Speculative execution mechanism	Out of order issue/commit of 4 operations per cycle, 32 entry reorder buffer, 32 entry load/store queue. Maximum of 8 unresolved branches. Loads execute only after all the preceding store addresses are known. Values bypassed to loads from matching stores ahead in load/store queue.
Architected Registers	32 integer, hi, lo, 32 floating point, fcc.
Functional units	4-integer ALUs, 2-load/store units, 4-FP adders, 1-integer MULT/DIV, 1-FP MULT/DIV
Functional unit latency (total/issue)	integer ALU-1/1, load/store 1/1, integer MULT 3/1, integer DIV 20/19, FP adder 2/1, FP MULT 4/1, FP DIV 12/12, FP SQRT 24/24.
Data cache	16K 2-way set associative, 32 bytes block, 6 cycles miss latency. Dual ported, non-blocking interface, one outstanding miss per register.

Table 1: *Details of the base simulator*

some key initial results for some sample configurations of the proposed mechanisms: how much dynamic reuse of instructions is there (as captured by our reuse schemes), what types of instructions are reused, how does it vary with RB size, and how much speedup results. We categorize total instruction reuse into squash reuse and general reuse, and show the contribution of either category to total speedup. We also evaluate the impact of associativity and the effectiveness of instruction reuse in alleviating dependences.

For most of our experiments we use fully-associative RBs of three different sizes: 32, 128, and 1024 entries with a FIFO replacement policy. As mentioned earlier, we make no attempt to be selective about what instructions get inserted into the RB; that will be the subject of future work. We expect that with clever RB management policies, small RBs will be able to achieve the same performance as the larger RBs presented in the next several sections.

5.2.1 Instructions Reused

Figure 9 shows the percentage of total dynamic instructions reused for the three different schemes, with 3 different RB sizes for each scheme. The harmonic mean (HM) over all benchmarks for each RB size is also shown in the figure. All the analyzed benchmarks exhibit significant instruction reuse, especially for the larger buffer sizes. For scheme S_v with 1024 entries the percentage of instructions reused are 63% for eqntott, 39% for espresso, 76% for yacr2 and 34% for xlisp. Even for small RB sizes the instructions reused are significant (21% for eqntott, 24% for espresso, 26% for yacr2). For other benchmarks and for other reuse schemes the percentage of instruction reuse is also appreciable.

For larger RB sizes, scheme S_n does not reuse as many instructions as schemes S_v and S_{n+d}. This is because invalidations are more frequent in scheme S_n (being done every time a register or memory location is written), which limit the number of reusable instructions irrespective of the RB size (for large RB sizes). Frequent invalidations help small size RBs (32 entries); the instructions which are more likely to be reused remain in the RB, resulting in better utilization. Thus, S_n performs better than other two schemes for RB with 32 entries.

In scheme S_v, invalidations are infrequent: only stores that match loads cause invalidations. Accordingly, larger buffers are able to retain more reusable instructions, resulting in S_v performing better than S_n and S_{n+d} for RB with 1024 entries. The smaller number of invalidations also means that instructions which are not likely to be reused remain in RB. This phenomenon results in scheme S_v performing worse than S_n and S_{n+d} for an RB size of 32 entries.

Since scheme S_{n+d} uses selective invalidations (only independent instructions are invalidated), the frequency of invalidations is reduced while still retaining the ability to purge unusable instructions from the RB. Thus, S_{n+d} not only continues to benefit as the RB size is increased to 1024 entries but also out performs other two schemes for RB with 128 entries.

To study the reuse characteristics of different instruction types, we divide the instructions into the following broad categories: *loads*, *address calculations*, *control* and *integer*. The category *address calculations* consists of loads and stores for which only the address calculation part is reused. (As noted earlier, for

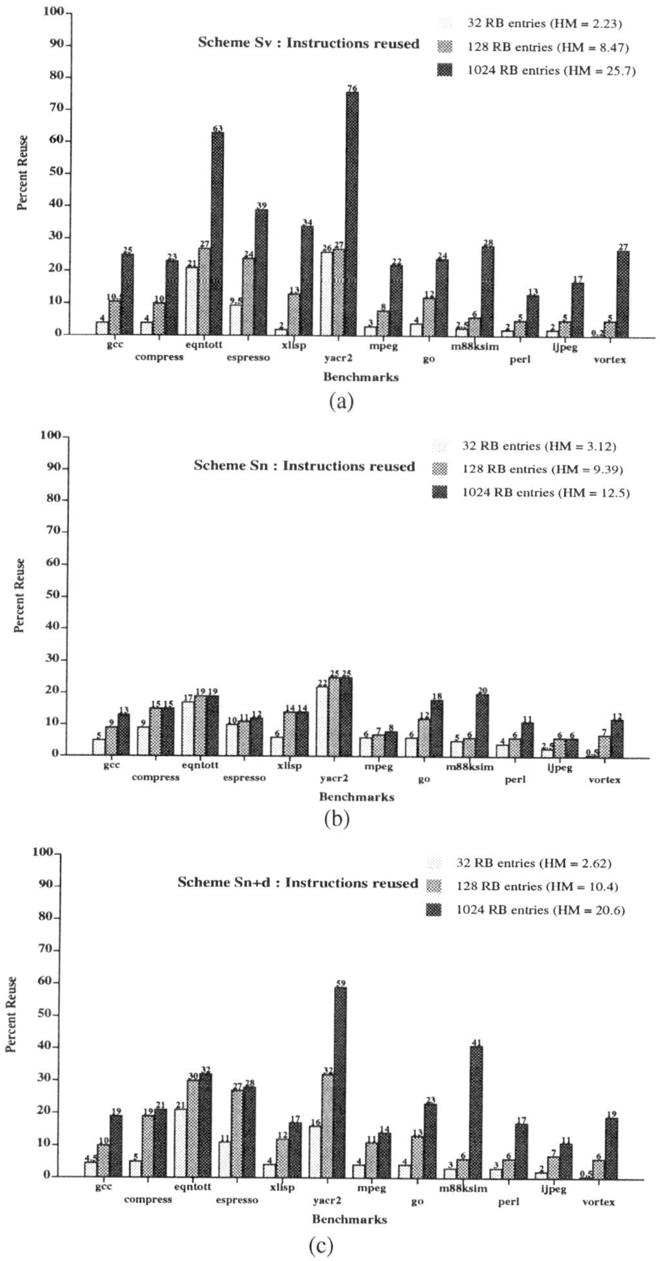

Figure 9. *Percentage of instructions reused for RB sizes: 32, 128 and 1024 entries. The RB in these experiments was fully associative. (a) Scheme S_v (b) Scheme S_n (c) Scheme S_{n+d}. HM stands for harmonic mean.*

stores we reuse only address calculation, and not the actual memory operation). The integer instructions are further divided into three subcategories based on the type of operands: *two reg operands, one reg operands* and *immediate*. Table 3 shows the percentage of instructions reused (average over all benchmarks) from each category using a 1024 entry RB (e.g. 36.9% of all integer instructions with two register operands are reused). As expected, most computation involving immediate constants is reused. Likewise, reuse of address calculation is also not very surprising. Somewhat surprising is that a large number of load instructions could be reused (an average of 21.2% for scheme S_v). This reduces the demand for data cache bandwidth, which can possibly be exploited by reducing the number of data cache ports.

Figure 10 shows the contribution of each instruction category to the total instruction reuse (averaged over all benchmarks), for 3 different RB sizes. We observe that each instruction category makes a measurable contribution to the total instruction reuse; reuse is not limited to some particular instruction type. However, it is worth noting that almost 40-50% of the reuse comes from the load instructions (about 15%) and address calculations (25-35%).

5.2.2 Speedups

Figure 11 shows the speedups ($IPC_{withRB}/IPC_{withoutRB}$) obtained with the different reuse schemes for varying RB sizes. The harmonic mean (HM) over all the benchmarks for each RB size is also shown in the figure. The speedups are not as impressive as the percentage of instructions reused, however, they are still significant in many cases; they range from no speedup to 19% for a 32 entry RB, from 2% to 28% for a 128 entry RB, and from 3% to 43% for a 1024 entry RB. The speedups are not as impressive because there are many other parameters that contribute to overall performance (e.g., cache misses) and reducing the instruction execution component of the execution time may not result in a proportionate decrease in the overall time. With more ideal system parameters (for which instruction issuing and/or the lengths of dependence paths are more important), the speedups will mirror the percentage of instructions reused more closely.

Comparing the harmonic means of the speedups we can see that S_n performs best (among the three schemes) for a 32 entry RB (harmonic mean 4.3), S_{n+d} performs best for a 128 entry RB (harmonic mean 7.2), S_v works best for a 1024 entry RB (harmonic mean 14.9). Comparing percent instruction reuse (section 5.2.1) with the resulting speedups, we see that the scheme that reuses more instructions also delivers better overall speedup.

Instruction Categories		Instruction Reused (%)		
		S_v	S_n	S_{n+d}
Loads (value)		21.2	6.7	11.9
Address Calculations		20.8	10.3	11.9
Control		35.1	1.8	20.2
integer	two reg operands	36.9	26.8	32.0
	one reg operand	38.6	17.9	30.9
	immediate	51.0	98.1	90.4

Table 3: *Percent reuse per instruction category for a 1024 entry RB*

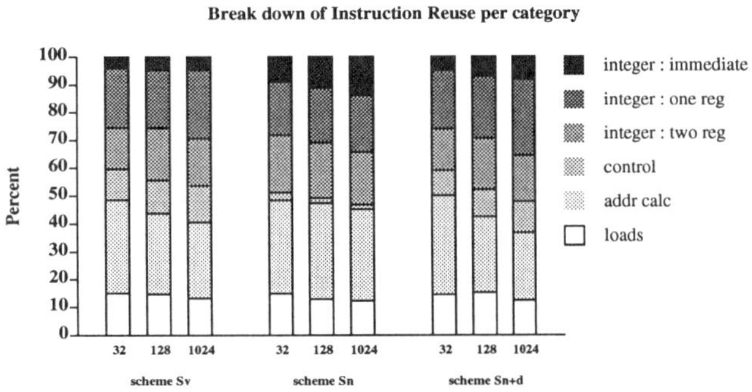

Figure 10. *Contribution of each instruction category to total reuse. These numbers are average over all benchmarks for full associative RB.*

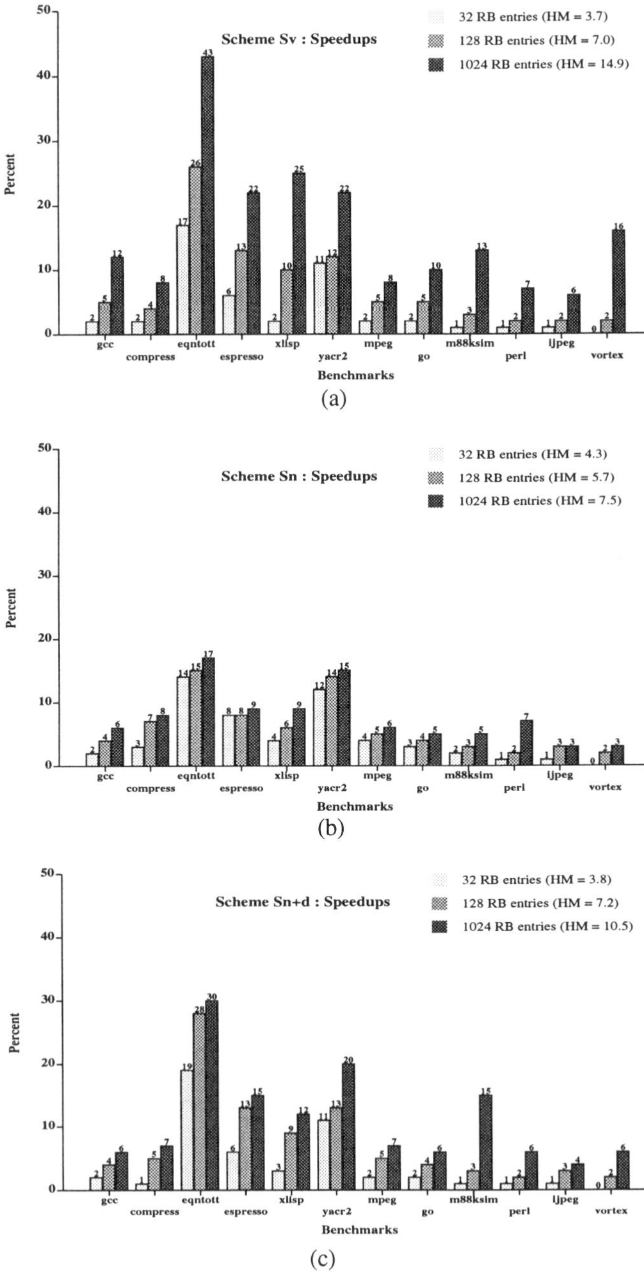

Figure 11. *Speedups obtained due to instruction reuse. The numbers are presented for RB entries 32, 128 and 1024. (a) Scheme S_v (b) Scheme S_n (c) Scheme S_{n+d}. HM stands for harmonic mean.*

5.2.3 Squash Reuse vs. General Reuse

Figure 12 gives a break down of the number of instructions reused into two categories: *squash reuse* and *general reuse*. Squash reuse and general reuse have been illustrated in Figure 1 and Figure 2 respectively. Due to a lack of space, we do not present the breakdown for all three schemes; Figure 12 contains the information only for scheme S_{n+d}. The figure suggests that, as one might expect (with a couple of exceptions), smaller RB sizes have a larger percentage of squash reuse. This is also true for the other schemes.

Figure 13 separates the performance obtained by squash reuse from that obtained by general reuse for each benchmark for scheme S_{n+d} with the three different RB sizes. Observe that the fraction of the speedup attributed to squash reuse is greater than the contribution of squash reuse to the total number of instructions reused (compare with Figure 12). This suggests that squash reuse is more time critical than general reuse — the squash penalty impacts the bottom line more than the latency of an instruction (or a set of instructions), especially in a dynamically scheduled processor.

5.2.4 Set Associative RB

Figure 14 presents the results for a 4-way set associative, 128 entry RB, for scheme S_v. (Figure 14(a) presents the instruction reuse and Figure 14(b) presents the speedups.) Other schemes and buffer sizes show similar results. As we can see, the performance is comparable in either case. For some programs (e.g., *eqntott*, *espresso*, and *compress*) set associativity actually improves performance. This is due to the fact that the FIFO replacement policy that we use does not discriminate between reusable and not reusable instructions. Reusable entries are evicted even though non-reusable entries are present (the non-reusable entries are evicted in the set-associative case because of limited choice).

5.2.5 Early resolution of data dependence

We now evaluate the effectiveness of instruction reuse in reducing the length of dependence chains. To do so, we measure the average number of cycles an instruction spends waiting for its operands to be ready (this is called the *data dependence resolution latency* [5]). Figure 15 plots the data dependence resolution latency with instruction reuse, normalized to that without instruction reuse. The data in the figure is for 4-way set associative RB implementing reuse scheme S_v. As is evident from the figure, instruction reuse causes significant reduction in operand waiting times. For *eqntott* and *espresso*, the waiting time is cut down by 40% and 32%, respectively, for an RB size of 128 entries, suggesting that dynamic instruction reuse is quite effective in collapsing true dependences.

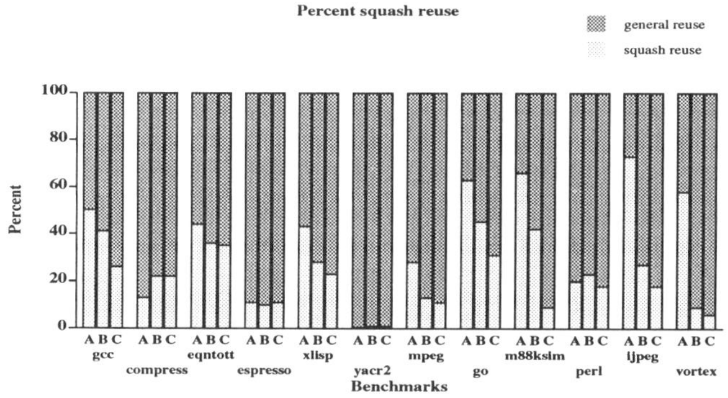

Figure 12. *Reuse break down in terms of general and squash reuse using scheme S_{n+d}. Bar 'A' stands for a 32 entry RB, 'B' stands for a 128 entry RB, and 'C' stands for a 1024 entry RB.*

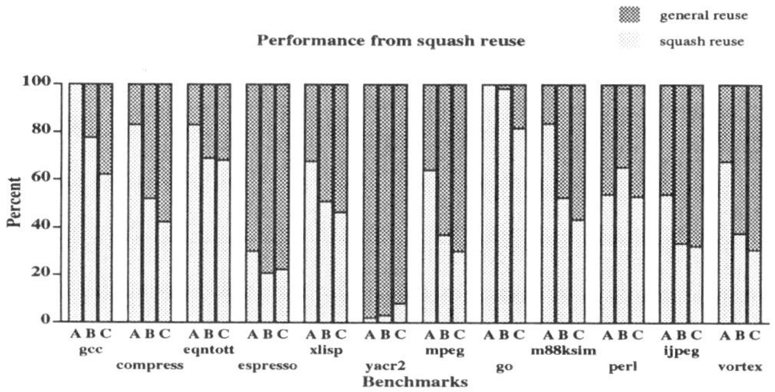

Figure 13. *Performance break down in terms of general and squash reuse using scheme S_{n+d}. Bar 'A' for a 32 entry RB, 'B' for a 128 entry RB, and 'C' for a 1024 entry RB*

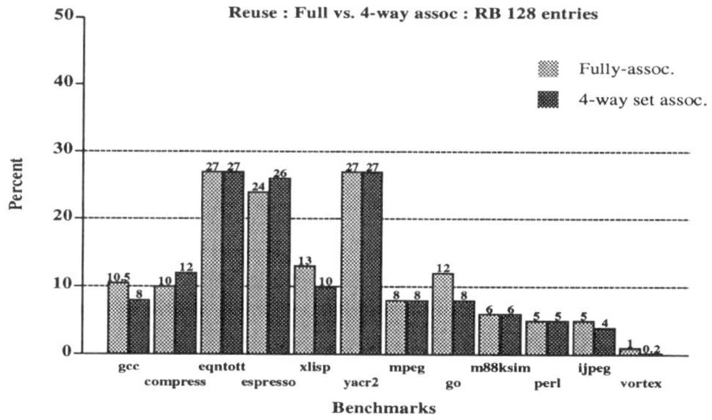

(a)

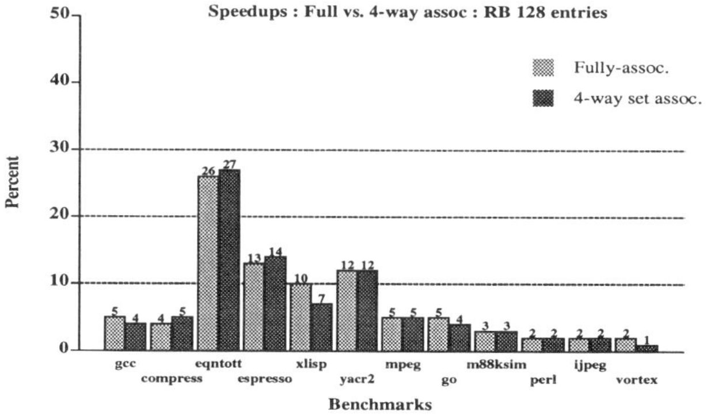

(b)

Figure 14. *Comparison of 4-way set associative RB against fully-associative RB. (a) Percentage instruction reused, (b) Speedups. The results are for RB with 128 entries using Scheme S_v.*

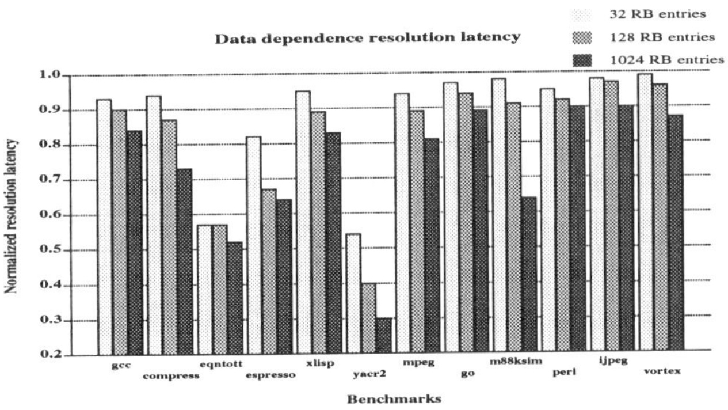

Figure 15. *Data dependence resolution latency with instruction reuse normalized to that without instruction reuse. The result is shown for scheme S_v using 4-way set associative RBs of three different sizes.*

6 Related Work and Discussion

The idea of not having to redo computation is not a new one — it has been used before in several different contexts. A technique called *memoization* has been used for functional and logic programs. The outcome of a function (or a rule) is saved in a table. If the function or the rule is encountered again with the same parameters then the result from the table is used instead of re-evaluation. Memoization is also used to reduce the running time of optimizing compilers, where the same data dependence test is carried out repeatedly.

Harbison in [2][3] proposes a stack-oriented architecture, the *Tree Machine*, which uses a hardware mechanism, the *value cache*, for eliminating common subexpressions and loop invariant expressions. He keeps the result of a computation (called a *phrase*) in the *value cache*. A bit vector, called a *dependency set*, is associated with each result in the value cache to indicate the variables used in computing the result; the bit positions are determined by the address of the variables. When an address is overwritten, all the results in the value cache which have the bit set for that address are invalidated. If a phrase is encountered again, recomputation is avoided by reading the result from the value cache. This approach is similar to our second reuse scheme, scheme S_n. Both perform reuse based on the architectural names of the operands (scheme S_n uses the register specifier, while the value cache uses the memory address). The differences are highlighted later in this section.

Richardson [7] introduces the notion of redundant computation, which is computation that produces the same result repeatedly because it gets the same value for its operands. In this work, the results of floating point operations are stored in a cache, called *result cache*. The index of the cache is obtained by hashing the operand values. The result cache is accessed in parallel with executing an floating point operation. If the result is found in the result cache then the operation is halted.

In [6], Oberman and Flynn, propose the use of *division caches* and *reciprocal caches* for capturing the redundancy in the division and square root computation. The division caches are similar to Richardson's result cache, but for divisions only. The reciprocal caches hold the reciprocals of the divisors. They help convert the high latency division operation to relatively low latency multiply operation. These caches are accessed using the bits from the mantissa of the operands.

There are several differences between our work and the work mentioned above. First, the above techniques are more special purpose. The value cache [2][3] approach is tailored for an architecture which expresses computation in the form of *parse trees* (Tree Machine). The result caches [7], and the division and reciprocal caches[6] target only floating point operations. Our approach is general purpose in that it does not assume any special architecture, and it captures reuse of any type of instruction (except stores). Second, the techniques referred to above access their respective result buffers (value cache in [3], result cache in [7] and division and reciprocal caches in [6]) by using either the operand address [3] or operand values [7][6], which are only available later in the pipeline. Thus, the result buffer access is delayed till the execute stage, which restricts the usefulness of these techniques only to instructions which have multi-cycle latency ([7] uses it for floating point instruction, while [6] uses it for floating point divides only). In contrast, the reuse schemes presented in this paper access the RB using the instruction address, and hence reuse occurs while the instruction is still in the decode stage. This has two advantages: first, even single cycle instructions benefit from reuse; second, the reused instruction need not flow down the pipeline, which frees machine resources for other instructions to use. The third difference is, since other techniques use operand values for indexing in the result buffer, unlike our schemes, they cannot reuse multiple dependent instructions simultaneously (the result of one instruction would be needed to form the index for the dependent instruction)

One of the benefits of instruction reuse is that it collapses true dependencies. Other techniques based on prediction have been proposed to achieve the same effect [4][5]. In [5], Lipasti et. al. propose predicting the value of loads to collapse the true dependencies. In [4] they extend this concept to predict the value of registers. The fundamental difference from our schemes is that these approaches are based on prediction. The instructions still must execute to generate result for later verification. Our schemes are not based on prediction, and the reused result is guaranteed to be correct.

7 Conclusions

In this paper we introduced and studied the concept of dynamic instruction reuse. Empirical observations suggest that in a program execution, many instructions (and groups of instructions) are executed repeatedly with the same inputs, generating the same results. We discussed two causes of this behavior: (i) the re-execution of (control-independent) computation when recovering from a branch mis-prediction, and (ii) the generic nature of programs which are written to operate on a variety of data inputs.

We presented three schemes for exploiting the phenomenon. All three schemes buffer the outcome of an instruction in a *reuse buffer* from where future instructions can access it (if the operands match). The schemes differ in the way that they track the reuse status of an instruction: scheme S_v uses operand values, scheme S_n uses operand names, and scheme S_{n+d} uses operand names as well as dependence information. By dynamically reusing instruction results, we are able to (i) cut down on the resources required to execute the instructions, and (ii) cut down on the time that it takes to know the outcomes of sequences of dependent instructions, i.e., reduce the length of critical paths of computation.

We evaluated the effectiveness of the proposed schemes using 3 different buffer sizes: 32, 128, and 1024 entries, using execution-driven simulation. Significant instruction reuse was found in many cases, with as many as 76% of the instructions being reused in one case. Furthermore, reuse was not limited to a particular category of instructions; a significant number of instructions were reused from all the broad categories of instructions considered. We also measured the resulting speedup in the program execution time. The speedup is not as pronounced as the percentage of instructions reused, but it is still quite significant, with as much as 43% speedup in one case. We also observed that a 4-way set associative reuse buffer compared favorably in performance for the cases considered. Finally, we measured the effectiveness of reuse in cutting down data dependence path lengths by measuring the average time that an instruction waits for operands. We found that the waiting time was cut down by 40% in one case.

This paper represents only a first attempt at studying a phenomenon (and associated means to exploit it) that could have significant implications for the microarchitecture of the future processors. There is a great deal of work that remains to be done; this work can broadly be classified into two-related categories: (i) better exploiting the reuse phenomenon, and (ii) impact of reuse on other microarchitectural components. Several issues need to be investigated in either category. In the former, we have observed that only about 20% of the instructions inserted into the RB constitute all the reuse. This calls for selective insertion policies that result in better reuse characteristics with small reuse structures. Another issue that needs to be investigated is better invalidation mechanisms (for schemes S_n and S_{n+d}) such as invalidation using time-stamps. Software transformations that facilitates reuse are also an area that deserves study. Considerable work is also needed in the second category. Success at instruction reuse might cause us to rethink the need for aggressive speculation structures: there might be no need to predict the outcome of a branch if its outcome can be determined from a reuse buffer. Likewise, there might be no need to carry out value prediction, if the value can be determined from the reuse buffer. In this case, resources that would otherwise be spent in making more powerful speculation structures might be better spent in structures that improve instruction reuse, backed up by less powerful speculation structures.

Acknowledgments

We thank Scott Breach, Doug Burger, Andy Glew, Andreas Moshovos, Shubu Mukherjee, Subbarao Palacharla and the anonymous referees for their comments on earlier drafts of the paper. We would also like to thank Haitham Akkary and Todd Austin for their comments on this work.

This work was supported in part by NSF Grants CCR-9303030 and MIP-9505853, the U.S. Army Intelligence Center and Fort Huachuca under contract DABT63-95-C-0127 and ARPA order no. D346, a donation from Intel Corp, and an equipment donation from Sun Microsystems. The views and conclusions contained herein are those of the authors and should not be interpreted as necessarily representing the official policies or endorsements, either expressed or implied, of the U.S Army Intelligence Center and Fort Huachuca, or the U.S. Government.

References

[1] D. Burger, T. M. Austin, and S. Bennett. Evaluating Future Microprocessors: The SimpleScalar Tool Set. Technical Report CS-TR-96-1308, University of Wisconsin-Madison, July 1996. (URL: http://www.cs.wisc.edu/~mscalar/simplescalar.html)

[2] S. P. Harbison. *A Computer Architecture for the Dynamic Optimization of High-Level Language Programs*. Ph.D. thesis, Carnegie Mellon University, Sept. 1980.

[3] S. P. Harbison. An architectural alternative to optimizing compilers. In *Proc. International Conference on Architectural Support for Programming Languages and Operating Systems (ASPLOS)*, page 57 65, Mar. 1982.

[4] M. H. Lipasti and J. P. Shen. Exceeding the dataflow limit via value prediction. In *Proc. of 29th International Symposium on Microarchitecture*, pages 226–237, Dec. 1996.

[5] M. H. Lipasti, C. B. Wilkerson, and J. P. Shen. Value locality and load value prediction. In *Proc. of ASPLOS VII*, pages 138–147, Sept. 1996.

[6] S. F. Oberman and M. J. Flynn. On Division and Reciprocal Caches. Technical Report CSL-TR-95-666, Stanford University, Apr. 1995.

[7] S. E. Richardson. Caching function results: Faster arithmetic by avoiding unnecessary computation. Technical Report SMLI TR-92-1, Sun Microsystems Laboratories, Sept. 1992.

[8] J. Smith and A. Pleszkun. Implementing precise interrupts in pipelined processors. *IEEE Transactions on Computers*, 37(5):562–573, May 1988.

Complexity-Effective Superscalar Processors

Subbarao Palacharla
Computer Sciences Department
University of Wisconsin-Madison
Madison, WI 53706, USA
subbarao@cs.wisc.edu

Norman P. Jouppi
Western Research Laboratory
Digital Equipment Corporation
Palo Alto, CA 94301, USA
jouppi@pa.dec.com

J. E. Smith
Dept. of Electrical and Computer Engg.
University of Wisconsin-Madison
Madison, WI 53706, USA
jes@ece.wisc.edu

Abstract

The performance tradeoff between hardware complexity and clock speed is studied. First, a generic superscalar pipeline is defined. Then the specific areas of register renaming, instruction window wakeup and selection logic, and operand bypassing are analyzed. Each is modeled and Spice simulated for feature sizes of $0.8\mu m$, $0.35\mu m$, and $0.18\mu m$. Performance results and trends are expressed in terms of issue width and window size. Our analysis indicates that window wakeup and selection logic as well as operand bypass logic are likely to be the most critical in the future.

A microarchitecture that simplifies wakeup and selection logic is proposed and discussed. This implementation puts chains of dependent instructions into queues, and issues instructions from multiple queues in parallel. Simulation shows little slowdown as compared with a completely flexible issue window when performance is measured in clock cycles. Furthermore, because only instructions at queue heads need to be awakened and selected, issue logic is simplified and the clock cycle is faster – consequently overall performance is improved. By grouping dependent instructions together, the proposed microarchitecture will help minimize performance degradation due to slow bypasses in future wide-issue machines.

1 Introduction

For many years, a major point of contention among microprocessor designers has revolved around complex implementations that attempt to maximize the number of instructions issued per clock cycle, and much simpler implementations that have a very fast clock cycle. These two camps are often referred to as "brainiacs" and "speed demons" – taken from an editorial in Microprocessor Report [7]. Of course the tradeoff is not a simple one, and through innovation and good engineering, it may be possible to achieve most, if not all, of the benefits of complex issue schemes, while still allowing a very fast clock in the implementation; that is, to develop microarchitectures we refer to as *complexity-effective*. One of two primary objectives of this paper is to propose such a complexity-effective microarchitecture. The proposed microarchitecture achieves high performance, as measured by instructions per cycle (IPC), yet it permits a design with a very high clock frequency.

Supporting the claim of high IPC with a fast clock leads to the second primary objective of this paper. It is commonplace to measure the effectiveness (i.e. IPC) of a new microarchitecture, typically by using trace driven simulation. Such simulations count clock cycles and can provide IPC in a fairly straightforward manner. However, the complexity (or simplicity) of a microarchitecture is much more difficult to determine – to be very accurate, it requires a full implementation in a specific technology. What is very much needed are fairly straightforward measures of complexity that can be used by microarchitects at a fairly early stage of the design process. Such methods would allow the determination of complexity-effectiveness. It is the second objective of this paper to take a step in the direction of characterizing complexity and complexity trends.

Before proceeding, it must be emphasized that while complexity can be variously quantified in terms such as number of transistors, die area, and power dissipated, in this paper complexity is measured as the delay of the critical path through a piece of logic, and the longest critical path through any of the pipeline stages determines the clock cycle.

The two primary objectives given above are covered in reverse order – first sources of pipeline complexity are analyzed, then a new complexity-effective microarchitecture is proposed and evaluated. In the next section we describe those portions of a microarchitecture that tend to have complexity that grows with increasing instruction-level parallelism. Of these, we focus on instruction dispatch and issue logic, and data bypass logic. We analyze potential critical paths in these structures and develop models for quantifying their delays. We study the variation of these delays with microarchitectural parameters of window size (the number of waiting instructions from which ready instructions are selected for issue) and the issue width (the number of instructions that can be issued in a cycle). We also study the impact of the technology trend towards smaller feature sizes. The complexity analysis shows that logic associated with the issue window and data bypasses are likely to be key limiters of clock speed since smaller feature sizes cause wire delays to dominate overall delay [20, 3].

Taking sources of complexity into account, we propose and evaluate a new microarchitecture. This microarchitecture is called *dependence-based* because it focuses on grouping dependent instructions rather than independent ones, as is often the case in superscalar implementations. The dependence-based microarchitecture simplifies issue window logic while exploiting similar levels of parallelism to that achieved by current superscalar microarchitectures using more complex logic.

The rest of the paper is organized as follows. Section 2 describes the sources of complexity in a baseline microarchitecture. Section 3 describes the methodology we use to study the critical pipeline

ISCA '97 Denver, CO, USA
© 1997 ACM 0-89791-901-7/97/0006...$3.50

structures identified in Section 2. Section 4 presents a detailed analysis of each of the structures and shows how their delays vary with microarchitectural parameters and technology parameters. Section 5 presents the proposed dependence-based microarchitecture and some preliminary performance results. Finally, we draw conclusions in Section 6.

2 Sources of Complexity

In this section, specific sources of pipeline complexity are considered. We realize that it is impossible to capture all possible microarchitectures in a single model, however, and any results have some obvious limitations. We can only hope to provide a fairly straightforward model that is typical of most current superscalar processors, and suggest that analyses similar to those used here can be extended to other, more advanced techniques as they are developed.

FETCH	DECODE	RENAME	WAKEUP SELECT	REG READ	EXECUTE BYPASS	DCACHE ACCESS	REG WRITE COMMIT

Figure 1: Baseline superscalar model.

Figure 1 shows the baseline model and the associated pipeline. The fetch unit reads multiple instructions every cycle from the instruction cache, and branches encountered by the fetch unit are predicted. Next, instructions are decoded and their register operands are renamed. Renamed instructions are dispatched to the instruction window, where they wait for their source operands and the appropriate functional unit to become available. As soon as these conditions are satisfied, instructions are issued and executed in the functional units. The operand values of an instruction are either fetched from the register file or are bypassed from earlier instructions in the pipeline. The data cache provides low latency access to memory operands.

2.1 Basic Structures

As mentioned earlier, probably the best way to identify the primary sources of complexity in a microarchitecture is to actually implement the microarchitecture in a specific technology. However, this is extremely time consuming and costly. Instead, our approach is to select certain key structures for study, and develop relatively simple delay models that can be applied in a straightforward manner without relying on detailed design.

Structures to be studied were selected using the following criteria. First, we consider structures whose delay is a function of issue window size and/or issue width; these structures are likely to become cycle-time limiters in future wide-issue superscalar designs. Second, we are interested in dispatch and issue-related structures because these structures form the core of a microarchitecture and largely determine the amount of parallelism that can be exploited. Third, some structures tend to rely on broadcast operations over long wires and hence their delays might not scale as well as logic-intensive structures in future technologies with smaller feature sizes.

The structures we consider are:

- *Register rename logic.* This logic translates logical register designators into physical register designators.
- *Wakeup logic.* This logic is part of the issue window and is responsible for waking up instructions waiting for their source operands to become available.
- *Selection logic.* This logic is another part of the issue window and is responsible for selecting instructions for execution from the pool of ready instructions.
- *Bypass logic.* This logic is responsible for bypassing operand values from instructions that have completed execution, but have not yet written their results to the register file, to subsequent instructions.

There are other important pieces of pipeline logic that are not considered in this paper, even though their delay is a function of dispatch/issue width. In most cases, their delay has been considered elsewhere. These include register files and caches. Farkas et. al. [6] study how the access time of the register file varies with the number of registers and the number of ports. The access time of a cache is a function of the size of the cache and the associativity of the cache. Wada et. al. [18] and Wilton and Jouppi [21] have developed detailed models that estimate the access time of a cache given its size and associativity.

2.2 Current Implementations

The structures identified above were presented in the context of the baseline superscalar model shown in Figure 1. The MIPS R10000 [22] and the DEC 21264 [10] are real implementations that directly fit this model. Hence, the structures identified above apply to these two processors.

On the other hand, the Intel Pentium Pro [9], the HP PA-8000 [12], the PowerPC 604 [16], and the HAL SPARC64 [8] do not completely fit the baseline model. These processors are based on a microarchitecture where the reorder buffer holds non-committed, renamed register values. In contrast, the baseline microarchitecture uses the physical register file for both committed and non-committed values. Nevertheless, the point to be noted is that the basic structures identified earlier are present in both types of microarchitectures. The only notable difference is the size of the physical register file.

Finally, while the discussion about potential sources of complexity is in the context of an out-of-order baseline superscalar model, it must be pointed out that some of the critical structures identified apply to in-order processors, too. For example, part of the register rename logic (to be discussed later) and the bypass logic are present in in-order superscalar processors.

3 Methodology

The key pipeline structures were studied in two phases. In the first phase, we selected a representative CMOS circuit for the structure. This was done by studying designs published in the literature (e.g. ISSCC [1] proceedings) and by collaborating with engineers at Digital Equipment Corporation. In cases where there was more than one possible design, we did a preliminary study of the designs to decide in favor of one that was most promising. By basing our circuits on designs published by microprocessor vendors, we believe the studied circuits are similar to circuits used in microprocessor designs. In practice, many circuit tricks could be employed to optimize critical paths. However, we believe that the relative delays between different structures should be more accurate than the absolute delays.

[1] International Solid-State and Circuits Conference.

In the second phase we implemented the circuit and optimized the circuit for speed. We used the Hspice circuit simulator [14] from Meta-Software to simulate the circuits. Primarily, static logic was used. However, in situations where dynamic logic helped in boosting the performance significantly, we used dynamic logic. For example, in the wakeup logic, a dynamic 7-input NOR gate is used for comparisons instead of a static gate. A number of optimizations were applied to improve the speed of the circuits. First, all the transistors in the circuit were manually sized so that overall delay improved. Second, logic optimizations like two-level decomposition were applied to reduce fan-in requirements. We avoided using static gates with a fan-in greater than four. Third, in some cases transistor ordering was modified to shorten the critical path. Wire parasitics were added at appropriate nodes in the Hspice model of the circuit. These parasitics were computed by calculating the length of the wires based on the layout of the circuit and using the values of R_{metal} and C_{metal}, the resistance and parasitic capacitance of metal wires per unit length.

To study the effect of reducing the feature size on the delays of the structures, we simulated the circuits for three different feature sizes: $0.8\mu m$, $0.35\mu m$, and $0.18\mu m$ respectively. Layouts for the $0.35\mu m$ and $0.18\mu m$ process were obtained by appropriately shrinking the layouts for the $0.8\mu m$ process. The Hspice models used for the three technologies are tabulated in [15].

4 Pipeline Complexity

In this section, we analyze the critical pipeline structures. The presentation for each structure begins with a description of the logical function being implemented. Then, possible implementation schemes are discussed, and one is chosen. Next, we summarize our analysis of the overall delay in terms of the microarchitectural parameters of issue width and issue window size; a much more detailed version of the analysis appears in [15]. Finally, Hspice circuit simulation results are presented and trends are identified and compared with the earlier analysis.

4.1 Register Rename Logic

Register rename logic translates logical register designators into physical register designators by accessing a map table with the logical register designator as the index. The map table holds the current logical to physical mappings and is multi-ported because multiple instructions, each with multiple register operands, need to be renamed every cycle. The high level block diagram of the rename logic is shown in Figure 2. In addition to the map table, dependence check logic is required to detect cases where the logical register being renamed is written by an earlier instruction in the current group of instructions being renamed. The dependence check logic detects such dependences and sets up the output MUXes so that the appropriate physical register designators are selected. At the end of every rename operation, the map table is updated to reflect the new logical to physical mappings created for the result registers written by the current rename group.

4.1.1 Structure

The mapping and checkpointing functions of the rename logic can be implemented in at least two ways. These two schemes, called the RAM scheme and the CAM scheme, are described next.

- *RAM scheme*
  In the RAM scheme, implemented in the MIPS R10000 [22], the map table is a register file where the logical register designator directly accesses an entry that contains the physical register to which it is mapped. The number of entries in the map table is equal to the number of logical registers.

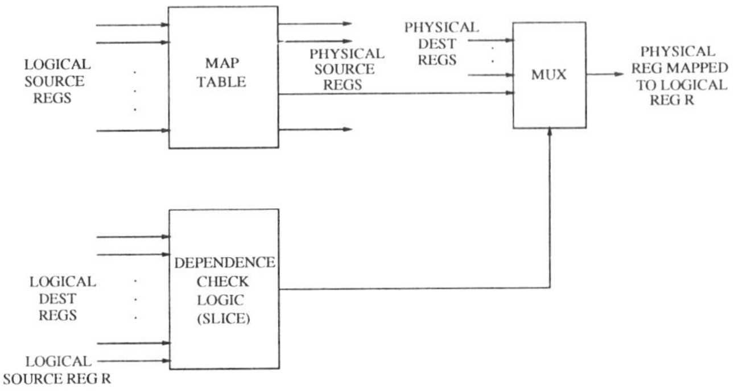

Figure 2: Register rename logic.

- *CAM scheme*
  An alternate scheme for register renaming uses a CAM (content-addressable memory) [19] to store the current mappings. Such a scheme is implemented in the HAL SPARC [2] and the DEC 21264 [10]. The number of entries in the CAM is equal to the number of physical registers. Each entry contains two fields: the logical register designator that is mapped to the physical register represented by the entry and a valid bit that is set if the current mapping is valid. Renaming is accomplished by matching on the logical register designator field.

In general, the CAM scheme is less scalable than the RAM scheme because the number of CAM entries, which is equal to the number of physical registers, tends to increase with issue width. Also, for the design space we are interested in, the performance was found to be comparable. Consequently, we focus on the RAM method below. A more detailed discussion of the trade-offs involved can be found in [15].

The dependence check logic proceeds in parallel with the map table access. Every logical register designator being renamed is compared against the logical destination register designators of earlier instructions in the current rename group. If there is a match, then the physical register assigned to the result of the earlier instruction is used instead of the one read from the map table. In the case of multiple matches, the register corresponding to the latest (in dynamic order) match is used. Dependence check logic for issue widths of 2, 4, and 8 was implemented. We found that for these issue widths, the delay of the dependence check logic is less than the delay of the map table, and hence the check can be hidden behind the map table access.

4.1.2 Delay Analysis

As the name suggests, the RAM scheme operates like a standard RAM. Address decoders drive word lines; an access stack at the addressed cell pulls a bitline low. The bitline changes are sensed by a sense amplifier which in turn produces the output. Symbolically the rename delay can be written as,

$$T_{rename} = T_{decode} + T_{wordline} + T_{bitline} + T_{senseamp}$$

The analysis presented here and in following subsections focuses on those parts of the delay that are a function of the issue width and window size. All sources of delay are considered in detail in [15]. In the rename logic, the window size is not a factor, and the issue width affects delay through its impact on wire lengths. Increasing the issue width increases the number of bitlines and wordlines in each cell thus making each cell bigger. This in turn increases the length of the predecode, wordline, and bitline wires and the associated wire delays. The net effect is the following relationships for the delay components:

$$T_{decode}, T_{wordline}, T_{bitline} = c_0 + c_1 \times IW + c_2 \times IW^2$$

where IW is the issue width and c_0, c_1, and c_2 are constants that are fixed for a given technology and instruction set architecture; derivation of the constants for each component is given in [15]. In each case, the quadratic component, resulting from the intrinsic RC delay of wires, is relatively small for the design space and technologies we explored. Hence, the decode, wordline, and bitline delays are effectively linear functions of the issue width.

For the sense amplifier, we found that even though its structural constitution is independent of the issue width, its delay is a function of the slope of the input – the bitline delay – and therefore varies linearly with issue width.

4.1.3 Spice Results

For our Hspice simulations, Figure 3 shows how the delay of the rename logic varies with the issue width i.e. the number of instructions being renamed every cycle for the three technologies. The graph includes the breakdown of delay into components discussed in the previous section.

A number of observations can be made from the graph. The total delay increases linearly with issue width for all the technologies. This is in conformance with our analysis, summarized in the previous section. Furthermore, each of the components shows a linear increase with issue width. The increase in the bitline delay is larger than the increase in the wordline delay as issue width is increased because the bitlines are longer than the wordlines in our design. The bitline length is proportional to the number of logical registers (32 in most cases) whereas the wordline length is proportional to the width of the physical register designator (less than 8 for the design space we explored).

Another important observation that can be made from the graph is that the relative increase in wordline delay, bitline delay, and hence, total delay as a function of issue width worsens as the feature size is reduced. For example, as the issue width is increased from 2 to 8, the percentage increase in bitline delay shoots up from 37% to 53% as the feature size is reduced from $0.8\mu m$ to $0.18\mu m$. Logic delays in the various components are reduced in proportion to the feature size, while the presence of wire delays in the wordline and bitline components cause the wordline and bitline components to fall at a slower rate. In other words, wire delays in the wordline and bitline structures will become increasingly important as feature sizes are reduced.

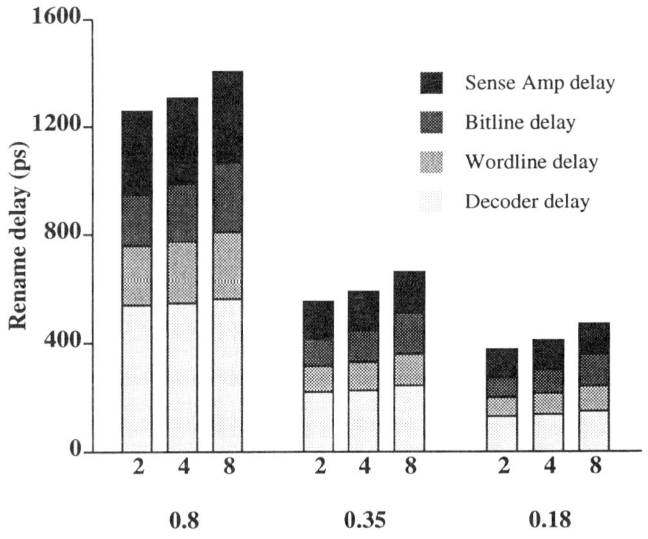

Figure 3: Rename delay versus issue width.

4.2 Wakeup Logic

Wakeup logic is responsible for updating source dependences for instructions in the issue window waiting for their source operands to become available.

4.2.1 Structure

Wakeup logic is illustrated in Figure 4. Every time a result is produced, a tag associated with the result is broadcast to all the instructions in the issue window. Each instruction then compares the tag with the tags of its source operands. If there is a match, the operand is marked as available by setting the rdyL or rdyR flag. Once all the operands of an instruction become available (both rdyL and rdyR are set), the instruction is ready to execute, and the ready flag is set to indicate this. The issue window is a CAM array holding one instruction per entry. Buffers, shown at the top of the figure, are used to drive the result tags $tag1$ to $tagIW$, where IW is the issue width. Each entry of the CAM has $2 \times IW$ comparators to compare each of the results tags against the two operand tags of the entry. The OR logic ORs the comparator outputs and sets the rdyL/rdyR flags.

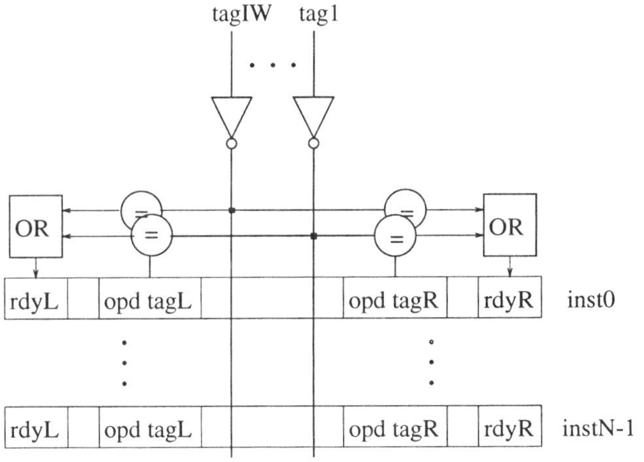

Figure 4: Wakeup logic.

4.2.2 Delay Analysis

The delay consists of three components: the time taken by the buffers to drive the tag bits, the time taken by the comparators in a pull-down stack corresponding to a mismatching bit position to pull the matchline low [2], and the time taken to OR the individual match signals (matchlines). Symbolically,

$$Delay = T_{tagdrive} + T_{tagmatch} + T_{matchOR}$$

The time taken to drive the tags depends on the length of the tag lines and the number of comparators on the tag lines. Increasing the window size increases both these terms. For a given window size,

[2] We assume that only one pull-down stack is turned on since we are interested in the worst-case delay.

increasing issue width also increases both the terms in the following way. Increasing issue width increases the number of matchlines in each cell and hence increases the height of each cell. Also, increasing issue width increases the number of comparators in each cell. Note that we assume the maximum number of tags produced per cycle is equal to the maximum issue width.

In simplified form (see [15] for a more detailed analysis), the time taken to drive the tags is:

$$T_{tagdrive} = c_0 + (c_1 + c_2 \times IW) \times WINSIZE + (c_3 + c_4 \times IW + c_5 \times IW^2) \times WINSIZE^2$$

The above equation shows that the tag drive time is a quadratic function of the window size. The weighting factor of the quadratic term is a function of the issue width. The weighting factor becomes significant for issue widths beyond 2. For a given window size, the tag drive time is also a quadratic function of the issue width. For current technologies ($0.35\mu m$ and longer) the quadratic component is relatively small and the tag drive time is largely a linear function of issue width. However, as the feature size is reduced to $0.18\mu m$, the quadratic component also increases in significance. The quadratic component results from the intrinsic RC delay of the tag lines.

In reality, both issue width and window size will be simultaneously increased because a larger window is required for finding more independent instructions to take advantage of wider issue. Hence, the tag drive time will become significant in future designs with wider issue widths, bigger windows, and smaller feature sizes.

The tag match time is primarily a function of the length of the matchline, which varies linearly with the issue width. The match OR time is the time taken to OR the match lines, and the number of matchlines is a linear function of issue width. Both of these (refer to [15]) have a delay:

$$T_{tagmatch}, T_{matchOR} = c_0 + c_1 \times IW + c_2 \times IW^2$$

However, in both cases the quadratic term is very small for the design space we consider, so these delays are linear functions of issue width.

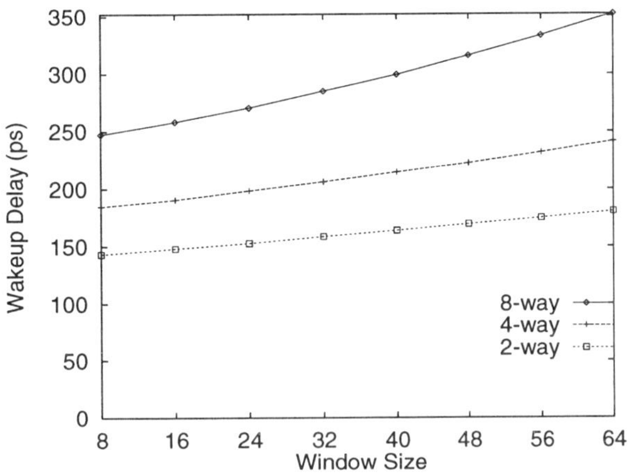

Figure 5: Wakeup logic delay versus window size.

4.2.3 Spice Results

The graph in Figure 5 shows how the delay of the wakeup logic varies with window size and issue width for $0.18\mu m$ technology. As expected, the delay increases as window size and issue width are increased. The quadratic dependence of the total delay on the window size results from the quadratic increase in tag drive time as discussed in the previous section. This effect is clearly visible for issue width of 8 and is less significant for issue width of 4. We found similar curves for $0.8\mu m$ and $0.35\mu m$ technologies. The quadratic dependence of delay on window size was more prominent in the curves for $0.18\mu m$ technology than in the case of the other two technologies.

Also, issue width has a greater impact on the delay than window size because increasing issue width increases all three components of the delay. On the other hand, increasing window size only lengthens the tag drive time and to a small extent the tag match time. Overall, the results show that the delay increases by almost 34% going from 2-way to 4-way and by 46% going from 4-way to 8-way for a window size of 64 instructions. In reality, the increase in delay is going to be even worse because in order to sustain a wider issue width, a larger window is required to find independent instructions.

Figure 6 shows the effect of reducing feature sizes on the various components of the wakeup delay for an 8-way, 64-entry window processor. The tag drive and tag match delays do not scale as well as the match OR delay. This is expected since tag drive and tag match delays include wire delays whereas the match OR delay only consists of logic delays. Quantitatively, the fraction of the total delay contributed by tag drive and tag match delay increases from 52% to 65% as the feature size is reduced from $0.8\mu m$ to $0.18\mu m$. This shows that the performance of the broadcast operation will become more crucial in future technologies.

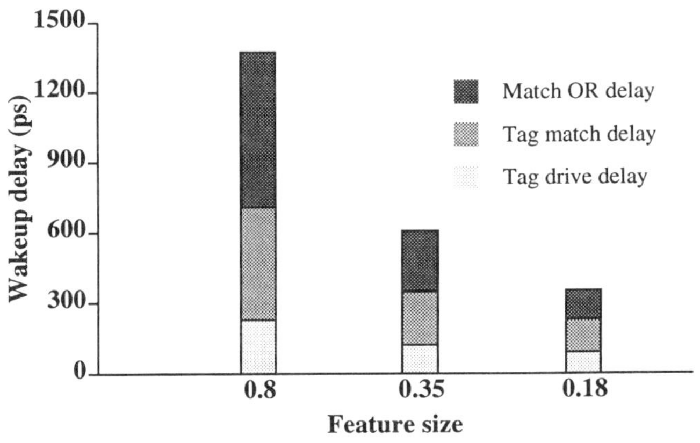

Figure 6: Wakeup delay versus feature size.

4.3 Selection Logic

Selection logic is responsible for choosing instructions for execution from the pool of ready instructions in the issue window. Some form of selection logic is required because the number and types of ready instructions may exceed the number and types of functional units available to execute them.

Inputs to the selection logic are request (REQ) signals, one per instruction in the issue window. The request signal of an instruction is raised when the wakeup logic determines that all its operands are available. The outputs of the selection logic are grant (GRANT) signals, one per request signal. On receipt of the GRANT signal, the associated instruction is issued to the functional unit.

A *selection policy* is used to decide which of the requesting instructions is granted. An example selection policy is *oldest first* - the ready instruction that occurs earliest in program order is granted the functional unit. Butler and Patt [5] studied various policies for scheduling ready instructions and found that overall performance is largely independent of the selection policy. The HP PA-8000 uses a selection policy that is based on the location of the instruction in the window. We assume the same selection policy in our study.

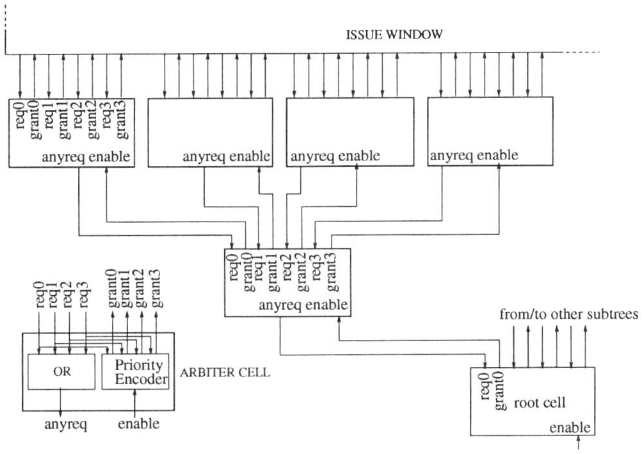

Figure 7: Selection logic.

4.3.1 Structure

The basic structure of selection logic is shown in Figure 7. Modifications to this scheme for handling multiple functional units of the same type are discussed in [15]. Selection logic consists of a tree of arbiters that works in two phases. In the first phase, request signals are propagated up the tree. Each cell raises the $anyreq$ signal if any of its input request signals is high. This in turn raises the input request signal of its parent arbiter cell. At the root cell one or more of the input request signals will be high if there are one or more instructions that are ready. The root cell grants the functional unit to one of its children by raising one of its grant outputs. This initiates the second phase where the grant signal is propagated down the tree to the instruction that is selected. The enable signal to the root cell is high whenever the functional unit is ready to execute an instruction.

The selection policy implemented is static and based strictly on location of the instruction in the issue window. The leftmost entries in the window have the highest priority. The *oldest first* policy can be implemented using this scheme by compacting the issue window to the left every time instructions are issued and by inserting new instructions at the right end. However, it is possible that the complexity of compaction could degrade performance. In this case, some restricted form of compacting can be used – so that overall performance is not affected. We did not analyze the complexity of compacting in this study.

4.3.2 Delay Analysis

The delay of the selection logic is the time it takes to generate the grant signal after the request signal has been raised. This is equal to the sum of three terms: the time taken for the request signal to propagate to the root of the tree, the delay of the root cell, and the time taken for the grant signal to propagate from the root to the selected instruction. Hence, the selection delay depends on the height of the arbitration tree and can be written as (see [15] for a more detailed analysis):

$$T_{selection} = c_0 + c_1 \times log_4(WINSIZE)$$

where c_0 and c_1 are constants determined by the propagation delays of a single arbiter. We found the optimal number of arbiter inputs to be four in our case, so the logarithm is base 4. The selection logic in the MIPS R10000, described in [17], is also based on four-input arbiter cells.

4.3.3 Spice Results

Figure 8 shows the delay of the selection logic for various window sizes and for the three feature sizes assuming a single functional unit is being scheduled. The delay is broken down into the three components. From the graph we can see that for all the three technologies, the delay increases logarithmically with window size. Also, the increase in delay is less than 100% when the window size is increased from 16 instructions to 32 instructions (or from 64 instructions to 128 instructions) since one of the components of the total delay, the delay at the root cell, is independent of the window size.

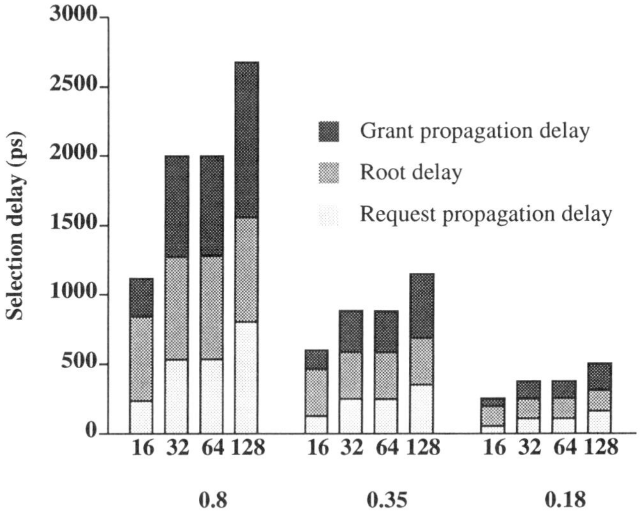

Figure 8: Selection delay versus window size.

The various components of the total delay scale well as the feature size is reduced. This is not surprising since all the delays are logic delays. It must be pointed out that we do not consider the wires in the circuit, so the selection delays presented here are optimistic, especially if the request signals (the ready flags discussed in the wakeup logic) originate from the CAM entries in which the instructions reside. On the other hand, it might be possible to minimize the effect of these wire delays if the ready signals are stored in a smaller, more compact array.

4.4 Data Bypass Logic

Data bypass logic is responsible for forwarding result values from completing instructions to dependent instructions, bypassing the register file. The number of bypass paths required is determined by the depth of the pipeline and the issue width of the microarchitecture. As pointed out in [1], if IW is the issue width, and if there are S pipestages after the first result-producing stage, then a fully bypassed design would require $(2 \times IW^2 \times S)$ bypass paths assuming 2-input functional units. In other words, the number of bypass paths grows quadratically with issue width. This is of critical importance, given the current trends toward deeper pipelines and wider issue.

Bypass logic consists of two components: datapath and control. The datapath comprises result busses, that are used to broadcast bypass values from each functional unit source to all possible destinations. Buffers are used to drive the bypass values on the result busses. In addition to the result busses, the datapath comprises operand MUXes. Operand MUXes are required to gate in the appropriate result on to the operand busses. The control logic is responsible for controlling the operand MUXes. It compares the tags of the result values with the tag of source value required at each functional unit. If there is a match, the MUX control is set so that the result value is driven on the appropriate operand bus. The key factor that determines the speed of the bypass logic is the delay of the result wires that are used to transmit bypassed values, not the control.

4.4.1 Structure

A commonly used structure for bypass logic is shown in Figure 9. The figure shows a bit-slice of the datapath. There are four functional units marked FU0 to FU3. Consider the bit slice of FU0. It gets its two operand bits from the *opd0-l* and *opd0-r* wires. The result bit is driven on the *res0* result wire by the result driver. Tristate buffers are used to drive the result bits on to the operand wires from the result wires of the functional units. These buffers implement the MUXes shown in the figure. To bypass the result of functional unit FU1 to the left input of functional unit FU0, the tristate driver marked A is switched on. The driver A connects the *res1* wire and the *opd0-l* wire. In the case where bypasses are not activated, operand bits are placed on the operand wires by the register file read ports [3]. The result bits are written to the register file in addition to being bypassed.

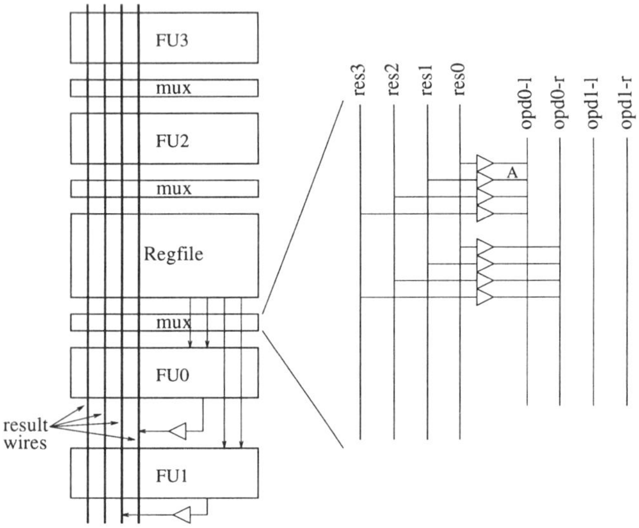

Figure 9: Bypass logic.

4.4.2 Delay Analysis

The delay of the bypass logic is largely determined by the amount of time it takes for the driver at the output of each functional unit to drive the result value on the corresponding result wire. This in turn depends on the length of the result wires. From the figure it is apparent that the length of the wires is a function of the layout. For the layout presented in the figure, the length of the result wires is determined by the height of the functional units and the register file.

[3] In a reservation-station based microarchitecture, the operand bits come from the data field of the reservation station entry.

Issue width	Wire length (λ)	Delay (ps)
4	20500	184.9
8	49000	1056.4

Table 1: Bypass delays for a 4-way and a 8-way processor.

Considering the result wires as distributed RC lines, the delay is given by

$$T_{bypass} = 0.5 \times R_{metal} \times C_{metal} \times L^2$$

where L is the length of the result wires, and R_{metal} and C_{metal} are the resistance and parasitic capacitance of metal wires per unit length respectively.

Increasing issue width increases the length of the result wires, and hence causes the bypass delay to grow quadratically with issue width. Increasing the depth of the pipeline also increases the delay of the bypass logic in the following manner. Making the pipeline deeper increases the fan-in of the operand MUXes connected to a given result wire. This in turn increases the amount of capacitance on the result wires, and hence adds to the delay of the result wires. However, this component of the delay is not captured by our simple model. This component of the delay is likely to become relatively less significant as feature size is reduced.

4.4.3 Spice Results

We computed the wire delays for hypothetical 4-way and 8-way machines assuming common mixes of functional units and functional unit heights reported in the literature. Table 1 shows the results. Wire lengths are shown in terms of λ, where λ is half the feature size. The delays are the same for the three technologies since wire delays are constant according to the scaling model assumed. See [15] for the detailed data and analysis.

4.4.4 Alternative Layouts

The results presented above assume a particular layout; the functional units are placed on either side of the register file. However, as mentioned before, the length of the result wires is a function of the layout. Hence, VLSI designers will have to study alternative layouts in order to reduce bypass delays. Alternative layouts alone will only decrease constants; the quadratic delay growth with number of bypasses will remain.

In the long term, microarchitects will have to consider *clustered* organizations where each cluster of functional units has its own copy of the register file and bypasses within a cluster complete in a single cycle while inter-cluster bypasses take two or more cycles. The hardware or the compiler or both will have to ensure that inter-cluster bypasses occur infrequently. In addition to mitigating the delay of the bypass logic, this organization also has the advantage of faster register files since there are fewer ports on each register file.

4.5 Summary of Delays and Pipeline Issues

We now summarize the pipeline delay results and consider the implications for future complexity-effective microarchitectures. It is easiest to frame this discussion in terms of satisfying the goal of permitting a very fast pipeline clock while, at the same time, exploiting high ILP through relatively wide, out-of-order superscalar operation.

Issue width	Window size	Rename delay (ps)	Wakeup+Select delay (ps)	Bypass delay (ps)
0.8μm technology				
4	32	1577.9	2903.7	184.9
8	64	1710.5	3369.4	1056.4
0.35μm technology				
4	32	627.2	1248.4	184.9
8	64	726.6	1484.8	1056.4
0.18μm technology				
4	32	351.0	578.0	184.9
8	64	427.9	724.0	1056.4

Table 2: Overall delay results.

To aid in this discussion, consider the overall results for a 4-way and a 8-way microarchitecture in $0.18\mu m$ technology shown in Table 2. We chose the $0.18\mu m$ technology because of our interest in future generation microarchitectures. For the 4-way machine, the window logic (wakeup + select) has the greatest delay among all the structures considered, and hence determines the critical path delay. The register rename delay comes next; it is about 39% faster than the delay of the window logic. The bypass delay is relatively small in this case. The results are similar for the 8-way machine, with one very notable exception: the bypass delay grows by a factor of over 5, and is now worse than the (wakeup + select) delay.

Now, let's turn to the problem of designing a future generation microarchitecture with a faster clock cycle. Of the structures we have examined here, the window logic and the bypasses seem to pose the largest problems. Moreover, both of these cause difficulties if we wish to divide them into more pipeline segments; these difficulties will be discussed in the following paragraphs. All the other structures either will not cause a clock cycle problem, or if they do, they can be pipelined. The pipelining aspects of these structures is discussed in [15]. This additional pipelining can cause some performance impact, although it is beyond the scope of this paper to evaluate the exact impact.

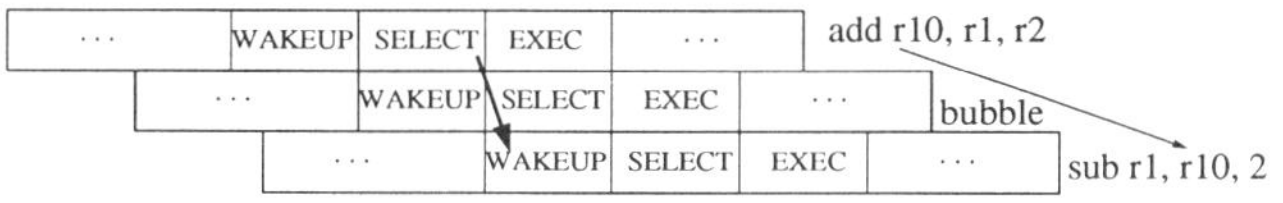

Figure 10: Pipelining wakeup and select.

Wakeup and select together constitute what appears to be an *atomic* operation. That is, if they are divided into multiple pipeline stages, dependent instructions cannot issue in consecutive cycles. Consider the pipeline example shown in Figure 10. The `add` and the `sub` instructions cannot be executed back-to-back because the result of the select stage has to feed the wakeup stage. Hence, wakeup and select together constitute an atomic operation and must be accomplished in a single cycle, at least if dependent instructions are to be executed on consecutive cycles.

Data bypassing is another example of what appears to be an atomic operation. In order for dependent operations to execute in consecutive cycles, the bypass value must be made available to the dependent instruction within a cycle. Results presented in table Table 2 show that this is feasible for a 4-way machine. However, bypass delay can easily become a bottleneck for wider issue-widths.

One solution is to include only a proper subset of bypass paths [1], and take a penalty for those that are not present. For an 8-way machine with deep pipelines, this would exclude a large number of bypass paths. Another solution is to generalize the method used in the DEC 21264 [10] and use multiple copies of the register file. This is the "cluster" method referred to in Section 4.4.

In the following section we tackle both the window logic and bypass problems by proposing a microarchitecture that simplifies window logic and which naturally supports clustering of functional units.

5 A Complexity-Effective Microarchitecture

From the analysis presented in the previous sections we see that the issue window logic is one of the primary contributors of complexity in typical out-of-order microarchitectures. Also, as architects employ wider issue-widths and deeper pipelines, the delay of the bypass logic becomes even more critical. In this section, we propose a *dependence-based* microarchitecture that replaces the issue window with a simpler structure that facilitates a faster clock while exploiting similar levels of parallelism. In addition, the proposed microarchitecture naturally lends itself to clustering and helps mitigate the bypass problem to a large extent.

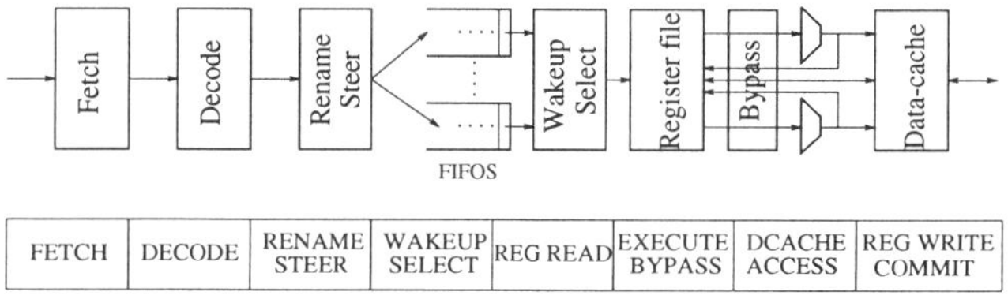

Figure 11: Dependence-based microarchitecture.

The idea behind the dependence-based microarchitecture is to exploit the natural dependences among instructions. A key point is that dependent instructions cannot execute in parallel. In the proposed microarchitecture, shown in Figure 11, the issue window is replaced by a small number of FIFO buffers. The FIFO buffers are constrained to issue in-order, and dependent instructions are steered to the same FIFO. This ensures that the instructions in a particular FIFO buffer can only execute sequentially. Hence, unlike the typical issue window where result tags have to be broadcast to all the entries, the register availability only needs to be fanned out to the heads of the FIFO buffers. The instructions at the FIFO heads monitor reservation bits (one per physical register) to check for operand availability. This is discussed in detail later. Furthermore, the selection logic only has to monitor instructions at the heads of the FIFO buffers.

The steering of dependent instructions to the FIFO buffers is performed at run-time during the rename stage. Dependence information between instructions is maintained in a table called the `SRC_FIFO` table. This table is indexed using logical register designators. `SRC_FIFO(Ra)`, the entry for logical register `Ra`, contains the identity of the FIFO buffer that contains the instruction that will write register `Ra`. If that instruction has already completed i.e. register `Ra` contains its computed value, then `SRC_FIFO(Ra)` is invalid. This table is similar to the map table used for register renaming and can be accessed in parallel with the rename table. In order to steer an instruction to a particular FIFO, the `SRC_FIFO` table is accessed with the register identifiers of the source operands of an instruction. For example, for steering the instruction `add r10,r5,1` where `r10` is the destination register, the SRC_FIFO table is indexed with 5. The entry is then used to steer the instruction to the appropriate FIFO.

5.1 Instruction Steering Heuristics

A number of heuristics are possible for steering instructions to the FIFOs. A simple heuristic that we found to work well for our benchmark programs is described next.

Let I be the instruction under consideration. Depending upon the availability of I's operands, the following cases are possible:

- All the operands of I have already been computed and are residing in the register file. In this case, I is steered to a new (empty) FIFO acquired from a pool of free FIFOs.
- I requires a single outstanding operand to be produced by instruction Isource residing in FIFO Fa. In this case, if there is no instruction behind Isource in Fa then I is steered to Fa, else I is steered to a new FIFO.
- I requires two outstanding operands to be produced by instructions Ileft and Iright residing in FIFOs Fa and Fb respectively. In this case, apply the heuristic in the previous bullet to the left operand. If the resulting FIFO is not suitable (it is either full or there is an instruction behind the source instruction), then apply the same heuristic to the right operand.

If all the FIFOs are full or if no empty FIFO is available then the decoder/steering logic stalls. A FIFO is returned to the free pool when the last instruction in the FIFO is issued. Initially, all the FIFOs are in the free pool. Figure 12 illustrates the heuristic on a code segment from one of the SPEC benchmarks.

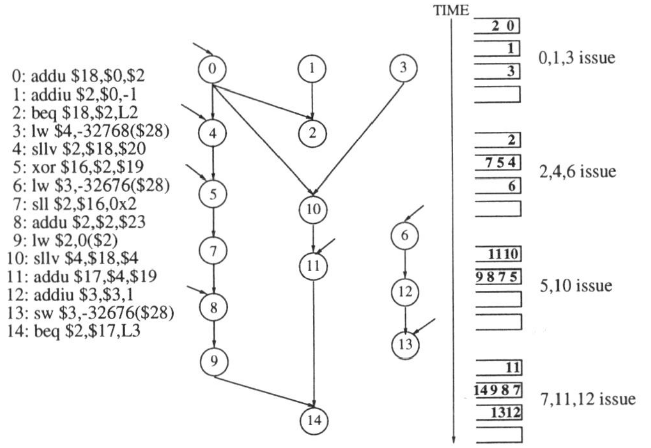

Figure 12: Instruction steering example.

This figure shows how instructions are steered to FIFOs using the heuristic presented in Section 5.1 for a sample code segment. Instructions can issue only from the heads of the four FIFOs. The steering logic steers four instructions every cycle and a maximum of four instructions can issue every cycle.

5.2 Performance Results

We compare the performance of the dependence-based microarchitecture against that of a typical microarchitecture with an issue window. The proposed microarchitecture has 8 FIFOs, with each FIFO having 8-entries. The issue window of the conventional processor has 64 entries. Both microarchitectures can decode, rename, and execute a maximum of 8 instructions per cycle. The timing simulator, a modified version of SimpleScalar [4], is detailed in Table 3.

Fetch width	any 8 instructions
I-cache	Perfect instruction cache
Branch Predictor	McFarling's gshare [13] 4K 2-bit counters, 12 bit history unconditional control instructions predicted perfectly
Issue window size	64
Max. in-flight instructions	128
Retire width	16
Functional Units	8 symmetrical units
Functional Unit Latency	1 cycle
Issue Mechanism	out-of-order issue of up to 8 ops/cycle loads may execute when all prior store addresses are known
Physical Registers	120 int/120 fp
D-cache	32KB, 2-way SA write-back, write-allocate 32 byte lines,1 cycle hit,6 cycle miss four load/store ports

Table 3: Baseline simulation model.

An aggressive instruction fetch mechanism is used to stress the issue and execution subsystems. We ran seven benchmarks from the SPEC'95 suite, using their training input datasets. Each benchmark was run for a maximum of 0.5B instructions.

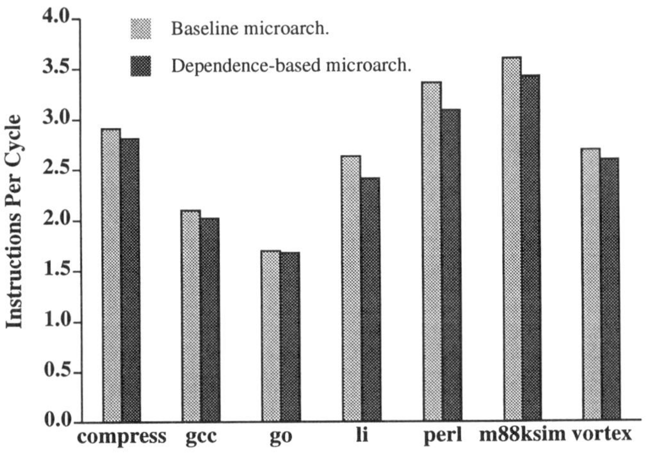

Figure 13: Performance (IPC) of dependence-based microarchitecture.

The performance results (in terms of instructions committed per cycle) are shown in Figure 13. The dependence-based microarchitecture is nearly as effective (extracts similar parallelism) as the typical window-based microarchitecture. The cycle count numbers are within 5% for five of the seven benchmarks and the maximum performance degradation is 8% in the case of *li*.

5.3 Complexity Analysis

First, consider the delay of the wakeup and selection logic. Wakeup logic is required to detect cross-FIFO dependences. For example, if the instruction Ia at the head of FIFO Fa is dependent on an instruction Ib waiting in FIFO Fb, then Ia cannot issue until Ib completes. However, the wakeup logic in this case does not involve broadcasting the result tags to all the waiting instructions. Instead, only the instructions at the FIFO heads have to determine when all

Issue width	No. physical registers	No. table entries	Bits per entry	Total delay (ps)
4	80	10	8	192.1
8	128	16	8	251.7

Table 4: Delay of reservation table in $0.18\mu m$ technology.

their operands are available. This is accomplished by interrogating a table called the *reservation table*. The reservation table contains a single bit per physical register that indicates whether the register is waiting for its data. When an instruction is dispatched, the reservation bit corresponding to its result register is set. The bit is cleared when the instruction executes and the result value is produced. An instruction at the FIFO head waits until the reservation bits corresponding to its operands are cleared. Hence, the delay of the wakeup logic is determined by the delay of accessing the reservation table. The reservation table is relatively small in size compared to the rename table and the register file. For example, for a 4-way machine with 80 physical registers, the reservation table can be laid out as a 10-entry table with each entry storing 8 bits [4]. Table 4 shows the delay of the reservation table for 4-way and 8-way machines. For both cases, the wakeup delay is much smaller than the wakeup delay for a 4-way, 32-entry issue window-based microarchitecture. Also, this delay is smaller than the corresponding register renaming delay. The selection logic in the proposed microarchitecture is simple because only the instructions at the FIFO heads need to be considered for selection.

Instruction steering is done in parallel with register renaming. Because the SRC_FIFO table is smaller than the rename table, we expect the delay of steering to be less than the rename delay. In case a more complex steering heuristic is used, the extra delay can easily be moved into the wakeup/select stage, or a new pipestage can be introduced – at the cost of an increase in branch mispredict penalty.

In summary, the complexity analysis presented above shows that by reducing the delay of the window logic significantly, it is likely that the dependence-based microarchitecture can be clocked faster than the typical microarchitecture. In fact, from the overall delay results shown in Table 2, if the window logic (wakeup + select) is reduced substantially, register rename logic becomes the critical stage for a 4-way microarchitecture. Consequently, the dependence-based microarchitecture can improve the clock period by as much as (an admittedly optimistic) 39% in $0.18\mu m$ technology. Of course, this may require that other stages not studied here be more deeply pipelined. Combining the potential for a much faster clock with the results in Figure 13 indicates that the dependence-based microarchitecture is capable of superior performance relative to a typical superscalar microarchitecture.

5.4 Clustering the Dependence-based Microarchitecture

The real advantage of the proposed microarchitecture is for building machines with issue widths greater than four where, as shown by Table 2, the delay of both the large window and the long bypass busses can be significant and can considerably slow the clock. Clustered microarchitectures based on the dependence-based microarchitecture are ideally suited for such situations because they simplify both the window logic and the bypass logic. We describe one such microarchitecture for building an 8-way machine next.

[4]A column MUX is used to select the appropriate bit from each entry.

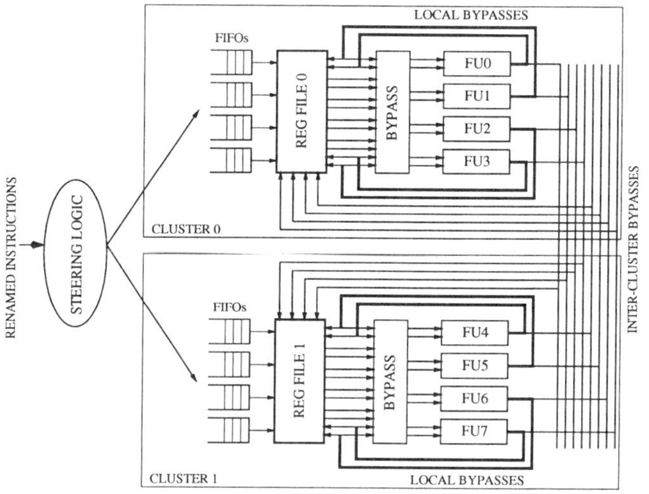

Figure 14: Clustering the dependence-based microarchitecture: 8-way machine organized as two 4-way clusters (2 X 4-way).

Consider the 2x4-way clustered system shown in Figure 14. Two clusters are used, each of which contains four FIFOs, one copy of the register file, and four functional units. Renamed instructions are steered to a FIFO in one of the two clusters. Local bypasses within a cluster (shown using thick lines) are responsible for bypassing result values produced in the cluster to the inputs of the functional units in the same cluster. As shown by the delay results in Table 2, local bypassing can be accomplished in a single cycle. Inter-cluster bypasses are responsible for bypassing values between functional units residing in different clusters. Because inter-cluster bypasses require long wires, it is likely that these bypasses will be relatively slower and take two or more cycles in future technologies. The two copies of the register file are identical, except for the one or more cycles difference in propagating results from one cluster to another.

This clustered, dependence-based microarchitecture has a number of advantages. First, wakeup and selection logic are simplified as noted previously. Second, because of the heuristic for assigning dependent instructions to FIFOs, and hence indirectly to clusters, local bypasses are used much more frequently than inter-cluster bypasses, reducing overall bypass delays. Third, using multiple copies of the register file reduces the number of ports on the register file and will make the access time of the register file faster.

5.5 Performance of Clustered Dependence-based Microarchitecture

The graph in Figure 15 compares performance, in terms of instructions committed per cycle (IPC), for the 2x4-way dependence-based microarchitecture against that of a conventional 8-way microarchitecture with a single 64-entry issue window. For the dependence-based system, instructions are steered using the heuristic described in Section 5.1 with a slight modification. Instead of using a single free list of empty FIFOs, we maintain two free lists of empty FIFOs, one per cluster. A request for a free FIFO is satisfied if possible from the *current* free list. If the current free list is empty, then the second free list is interrogated for a new FIFO and the second free list is made current. This scheme ensures that instructions adjacent in the dynamic stream are assigned to the same cluster to minimize inter-cluster communication. Local bypasses take one cycle while inter-cluster bypasses take 2 cycles. Also, in the conventional 8-way system, all bypasses are assumed to complete in a single cycle. From the graph we can see that for most of the benchmarks, the dependence-based microarchitecture is nearly as effective as the window-based microarchitecture even though the dependence-based microarchitecture is handicapped by slow inter-cluster bypasses that take 2 cycles. However, for two of the benchmarks, *m88ksim* and *compress*, the performance degradation is close to 12% and 9% respectively. We found that this degradation is mainly due to extra latency introduced by the slow inter-cluster bypasses.

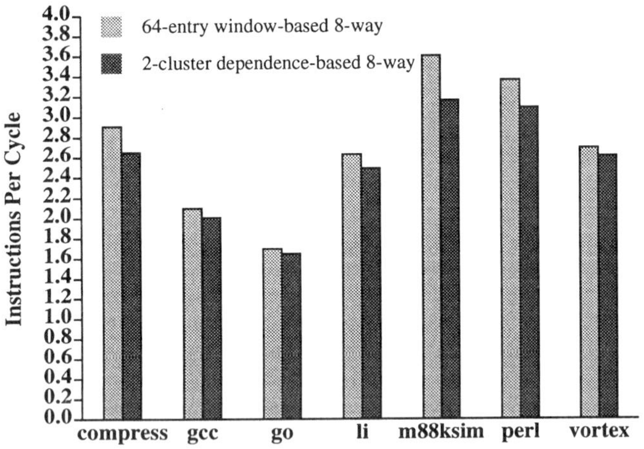

Figure 15: Performance of clustered dependence-based microarchitecture.

Because the dependence-based microarchitecture will facilitate a faster clock, a fair performance comparison must take clock speed into account. The local bypass structure within a cluster is equivalent to a conventional 4-way superscalar machine, and inter-cluster bypasses are removed from the critical path by taking an extra clock cycle. Consequently, the clock speed of the dependence-based microarchitecture is at least as fast as the clock speed of a 4-way, 32-entry window-based microarchitecture, and is likely to be significantly faster because of the smaller (wakeup + selection) delay compared to a conventional issue window as discussed in Section 5.3. Hence, if C_{dep} is the clock speed of the dependence-based microarchitecture, and C_{win} is the clock speed of the window-based microarchitecture, then from Table 2 for 0.18μm technology:

$$\frac{C_{dep}}{C_{win}} \geq \frac{delay\ of\ 8\,way\ 64\,entry\ window}{delay\ of\ 4\,way\ 32\,entry\ window} = 1.252$$

In other words, the dependence-based microarchitecture is capable of supporting a clock that is 25% faster than the clock of the window-based microarchitecture. Taking this factor into account (and ignoring other pipestages that may have to be more deeply pipelined), we can estimate the potential speedup with a dependence-based microarchitecture. The performance improvements vary from 10% to 22% with an average improvement of 16%.

5.6 Other Clustered Microarchitectures

The microarchitecture presented in the previous section is one point in the design space of clustered superscalar microarchitectures. The dependence-based microarchitecture simplifies both the window logic and naturally reduces the performance degradation due to slow inter-cluster bypass paths. In order to further explore the space, we studied the performance of some other interesting designs. In each case there are two clusters with inter-cluster bypasses taking an extra cycle to complete.

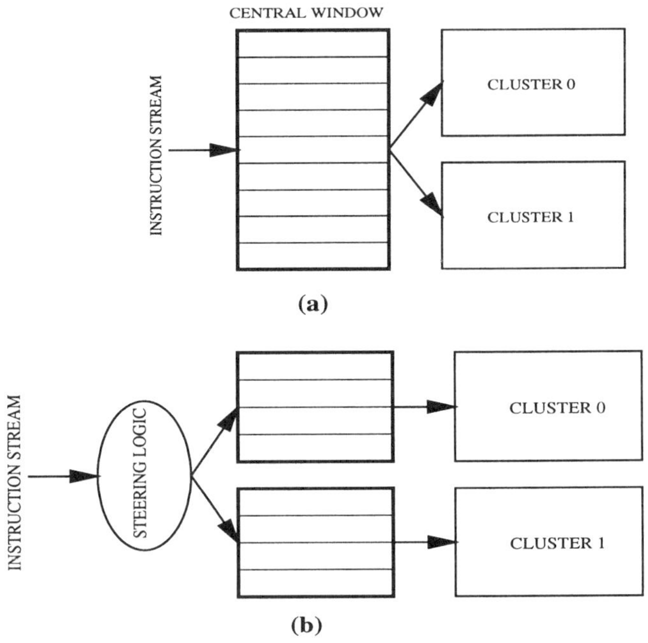

Figure 16: Clustered microarchitectures.

5.6.1 Single Window, Execution-Driven Steering

In the dependence-based microarchitecture described above, instructions are pre-assigned to a cluster when they are dispatched; we refer to this as *dispatch-driven* instruction steering. In contrast, Figure 16(a) illustrates a microarchitecture where instructions reside in a central window while waiting for their operands and functional units to become available. Instructions are assigned to the clusters at the time they begin execution; this is *execution-driven* instruction steering.

With this method, cluster assignment works as follows. The register values in the clusters become available at slightly different times; that is, the result register value produced by a cluster is available in that cluster one cycle earlier than in the other cluster. Consequently, an instruction waiting for the value may be *enabled* for execution one cycle earlier in one cluster than in the other. The selection logic monitors the instructions in the window and attempts to assign them to the cluster which provides their source values first (assuming there is a free functional unit in the cluster). Instructions that have their source operands available in both clusters are first considered for assignment to cluster 0. Static instruction order is used to break ties in this case.

The execution-driven approach uses a greedy policy to minimize the use of slow inter-cluster bypasses while maintaining a high utilization of the functional units. It does so by postponing the assignment of instructions to clusters until execution time. While this greedy approach may gain some IPC advantages, this organization suffers from the previously discussed drawbacks of a central window and complex selection logic.

5.6.2 Two Windows, Dispatch-Driven Steering

This microarchitecture, shown in Figure 16(b), is identical to the dependence-based clustered microarchitecture except that each cluster has a completely flexible window instead of FIFOs. Instructions are steered to the windows using a heuristic that takes both dependences between instructions and the relative load of the clusters into account. We tried a number of heuristics and found a simple extension of the FIFO heuristic presented in Section 5.1 to work best. In our scheme the window is modeled as if it is a collection of FIFOs with instructions capable of issuing from any slot within each individual FIFO. In this particular case, we treat each 32-entry window as eight FIFOs with four slots each. Note that these FIFOs are a conceptual device used only by the assignment heuristic – in reality, instructions issue from the window with complete flexibility.

Kemp and Franklin [11] studied an organization called PEWs (Parallel Execution Windows) for simplifying the logic associated with a central window. PEWs simplifies window logic by splitting the central instruction window among multiple windows much like the clustered microarchitecture described above. Register values are communicated between clusters (called pews) via hardware queues and a ring interconnection network. In contrast, we assume a broadcast mechanism for the same purpose. Instructions are steered to the pews based on instruction dependences with a goal to minimize inter-pew communication. However, for their experiments they assume that each of the pews has as many functional units as the central window organization. This assumption implies that the reduction in complexity achieved is limited since the wakeup and selection logic of the windows in the individual pews still have the same porting requirements as the central window.

5.6.3 Two Windows, Random Steering

This microarchitecture, using the structure presented in Figure 16(b), is a basis for comparisons. Instructions are steered randomly to one of the clusters. If the window for the selected cluster is full, then the instruction is inserted into the other (free) cluster. This design point was evaluated in order to determine the degree to which clustered microarchitectures are capable of tolerating the extra latency introduced by slow inter-cluster bypasses and the importance of dependence-aware scheduling. Each window has 32 entries in this case.

5.6.4 Performance of Clustered Microarchitectures

The top graph in Figure 17 shows the performance of various microarchitectures in terms of instructions committed per cycle (IPC). The leftmost bar in each group shows the performance of the ideal microarchitecture: a single 64-entry window with single cycle bypass between all functional units. A number of observations can be made from the figure. First, random steering consistently performs worse than the other schemes. The performance degradation with respect to the ideal case varies from 17% in the case of *vortex* to 26% in the case of *m88ksim*. Hence, it is essential for the steering logic to consider dependences when routing instructions. Second, the microarchitecture with a central window and execution-driven steering performs nearly as well as the ideal microarchitecture with a maximum degradation of 6% in the case of *m88ksim*. However, as discussed earlier in Section 5.6.1, this microarchitecture requires a centralized window with complex selection logic. Third, both the dependence-based microarchitecture and the flexible window microarchitecture using dispatch-driven steering perform competitively in comparison to the ideal microarchitecture.

The bottom graph in Figure 17 shows the frequency of inter-cluster communication for each organization. We measure inter-cluster communication in terms of the fraction of total instructions that exercise inter-cluster bypasses. This does not include cases where an instruction reads its operands from the register file in the cluster i.e. cases in which the operands arrived from the remote cluster in advance. As expected, we see that there is a high correlation between the frequency of inter-cluster communication and performance - organizations that exhibit higher inter-cluster communication commit fewer instructions per cycle. The inter-cluster communication is particularly high in the case of random steering, reaching as high as 35% in the case of *m88ksim*.

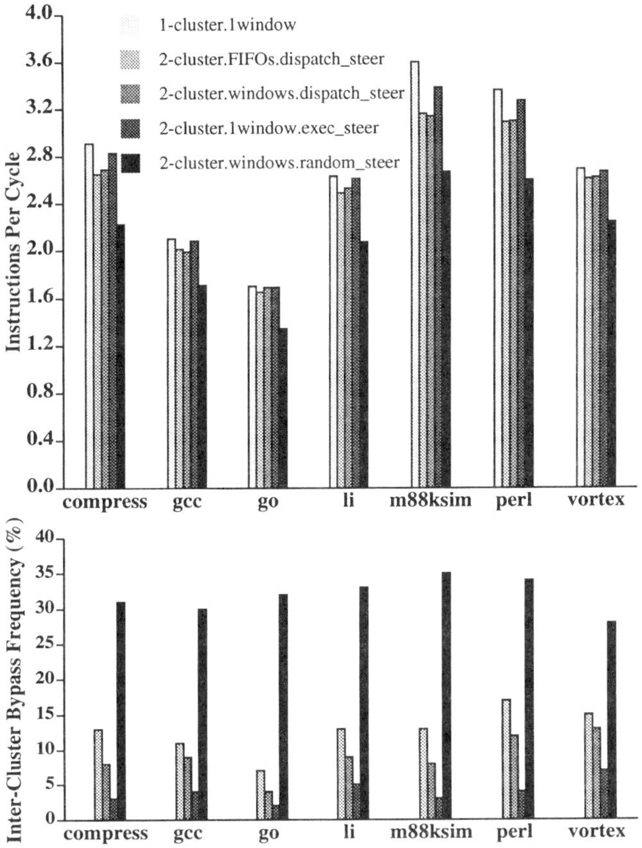

Figure 17: Performance of clustered microarchitectures.

Overall, the above results show that clustered microarchitectures using distributed windows coupled with dispatch-driven steering can deliver performance similar, in terms of instructions committed per cycle, to that of an ideal microarchitecture with a large window and uniform single cycle bypasses between all functional units.

6 Conclusions

We studied the variation of delays of key structures in a generic superscalar processor with two important microarchitectural parameters: issue width and issue window size. We also analyzed the impact of advanced technologies with smaller feature sizes on the delay of these structures. Our results show that the logic associated with the issue window and the data bypass logic are going to become increasingly critical as future designs employ wider issue widths, bigger windows, and smaller feature sizes. Furthermore, both of these structures rely on broadcasting values on long wires, and in future technologies wire delays will increasingly dominate total delay.

This is not to say that the delay of other structures, for example register files and caches, will not cause problems. However, these structures can be pipelined to some extent. In contrast, window logic and data bypass logic implement atomic operations that cannot be pipelined while allowing dependent instructions to execute in successive cycles. This characteristic makes the delay of the window logic and the data bypass logic even more crucial.

Hence, as architects build machines with wider issue widths and larger window sizes in advanced technologies, it is essential to consider microarchitectures that are complexity-effective i.e. microarchitectures that facilitate a fast clock while exploiting similar levels of ILP as an ideal large-window machine.

In the second half of the paper, we proposed one such microarchitecture called the dependence-based microarchitecture. The dependence-based microarchitecture detects chains of dependent instructions and steers the chains to FIFOs which are constrained to execute in-order. Since only the instructions at the FIFO heads have to be monitored for execution, the dependence-based microarchitecture simplifies window logic. Furthermore, the dependence-based microarchitecture naturally lends itself to clustering by grouping dependent instructions together. This grouping of dependent instructions helps mitigate the bypass problem to a large extent by using fast local bypasses more frequently than slow inter-cluster bypasses. We compared the performance of a 2x4-way dependence-based microarchitecture with a typical 8-way superscalar. Our results show two things. First, the proposed microarchitecture has IPC performance close to that of a typical microarchitecture (average degradation in IPC performance is 6.3%). Second, when taking the clock speed advantage of the dependence-based microarchitecture into account the 8-way dependence-based microarchitecture is 16% faster than the typical window-based microarchitecture on average.

Acknowledgements

This work was supported in part by an internship at DEC Western Research Laboratory, and by grants from the NSF Grant MIP-9505853, and the U.S. Army Intelligence Center and Fort Huachuca under Contract DABT63-95-C-0127 and ARPA order no. D346. The views and conclusions contained herein are those of the authors and should not be interpreted as necessarily representing the official policies or endorsements, either expressed or implied, of the U. S. Army Intelligence Center and Fort Huachuca, or the U.S. Government.

We thank the staff at DEC-WRL, especially Annie Warren and Jason Wold, for providing us with the CAD tools used in this study. Thanks to Andy Glew for answering specific questions regarding the implementation of the Intel Pentium Pro and for related discussions. Thanks also to Todd Austin, Scott Breach, and Shamik Das Sharma for comments on a draft of this paper.

References

[1] P. S. Ahuja, D. W. Clark, and A. Rogers. The Performance Impact of Incomplete Bypassing in Processor Pipelines. In *Proceedings of the 28th Annual International Symposium on Microarchitecture*, November 1995.

[2] C. Asato, R. Montoye, J. Gmuender, E. W. Simmons, A. Ike, and J. Zasio. A 14-port 3.8ns 116-word 64b Read-Renaming Register File. In *1995 IEEE International Sold-State Circuits Conference Digest of Technical Papers*, pages 104–105, February 1995.

[3] Mark T. Bohr. Interconnect Scaling - The Real Limiter to High Performance ULSI. In *1995 International Electron Devices Meeting Technical Digest*, pages 241–244, 1995.

[4] Doug Burger, Todd M. Austin, and Steve Bennett. Evaluating Future Microprocessors: The Simplescalar Tool Set. Technical Report CS-TR-96-1308 (Available from http://www.cs.wisc.edu/trs.html), University of Wisconsin-Madison, July 1996.

[5] M. Butler and Y. N. Patt. An Investigation of the Performance of Various Dynamic Scheduling Techniques. In *Proceedings of the 25th Annual International Symposium on Microarchitecture*, pages 1–9, December 1992.

[6] Keith I. Farkas, Norman P. Jouppi, and Paul Chow. Register File Design Considerations in Dynamically Scheduled Processors. In *Proceedings of the Second IEEE Symposium on High-Performance Computer Architecture*, February 1996.

[7] Linley Gwennap. Speed Kills? Not for RISC Processors. *Microprocessor Report*, 7(3):3, March 1993.

[8] Linley Gwennap. HAL Reveals Multichip SPARC Processor. *Microprocessor Report*, 9(3), March 1995.

[9] Linley Gwennap. Intel's P6 Uses Decoupled Superscalar Design. *Microprocessor Report*, 9(2), February 1995.

[10] Jim Keller. The 21264: A Superscalar Alpha Processor with Out-of-Order Execution, October 1996. 9th Annual Microprocessor Forum, San Jose, California.

[11] Gregory A. Kemp and Manoj Franklin. PEWs: A Decentralized Dynamic Scheduler for ILP Processing. In *Proceedings of the International Conference on Parallel Processing*, volume I, pages 239–246, 1996.

[12] Ashok Kumar. The HP-PA8000 RISC CPU: A High Performance Out-of-Order Processor. In *Proceedings of the Hot Chips VIII*, pages 9–20, August 1996.

[13] Scott McFarling. Combining Branch Predictors. DEC WRL Technical Note TN-36, DEC Western Research Laboratory, 1993.

[14] Meta-Software Inc. *HSpice User's Manual*, June 1987.

[15] Subbarao Palacharla, Norman P. Jouppi, and James E. Smith. Quantifying the Complexity of Superscalar Processors. Technical Report CS-TR-96-1328 (Available from http://www.cs.wisc.edu/trs.html), University of Wisconsin-Madison, November 1996.

[16] S. Peter Song, Marvin Denman, and Joe Chang. The PowerPC 604 RISC Microprocessor. In *IEEE Micro*, pages 8–17, October 1995.

[17] N. Vasseghi et al. 200 MHz Superscalar RISC Processor Circuit Design Issues. In *1996 IEEE International Sold-State Circuits Conference Digest of Technical Papers*, pages 356–357, February 1996.

[18] Tomohisa Wada, Suresh Rajan, and Steven A. Przybylski. An Analytical Access Time Model for On-Chip Cache Memories. *IEEE Journal of Solid-State Circuits*, 27(8):1147–1156, August 1992.

[19] Neil H.E. Weste and Kamran Eshraghian. *Principles of CMOS VLSI Design*. Addison Wesley, second edition, 1993.

[20] Neil C. Wilhelm. Why Wire Delays Will No Longer Scale for VLSI Chips. Technical Report SMLI TR-95-44, Sun Microsystems Laboratories, August 1995.

[21] Steven J. E. Wilton and Norman P. Jouppi. An Enhanced Access and Cycle Time Model for On-Chip Caches. Technical Report 93/5, DEC Western Research Laboratory, July 1994.

[22] K. C. Yeager. MIPS R10000 Superscalar Microprocessor. In *IEEE Micro*, April 1996.

Coherence Controller Architectures for SMP-Based CC-NUMA Multiprocessors*

Maged M. Michael[†], Ashwini K. Nanda[‡], Beng-Hong Lim[‡], and Michael L. Scott[†]

[†]University of Rochester
Department of Computer Science
Rochester, NY 14627
{michael,scott}@cs.rochester.edu

[‡]IBM Research
Thomas J. Watson Research Center
Yorktown Heights, NY 10598
{ashwini,bhlim}@watson.ibm.com

Abstract

Scalable distributed shared-memory architectures rely on coherence controllers on each processing node to synthesize cache-coherent shared memory across the entire machine. The coherence controllers execute coherence protocol handlers that may be hardwired in custom hardware or programmed in a protocol processor within each coherence controller. Although custom hardware runs faster, a protocol processor allows the coherence protocol to be tailored to specific application needs and may shorten hardware development time. Previous research show that the increase in application execution time due to protocol processors over custom hardware is minimal.

With the advent of SMP nodes and faster processors and networks, the tradeoff between custom hardware and protocol processors needs to be reexamined. This paper studies the performance of custom-hardware and protocol-processor-based coherence controllers in SMP-node-based CC-NUMA systems on applications from the SPLASH-2 suite. Using realistic parameters and detailed models of existing state-of-the-art system components, it shows that the occupancy of coherence controllers can limit the performance of applications with high communication requirements, where the execution time using protocol processors can be twice as long as using custom hardware.

To gain a deeper understanding of the tradeoff, we investigate the effect of varying several architectural parameters that influence the communication characteristics of the applications and the underlying system on coherence controller performance. We identify measures of applications' communication requirements and their impact on the performance penalty of protocol processors, which can help system designers predict performance penalties for other applications. We also study the potential of improving the performance of hardware-based and protocol-processor-based coherence controllers by separating or duplicating critical components.

*This work was supported and performed at IBM Thomas J. Watson Research Center. Michael Scott was supported in part by NSF grants (CDA–9401142 and CCR–9319445).

1 Introduction

Previous research has shown convincingly that scalable shared-memory performance can be achieved on directory-based cache-coherent multiprocessors such as the Stanford DASH [6] and MIT Alewife [1] machines. A key component of these machines is the coherence controller on each node that provides cache coherent access to memory that is distributed among the nodes of the multiprocessor. In DASH and Alewife, the cache coherence protocol is hardwired in custom hardware finite state machines (FSMs) within the coherence controllers. Instead of hardwiring protocol handlers, the Sun Microsystems S3.mp [10] multiprocessor uses hardware sequencers for modularity in implementing protocol handlers.

Subsequent designs for scalable shared-memory multiprocessors, such as the Stanford FLASH [5] and the Wisconsin Typhoon machines [12], have touted the use of programmable protocol processors instead of custom hardware FSMs to implement the coherence protocols. Although a custom hardware design generally yields better performance than a protocol processor for a particular coherence protocol, the programmable nature of a protocol processor allows one to tailor the cache coherence protocol to the application [2, 8], and may lead to shorter design times since protocol errors may be fixed in software. The study of the performance advantage of custom protocols is beyond the scope of this paper.

Performance simulations of the Stanford FLASH and Wisconsin Typhoon systems find that the performance penalty of protocol processors is small. Simulations of the Stanford FLASH, which uses a customized protocol processor optimized for handling coherence actions, show that the performance penalty of its protocol processor in comparison to custom hardware controllers is within 12% for most of their benchmarks [3]. Simulations of the Wisconsin Typhoon Simple-COMA system, which uses a protocol processor integrated with the other components of the coherence controller, also show competitive performance that is within 30% of custom-hardware CC-NUMA controllers [12] and within 20% of custom-hardware Simple-COMA controllers [13].

Even so, the choice between custom hardware and protocol processors for implementing coherence protocols remains a key design issue for scalable shared-memory multiprocessors. The goal of this research is to examine in detail the performance tradeoffs between these two alternatives in designing a CC-NUMA multiprocessor coherence controller. We consider symmetric multiprocessor (SMP) nodes as well as uniprocessor nodes as the building block for a multiprocessor. The availability of cost-effective SMPs, such as those based on the Intel Pentium Pro [11] makes SMP nodes an attractive choice for CC-NUMA designers [7]. However, the added load presented to the coherence controller by multiple SMP processors may affect the choice between custom hardware FSMs and protocol processors.

We base our experimental evaluation of the alternative coherence controller architectures on realistic hardware parameters for state-of-the-art system components. What distinguishes our work from previous research is that we consider commodity protocol processors on SMP-based CC-NUMA and a wider range of architectural parameters. We simulate eight applications from the SPLASH-2 benchmark suite [14] to compare the application performance of the architectures. The results show that for a 64-processor system based on four-processor SMP nodes, protocol processors result in a performance penalty (increase in execution time relative to that of custom hardware controllers) of 4% – 93%.

The unexpectedly high penalty of protocol processors occurs for applications that have high-bandwidth communication requirements, such as Ocean, Radix, and FFT. The use of SMP nodes exacerbates the penalty. Previous research did not encounter such high penalties because they were either comparing customized protocol processors in uniprocessor nodes, or they did not consider such high-bandwidth applications. We find that under high-bandwidth requirements, the high occupancy of the protocol processor significantly degrades performance relative to custom hardware.

We also study the performance of coherence controllers with two protocol engines. Our results show that for applications with high communication requirements on a 4×16 CC-NUMA system, a two-engine hardware controller improves performance by up to 18% over a one-engine hardware controller, and a controller with two protocol processors improves performance by up to 30% over a controller with a single protocol processor

This paper makes the following contributions:

- It provides an in-depth comparison of the performance tradeoffs between using custom hardware and protocol processors, and demonstrates situations where protocol processors suffer a significant penalty.
- It characterizes the communication requirements for eight applications from SPLASH-2 and shows their impact on the performance penalty of protocol processors over custom hardware. This provides an understanding of application requirements and limitations of protocol processors.
- It evaluates the performance gains of using two protocol engines for custom hardware and protocol-processor-based coherence controllers.
- It introduces a methodology for predicting the impact of protocol engine implementation on the performance of important large applications through the detailed simulation of simpler applications.

The rest of this paper is organized as follows. Section 2 presents the multiprocessor system and details the controller design alternatives and parameters. Section 3 describes our experimental methodology and presents the experimental results. It demonstrates the performance tradeoffs and provides analysis of the causes of the performance differences between the architectures. Section 4 discusses related work. Finally, Section 5 presents the conclusions drawn from this research and gives recommendations for custom hardware and protocol processor designs in future multiprocessors.

2 System Description

To put our results in the context of the architectures we studied, this section details these architectures and their key parameters. First we describe the organization and the key parameters of the common system components for the architectures. Then, we describe the details of the alternative coherence controller architectures. Finally, we present key protocol and coherence controller latencies and occupancies.

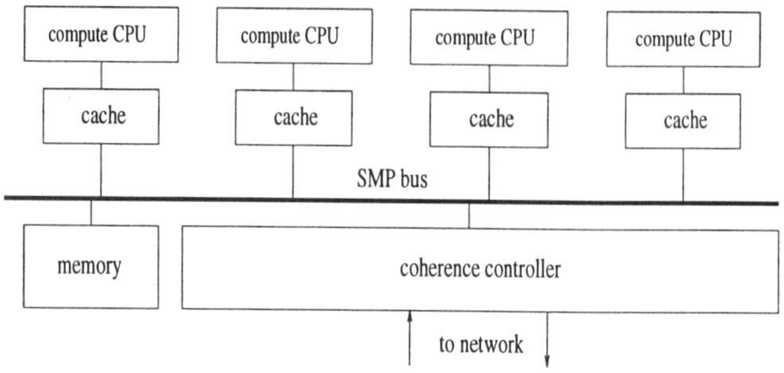

Figure 1: A node in a SMP-based CC-NUMA system.

Event	Latency
L1 to processor	1
L1 to L2	8
L2 to L1	4
L2 miss to address strobe on bus	4
Bus address strobe to bus response	14
Bus address strobe to start of cache-to-cache data response	18
Bus address strobe to next address strobe	4
Bus address strobe to start of data transfer from memory	20
Network point-to-point	14

Table 1: Base system no-contention latencies in compute processor cycles (5 ns.).

2.1 General System Organization and Parameters

The base system configuration is a CC-NUMA multiprocessor composed of 16 SMP nodes connected by a 32 byte-wide fast state-of-the-art IBM switch. Each SMP node includes four 200 MHz PowerPC compute processors with 16 Kbyte L1 and 1 Mbyte L2 4-way-associative LRU caches, with 128 byte cache lines. The SMP bus is a 100 MHz 16 byte-wide fully-pipelined split-transaction separate-address-and-data bus. The memory is interleaved and the memory controller is a separate bus agent from the coherence controller. Figure 1 shows a block diagram of an SMP node. Table 1 shows the no-contention latencies of key system components. These latencies correspond to those of existing state-of-the-art components. Note that memory and cache-to-cache data transfers drive the critical quad-word first on the bus to minimize latency.

2.2 Coherence Controller Architectures

We consider two main coherence controller designs: a custom hardware coherence controller similar to that in the DASH [6] and Alewife [1] systems, and a coherence controller based on commodity protocol processors similar to those in the Typhoon [12] system and its prototypes [13].

The two designs share some common components and features (see Figures 2 and 3). Both designs use duplicate directories to allow fast response to common requests on the pipelined SMP bus (one directory lookup per 2 bus cycles). The bus-side copy is abbreviated (2-bit state per cache line) and uses fast SRAM memory. The controller-side copy is full-bit-map and uses DRAM memory. Both designs use write-through directory caches for reducing directory read latency. Each directory cache holds up to 8K full-bit-map directory entries (e.g. approximately 16 Kbytes for a 16 node CC-NUMA system). The hardware-based design uses a custom on-chip cache, while the protocol-processor-based design uses the

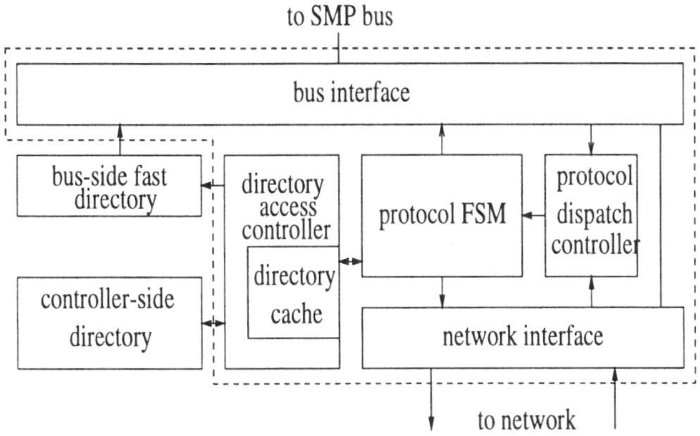

Figure 2: A custom-hardware-based coherence controller design (HWC).

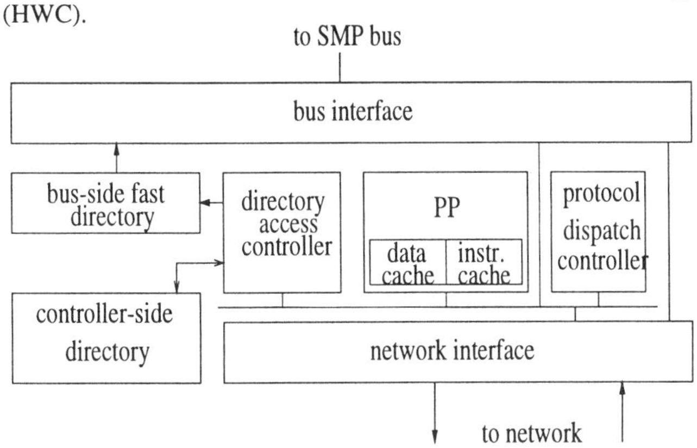

Figure 3: A commodity PP-based coherence controller design (PPC).

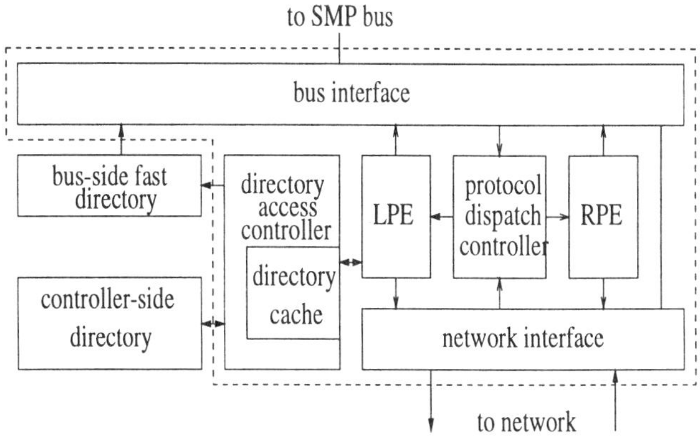

Figure 4: A custom hardware coherence controller design with local and remote protocol FSMs (2HWC).

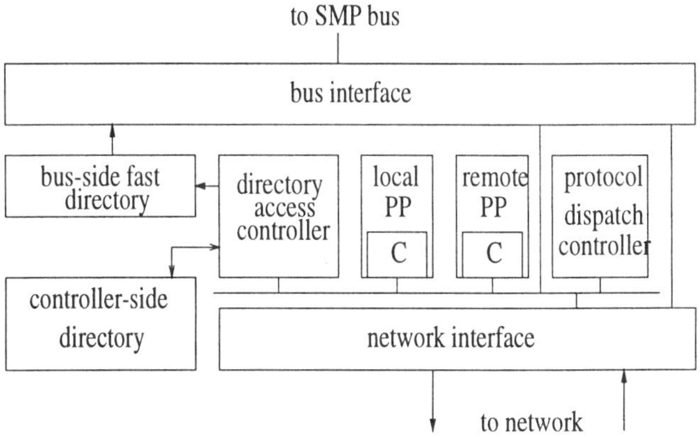

Figure 5: A commodity PP-based coherence controller design with local and remote protocol processors (2PPC).

commodity processor's on-chip data caches. [1] We assume perfect instruction caches in the protocol processors, as the total size of all protocol handlers in our protocol is less than 16 Kbytes.

Both designs include a custom directory access controller for keeping the bus-side copy of the directory consistent with the controller-side copy, and a custom protocol dispatch controller for arbitration between the request queues from the local bus and the network. There are 3 input queues for protocol requests: bus-side requests, network-side requests, and network-side responses. The arbitration strategy between these queues is to let the network transaction nearest to completion be handled first. Thus, the arbitration policy is that network-side responses have the highest priority, then network-side requests, and finally bus-side requests. In order to avoid live-lock, the only exception to this policy is to allow bus-side requests which have been waiting for a long time (e.g. four subsequent network-side requests) to proceed before handling any more network-side requests.

Figure 2 shows a block diagram of a custom hardware coherence controller design (HWC). The controller runs at 100 MHz, the same frequency as the SMP bus. All the coherence controller components are on the same chip except the directories. Figure 3 shows a block diagram of a protocol-processor-based coherence controller (PPC). The protocol processor (PP) is a PowerPC running at 200 MHz. The other controller components run at 100 MHz. The protocol processor communicates with the other components of the controller through loads and stores on the local (coherence controller) bus to memory-mapped off-chip registers in the other components. The protocol processor access to the protocol dispatch controller register is read-only. Its access to the network interface registers is write-only (for sending network messages and starting direct data transfer from the bus interface), since reading the headers of incoming network messages is performed only by the protocol dispatch controller.

Both HWC and PPC have a direct data path between the bus interface and the network interface. The direct data path is used to forward write-backs of dirty remote data from the SMP bus directly to the network interface to be sent to the home node without waiting for protocol handler dispatch. Also, in the case of PPC, the PP only needs to perform a single write to a special register on either the bus interface or the network interface to invoke direct data transfer, without the need for the PP to read and write the data to perform the transfer.

In order to increase the bandwidth of the coherence controller we also consider the use of two protocol processors in the PPC implementation and two protocol FSMs in the HWC implementation. We use the term "protocol engine" to refer to both the protocol processor in the PPC design and the protocol FSM in the HWC design. For distributing the protocol requests between the two engines, we use a policy similar to that used in the S3.mp system [10], where protocol requests for memory addresses on the local node are handled by one protocol engine (LPE) and protocol requests for memory addresses on remote nodes are handled by the other protocol engine (RPE). Only the LPE needs to access the directory. Figures 4 and 5 show the two-engine HWC design (2HWC), and the two PP controller design (2PPC), respectively.

[1] Although most processors use write-back caches, current processors (e.g. Pentium Pro [11]) allow users to designate regions of memory to be cached write-through.

Sub-operation	HWC	PPC
Issue request to bus	2	8
Detect response from bus	2	8
Issue network message	2	9
Read special bus interface associative registers	4	10
Write special bus interface registers	2	4
Directory read (cache hit)	2	2
Directory read (cache miss)	22	22
Directory write	2	2
Handler dispatch	2	12
Condition	2	2
Loop (per iteration)	2	5
Clear bit field	–	3
Extract bit field	–	2
Other bit operations	–	1

Table 2: Protocol engine sub-operation occupancies for HWC and PPC in compute processor cycles (5 ns.).

Step	HWC	PPC
detect L2 miss	8	8
issue bus read request	4	4
bus response	14	14
dispatch handler	2	12
extract home id	-	2
send message to home node	2	9
network latency	14	14
dispatch handler	2	12
read directory entry (cache hit)	2	2
conditions	2	6
issue bus read request	6	12
memory latency	20	20
detect bus response	2	8
extract requester's id	-	2
send message to the requester	2	9
network latency	14	14
dispatch handler	2	12
issue response to bus	6	12
L2 reissues read request	18	18
bus response	14	14
bus interface issues data	4	4
L1 fill	4	4
total	142	212

Table 3: Breakdown of the no-contention latency of a read miss to a remote line clean at home in compute processor cycles (5 ns.).

2.3 Controller Latencies and Occupancies

We modeled HWC and PPC accurately with realistic parameters. Table 2 lists protocol engine sub-operations and their occupancies [2] for each of the HWC and PPC coherence controller designs, assuming a 100 MHz HWC and a 100 MHz PPC with a 200 MHz off-the-shelf protocol processor. The occupancies in the table assume no contention on the SMP bus, memory, and network, and all directory reads hit in the protocol engine data cache. The other assumptions used in deriving these numbers are:

- Accesses to on-chip registers for HWC take one system cycle (2 CPU cycles).
- Bit operations on HWC are combined with other actions, such as conditions and accesses to special registers.
- PP reads to off-chip registers on the local PPC bus take 4 system cycles (8 CPU cycles). Searching a set of associative registers takes an extra system cycle (2 CPU cycles).
- PP writes to off-chip registers on the local PPC bus take 2 system cycles (4 CPU cycles) before the PP can proceed.
- PP compute cycles are based on the PowerPC instruction cycle counts produced by the IBM XLC C compiler.
- HWC can decide multiple conditions in one-cycle.

[2] Occupancy of sub-operations is the time a protocol engine is occupied by the sub-operation and cannot service other requests.

To gain insight into the effect of these occupancies and delays on the latency of a typical remote memory transaction, Table 3 presents the no-contention latency breakdown of a read miss from a remote node to a clean shared line at the home node. The relative increase in latency from HWC to PPC is only 49%, which is consistent with the 33% increase reported for Typhoon [13], taking into account that we consider a more decoupled coherence controller design and we use a faster network than that used in the Typhoon study. It is worth noting that in Table 3 there is no entry for updating the directory state at the home node. The reason is that updating the directory state can be performed after sending the response from the home node, thus minimizing the read miss latency. In our protocol handlers, we postpone any protocol operations that are not essential for responding to requests until after issuing responses.

Finally, in order to gain insight into the relative occupancy times of the HWC and PPC coherence controller designs, Table 4 presents the no-contention protocol handler occupancies for the most frequently used handlers. Handler occupancy times include: handler dispatch time, directory reference time, access time to special registers, SMP bus and local memory access times, and bit field manipulation for PPC. Note that memory is sequentially consistent, and that we use the same full-map directory, invalidation-based, write-back protocol, for both HWC and PPC. In our protocol, we allow remote owners to respond directly to remote requesters with data, but invalidation acknowledgments are collected only at the home node.

3 Experimental Results

In this section, we present simulation results of the relative performance of the different coherence controller architectures with several variations of communication-related architectural parameters. Then, we present analysis of the key statistics and communication measures collected from these simulations, and we conclude this section by presenting statistics and analysis of the utilization and workload distribution on two-protocol-engine coherence controllers. We start with the experimental methodology.

3.1 Experimental Methodology

We use execution-driven simulation (based on a version of the Augmint simulation toolkit [9] that runs on the PowerPC architecture) to evaluate the performance of the four coherence controller designs, HWC, PPC, 2HWC, and 2PPC. Our simulator includes detailed contention models for SMP buses, memory controllers, interleaved memory banks, protocol engines, directory DRAM, and external point contention for the interconnection network. Protocol handlers are simulated at the granularity of the sub-operations in Table 2, in addition to accurate timing of the interaction between the coherence controller and the SMP bus, memory, directory, and

Handler	HWC	PPC
bus read remote	4	23
bus read exclusive remote	4	23
bus read local (dirty remote)	10	33
bus read excl. local (cached remote)	10 + 4/inv.	32 + 16/inv.
remote read to home (clean)	38	73
remote read to home (dirty remote)	10	29
remote read excl. to home (uncached remote)	38	73
remote read excl. to home (shared remote)	10 + 4/inv.	32 + 16/inv.
remote read excl. to home (dirty remote)	10	30
read from remote owner (request from home)	32	81
read from remote owner (remote requester)	34	90
read excl. from remote owner (request from home)	32	81
read excl. from remote owner (remote requester)	34	90
data response from owner to a read request from home	8	21
write back from owner to home in response to a read req. from remote node	8	24
data response from owner to a read excl. request from home	6	16
ack. from owner to home in response to a read excl. request from remote node	4	17
invalidation request from home to sharer	26	49
inv. acknowledgment (more expected)	8	23
inv. ack. (last ack, local request)	10	33
inv. ack. (last ack, remote request)	36	75
data in response to a remote read request	4	16
data in response to a remote read excl. request	6	20

Table 4: Protocol engine occupancies in compute processor cycles (5 ns.).

network interface. All coherence controller implementations use the same cache coherence protocol.

We use eight benchmarks from the SPLASH-2 suite [14], (Table 5) to evaluate the performance of the four coherence controller implementations. All the benchmarks are written in C and compiled using IBM XLC C compiler with optimization level -O2. All experimental results reported in this paper are for the parallel phase only of these applications. We use a round-robin page placement policy except for FFT where we use an optimized version with programmer hints for optimal page placement. We observed slightly inferior performance for most applications when we used a first-touch-after-initialization page placement policy, due to load imbalance, and memory and coherence controller contention as a result of uneven memory distribution. LU and Cholesky are run on 32-processor systems (8 nodes $\times$ 4 processors each) as they suffer from load imbalance on 64 processors with the data sets used [14]. We ran all the applications with data sizes and systems sizes for which they achieve acceptable speedups.

Application	Type	Problem size
LU	Blocked dense linear algebra	512×512 matrix, 16x16 blocks
Water-Spatial	Study of forces and potentials of water molecules in a 3-D grid	512 molecules
Barnes	Hierarchical N-body	8K particles
Cholesky	Blocked sparse linear algebra	tk15.O
Water-Nsquared	$O(n^2)$ study of forces and potentials in water molecules	512 molecules
Radix	Radix sort	1M integer keys, radix 1K
FFT	FFT computation	64K complex doubles
Ocean	Study of ocean movements	258×258 ocean grid

Table 5: Benchmark types and data sets.

3.2 Performance Results

In order to capture the main factors influencing PP performance penalty (the increase in execution time on PPC relative to the execution time on HWC), we ran experiments on the base system configuration with the four coherence controller architectures. We then varied some key system parameters to investigate their effect on the PP performance penalty.

Base Case

Figure 6 shows the execution times for the four coherence controller architectures on the base system configuration normalized by the execution time of HWC. We notice that the PP penalty can be as high as 93% for Ocean and 52% for Radix, and as low as 4% for LU. The significant PP penalties for Ocean, Radix and FFT indicate that commodity PP-based coherence controllers can be the bottleneck when running communication-intensive applications. This result is in contrast to the results of previous research, which showed the cases where custom PP-based coherence controllers suffer small performance penalties relative to custom hardware.

Also, we observe that for applications with high bandwidth requirements, using two protocol engines improves performance significantly relative to the corresponding single engine implementation, up to 18% on HWC and 30% on PPC, for Ocean.

We varied other system and application parameters that are expected to have a big impact on the communication requirements of the applications. We start with the cache line size.

Smaller cache line size

With 32 byte cache lines, we expect the PP penalty to increase from that experienced with 128 byte cache lines, especially for applications with high spatial locality, due to the increase in the rate of requests to the coherence controller. Figure 7 shows the execution times normalized to the execution time of HWC on the base configuration. We notice a significant increase in execution time (regardless of the coherence controller architecture) relative to the corresponding execution times on the base system, for FFT, Cholesky, Radix, and LU, which have high spatial locality [14], and a minor increase in execution time for the other benchmarks.

Also, we notice a significant increase in the PP penalty (compared to the PP penalty on the base system) for applications with high spatial locality, due to the increase in the number of requests to the coherence controllers, which increases the demand on PP occupancy. For example, the PP penalty for FFT increases from 45% to 68%.

Slower network

To determine the impact of network speed on the PP performance penalty, we simulated the four applications with the largest PP penalties on a system with a slow network (1 μs. latency). Figure 8 shows the execution times normalized to the execution time of HWC on the base configuration. We notice a significant decrease in the PP penalty from that for the base system. The PP penalty for Ocean drops from 93% to 28%. Accordingly, systems designs with slow networks can afford to use commodity protocol processors instead of custom hardware, without significant impact on performance, when cache line size is large.

Also, we notice a significant increase in execution time (regardless of the coherence controller architecture) relative to the corresponding execution times on the base system, for Ocean and Radix, due to their high communication rates.

Larger data size

To determine the effect of data size on the PP penalty, we simulated Ocean and FFT on the base system with larger data sizes, 256K complex doubles for FFT, and a 514×514 grid for Ocean. Figure 9 shows the execution times normalized by the execution time of HWC for each data size. We notice a decrease in the PP penalty in comparison to the penalty with the base data sizes, since the communication-to-computation ratios for Ocean and FFT decrease with the increase of the data size [3]. The PP penalty for FFT drops from 46% to 33%, and for Ocean from 93% to 67%.

However, since communication rates for applications like Ocean increase with the number of processors at the same rate that they decrease with larger data sizes, we can think of high PP performance penalties as limiting the scalability of such applications on systems with commodity PP-based coherence controllers.

Number of processors per SMP node

Varying the number of processors per SMP node (i.e. per coherence controller), proportionally varies the demand on the coherence controller occupancy, and thus is expected to impact the PP performance penalty. Figure 10 shows the execution times on 64-processor systems (32 for LU and Cholesky) with 1, 2, 4, and 8 processors per SMP node, normalized to the execution time of HWC on the base configuration (4 processors/node).

We notice that for applications with low communication rates, the increase in the number of processors per node has only a minor effect on the PP performance penalty. For applications with high communication rates, the increase in the number of processors increases the PP performance penalty (e.g. the PP penalty increases from 93% for Ocean on 4 processors per node to 106% on 8 processors per node). However, the PP penalty can be as high as 79% (for Ocean) even on systems with one processor per node.

[3] Applications like Radix maintain a constant communication rate with different data sizes [14].

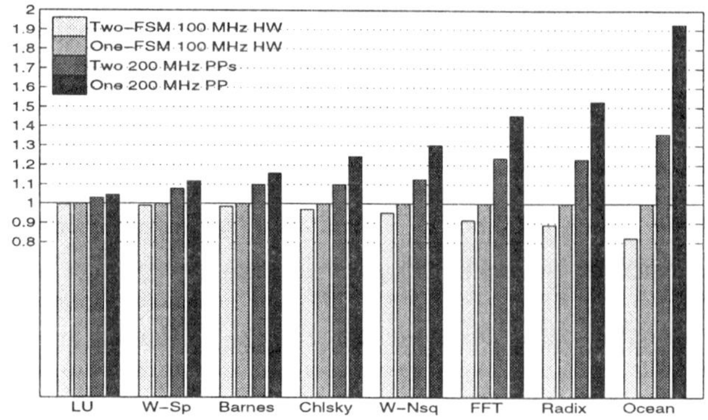

Figure 6: Normalized execution time on the base system configuration.

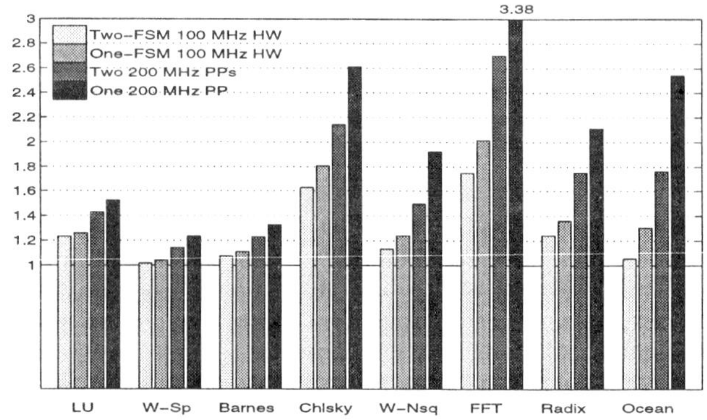

Figure 7: Normalized execution time for system with small (32 byte) cache lines.

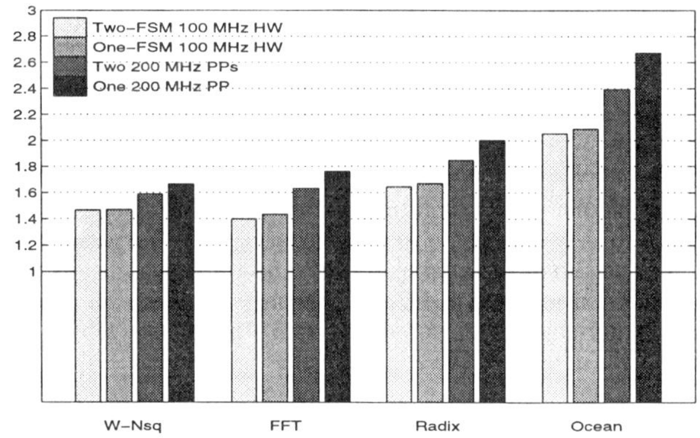

Figure 8: Normalized execution time for system with high (1 μs.) network latency.

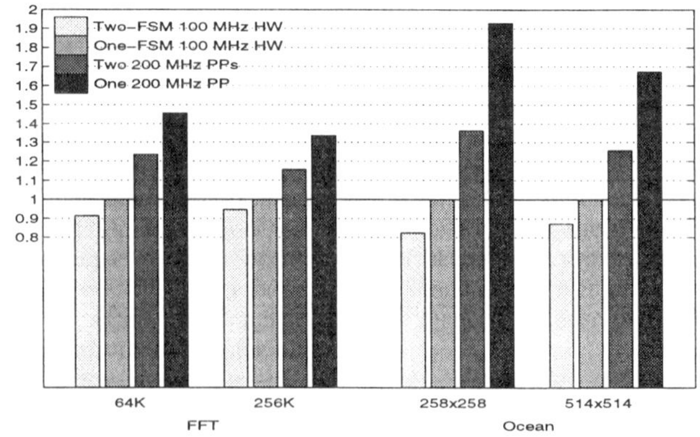

Figure 9: Normalized execution time for base system with base and large data sizes.

For each of the coherence controller architectures, performance of applications with high communication rates degrades with more processors per node, due to the increase in occupancy per coherence controller, which are already critical resources on systems with fewer processors per node.

Also, we observe that for applications with high communication rates (except FFT), the use of two protocol engines in the coherence controllers achieves similar or better performance than controllers with one protocol engine with half the number of processors per nodes. In other words, using two protocol engines in the coherence controllers, allows integrating twice as many processors per SMP node, thus saving the cost of half the SMP buses, memory controllers, coherence controllers, and I/O controllers.

3.3 Communication Statistics and Measures

In order to gain more insight into quantifying the application characteristics that affect PP performance penalty, we present some of the statistics generated by our simulations. Table 6 shows communication statistics collected from simulations of HWC and PPC on the base system configuration (except that Cholesky and LU are run on 32 processors). The statistics are:

- PP penalty: The increase in the execution time of PPC relative to the execution time of HWC.
- RCCPI (Requests to Coherence Controller Per Instruction) is the total number of requests to the coherence controllers divided by the total number of instructions.
- The total of the occupancies of all coherence controllers for PPC divided by that for HWC.
- Average HWC (PPC) utilization is the average HWC (PPC) occupancy divided by execution time.
- Average HWC (PPC) queuing delay is the average time a request to the coherence controller waits in a queue while the controller is occupied by other requests.
- Arrival rate of requests to HWC (PPC) per μs. (200 CPU cycles) is derived from the reciprocal of the mean inter-arrival time of requests to each of the coherence controllers.

In Table 6 we notice that as RCCPI increases, the PP performance penalty increases proportionally except for Cholesky. In the case of Cholesky, the high load imbalance inflates the execution time with both HWC and PPC. Therefore, the PP penalty which is measured relative to the execution time with HWC is less than the PP penalty of other applications with similar RCCPI but with better load balance.

Also, as RCCPI increases, the arrival rate of requests to the coherence controller per cycle for PPC diverges from that of HWC, indicating that the PPC has saturated, and that the coherence controller is the bottleneck for the base system configuration. This is also supported by the observation of the high utilization rates of HWC with Ocean, and of PPC with Ocean, Radix, and FFT, indicating that the coherence controller has saturated these cases, and it is the main bottleneck.

However, we notice that the queuing delays do not increase proportionally with the increase in RCCPI, since the queuing effect of the coherence controller behaves like a negative feedback system where the increase in RCCPI (the input) increases the queuing delay in proportion to the difference between the queuing delay and a saturation value, thus limiting the increase in queuing delay. Note that the high queuing delay for FFT is attributed to its bursty communication pattern [14].

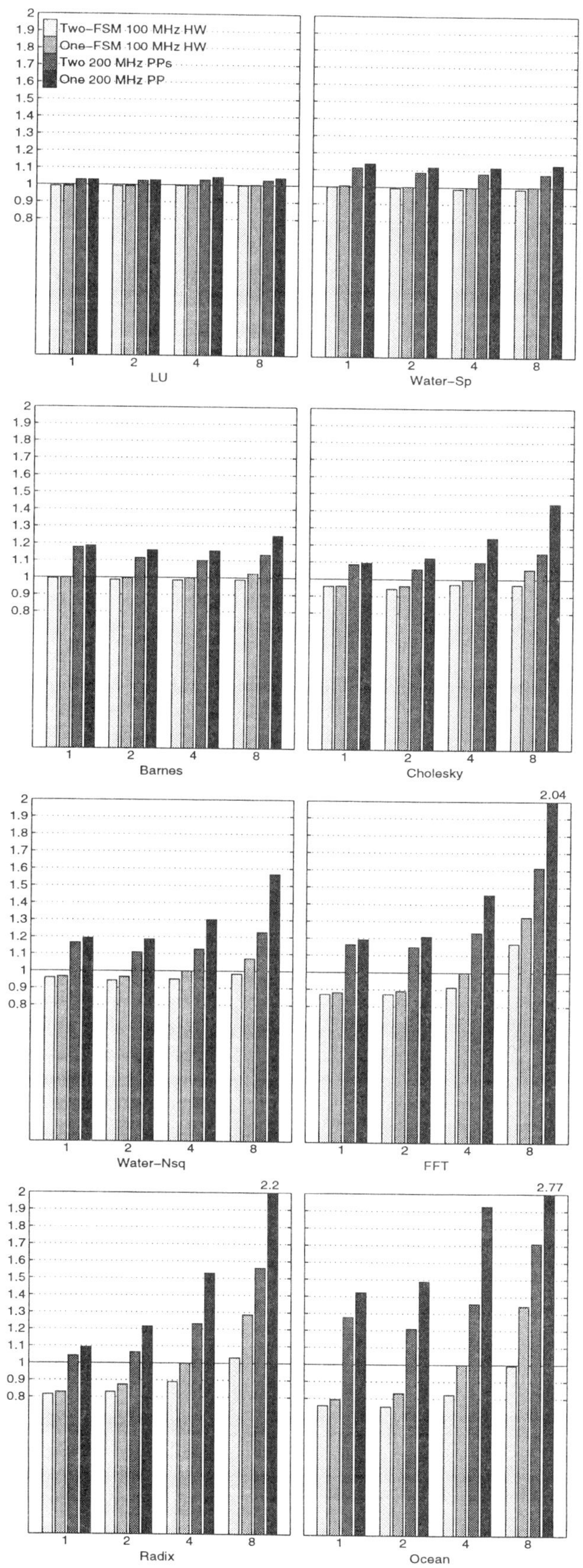

Figure 10: Normalized execution time with 1,2,4, and 8 processors per SMP node.

Application	PP Penalty	1000 × RCCPI	PPC/HWC occupancy	HWC utilization	PPC utilization	HWC queu-ing delay (ns.)	PPC queu-ing delay (ns.)	Average requests to HWC per μs.	Average requests to PPC per μs.
LU	4.37%	1.3	2.37	4.21%	9.58%	101	305	0.41	0.40
Water-Sp	11.69%	1.8	2.65	10.95%	25.99%	100	375	1.19	1.06
Barnes	15.81%	2.3	2.52	13.26%	28.88%	67	266	1.26	1.09
Cholesky	24.38%	4.1	2.23	26.38%	47.37%	113	365	2.34	1.86
Water-Nsq	30.15%	3.3	2.69	17.86%	36.87%	157	626	1.85	1.43
FFT-256K	33.44%	3.7	2.38	22.13%	39.54%	289	837	1.83	1.38
FFT-64K	45.59%	6.3	2.31	29.61%	46.96%	340	864	2.58	1.77
Radix	52.83%	9.8	2.36	36.82%	56.75%	229	640	3.66	2.33
Ocean-514	67.26%	14.0	2.29	47.54%	65.07%	226	648	3.87	2.31
Ocean-258	92.88%	23.2	2.47	52.89%	67.72%	232	720	4.69	2.41

Table 6: Communication statistics on the base system configuration.

Also, we observe that the ratio between the occupancy of PPC and the occupancy of HWC is more or less constant for the different applications, approximately 2.5.

Figure 11 plots the arrival rate of requests to each of the coherence controller architectures against RCCPI for all the applications on the base system configuration (except Cholesky and LU as they were run on 32 processors) including Ocean and FFT with large data sizes. The dotted lines show the trend for each architecture. The figure shows clearly the saturation levels of the different coherence controller architectures. The divergence in the arrival rates demonstrates that the coherence architecture is the performance bottleneck of the base system.

Figure 12 shows the effect of RCCPI on the PP penalty for the same experiments as those in Figure 11. We notice a clear proportional effect of RCCPI on the PP penalty. The gradual slope of the curve can be explained by the fact that the queuing model of the coherence controller resembles a negative feedback system. Without the negative feedback, the PP penalty would increase exponentially with the increase in RCCPI. The lower PP penalty for applications with low RCCPI such as Barnes and Water-Spatial is due to the fact that in those cases the coherence controller is under-utilized.

The previous analysis can help system designers predict the relative performance of alternative coherence controller designs. They can obtain the RCCPI measure for important large applications using simple simulators (e.g. PRAM) and relate that RCCPI to a graph similar to that in Figure 12 that can be obtained through the detailed simulation of simpler applications covering a range of communication rates similar to that of the large application. Although RCCPI is not necessarily independent of the implementation of the coherence controller, for practical purposes the effect of the architecture on RCCPI can be ignored. In our experiments the difference in RCCPI between the four implementations (HWC, PPC, 2HWC, and 2PPC) is less than 1% for all applications.

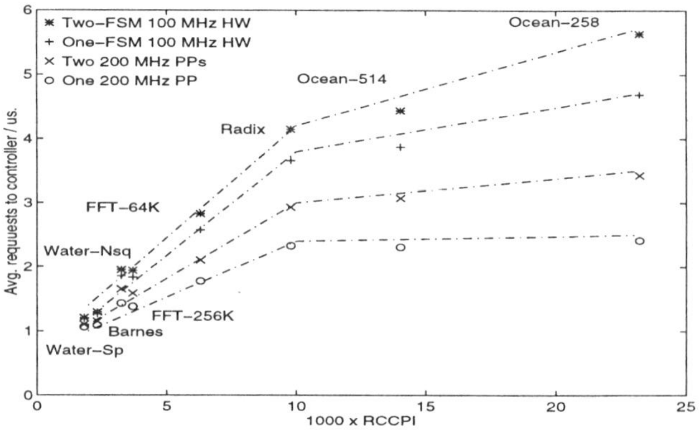

Figure 11: Coherence controller bandwidth limitations.

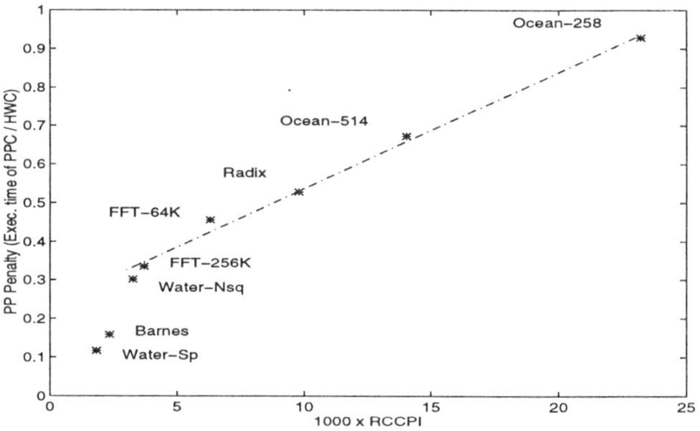

Figure 12: Effect of communication rate on PP penalty.

3.4 Utilization of Two-Engine Controllers

For coherence controller architectures with two protocol engines, there is more than one way to split the workload between the two protocol engines. In this study, we use a policy where protocol requests for memory addresses on the local node are handled by one protocol engine (LPE) and protocol requests for memory addresses on remote nodes are handled by the other protocol engine (RPE). In order to quantify the effectiveness of this policy, Table 7 shows the communication statistics collected from simulations of 2HWC and 2PPC on the base system configuration (except Cholesky and LU are run on 32 processors).

We observe that although most requests are handled by RPE (53-63%), the occupancy of LPE is up to 3 times that of RPE for 2HWC, and up to 2 times for 2PPC (derived from the utilization numbers). This is because the average occupancy of protocol handlers performed on LPE are more than those on RPE, since the former are more likely to access the directory and main memory. Also, we observe that the sum of the average utilization numbers for LPE and RPE is more than the average utilization for the corresponding one-engine coherence controller (Table 6). This is due to the fact that the sum of the occupancies of LPE and RPE are almost the same as that for the one-engine controller, but the execution time decreases with the use of two protocol engines.

Due to the imbalance between the utilization figures of LPE and RPE, the queuing delays for RPE are lower than those for the corresponding one-engine controllers, while those for LPE are higher

Application	Architecture	Utilization		Request distribution		Queuing delay (ns.)	
		LPE	RPE	LPE	RPE	LPE	RPE
LU	2HWC	3.20%	1.09%	35.67%	64.33%	182	2
	2PPC	5.66%	3.92%	35.74%	64.26%	501	14
Water-Sp	2HWC	6.82%	4.29%	38.09%	61.91%	60	40
	2PPC	14.66%	12.38%	38.08%	61.92%	263	78
Barnes	2HWC	8.43%	5.22%	39.38%	60.62%	67	11
	2PPC	16.64%	13.85%	39.41%	60.59%	237	53
Cholesky	2HWC	20.26%	7.48%	38.27%	61.73%	128	8
	2PPC	30.34%	19.99%	38.27%	61.73%	348	36
Water-Nsq	2HWC	11.30%	7.89%	39.26%	60.74%	82	49
	2PPC	22.87%	19.81%	39.22%	60.78%	384	167
FFT-256K	2HWC	17.93%	5.92%	46.33%	53.67%	378	10
	2PPC	30.64%	15.05%	46.33%	53.67%	934	38
FFT-64K	2HWC	25.63%	7.45%	41.40%	58.60%	478	8
	2PPC	36.35%	19.17%	41.40%	58.60%	1137	39
Radix	2HWC	21.63%	21.32%	39.95%	60.05%	138	91
	2PPC	30.70%	40.86%	39.94%	60.06%	243	366
Ocean-514	2HWC	38.10%	18.33%	41.03%	58.97%	210	35
	2PPC	50.42%	36.59%	41.02%	58.98%	480	138
Ocean-258	2HWC	40.02%	25.97%	40.45%	59.55%	173	48
	2PPC	52.60%	44.19%	40.39%	59.61%	476	185

Table 7: Communication statistics for controllers with two protocol engines on the base system configuration.

for most applications despite the decrease in demand, due to the exclusion of the requests to RPE which typically have low occupancy requirements.

The large imbalance in the distribution of occupancy between LPE and RPE (derived from the utilization statistics) for most applications indicate that there is potential for further improvement in performance by using a more even policy for distributing the workload on the two (or possibly more) protocol engines. However, it is worth noting that in the design used in this paper, only one protocol engine, LPE, needs to access the directory. Furthermore, in the case of custom hardware, none of the handlers in the LPE FSM needs to be duplicated in the RPE FSM, and vice versa, thus minimizing the hardware overhead of two-engine HWC over one-engine HWC. Alternative distribution policies, such as splitting the workload dynamically or based on whether the request is from the local bus or another node, might lead to a more balanced distribution of protocol workloads on the protocol engines, but would also require allowing multiple protocol engines to access the directory, which increases the cost and complexity of coherence controllers.

4 Related Work

The proponents of protocol processors argue that the performance penalty of protocol processors is minimal, and that the additional flexibility is worth the performance penalty. The Stanford FLASH designers find that the performance penalty of using a protocol processor is less than 12% for the applications that they simulated, including Ocean and Radix [3]. Their measured penalties are significantly lower than ours for the following reasons: 1) FLASH uses a protocol processor that is highly customized for executing protocol handlers, 2) they consider only uniprocessor nodes in their experiments, and 3) they assume a slower network latency of 220 ns., as opposed to 70 ns. in our base parameters.

In [12], Reinhardt *et al.* introduce the Wisconsin Typhoon architecture that relies on a SPARC processor core integrated with the other components of the coherence controller to execute coherence handlers that implement a Simple COMA protocol. Their simulations show that Simple COMA on Typhoon is less than 30% slower than a custom hardware CC-NUMA system. It is hard to compare our results to theirs because of the difficulty in determining what fraction of the performance difference is due to Simple COMA vs. CC-NUMA, and what fraction is due to custom hardware vs. protocol processors.

In [13], Reinhardt *et al.* compare the Wisconsin Typhoon and its first-generation prototypes with an idealized Simple COMA system. Here, their results show that the performance penalty of using integrated protocol processors is less than 20%. In contrast, we find larger performance penalties of up to 106%. There are two main reasons for this difference: 1) we are considering a more decoupled design than Typhoon, and 2) the application set used in the studies. Our results largely agree with theirs for Barnes, the only application in common between the two studies. However, we also consider applications with higher bandwidth requirements, such as Ocean, Radix, and FFT. Other differences between the two studies are: a) they compare Simple COMA systems, while we compare CC-NUMA systems, b) they assume a slower network with a latency of 500 ns., which mitigates the penalty of protocol processors, and c) they consider only uniprocessor nodes.

Holt *et al.* [4] perform a study similar to ours. They also find that the occupancy of coherence controllers is critical to the performance of high-bandwidth applications. However, their work uses abstract parameters to model coherence controller performance, whereas our work considers practical, state-of-the-art controller designs. Also, our work provides strong insight into coherence controller bottlenecks, and we study the effect of having multiple processors per node and two protocol engines per coherence controller.

5 Conclusions

The major focus of our research is on characterizing the performance tradeoffs between using custom hardware versus protocol processors to implement cache coherence protocols. By comparing designs that differ only in features specific to either approach and keeping the rest of the architectural parameters identical, we are able to perform a systematic comparison of both approaches. We find that for applications with high bandwidth requirements, like Ocean, Radix, and FFT, the occupancy of off-the-shelf protocol processors significantly degrades performance by up to 106% for the applications we studied. On the other hand, the programmable nature of protocol processors allows one to tailor the cache coherence protocol to the application, and may lead to shorter design times since protocol errors may be fixed in software.

We also find that using a slow network or large data sizes results in tolerable protocol processor performance, and that for communication-intensive applications, performance degrades with the increase in the number of processors per node, as a result of the decrease in the number of coherence controllers in the system.

Our results also demonstrate the benefit of using two protocol engines in improving performance or maintaining the same performance of systems with larger number of coherence controllers. We are investigating other optimizations such as using more protocol engines for different regions of memory, and using custom hardware to implement accelerated data paths and handler paths for simple protocol handlers, which usually incur the highest penalties on protocol processors relative to custom hardware.

Our analysis of the application characteristics captures the communication requirements of the applications and their impact on performance penalty. Our characterization–RCCPI–can help system designers predict the performance of coherence controllers with other applications.

The results of our research imply that it is crucial to reduce protocol processor occupancy in order to support high-bandwidth applications. One approach is to custom design a protocol processor that is optimized for executing protocol handlers, as in the Stanford FLASH multiprocessor. Another approach is to customize coherence protocols to the communication requirements of particular applications. We are currently investigating an alternative approach: to add incremental custom hardware to a protocol-processor-based design to accelerate common protocol handler actions.

Acknowledgments

We would like to thank several colleagues at IBM Research for their help in this research: Moriyoshi Ohara for his valuable insights and his generosity with his time and effort, Mark Giampapa for porting Augmint to the PowerPC, Kattamuri Ekanadham for useful discussions on coherence controller architectures, and Michael Rosenfield for his support and interest in this work. We also thank Steven Reinhardt at the University of Wisconsin for providing us with information about Typhoon performance, and Mark Heinrich and Jeffrey Kuskin at Stanford University for providing us with information about custom protocol processors.

References

[1] A. Agarwal, R. Bianchini, D. Chaiken, K. Johnson, D. Kranz, J. Kubiatowicz, B.-H. Lim, K. Mackenzie, and D. Yeung. The MIT Alewife Machine: Architecture and Performance. In *Proceedings of the 22nd Annual International Symposium on Computer Architecture*, pages 2–13, June 1995.

[2] B. Falsafi, A. Lebeck, S. Reinhardt, I. Schoinas, M. Hill, J. Larus, and D. Wood. Application-Specific Protocols for User-Level Shared Memory. In *Proceedings of Supercomputing '94*, November 1994.

[3] M. Heinrich, J. Kuskin, D. Ofelt, J. Heinlein, J. P. Singh, R. Simoni, K. Gharachorloo, J. Baxter, D. Nakahira, M. Horowitz, A. Gupta, M. Rosemblum, and J. Hennessy. The Performance Impact of Flexibility in the Stanford FLASH Multiprocessor. In *Proceedings of the Sixth International Conference on Architectural Support for Programming Languages and Operating Systems*, pages 274–285, October 1994.

[4] C. Holt, M. Heinrich, J. P. Singh, E. Rothberg, and J. Hennessy. The Effects of Latency, Occupancy, and Bandwidth in Distributed Shared Memory Multiprocessors. Technical Report CSL-TR-95-660, Stanford University, January 1995.

[5] J. Kuskin, D. Ofelt, M. Heinrich, J. Heinlein, R. Simoni, K. Gharachorloo, J. Chapin, D. Nakahira, J. Baxter, M. Horowitz, A. Gupta, M. Rosenblum, and J. Hennessy. The Stanford FLASH Multiprocessor. In *Proceedings of the 21st Annual International Symposium on Computer Architecture*, pages 302–313, April 1994.

[6] D. Lenoski, J. Laudon, K. Gharachorloo, W. Weber, A. Gupta, J. Hennessy, M. Horowitz, and M. Lam. The Stanford DASH Multiprocessor. *IEEE Computer*, 25(3):63–79, March 1992.

[7] T. Lovett and R. Clapp. STiNG: A CC-NUMA Computer System for the Commercial Marketplace. In *Proceedings of the 23rd Annual International Symposium on Computer Architecture*, pages 308–317, May 1996.

[8] S. Mukherjee, S. Sharma, M. Hill, J. Larus, A. Rogers, and J. Saltz. Efficient Support for Irregular Applications on Distributed-Memory Machines. In *Proceedings of the Fifth ACM Symposium on Principles and Practice of Parallel Programming*, pages 68–79, July 1995.

[9] A.-T. Nguyen, M. Michael, A. Sharma, and J. Torrellas. The Augmint Multiprocessor Simulation Toolkit for Intel x86 Architectures. In *Proceedings of the 1996 IEEE International Conference on Computer Design*, pages 486–490, October 1996.

[10] A. Nowatzyk, G. Aybay, M. Browne, E. Kelly, M. Parkin, B. Radke, and S.Vishin. The S3.mp Scalable Shared Memory Multiprocessor. In *Proceedings of the 1995 International Conference on Parallel Processing*, August 1995.

[11] *Pentium Pro Family Developer's Manual.* Intel Corporation, 1996.

[12] S. Reinhardt, J. Larus, and D. Wood. Tempest and Typhoon: User-Level Shared Memory. In *Proceedings of the 21st Annual International Symposium on Computer Architecture*, pages 325–336, April 1994.

[13] S. Reinhardt, R. Pfile, and D. Wood. Decoupled Hardware Support for Distributed Shared Memory. In *Proceedings of the 23rd Annual International Symposium on Computer Architecture*, pages 34–43, May 1996.

[14] S. C. Woo, M. Ohara, E. Torrie, J. P. Singh, and A. Gupta. The SPLASH-2 Programs: Characterization and Methodological Considerations. In *Proceedings of the 22nd Annual International Symposium on Computer Architecture*, pages 24–36, June 1995.

Reactive NUMA: A Design for Unifying S-COMA and CC-NUMA

Babak Falsafi and David A. Wood
Computer Sciences Department
University of Wisconsin, Madison
1210 W. Dayton Street
Madison, WI 53706
{babak,david}@cs.wisc.edu

Abstract

This paper proposes and evaluates a new approach to directory-based cache coherence protocols called *Reactive NUMA* (R-NUMA). An R-NUMA system combines a conventional CC-NUMA coherence protocol with a more-recent Simple-COMA (S-COMA) protocol. What makes R-NUMA novel is the way it dynamically reacts to program and system behavior to switch between CC-NUMA and S-COMA and exploit the best aspects of both protocols. This reactive behavior allows each node in an R-NUMA system to independently choose the best protocol for a particular page, thus providing much greater performance stability than either CC-NUMA or S-COMA alone. Our evaluation is both qualitative and quantitative. We first show the theoretical result that R-NUMA's worst-case performance is bounded within a small constant factor (i.e., two to three times) of the best of CC-NUMA and S-COMA. We then use detailed execution-driven simulation to show that, in practice, R-NUMA usually performs better than either a pure CC-NUMA or pure S-COMA protocol, and no more than 57% worse than the best of CC-NUMA and S-COMA, for our benchmarks and base system assumptions.

1 Introduction

Clusters of symmetric multiprocessors, or SMPs, have emerged as a promising approach to building large-scale shared-memory parallel machines [15,16]. The relatively high volumes of these small-scale parallel servers make them extremely cost-effective as building blocks. By connecting these low-cost nodes, system designers hope to construct large-scale parallel machines with better cost-performance than has been previously possible [3].

This work is supported in part by Wright Laboratory Avionics Directorate, Air Force Material Command, USAF, under grant #F33615-94-1-1525 and ARPA order no. B550, NSF PYI Award CCR-9157366, NSF Grants MIP-9225097 and MIP-9625558, an IBM graduate fellowship, and donations from A.T.&T. Bell Laboratories, Hewlett Packard, IBM Corporation, and Sun Microsystems. The U.S. Government is authorized to reproduce and distribute reprints for Governmental purposes notwithstanding any copyright notation thereon. The views and conclusions contained herein are those of the authors and should not be interpreted as necessarily representing the official policies or endorsements, either expressed or implied, of the Wright Laboratory Avionics Directorate or the U.S. Government.

To preserve software compatibility, these clusters use a directory-based cache coherence protocol to support a shared-memory abstraction despite having memory physically distributed across the nodes. Such systems have previously employed either a cache-coherent non-uniform memory access (CC-NUMA) protocol [15,16], a Simple-COMA (S-COMA) protocol [11], or provided support for both [22,8]. In a CC-NUMA system, remote data may be cached in a CPU's cache or a per-node cluster cache. References not satisfied by these hardware caches must be sent to the referenced page's home node to obtain the requested data (and enforce any necessary coherence actions). An S-COMA system uses the exact same coherence protocol, but allocates part of the local node's main memory to act as a large cache for remote pages. S-COMA is much cheaper and simpler to implement than earlier COMA systems [10,12] because it uses standard address translation hardware as "tags" for the page cache. Because S-COMA requires only incrementally more hardware than CC-NUMA, some systems have proposed providing support for both protocols [22,8].

A potential disadvantage of DSM clusters is the relatively large ratio of remote to local miss times. For example, the Sequent STiNG's remote misses are roughly ten times slower than local misses [16]. Conversely, in a full-integrated implementation like the recently-announced SGI Origin2000 [1], the ratio can be as small as two to three times. Thus an application's performance on a DSM cluster will be very sensitive to the frequency of remote misses.

S-COMA can potentially perform much better than CC-NUMA on these machines. This is because the S-COMA page cache is part of main memory, and can be much larger than a CC-NUMA cluster cache. Thus, S-COMA potentially results in significantly fewer remote misses, and achieves better performance. CC-NUMA machines can reduce this difference by allocating pages on the same node as the processor that uses them [17], dynamically migrating pages [4,24], and replicating read-only pages [24]. These techniques have been shown to dramatically reduce the number of remote misses for some applications. Unfortunately, they provide no help for read-write shared data, which are quite frequent in other applications. For example, Verghese, et al., found that 90% of user data misses in a commercial relational database application were to read-write shared pages [24]. S-COMA permits replication of these read-write pages, thus eliminating unnecessary remote references.

Conversely, S-COMA is not without its costs. Allocating space in the S-COMA page cache incurs substantial overhead, in the form of operating system intervention to set up the local translation. The page cache must eliminate many misses to amortize this initial overhead (and the subsequent replacement overhead). This is further complicated by the large—i.e., page—granularity. Programs with large sparse data sets may see severe internal fragmentation and thrash the S-COMA page cache. Thus CC-NUMA may have

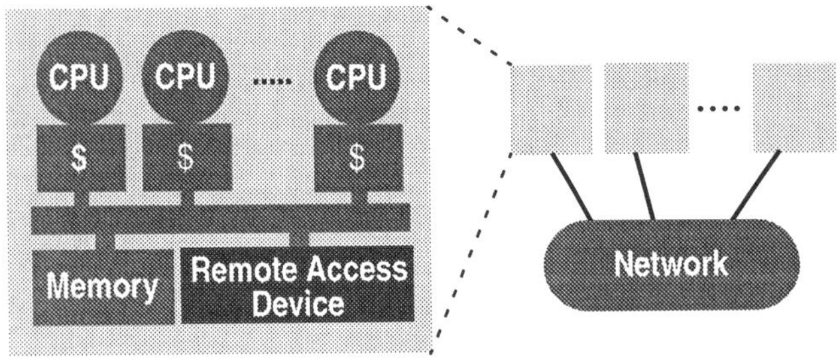

FIGURE 1. A distributed shared-memory machine.

substantially better performance for some applications and reference patterns.

In this paper, we propose a Reactive NUMA (R-NUMA) protocol that dynamically reacts to program and system behavior to switch between CC-NUMA and S-COMA protocols. This reactive behavior provides much greater performance stability than either CC-NUMA or S-COMA alone, by allowing each node in an R-NUMA system to independently choose the best protocol for a particular page. The algorithm initially allocates all remote pages as CC-NUMA, but maintains a per-node, per-page count of the number of times a block is refetched as a result of a conflict or capacity miss. When the refetch count exceeds a threshold, the operating system intervenes and reallocates the page in the S-COMA page cache. R-NUMA requires very little additional hardware—primarily a set of per-node, per-page counters—beyond what is needed to support both CC-NUMA and S-COMA.

We evaluate the protocol both qualitatively and quantitatively. We first present a simple analytical model indicating that R-NUMA performs competitively with respect to CC-NUMA and S-COMA. This result guarantees that R-NUMA never performs much worse than the best of either S-COMA or CC-NUMA. We then use detailed execution-driven simulation to show that, in practice, R-NUMA's reactive behavior often leads to better performance than either a pure CC-NUMA or pure S-COMA protocol. Quantitative results also confirm our theoretical result: R-NUMA performs no more than 57% worse than the best of the two underlying protocols. Conversely, for one application CC-NUMA was 179% slower than S-COMA; for another S-COMA was 315% slower than CC-NUMA. Thus, for our benchmarks and system assumptions, R-NUMA often achieves the best performance, and is never much worse than the best possible. This superior performance stability makes R-NUMA a very attractive alternative for future shared-memory machines.

The next section describes the basic distributed shared-memory machine structure that we study in this paper, and provides more details of the CC-NUMA and S-COMA protocols. Section 3 presents the Reactive NUMA protocol and its qualitative analysis. Section 4 and Section 5 describe the simulation methodology we use to quantitatively evaluate the protocols and the results, respectively. Finally, Section 6 summarizes the results and conclusions in this paper.

2 DSM Hardware Support

Figure 1 illustrates the basic distributed shared-memory machine organization that we study in this paper. Each node is a symmetric multiprocessor (SMP) workstation with four processors connected via a coherent bus to an interleaved memory. A *Remote Access*

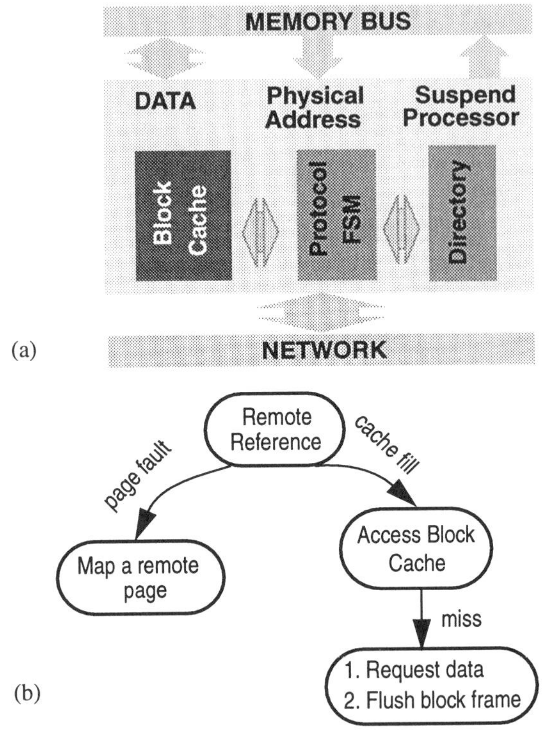

FIGURE 2. Caching remote data in CC-NUMA: (a) anatomy of a CC-NUMA RAD, (b) flow of a remote miss.

Device (RAD) implements a directory-based cache coherence protocol to extend the shared-memory abstraction across the nodes. This device implements the same basic coherence protocol in all systems; CC-NUMA, S-COMA, and R-NUMA simply differ in where remote data is cached.

All systems implement a global physical address space, where the high-order bits encode the node id. CC-NUMA systems reference global addresses directly; S-COMA uses a simple SRAM mapping table to translate local physical addresses to global physical addresses. R-NUMA does both, since it supports both protocols. All systems run a single operating system image, but maintain separate per-node page tables to permit independent allocation decisions and reduce TLB fill latency and contention.

2.1 CC-NUMA

Most previous distributed shared-memory machines have been CC-NUMA machines [15,2,16,5,18]. Figure 2(a) illustrates the CC-NUMA RAD we consider in this paper. Like the Sequent STiNG [16], our CC-NUMA RAD is equipped with a remote cluster cache for maintaining recently referenced remote data blocks. This cache acts as another level in the node's cache hierarchy, but unlike the processor caches, only holds remote data. In the remainder of this paper, we refer to this CC-NUMA cache as a *block cache* to differentiate it from S-COMA's page-granularity cache. A hardware protocol controller manages accesses to the block cache and directory, services messages from remote nodes, and requests remote data on the behalf of the node.

Figure 2 (b) illustrates the flow of events on a remote reference in CC-NUMA. The first processor to access a remote page within each node results in a (soft) page fault. The operating system's page fault handler maps the page to a CC-NUMA global physical address, updating the node's page table. Subsequent references to the same page by any processor within the SMP node result in cache block fills on the memory bus. The CC-NUMA RAD snoops for global physical addresses on the bus and satisfies the cache fill requests if the data resides in the block cache. Upon a miss in the block cache, the RAD allocates a block frame, writing back a dirty block if necessary, and sends a request for the data to the remote node.

The block cache improves CC-NUMA's performance by reducing the number of remote misses. Block caches can either be small, fast, and built with SRAM, or large, slow, and built with DRAM. The latter reduces the number of remote misses, but at the expense of increasing the remote miss latency and controller occupancy. To keep latencies and occupancies comparable between CC-NUMA and S-COMA we consider only relatively small, fast block caches in this paper.

Because the block cache is still relatively small, CC-NUMA's performance is very sensitive to data allocation and placement. LaRowe, et al. [14] have shown that a good initial allocation works well for many scientific applications. We use a first-touch migration policy which is both simple and has been shown to substantially eliminate unnecessary traffic [17]. In this policy, a user-invoked directive on every node initiates page migration at the start of the parallel phase of the program. Upon the first request for each page, the home node migrates the page to the requester, assuming the first requester is likely to prove a frequent requester. This is especially true for some regular scientific applications that specifically "touch" pages to ensure their proper placement [26]. Dynamic replication/migration can further improve performance by replicating code and read-only data pages, and migrating pages that are mostly accessed by a single processor [24]. Unfortunately, these techniques fail for data pages that are actively shared among multiple processors.

2.2 S-COMA

Cache-Only Memory Architectures (COMA) allow remote data to reside in both the node's cache hierarchy and main memory. For example, the SICS DDM [10] and Kendall Square Research KSR1 [19] replicate and migrate data at cache block granularities among the node's memories. Because data is allocated at subpage granularities, these machines require the use of significant additional hardware to determine the physical location of a datum.

Simple COMA (S-COMA) [11,21] greatly simplifies the original COMA approach by decoupling data allocation and naming from coherence. Remote data is allocated and mapped at page granularity using standard virtual address translation hardware, much like page-based DSMs [7]. A region of main memory is set aside as a *page cache* for remote data pages. An S-COMA remote access device (RAD), Figure 3 (a), maintains coherence using the same basic coherence protocol as the CC-NUMA RAD. The essential extra hardware is a set of fine-grain access control tags—two bits per block to detect when the RAD must inhibit memory and intervene—and an auxiliary SRAM translation table with one entry per page—to convert between local physical addresses (i.e., the page cache) and global physical addresses (i.e., the home address). Because operating system software handles the more complex operations of allocation and migration, S-COMA is much simpler than "full" COMA implementations.

Figure 3 (b) illustrates the S-COMA algorithm. On a node's first reference to a remote page, a page fault occurs and is handled by

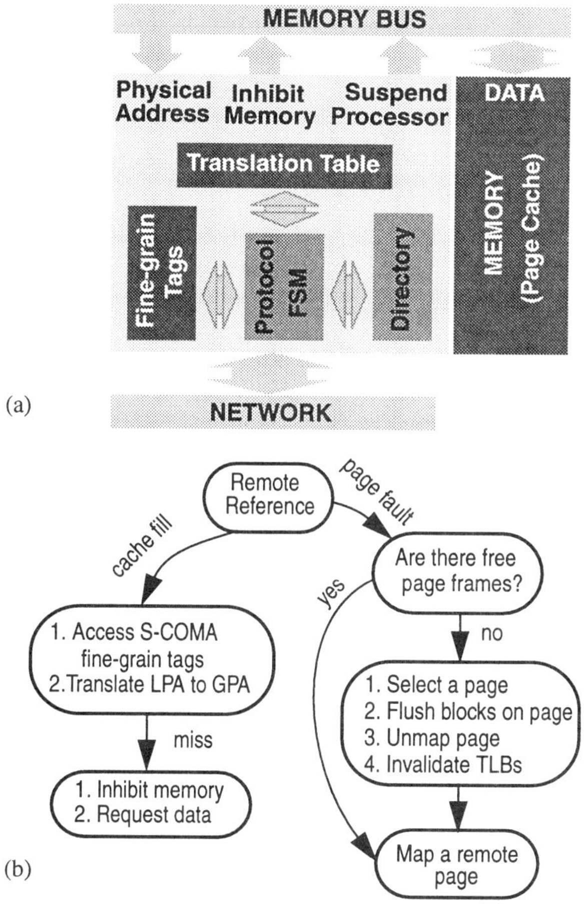

FIGURE 3. Caching remote data in S-COMA: (a) anatomy of an S-COMA RAD, (b) flow of a remote miss.

the operating system. If there are no free page frames available in the page cache, the operating system selects a victim, unmaps and flushes all dirty blocks back to home node, and shoots down the TLBs on the *local* node. When a page frame is available, the operating system initializes the page table, the RAD's auxiliary translation table, and fine-grain access control tags. Subsequent references find the page mapped, and hits and misses are detected by the fine-grain access control tags. Hits are serviced by local memory. Misses are detected by the RAD, which inhibits memory, translates to the corresponding global physical address, and communicates with the home node to obtain the requesting block.

S-COMA can potentially outperform CC-NUMA because it can exploit the node's large main memory to cache remote data. S-COMA can dynamically tailor the fraction of memory used to cache remote data, in response to an application's needs. S-COMA's remote cache is also fully-associative, because S-COMA uses the standard virtual address translation hardware to locate remote pages.

S-COMA's simplicity and fully-associative page cache come at a cost, however. Many parallel applications do not have sufficient spatial locality to fully utilize remote pages, leading to internal fragmentation. Irregular applications and regular applications with large strides are particularly susceptible to this problem. These applications may incur significant internal fragmentation, and require a prohibitively large page cache to fit their remote working sets. If the page cache is not sufficiently large, the result is frequent S-COMA page replacement (i.e., thrashing) and a rapid decrease in performance.

3 Reactive NUMA

Reactive NUMA (R-NUMA) tries to combine the best aspects of both CC-NUMA and S-COMA. R-NUMA is based on the observation that remote data pages can be classified into two groups. *Reuse* pages contain data structures that are accessed many times within the same node, and thus exhibit substantial remote traffic due to capacity and conflict misses in the node's cache hierarchy. Conversely, *communication* pages are used primarily to exchange data between nodes, and thus mainly exhibit coherence misses. R-NUMA attempts to distinguish between these two types of pages, and store reuse pages in an S-COMA-like page cache, while limiting communication pages to the node's cache hierarchy and CC-NUMA-like block cache. R-NUMA dynamically detects when communication pages become reuse pages, and vice versa.

3.1 Mechanisms for R-NUMA

An R-NUMA machine must provide mechanisms for caching remote data pages both as CC-NUMA and S-COMA pages. The operating system maps CC-NUMA pages directly to a remote global physical address and S-COMA pages to a local physical address in the page cache. The R-NUMA RAD snoops for both CC-NUMA global physical addresses and (local) physical addresses in the S-COMA page cache. Note that R-NUMA need not require any additional hardware. For example, s3.mp [18] and the Stanford FLASH [13] already provide sufficient mechanisms to implement both CC-NUMA and S-COMA. Because they use programmable controllers, implementing R-NUMA should just be a software change.

Figure 4 (a) illustrates that an R-NUMA RAD looks like a combination of an S-COMA RAD and a CC-NUMA RAD. A block cache serves as a backup device for CC-NUMA-mapped pages, a set of S-COMA fine-grain tags provide access control for S-COMA-mapped pages, a simple SRAM mapping table translates local S-COMA physical addresses to the corresponding global physical addresses, and a directory maintains coherence information for each page for which a node is the designated home.

The R-NUMA protocol separates data allocation from coherence. Coherence is a *global* operation, where all nodes cooperate to enforce the shared-memory abstraction. Data allocation is a *local* decision, which determines whether a particular cache block (page) should be replicated in the S-COMA page cache or CC-NUMA block cache. This separation allows each node to independently decide whether to manage a particular shared page as CC-NUMA or S-COMA.

R-NUMA requires a mechanism to decide when to switch between CC-NUMA and S-COMA. The key difference between reuse and communication pages is the number of remote capacity and conflict misses a page incurs in the block cache. When a block gets evicted from the block cache due to its limited capacity or a set conflict, the next subsequent reference to that block will miss, causing a *refetch* from the home node. The directory can detect refetches by simply keeping track of when a node requests a block that the directory state indicates it already has. Assuming a non-notifying protocol, this is trivial for read-only blocks. Handling read-write blocks generally requires adding an additional state to indicate that a processor previously held an exclusive block, but voluntarily wrote it back. The system then keeps track of the number of refetches on a per-node, per-page basis. The directory can either maintain the counts itself, similar to the page migration counts in the SGI Origin2000 [1], or communicate the information back to the requester on the reply message. We assume that each R-NUMA RAD maintains a set of per-page counters for its node and generates an interrupt when the count exceeds a preset threshold.

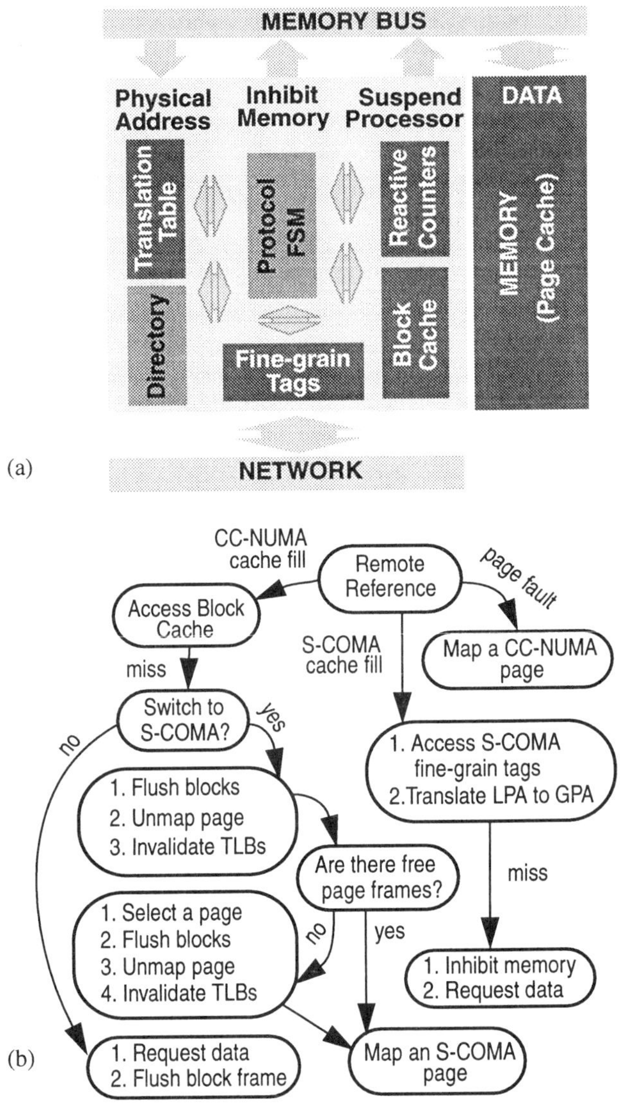

FIGURE 4. Caching remote data in R-NUMA: (a) anatomy of an R-NUMA RAD, (b) flow of a remote miss.

Figure 4 (b) illustrates the flow of events for caching remote data in R-NUMA. The first reference to an unmapped page results in a page fault. The operating system initially maps the page CC-NUMA. Further references are handled by the R-NUMA RAD, either supplying them from the block cache or fetching them from the home node. The RAD uses the per-page counters to detect when the number of refetches exceeds the threshold. When this occurs, the operating system is invoked to relocate the page from CC-NUMA to S-COMA. Relocation requires unmapping the CC-NUMA page, flushing all locally cached blocks from that page, and allocating and mapping a new S-COMA page (possibly cleaning a page, if no free ones exist).

3.2 Qualitative Performance

R-NUMA's performance depends upon how well it selects the appropriate mapping for a given page. If an off-line oracle selects the mapping, then the R-NUMA protocol always performs at least as well as either CC-NUMA or S-COMA, since it combines the hardware resources of both. Unfortunately, real systems must rely on on-line algorithms.

Instead, we present a simple intuitive model to analyze the worst-case behavior of R-NUMA. Our model shows that an application's execution time under R-NUMA is always within a small constant factor of the execution time under the best of CC-NUMA and S-COMA.

In the interest of brevity and clarity, we make several simplifying assumptions about the behavior of the system. We compare performance relative to an "ideal" CC-NUMA machine with an infinite capacity block cache. The finite capacities of the actual block and page caches result in extra overheads due to refetches in the block cache, replacements in the page cache, and relocation of pages between the block and page caches. We limit our analysis to these extra overheads for a single remote page. The results generalize to multiple pages because they hold for worst-case reference patterns.

Assume a CC-NUMA with a block cache of a given size, an S-COMA with a page cache of a given size, and an R-NUMA with block and page caches equal in size to their counterparts in the CC-NUMA and S-COMA. Also assume that the cost of fetching a block from a remote node is much higher than a local memory access. Our results remain qualitatively valid for systems that violate these assumptions, however, a further discussion is beyond the scope of this paper.

Parameter	Description
$C_{refetch}$	Cost of refetching a remote block
$C_{allocate}$	Cost of allocating/replacing a page
$C_{relocate}$	Cost of relocating a page
T	Relocation threshold value
$O_{CC\text{-}NUMA}$	Per-page overhead of CC-NUMA
$O_{S\text{-}COMA}$	Per-page overhead of S-COMA
$O_{R\text{-}NUMA}$	Per-page overhead of R-NUMA

TABLE 1. Parameters for the performance model.

Table 1 depicts the parameters we use in our performance model. $C_{refetch}$ is the cost of refetching a block from a remote node; $C_{allocate}$ is the cost of allocating and later replacing a page; $C_{relocate}$ is the cost of relocating a page from CC-NUMA to S-COMA; T is the number of refetches before R-NUMA relocates a CC-NUMA page to an S-COMA page. Our model uses these parameters to compute $O_{CC\text{-}NUMA}$, $O_{S\text{-}COMA}$ and $O_{R\text{-}NUMA}$, which represent the additional per-page overheads of the three machines as compared to our ideal machine respectively.

R-NUMA's per-page behavior digresses from CC-NUMA's when a page incurs more refetches than specified by the threshold T. R-NUMA relocates such a page to the page cache in order to convert remote block fetches to local memory accesses. R-NUMA performs worst when a page relocates from the block cache to the page cache and is not referenced again before being replaced. In this case, CC-NUMA's overhead ($O_{CC\text{-}NUMA}$) is only $TC_{refetch}$ whereas R-NUMA would incur additional overheads of relocating the blocks on the CC-NUMA page, and allocating and subsequently replacing an S-COMA page for a total of $O_{R\text{-}NUMA} = TC_{refetch} + C_{relocate} + C_{allocate}$. Therefore, R-NUMA's performance is worse than CC-NUMA by at most

$$\frac{O_{R\text{-}NUMA}}{O_{CC\text{-}NUMA}} = \frac{TC_{refetch} + C_{relocate} + C_{allocate}}{TC_{refetch}} . \quad \text{(EQ 1)}$$

R-NUMA's worst-case performance with respect to S-COMA also occurs for the same case. S-COMA's per-page overhead ($O_{S\text{-}COMA}$) would be simply $C_{allocate}$ whereas R-NUMA's overhead ($O_{R\text{-}NUMA}$) would include the additional overheads of refetching T blocks and relocating a page, i.e., $TC_{refetch} + C_{relocate} + C_{allocate}$. Hence, S-COMA will outperform R-NUMA by at most

$$\frac{O_{R\text{-}NUMA}}{O_{S\text{-}COMA}} = \frac{TC_{refetch} + C_{relocate} + C_{allocate}}{C_{allocate}} . \quad \text{(EQ 2)}$$

Our goal is to minimize the worst-case performance of R-NUMA with respect to both CC-NUMA and S-COMA. The right hand sides of the above two equations are intersecting functions of T. At the point of intersection, R-NUMA's relative worst-case performance is equal to

$$\frac{O_{R\text{-}NUMA}}{O_{CC\text{-}NUMA}} = \frac{O_{R\text{-}NUMA}}{O_{S\text{-}COMA}} = 2 + \frac{C_{relocate}}{C_{allocate}} \quad \text{(EQ 3)}$$

at the threshold value of $T = \frac{C_{allocate}}{C_{refetch}}$.

Equation 3 indicates that the bound on worst-case performance of R-NUMA depends on the cost of relocation relative to the cost of page allocation/replacement. Relocation includes generating an interrupt when the number of refetches reaches the threshold, and moving the blocks from the block cache to the page cache. In a high-performance implementation with support for fast interrupts and mechanisms for (locally) relocating blocks, $C_{relocate}$ will be small compared to $C_{allocate}$, and the worst-case performance bound will be close to 2. In a less aggressive implementation, the cost of relocation will be dominated by interrupt overhead and flushing the blocks from the block cache, $C_{relocate}$ will be approximately equal to $C_{allocate}$, and the worst-case performance will be close to 3.

Equation 3 also indicates that the threshold value at the point of intersection simply depends on the per-page overheads of CC-NUMA and S-COMA. As such, the value is a function of the cost of page allocation/replacement and the cost of a remote block fetch, and is independent of the cost of relocation.

In practical terms, the worst-case performance analysis proves that R-NUMA performs no more than three times worse than either a vanilla CC-NUMA or S-COMA system. In fact, since block refetch, page allocation/replacement, and page relocation over-

Application	Problem	Input Data Set
barnes	Barnes-Hut N-body simulation [26]	16K particles
cholesky	Blocked sparse Cholesky factorization [26]	tk16.O
em3d	3-D electromagnetic wave propagation [9]	76800 nodes, 15% remote, 5 iters
fft	Complex 1-D radix-$\sqrt{n}$ six-step FFT [26]	64K points
fmm	Fast Multipole N-body simulation [26]	16K particles
lu	Blocked dense LU factorization [26]	512x512 matrix, 16x16 blocks
moldyn	Molecular dynamics simulation [6]	2048 particles, 15 iters
ocean	Ocean simulation [26]	258x258 ocean
radix	Integer radix sort [26]	1M integers, radix 1024
raytrace	3-D scene rendering using ray-tracing [26]	car

TABLE 3. Applications and input parameters.

heads are only a few out of many components of execution time, the practical "bound" is much less than three. However, while bounding worst-case performance is important for some applications, e.g., on-line transaction processing and process control, most users focus on average performance. Moreover, the threshold value that maximizes R-NUMA's performance in practice may be different from the one that minimizes worst-case performance. In the remainder of this paper, we show that R-NUMA's ability to dynamically allocate some pages to the S-COMA page cache and others to the CC-NUMA block cache can significantly improve performance. We also show that R-NUMA performs well even with a much smaller block cache than CC-NUMA. Finally, we present results on the sensitivity of R-NUMA's performance on relocation threshold value and overhead.

4 Methodology

To compare practical implementations of R-NUMA, CC-NUMA, and S-COMA, we simulate a distributed shared-memory machine consisting of a network of eight SMP nodes (Figure 1). Each node is a 4-way multiprocessor with 400 MHz dual-issue statically scheduled processors—modeled after the Ross HyperSparc—interconnected by a 100 MHz split-transaction bus. A snoopy MOESI coherence protocol—modeled after Sparc's MBus protocol—keeps the caches within each node consistent. We assume perfect instruction caches[1] but model data caches and their contention at the memory bus accurately. We further assume a point-to-point network with a constant latency of 100 cycles but model contention at the network interfaces.

Our block cache is a writeback direct-mapped SRAM cache. The cache maintains inclusion—with respect to the node's cache hierarchy—for remote blocks cached in the read-write state but not for those cached in the read-only state. Cache inclusion for read-write blocks greatly simplifies the interaction between the DSM CC-NUMA protocol and the commodity workstation MOESI protocol. Maintaining inclusion for the remote blocks in the read-only state would require a very large block cache. Instead we opted for not maintaining inclusion for read-only blocks. However, since MBus does not implement cache-to-cache transfer for blocks that are not owned by a processor, read requests to read-only remote blocks that miss in the block cache are forwarded to the home node even if there are copies of the block in other processor caches on the node.

1. The scientific codes we study have low instruction cache miss ratios. This assumption may not hold for all applications.

Operation	Cost (processor cycles)
block operations	
SRAM access	8
DRAM access	56
local cache fill	69
remote fetch	376
page operations	
soft traps	2000
TLB shootdown	200
allocation/replacement or relocation	3000~11500

TABLE 2. Base line system assumptions.

Both S-COMA and R-NUMA implement a simple *Least Recently Missed* page replacement policy. This policy is similar to classical LRU, but the page frame list is re-ordered only on remote misses rather than on each reference. This can be approximated in practice by maintaining per-page hardware miss counters which the operating system periodically samples. However, since page replacement policies are beyond the scope of this paper, our model of S-COMA hardware simply maintains the necessary information and communicates it to the operating system at the time of a page fault.

Table 2 presents the costs of block and page operations in processor cycles for our base system assumptions. SRAM devices include the block cache, S-COMA fine-grain tags and translation table, and R-NUMA reactive counters. DRAM accesses correspond to accesses to the page cache. Soft traps include page faults and R-NUMA relocation interrupts. Page allocation/replacement involves taking a soft trap, invalidating the (local) TLBs, and flushing the blocks back to the home node. The overhead varies depend-

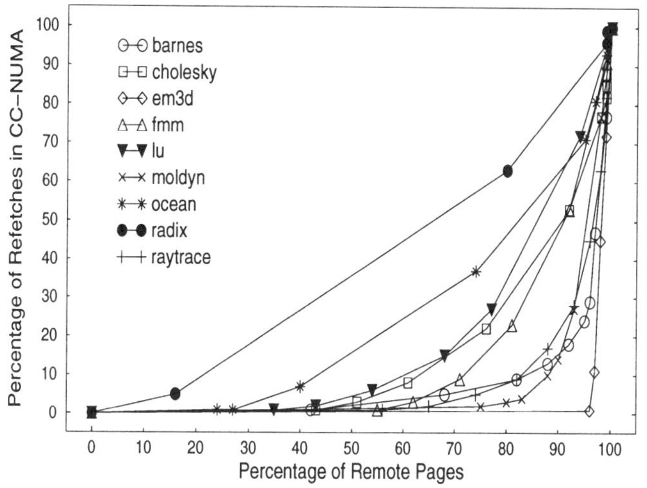

FIGURE 5. Characterizing remote pages.

The figure plots the cumulative distribution of refetches as a function of the fraction of remote pages in a CC-NUMA machine with a 32-Kbyte block cache. The figure omits *fft*, because it fits in the node's cache hierarchy and incurs no capacity or conflict misses.

ing on the number of blocks flushed. Page relocation uses similar mechanisms as page allocation/replacement and incurs the same overheads.

Table 3 presents the applications we use in this study and the corresponding input parameters. *Barnes*, *cholesky*, *fft*, *fmm*, *lu*, *ocean*, *radix* and *raytrace* are from the SPLASH-2 [26] benchmark suite. *Em3d* is a shared-memory implementation of the Split-C benchmark [9]. Moldyn is a shared-memory implementation of a CHARMM-like [6] molecular dynamics application.

Our application data set sizes are selected to be small enough so as to not require prohibitive simulation cycles, while being large enough to maintain the intrinsic communication and computation characteristics of the parallel application. Woo, et al., characterize the behavior of SPLASH-2 applications in terms of working sets and show that for most of the applications, the data sets provided have a primary working set that fits in an 8-Kbyte cache [26]. We, therefore, assume 8-Kbyte (direct-mapped) processor caches to compensate for the small size of the data sets.

In this study, our base system assumes a CC-NUMA block cache equal in size to the sum of all the processor cache sizes. This assumption helps mitigate any adverse effects due to the inclusion requirement of read-write blocks. Consequently, a four-processor node will have a 32-Kbyte CC-NUMA block cache. To compensate for the lower cost of DRAM as compared to SRAM, our base system assumes an S-COMA page cache of 320 Kbytes, a factor of 10 larger than our CC-NUMA block cache. We further assume a much smaller 128-byte block cache in R-NUMA than that in CC-NUMA. We present results in Section 5 that indicate that R-NUMA performs well even with such a small block cache.

5 Results

In this section, we present results from our simulation experiments. We first motivate the results by presenting a characterization of remote pages in a CC-NUMA machine. Next, we present numbers comparing the performance of CC-NUMA, S-COMA, and R-NUMA. In the rest of the section, we study the sensitivity of R-NUMA's performance to block cache size, relocation threshold value and overhead.

	CC-NUMA	R-NUMA	
Application	RW pages	refetches	replacements
barnes	97%	21%	2%
cholesky	28%	30%	15%
em3d	100%	0%	0%
fmm	99%	142%	2%
lu	82%	21%	70%
moldyn	98%	0%	0%
ocean	96%	36%	4%
radix	15%	125%	1%
raytrace	5%	41%	5%

TABLE 4. Characterizing block refetches and page replacements in CC-NUMA and R-NUMA.

The table presents the fraction of block refetches due to pages that incur both read and write coherence misses in CC-NUMA, and block refetches and page replacements in R-NUMA as a percentage of those in CC-NUMA and S-COMA. The table omits *fft* because it incurs no capacity or conflict misses in CC-NUMA and only a small number of page replacements in S-COMA. The numbers correspond to a CC-NUMA with a 32-Kbyte block cache, an S-COMA with 320-Kbyte page cache, and an R-NUMA with 128-byte block cache and a 320-Kbyte page cache and threshold value of 64.

5.1 Characterizing Pages in CC-NUMA

R-NUMA offers a performance advantage over CC-NUMA if an application incurs a large number of capacity and conflict misses on remote data in a CC-NUMA machine. R-NUMA also outperforms S-COMA when the majority of the capacity and conflict misses in CC-NUMA are due to a small fraction of remote pages that can fit in the page cache. Conversely, R-NUMA can perform worse, if the page cache is too small to accommodate the set of remote pages that account for most of the capacity and conflict misses in CC-NUMA. Therefore, R-NUMA's performance relative to CC-NUMA and S-COMA depends on the fraction of reuse and communication remote pages in the application.

Figure 5 illustrates the fraction of remote pages that are responsible for a given percentage of block refetches in CC-NUMA—due to capacity and conflict misses. The graphs indicate that in four of the applications, less than 10% of the remote pages account for over 80% of the capacity and conflict misses in CC-NUMA. With the exception of *radix*, an additional 20% of remote pages (for a total of 30%) account for just under 70% of the refetches in all of the applications. *Radix* performs an all-to-all communication, where processors march through a large number of remote pages writing to small number of blocks. As such, the remote pages for the most part exhibit similar behavior, and the capacity and conflict misses are evenly distributed among the pages.

Table 4 (second column from left) presents the fraction of block refetches in CC-NUMA due to pages that incur both read and write sharing traffic. The table indicates that with the exception of some of the kernels and *raytrace*, read-write remote pages account for over 80% of the block refetches in all of the applications. This result indicates that our first-touch migration is very effective in eliminating block refetch traffic due to pages that are not shared—i.e., pages that are always used by one node but initially allocated on another node. Moreover, simple replication of (read-only) remote pages which has been shown to be effective in mulitiprogammed workloads [24], will not help pages with read-write traffic. *Raytrace*, is the only application that proves to be a good candidate for replication schemes because most of the remote pages contain read-only data structures.

Not surprisingly, two of the kernels (*cholesky* and *radix*) also exhibit a large fraction of remote pages with read-only traffic. The kernels are representative of common computations that are typically found in larger applications. As such, much of the data structures that appear as read-only remote data in the kernel, are in fact the results of other intermediate stages of computation. Depending on the read-write sharing behavior of the data throughout the application, dynamic read-only replication schemes may or may not be effective. R-NUMA's relocation overheads are relatively small—only referenced blocks are replicated—and as such R-NUMA can help reduce read-only traffic even in small kernel computations.

5.2 Base System Results

R-NUMA's performance depends on the relative frequency of block refetches in the R-NUMA and CC-NUMA block caches, as well as page replacements in the R-NUMA and S-COMA page caches. Table 4 also presents the number of block refetches and page replacements in R-NUMA as a fraction of those in CC-NUMA and S-COMA. The numbers compare a CC-NUMA with a 32-Kbyte block cache, an S-COMA with a 320-Kbyte page cache, and an R-NUMA with a 128-byte block cache, a 320-Kbyte page cache, and a relocation threshold value of 64.

The table indicates that R-NUMA substantially reduces the block refetch traffic relative to CC-NUMA in all but two of the applications. R-NUMA also virtually eliminates the page replacement traffic relative to S-COMA in most of the applications. R-NUMA increases block refetches in *fmm* and *radix* relative to CC-NUMA because of its small block cache. Moreover, R-NUMA's page cache is too small to accommodate all the reuse pages, causing the pages to bounce between the block and page caches. The combined effect of a small block cache and page cache too small to contain all the reuse pages increases the overall number of refetches in these applications.

Figure 6 compares the performance of CC-NUMA, S-COMA, and R-NUMA. The graphs present the execution times on a CC-NUMA with a 32-Kbyte block cache, an S-COMA with a 320-Kbyte page cache, and an R-NUMA with 128-byte block cache, a 320-Kbyte page cache and a relocation threshold value of 64. The graphs are normalized to a CC-NUMA with an infinite block cache—i.e., one in which the block cache is large enough to hold all of the remote data.

Not surprisingly, the performance of CC-NUMA and S-COMA varies across applications. Applications whose sharing occurs in a small number of localized regions fit well in the node's cache hierarchy and the block cache. In contrast, a page cache favors applications with dense sharing patterns, because the overhead of allocation/replacement of a page can be amortized over a large number of blocks per page. Dense sharing patterns also result in lower page fragmentation, and thus place less pressure on the page cache.

The graphs corroborate our intuition (from Section 3.2) that R-NUMA either outperforms or is competitive with CC-NUMA and S-COMA. In the best case, R-NUMA reduces execution time by

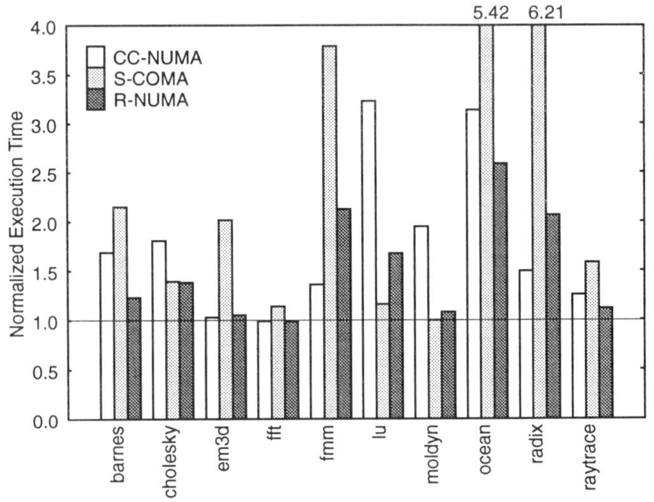

FIGURE 6. Comparing performance of CC-NUMA, S-COMA and R-NUMA.

The figure plots execution times on a CC-NUMA with a 32-Kbyte block cache, S-COMA with 320-Kbyte page cache, and R-NUMA with a 128-byte block cache, a 320-Kbyte page cache, and a relocation threshold value of 64. The numbers are normalized to a CC-NUMA with an infinite block cache, i.e., a block cache that can hold all of the referenced remote data.

37% in the best of CC-NUMA and S-COMA. In the worst case, R-NUMA increases execution time by only 57% in the best of the two protocols. In comparison, CC-NUMA performs as much as 179% worse than S-COMA, and S-COMA performs as much as 315% worse than CC-NUMA. Thus, R-NUMA exhibits much less sensitivity to a particular application's behavior and provides superior performance stability over either CC-NUMA or S-COMA alone.

We now examine the individual applications in more detail. In *em3d* and *fft* communication is of producer-consumer nature, where remote pages primarily exchange recently produced data. These applications incur minimal number of capacity and conflict misses in the 32-Kbyte block cache and hence perform well in CC-NUMA. S-COMA fails to provide enough page frames to hold all the remote pages for either of these applications, thus resulting in lower performance. Much like CC-NUMA, R-NUMA's block cache provides enough (temporary) storage for the remote data, and thus R-NUMA performs as well as CC-NUMA.

Moldyn performs well in S-COMA because the page cache can capture the complete set of remote pages in this application. In *moldyn*, a small number of reuse pages account for most of the capacity and conflict misses in CC-NUMA. R-NUMA simply relocates these pages into the page cache and performs much like S-COMA.

Cholesky, fmm, lu, ocean and *radix* are examples of applications in which a large fraction of remote pages are responsible for the capacity and conflict misses in CC-NUMA's block cache. S-COMA's (R-NUMA's) page cache is large enough to accommodate a large fraction of the remote pages in *cholesky* and *lu*. R-NUMA reduces most of the refetches in these applications and therefore outperforms CC-NUMA. R-NUMA also reduces most of the page replacements for *cholesky*. However, because of load-imbalance in *lu* [26], page replacements occur more frequently on the critical path, so the decrease is not as great as might be expected. Likewise, a small fraction of *lu*'s remote pages bounce between R-NUMA's block cache and page cache. Page replacements incur larger overheads in R-NUMA than in S-COMA because a page must reach the threshold value before relocation. Nevertheless, R-NUMA improves performance up to a factor of two over CC-NUMA and stays competitive with S-COMA in these applications.

Remote data in *fmm*, *ocean* and *radix* are too large to fit in the page cache. S-COMA's performance suffers for these applications because of frequent replacements in the page cache. In *fmm* and *radix,* CC-NUMA improves performance over S-COMA by up to a factor of 4 because the remote working sets of these applications fit in the 32-Kbyte block cache. R-NUMA eliminates much of the page replacements in S-COMA (Table 4), but increases the number of refetches in CC-NUMA because the 320-Kbyte page cache cannot contain the large number of reuse pages in these applications. R-NUMA remains competitive with CC-NUMA, increasing execution time by at most 57% in these applications. *Ocean* exhibits a large remote working set which does not even fit in CC-NUMA's block cache. Although R-NUMA outperforms both CC-NUMA and S-COMA for this application, block and page traffic remain high.

R-NUMA performs best when an application exhibits a small number of reuse remote pages that frequently miss in CC-NUMA's block cache, but the application's overall set of remote pages is too large to fit in S-COMA's page cache. R-NUMA can detect and relocate the reuse pages into the page cache, thereby eliminating much of the capacity and conflict misses in the block cache. This is the case for *barnes* and *raytrace*. In these applications, R-NUMA virtually eliminates all of the refetches and replacements in CC-NUMA and S-COMA and outperforms both.

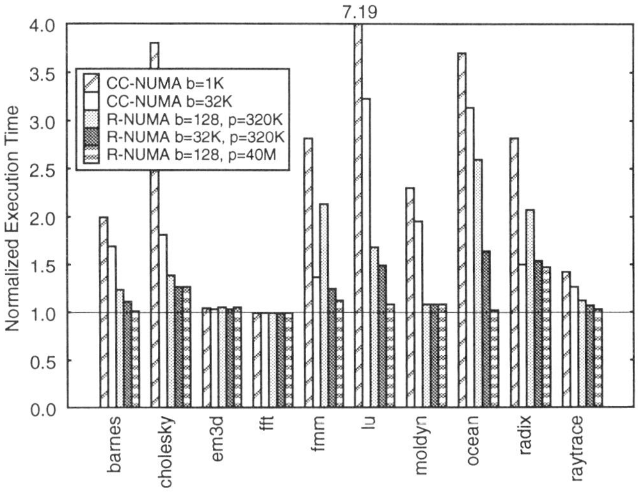

FIGURE 7. Performance sensitivity of CC-NUMA and R-NUMA to cache size.

The figure compares the performance sensitivity of CC-NUMA and R-NUMA to cache sizes. The figures plot execution times normalized to a CC-NUMA with an infinite block cache. CC-NUMA numbers correspond to a 1-Kbyte block cache (b=1K) and a 32-Kbyte block cache (b=32K). R-NUMA numbers correspond to a 128-byte block cache with a 320-Kbyte page cache (b=128, p=320K), a 32-Kbyte block cache with a 320-Kbyte page cache (b=32K, p=320K), and a 128-byte block cache with a 40-Mbyte page cache (b=128, p=40M). R-NUMA uses a relocation threshold value of 64.

5.3 Cache Size Sensitivity

CC-NUMA's performance lies in its ability to cache the (remote) working set of data in the node's processors caches and the block cache. Many classes of applications exhibit large temporal localities and small primary working set sizes [26,20]. Small CC-NUMA caches typically result in high performance because they are adequate to hold the primary working set of these applications.

Unfortunately, there are classes of applications that exhibit poor temporal locality and large primary working sets—e.g., commercial databases [16]. CC-NUMA's inability to cache these application's working sets severely degrades performance. R-NUMA can mitigate this problem by allowing portions of the working set with small temporal but large spatial localities to relocate to a large page cache. R-NUMA's performance, like S-COMA's, lies in its ability to cache these application's large working sets. In this section we study the sensitivity of CC-NUMA's and R-NUMA's performance to cache sizes.

Figure 7 plots CC-NUMA and R-NUMA execution times normalized to a system with an infinite block cache. We present CC-NUMA numbers for a small 1-Kbyte block cache and a 32-Kbyte block cache large enough to hold the primary working sets of most of the applications. R-NUMA numbers correspond to our base system assumptions of a 128-byte block cache with a 320-Kbyte page cache, a system with a larger 32-Kbyte block cache and a 320-Kbyte page cache, and a system with a 128-byte block cache and 40-Mbyte page cache, which is large enough to hold the working sets of all of the applications.

The graphs indicate that the applications can be grouped into three categories based on their working set sizes of reuse pages. *Em3d* and *fft* are examples of applications with small reuse working sets. In these applications, communication primarily consists of exchanging data between a producer and a consumer. The graphs indicate that these applications achieve high performance even with a 1-Kbyte block cache. Similarly, *barnes*, *moldyn,* and *raytrace* all have primary reuse working sets that fit in a very small block cache but require a much larger (> 32 Kbytes) cache to capture the complete set of remote data. R-NUMA achieves high performance in these applications even with a small (128-byte) block cache by moving the large portions of the reuse working sets into the page cache.

In the second category are those applications whose primary reuse working sets do not fit in a small 1-Kbyte cache, but do fit in a larger 32-Kbyte cache. *Cholesky*, *fmm,* and *radix* fall in this category. A small block cache severely impacts CC-NUMA's performance in these applications and increases execution time by up to a factor of 2. R-NUMA exhibits performance sensitivity to block cache size only when the reuse working set does not fit in the page cache. *Fmm* and *radix* have large and sparse working sets which result in fragmentation in the page cache. R-NUMA's performance improves up to 90% with either a large 32-Kbyte block cache or a large 40-Mbyte page cache. R-NUMA manages to capture *cholesky*'s reuse working set in a 320-Kbyte page cache, and hence shows no sensitivity to block cache size.

Lu and *ocean* comprise the third category of applications. In these applications, the primary reuse working set does not fit even in the larger 32-Kbyte block cache. In these applications, CC-NUMA's performance exhibits very high sensitivity to block cache size; execution times in CC-NUMA increase by up to a factor of 7 compared to a machine with an infinite size block cache. Much as in the second category of applications, R-NUMA's performance becomes sensitive to block cache size for applications whose reuse working set does not fit in the page cache, as in *ocean*.

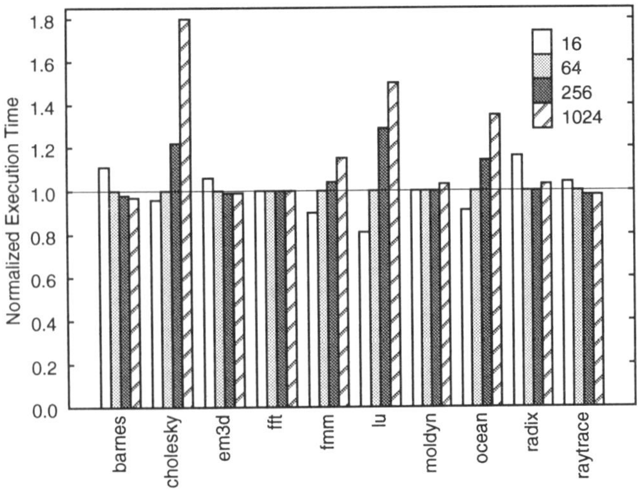

FIGURE 8. Performance sensitivity of R-NUMA to relocation threshold value.

The figure plots R-NUMA's performance sensitivity to relocation threshold value. R-NUMA relocates a page from the block cache into the page cache when it incurs as many capacity and conflict misses as specified by the threshold value. The numbers correspond to execution times on an R-NUMA with a 128-byte block cache and a 320-Kbyte page cache. The numbers are normalized to an R-NUMA with a relocation threshold value of 64.

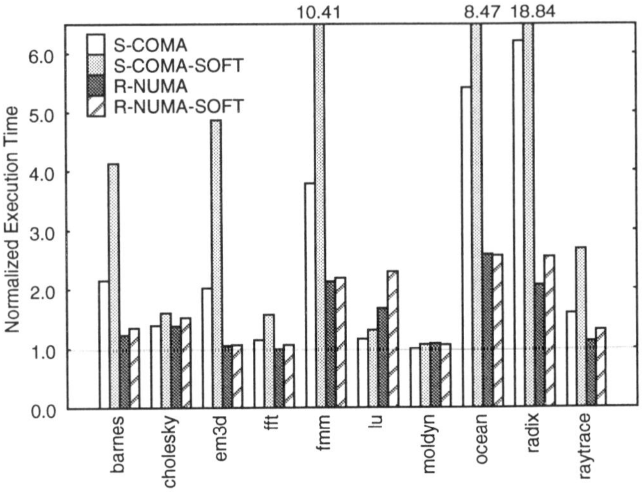

FIGURE 9. Performance sensitivity of S-COMA and R-NUMA to page-fault and TLB invalidation overheads.

The figure compares the sensitivity of S-COMA's and R-NUMA's performance to TLB invalidation and page fault overheads. Our base systems, S-COMA and R-NUMA, assume page fault handling times of 5 μs, and TLB hardware invalidation times of 0.5 μs. The slower systems, S-COMA-SOFT and R-NUMA-SOFT, assume a higher page fault handling time of 10 μs, and TLB software invalidation times of 5 μs. The page caches are of size 320 Kbytes. R-NUMA uses a 128-byte block cache and a relocation threshold value of 64. The numbers are normalized to execution times on a CC-NUMA with an infinite block cache.

5.4 Threshold Sensitivity

Worst-case performance analysis (Section 3.2) dictates that the relocation threshold be determined so as to bound the performance of the worst-case reference stream by a small constant. However, real applications rarely exhibit such worst-case behavior, so the threshold that gives the best performance in practice may be different. We would like to select a relocation threshold value which is low enough to allow reuse pages to relocate as quickly as possible, while high enough to prevent pages with low capacity and conflict miss rates from relocation. Performance sensitivity of R-NUMA to the threshold value is therefore directly related to the fraction of reuse pages in the remote working set of an application; a large fraction of reuse pages can benefit from low threshold values and vice versa.

Figure 8 plots R-NUMA's performance for various relocation threshold values. The R-NUMA configuration is a 128-byte block cache and 320-Kbyte page cache. The numbers are normalized to execution times on an R-NUMA with threshold value of 64—i.e., a page is selected for relocation when it incurs 64 capacity or conflict misses in the block cache. The graphs indicate that in all but three of the applications, R-NUMA's performance varies by at most 27%.

The figure also corroborates our intuition that a larger fraction of reuse pages in an application favor a smaller threshold value. *Cholesky*, *fmm*, *lu* and *ocean* all exhibit a large fraction of remote pages with high capacity and conflict miss rates in CC-NUMA (Figure 5). A threshold value of 16 can improve performance by up to 25% over a threshold value of 64 in these applications.

5.5 Relocation Overhead Sensitivity

Another factor that has a first order effect on the performance of a reactive protocol is the page relocation overhead: a larger overhead requires a higher threshold to keep R-NUMA competitive with CC-NUMA and S-COMA. Relocation of remote data from the block cache to the page cache involves taking a page fault (when the number capacity and conflict misses on a page reaches the threshold), allocating/replacing a page frame, and relocating the blocks to it. Page fault handling times can vary depending on the implementation and can take thousands of cycles on many commodity workstations [23]. Replacement requires invalidating the TLBs on a node, which may involve (slow) inter-processor interrupts if the processors are not equipped with the necessary hardware support—such as TLB invalidate transactions on the memory bus [25]. In this section we study the sensitivity of R-NUMA's performance to page fault and TLB invalidation overheads.

Figure 9 compares the sensitivity of S-COMA's and R-NUMA's performance to page fault and TLB invalidation overheads. S-COMA and R-NUMA correspond to our base case assumptions of 5 μs for page fault handling and 0.5 μs for (fast) TLB hardware invalidation. S-COMA-SOFT and R-NUMA-SOFT correspond to our slower systems with a 10 μs page fault handling time and a much higher 5 μs for a TLB software invalidation using inter-processor interrupts. The per-page allocation/replacement and relocation overheads are therefore approximately 3 times higher in the slower systems. The page caches are all of size 320 Kbytes, and R-NUMA's block cache is 128 bytes.

The graphs indicate that the performance of S-COMA is highly sensitive to page fault and TLB invalidation overheads. This is not surprising, because applications whose remote working sets are larger than the page cache exhibit high page replacement rates. In these cases, an increase in replacement overhead directly impacts performance; the execution time in more than half of the applications increases by up to a factor of 3 with a 3-fold increase in per-page relocation overhead.

R-NUMA's performance, however, is much less sensitive to page fault and TLB invalidation overheads. The execution time in R-NUMA-SOFT increases by at most 25% for all of but one of our applications. Because R-NUMA substantially reduces the replacement rate in the page cache (Table 4), its performance is not as sensitive to an increase in overhead.

Lu is our only application whose execution time on R-NUMA-SOFT increases by 40%. *Lu*'s working set of remote data primarily consist of reuse pages. Working set sizes significantly vary across nodes because of load-imbalance inherent to the blocking algorithm in this application for small data sets [26]; in *lu,* two nodes are responsible for more than 50% of the page replacements in the system. Because these slow nodes are on the critical path of the execution, an increase in the relocation overhead directly impacts execution time.

6 Conclusions

In this paper, we proposed and evaluated R-NUMA, a design for combining a conventional CC-NUMA with a more recent Simple-COMA in a single distributed shared-memory machine. R-NUMA's novelty lies in its ability to dynamically react to program and system behavior and select between CC-NUMA and S-COMA to exploit the best remote caching strategy on a per-page basis. CC-NUMA capitalizes on short-term temporal locality and small-scale spatial locality. Conversely, S-COMA's large page cache can exploit longer-term temporal localities, but only for applications with large-granularity spatial localities. R-NUMA monitors per-page miss behavior to determine when a page should be switched to the other protocol. R-NUMA's reactive behavior provides much greater performance stability than either CC-NUMA or S-COMA alone.

We presented a simple qualitative result that R-NUMA's worst-case performance is bounded within a small constant factor of the best of CC-NUMA and S-COMA. We then presented quantitative results based on execution-driven simulation of a distributed shared-memory system. Our results indicated that in practice: (i) R-NUMA usually outperforms or performs as well as the best of either CC-NUMA or S-COMA, (ii) when R-NUMA performs worse than the best protocol, the performance gap is much smaller than that predicted by our qualitative analysis, and (iii) R-NUMA never performs worse than both CC-NUMA and S-COMA. For the shared-memory applications we studied, R-NUMA was either best or within a few percent of best for seven of the ten; for the others it performed worst than the best protocol by at most 57%. In comparison CC-NUMA's and S-COMA's performance differed by as much as 315%.

We also investigated the sensitivity of R-NUMA's performance to cache sizes, relocation threshold, and relocation overhead. The results indicated that R-NUMA performs well with a very small block cache unless the working set of reuse pages is too large to fit in the page cache, which was the case in three of the applications we studied. In comparison, CC-NUMA exhibited very high sensitivity in seven of the applications when the primary working set was too large to fit in the block cache. R-NUMA did not exhibit significant sensitivity to relocation threshold or relocation—i.e., page allocation/replacement—overhead. In contrast, S-COMA's performance in half of the applications was highly sensitive to an increase in page allocation/replacement overhead.

The quantitative results we presented in this paper are closely tied to the application workload and system characteristics we studied. Many of the applications were extensively tuned to take advantage of locality in small caches. The relative performance of a reactive system may vary with both application (e.g., working set size) and system (e.g., cache sizes) characteristics. Our qualitative result on the reactive system's competitiveness, however, holds across a wide range of applications and systems.

Acknowledgements

We would like to thank Steve Reinhardt for helping with the development of our simulator, Beng-Hong Lim and Sandra Irani for their comments on our performance models, and Scott Breach, Erik Hagersten, Mark Hill, Andreas Moshovos, Jon Wade, and Bob Zack for their comments on earlier drafts of this paper.

References

[1] Silicon Graphics Origin Technology. http://www.sgi.com/Products/hardware/servers/technology/index.html.

[2] Anant Agarwal, Ricardo Bianchini, David Chaiken, Kirk L. Johnson, David Kranz, John Kubiatowicz, Beng-Hong Lim, Kenneth Mackenzie, and Donald Yeung. The MIT Alewife Machine: Architecture and Performance. In *Proceedings of the 22nd Annual International Symposium on Computer Architecture*, pages 2–13, June 1995.

[3] Tom Anderson, David Culler, and David Patterson. A Case for NOW (Networks of Workstations). *IEEE Micro*, 15(1):54–64, February 1995.

[4] David Black, Anoop Gupta, and Wolf-Dietrich Weber. Competitive management of distributed shared memory. In *Proceedings of COMPCON*, March 1989.

[5] Tony Brewer. A Highly Scalable System Utilizing up to 128 PA-RISC Processors. http://www.convex.com/tech_cache/ps/SPP_Arch.times.ps.

[6] B. R. Brooks, R. E. Bruccoleri, B. D. Olafson, D . J. States, S. Swamintathan, and M. Karplus. Charmm: A program for macromolecular energy, minimization, and dynamics calculation. *Journal of Computational Chemistry*, 4(187), 1983.

[7] John B. Carter, John K. Bennett, and Willy Zwaenepoel. Implementation and Performance of Munin. In *Proceedings of the 13th ACM Symposium on Operating System Principles (SOSP)*, pages 152–164, October 1991.

[8] John B. Carter, Al Davis, Ravindra Kuramkote, Chei-Chi Kuo, Leigh B. Stoller, and Mark Swanson. Avalanche: A Communication and Memory Architecture for Scalable Parallel Computing. In *Workshop on Scalable Shared-Memory Multiprocessors*, 1995. http://www.cs.utah.edu:80/projects/avalanche/.

[9] D. E. Culler, A. Dusseau, S. C. Goldstein, A. Krishnamurthy, S. Lumetta, T. von Eicken, and K. Yelick. Parallel Programming in Split-C. In *Proceedings of Supercomputing '93*, pages 262–273, November 1993.

[10] Erik Hagersten, Anders Landin, and Seif Haridi. DDM–A Cache-Only Memory Architecture. *IEEE Computer*, 25(9):44–54, September 1992.

[11] Erik Hagersten, Ashley Saulsbury, and Anders Landin. Simple COMA Node Implementations. In *Proceedings of the 27th Hawaii International Conference on System Sciences*, January 1994.

[12] Kendall Square Research. Kendall Square Research Technical

Summary, 1992.

[13] Jeffrey Kuskin et al. The Stanford FLASH Multiprocessor. In *Proceedings of the 21st Annual International Symposium on Computer Architecture*, pages 302–313, April 1994.

[14] Rick LaRowe and Carla Ellis. Experimental Comparison of Memory Management Policies for NUMA multiprcessors. *ACM Transactions on Computer Systems*, 9(4):319–363, November 1991.

[15] Daniel Lenoski, James Laudon, Kourosh Gharachorloo, Wolf-Dietrich Weber, Anoop Gupta, John Hennessy, Mark Horowitz, and Monica Lam. The Stanford DASH Multiprocessor. *IEEE Computer*, 25(3):63–79, March 1992.

[16] Tom Lovett and Russel Clapp. STiNG: A CC-NUMA Compute System for the Commercial Marketplace. In *Proceedings of the 23rd Annual International Symposium on Computer Architecture*, May 1996.

[17] Michael Marchetti, Leonidas Kontothanassis, Ricardo Bianchini, and Michael L. Scott. Using Simple Page Placement Policies to Reduce the Cost of Cache Fills in Coherent Shared-Memory Systems. In *Proceedings of the Nineth International Parallel Processing Symposium*, April 1995.

[18] A. Nowatzyk, M. Monger, M. Parkin, E. Kelly, M. Borwne, G. Aybay, and D. Lee. S3.mp: A Multiprocessor in a Matchbox. In *Proc. PASA*, 1993.

[19] E. Rosti, E. Smirni, T.D. Wagner, A.W. Apon, and L.W. Dowdy. The KSR1: Experimentation and Modeling of Poststore. In *Proceedings of the 1993 ACM Sigmetrics Conference on Measurement and Modeling of Computer Systems*, pages 74–85, May 1993.

[20] Edward Rothberg, Jaswinder Pal Singh, and Anoop Gupta. Working Sets, Cache Sizes, and Node Granularity Issues for Large-Scale Multiprocessors. In *Proceedings of the 20th Annual International Symposium on Computer Architecture*, pages 14–25, June 1993.

[21] Ashley Saulasbury, Tim Wilkinson, John Carter, and Anders Landin. An Argument for Simple COMA. In *Proceedings of the First IEEE Symposium on High-Performance Computer Architecture*, pages 276–285, January 1995.

[22] Ashley Saulsbury and Andreas Nowatzyk. Simple COMA on S3.MP. http://playground.Sun.COM/pub/S3.mp/simple-coma/isca-95/present.html.

[23] Chandramohan A. Thekkath and Henry M. Levy. Hardware and Software Support for Efficient Exception Handling. In *Proceedings of the Sixth International Conference on Architectural Support for Programming Languages and Operating Systems*, pages 110–119, San Jose, California, 1994.

[24] Ben Verghese, Scott Devine, Anoop Gupta, and Mendel Rosenblum. Operating System Support for Improving Data Locality on CC-NUMA Compute Servers. In *Proceedings of the Seventh International Conference on Architectural Support for Programming Languages and Operating Systems (ASPLOS VII)*, October 1996.

[25] Shlomo Weiss and James E. Smith. *Power and PowerPC*. Morgan Kaufmann Publishers, Inc., 1994.

[26] Steven Cameron Woo, Moriyoshi Ohara, Evan Torrie, Jaswinder Pal Singh, and Anoop Gupta. The SPLASH-2 Programs: Characterization and Methodological Considerations. In *Proceedings of the 22nd Annual International Symposium on Computer Architecture*, pages 24–36, July 1995.

The SGI Origin: A ccNUMA Highly Scalable Server

James Laudon and Daniel Lenoski
Silicon Graphics, Inc.
2011 North Shoreline Boulevard
Mountain View, California 94043
laudon@sgi.com lenoski@sgi.com

Abstract

The SGI Origin 2000 is a cache-coherent non-uniform memory access (ccNUMA) multiprocessor designed and manufactured by Silicon Graphics, Inc. The Origin system was designed from the ground up as a multiprocessor capable of scaling to both small and large processor counts without any bandwidth, latency, or cost cliffs.The Origin system consists of up to 512 nodes interconnected by a scalable Craylink network. Each node consists of one or two R10000 processors, up to 4 GB of coherent memory, and a connection to a portion of the XIO IO subsystem. This paper discusses the motivation for building the Origin 2000 and then describes its architecture and implementation. In addition, performance results are presented for the NAS Parallel Benchmarks V2.2 and the SPLASH2 applications. Finally, the Origin system is compared to other contemporary commercial ccNUMA systems.

1 Background

Silicon Graphics has offered multiple generations of symmetric multiprocessor (SMP) systems based on the MIPS microprocessors. From the 8 processor R3000-based Power Series to the 36 processor R4000-based Challenge and R10000-based Power Challenge systems, the cache-coherent, globally addressable memory architecture of these SMP systems has provided a convenient programming environment for large parallel applications while at the same time providing for efficient execution of both parallel and throughput based workloads.

The follow-on system to the Power Challenge needed to meet three important goals. First, it needed to scale beyond the 36 processor limit of the Power Challenge and provide an infrastructure that supports higher performance per processor. Given the factor of four processor count increase between the Power Series and Power Challenge lines, it was desired to have the next system support at least another factor of four in maximum processor count. Second, the new system had to retain the cache-coherent globally addressable memory model of the Power Challenge. This model is critical for achieving high performance on loop-level parallelized code and for supporting the existing Power Challenge users. Finally, the entry level and incremental cost of the system was desired to be lower than that of a high-performance SMP, with the cost ideally approaching that of a cluster of workstations.

Simply building a larger and faster snoopy bus-based SMP system could not meet all three of these goals. The second goal might be achievable, but it would surely compromise performance for larger processor counts and costs for smaller configurations.

Therefore a very different architecture was chosen for use in the next generation Origin system. The Origin employs distributed shared memory (DSM), with cache coherence maintained via a directory-based protocol. A DSM system has the potential for meeting all three goals: scalability, ease of programming, and cost. The directory-based coherence removes the broadcast bottleneck that prevents scalability of the snoopy bus-based coherence. The globally addressable memory model is retained, although memory access times are no longer uniform. However, as will be shown in this paper, Origin was designed to minimize the latency difference between remote and local memory and to include hardware and software support to insure that most memory references are local. Finally, a low initial and incremental cost can be provided if the natural modularity of a DSM system is exploited at a relatively fine granularity by the product design.

In the following section of this paper, the scalable shared-memory multiprocessing (S^2MP) architecture of the Origin is presented. Section 3 details the implementation of the Origin 2000. Performance of the Origin 2000 is presented in Section 4. Section 5 compares the Origin system with other contemporary ccNUMA systems. Finally, Section 6 concludes the paper.

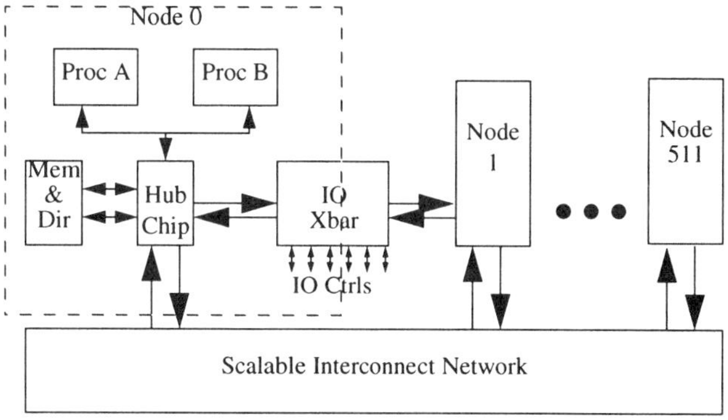

Figure 1 Origin block diagram

2 The Origin S^2MP Architecture

A block diagram of the Origin architecture is shown in Figure 1. The basic building block of the Origin system is the dual-processor node. In addition to the processors, a node contains up to 4 GB of main memory and its corresponding directory memory, and has a connection to a portion of the IO subsystem.

The architecture supports up to 512 nodes, for a maximum configuration of 1024 processors and 1 TB of main memory. The nodes can be connected together via any scalable interconnection network. The cache coherence protocol employed by the Origin system does not require in-order delivery of point-to-point messages to allow the maximum flexibility in implementing the interconnect network.

The DSM architecture provides global addressability of all memory, and in addition, the IO subsystem is also globally addressable. Physical IO operations (PIOs) can be directed from any processor to any IO device. IO devices can DMA to and from all memory in the system, not just their local memory.

While the two processors share the same bus connected to the Hub, they do not function as a snoopy cluster. Instead they operate as two separate processors multiplexed over the single physical bus (done to save Hub pins). This is different from many other ccNUMA systems, where the node is a SMP cluster. Origin does not employ a SMP cluster in order to reduce both the local and remote memory latency, and to increase remote memory bandwidth. Local memory latency is reduced because the bus can be run at a much higher frequency when it needs to support only one or two processor than when it must support large numbers of processors. Remote memory latency is also reduced by a higher frequency bus, and in addition because a request made in a snoopy bus cluster must generally wait for the result of the snoop before being forwarded to the remote node[7]. Remote bandwidth can be lower in a system with a SMP cluster node if memory data is sent across the remote data bus before being sent to the network, as is commonly done in DSM systems with SMP-based nodes[7][8]. For remote requests, the data will traverse the data bus at both the remote node and at the local node of the requestor, leading to the remote bandwidth being one-half the local bandwidth. One of the major goals for the Origin system was to keep both absolute memory latency and the ratio of remote to local latency as low as possible and to provide remote memory bandwidth equal to local memory bandwidth in order to provide an easy migration path for existing SMP software. As we will show in the paper, the Origin system does accomplish both goals, whereas in Section 6 we see that all the snoopy-bus clustered ccNUMA systems do not achieve all of these goals.

In addition to keeping the ratio of remote memory to local memory latency low, Origin also includes architectural features to address the NUMA aspects of the machine. First, a combination of hardware and software features are provided for effective page migration and replication. Page migration and replication is important as it reduces effective memory latency by satisfying a greater percentage of accesses locally. To support page migration Origin provides per-page hardware memory reference counters, contains a block copy engine that is able to copy data at near peak memory speeds, and has mechanisms for reducing the cost of TLB updates.

Other performance features of the architecture include a high-performance local and global interconnect design, coherence protocol features to minimize latency and bandwidth per access, and a rich set of synchronization primitives. The intra-node interconnect consists of single Hub chip that implements a full four-way crossbar between processors, local memory, and the I/O and network interfaces. The global interconnect is based on a six-ported router chip configured in a multi-level fat-hypercube topology.

The coherence protocol supports a clean-exclusive state to minimize latency on read-modify-write operations. Further, it allows cache dropping of clean-exclusive or shared data without notifying the directory in order to minimize the impact on memory/directory bandwidth caused by directory coherence. The architecture also supports request forwarding to reduce the latency of interprocessor communication.

For effective synchronization in large systems, the Origin system provides fetch-and-op primitives on memory in addition to the standard MIPS load-linked/store-conditional (LL/SC) instructions. These operations greatly reduce the serialization for highly contended locks and barrier operations.

Origin includes many features to enhance reliability and availability. All external cache SRAM and main memory and directory DRAM are protected by a SECDED ECC code. Furthermore, all high-speed router and I/O links are protected by a full CRC code and a hardware link-level protocol that detects and automatically retries faulty packets. Origin's modular design provides the overall

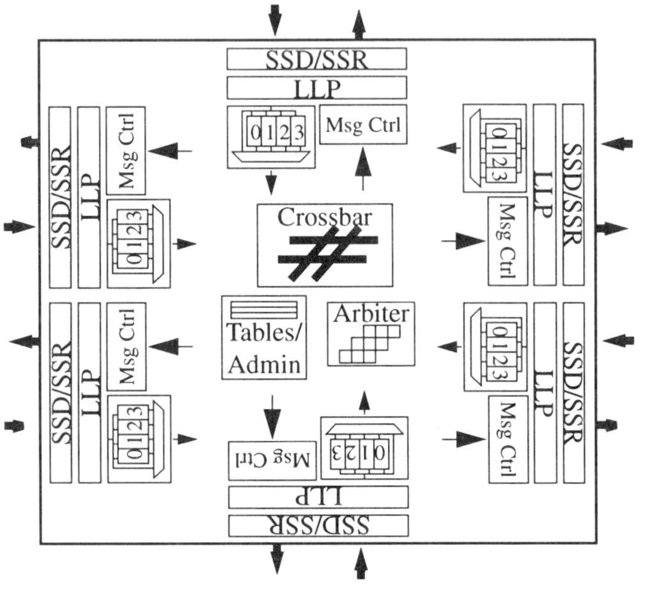

Figure 2 SPIDER ASIC block diagram

basis for a highly available hardware architecture. The flexible routing network supports multiple paths between nodes, partial population of the interconnect, and the hot plugging of cabled-links that permits the bypass, service, and reintegration of faulty hardware.

To address software availability in large systems, Origin provides access protection rights on both memory and IO devices. These access protection rights prevent unauthorized nodes from being able to modify memory or IO and allows an operating system to be structured into cells or partitions with containment of most failures to within a given partition[10][12].

3 The Origin Implementation

While existence proofs for the DSM architecture have been available in the academic community for some time[1][6], the key to commercial success of this architecture will be an aggressive implementation that provides for a truly scalable system with low memory latency and no unexpected bandwidth bottlenecks. In this section we explore how the Origin 2000 implementation meets this goal. We start by exploring the global interconnect of the system. We then present an overview of the cache coherence protocol, followed with a discussion of the node design. The IO subsystem is explored next, and then the various subsystems are tied together with the presentation of the product design. Finally, this section ends with a discussion of interesting performance features of the Origin system.

3.1 Network Topology

The interconnect employed in the Origin 2000 system is based on the SGI SPIDER router chip[4]. A block diagram of this chip is shown in Figure 2. The main features of the SPIDER chip are:

- six pairs of unidirectional links per router
- low latency (41 ns pin-to-pin) wormhole routing
- DAMQ buffer structures[4] with global arbitration to maximize utilization under load.
- four virtual channels per physical channel
- congestion control allowing messages to adaptively switch between two virtual channels

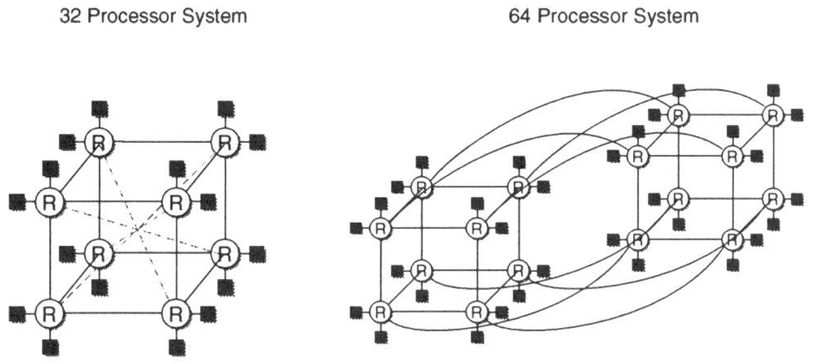

Figure 3 32P and 64P Bristled Hypercubes

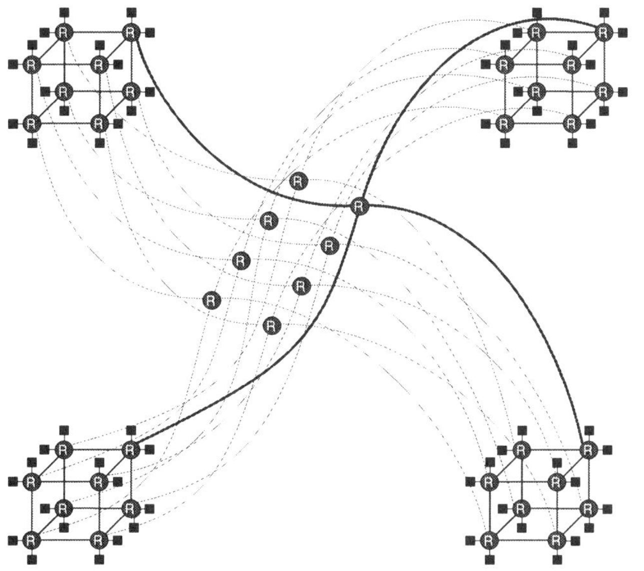

Figure 4 128P Heirarchical Fat Bristled Hypercube

- support for 256 levels of message priority with increased priority via packet aging
- CRC checking on each packet with retransmission on error via a go-back-n sliding window protocol
- software programmable routing tables

The Origin 2000 employs SPIDER routers to create a bristled fat hypercube interconnect topology. The network topology is bristled in that two nodes are connected to a single router instead of one. The fat hypercube comes into play for systems beyond 32 nodes (64 processors). For up to 32 nodes, the routers connect in a bristled hypercube as shown in Figure 3. The SPIDER routers are labeled using R, the nodes are the block boxes connecting to the routers. In the 32 processor configuration, the otherwise unused SPIDER ports are shown as dotted lines being used for Express Links which connect the corners of the cube, thereby reducing latency and increasing bisection bandwidth.

Beyond 64 processors, a hierarchical fat hypercube is employed. Figure 4 shows the topology of a 128 processor Origin system. The vertices of four 32-processor hypercubes are connected to eight *meta*-routers. To scale up to 1024 processors, each of the single meta-routers in the 128 processor system is replaced with a 5-D hypercubes.

3.2 Cache Coherence Protocol

The cache coherence protocol employed in Origin is similar to the Stanford DASH protocol[6], but has several significant performance improvements. Like the DASH protocol, the Origin cache coherence protocol is non-blocking. Memory can satisfy any incoming request immediately; it never buffers requests while waiting for another message to arrive. The Origin protocol also employs the request forwarding of the DASH protocol for three party transactions. Request forwarding reduces the latency of requests which target a cache line that is owned by another processor.

The Origin coherence protocol has several enhancements over the DASH protocol. First, the Clean-exclusive (CEX) processor cache state (also known as the exclusive state in MESI) is fully supported by the Origin protocol. This state allows for efficient execution of read-modify-write accesses since there is only a single fetch of the cache line from memory. The protocol also permits the processor to replace a CEX cache line without notifying the directory. The Origin protocol is able to detect a rerequest by a processor that had replaced a CEX cache line and immediately satisfy that request from memory. Support of CEX state in this manner is very important for single process performance as much of the gains from the CEX state would be lost if directory bandwidth was needed each time a processor replaced a CEX line. By adding protocol complexity to allow for the "silent" CEX replacement, all of the advantages of the CEX state are realized.

The second enhancement of the Origin protocol over DASH is full support of upgrade requests which move a line from a shared to exclusive state without the bandwidth and latency overhead of transferring the memory data.

For handling incoming I/O DMA data, Origin employs a write-invalidate transaction that uses only a single memory write as opposed to the processor's normal write-allocate plus writeback. This transaction is fully cache coherent (i.e., any cache invalidations/interventions required by the directory are sent), and increases I/O DMA bandwidth by as much as a factor of two.

Origin's protocol is fully insensitive to network ordering. Messages are allowed to bypass each other in the network and the protocol detects and resolves all of these out-of-order message deliveries. This allows Origin to employ adaptive routing in its network to deal with network congestion.

The Origin protocol uses a more sophisticated network deadlock avoidance scheme than DASH. As in DASH, two separate networks are provided for requests and replies (implemented in Origin via different virtual channels). The Origin protocol does have requests which generate additional requests (these additional requests are referred to as *interventions* or *invalidations*). This request-to-request dependency could lead to deadlock in the request network. In DASH, this deadlock was broken by detecting a potential deadlock situation and sending negative-acknowledgments (NAKs) to all requests which needed to generate additional requests to be serviced until the potential deadlock situation was resolved. In Origin, rather than sending NAKs in such a situation, a *backoff* intervention or invalidate is sent to the requestor on the reply network. The backoff message contains either the target of the intervention or the list of sharers to invalidate, and is used to signal the requestor that the memory was unable to generate the intervention or invalidation directly and therefore the requestor must generate that message instead. The requestor can always sink the backoff reply, which causes the requestor to then queue up the intervention or invalidate for injection into the request network as soon as the request network allows. The backoff intervention or invalidate changes the request-intervention-reply chain to two request-reply chains (one chain being the request-backoff message, one being the intervention-reply chain), with the two networks preventing deadlock on these two request-reply chains. The ability to generate backoff interventions and invalidations allows for better forward progress in the face of very heavily loaded systems since the deadlock detection in both DASH and Origin is conservatively done based on local information, and a processor that receives a backoff is guaranteed that it will eventually receive the data, while a processor that receives a NAK must retry its request.

Since the Origin system is able to maintain coherence over 1024 processors, it obviously employs a more scalable directory scheme than in DASH. For tracking sharers, Origin supports a bit-vector directory format with either 16 or 64 bits. Each bit represents a node, so with a single bit to node correspondence the directory can track up to a maximum of 128 processors. For systems with greater than 64 nodes, Origin dynamically selects between a full bit vector and coarse bit vector[12] depending on where the sharers are located. This dynamic selection is based on the machine being divided into up to eight 64 node *octants*. If all the processors sharing the cache line are from the same octant, the full bit vector is used (in conjunction with a 3-bit octant identifier). If the processors sharing the cache line are from different octants, a coarse bit vector where each bit represents eight nodes is employed.

Finally, the coherence protocol includes an important feature for effective page migration known as *directory poisoning*. The use of directory poisoning will be discussed in more detail in Section 3.6.

A slightly simplified flow of the cache coherence protocol is now presented for both read, read-exclusive, and writeback requests. We start with the basic flow for a read request.

1. Processor issues read request.
2. Read request goes across network to home memory (requests to local memory only traverse Hub).
3. Home memory does memory read and directory lookup.
4. If directory state is Unowned or Exclusive with requestor as owner, transitions to Exclusive and returns an exclusive reply to the requestor. *Go to 5a.*
   If directory state is Shared, the requesting node is marked in the bit vector and a shared reply is returned to the requestor. *Go to 5a.*
   If directory state is Exclusive with another owner, transitions to Busy-shared with requestor as owner and send out an intervention shared request to the previous owner and a speculative reply to the requestor. *Go to 5b.*
   If directory state is Busy, a negative acknowledgment is sent to the requestor, who must retry the request. QED

5a. Processor receives exclusive or shared reply and fills cache in CEX or shared (SHD) state respectively. QED

5b. Intervention shared received by owner. If owner has a dirty copy it sends an shared response to the requestor and a sharing writeback to the directory. If owner has a clean-exclusive or invalid copy it sends an shared ack (no data) to the requestor and a sharing transfer (no data) to the directory.

6a. Directory receives shared writeback or shared transfer, updates memory (only if shared writeback) and transitions to the shared state.

6b. Processor receives both speculative reply and shared response or ack. Cache filled in SHD state with data from response (if shared response) or data from speculative reply (if shared ack). QED

The following list details the basic flow for a read-exclusive request.

1. Processor issues read-exclusive request.
2. Read-exclusive request goes across network to home memory (only traverses Hub if local).
3. Home memory does memory read and directory lookup.
4. If directory state is Unowned or Exclusive with requestor as owner, transitions to Exclusive and returns an exclusive reply to the requestor. *Go to 5a.*
   If directory state is Shared, transitions to Exclusive and a exclusive reply with invalidates pending is returned to the requestor. Invalidations are sent to the sharers. *Go to 5b.*
   If directory state is Exclusive with another owner, transitions to Busy-Exclusive with requestor as owner and sends out an intervention exclusive request to the previous owner and a speculative reply to the requestor. *Go to 5c.*
   If directory state is Busy, a negative acknowledgment is sent to the requestor, who must retry the request. QED

5a. Processor receives exclusive reply and fills cache in dirty exclusive (DEX) state. QED

5b. Invalidates received by sharers. Caches invalidated and invalidate acknowledgments sent to requestor. *Go to 6a.*

5c. Intervention shared received by owner. If owner has a dirty copy it sends an exclusive response to the requestor and a dirty transfer (no data) to the directory. If owner has a clean-exclusive or invalid copy it sends an exclusive ack to the requestor and a dirty transfer to the directory. *Go to 6b.*

6a. Processor receives exclusive reply with invalidates pending and all invalidate acks. (Exclusive reply with invalidates pending has count of invalidate acks to expect.) Processor fills cache in DEX state. QED

6b. Directory receives dirty transfer and transitions to the exclusive state with new owner.

6c. Processor receives both speculative reply and exclusive response or ack. Cache filled in DEX state with data from response (if exclusive response) or data from speculative reply (if exclusive ack). QED

The flow for an upgrade (write hit to SHD state) is similar to the read-exclusive, except it only succeeds for the case where the directory is in the shared state (and the equivalent reply to the exclusive reply with invalidates pending does not need to send the memory data). In all other cases a negative acknowledgment is sent to the requestor in response to the upgrade request.

Finally, the flow for a writeback request is presented. Note that if a writeback encounters the directory in one of the busy states, this means that the writeback was issued before an intervention targeting the cache line being written back made it to the writeback issuer. This race is resolved in the Origin protocol by "bouncing" the writeback data off the memory as a response to the processor that caused the intervention, and sending a special type of writeback acknowledgment that informs the writeback issuer to wait for (and then ignore) the intervention in addition to the writeback acknowledgment.

1. Processor issues writeback request.
2. Writeback request goes across network to home memory (only traverses Hub if local).
3. Home memory does memory write and directory lookup.
4. If directory state is Exclusive with requestor as owner, transitions to Unowned and returns a writeback exclusive acknowledge to the requestor. *Go to 5a.*
   If directory state is Busy-shared, transitions to Shared, a shared response is returned to the owner marked in the directory. A writeback busy acknowledgment is also sent to the requestor. *Go to 5b.*
   If directory state is Busy-exclusive, transitions to Exclusive, an exclusive response is returned to the owner marked in the directory. A writeback busy acknowledgment is also sent to the requestor. *Go to 5b.*

5a. Processor receives writeback exclusive acknowledgment. QED

5b. Processor receives both a writeback busy acknowledgment and an intervention. QED

3.3 Node Design

The design of an Origin node fits on a single 16" x 11" printed circuit board. A drawing of the Origin node board is shown in Figure

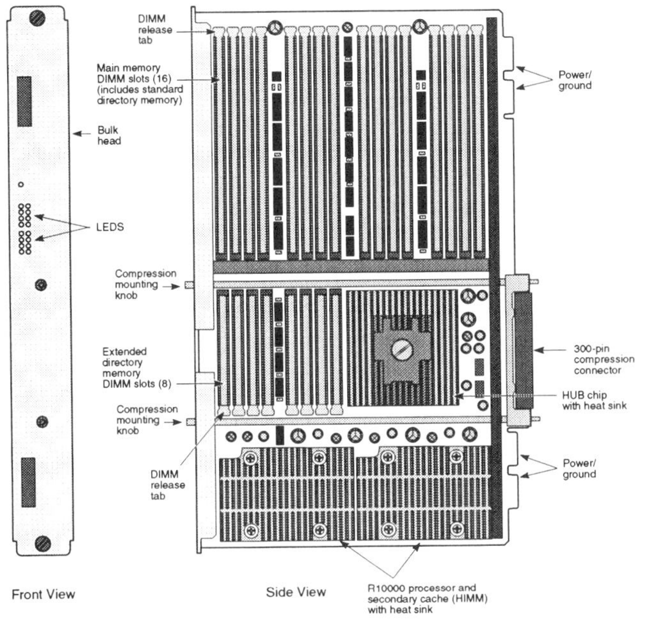

Figure 5 An Origin node board

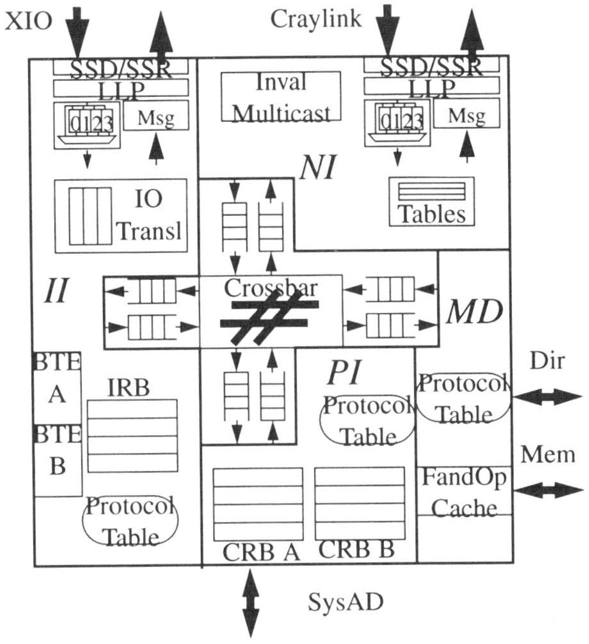

Figure 6 Hub ASIC block diagram

5. At the bottom of the board are two R10000 processors with their secondary caches. The R10000 is a four-way out-of-order superscalar processor[14]. Current Origin systems run the processor at 195 MHz and contain 4 MB secondary caches. Each processor and its secondary cache is mounted on a horizontal in-line memory module (HIMM) daughter card. The HIMM is parallel to the main node card and connects via low-inductance fuzz-button processor and HIMM interposers. The system interface buses of the R10000s are connected to the Hub chip. The Hub chip also has connections to the memory and directory on the node board, and has two ports that exit the node board via the 300-pin CPOP (compression pad-on-pad) connector. These two ports are the Craylink connection to router network and the XIO connection to the IO subsystem.

As was mentioned in Section 3.2, a 16 bit-vector directory format and a 64 bit-vector format are supported by the Origin system. The directory that implements the 16-bit vector format is located on the same DIMMs as main memory. For systems larger than 32 processors, additional expansion directory is needed. These expansion directory slots, shown to the left of the Hub chip in Figure 5, operate by expanding the width of the standard directory included on the main memory boards. The Hub chip operates on standard 16-bit directory entries by converting them to expanded entries upon their entry into the Hub chip. All directory operations within the Hub chip are done on the expanded directory entries, and the results are then converted back to standard entries before being written back to the directory memory. Expanded directory entries obviously bypass the conversion stages.

Figure 6 shows a block diagram of the Hub chip. The hub chip is divided into five major sections: the crossbar (XB), the IO interface (II), the network interface (NI), the processor interface (PI), and the memory and directory interface (MD). All the interfaces communicate with each other via FIFOs that connect to the crossbar.

The IO interface contains the translation logic for interfacing to the XIO IO subsystem. The XIO subsystem is based on the same low-level signalling protocol as the Craylink network (and uses the same interface block to the XIO pins as in the SPIDER router of Figure 2), but utilizes a different higher level message protocol. The IO section also contains the logic for two block transfer engines (BTEs) which are able to do memory to memory copies at near the peak of a node's memory bandwidth. It also implements the IO request tracking portion of the cache coherence protocol via the IO request buffers (IRB) and the IO protocol table. The IRB tracks both full and partial cache line DMA requests by IO devices as well as full cache line requests by the BTEs.

The network interface takes messages from the II, PI, and MD and sends them out on the Craylink network. It also receives incoming messages for the MD, PI, II, and local Hub registers from the Craylink network. Routing tables for outgoing messages are provided in the NI as the software programmable routing of the SPIDER chip is pipelined by one network hop[4]. The NI also is responsible for taking a compact intra-Hub version of the invalidation message resulting from a coherence operation (a bit-vector representation) and generating the multiple unicast invalidate messages required by that message.

The processor interface contains the logic for implementing the request tracking for both processors. Read and write requests are tracked via a coherent request buffer (CRB), with one CRB per processor. The PI also includes the protocol table for its portion of the cache coherence protocol. The PI also has logic for controlling the flow of requests to and from the R10000 processors and contains the logic for generating interrupts to the processors.

Finally, the memory/directory section contains logic for sequencing the external memory and directory synchronous DRAMs (SDRAMs). Memory on a node is banked 4-32 way depending on how many memory DIMMs are populated. Requests to different banks and requests to the same page within a bank as the previous request can be serviced at minimum latency and full bandwidth. Directory operations are performed in parallel with the memory data access. A complete directory entry (and page reference counter, as will be discussed in Section 3.6) read-modify-write can be performed in the same amount of time it takes to fetch the 128B cache line from memory. The MD performs the directory portion of the cache coherence protocol via its protocol table and generates the appropriate requests and/or replies for all incoming messages.

The MD also contains a small fetch-and-op cache which sits in front of the memory. This fetch-and-op cache allows fetch-and-op variables that hit in the cache to be updated at the minimum net-

Port	SysAD	Mem	XIO	Craylink
GB/s	0.78	0.78	1.56	1.56

Table 1 Hub ASIC port bandwidths

Section	XB	IO	NI	PI	MD
K gates	246	296	56	133	77

Table 2 Hub ASIC gate count

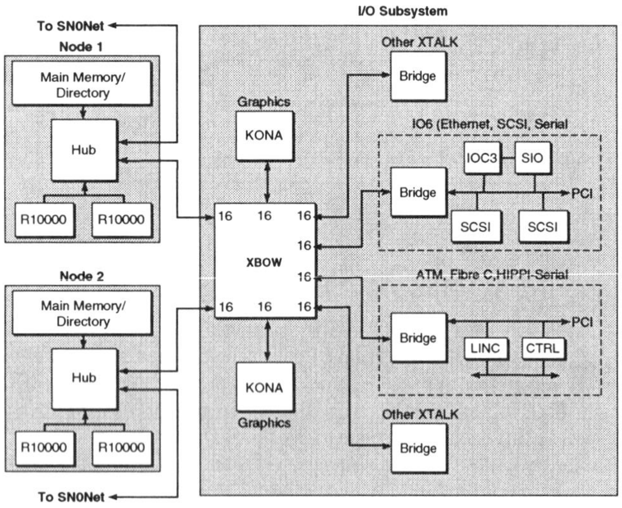

Figure 7 Example IO subsystem block diagram

work reply serialization rate of 41 ns instead of at the much slower SDRAM read-modify-write timing.

Note that all the protocol tables in the Hub are hard-wired. While programmable protocol engines can come close to achieving the performance of a hard-wired protocol state machine[5][9], we opted for hard-wiring the protocol to minimize latency and maximize bandwidth. We were also concerned about the variability in latency and bandwidth given the caching of directory information used by most programmable approaches. To ensure that the cache coherence protocol implemented in the tables was correct, we employed formal verification[3]. Formal verification worked extremely well; no bugs have been found in the Origin cache coherence protocol since the formal verification was completed.

The raw data bandwidth of the Hub chip ports is listed in Table 1. A summary of the sizes of the units is shown in Table 2. Note that most of the chip is allocated either to interfacing to the IO subsystem or in the crossbar itself, rather than in implementing global cache coherence.

3.4 IO Subsystem

Not too surprisingly, the Origin system also utilizes crossbars in its IO subsystem. Figure 7 shows one possible configuration of IO cards connected to two nodes. Using the same link technology as in the Craylink interconnect, each Hub link provides a peak of 1.56 GB/sec of bandwidth to the six XIO cards connected to it (actually limited to half this amount if only local memory bandwidth is considered). At the heart of the IO subsystem is the Crossbow (Xbow) ASIC, which has many similarities with the SPIDER router. The primary differences between the Xbow and the router is a simplification of the Xbow buffering and arbitration protocols given the chips more limited configuration. These simplifications reduce costs and permit eight ports to be integrated on a single chip. Some of the main features of the Xbow are:

- eight XIO ports, connected in Origin to 2 nodes and 6 XIO cards.
- two virtual channels per physical channel
- low latency wormhole routing
- support for allocated bandwidth of messages from particular devices
- CRC checking on each packet with retransmission on error via a go-back-n sliding window protocol

The Crossbow has support in its arbiter for allocating a portion of the bandwidth to a given IO device. This feature is important for certain system applications such as video on demand.

A large number of XIO cards are available to connect to the Crossbow. Table 3 contains a listing of the common XIO cards. The highest performance XIO cards connect directly to the XIO, but most of the cards bridge XIO to an embedded PCI bus with multiple external interfaces. The IO bandwidth together with integration provide IO performance which is effectively added as a PCI-bus at a time versus individual PCI cards.

Board	Number of Ports
Base IO	2 Ultra SCSI, 1 Fast Enet, 2 serial
Ultra SCSI	4
10/100 Enet	4
HiPPI	1 serial
Fibre Channel	2 Cu loops
ATM OC3	4
Infinite Reality Gfx	1
Standard PCI Cage	3
VME Adapter	1

Table 3 Origin IO boards

3.5 Product Design

The Origin 2000 is a highly modular design. The basic building block is the deskside module, which has slots for 4 node boards, 2 router boards, and 12 XIO boards. The module also includes a CDROM and up to 5 Ultra SCSI devices. Figure 8 shows a block diagram of the deskside module, while Figure 9 shows a rear-view perspective of a deskside system. The system has a central midplane, which has two Crossbow chips mounted on it. The 4 node and 12 XIO boards plug into the midplane from the rear of the system, while the 2 router boards, the power supply and the UltraSCSI devices plug into the midplane from the front of the system.

A module can be used as a stand-alone deskside system or two modules (without the deskside plastic skins) can be mounted in a rack to form a 16 processor system. In addition to the two modules, the rack also includes a disk bay for up to 8 additional disks. One of the modules can be replaced with an Infinite reality graph-

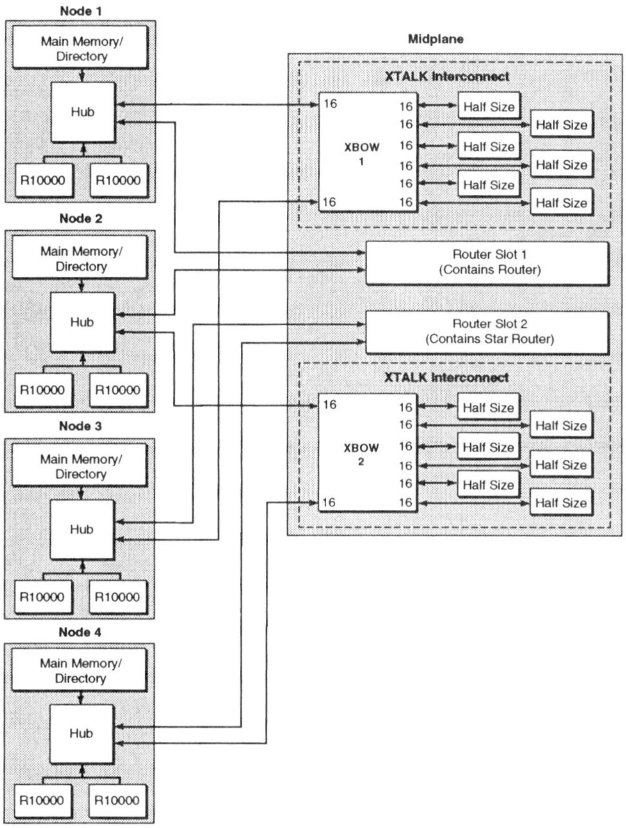

Figure 8 Deskside module block diagram

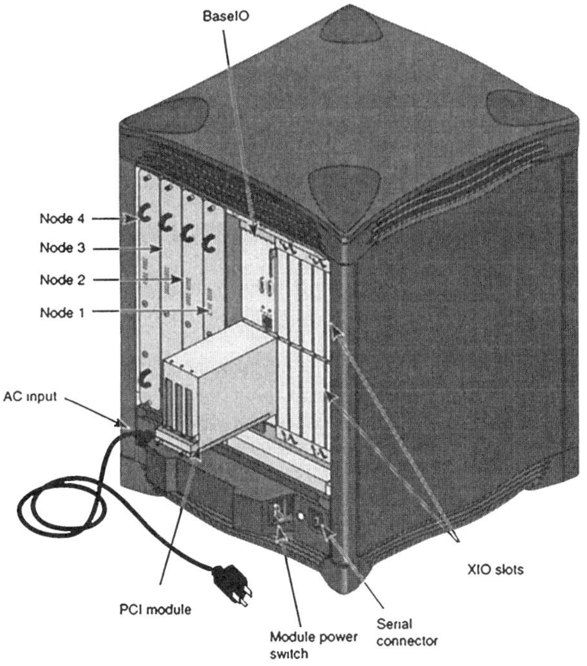

Figure 9 Deskside module, rear view

ics module or with 4 additional 8-disk bays. An Origin Vault which contains 9 8-disk bays in a single rack is also available. Figure 10 depicts a configured rack supporting 16 processors, 24 XIO boards, and 18 UltraSCSI devices.

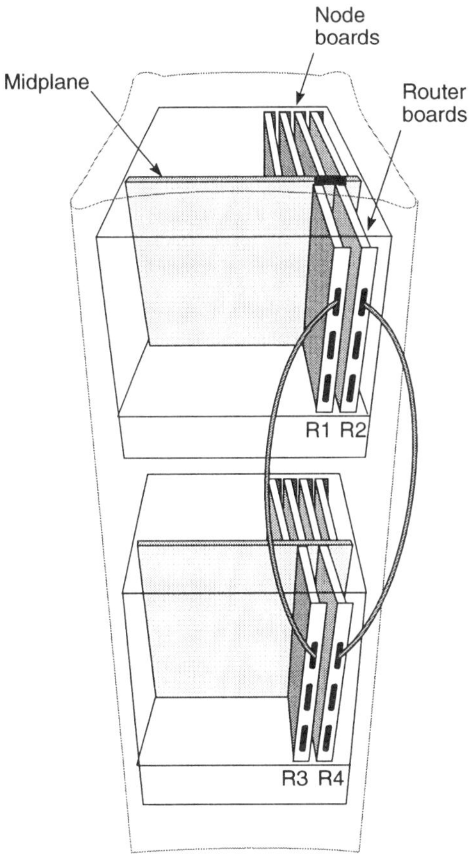

Figure 10 16 processor Origin system.

3.6 Performance Features

The Origin system has two features very important for achieving good performance in a highly scalable system. First, fetch-and-op primitives are provided as uncached operations that occur at the memory. Fetch-and-op variables are used for highly contended locks, barriers, and other synchronization mechanisms. The typical serialization rate (the rate at which a stream of requests can be serviced) for fetch-and-op variables is 41 ns. In Section 4.1 we will show how fetch-and-op variables can improve the performance of highly contended objects.

Second, Origin provides hardware and software support for page migration. Page migration is important for NUMA systems as it changes many of the cache misses which would have gone to remote memory to local misses. To help the OS in determining when and which page to migrate the Origin system provides an array of per-page memory reference counters, which are stored in the directory memory. This array is indexed by the nodes in a system (up to 64 nodes, beyond this 8 nodes share a single counter). When a request comes in, its reference counter is read out during the directory lookup and incremented. In addition, the reference counter of the home node is read out during the same directory lookup. The requestor's count and home count are compared and if the difference exceeds a software programmable threshold register (and the migration control bits stored with the requestor's reference counter says that this page is a candidate for migration), an interrupt is generated to the home node. This interrupt signals a potential migration candidate to the operating system.

When the operating system determines it does indeed want to migrate the page[13], two operations need to be performed. First, the OS needs to copy the page from its current location to a free memory page on the requestor's node. Second, the OS needs to invali-

Memory level	Latency (ns)
L1 cache	5.1
L2 cache	56.4
local memory	310
4P remote memory	540
8P avg. remote memory	707
16P avg. remote memory	726
32P avg. remote memory	773
64P avg. remote memory	867
128P avg. remote memory	945

Table 4 Origin 2000 latencies

date all the translations to the old page cached in processor's TLBs and then update the translation for the migrated page to point to the new page.

The block transfer engine allows a 16 KB page to be copied from one node's memory to another in under 30 microseconds. Unfortunately, in a very large Origin system, the cost to invalidate all the TLBs and update the translation using a conventional TLB shootdown algorithm can be 100 microseconds or more, removing much of the benefit of providing a fast memory to memory copy. Recent page migration research has also identified TLB shootdown as a significant cost of page migration[11]. To solve the TLB update problem, the directory supports a block transfer copy mode known as directory poisoning, which works as follows.

During the read phase of the poisoning block copy, in addition to reading the data, the directory protocol makes sure the latest copy of the data is written back to memory, and the directory is placed in the POISON state. Any access by a processor to a poisoned directory entry during the copy will result in a synchronous bus error. The bus error handler is able to quickly determine that the bus error was due to page migration, and the handler invalidates the processor's TLB entry for the page, and then has the process wait for the new translation to be produced.

Once the poisoning block copy has completed, the new translation is updated and all processors that took the poison bus error will load their TLB with the new translation. The poisoned page is now placed on a poisoned list to "age". The operating system invalidates one sequential TLB entry per scheduler tick, so after a time equal to the number of per-processor TLB entries times the period between scheduler ticks, the page can be moved off the poisoned list and onto the free list. This directory poisoning allows the TLB shootdown and page copy to proceed in parallel, and as a result the cost to migrate a page is much lower than if a standard TLB shootdown were invoked. This low cost of migration enables the operating system to be fairly aggressive in determining when to migrate a page.

4 Origin Performance

This section examines the performance of the Origin system using both microbenchmarks to measure latencies and bandwidths, and by using the NAS Parallel Benchmarks V2.2 and the SPLASH2 suite to measure performance of a set of parallel applications.

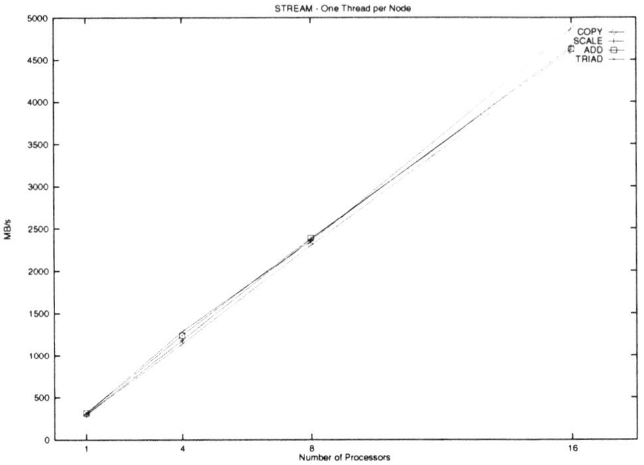

Figure 11 STREAM results - one thread per node

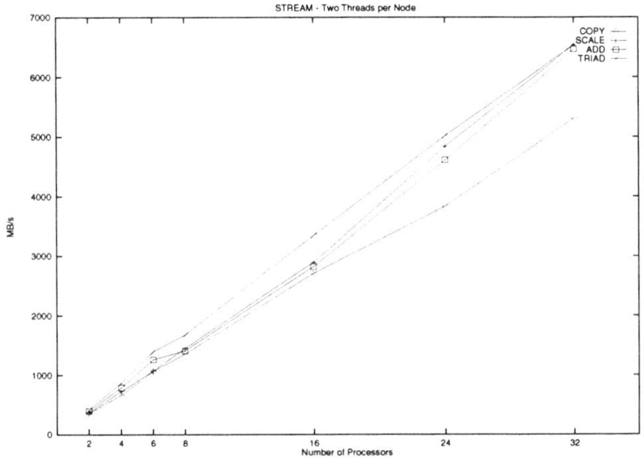

Figure 12 STREAM results - two threads per node

4.1 Microbenchmarks

The first microbenchmarks examine the latency and bandwidth of the Origin memory system. Table 4 shows the latency measured for a memory reference in isolation. This is the time from when the L1 cache is accessed until the instruction associated with the cache miss can graduate. The remote latency numbers for 16 and 32 processors assume that express links are employed.

The STREAM benchmark is the standard memory bandwidth benchmark for the high performance computing industry. STREAM measures the performance of four simple long vector kernels, which are sized to eliminate cache re-use, and reports the results in terms of sustained memory bandwidth. On parallel systems, STREAM is essentially completely parallel; the only communication required is for synchronization at the end of execution of each kernel.

On the Origin 2000, each processor can effectively utilize more than half of the memory bandwidth available on a node. Thus, we've included STREAM results in MB/s with only one thread running per node in Figure 11, and with two threads running per node in Figure 12.

Table 5 shows the effectiveness of the fetch-and-increment operations in implementing a globally shared counter. Note that LL/SC does much better for a single processor, at 6.9 million increments/ second, since the counter variable and the lock surrounding it (which are allocated from the same cache line) stays loaded in the processor's cache, whereas the fetch-and-increment variable is always accessed via an uncached reference to local memory, and de-

M op/s	1 P	2 P	4 P	8 P	16 P	32 P
fch-inc	4.0	7.4	6.1	10.0	19.3	23.0
LL/SC	6.9	2.3	0.84	0.23	0.12	0.09

Table 5 Comparison of LL/SC and fetch-and-op for atomic increments

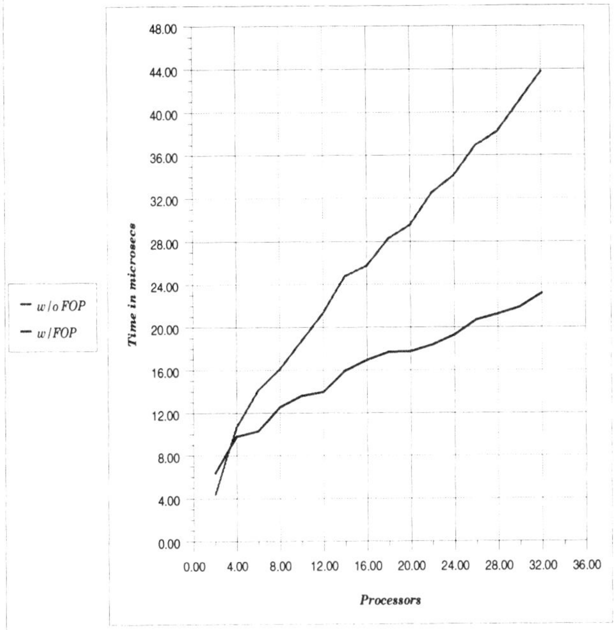

Figure 13 Comparison of LL/SC and fetch-and-op for a null doacross loop

livers only 4.0 million increments/sec. As more processors are added, however, the number of increments on the fetch-and-increment variable is able to increase to near the fetch-and-op cache throughput limit of 24.4 million/sec (one every 41 ns), while the number of increments on the LL/SC variable falls off dramatically, to under 100 thousand increments/second with 32 processors. Also note the drop off in fetch-and-op increments/second between two and four processors. With a small number of processors, the number of fetch-and-increments achievable per second is limited by the fetch-and-increment latency, since each R10000 processor can only have a single uncached read outstanding. Therefore with two processors, the fetch-and-increment can be allocated locally, whereas with four processors, only two of the processors can access the fetch-and-increment variable from local memory, and the other two processors must pay the longer remote latency.

Figure 13 shows the advantages of using fetch-and-op for barrier implementation. The graph shows the time to execute a null FORTRAN doacross statement. In addition to the barrier time, the null doacross includes the time to perform the work dispatch to the slaves and the execution of one iteration of an empty do-loop. Therefore the graph actually understates the performance benefits of fetch-and-ops in implementing the barrier itself.

4.2 Applications

In this section we examine the performance of the Origin system using the NAS Parallel Benchmarks V2.2 Class A and the SPLASH2 suite. Application and operating system tuning is ongoing, so these results are a snapshot as of late February, 1997.

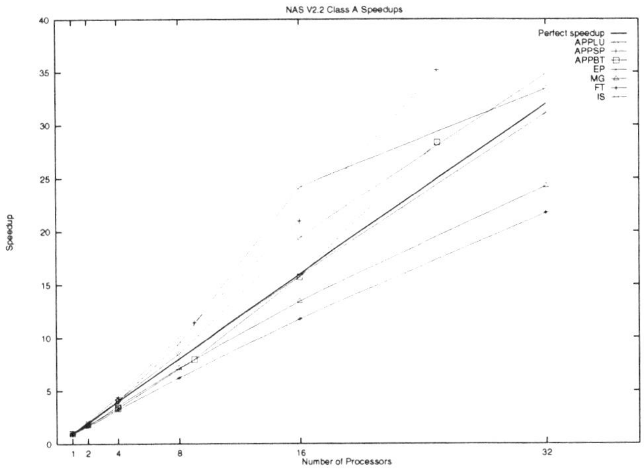

Figure 14 NAS Parallel V2.2 Speedups

Application	Command Line
radiosity	-batch -room
raytrace	balls4.env
lu	-n2048 -b16
ocean	-n 1026
barnes	< input.512

Table 6 SPLASH2 Applications

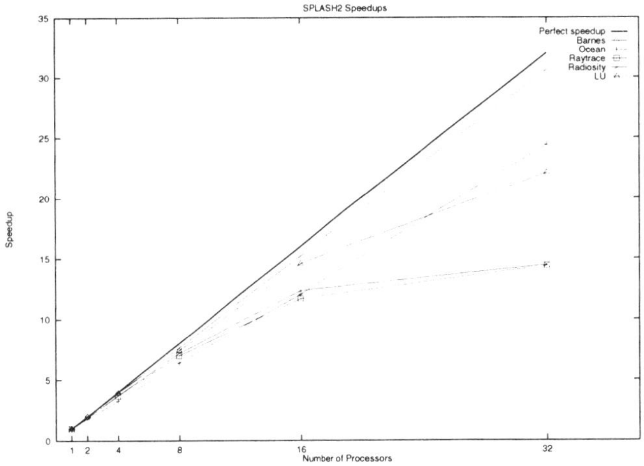

Figure 15 SPLASH2 Speedups

Figure 14 shows the performance of the NAS parallel benchmarks using the Class A datasets for up to 32 processors. Overall, speedup on the NAS benchmarks is very good. For several of the benchmarks, superlinear speedups are achieved due to the larger total cache size and memory bandwidth available as the number of processors (and therefore the number of nodes) increases.

Table 6 lists the applications run from the SPLASH2 suite along with their command line arguments. Figure 15 shows speedups for the four SPLASH2 applications and one SPLASH2 kernel on the Origin system. Barnes and Ocean get good speedups to 32 processors, while Lu starts to roll off beyond 16 processors. Radiosity and Raytrace both begin to have speedup fall-off after 8 processors, and show very small increases between 16 and 32 processors. We have just started our investigation into the performance of the SPLASH suite, so we are not certain of the exact cause of the speedup roll-off for Lu, Radiosity, and Raytrace. Our benchmark machine had a limited amount of total memory, so the small data sets for these applications may be a contributor to the limited speedup at 32 processors.

5 Related Systems

The Origin system benefitted from the many lessons the authors learned in designing the Stanford DASH[7], so we start by discussing the major differences between Origin and DASH. We then contrast the Origin with three contemporary ccNUMA systems: the Sequent NUMAQ, the Data General NUMALiiNE, and the Convex Exemplar X.

5.1 Stanford DASH

The differences between the Origin and DASH coherence protocols was already explored in Section 3.2. The main architectural difference between the Origin and DASH systems is that DASH employed a four processor SMP cluster as its node[7], while Origin uses a two processor node where coherence between the processors in the node is handled by the directory-based protocol.

The major advantage of a SMP-based node is the potential for cache-to-cache sharing within the node. In [7] the 4-way intranode sharing of DASH is shown to produce small performance gains for 3 out of 4 SPLASH applications with only the Barnes application showing significant performance gains.

On the other hand, the disadvantages of the SMP-based nodes are three-fold. First, to get to the number of processors where intranode sharing will be significant the bus will most likely not be able to be on a single board. This causes local memory latency to be longer as the bus must run slower to support the large number of devices connected to it and more ASIC crossings will generally be between the processor and local memory. In addition, this makes the initial cost of the SMP node much higher since even a single processor node requires several boards. Second, remote latency also increases as requests to remote memory will generally have to wait for the results of the local processor snoops before being able to issue to the remote memory. Finally, as discussed earlier, the remote memory bandwidth for a SMP-based node is half the local memory bandwidth. In fact, in DASH, the remove memory bandwidth was reduced by a factor of three since each remote memory reference needed to traverse the local bus for the initial request, the home memory bus to get the data, and the local bus again to return the data to the processor.

While the DASH prototype did suffer increased latency on it's local memory access time due to the snoopy bus, it did manage to have a 3:1 best case (nearest-neighbor) remote to local latency, which as we will see when we examine some commercial contemporary systems is quite good for a SMP-based ccNUMA machine. Despite being much better than other SMP-based node solutions, this ratio is still less than the 2:1 best case (nearest-neighbor) remote to local latency achieved by Origin.

5.2 Sequent NUMAQ and DG NUMALiiNE

The Sequent NUMAQ consists of up to 63 nodes, where each node is a 4-processor Pentium Pro-based SMP[8] referred to as a *quad*. The nodes are connected together via an SCI-based ring. Both the low-level transport layers and the higher-level coherence protocol of the SCI are utilized in the NUMAQ. A programmable protocol engine is used to implement the SCI coherence protocol. A full board (the Lynx Board) implements the complete interface between the Pentium Pro based quad.

The Sequent NUMAQ is architecturally similar to the Stanford DASH, albeit with a different processor, a simpler network topology, and the SCI coherence protocol instead of the DASH coherence protocol. It has the same advantages and disadvantages of DASH: the local memory latency is good, around 250 ns, but the best case remote memory latency is around 8 times the local latency[8]. The choice of a ring with its low bisection bandwidth as the interconnect network causes large degradation in remote latency as the system interconnect becomes loaded.

The Data General NUMALiiNE is architecturally very similar to the Sequent NUMAQ. The node is a Pentium-Pro quad, and the nodes are connected via a SCI-based ring. As such it suffers from the same limitations in remote latency and network performance as the NUMAQ.

5.3 Convex Exemplar X

The Convex Exemplar X is similar to earlier Exemplar systems implementing a crossbar connected set of hyper-nodes that are then connected by parallel ring interconnects that implement a modified version of the SCI protocol[2]. In the X-class machines the hypernode size has increased from 8 to 16 processors and the four 1-D rings have been replaced by eight sets of 2-D rings. Initial configurations support 64 processors (4 hypernodes), but the machine can architecturally scale to 512 processors in an 8x4 torus configuration.

The use of a crossbar intra-connect for the hypernode does reduce the bandwidth penalty of using an SMP node compared with the NUMAQ or NUMALiiNE machines, but still adds to latency in comparison with the smaller, more integrated nodes in Origin. While no latency data has been published to date, the ratio of local to remote in the Exemplar is likely to be similar to previous machines (5:1 without loading on small configurations), whereas the base numbers in the Origin start at 2:1 in small configurations and grow very slowly.

Another major difference is the use of a third-level cluster cache in the Exemplar. This mechanism is in contrast to Origin's page migration mechanism. The cluster cache can adapt to capacity misses more quickly then Origin's migration mechanism, but does this at the cost of increased latency for communication misses and misses that result from conflicts in the cluster cache. The cluster cache also hurts remote bandwidth because it implies that at least three DRAM accesses be made per remote miss (one in the local cluster cache, one at the home, an additional one or two if the line is held dirty in another cluster cache, and a final access to allocate into the local cluster cache), leading to remote bandwidth being one-third of the local bandwidth.

5.4 Overall Comparison of DSM Systems

The major difference between the Convex, Sequent and DG machines and the Origin is that the Origin has a much more tightly integrated DSM structure with the assumption of treating local accesses as an optimization of a general DSM memory reference. The other commercial DSM machines add a DSM mechanism on top of a relatively large SMP node in which local communication and memory accesses are optimized over performance of the general DSM structure. Which one of these models is more appropriate depends upon a number of factors:

1. Is scaling the system down in size and cost important? The overhead of the SMP nodes sets a minimum on how effective such machines can be in small configurations (one to two processors).

2. Is the workload primarily throughput oriented, with only a small degree of parallelism? If so, the SMP solutions might achieve higher performance due to lower communication costs between processors within the same SMP node. Oppositely, if parallelism beyond the size of the SMP node is important, then the latency and bandwidth overheads are likely to be very high in comparison to Origin.
3. Is I/O structured as a global resource or must nodes treat I/O as a local resource similar to a distributed memory system? If the goal is global accessibility then the tight DSM integration of Origin would also be preferred.

6 Conclusions

The Origin 2000 is a highly scalable server designed to meet the needs of both the technical and commercial marketplaces. This is accomplished by providing a highly modular system with a low-entry point and incremental costs. A bristled fat hypercube network is used to provide a high bisection bandwidth, low-latency interconnect. Low latency to local memory and a low remote to local memory latency ratio allow the existing application base to easily migrate their applications from the uniform access of the existing SMP Challenge and Power Challenge systems to the NUMA Origin systems. Origin also includes several features to help the performance of these applications including hardware and software support for page migration and fast synchronization.

7 Acknowledgments

The Origin system design resulted from the very hard work of a top-notch team of chip, board, and system engineers. Major contributors on the core logic design/verification team besides the authors included: Michael Anderson, John Andrews, Rick Bahr, John Burger, John Carlson, Hansel Collins, Pat Conway, Ken Choy, Asgeir Eiriksson, Paul Everhardt, Mike Galles, Sameer Gupta, Gary Hagensen, Dick Hessel, Roger Hu, Lee Jones, George Kaldani, John Keen, Ron Kolb, Yuval Koren, Waidy Lee, Viranjit Madan, John Manton, Greg Marlan, Dawn Maxon, David McCracken, Ali Moyedian, Bob Newhall, Kianoosh Naghshineh, Chuck Narad, Ron Nikel, Steve Padnos, Dave Parry, Ed Priest, Azmeer Salleh, Ken Sarocky, Chris Satterlee, Alex Silbey, Doug Solomon, Jim Smith, Tuan Tran, Swami Venkataraman, Rich Weber, Eric Williams, Mike Woodacre, and Steve Yurash.
The authors would also like to thank Jaswinder Pal Singh and Dongming Jiang for their help in getting the SPLASH performance numbers on Origin, John McCalpin for providing the NAS Parallel Benchmark and STREAM results, and the anonymous referees for their comments which helped to improve the final version of this paper.

References

[1] Anant Agarwal, Ricardo Bianchini, David Chaiken, Kirk L. Johnson, David Kranz, John Kubiatowicz, Beng-Hong Lim, Kenneth Mackenzie, and Donald Yeung. The MIT Alewife machine: Architecture and Performance. In *Proceedings of the 22nd Annual International Symposium on Computer Architecture*, pages 2-13, June 1995.

[2] Tony Brewer and Greg Astfalk. The evolution of the HP/Convex Exemplar. In *Proceedings of COMPCON Spring '97: Forty-Second IEEE Computer Society International Conference*, pages 81-86, February 1997.

[3] Asgeir Th. Eiriksson and Ken L. McMillan, Using formal verification/analysis methods on the critical path in system design: A case study. In *Proceedings of Computer Aided Verification Conference*, Liege Belgium, LNCS 939, Springer Verlag, 1995.

[4] Mike Galles. Scalable Pipelined Interconnect for Distributed Endpoint Routing: The SGI SPIDER chip. In *Hot Interconnects '96.*

[5] Mark Heinrich, Jeffrey Kuskin, David Ofelt, John Heinlein, Joel Baxter, Jaswinder Pal Singh, Richard Simoni, Kourosh Gharachorloo, David Nakahira, Mark Horowitz, Anoop Gupta, Mendel Rosenblum, and John Hennessy. The performance impact of flexibility in the Stanford FLASH multipocessor. In *Proceedings of the 6th International Conference on Architectural Support for Programming Languages and Operating Systems*, pages 274-285, October 1994.

[6] Daniel Lenoski, James Laudon, Kourosh Gharachorloo, Anoop Gupta, and John Hennessy. The directory-based cache coherence protocol for the DASH multiprocessor. In *Proceedings of the 17th Annual International Symposium on Computer Architecture*, pages 148-159, May 1990.

[7] Daniel Lenoski, James Laudon, Truman Joe, David Nakahira, Luis Stevens, Anoop Gupta, and John Hennessy. The DASH prototype: Logic overhead and performance. *IEEE Transactions on Parallel and Distributed Systems*, 4(1):41-61, January 1993.

[8] Tom Lovett and Russell Clapp, STiNG: A CC-NUMA computer system for the commercial marketplace. In *Proceedings of the 23rd Annual International Symposium on Computer Architecture*, pages 308-317, May 1996.

[9] Steven K. Reinhardt, James R. Larus, and David A. Wood. Tempest and Typhoon: User-level shared memory. In *Proceedings of the 21st Annual International Symposium on Computer Architecture*, pages 325-336, April 1994.

[10] Mendel Rosenblum, John Chapin, Dan Teodosiu, Scott Devine, Tirthankar Lahiri, and Anoop Gupta. Implementing efficient fault containment for multiprocessors. *Communications of the ACM*, 39(3):52-61, September, 1996.

[11] Ben Verghese, Scott Devine, Anoop Gupta, and Mendel Rosenblum. Operating system support for improving data locality on CC-NUMA compute servers. In *Proceedings of the 7th International Conference on Architectural Support for Programming Languages and Operating Systems*, pages 279-289, October 1996.

[12] Wolf-Dietrich Weber, *Scalable Directories for Cache-Coherent Shared-Memory Multiprocessors*. Ph.D.thesis, Stanford University, Stanford, California, January 1993.

[13] Steve Whitney, John McCalpin, Nawaf Bitar, John L. Richardson, and Luis Stevens. The SGI Origin software environment and application performance. In *Proceedings of COMPCON Spring '97: Forty-Second IEEE Computer Society International Conference*, pages 165-170, February 1997.

[14] Kenneth Yeager, The MIPS R10000 Superscalar Microprocessor, *IEEE Micro*, 16(2):28-40, April, 1996.

Prefetching using Markov Predictors

Doug Joseph
IBM T. J. Watson Research Lab
P.O. Box 218
IBM. T. J. Watson Research
Yorktown Heights, NY 10598
djoseph@watson.ibm.com

Dirk Grunwald
Department of Computer Science
University of Colorado
Boulder, Colorado, 80309-0430
grunwald@cs.colorado.edu

Abstract

Prefetching is one approach to reducing the latency of memory operations in modern computer systems. In this paper, we describe the *Markov prefetcher*. This prefetcher acts as an interface between the on-chip and off-chip cache, and can be added to existing computer designs. The Markov prefetcher is distinguished by prefetching *multiple reference predictions* from the memory subsystem, and then prioritizing the delivery of those references to the processor.

This design results in a prefetching system that provides good coverage, is accurate and produces timely results that can be effectively used by the processor. In our cycle-level simulations, the Markov Prefetcher reduces the overall execution stalls due to instruction and data memory operations by an average of 54% for various commercial benchmarks while only using two thirds the memory of a demand-fetch cache organization.

1 Introduction

Processors normally fetch memory using a demand-fetch model: when the processor issues a load instruction, the specified datum is fetched from memory. If the datum is not in the cache, a request is made to the external memory system to fetch the datum. By comparison, a memory prefetching mechanism attempts to provide data *before* the processor requests that data. We assume that the the data is placed in a *prefetch buffer* where it can be accessed by the processor, or uses some other mechanism to perform a *non-binding* prefetch that avoids disturbing the current cache contents.

There are three important metrics used to compare memory prefetchers: coverage, accuracy and timeliness. Coverage indicates the fraction of memory requests that were supplied by the prefetcher rather than being demand-fetched. Accuracy indicates the fraction of the prefetched cache lines offered to the processor that were actually used. Unless prefetched memory references are provided to the processor before they are needed, the processor may still stall during execution. Timeliness indicates if the data offered by the prefetcher arrives before it is needed, but not so early that the data must be discarded before it can be used. The ideal prefetcher has large coverage, large accuracy and produces timely data – the prefetcher offers the processor all the data it needs, only the data it needs and before the processor needs the data.

ISCA '97 Denver, CO, USA

We believe prefetching mechanisms are designed in a two-step process: first, the architect envisions a "model" describing the way that programs behave when accessing memory, and then attempts to construct a physical realization of that model that provides suitable prefetch coverage. In this paper, we describe a hardware prefetch mechanism that offers better performance than other prefetch mechanisms. In memory-level simulations, we find that this prefetching mechanism can reduce the memory overhead to the cycles-per-instruction by 54%, greatly reducing the memory stalls encountered by our model processor. Moreover, although we devote one MByte of memory to the prefetcher data structures, our prefetcher reduces the memory stalls while reducing the total amount of memory devoted to the combination of the prefetcher and second level cache – using 3 MBytes of memory, our prefetcher outperforms a demand-fetch memory system that uses 4 MBytes of memory.

We first describe the memory access model assumed by our prefetcher and how the prefetcher is physically implemented. We then briefly survey alternative prefetcher designs. We follow this by with a description of the experimental design and analysis we used to estimate the performance of this prefetcher.

2 Prefetcher Design and Implementation

Hardware prefetching is a prediction process: given some current prediction state, the prefetcher guesses what a future memory reference may be and requests that location from the memory subsystem. There are a number of possible sources of prediction information. One such source is the address reference stream, or the sequence of addresses referenced by the processor. However, using this prediction source requires that the prefetching hardware be on the same chip as the processor. The prefetcher would need to be very efficient, since it may then need to analyze many references per cycle.

The prefetchers we examine use the *miss address stream* as a prediction source. These references are presented to the external memory subsystem and, due to the first-level caches, these miss references occur much less frequently than memory references. Figure 1 shows a schematic design for the prefetcher, which can be built as an external part of the memory subsystem. We'll see that this is important because the prefetcher may need to use considerable state information to be effective. As shown in Figure 1, we assume the processor has on-chip prefetch buffers that are examined concurrently with the first level caches. Thus, prefetched data items do not displace data resident in the cache. The prefetched data only contends with the normal demand-fetched memory references for the processor bandwidth.

Prefetch mechanisms usually assume that programs access

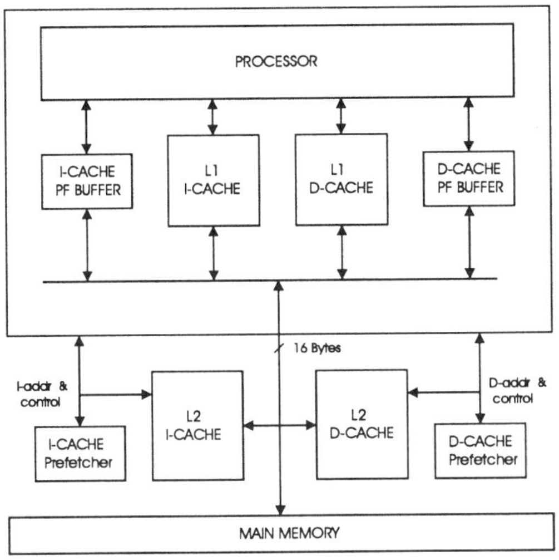

Figure 1: System design

A, B, C, D, C, E, A, C, F, F, E, A, A, B, C, D, E, A, B, C, D, C

Figure 2: Sample miss address reference string. Each letter indicates a cache miss to a different memory location.

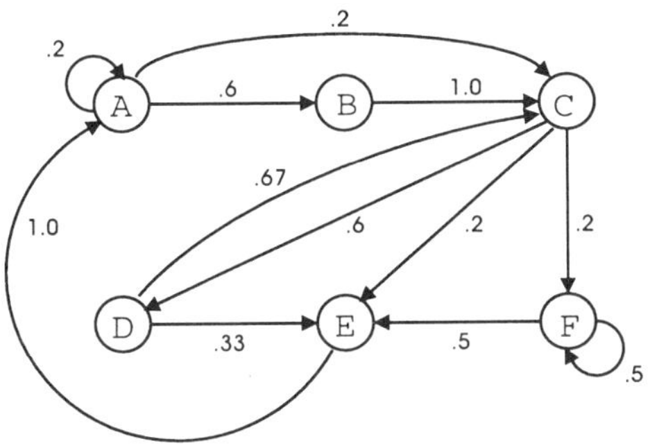

Figure 3: Markov model representing the previous reference string *via* transition probabilities.

memory using a particular pattern or access model. For example, stream buffers [7] assume that memory is accessed as a linear stream, possibly with a non-unit stride. Once an access model has been determined, architects design a hardware mechanism to capture or approximate that reference stream. In the next section, we describe the access model we assume and a hardware implementation that captures that access model.

2.1 Modeling Memory References via Markov Processes

We assume that the miss reference stream can be approximated by an observed Markov model. Assume that our miss reference stream is that shown in Figure 2. In this example, different memory locations are identified by different letters. Thus, this reference sequence indicates a missing reference to memory location "A", followed by a miss for "B" and so on. Using this reference string, we can build a Markov model, shown in Figure 3, that approximates the reference string using a transition frequency. Each transition from node X to node Y in the diagram is assigned a

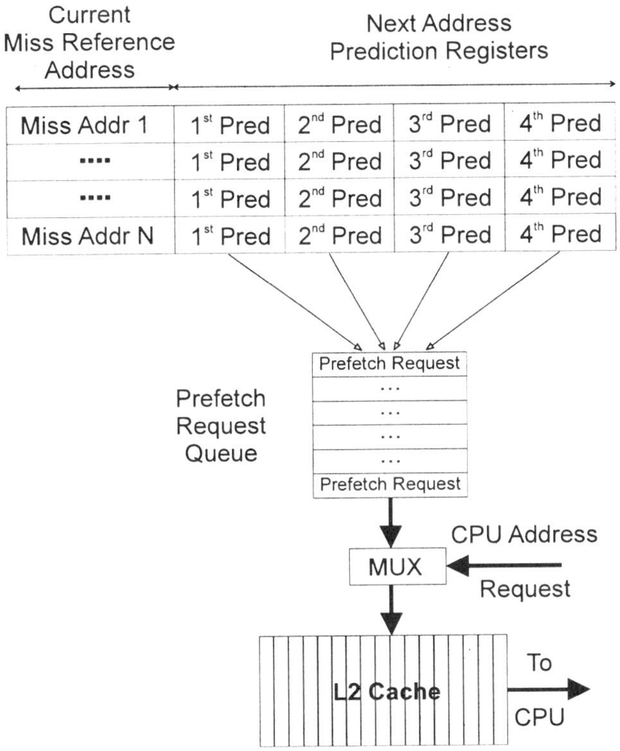

Figure 4: Hardware Used to Approximate Markov Prediction Prefetcher

weight representing the fraction of all references X that are followed by a reference Y. For example, there are five references to node A in the the example miss reference sequence. Of these, we see the pattern "A, A" 20% of the time, the pattern "A, C" 20% of the time and the pattern "A, B" 60% of the time. This example uses one previous reference to predict the next reference. Intuitively, if the program were to execute again and issue the same memory references, the Markov model could be used to predict the miss reference following each missing reference. For example, on re-execution, the appearance of an A may lead the hardware to predict that A, C or B will be the next missing reference and issue prefetch requests for each address. In general, a n-history Markov model can use more history information – for example, given the training sequence A, B, C, the prefetcher would predict C if the miss sequence A, B was seen. We have examined the performance of general n-history models and found little added benefit from the additional information, and thus focus on 1-history models in this paper.

2.2 Realizing the Markov Prefetcher in Hardware

There are several problems encountered in assuming a "pure" Markov model of memory references. In practice programs don't repeat exactly the same reference patterns from one execution to another, and the transition probabilities "learned" in one execution may not benefit another. Furthermore, it is difficult to efficiently represent a pure Markov model in hardware because each node may have an arbitrary degree and the transition probabilities are represented as real values. Lastly, programs reference millions of addresses and it may not be possible to record all references in a single table. Despite these drawbacks, our later data will show that a

"Markov-like" model of memory references is an effective prefetch mechanism. Thus, we need to make a set of design choices that address the problem of representing a Markov transition diagram in hardware. We first describe the design of the Markov predictor and then justify those decisions with simulation studies.

The first decision is to continuously rebuild and use the Markov model as a program is executing. Thus, the approximate Markov model captures the *past activity* of all programs on a system and uses that information to predict the future references. We limit the number of possible nodes in the transition diagram and limit their maximal out-degree. More concretely, we represent the Markov transition diagram using a table such as shown in Figure 4. In this sample configuration, each state in the Markov model occupies a single line in the prediction table, and can have up two to four transitions to other states. The total size of the table is determined by the memory available to the prefetcher. When the current miss address matches the index address in the prefetch table, all of the next address prediction registers are eligible to issue a prefetch, subject to mechanisms described later intended to improve prefetch accuracy. However, not all possible prefetches actually result in a transfer from the L2 cache. Each prefetch request has an associated *priority*. Prefetch addresses are stored in the prefetch request queue, and higher priority requests can dislodge lower-priority requests. The prefetch request queue contends with the processor for the L2 cache, and the demand fetches from the processor have higher priority. Thus, after a series of prefetches, the prefetch request queue may be full, and lower-priority requests will be discarded.

Once a fetch request is satisfied by the L2 cache, it is placed in the on-chip prefetch buffers. Demand-fetch requests are directly stored in the cache. We model the on-chip prefetch buffers as a 16 entry fully associative FIFO buffer. When the processor queries it, all entries are associatively searched in one cycle. If a match is found, it is relocated to the head of the FIFO, and all the entries from the head to the vacated slot are shifted down by one. The FIFO is also searched when updated to avoid duplicate entries. If there are no duplicates when adding an entry, an empty slot is filled, or if there are no empty slots the last slot (the least recently used entry) is replaced. This design is similar to the stream buffer design of Farkas *et.al.* [6]. The primary difference is that in [6], the entire buffer is shifted, discarding all the entries above the matching one.

There are many other parameters that affect the performance of this hardware configuration. We used trace-driven simulation and a memory-level performance model to determine the importance of those parameters and to compare the performance of the Markov prefetcher to previously suggested prefetchers. We next describe prior work on prefetchers and then describe the experimental design to compare the performance of Markov prefetchers to previous designs. We then show the effect of the various parameters in the Markov prefetcher implementation.

3 Prior Work

Hardware and software prefetching schemes have been devised that are effective on structured workloads [14, 4, 12, 8]. However research on prefetching for unstructured workloads is not nearly as common and only recently have results in this area begun to appear [17, 3, 9, 13]. The section on *correlation-based prefetching* is especially relevant since Markov prefetching is an evolution of correlation based prefetching.

Static predictors Almost all static predictors rely on the compiler to determine possible L1 cache misses and embed the information into the code in the form of prefetch instructions. Mowry *et.al.* [12] show that structured scientific codes are very amenable to this approach. However, they also show that their techniques failed to improve performance of the pointer intensive applications used in their study. In terms of hardware resources, compiler based schemes are inexpensive to implement. However, since prediction information is embedded in the program at compile time, compiler based schemes lack the flexibility to account for the dynamic behavior of a workload. Compiler based techniques have been proposed which insert prefetch instructions at sites where pointer dereferences are anticipated. Lipasti *et. al.* [9] developed heuristics that consider pointers passed as arguments on procedure calls and insert prefetches at the call sites for the data referenced by the pointers. Ozawa *et.al.* [13] classify loads whose data address comes from a previous load as *list accesses*, and perform code motions to separate them from the instructions that use the data fetched by list accesses.

Stride Prefetchers Chen and Baer investigate a mechanism for prefetching data references characterized by regular strides [4]. Their scheme is based on a *reference prediction table* (RPT) and *look-ahead program counter* (LPC). The RPT is a cache, tagged with the instruction address of load instructions. The entries in the RPT hold the previous address referenced by the corresponding load instruction, the offset of that address from the previous data address referenced by that instruction, and some flags. When a load instruction is executed that matches an entry in the RPT, the offset of the data address of that load from the previous data address stored in the RPT is calculated. When this matches the offset stored in the table, a prefetch is launched for the data address one offset ahead of the current data address. In [4], the *reference address stream* was used to index the reference prediction table. In practice, we found little performance difference between using the reference addresses or the miss address stream. Our later simulations of stride prefetchers use the miss address stream.

Stream Buffers Jouppi introduced *stream buffers* as one of two significant methods to improved direct mapped cache performance [7]. In contrast to stride prefetchers, stream buffers are designed to prefetch sequential streams of cache lines, independent of program context. The design presented by Jouppi is unable to detect streams containing non-unit strides. Palacharla and Kessler [14] extended the stream buffer mechanism to also detect non-unit strides without having direct access to the program context. They also introduced a noise rejection scheme for improving the accuracy of stream buffers. Farkas *et.al.* [6] further enhanced stream buffers by providing them with an associative lookup capability and a mechanism for detecting and eliminating the allocation of stream buffers to duplicate streams. Later, we compare the performance of the design of Farkas *et. al.* to Markov prefetchers.

Stream buffers are used like a prefetch fill buffer for servicing L1 cache misses in this paper. Prefetches are placed in the stream buffer itself rather than a separate prefetch buffer. Stream buffers are *allocated* on L1 cache misses. If any stream buffer contains an entry that matches the current L1 miss reference address, it is taken from the stream buffer, the entries below the one removed are all shifted up to the head of the buffer, and prefetches are launched to sequentially consecutive cache line addresses to fill the vacancies that open up in the bottom part of the stream buffer. If there is no match in any stream buffer, a new stream buffer is allocated to the new stream. In the model employed in this paper, an empty or least recently used buffer is selected for replacement. The noise rejection scheme introduced by Palacharla [14] is also employed in the allocation of stream buffers used in this research. It is a simple filtering mechanism that waits for two consecutive L1 misses to sequential cache line addresses before allocating a stream buffer to the stream.

Stride prefetchers and stream buffers complement one another is various ways. Stream buffers generally exhibit greater prefetch coverage than stride prefetchers, but also are much more inaccurate, even when using allocation filters. However, while detecting non-unit strides is natural for stride prefetchers, providing non-unit stride detection to stream buffers is more difficult [6].

Stream buffers tend to be more efficient in use of resources than stride prefetchers. For example, given the following program fragment:

```
for (i = 0; i < N; ++i)
{
   b = x[i+20];
   c = x[i+22];
}
```

a stride prefetcher will consume two resources in the stride detection table, while only one stream buffer would be allocated. In our studies we have found that using a stride prefetcher in *series* with stream buffers works well. That is, we allow the more accurate stride prefetcher to issue a prefetch first if it is able and otherwise allocate a stream buffer. The combination provides better coverage than either mechanism alone, and is generally more accurate than stream buffers alone (although less accurate than a stride prefetcher alone).

Indirect Stream Detectors Mehrota [11] describes a hardware data prefetching scheme based on the recursion that occurs in linked list traversals. We also simulated this design, but do not present the performance since it was uniformly worse than correlation-based prefetching.

Correlation-Based Prefetching Markov prefetching is a continuing evolution of what has been called *correlation-based prefetching* [3]. The basic concept of correlation-based prefetching was introduced by Baer [2] in the context of paged virtual memory systems. Baer associated a single prefetch address with each memory address referenced and developed algorithms for updating the prefetch address based upon observed reference patterns. When a reference occurs, the associated prefetch address is checked for residence in physical memory. If the prefetch page is not resident, then it is paged in. This pairing of two temporally related related events, such as a current address with a prefetch address, is the essence of correlation-based prefetching. The first address of the pair is referred to as the *parent* or *key* that is used to select a child prefetch address.

The first instance of correlation-based prefetching being applied to data prefetching is presented in a patent application by Pomerene and Puzak [15]. A hardware cache is used to hold the parent-child information. A further innovation they introduce is to incorporate other information into the parent key. They suggest the use of bits from the instruction causing the miss, and also bits from the last data address referenced. They also introduce a confirmation mechanism that only activates new pairs when data that would have been prefetched would also have been used. This mechanism is very much like the *allocation filters* introduced by Palacharla *et.al.* [14] to improve the accuracy of stream buffers and serves a similar purpose here.

Charney and Reeves [3] extend the Pomerene and Puzak mechanism and apply it to the L1 miss reference stream rather than directly to the load/store stream. Besides being the first to publish results on the Pomerene and Puzak scheme, this work improved upon the mechanism in two significant ways. One was to introduce greater lead time into the prefetching with the use of a FIFO history buffer. Instead of entering parent-child pairs into the pair cache, ancestors older than the parent can be paired with the child and entered in the pair cache. Although no results are reported in the impact this had on CPU stalls, it was demonstrated that prefetch lead time could be significantly improved at the expense of lower prefetch accuracy. The other contribution was a study of various alternate structures for the parent key. This study focused primarily on using different combinations of bits from the instruction and data addresses of L1 miss references. In general, there was marginal improvement in prefetch accuracy or coverage in those attempts.

Another important contribution by Charney and Reeves was to show that stride based prefetching could be combined with correlation based prefetching to provide significant improvements in prefetch coverage over using either approach alone, on certain benchmarks. In this scheme, a stride prefetcher is placed at the front end of a correlation-based prefetcher. If the stride prefetcher could make a prediction it would, and the miss references associated with the stride prediction would be filtered out of the miss reference stream presented to the correlation-based prefetcher. Coverage improved for two reasons. One is correlation-prefetchers (and Markov prefetchers) must see a miss reference repeat before it can predict a future miss reference. Stride prefetchers do not have that limitation. The other is that better utilization of the pair cache is achievable when the stride references are filtered out. For the workloads used in this paper, we find that there are insufficient stride references in the applications we examined for this scheme to offer much improvement in prefetch coverage. However, in the case of very "stridy" workloads, it seems clear this approach is advantageous.

Alexander and Kedem [1] proposed a mechanism similar to correlation-based prefetching but used a *distributed* prediction table. In their variation, a correlation-based table was used to predict bit-line accesses in an Enhanced DRAM, and was used to prefetch individual bit lines from the DRAM to the SRAM array.

4 Experimental Design and Simulation Study

There are three important factors that influence the performance of a prefetching scheme: coverage, accuracy and timeliness. Prefetch coverage and accuracy are less dependent on a specific memory system configuration, while timeliness depends greatly on the memory reference penalties of a particular system. In this study, we use a single metric, the fraction of first-level cache misses, to characterize *both* coverage and accuracy. For each application, we record the number of demand-cache misses encountered without any prefetching and normalize these values. Then, we measure and normalize the number of cache misses for different prefetching schemes. We define "coverage" to be the fraction of the miss references satisfied by the prefetch mechanism. A prefetch mechanism will fetch more data from memory than a simple demand-fetch mechanism, and many of those references may be mispredicted fetches. We record the additional references relative to the normalized demand-fetch references, and define this to be a measure of the *inaccuracy* of a prefetcher. We measured timeliness by simulating a non-speculative processor with a detailed memory model and comparing the *memory cycles-per-instruction* (MCPI). This represents the average number of CPU stalls attributed to the memory subsystem. Both simulation studies used the same cache configurations, described below.

We assume that all non-memory instructions execute in one cycle. The model processor has a single-cycle on-chip 8KB L1 data cache and an 8KB L1 instruction cache. Each cache has 8-entry single-cycle victim buffers and 32-byte lines. The L1 data cache also has a single-cycle 8-entry write buffer and uses a write-around policy. The second-level (L2) cache were multi-cycle, multi-bank, direct mapped, lockup-free 4MB I and D caches, with 128 byte lines. The L2 data cache uses a write-back with write allocate policy and had one 8-entry address request queue per bank. We model four synchronous SRAM cache banks in the baseline model. The address and data busses have a latency of four cycles. When combined with the four cycle memory latency, and the four cycles to return the data to the processor, the total cache miss penalty is twelve cycles, but new requests can be pipelined every four cycles. Each cache bank has a separate address bus to each L2 cache bank but just one L2 data bus shared by all banks. Thus, there is never address bus contention, but there may be considerable contention for the data bus. The L1-L2 bus bandwidth is 8 bytes/cycle. We used a multi-cycle, multi-banked memory model with one 8 entry address request queue per bank and 4 memory banks. Address and data busses have a latency of 4 cycles. The access latency of a bank is 24 cycles and the L2-L3 bus bandwidth is 4 bytes/cycle.

When simulating stream buffers, we used eight three-entry stream buffers, with associative lookup, non-overlapping stream allocation, and allocation filters. Each stream buffer has single cycle access. When simulating stride prefetchers, we used a stride prefetcher with a 16 entry fully associative *stride detection table*. Access is also single cycle. We also experimented with larger stride tables using four-way set associative tables taking 32-KBytes of storage. There was no advantage to tables larger than 2KBytes for the traces we considered, and there was little difference between a 4-way associative table larger than 2-KBytes or the 16-entry fully-associative table. In earlier work on stream buffers, Farkas *et. al.* [6] used four three-entry stream buffers. We used eight because there was a small, but noticable improvement in coverage up to that point. We also varied the number of entries in the stream buffer and reached the same conclusions stated in [6]: below three entries, prefetches have insufficient lead time and above three entries, accuracy begins to fall off rapidly..

The Correlation and Markov prefetchers are combined with the second-level cache. When modeling the Correlation and Markov prefetchers, we used a bounded or constant amount of storage for the combined prefetch and cache subsystem, but that was not possible while continuing to use direct mapped caches. Thus, we configured the Markov and Correlation prefetchers to use less memory than the corresponding demand-fetch cache or the stride and stream prefetchers. For the Markov and Correlation prefetchers, we used a one MByte data prefetch table and a 2MByte data cache. For the demand-fetch model, we used a 4-MByte data cache. In other words, the prefetch implementations would require two thirds the memory of stride or stream prefetchers when implemented. For the data cache, we also used a 2MB instruction cache and 1MByte prefetch table for the prefetch configurations, and a 4-MBbyte instruction cache for the demand-fetch model.

4.1 Benchmark Applications

There is a deficiency in the most widely used benchmarks for simulation studies (e.g. the SPEC programs suite). Past research has indicated that operating system activity and multi-programming can significantly effect cache performance [10, 5]. However, little has been reported on the impact these factors have on prefetching strategies. At the same time, the cache performance on such workloads tends to be significantly worse than other workloads, making the need for latency reducing methods such as prefetching even more important.

Many important technical and commercial applications give rise to unstructured workloads. Technical applications involving large sparse arrays of data often store such data in a compressed format and access that data via indirection arrays (i.e. $a[b[i]]$). Usually the organization of sparse arrays is not known till run time and may evolve during execution. Another common source of unstructured access patterns in technical and commercial workloads is the use of pointer connected structures. Large graphs or trees of structures are often dynamically generated and may evolve during execution. Algorithms in the application may jump from one part of a tree or graph to another. Consequently, pointers are not always accurate indicators of access patterns. Unstructured technical workloads include such important examples as event driven simulators and wire routing tools for VLSI design, unstructured grid algorithms in computational fluid dynamics, modeling of molecular dynamics, DRAM device level simulation, and structural dynamics analysis. Commercial environments tend to be unstructured because of high process switch rates, high random I/O rates, and they typically involve a large number of user processes [10]. Transaction processing also utilize searching and sorting algorithms that give rise to unstructured access patterns. Examples of commercial workloads include: transaction processing, multi-user software development environments, network and file server kernels, desktop publishing tools, and compilers.

The simulations of this work are based on address traces of technical and commercial industry-standard benchmarks. They were captured on an **IBM RS/6000** running **AIX** using a proprietary tracing tool developed at **IBM**. Cache performance characteristics on most of the traces we used were presented by Maynard *et.al.* [10]. The traces include both instruction and data references obtained throughout the execution of multiple processes containing kernel, user and shared library activity. Four of the traces used were generated from unstructured technical codes, and four were from commercially oriented workloads. Table 1 provides a brief summary of all eight. More information on the benchmarks can be found in [10] and the appendix.

Table 2 shows statistics indicative of the impact of these differences. The first two columns show the percentage of the instructions that are branches and the percentage of these that are taken branches. An analysis of branching behavior helps explain one of the reasons I-cache miss rates tend to be higher for commercial workloads than technical workloads. Typical technical workloads are dominated by short to medium length loops. For such a workload where most branch instructions return control to the head of the loop, the percentage of taken branches is much higher. Also, if the longest instruction loops fit in the I-cache, the I-cache miss rate is very low. In contrast, the percentage of taken branches in commercial workloads is relatively low, indicating that these workloads execute relatively few iterations per loop. The lack of dominant loops is why these commercial workloads have a lower probability of re-executing recent instructions, leading to higher miss rates [10]. We note that Spice is anomalous in this trend, yet still has a very low I-miss rate. As with all the SPEC92 and SPEC95 benchmarks, the instruction working set for Spice is very small and fits comfortably in the I-cache.

The average sequential block size also shows the "branchy" nature of commercial workloads. Block sizes in commercial workloads tend to be much shorter than in technical codes. The last column in Figure 2 shows the fraction of the total number of instructions executed in the operating system. These numbers indicate that much of the work in commercial workloads is actually done by the operating system. One reason for this is the relatively high usage is that there is frequent movement of small amounts of data between the different levels of the system, with few arithmetic operations on the data. In technical workloads, the operating system brings data into application space, and the application performs extensive arithmetic manipulation before handing it back to the operating system to store.

Benchmark	Description
Sdet	Multi-User software development environment from the SPEC SDM benchmark suite.
Laddis	*NFS* file server: basis of the SPEC system-level File Server (SFS) benchmark suite.
Netperf	TCP/IP benchmark for system communication performance.
TPCB	Transaction Processing Performance Council-B benchmark; users connected in client-server configurations, data base server traced.
Abaqus	Structural dynamics analysis tool (**HKS** Inc.)
G92	Computation Chemistry Code (**Gaussian** Inc.)
MM4	Local-Weather model (**Pitt/NCAR**)
Spice	Electronic circuit simulation (from SPEC92, kernel activity not traced).

Table 1: Workloads Focus

Benchmark	% Branches	%Branches Taken	Avg Seq Block Size	% Instrs in OS
Sdet	17.8	66.5	8.4	50
Laddis	18.9	68.7	7.7	100
Netperf	18.6	66.2	8.1	97
TPCB	16.7	68.1	8.9	42
Abaqus	23.9	97.3	4.3	7
G92	39.6	97.6	2.6	0
MM4	8.5	74.4	15.8	4
Spice	16.8	39.7	15.0	0

Table 2: Workload Characteristics

Program	I-Refs (Mil.)	D-Refs (Mil)	L1-I MR	L1-D MR	L2-I MR	L2-D MR
Sdet	32.1	11.1	.067	.102	.001	.010
Laddis	32.5	11.2	.101	.203	.001	.009
Netperf	32.9	11.0	.145	.153	.001	.017
TPCB	31.5	11.4	.130	.198	.002	.027
Abaqus	77.4	26.3	.054	.188	.001	.028
G92	58.8	19.2	.041	.170	.003	.013
MM4	31.8	9.7	.026	.412	.004	.054
Spice	37.1	11.9	.0001	.144	.000	.001

Table 3: 8KB Cache Reference Counts and Miss Rates

Table 3 provides a summary of the number of instruction and data references in each trace and the miss rates obtained with the memory subsystem described above.

5 Performance Comparison

Most of the physical parameters influencing the performance of the Markov predictor have been specified in the simulation environment. However, there are two important parameters that simplify the implementation of a "pure Markov" model. A node or state in a pure Markov model can have an arbitrary fan-out, and each outgoing edge has a transition probability that indicates the likelihood of moving to a particular next state. This transition probability is used to prioritize memory prefetches.

We choose to limit the fanout for each state in the prediction table and to approximate the transition probabilities using an LRU mechanism. Figure 5 shows the effect of varying the maximal fanout for one, two, four and eight prefetch address predictors. This graph shows both the prediction accuracy and coverage on a single axis. The vertical axis is the percentage of cache misses normalized to the same application and cache organization using a demand-fetch organization. Four bars, indicating the different configurations being considered, are shown for each application. Each bar has three components. The lower component represents the *coverage*, or the fraction of miss references that were prefetched and then used by the processor. Larger values are better, but never exceed 100% of the normalized miss references. The middle component represents the fraction of miss references that were not satisfied by prefetch references and had to be demand-fetched. The upper component represents the fraction of miss references that were incorrectly predicted and result in wasted bandwidth. Smaller values are better for this component. The upper component indicates the *accuracy* of the prefetcher, because a more accurate prefetcher would fetch fewer references that were not used.

Clearly, the accuracy decreases and the coverage increases as more prefetch address predictors are added, because *every* predicted address can be fetched fetched when a matching parent key is found in the prefetch table. A larger number of prefetch addresses results in a considerably decreased accuracy with little improvement in coverage. For example, when the TCPB benchmark is simulated, the prefetcher fetches twice as many wasted cache lines when using eight rather than four prefetch predictors, but only increases the coverage by $\approx$10%. In most applications that we examined, four prefetch predictors provided a reasonable balance between coverage and accuracy for the data cache, and we use that configuration for the remainder of the paper. Only two prefetchers were needed for the instruction cache, because there are fewer successors for a given instruction reference.

Since the performance of the Markov prefetcher is dependent on the size of the prefetcher tables, we also investigated a two-tiered allocation strategy, where records are initially allocated to a table with two prefetch address predictors. If more than two addresses are needed, the entry is moved to a separate four-entry table. Although we do not report the results here, this design afforded better performance for a given table size at the expense of a slightly more complex design.

As mentioned, *every* predicted prefetch address is fetched when the parent key is found in the prefetcher. To improve performance, individual references are prioritized based on the likelihood of satisfying the request. We considered two methods to prioritize the references. In the first, we used the true transition probability and in the second, we used a simple LRU algorithm. The LRU algorithm out-performed the true transition probability in every application, and is much easier to implement. Table 4 shows the reference fre-

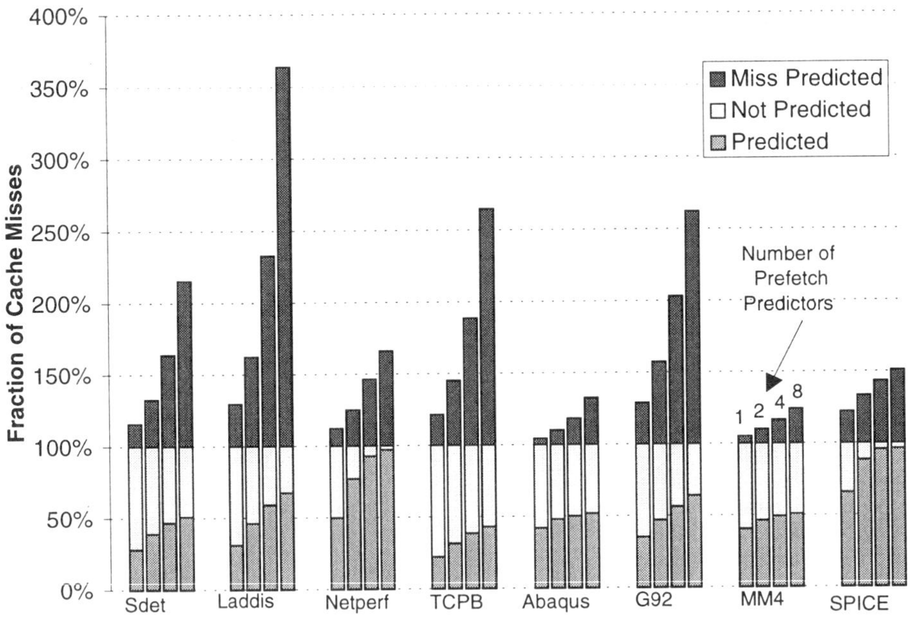

Figure 5: Changes in prefetch accuracy and coverage for the Markov prefetcher as the number of prefetch addresses is increased. Each bar shows the normalized percentage of L1 data cache misses when using one, two, four or eight prefetch address predictors.

Benchmark	Address Predictor			
	0	1	2	3
Sdet	0.342	0.200	0.13	0.097
Laddis	0.344	0.239	0.172	0.123
Netperf	0.754	0.335	0.157	0.107
TPCB	0.511	0.397	0.238	0.205
Abaqus	0.756	0.227	0.103	0.066
G92	0.501	0.256	0.153	0.116
MM4	0.691	0.202	0.093	0.062
Spice	0.606	0.262	0.082	0.034

Table 4: Reference frequency for each data cache prediction address entry for different applications

Benchmark	Address Predictor			
	0	1	2	3
Sdet	152	313	439	581
Laddis	33	56	90	123
Netperf	46	129	320	560
TPCB	34	72	140	204
Abaqus	54	272	486	939
G92	226	431	584	1,264
MM4	97	824	991	1,546
Spice	41	76	230	418

Table 5: Reference lead time for each data cache prediction address entry for different applications.

quency for each predictor address in a Markov prefetcher with four prediction addresses. The columns represent the relative age of the predictor reference and predictor "0" is always the most recently used address predictor. For example, 34.2% of the references correctly prefetched for the Sdet application were predicted by the first predictor address. The large difference in reference frequency for the first and second predictors indicates that an LRU policy is very effective.

The LRU prioritization also orders the data to improve the *lead time*, or the time until the data is needed in our model memory simulator. Table 5 shows the average number of cycles between the time a prefetch is issued and when it is used, for those prefetch requests that are actually used. Larger values indicate a longer "lead time", meaning there is more time to actually provide the data to the processor. In each case, the lead time increases from the most recently used reference (the first column) to the least recently used (the last column). This indicates that the LRU prioritization method not only requests the most frequently needed items, but that it also requests those that are needed soonest.

We compared the performance of the Markov prefetcher using four prefetch addresses and an LRU prioritization policy against other prefetch mechanisms. Figure 6 shows the normalized memory transfers for the different methods. From left to right, each column shows the performance for: stream prefetching, stride prefetching correlation prefetching, Markov prefetching, stride, stream and Markov in parallel and stride, stream and Markov in series. The stride, stream and correlation prefetchers are simulated as described in §3.

Figure 6 shows that stream prefetchers provide better coverage than stride prefetchers, but do so by using considerably more bandwidth. The correlation prefetcher (column 3) provides still better coverage and the Markov prefetcher (column 4) provides the best coverage over the set of applications. However, as with stream buffers, this increase in coverage comes at the price of in-

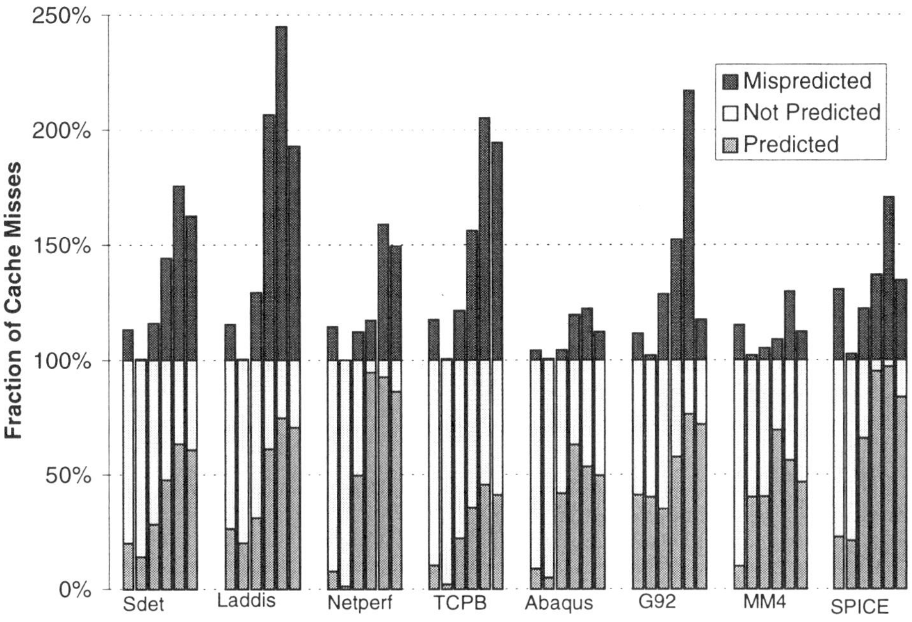

Figure 6: Simulation-based study comparing prefetcher accuracy. From left to right, each column shows the performance for: stream prefetching, stride prefetching correlation prefetching, Markov prefetching, stride, stream and Markov in parallel and stride, stream and Markov in series.

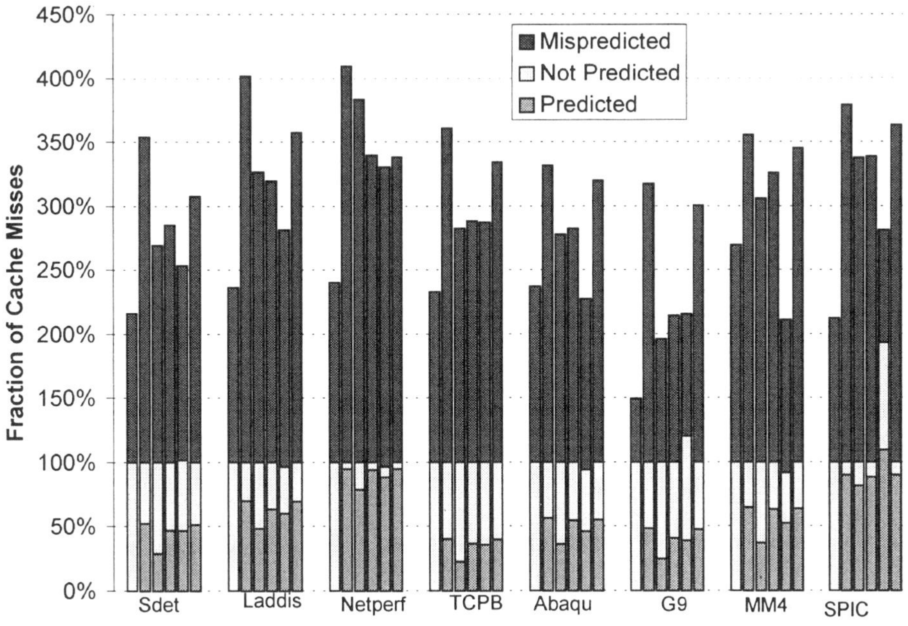

Figure 7: Memory reference overhead for different bandwidth reduction techniques. In this figure, the vertical axis shows the the fraction of *words* transfered, rather than cache lines. In the group for each program, the first bar is for demand fetching (no prefetched), followed by Markov prefetching, Markov prefetching with noise rejection, accuracy-based adaptivity and CNA-based adaptivity. The last bar shows the memory references if the L1-cache is queried prior to prefetching.

creased memory bandwidth demands, often five-fold that of the stream buffers. The last two columns indicate alternative designs that attempt to either improve coverage or improve accuracy. In the fifth column, we use a combination of stride, stream and Markov prefetchers in parallel. This typically results in a large increase in mispredicted references that waste bandwidth, but with a modest improvement in coverage. At times, the coverage actually *decreases*. When the predictors are used in series, the coverage improves again, but by a smaller amount. Likewise, the mispredictions increase, wasting more bandwidth. In part, this occurs because references handled by the stream and stride mechanisms are not used to "train" the Markov predictor, since they are not misses. A more important factor in the "parallel" configuration is interference and contention for the prefetch buffers. For example, both the stream buffer and the Markov prefetcher may predict a specific, yet different address. These differing predicitons must contend for a small number of prefetch buffers and the limited memory bandwidth.

5.1 Limiting the Prefetch Bandwidth

In general, the increased need for bandwidth provides the greatest limitation to effective prefetcher implementations. The additional demand increases contention for the processor bus, possibly blocking demand fetches or later prefetched requests. We examined four techniques to improve the accuracy of the Markov prefetcher and thus reduce the bandwidth consumed by prefetching. Figure 7 shows the performance of these techniques using a variant of the previous presentations. In this figure, we show that fraction of subblock cache misses, where each sub-block is a four-byte word. In the group for each program, the first bar is for demand fetching, where no prefetching is used. Figure 7 indicates that $\approx$50% of the bandwidth for demand-fetched references is wasted, because the part of the data stored in the 32-byte cache line is not references. The second bar shows the same information for Markov prefetching, using four addresses predictors and an LRU prioritization policy. The third bar shows the bandwidth reduction that occurs when a simple "noise rejection" filter is used. This filter was proposed by Pomerene and Puzak [15] and also examined by Charney and Reeves [3]. It is similar to the filter used by Kessler [14] to improve the accuracy of stream buffers – a prefetch request is not dispatched until the prefetch pattern has been seen twice. The fourth column shows the performance for *accuracy based adaptivity*. In this scheme, two bit saturation counters are added to each prediction address, and a link back to the prediction address that was used to make a prefetch is added to each prefetch buffer entry. When a prefetch is discarded from the prefetch buffer without ever being used, the corresponding counter in the prediction address is incremented. When a prefetch in the prefetch buffer is used, the corresponding counter is decremented. When the sign bit of the counter is set, the associated prefetch address is disabled. Prefetch requests from disabled prefetches are placed in a "pseudo-prefetch buffer" so the predictions can be compared against actual prefetch requests, allowing a "disabled" prefetcher to become enabled once again. The fifth column shows the effect of using an automatic *cache-noallocate* (CNA) policy to reduce the portion of the cache line that is actually placed in the prefetch buffer. This design is based on the CNA mechanism of Tyson *et. al.* [16]. As in [16], we use a table of two bit counters to determine if a specific memory instruction should use a CNA policy. The prefetcher records information both about the predicted address and the instruction predicted to issue the memory reference. If that instruction is marked CNA, only the requested word, rather than the full cache line, is prefetched. The last bar in each group shows the effect of querying the L1-cache prior to prefetching. Some number of prefetch requests are already valid in the cache, but the external prefetch mechanism may not know that unless an external shadow tag table is used.

Of these techniques, only querying the L1 cache can be implemented as a completely external subsystem. The others require modifications to the prefetch mechanisms or interaction between the prefetcher and the processor. In general the CNA-based adaptivity provides the greatest performance improvement, but the CNA mechanism isn't directly applicable to the instruction cache. Instruction references tend to use most of a cache line, and techniques that either accept or reject and entire cache lines (such as the accuracy-based adaptivity) work better than the CNA method, which prefetches only a portion of the cache line. Figure 7 shows that the CNA mechanism changes the number of cache misses used as a "baseline" for some programs (G92, MM4 and Spice). The CNA mechanism improves the basic cache performance for MM4, but decreases the performance for G92 and SPICE. This is an artifact of the CNA bandwidth reduction technique [16].

5.2 Comparison Using a Memory-system Simulator

We have seen that the Markov predictor provides better prefetch coverage than the other prefetchers we examined. We used a memory-level simulator to determine if that improved coverage resulted in better performance for the memory subsystem. Our memory simulator models the contention for the system resources shown in Figure 1. In particular, we wanted to insure that the additional bandwidth consumed by the Markov prefetcher did not reduce the overall memory performance.

Figure 8(a) shows the memory CPI when different prefetchers are used for only the data cache and Figure 8(b) shows the memory CPI when prefetchers are used for the instruction and data caches. In each case, we used the accuracy-based adaptivity bandwidth filter for each Markov prefetcher. The correlation prefetcher uses the filter suggested by Charney and Reeves, and the stream buffers use the filter proposed by Kessler. From left-to-right, the individual bars indicate the performance of stream, stride, correlation and Markov prefetchers. The segments of each bar indicate the fraction of the overall MCPI attributed to individual parts of the memory system. From bottom to top, the segments indicates the delay due to fetching instructions into the L1 cache, fetching data into the L1 cache, fetching data into the L2 cache and the additional delay incurred by a pure demand-fetch model.

The Markov prefetcher provides the best performance across all the applications, particularly when applied to both the instruction and data caches. Recall that the correlation and Markov prefetchers require *fewer* resources than the stream and stride buffers – the Markov prefetcher used a 2MByte cache and a 1MByte prefetch table, *vs.* the 4MByte cache used in the demand-fetch model.

6 Conclusion

We have presented the Markov prefetcher, and simulated its performance over a number of significant applications. Although the Markov prefetcher can be characterized as an extension to the correlation prefetcher previously described by Pomerene and Puzak [15] and Charney and Reeves [3], there are a number of design issues presented by the Markov prefetcher. The prefetcher must be able to launch multiple prefetch requests and prioritize them, and the prefetcher must consider some mechanism to limit the bandwidth devoted to prefetching.

Our study has shown that a simple, effective and realizable Markov prefetcher can be built as an off-chip component of the memory subsystem. The design we present takes fewer resources than a normal demand-fetch cache, yet reduced the memory CPI

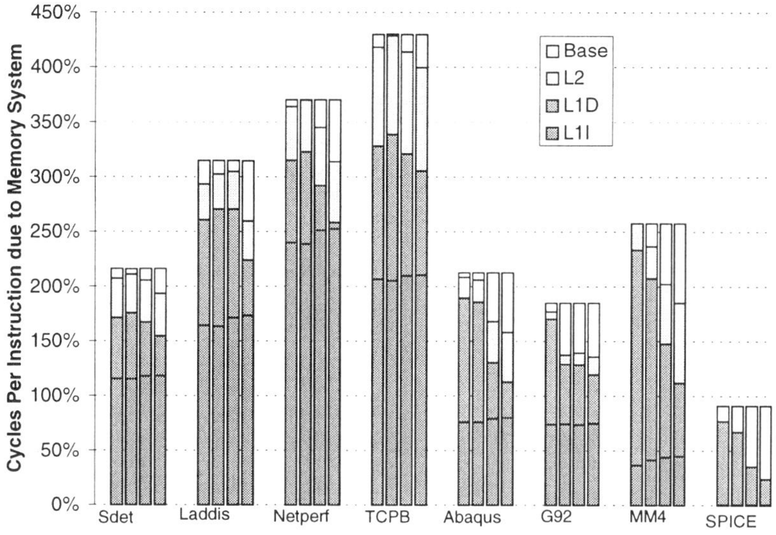

(b) Data and Instruction References

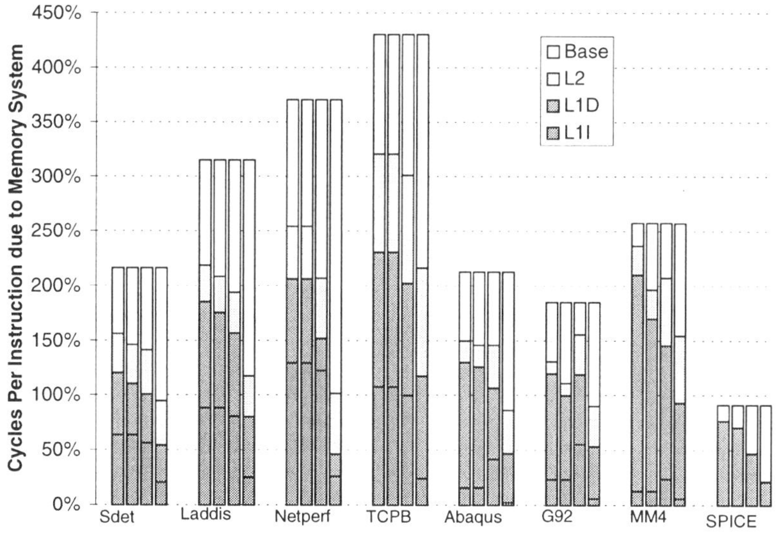

(b) Data and Instruction References

Figure 8: The average number of CPU stalls attributed to the memory subsystem (MPCI) when using different prefetchers for just the data references and both data and instructions. Across each application, the vertical bars indicate the MCPI for a demand-fetch model. From left-to-right, the individual bars indicate the performance of stream, stride, correlation and Markov prefetchers. The segments of each bar indicate the fraction of the overall MCPI attributed to individual parts of the memory system.

by an average of 54% over the applications we examined. The Markov prefetchers we examined provide better prefetch coverage and more timely prefetches than other prefetchers at the expense of reduce accuracy. However, the combination of bandwidth reduction filters and prioritization of the prefetch requests makes the Markov prefetcher the most effective prefetcher we examined.

There are a number of ways the Markov prefetcher can be improved. In particular, both the Markov and correlation prefetchers must observe a reference sequence prior to predicting references. It would be desirable to abstract a *reference pattern* from several instances of reference sequences. Likewise, it would be useful to have some mechanism to issue prefetch requests for patterns or sequences that have not yet occurred, eliminating the training period needed by the Markov predictor.

References

[1] T. Alexander and G. Kedem. Distributed predictive cache design for high performance memory system. In *Second International Symposium on High-Performance Computer Architecture*, Feb 1996.

[2] J.L. Baer. Dynamic improvements of locality in virtual memory systems. *IEEE Transactions on Software Engineering*, 2, March 1976.

[3] M.J. Charney and A.P. Reeves. Generalized correlation based hardware prefetching. Technical Report EE-CEG-95-1, Cornell University, Feb 1995.

[4] T.F. Chen and J.L. Baer. Reducing memory latency via non-blocking and prefetching caches. In *ASPLOS-V*, pages 51–61, Oct 1992.

[5] Z. Cvetanovic and D. Bhandakar. Characterization of alpha axp using tp and spec workloads. In *21th Annual International Symposium on Computer Architecture*, pages 60–70, April 1994.

[6] K.I. Farkas and N.P. Jouppi. Complexity/performance tradeoffs with non-blocking loads. In *21th Annual International Symposium on Computer Architecture*, pages 211–222, April 1994.

[7] N. Jouppi. Improving direct-mapped cache performance by the addition of a small fully associative cache and prefetch buffers. In *17th International Symposium on Computer Architecture*, May 1990.

[8] A.C. Klaiber and H.M. Levy. An architecture for software controlled data prefetching. In *18th International Symposium on Computer Architecture*, May 1991.

[9] M.H. Lipasti and et.al. Spaid: Software prefetching in pointer and call intensive enviornments. In *Proceedings of 28th Annual International Symposium on Microarchitecture*, pages 231–236, Nov 1995.

[10] A.M. Maynard, C.M. Donnelly, and B.R. Olszewski. Contrasting characteristics and cache performance of technical and multi-user commercial workloads. In *ASPOS-VI*, Apr 1994.

[11] S. Mehrota and H. Luddy. Examination of a memory access classification scheme for pointer-intensive and numeric programs. Technical Report CRSD tech report 1351, CRSD University of Illinois, Dec 1995.

[12] T.C. Mowry, M.S. Lam, and A. Gupta. Design and evaluation of a compiler algorithm for prefetching. In *ASPLOS-V*, pages 62–73, Oct 1992.

[13] T. Ozawa and et.al. Cache miss heuristics an preloading techniques for general-purpose programs. In *Proceedings of 28th Annual International Symposium on Microarchitecture*, pages 243–248, Nov 1995.

[14] S. Palacharla and R.E. Kessler. Evaluating stream buffers as a secondary cache replacement. In *21th Annual International Symposium on Computer Architecture*, pages 24–33, April 1994.

[15] J. Pomerene and et.al. Prefetching system for a cache having a second directory for sequentially accessed blocks. Technical Report 4807110, U.S. Patent Office, Feb 1989.

[16] Gary Tyson, Matt Farrens, and Andrew Pleszkun. A modified approach to data cache management. In *Proceedings of 28th Annual International Symposium on Microarchitecture*, pages 93–105, Nov 1995.

[17] Z. Zhang and T. Torrellas. Speeding up irregular applications in shared memory multiprocessors: Memory binding and group prefetching. In *22th Annual International Symposium on Computer Architecture*, pages 1–19, June 1995.

A.Benchmark Descriptions

The System Evaluation Corporation (SPEC SDM) suite includes two benchmarks: Sdet and Kenbus. Sdet is intended to represent a general purpose computing environment. A large number of users run concurrently with commands separated by little or no think time. Commands executed by the users include: edit, compile, bind, ksh, grep, ls, cp, rm and mkdir. The benchmark is run with multiple user levels to show throughput as a function of number of users. The benchmark is traced consists of 64 users and includes kernel, user and shared library activity.

The Laddis benchmark measures the capacity of a file server running NFS. It is essentially a re-packaging of the NHFSSTONES benchmark created by Legato Systems. It runs by having one or more client workstations submit NFS requests to the server. The requests must be completed with an average response time of 50 milliseconds. The benchmark was run using a single client with a load of 20 transactions per second, and six processes submitting requests.

The Netperf benchmark measures the performance of system communications. It important because it mimics interactive network environments, such as telnet, where response time is critical. As currently implemented Netperf provides a simple representation of interactive workloads and data xfers. The benchmark traced consisted of a single machine sending packets to it self. In this scenario a single one byte packet was "ping-ponged" between two processes 10,000 times. The metric was the latency of the transfers in elapsed time.

The Transaction Processing Performance Council (TPC) benchmarks are the best known and most frequently cited measures of commercial performance. The TPC is a collection of representatives from many system and database vendors. At the time of this writing the TPC has released three benchmarks called TPC-A, TPC-B and TPC-C, along with rules for running them and for reporting results. Although some simulations in this thesis research were executed with all three benchmarks, only one was selected for every test case: TPC-B. TPC-B simulates a banking application where users submit many simple debit or credit transactions from automated teller machines. The system is expected to respond within two seconds. The number of users and size of the database are scaled with the reported performance metric: transactions per second (TPS). For example, a system which reports a TPS rating of 80 would have a database roughly eight times as large as a system with a rating of 10. The benchmark used in this thesis was traced with 60 users in a client-server configuration.

Abaqus is a structural dynamics analysis product, like NASTRAN and ANSYS. This particular application is from the set of timing runs provided by HKS, Inc.. It is described as: "This is a large linear analysis consisting of a 40x40 mesh of shell elements of type S8R5. The total number of degrees of freedom is 39366; the maximum wavefront is 522 and the RMS wavefront is 503. Most of the time is spent in the inner loop in the solver, so that computers with fast vector processors should run this problem quickly."

G92 is a computational chemistry application from the Gaussian '92 Application Test Suite from Gaussian,Inc. Since the runtime of this test is about 8 minutes and consists of many processes (none running concurrently with the other), the tracing effort concentrated on user mode only of the top two processes: l703.exe and l1002.exe. These processes accounted for over 70% of the total runtime and almost 77% of the total user-mode runtime.

MM4 is a local-weather model owned by NOAA (National Oceanic and Atmospheric Administration). It uses Navier-Stokes equations to solve a finite element grid.

Spice is a floating point intensive electronic circuit simulation benchmark from the SPEC92 suite. Only the user activity was traced for this benchmark.

Data Prefetching on the HP PA-8000

Vatsa Santhanam, Edward H. Gornish and Wei-Chung Hsu
Hewlett-Packard Company
{vatsa,egornish,wei}@cup.hp.com

Abstract

Memory latency is a major issue for many modern microprocessor based systems, including the Hewlett-Packard PA-8000. Due to its fast clock rate and wide issue capability, cache misses in the PA-8000 are very expensive. The PA-8000 combines out-of-order execution with multiple outstanding memory requests to tolerate memory latency; however, this approach has its limitations. In order to substantially reduce much of the memory latency penalty, the PA-8000 uses software-based data cache prefetching. In this paper, we discuss the implementation of the data prefetch generation algorithm in the Hewlett-Packard Precision Architecture (HP-PA) compiler. We present performance results for SPECfp95 on a PA-8000 system that show speedups, due to data prefetching, of up to 100%.

1 Introduction

Memory latency has always been a major issue in high-performance systems. This is particularly true as the gap between processor and memory speeds continues to grow. The HP PA-8000 [Gwen94, Hunt95] is a 4-way superscalar microprocessor, and a 180MHz PA-8000 has a minimum memory latency of 50+ cycles. Conceivably, a cache miss can cause the processor to stall for the equivalent of over 200 (50*4) instructions!

Placing caches between processors and memory modules is an obvious first step towards reducing average memory latencies; however, caches alone are insufficient. Other hardware techniques, such as non-blocking caches [Krof81] and write buffers [Smit82], and software techniques, such as locality transformations [Wolf91] have also been used to reduce the memory latency penalty. Even with these methods, however, memory access stall time can still account for a large fraction of a program's execution. The HP PA-8000 uses a non-blocking cache, out-of-order execution and multiple outstanding cache misses to reduce some memory access stall time. Ultimately, however, this technique is limited by the size of the memory buffer (see Figure 1), and increasing the buffer size beyond a certain limit becomes impractical.

Data prefetching---moving data from a higher level of the memory hierarchy to a lower level of the memory hierarchy before the data is actually needed---is a method that can further reduce the memory latency penalty. There are two main classes of data prefetching. In hardware data prefetching [Smit82, Baer91], the hardware alone decides what data to prefetch and when and where to prefetch the data. In software data prefetching [Call91, Mowr92, Bern95], the compiler, or possibly the user, directs prefetching by inserting prefetch instructions into the code. The PA-8000 provides a software mechanism for prefetching a 32-byte block of data from main memory to the d-cache (i.e. a single cache line)[1]. The HP-UX 10.2 version of the HP-PA compilers implement a data prefetch generation algorithm, that is under the control of a compiler option. Performance results on a PA-8000 system show data prefetching speeding up programs by as much as 100%.

The remainder of this paper is organized as follows. Section 2 describes the features of the PA-8000 that are relevant to data prefetching. Section 3 discusses the architectural interactions of data prefetching on the PA-8000, using a simple program as an example. Section 4 describes the HP-PA compiler implementation of data prefetch generation and presents performance results for several facets of the compiler algorithm. Section 5 presents the overall performance impact of data prefetching. Finally, Section 6 presents our conclusions.

All the results shown in this paper were gathered on a 180MHz PA-8000 system, with a 1Mb data cache. Unless otherwise specified, each benchmark was compiled with the set of compiler options that yielded peak results for the individual benchmark.

2 PA-8000

Figure 1 shows a block diagram of the PA-8000. The PA-8000 is Hewlett-Packard's first processor to implement the new 64-bit PA-RISC 2.0 architecture [Kane96], which includes instructions defined for data cache prefetching. The PA-8000 is a 4-way superscalar processor, supporting out-of-order execution. As many as 28 Arithmetic and Logic Unit (ALU) instructions and 28 memory instructions can be in the process of execution, and up to 2 ALU and 2 memory instructions can be retired in a given cycle.

The PA-8000 has a direct-mapped, single-level data cache that may be up to 4Mb in size. Since this cache is off-chip, it is typically fairly large. The cache has a latency of 2 cycles. Cache misses in a 180MHz PA-8000 incur a minimum miss penalty of 50+ cycles, and the PA-8000 can support up to 10 outstanding cache misses. If a non-resident cache line is accessed multiple times, only one physical access to memory is actually generated. The PA-8000 processor and its memory are connected by the Runway bus: a synchronous, split-transaction, time multiplexed

1. The PA-8000 also employs hardware instruction cache prefetching, but this feature is not addressed in this paper.

ISCA '97 Denver, CO, USA

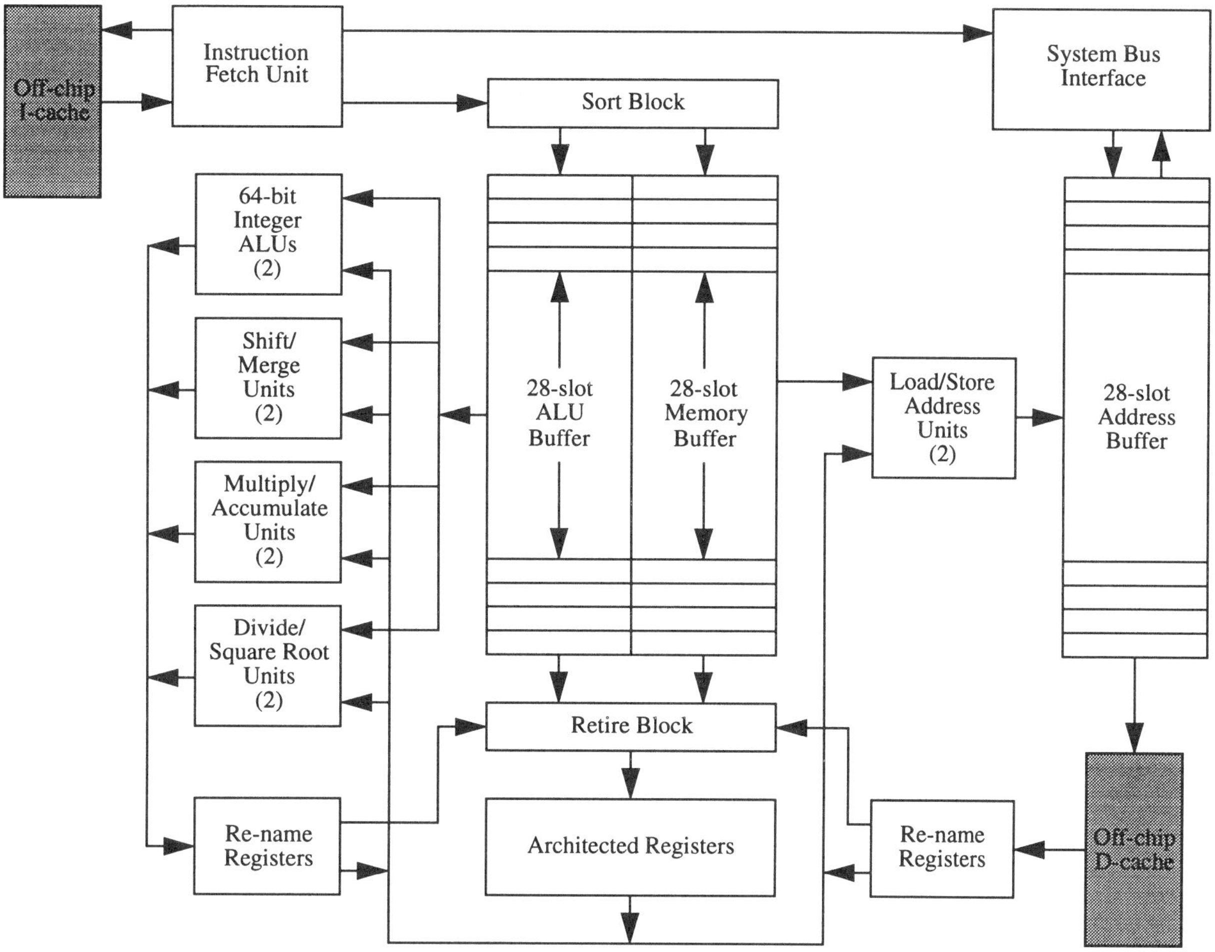

Figure 1: PA-8000 Block Diagram

address and data bus [Bryg96]. Running at 120 MHz, the Runway bus can sustain memory bandwidths of up to 768 Mbytes per second. The performance benefit of software prefetching would be limited without such a high bandwidth system bus.

Several features have been added to the PA2.0 architecture to support data prefetching. An ordinary load to general register zero is defined as a prefetch instruction, which brings the addressed line into the cache. Unlike ordinary loads, a load to general register zero can retire before a data cache miss it has initiated has been returned from memory. Prefetch instructions will not cause any traps. Both Load Word (LDW) and Load Word Indexed (LDWX) instructions can be used as prefetches. This flexibility allows the compiler to more efficiently generate prefetch instructions.

3 Software Directed Data Prefetching on the PA-8000

The PA-8000 integrates architecture (PA2.0), implementation (a non-blocking cache and a split transaction bus), and compiler optimizations (prefetch instruction insertion) into a real system. Some aspects of data prefetching research now can be verified on PA-8000-based systems. In this section, we use the simple loop in Example 1 to verify some traditional wisdom on software-directed data cache prefetching on the PA-8000 system. Using a simple loop makes the explanation of performance issues easier to understand. We will report the evaluation of software prefetching on the complete SPECfp95 suite in Section 5.

Example 1

```
subroutine example(X,Y,Z,B,n)
real *4 X(1), Y(1), Z(1), B
do i = 1, n
   X(i) = Y(i) + B*Z(i)
enddo
```

The loop shown in Example 1 is similar to a single precision saxpy. Arrays are declared in the main program with various sizes (and passed to the subroutine) in order to control cache hit/miss rate as well as cache/memory-bank conflicts. The executable is compiled at the default optimization level (O2), along with an option to turn on/off data prefetching related optimizations.

3.1 Prefetching Speedup

When the arrays are dimensioned sufficiently large enough to cause capacity misses in the 1MB d-cache, the prefetched version of the loop is 70% faster than the non-prefetched version. There are two loads, one FMAC (floating point multiply and accumulate) and one store instruction generated for each iteration of the loop. The best achievable performance for this loop is about 1.5 cycles per iteration assuming all latencies are hidden. The FMAC latency is relatively easy to hide, either by the PA-8000's out-of-order execution capability or by compiler instruction scheduling. Since a cache miss would cost 50+ cycles, and since there will be at least

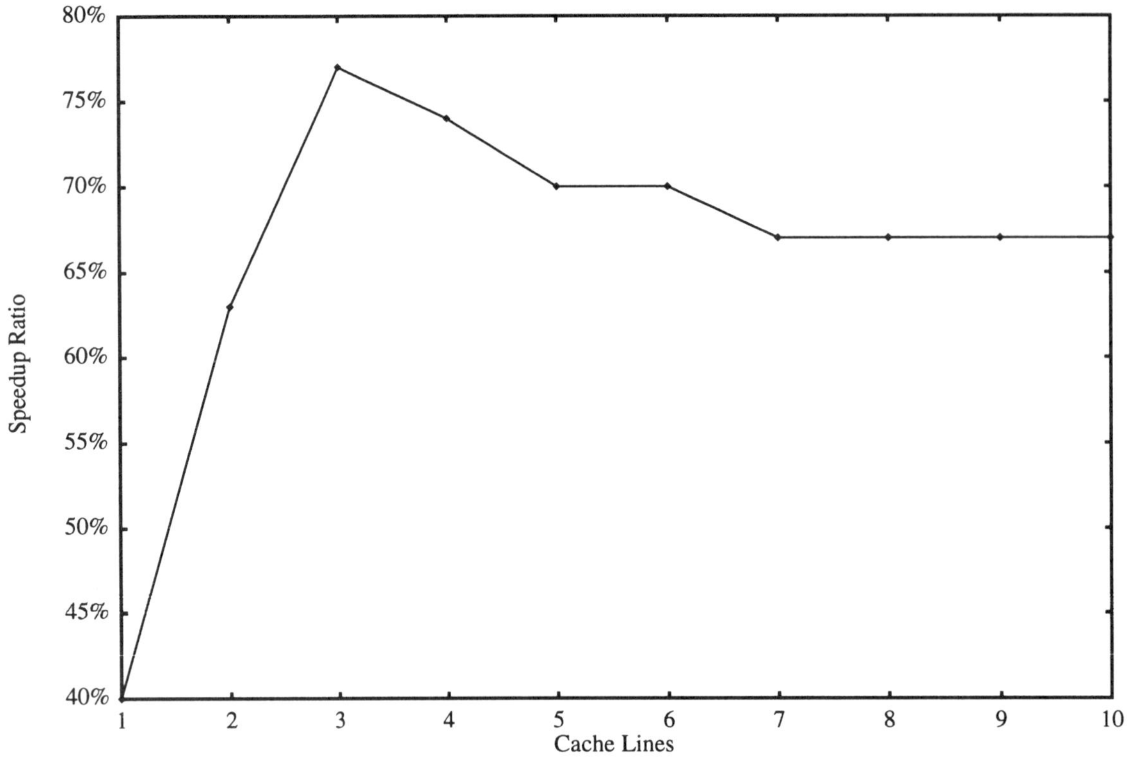

Figure 2: Speedup Ratio for Different Prefetch Distances

one cache miss per array every 8 iterations (4 bytes per access and the line size is 32 bytes), one may think the prefetched version could potentially be over 4 times faster (i.e. 50 / (1.5*8)). Therefore, is the 70% speedup too low?

First of all, the peak performance of 1.5 cycles per iteration will not be attained if all data reads and writes must come from or go to the memory. Each iteration will read 8 bytes and write 4 bytes. At 180 MHz, the memory bandwidth requirement would be 1.44GB per second, which exceeds the Runway bus's capacity (768MB per second). Hence the best execution time of each iteration will take about 3 cycles per iteration when all arrays have capacity misses.

Second, the PA-8000 can overlap multiple cache misses even without prefetch instructions. In our example, the 28-entry memory queue (Fig 1) in the PA-8000 can hold 9 loop iterations worth of memory operations (3 memory ops x 9= 27). When the three arrays all have capacity misses, there will be up to six cache misses comprising the 9 iterations worth of memory operations in the queue. The multiple cache misses in the same window will be processed in parallel because of the PA-8000's out-of-order execution and non-blocking cache design. Such overlap can significantly reduce clustered miss penalties. However, without prefetch instructions, the PA-8000 can only overlap cache misses simultaneously residing in the queue. When prefetch instructions are inserted, the PA-8000 can overlap cache misses beyond the 9-iteration window. This is because prefetch instructions do not stall the pipeline at retirement stage, allowing instructions to flow through the queue more smoothly. Such "cross window" miss overlap provides an additional 70% speed up for the example loop.

3.2 Prefetch Distance

The prefetch distance is generally computed as the memory latency divided by the estimated execution time of one iteration of the loop multiplied by the stride of a prefetched reference [Mowr92]. For our example, assuming one iteration latency is 1.5 cycles and a memory latency of 50 cycles, the suggested prefetch distance would be 132 bytes ((50/1.5)*4), which is about 4 cache lines in the PA-8000 system. Figure 2 shows the speedup ratio with different prefetch distances.

Since memory latency is usually non-deterministic, especially in a multi-processor, multiprogramming environment, one approach is to assume that memory latency will be greater than the minimum memory latency. This is a reasonable assumption since a cache miss return could be greatly delayed by insufficient memory/bus bandwidth and memory bank conflicts. If we assume that the memory latency is 70 cycles instead of 50, our formula would suggest a prefetch distance of 5 lines. However, as discussed in the previous section, the actual execution time will be greater than our optimistic estimation. So a more reasonable estimation that considers memory/bus bandwidth capacity, would yield 93 bytes ((70/3)*4), which is 3 lines. As shown in Figure 2, prefetching 3 lines ahead gives the best performance, and prefetching farther ahead yields less than optimal speedup.

One factor that has not been accounted in the formula is the degree of non-blocking -- the PA-8000 allows up to 10 outstanding misses. Once there are 10 outstanding misses, no further misses can be serviced until one of the outstanding misses has returned. For our example, prefetching four cache lines ahead accounts for more than 32 iterations, which will generate more than 10 outstanding misses. Hence prefetching farther than 3 lines exceeds the non-blocking degree, and results in no further performance gain.

3.3 Prefetch Instruction Minimization

In the compiler implementation, we try to maximize prefetch coverage of cache misses with minimal cost. For example, our compiler unrolls [Dong79] the example loop eight times and generates only one prefetch per cache line by exploiting *self-spatial locality* [Wolf91]. If we do not exploit this spatial locality, eight prefetches will be generated per cache line for each array. Table 1 shows the speedup ratio with/without minimizing prefetch instructions to exploit spatial locality.

	With cache capacity misses	With cache hits
With prefetch instruction minimization	70%	-13%
Without prefetch instruction minimization	70%	-55%

Table 1: Speedup with/without Prefetch Minimization

When all array references hit in the cache without prefetching, the generated prefetch instructions will consume valuable instruction and cache access bandwidth, while yielding no benefit. Thus, they degrade performance. In such cases, minimizing the number of prefetch instructions inserted is critical. For instance, the example loop shows that without prefetch minimization, the degradation could be as high as 55%. However, when there are intensive capacity misses, the performance of a prefetched code will be so dominated by memory bus bandwidth and other memory related resources that the extra prefetch instructions may be launched and retired for free. In such cases, prefetch minimization is not as critical. Since the compiler does not know exactly which loop will have intensive misses, it tries to minimize prefetch instructions for all loops.

3.4 Prefetch Instruction Scheduling

Since prefetch instructions have no direct consumers in the code stream and do not raise exceptions, they provide considerable freedom to the instruction scheduler. They are typically assigned lower scheduling priorities than most of the other instructions in the code stream. This tends to cause all the prefetch instructions to be placed close together in the final schedule - often times towards the end of basic blocks. Table 2 shows the speed up ratio if the scheduler evenly distributes prefetch instructions over the loop body rather than scheduling them in clumps.

	Scheduling prefetches in clumps	Spreading prefetches evenly
Speed up ratio	57%	70%

Table 2: Speedup Ratio with/without Prefetch Spreading

Table 2 indicates that spreading prefetches evenly has a significant performance advantage over traditional scheduling. This is because dirty misses incur additional overhead on the PA-8000. Specifically, the write-back triggered by a dirty miss makes the cache/memory interface unavailable for some number of cycles. A burst of dirty misses can delay the processing of subsequent cache misses. The loop in our example generates dirty misses frequently because the stores to array *X* make cache lines dirty. In a loop with data prefetching, most of the misses are generated by the prefetches, hence it is efficient to spread prefetches evenly throughout the loop body to ensure some room for such potential resource contention.

3.5 Prefetching and Conflict Misses

Conflict misses are particularly expensive on the PA-8000. Capacity misses and compulsory misses can often be overlapped because the cache is non-blocking. However, conflict misses need to be handled serially. When references to a pair of arrays thrash in the cache, prefetching may exacerbate the situation. Table 3 shows the relative performance for our loop when the three arrays are dimensioned to force conflict misses.

	With conflict Misses	Without conflict misses
Without prefetching	8.40	1.00
With prefetching	9.07	0.60

Table 3: Relative Execution Time with/without Conflict Misses

In Table 3, execution time of each case is normalized to the case having no conflict misses and no prefetching. With intensive conflict misses where all three arrays map to the same set of cache lines, the execution time slowed down by over 8 times. If prefetch instructions are also generated (and prefetches will also conflict with each other), the degradation increases to 9 times. The HP-PA compiler implements some array padding optimizations to avoid expensive conflict misses.

3.6 Prefetching and Memory Bank Conflicts

Memory bank conflicts will significantly increase the cache line return time. In a high performance cache based system, the memory is usually cache-line interleaved[1] to deliver high memory bandwidth. Assuming a 32-byte cache line size and an 8-way interleaved memory system, two cache misses separated by a multiple of 512 bytes will access the same memory bank. In this case, the second miss will be returned much later than the first miss. Table 4 shows the impact of memory bank conflict and its interaction with cache prefetching.

	With memory bank conflicts	Without memory bank conflicts
Without prefetch	1.32	1.00
With prefetch	0.95	0.60

Table 4: Relative Execution Time when Memory Bank Conflicts are Presented

In Table 4, execution time of each case is normalized to the case having no bank conflicts and no prefetching. With frequent bank conflicts, where all three arrays are allocated starting at the same memory bank, the execution time is slowed down by 32%. Prefetching is still effective but not as much as without bank conflicts.

1. The memory system in vector supercomputers is usually double word interleaved since vector computers are in general not cache based.

4 Compiler Implementation

The algorithm used to guide the insertion of explicit prefetch instructions in the production compilers for the PA-8000 systems is described below.

4.1 General Strategy

There are two main issues that need to be addressed in designing a compiler prefetch algorithm:

- Identifying the memory references that are candidates for explicit data prefetching.
- Reducing the prefetch overhead for the candidate memory references without sacrificing *prefetch coverage*[1].

Accurately identifying the memory references that may incur a d-cache miss (and are hence prefetch candidates) at compile-time is a very difficult task. Previous compiler algorithms have attempted to do this for memory references found in loops using heuristics based on the size of the data accessed in loop iterations compared to the d-cache size [Mowr92][Bern95]. However, often times, loop bounds are not known at compile-time, hindering accurate prediction of the volume of data that is accessed within loops, which in turn makes it difficult to identify the memory references that are prefetching candidates. This is borne out in Table 5 which indicates the percentage of innermost loops in the SPECfp95 suite that have compile-time constant loop bounds.

Benchmark	**% Innermost Loops With Constant Bounds**
101.tomcatv	0.0%
102.swim	0.0%
103.su2cor	13.2%
104.hydro2d	9.7%
107.mgrid	5.7%
110.applu	63.9%
125.turb3d	0.0%
141.apsi	0.8%
145.fpppp	22.2%
146.wave5	0.2%

Table 5: Innermost Loops with Constant Bounds

The approach adopted in the PA-8000 compilers for identifying prefetch candidates is to rely on a user-specified option to enable explicit data prefetching for memory references found in innermost program loops. All memory accesses found in innermost loops that specify an address with a uniform 'stride' are considered candidates for data prefetching when the +Odataprefetch compiler option is specified. The analysis performed to discover whether a memory reference specifies an address with a uniform stride is discussed below.

With regard to the second issue, our compiler algorithm performs simple re-use analysis based on the symbolic address expressions associated with the candidate memory references to avoid inserting redundant prefetch instructions. However, the algorithm inserts enough prefetch instructions to accommodate poor cache line alignment of candidate memory references. Loop unrolling [Dong79] is also performed by the compiler which tends to reduce prefetch overhead for memory references that exhibit *self-spatial locality*[Wolf91][2].

The compiler prefetch algorithm is implemented in the low-level optimizer of the production compilers for the PA-8000. Because the algorithm is focused on prefetching memory references found in loops, it is integrated with the loop optimization phase, which performs loop unrolling, dependence analysis, and register reassociation which exploits the addressing modes available on PA-RISC systems [Sant92]. Much of the symbolic memory address expression analysis performed by the loop optimization phase is leveraged by the prefetch algorithm.

4.2 Memory Address Analysis

The prefetch algorithm leverages the memory address expression analysis performed by the compiler. The address expressions feeding into memory references found in loops are traced back and re-expressed, if possible, as a simple linear function of a basic loop induction variable (BIV), of the form:

$$\text{memory address} = (\alpha \times \text{BIV}) + \beta$$

where the coefficient, α, and the addend, β, are loop invariant quantities that are reduced into a canonical *sum-of-products* representation. If the BIV is updated in constant steps of Δ on each loop iteration, the memory address is said to have a uniform stride of ($\alpha \times \Delta$) bytes. For example, in the FORTRAN code fragment shown in Example 2

Example 2

```
subroutine example (A)
real *4 A(10,10)
do i = 1, 9
   do j = 1, 10, 2
      A(i+1, j) = 0
   enddo
enddo
```

the symbolic address expression for the store in the loop would be represented as:

$$\text{address}[A(i+1,j)] = (40*j) + (4 * i) + 4 + A_{start}$$

where A_{start} represents the starting memory location of the array parameter A. In other words, $\alpha = 40$ and $\beta = (4*i + 4 + A_{start})$ and the BIV, j, would have a $\Delta = 2$, implying that the memory address has a stride of 40 x 2 = 80 bytes.

4.3 Loop Unrolling

Loop unrolling can help reduce the prefetch overhead for loops containing memory references with self-spatial locality. As discussed in Section 3.3, this can be an important performance factor when memory references actually hit in the cache.

In the PA compiler, loop unrolling is performed *before* the cache prefetch algorithm is invoked. The loop unroller determines the

1. Prefetch coverage refers to the percentage of dynamic candidate memory references that used to incur a d-cache miss, which actually benefit from explicit data prefetching (by experiencing fewer stall cycles).

2. A memory reference has *self-spatial locality* if multiple executions of that memory reference (e.g. in different loop iterations) access locations that map to the same cache line.

number of times to unroll innermost loops based on a variety of factors including the loop trip count (if it is a compile-time constant) and the size of the loop body. Cache prefetching needs are also considered in determining the loop unroll factor.

We tried to isolate the impact of loop unrolling on cache prefetch efficiency by comparing the observed performance for the benchmarks shown in Table 6 with loop unrolling enabled and the prefetch algorithm modified to always insert a separate prefetch instruction for every candidate memory reference (in effect forcing the algorithm to ignore cache locality of memory references altogether). The 6% improvement indicated in Table 6, exaggerates the improvement in prefetch efficiency due to loop unrolling since cache locality can be exploited to reduce prefetch overhead even when loop unrolling is not performed. However, for benchmarks that are already constrained by memory retirement bandwidth, loop unrolling clearly helps minimize the incremental prefetching overhead. Note that the 101.tomcatv benchmark is not limited by memory retirement bandwidth, and hence the prefetch overhead is negligible even without loop unrolling. The slight decrease in prefetching benefit caused by loop unrolling is due to the reduction in the number of prefetch instructions triggering different scheduling heuristics.

BENCHMARK	SPEEDUP
101.tomcatv	0.98
102.swim	1.04
103.su2cor	1.10
104.hydro2d	1.08
107.mgrid	1.04
110.applu	1.06
146.wave5	1.09
harmonic mean	1.06

Table 6: Data Prefetching Speedup Attributable to Loop Unrolling

4.4 Prefetch Iteration Distance

After loop unrolling, the prefetch iteration distance, PFID, which represents the number of loop iterations in advance to prefetch data, is computed based on the formula:

$$\text{PFID} = \left\lceil \frac{\text{average cache miss latency}}{\text{average latency per loop iteration}} \right\rceil$$

The average latency per loop iteration is estimated assuming that there is sufficient parallelism in the code stream to make resource utilization the determining factor. In the absence of loop carried dependencies, this is a reasonable estimate for an implementation such as the PA-8000 processor that can overlap instruction latencies through out-of-order execution. A lower-bound on the retirement cycles needed to complete a loop iteration is computed, based on this assumption, and this value is used as the loop iteration latency.

Figure 3 plots the relative speedup observed for some SPECfp95 benchmarks as the cache miss latency assumed by the compiler is varied. As the assumed miss latency is increased, the PFID computed increases proportionally. Figure 3 indicates that the performance impact of over-estimating the PFID is not very significant on the PA-8000. Prefetching data in advance beyond a certain point is ineffective due to the limitation on the number of outstanding memory requests that can be concurrently serviced. Moreover, a larger PFID results in a larger prefetch distance which increases the number of active prefetched lines in the d-cache. This in turn risks displacing data prematurely from the d-cache and can potentially degrade performance.

4.5 Memory Reference Classification

The prefetch candidate memory reference instructions in the (unrolled) loop are classified into disjoint partitions based on their symbolic address expressions. Two memory reference instructions are placed in the same partition if their respective address expressions are linear functions of the same BIV, with identical α values and β terms that differ by a known compile-time constant. Only memory references whose address expressions have a non-zero α value and whose BIV has a Δ value that is a compile-time constant are considered candidates for prefetching and hence placed in a partition.

Each partition is then analyzed independently to determine its prefetching needs. The memory references within a partition are sorted in increasing (or decreasing if $\Delta < 0$) order of their relative β terms to facilitate analysis.

Note that all memory references that are placed in a partition will have the same stride (given by: $\alpha \times \Delta$). The prefetch memory distance, PFMD, which is the number of bytes in advance to prefetch data, is computed for each partition as the product of the stride and the PFID, rounded up to an integral multiple of the cache line size.

4.6 Prefetches for Small Strides

If the stride for the memory references in a partition is no greater than the cache line size, then a fairly simple prefetching strategy is adopted. The memory references in such a partition are scanned in reverse sort order to identify *leading references*. If M_i and M_{i+1} are two consecutive memory references in a 'small-stride' partition, M_i is considered to be a leading reference if the absolute difference between the β terms for M_{i+1} and M_i exceeds PFMD. The memory reference in a small-stride partition with the largest relative β value is considered a leading reference by default.

A prefetch instruction is then generated for each leading reference in the small-stride partition. The memory address for the prefetch instruction is formed by summing the memory address specified by the leading reference with the PFMD for the small-stride partition.

4.6.1 Example

To better understand how prefetch instructions are generated for small-stride partitions, consider the FORTRAN code fragment in Example 3.

Example 3

```
subroutine smallStride(A)
real *8 A(100,100)
do i = 1, 99
   do j = 2, 99
      ...A(j-1,i)...        : reference M0
      ...A(j,i)...          : reference M1
      ...A(j,i+1)...        : reference M2
      ..A(j+1,i+1)...       : reference M3
   enddo
enddo
```

The inner loop contains four memory references, marked M0 through M3. All four of these memory references will be placed in

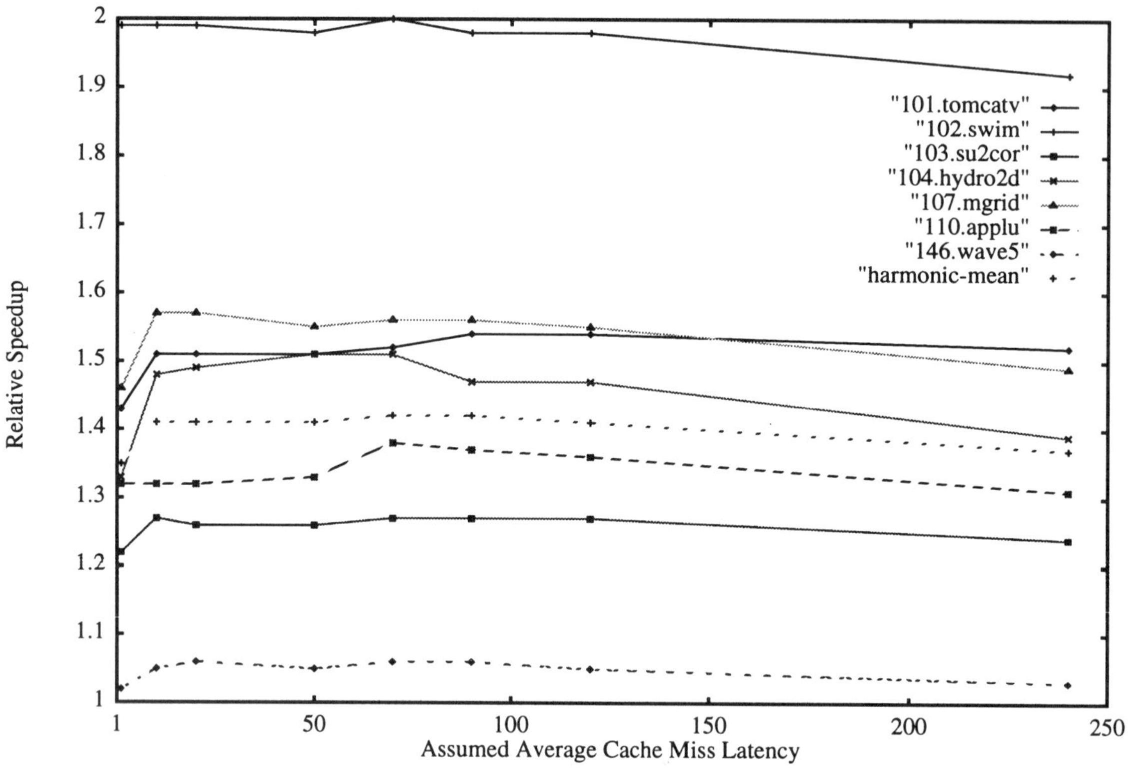

Figure 3: Relative Speedup for Different Assumed Average Cache Miss Latencies

the same partition, since their symbolic address expressions are linear functions of the same BIV (i.e. variable 'j'), and have an identical α value of 8. The stride for the partition members would be 8 bytes since the BIV has a unit increment. This partition would be considered to have a 'small' stride given 32-byte cache lines. The four memory references will be sorted in increasing order of their relative β terms into the sequence M0, M1, M2, M3. If we assume that the PFID was computed to be 16, then the PFMD for the partition would be 16 x 8 = 144 bytes, or 4 cache lines. Now, considering the partition members backwards starting with M3, we would end up identifying M3 and M1 as the leading references in the partition. Hence two prefetch instructions would be inserted into the code stream, that prefetch the cache lines containing the array elements A(j+17,i+1) and A(j+16,i).[1]

4.7 Prefetches for Large Strides

The analysis to determine the prefetch instructions needed for a partition with a stride that is larger than the cache line size is complicated by the need to account for poor cache line alignment of data references. This issue is illustrated by Example 4.

1. One could argue that for this example, prefetching A(j+16,i) is unnecessary, since the corresponding cache line would have been fetched into the d-cache on the previous iteration of the outer i-loop. However, that line may be displaced from the cache in the interim. Our algorithm takes the conservative approach of generating two prefetches.

Example 4

```
subroutine largeStride(A)
real *8 A(100,100)
do i = 1, 99
   do j = 1, 100
      ...A(i,j)...          : reference M0
      ...A(i+1,j)...        : reference M1
   enddo
enddo
```

For this example, both memory references M0 and M1 will be placed in the same partition, and have a stride of 800 bytes which far exceeds a 32-byte cache line size. If we applied the simple leading reference identification algorithm described earlier, only M1 would be classified as a leader and a single prefetch instruction would be accordingly generated. In general, this may not ensure full prefetch coverage. Specifically, if cache lines are not re-used across iterations of the outer i-loop, on every fourth iteration of the outer i-loop, the M0 and M1 references would straddle a cache-line boundary. When this is the case, the prefetch corresponding to the M1 reference will not bring in the cache line needed by the M0 reference in later iterations of the inner j-loop (for a given iteration of the i-loop). In this case the M0 reference could potentially incur a cache-miss on every iteration of the inner j-loop.

To ensure full prefetch coverage for memory references with strides greater than the cache line size, a separate two-pass algorithm is used to generate prefetch instructions for partitions with 'large strides.'

The first pass sub-divides the memory references in a large-stride partition into smaller groups called *clusters* where the memory references in each cluster exhibit group spatial locality. A group of memory references, M0, M1...Mn that are adjacent in a large-stride partition are placed in the same cluster provided that the difference in the β terms between the *cluster leader,* Mn, and the cluster trailer, M0, is no greater than the stride. In addition, no pair of adjacent memory references within the cluster are allowed to have a β difference greater than the cache line size.

The intent of identifying clusters in this manner is to then insert prefetch instructions that are offset from the cluster leader and spaced a cache-line apart from each other, spanning down to the cluster trailer. This avoids prefetch coverage loss regardless of the relative cache line alignment of the memory references within the cluster. Now if we define the *span* of a cluster, represented as C_s, to be the difference in the β terms of the cluster leader and cluster trailer, and if L is the cache line size, the number of prefetch instructions, C_p, required for a cluster can be computed as

$$C_p = \lceil C_s / L \rceil + 1$$

Before inserting prefetch instructions for each cluster in the manner described above, the second pass of the algorithm is invoked to exploit group temporal locality *across* clusters in a large-stride partition. If two adjacent clusters in a large-stride partition are less than PFMD apart (measured as the difference in the β terms of the leading cluster's trailing memory reference and the trailing cluster's leading memory reference), then we may consider *merging* the two clusters to reduce the aggregate number of the prefetch instructions required for the two clusters. To merge a trailing cluster into a leading cluster, we project the span of the trailing cluster forwards in increments of the memory stride (but no more than PFID times), until we achieve maximum overlap with the span of the leading cluster. Merging two clusters, C^i and C^{i+1}in this way into a single cluster, C^m is deemed profitable only if $C^m{}_p <= (C^i{}_p + C^{i+1}{}_p)$. If this is the case, the merged cluster's span is adjusted based on the extent of the overlap between the projected trailing cluster's span and the leading cluster's span. The trailing cluster is removed from the partition and the merged cluster is re-considered for further merging with other leading clusters in the partition.

Finally, prefetch instructions are generated for each of the remaining clusters in a large-stride partition. If a cluster spans over β terms ranging from β_T through β_L then the prefetch instructions that are generated for the cluster would specify the following memory addresses, where L represents the cache line size (which is subtracted from the prefetch address if the stride is positive and added otherwise):

$$(\alpha \times BIV) + \beta_L + PFMD$$
$$(\alpha \times BIV) + \beta_L + PFMD -/+ L$$
$$(\alpha \times BIV) + \beta_L + PFMD -/+ (2xL)$$
$$\vdots$$
$$(\alpha \times BIV) + \beta_T + PFMD$$

4.7.1 Example

The prefetching algorithm for large-stride partitions can be better understood by considering Example 5.

Example 5

```
subroutine largeStride2(A)
real *8 A(100,100)
do i = 1, 99
   do j = 2,99
      ...A(i+1,j-1)...      : reference M0
      ...A(i-1,j)...        : reference M1
      ...A(i,j+1)...        : reference M2
   enddo
enddo
```

References M0, M1, and M2 each have a large stride (800 bytes) and will be placed in the same partition. Again assuming a cache line size of 32-bytes, M0, M1, and M2 will each be placed in a different cluster, say respectively, C0, C1, and C2 by the first-pass of our algorithm. The second-pass of the algorithm will proceed by merging cluster C0 into C1 by projecting C0 ahead one j-loop iteration. The merged cluster would span from the address of A(i+1,j) down to the address of A(i-1,j). This merged cluster would then be merged into C2, yielding a single merged cluster for the entire partition that spans from the address of A(i+1,j+1) down to the address of A(i-1,j+1). Since the span of this merged cluster is 16-bytes which is less than the cache line size (32-bytes), only 2 prefetch instructions would be needed for the partition. If the PFID is computed to be 4, then the memory addresses that get prefetched would correspond to A(i+1,j+5) and A(i-1,j+5). Note that without the cluster merging pass, we would have had to insert 3 prefetch instructions instead of 2.

4.8 Extensions

In the PA-8000 production compiler, the prefetch generation algorithm has been extended to handle prefetching memory references in loops with control-flow as well as memory references with strides that are not compile-time constants. Based on profile information that's either heuristically generated or fed back from previous runs of the application, only those memory references whose execution frequencies exceed half the innermost loop iteration count are considered prefetching candidates. If the innermost loop trip count is relatively low, data prefetching is also performed for memory references located in the enclosing outer loop.

For run-time dimensioned array references in FORTRAN, the stride may not be a compile-time constant. In such cases, to facilitate the locality analysis, the run-time variables in the stride expression are assumed to be large values. The PFMD is computed symbolically to determine the addresses specified by the prefetch instructions.

4.9 Instruction Scheduling

As explained in Section 3.4, scheduling prefetch instructions in clumps can reduce the effectiveness of data prefetching when the prefetch instructions cause dirty misses.Table 7 shows the speedup obtained when the prefetches are spread apart in the generated schedule. The performance speedup is as high as 10% in at least one benchmark (110.applu), and, overall, the improvement is 3% for these benchmarks that benefit from prefetching.

BENCHMARK	SPEEDUP
101.tomcatv	1.03
102.swim	1.04
103.su2cor	1.01
104.hydro2d	1.02
107.mgrid	1.01
110.applu	1.10
146.wave5	1.02
harmonic mean	1.03

Table 7: Data Prefetching Speedup Attributable to Prefetch Spreading

4.10 Prefetching And Array Padding

The relative alignment of array variables can significantly impact the performance of a program due to cache and memory bank conflicts as illustrated in Section 3.5 and Section 3.6. In the PA-8000 compiler, the +Ocachepadcommon option adjusts the separation between arrays in FORTRAN common blocks to alleviate this problem[1]. This option is beneficial by itself for the 102.swim benchmark, which suffers from memory bank conflicts, but also improves the effectiveness of prefetching.

Table 8 shows the performance speedup for this benchmark when compiled with and without cache prefetching and common block padding enabled. Both padding and prefetching individually improve 102.swim's performance. However, when combined, the performance speedup clearly exceeds the sum of the individual performance contributions. These results correlate with the results shown in Table 4. In Table 4, prefetching was somewhat effective even though there were memory bank conflicts. However, when the memory bank conflicts were removed, prefetching effectiveness significantly increased.

102.swim	No Padding	Padding
No Prefetching	1.00	1.25
Prefetching	1.39	2.51

Table 8: Speedup Due to Data Prefetching and Cache Padding of Commons

5 Overall SPECfp95 Results

The middle column of Table 9 shows the speedups due to data prefetching for the SPECfp95 suite on a PA-8000. The results indicate that data prefetching is a very effective technique. There are only three benchmarks that do not benefit from prefetching, and only in 125.turb3d is there any significant performance degradation. This benchmark contains sufficient interprocedural data reuse. Hence, many unnecessary prefetches are generated causing significant instruction overhead.

Recall that prefetch generation is controlled by a user option. This implies that any performance degradations for an application caused by data prefetching can be regained, simply by not requesting prefetching. The right most column of Table 9 shows the prefetching speedups using this latter approach. As can be seen, the harmonic means are higher when we disable data prefetching for benchmarks where it degrades performance.

BENCHMARK	SPEEDUP	SPEEDUP (assuming no degradation)
101.tomcatv	1.52	1.52
102.swim	2.00	2.00
103.su2cor	1.27	1.27
104.hydro2d	1.50	1.50
107.mgrid	1.56	1.56
110.applu	1.38	1.38
125.turb3d	0.75	1.00
141.apsi	0.98	1.00
145.fpppp	1.00	1.00
146.wave5	1.06	1.06
harmonic mean	1.21	1.26

Table 9: Data Prefetching Speedup for SPECfp95

6 Conclusions and Future Directions

To more effectively utilize high-speed systems, it is necessary to provide methods for coping with high memory latencies. To this end, the HP PA-8000 provides support for data cache prefetching, coupled with out-of-order execution and support for multiple outstanding memory requests. A prefetch generation algorithm has been implemented in the HP-PA production compiler. When compiling with prefetch generation enabled, we are able to obtain speedups of 26% for the SPECfp95 benchmark suite and up to 100% for some SPECfp95 programs. This integration of architecture, micro-architecture, and compiler optimizations in PA-8000 systems has shown to be very effective in reducing the cost of cache misses.

In this paper we focused on data prefetching for numerical programs. Data prefetching for non-numerical programs introduces new complexities and is an area for future research. This area has been addressed in the context of pointer-based applications containing recursive data structures [Luk96].

Future micro-processors are more likely to employ multi-level cache hierarchies, for example, a fast on-chip cache plus a large off-chip cache. In order to support software prefetching more effectively, processor architectures should include provisions in memory operations for the compiler to direct prefetching in a multi-level cache hierarchy.

7 References

[Baer91] Baer, J. L. and T. F. Chen, "An Effective On-Chip Preloading Scheme to Reduce Data Access Penalty," *Supercomputing*, pp. 176—186, 1991.

[Bern95] Bernstein, David, Doron Cohen and Ari Freund, "Compiler Techniques for Data Prefetching on the PowerPC," *PACT-95.*

[Bryg96] Bryg, W. R., et al., "A High-Performance, Low-Cost Multiprocessor Bus for Workstations and Midrange Servers," *Hewlett-Packard Journal*, February, 1996.

1. The high-level optimizer, which is enabled at optimization level 3, pads large local arrays to avoid cache conflicts even without the +Ocachepadcommon option.

[Call91] Callahan, D., Ken Kennedy and Allan Porterfield, "Software Prefetching,", *Proceedings of the Fourth International Conference on Architectural Support for Programming Languages and Operating Systems*, pp. 40—52, 1991.

[Dong79] Dongarra, J. J. and A. R. Hinds, "Unrolling Loops in FORTRAN," *Software—Practice and Experience* 9, 3, pp. 219—226, March 1979.

[Gwen94] Gwennap, Linley, "PA-8000 Combines Complexity and Speed," *Microprocessor Report* 8, 15, pp. 5—9, November 1994.

[Hunt95] Hunt, D. "Advanced Performance Features of the 64-bit PA-8000," *COMPCON* '95 Digest of Papers, pp. 123—128, March 1995.

[Kane96] Kane, Gerry, PA-RISC 2.0 Architecture, ISBN 0-13-182734-0, *Prentice-Hall*, Englewood Cliffs, NJ, 1996.

[Krof81] Kroft, D. "Lockup-free Instruction Fetch/Prefetch Cache Organization," *International Symposium on Computer Architecture*, pp. 81—87, 1981.

[Luk96] Luk, Chi-Keung and Todd C. Mowry, "Compiler-Based Prefetching for Recursive Data Structures," *Proceedings of the Seventh International Conference on Architectural Support for Programming Languages and Operating Systems,* pp. 222—233, September 1996.

[Mowr92] Mowry, T. C., Monica S. Lam and Anoop Gupta, "Design and Evaluation of a Compiler Algorithm for Prefetching," *Proceedings of the Fifth International Conference on Architectural Support for Programming Languages and Operating Systems*, pp. 62—73, September 1992.

[Sant92] Santhanam, V., "Register Reassociation in PA-RISC Compilers, *Hewlett-Packard Journal*, vol. 43, pp. 33—38, June 1992.

[Smit82] Smith, A. J., "Cache Memories," *Computing Surveys*, vol. 14, pp. 473—530, September 1982.

[Wolf91] Wolf, M. E. and Monica S. Lam, "A Data Locality Optimizing Problem," *Proceedings of the SIGPLAN '91 Conference on Programming Language Design and Implementation*, pp. 30—44, June 1991.

Target Prediction for Indirect Jumps

Po-Yung Chang Eric Hao Yale N. Patt

Department of Electrical Engineering and Computer Science
The University of Michigan
Ann Arbor, Michigan 48109-2122
email: {pychang,ehao,patt}@eecs.umich.edu

Abstract

As the issue rate and pipeline depth of high performance superscalar processors increase, the amount of speculative work issued also increases. Because speculative work must be thrown away in the event of a branch misprediction, wide-issue, deeply pipelined processors must employ accurate branch predictors to effectively exploit their performance potential. Many existing branch prediction schemes are capable of accurately predicting the direction of conditional branches. However, these schemes are ineffective in predicting the targets of indirect jumps achieving, on average, a prediction accuracy rate of 51.8% for the SPECint95 benchmarks. In this paper, we propose a new prediction mechanism, the target cache, for predicting indirect jump targets. For the perl and gcc benchmarks, this mechanism reduces the indirect jump misprediction rate by 93.4% and 63.3% and the overall execution time by 14% and 5%.

1 Introduction

As the issue rate and pipeline depth of high performance superscalar processors increase, the amount of speculative work issued also increases. Because speculative work must be thrown away in the event of a branch misprediction, wide-issue, deeply pipelined processors must employ accurate branch predictors to effectively exploit their performance potential.

A program's branches can be categorized as conditional or unconditional and direct or indirect, resulting in four classes. A conditional branch conditionally redirects the instruction stream to its target whereas an unconditional branch always redirects the instruction stream to its target. A direct branch has a statically specified target which points to a single location in the program whereas an indirect branch has a dynamically specified target which may point to any number of locations in the program. Although these branch attributes can combine into four classes, only three of the classes – conditional direct, unconditional direct, and unconditional indirect – occur with significant frequency.

In the past, branch prediction research has focused on accurately predicting conditional and unconditional direct branches [11, 7, 15, 6, 2, 8]. To predict such branches, the prediction mechanism predicts the branch direction (for unconditional branches, this part is trivial) and then generates the target associated with that direction. To generate target addresses, a branch target buffer (BTB) is used. The BTB stores the fall-through and taken address for each branch. For indirect jumps, the taken address is the last computed target for the indirect jump. (For a jump-to-subroutine, the fall-through address is needed so that it can be pushed onto the return address stack, even though the jump-to-subroutine will never jump to the fall-through address.) Unfortunately, BTB-based prediction schemes perform poorly for indirect branches. Because the target of an indirect branch can change with every dynamic instance of that branch, predicting the target of an indirect branch as the last computed target for that branch will lead to poor prediction accuracy. Figures 1 through 8 show the number of different dynamic targets seen for each indirect branch in the SPECint95 benchmarks. Table 1 lists the indirect branch target misprediction counts achieved by a 1K-entry 4-way set-associative BTB for the SPECint95 benchmarks. For gcc and perl, the two benchmarks with significant numbers of indirect branches, the misprediction rates for indirect branches were 66.0% and 76.4%.

In this paper, we propose a new prediction mechanism, the target cache, for predicting the targets of indirect jumps[1]. The target cache uses a concept central to the 2-level branch predictor: branch history is used to distinguish different dynamic occurrences of each indirect branch. When fetching an indirect jump, the fetch address and the branch history are used to form an index (A) into the target cache. The target cache is then accessed for the indirect jump. Later, when the indirect branch retires, the target cache is accessed again using index A, and the computed target for the indirect jump is written into the target cache. As the program executes, the target cache records the target for each indirect jump target encountered. When fetching an indirect jump,

[1] Although return instructions technically are indirect jumps, they are not handled with the target cache because they are effectively handled with the return address stack [13, 4].

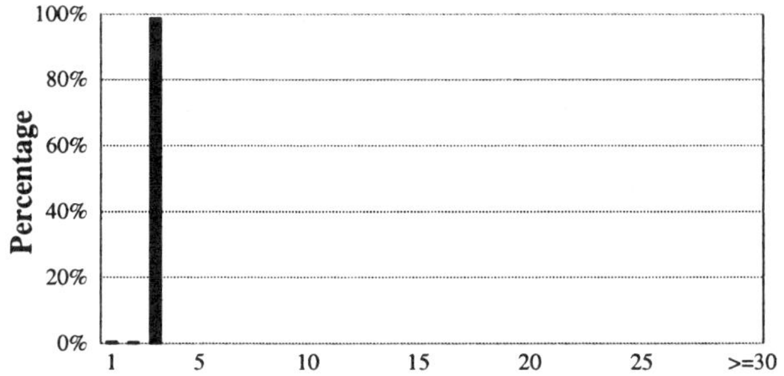

Figure 1: Number of Targets per Indirect Jump (compress)

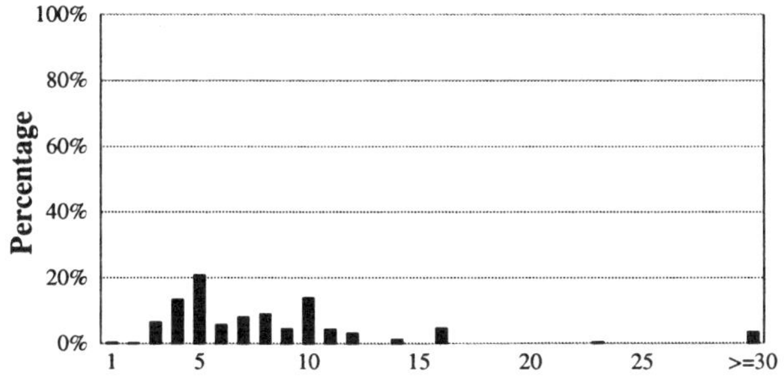

Figure 2: Number of Targets per Indirect Jump (gcc)

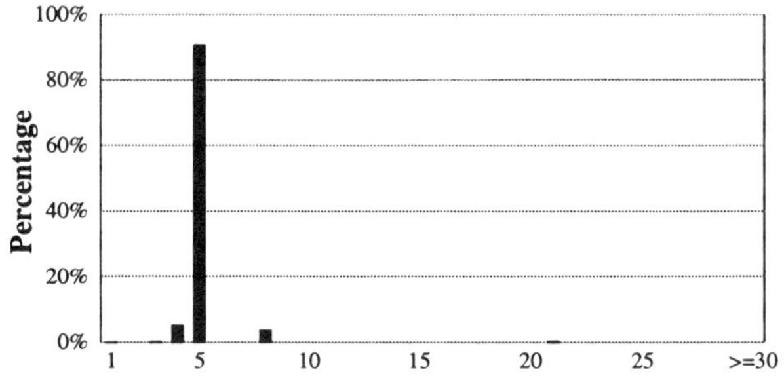

Figure 3: Number of Targets per Indirect Jump (go)

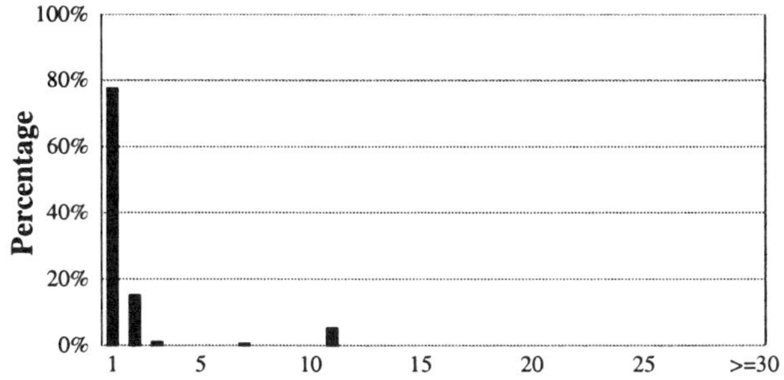

Figure 4: Number of Targets per Indirect Jump (ijpeg)

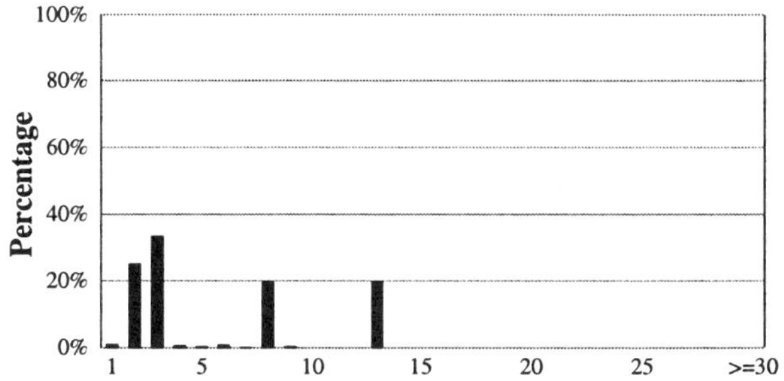

Figure 5: Number of Targets per Indirect Jump (m88ksim)

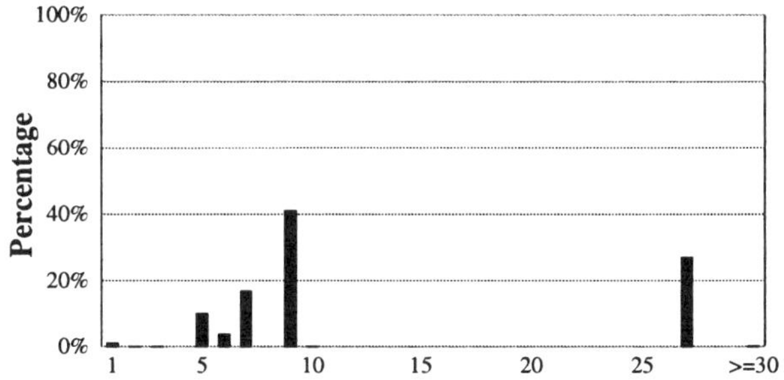

Figure 6: Number of Targets per Indirect Jump (perl)

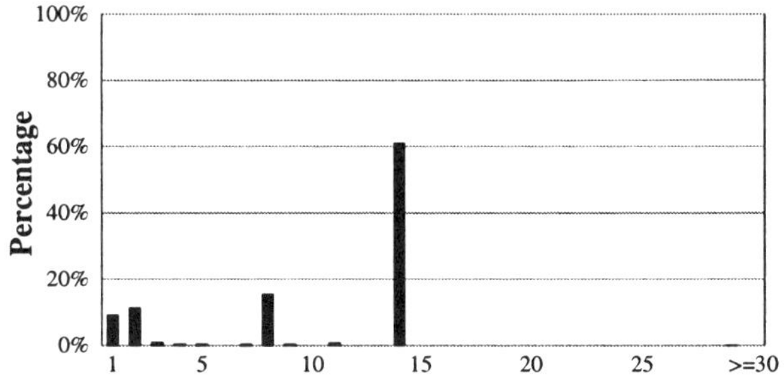

Figure 7: Number of Targets per Indirect Jump (vortex)

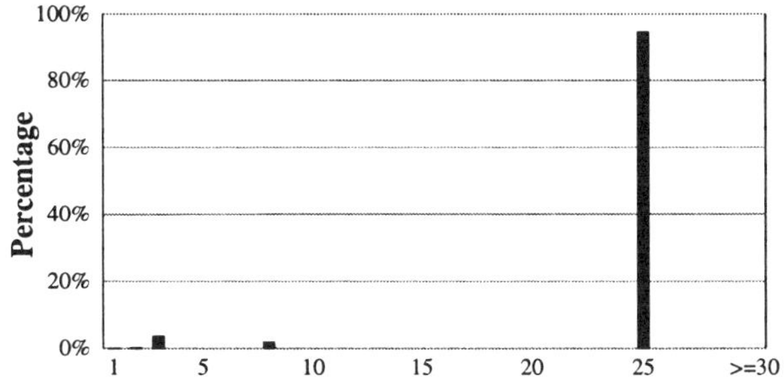

Figure 8: Number of Targets per Indirect Jump (xlisp)

Benchmark	Input	#Instructions	#Branches	#Indirect Jumps	Ind. Jump Mispred. Rate
compress	test.in[2]	125,162,687	17,460,753	590	61.7%
gcc	jump.i	172,328,834	35,979,748	939,417	66.0%
go	2stone9.in[3]	125,637,006	23,378,150	173,719	37.6%
ijpeg	specmun.ppm[4]	206,802,135	23,449,572	103,876	14.3%
m88ksim	dcrand.train.big	131,732,141	23,840,021	186,285	37.3%
perl	scrabbl.pl[5]	106,140,733	16,727,047	588,136	76.4%
vortex	vortex.in[6]	236,081,621	44,635,060	243,706	11.3%
xlisp	train.lsp	192,569,022	40,909,525	114,789	80.7%

Table 1: Misprediction counts for indirect jumps in the SPECint95 benchmarks

the target cache is accessed with the fetch address and the branch history to produce the predicted target address. The target cache improves on the prediction accuracy achieved by BTB-based schemes for indirect jumps by choosing its prediction from (usually) all the targets of the indirect jump that have already been encountered rather than just the target that was most recently encountered. We will show that for the perl and gcc benchmarks, a target cache can reduce the indirect jump misprediction rate by 93.4% and 63.3% and the overall execution time by 14% and 5%.

This paper is organized into five sections. Section 2 discusses related work. Section 3 introduces the concept of a target cache. Section 4 shows the performance benefits of target caches. Section 5 provides some concluding remarks.

2 Related Work

To address the problem of target prediction for indirect jumps in C++ programs, Calder and Grunwald proposed a new strategy, the 2-bit strategy, for updating BTB target addresses [1]. The default strategy is to update the BTB on every indirect jump misprediction, Calder and Grunwald's 2-bit strategy does not update a BTB entry's target address until two consecutive predictions with that target address are incorrect. This strategy was shown to achieve a higher target prediction accuracy than that achieved by the default strategy.

The 2-bit strategy is not very successful in predicting the targets of indirect branches in C programs such as the SPECint95 benchmarks. Table 2 compares the indirect branch target misprediction rate achieved by a 1K entry, 4-way set-associative BTB that uses the 2-bit strategy to that achieved by an identically configured BTB that uses the default target update strategy. The 2-bit strategy reduced the misprediction rates for the compress, gcc, ijpeg, and perl benchmarks, but increased the misprediction rates for the m88ksim, vortex, and xlisp benchmarks. The target prediction scheme proposed by this paper, the target cache, has significantly lower indirect jump misprediction rates than those achieved by the 2-bit strategy. For example, a 512-entry target cache achieve the misprediction rates of 30.4% and 30.9% for gcc and perl respectively.

Benchmark	Misprediction Rate	
	BTB	2-bit BTB
compress	61.7%	44.4%
gcc	66.0%	64.1%
go	37.6%	36.4%
ijpeg	14.3%	9.36%
m88ksim	37.3%	38.1%
perl	76.4%	67.5%
vortex	11.3%	14.6%
xlisp	80.7%	85.4%

Table 2: Performance of 2-bit BTB

Kaeli et al. proposed a hardware mechanism, the case block table (CBT), to speed up the execution of SWITCH/CASE statements [5]. Figure 9 gives an example of a SWITCH/CASE statement and the corresponding assembly code for that statement. The assembly code consists of a series of conditional branches that determine which case of the SWITCH/CASE statement is to be executed. Because a single variable, the case block variable, specifies the case to be executed, this series of conditional branches can be avoided if the instruction stream could be directly redirected to the appropriate case. The CBT enables this redirection by recording, for each value of the case block variable, the corresponding case address. This mapping of case block variable values to case addresses is dynamically created. When a SWITCH/CASE statement is encountered, the value of the case block variable is used to search the CBT for the next fetch address. In effect, the CBT is dynamically generating a jump table to replace the SWITCH/CASE statements.

The study done by Kaeli et al. showed that an oracle CBT, that is, a CBT which always selects the correct case to execute, can reduce significantly the number of conditional branches in the instruction stream. However, the CBT's usefulness is limited by two factors. First, modern day compilers are capable of directly generating jump tables for SWITCH/CASE statements at compile-time, eliminating the need for the CBT to generate the tables dynamically.

[2] Abbreviated version of the SPECint reference input set bigtest.in. The initial list consists of 30000 elements.

[3] Abbreviated version of the SPECint training input set 2stone9.in using 19 levels instead of 50 levels.

[4] Abbreviated version of the SPECint test input set specmun.ppm where the compression quality is 50 instead of 90.

[5] Abbreviated version of the SPECint reference input set.

[6] Abbreviated version of the SPECint test input set. PART_COUNT = 100 and LOOKUPS = DELETES = STUFF_PARTS = 10

```
High-Level
Construct                  Assembly Code
----------                 -------------

switch(v) {                    r1 <- compare v, 1
 case 1:                       beq r1, L1
                                ; beq == branch if equal
   char = 'a';                 r1 <- compare v, 2
   break;                      beq r1, L2
 case 2:                       r1 <- compare v, 3
   char = 'b';                 beq r1, L3
   break;                      goto L4
 case 3:                   L1: char <- 'a'
   char = 'c';                 goto L5
   break;                  L2: char <- 'b'
 default:                      goto L5
   char = 'd';             L3: char <- 'c'
}                              goto L5
                           L4: char <- 'd'
                           L5:
```

Figure 9: An Example of a SWITCH/CASE Construct

Second, for processors with out-of-order execution, the value of the case block variable is often not yet known when the instruction corresponding to the SWITCH/CASE statement is fetched. As a result, the CBT cannot redirect the instruction stream to the appropriate case until that value is computed.

The target cache proposed in this paper has some similarities to the CBT. Like the CBT, the target cache dynamically records the case addresses for a program's SWITCH/CASE statements. However, the target cache differs from the CBT in two significant ways. First, the purpose of the target cache is to accurately predict the target of the indirect jumps used to implement the jump tables, not to dynamically construct jump tables. The target cache assumes that the compiler has generated jump tables for the SWITCH/CASE statements. Second, the target cache was designed for highly speculative machines, where the value of the case block variable is likely to be unknown when the prediction is made; therefore, a branch history is used to make the prediction instead.

3 Target Cache

The target cache improves on the prediction accuracy achieved by BTB-based schemes for indirect jumps by choosing its prediction from (usually) all the targets of the indirect jump that have already been encountered rather than just the target that was most recently encountered. When fetching an indirect jump, the target cache is accessed with the fetch address and other pieces of the machine state to produce the predicted target address. As the program executes, the target cache records the target for each indirect jump target encountered.

3.1 Accessing Target Cache

In our study, we consider using branch history along with the branch address to index into the target cache. Two types of branch history information are used to decide which target of the indirect jump will be predicted – pattern history and path history.

- **Branch History**

  It is now well known that the 2-level branch predictor improves prediction accuracy over previous single-level branch predictors [14]. The 2-level predictors attain high prediction accuracies by using pattern history to distinguish different dynamic occurrences of a conditional branch. To predict indirect jumps, the target cache is indexed using branch address and global pattern history. Global pattern history is a recording of the last n conditional branches. No extra hardware is required to maintain the branch history for the target cache if the branch prediction mechanism already contains this information. The target cache can use the branch predictor's branch history register.

- **Path History**

  Previous research [16, 8] has shown that path history can also provide useful correlation information to improve branch prediction accuracy. Path history consists of the target addresses of branches that lead to the current branch. This information is also useful in predicting indirect branch targets.

  In this study, two different types of path history can be associated with each indirect jump – global or per-address. In the per-address scheme, one path history register is associated with each distinct static indirect branch. Each n-bit path history register records the last k target addresses for the associated indirect jump. That is, when an indirect branch is resolved, n/k bits from its target address are shifted into the path history register.

  In the global scheme, one path history register is used for all indirect branches. Because the history register has a fixed length, it can record a limited number of branches in the past history. Thus, the history register may be better utilized by only recording a particular type of branch instruction. For example, if a sequence of conditional branches is sufficient to distinguish the different paths of each indirect jump, then there is no need to include other types of branches in the path history. Four variations of the global scheme were considered – `Control`, `Branch`, `Call/ret`, `Ind jmp`. The `Control` scheme records the target address of all instructions that can redirect the instruction stream. The `Branch` scheme only records the targets of conditional branches. The `Call/ret` scheme records only the targets of procedure calls and returns. The `Ind jmp` scheme records only the targets of indirect jumps.

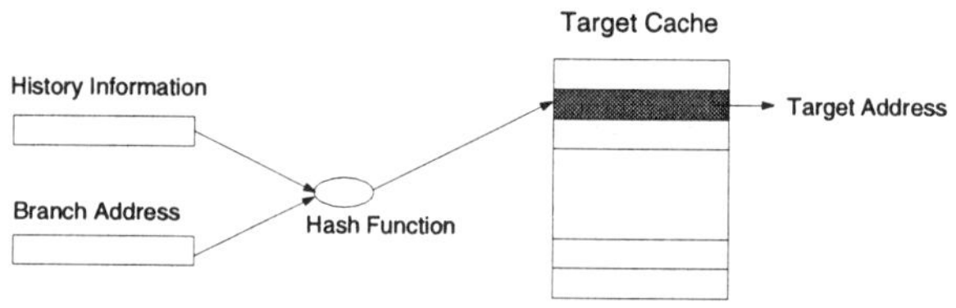

Figure 10: Structure of a Tagless Target Cache

3.2 Target Cache Structure

In addition to varying the type of information used to access the target cache, we also studied tagged and tagless target caches.

- **Tagless Target Cache**

  Figure 10 shows the structure of a tagless cache. The target cache is similar to the pattern history table of the 2-level branch predictor; the only difference is that a target cache's storage structure records branch targets while a 2-level branch predictor's pattern history table records branch directions.

  The target cache works as follows: during instruction fetch, the BTB and the target cache are examined concurrently. If the BTB detects an indirect branch, then the selected target cache entry is used for target prediction. When the indirect branch is resolved, the target cache entry is updated with its target address.

  Several variations of the tagless target cache can be implemented. They differ in the ways that branch address and history information are hashed into the target cache. For example, the branch address can be XORed with the history information for selecting the appropriate entry. Section 4 will describe the different hashing schemes considered.

- **Tagged Target Cache**

  Like the previous 2-level branch predictors, interference occurs in the target cache when a branch uses an entry that was last accessed by another branch. Interference is particularly detrimental to the target cache because each entry in the target cache stores the branch target address. Since the targets of two different indirect branches are usually different, interference will most likely cause a misprediction.

  To avoid predicting targets of indirect jumps based on the outcomes of other branches, we propose the tagged target cache where a tag is added to each target cache entry (see Figure 11). The branch address and/or the branch history are used for tag matching. When an indirect branch is fetched, its instruction address and the associated branch history are used to select the appropriate target cache entry. If an entry is found, the instruction stream is redirected to the associated target address.

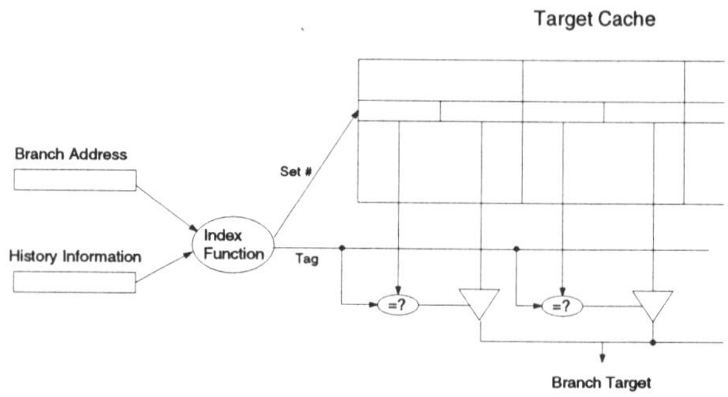

Figure 11: Structure of a Tagged Target Cache

4 Results

4.1 Experimental Methodology

The experimental results presented in this paper were measured by trace-driven simulations using an instruction level simulator. The benchmarks simulated were the SPECint95 benchmarks and they were all simulated to completion. Table 1 (see Section 1) lists the input data set used for each benchmark and the dynamic instruction counts. We will concentrate on the gcc and perl benchmarks, the two benchmarks with the largest number of indirect jumps.

The machine model simulated is the HPS microarchitecture [9] [10]. HPS is a wide-issue out-of-order execution machine, using Tomasulo algorithm for dynamic scheduling [12]. Checkpointing [3] is used to maintain precise exceptions. Checkpoints are established for each branch; thus, once a branch misprediction is determined, instructions from the correct path are fetched in the next cycle.

The HPS processor simulated in this paper supports 8 wide issue with a perfect instruction cache and a 16KB data cache. Latency for fetching data from memory is 10 cycles. Table 3 shows the instruction classes and their simulated execution latencies, along with a description of the instructions that belong to that class. In the processor simulated, each functional unit can execute instructions from any of the instruction classes. The maximum number of instructions that can exist in the machine at one time is 128. An instruction is considered in the machine from the time it is issued until it is retired.

Instruction Class	Exec. Lat.	Description
Integer	1	INT add, sub and logic OPs
FP Add	3	FP add, sub, and convert
FP/INT Mul	3	FP mul and INT mul
FP/INT Div	8	FP div and INT div
Load	2	Memory loads
Store	-	Memory stores
Bit Field	1	Shift, and bit testing
Branch	1	Control instructions

Table 3: Instruction classes and latencies

4.2 Tagless Target Cache

This section examines the performance of tagless target caches. The size of every target cache considered in this section is 512 entries. Since the BTB has 256 sets and is 4-way set-associative, the target cache increases the predictor hardware budget by 10 percent. The cost of the predictor is estimated using the following equations:

$$\begin{aligned} \text{BTB}^{\dagger} &= 77 \times 2048 \ \texttt{bits} \\ \text{target cache}(n) &= 32 \times n \ \texttt{bits} \\ \text{predictor budget} &= \text{BTB} + \text{target cache}(n) \ \texttt{bits} \end{aligned}$$

where n is the number of target cache entries.

4.2.1 Hashing Function

With the tagless schemes, branch history information and address bits are hashed together to select the appropriate target cache entry. An effective hashing scheme must distribute the cache indexes as widely as possible to avoid interference between different branches.

Table 4 shows the performance benefit of tagless target caches using different history information for indexing into the storage structure. The GAg(9) scheme uses 9 bits of branch pattern history to select the appropriate target cache entry. In the GAs schemes, the target cache is conceptually partitioned into several tables. The address bits are used to select the appropriate table and the history bits are used to select the entry within the table. The GAs(8,1) scheme uses 8 history bits and 1 address bit while the GAs(7,2) scheme uses 7 history bits and 2 address bits. For the perl benchmark, GAg(9) outperforms GAs(8,1), showing that branch pattern history provides marginally more useful information than branch address. This is because the perl benchmark executes only 22 static indirect jumps. On the other hand, GAs(8,1) is competitive with GAg(9) for the gcc benchmark, a benchmark which executes a large number of static indirect jumps. In the gshare scheme, the branch address is XORed with the branch history to form the target cache index. Like the previous 2-level branch predictors, the gshare scheme outperforms the GAs scheme because it effectively utilizes more of the entries in the target cache. In the following sections, we will use the gshare scheme for tagless target caches.

†each BTB entry consists of 1 valid bit, 2 least-recently-used bits, 23 tag bits, 32 target address bits, 2 branch type bits, 4 fall-thru address bits, and 13 branch history bits.

Perl		
config	Misprediction Rate	Reduction in Exec. Time
gshare(9)	30.9%	8.92%
GAg(9)	31.2%	8.87%
GAs(8,1)	33.4%	8.36%
GAs(7,2)	48.1%	5.17%
Gcc		
config	Misprediction Rate	Reduction in Exec. Time
gshare(9)	30.4%	4.27%
GAg(9)	35.8%	3.61%
GAs(8,1)	35.7%	3.62%
GAs(7,2)	36.7%	3.48%

Table 4: Performance of Pattern History Tagless Target Caches

4.2.2 Branch Path History: Tradeoffs

Path history consists of the target addresses of branches that lead to the current branch. Ideally, each path leading to a branch should have a unique representation in the path history register. However, since only a few bits from each target are recorded in the path history register, different targets may have the same representation in the path history. When this occurs, the path history may not be able to distinquish between different paths leading to a branch. Thus, the performance of a path based target cache depends on the address bits from each target used to form the path history. Table 5 shows that the lower address bits provide more information than the higher address bits. In the following experiments, the least significant bits from each target are recorded in the path history register; the 2 least significant bits from each address are ignored because instructions are aligned on word boundaries.

Because the length of the history register is fixed, there is also a tradeoff between identifying more branches in the past history and better identifying each branch in the past history. Increasing the number of bits recorded per address results in fewer branch targets being recorded in the history register. Table 6 shows the performance of target caches

Perl					
addr bit no.	Reduction in Execution Time				
	Per-addr	Global			
		branch	control	ind jmp	call/ret
2	7.64%	7.41%	4.70%	12.36%	8.45%
3	10.09%	6.85%	3.41%	11.00%	9.75%
4	5.52%	5.97%	4.88%	10.50%	9.97%
5	7.34%	9.13%	4.31%	9.24%	10.82%
7	6.17%	6.89%	4.22%	11.34%	11.16%
10	6.19%	6.60%	3.94%	12.82%	10.42%
15	1.87%	2.98%	2.30%	10.97%	9.92%
20	0.00%	0.00%	0.00%	0.00%	0.00%
Gcc					
addr bit	Reduction in Execution Time				
	Per-addr	Global			
		branch	control	ind jmp	call/ret
2	2.57%	3.82%	3.75%	2.68%	2.52%
3	2.46%	3.71%	3.81%	2.63%	2.24%
4	2.67%	3.88%	3.63%	2.69%	2.80%
5	2.02%	3.75%	3.82%	2.37%	2.63%
7	2.60%	3.57%	3.76%	2.72%	2.98%
10	1.34%	3.24%	3.14%	1.83%	2.60%
15	0.01%	1.05%	0.78%	1.06%	1.56%
20	-0.02%	0.26%	0.14%	0.24%	0.78%

Table 5: Path History: Address Bit Selection

Perl					
bits	Reduction in Execution Time				
per	Per-addr	Global			
addr		branch	control	ind jmp	call/ret
1	7.64%	7.41%	4.70%	12.36%	8.45%
2	9.17%	3.12%	0.88%	11.81%	8.40%
3	7.19%	0.30%	0.74%	10.99%	6.24%
Gcc					
bits	Reduction in Execution Time				
per	Per-addr	Global			
addr		branch	control	ind jmp	call/ret
1	2.57%	3.82%	3.75%	2.68%	2.52%
2	2.96%	2.60%	2.21%	3.35%	2.66%
3	3.57%	2.02%	1.66%	3.83%	2.63%

Table 6: Path History: Address Bits per Branch

using different numbers of bits from each target in the path history. In general, with nine history bits, the performance benefit of the target cache decreases as the number of address bits recorded per target increases. This is especially true for the `Control` and `Branch` schemes. With the `Control` scheme, we record the target of all instructions that can redirect the instruction stream, which may include branches that provide little or no useful information, e.g. unconditional branches. Each of these uncorrelated branches takes up history bits, possibly displacing useful history. As a result, the performance benefit of the `Control` scheme drops even more significantly when the number of bits to be recorded for each target increases from 1 to 2; for perl, the reduction in execution time dropped from 4.7% to 0.9%.

4.2.3 Pattern History vs. Path History

Table 4 and Table 6 show that using pattern history results in better performance for gcc and using global path history results in better performance for perl. Using the `Indirect Jmp` scheme, the execution time for perl was reduced by 12.34%, as compared to 8.92% for the best pattern history scheme. The branch path history was able to perform extremely well for the perl benchmark because it is an interpreter. The main loop of the interpreter parses the the perl script to be executed. This parser consists of a set of indirect jumps whose targets are decided by the tokens (i.e. components) which make up the current line of the perl script. The perl script used for our simulations contains a loop that executes for many iterations. As a result, when the interpreter executes this loop, the interpreter will process the same sequence of tokens for many iterations. By capturing the path history in this situation, the target cache is able to accurately predict the targets of the indirect jumps which process these tokens.

4.3 Tagged Target Caches

This section examines the performance of tagged target caches. While the degree of associativity was varied, the total size of each target cache simulated was kept constant at 256 entries. The tagged target caches have half the number of entries as that of tagless target caches to compensate for the hardware used to store tags.

4.3.1 Indexing Function

Since there can be several targets for each indirect branch and each target may be reached with a different history, a large number of target cache entries may be needed to store all the possible combinations. Thus, the indexing scheme into a target cache must be carefully selected to avoid unnecessary trashing of useful information.

Three different indexing schemes were studied – **`Address`**, **`History Concatenate`**, and **`History Xor`**. The **`Address`** scheme uses the lower address bits for set selection. The higher address bits and the global branch pattern history are XORED to form the tag. The **`History Concatenate`** scheme uses the lower bits of the history register for set selection. The higher bits of the history register are concatenated with the address bits to form the tag. The **`History Xor`** scheme XORs the branch address with the branch history; it uses the lower bits from the result of the XOR for set selection and the higher bits for tag comparison. Table 7 shows the performance of the different indexing schemes. Global pattern history is used in these experiments. The **`Address`** selection scheme results in a significant number of conflict misses in target caches with a low degree of set-associativity because all targets of an indirect jump are mapped to the

Perl			
	Reduction in Exec Time		
	Addr	History	
set-assoc.		Conc	Xor
1	0.00%	8.31%	7.42%
2	0.21%	8.30%	7.24%
4	2.76%	8.71%	7.76%
8	6.82%	9.11%	7.73%
16	8.67%	9.14%	8.17%
32	8.67%	9.14%	8.20%
64	9.10%	9.14%	8.10%
128	9.06%	9.14%	8.10%
256	8.10%	9.14%	8.10%
Gcc			
	Reduction in Exec Time		
	Addr	History	
set-assoc.		Conc	Xor
1	0.00%	3.51%	3.56%
2	0.30%	3.85%	3.92%
4	1.27%	4.01%	4.13%
8	2.54%	4.19%	4.24%
16	3.48%	4.30%	4.28%
32	4.22%	4.32%	4.30%
64	4.16%	4.38%	4.31%
128	4.26%	4.52%	4.31%
256	4.31%	4.59%	4.31%

Table 7: Performance of Tagged Target Cache using 9 pattern history bits

same set. Since there are several targets for each indirect jump for gcc and perl as shown in Section 1, a high degree of set-associativity is required to avoid trashing of useful information due to conflict misses. The `History Concatenate` and `History Xor` schemes suffer a much smaller number of conflict misses because they can map the targets of an indirect jump into any set in the target cache, removing the need for a high degree of associativity in the target cache.

In the following sections, we will use the `History Xor` scheme for tagged target caches.

4.3.2 Pattern History vs. Path History

Table 8 shows the performance of tagged target caches that use branch path histories. The path history schemes reported in this section record one bit from each target address into the 9-bit path history register. This design choice resulted in the best performance for most of the path history schemes. As in the tagless schemes, using pattern history results in better performance for gcc and using global path history results in better performance for perl.

Perl					
	Reduction in Execution Time				
set assoc	Per-addr	Global			
		branch	control	ind jmp	call/ret
1	7.13%	6.20%	2.98%	10.71%	7.59%
2	8.20%	6.34%	4.15%	11.62%	7.91%
4	9.15%	7.21%	4.30%	12.29%	7.91%
8	9.46%	7.21%	4.70%	13.38%	8.79%
16	9.69%	7.21%	4.70%	13.78%	8.69%
32	9.77%	7.21%	4.70%	13.97%	8.83%
64	9.77%	7.21%	4.70%	14.14%	8.78%
128	9.77%	7.21%	4.70%	14.15%	8.98%
256	9.77%	7.21%	4.70%	14.15%	8.66%
Gcc					
	Reduction in Execution Time				
set assoc	Per-addr	Global			
		branch	control	ind jmp	call/ret
1	2.45%	3.28%	2.88%	2.15%	2.07%
2	2.72%	3.35%	3.28%	2.46%	2.25%
4	2.90%	3.59%	3.58%	2.65%	2.42%
8	3.01%	3.73%	3.55%	2.76%	2.56%
16	3.05%	3.76%	3.58%	2.86%	2.58%
32	3.11%	3.76%	3.59%	2.90%	2.63%
64	3.12%	3.77%	3.59%	2.92%	2.64%
128	3.14%	3.79%	3.57%	2.92%	2.65%
256	3.14%	3.79%	3.57%	2.94%	2.65%

Table 8: Performance of Tagged Target Caches using 9 path history bits

4.3.3 Branch History Length

For tagged target caches, the number of branch history bits used is not limited to the size of the target cache because additional history bits can be stored in the tag fields. Using more history bits may enable the target cache to better identify each occurrence of an indirect jump in the instruction stream.

Table 9 compares the performance of 256-entry tagged target caches using different numbers of global pattern history bits. For caches with a high degree of set-associativity, using more history bits results in a significant performance improvement. For example, when using 16 history bits, an 8-way tagged target cache reduces the execution time of perl and gcc by 10.27% and 4.31% respectively, as compared to 7.73% and 4.28% when using 9 history bits. Greater improvements are seen for caches with higher set associativity. For a 16-way tagged target cache, using 16 history bits results in 12.66% and 4.74% reduction in execution time for perl and gcc while using 9 history bits results in 8.17% and 4.28% reduction in execution time.

For target caches with a small degree of set-associativity, using more history bits degrades performance. Using more history bits enables the target cache to better identify each occurrence of an indirect jump in the instruction stream; however, more entries are required to record the different occurrences of each indirect jump. The additional pressure on the target cache results in a significant number of conflict misses. The performance loss due to conflict misses outweighs the performance gain due to better identification of each indirect jump.

Perl		
	Reduction in Exec Time	
set-assoc.	9 bits	16 bits
1	7.42%	7.07%
2	7.24%	8.39%
4	7.76%	10.02%
8	7.73%	10.27%
16	8.17%	12.66%
32	8.20%	12.71%
64	8.10%	12.83%
128	8.10%	12.84%
256	8.10%	12.85%
Gcc		
	Reduction in Exec Time	
set-assoc.	9 bits	16 bits
1	3.56%	2.35%
2	3.92%	2.99%
4	4.13%	3.62%
8	4.24%	4.31%
16	4.28%	4.74%
32	4.30%	4.87%
64	4.31%	5.11%
128	4.31%	5.19%
256	4.31%	5.24%

Table 9: Tagged Target Cache: 9 vs 16 pattern history bits

4.4 Tagless Target Cache vs Tagged Target Cache

A tagged target cache requires tags in its storage structure for tag comparisons while a tagless target cache does

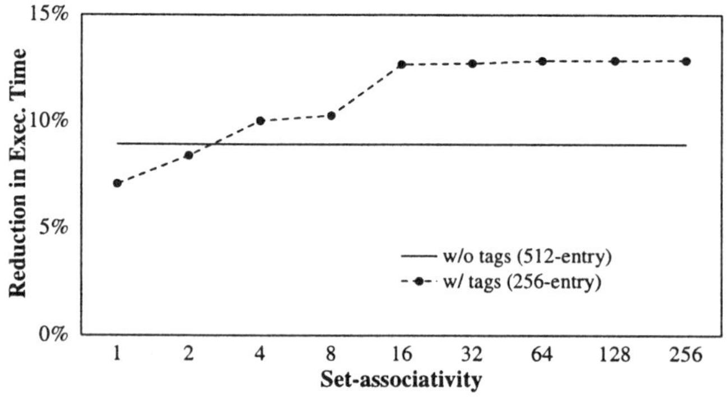

Figure 12: Tagged vs. tagless target cache – perl

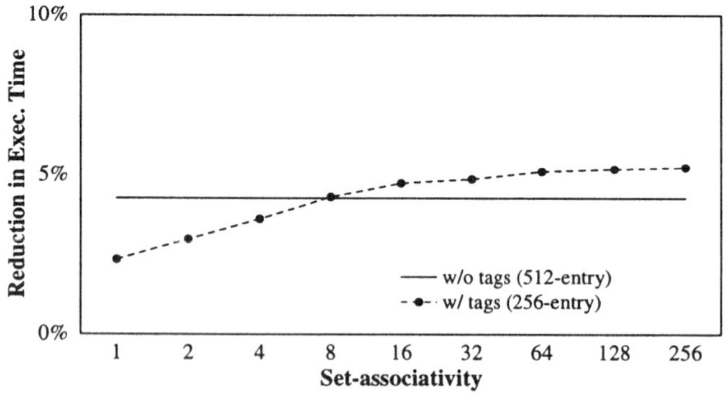

Figure 13: Tagged vs. tagless target cache – gcc

not. Thus, for a given implementation cost, a tagless target cache can have more entries than a tagged target cache. On the other hand, interference in the storage structure can degrade the performance of a tagless target cache.

Figures 12 and 13 compare the performance of a 512-entry tagless target cache to that of several 256-entry target caches, with various degrees of set-associativity. The tagless target cache outperforms tagged target caches with a small degree of set-associativity. On the other hand, a tagged target cache with 8 or more entries per set outperforms the tagless target cache.

5 Conclusions

Current BTB-based branch prediction schemes are not effective in predicting the targets of indirect jumps. These schemes have a 48% misprediction rate for the indirect jumps in the SPEC95 integer benchmarks. To address this problem, this paper proposes the target cache, a prediction mechanism that significantly improves the accuracy of predicting indirect jump targets. The target cache uses concepts embodied in the 2-level branch predictor.

By using branch history to distinguish different dynamic occurrences of indirect branches, the target cache was able to reduce the total execution time of perl and gcc by 8.92% and 4.27% respectively.

Like the pattern history tables of the 2-level branch predictors, interference can significantly degrade the performance of a target cache. To avoid predicting targets of indirect jumps based on the outcomes of uncorrelated branches, tags are added to the target cache. However, with the tagged target cache, useful information can be displaced if different branches are mapped to the same set. Thus, set-associative caches may be required to avoid mispredictions due to conflict misses.

Our experiments showed that a tagless target cache outperforms a tagged target cache with a small degree of set-associativity. On the other hand, a tagged target cache with 8 or more entries per set outperforms a tagless target cache. For example, a 512-entry tagless target cache can reduce the execution time of perl and gcc by 8.92% and 4.27% respectively, as compared to 7.42% and 3.56% for a direct mapped 256-entry tagged target cache. A 16-way set-associative tagged target cache can reduce the execution of gcc and perl by 12.66% and 4.74% respectively.

We examined the SPEC95 integer benchmarks where only a small fraction of instructions are indirect branches; e.g. 0.5% in gcc and 0.6% in perl. For object oriented program where more indirect branches may be executed, tagged caches should provide even greater performance benefits. In the future, we will evaluate the performance benefit of target caches for C++ benchmarks.

6 Acknowledgments

We gratefully acknowledge the support of our industrial partners, without which it would not have been possible to undertake this work, in particular Intel Corporation. In addition, we wish to gratefully acknowledge the other members of our HPS research group for the stimulating environment they provide, in particular, Marius Evers, Sanjay Patel and Jared Stark for their comments and suggestions on this work.

References

[1] Brad Calder and Dirk Grunwald. Reducing indirect function call overhead in c++ programs. In *Proceedings of the 6th International Conference on Architectural Support for Programming Languages and Operating Systems*, 1994.

[2] Po-Yung Chang, Eric Hao, Tse-Yu Yeh, and Yale N. Patt. Branch classification: A new mechanism for improving branch predictor performance. In *Proceedings of the 27th Annual ACM/IEEE International Symposium on Microarchitecture*, pages 22–31, 1994.

[3] W. W. Hwu and Yale N. Patt. Checkpoint repair for out-of-order execution machines. In *Proceedings of the 14th Annual International Symposium on Computer Architecture*, pages 18–26, 1987.

[4] David R. Kaeli and Philip G. Emma. Branch history table prediction of moving target branches due to subroutine returns. In *Proceedings of the 18th Annual International Symposium on Computer Architecture*, pages 34–41, 1991.

[5] David R. Kaeli and Philip G. Emma. Improving the accuracy of history-based branch prediction. Submitted to IEEE Transactions on Computers, 1994.

[6] Scott McFarling. Combining branch predictors. Technical Report TN-36, Digital Western Research Laboratory, June 1993.

[7] Scott McFarling and John Hennessy. Reducing the cost of branches. In *Proceedings of the 13th Annual International Symposium on Computer Architecture*, pages 396–403, 1986.

[8] Ravi Nair. Dynamic path-based branch correlation. In *Proceedings of the 28th Annual ACM/IEEE International Symposium on Microarchitecture*, pages 15–23, 1995.

[9] Yale Patt, W. Hwu, and Michael Shebanow. HPS, a new microarchitecture: Rationale and introduction. In *Proceedings of the 18th Annual ACM/IEEE International Symposium on Microarchitecture*, pages 103–107, 1985.

[10] Yale N. Patt, Steven W. Melvin, W. Hwu, and Michael C. Shebanow. Critical issues regarding HPS, a high performance microarchitecture. In *Proceedings of the 18th Annual ACM/IEEE International Symposium on Microarchitecture*, pages 109–116, 1985.

[11] James E. Smith. A study of branch prediction strategies. In *Proceedings of the 8th Annual International Symposium on Computer Architecture*, pages 135–148, 1981.

[12] R. M. Tomasulo. An efficient algorithm for exploiting multiple arithmetic units. *IBM Journal of Research and Development*, 11:25–33, January 1967.

[13] C. F. Webb. Subroutine call/return stack. *IBM Technical Disclosure Bulletin*, 30(11), April 1988.

[14] Tse-Yu Yeh and Yale N. Patt. Two-level adaptive branch prediction. In *Proceedings of the 24th Annual ACM/IEEE International Symposium on Microarchitecture*, pages 51–61, 1991.

[15] Tse-Yu Yeh and Yale N. Patt. A comparison of dynamic branch predictors that use two levels of branch history. In *Proceedings of the 20th Annual International Symposium on Computer Architecture*, pages 257–266, 1993.

[16] Cliff Young and Michael D. Smith. Improving the accuracy of static branch prediction using branch correlation. In *Proceedings of the 6th International Conference on Architectural Support for Programming Languages and Operating Systems*, pages 232–241, 1994.

The Agree Predictor: A Mechanism for Reducing Negative Branch History Interference

Eric Sprangle‡† Robert S. Chappell†‡ Mitch Alsup‡ Yale N. Patt†

Advanced Computer Architecture Laboratory †
Department of Electrical Engineering and Computer Science
The University of Michigan
Ann Arbor, Michigan 48109-2122
{robc, patt}@eecs.umich.edu

ROSS Technology, Inc. ‡
5316 Hwy 290 West Austin, Texas 78735
{sprangle, mitch}@ross.com

Abstract

Deeply pipelined, superscalar processors require accurate branch prediction to achieve high performance. Two-level branch predictors have been shown to achieve high prediction accuracy. It has also been shown that branch interference is a major contributor to the number of branches mispredicted by two-level predictors.

This paper presents a new method to reduce the interference problem called agree prediction, which reduces the chance that two branches aliasing the same PHT entry will interfere negatively. We evaluate the performance of this scheme using full traces (both user and supervisor) of the SPECint95 benchmarks. The result is a reduction in the misprediction rate of gcc ranging from 8.62% with a 64K-entry PHT up to 33.3% with a 1K-entry PHT.

Keywords: *branch prediction, superscalar, speculative execution, two-level branch prediction.*

1 Introduction

The link between changes in branch misprediction rate and changes in performance has been well documented [1–4, 6]. Yeh and Patt have shown that a two-level branch predictor can achieve high levels of branch prediction accuracy [4]. In a two-level predictor, the first level generates an index into a Pattern History Table (PHT) using some function of the outcomes of preceding branches. The first level function was originally the value of an N-bit shift register, called the Branch History Register (BHR), that kept track of the directions of the previous N branches. The second level is an array of PHT entries (in this paper, 2-bit saturating counters) which tracks the outcomes of branches mapped to it by the first level's indexing function. Figure 1 depicts a general two-level predictor.

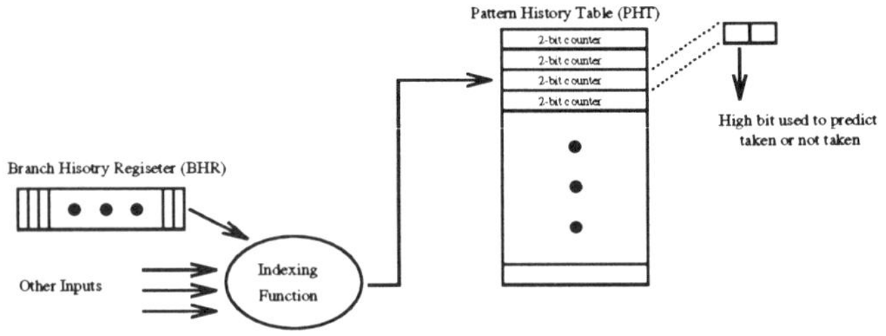

Figure 1: A general two-level predictor.

Since the number of PHT entries is finite, it sometimes is the case that two unrelated branches in the instruction stream are mapped to the the same PHT entry by the predictor's indexing function. This phenomenon is known as PHT interference, since the outcome of one branch is interfering with the subsequent prediction of another completely unrelated branch. Figure 2 shows a case of interference in a general two-level predictor.

2 Interference in Two-Level Predictors

We define an instance of PHT interference as a branch accessing a PHT entry that was previously updated by a different branch. In most cases, this does not change the direction of the prediction. We refer to this as neutral interference, since the presence of interference had no effect on that prediction. However, it is possible for the influence of the previous branches to change the prediction of the current branch. This effect can cause a correct prediction where there would be a misprediction otherwise. This is referred to as positive interference, since the introduction of interference causes a positive effect on performance by removing a misprediction. It is also possible that interference can cause a misprediction where there would not be otherwise. We refer to this as negative interference, since it has a negative effect on performance. We will confirm that negative interference is a substantial contributor to the number of branch mispredictions [7, 8].

Given that negative interference has a substantial impact

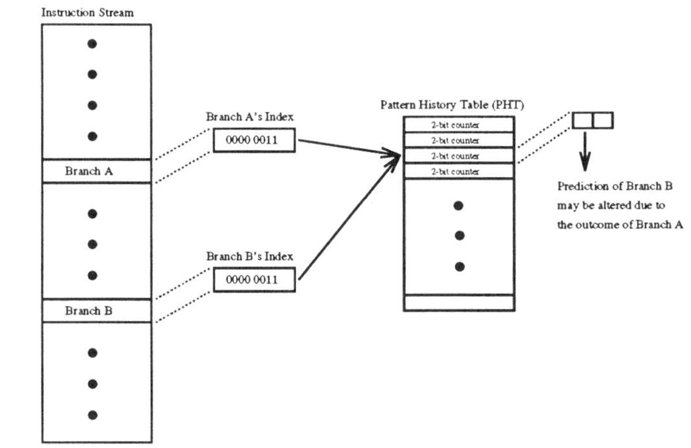

Figure 2: Interference in a two-level predictor.

on performance, it is worthwhile to attempt to reduce it. Most previous studies have examined three basic ways to counteract the interference problem:

1) Increasing predictor size, causing conflicting branches to map to different table locations.

2) Selecting a history table indexing scheme that best distributes history state among the available counters.

3) Separating different classes of branches so that they do not use the same prediction scheme, and thus cannot possibly interfere.

The first, and somewhat obvious, approach is to increase the number of entries in the PHT. This allows interfering branches to be mapped by the indexing function to different PHT entries. The fewer branches using the same PHT entry, the less interference and the less opportunity for negative interference to occur. Of course, this approach is limited by the number of transistors available to devote to the PHT.

Another means of reducing interference is to choose an indexing function that more effectively utilizes the PHT entries. For example, the gshare predictor [9] XORs the Branch History Register (BHR) with the lower bits of the branch address to generate the index into the PHT. Since BHR histories are not uniformly distributed, the introduction of address bits into the index gives a more useful distribution across all PHT entries.

Chang et al introduced *filtering*, another method of reducing PHT interference [10]. By using a simple predictor for easily predicted branches, these branches can be "filtered" out of the PHT, reducing the number of branches that are using PHT entries. This leads to a reduction in PHT interference.

3 The Agree Predictor

This paper introduces a new method of reducing negative branch interference called *agree prediction*. All of the methods discussed above focus on reducing the harmful effects of negative interference by reducing overall interference. Rather than attempting to reduce interference as a whole, the agree scheme converts instances of negative interference into either positive or neutral interference. This is done by modifying the structure and the use of the PHT.

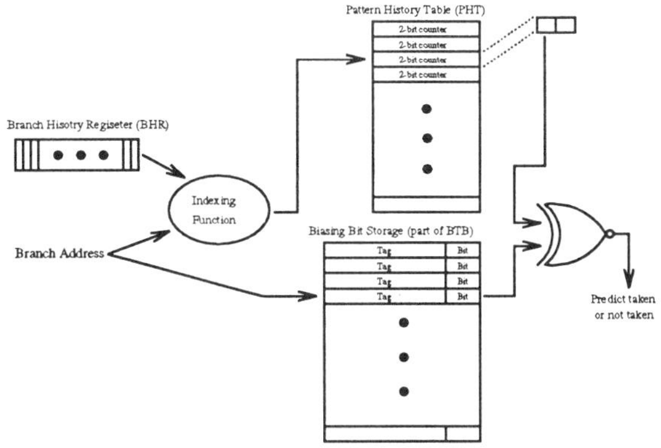

Figure 3: Agree predictor operation.

In a traditional two-level branch predictor, each PHT entry is a 2-bit saturating counter that is used to predict whether branches using that entry are taken or not taken. The counter's state is updated using the resolved direction of the branch. If the branch was taken, the PHT entry's counter is incremented. If the branch was not taken, the counter is decremented. In this manner, future occurrences using that PHT entry are more likely to predict the correct directions.

In an agree predictor (shown in figure 3), we attach a biasing bit to each branch (for example, in the instruction cache or in a BTB) that predicts the most likely outcome of the branch. Rather than predicting the direction of a given branch, the 2-bit counters predict whether or not the branch will go in the direction indicated by the biasing bit. In effect, this scheme predicts if the branch's direction *agrees* with the biasing bit. Like a traditional predictor, the 2-bit counter is updated when the branch has been resolved. However, in the agree scheme, the counter is incremented if the branch's direction agreed with the biasing bit. The counter is decremented if the branch did not agree with the biasing bit.

This agree scheme effectively reduces negative interference. If the biasing bit is well chosen, two branches using the same PHT entry are more likely to update the counter in the same direction—towards the agree state. This fundamental change in the PHT interpretation results in negative interference being converted to positive and neutral interference, thus increasing overall prediction accuracy.

To illustrate, assume two branches have respective taken rates of 85% and 15%. In a conventional scheme, the probability that any combination of these two branches has opposite outcomes is given by:

$$(br1taken, br2nottaken) + (br1nottaken, br2taken) = (85\% * 85\%) + (15\% * 15\%) = \mathbf{74.5\%}$$

In our agree predictor experiments, we set the biasing bit to the direction the branch goes the first time it is executed. This biasing bit represents the correct direction of the branch about 85% of the time, on average. Assuming that the biasing bits are optimally determined for the branches in the previous example (taken for the first branch, not taken for the second), the probability that any combination of these two branches has opposite outcomes becomes:

$$(br1agrees, br2disagrees) + (br1disagrees, br2agrees) = (85\% * 15\%) + (15\% * 85\%) = \mathbf{25.5\%}$$

Therefore, the PHT entries in the agree predictor are less likely to be different for two different branches, and negative interference is decreased.

Another important side-effect of this change is the potential for increased prediction accuracy during a new branch's warm-up period. Any new branch is more likely to have it's PHT entries already in the warmed-up state—the agree state. Details of both of these effects are studied below. Finally, we should point out that the agree predictor modifies only the PHT. Any of the first level history structures can be used with this scheme. In this paper, we restrict the first level history mechanism to that of gshare.

4 Experiments

The experimental results presented in this paper were generated using SoSS, a full system simulator designed to model a Sun 4m workstation. SoSS models the CPU, MMU, memory system, disk, and other I/O devices in a Sun 4m in enough detail to allow it to boot and run SunOS 4.1.4. Users can then log into the simulated machine's console and run arbitrary user processes on it. SoSS provides mechanisms for gathering a wide variety of statistics on both the user and operating system code that are executed in a given process. These include full symbolic breakpoints, conditional counter enabling and resetting, and full disassembly of all or part of the executed code.

Without the overhead of simulating the branch predictors, the current implementation of SoSS is capable of executing at approximately 1/30th the speed of the host machine. SoSS is able to achieve this level of performance through a number of optimizations. Two of the most important sources of speed are a special fetch-decode cache (FD-cache) and host pointer entries in the simulated TLB. The FD-cache, instead of caching the instruction binary to be simulated, caches a pointer to a segment of code that simulates the instruction on the host machine. Most instructions can be simulated in less than ten host instructions. Host pointers in TLB lines allow target machine virtual addresses to be translated directly to pointers on the host machine without having to be translated to target machine physical addresses as an intermediate step.

For this paper, we ran the SPECint95 benchmarks on SoSS for 2 billion instructions, or to completion. All benchmarks were compiled to the SunOS operating system using the gcc compiler with the -O3 option. The biasing bit was set to the direction of the branch the first time it was brought into the Branch Target Buffer (BTB). Since this bit is unknown on the first prediction after a BTB fill, the agree predictor uses the sign of the branch's offset as the biasing bit. The biasing bits were recorded in a 4K–entry direct-mapped BTB.

4.1 Interference Study

As the number of PHT entries is increased, three factors affect prediction accuracy:

1) Interference decreases. This increases prediction accuracy.

2) Better branch correlation. Increasing PHT size means it is more likely for an indexing function to map only those branches with similar behavior to the same PHT entry. This also increases prediction accuracy.

3) Training time increases. Larger PHT sizes require larger indices. This typically translates to more pattern history bits being used in the address, resulting in a longer warm-up period for new branches. A longer training period reduces prediction accuracy.

These first experiments model the performance of a hypothetical interference-free predictor versus the performance of conventional and agree predictors of increasing PHT sizes. Since the interference-free predictor is not affected by the first of the above three factors, we can gain use its results to gain insight into the relative magnitudes of the other two forces. We model 1K, 2K, 4K, 8K, 16K, 32K, and 64K–PHT entry predictors.

Figures 4 to 9 show the prediction accuracy for the SPECint95 benchmarks using three versions of the gshare predictor. All three predictors use the same gshare indexing function; the lower N bits of the address are XORed with the BHR. The first version, conventional, updates the PHT entries in a conventional manner. The second version, agree, uses the agree scheme to update the PHT entries. The third version, interference-free, allocates a separate 2-bit counter for each branch/BHR index combination. All three predictors are simulated with 10-16 bit BHRs (1K to 64K–entry PHT entries, respectively).

The results show that the interference-free predictor consistently outperforms both the conventional and agree predictors, implying that negative interference dominates positive interference. In addition, the interference-free predictor gains only a slight improvement in performance as the PHT size is increased. This affirms our hypothesis that interference is the major contributor to reducing prediction accuracy.

The agree predictor clearly outperforms the conventional two-level scheme, especially in the smaller predictors and on certain benchmarks. Smaller predictors naturally have more contention for the PHT entries. The agree predictor attacks this interference and is able to increase performance. However, as the PHT size becomes very large, the agree predictor becomes less and less effective, since there is less opportunity to remove negative interference. In addition, secondary effects, such as misses in the BTB (where the biasing bits are stored) become more significant.

The agree predictor also seems to perform better on some benchmarks than on others. Benchmarks such as gcc and go have a larger branch "footprint"; they have a large number of static branches that are frequently executed. Figure 10 plots the percentage of total branches executed by each benchmark versus the number of static branches in each benchmark. We can see that some benchmarks, such as gcc and go, have much larger branch footprints than others. In general, these benchmarks are the ones that benefit the most from interference reduction. While the branch footprint is not directly representative of the amount of interference that occurs in a benchmark, it is a good first-order indicator.

Table 1 lists the improvement in prediction accuracy when moving from a 1K–entry PHT to a 64K–entry PHT, for each predictor class. All of the predictors achieve higher prediction accuracies as the number of PHT entries is increased. For the interference-free predictor, the change in performance is due solely to the combination of better correlation and greater training time. Since the plot for the interference-free predictor is monotonically increasing, we can conclude that the increase in performance due to better correlation is greater than the decrease due to increased training time.

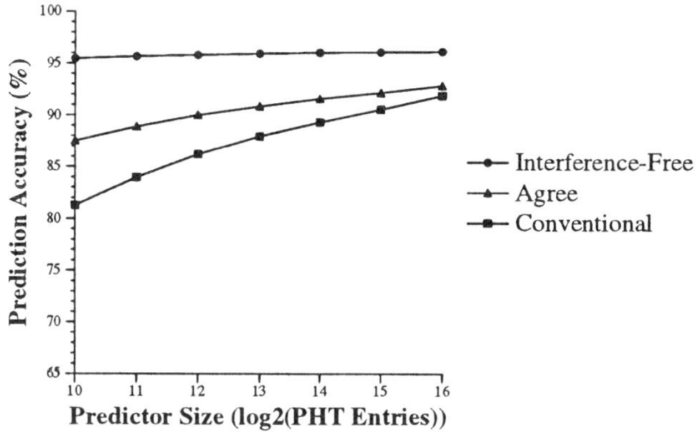

Figure 4: Prediction accuracy versus predictor size for gcc.

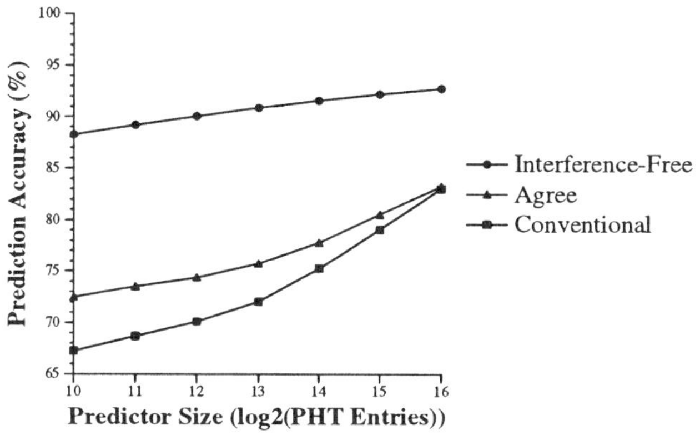

Figure 5: Prediction accuracy versus predictor size for go.

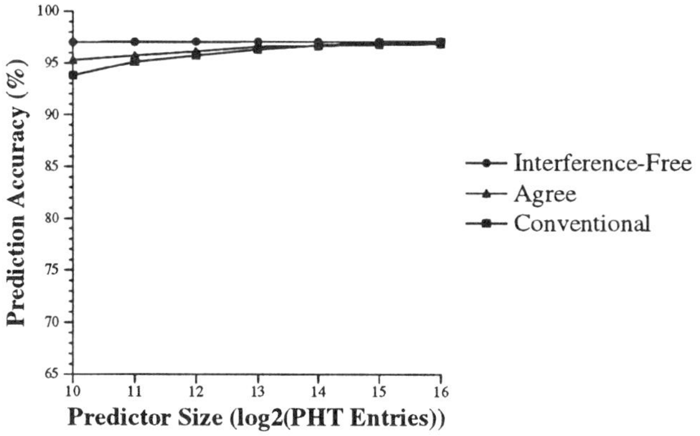

Figure 6: Prediction accuracy versus predictor size m88ksim.

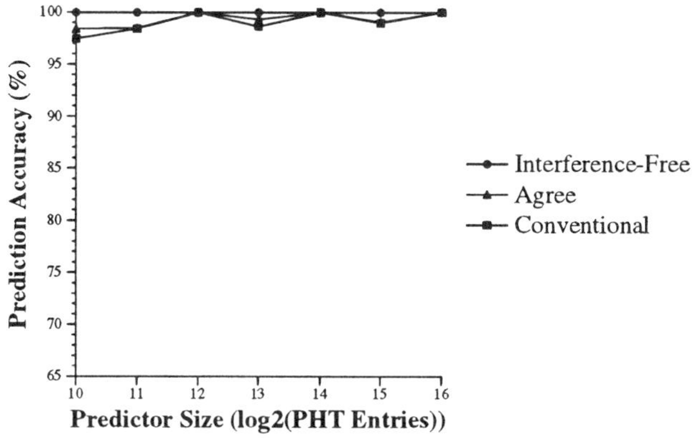

Figure 7: Prediction accuracy versus predictor size for perl.

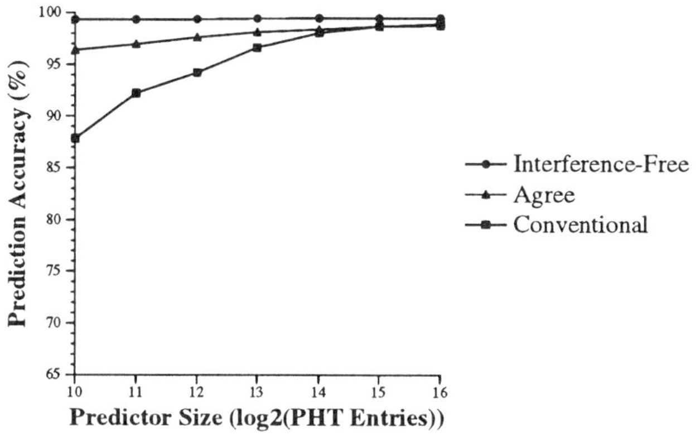

Figure 8: Prediction accuracy versus predictor size for vortex.

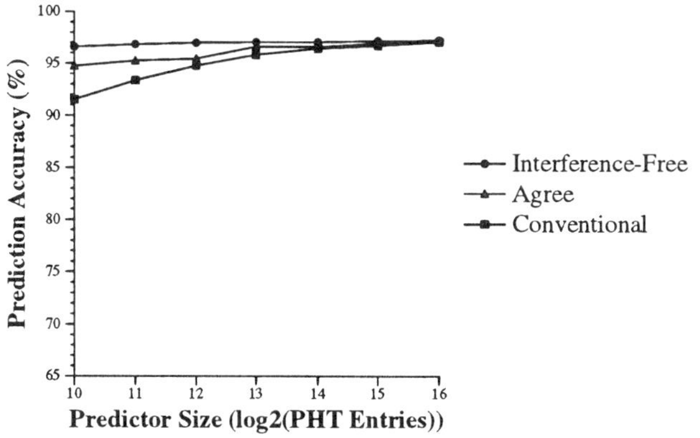

Figure 9: Prediction accuracy versus predictor size for xlisp.

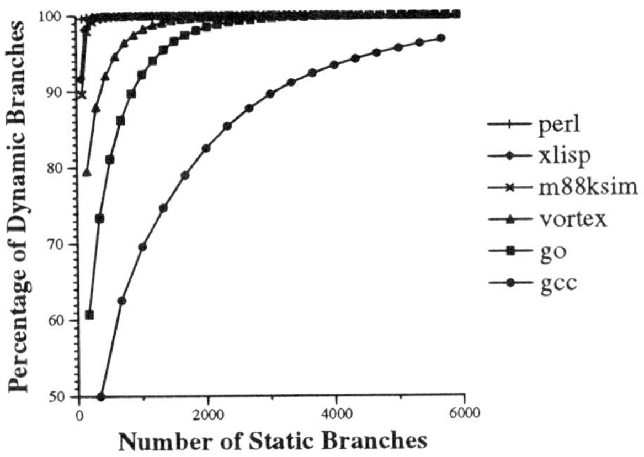

Figure 10: Percentage of static branches accounting for dynamic branches by benchmark.

Table 1: Improvement in accuracy from 1K to 64K–entry PHT.

Benchmark	Interference-Free	Agree	Conventional
gcc	.67%	5.22%	10.63%
go	4.50%	10.77%	15.77%
m88ksim	.13%	1.60%	3.32%
perl	.00%	1.57%	2.52%
vortex	.16%	2.36%	11.10%
xlisp	.60%	2.35%	5.51%

As the predictor size is increased, both the agree and conventional predictors achieve greater improvements in accuracy than the interference-free predictor. This implies that interference is a much greater factor in predictor performance than is correlation. We can estimate the improvement in accuracy due to interference reduction (as the PHT size is increased) by examining the equation:

$$ChangeinAccuracy = InterferenceReduction + (BetterCorrelation - TrainingTimeIncrease)$$

The sum *(Better Correlation – Training Time Increase)* can be approximated by the increase in performance of interference-free predictor. By subtracting this term from the total change in PHT accuracy, we are left with the change in accuracy due to interference reduction. Table 2 lists estimates of what percentage of total improvement in accuracy is due to reduced interference as predictor size is increased from 1K to 64K–entries. These calculations imply that, as the PHT size is increased, interference reduction is responsible for most (over 71%) of the improvement in prediction accuracy.

4.2 Characterizing Positive, Neutral, Negative Interference

There are three classes of interference: positive, neutral and negative. We define an occurrence of positive interference as a branch being predicted correctly by a predictor when it would have been mispredicted by a similar predictor with no interference. Neutral interference occurs when the realistic predictor and interference-free predictor are both correct or both incorrect. Negative interference occurs if the interference-free predictor is correct, but the realistic predictor mispredicts.

Table 2: Estimated percent of improvement from reduced interference when going from a 1K– entry PHT to a 64K–entry PHT conventional scheme.

Benchmark	
gcc	93.70%
go	71.46%
m88ksim	96.08%
perl	100.0%
vortex	98.56%
xlisp	89.10%

Table 3 shows the percentage of occurrences of positive, neutral, and negative interference for conventional and agree predictors for each benchmark and predictor size.

This table confirms many of our hypotheses. In general, as the predictor size is increased, most of the interference ends up being neutral. We also see that negative interference occurs much more often than positive interference. Finally, these figures show the agree predictor effectively converts negative interference into positive and neutral interference. As with overall prediction accuracy, the reduction of negative interference lessens as the predictor size increases.

4.3 Warm-up Study

One of the problems with two-level branch prediction is the number of times a new branch instruction must execute before the predictor "warms up". This section studies the relative performance of the agree predictor versus the conventional two-level predictor for branches seen 1 to 16 times previously (we choose the first 16 branches because that is the length of the largest BHR simulated). We refer to this as the predictor's *warm-up period* for a new branch. The agree predictor achieves a higher accuracy than the conventional predictor during this period due to the increased likelihood that the PHT entry in the agree predictor will already be in a trained (agree) state. Figures 11 and 12 show the prediction accuracies of each predictor for all branches encountered exactly N times. Recall that for branches seen for the very first time (N = 1), the agree predictor is using the branch offset's sign for the biasing bit. Because of this, for some benchmarks, the conventional two-level predictor sometimes achieves higher accuracy on the first prediction for a new branch.

These results demonstrate the ability of an agree predictor to, in effect, warm up more quickly than a conventional predictor of the same history length. This is an advantage for prediction in the presence of context switches, as an agree predictor would adapt more quickly.

4.4 Choosing the Biasing Bit

In these experiments, we use the direction of the branch the first time it was executed after being placed in the BTB as the biasing bit. Once it is defined, it does not change over the course of the program, unless the branch is replaced in the BTB and later retrieved. We refer to this as the "first time" selection mechanism. It has been suggested that a better biasing bit selection mechanism would be to set the biasing bit to the direction most often taken by that branch

Table 3: Percentage of total interference classified as positive, neutral, and negative.

Benchmark	Positive (conv,agree)	Neutral (conv,agree)	Negative (conv,agree)
gcc			
1K	1.15%,1.23%	83.51%,89.59%	15.35%,9.18%
2K	.99%,1.11%	86.29%,90.99%	12.71%,7.90%
4K	.91%,1.03%	88.53%,92.09%	10.56%,6.88%
8K	.83%,.98%	90.29%,92.88%	8.88%,6.14%
16K	.79%,.96%	91.60%,93.56%	7.61%,5.48%
32K	.75%,.96%	92.77%,94.03%	6.48%,5.01%
64K	.72%,.96%	93.90%,94.49%	5.37%,4.55%
go			
1K	4.15%,4.10%	70.68%,76.03%	25.17%,19.87%
2K	3.60%,3.62%	72.31%,77.09%	24.09%,19.29%
4K	3.10%,3.13%	73.85%,78.05%	23.05%,18.82%
8K	2.59%,2.65%	75.97%,79.55%	21.43%,17.79%
16K	2.11%,2.21%	79.39%,81.75%	18.50%,16.04%
32K	1.68%,1.83%	83.45%,84.61%	14.87%,13.56%
64K	1.29%,1.51%	87.63%,87.43%	11.08%,11.06%
m88ksim			
1K	.18%,.19%	96.41%,97.90%	3.40%,1.91%
2K	.10%,.08%	97.86%,98.51%	2.04%,1.40%
4K	.09%,.07%	98.51%,98.93%	1.41%,1.00%
8K	.03%,.03%	99.19%,99.47%	.78%, .50%
16K	.01%,.01%	99.60%,99.57%	.38%, .42%
32K	.02%,.02%	99.85%,99.64%	.13%, .33%
64K	.01%,.01%	99.91%,99.76%	.08%, .22%
vortex			
1K	.12%,.18%	88.25%,96.69%	11.63%,3.12%
2K	.11%,.12%	92.68%,97.38%	7.21%,2.50%
4K	.09%,.09%	94.69%,98.10%	5.22%,1.81%
8K	.07%,.08%	97.06%,98.53%	2.87%,1.39%
16K	.02%,.04%	98.54%,98.83%	1.44%,1.13%
32K	.04%,.05%	99.06%,99.06%	.91%, .88%
64K	.03%,.04%	99.27%,99.20%	.70%, .76%
xlisp			
1K	.21%,.23%	94.53%,97.70%	5.26%,2.07%
2K	.10%,.08%	96.34%,98.48%	3.55%,1.44%
4K	.13%,.15%	97.53%,98.10%	2.34%,1.75%
8K	.04%,.03%	98.67%,99.49%	1.28%, .47%
16K	.10%,.03%	99.11%,99.40%	.79%, .56%
32K	.02%,.02%	99.28%,99.61%	.70%, .37%
64K	.08%,.04%	99.54%,99.76%	.39%, .20%

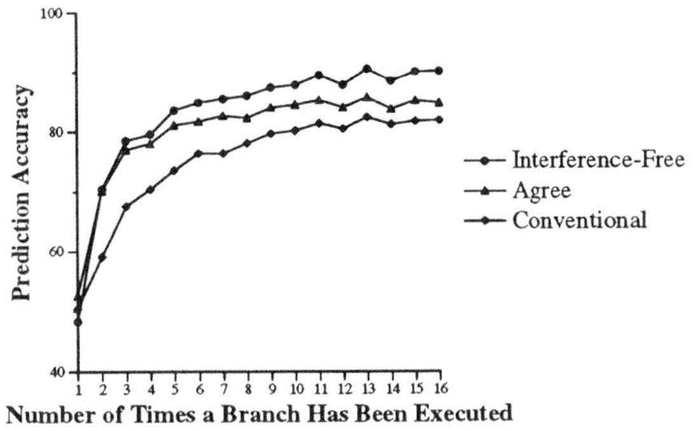

Figure 11: Prediction of branches during warm-up period with a 16-bit BHR for gcc.

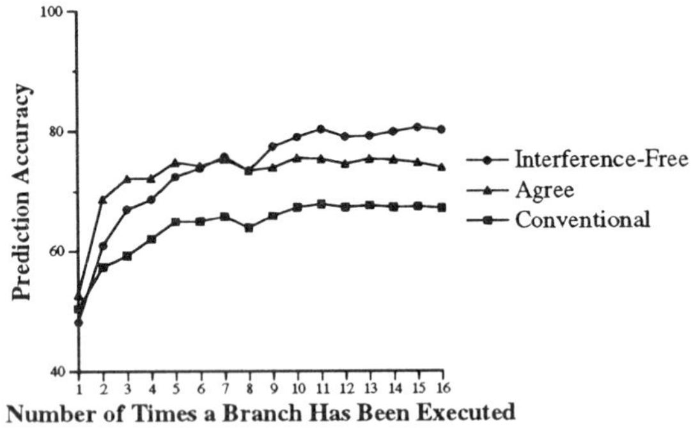

Figure 12: Prediction of branches during warm-up period with a 16-bit BHR for go.

over run of the entire benchmark. We refer to this hypothetical mechanism as "most often". As a first step toward determining an optimal biasing bit selection mechanism, we compare the agree predictor's performance using "first time" selection to the performance using "most often" selection.

We simulate the hypothetical "most often" selection scheme by running the benchmark twice. The first run records, for each static branch in the benchmark's instruction stream, whether the branch is more often taken or not taken. This information is used to set the biasing bits for the second run. Table 4 shows the results of this experiment. Our heuristic of "first time" is comparable to the hypothetical "most often" mechanism. Future agree predictor studies will examine other dynamic schemes for selecting biasing bits.

Table 4: Comparison of prediction accuracies for "first time" versus "most often" biasing bit selection for gcc.

PHT Entries	First Time	Most Often	Difference
1K	87.52%	89.44%	1.92%
2K	88.88%	90.43%	1.55%
4K	89.99%	91.29%	1.30%
8K	90.84%	92.01%	1.17%
16K	91.59%	92.66%	1.07%
32K	92.17%	93.17%	1.00%
64K	92.84%	93.81%	.97%

5 Conclusions

This paper proposes a new method for reducing negative interference in two-level branch predictors. We have shown that an interference-free predictor performs much better than a conventional two-level predictor scheme. By redefining the operation of the PHT in a two-level predictor, we can recover some of the lost prediction accuracy due to interference. The agree scheme, while relatively simple to implement, achieves a significant improvement in branch prediction accuracy. This improvement stems from two sources. First, the agree scheme effectively converts negative PHT interference to positive and neutral interference. Second, prediction accuracy during warm-up periods is improved. The most dramatic improvements by the agree scheme over the conventional predictors can be seen in benchmarks with large branch footprints and in predictors with small PHT sizes. The agree predictor reduces misprediction rates in gcc ranging from 8.62% with a 64K–entry PHT up to 33.3% with a 1K–entry PHT.

6 Acknowledgments

This work is the result of collaborative research performed jointly by researchers at the University of Michigan and at Ross Technology and was funded in part by a gift from Ross Technology. We gratefully acknowledge their support. We also acknowledge the contributions of Sanjay Patel, Jared Stark, and Daniel Friendly, PhD students at Michigan who have been very helpful to our work.

References

[1] B. Calder and D. Grunwald, "Fast and Accurate Instruction Fetch and Branch Prediction", Proceedings of the 21st International Symposium on Computer Architecture, (April 1994), pp. 2-11.

[2] S. McFarling and J. Hennessy, "Reducing the Cost of Branches", Proceedings of the 13th International Symposium on Computer Architecture, (1986), pp. 396-403.

[3] J. A. Fisher and S. M. Freudenberfer, "Predicting Conditional Branch Directions from Previous Runs of a Program", Proceedings 5th Annual International Conference on Architectural Support for Programming Languages and Operating Systems, (October 1992).

[4] T-Y. Yeh and Y. N. Patt, "Two-Level Adaptive Training Branch Prediction", 24th ACM/IEEE International Symposium on Microarchitecture, (November 1991), pp. 51-61.

[5] T-Y. Yeh and Y. N. Patt, "A Comprehensive Instruction Fetch Mechanism for Processor Supporting Speculative Execution", 25th ACM/IEEE International Symposium on Microarchitecture, (December 1992), pp. 129-139.

[6] B. Calder, D. Grunwald, and J. Emer, "A System Level Perspective on Branch Architecture Performance," 28th ACM/IEEE International Symposium on Microarchitecture, (November 1995).

[7] A. R. Talcott, M. Nemirovsky, and R. C. Wood. "The Influence of Branch Prediction Table Interference on Branch Prediction Scheme Performance", International Conference on Parallel Architectures and Compilation Techniques, (1995).

[8] C. Young, N. Gloy, and M. D. Smith, "A Comparative Analysis of Schemes for Correlated Branch Prediction", Proceedings of the 22nd Annual International Symposium on Computer Architecture, (1995), pp. 276-286.

[9] S. McFarling, "Combining Branch Predictors", Technical Report TN-36, Digital Western Research Laboratory, (June 1993).

[10] P-Y. Chang, M. Evers, and Y.N. Patt, "Improving Branch Prediction Accuracy by Reducing Pattern History Table Interference", International Conference on Parallel Architectures and Compilation Techniques, (October 1996).

Trading Conflict and Capacity Aliasing in Conditional Branch Predictors

Pierre Michaud
pmichaud@irisa.fr

André Seznec
seznec@irisa.fr

Richard Uhlig *
ruhlig@ichips.intel.com

IRISA/INRIA
Campus de Beaulieu
35042 Rennes, France
http://www.irisa.fr/caps/

Abstract

As modern microprocessors employ deeper pipelines and issue multiple instructions per cycle, they are becoming increasingly dependent on accurate branch prediction. Because hardware resources for branch-predictor tables are invariably limited, it is not possible to hold all relevant branch history for all active branches at the same time, especially for large workloads consisting of multiple processes and operating-system code. The problem that results, commonly referred to as aliasing *in the branch-predictor tables, is in many ways similar to the misses that occur in finite-sized hardware caches.*

In this paper we propose a new classification for branch aliasing based on the three-Cs model for caches, and show that conflict aliasing is a significant source of mispredictions. Unfortunately, the obvious method for removing conflicts – adding tags and associativity to the predictor tables – is not a cost-effective solution.

To address this problem, we propose the skewed branch predictor*, a multi-bank, tag-less branch predictor, designed specifically to reduce the impact of conflict aliasing. Through both analytical and simulation models, we show that the skewed branch predictor removes a substantial portion of conflict aliasing by introducing redundancy to the branch-predictor tables. Although this redundancy increases capacity aliasing compared to a standard one-bank structure of comparable size, our simulations show that the reduction in conflict aliasing overcomes this effect to yield a gain in prediction accuracy. Alternatively, we show that a skewed organization can achieve the same prediction accuracy as a standard one-bank organization but with half the storage requirements.*

Keywords

Branch prediction, aliasing, 3 C's classification, skewed branch predictor.

* Now with Intel Microcomputer Research Lab, Oregon

1 Introduction and Related Work

In processors that speculatively fetch and issue multiple instructions per cycle to deep pipelines, dozens of instructions might be in flight before a branch is resolved. Under these conditions, a mispredicted branch can result in substantial amounts of wasted work and become a bottleneck to exploiting instruction-level parallelism. Accurate branch prediction has come to play an important role in removing this bottleneck.

Many dynamic branch prediction schemes have been investigated in the past few years, with each offering certain distinctive features. Most of them, however, share a common characteristic: they rely on a collection of 1- or 2-bit counters held in a *predictor table*. Each entry in the table records the recent outcomes of a given branch *substream* [21], and is used to predict the direction of future branches in that substream. A branch substream might be defined by some bits of the branch address, by a bit pattern representing previous branch directions (known as a *branch history*), by some combination of branch address and branch history, or by bits from target addresses of previous branches [14, 7, 18, 10, 8, 9].

Ideally, we would like to have a predictor table with infinite capacity so that every unique branch substream defined by an (address, history) pair will have a dedicated predictor. Chen et al. have shown that two-level predictors are close to being optimal, provided unlimited resources for implementing the predictors [3]. Real-world constraints, of course, do not permit this. Chip die-area budgets and access-time constraints limit predictor-table size, and most tables proposed in the literature are further constrained in that they are direct-mapped and without tags.

Fixed-sized predictor tables lead to a phenomenon known as *aliasing* or *interference* [21, 16], in which multiple (address, history) pairs share the same entry in the predictor table, causing the predictions for two or more branch substreams to intermingle. Aliasing has been classified as either *destructive* (i.e., a misprediction occurs due to sharing of a predictor-table entry), *harmless* (i.e., it has no effect on the prediction) or *constructive* (i.e., aliasing occasionally provides a good prediction, which would have been wrong otherwise) [21]. Young et al. have shown that constructive aliasing is much less likely than destructive aliasing [21].

Recent studies have shown that large or multi-process workloads with a strong OS component exhibit very high degrees of aliasing [11, 5], and require much larger predictor tables than previously thought necessary to achieve a level of accuracy close to an ideal, unaliased predictor table [11]. We therefore expect that new techniques for removing conflict aliasing could provide important gains towards increased branch-prediction accuracy.

Branch aliasing in fixed-size, direct-mapped predictor tables is in many ways analogous to instruction-cache or data-cache misses.

This suggests an alternative classification for branch aliasing based on the *three-Cs model* of cache performance first proposed by Hill [6]. As with cache misses, aliasing can be classified as *compulsory*, *capacity* or *conflict* aliasing. Similarly, as with caches, larger predictor tables reduce capacity aliasing, while associativity in a predictor table could remove conflict aliasing.

Unfortunately, a simple-minded adaptation of cache associativity would require the addition of costly tags, substantially increasing the cost of a predictor table. In this paper we examine an alternative approach, called skewed branch prediction, which borrows ideas from skewed-associative caches [12]. A *skewed branch predictor* is constructed from an odd number (typically 3 or 5) of *predictor-table banks*, each of which functions like a standard tag-less predictor table. When performing a prediction, each bank is accessed in parallel but with a different indexing function, and a majority vote between the resulting lookups is used to predict the direction of the branch.

In the next section we explain in greater detail our aliasing classification. In section 3, we quantify aliasing and assess the effect of conflict aliasing on overall branch-prediction accuracy. In section 4, we introduce the skewed branch predictor, a hardware structure designed specifically to reduce conflict aliasing. In section 5, we show how and why the skewed branch predictor removes conflict aliasing effects at the cost of some redundancy. Our analysis includes both simulation and analytical models of performance, and considers a range of possible skewed predictor configurations driven by traces from the instruction-benchmark suite (IBS) [17], which includes complete user and operating-system activity. Section 6 proposes the enhanced skewed branch predictor, a slight modification to the skewed branch predictor, which enables more attractive tradeoffs between capacity and conflict aliasing. Section 7 concludes this study and proposes some future research directions.

2 An Aliasing Classification

Throughout this paper, we will focus on global-history prediction schemes for the sake of conciseness. Global-history schemes use both the branch address and a pattern of global history bits, as described in [18, 19, 20, 10, 8]. Previously-proposed global-history predictors are all direct-mapped and tag-less. Given a history length, the distinguishing feature of these predictors is the hashing function that is used to map the set of all (address, history) pairs onto the predictor table.

The *gshare* and *gselect* schemes [8] have been the most studied global schemes (*gselect* corresponds to GAs in Yeh and Patt's terminology [18, 19, 20]). In *gshare*, the low-order address bits and global history bits are XORed together to form an index value[1], whereas in *gselect*, low-order address bits and global history bits are concatenated.

Aliasing occurs in direct-mapped tag-less predictors when two or more (address, history) pairs map to the same entry. To measure aliasing for a particular global scheme and table, we simulate a structure having the same number of entries and using the same indexing function as the predictor table considered. However, instead of storing 1-bit or 2-bit predictors in the structure, we store the identity of the last (address, history) pair that accessed the entry. Aliasing occurs when the indexing (address, history) pair is different from the stored pair. The *aliasing ratio* is the ratio between the number of aliasing occurrences and the number of dynamic conditional branches. When measured in this way, we can see the relationship between branch aliasing and cache misses. Our simulated tagged table is like a cache with a line size of one datum, and an aliasing occurrence corresponds to a cache miss.

[1] When the number of history bits is less than the number of index bits, the history bits are XORed with the *higher-order* end of the section of low-order address bits, as explained in [8]

benchmark	conditional branch count	
	dynamic	static
groff	11568181	5634
gs	14288742	10935
mpeg_play	8109029	4752
nroff	21368201	4480
real_gcc	13940672	16716
verilog	5692823	3918

Table 1: Conditional branch counts

A widely-accepted classification of cache misses is the three-Cs model, first introduced by Hill [6] and later refined by Sugumar and Abraham [15]. The three-Cs model divides cache misses into three groups, depending on their causes.

- **Compulsory misses** occur when an address is referenced for the first time. These unavoidable misses are required to fill an empty or "cold" cache.
- **Capacity misses** occur when the cache is not large enough to retain all the addresses that will be re-referenced in the future. Capacity misses can be reduced by increasing the total size of the cache.
- **Conflict misses** occur when two memory locations contend for the same cache line in a given window of time. Conflict misses can be reduced by increasing the associativity of a cache, or improving the replacement algorithm.

Aliasing in branch-predictor tables can be classified in a similar fashion:

- **Compulsory aliasing** occurs when a branch substream is encountered for the first time.
- **Capacity aliasing**, like capacity cache misses, is due to a program's working set being too large to fit in a predictor table, and can be reduced by increasing the size of the predictor table.
- **Conflict aliasing** occurs when two concurrently-active branch substreams map to the same predictor-table entry. Methods for reducing this component of aliasing have not yet, to our knowledge, appeared in the published literature.

3 Quantifying Aliasing

3.1 Experimental Setup

We conducted all of our trace-driven simulations using the IBS-Ultrix benchmarks [17]. These benchmarks were traced using a hardware monitor connected to a MIPS-based DECstation running Ultrix 3.1. The resulting traces include activity from all user-level processes as well as the operating-system kernel, and have been determined by other researchers to be a good test of branch-prediction performance [5, 11]. Conditional branch counts[2] derived from these traces are given in Table 1.

Although we simulated the *sdet* and *video_play* benchmarks, they exhibited no special behavior compared with the other benchmarks. We therefore omit *sdet* and *video_play* results from this paper in the interest of saving space.

[2] **beq r0,r0** is used as an unconditional relative jump by the MIPS compiler, therefore we did not consider it as conditional. This explains the discrepancy with the branch counts reported in [5, 11]

4-bit history				
benchmark	**substream ratio**	**compulsory aliasing**	**misprediction**	
			1-bit	**2-bit**
groff	1.82	0.09 %	5.47 %	3.77 %
gs	1.91	0.15 %	7.03 %	5.28 %
mpeg_play	1.83	0.11 %	9.08 %	7.24 %
nroff	1.79	0.04 %	4.99 %	3.72 %
real_gcc	2.36	0.28 %	9.38 %	7.16 %
verilog	1.96	0.13 %	6.48 %	4.57 %

12-bit history				
benchmark	**substream ratio**	**compulsory aliasing**	**misprediction**	
			1-bit	**2-bit**
groff	7.14	0.35 %	3.63 %	2.56 %
gs	7.95	0.61 %	3.71 %	2.77 %
mpeg_play	6.27	0.37 %	5.85 %	4.52 %
nroff	5.71	0.12 %	3.04 %	2.20 %
real_gcc	12.90	1.55 %	4.90 %	3.93 %
verilog	9.24	0.64 %	3.74 %	2.66 %

Table 2: Unaliased predictor

We first simulated an ideal unaliased scheme (i.e., a predictor table of infinite size). The misprediction ratios that we obtained are shown in Table 2 for history lengths of 4 and 12 bits, and for both 1-bit and 2-bit predictors (we include unconditional branches as part of the global-history bits). When an (address, history) pair is encountered for the first time, we do not count it as a misprediction, so compulsory miss contribution to mispredictions is not reported in the last two columns of Table 2.

The 2-bit saturating counter gives better prediction accuracy in an unaliased predictor table than the 1-bit predictor. Our intuition is that this difference is due mainly to loop branches. We also measured the *substream ratio*, which we define as the average number of different history values encountered for a given conditional branch address (see first column of Table 2).

The compulsory-aliasing percentage was computed from the number of different (address, history) pairs referenced throughout the trace divided by the total number of dynamic conditional branches. From Table 2, we observe that compulsory aliasing, with a 12-bit history length, generally constitutes less than 1% of the total of all dynamic conditional branches, except in the case of *real_gcc*, which exhibits a compulsory-aliasing rate of 1.55%.

3.2 Quantifying Conflict and Capacity Aliasing

To quantify conflict and capacity aliasing, we simulated tagged predictor tables holding (address, history) pairs. Figures 1 and 2 show the miss ratio in direct-mapped (DM) and fully-associative (FA) tables using 4 bits and 12 bits of global history, respectively. The two direct-mapped tables are indexed with a *gshare*- and a *gselect*-like function. The fully-associative table uses a least-recently-used (LRU) replacement policy.

The miss ratio for the fully-associative table gives the sum of compulsory and capacity aliasing. The difference between *gshare* or *gselect* and the fully-associative table gives the amount of conflict aliasing in the corresponding *gshare* and *gselect* predictors. It should be noted that LRU is not an optimal replacement policy [15]. However, because it bases its decisions solely on past information, the LRU policy gives a reasonable base value of the amount of conflict aliasing that can be removed by a hardware-only scheme.

It appears that for our benchmarks, *gselect* has a higher aliasing rate than *gshare*. This explains why, for a given table size and history length, *gshare* has a lower misprediction rate than *gselect*, as claimed in [8]. This difference is very pronounced with 12 bits of global history, because in this case, *gselect* uses only a very small number of address bits (e.g., only 4 address bits for a 64K-entry table).

Figure 1 shows that when the number of entries is larger than or equal to 4K, capacity aliasing nearly vanishes, **leaving conflicts as the overwhelming cause of aliasing**. The same condition holds in Figure 2 for table sizes greater than about 16K. This leads us to conclude that some amount of associativity in branch prediction tables is needed to limit the impact of aliasing.

3.3 Problems with Associative Predictor Tables

Associativity in caches introduces a degree of freedom for avoiding conflicts. In a direct-mapped cache, tag bits are used to determine whether a reference hits or misses. In an associative cache, the tag bits also determine the precise location of the requested data in the cache.

Because of its speculative nature, a direct-mapped branch prediction table can be tag-less. To implement associativity, however, we must introduce tags identifying (address, history) pairs. Unfortunately, the tag width is disproportionately large compared to the width of the individual predictors, which are usually 1 or 2 bits wide.

Another method for achieving the benefits of associativity, without having to pay the cost of tags is needed. The skewed branch predictor, described in the next section, is one such method.

4 The Skewed Branch Predictor

We have previously noted that the behaviors of *gselect* and *gshare* are different even though these two schemes are based on the same (address, history) information. This is illustrated on Figure 3 where we represent a *gshare* and a *gselect* table with 16 entries. In this example, there is a conflict both with *gshare* and *gselect*, but the (address, history) pairs that conflict are not the same. We can conclude that the precise occurrence of conflicts is strongly related to the mapping function. The skewed branch predictor is based on this observation.

The basic principle of the skewed branch predictor is to use several branch-predictor banks (3 banks in the example illustrated in Figure 4), but to index them by different and independent hashing functions computed from the same vector V of information (e.g., branch address and global history). A prediction is read from each of the banks and a majority vote is used to select a final branch direction.

The rationale for using different hashing functions for each bank is that two vectors, V and W, that are aliased with each other in one bank are unlikely to be aliased in the other banks. A destructive aliasing of V by W may occur in one bank, but the overall prediction on V is likely to be correct if V does not suffer from destructive aliasing in the other banks.

4.1 Execution Model

We consider two policies for updating the predictors across multiple banks:

- A **total update** policy: each of the three banks is updated as if it were a sole bank in a traditional prediction scheme.
- A **partial update** policy: when a bank gives a bad prediction, it is not updated when the overall prediction is good. This

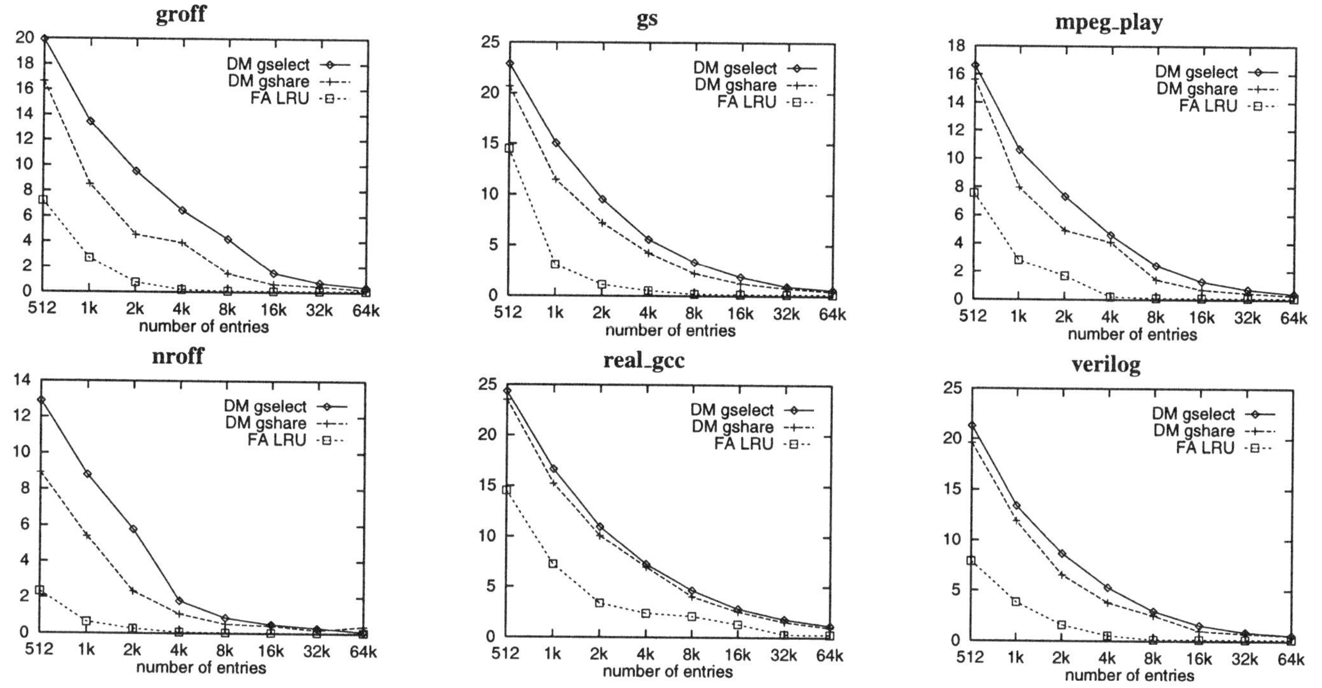

Figure 1: Miss percentages in tables tagged with (address, history) pairs (4-bit history)

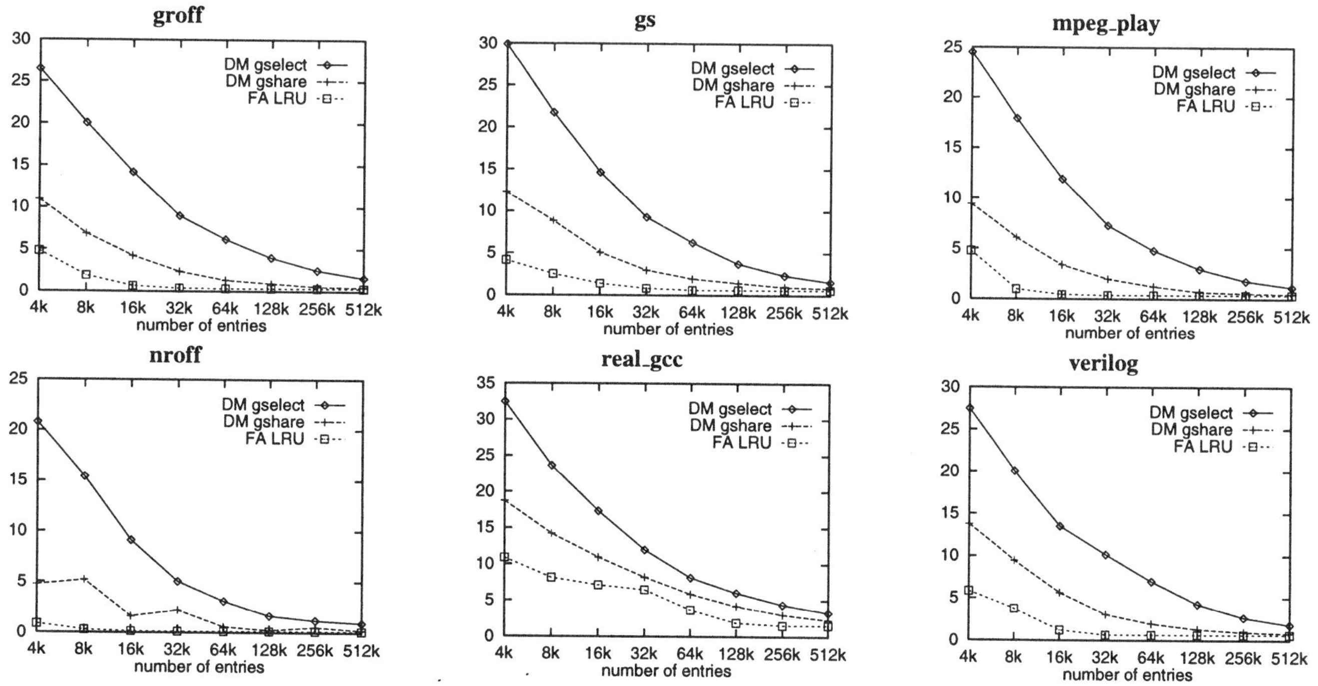

Figure 2: Miss percentages in tables tagged with (address, history) pairs (12-bit history)

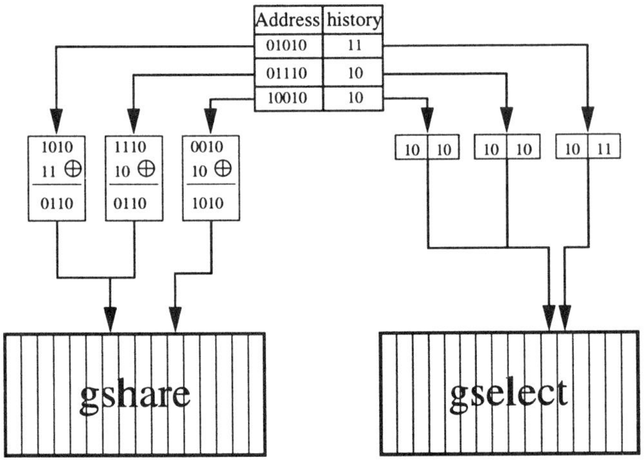

Figure 3: Conflicts depend on the mapping function

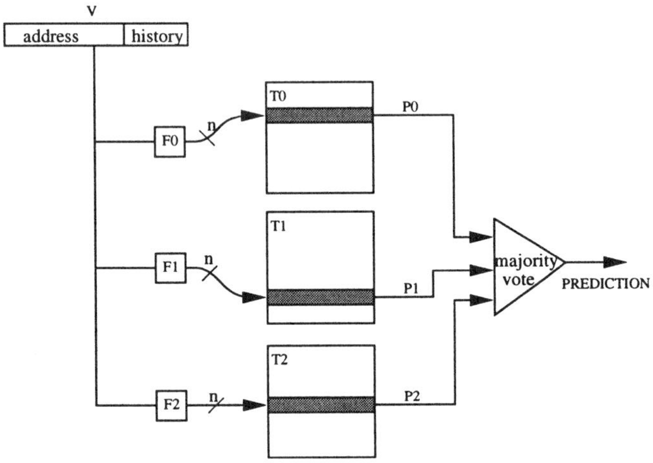

Figure 4: A Skewed Branch Predictor

wrong predictor is considered to be attached to another (address, history) pair. When the overall prediction is wrong, all banks are updated as dictated by the outcome of the branch.

4.2 Design Space

Chosing the information (branch address, history, etc.) that is used to divide branches into substreams is an open problem. The purpose of this section is not to discuss the relevance of using some combination of information or the other, but to show that most conflict aliasing effects can be removed by using a skewed predictor organization. For the remainder of this paper, the vector of information that will be used for recording branch-prediction information is the concatenation of the branch address and the k bits of global history: $V = (a_N, ...a_2, h_k, ...h_1)$. Let $\mathcal{V}$ be the set of all V's.

The functions f_0, f_1 and f_2 used for indexing the three 2^n-entry banks in the experiments are the same as those proposed for the skewed-associative cache in [13]. Consider the decomposition of the binary representation of vector V in bit substrings (V_3,V_2,V_1), such that V_1 and V_2 are two n-bit strings. Now consider the function H defined as follows:

$$H: \begin{array}{ccc} \{0,..,2^n-1\} & \longrightarrow & \{0,..,2^n-1\} \\ (y_n, y_{n-1},..,y_1) & \longmapsto & (y_n \oplus y_1, y_n, y_{n-1},..,y_3,y_2) \end{array}$$

where $\oplus$ is the XOR (exclusive or) operation. We can now define three different mapping functions as follows:

$$f_0: \begin{array}{ccc} \mathcal{V} & \longrightarrow & \{0,..,2^n-1\} \\ (V_3,V_2,V_1) & \longmapsto & H(V_1) \oplus H^{-1}(V_2) \oplus V_2 \end{array}$$

$$f_1: \begin{array}{ccc} \mathcal{V} & \longrightarrow & \{0,..,2^n-1\} \\ (V_3,V_2,V_1) & \longmapsto & H(V_1) \oplus H^{-1}(V_2) \oplus V_1 \end{array}$$

$$f_2: \begin{array}{ccc} \mathcal{V} & \longrightarrow & \{0,..,2^n-1\} \\ (V_3,V_2,V_1) & \longmapsto & H^{-1}(V_1) \oplus H(V_2) \oplus V_2 \end{array}$$

Further information about these functions can be found in [13]. The most interesting property of these functions is that if two distinct vectors $(V3, V2, V1)$ and $(W3, W2, W1)$ map to the same entry in a bank, they will not conflict in the other banks if $(V2, V1) \neq (W2, W1)$. Any other function family exhibiting the same property might be used.

Having defined an implementation of the skewed branch predictor, we are now in a position to evaluate it and check its behavior against conventional global-history schemes.

For the purposes of comparison, we will use the *gshare* global scheme for referencing the standard single-bank organization. The skewed branch predictor described earlier will also be referred to as *gskewed* for the remainder of this paper.

5 Analysis

5.1 Simulation Results

The aim of this section is to evaluate the cost-effectiveness of the skewed branch predictor via simulation. In the skewed branch predictor, a prediction associated with a (branch, history) pair is recorded up to three times. It is intuitive that the impact of conflict aliasing is lower in a skewed branch predictor than in a direct-mapped *gshare* table. However, if the same total number of predictor storage bits is allocated to each scheme, it is not clear that *gskewed* will yield better results – the redundancy that makes *gskewed* work also has the effect of increasing the degree of capacity aliasing among a fixed set of predictor entries. Said differently, it may be better to simply build a one-bank predictor table 3 times as large, rather than a 3-bank skewed table.

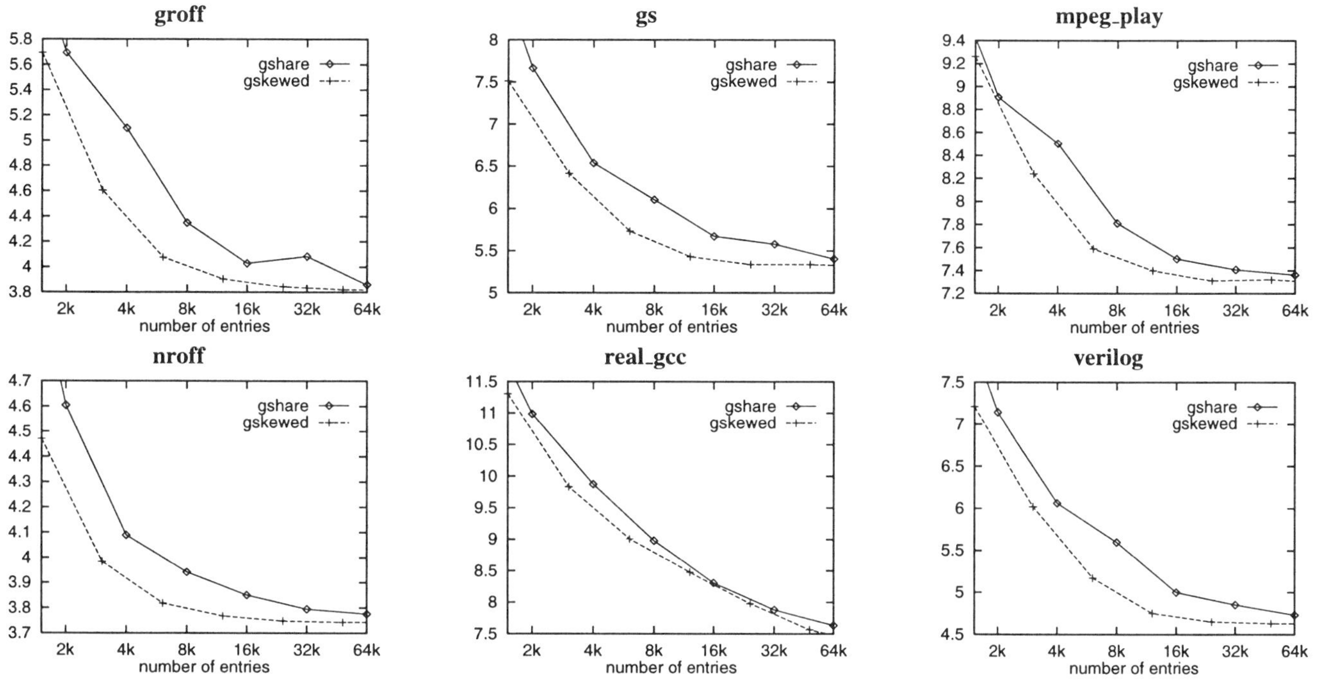

Figure 5: Misprediction percentage with 4-bit history

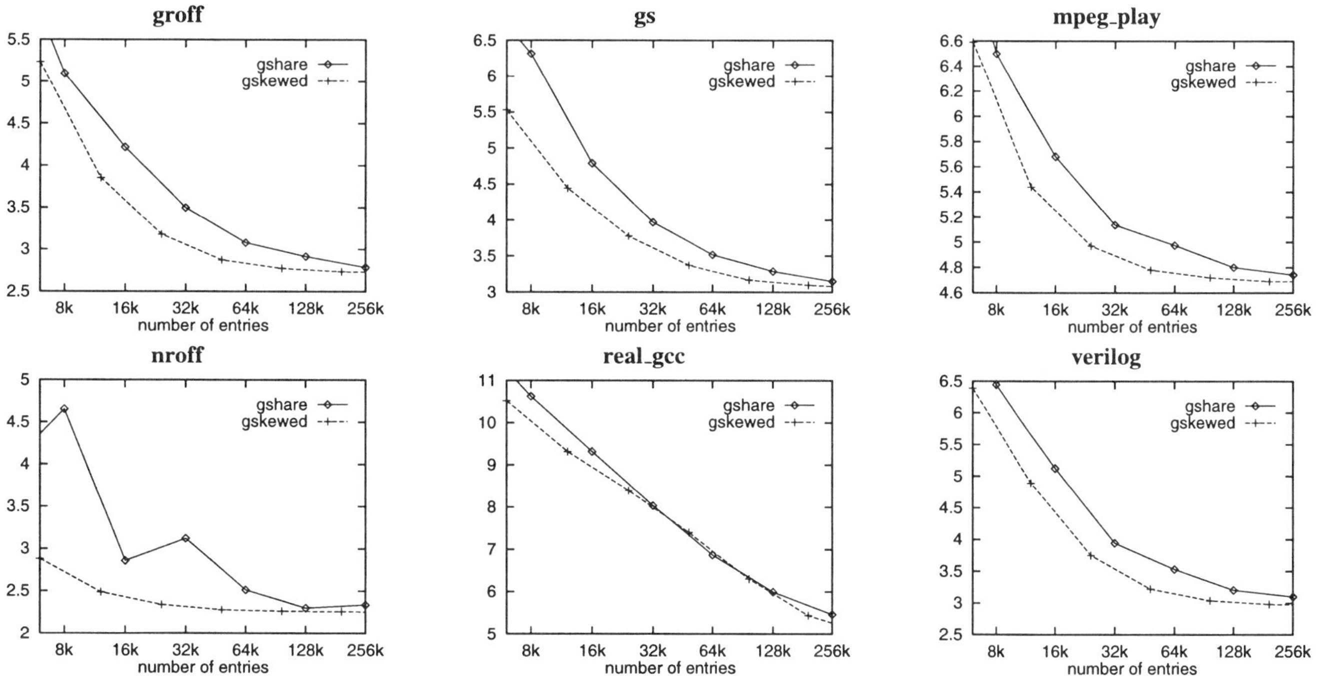

Figure 6: Misprediction percentage with 12-bit history

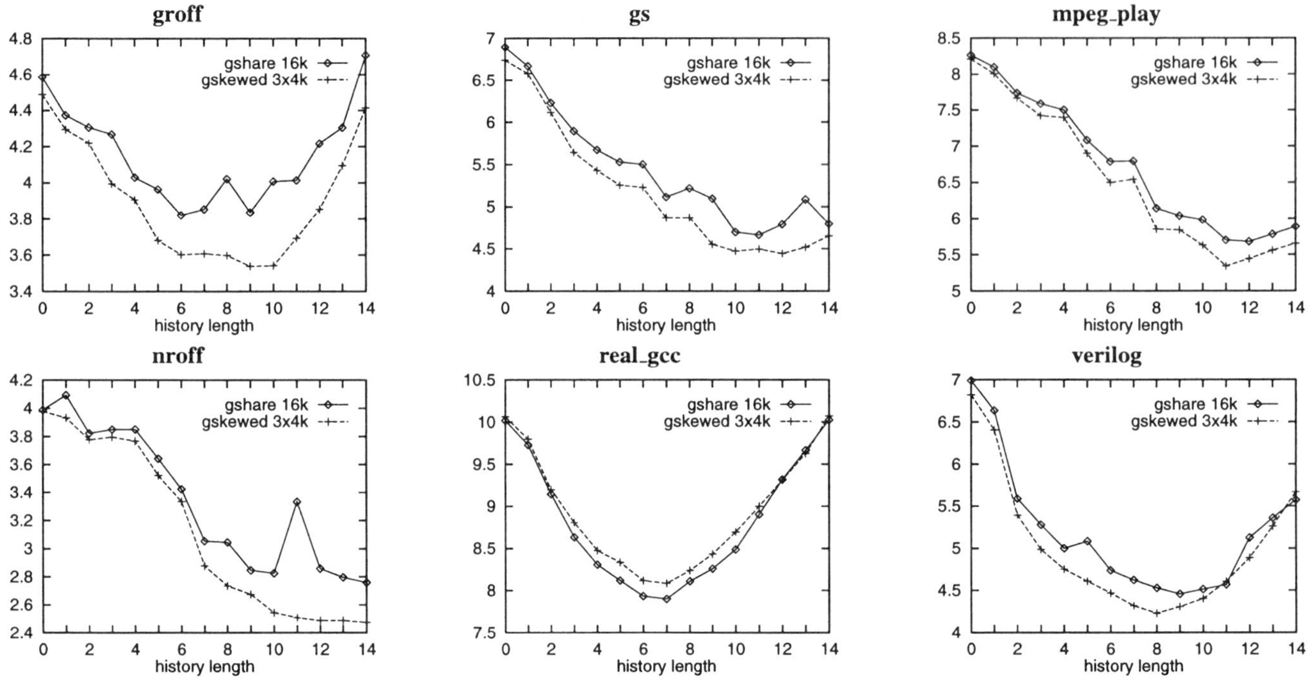

Figure 7: Misprediction percentage of 3x4k-gskewed vs. 16k-gshare

For the direct comparison between *gshare* and *gskewed*, we used 2-bit saturating counters and a *partial update* policy for *gskewed*.

Varying prediction table size The results for a history size of 4 bits and 12 bits are plotted in Figures 5 and 6, respectively, for a large spectrum of table sizes.

The interesting region of these graphs is where capacity aliasing for *gshare* has vanished. In this region,

> *a skewed branch predictor with a partial update policy achieves the same prediction accuracy as a 1-bank predictor, but requires approximately half the storage resources.*

For all benchmarks and for a wide spectrum of predictor sizes, the skewed branch predictor consistently gives better prediction accuracy than the 1-bank predictor. It should be noted that when using the skewed branch predictor and a history length of 4 (12), there is very little benefit in using more than 3x4k (3x16k) entries, while increasing the number of entries to 64k (256k) on *gshare* still improves the prediction accuracy.

Notice that the skewed branch predictor is more able to remove pathological cases. This appears clearly on Figure 6 for *nroff*.

Varying history length For any given prediction table size, some history length is better than others. Figure 7 illustrates the miss rates of a 3x4k-entry *gskewed* vs. a 16k-entry *gshare* when varying the history length. The plots show that despite using 25 % less storage resources, *gskewed* outperforms *gshare* on all benchmarks except *real_gcc*.

Varying number of predictor banks We also considered skewed configurations with five predictor banks. Our simulations results (not reported here) showed that there is very little benefit to increasing the number of banks to five; it appears that a 3-bank skewed branch predictor removes the most significant part of conflict aliasing, and a more cost-effective use of resources would be to increase the size of the banks rather than to increase their number.

Update policy To verify that *gskewed* is effective in removing conflict aliasing, we compare a 3∗N-entry *gskewed* branch predictor with a fully-associative N-entry LRU table. Figure 8 illustrates this experiment for a global history length of 4 bits and 2-bit saturating counters. For (address, history) pairs missing in the fully-associative table, a static prediction *always taken* was assumed. For *gskewed*, both partial-update and total-update policies are shown.

It appears that a 3*N-entry *gskewed* table with partial update delivers slightly better behavior than the N-entry fully-associative table, but when it uses total-update policy, it exhibits slightly worse behavior. We conclude that a 3xN-entry *gskewed* predictor with partial update delivers approximately the same performance as an N-entry fully-associative LRU predictor.

The reason why *partial update* is better than *total update* is intuitive. For partial update, when 2 banks give a good prediction and the third bank gives a bad prediction, we do not update the third bank. By not updating the third bank, we enable it to contribute to the correct prediction of a different substream and effectively increase the capacity of the predictor table as a whole.

5.2 Analytical Model

Although our simulation results show that a skewed predictor table offers an attractive alternative to the standard one-bank predictor structure, they do not provide much explanation as to why a skewed organization works. In this section, we present an analytical model that helps to better understand why the technique is effective.

To make our analytical modeling tractable, we make some simplifying assumptions: we assume 1-bit automatons and the total update policy. We begin by defining the table *aliasing probability*. Consider a hashing function F which maps (address, history)

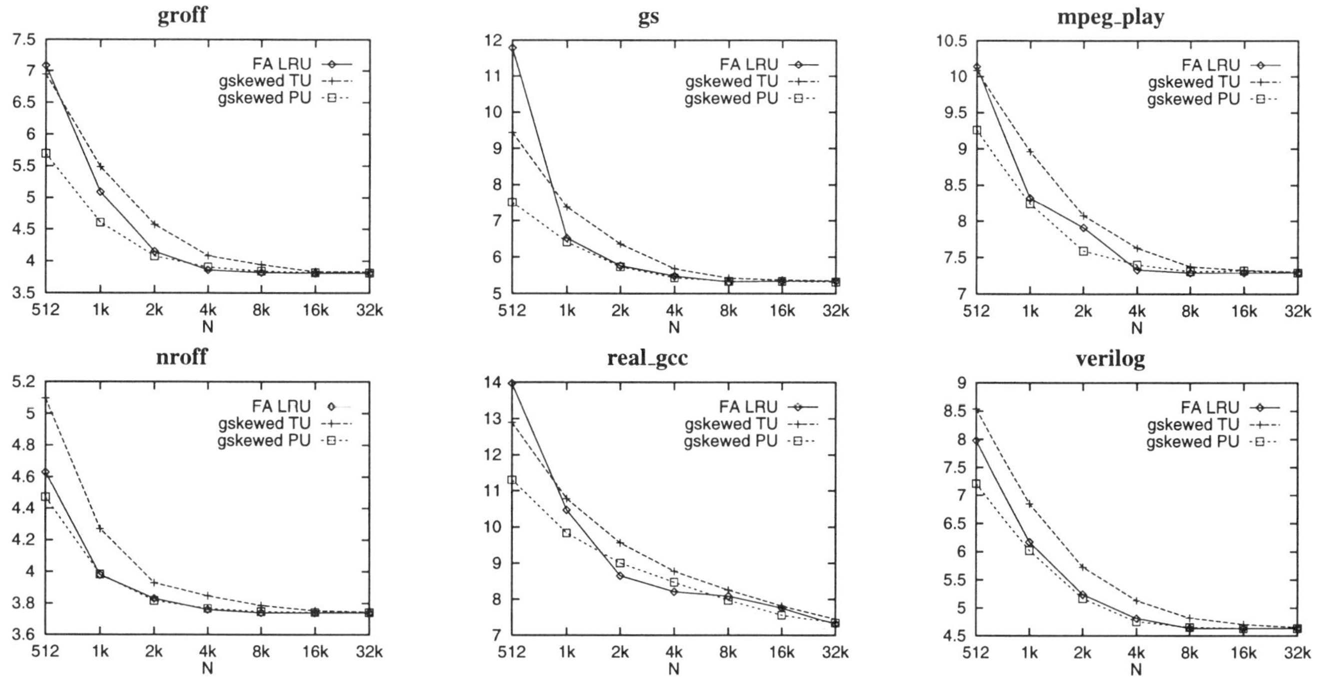

Figure 8: Misprediction percentage of 3N-entry gskewed vs. N-entry fully-associative LRU

pairs onto a N-entry table. The aliasing probability for a dynamic reference V = (address, history) is defined as follows:

Let D be the last-use distance of V, i.e. the number of distinct (address, history) pairs that have been encountered since the last occurrence of V. Assuming F distributes these D vectors equally in the table (i.e., assuming F is a good hashing function), the aliasing probability for dynamic reference V is

$$p_N = 1 - (1 - \frac{1}{N})^D \tag{1}$$

When N is much greater than 1, we get a good approximation with

$$p_N = 1 - e^{-\frac{D}{N}} \tag{2}$$

The aliasing probability is a function of the ratio between the last-use distance and the number of entries.

Let p represent the per-bank aliasing probability, and b be the probability that an (address, history) pair is biased *taken*. With 1-bit predictors, when an entry is aliased, the probability that the prediction given by that entry differs from the unaliased prediction is $2b(1-b)$. It should be noted that the aliasing is less likely to be destructive if b is close to 0 or 1 than if b is close to 1/2.

Assuming a *total update policy*, and because we use different hashing functions for indexing the three banks, the events in a bank are not correlated with the events in an other bank. Now consider a particular dynamic reference V. Four cases can occur:

1. With probability $(1-p)^3$, V is not aliased in any of the three banks: the prediction will be the same as the unaliased prediction.

2. With probability $3p(1-p)^2$, V is aliased in one bank, but not in the other two banks: the resulting majority vote will be in the same direction as the unaliased prediction.

3. With probability $3p^2(1-p)$, V is aliased in two banks, but not in the remaining one.
   With probability $b(1-b)^2 + (1-b)b^2$, predictions for both aliased banks are different from the unaliased prediction: the overall prediction is different from the unaliased prediction.

4. With probability p^3, V is aliased in all three banks.
   With probability $b((1-b)^3+3b(1-b)^2)+(1-b)(b^3+3(1-b)b^2)$, the predictions are different from the unaliased prediction in at least two prediction banks: the skewed prediction is different from the unaliased prediction.

In summary, the probability that a prediction in our 3-bank skewed predictor differs from the unaliased prediction is :

$$\begin{aligned} P_{sk} = \; & 3p^2(1-p)b(1-b) \\ & +p^3b[3b(1-b)^2 + (1-b)^3] \\ & +p^3(1-b)[3(1-b)b^2 + b^3] \end{aligned} \tag{3}$$

In contrast, the formula for a direct-mapped 1-bank predictor table is:

$$P_{dm} = [b(1-b) + (1-b)b]p = 2b(1-b)p \tag{4}$$

P_{dm} and P_{sk} are plotted in Figure 9 for the worst case $b = 50$ %. We have

$$P_{sk} = \frac{3}{4}p^2(1-p) + \frac{1}{2}p^3$$

$$P_{dm} = \frac{1}{2}p$$

The main characteristic of the skewed branch predictor is that its mispredict probability is a polynomial function of the aliasing probability. The most relevant region of the curve is where the per-bank aliasing probability, p, is low (Figure 10 magnifies the curve for small aliasing probabilities).

At comparable storage resources, a 3-bank scheme has a greater per-bank aliasing probability than a 1-bank scheme, because each bank has a smaller number of entries. By taking into account formula (1), we find that for a 3x(N/3)-entry *gskewed*, P_{sk} is lower than P_{dm} in a N-entry direct-mapped table when the last-use distance D is less than approximately $\frac{N}{10}$, while for $D > \frac{N}{10}$, P_{sk} exceeds P_{dm}.

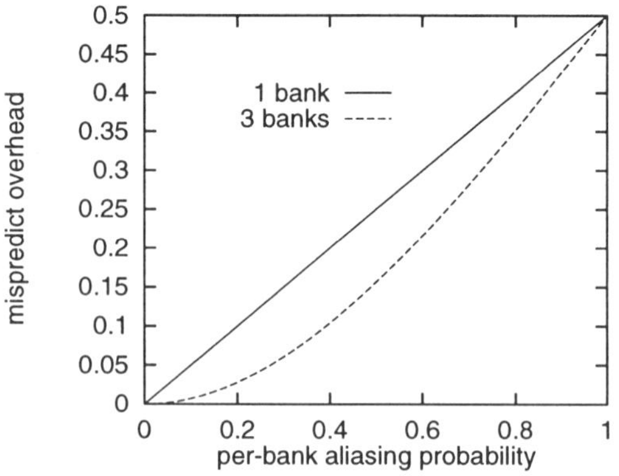

Figure 9: destructive aliasing

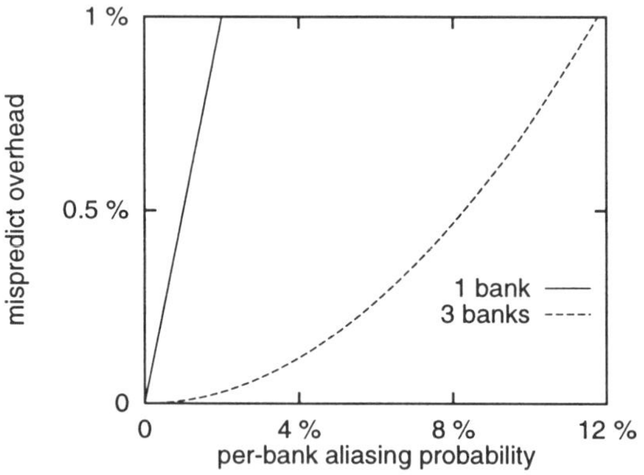

Figure 10: destructive aliasing

This highlights the tradeoff that takes place in the skewed branch predictor: a gain on short last-use distance references is traded for a loss on long last-use distance references. Now consider a N-entry fully-associative LRU table. When the last-use distance D is less than N, there is a hit, otherwise there is a miss. Hence, in a predictor table, aliasing for short last-use distance references is conflict aliasing, and aliasing for long last-use distance references is capacity aliasing.

In other words, **the skewed branch predictor trades conflict aliasing for capacity aliasing**.

To verify if our mathematical model is meaningful, we extrapolated the misprediction rate for *gskewed* by measuring D for each dynamic (address, history) pair and applied formulas (1) and (3). When an (address, history) pair was encountered for the first time, we applied formula (3) with $p = 1$. The bias probability b was evaluated for the entire trace by measuring the density of static (address, history) pairs with bias *taken*, and the value found was then fed back to the simulator when applying formula (3) on the same trace. Finally, we added the unaliased misprediction rate of table 2 (the contribution of compulsory aliasing to mispredictions appears only in the mispredict overhead).

The results are shown in Figure 11 for a history length of 4. It should be noted that our model always slightly overestimates the misprediction rate. This can be explained by the *constructive* aliasing phenomenon that is reported in [21].

As noted above, we made some simplifying assumptions when we devised our analytical model. The difficulty with extending the model to a partial-update policy is that occurrences of aliasing in a bank depend on what happens in the other banks. Modeling the effect of using 2-bit automatons is also difficult because a 2-bit automaton by itself removes some part of aliasing effects on prediction.

Despite the limitations of the model, it effectively explains why skewed branch prediction works: in a standard one-bank table, the mispredict overhead increases linearly with the aliasing probability, but in an M-bank skewed organization, it increases as an M-th degree polynomial. Because we deal with per-bank aliasing probabilities, which range from 0 to 1, a polynomial growth rate is preferable to a linear one.

6 An Enhanced Skewed Branch Predictor

Using a short history vector limits the number of (address, history) pairs (see the *substream ratio* column of Table 2) and therefore the amount of capacity aliasing. On the other hand, using a long history length leads to better intrinsic prediction accuracy on unaliased predictors, but results in a large number of (address, history) pairs. Ideally, given a fixed transistor budget, one would like to benefit from the better intrinsic prediction accuracy associated with a long history, and from the lower aliasing rate associated with a short history. Selecting a good history length is essentially a tradeoff between the accuracy of the unaliased predictor and the aliasing probability.

While the effect of conflict aliasing on the skewed branch predictor has been shown to be negligible, capacity aliasing remains a major issue. In this section we propose an enhancement to the skewed branch predictor that removes a portion of the capacity-aliasing effects without suffering from increased conflict aliasing.

In the *enhanced skewed branch predictor*, the complete information vector (i.e., branch history and address) is used with the hashing functions f_1 and f_2 for indexing bank 1 and bank 2, as in the previous *gskewed* scheme. But for function f_0, which indexes bank 0, we use the usual bit truncation of the branch address ($address \bmod 2^n$).

The rationale for this modification is as follows:
Consider an *enhanced gskewed* and *gskewed* using the same history length L, and (address, history) pair (A, H).

(A, H) has the same last-use distance D_L on the three banks of *gskewed* and on banks 1 and 2 of *enhanced gskewed*. But for *enhanced gskewed*, only the address is used for indexing bank 0, so the last-use distance D_S of the address A on bank 0 is shorter than D_L.

Two situations can occur:

1. When D_L is small compared with the bank size, the aliasing probability on a bank in either *gskewed* or *enhanced gskewed* is small, and both *gskewed* and *enhanced gskewed* are likely to deliver the same prediction as the unaliased predictor for history length L, because these predictions will be present in at least two banks.

2. When D_L becomes large compared with the bank size, the aliasing probability p_L on a any bank of *gskewed* or banks 1 and 2 of *enhanced gskewed* becomes close to 1 (formula (2) in the previous section).

   For both designs, when predictions on banks 1 and 2 differ, the overall prediction is equal to the prediction on bank 0. Now, since $D_S < D_L$, the aliasing probability p_S on bank 0 of *enhanced gskewed* is lower than the aliasing probability p_L on bank 0 of *gskewed*. When D_L is too high, the better intrinsic prediction accuracy associated with the long history on bank 0 in *gskewed* cannot compensate for the increased aliasing probability in bank 0.

Our intuition is that when the history length is short, the first situation will dominate and both predictors will deliver equivalent

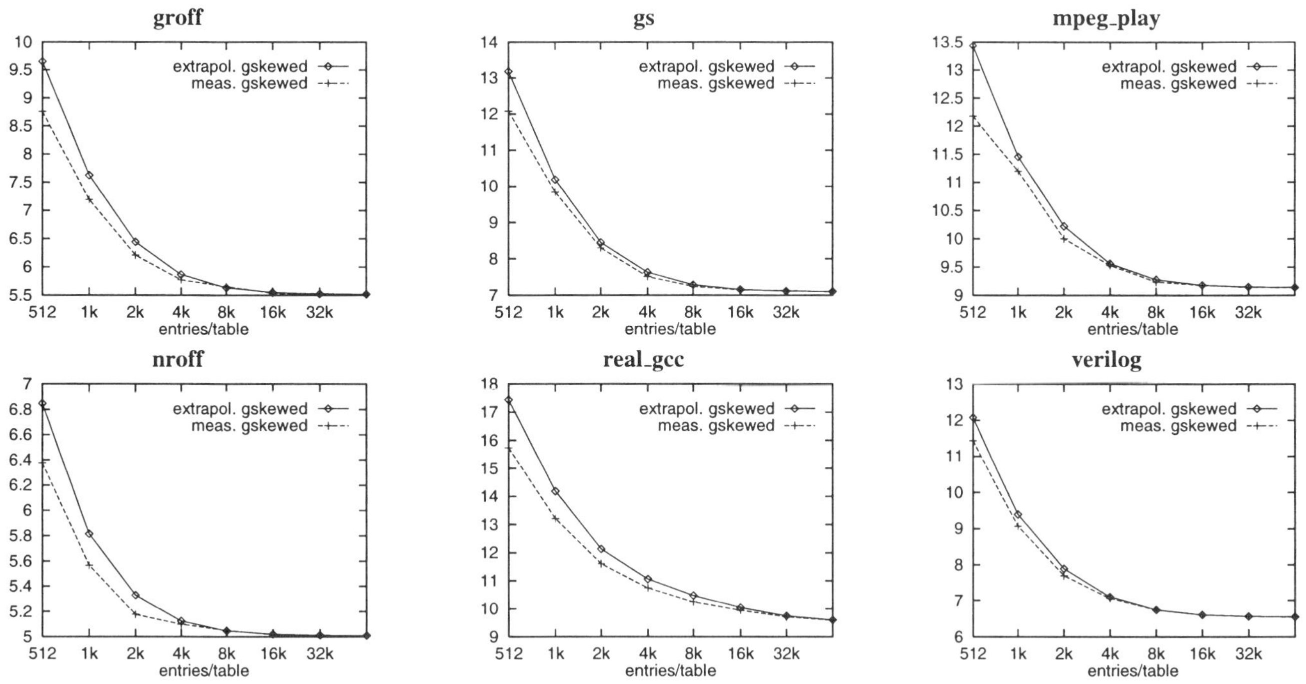

Figure 11: Extrapolated vs. measured misprediction percentage

prediction, but for a longer history length, the second situation will occur more often and *enhanced gskewed* will deliver better overall prediction than *gskewed.*

Simulation results: Figure 12 plots the results of simulations that vary the history length for a 3x4K-entry *enhanced gskewed*, a 3x4K-entry *gskewed* and a 32K-entry *gshare*. A partial-update policy was used in these experiments.

The curves for *gskewed* and *enhanced gskewed* are nearly indistinguishable up to a certain history length. After this point, which is different for each benchmark, the curves begin to diverge, with *enhanced gskewed* exhibiting lower mispredication rates at longer history lengths.

Based on our simulation results, 8 to 10 seems to be a reasonable choice for history length for a 3x4K-entry *gskewed* table, while for *enhanced gskewed*, 11 or 12 would be a better choice.

Notice that the 3x4K-entry *enhanced gskewed* performs as well as the 32K-entry *gshare* on all our benchmarks and for all history lengths, but with less than half of the storage requirements.

7 Conclusions and Future Work

Aliasing effects in branch-predictor tables have been recently identified as a significant contributor to branch-misprediction rates. To better understand and minimize this source of prediction error, we have proposed a new branch-aliasing classification, inspired by the three-Cs model of cache performance.

Although previous branch-prediction research has shown how to reduce compulsory and capacity aliasing, little has been done to reduce conflict aliasing. To that end, we have proposed *skewed branch prediction*, a technique that distributes branch predictors across multiple banks using distinct and independent hashing functions; multiple predictors are read in parallel and a majority vote is used to arrive at an overall prediction.

Our analytical model explains why skewed branch prediction works: in a standard one-bank table, the misprediction overhead increases linearly with the aliasing probability, but in an M-bank skewed organization, it increases as an M-th degree polynomial. Because we deal with per-bank aliasing probabilities, which range from 0 to 1, a polynomial growth rate is preferable to a linear one.

The redundancy in a skewed organization increases the amount of capacity aliasing, but our simulation results show that this negative effect is more than compensated for by the reduction in conflict aliasing when using a partial-update policy.

For tables of 2-bit predictors and equal lengths of global history, a 3-bank skewed organization consistently outperforms a standard 1-bank organization for all configurations with comparable total storage requirements. We found the update policy to be an important factor, with partial update consistently outperforming total update. Although 5-bank (or greater) configurations are possible, our simulations showed that the improvement over a 3-bank configuration is negligible. We also found skewed branch prediction to be less sensitive to pathological cases (e.g., *nroff* in Figure 6).

To reduce capacity aliasing further, we proposed the enhanced skewed branch predictor, which was shown to consistently reach the performance level of a conventional *gshare* predictor of more than twice the same size.

In addition to these performance advantages, skewed organizations offer a chip designer an additional degree of flexibility when allocating die area. Die-area constraints, for example, may not permit increasing a 1-bank predictor table from 16K to 32K, but a skewed organization offers a middle point: 3 banks of 8K entries apiece for a total of 24K entries.

In this paper, we have only addressed aliasing on prediction schemes using a global history vector. The same technique could be applied to remove aliasing in other prediction methods, including per-address history schemes [18, 19, 20], or hybrid schemes [8, 2, 1, 4].

Skewed branch prediction raises some new questions:

- **Update Policies:** Are there policies other than partial-update and total-update that offer better performance in skewed or enhanced skewed branch predictors?

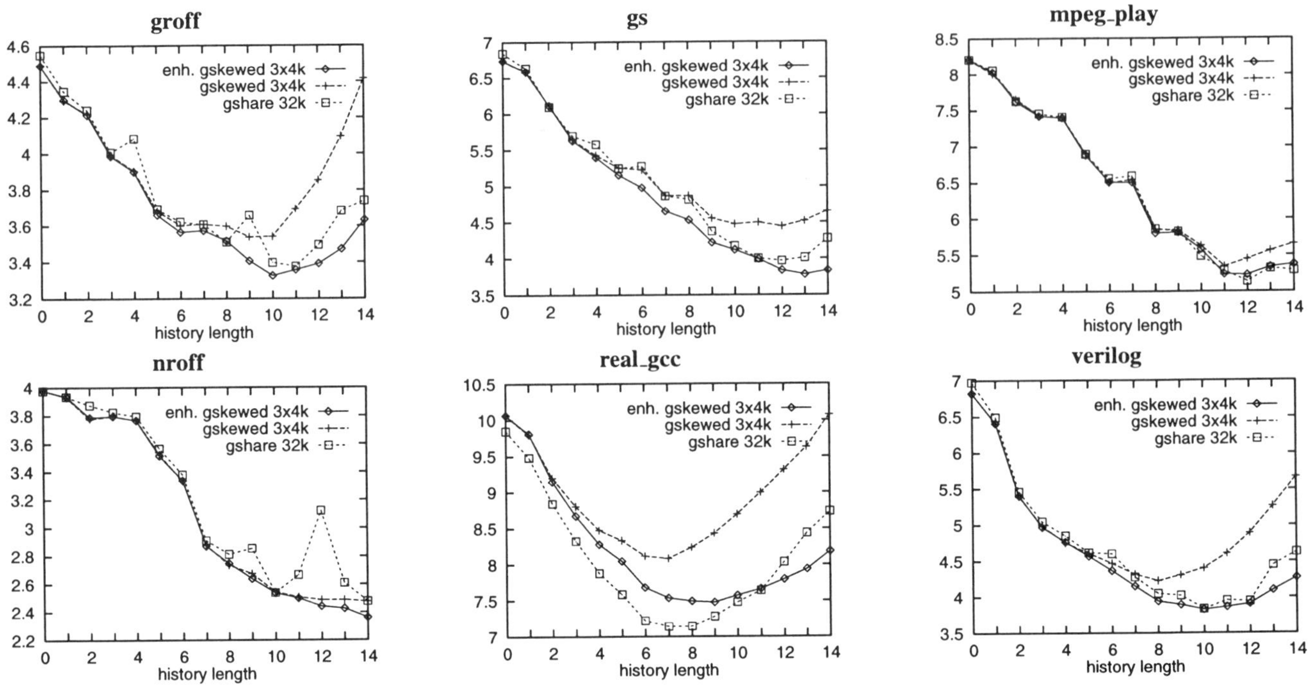

Figure 12: Misprediction percentage of *enhanced gskewed*

- **Distributed Predictor Encodings:** In our simulations we adopted the standard 2-bit predictor encodings and simply replicated them across 3 banks. Do there exist alternative "distributed" predictor encodings that are more space efficient, and more robust against aliasing?
- **Minimizing Capacity Aliasing**: Skewed branch predictors are very effective in reducing conflict-aliasing effects, but they do so at the expense of increased capacity aliasing. Do there exist other techniques, like those used in the enhanced skewed predictor, that could minimize these effects?

References

[1] P.-Y. Chang, E. Hao, and Y.N. Patt. Alternative implementations of hybrid branch predictors. In *Proceedings of the 28th International Symposium on Microarchitecture*, 1995.

[2] P.-Y. Chang, E. Hao, T.-Y. Yeh, and Y.N. Patt. Branch classification: a new mechanism for improving branch predictor performance. In *Proceedings of the 27th International Symposium on Microarchitecture*, 1994.

[3] I.-C.K. Chen, J.T. Coffey, and T.N. Mudge. Analysis of branch prediction via data compression. In *Proceedings of the 7th International Conference on Architectural Support for Programming Languages and Operating Systems*, Oct. 1996.

[4] M. Evers, P.-Y. Chang, and Y.N. Patt. Using hybrid branch predictors to improve branch prediction accuracy in the presence of context switches. In *Proceedings of the 23rd Annual International Symposium on Computer Architecture*, May 1996.

[5] N. Gloy, C. Young, B. Chen, and M.D. Smith. An analysis of dynamic branch prediction schemes on system workloads. In *Proceedings of the 23rd Annual International Symposium on Computer Architecture*, May 1996.

[6] M.D. Hill. *Aspects of Cache Memory and Instruction Buffer Performance*. PhD thesis, University of California, Berkeley, 1987.

[7] J.K.F. Lee and A.J. Smith. Branch prediction strategies and branch target buffer design. *IEEE Computer*, pages 6–22, January 1984.

[8] Scott McFarling. Combining branch predictors. Technical report, DEC, 1993.

[9] R. Nair. Dynamic path-based branch correlation. In *Proceedings of the 28th Annual International Symposium on Microarchitecture*, 1995.

[10] S.T. Pan, K. So, and J.T. Rahmeh. Improving the accuracy of dynamic branch prediction using branch correlation. In *Proceedings of the 5th International Conference on Architectural Support for Programming Languages and Operating Systems*, 1992.

[11] S. Sechrest, C.C. Lee, and T. Mudge. Correlation and aliasing in dynamic branch predictors. In *Proceedings of the 23rd Annual International Symposium on Computer Architecture*, May 1996.

[12] A. Seznec. A case for two-way skewed-associative caches. In *Proceedings of the 20th Annual International Symposium on Computer Architecture*, May 1993.

[13] A. Seznec and F. Bodin. Skewed associative caches. In *Proceedings of PARLE' 93*, May 1993.

[14] J.E. Smith. A study of branch prediction strategies. In *Proceedings of the 8th Annual International Symposium on Computer Architecture*, May 1981.

[15] R.A. Sugumar and S.G. Abraham. Efficient simulation of caches under optimal replacement with applications to miss

characterization. In *Proceedings of the ACM SIGMETRIC Conference*, 1993.

[16] A.R. Talcott, M. Nemirovsky, and R.C Wood. The influence of branch prediction table interference on branch prediction scheme performance. In *Proceedings of the 3rd Annual International Conference on Parallel Architectures and Compilation Techniques*, 1995.

[17] R. Uhlig, D. Nagle, T. Mudge, S. Sechrest, and J. Emer. Coping with code bloat. In *Proceedings of the 22nd Annual International Symposium on Computer Architecture*, June 1995.

[18] T.-Y. Yeh and Y.N. Patt. Two-level adaptive branch prediction. In *Proceedings of the 24th International Symposium on Microarchitecture*, Nov. 1991.

[19] T.-Y. Yeh and Y.N. Patt. Alternative implementations of two-level adaptive branch prediction. In *Proceedings of the 19th Annual International Symposium on Computer Architecture*, May 1992.

[20] T.-Y. Yeh and Y.N. Patt. A comparison of dynamic branch predictors that use two levels of branch history. In *Proceedings of the 20th Annual International Symposium on Computer Architecture*, May 1993.

[21] C. Young, N. Gloy, and M.D. Smith. A comparative analysis of schemes for correlated branch prediction. In *Proceedings of the 22nd Annual International Symposium on Computer Architecture*, June 1995.

A Language for Describing Predictors and its Application to Automatic Synthesis

Joel Emer
Digital Equipment
Hudson, MA 01749
emer@vssad.hlo.dec.com

Nikolas Gloy
Harvard University
Cambridge, MA 02138
ng@eecs.harvard.edu

Abstract

As processor architectures have increased their reliance on speculative execution to improve performance, the importance of accurate prediction of what to execute speculatively has increased. Furthermore, the types of values predicted have expanded from the ubiquitous branch and call/return targets to the prediction of indirect jump targets, cache ways and data values. In general, the prediction process is one of identifying the current state of the system, and making a prediction for some as yet uncomputed value based on that state. Prediction accuracy is improved by learning what is a good prediction for that state using a feedback process at the time the predicted value is actually computed. While there have been a number of efforts to formally characterize this process, we have taken the approach of providing a simple algebraic-style notation that allows one to express this state identification and feedback process. This notation allows one to describe a wide variety of predictors in a uniform way. It also facilitates the use of an efficient search technique called genetic programming, which is loosely modeled on the natural evolutionary process, to explore the design space. In this paper we describe our notation and the results of the application of genetic programming to the design of branch and indirect jump predictors.

1. Introduction

In the quest for more CPU performance, there is ever greater use of strategies to increase instruction-level parallelism, including deep pipelines, super-scalar issue, and out-of-order issue. In order to achieve a performance benefit, these techniques have resulted in an increasing reliance on **speculative execution**, that is, executing operations before all the input values are known.

ISCA '97 Denver, CO, USA
© 1997 ACM 0-89791-901-7/97/0006...$3.50

The standard technique for coping with unknown input values is guessing the value, using the guessed value in the speculative operation, and eventually resolving whether the guess was right or not. If the guess was right, then the computation can proceed. If the guess was wrong, however, the processor needs to reset its state back to the point before the guess, and resume with the correct input values. This process of generating a guess is more formally called **prediction**.

Branch prediction is the most commonly seen form of prediction [14,17,18,11]. In this case, the value being predicted is the instruction to execute after a branch instruction, e.g., either the target of the branch or the next sequential instruction. This information is needed very early in the pipeline, so that instruction fetch can be directed to fetch the correct instruction. On the other hand, the branch result will not be determined until the branch executes far down the pipeline. Thus, accurate branch prediction can substantially improve performance by allowing for the speculative execution of instructions following the branch before the branch resolves.

While branch prediction is probably the best known form of prediction, there are many other cases where one can predict either architectural or implementation values. Some examples are: indirect jump target prediction [6,8], return instruction target prediction [5], cache way prediction [2], cache miss prediction, and data value prediction [9]. In each of these cases, a value is predicted and used speculatively pending actual computation of the value.

Previous work on categorizing and characterizing predictors has been based on the high-level constructs from earlier research on branch prediction mechanisms, such as global-history components or tables of saturating counters [12,13,18,19]. This seems logical, particularly for an automated search, because a predictor composed from such constructs is quite likely to resemble a known good predictor, whereas a predictor built arbitrarily from lower-level primitives is less likely to be useful.

Using higher-level constructs, however, means that the only predictors we are ever going to see are made from

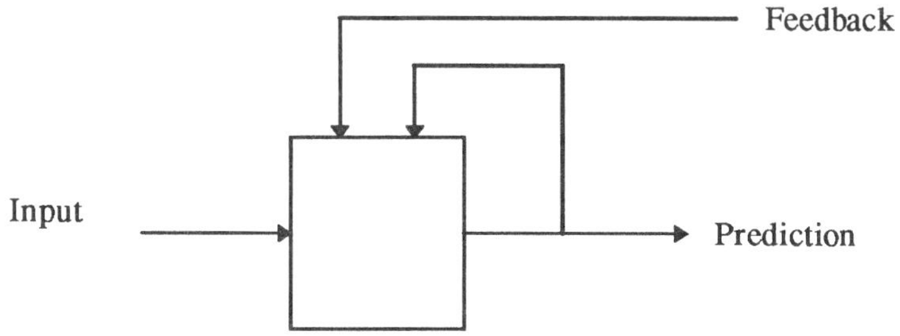

Figure 1 - Basic Prediction Feedback Loop

these familiar building blocks. We are therefore losing the chance to find interesting new components of predictors that we had not previously thought of. Another drawback is that while we know many good building blocks for branch predictors, this may not be the case for other prediction problems. So for those problems, we would likely be more successful starting from lower-level primitives. Therefore, rather than base a model of prediction on the various existing predictors, we define a simple primitive predictor.

The model we have developed allows a large variety of predictors to be described using a language with a simple algebraic-style syntax. Our aim is to formalize the process of specification of predictors in part to facilitate the search of the design space. Previously, this has been essentially a manual process, i.e., dependent on the creativity of the researcher. We aim to provide automatic help.

Thus, given this algebraic-style description for predictors, we can employ automated search techniques in order to find new predictors. In particular, the set of techniques known as genetic programming allows one to search a general expression design space [7]. It is a stochastic technique that is well suited to situations where we do not know much about what solutions might look like, since it finds increasingly better solutions from a starting point that can be completely randomly generated.

In Section 2 we provide a framework that can be used to describe a wide variety of predictors, and a corresponding algebraic notation that can be used to simply describe these predictors. In Section 3 we provide an overview of genetic programming, and in Section 4 we describe how we apply it to the task of finding predictors. In section 5 we describe the results of our genetic programming experiments to find branch predictors and indirect jump predictors. Then finally in Section 6 we conclude with some observations.

2. Predictor Notation

The principal function of any predictor is to take an input, corresponding to the current state of the system, and generate an output that predicts some as yet uncomputed value. Note that this input can be as all-encompassing of system state as desired. Thus, while most branch predictor studies have been based on just the current program counter, PC, as the input for the predictor, there is no reason not to use other information, such as the opcode or sign of the branch offset (since backward branches are likely to be part of loops, and hence more likely taken). So in general one should consider using all the information available in earlier pipe stages of the current or later instructions as well as information available from earlier instructions in later pipe stages [2].

Predictors can be divided into two classes: **static** and **dynamic.** In the case of a **static** predictor the prediction is always the same logical function of the input to the predictor. On the other hand, **dynamic** predictors *learn* to make better predictions from information that is only available after the prediction is made. Dynamic predictors thus use feedback to learn from past behavior and hence make better predictions in the future.

The natural, but not necessarily required, time to feed information back to the predictor is when it is determined whether the prediction was correct or not. This is referred to as the time the prediction **resolves.** Thus, frequently, the information fed back to the predictor is simply the accuracy of the prediction. So, in the case of a branch predictor, whether the branch was taken or not can be fed back to the predictor to help it improve its predictions. In addition, however, other information might also be provided. This overall dynamic prediction scheme can be viewed as a feedback control system as illustrated in Figure 1.

In order for such a feedback control system to learn, it needs some sort of memory. To provide this memory we define, as a primitive, the structure in Figure 2. This primitive is basically a memory that is w bits wide and d entries deep. As with a typical memory, it has two operations. For our purposes, however, rather than read and write, the two operations are called **predict** and **update**, and furthermore these two operations are always used as a pair. Thus, in our example, the operation of the predictor consists of a **predict** step in which the memory is accessed at address index, I, and the value read is used as the prediction, P. Some time later, when the prediction resolves, an update value, U, is delivered to the predictor

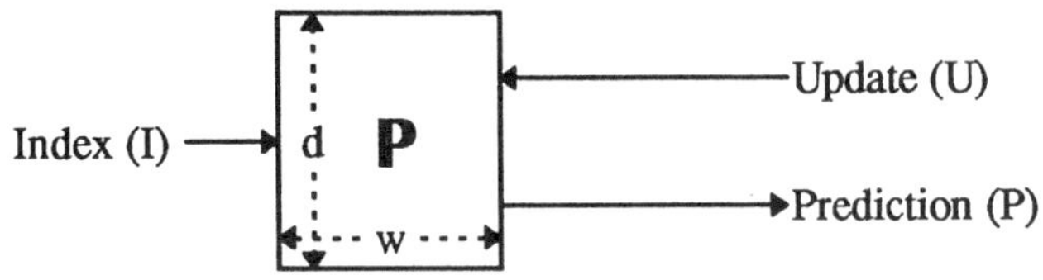

Figure 2 - Primitive Predictor

and written into the same location indexed by I. A trivial extension might involve writing back to a different location, but we will not consider that case. Similarly, we do not consider the case where there might be multiple predictions before there is an update.

We will represent the primitive predictor in Figure 2 as an algebraic expression:

P[w, d](I; U)

where,
w = width
d = depth
I = index for prediction and update
U = update value

Note that we use a notation in which the static configuration parameters of the predictor are enclosed in square brackets ([]). These parameters allow us to describe a class of predictors of various sizes with one definition. A specific instance of a predictor has constant values specified for these parameters.

Following the configuration parameters are the dynamic arguments used to generate predictions. These are enclosed in parentheses (()). These arguments are in turn partitioned between the input arguments, listed first, and the update arguments, listed after the semicolon (;). Other predictors defined in terms of this primitive predictor will also follow this notation.

Use of this predictor can be thought of as inputting a series of index, I, and update, U, values and generating a series of predictions, P. By using specific values or expressions as the inputs to the predictor, we can create a variety of predictors. Thus a simple 1-bit branch predictor that predicts a branch will behave the same this time as it did last time can be represented as:

Onebit[d](PC; T) = P[1, d](PC; T);

where,
PC = current program counter
T = branch resolution
(0 -> not taken, 1 -> taken)

This expression defines the predictor "Onebit" with parameter d, input PC and update expression T as the expression on the right of the equal sign (=). The expression on the right describes the size and how to "wire up" the primitive predictor P to create "Onebit." Note that this predictor is parameterized by its depth, d. Therefore, to specify a specific predictor, like that in the DEC Alpha 21064, we can use Onebit as follows:

A21064[](PC; T) = Onebit[2K](PC; T);

We can also build up more complex components out of the simple predictor that can be used to build even more sophisticated predictors. Thus we can define an array of n-bit saturating counters each of which counts up or down based on their update value, such as described in [14] as:

Counter[n,d](I; T) = P[n, d](I; if T then P+1 else P-1);

Note that in this case we use the value generated by the predictor, P in this example, as part of the expression for the update expression. We also have assumed that our addition and subtraction operations are saturating operations. Using this predictor and a function MSB that returns the most-significant bit of a value, we can easily create the ubiquitous 2-bit counter predictor as:

Twobit[d](PC; T) = MSB(Counter[2,d](PC;T));

Another useful primitive is one that keeps a history of some value by concatenating the current history value with the update value. The following expression describes a predictor that maintains an array of histories of values:

Hist[w, d](I;V) = P[w,d](I; P || V);

Using this primitive one can create a variety of predictors such as these global and local history or two-level adaptive branch predictors from Yeh and Patt [18]:

GAg[n](;T) = Twobit[2^n](Hist[n, 1](0; T); T);

PAg[n, d](PC; T) = Twobit[2^n](Hist[n, d](PC; T); T);

A simple modification of the index expression leads to the PAp scheme from Pan, So and Rameh [11]:

PAp[n, m, d](PC; T) =
Twobit[2^m](PC || Hist[n, d](PC; T); T);

Similarly, McFarling's GShare predictor [10] can be expressed as:

GShare[m](PC; T) =
Twobit[2^m](PC $\oplus$ Hist[m, 1](0; T); T);

Finally, what may be the most complex commercially implemented predictor, the choosing predictor [10] used in the DEC Alpha 21264. This predictor consists of a local history predictor and a global history predictor that are selected between by a global history based chooser:

Lhist[](PC;T) = Threebit[1K](Hist[10,1K](PC;T); T);
Ghist[](;T) = Twobit[4K](Hist[12,1](0;T); T);

A21264[](PC; T) =
if (MSB(P[2,4K](Hist[12,1](0;T);
P + (Lhist==T) - (Ghist == T)))
then Lhist[](PC;T)
else Ghist[](;T);

Where Threebit is the obvious extension of Twobit to three bit counters.

Through the composition of predictors and various logic expressions a large variety of predictors can be created. Note, furthermore, that the predictors need not be restricted to generating single bit predictions. For example, one can specify a predictor for indirect jumps. Following is an expression that builds a table for indirect jumps that predicts that each indirect jump instruction will jump to the same target it jumped to last time:

Jump[d](PC; Target) = P[32, d](PC; Target);

We have developed a parser for a version of this notation called the **BP language.** This BP language parser understands the predictor primitive and a variety of functions. It also understands another primitive, which we do not use here, that represents a set-associative tag store.

The parser translates BP language expressions into a set of subroutines that simulate the predictor that the expression describes. From there it is easy to link the predictor subroutines to a trace reader to simulate the performance of the specified predictor.

In the next section, we describe a search technique that can automatically generate predictors.

3. Genetic Programming

We base our automatic search for predictors on genetic programming [7]. Genetic programming is derived from genetic algorithms [4], so we will describe those first. Genetic algorithms are a method for efficiently searching extremely large problem spaces. Their behavior has some similarities to the way in which natural selection enables evolution to produce species that are adapted to their environment.

A genetic algorithm encodes potential solutions to a given problem as fixed-length bit strings. Initially, we generate a set of random bit strings, each of which is called an **individual** by analogy to the evolution paradigm. This set is our initial **population** or **generation**. We evaluate the **fitness** of each individual by computing a metric that reflects how well the solution encoded by its bit string solves the problem. This metric might be the cost of the solution, or a measure of how close an individual gets to achieving a particular task.

To create the next generation in the evolutionary process, we create new individuals from old ones by applying **genetic operations** that recombine the components of the old individuals in different ways. Thus, structures that are part of a good solution that have developed in some individuals can be combined with structures developed in other individuals. The resulting offspring might be an individual combining several good components and potentially achieving a higher fitness value.

This process of combining pieces of solutions to form new solutions is one of the key features of genetic algorithms. The other key feature is the way in which the fitness of an individual influences its propagation in future generations: The individuals that serve as input to the genetic operations are chosen with a probability based on their fitness value. Individuals with a higher fitness value have a higher probability of being chosen, so that they may appear many more times than individuals of lower fitness value. This means that the next generation will contain many individuals that contain one or more components from successful individuals of the previous generations, which makes it likely that the average fitness of the new generation will be better than that of the previous generation. By repeating this process many times, we produce a sequence of successive generations.

The first generation, being a set of random points in the search space, will usually not contain any reasonable solutions. The fitness-based selection method will, however, try out many modifications and combinations of the slightly better individuals, which generally leads to much improved solutions within a few generations.

Genetic algorithms often work very well for problems where solutions can be encoded in fixed-length strings. They are too constraining for problems, such as prediction, where the solutions are general algebraic expressions or programs. Genetic programming, which is closely related to genetic algorithms, is better suited to these problems. The only change is that the individuals are not encoded as fixed-length strings, but as tree structures, and the genetic operations are adapted to perform analogous operations on tree structures. This allows us to easily represent algebraic expressions or parse-tree representations of programs, and it allows the individuals to grow as needed. In our application of this method, the individuals are BP language expressions that describe predictors.

4. Genetic Programming Search

To apply genetic programming to automatically synthesize predictors, we created a set of programs and scripts to perform the genetic programming search as follows:

1. Create initial population of randomly generated individuals
2. Rank fitness of individuals in the population by simulation
3. Apply genetic operations to create new generation
4. Repeat steps 2 and 3

More specifically, however, to apply genetic programming to predictors one needs to map the predictor problem into the appropriate structure. First, we will describe how we represent expressions in the BP language as tree data structures. Next, we present the genetic operations that are used to produce new individuals from old ones. Then, we describe how these operations are applied to a generation of individuals to create the next generation. We also need to place some constraints on the expressions that are produced by genetic operations to ensure that the results are valid BP expressions, that they do not grow unreasonably large, and that they satisfy certain other constraints that simplify the implementation of some aspects of the operations. Finally, we present the method we use to determine the fitness of the individuals in the population.

4.1 Representation of expressions

Individuals are represented by a tree structure which is easily translated into a corresponding expression in the BP language. The tree nodes are divided into the following categories:

Predictors

A predictor node represents a primitive predictor of the BP language. It contains the width and height of the predictor, and has two descendants: The first one corresponds to the expression used to compute the index of the predictor, and the second one corresponds to the expression used to update the state of the predictor.

Functions

We currently use the following functions: XOR, CAT (concatenation), MASKHI/MASKLO (which return a given number of the high or low bits), MSB (returns the highest bit), SATUR (performs a saturating add of a given width), IF (selects one of two inputs depending on the value of a third input). If desired, it is very easy to extend this set, since the BP language contains many additional functions.

Terminals

Input values: For each class of prediction problem, there is a list of the arguments to a predictor. Arguments are separated into two classes: the **input** values that are available immediately, and the **update** values that are available after the value being predicted has been computed. For branch prediction, the **inputs** usually include the PC of the branch instruction, but other processor state can also be useful, such as the branch direction (the sign bit of the branch offset). The **update** value for branch prediction is typically the branch outcome.

Value of a predictor: An expression can be a reference to the value of another predictor node. To simplify the implementation of other parts of the system, it was expedient to allow only references to the nearest enclosing predictor. This restricts the class of predictors that can be generated, and we plan to remove this restriction in the future.

Integer constants: We allow small integer constants to be available in expressions.

4.2 Genetic Operations

In this section, we describe the genetic operations that are used to populate a new generation.

Replication

To ensure that the very best individuals of a generation are not lost or destroyed by other operations, we copy a certain number of the best individuals to the next generation.

Crossover

The most important operation is one that combines the components of two predictors in a different way to form two new predictors. To perform a crossover operation on two individuals, we randomly choose a node in each of the two, and exchange the subtrees defined by the two nodes.

Mutation

There are two kinds of mutation operations; their purpose is to make small changes to individuals, which can sometimes be needed to prevent the entire generation from converging to identical individuals. We apply mutation operations to the offspring generated by crossover operations.

For a node mutation, we randomly choose a node within the expression tree of the individual, and modify the node as follows: If it is a function node, we replace it with a different function; if that function needs more arguments than the original function, we create random expression trees as needed. If it is a terminal node, we replace it with another terminal. If it is a predictor node, we change the width and/or height of the predictor.

For a subtree mutation, we randomly choose a node and replace the subtree defined by the node with a randomly generated subtree of identical height.

Encapsulation

Crossover operations are necessary to combine useful components of individuals, but they can also be destructive: They may break up a useful component of an individual into parts that are meaningless by themselves. An encapsulation operation makes a randomly chosen subtree of an individual into an indivisible unit that cannot be broken apart by a crossover operation or mutation, although it can still be moved in its entirety [1]. For a randomly chosen encapsulation point, there is no way to know that this encapsulated component is actually useful. However, if it is useful, then individuals that receive this component through crossover will tend to improve, and the fitness-based selection and replication will make those individuals more frequent in the next generation. On the other hand, if the component is useless, then individuals incorporating it will tend not to be successful, and the component will not propagate and eventually die out.

There is an opposite operation, called expansion, that turns an encapsulated subtree back into a regular subtree. This way, encapsulated expressions still have a chance to improve by taking part in other operations.

For each of these operations, the individuals serving as inputs are chosen using a method called **tournament selection**. To choose one individual by this method, we first choose a set of individuals randomly and uniformly from all the individuals of the current generation; the size of this set is a parameter called the **tournament size**. Then we find the individual in that set that has the best fitness value, and discard all the other individuals. The result is that individuals are chosen according to a probability distribution that gives higher probability to individuals with higher fitness values, while less fit individuals still have some chance to be chosen occasionally. How much this probability distribution is biased towards better individuals is determined by the tournament size parameter. For a generation size of 400 individuals, we typically use a tournament size of 8.

4.3 Constraints

In order to produce legal and usable individuals, we need to impose certain constraints on the results of genetic operations. In most cases, we achieve this by first allowing the operations to proceed oblivious to the constraints. We then check the result for compliance with these constraints, and modify the individuals where necessary.

Our first constraint is to avoid generating predictors of excessive implementation size (i.e. the number of storage bits it takes to implement the predictor). To keep the predictors from growing indefinitely, we limit the implementation size of any predictor to 512K bits of storage. When a predictor exceeds this bound, we reduce its size until it falls below this limit: we randomly choose a predictor node within the expression tree, and reduce either its width or its height by one step. Experience has shown that many of the predictors that are created do not use their implementation size efficiently; for example, many predictors contain subexpressions that contain a large predictor table whose value does not affect the output of the entire expression. Therefore, the somewhat generous limit of 512K bits was deemed appropriate.

Our second constraint is making sure that the expression is a legal BP expression. For example, during crossover a terminal node that refers to the value of an enclosing predictor may be moved outside of the update subtree of that predictor. In this case, if there is another predictor enclosing the new location, the node will now automatically refer to the nearest enclosing predictor in its new context. If there is no such predictor, the node is changed to a constant value of 1. Another problem occurs when a terminal node that represents an update value is in a context where that value is not available, e.g., the branch outcome cannot be used in an indexing expression of a branch predictor.

Because the widths of values in the BP system are important, when generating predictors the system must explicitly specify the widths of each expression. As a simplification, we currently only allow expressions whose width can be statically determined. In most cases, these can be determined from the widths of the subexpressions, except where there is a recursion. In those cases, we pick a width at random.

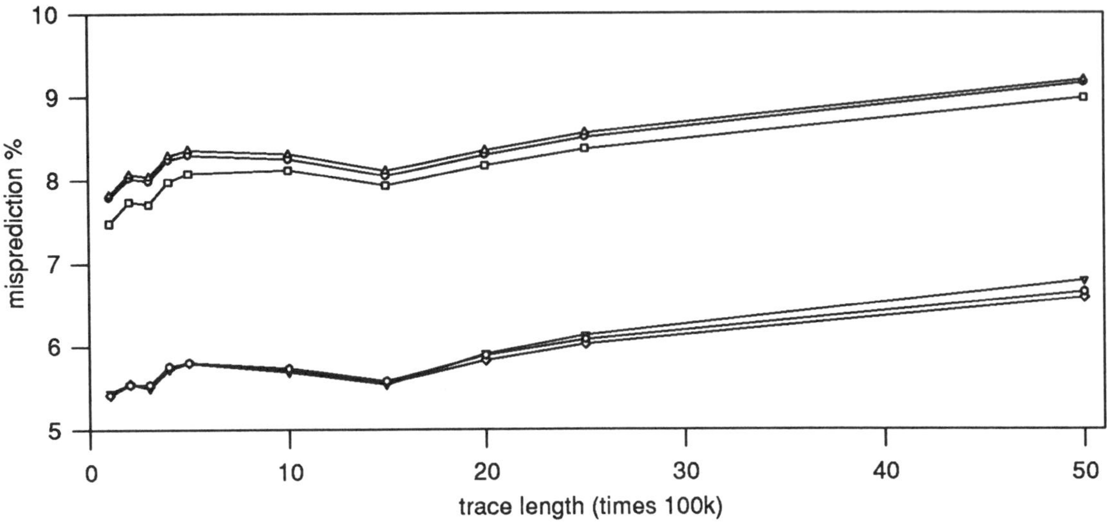

Figure 3- Performance of Branch Predictors vs. Trace Length

As Koza [7] notes, one often needs to coerce results into a particular form for the problem being studied. We found this to be true, so we developed a way of using templates for the individuals of the initial generation, to provide a reasonable starting point. For example, one could use a template that is a predictor with a random indexing expression and 2-bit saturating counter as the update expression. It is possible to have templates where the user-provided components are forever fixed, or the entire individual may be changed by genetic operations. Usually, generating the more complex forms of branch predictors depended on starting with more advanced structures in the template.

4.4 Fitness

For the predictors we study, we use the accuracy of the predictor, expressed as a misprediction rate, as the fitness metric. To calculate the misprediction rate, we use the BP language parser to create simulators of predictors from these BP language expressions. We run those simulators over instruction traces with a parameterizable training period to avoid startup effects. In our experiments, we used Atom [3] generated traces from some SPEC92 and SPEC95 [15] integer benchmarks (compress, eqntott, gcc, go, m88ksim, xlisp) compiled for the DEC Alpha on Digital Unix with the switches set as submitted to SPEC. We also used some traces from the IBS benchmark suite [16]. The simulation output consists of a prediction accuracy and fitness ranking for each predictor.

Simulating the execution of an entire benchmark every time we need to evaluate the fitness of the hundreds of predictors in a generation would make it unbearably slow to produce the 20-30 generations that are usually needed to obtain good results. Thus, we use shortened runs to generate fitness values.

Fortunately, the fitness measure is used only as an input for the tournament selection process, which needs only the relative ranking of the individuals and furthermore is a probabilistic process that is unlikely to be affected by slight inaccuracies in the rankings. Therefore, we do not need a perfectly accurate fitness value, but only a roughly accurate ranking of the individuals in a generation. To generate this ranking, we simulate until we find a ranking order that is reasonably stable. Typically, this requires simulating about one million branches.

Note, however, that if we use a single trace for an entire benchmark, we would repeatedly use only the first million events from the trace. Instead, we use several shorter samples from the entire trace. Each sample contains 5 million predicted events, and for our experiments we had 2 or 3 samples from each benchmark.

In our experiments, we used two different methods for ranking predictors. In the first method, we ranked the individuals in a generation based on just one randomly selected benchmark, i.e., one benchmark per generation. This method was relatively fast, and might correspond to looking for individuals that can survive though successive eras of drought, flood and temperate weather.

In our second method, we determine the rankings for each benchmark in a set of benchmarks and then combine the rankings for each benchmark into a single average ranking. This second approach is much more time-consuming, but it avoids the problem of only one benchmark influencing the outcome of the next generation. In either case, final evaluations of the predictors are based on longer runs of the SPEC benchmarks and IBS traces.

It remains to be shown that the relative fitness determined using short traces is actually a good measure

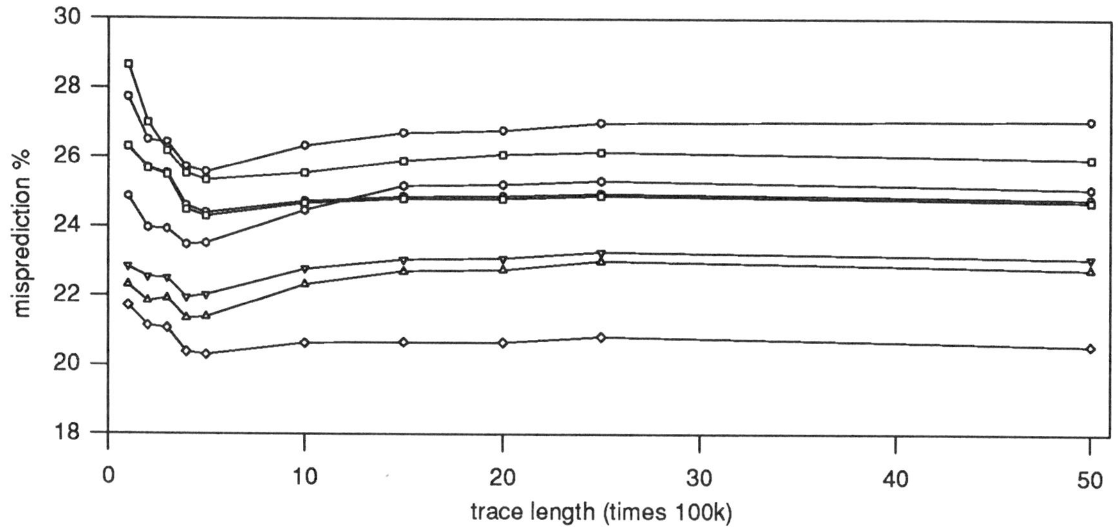

Figure 4 - Performance of Indirect Jump Predictors vs. Trace Length

of the relative fitness for longer traces of benchmark execution. We verified this by selecting some of the better predictors from our experiments, and evaluating their performance over traces of varying length.

The results of these experiments are presented in Figures 3 and 4. These figures show the absolute and relative performance for several branch and indirect jump predictors as a function of the number of predicted events in the trace. Each line represents a different predictor, where each point is calculated by averaging the results of 4 benchmarks: compress, gcc, go, xlisp.

These curves show that over time the relative ranking of the predictors is quite stable (or indistinguishably close), even though the absolute performance varies due to the differing behavior of the benchmark programs over time. Thus, we believe that rankings generated from the short traces form an adequate input to the tournament selection process.

5. Results

5.1 Branch Predictors

We chose branch prediction as the first test case for automated synthesis of predictors. Because we had previous knowledge of branch predictors, we knew what kinds of structures are promising and what kind of prediction accuracy can be achieved by a good predictor. This gave us the opportunity to tune the system to get generation to generation improvements. On the other hand, given the many years of research on human designed branch predictors, the task of finding new ones is more difficult.

Figure 5 shows the development of the best and average individuals over 16 generations of one experiment; fitness calculations were based on the average of 8 SPEC traces, and the resulting average misprediction percentages are shown for each generation. Each generation contains 400 individuals.

The graph shows a steady improvement in the performance of the best predictor. As in this example, somewhere between 15 and 30 generations the experiments usually converge to a few distinct predictors, and the subsequent generations do not achieve any significant improvement. Typically, this indicates that the predictors that can be created from the population using crossover and mutation do not show any improvement over the best predictors in the population. Note that the average performance of a population is more variable and can even get worse if crossover and mutation generate a number of useless predictors.

To see how well our automatically generated predictors fared, we have taken 6 of the better predictors produced in the course of our experiments, called GP1 through GP6, and 6 well-known human-discovered predictors. The configurations for the human-made predictors are specified using the predictor definitions from Section 2. In all cases we tried to size the predictors to about 512K bits. Table 1 shows the average performance of each predictor for the SPEC benchmarks we studied (either full runs or 50M branches whichever came first), and the average for the IBS traces.

The results show that the automatically generated predictors compared favorably to the human-generated versions. In fact, three of the predictors were better than all but the GShare predictor. Note, however, that we were not yet able to create any choosing style predictors, due to the current limitations of our crossover operation.

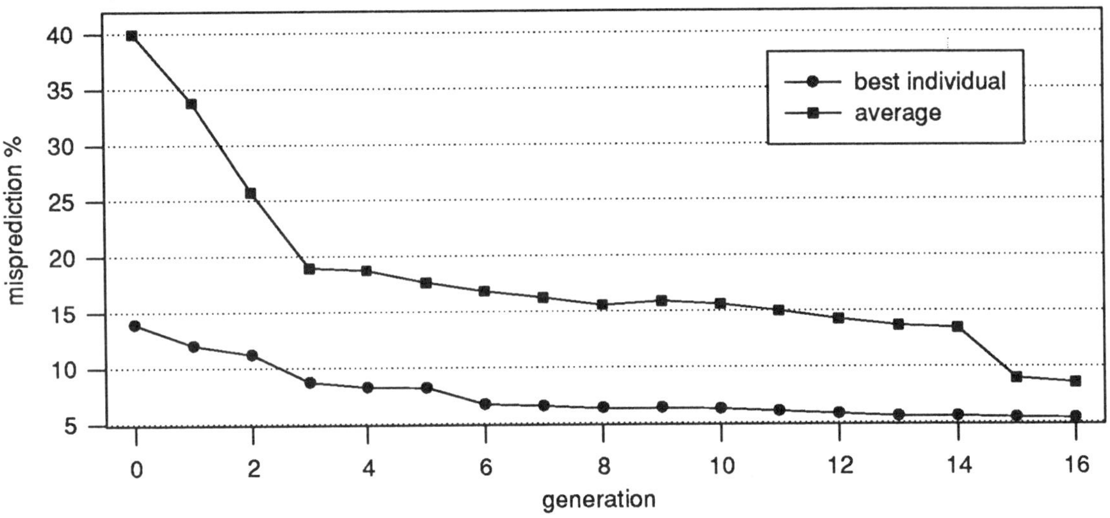

Figure 5 - Fitness vs. Generation

We have not shown the predictor expressions for GP1 to GP6, because the predictors that are generated tended to grow to the point where they consist of very deep tree structures. Thus, even though in size these predictors are comparable to the human-designed predictors they are logically much more complex, and probably not directly implementable.

The complexity of these automatically-created predictors is actually a natural consequence of the genetic programming process. Genetically created solutions are typically not very efficient, consisting of many apparently useless expressions. These expressions, called "introns" in the genetic programming literature, appear to be needed to protect the developing expression from crossovers. Thus, defining a fitness function biased against this sort of complexity may not work. In any case, we believe that there is value in just manually identifying the pieces of the solution that might be contributing to their effectiveness, and manually creating better predictors.

In fact, we were able to find numerous interesting subcomponents of these synthesized predictors. Over a variety of runs of the experiment, we found the system "invented" many familiar components of branch predictors: saturating counters, global and local branch histories as well as indirect histories.

There were also some apparently new structures that could form the basis for practical predictors. Invariably these were used as part of something like a GShare-style index (a global history xor'ed with the PC [10]) for a set of two or three bit counters. Below are some examples of such predictor components.

First is a global history indexed by a global history, which keeps around a portion of the older global history when there is a series of taken or not taken branches.

P0[14,16384](P1[14,1](0; P1 || T); P0 || T)

Next is a global history biased by the direction of the branch. If one assumes that backwards branches are normally taken, and forward branches normally not taken, then this keeps a history of "unexpected" branch actions:

P[14,1](0; (P || (DIR ⊕ T))

Next is a predictor that keeps separate global histories for forward and backward branches, maybe indicating that it is useful to separate the behaviors of loop branches from non-loop branches:

P[5,2](DIR; P || T)

Finally, we found a predictor that keeps a short history of PC values, which could be useful for tracking the history of the program:

P0[11,32](P1[5,1024](PC<10:0>; PC<5:0>);
P0 || PC<4:0>)

5.2 Jump Predictors

In contrast to branch prediction, there has been little research on predicting the target addresses of jump instructions that use a register as the target address. We therefore have little knowledge of what a good jump predictor looks like. For the same reason, this is a more interesting search space because we can expect to find

Table 1 - Branch Predictor Performance					
Predictor	Mispredict Rate (SPEC)	Mispredict Rate (IBS)	Predictor	Mispredict Rate (SPEC)	Mispredict Rate (IBS)
Onebit[1, 512K]	17.7	10.0	GP1	9.7	5.7
Twobit[2, 256K]	13.1	6.7	GP2	9.5	5.0
GShare[18]	6.7	2.7	GP3	9.7	5.7
GAg[18]	7.9	4.0	GP4	7.2	3.0
PAg[18, 8K]	7.9	4.5	GP5	7.0	2.9
PAp[9, 18, 8K]	11.2	5.5	GP6	7.1	2.9

predictors that are better than the ones that we already know.

The inputs that are available to a jump predictor are: PC, SP (stack pointer), TREG (number of register containing the jump target), and the target itself (after the address has been resolved). The benchmarks we used for this study were: gcc, go, xlisp and m88ksim.

Table 2 below shows some of the jump prediction mechanisms that one might think of; note that we only need to predict the lower 12 bits of the word address because only targets that are in the instruction cache need to be predicted.

The best predictors seen during our genetic programming experiments achieve average misprediction percentages as low as 15% on long runs of the same set of programs; this represents a significant improvement over the three predictors in Table 2. Since the genetic programming system had already been developed and refined using branch prediction as a test case, producing these jump predictors required very little effort.

One of the simplest predictors that gets significantly better performance than the simple predictors above is shown below. The average misprediction percentage of this predictor for full runs of the 4 SPEC traces of 1 to 21 million jumps is 33.4%.

```
P0[16, 16384](PC<3:0> ⊕ SP
              P1[12,16](TREG; TARGET);
              TARGET);
```

This expression contains a predictor that stores a previous target, indexed by the target register; this is XORed with the PC and the SP to form an index into a table of previous targets.

Another example is the following more complicated predictor; its misprediction rate is 30.0%.

```
P0[16, 16384](
      SP ⊕ PC ⊕
      P1[12,32](TREG; TARGET<11:2>) ⊕
      P2[15,32](P3[5,2](1; PC<4:0>);
                SP ⊕ TARGET ⊕
                P4[12,32](P3;TARGET));
      TARGET);
```

While maybe too complex to implement, this expression shows some interesting subcomponents that might be useful for creating more practical predictors.

6. Conclusions

In this paper, we have presented a new language for describing predictors. This language provides a concise and unambiguous way for describing a large variety of predictors. Furthermore, it allows for their automatic manipulation, including generating simulators and automated synthesis. In particular, we have used the search technique called genetic programming to search the design space for branch and jump predictors.

The result of these experiments has been the creation of branch predictors comparable to the best non-choosing

Table 2 - Indirect Jump Predictor Performance		
Description	BP expression	Misprediction percentage: average of 4 traces, 35M jumps
use the target of the previous jump	p[12,1](1: target)	63%
table of previous targets, indexed by PC	p[12,4096](PC : target)	47%
table of previous targets, indexed by PC and SP	p[12,4096](PC[9..0] || SP[4..0] : target)	54%

predictors that have been published. Although these predictors are logically complex, analysis of their structure revealed a number of interesting subcomponents that might be used to develop implementable predictors. In addition, we created relatively simple indirect jump target predictors significantly better than those typically used today.

Given the base system developed for branch prediction, generating the indirect jump predictors was a straightforward one week task. The positive results for these predictors, and the ease of adaptation of the system, make trying this technique for other types of predictors promising.

While we have been encouraged by our results, the genetic programming search often generates rather verbose predictors with portions that contribute little. While this is a necessary characteristic of genetic programming, the opportunity still remains for the automatic reduction of expressions to reduce complexity. This can include eliminating unused memory as well extracting the useful subcomponents of the more accurate predictors and applying them in a more cost-effective manner.

Acknowledgments

The authors would like to thank Simon Steely for his initial encouragement to consider genetic programming for our search. Thanks also to Addison Chen who implemented the initial version of the BP language parser. We also owe thanks to several of our colleagues who reviewed this paper, especially Rebecca Stamm and Geoff Lowney, as well as the anonymous referees. Finally, special thanks go to one of our managers, Tryggve Fossum, for his ever present support and encouragement of this work.

Bibliography

[1] P.J. Angeline and J.B. Pollack, "The Evolutionary Induction of Subroutines", *14th Annual Conference of the Cognitive Science Society*, 1992.

[2] B. Calder, D. Grunwald, J. Emer, "Predictive Associative Cache", *2nd International Symposium on High-Performance Computer Architecture*, Feb 1996.

[3] A. Eustace and A. Srivastava, "ATOM: A Flexible Interface for Building High Performance Program Analysis Tools", *Winter 1995 USENIX Technical Conference on UNIX and Advanced Computing Systems*, Jan 1995.

[4] J.H. Holland, *Adaptation in Natural and Artificial Systems*, University of Michigan Press, 1975.

[5] D.R. Kaeli and P.G. Emma, "Branch History Table Prediction of Moving Target Branches Due to Subroutine Returns", *18nd International Symposium on Computer Architecture*, May 1991.

[6] Q. Jacobson, S. Bennett, N. Sharma and J. Smith, "Control Flow Speculation in Multiscalar Processors", 3rd International Symposium on High-Performance Computer Architecture, Feb 1997.

[7] J.R. Koza, *Genetic Programming*, MIT Press, 1992.

[8] J. Lee and A. Smith, "Branch Prediction Strategies and Branch Target Buffer Design", *Computer*, 17(1), Jan 1984.

[9] M.H. Lipasti, C.B. Wilkerson, and J.P. Shen, "Value Locality and Load Value Prediction", *7th International Conference on Architectural Support for Programming Languages and Operating Systems*, Oct 1996.

[10] S. McFarling, "Combining Branch Predictors", WRL Technical Note TN-36, Digital Equipment Corporation, June 1993.

[11] S. Pan, K. So, and J. Rahmeh, "Improving the Accuracy of Dynamic Branch Prediction Using Branch Correlation", *5th International Conference on Architectural Support for Programming Languages and Operating Systems*, Oct 1992.

[12] S. Sechrest, C-C Lee and T. Mudge, "The Role of Adaptivity in Two-level Adaptive Branch Prediction", *28th ACM/IEEE International Symposium on Microarchitecture*, Nov 1995.

[13] S. Sechrest, C-C Lee and T. Mudge, "Correlation and Aliasing in Dynamic Branch Predictors", *23nd International Symposium on Computer Architecture*, May 1996.

[14] J.E. Smith, "A Study of Branch Prediction Strategies", *8th International Symposium on Computer Architecture*, June 1981.

[15] SPEC. "Spec Benchmark Specifications", SPEC95 Benchmarks Release, 1995.

[16] R. Uhlig, D. Nagle, T. Mudge, S. Sechrest and J. Emer, "Instruction Fetching: Coping with Code Bloat", *22nd International Symposium on Computer Architecture*, Jun 1995.

[17] T.-Y. Yeh and Y.N. Patt, "Two-level Adaptive Branch Prediction", *24th ACM/IEEE International Symposium on Microarchitecture*, Nov 1991.

[18] T.-Y. Yeh and Y.N. Patt, "Alternative Implementation of Two-level Adaptive Branch Prediction", *19th Annual International Symposium on Computer Architecture*, May 1992.

[19] C. Young, N. Gloy and M. Smith, "A Comparative Analysis of Schemes for Correlated Branch Prediction", *22nd International Symposium on Computer Architecture*, Jun 1995.

Run-time Adaptive Cache Hierarchy Management via Reference Analysis

Teresa L. Johnson Wen-mei W. Hwu

Center for Reliable and High-Performance Computing
University of Illinois
Urbana-Champaign, IL 61801
{tjohnson,hwu}@crhc.uiuc.edu

Abstract

Improvements in main memory speeds have not kept pace with increasing processor clock frequency and improved exploitation of instruction-level parallelism. Consequently, the gap between processor and main memory performance is expected to grow, increasing the number of execution cycles spent waiting for memory accesses to complete. One solution to this growing problem is to reduce the number of cache misses by increasing the effectiveness of the cache hierarchy. In this paper we present a technique for dynamic analysis of program data access behavior, which is then used to proactively guide the placement of data within the cache hierarchy in a location-sensitive manner. We introduce the concept of a macroblock, which allows us to feasibly characterize the memory locations accessed by a program, and a Memory Address Table, which performs the dynamic reference analysis. Our technique is fully compatible with existing Instruction Set Architectures. Results from detailed simulations of several integer programs show significant speedups.

1 Introduction

As improvements in processor performance outpace that of main memory performance [1], the cache miss penalty will dominate the cycle counts of many applications. The large improvements in processor performance are due both to better circuit design and fabrication technology, which reduce the cycle time, and to better *Instruction-Level Parallelism* (ILP) techniques, which increase the instructions executed per cycle. The growing disparity between processor and memory performance will make cache misses increasingly expensive. Not only do the cache misses result in more processor stall cycles, but in processors with dynamic scheduling, they can also disrupt the compiler-generated ILP schedule. Additionally, data caches are not always used efficiently. In numeric programs there are several known compiler techniques for optimizing data cache performance. However, integer programs often have irregular access patterns that are more difficult for the compiler to optimize. This paper focuses on data cache performance optimization for integer programs.

In order to increase data cache effectiveness for integer programs we have investigated methods of *adaptive cache hierarchy management*, where we proactively control the movement and placement of data in the hierarchy based on the data usage characteristics. In this paper we present a microarchitecture scheme where the hardware determines data placement based on dynamic referencing behavior. This scheme is fully compatible with existing Instruction Set Architectures.

Our scheme seeks to manage the cache in a manner that is sensitive to the usage patterns of the memory locations accessed. Since the number of memory locations is excessively large, we introduce the notion of a *macroblock*. A macroblock is a contiguous block of memory that is large enough so that the maintainance overhead is reasonable, but small enough so that the access pattern of the memory addresses within each macroblock is statistically uniform. A hardware mechanism called the *Memory Address Table* (*MAT*) is introduced to maintain and utilize the access patterns of the macroblocks to direct data placement in the cache hierarchy. We show that this extension to the cache microarchitecture significantly improves the overall performance of integer applications. The improvements are due to increased cache hit rates and reduced cache handling latencies.

The remainder of this paper is organized as follows: Section 2 discusses related work; Section 3 contains a case study of a particular benchmark as well as some main concepts used to motivate and develop this work; Section 4 discusses the hardware implementation; Section 5 presents simulation results and performs a cost analysis of the added hardware; and Section 6 concludes with future directions.

2 Related Work

Several methods exist to overlap memory accesses with other computation in the processor, attempting to hide the memory latency. Write buffers can often successfully hide the latency of write misses by buffering the write data until the bus is idle. Non-blocking caches allow multiple outstanding load misses without stalling the processor, in order to overlap load miss latency with other computation that does not consume the result of an outstanding load miss [2]. Prefetching attempts to fetch data from main memory to the cache before it is needed, which also overlaps the load miss latency with other computation. Both hardware [3][4][5][6][7] and software [8][9][10][11][12] prefetching methods for uniprocessor machines have been proposed. However, many of these methods focus on prefetching regular array accesses within well-structured loops[1], which are access patterns primarily found in numerical applications. There is also a great deal of prior work on prefetching in multiprocessors, but since their focus is even more on optimizing numerical applications, we will not review them here.

While these schemes attempt to hide the latency of load misses, our work focuses on reducing the effective memory latency seen by the processor through the reduction of both conflict and capacity misses, and their effects. Victim caches also attempt to reduce conflict miss effects in caches with low associativity [4]. While victim caches work well for some programs, as we will show in Section 5.2, they do not greatly improve programs that have large working sets.

Methods for both static and dynamic cache bypassing have also been investigated. In their pioneer work [13], Tyson *et al.* proposed a method where loads are marked for cache bypass either statically by the compiler, or dynamically at runtime. While we also investigate cache bypassing, our work differs in several key aspects. First, Tyson *et al.* use miss behavior of the load as the main decision metric, and reuse behavior as a secondary metric, for determining whether to bypass that load's data. Our work focuses on the reuse behavior, because data that tend to miss may still have high locality that would result in reuse while in the cache. Secondly, they decide whether to bypass data based on the particular load referencing that data. As we will show in Section 3.1, a single load instruction may reference data with widely varying access patterns. Therefore, we designed a mechanism to determine whether to bypass based on the data address. As a result, we see an increase in cache hit ratios, a decrease in the bus traffic and a decrease in total cycle counts, while they achieve a decrease in the bus traffic at the expense of a small drop in the cache hit ratios, which may result in performance degradation.

Another study [14] presented a hardware bypassing mechanism based on reuse behavior of cached locations, and was proven effective for numeric programs. Their mechanism only performs bypassing of the first-level data cache, whereas we study bypassing of both cache levels. It is important to improve second-level cache performance, since system bus latencies are large. Also, their scheme marks a cache block for bypass permanently until the corresponding block is replaced from the second-level cache, at which time all reuse information is lost. We overcome this limitation by keeping track of reuse behavior in a separate structure, and by allowing bypass decisions to vary based on dynamic accessing behavior.

Some of our techniques, in particular the bypass buffer presented in Section 4.2, could be used in synergy with both of these schemes to obtain improved performance.

[1]By *regular* we mean arrays indexed by the loop iteration variable, or some other induction variable.

3 Concepts

3.1 Case Study

To understand some of the inefficiencies of current cache hierarchies it is helpful to first examine the accessing behavior of a particular application in detail. Figure 1 shows the main loop body of the *026.compress* program from the *SPEC92* benchmark suite [15]. Over 90% of *compress'* execution time is in this loop body. Many of the memory accesses in *compress* are to its hash tables, *htab* and *codetab* (the lines containing the hash table load accesses are numbered[2]). Due to the large hash table sizes (*htab* and *codetab* are roughly 270K and 135K bytes, respectively) and the fact that the hash table accesses have little temporal or spatial locality, there is very little reuse in a first-level data cache.

Table 1 shows the hash table loads' dynamic execution counts, miss ratios and reuse ratios obtained via memory access profiling. A simple cache simulation was performed to determine whether each of the accesses was a first-level cache hit or miss in a direct-mapped 16K cache with 32-byte lines[3]. Also, the profiler kept track of reuse ratios[4]. The table shows that, indeed, the hash table load accesses have high miss ratios and little reuse of the accessed data.

In order to obtain a clearer picture of how the hash tables are accessed throughout the dynamic execution of the program, we profiled the accesses as explained above and plotted the address distribution for a given execution phase. The profiling results for a 100000-cycle sample of *compress* are shown in Figure 2. The memory access distribution for *htab* is shown in Figure 2a, where *htab* starts at address 171680 (all addresses are offsets from a base address of 1073741824, or 1G). As the *htab* distribution shows, much of *htab* is relatively sparsely accessed, except for two bands that are heavily accessed. These bands are located roughly from addresses 200000 to 220000 and 257000 to 300000. Looking at several other execution phases of *compress* shows that this pattern remains the same throughout the execution.

Analogous to Figure 2a, Figure 2b shows the access distribution for codetab. The access patterns of the two figures look similar since *codetab* is accessed with the same index as *htab*.

The memory access distributions of Figure 2 illustrate the

[2]The other load accesses to *htab* in this loop can be eliminated through load elimination optimizations

[3]This profiler is a simplified version of the detailed simulator used to generate the results presented in Section 5.2. Unlike the simulator, the profiler assumes a single-issue, in-order machine and zero-cycle load latencies to simplify handling back-to-back accesses to the same cache block. More details on the simulator are given in Section 5.1.3.

[4]The reuse ratio is calculated in the following way. If load A accesses a cache block (whether a hit or miss), on a following hit by load B to that cache block the reuse counter for load A is incremented once. If another access by load C is a hit to the same cache block, the counter for load B is incremented, and so on. The total number of reuses counted for a load, divided by its dynamic execution count, is that load's reuse ratio. Therefore, some of the hits will have reuse, as will some of the misses.

```
    while ( (c = getchar()) != EOF ) {
        in_count++;
        fcode = (long) (((long) c << maxbits) + ent);
        i = ((c << hshift) ^ ent);
1.      if ( htabof (i) == fcode ) {
2.          ent = codetabof (i);
            continue;
        } else if ( (long)htabof (i) < 0 ) goto nomatch;
        disp = hsize_reg - i;
        if ( i == 0 ) disp = 1;
probe:
        if ( (i -= disp) < 0 ) i += hsize_reg;
3.      if ( htabof (i) == fcode ) {
4.          ent = codetabof (i);
            continue;
        }
        if ( (long)htabof (i) > 0 ) goto probe;
nomatch:
        output ( (code_int) ent );
        out_count++;
        ent = c;
        if ( free_ent < maxmaxcode ) {
            codetabof (i) = free_ent++;
                                /* code -> hashtable */
            htabof (i) = fcode;
        }
        else if ( (count_int)in_count >= checkpoint
                                    && block_compress )
            cl_block ();
    }
```

Figure 1: Compress Main Loop Code

Line	Hash Table	Dynamic Execution Count	Miss Ratio	Reuse Ratio
1	htab	999999	78.9%	29.2%
2	codetab	566776	70.8%	30.0%
3	htab	1803911	91.4%	15.6%
4	codetab	182336	89.1%	11.5%

Table 1: Profiling Statistics for Hash Table Load Accesses (direct-mapped, 16K-byte data cache with 32-byte lines, single-issue processor). Two-way and four-way cache profiles exhibit similar behavior.

inherent problem with schemes that determine how to handle data based on the particular load instruction that requested the access [13]. In *compress* there are only two load instructions in the main loop body that access *htab*. However, from the distributions we see that these loads can access data with dramatically different usage patterns, even during small time intervals. Schemes that decide where to place the data in the cache hierarchy based on the load instruction accessing that data, whether in a static or dynamic manner, must face the challenge of giving each dynamic instance of a load instruction different treatment. Otherwise, information is lost and some data will be mishandled.

Figure 3 shows how we would like to handle accesses to data with different usage frequencies. In Figure 3a accesses to differently accessed regions of memory will map into the same cache lines, causing conflict or capacity misses. Assume that an access to a block in an infrequently accessed region of the memory misses in cache and that the conflicting block that would be replaced from the cache under a normal cache management policy is from a heavily accessed region. Instead of replacing the heavily accessed block, which has a much greater chance of being reused in the near future, we would like the missing block to bypass the cache. In this case the missing block would not be placed in the cache, as illustrated in Figure 3b. Bypassing infrequently accessed data when it conflicts with much more frequently accessed data will result in less cache pollution, and therefore increased reuse of more frequently accessed data, resulting in an overall increase in the hit ratio. To perform this selective cache bypassing, we need some method of tracking the access behavior of different memory regions.

3.2 Macroblocks

Ideally, we would like to keep track of the usage frequencies of all cache block size data in memory. While this would give us the most accurate information, it would result in an unmanageably large amount of information. Instead, we combine groups of adjacent cache block size data into larger blocks called *macroblocks*. The size of the macroblocks should be large enough so that the total number of macroblocks residing in the accessed portion of memory is not excessively large, but small enough so that the accessing frequency of the cache blocks contained within each macroblock is relatively uniform. If we can keep track of each macroblock's accessing frequency through some hardware mechanism, then we can determine on a macroblock basis whether or not to cache the contained data.

In order to determine the best size of a macroblock in practice, we studied the uniformity of cache block access frequencies within the macroblocks for several macroblock sizes. The number of accesses to each cache block in memory was first profiled. Then, for each macroblock size, the mean and standard deviation of the number of accesses to the cache blocks contained within each macroblock in memory were computed. For a high intra-macroblock accessing uniformity most of the macroblocks should have relatively small standard deviations.

Figure 4 shows the results for macroblock sizes of 256, 1K, 4K and 16K-bytes for *compress*. The y-axis is a log_{10} scale of the standard deviation divided by the mean (in order to normalize the results), and the x-axis is the percentage of macroblocks with a standard deviation divided by mean less than or equal to the plotted value. The curve for 256-byte macroblocks has the lowest standard deviations, however using 256-byte macroblocks may result in too many total macroblocks to feasibly track. Using 1K-byte macroblocks, which would include four times as many cache blocks per macroblock, may be much more feasible and still result in most macroblocks having high uniformity. For this size, about 60% of the macroblocks lie within 20% of the mean, with almost 90% within 50% of the mean. The 4K-byte curve is only slightly higher, but the 16K-byte curve does not look quite as good. The curves for other benchmarks have similar characteristics, and will not be presented here due to space constraints. A large number of simulations confirm that 1K-byte macroblocks provide the best cost-performance tradeoff. Therefore, we chose 1K-byte macroblocks for all experiments presented in this paper.

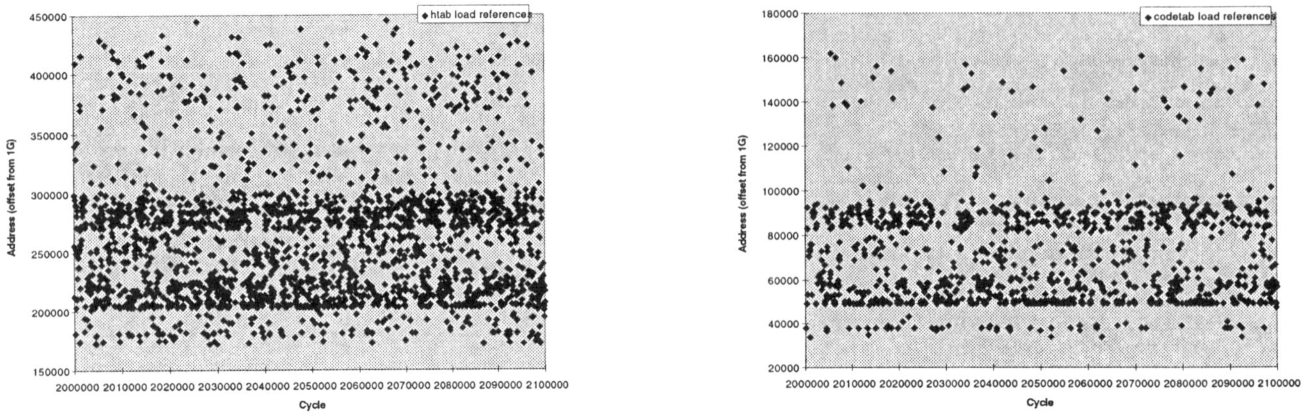

(a) htab (b) codetab

Figure 2: Memory Access Distributions for htab and codetab

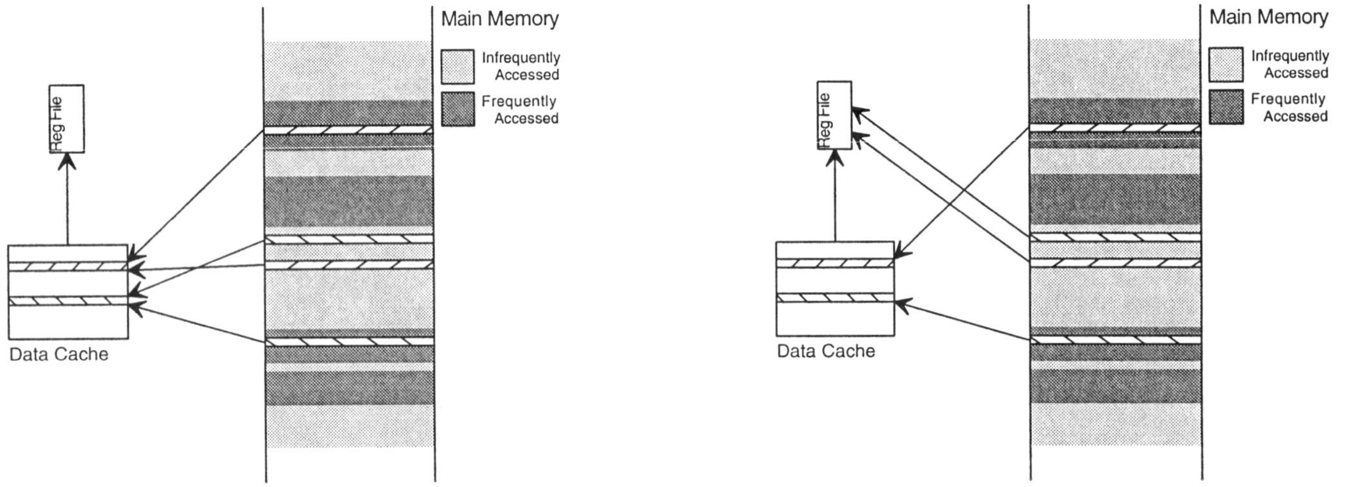

(a) Conflicts Between Data with Different Usage Patterns (b) Bypassing Less Frequently Accessed Addresses

Figure 3: Conflict Misses in Compress.

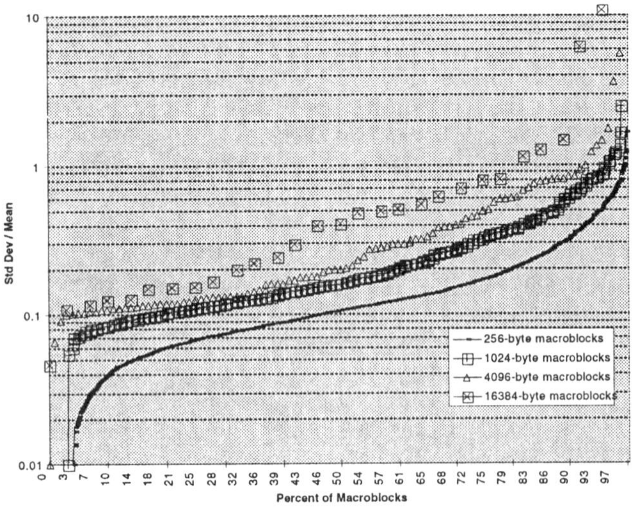

Figure 4: Macroblock Access Uniformity

4 Hardware

4.1 Memory Address Table

In order to keep track of the macroblocks at run time we use a table in hardware called a *Memory Address Table*, or *MAT*. The MAT ideally contains an entry for each macroblock. Each entry in the table contains a saturating counter, where the counter value represents the frequency of accesses to the corresponding macroblock.

On a memory access, a lookup in the MAT of the corresponding macroblock entry is performed in parallel with the data cache access. If no entry is found, a new entry is allocated and initialized, as will be discussed later. If an entry is found, the counter is incremented. Also, the counter value (*ctr1*) must be saved in a register for possible use in the next step. An example of this operation is shown in Figure 5a, where data in macroblock A is accessed.

If the data cache access resulted in a hit, the access proceeds as normal, and the counter value is ignored. If the access resulted in a cache miss, the cache controller must look up the MAT counter corresponding to the cache block that

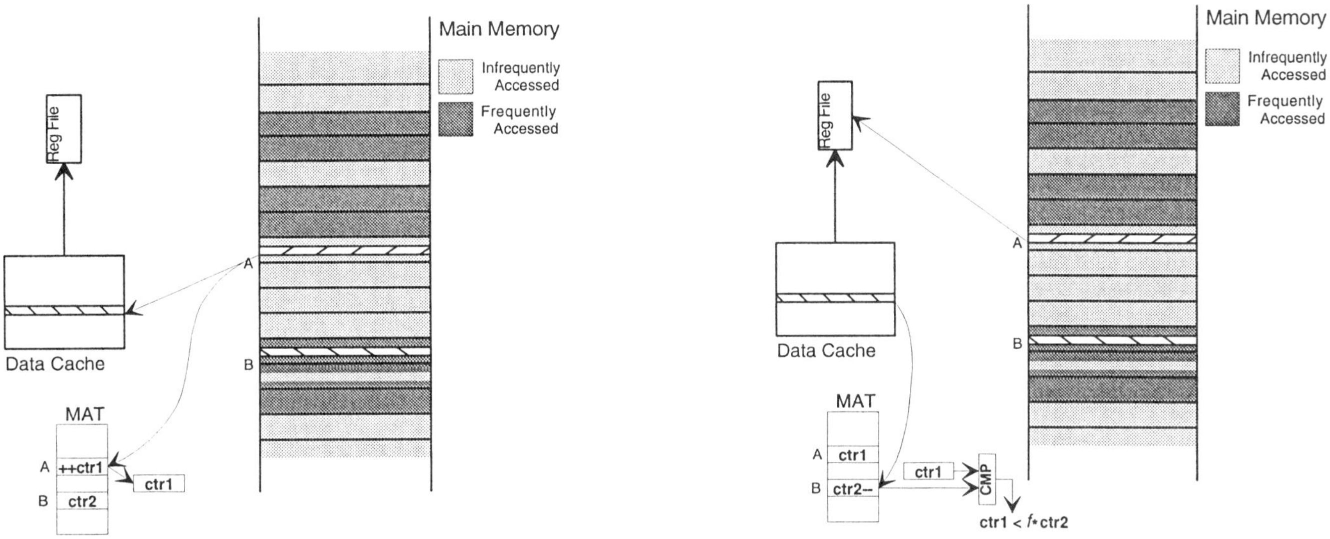

(a) Accessing *ctr1* (b) Accessing *ctr2*

Figure 5: MAT Operation.

would be replaced to determine which data is more heavily accessed, and therefore more likely to be reused in cache, as shown in Figure 5b where data in macroblock B would be replaced. This counter value (*ctr2*) is then decremented and compared to the counter value corresponding to the missing access. The actual comparison performed is:

$$ctr1 < f * ctr2 \tag{1}$$

where *f* is some fraction. If the above inequality is satisfied the fetched data will bypass the cache. Otherwise, it replaces the existing cached data as normal.

As mentioned above, the counter corresponding to the currently cached block (*ctr2*) is decremented. This is to ensure that the counter values will eventually decrease, so that after a transition to another phase of the program execution, new data can replace data that is now unused. The rationale for decrementing counters on missing accesses to conflicting data is that the data currently residing in the cache must justify remaining cached when there is heavy contention for that cache location. Therefore, the heavier the contention for a particular cache location, the more the cached data must be reused to maintain a counter large enough to satisfy Equation 1.

Rather than compare *ctr1* and *ctr2* exactly, in Equation 1 we compare *ctr1* to some fraction *f* of *ctr2*. Choosing *f* less than 1.0 will conservatively prevent bypassing when the counter values are almost the same.

Also, we do not want to bypass when the MAT contains no entry for one of the macroblocks, so that the cache will then default to its normal replacement behavior when there is insufficient information. In the case where there is no counter for the address being accessed this can be achieved by setting all bits to 1 in the register which holds *ctr1* for the comparison. When there is no counter found for the data residing in cache (*ctr2*), we compare to 0. Both of these are simply a matter of multiplexing in either the counter value read from the MAT or the appropriate constant, using the valid bit as a selector.

When a new entry is allocated, the counter value must be initialized to some value. One possibility is to initialize it to 0. This will result in more aggressive bypassing, since it will take longer for the new counter to "catch up" to the older cached data's counter. Another possibility is to initialize to the conflicting data's counter value, as shown in Figure 6a. The new counter will start at an equal position, resulting in more selective bypassing. Simulations verified that initialization to 0 is optimal for an L1 data cache MAT, since the L1-L2 latency is small. The small latency means that the shorter bypass fetch size can be just as important as reducing the number of fetches, and that there will be less penalty when the decision to bypass was incorrect. Simulations also verified that initialization of *ctr1* with *ctr2* is optimal for an L2 data cache MAT, since the system bus latency is long. In this case reducing the length of data transferred is not critical, and although bypassing is still beneficial, it is much more important to make very careful bypassing decisions.

The second MAT access and the comparison are needed only during a cache miss to determine the data size requested, since only the element size[5] needs to be fetched on a bypass. It is unlikely that both MAT accesses can be performed in one cycle, so this information will be available the cycle after the miss is detected. However, the size can be sent to the next level of the cache hierarchy the cycle after the address is sent, as the access to the L2 cache or main memory will take at least one cycle before the data can be returned. In some current processors the system bus request takes two cycles, with the address sent the first cycle and the data request size the second [16], which matches the MAT timing.

4.2 Temporal Locality in Bypassed Data

Another issue is that there can be some temporal locality even when the total accessing frequency is relatively low. In

[5] In this paper the *element size* refers to the maximum element size allowed by the ISA, which in our system is 8 bytes.

this case the MAT scheme will bypass some data which may have otherwise had a few hits before being displaced from the cache. More than one additional miss will be incurred by not caching that data, whereas only one miss is removed by not displacing the much more frequently accessed data.

To optimize performance in this situation, we place bypassing data in a small set-associative buffer, as shown in Figure 6b. This bypass buffer will be accessed in the same manner as a victim cache. As a result, the bypassed data is held close to the processor for a short time, allowing much of the temporal locality of the infrequently accessed data to be exploited.

4.3 Spatial Locality in Bypassed Data

Spatial locality may also exist in the bypassed data. It is only necessary to fetch the element size on a bypass, which can be effective in reducing the bus transfer time. However, simulations show that when simulating the MAT scheme with a small bypass fetch size, around 15% of the L1 data cache misses in several benchmarks are a result of the lost spatial reuse opportunities when fetching only the element on a bypass. These misses are accesses to another element in the same cache block as some element in the bypass buffer. Fetching the entire cache block on a bypass would eliminate these misses.

However, fetching the entire cache block for benchmarks with little spatial locality in bypassed data will unnecessarily increase bus traffic. Therefore, it is beneficial to implement some means of dynamically choosing the optimal bypass fetch size. The choice of bypass fetch size should depend on the spatial locality detected, and can be determined at the macroblock granularity.

This optimization could be implemented using subblock support in the bypass buffer. However, subblocks can result in underutilized lines, when only the element size is fetched. Instead, we use a bypass buffer with small lines, equal to the element size, and optionally fill in consecutive blocks when the larger bypass fetch size is chosen. This approach is similar to that used in some prefetching strategies [17].

To facilitate spatial locality detection, a new counter, *sctr*, will be added to each macroblock entry. In addition, an *sr* (*spatial reuse*) bit and an *fi* (*fetch initiator*) bit are added to each bypass buffer tag. When a new entry is allocated in the bypass buffer, its *sr* bit is reset to 0. On a miss in the bypass buffer, if the upper bits of another tag indicate that data from the same full L1 data cache block resides in the bypass buffer, then the missing data's *sr* bit is set and the corresponding macroblock's *sctr* is incremented. However, in a set-associative bypass buffer we may need to access additional sets, or a separate structure which tracks this information. If the entire cache block was fetched into the bypass buffer, the *sr* bit is set on a hit access to any element other than the element which caused the block to be loaded. This is implemented by setting the *fi* bit to 1 during the cache refill for the bypass buffer block which contains the missing element, otherwise resetting it to 0. Then the *sr* bit is set to 1 on a hit to a block with a *fi* bit of 0. When the bypass buffer block is replaced, the corresponding macroblock's *sctr* is decremented if the *sr* bit is not set for any of the blocks in the same full L1 data cache block.

On a cache bypass, the full cache block is fetched if the *sctr* is saturated, otherwise the element size is fetched. Simulations showed that a 1-bit *sctr* is optimal.

The cost of the MAT hardware will be analyzed in Section 5.3, following the presentation of experimental results.

5 Experimental Evaluation

5.1 Experimental Environment

In this section, the environment used for experimental evaluation of our technique is presented. The applications for this study consist of several integer benchmark programs, that will be discussed below in Section 5.1.1. The experimental environment also includes compiler support, emulation to verify transformation correctness, and the simulation techniques used to generate experimental results.

5.1.1 Benchmarks

Ten benchmarks were simulated under each of the configurations from Section 5.1.5. The first, *026.compress*, is from the *SPEC92* benchmark suite, and was discussed in detail in Section 3.1. *072.sc* and *085.cc1*, also from the *SPEC92* benchmark suite, are simulated. *099.go*, *147.vortex*, *130.li* and *134.perl*, from the *SPEC95* benchmark suite, are simulated using the training inputs. The next two benchmarks consist of modules from the *IMPACT* compiler [18] that we felt were representative of many real-world integer applications. *Pcode*, the front end of *IMPACT*, is run performing dependence analysis with the internal representation of the *combine.c* file from GNU CC as input. *lmdes2_customizer*, a machine description optimizer, is run optimizing the SuperSPARC machine description for efficient use by the *IMPACT* compiler. These optimizations operate over linked list and complex data structures, and utilize hash tables for efficient access to the information. The last benchmark is the *java* interpreter. It is run interpreting the compress benchmark which was hand-translated to java code, with the *SPEC92* compress input. The experimental environment for *java* is slightly different from that of the other benchmarks, and will be discussed in Section 5.1.4.

5.1.2 Compiler and Architecture

In order to provide a realistic evaluation of our technique, we first optimized the code using the *IMPACT* compiler [18]. Classical optimizations were applied, then optimizations were performed which increase instruction level parallelism such as loop unrolling and superblock formation [19]. The code was scheduled, register allocated and optimized for an eight-issue, scoreboarded, superscalar processor with register renaming. The Instruction Set Architecture is an extension of the HP PA-RISC instruction set to support compile-time speculation. Up to four memory accesses can be executed per cycle. The register file contains 64 integer registers and 64 double-precision floating-point registers.

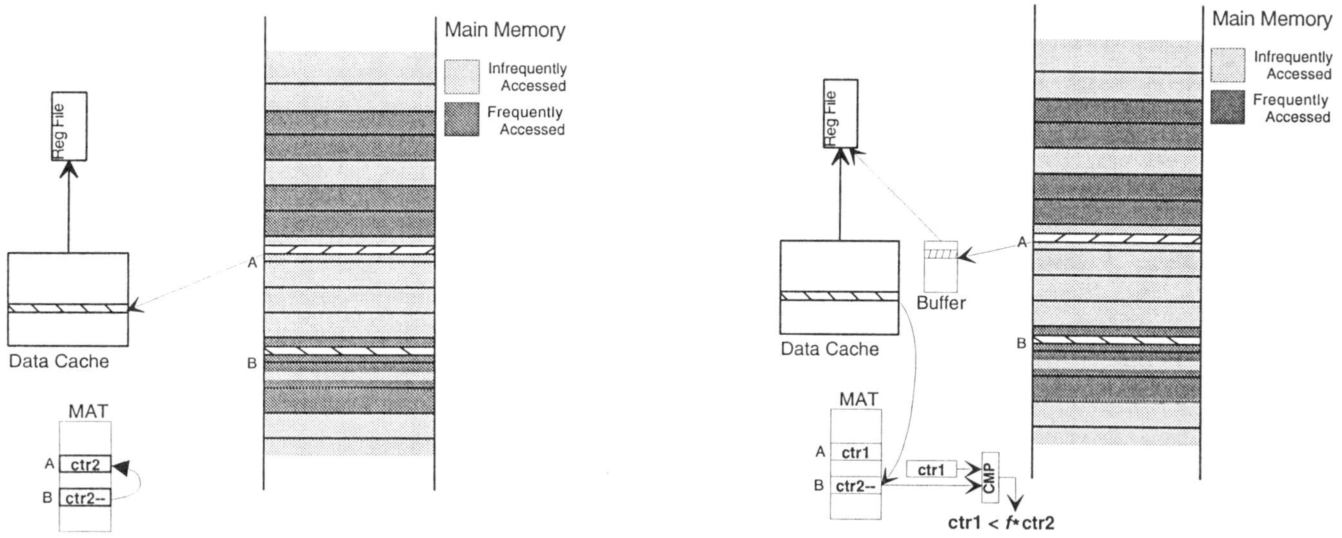

(a) Counter Initialization to *ctr2* Value

(b) Accessing MAT Operation with a Buffer

Figure 6: MAT Operation Details.

Function	Latency	Function	Latency
Int ALU	1	FP ALU	2
memory load	2	FP multiply	2
memory store	1	FP divide (single prec.)	8
branch	1 + 1 slot	FP divide (double prec.)	15

Table 2: Instruction latencies for simulation experiments.

5.1.3 Simulation Parameters and Techniques

To verify the correctness of the code transformations, emulation of the target processor architecture was performed for all input programs on a Hewlett-Packard *PA-RISC 7100* workstation.

The emulator drives the simulator that models on a cycle-by-cycle basis the processor and the memory hierarchy (including all related busses) to determine application execution time, cache performance and bus utilization. The instruction latencies used are those of a Hewlett-Packard *PA-RISC 7100* microprocessor, as given in Table 2.

The memory hierarchy includes separate L1 instruction and data caches. The L1 instruction cache is a direct-mapped, 32K-byte split-block cache with a 64-byte block size. The L1 data cache is a direct-mapped[6], 16K-byte non-blocking cache with a 32-byte block size. The data cache is a multiported, write-back, no write-allocate cache that satisfies up to four load or store requests per cycle from the processor and has streaming support. Up to 50 load misses can be outstanding simultaneously on the bus connecting the L1 and L2 data caches. An 8-entry write buffer combines write requests to the same cache block. The instruction cache and data cache share a common, split-transaction L1-L2 bus, with a 4 cycle latency and 8 bytes/cycle data bandwidth. The memory hierarchy also includes a direct-mapped, 256K-byte non-blocking L2 data cache with a 64-byte block size. This cache is also write-back and no write allocate. Up to 50 load misses can be outstanding simultaneously from the L2 data cache on the system bus, which is split-transaction with a 50 cycle latency to memory and 8 bytes/cycle data bandwidth.

A direct-mapped branch target buffer with 1024 entries is used to perform dynamic branch prediction using a 2-bit counter. Hardware speculation is supported, and the branch misprediction penalty is approximately two cycles.

Since simulating the entire applications at this level of detail would be impractical, uniform sampling is used to reduce simulation time [20], however emulation is still performed between samples. The simulated samples are 200,000 instructions in length and are spaced evenly every 20,000,000 instructions, yielding a 1% sampling ratio. For smaller applications, the time between samples is reduced to maintain at least 50 samples (10,000,000 instructions). From experience with the emulation-driven simulator, we have determined that sampling with at least 50 samples introduces typically less than 1% error in generated performance statistics.

The current versions of HPUX sometimes allocate the stack frame differently in memory across runs of the same program, which can cause the cache performance to vary. This effect is most noticeable when running the same executable on different machines. To obtain the typical performance benefit of our techniques, we emulated each configuration for every benchmark on three different HP workstations and recorded the median speedup. However, the speedups generally varied less than one percent.

5.1.4 Java

The *java* benchmark was simulated on a Pentium system running Linux, for which we do not yet support virtual machine emulation. Therefore, *java* was optimized for a Pentium machine [16], and x86 machine code was generated and run to ensure correctness, as well as to drive the simulator. The machine model simulated is that of the Pentium, rather than the virtual machine described in Section 5.1.2, except for the memory system which is identical to that explained in Section 5.1.3.

[6]Initially both data caches are direct-mapped, but in a later section we examine the affects of set-associative data caches.

5.1.5 Experimental Configurations

The first set of configurations use the MAT scheme presented in Section 4.1. In this scheme, two independent MATs are used, an L1 MAT and an L2 MAT. Each MAT operates independently of the other, so the L2 MAT only reflects the accesses that missed in the L1 cache and therefore accessed the L2 cache. Both MATs use the same value of f and 1K-byte macroblocks. After a large number of simulations[7] f = 1.0 was shown to have the best performance across all the benchmarks, and will be used throughout the rest of this paper. The bypass buffer allows aggressive bypassing from f = 1.0 to occur without much effect from any incorrect bypassing decisions made by the higher f value.

The 4-way set-associative buffers used to hold the bypassed data at the L1 and L2 caches contain 32 and 256 entries, respectively, in the first configuration. We fetch the L1 block size on an L2 bypass because the L1 access may not have been a bypass. The next several experimental configurations explore the effects of varying the bypass fetch sizes. Unless noted otherwise, the bypass buffer line sizes will be the maximum bypass fetch size used.

We first present results for an infinite-entry MAT, then study the effects of limiting the number of MAT entries.

5.2 Results

Figure 7a shows the speedup of each benchmark for the MAT scheme, which places the bypassing data in a small buffer, using an infinite MAT with 1K macroblocks and f = 1. The leftmost speedup bar for each benchmark, labeled (8,32) to denote an 8-byte L1 bypass fetch size and a 32-byte L2 bypass fetch size, fetches the minimum data necessary on a bypass. Most benchmarks achieve good performance improvement, with *compress* and *Pcode* improving the most, yielding 12% improvement each.

The next three configurations shown in Figure 7a consist of the various combinations of fetching either the minimum size or the cache block size on a bypass. Several observations can be made from this figure. First, all benchmarks perform better using an L2 bypass fetch size of 64, or the entire L2 cache block, compared to the minimum fetch size of 32. This is due to the long system bus latency (50 cycles), which means that the time necessary to transfer the 32 or 64 bytes is small in comparison to the latency of accessing main memory. Therefore, it is better to fetch more data, and reduce the likelihood of needing another fetch for the other data in the cache block.

Comparing L1 bypass fetch sizes of 8 and 32, the trend is not as clear. Some benchmarks (*026.compress*, *072.sc*, *Pcode*) perform better when fetching only the element on an L1 bypass, due to an overall lack of spatial locality in these benchmarks. Other benchmarks, such as *134.perl*, perform much better when fetching the full 32-byte L1 cache block on a bypass. Because the L1-L2 latency is much shorter, the data transfer time is very close to the L2 access latency, and it is not as clear which aspect to optimize. Therefore, the spatial reuse optimization discussed in Section 4.3 was simulated, with results shown by the rightmost speedup bar for each benchmark in Figure 7a. In this case the number of entries in the L1 bypass buffer was increased to 128. However, due to the smaller line size of 8 bytes, the size of the bypass buffer is the same as the 32-entry buffer with a bypass fetch size of 32 bytes. The benchmarks achieve speedups better than, or very close to, the best speedup achieved by the other configurations.

Figure 7b shows the utilization of the system bus (connecting the L2 cache with the main memory) for the MAT scheme with an infinite number of entries. Only the 64-byte L2 bypass fetch size configurations are shown. The reduction in system bus traffic is due to the improvements in hit ratio.

The L1 data cache read hit ratios for the same configurations are shown in Figure 7c. Surprisingly, the hit ratios for *compress* improve the least, while *compress* achieved the largest speedup. From the memory access distributions of Figure 2 we see that the heavily accessed portions of htab and codetab alone total much more than 16K bytes, so although the MAT allows us to keep only heavily accessed data cached, different blocks from the heavily accessed regions will still replace each other frequently.

Non-blocking caches can result in different amounts of effective memory latency seen by the processor, depending on how many miss requests are outstanding when an access occurs. Therefore, the hit ratios may not be indicative of the overall performance. A more meaningful metric is the *average miss penalty*, or the average number of cycles the processor is stalled on the data cache per load access. Figure 7d shows that the average miss penalties correspond better than the hit ratios with the speedup results shown in Figure 7a.

Figure 8 suggests that the MAT is correctly deciding which data to bypass for *compress*. Figure 8a shows the memory access distribution for both htab and codetab, for the same execution phase shown in Figure 2. Figure 8b has the same y-axis, and lines up with Figure 8a. The x-axis of Figure 8b is the ratio of times that a missing access was instructed by the MAT to bypass the cache. Figure 8 shows that the very heavily accessed portions of the hash table bypass very rarely. The sparsely accessed portion of codetab, roughly between address offsets 100000 and 170000, bypasses almost 100% of the time.

5.2.1 Set-associative Data Caches

Increasing the set-associativity of the data caches can reduce the number of conflict misses, which may in turn reduce the advantage offered by the MAT. To investigate these effects, the data cache configuration discussed in Section 5.1.3 was slightly modified to have a 2-way set-associative L1 data cache and a 4-way set-associative L2 data cache.

Figure 9 shows the new speedup for two MAT configurations. The first configuration is the same shown in the previous section, with a 64-byte L2 bypass fetch size and the dynamically varying L1 bypass fetch size. Because the higher associativity filters out some of the conflict misses that were bypassed in the case of direct-mapped caches, it may be beneficial to bypass less aggressively. One way in which to bypass less frequently is to have fewer bits in the MAT access

[7] Due to space constraints these results will not be shown here.

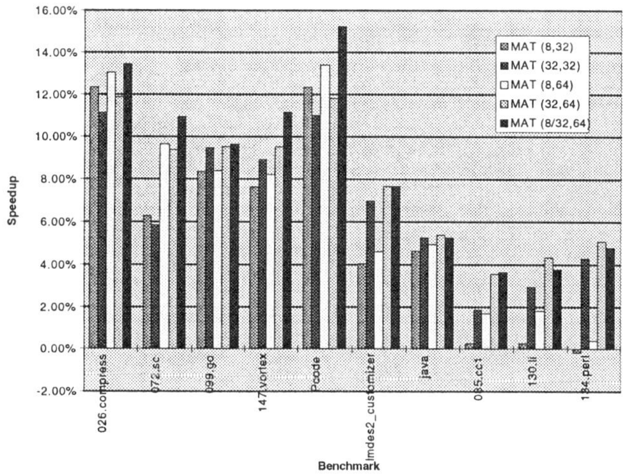

(a) Speedup

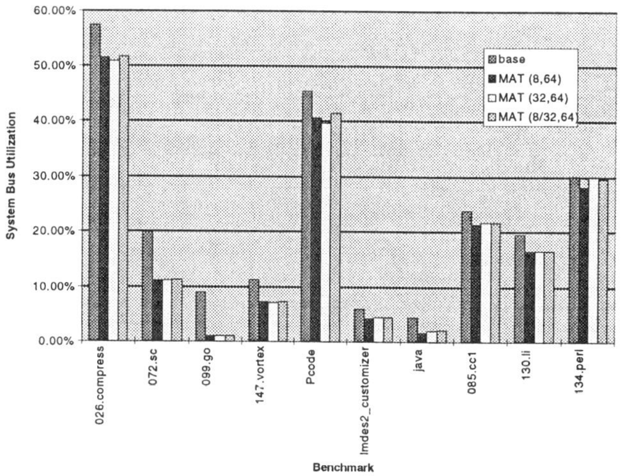

(b) System Bus Utilization

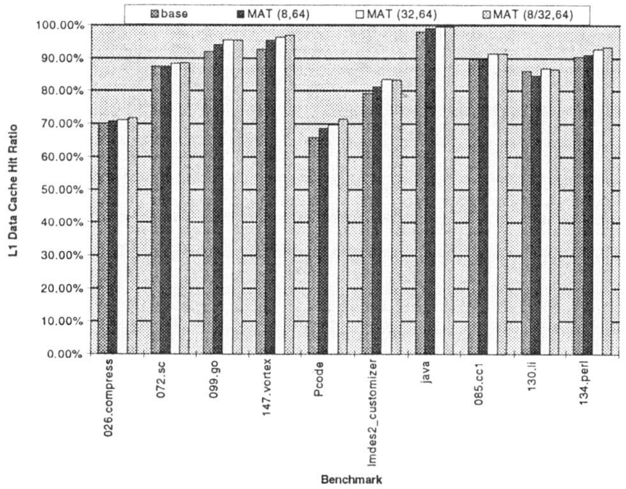

(c) L1 Data Cache Read Hit Ratio

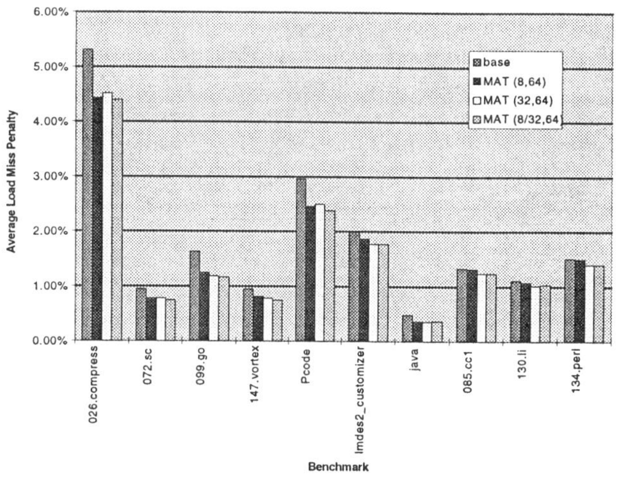

(d) Average Miss Penalty per Load Access

Figure 7: Performance data for the MAT Scheme (infinite-entry MAT). The legend denotes (L1 bypass fetch size, L2 bypass fetch size), where an L1 bypass fetch size of 8/32 denotes the dynamically varying scheme.

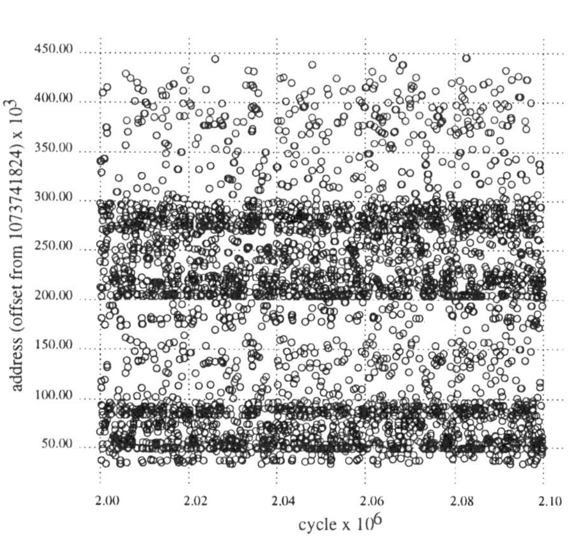

(a) Memory Access Distribution

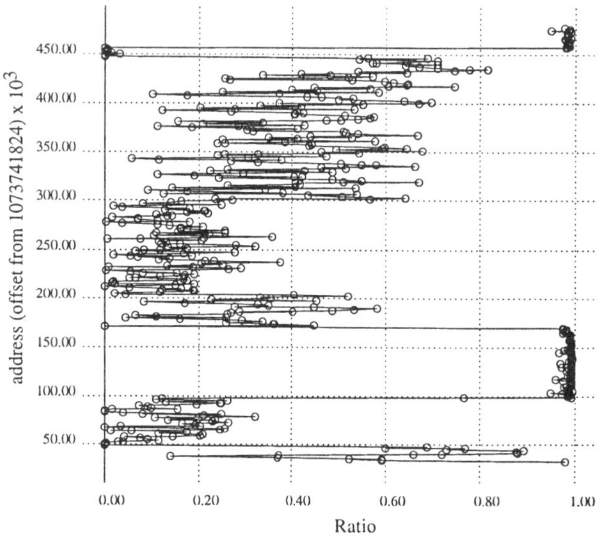

(b) Bypassing Ratio

Figure 8: Compress Distribution and Bypassing Ratio Comparison (MAT Scheme, infinite-entry MAT).

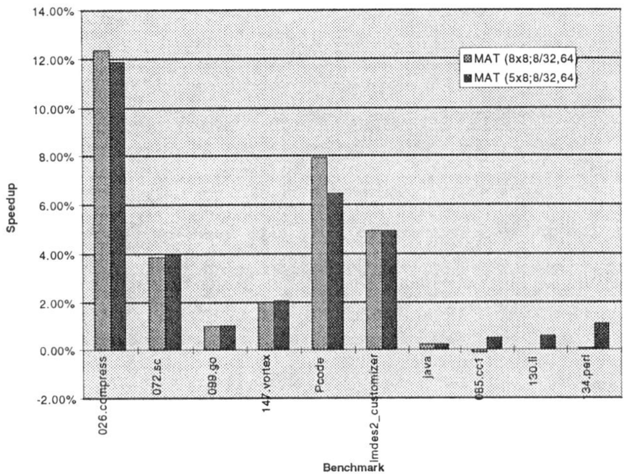

Figure 9: Speedup for 2-way and 4-way set-associative L1 and L2 data caches, respectively, with the MAT Schemes using dynamically-varying L1 bypass fetch sizes (infinite-entry MAT) and various numbers of bits per L1 MAT *ctr*. The legend denotes ({bits/L1 MAT *ctr*}x{bits/L2 MAT *ctr*}; L1 bypass fetch size, L2 bypass fetch size), where an L1 bypass fetch size of 8/32 denotes the dynamically varying scheme.

counter. Because the counters will saturate faster, and at a lower value, it is less likely that one macroblock will have a much larger *ctr* value for very long. As a simple preliminary investigation we modified the previous configuration so the L1 MAT had a 5-bit (rather than 8-bit) *ctr*. This configuration, denoted (5x8;8/32,64) to reflect the 5-bit L1 MAT *ctr* and 8-bit L2 MAT *ctr*, is also shown in Figure 9.

As noted in Section 3.1, *compress* has very large hash tables, resulting in many capacity misses. For this reason, its speedup using a MAT decreases little when increasing the data cache associativity, seen by comparing Figure 9 to Figure 7a. Other benchmarks decrease in varying amounts. However, using a 5-bit L1 MAT *ctr* the MAT still achieves speedup for all benchmarks. With increasing memory latency these speedups are likely to increase.

5.2.2 Finite-size MAT

To study the effects of a finite-size MAT we chose to simulate the MAT scheme with both 512 and 1K-entry direct-mapped MATs. These sizes were chosen because their hardware cost is reasonable, as will be discussed in Section 5.3, yet they were large enough to hold most of the macroblocks for each of the benchmarks. The bypassing choices should be more conservative as the number of entries in the MAT is decreased, since we do not bypass unless both counters are found in the MAT, as discussed in Section 4.1. Table 3 shows the number of macroblocks accessed by each benchmark for a 1K-byte macroblock size. Figure 10 shows speedups achieved by the MAT scheme for direct-mapped data caches using differing numbers of entries per MAT. Some benchmarks degrade slightly when the entries per MAT are decreased. One anomaly is that several benchmarks have slight performance improvements from reducing the MAT entries. This is due to the more conservative bypassing choices avoiding some incorrect bypasses. In general, the performance effects of restricting the number of MAT entries is small.

	Macroblocks Accessed
026.compress	548
072.sc	321
099.go	238
147.vortex	2275
Pcode	2955
lmdes2_customizer	342
java	527
085.cc1	1864
130.li	670
134.perl	4581

Table 3: Number of Macroblocks Accessed.

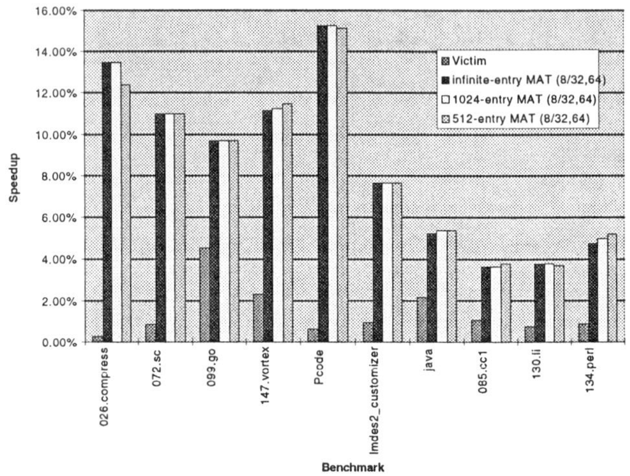

Figure 10: Speedup for the MAT Scheme with infinite, 1024 and 512-entries per MAT. All have 4-way set-associative bypass buffers and dynamically-varying L1 and 64-byte L2 bypass fetch sizes. The L1 and L2 fully-associative victim caches have 64 and 512 entries, respectively.

Also shown in Figure 10 are the speedups attained by the traditional victim caches. A 64-entry fully-associative L1 victim cache and a 512-entry fully-associative L2 victim cache are used in this configuration. Although the victim caches are large and have full associativity, they attain smaller speedups than those obtained by the MAT scheme with 4-way set-associative bypass buffers, using similar amounts of hardware, as will be shown in Section 5.3. The fact that *compress* uses large hash tables, resulting in many capacity misses, is underlined by the extremely small speedup achieved by the victim caches (0.26%). Thus, the combination of a 64-entry L1 victim cache and a 512-entry L2 victim cache is still too small to hold a significant portion of the conflicting data.

5.2.3 Growing Memory Latency Effects

As discussed in Section 1, memory latencies are increasing, and this trend is expected to continue. Figure 11 shows the speedups of the MAT scheme applied to direct-mapped data caches for three different latencies, the 50-cycle latency used in all previous configurations, as well as 100-cycle and 200-cycle latencies. Most of the benchmarks see much higher performance improvements from the MAT scheme when the memory latencies increase, with speedups close to 25% for *072.sc* and *099.go* for a 200-cycle memory latency. This is to be expected, as the number of cycles spent waiting for out-

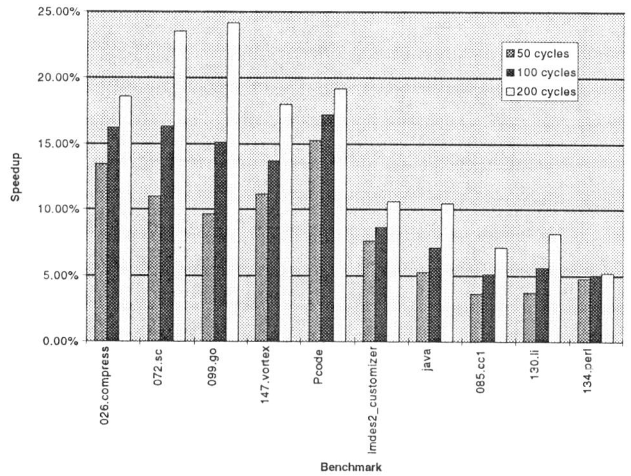

Figure 11: Speedup for the MAT Scheme with varying memory latency. All have dynamically-varying L1 and 64-byte L2 bypass fetch sizes.

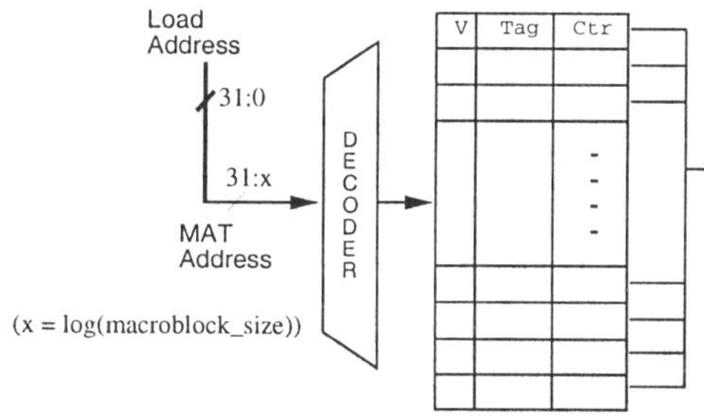

Figure 12: MAT Design.

standing cache misses will increase, and optimizations which decrease the number of cache misses will become increasingly important.

5.3 Design Considerations

The additional hardware cost incurred by the MAT scheme is small compared to doubling the cache sizes at each level, particularly for the L2 cache. For the 16K-byte direct-mapped L1 cache used to generate the results of Section 5.2, 18 bits of tag are used per entry (assuming 32-bit addresses). Doubling this cache will result in 17-bit tags. Because the line size is 32 bytes, the total additional cost of the increased tag array will be $17 * 2^{10} - 18 * 2^{9}$, which is 1K bytes[8]. In addition, an extra 16K of data is needed.

For a direct-mapped MAT with 8-bit access counters and 1-bit spatial counters, Table 4 gives the hardware cost of the data and tags for the MAT and macroblock sizes discussed in Section 5.2. Since all addresses within a macroblock map to the same MAT counter, a number of lower address bits are thrown away when accessing the MAT, as shown in Figure 12. The size of the resulting *MAT address*, used to access the MAT, is shown in column 3 of Table 4.

[8]We are ignoring the valid bit and other state, which is conservative since the number of these bits per entry is the same or less in the MAT, and because the number of entries created when doubling the cache is larger than the number of entries in the MAT.

MAT Entries	Data Cost (bytes)	Size of MAT Address (bits)	Tag Size (bits)	Tag Cost (bytes)
512	576	22	13	832
1K	1152	22	12	1536

Table 4: Hardware Cost of 512 and 1K entry MATs.

Entries	Bypass Fetch Size (bytes)	Block Size (bytes)	Data Cost (bytes)	Tag Size (bits)	Tag Cost (bytes)
32	8	8	256	26	104
	32	32	1024	24	96
128	8/32	8	1024	26	416

Table 5: Hardware Cost of L1 Bypass Buffer.

Entries	Block Size (bytes)	Data Cost (bytes)	Tag Size (bits)	Tag Cost (bytes)
64	32	2048	27	216

Table 6: Hardware Cost of L1 Victim Cache.

The cost for the L1 buffer, which is a 4-way set-associative cache with 8 or 32 byte lines, depending on the bypass fetch size chosen, is shown in Table 5. The total cost of the additional tag and data arrays for the MAT scheme is much less than that of increasing the data cache size. If the varying bypass size scheme of Section 4.3 is used, then spatial locality detection support is necessary in the L1 bypass buffer, which will require a small amount of additional hardware. This is reflected by the 8/32 entry in Table 5, where an extra 2 bits of tag are needed per entry (1-bit *spatial reuse bit* and 1-bit *fetch initiator bit*).

Table 6 shows the costs for a 64-entry L1 victim cache. Adding the costs from Tables 4 and 5 and comparing to Table 6 shows that the MAT configurations are only slightly more expensive in tag and data costs. However, the victim caches are fully-associative, which may make the MAT scheme with 4-way set-associative buffers less costly overall. For a similar cost of tags and data, the results presented in Figure 10 show that the MAT scheme always performs better than victim caching with higher associativity.

Similar calculations will show that all L2 MAT configurations are much less expensive than the L2 victim cache configuration used to generate the results of Section 5.2.

To reduce the hardware cost, we could potentially integrate the L1 MAT with the TLB and page tables. For a macroblock size larger than or equal to the page size, each TLB entry will need to hold only one 8-bit counter value. For a macroblock size less than the page size, each TLB entry needs to hold several counters, one for each of the macroblocks within the corresponding page. In this case a small amount of additional hardware is necessary to select between the counter values. However, further study is needed to determine the full effects of TLB integration.

6 Conclusion

In this paper, we presented a method to improve the efficiency of the caches in the memory hierarchy, by bypassing data that is expected to have little reuse in cache. This allows more frequently accessed data to remain cached longer, and therefore have a larger chance of reuse. The bypassing choices are made by a Memory Address Table (MAT), which performs dynamic reference analysis in a location-sensitive manner. An MAT scheme was investigated, which places bypassing data in a small 4-way set-associative buffer, allowing exploitation of small amounts of temporal locality which may exist in the bypassed data. We also introduced the concept of a macroblock, which allows the MAT to feasibly characterize the accessed memory locations.

Variations in the amount of data fetched on a bypass were investigated, including a dynamically-varying bypass fetch size. Additionally, the effects of increasing the data cache associativities and reducing the number of MAT entries were examined.

Cycle-by-cycle simulations of several benchmarks show that significant speedups can be achieved by this technique. The speedups are due to the improved miss ratios and reduced bus traffic, which also result in a reduction in the average miss penalty per load. The MAT scheme was shown to outperform large victim caches, even for a finite-size MAT of a similar hardware cost and less associativity. In addition, we showed that the speedups achieved by the MAT scheme increase as the memory latency increases.

For future work we will examine more sophisticated MAT counter algorithms, beyond the simple reference count of this design, as well as adaptive cache remapping schemes. TLB integration is another area of future investigation, as mentioned earlier. In general, we believe that the schemes presented in this paper can be extended into a more general framework for intelligent runtime management of the cache hierarchy.

Acknowledgements

The authors would like to thank all the members of the IMPACT research group whose comments and suggestions helped to improve the quality of this research, in particular Dave August for proofreading various drafts of this paper. The authors would also like to thank Santosh Abraham and Balas Natarajan at HP Labs for helpful discussions concerning the behavior of the compress benchmark. We would also like to thank the anonymous referees for their constructive comments.

This research has been supported by the National Science Foundation (NSF) under grant CCR-9629948, Intel Corporation, Advanced Micro Devices Hewlett-Packard, SUN Microsystems, NCR, and the National Aeronautics and Space Administration (NASA) under Contract NASA NAG 1-613 in cooperation with the Illinois Computer laboratory for Aerospace Systems and Software (ICLASS).

References

[1] K. Boland and A. Dollas, "Predicting and precluding problems with memory latency," *IEEE Micro*, pp. 59–66, August 1994.

[2] G. S. Sohi and M. Franklin, "High-bandwidth data memory systems for superscalar processors," in *Fourth International Conference on Architectural Support for Programm ing Languages and Operating Systems*, pp. 53–62, April 1991.

[3] A. J. Smith, "Cache memories," *Computing Surveys*, vol. 14, no. 3, pp. 473–530, 1982.

[4] N. P. Jouppi, "Improving direct-mapped cache performance by the addition of a small fully-associative cache and prefetch buffers," in *Proceedings of the 17th International Symposium on Computer Architecture*, pp. 364–373, June 1990.

[5] J.-L. Baer and T.-F. Chen, "An effective on-chip preloading scheme to reduce data access penalty," in *Proceeding of Supercomputing '91*, pp. 176–186, Nov. 1991.

[6] T.-F. Chen and J.-L. Baer, "Reducing memory latency via non-blocking and prefetching caches," Tech. Rep. 92-06-03, Department of Computer Science and Engineering, University of Washington, Seattle, WA, June 1992.

[7] S. Mehrotra and L. Harrison, "Quantifying the performance potential of a data prefetch mechanism for pointer-intensive and numeric programs," Tech. Rep. 1458, CSRD, Univ. of Illinois, November 1995.

[8] A. K. Porterfield, *Software Methods for Improvement of Cache Performance on Supercomputer Applications.* PhD thesis, Department of Computer Science, Rice University, Houston, TX, 1989.

[9] A. C. Klaiber and H. M. Levy, "An architecture for software-controlled data prefetching," in *Proc. 18th Ann. Int'l Symp. Computer Architecture*, (Toronto, Canada), pp. 43–53, May 1991.

[10] T. C. Mowry, M. S. Lam, and A. Gupta, "Design and evaluation of a compiler algorithm for prefetching," in *Proc. Fifth Int'l Conf. on Architectural Support for Prog. Lang. and Operating Systems.*, pp. 62–73, Oct. 1992.

[11] W. Y. Chen, S. A. Mahlke, P. P. Chang, and W. W. Hwu, "Data access microarchitectures for superscalar processors with compiler-assisted data prefetching," in *Proceedings of the 24th Annual International Symposium on Microarchitecture*, pp. 69–73, November 1991.

[12] W. Y. Chen, S. A. Mahlke, W. W. Hwu, T. Kiyohara, and P. P. Chang, "Tolerating data access latency with register preloading," in *Proceedings of the 6th International Conference on Supercomputing*, July 1992.

[13] G. Tyson, M. Farrens, J. Matthews, and A. R. Pleszkun, "A modified approach to data cache management," in *Proceedings of the 28th Annual International Symposium on Microarchitecture*, pp. 93–103, December 1995.

[14] J. A. Rivers and E. S. Davidson, "Reducing conflicts in direct-mapped caches with a temporality-based design," in *Proceedings of the 1996 International Conference on Parallel Processing*, pp. 151–162, August 1996.

[15] "SPEC newsletter," 1991. SPEC, Fremont, CA.

[16] Intel, *Pentium Pro Processor at 150 MHz, 166 MHz, 180 MHz and 200 MHz.* Intel Corporation, Santa Clara, CA, 1995.

[17] J. W. C. Fu and J. H. Patel, "Data prefetching in multiprocessor vector cache memories," in *Proc. 18th Ann. Int'l Symp. Computer Architecture*, (Toronto, Canada), pp. 54–63, June 1991.

[18] P. P. Chang, S. A. Mahlke, W. Y. Chen, N. J. Warter, and W. W. Hwu, "IMPACT: An architectural framework for multiple-instruction-issue processors," in *Proceedings of the 18th International Symposium on Computer Architecture*, pp. 266–275, May 1991.

[19] W. W. Hwu, S. A. Mahlke, W. Y. Chen, P. P. Chang, N. J. Warter, R. A. Bringmann, R. G. Ouellette, R. E. Hank, T. Kiyohara, G. E. Haab, J. G. Holm, and D. M. Lavery, "The superblock: An effective structure for VLIW and superscalar compilation," tech. rep., Center for Reliable and High-Performance Computing, University of Illinois, Urbana, IL, February 1992.

[20] J. W. C. Fu and J. H. Patel, "How to simulate 100 billion references cheaply," Tech. Rep. CRHC-91-30, Center for Reliable and High-Performance Computing, University of Illinois, Urbana, IL, 1991.

The Energy Efficiency of IRAM Architectures

Richard Fromm, Stylianos Perissakis, Neal Cardwell, Christoforos Kozyrakis,
Bruce McGaughy, David Patterson, Tom Anderson, Katherine Yelick

Computer Science Division, University of California–Berkeley

Abstract

Portable systems demand energy efficiency in order to maximize battery life. IRAM architectures, which combine DRAM and a processor on the same chip in a DRAM process, are more energy efficient than conventional systems. The high density of DRAM permits a much larger amount of memory on-chip than a traditional SRAM cache design in a logic process. This allows most or all IRAM memory accesses to be satisfied on-chip. Thus there is much less need to drive high-capacitance off-chip buses, which contribute significantly to the energy consumption of a system. To quantify this advantage we apply models of energy consumption in DRAM and SRAM memories to results from cache simulations of applications reflective of personal productivity tasks on low power systems. We find that IRAM memory hierarchies consume as little as 22% of the energy consumed by a conventional memory hierarchy for memory-intensive applications, while delivering comparable performance. Furthermore, the energy consumed by a system consisting of an IRAM memory hierarchy combined with an energy efficient CPU core is as little as 40% of that of the same CPU core with a traditional memory hierarchy.

1 Introduction

Energy efficient computing is growing in importance. Sales of laptop and notebook computers have been steadily climbing, and applications for portable computing are likely to continue to grow in the near future, in areas such as PDAs (personal digital assistants), smart phones, GPS (global positioning system) receivers, and other "anywhere-anytime" consumer computing devices [17][10]. The increasing prevalence of portable computing has promoted energy efficiency from a concern primarily of circuit designers to an issue of general interest to the computer architecture community [30][28]. Hence this area has received significant research attention [3][16][4][5][21].

Due to recent advances in flat-panel displays and disk power management, the share of the energy in portable systems consumed by the processor and external memory is growing [20]. Within processors, often a large percentage of energy is devoted to on-chip memory [25][38][39][16].

Our goal is to reduce the energy consumed by the memory system. Integrating a microprocessor and DRAM memory on the same die, an idea that we call Intelligent RAM (IRAM)[31], offers the potential for dramatic improvements in the energy consumption of the memory system. DRAM is much denser than SRAM, which is traditionally used for on-chip memory. Therefore, an IRAM will have much fewer external memory accesses, which consume a great deal of energy to drive high-capacitance off-chip buses. Even on-chip accesses will be more energy efficient, since on-chip DRAM consumes less energy than either SRAM or off-chip DRAM.

Previous work has examined how IRAM can be utilized to improve performance [33][40]. This has been motivated by the exponentially growing performance gap between processors, which are increasing in performance at a rate of 60% per year, and memory access times, which are only getting approximately 7% faster per year [18][46]. An IRAM has both lower latency and higher bandwidth between the processor and the memory compared to a conventional architecture, offering the potential for high performance. A potential challenge to the performance of IRAM implementations is the speed of logic in a DRAM process.

The contribution of this paper is to evaluate to what extent an IRAM design reduces the energy consumption of the memory system. We compare an IRAM to a conventional approach for two different die sizes, using appropriate ranges to account for the potential differences in area between DRAM and SRAM and the speed of a processor in a DRAM process. Using cache simulations of several applications reflective of personal productivity tasks on low-power systems and models of the energy consumption in DRAM and SRAM memories, we calculate the energy consumption of the memory hierarchy and performance for the various architectures. We find that the IRAM memory hierarchy consumes as little as 22% of the energy compared to a conventional implementation for memory-intensive applications, while delivering comparable performance. Furthermore, the energy consumed by a system consisting of an IRAM memory hierarchy combined with an energy efficient CPU core is as little as 40% of that of the same CPU core with a traditional memory hierarchy.

The remainder of the paper is organized as follows: Section 2 discusses various system metrics, including power and energy. Section 3 discusses potential energy and performance benefits of IRAM. Section 4 presents several alternative architectures and our methodology for evaluating them. Section 5 presents the results of our evaluations. Section 6 summarizes related work, Section 7 suggests future work, and Section 8 presents our conclusions. A more detailed discussion of the energy consumption models used

This research was supported by DARPA (DABT63-C-0056), the California State MICRO Program, and by research grants from Intel and Sun Microsystems. The authors can be contacted at `http://iram.cs.berkeley.edu` or `{rfromm, sper, neal, kozyraki, brucemcg, patterson, tea, yelick}@cs.berkeley.edu`.

ISCA '97 Denver, CO, USA

for our evaluations is included as an Appendix.

2 Metrics

Various metrics provide different perspectives on the characteristics of a portable computer system.

2.1 Power

Traditionally, the unit of concern for portable devices has been power, measured in Watts. Power represents the amount of energy consumed per unit time: $Power = Energy/Time$.

Power is a useful metric for certain concerns. The amount of power required by a system determines, for a fixed voltage, how much current a battery or other power source must be able to deliver. Also, higher power leads to high temperature, which in turn leads to more expensive packaging and a cooling system that can be more expensive, larger, and heavier.

2.2 Energy

As anyone who has ever used a portable computer can attest, the overriding concern for a user of such a system is battery life. Battery life is measured in units of energy, not power. Energy is the product of power and time, i.e., $Energy = Power \cdot Time$. For a given amount of work, what matters most to the user is how much energy is required to do that work.

Thus energy efficiency, measured in energy consumed per instruction, or MIPS per Watt, is a better metric than power for measuring how a given machine best utilizes limited battery life [6][45][16]. Energy per instruction and MIPS per Watt are inversely proportional to each other, as can be seen from the following relationship:

$$\frac{Energy}{Instruction} = \frac{Energy/Sec}{Instruction/Sec} \propto \frac{Watts}{MIPS}$$

Power can be a deceiving metric, since it does not directly relate to battery life. For instance, if the clock rate of a processor is cut in half, then the processor will consume approximately half the amount of power, assuming that the voltage is held constant, since $Power = Frequency \cdot Capacitance \cdot Voltage^2$. However, if all else is kept equal, it will now take approximately twice as long to execute a sequence of instructions. Thus the energy consumed by the processor for some given amount of work will be roughly the same.[1] Even worse, since the task will take longer, the energy consumed by the display and other components of the system will be greater.

At the extreme, slowing the frequency down to zero and putting the processor in sleep mode wins if processor power consumption is the only metric, yet this allows no work to be accomplished.

2.3 Performance

Besides energy efficiency, users are also concerned about performance. Users of portables are willing to tolerate lower performance than a desktop system has, but performance still matters. Portable systems are being used increasingly for more demanding applications that require higher performance. Examples include preparing large, graphical presentations, audio and video playback, handwriting recognition, and speech recognition. The goal is to be able to deliver high performance while still maintaining energy efficiency.

[1] Reducing the clock rate may also make it possible to lower the voltage [45], which would reduce both energy and power consumption, at the cost of decreased performance.

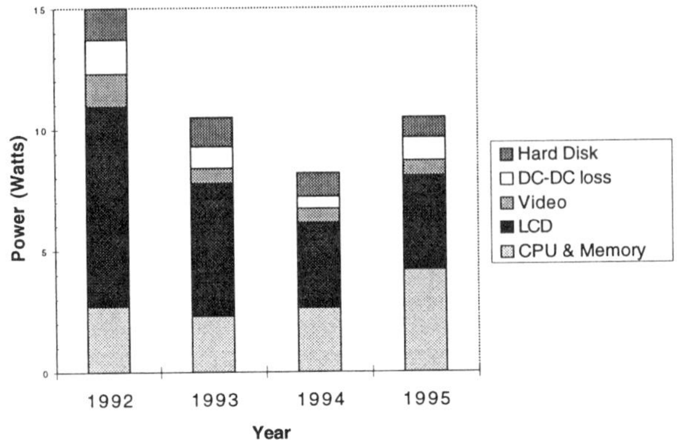

Figure 1: Notebook Power Budget Trends

In general, performance is measured by the execution time of a workload. However, we use MIPS to compare the performance of different systems on a given application since we limit our consideration to a single executable for a single instruction set architecture[18].

3 Benefits of Processor-Memory Integration

3.1 Energy Components of Current Systems

Given that portable devices, and hence energy efficient systems, are becoming more prevalent, it is useful to examine where the energy is consumed in such a device. Figure 1 shows the breakdown of the power consumption over time in IBM ThinkPad notebook computers [20]. Whereas the power used to be dominated by the screen, over time the CPU and memory are becoming an increasingly significant portion of the power budget. In smaller handheld portable devices, such as the Apple Newton and U.S. Robotics Pilot, there is no disk and the screen consumes much less power. The LCD on the original Newton consumed only 5 mW for static images, for example [6]. Hence, for these systems the power consumption of the CPU and memory is an even larger fraction of the total.

There are three parts to the portion labeled "CPU and Memory" in Figure 1: CPU core, on-chip caches, and external memory. The introduction of low power CPU cores places an even greater emphasis on the energy consumed by the memory system, both on-chip and off-chip. Considering only the on-chip costs, several studies show a roughly equal division of power or energy (different studies used different metrics) between CPU and memory.

StrongARM [25][38], a microprocessor by Digital that implements the ARM instruction set, delivers 183 Dhrystone MIPS at 160 MHz while dissipating less than 0.5 W. The 32 KB of on-chip caches consume 43% of the CPU power.

Sato, Nagamtsu, and Tago [39] used a power simulator of a generic RISC processor, examining both the current drawn by the various components and the percentage of time those components are used. Their results indicate that the instruction and data caches consume 60% of the total processor power.

Gonzalez and Horowitz [16] show in their simulations that 25-40% of the energy on a microprocessor is dissipated by the on-chip caches. They note that although each individual memory cell dissipates very little energy, the total represents a very significant sum. They are pessimistic that the combined goals of energy efficiency and performance can improve significantly since the energy is dissipated in so many small units. They feel that only a "radical new architecture" can significantly improve this situation.

die size	Small		Large	
implementation	Conventional	IRAM	Conventional	IRAM
CPU frequency	160 MHz	120 MHz *(0.75* **X***)* to 160 MHz *(1.0* **X***)*	160 MHz	120 MHz *(0.75* **X***)* to 160 MHz *(1.0* **X***)*
technology	0.35 μm logic	0.35 μm DRAM	0.35 μm logic	0.35 μm DRAM
L1 config	16 KB I + 16 KB D	8 KB I + 8 KB D	8 KB I + 8 KB D	8 KB I + 8 KB D
L1 associativity	32-way	32-way	32-way	32-way
L1 write policy	write-back	write-back	write-back	write-back
L1 block size	32 Bytes	32 Bytes	32 Bytes	32 Bytes
L1 type	SRAM on-chip	SRAM on-chip	SRAM on-chip	SRAM on-chip
L1 access time	1 cycle	1 cycle	1 cycle	1 cycle
L2 config	–	256 KB *(16:1)* to 512 KB *(32:1)* unified	256 KB *(32:1)* to 512 KB *(16:1)* unified	–
L2 associativity	–	direct-mapped	direct-mapped	–
L2 write policy	–	write-back	write-back	–
L2 block size	–	128 Bytes	128 Bytes	–
L2 type	–	DRAM on-chip	SRAM on-chip	–
L2 access time	–	30 ns	3 cycles (18.75 ns)	–
main memory	8 MB DRAM off-chip	8 MB DRAM off-chip	8 MB DRAM off-chip	8 MB DRAM on-chip
memory latency	180 ns	180 ns	180 ns	30 ns
bus width	narrow (32 bits)	narrow (32 bits)	narrow (32 bits)	wide (32 Bytes)

Table 1: **Architectural Models Used for Evaluation.** The SMALL and LARGE models roughly correspond to the die sizes given in Table 2. It is economically feasible to build large memory arrays by using redundancy. StrongARM's caches, in contrast, use no redundancy. Memory capacity and speed differentials between the CONVENTIONAL and IRAM models, including the variations in CPU frequency and L2 cache size, are based on the arguments presented in Sections 4.1 and 4.2 respectively. All caches are write-back to minimize energy consumption from unnecessarily switching internal and/or external buses. The 30 ns on-chip DRAM access time is based on [24], the 180 ns off-chip access time is based on [11], and the 18.75 ns on-chip L2 SRAM cache access time is chosen to be slightly larger than the on-chip L2 cache of the Alpha 21164A [8], which is slightly smaller (96 KB). The "narrow" bus width matches StrongARM, and the "wide" bus width takes advantage of the additional bandwidth available to main memory in an IRAM configuration. Note that it is only sensible to perform comparisons between SMALL-CONVENTIONAL and SMALL-IRAM and between LARGE-CONVENTIONAL and LARGE-IRAM. The SMALL and LARGE models correspond to different die sizes and are not meant to be compared to one another.

3.2 IRAM Energy Benefits

Although the concept of IRAM may represent a somewhat "radical" implementation, the integration of processor and memory has the potential to improve energy efficiency with a relatively simple system architecture.

There are numerous ways in which processor and memory can be integrated: 1) putting SRAM memory with a CPU in a logic process; 2) putting CPU logic with memory in a DRAM process; 3) putting DRAM memory with a CPU in a logic process. The first idea represents the conventional approach, using SRAM caches for on-chip memory. The second idea is what we are suggesting for IRAM. The third idea has a number of technological disadvantages, including a significant loss in memory density and a much higher refresh rate for the DRAM, due to DRAM process optimizations which are not present in a logic process [12]. Therefore, we only consider the first two approaches.

IRAM has a number of advantages over a conventional approach in achieving energy efficiency. First, DRAM is more energy efficient than SRAM per memory access, so accesses to the on-chip memory consume less energy. More importantly, since DRAM is much denser (see Section 4.1), more memory can reside on-chip, allowing some applications to become entirely chip-resident and significantly reducing the frequency of off-chip accesses for other applications. Driving high-capacitance off-chip buses requires a large amount of energy, so significantly reducing the number of off-chip accesses dramatically reduces the overall energy consumption.

3.3 IRAM Performance Benefits and Challenges

IRAM also has the potential for higher performance than a conventional approach. Even without considering architectural models specifically tailored to exploit the low-latency, high-bandwidth characteristics possible from an IRAM organization, the significant density improvement for DRAM over SRAM can result in higher performance for IRAM. As with the energy efficiency advantages, the big win for IRAM is that many more memory accesses can stay on-chip, which can significantly reduce the average memory access time. However, there are two limitations which might offset this benefit. First, access to a DRAM array is somewhat slower than an SRAM array. Second, logic in a DRAM process may initially be slower than logic in a state-of-the-art logic processes, leading to a slower CPU (see Section 4.2). The improvements due to the reduction in off-chip memory accesses will have to be greater than these slowdowns for there to be an overall increase in performance.

4 Methodology

To quantitatively investigate the energy efficiency and performance merits of IRAM, we compared the architectures listed in Table 1. The models assume commercially available logic and DRAM semiconductor processes. We use the models to estimate the behavior of a small, conventional CPU in a logic process (SMALL-CONVENTIONAL); that same CPU implemented in a DRAM process (SMALL-IRAM); a large DRAM die with a CPU added (LARGE-IRAM); and a similarly large die implemented in a logic process (LARGE-CONVENTIONAL).

In order to determine the characteristics of the models used to evaluate IRAM versus conventional architectures, two questions that need to be addressed are the area differences of DRAM and SRAM and the speed differences of logic in a DRAM versus logic process.

	StrongARM	64 Mb DRAM
process	0.35 μm CMOS	0.40 μm CMOS
memory cell size	26.41 μm^2	1.62 μm^2
number of memory bits	32 KB + tags = 287,744	64 Mb = 67,108,864
total chip area	49.9 mm^2	186.0 mm^2
total area of memory	27.9 mm^2	168.2 mm^2
Kbits per mm^2	10.07	389.6

Table 2: Memory Cell Parameters For Typical Microprocessor [25][37] and DRAM Chips[24]

4.1 Area Differences

As mentioned previously, the density of a DRAM array in a DRAM process is *much* higher than that of SRAM in a logic process. The ratio of the number of cells per unit area for DRAM versus SRAM is much greater than the 4:1 or 6:1 figure that one would assume if the only relevant factor was the number of transistors, four or six for an SRAM cell versus a single transistor for a DRAM cell [12]. DRAM storage cells use pseudo-3-dimensional trench or stacked capacitors to achieve very small cell sizes [35]. As Table 2 shows, the DRAM cell size for a 64 Mb DRAM implemented in a 0.4 μm CMOS process [24] is 16 times smaller than the SRAM cell size for StrongARM [37]. If the DRAM feature size is scaled down so that the comparison is for the same size process (0.35 μm), then the cell size is 21 times smaller.

What is more important, however, is to compare the total amount of memory that can fit in a given area when all circuits and interconnect that make up the entire memory array are taken into account. Examining the cell efficiency (bits of memory per unit area) shows that the 64 Mb DRAM is effectively 39 times more dense than the StrongARM. After again scaling the DRAM parameters to make an equal process comparison, the DRAM is 51 times more dense!

These numbers can be used to obtain an approximate value for the differences in memory capacity of a conventional and an IRAM architecture, given a fixed chip area. However, it is difficult to precisely quantify this for all cases, due to a number of extenuating circumstances. The comparisons above use chips with very different die areas, and the actual ratio obtained between two implementations is somewhat dependent on implementation-specific design decisions as well as the absolute size of the array – it is easier to make a memory array denser as it gets larger. Also, logic circuits in a DRAM process will be somewhat larger than logic circuits in a corresponding logic process. Therefore, to obtain equal total area, somewhat less area will be available for the memory array. This situation is likely to improve as future DRAM generations add additional metal layers, enabling more optimal layout of logic. Recognizing these factors, we are conservative when picking DRAM to SRAM capacity ratios used in the models, and instead of limiting our analysis to a single value, we use a range. The bounds of this range are obtained by rounding down the cell size and bits per unit area ratios to the nearest powers of 2, namely 16:1 and 32:1.

4.2 Speed Differences

Logic processes are optimized for fast transistors and interconnect, and DRAM processes are optimized for density and retention. Due to these different process characteristics, logic gates are currently slower in a standard DRAM process than a standard logic process, resulting in a CPU speed that may be slower in an IRAM than a conventional processor [19]. The precise slowdown varies by the manufacturer and the process generation. While logic circuits implemented in a DRAM currently have a speed disadvantage, ongoing trends in the DRAM industry will likely alleviate this difficulty. DRAM processes are beginning to incorporate faster transistors to support synchronous DRAM, and some DRAM manufacturers are already developing merged logic and DRAM processes in an attempt to get the best features of both on a single die. A panel of DRAM experts at the 1997 ISSCC [23] agreed that soon it will be possible to achieve the same performance from logic transistors in a DRAM process compared to a logic process, albeit at a modest (20-30%) increase in cost per wafer.

To address the question of transistor speeds in DRAM versus logic processes, we calculate our performance results for a range of CPU speeds for the architectures implemented in DRAM technologies. We vary the CPU speed from 0.75 as fast to equal in speed to the architectures implemented in logic processes. We expect that the low end of the range characterizes what an IRAM implementation might face today, while the high end of the range reflects DRAM processes likely to be available in the future.

4.3 Architectural Models

The SMALL-CONVENTIONAL design is architecturally similar to StrongARM [25][38], a low-power implementation of the ARM architecture by Digital that delivers 183 Dhrystone MIPS while dissipating under 0.5 W at 160 MHz.[2]

The SMALL-IRAM model addresses what the SMALL-CONVENTIONAL CPU would look like if implemented in a DRAM process given current technology, and if the overall chip area was kept constant. Since a single-cycle first level cache access is desirable for good performance, and access to an on-chip DRAM array is slower than that, we chose *not* to simply change the 32 KB of SRAM cache into a DRAM cache of similar area for the SMALL-IRAM model. Instead, we split the area originally allocated for the cache into two. Half of the area is allocated to a conventional L1 SRAM cache, and the remaining area is implemented as DRAM, organized as an L2 cache.

We consider L2 cache sizes of 256 KB and 512 KB, which corresponds to a density increase for DRAM compared to SRAM of 16:1 and 32:1 respectively (see Section 4.1). We consider CPU speeds between 120 and 160 MHz, which cover a range of speeds for logic in a DRAM process from 0.75 as fast to no slowdown (see Section 4.2).

The LARGE-IRAM model approaches the problem from a different angle: instead of starting with an existing CPU architecture and modifying it to be implemented in a DRAM process (with comparable total area), we start with a DRAM chip and add a CPU. We choose a 64 Mb DRAM chip, which is roughly comparable to 0.35 μm logic technology; both represent the state of the art available today in commercial implementations. This gives 8 MB of DRAM memory on-chip, which is large enough to be considered the main memory for many applications, especially in portable systems. We therefore assume that the on-chip DRAM array is main memory rather than an L2 cache. All memory references are assumed to be satisfied on-chip. Just as in the previous case (SMALL-IRAM), we desire for the CPU to be able to access most memory references in 1 cycle, so we again add a first level SRAM cache (again, 8 KB I + 8 KB D). Based on the same arguments as before (see Section 4.2), we consider CPU speeds of 120 and 160 MHz to address the potential speed differential between logic in DRAM and logic processes.

The LARGE-CONVENTIONAL model rounds out the four architectures studied by assuming roughly the same die area as the LARGE-IRAM model, but using a logic process instead. The large, on-chip memory array is therefore composed of SRAM cells. Based on the

[2] While 32-way set associativity may seem somewhat excessive, the StrongARM designers note that only 4-way associativity was desired for performance goals. Additional design requirements of single cycle access and bank selection led to the highly associative cache as a result. See [38] for details. We choose to keep the same 32-way set associativity for the L1 cache for all of our models to enable fair comparisons.

benchmark	instructions	16K L1 I miss	16K L1 D miss	% mem ref	description
hsfsys	1.8 billion	0.01%	5.2%	27%	Form-based handwriting recognition system; 1 page (55 MB)
noway	83 billion	0.02%	5.7%	31%	Continuous speech recognition system; 500 words (20.6 MB)
nowsort	48 million	0.0031%	6.9%	34%	Quicksorts 100-byte records with 10-byte keys (6 MB)
gs	3.1 billion	0.70%	3.0%	22%	Postscript interpreter; 9-chapter text book (7 MB)
ispell	26 billion	0.02%	2.0%	13%	Spelling checker; histories and tragedies of Shakespeare (2.9 MB)
compress	49 billion	0.000003%	9.3%	30%	Compresses and decompresses files; 16 MB
go	102 billion	1.3%	3.0%	31%	Plays the game of Go against itself three times
perl	47 billion	0.33%	0.63%	38%	Manipulates 200,000 anagrams and factors 250 numbers in Perl

Table 3: **Benchmarks and Data Sets Used For Evaluation.** Hsfsys [14] is from the National Institute of Standards and Technology (NIST), and noway [36] was written at the University of Sheffield. Nowsort was developed at the University of California-Berkeley. Ghostscript (gs) and ispell are well-known utilities. The final three benchmarks are from the SPECint95 benchmark suite [42]. Cache miss rates are for the SMALL-CONVENTIONAL model only and are meant, along with the percentage of instructions which are memory references (loads/stores), to give an overview of the memory behavior of each program.

	DRAM	SRAM	
		L1	L2
Internal power supply	2.2V	1.5V	1.5V
Bank width	256 bits	128 bits	128 bits
Bank height	512 bits	64 bits	512 bits
Bit line swing (read)	1.1V	0.5V	0.5V
Bit line swing (write)	1.1V	1.5V	1.5V
Sense amplifier current	–	150μA	150μA
Bit line capacitance	250fF	160fF	1280fF

Table 4: **Major Technology Parameters Used in Memory Hierarchy Models**

same arguments as before (see Section 4.1), we model both a 16:1 and 32:1 ratio of DRAM to SRAM array areas. This gives SRAM array sizes of 512 KB and 256 KB respectively. This is unlikely to be adequate for main memory, even for portable applications. Consequently, we assume that this is treated as an L2 cache, with conventional (off-chip) DRAM main memory as the next level in the memory hierarchy.

4.4 Simulations

Table 3 shows the applications we used for our evaluations. Each of these benchmarks is representative of current or potential future applications for a portable computing device. For each of these benchmarks and each of the architectural models in Table 1 we calculated the performance of the system as well as the energy consumed by the memory hierarchy, including caches, memory buses, and main memory.

The benchmarks were simulated using the multilevel cache simulator `cachesim5` included with `shade` [43], a tool from Sun which integrates instruction set simulation and trace generation with custom trace analysis. Activity at each of the levels of the memory hierarchy was recorded. Additionally, the base cycles per instruction (CPI), as if there were no stalls due to memory references, was determined using `spixcounts` and `ifreq`, dynamic instruction frequency profiling utilities also included with `shade`. Final performance numbers were computed by combining the base CPI with the miss rates and latencies at the various levels of the memory hierarchy.

The models for memory system energy consumption capture the dominant effects in DRAM and SRAM memories. Technology parameters were taken from typical DRAM circuits of the 64 Mb generation [24][47][44][27] and contemporary microprocessor SRAM cache generations [11][26][9] (see Table 4), which represent the state of the art commercially available in 1997. See the Appendix for a more detailed explanation of how energy consumption was calculated.

Our CPU model is similar to StrongARM, a single-issue, in-order CPU that achieves remarkable energy efficiency. The off-chip latency is the time to return the critical word. The CPU initially stalls on cache read misses, then continues execution while the rest of the cache block is fetched. We assume a write buffer big enough so that the CPU does not have to stall on write misses.

It should be noted that our energy models only address the energy consumed by the memory hierarchy, and not by the CPU core. Previous work [3][10] has already addressed techniques for reducing the CPU energy consumption; it is presumed that any system employing IRAM for reasons of energy efficiency will employ many of these techniques. Section 5.1 compares our results for the energy consumption of the memory hierarchy to the energy consumption of a low power CPU.

5 Evaluation

5.1 Energy

Figure 2 shows the energy consumption of the memory hierarchy for each of the benchmarks for each of the models. The energy consumption is divided into its various components, including L1 instruction and data caches, L2 cache, main memory, and the energy to drive the buses to access the various levels. Only a single value is given for each configuration, including the DRAM configurations where the CPU speed is varied, since the energy consumed by the memory system, for a given voltage, does *not* depend on CPU frequency.

As can be seen from the figure, the various IRAM configurations can significantly reduce the amount of energy consumed per instruction compared to the corresponding conventional cases. For the small chips, the memory hierarchy of the IRAM architectures consumes as little as 29% of the energy of the corresponding conventional architectures; for the large chips IRAM consumes as little as 22% of the conventional cases. In the worst case, the energy consumption of the IRAM memory hierarchy is comparable to that of the conventional models – either 116% or 76% for the small and large chips respectively. Note that the valid comparisons here are between the SMALL-CONVENTIONAL and SMALL-IRAM models, and between the LARGE-CONVENTIONAL and LARGE-IRAM models. The SMALL and LARGE models correspond to different die sizes and are not meant to be compared to one another.

The results can be understood by considering the following equation that relates the energy consumption at each level of the memory hierarchy with the frequency of accesses to the various

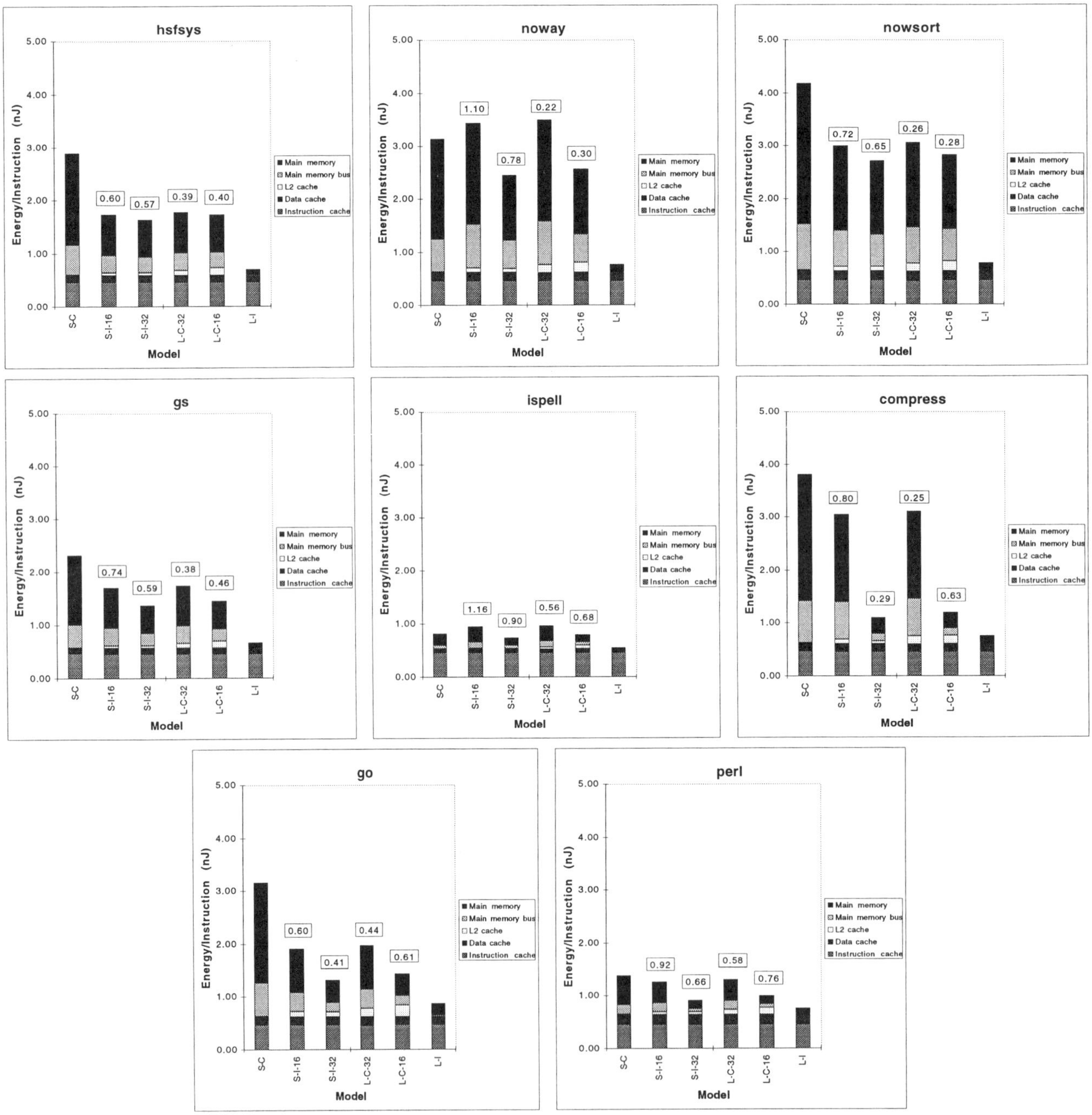

Figure 2: **Energy Consumption of Memory Hierarchy.** The labels for the models are as follows: S-C = SMALL-CONVENTIONAL; S-I-16 = SMALL-IRAM with 16:1 DRAM to SRAM-cache area density ratio (i.e. 256 KB L2 cache); S-I-32 = SMALL-IRAM with 32:1 ratio (512 KB L2); L-C-32 = LARGE-CONVENTIONAL with 32:1 ratio (256 KB L2); L-C-16 = LARGE-CONVENTIONAL with 16:1 ratio (512 KB L2); and L-I = LARGE-IRAM. The values atop the IRAM bars show the ratios of energy consumption compared to the CONVENTIONAL implementations. Ratios less than 1.0 indicate that IRAM consumes less energy per instruction.

	Small		Large	
	Conven-tional	IRAM	Conven-tional	IRAM
L1 access	0.447	0.447	0.447	0.447
L2 access	–	1.56	2.38	–
MM access (L1 line)	98.5	–	–	4.55
MM access (L2 line)	–	316	318	–
L1 to L2 Wbacks	–	1.89	2.71	–
L1 to MM Wbacks	98.6	–	–	4.65
L2 to MM Wbacks	–	321	323	–

Table 5: **Energy (in nanoJoules) Per Access to Levels of Memory Hierarchy.** Note that this table is somewhat of an approximation. For instance, the L2 cache access values vary somewhat depending on whether the access is a read or a write, as well as on the size of the cache. The average is shown.

levels (see Table 5). It is closely modeled after the familiar equation for average memory access time [18]:

$$\textit{Energy per instruction} = AE_{L1} + (MR_{L1} \times (1 + DP_{L1}) \times (AE_{L2} + (MR_{L2} \times (1 + DP_{L2}) \times AE_{\textit{off-chip}})))$$

where AE = access energy,
MR = miss rate,
and DP = dirty probability.

It is clear from this equation that there are two ways to reduce the energy consumption per instruction: 1) reduce the energy to access various levels of the memory hierarchy; 2) reduce the frequency of accesses to lower levels (i.e. reduce the miss rate). IRAM has the ability to deliver both.

There are two major sets of reductions of energy per access for a given level of an IRAM memory hierarchy – the differences between DRAM and SRAM and the differences between on-chip and off-chip accesses. For accesses that hit in the second level cache, accessing a DRAM array is more energy efficient than accessing a much larger SRAM array of the same capacity (see Table 5), mostly because the interconnect lines are shorter and the related parasitic capacitances are smaller. More striking is the comparison between on-chip and off-chip main memory, which is DRAM in both cases. Having the DRAM on-chip saves energy in three ways. First, accesses to the high-capacitance, off-chip bus are avoided. Second, with the multiplexed address scheme of conventional DRAMs, the short row address will select a larger number of DRAM arrays than needed to deliver the desired number of bits. On an IRAM, the entire address is available at the same time, which allows the minimum required number of arrays to be selected.[3] Finally, an external DRAM with a narrow pin interface will need to go through a number of column cycles to deliver an entire cache block, using additional energy to decode the column address and drive the long column select lines and multiplexers in every cycle. This energy is saved with an on-chip DRAM, which can deliver the entire cache line in one cycle.

The big win for IRAM comes from reducing the frequency of accesses to lower levels of the memory hierarchy. By having a DRAM array on-chip instead of an SRAM array, the on-chip memory can be *much* larger. Consequently, the IRAM configurations will have much lower off-chip miss rates and will not have to pay the significant energy penalty for going off-chip as frequently. For example, the off-chip (L1) miss rate for the go benchmark is 1.70% on the SMALL-CONVENTIONAL resulting in an off-chip energy cost of 2.53 nanoJoules/instruction and a total memory system energy consumption of 3.17 nJ/I. For the SMALL-IRAM case with a 32:1 DRAM to SRAM density ratio, although the local L1 miss rate rises to 3.95% (the L1 caches are only 8 KB each instead of 16 KB), the large L2 cache reduces the global off-chip (L2) miss rate to 0.10%. This contributes to the result of an off-chip energy cost of 0.59 nJ/I and a total memory system energy consumption of 1.31 nJ/I. These are respectively 23% and 41% of the conventional values. In the LARGE-IRAM case, where the main memory array is on-chip, all memory accesses can be satisfied without paying this high energy cost, offering the potential to even further reduce the energy consumption. The degree of improvement for IRAM depends on the nature of the application. Memory-intensive applications are much more likely to benefit by having access to much more memory than compute-intensive applications. If an application already fits within the available on-chip memory in a conventional approach, having still more memory will not provide a significant benefit.

There are some minor offsetting factors. For example, the SMALL-IRAM configuration has an L1 cache that is half of the size of the SMALL-CONVENTIONAL configuration, giving it a higher L1 miss rate and forcing it to access its next level (L2 DRAM cache) on some occasions in which the SMALL-CONVENTIONAL case hits in its L1 cache. This factor is small enough compared to the savings from going off-chip less often that, in most cases, there is a significant reduction in the energy consumption of the memory hierarchy by integrating the processor with DRAM.

Another offsetting factor arises from the particulars of the architectural models that we chose for our simulations. The L1 cache block sizes are 32 Bytes, while the L2 block sizes are 128 Bytes. As a result of this, main memory accesses that have to perform a cache fill consume more energy on the SMALL-IRAM model than they do for SMALL-CONVENTIONAL(see Table 5). This causes some anomalous cases (See noway and ispell in Figure 2) in which the energy consumption of the memory hierarchy for an IRAM implementation is actually greater than for a corresponding conventional model. This illustrates that the choice of block size is important for energy efficiency. While there has been a trend over time towards larger block sizes, fetching potentially unneeded words from memory may not be the best choice, depending on the memory access patterns of a given application, when energy consumption is taken into account.

By comparing our energy results to some known values from StrongARM, we can perform a quick validation of a portion of our energy consumption models. StrongARM dissipates 336 mW while delivering 183 Dhrystone MIPS. Of this, 27% of the power consumption comes from the ICache [25]. This translates into 0.50 nanoJoules per instruction. The energy consumption of the ICache in our simulations is fairly consistent across all of our benchmarks, at 0.46 nJ/I.

Our results presented so far only include the energy consumption of the memory hierarchy. Using an analysis similar to that above, we can place our results in the context of the energy consumption of a CPU combined with memory. As stated earlier, the on-chip caches on StrongARM consume 43% of the power, leaving 57% for the CPU core. Based on the same 336 mW and 183 MIPS figures noted above, this translates into 1.05 nanoJoules per instruction. For a memory-intensive application, this is a small portion of the energy consumed by the CPU and external memory. Thus, improving the energy of the memory hierarchy leads to a noticeable reduction in the energy dissipated by the CPU and memory. For example, for noway, comparing the energy consumption of LARGE-CONVENTIONAL (with 32:1 DRAM to SRAM density ratio)

[3] This might mean a corresponding increase in the number of cycles needed to refresh the entire memory, but with a minor increase in complexity an on-chip DRAM could separate the refresh operation from the read and write accesses and make it as wide as needed to keep the number of cycles low.

to LARGE-IRAM, and adding 1.05 nJ/I for the CPU core, shows that IRAM (1.82 nJ/I) uses only 40% of the energy of the conventional model (4.56 nJ/I). For more compute-intensive applications, the energy consumed by the CPU dominates that of the memory hierarchy. However, even for compute-intensive applications, the memory hierarchy is still relevant and represents a significant portion of the total energy consumption, especially when on-chip accesses are considered. Even if an application is entirely cache-resident, some energy will be consumed to access the caches.

5.2 Performance

While the primary motivation for this study is energy efficiency, it is also important to ensure that energy efficiency can be obtained while demonstrating comparable performance.

Table 6 shows the performance of each of the models, assuming a 32:1 DRAM to SRAM-cache area density ratio, on each of the benchmarks. This is shown for the range of frequencies for the CPU core implemented in a DRAM process compared to a logic process discussed earlier, from 0.75 times as slow for the CPU in a logic process to equal in speed. For the small chips, the IRAM architectures range from 0.78 to 1.50 times the performance of the corresponding conventional cases. For the large chips, IRAM ranges from 0.76 to 1.09 times the performance.

There are two opposing factors that determine the speed of the IRAM architectures relative to the conventional architectures. Which of these factors will dominate is a function of both the physical organization and the application. For an application that is compute-intensive and is not heavily dependent on the memory hierarchy, it is possible that a naive IRAM architecture will have lower performance than a conventional processor. The processor's operating frequency may initially be limited by the DRAM process in which it is implemented, and a compute-intensive application will likely be adversely impacted by such a slowdown.

For an application that is heavily dependent on the memory hierarchy and is already not fully utilizing the CPU, however, IRAM has the potential for a large performance gain. Many more of the memory accesses can be satisfied in the low-latency, high-bandwidth on-chip memory, due to the much higher density of DRAM than SRAM. For instance, Cvetanovic and Bhandarkar [7] found that a 300 MHz Alpha 21164 microprocessor spends about 75% of its time in the memory hierarchy for database and matrix computations. As the performance gap between processors and memory continues to increase, as applications have more demanding memory requirements, and as DRAM capacities continue to increase beyond the 64 Mb used in this study, the performance advantages of IRAM will grow.

The performance results of this study are, unfortunately, not impressive. One important conclusion from this is that, for these benchmarks, an IRAM implementation of a conventional architecture is not likely to lead to dramatic performance gains. This is consistent with other preliminary IRAM investigations [33][32][22]. This illustrates the importance of investigating new performance-oriented architectural ideas and organizations that can take better advantage of the lower latency and dramatically higher bandwidth between the processor and memory that IRAM offers.

6 Related Work

Other researchers have investigated a close integration of processors and memory. However, previous discussions have concentrated on the potential performance benefits. This paper is the first to quantify the energy efficiency advantages of IRAM.

Commercial products integrating DRAM and logic include graphics accelerators from NeoMagic [29] and Accelerix [1], and a chip from NEC that combines 16 Mb of DRAM with 128 8-bit processors for image-processing applications [2]. In addition, Mitsubishi has announced the M32R/D, which integrates a processor, 2KB of SRAM cache, and 2 MB of DRAM and is targeted at personal digital assistants [41][22]. They state that integrating a processor with memory significantly reduces power dissipation.

Researchers at Sun [40] evaluated the performance of a RISC processor on a 256 Mb DRAM, using the sense amps as caches. They arbitrarily limited their additions to be about 10% of the DRAM size, and found that they could achieve comparable integer performance and about half the floating point performance compared to a 1995 DEC Alpha. Other research projects investigating processor-memory integration include the Galileo project at the University of Wisconsin [13], the PPRAM project at Kyushu University in Japan [34], and the Processor-in-Memory Technology Infrastructure Development project at the University of Notre Dame.

7 Future Work

There is much more work to be done in this area, concerning both low level circuit issues and high level architectural issues. The physical implications (including temperature and noise) of closely integrating logic and memory need to be studied. For instance, as a rule of thumb, for every increase of 10 degrees Celsius, the minimum refresh rate of a DRAM is roughly doubled [15]. Research in process development would be useful in this and other areas. Perhaps the best realization of processor-memory integration can be achieved in a hybrid CMOS process that incorporates the best features of both logic and DRAM processes.

Also, as we suggested in Section 5.1, it would be useful to quantify the energy dissipation impact of cache design choices, including block size and associativity.

Finally, an IRAM organization gives us the opportunity for both lower latency and dramatically higher bandwidth between the processor and memory. Investigating new ideas and organizations that can turn these opportunities into significantly increased performance is an exciting and open area of research in architecture as well as compilers and operating systems. While this study concentrated on the benefits of IRAM for energy-conscious systems, this is certainly not the only realm in which IRAM may play an important role in redefining our notion of processor and memory system design.

8 Conclusion

We have quantified the energy efficiency advantages of IRAM memory hierarchies, relative to traditional memory hierarchies, by applying models of energy consumption in DRAM and SRAM memories to results of cache simulations of several applications reflective of personal productivity tasks on low power systems.

We found that IRAM memory hierarchies consume as little as 22% of the energy consumed by a conventional memory hierarchy (with on-chip L1 and L2 caches) for memory-intensive applications. They do so while delivering comparable system performance. When placed in the context of the energy dissipated by a high performance, low power CPU, we found that the energy consumed by an IRAM memory hierarchy combined with an energy efficient CPU core is as little as 40% of that consumed by that same CPU core combined with a traditional memory hierarchy.

Acknowledgments

We are grateful to Dan Dobberpuhl, Dan Murray, and Sribalan Santhanam of Digital Equipment Corporation for their helpful an-

benchmark	Small Conventional	Small IRAM (.75 **X**)	Small IRAM (1.0 **X**)	Large Conventional	Large IRAM (.75 **X**)	Large IRAM (1.0 **X**)
hsfsys	138	112 *(0.81)*	150 *(1.08)*	149	114 *(0.77)*	152 *(1.02)*
noway	111	99 *(0.89)*	132 *(1.19)*	127	104 *(0.82)*	139 *(1.09)*
nowsort	109	104 *(0.95)*	138 *(1.27)*	136	110 *(0.81)*	147 *(1.08)*
gs	119	107 *(0.90)*	142 *(1.20)*	141	109 *(0.78)*	146 *(1.04)*
ispell	145	113 *(0.78)*	151 *(1.04)*	149	115 *(0.77)*	153 *(1.03)*
compress	91	102 *(1.13)*	137 *(1.50)*	127	104 *(0.82)*	139 *(1.09)*
go	97	96 *(0.99)*	128 *(1.31)*	128	98 *(0.76)*	130 *(1.02)*
perl	136	106 *(0.78)*	141 *(1.04)*	140	107 *(0.76)*	142 *(1.01)*

Table 6: **Performance (in MIPS) of IRAM versus conventional processors, as a function of processor slowdown in a DRAM process.** Only the models with the 32:1 DRAM to SRAM-cache area density ratio are shown. The values in parentheses are the ratios of performances of the IRAM models compared to the CONVENTIONAL implementations. Ratios greater than 1.0 indicate that IRAM has higher performance.

swers to our questions about StrongARM. Thanks to Krste Asanovic for his role as an indispensable technical reference and to Noah Treuhaft, Randi Thomas, and Scott McPeak for useful feedback on earlier drafts of this paper.

Appendix

Energy dissipation modeling

The dominant factors of energy consumption in SRAM caches, DRAM caches, and external memory were captured in a spreadsheet. Typical values of circuit parameters, such as bit and word line capacitances and memory bank dimensions, were used [24][47][21][27][44][11][26][9] (see Table 4).

The dominant factor in DRAM energy dissipation is the capacitance of the bit lines being driven to the power supply rails. SRAM power dissipation is dominated by the sense amplifiers when reading, because the swing of the bit lines is low. However, to write the SRAM, the bit lines are driven to the rails, so their capacitance becomes the dominant factor when writing. For large arrays of SRAM and DRAM, driving the data into or out of the array and distributing the address to the row decoders also plays a significant role. Current-mode signaling is used for the data I/O, which is more energy efficient than voltage-mode [44]. Finally, there is some "background" power consumption, which is mostly cell leakage for SRAM and refresh power in the case of DRAM. This is normally very small, but can become non negligible when a memory is accessed rarely.

For all architectural models, the first-level instruction and data caches were closely modeled after the StrongARM caches, which are 32-way set-associative and are implemented as 16 banks. The tag arrays are implemented as Content-Addressable Memories (CAMs). This was done mainly to reduce power, since the conventional way of accessing a set-associative cache, reading all the lines in a set and then discarding all but one, is clearly wasteful. The second level unified cache is assumed to consist of the appropriate number of 512-by-256 DRAM banks, or 512-by-128 SRAM banks. This is organized in the conventional way, since it is direct mapped.

The IRAM model consists of 512 128Kbit sub-arrays, like some high-density DRAMs [27]. On-chip L2 caches, as well as the on-chip main memory, have 256-bit wide interfaces to the first level caches. In the case of IRAM, this is a significant departure from the common 4- to 16-bit wide memories and one of the main performance and energy advantages of IRAM-based architectures.

For external memory, for a fair comparison we used a single 64Mbit chip. This of course assumes that such chips with 32-bit wide interfaces will be available. This choice clearly minimizes the external memory power, both in the DRAM chips themselves (just one in our case) and in the bus, which is as small as possible. If such chips are not available, external power consumption will be higher and the IRAM advantage more pronounced.

Having calculated the energy dissipated in the various parts of the memory system each time they are accessed, the energy required for each memory operation is easily computed. For example, a primary cache read miss that hits in the secondary cache consists of (unsuccessfully) searching the L1 tag array, reading the L2 tag and data arrays, filling the line into the L1 data array, updating the L1 tag and returning the word to the processor. In addition, a writeback may be needed. Individual energy components are summed to yield the total energy for this operation. Such results are combined with the miss rates, dirty probabilities and read/write frequencies reported by shade to calculate the average energy per instruction.

References

[1] Accelerix Incorporated. http://www.accelerix.com/.

[2] AIMOTO, Y., ET AL. A 7.68 GIPS, 3.84 GB/s 1W parallel image-processing RAM integrating a 16 Mb DRAM and 128 processors. In *Digest of Technical Papers, 1996 IEEE International Solid-State Circuits Conference* (San Francisco, CA, Feb 1996), vol. 39, pp. 372–373, 476.

[3] BURD, B., AND BRODERSEN, R. Energy efficient CMOS microprocessor design. In *Proroceedings of the Twenty-Eighth Hawaii International Conference on System Sciences* (Los Alamitos, CA, Jan. 1995), vol. 1, pp. 288–297.

[4] CHANDRAKASAN, A. *Low Power Digital CMOS Design.* PhD thesis, University of California at Berkeley, 1994.

[5] CHANDRAKASAN, A., ET AL. System design of a multimedia I/O terminal. In *Proceedings of IEEE Workshop on VLSI Signal Processing* (Veldhoven, Netherlands, October 1993), pp. 57–65.

[6] CULBERT, M. Low power hardware for a high performance PDA. In *Digest of Technical Papers, 1994 IEEE Symposium on Low Power Electronics* (San Diego, CA, Oct. 1994), pp. 28–31.

[7] CVETANOVIC, Z., AND BHANDARKAR, D. Performance characterization of the Alpha 21164 microprocessor using TP and SPEC workloads. In *Proceedings, Second International Symposium on High-Performance Computer Architecture* (San Jose, CA, Feb 1996), pp. 270–280.

[8] DIGITAL EQUIPMENT CORPORATION. *Alpha 21164 Microprocessor Hardware Reference Manual*, 1995.

[9] DIMARCO, D., ET AL. A 200MHz 256KB second-level cache with 1.6GB/s data bandwidth. In *Digest of Technical Papers, 1996 IEEE International Solid-State Circuits Conference* (San Francisco, CA, Feb 1996), vol. 39, pp. 158–159.

[10] DOBBERPUHL, D. The design of a high performance low power microprocessor. In *Digest of Technical Papers, 1996 International Symposium on Low Power Electronics and Design* (Montery, CA, Aug. 1996), pp. 11–16.

[11] DOBBERPUHL, D. Personal communication, Nov. 1996.

[12] FOSS, R. Implementing application specific memory. In *Digest of Technical Papers, 1996 IEEE International Solid-State Circuits Conference* (San Francisco, CA, Feb. 1996), pp. 260–261, 456.

[13] Galileo project. http://www.cs.wisc.edu/galileo/. Computer Sciences Department, University of Wisconin - Madison.

[14] GARRIS, M., ET AL. *Public Domain OCR: NIST Form-Based Handprint Recognition System*. National Institute of Standards and Technology, http://www.nist.gov/itl/div894/894.03/databases/defs/nist_ocr.html.

[15] GIACALONE, G., ET AL. A 1 MB, 100 MHz integrated L2 cache memory with 128b interface and ECC protection. In *Digest of Technical Papers, 1996 IEEE International Solid-State Circuits Conference* (San Francisco, CA, Feb. 1996), pp. 370–371.

[16] GONZALEZ, R., AND HOROWITZ, M. Energy dissipation in general purpose microprocessors. *IEEE Journal of Solid-State Circuits 31*, 9 (Sept. 1996), 1277–1284.

[17] HARRIS, E., ET AL. Technology directions for portable computers. In *Proceedings of the IEEE* (Apr. 1995), vol. 83, pp. 636–658.

[18] HENNESSY, J., AND PATTERSON, D. *Computer Architecture: A Quantitative Approach*. Morgan Kaufmann Publishers, Inc, San Francisco, CA, 1996.

[19] HOROWITZ, M. Merged DRAM/Logic. IEDM short course on "DRAMs in the 21st Century", San Francisco, CA, December 1996.

[20] IKEDA, T. Thinkpad low-power evolution. In *Digest of Technical Papers, 1995 IEEE Symposium on Low Power Electronics* (San Jose, CA, Oct. 1995), pp. 6–7.

[21] ITOH, K., SASAKI, K., AND NAKAGOME, Y. Trends in low-power RAM circuit technologies. In *Proceedings of the IEEE* (Apr. 1995), vol. 83, pp. 524–543.

[22] IWATA, S., SHIMIZU, T., ET AL. Performance evaluation of a microprocessor with on-chip DRAM and high bandwidth internal bus. In *Custom Integrated Circuits Conference* (1996), pp. 269–272.

[23] KIMURA, O., ET AL. Panel: DRAM + logic integration: Which architecture and fabrication process. In *IEEE International Solid-State Circuits Conference* (San Francisco, CA, Feb. 1997).

[24] KOIKE, H., ET AL. A 30ns 64Mb DRAM with built-in self-test and repair function. In *Digest of Technical Papers, 1996 IEEE International Solid-State Circuits Conference* (San Francisco, CA, Feb. 1996), pp. 150–151, 270.

[25] MONTANARO, J., ET AL. A 160MHz 32b 0.5W CMOS RISC microprocessor. In *Digest of Technical Papers, 1996 IEEE International Solid-State Circuits Conference* (San Francisco, CA, Feb. 1996), pp. 214–215, 447.

[26] MURRAY, D. Personal communication, Nov. 1996.

[27] NAKAMURA, M. TAKAHASHI, T., ET AL. A 29ns 64Mb DRAM with hierarchical array architecture. In *Digest of Technical Papers, 1995 IEEE International Solid-State Circuits Conference* (San Francisco, CA, Feb 1995), vol. 38, pp. 246–247.

[28] NSF workshop on critical issues in computer architecture research. http://www.cise.nsf.gov/mips/MSAWorkshop96/, May 1996.

[29] NeoMagic Corporation. http://www.neomagic.com/.

[30] PATTERSON, D. Panel: Research opportunities and critiques: An industrial perspective. In *1996 International Symposium on Computer Architecture* (Philadelphia, PA, May 1996).

[31] PATTERSON, D., ANDERSON, T., AND YELICK, K. A case for Intelligent DRAM: IRAM. In *HotChips VIII* (Stanford, CA, 1996), pp. 75–93.

[32] PATTERSON, D., ET AL. A case for Intelligent RAM: IRAM. In *IEEE Micro* (Apr. 1997).

[33] PATTERSON, D., ET AL. Intelligent RAM (IRAM): Chips that remember and compute. In *Digest of Technical Papers, 1997 IEEE International Solid-State Circuits Conference* (San Francisco, CA, Feb. 1997), pp. 224–225.

[34] PPRAM project. http://kasuga.csce.kyushu-u.ac.jp/~ppram/. Computer Science Division, Kyushu Univeristy, Japan.

[35] PRZYBYLSKI, S. A. *New DRAM Technologies: A Comprehensive Analysis of the New Architctures*. MicroDesign Resources, Sebastopol, California, 1994.

[36] RENALS, S., AND HOCHBERK, M. Decoder technology for connectionist large vocabulary speech recognition. Research Memorandum CS-95-17, Department of Computer Science, University of Sheffield, 1995.

[37] SANTHANAM, S. Personal communication, Oct. 1996.

[38] SANTHANAM, S. StrongARM SA110: A 160MHz 32b 0.5W CMOS ARM processor. In *HotChips VIII* (Stanford, CA, 1996), pp. 119–130.

[39] SATO, T., NAGAMATSU, M., AND TAGO, H. Power and performance simulator: ESP and its application for 100MIPS/W class RISC design. In *Digest of Technical Papers, 1994 IEEE Symposium on Low Power Electronics* (San Diego, CA, Oct. 1994), pp. 46–47.

[40] SAULSBURY, A., PONG, F., AND NOWATZYK, A. Missing the memory wall: The case for processor/memory integration. In *Proceedings of the 23rd Annual International Symposium on Computer Architecture* (Philadelphia, PA, May 1996), pp. 90–101.

[41] SHIMIZU, T., ET AL. A multimedia 32b RISC microprocessor with 16Mb DRAM. In *Digest of Technical Papers, 1996 IEEE International Solid-State Circuits Conference* (San Francisco, CA, Feb. 1996), pp. 216–217, 448.

[42] SPEC CPU95 benchmarks. http://www.specbench.org/osg/cpu95/.

[43] SUN MICROSYSTEMS LABORATORIES, INC. *Introduction to Shade*. Mountain View, CA, Apr 1993.

[44] TAGUCHI, M. TOMITA, H., ET AL. A 40ns 64Mb DRAM with current-sensing data-bus amplifier. In *Digest of Technical Papers, 1991 IEEE International Solid-State Circuits Conference* (San Francisco, CA, Feb 1991), vol. 34, pp. 112–113.

[45] WEISER, M., ET AL. Scheduling for reduced CPU energy. In *Proceedings of the First USENIX Symposium on Operating Systems Design and Implementation OSDI* (Monterey, CA, November 1994), pp. 13–23.

[46] WULF, W., AND MCKEE, S. Hitting the memory wall: Implications of the obvious. *Computer Architecture News 23*, 1 (Mar. 1995), 20–24.

[47] YAMADA, T., ET AL. A 64Mb DRAM with meshed power line and distributed sense-amplifier driver. In *Digest of Technical Papers, 1991 IEEE International Solid-State Circuits Conference* (San Francisco, CA, Feb 1991), vol. 34, pp. 108–109.

DataScalar Architectures

Doug Burger, Stefanos Kaxiras, and James R. Goodman

Computer Sciences Department
University of Wisconsin-Madison
1210 West Dayton Street
Madison, Wisconsin 53706 USA

galileo@cs.wisc.edu – http://www.cs.wisc.edu/galileo

Abstract

DataScalar architectures improve memory system performance by running computation redundantly across multiple processors, which are each tightly coupled with an associated memory. The program data set (and/or text) is distributed across these memories. In this execution model, each processor broadcasts operands it loads from its local memory to all other units. In this paper, we describe the benefits, costs, and problems associated with the DataScalar model. We also present simulation results of one possible implementation of a DataScalar system. In our simulated implementation, six unmodified SPEC95 binaries ran from 7% slower to 50% faster on two nodes, and from 9% to 100% faster on four nodes, than on a system with a comparable, more traditional memory system. Our intuition and results show that DataScalar architectures work best with codes for which traditional parallelization techniques fail. We conclude with a discussion of how DataScalar systems may accommodate traditional parallel processing, thus improving performance over a much wider range of applications than is currently possible with either model.

1 Introduction

Although microprocessor performance continues to grow at an exponential rate, not all microprocessor components improve similarly. Imbalances created by divergent rates of improvement are eliminated through microarchitectural innovations and altered assignations of resources. Specifically, the relative costs of communication are increasing relative to those of computation. This trend is resulting in successively larger caches with each processor generation, as well as more complex and expensive latency tolerance mechanisms.

As microprocessor clock improvements continue to outpace reductions in commodity DRAM access times and improvements in bus clocks, accesses to main memory grow more expensive. Techniques to reduce or tolerate this latency often do so by increasing the bandwidth requirements of the processor, which in turn increases the latency of memory accesses [4]. Processors that perform more parallel operations simultaneously may also increase queueing delays in the memory system.

This work is supported in part by NSF Grant CCR-9509589, an unrestricted grant from the Intel Research Council, and equipment donations from Sun Microsystems.

This paper describes an architecture that exploits comparatively inexpensive computation to reduce communication overheads. In a DataScalar architecture, multiple autonomous processing units are each tightly coupled with a fraction of a program's physical memory. Each unit runs the same program, asynchronously executing the same instructions on the same data. When a processor issues a load to an operand that is located in its memory (i.e., the operand is *owned* by that processor), it broadcasts the result of the load to the other processors. When a processor issues a load to an operand not contained in its memory, the load request is buffered until the operand arrives, broadcast by some other processor. Stores are completed only by the owning processor, and dropped by the others.[1]

By performing redundant computation, a processor that has a datum locally can compute the address of that datum, access that datum, and send that datum to the other nodes quickly. Since all physical memory is local to at least one processor, a request for a remote operand never need be made. This execution model eliminates off-chip request and write traffic, reduces memory access latencies, and creates opportunities for new optimizations.

Current technological parameters do not make DataScalar systems a cost-effective alternative to today's implementations. For a DataScalar system to be more cost-effective than the alternatives, the following three conditions must hold: (1) Processing power must be cheap; the dominant cost of each node should be memory. (2) Remote memory accesses should be much slower than local memory accesses. (3) Broadcasts should not be prohibitively expensive.

We believe that technological trends are driving commodity systems in a direction such that the aforementioned conditions will all eventually hold. We list three possible candidates for DataScalar systems, ordered in increasing levels of integration, below.

- **Networks of workstations**: DataScalar execution could perform as an alternative to paging to remote physical memories [15] on a network of workstations, provided broadcasts were sufficiently inexpensive. Some network topologies, such as fat trees, support efficient broadcasts. Alternatively, some implementations of optical networks render broadcasts virtually free, enabling efficient DataScalar execution [2].

- **IRAM-based systems**: the concept of a single-chip computer, in which processor logic and main memory are merged on the same die has existed for decades. Processor/memory integration has received much attention recently [3, 20, 21, 17]; acknowledging this current enthusiasm, we refer to implementation of such systems as IRAM [20]. Remote memory accesses (to other IRAM chips) will certainly be more expensive than on-chip memory accesses. IRAM chips connected by a bus or point-to-point ring would exhibit the needed parameters for a cost-effective DataScalar implementation.

1. Except when the data are cached, in which case the cache line is updated, and no write-through or write-back is required.

- **Chip multiprocessors (CMPs)**: Single commodity chips are projected to hold a billion logic transistors by 2010. Such copious silicon real estate will enable fabrication of single-chip multiprocessors containing substantial quantities of memory per processor—such a chip is in development even today [18]. Wiring delays on these chips will be substantial [6]; accessing an operand from a bank to which the requester is tightly coupled is likely to be much faster than requesting an operand from a memory bank across the chip (in essence, the former access would be "local" and the latter "remote," even though both requests are serviced on the same chip).

In this paper, we evaluate a DataScalar implementation in the IRAM context, since we believe that it is a promising technological match for these ideas. In Section 2, we describe the ideas and background in more detail. In Section 3, we describe the benefits of the base model and present some supportive simulation results. In Section 4, we describe one implementation of a DataScalar system and present timing simulation results comparing it against a traditional alternative. In Section 5, we discuss the potential for the interaction of DataScalar and parallel processing. Finally, we discuss related work and conclude in Section 6.

2 DataScalar overview

DataScalar architectures are intended to mitigate the dual constraints of (1) processors coupled with limited memories that may not easily be expanded—such as a finite on-chip or on-module capacity in a highly integrated system—and (2) existing uniprocessor programs that are not easily parallelized. This architecture exploits the availability of multiple processors to minimize memory latency by using the fact that any memory location is local to *some* processor. Thus each read operand can be quickly fetched by some processor. Each memory update can be achieved by means of only one write by the processor to which the store address is local.

DataScalar is based on the Massive Memory Machine (MMM) work from the early 1980s. The MMM was a synchronous, SISD architecture that connected a number of minicomputers with a global broadcast bus [13]. Each computer contained a very large memory, which was a fraction of the total program memory (each operand was thus *owned* by only one processor, i.e., it resides in the physical memory of only one processor). All computers ran the same program in lock-step, and the owner of each operand broadcast it on the global bus when accessed. This broadcast model was called *ESP* in the MMM work. We depict an example of synchronous ESP in Figure 1. One processor (the *lead* processor) is slightly ahead of the others while it is broadcasting (initially processor 3 in Figure 1). When the program execution accesses an operand that the lead processor does not own, a *lead change* occurs. All processors stall until the new lead processor catches up and broadcasts its operand (e.g., processor 2 broadcasting w_5 at cycle 7 in Figure 1).

Some advantages to ESP are: (1) that no requests need be sent, thus reducing access latency and bus traffic, since all communication is one-way. (2) Writes (or write-backs) never appear on the global bus, further reducing bus traffic (since all processors are running the same program, they all generate the same store values, which need complete only on the owning processor). (3) Since the MMM was synchronous, and all processors generated the address for each successive operand, no tags needed to be sent with the data on the global bus.

DataScalar architectures combine ESP with out-of-order execution, the combination of which is an asynchronous version of ESP. Each processor may access owned operands simultaneously. This asynchrony permits each processor to run ahead on computation involving operands that it owns, generating the total stream of broadcasts more quickly. We call this capability *datathreading*. Unlike synchronous ESP, however, each broadcast must contain an address or tag, since broadcasts occur in an unknown total order.

Because each processor executes the instructions in a different order, it is possible for a processor to temporarily deviate from the ESP model and execute a private computation, broadcasting only the result—not the operands—to the other processors. We call this technique *result communication*, and discuss it in more detail in Section 5.1. We note that this execution model—which we call Single-Program, Single Data stream (SPSD)—is a serial analogue to the Single-Program, Multiple Data stream (SPMD) execution model proposed by Darema-Rogers et al. in 1985 [5] (which extended Flynn's classification [11]).

Requiring every load to be broadcast would generate much more total traffic than current systems with cache memories. Interchip traffic can be reduced dramatically by replicating the frequently accessed portions of the address space both statically and dynamically at various granularities (word, cache line, and/or page).

We replicate data statically by duplicating the most heavily accessed pages[1] in each processor's local memory. Accesses to a replicated page will complete locally at every processor, requiring no off-chip traffic. The address space is thus divided into two categories: *replicated* and *communicated*. Replicated pages are mapped in each processor's local memory, and the communicated part of the address space is distributed among the processors.

Figure 2 shows how loads and stores differ for replicated and communicated memory; both processors issue a load and store to replicated memory (L1 and S1), which complete locally. Both processors also issue loads to L2 and S2, which are located in the communicated memory of processor **A** only. Processor **A** broadcasts L2, which processor **B** receives and consumes. S2 completes at processor **A**, but is dropped at processor **B**.

Static, coarse-grained replication of pages cannot capture locality that is fine-grained or identifiable only at run-time. We must therefore allow caching at each node, effectively replicating data dynamically for the period that they are cached. Dynamic replication of data, however, introduces some new consistency issues that we will discuss in Section 4.1.

The DataScalar execution model is a memory system optimization, not a substitute for parallel processing. When coarse-grain parallelism exists and is obtainable, the system should be run as a parallel processor (since a majority of the needed hardware is already present). We discuss the issues concerning hybrid execution models for multiprocessors further in Section 5.2.

3 DataScalar benefits

In this section, we describe the benefits associated with the base DataScalar model (ESP and datathreading) in detail. We show how ESP reduces about a third of off-chip traffic (on average), and we show how datathreading offers the potential for reductions in memory latency. We also present simulation results that address each of these benefits.

3.1 ESP and traffic reduction

DataScalar systems enjoy nearly the same benefits from ESP as did the MMM proposal. ESP reduces traffic—thereby increasing effective bandwidth—by eliminating both request traffic and write traffic from the global interconnect. ESP, asynchronous or otherwise, does not further reduce the number of read operands that must be communicated off-chip over that of a conventional architecture.

1. We assume a static partitioning at the page level, and thus this distinction would is in the page table. Other schemes are possible.

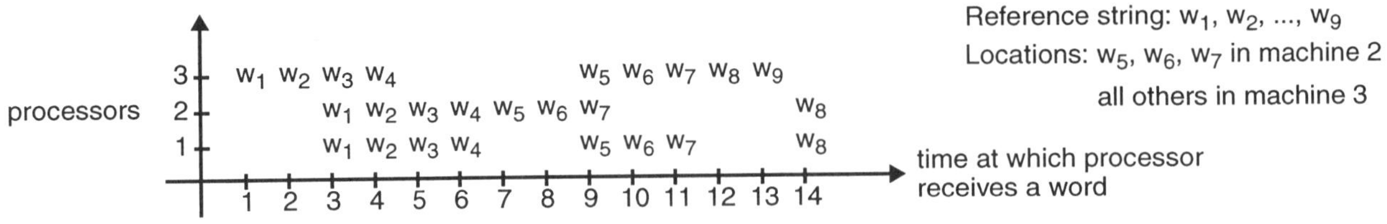

Figure 1. Operation of the ESP Massive Memory Machine (from [13])

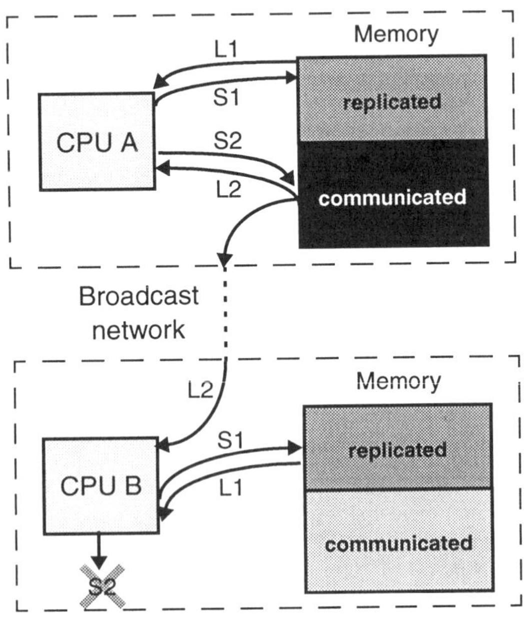

Figure 2. Replicated vs. communicated memory

ESP-based systems eliminate request traffic because ESP uses a *response-only* (or *data-pushing*) model. Since all processors run the same program, if one processor issues a load to an address, all the other processors will eventually issue that same load. The owner is therefore assured that when it broadcasts the load, all other processors will consume it. Conversely, when a processor issues a load to a datum that it does not own, it can buffer the request on-chip, and the matching data will eventually arrive. Thus, requests need never be sent off-chip. Similarly, when a store is generated at all nodes, only the owner of that address need complete the store on-chip. Since every chip is generating the value locally, created store values never need be sent off-chip. All processors will complete the store if the address is a replicated location. If the address is cached at all nodes, the store will complete in the cache, and the eventual write-back (or write-through) operation will be dropped at nodes that do not own that address. Note that there are none of the traditional cache consistency issues, since every processor is running the same program.

In a synchronous implementation of ESP, tags need not be broadcast with data—every processor is generating the same instruction stream in the same order, so tags can be inferred from the order in which the broadcasts are received. DataScalar systems do not enjoy this benefit; the out-of-order issue processors will all issue multiple broadcasts in an unpredictable order. In addition, more than one processor generally will be attempting to broadcast at any given time. This lack of predictability means that data must be broadcast along with their addresses and/or some other identifying tags (multiple instances of the same address may require supplementary tag information, such as a sequence number).

We measured the extent to which ESP reduces off-chip communication using cache simulation. We used the SimpleScalar tool set [1], which is an execution-driven set of processor simulators that simulate a MIPS-like instruction set architecture. We simulated a 64-Kbyte, two-way set-associative, write-allocate, write-back, on-chip level-one data cache (this size is consistent with typical cache sizes at the time that SPEC95 was released). We measured the aggregate miss traffic from the cache, and calculated the fraction of traffic that remained once write-backs and requests were eliminated. In Table 1, we show this measured fraction for fourteen of the SPEC95 benchmarks. We show both total traffic eliminated, and the reduction in the total number of distinct messages (we count a request/response pair as two transactions). The table shows that, for this cache size, ESP eliminates roughly 15% to 50% of the off-chip traffic in bytes, and from 52% to 75% of the individual transactions (because no requests are sent, the transaction reduction will always be at least 50%).

These results indicate that—for systems in which memory bandwidth is at a premium—implementing ESP is likely to improve performance, or reduce the required system cost to achieve the same performance. These results focus solely on bus traffic reduction—they do not address the performance penalties associated with necessitating broadcasts on interconnects other than buses. We address that issue in Section 4.4.

3.2 Datathreading and latency reduction

ESP-based systems reduce memory latency by making all off-chip communications one-way only. These savings might be large if the remote communication time dominates the memory request latency, or small if the memory access latency and/or memory system queueing delays dominate the request latency.

ESP-based systems offer the potential for further reductions in memory access latencies, however. Consider a stream of accesses to memory locations, each address of which is dependent on the value of the previous address (e.g., pointer chasing). When two or more dependent addresses reside in one processor's local memory, that processor may fetch those values without incurring any off-chip latencies. Those values may then be sent to the other processors by pipelining the broadcasts, incurring only one off-chip delay on the critical path. All processors thus complete the processing of those addresses faster than would a traditional system.

To illustrate this concept, we depict a simple example in Figure 3. Figure 3a shows a four-chip DataScalar system in which each IRAM chip contains a quarter of the program's physical memory. Figure 3b shows a more traditional organization, in which one IRAM chip holds a quarter of the program's memory and traditional DRAM chips hold the other three-quarters. In both systems, operands x_1, x_2, x_3 all reside on one chip, and operand x_4 resides on a different chip. The address of each x_{i+1} is dependent on x_i. One processor in the DataScalar system can access the first three without a single off-chip access, and then pipeline the broadcasts of those three operands to the other nodes (the broadcasts will be separated by the memory access time, of course). There will be a serialized off-chip access between x_3 and x_4 (analogous to a lead

Quantity eliminated:	tomcatv	swim	hydro2d	mgrid	applu	m88ksm	turb3d	gcc	compress	li	perl	fpppp	wave5	vortex
Traffic	.16	.39	.33	.31	.38	.14	.40	.19	.54	.39	.32	.17	.46	.21
Transactions	.52	.66	.62	.61	.65	.52	.66	.55	.74	.66	.62	.53	.70	.56

Table 1: Off-chip data traffic reduced by ESP

Shows reductions in off-chip data traffic due to ESP (removal of write and request traffic) for the SPEC95 benchmarks. Traffic is measured in two ways: fraction of bytes eliminated (top row) and fraction of transactions eliminated (second row).

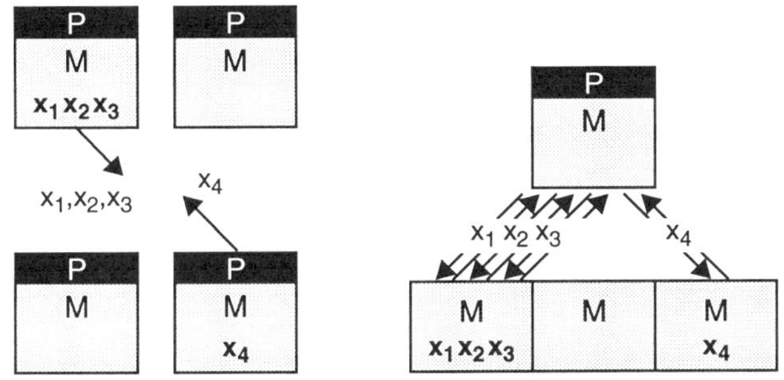

(a) DataScalar system:
Pipelined broadcasts
Serialized off-chip accesses: 2

(b) Traditional system:
Req./response each operand
Serialized off-chip accesses: 8

Figure 3. Comparing off-chip access serializations

change in the MMM), and then x_4 will be broadcast. The system thus incurs two serialized off-chip delays. The traditional system, conversely, incurs two serialized off-chip accesses (one request, one response) for each operand, for a total of eight in this example The traditional system would incur zero off-chip delays if all the operands happened to reside in the on-chip quarter of the memory, as opposed to a minimum of one for a DataScalar system.

We call a series of accesses to consecutive local dependent operands a *datathread*. If the operands are not dependent, then a traditional system could simply pipeline multiple non-blocking accesses, obtaining them in two serialized off-chip crossings. When a dependence spans two nodes, we view that point as initiating a datathread migration from one node to the other, beginning the access stream of that thread at the new node. The overhead of migrating this conceptual thread is one serialized off-chip access. The cost of maintaining inexpensive datathread migrations is precisely that of maintaining SPSD execution— broadcasting loads and performing computation redundantly at all nodes.

Another conceptual view of asynchronous ESP execution is that from each processor's perspective, it is the main processor, and the others are simply intelligent prefetch engines residing in the main memory modules. From this perspective, the broadcasts the processor sends are merely the state the prefetch engines need to continue performing the accurate prefetching. Since this is a homogenous system, each processor will have this view of the others, of course.

The Massive Memory Machine was able to exploit only one datathread at any time; when a lead change occurred, a new datathread began at the new leader (in Figure 1, operands w_1-w_4, w_5-w_7, and w_8-w_9 would constitute three datathreads, assuming each operand is dependent on the previous one). DataScalar systems, because they implement asynchronous ESP with out-of-order issue at each node, may have multiple datathreads running concurrently. DataScalar systems do not require special support for datathreads, since they transparently exploit the locality already inherent in reference streams. However, programs would benefit from special support to increase datathread length or raise the number of datathreads executing concurrently.

In Table 2 we show experimental results that measure the mean number of loads falling consecutively on a single node. This is an approximation of datathread length, since we do not account for dependences. All results presented here assumed a four-processor system. These simulations also used the SimpleScalar tools and assumed a cache configuration identical to that presented in Section 3.1. For each benchmark, we replicated 32 4-Kbyte pages on each node. We selected the pages to replicate by running the benchmark, saving the number of accesses to each page, sorting the pages by number of accesses, and choosing the 32 most heavily accessed pages. We distributed the communicated pages among the nodes round-robin, in blocks with sizes ranging from 4 to 32 pages. The sizes of the distributed blocks of data are shown for each benchmark in the first column of Table 2. For each benchmark, we tried to maximize the distribution block size (to improve datathread length) while still keeping it smaller than 1/4 of both the text and the largest data (globals, heap, stack) segment. This action prevented either segment from being completely contained at one processor, a situation which would make the datathread length equal to the number of references.)

The next four columns in Table 2 show the distribution of replicated pages among the four segments. Columns seven through nine show the mean (arithmetic) datathread lengths using three different definitions of datathreads. All three methods count consecutive references on a node, beginning the count upon the first reference to a communicated datum local to some node, ending (and restarting) the count upon the next reference to communicated data local to a different node. Column seven approximates datathread lengths using all references to memory (e.g., all cache misses). The second and third columns compute datathread length using only instruction and data references to memory, respectively.

The right-most column shows the average number of contiguous accesses to replicated pages in main memory. High numbers of references to replicated pages will extend average datathread lengths. If references to replicated data are frequent, the threads will tend to be long.

The average datathread lengths in Table 2 are generally high for instructions—over 20 in every case. These large numbers are partially due to the replication of a high percentage of the text pages, which is significant for most programs (`li`, `tomcatv`, `m88ksim`, `turb3d`, and `fpppp` have average code datathreads in the hundreds or thousands, and each has from 1/3 to 1/2 of the code replicated across all processors). Part of the explanation for the long datathreads, however, is the high spatial locality generally found in code reference streams.

Data reference thread lengths that we see tend to be shorter than the instruction thread lengths. They are low (less than 3) for some of the floating point codes (`swim`, `applu`, `turb3d`, `mgrid`, and `hydro2d`). Although floating-point codes tend to have high spatial locality, our approximation of datathreads is cut by interleaved accesses to arrays residing at different processors (*e.g.*, `c[i] = a[i] + b[i]`). Also, some of the spatial locality is filtered out by the cache. The three other floating-point codes have higher average datathread lengths, however, ranging from about 6 to 33. The integer codes tend to have higher datathread lengths than do the floating-point codes. The datathread length for `li` is high

Benchmark	Dist. size (Kb)	Replicated pages (128Kb)				Datathread length approximation			
		text	global	heap	stack	total	text	data	repl.
tomcatv	32	22	6	2	2	42.3	31486.7	6.7	21.7
swim	32	7	24	0	1	2.1	60.2	2.1	1.0
hydro2d	32	25	5	0	2	1.7	176.9	1.6	1.1
mgrid	32	4	27	0	1	1.5	31.4	1.5	1.0
applu	32	23	8	0	1	2.6	43.3	2.6	1.0
m88ksim	64	16	10	5	1	157.3	859.2	69.1	16.2
turb3d	64	19	12	0	1	1.7	1541.6	1.6	1.1
gcc	256	25	1	0	6	7.4	23.9	4.5	1.2
compress	16	6	25	0	1	103.5	41.7	134.7	1.3
li	16	17	2	12	1	841.2	777.2	2027.1	208.4
perl	128	26	2	3	1	7.6	34.5	4.1	2.1
fpppp	64	27	4	0	1	165.6	755.9	33.7	3.7
wave5	64	17	14	0	1	6.4	171.6	5.9	1.7
vortex	128	27	2	1	2	5.5	21.0	2.9	1.9

Table 2: Approximate datathread measurements for a four-processor system

Each row shows the experimental parameters for each benchmark, followed by the results. The first column contains the granularity at which communicated data are distributed round-robin around the processors. The second through fifth columns show the number of pages from each segment that were replicated for each benchmark. The right-most four columns show the arithmetic mean of our datathread length approximations for all reads, all reads to code and data separately, and reads to replicated memory, respectively.

because most of its data set is replicated. The others show average datathread lengths from about three to over 130.

These results show that many programs will be able to exploit datathreading. Ideally, each processor in a DataScalar system will run ahead of the others, finding multiple needed operands and instructions locally, and sending them to the other processors early—sometimes even before the other processors have resolved those addresses.

4 Performance of a DataScalar implementation

In this section we present simulation results comparing one implementation of a DataScalar architecture with a more traditional architecture. We first discuss the specific solution we implemented to enable caching under asynchronous ESP. We then describe our simulated architecture, simulation environment and parameters, and present our results.

4.1 Cache correspondence

In Section 2 we described static replication of data, in which heavily used pages are copied at each processor running as a DataScalar machine. Static replication is limited in that it cannot use run-time information to reduce off-chip accesses—caches are universally used precisely because this run-time information is so crucial. Dynamic replication, therefore, is crucial to the competitiveness of DataScalar systems.

Dynamic replication in a DataScalar system is analogous to caching in a uniprocessor; processors take a broadcast operand or block of data, and decide to cache the data locally for a period of time (the difference is that multiple processors are all caching the same data instead of just one). However, replicating data dynamically is more complicated than simple caching. The goal of replication is to improve average memory access latency by reducing the number of broadcasts (which are analogous to cache misses in a uniprocessor). If the owner of a datum decides not to broadcast it upon a load, assuming it to be replicated, *every other node must still have that operand*, or deadlock will result. Conversely, if the owner broadcasts the operand and other nodes already have that operand locally, superfluous messages may fill up the queues on the remote nodes (depending on the broadcasting/receiving implementation). Certainly unnecessary broadcasts will waste bandwidth.

All nodes in a DataScalar system must therefore keep exactly the same set of dynamically replicated data, all choosing to stop replicating a datum at the same point in the access stream. Furthermore, these nodes should ideally make the decisions about what to keep replicated and what to throw out based on *local information only*—requiring continuous remote communication solely to reduce the number of broadcasts would make DataScalar systems non-competitive.

While many solutions are conceivable, in this paper we describe only the one that we have implemented. Our solution is to fold the decisions about what to replicate dynamically into the first-level caches—a block is considered to be dynamically replicated so long as it is in those caches.[1] If a level one cache miss occurs for communicated data, the owner must broadcast that line to the other nodes. This solution implies that no node may ever miss on a communicated line if another node hits on that line for the same load. We call this the *cache correspondence* problem; data must be kept *correspondent* in the primary caches to prevent deadlocks.

Keeping the caches correspondent is a non-trivial problem. Dynamically scheduled processors will send loads to the cache in different orders, and will also send different sets of instructions (when branch conditions take longer to resolve at some processors than others, allowing more mis-speculated instructions to issue). If two loads to different lines in the same cache set are issued in a different order at two processors, that set will replace different lines, and the caches will cease to be correspondent.

Our solution is to update the primary cache state only when a memory operation is *committed*, not when it is issued. To maintain correct program semantics, instructions must be committed in the same order at all processors, even though they may be issued in

1. It is possible to use lower levels of a multi-level cache hierarchy to perform dynamic replication. We chose to use only the level-one caches because our particular solution requires a tight coupling of the cache tags and the load/store queue in the processor.

different orders. This solution also prevents mis-speculated instructions from affecting the cache contents.

We implement this solution with a structure called a *Commit Update Buffer* (CUB). We envision separate CUBs for instructions and data (ICUBs and DCUBs), but in this paper we only evaluate a DCUB. When a cache miss returns, rather than loading the data into the cache, the line is placed into an entry of the DCUB, and a pointer to that entry is placed in the load/store queue at the entry of the load that generated the miss. Memory operations to the same line are serviced by the data in the DCUB (loads may still be serviced by stores farther ahead in the load/store queue). When a memory operation is committed, the cache tags are updated, and, if necessary, the line is loaded from the DCUB into the cache. A DCUB entry is deallocated when the last entry in the load/store queue that uses that line is committed. In addition to a pointer to the DCUB entry, each entry in the load/store queue is extended with state that represents whether the instruction missed in the primary cache at issue time.

This extra state is necessary because updating the cache at commit time only is sufficient to guarantee cache correspondence, but not to guarantee identical hit/miss behavior at all processors. Since instructions may issue at different times across processors, the same instruction will issue at different commit points in the instruction stream across the processors, causing some to hit and others to miss in their caches. By saving whether a hit or miss occurred at issue time, we can compare that event with the correct commit-time event, and take corrective action if there is a disparity.

We show a simple example in Figure 4. Two addresses, **X** and **Y**, conflict in the cache. Instructions commit from left to right. The second load to **X** ($\mathbf{X_2}$) misses when issued, but would have hit at commit time if the instructions were issued in program order (because $\mathbf{X_1}$ would have already generated the miss). This is an example of a *false miss*. Analogously, $\mathbf{Y_2}$ hits at issue time because $\mathbf{Y_1}$ had just been committed, but should have missed at commit time (e.g., at another processor, $\mathbf{Y_2}$ might issue after $\mathbf{X_1}$ is committed, causing a miss at issue time instead of a hit). We call this a *false hit*, and deal with it by generating a reparative miss when this situation is detected at commit time (a reparative miss consists of a reparative broadcast by the owner, or a squash to the local BSHR by a non-owner of that datum). We deal with false misses by recognizing that any sequence of accesses to the same line will generate only one miss ($\mathbf{X_1}$ and $\mathbf{X_2}$ in this example). If $\mathbf{X_1}$ issues after $\mathbf{X_2}$, we can "assign" the miss generated by $\mathbf{X_2}$ to $\mathbf{X_1}$, thus ensuring that all processors will generate only one miss for that line.

This "cache correspondence protocol" does not currently handle speculative accesses; if we were to permit incorrect speculations in our simulations, we would have to buffer speculative broadcasts at the network interface. We would then allow them to proceed only when they were determined to be correct, and squash them locally otherwise. We are in the process of extending this correspondence protocol to support speculative broadcasts.

4.2 Simulated implementation

We evaluated a DataScalar system consisting of multiple integrated processor/memory (IRAM) modules connected via a global bus. In Figure 5 we show a diagram of the high-level datapaths present in our simulated DataScalar implementation. We assume split primary instruction and data caches. We replicate the program text at each node, obviating the need for dynamically replicated instructions (and therefore a speculative correspondence protocol). We do support dynamic replication of data, so a DCUB, not the accesses themselves, updates the data cache tags and storage. We assume a fast on-chip main memory, which is insufficiently large to hold an entire program data set, but which is fast enough to eliminate the need for a level-two cache.

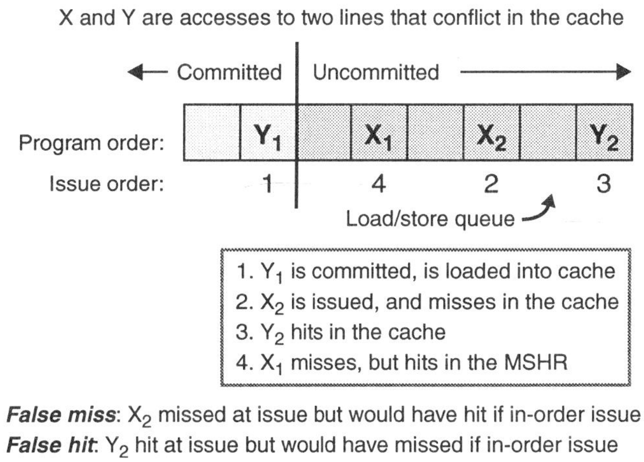

Figure 4. Cache correspondence example

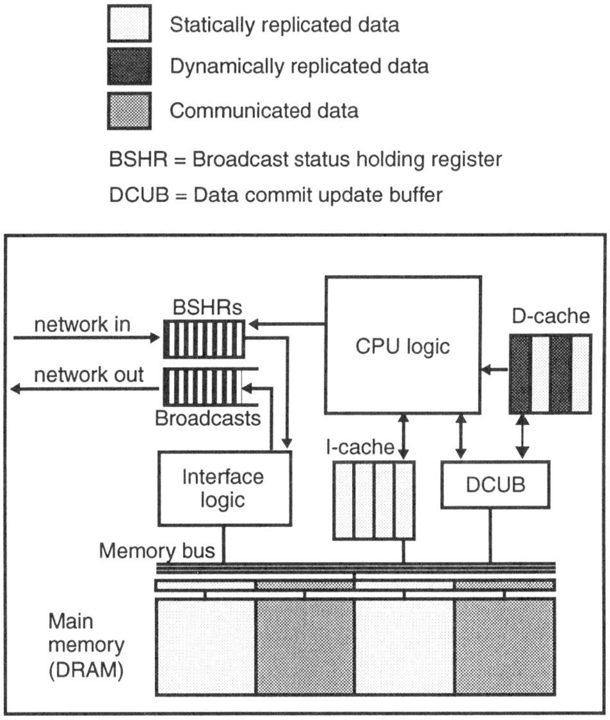

Figure 5. Simulated DataScalar chip datapath

We use a simple queue to buffer broadcasts being placed on the global bus. The process of receiving broadcasts is more involved. We call the broadcast-receiving structures that we simulate *Broadcast Status Holding Registers*, or BSHRs. We implement the BSHRs as a circular queue. When a broadcast arrives from the network, the BSHR performs an associative search on that address. If a match occurs, the earliest entry matching that address in the queue is freed and the data are forwarded to the processor. If no match occurs, the BSHR allocates the next entry in the queue and buffers the data. In this case, when the processor issues the request for the data, it finds them waiting in the BSHR, and effectively sees an on-chip hit.

Level-one cache misses become broadcasts if the missing cache line is in communicated memory, and the processor is the owner of that cache line. The miss allocates a BSHR entry if, at a given processor, the miss is to a line that is both communicated and unowned by that processor. In Figure 5 we show a datapath from the processor to the BSHR queue; this path is used to squash BSHR entries allocated due to false misses.

Our simulation platform was a substantially modified version of the SimpleScalar tools [1]. To simulate DataScalar systems, we extended the SimpleScalar out-of-order processor simulator with multiple target contexts. The simulator switches contexts after executing each cycle (i.e., it simulates cycle n for all contexts before simulating cycle $n + 1$ for any context).

We also implemented address translation, which was not present in the original version. We assume a single-level page table, locked in the low region of physical memory. We maintain the replicated vs. communicated state of each page with a bit in the page table entry. Each page table entry also has one bit that determines ownership of a communicated page (only one processor will have the ownership bit set for a communicated page; the bit for that page is cleared in the page table entries of all other processors).

Processor parameters

Evaluating future systems, particularly those five or ten years away, is always difficult. Simulating the processors of tomorrow on the machines of today (using the benchmarks of yesterday) makes choosing parameters that give meaningful results difficult. We opted for an aggressive processor model, coupled with a memory hierarchy that has cycle times matching the generation of our hypothetical future processor, but which is sized according to the year that the benchmarks were released.

For all our experiments, we targeted a processor that might be built about five years hence. We assumed an 8-way issue, 1 GHz, out-of-order issue processor. Our processor used a Register Update Unit (RUU) [24] to keep track of instruction dependencies. We simulated an instruction window size of 256 instructions (RUU entries). Our simulated processor also contains a load/store queue, to prevent loads from bypassing stores to the same address. Loads are sent from this queue to the cache at issue time, while stores are sent to the cache at commit time. Loads can be serviced in a single cycle by stores to the same address that are ahead in the queue. For all simulations, we simulated a load/store queue that had half as many entries as did the simulated RUU.

Modern branch predictors are already quite accurate, however, and we have no way of knowing what prediction techniques will be prevalent in future processors, or the extent to which these processors will engage in aggressive speculation. We therefore assumed perfect branch prediction in our simulations. This assumption simplified our handling of the BSHRs (since our cache correspondence protocol does not currently support speculative broadcasts). Assuming perfect branch prediction will also increase the measured IPC, due to the absence of branch misprediction penalties (the IPC of future processors is likely to be even higher as they engage in speculation that is much more aggressive than branch prediction [25]).

Memory system parameters

On-chip memories are likely to be significantly faster than DRAMs are today. Using sub-banking, with hierarchical word- and bit-lines, will enable DRAM banks to have access latencies that are comparable with those of cache memories. Current high-density (1 Gb) DRAM prototypes, the processes of which are optimized for density and not speed, have access latencies in the low 30's of nanoseconds [7, 8]. On-chip DRAM banks implemented in hybrid memory/logic processes are likely to be significantly faster.

For our simulations, we assume a memory hierarchy on-chip that is just two levels. The first level is split instruction and data caches, 64KB each with single-cycle access. The caches are direct-mapped (for speed) and the data cache implements a write-back, write-noallocate policy. We believe that this write policy is superior to write-allocate in an ESP-based system (with a write-allocate protocol, a write miss requires sending an inter-processor message, only to overwrite the received data). Both caches are fully non-blocking and can support an arbitrarily high number of outstanding requests. The second level of the hierarchy is composed of high-capacity, on-chip memory banks that can be accessed in 8 ns. They are connected with a 256 bit bus that is clocked at the processor frequency. We assume that our off-chip bus is 128 bits wide and is clocked at 200 MHz. Commodity parts that expect to do most of their computing and memory accesses on-chip are not likely to have support for extremely aggressive off-chip connections.

We assume BSHRs with 3-ns access latencies and 128 entries. We assume a broadcast queue for the DataScalar simulations, which incurs a two-cycle access penalty before broadcasting data onto the global interconnect (the traditional architecture, similarly, buffers off-chip requests at a network interface that functions as a connection between the local and global buses, also incurring a two-cycle penalty).

4.3 Performance results

As with the previous experiments, the benchmarks that we used were drawn from the SPEC95 suite [26]. We used the `test` input set in all cases, although we reduced the number of iterations in some programs (after performing experiments to ensure that the reduced number of iterations did not perturb our results).

We simulated six of the SPEC95 benchmarks: `go`, `mgrid`, `applu`, `compress`, `turb3d`, and `wave5`. We ran each benchmark for 200 million instructions or to completion, whichever came first. We did not statically replicate any data pages; all pages were distributed round-robin across all nodes. We ran simulations for both two-processor and four-processor DataScalar systems. Each processor has sufficient capacity to hold one-half and one-fourth of the data set, respectively, for each benchmark. Our target DataScalar system dynamically replicates remote data in the data cache, as described in Section 4.1.

We compared the Datascalar performance against two points: an identical processor with a perfect data cache (single-cycle access to any operand), and a more traditional system which has the same amount of on-chip memory as does one chip in each DataScalar experiment. We thus compare a two-processor DataScalar execution against a system which has the same processor, half the memory on-chip, and half off-chip (to make a fair comparison, the buses are the same, and both systems cache updates at instruction commit, not issue). We show an example of this comparison, assuming four processors, in Figure 6. A traditional system (Figure 6a) being compared against a four-processor DataScalar machine (Figure 6b) would thus have one-fourth of its main memory on-chip and three-fourths off-chip.

While the traditional system would certainly benefit if all of the on-chip memory was devoted to a large second- or third-level cache, measuring such a system against our simulated DataScalar implementation would be an unfair comparison. We consider the IRAM chip used in both types of system to be a commodity part, intended for stand-alone use, with the large on-chip memory functioning as main memory and not a cache.

In Figure 7 we plot the instructions per cycle for each experiment. We ran each benchmark assuming two and four DataScalar processors. The actual IPC value resides atop each bar. We see that the performance benefits that the DataScalar system has to offer are substantial. The results are particularly striking for `compress`, almost a doubling of IPC over the traditional architecture. That performance gain is so much higher because `compress` issues almost as many stores as loads, which never have to go off-chip in a DataScalar system. For all other benchmarks, the Data-

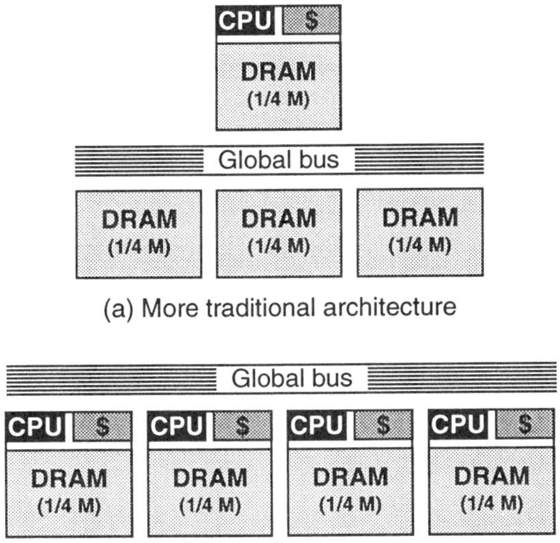

(a) More traditional architecture

(b) DataScalar architecture (4 nodes)

Figure 6. Comparing two IRAM organizations

Scalar system manages to capture much of the available ILP, approaching the IPC of the perfect data cache in some cases.

The DataScalar system deals with a finer-grain distribution of memory better than does the traditional system; the drops in DataScalar performance when going from two-processor to four-processor systems are less than 0.05 IPC (the comparable drops in performance on the traditional system range from 0.1 to 0.6 IPC). The IPC for `wave` actually improves when running on four processors instead of two (the benefits of more processors running datathreads concurrently outweigh the additional off-chip communication). In only two cases (`mgrid` and `turb3d` with two nodes) does the DataScalar system perform worse than the traditional system. This abnormality results from poor correspondence protocol performance (a high rate of false hits at one node causes the other node to stall frequently, waiting for the owner to commit the offending load and issue a reparative broadcast).

We present the results of a sensitivity analysis in Figure 8. The two benchmarks presented are `go` and `compress`, each of which was run to completion. For each benchmark, we plot results assuming the same parameters that we used for the experiments in Figure 7, except that we vary one parameter in each graph. The parameters we varied were: data cache size, main memory access time, global bus clock speed, width of the global bus, and number of RUU entries. On each graph, we plot the IPC for the same five systems as we measured in Figure 7 (perfect data cache, two- and four-processor DataScalar machines, and traditional systems assuming one-half and one-fourth of the main memory on-chip).

We see that the DataScalar runs consistently outperform the traditional runs over a wide range of parameters. As expected, the performance of the two types of systems converges when memory bank access times come to dominate the latency of a memory request (because DataScalar systems reduce the overhead of transmitting the data, not accessing them). Conversely, when the speed differential between the global and on-chip buses grows, so does the disparity between DataScalar and traditional performance.

In Table 3 we list a few of the BSHR and broadcast statistics from the two-processor runs. We list the percentage of broadcasts that were issued late, at commit time, due to false hits. These percentages will drop for larger caches, since the probability that a block will be replaced in between issue time and commit time is inversely proportional to cache size. The middle column lists the percentage of BSHR entries that were squashed due to false hits. The right-most column lists the percentage of remote accesses that were waiting in the BSHR for the local processor's request. Those values range from 2% to 9%, showing evidence that some effective datathreading is occurring, since a processor needs to be running fairly far ahead of another for that situation to occur.

4.4 Other implementation issues

In this subsection we describe other issues pertinent to DataScalar architectures—namely, the cost overheads of the extra processors, the expense of requiring broadcasts, speculation in DataScalar, and operating systems issues.

Cost

Conventional systems today typically consist of a single processor and a collection of memory chips. Each of these components comprise a significant fraction of the total cost of the system. A DataScalar system would consist of a collection of identical chips, each of which costs more than a conventional DRAM chip,

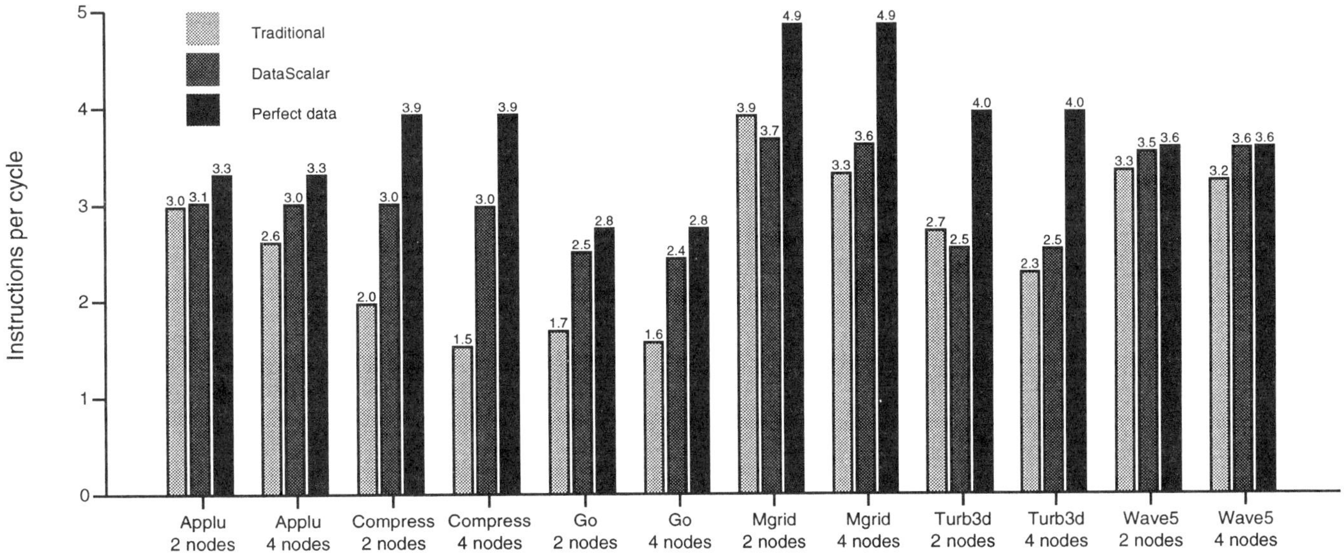

Figure 7. Timing simulation DataScalar results

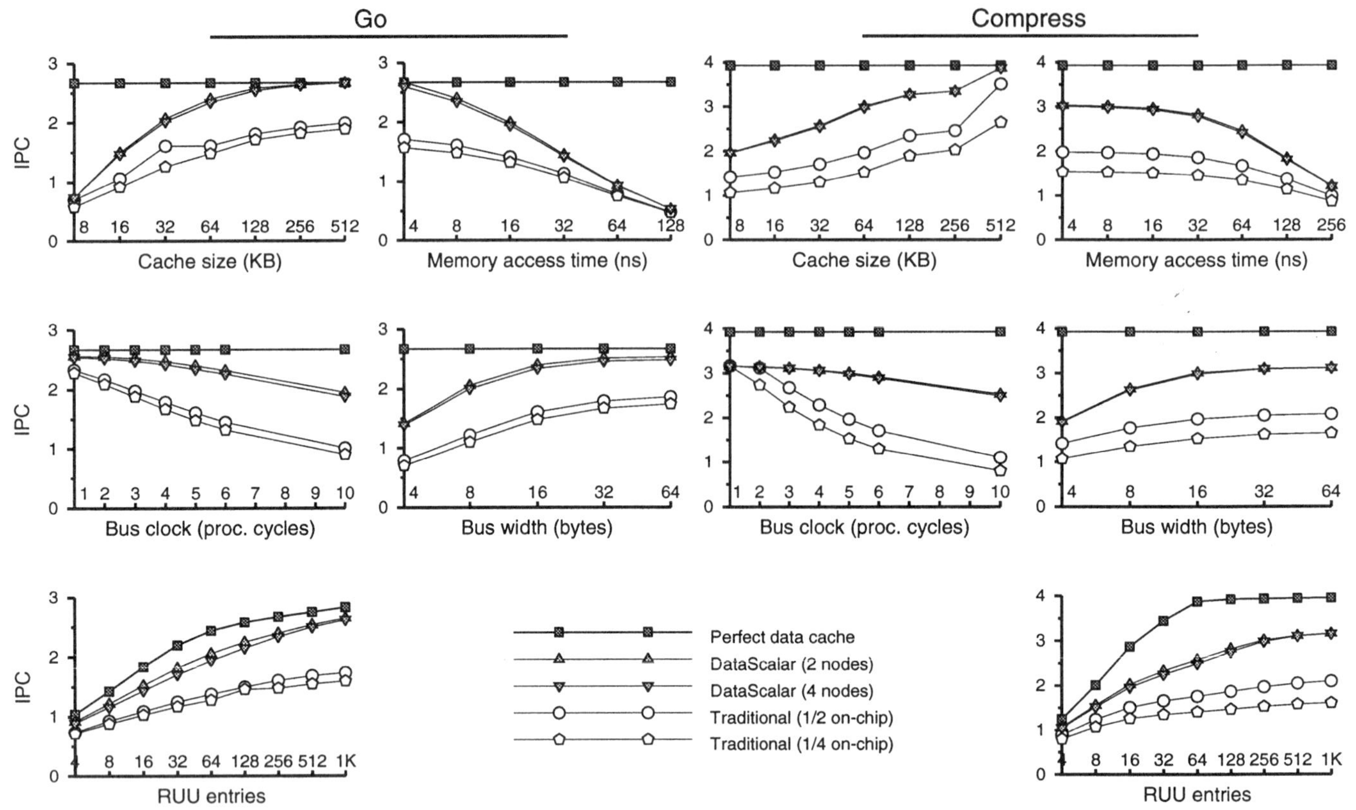

Figure 8. Sensitivity analysis of DataScalar experiments

Benchmark	Late broadcasts		BSHR squashes		Data found in BSHR	
(# of nodes)	2	4	2	4	2	4
applu	10%	9%	12%	12%	10%	7%
compress	11%	8%	16%	22%	8%	4%
go	9%	10%	12%	15%	19%	7%
mgrid	23%	21%	31%	31%	6%	4%
turb3d	38%	37%	59%	59%	3%	1%
wave5	9%	7%	11%	3%	3%	1%

Table 3: DataScalar broadcast statistics
The parameters are the same as for the experiments described in Section 4.3. The numbers are the arithmetic mean at all nodes. The percentages are out of total number of broadcasts (column one) and out of BSHR accesses (columns two and three).

but less than a processor chip. When comparing the cost of a DataScalar system and a traditional system with one processor and "dumb memory" (such as the comparison in Figure 6), the DataScalar system becomes cost-effective when the performance it adds outstrips the cost of the additional processors.

Wood and Hill showed [28] that for a parallel system to be cost-effective, the *costup* (the relative increase in total cost as more processors are added) should be less than the *speedup* (the relative increase in performance as more processors are added). When memory or interconnect costs dominate those of the additional processors, the system may still be cost-effective even if the speedups are comparatively small.

A majority of the die of most modern processors is devoted to memory, even though the total cache capacity for each is generally only in the tens of kilobytes. We believe that the ratio of on-chip memory area to total chip area will continue to grow in the future, making the relative expense of the processing logic shrink over time. If true, this trend will make memory and packaging the dominant costs of future systems. DataScalar architectures could thus be cost-effective, even though the speedups they provide are much less than linear.

Inter-chip communication

Because of the symmetric nature of the DataScalar model, all communicated values must be broadcast to all nodes. In general, broadcast operations are both expensive and not scalable. On certain interconnects—such as on a ring or bus—they may be effected with only minor additional cost, though reliable delivery and error recovery are inevitably more complicated for broadcast operations.

Broadcasts on a bus are free, since every bus transaction is an implicit broadcast. However, the very feature that makes broadcasts cheap—the centralized nature of a bus—makes the bus an unlikely candidate for the high-performance interconnect of the future. However, the demise of the bus has been much slower than predicted, and buses may persist for some time to come.

Ring operations, such as the IEEE/ANSI standard Scalable Coherent Interface [16, 23] seem well-suited for this kind of operation. On a ring, operations are observed by all nodes if the sender is responsible for removing its own message. We envision a ring interconnect because of the high-performance capability [22], but broadcast on a ring is complicated by the fact that operands originating at different processors are received at other nodes in different orders. A simple tag can sort out data to different addresses, but the issue is complicated when two accesses to the same datum are broadcast close in time. Complications also arise whenever certain data items must be rebroadcast (e.g., because a receive queue is full), or cancelled.

One technology that may be an excellent match for DataScalar programs running on large systems is optical interconnects. One of the properties of free-space optical interconnects is that they have extremely cheap (essentially free) broadcasts. For massively parallel systems that use optical interconnects, the SPSD execution model may be a good way to reduce the execution time spent in serialized code, thus improving scalability [2].

Speculative execution

Fine-grain speculative execution is now present in state-of-the-art processors, and a successful DataScalar architecture must be compatible with speculation. Much of the promise we see in DataScalar comes from out-of-order execution, which enables multiple processors to race ahead simultaneously on different instruction sequences. However, speculation must be tightly controlled: the broadcast of data may well be a critical limitation of this model, and frequent superfluous broadcasts would greatly hinder performance. The two endpoints for speculative policies are (1) to hold onto speculative broadcasts until the speculative condition is resolved, and (2) to send the broadcast immediately upon issue and then send a corresponding squash if the load that generated the broadcast is squashed.[1] The former conserves bandwidth at the expense of added latency, while the latter consumes bandwidth while reducing latency (bandwidth limitations add latency, however, so there is likely a crossover point at which one policy becomes better than the other). A promising approach is to assign confidence values to speculative loads; loads with high correctness confidence should be broadcast and squashed if incorrect, whereas loads with low confidence should be held locally until the speculative condition is resolved.

Operating systems issues

To the extent that an executing program is non-deterministic, operating system code can be executed in the same manner as user code. Synchronous exceptions, such as for an unaligned address, would be observed at slightly different times at different processors, but would cause no special problems. However, asynchronous events could potentially cause difficulty if they are not observed at precisely the same point by all processors. Consider the case in which a write causes a page fault. Since only one processor actually performs a write to communicated data—the other processors all simply discard their result—only the owning processor would observe the page fault. If the other processors did not recognize the page fault, they might proceed beyond the fault point indefinitely. While it is interesting to consider such a variation on the idea of an imprecise exception, the problem can be avoided by making sure that all processors have the same page table entries, and actually check for exceptions on every memory operation. Thus each processor would observe this page fault. External interrupts, likewise, must be injected into the system with care to assure that all processors observe them at the same point in their execution.

5 Exploiting parallelism with DataScalar

DataScalar is a memory system optimization, intended for codes that are (1) limited by the memory system and (2) difficult to parallelize. Every DataScalar machine is a *de facto* multiprocessor, however. When codes contain coarse-grain parallelism, the system should be run more like a traditional multiprocessor. We view DataScalar and multiprocessing as two endpoints on a spectrum: the former runs transparently and makes no attempt to exploit parallelism in the code; the latter requires compiler and/or programmer support, and its main focus is explicit exploitation of coarse-grain parallelism.

In this section we discuss some of the intermediate points along this spectrum. In Section 5.1 we describe new opportunities for exploiting medium-grain parallelism in a DataScalar architecture. In Section 5.2 we present some issues associated with running a mixed-mode program, in which some parts of the program run in DataScalar mode and others run as on a traditional MIMD machine.

5.1 Multiprocessing from a Datascalar perspective

DataScalar systems benefit from both ESP and datathreading transparently, without requiring recompilation. In many codes there is limited parallelism, which is insufficient to justify porting the code to a full-blown parallel processor, but which could improve DataScalar performance. We propose using software support to expose this parallelism in a DataScalar context.

When the programmer or compiler identifies an isolated block of code that can be executed on one node and not the others (requiring few or no remote operands), that processor may temporarily "peel off" from ESP mode. The processor will then compute some result, and either store the result locally, or communicate it to the other processors when the processor rejoins ESP execution. We call this technique *result communication*. Only the participating processor(s) must execute the code block in question; the others must branch around the code. The compiler must perform the analysis to ensure that the non-participating nodes do not need any of the intermediate results generated during the isolated computation.

Result communication has the potential to reduce global traffic as well as reduce the critical path at the non-participating nodes. We note that this is a special case of data parallel execution; if all nodes are independently performing computations and writing the results to communicated data that they own, the execution looks similar to traditional data parallel [5].

Performing this parallelizing analysis in a DataScalar context has distinct advantages. Hardware support in the processor, coupled with run-time system support (described below), can assist in making run-time checking efficient. When the data for a computation are scattered across all nodes, the system has an efficient fall-back case (asynchronous ESP). The compiler's job is therefore to provide the hardware with *options* (break from ESP *if* most or all of the data are local), not *guarantees* about where the data are located.

When a processor deviates from ESP, the code it executes must not perturb the state of the correspondent caches, if the caches are indeed used to implement dynamic replication. We may prevent such a perturbation by marking non-ESP accesses, and dropping them at commit time, rather than updating the caches. If, while in this mode, a processor requires a communicated datum that it does not own, either the compiler must have generated code to force the owning processor to send the operand, or the processor could fall back to a traditional request/response model. The most important guarantee the compiler must make, however, is that there are no side-effects in the isolated code that were supposed to have changed the state at every processor.

In the rest of this subsection we present an illustrative example of result communication. The branch test could be implemented by performing a test on a bit stored in the page table. We call this test the "local" function. A processor might take the branch if the `local` bit in the TLB for a given address was zero (the `local` bit corresponds to ownership of the operand). To make this run-time check efficient, however, the processors should not have to check

1. A squash is necessary because all incoming broadcasts are buffered in the BSHRs. Incorrectly speculated broadcasts would not always be matched with a request from the receiving processor, and would thus accumulate until the BSHR was full. An alternative solution is to periodically flush the BSHRs, cleansing them of stale broadcasts.

ownership of multiple addresses, the resolution of some of which the processors would need to run the code being parallelized to resolve. We can fold the check for multiple operands into a single check, by securing a guarantee from the run-time system that certain data items are placed local to the same processor. One technique for doing so is to modify the run-time storage allocator by both giving it an ownership assignation function and passing it an address on a request for storage. The storage allocator then ensures that the allocated storage was allocated at the same processor as the address that was passed to it. The goal is to ensure that all of an aggregate (either an array or a dynamically allocated structure) falls entirely on one node. Binding the aggregate to one node should be avoided if the aggregate is so large that it should be spread across multiple nodes.

The notion of placing data can be generalized so that pages containing parts of a structure are tagged with a class identifier. This would decouple structures from specific nodes, so that the number of processors (and page assignation) could change dynamically (the OS would ensure that all of the pages of a given class came to reside entirely on one processor).

In Figure 9 we depict an example that could make effective use of result communication. We show a chained hash table, the main array of which is distributed across multiple processors. Below the hash table we show the high-level code transformation that would alter the insertion routine. The additions to the code are marked with arrows. Whenever a collision occurs and an entry must be added to a chain, the run-time allocator (`malloc` in this example) is passed the address of the head of the chain, and it returns storage that is local to the same processor as is the head of the chain. When insertions or deletions into the hash table need to be made, the compiler places a branch around the insertion or deletion code. The processor that owns the head of the chain will thus own the entire chain, and can make the insertion or deletion without requiring any off-chip communication.

Since every part of the array resides local to some processor, *every* insertion and deletion can be made with *no remote communication*. The run-time test is efficient because the locality bit for the head of the table is obtained with a simple address translation, and the tests for every element in entire chain are subsumed by the locality test for the head of the list. Many such optimizations are possible, and are a promising area of research.

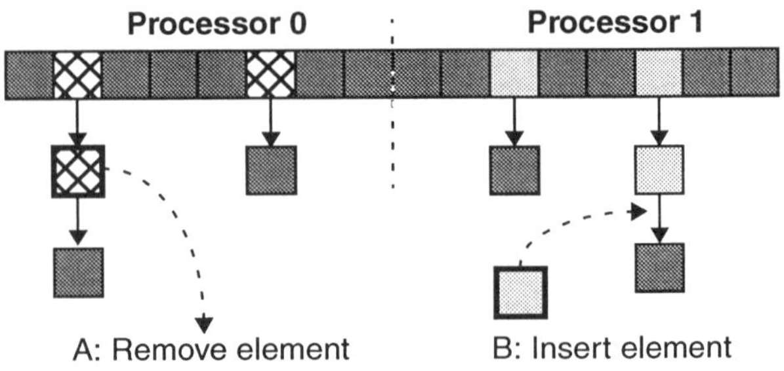


```
    struct t_entry *HASH_TABLE[SIZE];
    insert_entry(int key)
    {
      struct t_entry *entry;
      int h_index = HASH_FN(key);
      entry = (struct t_entry *)
              malloc(sizeof(struct t_entry),
→                    &HASH_TABLE[h_index]);
→     if (local(&HASH_TABLE[h_index])) {
        entry->key = key;
        entry->next = HASH_TABLE[h_index];
        HASH_TABLE[h_index] = entry;
→     }
    }
```

Figure 9. Medium-grain parallelism in a hash table

5.2 DataScalar from a multiprocessing perspective

If much coarse-grain parallelism is extractable from a program, the program should be run using the system as a multiprocessor rather than as a DataScalar architecture. Few codes are "embarrassingly parallel," however. Codes should perhaps be run on a hybrid architecture, which runs a program as a multiprocessor when there is sufficient coarse-grain parallelism, and as a DataScalar architecture when there is not (thereby reducing serial overheads). The program may either switch statically or dynamically between the two modes, or run both modes simultaneously, using tagged instructions or regions of data addresses to decide which mode to use at a given point.

Future microprocessors will soon have sufficient resources to put multiple processing units on a single chip. Whether chip multiprocessors (CMPs) will succeed is a subject of debate in the research community. Widespread use of CMPs is more likely if techniques are developed that speed up uniprocessor programs—particularly those that are not easily parallelizable—by running them on a tightly coupled multiprocessor. DataScalar architectures may be one such candidate, depending on the future disparity between the cost of near versus far intra-chip communication.

Given the wide variance of characteristics across important applications, CMPs may benefit by supporting multiple modes of execution, so as to execute the broadest possible range of applications efficiently. To this end, we propose a "three C's" model for CMP execution modes.[1] In our model, we characterize an application as being limited by either *computation*, *control*, or *communication*. We propose to run a CMP as a different organization for each limiting category.

- **Computation-bound**: the application has enough coarse-grain parallelism that functional unit throughput is the limiting factor. If enough work can be found to allow all processing units to be utilized, the CMP should be run as a conventional multiprocessor.
- **Control-bound**: limited instruction-level parallelism requires the CMP to perform coarse-grain speculation. Control dependencies prevent a single processor from running very far ahead. The program execution could therefore benefit from having the processors function as stages in a Multiscalar-like architecture [12, 25], wherein each processor speculatively executes large blocks of code. The processor thereby obtains a much larger instruction window in which to find sufficient ILP.
- **Communication-bound**: a single processor is limited by frequent, slow accesses to non-local (on-chip) memory banks. The program execution could benefit from an architecture that uses multiple processors to reduce communication overheads. DataScalar architectures are one such example, and may be a good match for this category.

Many applications are unlikely to fall squarely into one category or another; it is probable that an application will run alternately in two or all three of these modes. Both characterizing applications in this manner, and designing the mechanisms needed to support concurrent execution of multiple modes, are interesting research issues to be explored.

6 Future directions and conclusions

This work began as a solution for running programs on multiple single-chip computers, when the physical memory requirements exceeded the capacity available on a single chip. Other groups are

1. Our model is not to be confused with Mark Hill's "three C's" model that characterizes cache misses [14].

also working on issues associated with the integration of processors and main memory, notably the IRAM project at UC-Berkeley [20] and the PPRAM project at Kyushu University [18]. Some companies are already prototyping preliminary designs that incorporate processing logic with a substantial amount of memory on a single die; Sun Microsystems [21] and Mitsubishi [9] are two examples. Our proposal uses multiple processing units to enhance the performance of uniprocessor programs. Other groups are also exploiting this concept—Stanford Hydra [19] uses automatic parallelization, Wisconsin Multiscalar [12, 25] uses coarse-grain speculation, and both the M-machine [10] and the Simultaneous Multithreading work [27] use aggressive multithreading.

In this paper we have proposed a system organization that exploits cheap computation to reduce memory system overheads. DataScalar architectures combine dynamic execution and speculation with the Massive Memory Machine's ESP execution mode. This class of architectures works well when remote memory accesses are significantly more expensive than local memory accesses, when global broadcasts are relatively inexpensive, and when the cost of additional processors is a small addition to the total cost of the system. We evaluated one conceivable DataScalar implementation, and showed that these ideas can indeed improve performance when memory system performance is critical.

Our current research efforts include a performance decomposition of DataScalar execution, to determine the relative fractions of performance gains coming from the elimination of write traffic, the elimination of requests, and datathreading. We are extending our cache correspondence protocol to handle speculation. We are also studying the potential of static replication, both coarse- and fine-grained, the effectiveness of more coarse-grained dynamic replication, and software support for improving datathread length. Finally, a major effort underway addresses exploiting parallelism within the DataScalar context, both at a medium grain (compiler support for result communication) and at a coarser grain (mixed-mode execution of SPSD and MIMD).

Acknowledgments

The authors thank Alain Kägi, Scott Breach, Babak Falsafi, Mark Hill, Milo Martin, Steve Reinhardt, Mike Smith, T.N. Vijaykumar, David Wood, and Todd Bezenek for their helpful discussions and comments on drafts of this paper. We also thank Todd Austin, who developed the original SimpleScalar tool set.

References

[1] Doug Burger, Todd M. Austin, and Steven Bennett. Evaluating Future Microprocessors: the SimpleScalar Tool Set. Technical Report 1308, Computer Sciences Department, University of Wisconsin, Madison, WI, July 1996.

[2] Doug Burger and James R. Goodman. Exploiting Optical Interconnects to Eliminate Serial Bottlenecks. In *Proceedings of the Third International Conference on Massively Parallel Processing Using Optical Interconnects*, October 1996.

[3] Doug Burger, James R. Goodman, and Alain Kägi. The Declining Effectiveness of Dynamic Caching for General-Purpose Microprocessors. Technical Report 1261, Computer Sciences Department, University of Wisconsin, Madison, WI, January 1995.

[4] Doug Burger, James R. Goodman, and Alain Kägi. Memory Bandwidth Limitations of Future Microprocessors. In *Proceedings of the 23rd Annual International Symposium on Computer Architecture*, pages 79–90, May 1996.

[5] F. Darema-Rogers, V. A. Norton, and G. F. Pfister. Using a Single-Program Multiple-Data Computation Model for Parallel Execution of Scientific Applications. IBM Research Report RC 11552, November 1985.

[6] Don Draper, Jeff Yetter, Ahsan Bootehsaz, Michael A. Buckley, Charlie X. Huang, Yusuke Ohtomo, Jurij Paraszczak, and Donald A. Priore. Panel Discussion on the Interconnect Nightmare. In *Proceedings of the 1996 International Solid-State Circuits Conference*, pages 278–279, February 1996.

[7] J. H. Yoo et al. A 32-bank 1Gb DRAM with 1 GB/s Bandwidth. In *Proceedings of the 1996 International Solid-State Circuits Conference*, pages 378–379. Samsung Electronics Co., February 1996.

[8] Masashi Horiguchi et al. An Experimental 220MHz 1Gb DRAM. In *Proceedings of the 1995 International Solid-State Circuits Conference*, pages 252–253. Hitachi, February 1995.

[9] Toru Shimizu et al. A Multimedia 32b RISC Microprocessor with 16Mb DRAM. In *Proceedings of the 1996 International Solid-State Circuits Conference*, pages 216–217. Mitsubishi Electric Co., February 1996.

[10] Marco Fillo, Stephen W. Keckler, William J. Dally, Nicholas P. Carter, Andrew Chang, Yevgeny Gurevich, and Whay S. Lee. The M-Machine Multicomputer. In *Proceedings of the 28th International Symposium on Microarchitecture*, pages 146–156, November 1996.

[11] Michael J. Flynn. Some Computer Organizations and Their Effectiveness. *IEEE Transactions on Computers*, C-21:948–960, 1972.

[12] Manoj Franklin. *The Multiscalar Architecture*. Ph.D. thesis, University of Wisconsin, Madison, WI, December 1993.

[13] Hector Garcia-Molina, Richard J. Lipton, and Jacobo Valdes. A Massive Memory Machine. *IEEE Transactions on Computers*, C-33(5):391–399, May 1984.

[14] Mark D. Hill. *Aspects of Cache Memory and Instruction Buffer Performance*. Ph.D. thesis, University of California at Berkeley, November 1987.

[15] Liviu Iftode, Kai Li, and Karin Petersen. Memory Servers for Multicomputers. In *Proceedings of the 38thIEEE Computer Society International Conference (COMPCON)*, pages 538–547, February 1993.

[16] David V. James, Anthony T. Laundrie, Stein Gjessing, and Gurindar S. Sohi. Scalable Coherent Interface. *IEEE Computer*, 23(6):74–77, June 1990.

[17] Osamu Kimura, Richard Crisp, Michael Nagy, Henry Lie, Roelof Salters, Kenji Numata, Takao Watanabe, and Kazunori Saitoh. Panel Session: DRAM + Logic Integration: Which Architecture and Fabrication Process. In *Proceedings of the 1997 International Solid-State Circuits Conference*, February 1997.

[18] Kazuaki Murakami, Satoru Shirakawa, and Hiroshi Miyajima. Parallel Processing RAM Chip with 256Mb DRAM and Quad Processors. In *Proceedings of the 1997 International Solid-State Circuits Conference*, pages 228–229, February 1997.

[19] Basm A. Nayfeh, Lance Hammond, and Kunle Olukotun. Evaluation of Design Alternatives for a Multiprocessor Microprocessor. In *Proceedings of the 23rd Annual International Symposium on Computer Architecture*, May 1996.

[20] David Patterson, Tom Anderson, and Kathy Yelick. The Case for IRAM. In *Proceedings of HOT Chips 8*, Stanford, CA, August 1996.

[21] Ashley Saulsbury, Fong Pong, and Andreas Nowatzyk. Missing the Memory Wall: The Case for Processor/Memory Integration. In *Proceedings of the 23rd Annual International Symposium on Computer Architecture*, May 1996.

[22] Steven L. Scott, James R. Goodman, and Mary K. Vernon. Performance of the SCI Ring. In *Proceedings of the 19th Annual International Symposium on Computer Architecture*, pages 403–414, May 1992.

[23] IEEE Computer Society. Scalable Coherent Interface (SCI). ANSI/IEEE Std 1596-1992, August 1993.

[24] Gurindar S. Sohi. Instruction Issue Logic for High-Performance, Interruptible, Multiple Functional Unit, Pipelined Computers. *IEEE Transactions on Computers*, 39(3):349–359, March 1990.

[25] Gurindar S. Sohi, Scott E. Breach, and T. N. Vijaykumar. Multiscalar Processors. In *Proceedings of the 22nd Annual International Symposium on Computer Architecture*, pages 414–425, June 1995.

[26] Standard Performance Evaluation Corporation. *SPEC Newsletter*, Fairfax, VA, September 1995.

[27] Dean M. Tullsen, Susan J. Eggers, and Henry M. Levy. Simultaneous Multithreading: Maximizing On-Chip Parallelism. In *Proceedings of the 22nd Annual International Symposium on Computer Architecture*, pages 392–403, June 1995.

[28] David A. Wood and Mark D. Hill. Cost-Effective Parallel Computing. *IEEE Computer*, 28(2):69–72, February 1995.

Author Index

NOTES

NOTES

NOTES

NOTES

NOTES

NOTES

NOTES